T0215752

Lecture Notes of the Institute for Computer Sciences, Social Informatics and Telecommunications Engineering 312

More information about this series at http://www.springer.com/series/8197

Organization

Steering Committee

Chair

Imrich Chlamtac   Bruno Kessler Professor, University of Trento, Italy

Honorary Co-chairs

Changjun Jiang   Tongji University, China
Qing Nie   Shanghai University, China
R. K. Shyamasundar   Indian Institute of Technology, India

Organizing Committee

General Chairs

Jizhong Zhao   Xi'an Jiaotong University, China
Zhiyong Feng   Tianjin University, China
Jun Yu   Hangzhou Dianzi University, China

Technical Program Chairs

Honghao Gao   Shanghai University, China
Guangjie Han   Hohai University, China
Jun Wu   Tongji University, China
Wei Xi   Xi'an Jiaotong University, China

International Advisory Committee

Zhenhua Duan   Xidian University, China
Vladimir Zwass   Fairleigh Dickinson University, USA
Mohammad S. Obaidat   Fordham University, USA
Han-Chieh Chao   National Dong Hwa University, Taiwan
Tai-Wei Kuo   National Taiwan University, Taiwan
Minho Jo   Korea University, South Korea

Publicity Chairs

Congfeng Jiang   Hangzhou Dianzi University, China
Zijian Zhang   Beijing Institute of Technology, China

Social Media Chair

Jiang Deng   Shanghai University, China

Workshops Chairs

Yuyu Yin   Hangzhou Dianzi University, China
Xiaoxian Yang   Shanghai Polytechnic University, China

Sponsorship and Exhibits Chair

Honghao Gao   Shanghai University, China

Publications Chairs

Youhuizi Li   Hangzhou Dianzi University, China
Wenmin Lin   Hangzhou Dianzi University, China

Demos Chair

Rui Li   Xidian University, China

Posters and PhD Track Chairs

Yueshen Xu   Xidian University, China
Zhiping Jiang   Xidian University, China

Local Arrangement Chairs

Yihai Chen   Shanghai University, China
Yuan Tao   Shanghai University, China

Web Chair

Qiming Zou   Shanghai University, China

Conference Manager

Kristina Lappyova   European Alliance for Innovation, Belgium

Technical Program Committee

Amjad Ali   Korea University, South Korea
An Liu   Zhejiang University, China
Anand Nayyar   Duy Tan University, Vietnam
Anwer Al-Dulaimi   University of Toronto, Canada
Ao Zhou   Beijing University of Posts and Telecommunications,
                             China
Bin Cao   Zhejiang University of Technology, China
Buqing Cao   Hunan University of Science and Technology, China
Changai Sun   University of Shanghai for Science and Technology,
                             China
Congfeng Jiang   Hangzhou Dianzi University, China
Cui Ying   Shanghai Jiao Tong University, China
Dongjing Wang   Hangzhou Dianzi University, China

Dagmar Caganova	Slovak University of Technology, Slovakia
Elahe Naserianhanzaei	University of Exeter, UK
Fei Dai	Yunnan University, China
Fekade Getahun	Addis Ababa University, Ethiopia
Gaowei Zhang	Nanyang Technology University, Singapore
George Ubakanma	London South Bank University, UK
Guobing Zou	Shanghai University, China
Haolong Xiang	The University of Auckland, New Zealand
Haoqi Ren	Tongji University, China
Honghao Gao	Shanghai University, China
Imed Romdhani	Edinburgh Napier University, UK
Jian Wang	Wuhan University, China
Jianxun Liu	Hunan University of Science and Technology, China
Jie Wang	Tongji University, China
Jie Zhang	Nanjing University, China
Jiuyun Xu	China University of Petroleum, China
Jiwei Huang	Beijing University of Post and Telecommunications, China
Jun Zeng	Chongqing University, China
Junaid Arshad	University of West London, UK
Junhao Wen	Chongqing University, China
Kuangyu Qin	Wuhan University, China
Li Kuang	Central South University, China
Li Yu	Hangzhou Dianzi University, China
Liang Chen	University of West London, UK
Lianhai Liu	Central South University, China
Lianyong Qi	Nanjing University, China
Lin Meng	Ritsumeikan University, Japan
Malik Ahmad Kamran	COMSATS University Islamabad, Pakistan
Miriam Hornakova	Slovak University of Technology, Slovakia
Rui Li	Xidian University, China
Rui Wang	Tongji University, China
Rui Wang	South University of Science and Technology of China, China
Rui Wang	Tongji University, China
Ruyu Li	Tongji University, China
Shanchen Pang	China University of Petroleum, China
Shaohua Wan	Zhongnan University, China
Sheng Zhou	Zhejiang University, China
Shijun Liu	Shandong University, China
Shizhan Chen	Tianjin University, China
Shucun Fu	Nanjing University of Information Science and Technology, China
Shunmei Meng	Nanjing University of Science and Technology, China
Shunqing Zhang	Shanghai University, China
Stephan Reiff-Marganiec	University of Leicester, UK

Tao Huang	Silicon Lake University, China
Wenda Tang	Lancaster University, UK
Wenmin Lin	Hangzhou Dianzi University, China
Xiaobing Sun	Yangzhou University, China
Xiaoliang Fan	Fuzhou University, China
Xiaolong Xu	Nanjing University of Information Science and Technology, China
Xiaoxian Yang	Shanghai Polytechnic University, China
Xihua Liu	Nanjing University of Information Science and Technology, China
Xuan Liu	Southeast University, China
Xuan Zhao	Nanjing University, China
Yanmei Zhang	Central University of Finance and Economics, China
Yihai Chen	Shanghai University, China
Ying Chen	Beijing University of Information Technology, China
Yiping Wen	Hunan University of Science and Technology, China
Yirui Wu	Hohai University, China
Yiwen Zhang	Anhui University, China
Youhuizi Li	Hangzhou Dianzi University, China
Yu Weng	Minzu University of China, China
Yu Zheng	Nanjing University of Information Science and Technology, China
Yuan Yuan	Michigan State University, USA
Yu-Chun Pan	University of West London, UK
Yucong Duan	Hainan University, China
Yueshen Xu	Xidian University, China
Yunni Xia	Chongqing University, China
Yutao Ma	Wuhan University, China
Yuyu Yin	Hangzhou Dianzi University, China
Zhe Xing	Sichuan University, China
Zhixhi Xu	Tongji University, China
Zhongqin Bi	Shanghai University of Electric Power, China
Zhuofeng Zhao	North China University of Technology, China
Zijian Zhang	Beijing Institute of Technology, China

Contents – Part I

Antenna, Microwave and Cellular Communication

Wireless Communications and Networking

Network and Information Security

Communication QoS, Reliability and Modeling

Contents – Part II

Pattern Recognition and Signal Processing

Information Processing

DISA Workshop

Internet of Things, Edge and Fog

Pricing-Based Partial Computation Offloading in Mobile Edge Computing

Lanhui Li$^{(\boxtimes)}$ and Tiejun Lv

Beijing University of Posts and Telecommunications, Beijing 100876, China
{lilanhui,lvtiejun}@bupt.edu.cn

Abstract. For mobile devices (MDs) and Internet of Things (IoT) devices with limited computing capacity and battery, offloading part of tasks to the mobile edge computing (MEC) server is attractive. In this paper, we propose a joint partial computation offloading and pricing scheme in a multi-user MEC system. Firstly, we establish MD's cost model and MEC server's revenue model in terms of money. Secondly, we investigate MD's cost minimization partial offloading strategy to jointly control MD's task allocation, local CPU frequency and the amount of computational resource blocks (CRBs) requested. Finally, we formulate the revenue maximization problem for MEC server with limited computing capacity, a heuristic algorithm is proposed for MEC server to find the optimal service price. Numerical results verify the effectiveness of our proposed scheme in cost saving and pricing.

Keywords: Mobile edge computing · Partial computation offloading · MEC server · Pricing scheme

1 Introduction

Recent years, with the rapid development of mobile computing and communication techniques, more and more computation-demanding and latency-sensitive mobile applications are appearing, such as face recognition, argument reality and natural language processing [1]. However, due to the finite storage and computing capacity, mobile devices (MDs) are still not able to handle these tasks locally [2].

To meet these challenges, mobile edge computing (MEC), which works at the close proximity of MDs has been advocated [3,4]. MEC offloading has been recognized as a promising paradigm to enhance the computing capacity of MDs. For energy and computing capacity constrained MDs, offloading tasks to adjacent MEC server is effective in reducing latency, saving energy and extending the battery lifetime. Comparing with mobile cloud computing (MCC), MEC can reduce transmitting delay and alleviate network burden.

Recent years, many researches have investigated the computation offloading problem in mobile edge networks. The authors of [5] presented an energy-efficient computation offloading scheme in 5G heterogeneous networks. In [6], the authors

© ICST Institute for Computer Sciences, Social Informatics and Telecommunications Engineering 2020
Published by Springer Nature Switzerland AG 2020. All Rights Reserved
H. Gao et al. (Eds.): ChinaCom 2019, LNICST 312, pp. 3–14, 2020.
https://doi.org/10.1007/978-3-030-41114-5_1

investigated the cost and latency trade-off in the process of mobile code offloading. In [7], the authors studied the economic performance in the D2D assisted data offloading network. In [8], the authors proposed a distributed full computation offloading and resource allocation mechanism in heterogeneous networks, however, the service price has not been optimized in this paper. The authors of [9,10] investigated partial computation offloading in MEC system. Although there have been many studies working on the energy efficiency and resource allocation in MEC system, the economic performance has seldom been investigated. Moreover, none of these works jointly optimized the revenue of MEC server and the cost of MDs with partial computation offloading. As partial computation offloading offers MDs more flexibility in making offloading strategies, we adopt partial offloading in this paper.

As money expenditure is more intuitive for MDs and MEC server, we aim to investigate the economic performance of partial computation offloading in this paper. The main contributions of this paper are summarized as follows:

- Firstly, we establish MD's cost model in terms of money and formulate its computation offloading problem. In the problem, MDs optimize its cost by jointly adjusting local execution ratio, CPU speed and computational resource blocks (CRBs) rent from MEC server. The minimization problem is subjected to the delay and computing capacity limits.
- Secondly, we formulate the revenue maximization problem of MEC server and propose a heuristic optimal pricing algorithm. In the pricing algorithm, we take the limitation of CRBs in MEC server into consideration.
- Finally, we conduct simulations to verify the proposed MEC offloading scheme. The relationships between CRB renting price, number of CRBs rented by MDs and the revenue of MEC server are analyzed. Simulation results show that our pricing algorithm converges quickly. We also compare our proposed cost minimization partial computation offloading scheme with other two computation schemes, simulation results indicate that our proposed offloading mechanism is more effective in cost saving.

The rest of the paper is organized as follows. Section 2 presents our system model and computation model. In Sect. 3, we propose the cost minimization partial offloading scheme of MDs together with the optimal pricing scheme of MEC server. The simulation results are presented and analyzed in Sect. 4. Finally, we conclude this paper in Sect. 5.

2   System Model

As depicted in Fig. 1, we consider $\Im = \{1, 2, \ldots, I\}$ MDs and one MEC server in the system. We assume MDs have tasks need to be executed. The MEC server which is assumed to be deployed between the remote cloud server and MDs, generally near the small-cell base stations. MEC server's computing resource can be divided into multiple CRBs. The computing capacity of each CRB is f^c and the maximum number of CRBs is Q. If there are available CRBs at the MEC

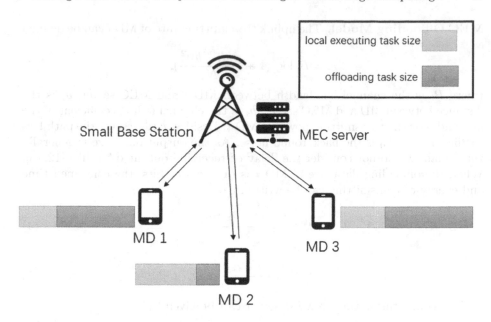

Fig. 1. System model

server, MDs can rent CRBs to compute its task. Note that the MEC server can handle different MDs' tasks independently. Thus, if errors happen in some tasks, these errors would not influence other tasks processed by the MEC server.

2.1 Computation Model

In this sub-section, we describe the local and offloading computation model of MD. We denote MD i' task as $T_i = \{m_i, c_i, t_i^{\max}\}$. Where m_i is the task size, c_i represents the number of CPU cycles required per bit; and $m_i c_i$ is the total CPU cycles needed by task T_i. $t_i^{\max}$ denotes the time limitation of task T_i, which means the task should be finished before $t_i^{\max}$. In this paper, we assume that MD's task can be divided. We define α_i $(0 \leq \alpha_i \leq 1)$ as the ratio of the task that MD i computes locally. Thus, $1 - \alpha_i$ is the ratio of task that MD i offloads to the MEC server.

Local Computation Model. Same with [11], the energy consumed per CPU cycle of MD i is denoted as $P = k_i f_i^2$, where k_i is a parameter related to the structure of device, f_i denotes the local CPU speed of MD i. With DVS technology, MD can reduce energy consumption by adjusting f_i. According to the task model described above, the time and energy consumption of local computing is

$$t_i^{\text{local}} = \frac{\alpha_i m_i c_i}{f_i}, \tag{1}$$

$$e_i^{\text{local}} = \alpha_i m_i c_i k_i f_i^2. \tag{2}$$

MEC Offloading Model. The uplink transmitting rate of MD i can be defined as

$$r_i = B_i \log_2(1 + \frac{p_i d_i^{-v}|h_i|^2}{N_0}), \tag{3}$$

where B_i is the channel bandwidth between MD i and MEC server, d_i is the distance between MD and MEC server, h_i is the channel fading coefficient of the link and p_i is the transmitting power of MD i. Besides, v represents the path loss coefficient and N_0 is the background noise. As the output data size is generally very small, we do not consider the delay of receiving output data, like [12,13]. When the offloading data size of MD i is $(1 - \alpha_i)m_i$ bits, the consumed time and energy of transmitting can be written as

$$t_i^{\text{trans}} = \frac{(1 - \alpha_i)m_i}{r_i}, \tag{4}$$

$$e_i^{\text{trans}} = \frac{(1 - \alpha_i)p_i m_i}{r_i}. \tag{5}$$

The computation time in MEC server can be given by

$$t_i^{\text{mec}} = \frac{(1 - \alpha_i)m_i c_i}{q_i f^c}, \tag{6}$$

where q_i is the number of CRBs MD i rents from MEC server, and f^c (in cycles/s) is the computing capacity of each CRB. Thus, the time consumption of computation offloading can be represented as

$$t_i^{\text{off}} = t_i^{\text{mec}} + t_i^{\text{trans}} = \frac{(1 - \alpha_i)m_i c_i}{q_i f^c} + \frac{(1 - \alpha_i)m_i}{r_i}. \tag{7}$$

In partial computation offloading, MD and MEC server cope with the task simultaneously. The total time and energy consumption of completing task T_i can be denoted as

$$t_i^{\text{total}} = \max\{\frac{\alpha_i m_i c_i}{f_i}, \frac{(1 - \alpha_i)m_i c_i}{q_i f^c} + \frac{(1 - \alpha_i)m_i}{r_i}\}. \tag{8}$$

$$e_i^{\text{total}} = \alpha_i m_i c_i k_i f_i^2 + \frac{(1 - \alpha_i)p_i m_i}{r_i}. \tag{9}$$

3   Computation Offloading and Pricing Scheme

3.1   Cost Minimization Computation Offloading for MDs

The cost function of MD i is defined as MD's payment for renting CRBs plus the consumed energy. Here, the consumed energy is transformed into monetary cost with λ_i, which represents the value of energy of MD i. Therefore, the cost function can be expressed as

$$C_i = \lambda_i e_i^{\text{total}} + s q_i t_i^{\text{mec}}, \tag{10}$$

where s (in cents/s) is the price per second for renting a CRB. Substituting (6) and (9) into (10), the cost function can be rewritten as

$$C_i(\alpha_i, f_i) = \lambda_i (\alpha_i m_i c_i k_i f_i^2 + \frac{p_i m_i (1 - \alpha_i)}{r_i}) + \frac{(1 - \alpha_i) m_i c_i s}{f^c}. \tag{11}$$

From (11), it is clear that once the service price s is given, C_i is affected by the local executing ratio α_i and frequency f_i. Therefore, α_i and f_i should be optimized. Thus, MD's cost minimization problem can be established as

$$\min_{\alpha_i, f_i} \quad C_i \tag{12a}$$

$$\text{s.t.} \quad t_i^{\text{total}} \leq t_i^{\text{max}}, \tag{12b}$$

$$0 \leq \alpha_i \leq 1, \tag{12c}$$

$$0 \leq f_i \leq f_i^{\text{max}}, \tag{12d}$$

where f_i^{max} is the largest computing speed of MD i. In the above problem, condition (12b) ensures the task can be finished within the deadline; (12c) limits the domain of α_i; and (12d) is the maximum local computation frequency constraint.

Based on (12b) and (12d), we have

$$\alpha_i \leq \frac{f_i^{\text{max}} t_i^{\text{max}}}{m_i c_i} \triangleq \alpha_i^{\text{u}}, \tag{13}$$

Thus, we have

$$\alpha_i^{\text{max}} = \min\{\alpha_i^{\text{u}}, 1\}, \tag{14}$$

Therefore, the new range of α_i is

$$0 \leq \alpha_i \leq \alpha_i^{\text{max}}. \tag{15}$$

From (11), we can know that $C_i(\alpha_i, f_i)$ increases monotonically with f_i. According to (12b), we have $t_i^{\text{local}} \leq t_i^{\text{max}}, t_i^{\text{off}} \leq t_i^{\text{max}}$ from which we can obtain $f_i \geq \frac{\alpha_i m_i c_i}{t_i^{\text{max}}}$ and $q_i \geq \frac{m_i c_i r_i (1 - \alpha_i)}{t_i^{\text{max}} r_i f^c - (1 - \alpha_i) m_i f^{\text{mec}}}$. Therefore, the optimal f_i is denoted as

$$f_i^*(\alpha_i) = \frac{\alpha_i m_i c_i}{t_i^{\text{max}}}. \tag{16}$$

The amount of CRBs requested by MD i is written as

$$q_i^* = \left\lceil \frac{m_i c_i r_i (1 - \alpha_i)}{t_i^{\max} r_i f^{\mathrm{c}} - (1 - \alpha_i) m_i f^{\mathrm{c}}} \right\rceil. \tag{17}$$

Taking (15) and (16) into (12a)–(12d), we can transform the problem into

$$\min_{\alpha_i} \quad C_i, \tag{18a}$$

$$\mathrm{s.t.}\, 0 \le \alpha_i \le \alpha_i^{\max}, \tag{18b}$$

where

$$C_i(\alpha_i) = \frac{k_i \lambda_i \alpha_i^3 m_i^3 c_i^3}{(t_i^{\max})^2} + \frac{\lambda_i p_i m_i (1 - \alpha_i)}{r_i} + \frac{(1 - \alpha_i) m_i c_i s}{f^{\mathrm{c}}}. \tag{19}$$

The first and second-order derivatives of C_i with respect to α_i can be denoted as

$$\frac{\partial C_i(\alpha_i)}{\partial \alpha_i} = \frac{3 k_i \lambda_i \alpha_i^2 m_i^3 c_i^3}{(t_i^{\max})^2} - \frac{\lambda_i p_i m_i}{r_i} - \frac{m_i c_i s}{f^{\mathrm{CRB}}}, \tag{20}$$

$$\frac{\partial C_i^2(\alpha_i)}{\partial \alpha_i^2} = \frac{6 k_i \lambda_i \alpha_i m_i^3 c_i^3}{(t_i^{\max})^2} \ge 0. \tag{21}$$

Let

$$\lim_{\alpha_i \to 0} \frac{\partial C_i(\alpha_i)}{\partial \alpha_i} = -\frac{\lambda_i p_i m_i}{r_i} - \frac{m_i c_i s}{f^{\mathrm{c}}} < 0, \tag{22}$$

$$\lim_{\alpha_i \to \alpha_i^{\max}} \frac{\partial C_i(\alpha_i)}{\partial \alpha_i} = \frac{3 k_i \lambda_i (\alpha_i^{\max})^2 m_i^3 c_i^3}{(t_i^{\max})^2} - \frac{\lambda_i p_i m_i}{r_i} - \frac{m_i c_i s}{f^{\mathrm{c}}}. \tag{23}$$

When (23) is smaller than zero, C_i is a decreasing function of α_i, the optimal local execution ratio is

$$\alpha_i^* = \alpha_i^{\max}. \tag{24}$$

If (23) is greater than zero, the cost function of MD i is a strict convex function of α_i, then

$$\alpha_i^* = \sqrt{\frac{\lambda_i p_i m_i f^{\mathrm{c}} (t_i^{\max})^2 + m_i c_i r_i s (t_i^{\max})^2}{3 r_i k_i \lambda_i m_i^3 c_i^3 f^{\mathrm{c}}}}. \tag{25}$$

Therefore, $C_i(\alpha_i)$ must have a minimum value when $0 \le \alpha_i \le \alpha_i^{\max}$. Now, we have obtained the optimal local execution ratio α_i^*. By taking it into (16) and (17), the local computing speed f_i^* and the number of CRBs MD should request q_i^* can be obtained.

3.2   Optimal Pricing Scheme for MEC Server

In the MEC offloading system, earn profit from computation offloading service is the motivation of MEC server. Thus, pricing strategy is very important to MEC server. We aim to design a dynamic pricing strategy for MEC server, where MEC server charges MDs according to the number of CRBs requested and the length of time occupied. Take the service cost into consideration, MEC server's revenue function can be given by

$$R(s) = (s - \varepsilon) \sum_{i=1}^{I} q_i t_i^{\text{mec}}. \tag{26}$$

where ε (in cents/s) is the cost to maintain CRB's service per second. Then, the revenue maximization problem is established as

$$\max_{s} \quad R \tag{27a}$$

$$\text{s.t. } 0 \leq \sum_{i=1}^{I} q_i \leq Q, \tag{27b}$$

$$s \geq 0, \tag{27c}$$

where Q is the maximum number of CRBs that MEC server can offer. In this problem, (27b) limits the total requested CRBs would not be more than Q, and (27c) guarantees the price is positive.

From (17) and (25), we can know that q_i^* is a decreasing function of s. It's obvious that when the service price s increases, MDs tend to request less CRBs from MEC server. As the number of CRBs is limited, we need to find the lowest price $s^{\min}$ that guarantees the requested CRBs would not be more than Q. In addition, we set $s^{\max} = 10 * \varepsilon$.

Inspired by the simulate anneal algorithm, we propose the following Optimal Pricing Algorithm. In the following algorithm, U and $U^{\min}$ are the initial and lowest temperature while g is the temperature decreasing factor. This algorithm runs while $U > U^{\min}$ holds. Firstly, the lowest price is got by step 2–7, where ω is a constant used to control the price. In step 8 and 9, MEC server obtains a random initial price s_1 ($s^{\min} < s_1 < s^{\max}$) and calculate the corresponding revenue according to MDs' offloading decisions. In step 11–13, we get the next price by $s_{n+1} = s_n + random$ and calculate R_{n+1}. In step 14–18, we compare R_n and R_{n+1}, if the revenue is improved, we get the new price s_{n+1} directly. If not improved, s_{n+1} can be used as new price if $P = e^{-\tau/U} > random$, where $\tau = R(n) - R(n+1)$. With this step, we can jump out of the local optimal price. As the current temperature is cooled by $U = g * U$ in each iteration, the iteration will end when $U < U^{\min}$.

Algorithm 1. Optimal Pricing Algorithm for MEC Server

1: **input:** s^{max}, Q, f^c, U, U^{min}, g, $n = 1$, ε
2: Set the initial service price as $s_0 = 0$ and announce vehicles
3: Calculate $\sum_{i=1}^{I} q_i$ according to MDs' reply
4: **while** $\sum_{i=1}^{I} q_i > Q$
5:     Increase the service price by $s = s + \omega$
6: **end while**
7: $s^{min} \leftarrow s$
8: Get the initial service price s_1 and announce MDs, $s^* \leftarrow s_1$
9: Calculate R_1 according to MDs' replies
10: **while** $U > U^{min}$
11:     Moves randomly to get a new service price $s_{n+1} = s_n + random$
12:     MDs calculate q_i^* based on s_{n+1} and reply to the server
13:     Calculate R_{n+1} by (26)
14:     **if** $R_{n+1} > R_n$
15:         $s^* \leftarrow s_{n+1}$
16:     **else if** $P > random$
17:         $s^* \leftarrow s_{n+1}$
18:     **end if**
19:     Announce s^* to MDs
20:     $U = g * U$
21:     $n = n + 1$
22: **end while**
23: **output:** s^*

---

4   Simulations

In this section, we present the simulation results of our computation offloading mechanism. We firstly list the simulation parameters used, then we discuss the experiment results.

4.1   Simulation Settings

We list the main parameter settings in Table 1.

4.2   Simulation Results

In this subsection, the simulation results of our proposed scheme is presented.

Figure 2 describes the relationship between the service price s and the number of CRBs required by MDs. When s increases from 0 cents/s to 3 cents/s, the number of CRBs rented by MDs decreases obviously. When s rises to an unacceptable value, MDs do not require any CRBs at all, which implies $\alpha_i = 1$.

Table 1. Simulation settings

Parameter	Description	Value
I	Number of MDs	3–6
m_i	Size of task	200 kB–1300 KB
c_i	Cycles needed per bit by task	600–1000 cycles/bit
$t_i^{\max}$	Latency constraint of task	5–10 s
$f_i^{\max}$	Maximum computing capacity of MD i	0.5–1 Gigacycles/s
p_i	Transmitting power of MD i	0.1–0.3 W
k	Local energy consumption coefficient	1×10^{-24}
λ_i	Energy-Money coefficient of MD i	1.5–2.4 cents/W
f^c	Computing capacity of CRB	0.1 Gigacycles/s
Q	Total number of CRBs	80
ε	MEC server's cost	0.3–1 cents/s

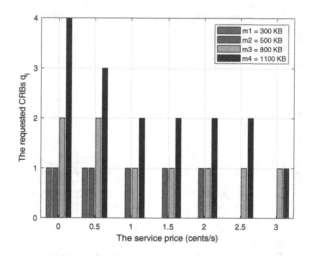

Fig. 2. The requested CRBs q_i versus service price s

The relationship between price s and revenue of MEC server is presented in Fig. 3. When $s = 0$ cents/s, the revenue of MEC server is not positive, which indicates the MEC server is in a loss state. Obviously, R rises with s in the beginning, after reaching the maximum value, R starts to decline with s. It's obvious that MEC server with higher service cost has relatively low revenue. For MEC server, reducing the service cost ε is an effective way to gain more profit.

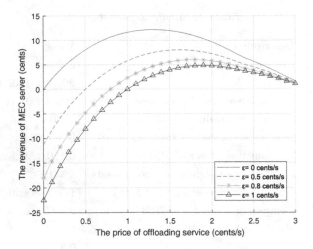

Fig. 3. The revenue R versus service price s

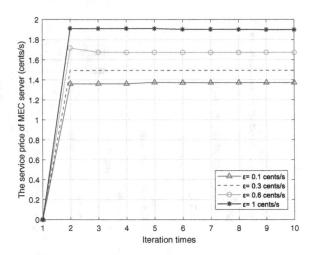

Fig. 4. Service price s versus iteration times

Figure 4 shows the service price got by the proposed Optimal Pricing Algorithm. As shown in the picture, the algorithm converges very fast, which implies that our proposed algorithm is very effective in pricing. When providing service to the same MDs, MEC server with higher cost has a higher service price correspondingly, which verifies the trend in Fig. 3.

In Fig. 5, we compare our computation scheme with other two schemes. (1) Local computation: MD computes the task locally and configures its local CPU speed to save cost. (2) Full computation offloading: MD chooses either local execution or full computation offloading according to the cost.

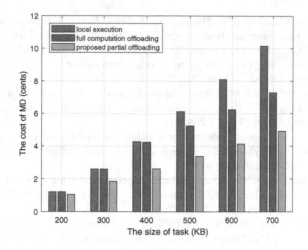

Fig. 5. Cost of MD i in different computing schemes

When the task size is not very large, the cost of the three execution mechanisms is similar. Nevertheless, the gap of cost between local execution and computation offloading becomes larger with the increase of task size. This is mainly because that the local energy is usually more valuable compared with the price of renting CRBs. It's obvious that our proposed offloading scheme keeps the lowest cost among the three schemes. Thus, we have proved the superiority of our proposed offloading strategy.

5   Conclusion

In this paper, we proposed a cost minimization offloading mechanism for MDs together with a price scheme for server. Firstly, we established the cost model of MDs. Then, the cost minimization partial offloading scheme was studied. After that, we formulated MEC server's revenue maximization problem and proposed the optimal pricing algorithm. Numerical results verified our scheme as compared to two benchmark schemes. In the future work, we will pay attention to the mobility of MDs.

Acknowledgements. This work is financially supported by the National Natural Science Foundation of China (NSFC) (Grant No. 61671072).

References

1. Huang, J., Xing, C., Wang, C.: Simultaneous wireless information and power transfer: technologies, applications, and research challenges. IEEE Commun. Mag. **55**(11), 26–32 (2017). https://doi.org/10.1109/MCOM.2017.1600806

2. Mao, Y., You, C., Zhang, J., Huang, K., Letaief, K.B.: A survey on mobile edge computing: the communication perspective. IEEE Commun. Surv. Tutor. **19**(4), 2322–2358 (2017). https://doi.org/10.1109/COMST.2017.2745201
3. Satyanarayanan, M.: The emergence of edge computing. Computer **50**(1), 30–39 (2017). https://doi.org/10.1109/MC.2017.9
4. Mach, P., Becvar, Z.: Mobile edge computing: a survey on architecture and computation offloading. IEEE Commun. Surv. Tutor. **19**(3), 1628–1656 (2017). https://doi.org/10.1109/COMST.2017.2682318
5. Zhang, K., et al.: Energy-efficient offloading for mobile edge computing in 5G heterogeneous networks. IEEE Access **4**, 5896–5907 (2016). https://doi.org/10.1109/ACCESS.2016.2597169
6. Kim, Y., Kwak, J., Chong, S.: Dual-side optimization for cost-delay tradeoff in mobile edge computing. IEEE Trans. Veh. Technol. **67**(2), 1765–1781 (2018). https://doi.org/10.1109/TVT.2017.2762423
7. Shang, B., Zhao, L., Chen, K., Chu, X.: An economic aspect of device-to-device assisted offloading in cellular networks. IEEE Trans. Wirel. Commun. **17**(4), 2289–2304 (2018). https://doi.org/10.1109/TWC.2018.2791518
8. Zhang, J., Xia, W., Yan, F., Shen, L.: Joint computation offloading and resource allocation optimization in heterogeneous networks with mobile edge computing. IEEE Access **6**, 19324–19337 (2018). https://doi.org/10.1109/ACCESS.2018.2819690
9. Ning, Z., Dong, P., Kong, X., Xia, F.: A cooperative partial computation offloading scheme for mobile edge computing enabled Internet of Things. IEEE Internet Things J. **6**(3), 4804–4814 (2019). https://doi.org/10.1109/JIOT.2018.2868616
10. Wang, Y., Sheng, M., Wang, X., Wang, L., Li, J.: Mobile-edge computing: partial computation offloading using dynamic voltage scaling. IEEE Trans. Wirel. Commun. **64**(10), 4268–4282 (2016). https://doi.org/10.1109/TCOMM.2016.2599530
11. Zhang, W., Wen, Y., Guan, K., Kilper, D., Luo, H., Wu, D.O.: Energy-optimal mobile cloud computing under stochastic wireless channel. IEEE Trans. Wirel. Commun. **12**(9), 4569–4581 (2013). https://doi.org/10.1109/TWC.2013.072513.121842
12. Chen, X., Jiao, L., Li, W., Fu, X.: Efficient multi-user computation offloading for mobile-edge cloud computing. IEEE/ACM Trans. Netw. **24**(5), 2795–2808 (2016). https://doi.org/10.1109/TNET.2015.2487344
13. Chen, M., Hao, Y.: Task offloading for mobile edge computing in software defined ultra-dense network. IEEE J. Sel. Areas Commun. **36**(3), 587–597 (2018). https://doi.org/10.1109/JSAC.2018.2815360

Dynamic Resource Allocation in High-Speed Railway Fog Radio Access Networks with Delay Constraint

Rui Wang[1,2,3]($\boxtimes$), Jun Wu[1], and Jun Yu[1]

[1] School of Electronics and Information Engineering, Tongji University,
Shanghai, China
{ruiwang,wujun,1610986}@tongji.edu.cn
[2] State Key Laboratory of Integrated Services Networks, Xidian University,
Xian, China
[3] Shanghai Institute of Intelligent Science and Technology, Tongji University,
Shanghai, China

Abstract. By applying caching resource at the remote radio heads (RRHs), the fog radio access network (Fog-RAN) has been considered as an promising wireless architecture in the future network to reduce the transmission delay and release the heavy burden of backhaul link for huge data delivery. In this paper, we propose to use the Fog-RAN to assist the data transmission in the high-speed railway scenario. In specific, we investigate the dynamic resource allocation in high-speed railway Fog-RAN systems by considering the delay constraint. The instantaneous power allocation at the RRHs and the instantaneous content delivery rate over the backhaul links are jointly optimized with an aim to minimize the total power consumed at the RRHs and over the backhaul links. An alternating optimization (AO) approach is used to find solutions of the instantaneous power and instantaneous content delivery rate in two separate subproblems. The closed-form solutions are derived in two subproblems under certain special conditions. Simulation results demonstrate that the proposed dynamic resource allocation is significantly superior to the constant resource allocation scheme.

Keywords: Fog radio access network · High-speed railway · Mobility · Power allocation

1 Introduction

Cloud radio access network (C-RAN) has been considered a promising wireless access network architecture to deal with the confronted explosive amount of traffic in the current cellular network to carry out the goal of the fifth generation (5G) wireless communication [1]. Thanks to the centralized wireless resource control ability at the base band unit (BBU) pool, the C-RAN can allocate the wireless resource of the network in a more efficient way. In C-RAN system,

© ICST Institute for Computer Sciences, Social Informatics and Telecommunications Engineering 2020
Published by Springer Nature Switzerland AG 2020. All Rights Reserved
H. Gao et al. (Eds.): ChinaCom 2019, LNICST 312, pp. 15–32, 2020.
https://doi.org/10.1007/978-3-030-41114-5_2

the uplink/downlink data transmission between BBU and the rate radio heads (RRHs) uses the backhaul links. However, the capacity of the backhaul links is still insufficient. As a result, when transmission data becomes large, the ginormous content demand creates heavy burden on backhaul links. To overcome this limitation, the fog radio access network (Fog-RAN) is proposed [2]. Compared to the C-RAN, certain caching resources are employed at RRHs. By caching some popular contents at RRHs, the requested data by users can be directly served by edge RRHs. This greatly alleviates the heavy traffic load pressure over the backhaul links and a significant portion of delay could be declined.

Although Fog-RAN is more efficient than C-RAN to achieve low-latency transmission and alleviate huge traffic burden on backhaul links, the configuration of network resources, including caching, power, computation etc., need further optimization to achieve better performance. A good number of studies have already been reported in this direction. For example, in literature [3], the authors investigated the problem of maximizing the delivery rate of Fog-RAN through content prefetching and improved precoding scheme. In literature [4], the authors investigated a proactive probabilistic caching optimization in wireless Fog-RAN by maximizing the successful transmission probability (STP). The authors in [5] studied the subchannel assignment and power control in mmWave-based fog radio access networks. In literature [6], the authors studied sparse beamforming design in a multicast Fog-RAN system.

All the aforementioned contributions show that great efforts have been paid to overcome the challenges of Fog-RAN architecture. However, the investigations are still insufficient as more different application scenarios may emerge in the upcoming 5G network domain. One important application is to employ the Fog-RAN architecture to assist the huge data transmission in high speed railway (HSR) scenario [7]. Recently, HSR is developing rapidly all over the world, especially in China. How to provide a reliable, high data rate and low latency HSR wireless communication has been identified as one of most important technologies needing to break though in the development. Moreover, HSR wireless communication has been categorized as a typical scenario in future 5G systems [8]. Undoubtedly, the Fog-RAN can be treated as an promising solution.

Different from traditional wireless communication problem, HSR wireless communication has to take the high-speed mobility condition into account, which greatly challenges the corresponding key technologies studies. High-speed mobility has already been considered in traditional wireless communication studies. For example, the authors in [9] studied a pilot aided joint channel and frequency offset estimation. In [10], the authors investigated the effect of distributed antenna techniques in HSR communications. In [11], a quality-of-service (QoS) based achievable rate region was characterized and a QoS distinguished power allocation algorithm was proposed to achieve the largest achievable rate region. In [12], the authors studied how to optimize the power to match user-data arrival process and time-varying channel service process with a delay constraint. The work in [13] studied the location-fair beamforming design by considering the Doppler shift. However, to the best of our knowledge, there are limited works studying the Fog-RAN in the HSR scenarios, which motivates the study of this work.

In this paper, we propose to use the Fog-RAN architecture to assist the data transmission in the HSR wireless communications to achieve low latency service. In the considered Fog-RAN system, the train is served by multiple RRHs and each RRH node has a local cache, which stores certain popular contents. When the contents requested by passengers has been cached at a given RRH, this RRH can directly serve the train; otherwise, the RRH needs to fetch the content from BBU pool via backhaul link. We investigate the dynamic resource allocation at Fog-RAN with an aim to minimize total power cost, including the power cost at RRHs and over backhaul links. The instantaneous power allocation at the RRHs and the instantaneous content delivery rate over backhaul links are simultaneously optimized under transmission delay constraint. By adopting smoothed l_0-norm approximation and other techniques, we propose an alternating optimization (AO) approach to find solutions of the instantaneous power and instantaneous content delivery rate in two separate subproblems. To reduce the computational complexity, we derive the closed-form solutions in two subproblem under certain special conditions. A constant resource allocation scheme is also provided as a benchmark to assess the performance of dynamic resource allocation scheme. Simulation results verify our analysis and demonstrate that the proposed dynamic resource allocation is significantly superior to the constant resource allocation scheme.

2   System Model

2.1   Channel Model

In a Fog-RAN served high speed railway wireless communication systems as illustrated in Fig. 1, BBU performs the resource allocation and the RRH selection to archive a high efficiency transmission. We consider the downlink transmission of a Fog-RAN system where a high speed train is served by uniformly deployed base stations (i.e., RRHs) along one side of the railway with equal intervals d. Assume that the distance between each RRH and railway is d_0, and the height of antenna equipped at each RRH is h_0. A high-speed train is traveling along the line railway with a constant velocity v_0. At the system time $t = 0$, the train passes the original point 0, and during time interval $t \in (0, T]$, the train is served by the same set of by N RRHs. Let $\mathcal{N} = \{1, ..., N\}$ denote the set of RRHs. The coordinate of the n-th RRH is denoted as (l_n, d_0). Then we can obtain the transmission distance between the n-th RRH antenna and the access point (AP) at train at time t as $d_n(t) = \sqrt{(v_0 t - l_n)^2 + d_0^2 + h_0^2}$ with $t \in (0, T]$. After the time $t = T$, the BBU will coordinate the handoff process and the train will be served by another set of N RRHs. Since the transmission process along the time is periodic, we only need to investigate the transmission problem during $t \in (0, T]$. Here we assume that the users in the train connect to the RRHs through the help of AP equipped on the roof the train to avoid severe penetration loss and large amounts of handoff operations. And the connection between the users and

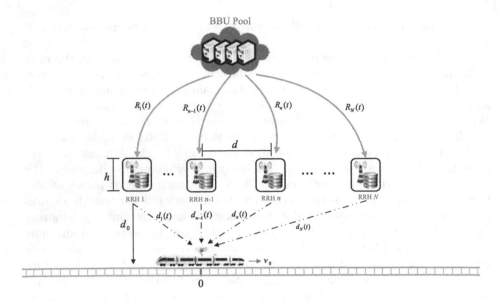

Fig. 1. Fog-RAN based high-speed railway communication system.

the AP is based on some other traditional reliable access networks, e.g. Wi-Fi etc. Therefore, in this study, we only focus on the transmission process between RRHs and AP.

It is supposed that the required data by the passengers in the train are grouped to F different contents. Contents have the same size of Q. We assume that the local storage size of RRH n is F_n and $F_n < QF$, which means that a RRH cannot store all the contents. Therefore, we define a cache placement matrix $C \in \mathbb{B}^{N \times F}$, where $c_{n,f} = 1$ means that the content f is cached in RRH n and $c_{n,f} = 0$ means the opposite. Note that $\forall n, \sum_{f=1}^{F} c_{n,f} Q \leq F_n$. At the beginning of each transmission time interval, the train submits a content request. According to the caching status of all RRHs, the BBU performs the dynamic resource allocation. Denote $x(t)$ the transmit signal from RRHs and $y_n(t)$ the received signal at the AP sent from RRH n. $x(t)$ can be considered as a stochastic process with zero mean and unit variance. Then, the baseband-equivalent instantaneous-time signal transmission between RRH n and AP can be represented as

$$y_n(t) = \sqrt{P_n(t)} h_n(t) x(t) + n_n(t) \tag{1}$$

where $P_n(t)$ is instantaneous transmit power at RRH n, $h_n(t)$ represents the instantaneous channel state information, and $n_n(t)$ denotes the additive complex cycle symmetric Gaussian noise at AP following a distribution of $CN(0, \sigma^2)$. It is noted that we here assume that the signal transmissions from RRHs are over orthogonal bandwidth, then at the receiver, maximal ratio combiner can be used to combine the signals. The corresponding instantaneous information capacity at time t can be expressed as

$$C(t) = B \log_2 \left(1 + \sum_{n=1}^{N} \frac{P_n(t)|h_n(t)|^2}{\sigma^2} \right) \tag{2}$$

where B is the bandwidth allocated for each channel between a RRH and the AP.

Consider that in HSR scenario, the train always runs in plain areas with less scatters. In this case, line-of-sight (LOS) component dominates the channel gain. Therefore, in this work a simple propagation attenuation model, i.e., $h_n(t) = \sqrt{\frac{G}{d_n^\alpha(t)}}$, is employed.

2.2 Problem Formulation

Our objective aims to minimize the total network power cost including total RRH power consumption and backhaul power consumption, while satisfying the delay constraint and individual RRH power constraint. Assume that the train request content F_f. If content F_f has been cached at RRH n, RRH n can directly transmit it to the AP without costing backhaul. Otherwise, content F_f needs to be fetched from the BBU via backhaul links. Assuming that instantaneous content delivery rate at time t over backhaul link connecting BBU and RRH n is $R_n(t)$, the total power cost for backhaul content delivery can be represented by

$$\text{Cost}_b = \int_0^T \sum_{n=1}^N \beta \left\| \int_0^T P_n(t)dt \right\|_0 (1 - c_{n,f}) R_n(t) dt. \tag{3}$$

In (3), we use term $| \int_0^T P_n(t)dt |_0$ to indicate the active RRH and term $1 - c_{n,f}$ to indicate the RRHs which do not cache the content F_f. It is noted that only the active RRHs which do not cache the content needs to cost backhaul links. Parameter β in (3) represents the ratio relationship between the rate $R_n(t)$ and the power cost.

On the other hand, the total power consumed by the RRHs over time period $(0, T]$ is represented by

$$\text{Cost}_p = \int_0^T \sum_{n \in \mathcal{N}} P_n(t) dt. \tag{4}$$

As a result, the network total power cost can be modeled as

$$\text{Cost} = \text{Cost}_b + \text{Cost}_p. \tag{5}$$

Regarding the delay consideration, as Fog-RAN based HSR system consists of two hops. One hop refers to the backhaul data transmission and the other refers to the content delivery over the wireless channel between the RRHs and the AP. Denote the set of active RRHs which do not cache content F_f as $\Theta = \{n ||| \int_0^T P_n(t)dt||_0 (1 - c_{n,f}) \neq 0\}$. The instantaneous transmission delay can be represented as

$$\tau_f(t) = \frac{1}{\min\{C(t), \min_{m \in \Theta} R_m(t)\}}. \tag{6}$$

In summary, the overall resource allocation problem is formulated as follows:

$$\min_{P_n(t), R_n(t)} \text{Cost} \tag{7a}$$

$$s.t \quad \frac{1}{T} \int_0^T P_n(t)dt \leq P_{n,\text{avg}} \quad \forall n \in \mathcal{N} \tag{7b}$$

$$\tau_f(t) \leq \tau_{\max} \tag{7c}$$

$$\int_0^T C(t)dt \geq Q, \quad \int_0^T R_n(t)dt \geq Q, n \in \Theta \tag{7d}$$

$$R_n(t) \leq b_n, \quad P_n(t) \geq 0 \tag{7e}$$

where (7b) indicates the average power constraint of each RRH, (7c) represents the instantaneous transmission delay constraint, (7d) means that the content needs to sent out though the network during the time period of T, constraint (7e) indicates that for each backhaul link, we have maximum instantaneous transmission rate, and for each RRH, instantaneous power should not be smaller than zero. Our final objective is to minimize the overall network cost by optimizing the instantaneous power at each RRH and the instantaneous transmission rate over each backhaul link.

3 Dynamic Resource Optimization for HSR with Delay Constraint

In this section, we try to solve problem (7) by using proper optimization techniques. It is noted that different from traditional resource allocation problem, the considered dynamic optimization problem involves integration, which makes the optimization more challenging. Also, as we instantaneously optimize the power at each RRH and the content delivery rates over backhaul links, optimization (7) is a non-convex problem. To find an efficient solution, we apply the alternating optimization to decouple $P_n(t)$ and $R_n(t)$ in optimization (7). Our contribution lies in that in each subproblem, we can approximately find the optimal solution.

3.1 Solving Power $P_n(t)$

With given $R_n(t)$, we optimize the power allocation by solving the following problem

$$\min_{P_n(t)} \text{Cost} \tag{8a}$$

$$s.t \quad \frac{1}{T} \int_0^T P_n(t)dt \leq P_{n,\text{avg}} \quad \forall n \in \mathcal{N} \tag{8b}$$

$$\frac{1}{C(t)} \leq \tau_{\max} \tag{8c}$$

$$\int_0^T C(t)dt \geq Q \tag{8d}$$

$$R_n(t) \leq b_n, \quad P_n(t) \geq 0 \tag{8e}$$

In (8), we observe that all constraints are convex with respect to $P_n(t)$. However, since Cost_b in the objective function includes a nonconvex l_0-norm function, the overall problem (8) is nonconvex. To deal with this problem, we approximate the discontinuous l_0-norm with a continuous smooth log-function, i.e., $||x||_0 \approx \frac{\log(\frac{x}{\theta}+1)}{\log(\frac{1}{\theta}+1)}$. Here the introduced parameter θ can control the smoothness of the approximation. In general, a larger value of θ leads to a smoother function but a worse approximation and vice versa. With this approximation, the term Cost_b in the objection function of (8) can be approximated as

$$\text{Cost}_b \approx c\beta \sum_{n=1}^{N}(1 - c_{n,f}) \log\left(\frac{\int_0^T P_n(t)dt + \theta}{\theta}\right) \int_0^T R_n(t)dt. \tag{9}$$

where $c = \frac{1}{\log(\frac{1}{\theta}+1)}$. Then the objective function in (8) changes to

$$\text{Cost}_{\text{appro1}} \approx \int_0^T \sum_{n \in \mathcal{N}} P_n(t)dt + \sum_{n \in \mathcal{N}} b_n \log\left(\frac{\int_0^T P_n(t)dt + \theta}{\theta}\right). \tag{10}$$

where $b_n = c\int_0^T \beta(1 - c_{n,f})R_n(t)dt$.

In (10), it is found that the objective function is still nonconvex as it is the sum of convex function and a concave function, which cannot be solved directly. We next use the majorization-minimization (MM) algorithm to further approximate it. The key idea is to minimize an upper bound. As the logarithmic function is a concave one, it is upper bounded by its first-order Taylor expansion. In MM algorithm, an optimal solution of problem (10) can be obtained by minimizing the upper-bounded function of objective in an iterative manner.

$$\text{Cost}_{\text{appro2}} \approx \int_0^T \sum_{n \in \mathcal{N}} P_n(t)dt + \sum_{n \in \mathcal{N}} b_n \left[\log\left(\frac{\theta + \int_0^T P_n^0(t)dt}{\theta}\right) \right.$$
$$\left. + \frac{\int_0^T P_n(t)dt - \int_0^T P_n^0(t)dt}{\theta + \int_0^T P_n^0(t)dt}\right] \tag{11}$$

where $\int_0^T P_n^0(t)dt$ is basis point of the Taylor expansion of $\log\left(\frac{\int_0^T P_n(t)dt+\theta}{\theta}\right)$.

Let $k_n = 1 + b_n\frac{1}{\theta+\int_0^T P_n^0(t)dt}$, we transfer (8) to the following MM problem:

$$\min_{P_n(t)} \int_0^T \left(\sum_{n\in\mathcal{N}} k_n P_n(t)\right) dt \tag{12a}$$

$$s.t \quad \frac{1}{T}\int_0^T P_n(t)dt \le P_{n,\text{avg}} \quad \forall n\in\mathcal{N} \tag{12b}$$

$$C(t) \ge \frac{1}{\tau_{\max}} \tag{12c}$$

$$\int_0^T C(t)dt \ge Q \tag{12d}$$

$$P_n(t) \ge 0 \tag{12e}$$

To solve (12), we first give the following theorem.

Theorem 1. *If $\frac{T}{\tau_{\max}} \ge Q$, we have $C(t) = \frac{1}{\tau_{\max}}$ at the optimal solution and optimal solution of (12) can be represented as*

$$P_n(t) = \beta_n \tilde{a}_n(t), \quad n = \{2,3,\cdots,N\}$$
$$P_1(t) = \tilde{a}_0(t) - \sum_{n=2}^N \tilde{a}_n(t)P_n(t) \tag{13}$$

where $\tilde{a}_n(t)$ is defined in (16), and optimal β_n with ordered form is given by

$$\beta_{[n]} = \begin{cases} \frac{TP_{[n],\text{avg}}}{A_{[n]}} & \text{if } n \le m-1 \\ \frac{b}{k_{[n]}A_{[n]}} & n = m \\ 0 & \text{Otherwise} \end{cases} \tag{14}$$

where $\beta_{[n]}$ is defined in (22), m and b are defined in (23).

Proof. It is found that if $\frac{T}{\tau_{\max}} \ge Q$, constraint (12d) is redundant as it must be satisfied if constraint (12c) is satisfied. In this case, constraint (12c) is active. Otherwise, we can always scale $P_n(t)$ using a positive and less than 1 value to activate constraint (12c) and simultaneously decreases the value of the objective function. With above analysis, problem (12) can be equivalently rewritten as:

$$\min_{P_n(t)} \int_0^T \left(\sum_{n\in\mathcal{N}} k_n P_n(t)\right) dt \tag{15a}$$

$$s.t \quad \int_0^T P_n(t)dt \le TP_{n,\text{avg}} \quad \forall n\in\mathcal{N} \tag{15b}$$

$$B\log_2\left(1 + \sum_{n\in\mathcal{N}} \frac{GP_n(t)}{d_n(t)^\alpha\sigma^2}\right) = \frac{1}{\tau_{\max}} \tag{15c}$$

$$P_n(t) \ge 0 \tag{15d}$$

To proceed, we re-express constraint (15c) as $\sum_{n=1}^{N} a_n(t)P_n(t) = 2^{\frac{1}{B\tau_{\max}}}$ where $a_n(t) = \frac{G}{d_n(t)^{\alpha}\sigma^2}$. With this relationship between $P_n(t)$, we have

$$P_1(t) = \tilde{a}_0(t) - \sum_{n=2}^{N} \tilde{a}_n(t)P_n(t) \tag{16}$$

where $\tilde{a}_0(t) = \frac{1}{a_1(t)}(2^{\frac{1}{B\tau_{\max}}} - 1)$ and $\tilde{a}_n(t) = \frac{a_n(t)}{a_1(t)}$. Substituting (16) into (15), we have

$$\min_{P_n(t)} \int_0^T \left(\sum_{n=2}^{N} k_n P_n(t) \right) dt + \int_0^T \left(k_1 \tilde{a}_0(t) - \sum_{n=2}^{N} k_1 \tilde{a}_n(t)P_n(t) \right) dt \tag{17a}$$

$$s.t \int_0^T P_n(t)dt \le TP_{n,\text{avg}} \quad \forall n \in \{2, 3, \cdots, N\} \tag{17b}$$

$$\int_0^T \left(\tilde{a}_0(t) - \sum_{n=2}^{N} \tilde{a}_n(t)P_n(t) \right) dt \le TP_{1,\text{avg}} \tag{17c}$$

$$P_n(t) \ge 0 \tag{17d}$$

From problem (17), we see that at the optimal solution, for given average power, the term $\int_0^T \tilde{a}_n(t)P_n(t)dt$ should be as large as possible. To obtain the optimal solution, using Cauchy-Schwarz inequality, we have

$$\int_0^T \tilde{a}_n(t)P_n(t)dt \le \sqrt{\int_0^T \tilde{a}_n^2(t)dt \int_0^T P_n^2(t)dt} \tag{18}$$

where the equality succeeds when $P_n(t) = \beta_n \tilde{a}_n(t)$ with β_n being an variable to control the average consumed power. With this observation, finding the optimal solution of problem (17) reduces to finding optimal variables of β_n via solving

$$\min_{\beta_n} \sum_{n=2}^{N} (k_n A_n - k_1 B_n) \beta_n \tag{19a}$$

$$s.t \ 0 \le \beta_n \le \frac{TP_{n,\text{avg}}}{A_n} \quad \forall n \in \{2, 3, \cdots, N\} \tag{19b}$$

$$\int_0^T \tilde{a}_0(t)dt - TP_{1,\text{avg}} \le \sum_{n=2}^{N} \beta_n B_n \le \int_0^T \tilde{a}_0(t)dt \tag{19c}$$

where $A_n = \int_0^T \tilde{a}_n(t)dt$ and $B_n = \int_0^T \tilde{a}_n^2(t)dt$. It is observed that problem (19) is a linear programming which can efficiently solved by interior point algorithm. We next derive the optimal analytical solution. It is noted that if ignoring constraint (19c), the optimal solution can be represented as

$$\beta_n = \begin{cases} \frac{TP_{n,\text{avg}}}{A_n} & \text{if } \ \text{Sign}(k_n A_n - k_1 B_n) < 0 \\ 0 & \text{Otherwise} \end{cases} \tag{20}$$

If the solution given in (20) satisfies constraint (19c), it is the optimal solution of (19). Otherwise, we should increase the values of β_n with corresponding $\text{Sign}(k_n A_n - k_1 B_n) > 0$ if $\sum_{n=2}^{N} \beta_n B_n < \int_0^T \tilde{a}_0(t)dt - TP_{1,\text{avg}}$ to make $\sum_{n=2}^{N} \beta_n B_n = \int_0^T \tilde{a}_0(t)dt - TP_{1,\text{avg}}$; or we should decrease the values of β_n with corresponding $\text{Sign}(k_n A_n - k_1 B_n) < 0$ if $\sum_{n=2}^{N} \beta_n B_n > \int_0^T \tilde{a}_0(t)dt$ to make $\sum_{n=2}^{N} \beta_n B_n = \int_0^T \tilde{a}_0(t)dt$. Then optimal β_n in (19) can be found by solving

$$\min_{\beta_n} \sum_{n=2}^{N} k_n A_n \beta_n \tag{21a}$$

$$s.t \ \ 0 \le \beta_n \le \frac{TP_{n,\text{avg}}}{A_n} \quad \forall n \in \{2, 3, \cdots, N\} \tag{21b}$$

$$\sum_{n=2}^{N} \beta_n B_n = a \tag{21c}$$

where $a = \int_0^T \tilde{a}_0(t)dt - TP_{1,\text{avg}}$ or $\int_0^T \tilde{a}_0(t)dt$ depending on the previous analysis. By replacing the variable β_n by a new variable $\beta'_n = k_n A_n \beta_n$, we transfer problem (21) to the one given by (19) can be found by solving

$$\min_{\beta_n} \sum_{n=2}^{N} \beta'_n \tag{22a}$$

$$s.t \ \ 0 \le \beta'_n \le \frac{k_n A_n TP_{n,\text{avg}}}{A_n} \quad \forall n \in \{2, 3, \cdots, N\} \tag{22b}$$

$$\sum_{n=2}^{N} \beta'_n \frac{B_n}{k_n A_n} = a \tag{22c}$$

To find the optimal solution of (22), we reorder $\left\{ \frac{B_n}{k_n A_n} \right\}$ as $\frac{B_{[2]}}{k_{[2]} A_{[2]}} \ge \frac{B_{[3]}}{k_{[3]} A_{[3]}} \ge \cdots \ge \frac{B_{[N]}}{k_{[N]} A_{[N]}}$. The optimal solution of $\beta'_{[n]}$ can be represented as

$$\beta'_{[n]} = \begin{cases} \frac{k_{[n]} A_{[n]} TP_{[n],\text{avg}}}{A_{[n]}} & \text{if } n \le m - 1 \\ b & n = m \\ 0 & \text{Otherwise} \end{cases} \tag{23}$$

where m is the smallest integer ensuring $\sum_{[n]=2}^{m} \frac{B_{[n]} TP_{[n],\text{avg}}}{A_{[n]}} > a$ and $b = a - \sum_{[n]=2}^{m-1} \frac{B_{[n]} TP_{[n],\text{avg}}}{A_{[n]}}$. This completes the proof of Theorem 1.

For s special case where $N = 1$, Lemma 1 reduces to the following lemma.

Lemma 1. *If $\frac{T}{\tau_{\max}} \ge Q$ and $N = 1$, we have $C(t) = \frac{1}{\tau_{\max}}$ at the optimal solution and optimal solution of (12) can be represented as*

$$P_1(t) = \left(2^{\frac{1}{B\tau_{\max}}} - 1 \right) \frac{d_1^{\alpha}(t)\sigma^2}{G}. \tag{24}$$

Proof. When $N = 1$, problem (12) can be written as

$$\min_{P_1(t)} \int_0^T \left(k_1 P_1(t) \right) dt \tag{25a}$$

$$s.t \quad \frac{1}{T} \int_0^T P_1(t) dt \leq P_{1,\text{avg}} \quad \forall n \in \mathcal{N} \tag{25b}$$

$$C(t) = \frac{1}{\tau_{\max}} \tag{25c}$$

$$P_1(t) \geq 0 \tag{25d}$$

If the problem is feasible, the solution is determined by constraint (25c), which completes the proof of Lemma 1.

If condition $\frac{T}{\tau_{\max}} \geq Q$ is not satisfied, the conclusions presented in Theorem 1 and Lemma 1 are not applicable. To find the solution, we decompose the power $P_n(t) = P_{n,1}(t) + P_{n,2}(t)$, where $P_{n,1}(t)$ is used to satisfy

$$\min_{P_{n,1}(t)} \int_0^T \left(\sum_{n \in \mathcal{N}} k_n P_{n,1}(t) \right) dt \tag{26a}$$

$$s.t \quad \frac{1}{T} \int_0^T P_{n,1}(t) dt \leq P_{n,\text{avg}} \quad \forall n \in \mathcal{N} \tag{26b}$$

$$B \log_2 \left(1 + \sum_{n=1}^N \frac{G P_{n,1}(t)}{d_n^\alpha(t)\sigma^2} \right) = \frac{1}{\tau_{\max}} \tag{26c}$$

$$P_{n,1}(t) \geq 0 \tag{26d}$$

It is noted that conclusions presented in Theorem 1 and Lemma 1 can be used to find $P_{n,1}(t)$. After determining optimal $P_{n,1}(t)$, denoted by $P_{n,1}^*(t)$, $P_{n,2}(t)$ can found by solving

$$\min_{P_{n,2}(t)} \int_0^T \left(\sum_{n \in \mathcal{N}} k_n P_{n,2}(t) \right) dt \tag{27a}$$

$$s.t \quad \frac{1}{T} \int_0^T P_{n,2}(t) dt \leq b_n(t) \quad \forall n \in \mathcal{N} \tag{27b}$$

$$\int_0^T B \log_2 \left(c_n(t) + \sum_{n=1}^N \frac{G P_{n,2}(t)}{d_n^\alpha(t)\sigma^2} \right) dt \geq Q \tag{27c}$$

$$P_{n,2}(t) \geq 0 \tag{27d}$$

where $b_n(t) = P_{n,\text{avg}} - \frac{1}{T} \int_0^T P_{n,1}^*(t) dt$ and $c_n(t) = 1 + \sum_{n=1}^N \frac{G P_{n,1}^*(t)}{d_n^\alpha(t)\sigma^2}$. As $P_{n,2}(t)$ is non-negative, constraint (12c) must be satisfied when solving $P_{n,2}(t)$ and thus it can be ignored.

It is easy to observe that problem (27) is a convex problem. To get the optimal solution, we next develop a algorithm based on Karush-Kuhn-Tucher (KKT) conditions. To proceed, we first present the Lagrangian function given as

$$L = \int_0^T \left(\sum_{n \in \mathcal{N}} \left(k_n P_{n,2}(t) + \mu_{1,n}(P_{n,2}(t) - Tb_n(t)) \right) \right.$$
$$\left. - \mu_2 \left(B \log_2(c_n(t) + \sum_{n=1}^N \frac{GP_{n,2}(t)}{d_n^\alpha(t)\sigma^2}) - Q \right) \right) dt$$

(28)

where $\mu_{1,n}$ and μ_2 are non-negative multiplier related to constraints (27b) and (27c), respectively. To minimize the Lagrangian function, it is necessary to differentiate the Lagrangian function with respect to $P_{n,2}(t)$ and set the derivative to zero for each time t, that is

$$\frac{\partial L}{\partial P_{n,2}(t)} = k_n + \mu_{1,n} - \frac{\mu_2 B}{\log 2} \frac{\frac{G}{d_n(t)^\alpha \sigma^2}}{c_n(t) + \sum_{n \in \mathcal{N}} \frac{GP_{n,2}(t)}{d_n(t)^\alpha \sigma^2} - Q} = 0$$

(29)

By combining with the constraint (27d), we can obtain the solution given by

$$P_{n,2}(t) = \left[\left(\frac{\mu_2 GB}{\log 2 d_n(t)^\alpha \sigma^2 (k_n + \mu_1)} + Q - c_n(t) - \sum_{m \neq n}^N \frac{GP_{m,2}(t)}{d_m(t)^\alpha \sigma^2} \right) \right.$$
$$\left. \times \frac{d_n(t)^\alpha \sigma^2}{G}, 0 \right]^+ .$$

(30)

(30) shows that $P_{n,2}(t)$ with different n are coupled with each other, the final solution of $P_{n,2}(t)$ can be obtained by iterative update them until convergence. During the iteration, Lagrangian multipliers $\mu_{1,n}$ and μ_2 can be obtained via subgradient technique.

3.2   Solving Content Delivery Rate $R_n(t)$

For given $P_n(t)$, we next optimize the content delivery rate $R_n(t)$ over backhaul link by solving

$$\min_{R_n(t)} \int_0^T \sum_{n \in \mathcal{N}} E(t) R_n(t) dt$$

(31a)

$$s.t \quad \frac{1}{\min_{n \in \Theta} R_n(t)} \leq \tau_{\max}$$

(31b)

$$\int_0^T R_n(t) dt \geq Q, n \in \Theta$$

(31c)

$$0 \leq R_n(t) \leq b_n$$

(31d)

where $E(t) = \beta || \int_0^T P_n(t) dt ||_0 (1 - c_{n,f})$. The optimal solution is given in the following lemma.

Lemma 2. *For problem* (31), *if* $\frac{T}{\tau_{\max}}$, *the optimal solution is*

$$\begin{cases} R_n(t) = \frac{1}{\tau_{\max}}, & n \in \Theta \\ R_n(t) = 0, & n \notin \Theta \end{cases} \tag{32}$$

Otherwise, the optimal solution is

$$\begin{cases} R_n(t) = \gamma \frac{1}{\tau_{\max}}, & n \in \Theta \\ R_n(t) = 0, & n \notin \Theta \end{cases} \tag{33}$$

where γ is chosen to activate constraint (31c).

Proof. To find optimal $R_n(t)$, we rewrite problem (31) as

$$\min_{R_n(t)} \int_0^T \sum_{n \in \mathcal{N}} E(t) R_n(t) dt \tag{34a}$$

$$s.t \ \ R_n(t) \geq \frac{1}{\tau_{\max}}, n \in \Theta \tag{34b}$$

$$\int_0^T R_n(t) dt \geq Q, n \in \Theta \tag{34c}$$

$$0 \leq R_n(t) \leq b_n \tag{34d}$$

If condition $\frac{T}{\tau_{\max}}$ is met, constraint in (34c) is redundant. The optimal solution is to activate constraint (34b) with the optimal solution given in (32). Otherwise, the optimal $R_n(t)$ should activate constraint (34c) with the optimal solution given in (33).

4 Invariant Resource Optimization for HSR with Delay Constraint

As another simple power allocation scheme, we consider a constant power optimization design where power does not vary with the channel. In this case, the overall optimization problem is modified as

$$\min_{P_n, R_n(t)} T \sum_{n=1}^N P_n + \int_0^T \sum_{n=1}^N \beta \|P_n\|_0 (1 - c_{n,f}) R_n(t) dt \tag{35a}$$

$$s.t \ 0 \leq P_n \leq P_{n,\text{avg}} \ \ \forall n \in \mathcal{N} \tag{35b}$$

$$\frac{1}{\min\{C(t), \min_{m \in \Theta} R_m(t)\}} \leq \tau_{\max} \tag{35c}$$

$$\int_0^T C(t) dt \geq Q, \ \int_0^T R_n(t) dt \geq Q, n \in \Theta \tag{35d}$$

$$R_n(t) \leq b_n \tag{35e}$$

where $\Theta = \{n| \ \|P_n\|_0 (1 - c_{n,f}) \neq 0\}$ and $C(t) = B \log_2 \left(1 + \sum_{n=1}^N \frac{G P_n}{d_n(t)^\alpha \sigma^2}\right)$. The alternating optimization approach is also used here to jointly solve P_n and

$R_n(t)$ in an iterative way. For given P_n, the optimization of $R_n(t)$ is the same with the dynamic case. In what follows, we mainly focus on the optimization of P_n by solving

$$\min_{P_n} \sum_{n=1}^{N} k'_n P_n \tag{36a}$$

$$s.t \ \ 0 \le P_n \le P_{n,\text{avg}} \ \ \forall n \in \mathcal{N} \tag{36b}$$

$$\frac{1}{C(t)} \le \tau_{\max} \tag{36c}$$

$$\int_0^T C(t) dt \ge Q \tag{36d}$$

where $k'_n = T + \frac{1}{\log(1/\theta+1)} \frac{\beta(1-c_{n,f}) \int_0^T R_n(t) dt}{\theta + P_n^0}$ with P_n^0 being a is basis point of the Taylor expansion.

To solve (36), we consider two specific cases. If $\frac{T}{\tau_{\max}} \ge Q$, we have $C(t) = \frac{1}{\tau_{\max}}$. Then constraint (36d) is redundant. P_n can be found by solving

$$\min_{P_n} \sum_{n=1}^{N} k'_n P_n \tag{37a}$$

$$s.t \ \ 0 \le P_n \le P_{n,\text{avg}} \ \ \forall n \in \mathcal{N} \tag{37b}$$

$$\sum_{n=1}^{N} \frac{GP_n}{d_n(t)^\alpha \sigma^2} \ge 2^{\frac{1}{\tau_{\max} B}} - 1 \tag{37c}$$

It is noted in (37), constraint (37c) should be satisfied for arbitrary t, which makes that problem (37) contains infinite constraints. To be feasible, we next sample the time period to generate certain discrete time points. If the time interval between two neighboring discrete points is small enough, the obtained solution can be approximately considered as an solution of (37). Denote the discrete time points $\{t_1, t_2, \cdots, t_M\}$, the power P_n can be efficient obtained by solving the following linear programming problem

$$\min_{P_{n,1}} \sum_{n=1}^{N} k'_n P_n \tag{38a}$$

$$s.t \ \ 0 \le P_n \le P_{n,\text{avg}} \ \ \forall n \in \mathcal{N} \tag{38b}$$

$$\sum_{n=1}^{N} \frac{GP_n}{d_n(t_i)^\alpha \sigma^2} \ge 2^{\frac{1}{\tau_{\max} B}} - 1, \forall i \tag{38c}$$

If $\frac{T}{\tau_{\max}} < Q$, similar to the dynamic case, we represent the power as $P_n = P_{n,1} + P_{n,2}$ where $P_{n,1}$ is used to activate the constraint (38c) in (38). Then $P_{n,2}$ can be obtained by solving

$$\min_{P_{n,2}} \sum_{n=1}^{N} k_n' P_n \tag{39a}$$

$$s.t \ \ 0 \le P_{n,2} \le P_{n,\text{avg}} - P_{n,1} \ \ \forall n \in \mathcal{N} \tag{39b}$$

$$\int_0^T B \log_2 \left(1 + \sum_{n=1}^{N} \frac{G P_{n,1}}{d_n(t)^\alpha \sigma^2} + \sum_{n=1}^{N} \frac{G P_{n,2}}{d_n(t)^\alpha \sigma^2} \right) dt \ge Q \tag{39c}$$

Problem (39) can be solved similarly to (36) by using Lagrangian method.

5 Numerical Results

In this section, we present some numerical results to illustrate the superiority of the proposed dynamic resource allocation. For the network shown in Fig. 1, it is assumed that we have 2 RRHs and the coordinates of them are $(-200, 100)$ and $(800, 100)$. The height of the RRH is 100 m. We assume that the periodic transmission time is 5 s and only consider the content service during $t \in (0, 5)$.

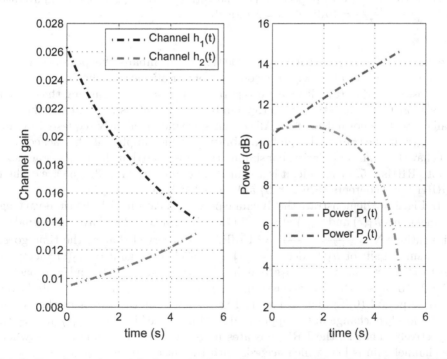

Fig. 2. Power varying with dynamic channel gains with $G = 2$ and average SNR $\frac{P_{1,\text{avg}}}{\sigma^2} = \frac{P_{2,\text{avg}}}{\sigma^2} = 10$ dB at $v_0 = 200$ km/h.

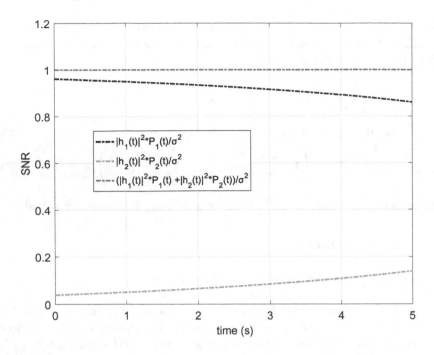

Fig. 3. SNR varying with respect to the time with $G = 10$, $\tau_{\max} = 0.005$ and average SNR $\frac{P_{1,\text{avg}}}{\sigma^2} = \frac{P_{2,\text{avg}}}{\sigma^2} = 10\,\text{dB}$ at $v_0 = 200\,\text{km/h}$.

The bandwidth of the frequency is 200 Hz. We compare the performance of dynamic power allocation with the constant power allocation scheme in terms of total cost defined in (5) with the ratio parameter $\beta = 2.8$. Regarding the cached contents at BBU, we assume that the number of contents is $F = 30$ and the size of all contents is normalized to 1. All contents are independently requested by the passengers in the train with equal probability $\frac{1}{F}$, which implies all the cached contents have the same popularity. For simplicity, we assume that the local storage size at both RRHs is 5. In specific, it is assumed that contents $\{1, 2, 3, 4, 5\}$ are cached at RRH 1 and contents $\{5, 6, 7, 8, 9\}$ are cached at RRH 2.

In Fig. 2, we demonstrate the dynamic power allocation with the time-varying channel gains $h_1(t)$ and $h_2(t)$ at $v_0 = 200\,\text{km/h}$ with $G = 2$ and average signal to noise ratio (SNR) $\frac{P_{1,\text{avg}}}{\sigma^2} = \frac{P_{2,\text{avg}}}{\sigma^2} = 10\,\text{dB}$. It is observed that as the time goes, the channel gain of $h_1(t)$ decreases while the channel gain of $h_2(t)$ increases due to the fact that the train gradually departs from RRH 1 and approaches RRH 2. To satisfy the delay constraint, the power is dynamically allocated over the time period $(0, T)$. The curves in Fig. 2 show that the values of the power $P_1(t)$ and $P_2(t)$ change in the opposite direction of the channels $h_1(t)$ and $h_2(t)$, respectively. That is, the RRH allocates more power to the time instant when the channel gain is low, which accords with the intuition.

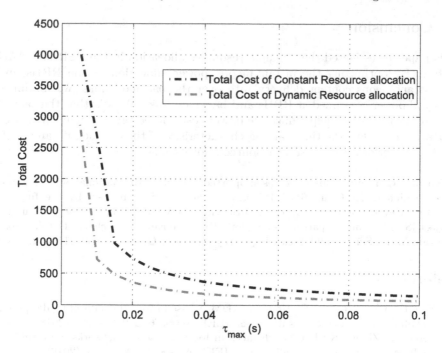

Fig. 4. Total cost comparison between the dynamic power allocation and constant power allocation with $G = 10$ and average SNR $\frac{P_{1,\text{avg}}}{\sigma^2} = \frac{P_{2,\text{avg}}}{\sigma^2} = 10\,\text{dB}$ at $v_0 = 200\,\text{km/h}$.

In Fig. 3, we illustrate the change of the instantaneous SNR over the time by considering a special case where the requested content is cached at both RRHs. With a slight abuse of the notation, we denote $\frac{|h_1(t)|^2 p_1(t)}{\sigma^2}$ and $\frac{|h_2(t)|^2 p_2(t)}{\sigma^2}$ as the instantaneous SNR at the time t over the channel links from RRH 1 to the train and from RRH 2 to the train, respectively. The final instantaneous SNR we obtain at the train after using the maximal ratio combiner is $\frac{|h_1(t)|^2 p_1(t)}{\sigma^2} + \frac{|h_2(t)|^2 p_2(t)}{\sigma^2}$. It is observed that although the values of SNR $\frac{|h_1(t)|^2 p_1(t)}{\sigma^2}$ and $\frac{|h_2(t)|^2 p_2(t)}{\sigma^2}$ vary over the time, their summation equals to a constant value, which is consistent with our analysis in Theorem 1, that is, to minimize the power cost, the constraint (12c) is active if $\frac{T}{\tau_{\max}} \geq Q$.

In Fig. 4, we compare the performance of the proposed dynamic resource allocation and the constant resource allocation with the change of $\tau_{\max}$. The curves show that the proposed dynamic resource allocation is significantly superior to the constant one. Constant resource allocation degrades the performance as it cannot fit the time-varying characteristic of the channel. It is also observed that as the increase of $\tau_{\max}$, the total cost decreases as less power is needed to meet the delay requirement.

6   Conclusion

This paper investigated the dynamic resources allocation in the HSR Fog-RAN system. By optimizing the instantaneous power allocation at the RRHs and the instantaneous content delivery rate over the backhaul links, we minimize the total power consumed at RRHs and backhaul links. We saw that the cached resource at RRHs can help reduce the power cost. Moreover, as dynamic resource allocation considers the time-varying characteristic of the channel, it can significantly outperform the constant resource allocation scheme.

Acknowledgement. This work was supported in part by the National Science Foundation China under Grant 61771345 and Grant 61831018, in part by the fund of the State Key Laboratory of Integrated Services Networks, Xidian University, under Project ISN19-01, and in part by Guangdong Province Key Research and Development Program Major Science and Technology Projects under Grant 2018B010115002.

References

1. Yan, D., Wang, R., Liu, E., Hou, Q.: ADMM-based robust beamforming design for downlink cloud radio access networks. IEEE Access **6**, 27912–27922 (2018)
2. Peng, M., Zhang, K.: Recent advances in fog radio access networks: performance analysis and radio resource allocation. IEEE Access **4**, 5003–5009 (2016)
3. Liu, J., Sheng, M., Quek, T.Q.S., Li, J.: D2D enhanced co-ordinated multipoint in cloud radio access networks. IEEE Trans. Wirel. Commun. **15**(6), 4248–4262 (2016)
4. Wang, R., Li, R., Wang, P., Liu, E.: Analysis and optimization of caching in fog radio access networks. IEEE Trans. Veh. Technol. **68**(8), 8279–8283 (2019)
5. Zhang, H., Zhu, L., Long, K., Li, X.: Energy efficient resource allocation in millimeter-wave-based fog radio access networks. In: 2nd URSI Atlantic Radio Science Meeting (AT-RASC), Meloneras, pp. 1–4 (2018)
6. Tao, M., Chen, E., Zhou, H., You, W.: Content-centric sparse multicast beamforming for cache-enabled cloud RAN. IEEE Trans. Wirel. Commun. **15**(9), 6118–6131 (2016)
7. Ai, B., et al.: Future railway services-oriented mobile communications network. IEEE Commun. Mag. **53**(10), 78–85 (2015)
8. Wu, J., Fan, P.: A survey on high mobility wirless communications: challenges, oppportunities and solutions. IEEE Access **4**, 450–476 (2016)
9. Muneer, P., Sameer, S.M.: Joint ML estimation of CFO and channel, and a low complexity turbo equalization technique for high mobility OFDMA uplinks. IEEE Trans. Wirel. Commun. **14**(7), 3642–3654 (2015)
10. Wang, J., Zhu, H., Gomes, N.J.: Distributed antenna systems for mobile communications in high speed trains. IEEE J. Sel. Areas Commun. **30**(4), 675–683 (2012)
11. Li, T., Xiong, K., Fan, P., Letaief, K.B.: Service-oriented power allocation for high-speed railway wireless communications. IEEE Access **5**, 8343–8356 (2017)
12. Zhang, C., Fan, P., Xiong, K., Fan, P.: Optimal power allocation with delay constraint for signal transmission from a moving train to base stations in high-speed railway scenarios. IEEE Trans. Veh. Technol. **64**(12), 5775–5788 (2015)
13. Liu, X., Qiao, D.: Location-fair beamforming for high speed railway communication systems. IEEE Access **6**, 28632–28642 (2018)

Distributed Task Splitting and Offloading in Mobile Edge Computing

Yanling Ren[1], Zhihui Weng[1], Yuanjiang Li[1], Zhibin Xie[1($\boxtimes$)], Kening Song[2], and Xiaolei Sun[3]

[1] Jiangsu University of Science and Technology, Zhenjiang, China
`xiezhibin@just.edu.cn`
[2] PLA AF 95829, Xiaogan, China
`skning@163.com`
[3] PLA Navy Submarine Academy, Qingdao, China
`msyl1211@163.com`

Abstract. With the rapid development of the mobile internet, many emerging compute-intensive and data-intensive tasks are extremely sensitive to latency and cannot be implemented on mobile devices (MDs). To solve this problem, mobile edge computing (MEC) appears to be a promising solution. In this paper, we propose a distributed task splitting and offloading algorithm (DSOA) for the scenario of multi-device and multi-MEC servers in ultra-dense networks (UDN). In the proposed scheme, the MDs can perform their tasks locally or offload suitable percentage of tasks to the MEC server. The optimization goal is to minimize the overall task computation time. Since the MDs are selfish, we propose a game theory approach to achieve optimal global computation time. Finally, the numerical simulation results verify that the algorithm can effectively reduce global computation time.

Keywords: Mobile edge computing · Offload strategy · Game theory

1 Introduction

In recent years, the mobile internet have developed rapidly, which has promoted the popularity of mobile devices (MDs) and the exponential growth of internet traffic [1]. Ultra-dense network (UDN) is considered to be one of the key technologies of the future mobile network [2]. However, many applications are computationally intensive and data intensive with strict time requirements such as virtual reality, face recognition, smart traffic and interactive games. The computing resources of existing MDs are often limited, and the processing capability is difficult to meet the requirements of these applications. Therefore, the deployment of UDN faces unprecedented challenges [3].

Cloud computing is an optional solution [4, 5]. However, the remotely offloading task to the cloud has some limitations that will still consume some unexpected excessive time and energy. Subsequently, some researchers began to pay attention to provide cloud computing ability at the edge of the wireless access network near MDs, which is

H. Gao et al. (Eds.): ChinaCom 2019, LNICST 312, pp. 33–42, 2020.
https://doi.org/10.1007/978-3-030-41114-5_3

named Mobile Edge Computing (MEC). MEC not only solves the problem of insufficient resources of the MDs, but also makes up for the shortcomings of long delays in cloud computing. The issues related to deployment, resource allocation, load balancing and fairness among multiple MDs in a mobile network are discussed in [6]. Some works have been done on the problem of offloading decision-making and resource allocation. The key technology is how to achieve low latency caused by communication and computation. In [7], cloud and wireless resource allocation are considered, and a convex optimization solution method is adopted. The model established in [7, 8] is a single model of multi-device and single MEC server. Guo et al. discussed the case of multiple servers and used potential games to solve the problem of offloading strategies, but the situation of task splitting was not taken into account [9]. The distributed joint computing offloading and resource allocation optimization problem in heterogeneous networks is considered in [10], but it is also directed to the case of single server offloading. Reference [11] combines the offloading task and the scheduling execution sequence to form a dynamic task offloading and scheduling problem, and use a logic-based bending decomposition technique to solve the problem.

Although, there are some excellent works in terms of offloading decisions and resource allocation, few literature has considered multi-device and multi-server offload scenarios to our knowledge. Most of the works are binary offloading choice, either the MDs performs computational tasks locally on its CPU or offloads its computationally intensive tasks to the MEC server [7]. In this paper, we propose an effective distributed task splitting and offloading algorithm (DSOA) for multi-device and multi-MEC server scenarios in UDN. In the proposed scheme, the change of the MEC server computing resources and the distance are considered. Based on these factors, the optimal server and the offload ratio are searched for realizing the goal of overall minimum computation time. Since the MDs are selfish, a game approach is proposed to find the optimal strategy. The numerical simulation results show the effectiveness of DSOA.

2   System Model

2.1   Network Model

As shown in Fig. 1, we consider a distributed UDN including multi-device and multi-MEC servers. In this network, there are $j \in M = \{1, 2, ..., M\}$ small base stations (BS), $i \in N = \{1, 2, ..., N\}$ MDs, the small BS and MDs are evenly distributed. The small BSs is connected to the core network through wired fibers. A lightweight MEC server is deployed around the small BS, so that the small BS has MEC capability. Assume that each MD has an intensive computing task to perform, they will choose to offload to the MEC server subject to their own resources and latency requirements. The small BSs can communicate with each other, and determine the MD's offloading decisions that minimize the overall computation time.

2.2   Communication Model

The data transmission rate r_i of MD i can be expressed as:

$$r_i = B \log_2(1 + \frac{p_i h_i}{\sigma^2}),$$

(1)

where B represents the bandwidth of the selected channel when the task is offloaded, p_i represents the transmission power of MD i, h_i is the channel gain between MD i and the BS, and σ^2 represents the thermal noise power.

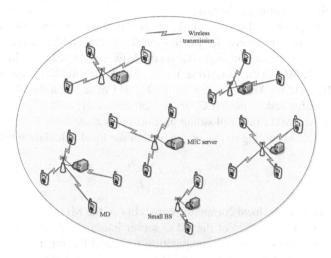

Fig. 1. Mobile edge computing model in ultra-dense network

2.3   Computation Model

If MD i selects MEC server j to offload, then the task transmission time is divided into three parts: uplink time, channel transmission time and downlink time. For each MD i, the size of task input data is b_i. Compared with b_i, the size of output data that calculation result from MEC servers is less, so the downlink time is set to be a constant α [7]. So the task transmission time is

$$t_i^{\text{trans}} = \frac{b_i}{r_i} + \frac{d_{i,j}}{v} + \alpha, \tag{2}$$

where $d_{i,j}$ is the distance from the MD i to the MEC server j, and v is the speed at which the electromagnetic wave propagates.

Assume that s_i is the required CPU cycles for finishing the task b_i, and f_i is the computing capability of the device, then the computation execution time can be expressed as

$$t = \frac{s_i}{f_i}. \tag{3}$$

3   Problem Formulation

Assume that each MD i is running a computing task, there are two possibilities for the execution location of these tasks. One is performed locally by the MD, and the other is offloaded to the MEC server for execution. Limited by their computation resources, the MDs will choose to offload computing tasks. However, if a lot of MDs offload its task, it will cause a certain amount of congestion and increase the task calculation time. The MD can make a decision whether to split the computation task according to its own needs and the characteristics of the task.

If the computing task is a detachable task, a part of the task is executed locally, and the rest is offloaded to the MEC server for calculation. That is, each MD can only select one MEC server to offload the computing task, and the MEC server j can provide computing service for multiple MDs at the same time. Let $\lambda_{i,j} \in \{0,1\}$ denote the offloading decision between the MD i and the MEC server j, where $\lambda_{i,j} = 1$ means that the MD i decides to offload the computing task to the MEC server j, otherwise $\lambda_{i,j} = 0$.

Suppose that the MD i task offloading proportion is x_i, and the locally calculating proportion is $(1-x_i)$. According to (3), we know that the local calculation time is

$$T_i^{\text{local}} = (1 - x_i)\frac{s_i}{f_i^{\text{local}}}, \tag{4}$$

where f_i^{local} represents the local computing capability of the MD i.

The computation time t_i^{cloud} of the MEC server is mainly divided into two parts, one is the transmission time of the computation task, and the other is the calculation execution time of the task processed by the MEC server. Combined with (2) (3), the task execution time on the MEC server side can be expressed as

$$T_i^{\text{cloud}} = \frac{x_i b_i}{r_i} + \frac{d_{i,j}}{v} + \alpha + \frac{x_i s_i}{f_{i,j}}, \tag{5}$$

where $f_{i,j}$ represents the computing capability allocated by the MEC server j to the MD i, and $f_{i,j} = f_j \Big/ \sum\limits_{i=1}^{N} \lambda_{i,j}$, where $\sum\limits_{i=1}^{N} \lambda_{i,j}$ indicates the number of MDs that all choose to offload the computing task to the MEC server j.

Therefore, the task computation time of the MD i is

$$T_i = \max\{T_i^{\text{local}}, T_i^{\text{cloud}}\}. \tag{6}$$

Based on this, the problem of minimizing overall computation time can be described as follows:

$$\min_{\{\lambda_{i,j}, x_i\}} \quad \sum_{i=1}^{N} T_i,$$
$$s.t. \quad \sum_{i=1}^{N} f_{i,j} \leq f_j^{\max},$$
$$T_i \leq T_i^{\max}, \tag{7}$$
$$0 < p_i \leq p_i^{\max},$$
$$f_i^{\text{local}} \geq 0.$$

In (7), the first constraint indicates that the sum of the computing resources allocated by the MEC server j for the MDs does not exceed its maximum computing capability;

the second constraint indicates that the total execution time of the computing task is lower than the sum of the maximum tolerable time $T_i^{\max}$ of each MD. In this paper, we set $T_i^{\max}$ as the time which all tasks are executed locally, because the selection task offloading execution time cannot be performed higher than the task locally; the third constraint represents the range of variation of the uplink transmission power of the MD i; the fourth constraint indicates that the MD i has a certain computing capability f_i^{local}.

4 Distributed Task Splitting and Offloading Algorithm

After one MEC server is selected, the proportion x_i of offloading task determines T_i^{local} and T_i^{cloud}. According to (6), we can know that the computation time of the MD i depends on the maximum value of the local computing time T_i^{local} and the MEC server side time T_i^{cloud}. The computation time of the MD i has three possible situations, i.e., $T_i^{\text{local}} < T_i^{\text{cloud}}$, $T_i^{\text{local}} > T_i^{\text{cloud}}$, $T_i^{\text{local}} = T_i^{\text{cloud}}$. Based on (4) and (5), we can find that the computation time of the MD i when $T_i^{\text{local}} > T_i^{\text{cloud}}$ or $T_i^{\text{local}} < T_i^{\text{cloud}}$ is more than when $T_i^{\text{local}} = T_i^{\text{cloud}}$. Therefore, when $T_i^{\text{local}} = T_i^{\text{cloud}}$, the optimal T_i^* exists and the task computation time reaches a minimum value, then

$$
x_i^* = \frac{\frac{s_i}{f_i^{\text{local}}} - \frac{d_{i,j}}{v} - \alpha}{\frac{b_i}{r_i} + \frac{s_i}{f_i^{\text{local}}} + \frac{s_i}{f_{i,j}}}. \tag{8}
$$

Based on (8), we can know that the time caused by computing locally of MD i is as fast as the MEC time for the transmission and calculate caused by offloading to the MEC server. Therefore, the problem (7) can be converted into

$$
\min_{\{\lambda_{i,j}\}} \sum_{i=1}^{N} (1 - x_i^*)\frac{s_i}{f_i^{\text{local}}},
$$
$$
s.t. \ \sum_{i}^{n} f_{i,j} \le f_j^{\max}, \tag{9}
$$
$$
T_i \le T_i^{\max},
$$
$$
f_i^{\text{local}} > 0.
$$

In order to solve the optimization problem of (9), we need to obtain the specific offloading ratio x_i according to the distance $d_{i,j}$ and the computing capability $f_{i,j}$ allocated by the MEC server j to the MD i. Therefore, the problem (9) can be transformed into an offloading decision problem. In order to solve the offloading decision problem, we adopt the game approach to find the optimal decision and achieve minimum global computation time.

Let a_i indicates the offloading decision of MD i, and let a_{-i} indicates the offloading decision of all other MDs except MD i. The goal of the game is to minimize the computational time of each MD, i.e.,

$$
\min_{\{\lambda_{i,j}\}} T(a_i, a_{-i}), \forall a_i, \tag{10}
$$

where $T(a_i, a_{-i})$ is the overall computing time for all MDs based on the current decision, i.e.,

$$T(a_i, a_{-i}) = \sum_i^N T_i(\lambda_{i,j}). \tag{11}$$

The offloading decision problem can be described as a distributed offloading decision game for multi-MD and multi-MEC servers. The game can be denoted by

$$\Gamma = (K, \{A_{i,j}\}_{i \in K}, \{T(a_i, a_{-i})\}_{i \in K}), \tag{12}$$

where K represents all game participants, $\{A_{i,j}\}_{i \in K}$ is the decision set of participant i, $\{T(a_i, a_{-i})\}_{i \in K}$ is the revenue function of MD i in the game, and this paper refers to the time function.

According to the Nash equalization (NE) existence theorem, there is at least one pure strategic NE in a finite number of repeated games [12]. Our distributed offloading decision game have finite players and offloading strategy space, and each player can choose a pure strategy from a limited set of offloading strategies, so have a NE. Thus, our game will get NE over a limited number of iterations. In this state of NE, none MD can further reduce computing time by changing its strategy. If the strategy of the equilibrium point is denoted as

$$a^* = (a_1^*, \ldots, a_{i-1}^*, a_i^*, a_{i+1}^*, \ldots, a_K^*), \tag{13}$$

where a^* is the optimal decision. According to the equilibrium point decision, the optimal computation time T_i can be expressed as

$$T(a_i^*, a_{-i}) \leq T(a_i, a_{-i}), \forall a_i. \tag{14}$$

Next, in order to get the equilibrium point decision a^*, we propose an effective DSOA. In this algorithm, it is assumed that the MDs can get all the information, including the distance, the computing capability of the MEC server, and the size of tasks that other MDs need to offload. First, each MD first selects the MEC server closest to itself as the offload destination, and the current decision is called the initial decision. Within each iteration, the MD can select a better decision based on the decisions of other MDs in the previous iteration, and calculate whether the decision is an overall better decision. If $T(a_i', a_{-i}) < T(a_i, a_{-i})$, store the updated $\mathbb{D}$, $\mathbb{T}$ and broadcast them to other MDs. Then, each iteration updates the decision that is the global optimum in the current $\mathbb{D}$. After a finite number of iterations, when the $\mathbb{D}$ is empty, i.e., all MDs have no better choice than current decisions, it indicates that the entire system has reached the NE, and the algorithm has converged to the global optimal solution.

Algorithm distributed task splitting and offloading algorithm (DSOA)

1: **Initialize:** $N, M, B, d, p_i, \sigma^2, b_i, s_i, f_j, f_i^{local}, \alpha$; an offloading decision space of the
    MDs $a_i = \{1, \cdots, M\}$; the initial offloading decision of the MD i is the MEC server j
    closest to it, i.e., (a_i, a_{-i}); the initial computation time $T(a_i, a_{-i})$ based on the ini-
    tial decision; the update set $\mathbb{D} = \varnothing$ of the MD i; the time update set $\mathbb{T} = \varnothing$;
2: for each iteration τ
3:    for all MD i do
4:        compute x_i, T_i, and compute whether $T_i(\lambda_{i,k}) < T_i(\lambda_{i,j})$ exists;

5:        if $T(a_i', a_{-i}) < T(a_i, a_{-i})$ then

6:            save $\lambda_{i,k}$ to $\mathbb{D}$ and save $T(a_i', a_{-i})$ to $\mathbb{T}$

7:        end if
8:    end for
9:    while $\mathbb{T} = \varnothing$ do
10:        find the minimum time $T(a_i^*, a_{-i})$ from the set of $\mathbb{T}$;

        update MD's decisions, let $a_i = a_i^*$;

11:    end while
12: end for

---

5 Simulation Results

In this section, the transmission distance between MDs to MEC server is in the [100, 1000] m following uniform distribution. The bandwidth of the wireless channel is $B = 1$ MHz. The transmit power of the MD i is 100 mW. The Gaussian thermal noise σ^2 is -100 dBm. The path fading factor γ is 3. The downlink backhaul time α of the calculated result is 0.5 μs. Each MD's computing task data size b_i is between 200 KB and 500 KB which follows uniform distribution, and the required CPU cycles range from 5,000 megacycles to 10,000 megacycles. The computing capability of the MEC server is 4 GHz, and the computing capability of the MD is 0.1 GHz.

In order to verify the DSOA, we use the exhaustive scheme as a benchmark for comparison, as shown in Fig. 2. Considering that the exhaustive algorithm has a large amount of computation and is not suitable for adopting more MDs and MEC servers, therefore the number of MEC servers is set to 4, and the number of MDs $N = 1, 2, \ldots$, 8. It can be found that the overall minimum computation time of our proposed DSOA scheme is very consistent with exhaustive scheme results. The numerical results confirm that the solution can provide a near-optimal solution to our problem.

In addition, we present the convergence behavior of the algorithm under different MD numbers, which are $N = 30, 50$ respectively. The number of MEC servers is 8. It can be easily observed from Fig. 3 that the overall computation time of the system gradually decreases as the number of iterations increases. After a finite number of iterations, the DSOA converges to a certain value. In addition, it can be found from the two curves that when $N = 30$, the number of iterations to reach equilibrium is 7, and when $N = 50$, the number of iterations is 13, indicating that the more devices, the more iterations are needed.

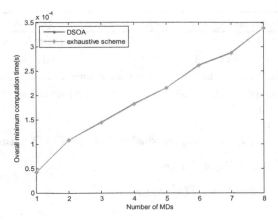

Fig. 2. Comparison between DSOA and exhaustive scheme

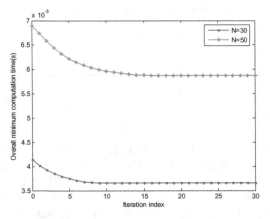

Fig. 3. Iteration comparison of DSOA with different number of MDs

In order to verify the performance of our proposed DSOA, we simulated the local computing strategy, all offloading computing strategies and our DSOA respectively, and the other two strategies also adopt game theory to get optimal decision. At this time, the number of MEC servers is set to 10. The comparison results are shown in Fig. 4. It can be seen from the simulation results that our solution can increase the calculation time by 43% and 63% respectively compared to all computing locally and all offloading to the MEC server. In the scheme of computing locally, all MDs perform calculations on the device itself, and the CPU consumption per unit is large, so the time of local execution of the computing task is significantly increased. The scheme of offloading all tasks to the MEC server, as the number of MDs increases, the latency will increase significantly. This is because the more MDs there are, the more tasks that need to be offloaded, the communication resources and MEC server resources are limited, so it will cause more time.

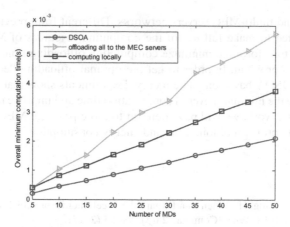

Fig. 4. Comparison results by adopting different offload strategies

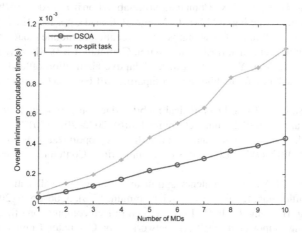

Fig. 5. Comparison results between task splitting and non-splitting

Finally, we compare DSOA with the scheme of no splitting the task. Under this scheme, the MD can choose to calculate locally or offload it to the MEC server and it also adopt game theory to get optimal decision. As can be seen from Fig. 5, as the number of MDs increases, DSOA will reduce the computation time by nearly 57% compared to the scenario without task splitting. Therefore, our DSOA has better flexibility and adaptability. Numerical results not only demonstrates the need to use multiple MEC servers for computational offloading in UDN, but also demonstrates that our DSOA can adopt multiple server selections and partially offload to reduce overall computation time.

6   Conclusions

Due to most of MDs have limited resources and mobile applications are sensitive to task computation time, we consider a minimizing the computational offloading time scheme for multi-device and multi-MEC servers networks. Different from previous works, the tasks can be splitted to make full use of the computing resources of MDs and MEC servers. Next, we transform the minimize computation offloading time problem to an offloading decision problem. In order to get the optimal offloading decision, we propose an effective DSOA based on game theory. Experiments show that the DSOA can effectively achieve the minimum overall computation time and improve network performance. In the future work, we will pay attention to more practical MEC scenarios and solve the weighting problem of joint time and energy consumption.

References

1. Sun, W., Liu, J., Zhang, H.: When smart wearables meet intelligent vehicles: challenges and future directions. IEEE Wirel. Commun. **24**(3), 58–65 (2017)
2. Zhang, S., Zhang, N., Zhou, S., Gong, J., Niu, Z., Shen, X.: Energy sustainable traffic steering for 5G mobile networks. IEEE Commun. Mag. **55**(11), 54–60 (2017)
3. Yang, T., Zhang, H., Ji, H., Li, X.: Computation collaboration in ultra dense network integrated with mobile edge computing. In: PIMRC, Montreal, Canada, pp. 1–5. IEEE (2017)
4. Zhang, W., Wen, Y., Wu, D.: Collaborative task execution in mobile cloud computing under a stochastic wireless channel. IEEE Trans. Wirel. Commun. **14**(3), 81–93 (2015)
5. Wang, J., Peng, J., Wei, Y., Liu, D., Lu, J.: Adaptive application offloading decision and transmission scheduling for mobile cloud computing. IEEE China Commun. **14**(3), 169–181 (2017)
6. Kiani, A., Ansari, N.: Toward hierarchical mobile edge computing: an auction-based profit maximization approach. IEEE Internet Things J. **4**(6), 2082–2091 (2017)
7. Zhang, J., et al.: Joint offloading and resource allocation optimization for mobile edge computing. In: GLOBECOM IEEE Global Communications Conference, Singapore, pp. 1–5. IEEE (2017)
8. Ren, J., Yu, G., Cai, Y., He, Y.: Latency optimization for resource allocation in mobile-edge computation offloading. IEEE Trans. Wirel. Commun. **17**(8), 5506–5519 (2018)
9. Guo, J., Zhang, H., Yang, L., Ji, H., Li, X.: Decentralized computation offloading in mobile edge computing empowered small-cell networks. In: Computer Communications. IEEE GlobeCom, Singapore, pp. 1–6. IEEE (2017)
10. Zhang, J., Xia, W., Yan, F., Shen, L.: Joint computation offloading and resource allocation optimization in heterogeneous networks with mobile edge computing. IEEE Access **6**, 19324–19337 (2018)
11. Alameddine, H., Sharafeddine, S., Sebbah, S., Ayoubi, S., Assi, C.: Dynamic task offloading and scheduling for low-latency IoT services in multi-access edge computing. IEEE J. Sel. Areas Commun. **37**(3), 668–682 (2019)
12. Nash, J.F.: Equilibrium points in N-person games. Proc. Nat. Acad. Sci. U.S.A. **36**(1), 48–49 (1950)

Evolution Computation Based Resource Allocation for Hybrid Visible-Light and RF Femtocell

Yuan Zhang[1], Yang Li[1], Liang Chen[1], Ning Wang[1], and Bo Fan[2(✉)]

[1] State Grid Information and Telecommunication Branch,
Beijing 100761, People's Republic of China
[2] Beijing University of Technology College of Metropolitan Transportation,
Beijing 100124, People's Republic of China
fanbo@bjut.edu.cn

Abstract. Incorporating visible light communication (VLC) with existing radio frequency (RF) access techniques has received widespread concern to enhance network coverage/capacity. This paper focuses on the joint downlink resource allocation (RA) in a hybrid VLC-RF network. The problem is formulated as utility maximization by jointly adjusting downlink sub-channel allocation. A Evolution Computation (EC) based centralized algorithm is developed to solve the problem. To reduce computation complexity, the algorithm is decoupled into two sub-steps. First, users are assigned to different VLC access points and the allocation is initialized in a proportional fair (PF) like method. Second, EC search procedures are iteratively operated until optimality. Through simulation, the algorithm outperforms classic PF and Round Robin RA methods in terms of throughput and user fairness.

Keywords: Visible light communication · Heterogeneous network · 5G

1 Introduction

Visible-light communication is considered as a promising technique to provide high-speed network access for future indoor users. Its main advantages include license-free operation, clean electro-magnetic interference and high network security. One primary research direction is to deploy indoor VLC attocells with symbols-based dc-biased optical discrete multi-tone modulation (DMT) signals [1]. VLC attocell refers to indoor femtocell-like VLC coverage with radius of 0.5–1.5 m. Such deployment enables VLC system to serve multiple mobile users, allowing them to move around inside a room with seamless connection to the best serving light bulb. Besides, DMT offers adaptability in modulation patterns, which have recently demonstrated excellent bit-rate performance [2].

In spite of above advantages, the main drawback of VLC is its limited coverage. Obstacles can easily cut off VLC links and then leave the service deprived.

H. Gao et al. (Eds.): ChinaCom 2019, LNICST 312, pp. 43–52, 2020.
https://doi.org/10.1007/978-3-030-41114-5_4

On the other hand, radio frequency (RF) can cover larger area up to several square kilometers. Therefore, next generation mobile communication (5G) envisions an ultra-dense small cell deployment network (UDN) on licensed and unlicensed spectrum, aggregating various access techniques including Wireless Local Area Network (WLAN), millimetre-wave, Optical Wireless (OW), etc.

Following this trend, VLC attocell may also work as part of future UDN. Many researchers have demonstrated the attraction of corporation VLC with RF because of their complementary nature in both coverage and capacity [3]. VLC provides wide bandwidth with limited coverage, while radio frequency (RF) covers large area with lower throughput. What' more, there exists no interference problem between VLC and RF. Therefore, this paper considers an indoor co-deployment of several VLC attocells and a classic RF femtocell.

Joint resource allocation (RA) is an important issue in such hybrid systems but there exist few related studies. [4] focuses on network capacity analysis in hybrid VLC-RF system. The study is built on queue theory and VLC channel is idealized as binary channel of transmission success or failure. The network capacity is evaluated by the spatial density of accessed queues. [5] proposes distributed algorithm to solve network selection problem in order to improve VLC-RF hybrid system capacity. Fundamentally, there remains missing pieces of the RA puzzle: (i) VLC channel-aware RA scheme should be elaborated with advanced modulation signals to improve RA efficiency. (ii) Small user number and less channel complexity in VLC network alleviate the backhaul load and make centralized RA possible. Compared to distributed RA, centralized RA enables flexible resource aggregation and absolves VLC APs from complex signalling process burden.

In order to address above issues, this paper proposes a joint subcarriers (subchannels) allocation of hybrid DMT-attocell and OFDM-femtocell system. A centralized algorithm based on Evolution Computation (EC) is developed to solve the problem. To reduce complexity, the algorithm is decoupled into two subsequential steps. The first step assigns users to different VLC APs and initializes the allocation in a proportional fair (PF) like method. The second step iteratively carries out EC search procedures to improve both network throughput and user fairness. The complexity is analyzed on the basis of the dimension of the searching space. Results are compared with classic RA methods of PF and Round Robin (RR).

The paper is organized as follows. Section 2 presents the system model. Problem formulation and optimization strategy are given in Sects. 3 and 4. Simulation results are presented in Sect. 5. Section 6 concludes the paper.

2   System Model

2.1   Scenario Description

In Fig. 1, several light-emitting diode (LED) APs and a RF femto are co-located to cover the whole room area. LED signal is DMT based: the whole bandwidth is divided into subcarriers that can be allocated to multiple users. In order to realize the full potential of DMT, subcarriers can be densely reused among different APs [6]. RF signal is OFDM based. In our model, mobile terminal (MT) is indexed by m and $\mathcal{M}$ denote total MT set. VLC AP is indexed by k and $\mathcal{K}$ denote total VLC AP set.

The work is based on following assumptions: (i) VLC APs and RF femto-cell are linked with each other through wired backbone for exchanging signalling information. (ii) The network is converged in Internet Protocol (IP) layer. So the physical difference between VLC and RF sub-channel is ignored. MTs are capable of scheduling multiple heterogeneous or homogeneous sub-channels simultaneously. (iii) Transmit power on every VLC and RF sub-channel is constant, subject to total power constraint.

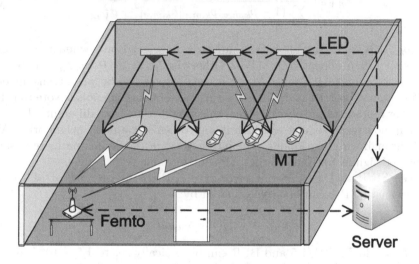

Fig. 1. Indoor VLC-RF hybrid network.

2.2   VLC Channel Model

VLC channel consists of two parts: line-of-sight (LOS) and non-line-of-sight (NLOS) components [7]. The LOS DC (Direct Current) gain between transmitter k and receiver m is given by:

$$h_{k,m} = \begin{cases} \frac{A}{d_{k,m}^2} I_w(\phi_{k,m}) \cos(\varphi_{k,m}), & 0 \leq \varphi_{k,m} \leq \varphi_c \\ 0, & \varphi_{k,m} > \varphi_c \end{cases} \tag{1}$$

where A is the size of the receiver, $d_{k,m}$ is the distance between transmitter k and receiver m. $\varphi_{k,m}$ is the angle of incidence of light at the receiver. φ_c is the receiver field-of-view (FOV). The light signal can be detected only when the incidence angle is no more than receiver's FOV. $I_w(\phi_{k,m})$ is the Lambertian radiant intensity profile of order w that models LED radiation pattern.

Reflective responses (NLOS channel) have similar forms with LOS components and can be calculated recursively in terms of (1). LOS and first-reflective path are considered in our work since these two components account for more than 97% of the total received energy. Readers may consult [8] for details.

3 Problem Formulation

3.1 User Rate Calculation

Subcarrier of VLC AP is indexed by v and $\mathcal{V}$ denote total VLC subcarrier resource set of the corresponding AP. The SINR of user m on channel v can be calculated by [6]:

$$
\gamma_{m,v} = \frac{\sum\limits_{k \in \mathcal{K}} \rho_{k,m,v} p_{k,m,v} |h_{k,m,v}|^2}{\sum\limits_{k \in \mathcal{K}} (1 - \rho_{k,m,v}) p_{k,m,v} |h_{k,m,v}|^2 + \sigma_{VLC}^2} \tag{2}
$$

where $\rho_{k,m,v}$ is subcarrier allocation indicator. $\rho_{k,m,v} = 1$ only when subcarrier v of transmitter k is allocated to MT m. Otherwise, $\rho_{k,m,v} = 0$. $p_{k,m,v}$ denotes the transmit power on subcarrier v, $h_{k,m,v}$ is the channel gain between transmitter k and MT m on subcarrier v. σ_{VLC}^2 is the variance of Gaussian noise. Note that the numerator represents the desired signal that might come from different VLC APs in synchronous time sequence, which is unproblematic among neighboring APs linked through wired backhauls. The interference in the denominator represents unexpected signals from interfering APs on the same sub-channel.

Given SINR and a target bit error rate (BER), the bit rate of MT m on subcarrier v of AP k can be approximated by:

$$
r_{m,v} \approx \log_2(1 + \gamma_{m,v}/\Gamma) \tag{3}
$$

where $\Gamma = -\ln(5\text{BER})/1.5$ and BER can be typically set to 1.5×10^{-3} [6].

RF femtocell sub-channel is indexed by f. $\mathcal{F}$ denote total RF femtocell channel resource set. The SNR of user m on channel f is calculated by:

$$
\gamma_{m,f} = \frac{\rho_{m,f} p_{m,f} |h_{m,f}|^2}{\sigma^2} \tag{4}
$$

where $\rho_{m,f}$ denotes channel allocation indicator. $p_{m,f}$ and $h_{m,f}$ respectively represent transmit power and channel gain of MT m on sub-channel f. The achievable rate $r_{m,f}$ can be estimated for a target BER under adaptive modulation.

3.2 Utility Function Definition

The utility function can be defined in (5a) as follows:

$$
u_m = r_m d_m \tag{5a}
$$

$$
r_m = \sum_{v \in \mathcal{V}} r_{m,v} + \sum_{f \in \mathcal{F}} r_{m,f} \tag{5b}
$$

$$
d_m = \overline{R}/(R_m + \delta) \tag{5c}
$$

$$
\overline{R} = \left(\sum_{m \in \mathcal{M}} R_m \right) / M \tag{5d}
$$

where r_m represents the total achievable data rate of MT m as defined in (5b). d_m indicates the service status of MT m in (5c). Note that δ in (5c) has a small value that prevents d_m from being ∞. R_m is the average throughput of MT m over a certain time-window. $\overline{R}$ is the average throughput across all MTs given in (5d). A rate deprived user will have higher service status indicator and vice versa.

Thus the problem is formulated as utility maximization by adjusting channel allocation indicator ρ:

$$\max_{\rho} \sum_{m \in \mathcal{M}} u_m$$

subject to:

$$\forall m \in \mathcal{M}, v \in \mathcal{V}, f \in \mathcal{F}, \tag{6}$$

$$\rho_{k,m,v} \in \{0,1\}, \sum_{m \in \mathcal{M}} \rho_{k,m,v} \leq 1$$

$$\rho_{m,f} \in \{0,1\}, \sum_{m \in \mathcal{M}} \rho_{m,f} \leq 1$$

where the constraints declare that each subcarrier or sub-channel can be simultaneously allocated to one MT at most. The problem in (6) includes the nonlinear optimization of both $|\mathcal{M}| \times |\mathcal{K}| \times |\mathcal{V}|$ integer variables $(\rho_{k,m,v})$ and $|\mathcal{M}| \times |\mathcal{F}|$ integer variables $(\rho_{m,f})$. Its optimal solution by means of an integer nonlinear programming solver is exceptionally complicated and computationally intractable for evaluation within reasonable time [8]. Note that $|\cdot|$ represents set's cardinality.

4 Evolution Computation Based RA Algorithm

In this part, Evolution Computation (EC) is introduced to solve problem (6). EC is widely adopted as a general concept for solving difficult discrete optimization problems. Though its global search characteristic has been confirmed, the computation task complexity is greatly increased. Therefore, the allocation algorithm is split into two sequential steps to reduce computation complexity, as given in Algorithm 1.

4.1 Initialization

The first step **Initialization** includes line 1–10 of Algorithm 1. Line 2 allocates MTs to the highest channel gain APs. Given MT m, its allocated AP is defined by: $\mathcal{M}_k = \left\{ m_k \in \mathcal{M}_k | k = \arg \max_k \sum_{v \in \mathcal{V}} |h_{k,m,v}|^2 \right\}$, where $\sum_{k \in \mathcal{K}} \mathcal{M}_k = \mathcal{M}$. Line 3–7 allocate VLC subcarriers of each AP to its assigned users. Line 8–10 allocate femto sub-channel resource to users.

4.2 Evolution Computation

The second step **Evolution Computation** includes line 11–18 of Algorithm 1. EC mimics the evolution process of a population of a certain species, driving its

Algorithm 1. Evolutionary Computation based RA Algorithm for VLC Heterogeneous Network

---

1: **Initialization:**
2: VLC AP assignment
3: **for** each $k \in \mathcal{K}$ **do**
4:     **for** each $v \in \mathcal{V}$ **do**
5:         Allocate subcarrier v to m_k of maximum u_m
            Update u_m
6:     **end for**
7: **end for**
8: **for** each $f \in \mathcal{F}$ **do**
9:     Allocate sub-channel f to m of maximum u_m
        Update u_m
10: **end for**
11: **Evolution Computation:**
12: $i = 0$
13: **repeat**
14:     $i + +$
15:     Selection(Ψ)
16:     Crossover(Ψ)
17:     Mutation(Ψ)
18: **until** $i == Generation\_number$

Table 1. Reflection relationship.

Parameters in our model	Reflection in evolution operators
Resource index: v or f	Gene: g
Resource set: $\underbrace{\{\mathcal{V}, \cdots, \mathcal{V}, F\}}_{\|\mathcal{K}\|}$	Individual: $\mathcal{G}$
Objective function	Fitness

individuals towards higher fitness for adaptation and survival. Generally speaking, EC is a periodical result of the population's selection, heredity and mutation in its genetic perspective.

The reflection relationship between model parameters and EC are given in Table 1. An individual is made up of the total genes. Each individual corresponds to a certain allocation scheme with respective fitness (objective function). The individual with the highest fitness in the population is of the optimal allocation strategy. A population Ψ consists of multiple individuals. For each generation, population Ψ carries out the following three EC operators:

Selection operator (line 15) can be used to generate new population, which emphasizes fitter individuals and preserves their genotypic information. Typically, selection can be implemented as a probabilistic operator, namely roulette wheel selection (RWS) in our paper. RWS utilizes the relative fitness (a single individual fitness divided by total individuals fitness) of the individuals within the population to determine the selection probability of generated individual. Individuals are mapped into new population based on the probability proportional to the relative fitness. Individuals with higher fitness is more likely to exist in next generation of population.

Crossover (line 16) is a basic operator for producing new individuals with differentiated genotypic information. Crossover can be described as a recombination of two parent individuals, producing offsprings that have some parts of both parent's genetic material. In this paper, a standard one-point crossover is utilized as defined in [9]. First, two individuals are chosen randomly from the population. Second, a position in the gene string is randomly determined as the crossover point. Third, an offspring is generated by concatenating the left substring of one parent and the right substring of the other parent. These procedures are executed with a fixed probability of 0.3 [9]. Crossover demonstrates disruptive nature, driving the search direction more diversified.

Maturation (line 17) is discussed as 'background operator', preventing good genetic material from getting lost during selection and crossover procedures [9]. Therefore, mutation probability should not be too high to avoid interfering with selection and crossover. In our paper, mutation probability $P_{mut} = 0.05$ [9].

4.3   Complexity Analysis

Since EC is an intelligent search algorithm, the searching space greatly influences its efficiency. So this part analyzes algorithm complexity based on the dimension of searching space. Following proves the complexity of our algorithm is less than traditional EC search. First, as for VLC:

$$
\begin{aligned}
g &= [1, 2, \cdots, |\mathcal{M}_k|][\rho_{k,1,v}, \rho_{k,2,v}, \cdots, \rho_{k,|\mathcal{M}_k|,v}]^T \\
Given &: \rho_{k,m,v} \in \{0,1\} \land \sum_{m \in \mathcal{M}} \rho_{k,m,v} = 1 \\
&= m_k \in \mathcal{M}_k
\end{aligned} \tag{7}
$$

Second, as for RF femtocell:

$$
\begin{aligned}
g &= [1, 2, \cdots, |\mathcal{M}|][\rho_{1,f}, \rho_{2,f}, \cdots, \rho_{|\mathcal{M}|,f}]^T \\
Given &: \rho_{m,f} \in \{0,1\} \land \sum_{m \in \mathcal{M}} \rho_{m,f} = 1 \\
&= m \in \mathcal{M}
\end{aligned} \tag{8}
$$

Third, the dimension of the searching space is:

$$
\begin{aligned}
Dim &= \sum_{k \in \mathcal{K}} |\mathcal{M}_k||\mathcal{V}| + |\mathcal{M}||\mathcal{F}| \\
&= |\mathcal{V}| \sum_{k \in \mathcal{K}} |\mathcal{M}_k| + |\mathcal{M}||\mathcal{F}| \\
Given &: \sum_{k \in \mathcal{K}} \mathcal{M}_k = \mathcal{M} \\
&= |\mathcal{V}||\mathcal{M}| + |\mathcal{M}||\mathcal{F}| \\
Given &: |K| > 1 \land |\mathcal{K}| \text{ is integer} \\
&= |\mathcal{M}|(|\mathcal{V}| + |\mathcal{F}|) < |\mathcal{M}|(|\mathcal{K}||\mathcal{V}| + |\mathcal{F}|)
\end{aligned} \tag{9}
$$

Table 2. Simulation configuration

VLC system	Femtocell system
LED power: 20 [w]	Femotcell BS power: 0.02 [w]
LED bandwidth: 20 [MHz]	Femtocell bandwidth: 5 [MHz]
FOV: 60 [deg.]	Fast-fading: Rician
Semi-angle: 80 [deg.]	Path-loss constant: 37 [dB]
MT's receive area: 1 [cm^2]	Path-loss exponent: 3

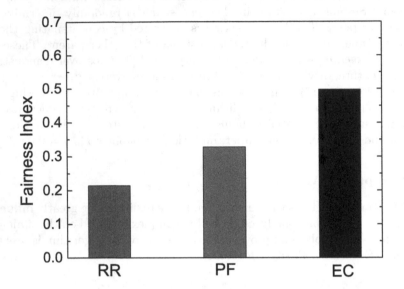

Fig. 2. Indoor VLC-RF hybrid network.

5　Simulation and Analysis

In the simulation, a 5 m × 5 m × 3 m room is considered. 30 terminals are served by 8 LED APs and a femtocell. Detailed parameters are listed in Table 2. Proportional Fair (PF) and Round Robin (RR) RA algorithms are introduced for comparison.

Figure 2 compares users' rate fairness. Fairness Index is defined as [10]:

$$F = \frac{\left(\sum_{m\in\mathcal{M}} r_m\right)^2}{|\mathcal{M}| \cdot \sum_{m\in\mathcal{M}} r_m^2} \tag{10}$$

F ranges from 0 (worst case) to 1 (best case). The best case corresponds to the situation that all users obtain equal data rate. Compared with RR and RF, the user fairness of our algorithm (EC) is improved 0.28 and 0.17 respectively.

Figure 3 compares system's average throughput. Compared with RR and RF, average system throughput of EC is improved 103.4% and 53.8% respectively.

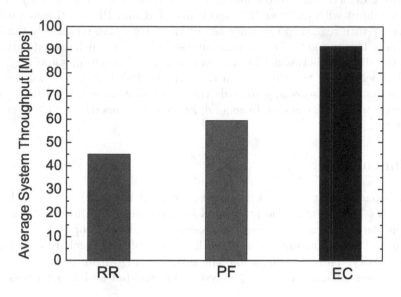

Fig. 3. Average system throughput.

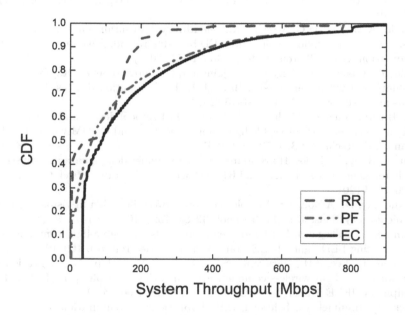

Fig. 4. Cumulative distribution function of the system throughput.

Figure 4 demonstrates the cumulative distribution function (CDF) of system throughput with different RA algorithms. RR and PF algorithms perform very poorly with regard to the lower tail of the CDF curve (especially the 30th percentile). This is due to the non-randomness of VLC channel, exceedingly subject to the distance between VLC receiver and AP. Therefore, some very poor VLC channels might be utilized by using RR and PF. On the other hand, EC promotes intelligent searching towards the point that users are allocated with possibly optimal VLC channel. In general, EC outperforms RR and PF in system throughput.

6   Conclusions

In this paper, a joint downlink resource allocation is investigated in a hybrid indoor VLC-RF network. The problem is formulated as non-linear integer optimization. An evolutionary computation based algorithm is proposed to solve the problem and the algorithm is decoupled into two subsequential steps to reduce the complexity. Through simulation, the proposed algorithm is proved to outperform classic allocation schemes in system throughput and user fairness.

References

1. Tsonev, D., Videv, S., Haas, H.: Light fidelity (Li-Fi): towards all-optical networking. In: SPIE Proceedings, pp. 1–10, February 2013. https://doi.org/10.1117/12.2044649
2. Khalid, A.M., Cossu, G., Corsini, R., Choudhury, P., Ciaramella, E.: 1-Gb/s transmission over a phosphorescent white LED by using rateadaptive discrete multitone modulation. IEEE Photon. J. **4**(5), 1465–1473 (2012)
3. Rufo, J., Rabadan, J., Delgado, F., Quintana, C., Perez-Jimenez, R.: Experimental evaluation of video transmission through LED illumination devices. IEEE Trans. Consum. Electron. **56**(3), 1411–1416 (2010)
4. Xu, B., Xiaorong, Z., Tiecheng, S., Yanqiu, O.: Protocol design and capacity analysis in hybrid network of visible light communication and OFDMA systems. IEEE Trans. Veh. Technol. **63**, 1770–1778 (2014)
5. Fan, J., Rong, Z., Lajos, H.: Resource allocation under delay-guarantee constraints for heterogeneous visible-light and RF femtocell. IEEE Trans. Wirel. Commun. **14**, 1020–1034 (2015)
6. Bykhovsky, D., Arnon, S.: Multiple access resource allocation in visible light communication systems. J. Light. Technol. **32**(8), 1594–1600 (2014)
7. Komine, T., Nakagawa, M.: Fundamental analysis for visible-light communication system using LED lights. IEEE Trans. Consum. Electron. **50**, 100–107 (2004)
8. Komine, T., Lee, J.H., Haruyama, S., Nakagawa, M.: Adaptive equalization system for visible light wireless communication utilizing multiple white LED lighting equipment. IEEE Trans. Wirel. Commun. **8**, 2892–2900 (2009)
9. Back, T., Hammel, U., Schwefel, H.P.: Evolutionary computation: comments on the history and current state. IEEE Trans. Evol. Comput. **1**(1), 3–17 (1997)
10. Jain, R., Durresi, A., Babic, G.: Throughput fairness index: an explanation. Technical report, Department of CIS, The Ohio State University (1999)

Deep Reinforcement Learning Based Computation Offloading for Mobility-Aware Edge Computing

Minyan Shi[1($\boxtimes$)], Rui Wang[1,2], Erwu Liu[1], Zhixin Xu[1], and Longwei Wang[3]

[1] School of Electronics and Information Engineering, Tongji University,
Shanghai, China
1832915@tongji.edu.cn
[2] Shanghai Institute of Intelligent Science and Technology, Tongji University,
Shanghai, China
[3] Department of Electrical Engineering, University of Texas at Arlington,
Arlington, TX 76013, USA

Abstract. Mobile Edge Computing (MEC) has become the most likely network architecture to solve the problems of mobile devices in terms of resource storage, computing performance and energy efficiency. In this paper, we first model the MEC system with the exploitation of mobility prediction. Considering the user's mobility, the deadline constraint and the limited resources in MEC servers, we propose a deep reinforcement learning approach named deep deterministic policy gradient (DDPG) to learn the power allocation policies for MEC servers users. Then, the aim of the policy is to minimize the overall cost of the MEC system. Finally, simulation results are illustrated that our proposed algorithm achieves performance gains.

Keywords: Mobile Edge Computing · Computation offloading · Mobility · Deep reinforcement learning

1 Introduction

The rapid development of the Internet has made future networks face the challenges of higher speed and lower latency. Although the processing capacity of the new mobile device's central processing unit (CPU) is becoming more and more powerful, it is unable to handle huge amounts of tasks in a short time [1].

In view of this, Mobile Edge Computing (MEC) has become the most likely network architecture to realize the 5G vision and has attracted wide attention [2, 3]. MEC refers to the deployment of computing and storage resources at the edge of the mobile network to provide Internet services and cloud computing capabilities for mobile networks, providing users with ultra-low latency and high bandwidth networks.

Computation offloading is one of the key technologies in MEC systems [4], which is the terminal device hands over some or all of the computing tasks to the

© ICST Institute for Computer Sciences, Social Informatics and Telecommunications Engineering 2020
Published by Springer Nature Switzerland AG 2020. All Rights Reserved
H. Gao et al. (Eds.): ChinaCom 2019, LNICST 312, pp. 53–65, 2020.
https://doi.org/10.1007/978-3-030-41114-5_5

cloud computing environment to solve the problems of mobile devices in terms of resource storage, computing performance and energy efficiency. For example, in the fields of automatic driving, vehicles must sense road conditions, obstacles, driving information of surrounding vehicles in real time, and these information can be quickly calculated and transmitted through MEC offloading technology.

Computation offloading strategies for MEC servers recently have been widely investigated in the literature in order to achieve higher energy efficiency or better computation experience. In [5], a dimensional search algorithm was studied to determine whether the buffer task is offloaded to the MEC servers with the goal of optimizing the time delay in each time slot. Considering the limited computing resources of the MEC servers for offloading decisions and resource allocation, the authors in [6] proposed a layered MEC deployment architecture and solved the multi-user offloading problem by using Stackelberg game theory. Moreover, with the dynamic voltage and frequency (DVFS) techniques, CPU-cycle frequency was flexibly controlled with other features in [7,8], where the system cost, defined as weighted sum of energy consumption and execution time, has been reduced. Additionally, exploiting users mobility for offloading strategies has also received much attention from researchers. In [9], the resource allocation policy is designed by considering the vehicles mobility and the hard service deadline constraint.

Machine learning has brought unprecedented algorithmic capabilities in providing adept solutions to a great span of complex learning and planning tasks. So there have been some attempts to adopt deep reinforcement learning (DRL) in the design of online resource allocation and scheduling in wireless networks, especially for some recent works targeting computation offloading in MEC servers. The authors in [10] proposed a continuous action space based DRL approach named deep deterministic policy gradient (DDPG) to learn efficient computation offloading policies independently at each mobile user. Most of the existing work is focused on the resource allocation of MEC without considering the insufficient resources of MEC. However, in some cases, it is very likely that there will not be enough MEC resources for computation offloading.

In this paper, we propose a continuous action space based algorithm named deep deterministic policy gradient (DDPG) to derive better power control of local execution and task offloading by considering the mobility of users and hard deadline delay. Specifically, the contributions of this paper can be summarized as follows.

(1) We model the MEC system with the exploitation of mobility prediction and design dynamic computation offloading policies, where both users and MEC servers have computing capabilities. The agent decides the dynamic power allocation of both local execution and computation offloading during the movement. In case the user offload the tasks to a MEC server with insufficient computing resources, the MEC server passes the unfinished tasks to the core network.

(2) We design a DRL framework based on DDPG to learn efficient policies for power allocation of both local execution and computation offloading with the goal of minimizing the cost of communication and computation.

(3) We present numerical simulations to illustrate the performance of the DDPG algorithm and analyze the effects of different parameters on the results.

The rest of this paper is organized as follows. Section 2 describes the MEC system model. We briefly introduce the deep reinforcement learning and formulate the power allocation optimization problem by using deep reinforcement learning in Sect. 3. Numerical results will be illustrated in Sect. 4. Last, Sect. 5 concludes the paper and outlines future work plans.

2 System Model

2.1 Network Model

We consider a hybrid network which includes one mobile user k, Q MEC servers and the core network as shown in Fig. 1. Let $Q = \{1, \ldots, q\}$ be the sets of the MEC servers. Note that every MEC server is equipped with N antennas and have the capability of computing and transmitting. For example, we set the scene to a vehicular network and regard mobile users as vehicles. The red vehicle can offload tasks to different MEC servers during its movement. In case several vehicles simultaneously offload tasks to the same MEC server and the requested MEC server lacks enough resources to process tasks from the user, it will transmit unprocessed tasks to the core network.

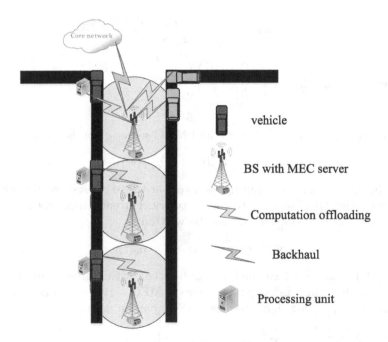

Fig. 1. Mobility-aware computation offloading system. (Color figure online)

2.2 Communication Model

Assume that the channel vector of vehicle-to-MEC links and MEC-to-core network are both time-varying and modeled as the finite-state Markov chain (FSMC). For each time slot $t \in \mathcal{T}$, the received signal of the MEC server q from user k can be written as

$$\mathbf{y}_q(t) = \mathbf{g}_{k,q}(t)x_k(t) + \mathbf{n}_q(t) \tag{1}$$

where $\mathbf{g}_{k,q}(t)$ is the $N \times 1$ channel matrix between user k and MEC server q, $x_k(t)$ is the data symbol with unit variance, and $\mathbf{n}_q(t)$ is a vector of additive white Gaussian noise with variance σ^2. Then the received signal for user k is

$$\mathbf{v}_{k,q}^T \mathbf{y}_q(t) = \mathbf{v}_{k,q}^T \mathbf{g}_{k,q}(t)x_k(t) + \mathbf{v}_{k,q}^T \mathbf{n}_q(t) \tag{2}$$

where $\mathbf{v}_{k,q}^T$ is the normalized Beamforming vector and $||\mathbf{v}_{k,q}|| = 1$.

Denoting $p_{k,q}^o$ as the transmission power of user k to MEC server q. Thus, the corresponding signal-to-noise (SNR) can be derived by

$$\gamma_{q,k}(t) = \frac{\mathbf{E}\left\{|\mathbf{v}_{k,q}^T \mathbf{g}_{k,q}x_k(t)|^2\right\}}{\mathbf{E}\left\{|\mathbf{v}_{k,q}^T \mathbf{n}_q|^2\right\}} = \frac{|\mathbf{v}_{k,q}^T \mathbf{g}_{k,q}|^2 p_{k,q}^o}{\sigma_0^2 ||\mathbf{v}_{k,q}||^2} \tag{3}$$

$$\max \ SNR = \frac{|\mathbf{v}_{k,q}^T \mathbf{g}_{k,q}|^2}{\sigma_0^2 ||\mathbf{v}_{k,q}||^2} \tag{4}$$

$$s.t. \quad ||\mathbf{v}_{k,q}|| = 1 \tag{5}$$

Then we can obtain that

$$\mathbf{v}_{k,q} = \frac{\mathbf{g}_{k,q}^*}{||\mathbf{g}_{k,q}||} \tag{6}$$

So, the communication rate of user k and MEC server q can be expressed as

$$r_{q,k}(t) = W_q log(1 + \gamma_{q,k}(t)) \tag{7}$$

Due to the limitations in computing resources at the MEC servers, tasks can be transferred from MEC server q to core network. For each time slot $t \in \mathcal{T}$, the received signal of the core network can be written as

$$\mathbf{y}_c(t) = \mathbf{g}_{q,c}^T(t)\mathbf{u}x_c(t) + \mathbf{n}_c(t) \tag{8}$$

where $\mathbf{g}_{q,c}(t)$ is the $N \times 1$ channel matrix between MEC server q and core network, $p_{q,c}^o$ is the transmission power between MEC server q and core network. Thus, the corresponding signal-to-noise (SNR) can be derived by

$$\gamma_{q,c}(t) = \frac{\mathbf{E}\left\{||\mathbf{g}_{q,c}^T \mathbf{u}(t)x_c(t)||^2\right\}}{\mathbf{E}\left\{n_c(t)\right\}} = \frac{|\mathbf{g}_{q,c}^T \mathbf{u}|^2 p_{q,c}^o}{\sigma_1^2} \tag{9}$$

$$\max \ SNR = \frac{|\mathbf{ug}_{q,c}^T|^2}{\sigma_1^2} \tag{10}$$

$$s.t. \quad ||\mathbf{u}||_2^2 \leq p_{q,c}^o \tag{11}$$

Thus, we can obtain that

$$\mathbf{u} = \sqrt{\alpha}\mathbf{g}_{q,c}^* \tag{12}$$

$$\alpha = \frac{p_{q,c}^o}{||\mathbf{g}_{q,c}||^2} \tag{13}$$

So, the communication rate of MEC q and core network can be expressed as

$$r_{q,c}(t) = W_c log(1 + \gamma_{q,c}(t)) \tag{14}$$

2.3   Computation Model

Let C_k and C_q be the number of CPU cycles required for user k and MEC server q to accomplish one task bit, respectively. Since the tasks can be computed locally or offloaded to MEC servers, we can obtain that

(1) *Local computing:* The CPU frequency at t-th slot can be written by

$$f_k^l(t) = \sqrt[3]{p_k^l(t)/k} \tag{15}$$

where $p_k^l(t)$ is the allocated power for computing locally, k is the effective switched capacitance depending on the chip architecture (CPUs per second). So the computing rate (bits computed per second) for user k locally is expressed as

$$R_k^l(t) = \frac{f_k^l(t)}{C_k} = \frac{\sqrt[3]{p_k^l(t)/k}}{C_k} \tag{16}$$

(2) *Edge computing:* The computing rate (bits computed per second) for MEC server q is expressed as

$$R_{q,k}^{mec}(t) = \frac{\sqrt[3]{p_{q,k}^{mec}(t)/k}}{C_q} \tag{17}$$

where $p_{q,k}^{mec}(t)$ is the allocated power for computation offloading.

2.4   Mobility Model

We model the mobility of users by contact time T_{con}^{mec} and user k keeps contact with the same MEC within T_{con}^{mec}. Besides, the number of contacts between user k and MEC server q follow the Poisson distribution with parameters of $\lambda_{q,k}$. Hence the connect frequency $\lambda_{q,k}$ accounts for mobility intensities [11].

The duration T_{con}^{mec} includes transmitting time and computing time, so we obtain

$$T_{con}^{mec} = \frac{H_{q,k}}{r_{q,k}} + \frac{\alpha_q H_{q,k}}{R_{q,k}^{mec}} + \frac{(1-\alpha_q)H_{q,k}}{r_{q,c}} \tag{18}$$

$$H_{q,k} = \frac{T_{con}^{mec}}{\frac{1}{r_{q,k}} + \frac{\alpha_q}{R_{q,k}^{mec}} + \frac{(1-\alpha_q)}{r_{q,c}}} \tag{19}$$

where $\alpha_q \in [0,1]$ is the weight of the bits of tasks computed in MEC server q, which can be learned from DDPG algorithm. $H_{q,k}^n$ is the maximum bits of offloading tasks from user k to MEC server q during one contact and $\lambda_{q,k}t$ is the number of contacts for user k with MEC server q. Then we can calculate the total offloading bits of user k within time slot t as

$$V_{k,q}(Z) = \sum_{n=1}^{\lambda_{q,k}t} H_{q,k}^n \tag{20}$$

Thus the probability distribution function (PDF) of variable $V_{k,q}(Z)$ can be expressed as

$$f_{V_{k,q}(Z)}(x) = \frac{x^{\lambda_{q,k}t-1}e^{-xH_{q,k}}}{(H_{q,k})^{-\lambda_{q,k}t}\Gamma(\lambda_{q,k}t)} \tag{21}$$

Denoting Z_q as the computation capacity of MEC server q, so the probability that user k offloads m bits tasks to MEC server q is

$$P_{k,q}(m) = \begin{cases} \int_m^{m+1} f_{V_{k,q}(Z)}(x)dx, & 0 \le m < Z_q \\ \int_m^\infty f_{V_{k,q}(Z)}(x)dx, & m = Z_q \\ 0, & otherwise \end{cases} \tag{22}$$

3   Deep Reinforcement Learning

In this section, we will briefly introduce the deep reinforcement learning and DDPG.

3.1   Deep Deterministic Policy Gradient

Reinforcement learning is learning how to map situations to actions by maximizing reward function. In reinforcement learning, the environment is typically formulated as a Markov decision process (MDP). So far, describe MDP with a tuple (S, A, P, R, γ) including an agent, a set of possible states S, a set of available actions A, transition probability matrix P, a reward function R and discount factor of returns γ. We can define the value of the current state s_t with the long-term expected discounted reward, called the value function

$$V_\pi(s_t) = \mathbb{E}_\pi\left[\sum_{t=0}^\infty \gamma^k R_{t+k+1}|s_t\right] \tag{23}$$

Further consider the value of each action, we can define state-action value function after taking action a_t in state s_t:

$$Q_\pi(s_t, a_t) = \mathbb{E}_\pi \left[\sum_{t=0}^{\infty} \gamma^k R_{t+k+1} | s_t, a_t \right] \tag{24}$$

The optimal state-action value function $Q^*(s_t, a_t)$ is the maximum among all policies and the optimal policy π^* can be calculated by maximizing $Q^*(s_t, a_t)$:

$$Q^*(s_t, a_t) = \max_{\pi} Q_\pi(s_t, a_t) \tag{25}$$

$$\pi^*(s_t) = \arg \max_{a_t \in A} Q^*(s_t, a_t) \tag{26}$$

One of the challenges that reinforcement learning faces is the estimation of value functions, but the development of deep learning solves the problems. Deep reinforcement learning combines deep learning and reinforcement learning, which employs deep convolutional neural networks to approximate $Q(s_t, a_t)$. DDPG has been proposed in [12] to solve problems in continuous action spaces. As shown in Fig. 2, DDPG uses an actor-critic algorithm framework that reduces the difficulty of learning by separating the policy network (the actor function) and the Q-value network (the critic function). DDPG is a policy-base algorithm which parameterizes the policy and describes policy $\pi_\theta(s)$ with parametric linear or nonlinear function. In order to maximize cumulative returns $J(\pi_\theta) = \mathbb{E}_{T \sim \pi_\theta} \left[R(T) \right]$, where T represents the trajectory of one episode. According to [13], the policy gradient of the actor can be expressed as

$$\nabla_\theta J(\mu_\theta) = \mathbb{E}_{s \sim \rho^\mu} \left[\nabla_\theta \mu_\theta(s) \nabla_a q^\mu(s, a)|_{a=\mu_\theta(s)} \right] \tag{27}$$

Then we can update the network parameter with a learning rate α as:

$$\theta_{k+1} = \theta_k + \alpha \nabla_\theta J(\mu_\theta) \tag{28}$$

Actor network is used for the interaction with the environment and critic network is responsible for policy evaluation. During the learning process, actor network adjusts the parameter θ to control the action, and critic network guides the actor network to converge toward a larger cumulative return. The detailed steps are shown in Algorithm 1.

3.2   The DDPG Framework

In this section, we will employ the DDPG algorithm to minimize the overall cost of transmission and computation. Thus, the three elements of the DDPG algorithm can be defined as follows:

- System State: At the beginning of time slot t, the bits of user k's tasks $l_k(t)$ will be updated with the rate of poisson distribution λ_k. Meanwhile, channel

---

Algorithm 1. The DDPG-based Computational Offloading

1: Randomly initialize the actor network μ_{θ^μ} and the critic network Q_{θ^Q} with weights θ^μ and θ^Q;
2: Initialize target network μ and Q with weights $\theta^{\mu'} \leftarrow \theta^\mu$, $\theta^{Q'} \leftarrow \theta^Q$;
3: Initialize the experience replay buffer B;
4: **for** each episode $m = 1, 2, ..., M$ **do**
5:      Reset simulation parameters for the environment;
6:      Randomly generate an initial state s_1;
7:      **for** each time slot $t = 1, 2, ..., T$ **do**
8:          Select an action $a_t = \mu(s_t|\theta^\mu) + \nabla\mu$ to determine the power for transmission and computation;
9:          Execute action a_t and receive reward r_t and observe the next state s_{t+1};
10:         Store the tuple (s_t, a_t, r_t, s_{t+1}) into B;
11:         Sample a random mini-batch of N transitions (s_t, a_t, r_t, s_{t+1}) from B;
12:         Update the critic network by minimizing the loss L :
$L = \frac{1}{N}\sum_{t=1}^{N}\left(r_t + \max_{a\in A} Q(s_t', a|\theta^{Q'}) - Q(s_t, a_t|\theta^Q)\right)^2$;
13:         Update the actor network by using the sampled policy gradient:
$\nabla_{\theta^\mu} J \approx \frac{1}{N}\sum_{t=1}^{N}\nabla_a Q(s_t, a|\theta^Q)|_{a=a_t}\nabla_{\theta^\mu}\mu(s_t|\theta^\mu)$;
14:         Update the target networks by:
$\theta^{\mu'} \leftarrow \tau\theta^\mu + (1-\tau)\theta^{\mu'}$;
$\theta^{Q'} \leftarrow \tau\theta^Q + (1-\tau)\theta^{Q'}$;
15:     **end for**
16: **end for**

---

vectors $\mathbf{g}_{k,q}(t)$ and $\mathbf{g}_{q,c}(t)$ will also be estimated. Thus the system state can be denoted as

$$s(t) = \left\{l_k(t), \mathbf{g}_{k,q}(t), \mathbf{g}_{q,c}(t)\right\} \tag{29}$$

- System Action: In the system, the agent has to decide the allocated powers for local execution and transmission, MEC servers' computation and transmission. The weight of the bits of tasks computed in the MEC server will also be included. So the system action can be expressed as

$$a(t) = \left\{p_k^l(t), p_{k,q}^o(t), p_{q,c}^o(t), p_{k,q}^{mec}(t), \alpha_q(t)\right\} \tag{30}$$

- Reward Function: We set the deadline t and assume that the transmission and computation must be accomplished within t. The overall cost of transmission and computation is regarded as the feedback of the system. In this way, the reward function $R(t)$ at time slot t can be written as

$$R(t) = -R_k^l * C^{user} - \sum_{m=1}^{l_k - R_k^l} P_k(m)(\alpha_q m C^{mec} + (1-\alpha_q)m C^{cloud}) - \omega(l_k - R_k^l - m) \tag{31}$$

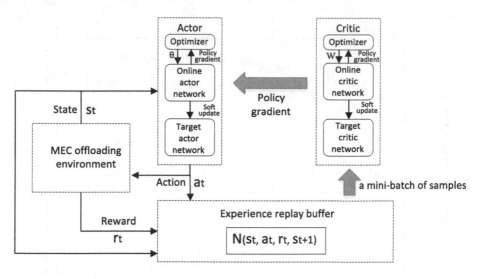

Fig. 2. The structure of DDPG

where ω is nonnegative weighted factor, and the agent will receive a negative reward if the transmission and computation are not completed within the deadline.

4   Numerical Results

In this section, we will present the numerical results to illustrate the performance of the proposed DDPG algorithm for power allocation. We assume that the bandwidth of the system is $1\,\mathrm{MHz}$, the path loss factor α is 2. On the other hand, the maximum transmission and computation power, that is, the constraint of actions is $2\,\mathrm{W}$. Additionally, the required CPU cycles per bit C_k and C_q is 500 cycles/bit, and $k = 10^{-27}$. Additionally, the cost of local computation C^{user} is 10, the cost of one task bit offloading including transmission and computation to MEC servers is 8, and the cost for one task bit transmitting to the core network is 15.

According to the results of the actual debugging experiment, the general training process of the deep reinforcement learning algorithm is summarized as follows: Firstly, the agent interacts with the environment with random actions, and explores the environment as much as possible. Then the agent chooses action based on a specific policy (obtained by the actor network or the greedy policy), and trains the agent according to the next state and reward that the environment feedbacks. Finally, the agent evaluates the performance of the learned policy and continues to train the network after evaluation. In order to receive the optimal policy, we set the learning rate of actor and critic as 0.0001 and 0.001 respectively. In Fig. 3, we show the training process of DDPG-based power allocation algorithm with $\lambda_{q,k} = 0.3$ and $\lambda_{q,k} = 2.5$. For different connect frequencies, the

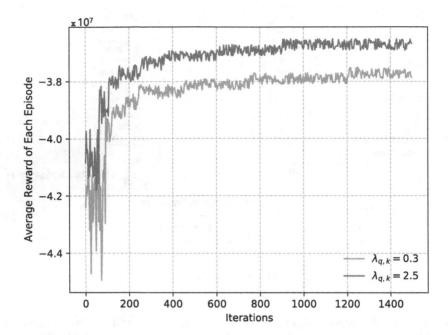

Fig. 3. Average reward of each episode for $\lambda_{q,k} = 0.3$ and $\lambda_{q,k} = 2.5$.

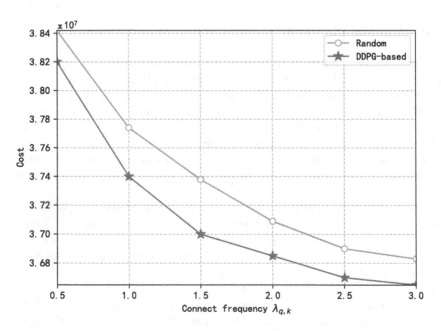

Fig. 4. Overall cost for DDPG-based and random power allocation with different connect frequency $\lambda_{q,k}$.

average reward both increases as the training time goes by, and reach a stable value. On the other hand, when the connect frequency is low, there are fewer tasks that the requested user can offload and then the overall cost increase.

We compare the performance of our proposed algorithm and random power allocation algorithm with different connect frequencies $\lambda_{q,k}$ in Fig. 4. The impact of connect frequency on the overall cost is shown in the figure. When the connect frequency increases, more tasks can be offloaded to MEC servers and the core network so the overall cost becomes lower. As expected, the DDPG-based algorithm presents a better power allocation scheme than random power allocation scheme.

It can be observed from Fig. 5 that when the task arrival rate increases, the overall cost will increase as well, which means that more tasks can be processed within the capabilities of the MEC offloading system. We can also find that the performance of our proposed DDPG-based algorithm acts better than random power allocation algorithm since the DDPG agent can adjust the power allocation and learn the optimal policy according to the current state after training.

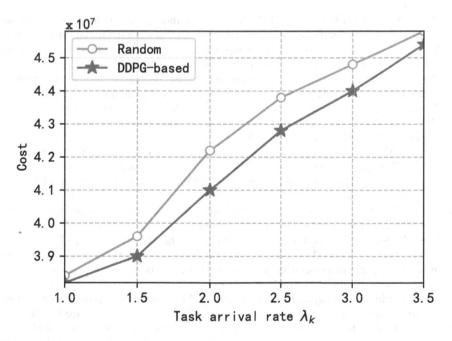

Fig. 5. Overall cost for DDPG-based and random power allocation with different task arrival rate λ_k.

5   Conclusion

In this paper, we developed a mobility-aware computation offloading system, where tasks can be processed locally and offloaded to MEC servers. By considering the limited resources at MEC servers, the unprocessed tasks can be handed over to the core network. Then we derive the offloading and computation rates under the condition of time-varying wireless channels and mobile users. We adopt the deep reinforcement learning algorithm named DDPG to learn the optimal power allocation policy with minimizing the overall consumption cost. Finally, it can be observed from numerical simulations that the DDPG-based algorithm presents a better power allocation scheme than existing method.

Acknowledgement. This work was supported in part by the National Science Foundation China under Grant 61771345 and Grant 61571330, and in part by the Fundamental Research Funds for the Central Universities.

References

1. Wang, Y., Chen, I.R., Wang, D.C.: A survey of mobile cloud computing applications: perspectives and challenges. Wirel. Pers. Commun. **80**(4), 1607–1623 (2015)
2. Yi, S., Li, C., Li, Q.: Mobile edge computing: a survey on architecture and computation offloading. IEEE Commun. Surv. Tutor. 1 (2017)
3. Ren, J., et al.: Exploiting mobile crowdsourcing for pervasive cloud services: challenges and solutions. IEEE Commun. Mag. **26**(1), 1–12 (2017)
4. Zhang, K., Mao, Y., Leng, S., He, Y., Zhang, Y.: Mobile-edge computing for vehicular networks: a promising network paradigm with predictive offloading. IEEE Commun. Mag. **12**(2), 36–44 (2017)
5. Liu, J., Mao, Y., Zhang, J., et al.: Delay-optimal computation task scheduling for mobile-edge computing systems. In: IEEE International Symposium on Information Theory, Barcelona, Spain, pp. 1451–1455 (2016). https://doi.org/10.1109/ISIT.2016.7541539
6. Zhang, K., Mao, Y., Leng, S., et al.: Optimal delay constrained offloading for vehicular edge computing networks. In: IEEE International Conference on Communications, Paris, France, pp. 1–6 (2017). https://doi.org/10.1109/ICC.2017.7997360
7. Du, J., Zhao, L., Feng, J., Chu, X.: Computation offloading and resource allocation in mixed fog/cloud computing systems with min-max fairness guarantee. IEEE Trans. Commun. **66**(4), 1594–1608 (2018)
8. Guo, H., Liu, J., Zhang, J., Sun, W., Kato, N.: Mobile-edge computation offloading for ultra-dense IoT networks. IEEE Internet Things J. **5**(6), 4977–4988 (2018)
9. Tan, L.T., Hu, R.Q.: Mobility-aware edge caching and computing in vehicle networks: a deep reinforcement learning. IEEE Trans. Veh. Technol. **67**(11), 10190–10203 (2018)
10. Chen, Z., Wang, X.: Decentralized computation offloading for multi-user mobile edge computing: a deep reinforcement learning approach. arXiv preprint arXiv: 1812.07394 (2015)
11. Ross, S.M.: Introduction to Probability Models, 11th edn. Academic Press, San Francisco (2000)

12. Lillicrap, T.P., et al.: Continuous control with deep reinforcement learning. arXiv preprint arXiv: 1509.02971 (2015)
13. Silver, D., Lever, G., Heess, N., Degris, T., Wierstra, D., Riedmiller, M.: Deterministic policy gradient algorithms. In: International Conference on Machine Learning, pp. 387–395 (2014)

Priority EDF Scheduling Scheme
for MANETs

Abel Mukakanya Muwumba[1]([⊠]), Godfrey Njulumi Justo[1],
Libe Valentine Massawe[1], and John Ngubiri[2]

[1] College of Information and Communication Technologies,
University of Dar es Saalam, Dar es Salaam, Tanzania
abelmuk@gmail.com, njulumi@gmail.com, massawe.libe@udsm.ac.tz,
liebetz@yahoo.co.uk
[2] Makerere University, Kampala, Uganda
ngubiri@cis.mak.ac.ug

Abstract. Analytical EDF Priority schedulers are not common in
Mobile Ad-hoc Networks (MANETs). Some researchers like Abhaya et
al. have proposed a classical preemptive Earliest Deadline First (EDF)
scheduler. The goal of this EDF scheduler was to favor higher priority packets thereby reducing their waiting times. Accordingly, favoring
higher priority queues end up increasing the waiting times of lower priority queues. We improve Abhaya's approach and adopt it to the MANETs
environment. We numerically study the performance of the Adopted and
Improved Adopted Abhaya Earliest Deadline First (IEDF) models for
different packet queues. Our analytical results show that the IEDF model
shortens the waiting times of packets of the different queues at various
system loads in comparison to the Adopted Abhaya EDF model.

Keywords: Deadline · Model · Packets · Preemptive · Waiting time

1 Introduction

Mobile Ad-hoc Networks consists of a set of mobile nodes that communicate with
one another across multiple hops in a distributed manner [1]. The traffic transmitted by the nodes in MANETs is real-time and some is non-real time. Both
delay-sensitive and non-delay-sensitive applications usually coexist in the same
network, making QoS provisioning to be a critical issue [2]. Real-time traffic is
delay sensitive, therefore, the design of an efficient priority scheduling scheme
that will ensure that the mobile nodes in MANETs transmit traffic to the desired
expectations of the users under strict deadline constraints becomes crucial. In
designing priority-based scheduling policies, the ultimate goal is to avoid job
starvation [3]. Unfortunately, MANETs technology does not specify any specific
scheduling scheme leaving it open to researchers and scholars to innovate in this
area. Whereas priority scheduling algorithms like Earliest Deadline First (EDF)

© ICST Institute for Computer Sciences, Social Informatics and Telecommunications Engineering 2020
Published by Springer Nature Switzerland AG 2020. All Rights Reserved
H. Gao et al. (Eds.): ChinaCom 2019, LNICST 312, pp. 66–76, 2020.
https://doi.org/10.1007/978-3-030-41114-5_6

have been sought to be among the viable solutions in transmitting traffic in wireless networking environments. Unfortunately, at the time of this study, we did not come across any specific EDF analytical models in MANETs. However, there exist a classical preemptive EDF model proposed by Abhaya et al. [4,5] that we have adopted to the MANETs environment. Therefore, in this paper, we study the Adopted Abhaya EDF model. The numerical results from the Adopted Abhaya EDF model show a performance degradation in waiting time for different packets in different priority queues at various system loads. We propose an Improved Adopted Abhaya Earliest Deadline First (IEDF) model that shortens the average waiting times of packets of the different queues. Therefore, in this paper we address the following specific gaps in the Adopted Abhaya EDF scheduler research. (i) the starvation of low priority queue packets. (ii) We address the poor performance of the Adopted Abhaya EDF model at high network traffic loads.

We use the Adopted and Improved EDF schemes to determine which packet in a particular queue of traffic should be served first among the set of waiting or remaining packets in different queues at a specific node in MANETs. The remainder of this paper is organized as follows: In Sect. 2 we describe the some Related Works. This is followed in Sect. 3 by the EDF schemes. Section 4 presents the Improved Adopted Abhaya EDF model. The Results and Discussions are presented in Sect. 5. Conclusion and Future Research are finally presented in Sect. 6.

2 Related Work

Liu and Layland [6] suggested the most popular real-time scheduling algorithms, EDF. The EDF policy assigns a deadline to each packet, which is used by the scheduler to define the order of service. The highest priority job is the one with the earliest deadline. It essentially schedules the jobs in a greedy manner which always picks the jobs with the closest deadline. An efficient Quality of Service architecture using inter layer communication with a highly efficient real time scheduler design at the network layer with improved Rate Monotonic Algorithm and Earliest Deadline First scheduling that efficiently schedules multiple real time applications without missing any of their deadline was proposed [7].

A number of EDF priority scheduling policies have been proposed in the previous works by altering the existing ones and adding new constraints to enhance performance [4,8–12]. An analytical method for approximating the performance of a two-class priority M/M/1 system was presented [8]. In this model the prioritized class-1 jobs were considered to be real-time and served according to the EDF scheduling policy, and the non real-time class-2 jobs were served according to the FIFO policy. One limitation with this model is that it is not an exact analytical solution for the analysis of EDF, even for a system with purely real-time jobs.

A multi-queue EDF and its variant Flexible Earliest Deadline First (F-EDF) was proposed [9]. The solution [10] investigated mean sojourn times in multi-class queues with feedback and their application to packet scheduling in communication networks. A Packet Scheduling algorithm consisting of EDF algorithm and

Least Slack Time algorithm is proposed for scheduling the various multimedia applications [11]. This Scheduling algorithm is used to reduce the transmission delay and to achieve better QoS requirements.

A preemptive M/M/1/EDF and non-preemptive M/M/m/EDF model is presented [10]. In this model exponentially distributed service times are assumed and these may not suitably represent web services workloads because the services could be used in exposing any type of system. A non-preemptive and work-conserving M/G/1/./EDF model which is supported by general workloads is proposed [12]. A preemptive EDF scheduling scheme that approximates the mean waiting time for a given class based on the higher and lower priority tasks receiving service prior to the target and the mean residual service time experienced was proposed [4,5]. The goal of this EDF scheduler was to favor higher priority packets thereby reducing their waiting times. The limitation with this approach is that favoring higher priority queues yielded increased waiting times of lower priority queues.

3   The EDF Schemes

3.1   The Preemptive EDF Model

Abhaya et al. [4,5] proposed an algorithm that applies on web services middleware. In the algorithm the requests, jobs and tasks are received by the middleware, and selected requests are serviced at each server using the EDF scheduling algorithm. The model considers mean waiting time of multiple streams of packets serviced by node that acts as server. When packets arrive at the node, the scheduler classifies the packets into high and low priority queues. Each packet in the priority queue is assigned a deadline and the packets with high priority and with short deadlines are serviced first. The generic expression of mean waiting time for any queue i is given in Eq. (1).

$$\overline{W}_i = [\frac{\overline{W^i}_0}{1 - \sigma_i} + \sum_{k=i+1}^{N} \rho_k max(0, \overline{W}_k - D_{k,i})] + \sum_{k=1}^{i-1} \rho_k min(\overline{W}_i, D_{i,k}) \quad (1)$$

According to Abhaya et al. [4,5] the symbols in Eq. 1 are explained as follows: $\overline{W}_i$, is mean waiting time for a packet of stream/priority i; $\overline{W}_k$, is mean waiting time for a packet of stream/priority k; $\overline{W}_0^i$ is mean time delay experienced by an arrival from stream i, from the packets already in progress; $D_{k,i}$ is the difference in the deadline offsets of streams i and k; $D_{i,k}$ is the difference in the deadline offsets of streams k and i; N is the number of independent streams through which requests arrive at the system following a Poisson process; and ρ_k is the system load due to queue k packets.

3.2   Adopting the Abhaya EDF Model to MANETs

MANETs have a unique characteristic behaviour, where within their network each node has the potential to act as a data source, a data sink, and/or a router

input : Consider a preemptive M/G/1 queue
output: Mean waiting time for any class i
For all incoming jobs classify into Priority Classes;
Assign a deadline to each job;
for $i = 1 \leftarrow N$ **do**
  for $j = i + 1 \leftarrow N$ **do**
  | $D_{i,j} = d_j - d_i$;
  end
  Compute the;
  Service times;
  Second moments;
  System loads;
  Mean residual service;
  Probability of a request from stream;
  Mean delay experienced by a new arrival;
  Mean waiting time;
end

Algorithm 1. The EDF Abhaya model

[13]. The basic structure of MANETs constitutes mobile nodes that are connected to transfer packets from source to destination mobile nodes, and there is an intermediary node between transmitting and receiving node acting as a router [14]. It is possible to have multiple servers in a single MANETs environment. We exploit this property of MANETs in the adopted EDF Abhaya model.

We make the following changes in the Abhaya model. (i) We adopt an M/G/m queue which is a multi-server system. Specifically, we use the M/M/m queueing system with arrival rates λ and service time $\overline{X}$. (ii) Compute the waiting probability following a non-preemptive M/M/m queue for server utilization. (iii) We compute the mean residual service time for a request of stream/priority i is for a M/M/m system. (iv) We change from preemptive scheduling to non-preemptive scheduling because all network data is useful and once it has been assigned a deadline, preempting an on-going job leads to several re-transmissions and results into wastage of resources.

We present the classic Adopted Abhaya EDF model in Algorithm 2. The Adopted Abhaya EDF scheduling algorithm determines the way packets are processed by the M/G/m scheduling system depending on deadline priority factor. Four priority queues i.e., $P1$-high, $P2$-medium, $P3$-normal and $P4$-low are considered at the intermediary node (router). Routers transmit packets by selecting the packet with shortest deadlines in the high priority queue. If any packet exists in the high priority queue, then it is selected and transmitted. Else, a packet with the shortest deadline is selected from the medium priority queue and transmitted. If there does not exist any packet in the medium priority queue also, then normal priority queue is considered. Finally, the low priority queue is taken into account. This procedure is continued for every packet in the MANET traffic.

The adopted generic expression of mean waiting time for any Queue i is given by Eq. (2).

input : Consider a non-preemptive M/G/m
output: Mean waiting time for any Queue i

For all incoming Jobs classify into Priority Queues;
Assign a deadline;
for $i = 1 \leftarrow N$ **do**
    for $j = i + 1 \leftarrow N$ **do**
       | $D_{i,j} = d_j - d_i;$
    end
    Compute the;
    Service times;
    Second moments;
    System loads;
    Waiting Probability of a request;
    Mean mean residual service time;
    Mean delay experienced by a new arrival;
    Mean waiting time;
end

Algorithm 2. The Adopted EDF Abhaya model

$$\overline{W}_i(Adp) = [\frac{\overline{W}^i_0}{m(1 - \sigma_i)} + \sum_{k=i+1}^{N} \rho_k max(0, \overline{W}_k - D_{k,i})] + \sum_{k=1}^{i-1} \rho_k min(\overline{W}_i(Adp), D_{i,k})$$

(2)

Like in Eq. 1, and according to Abhaya et al. [4,5] the symbols in Eq. 2 are explained as follows: $\overline{W}_i(Adp)$, is the mean waiting time for a packet of stream/priority i for Adopted EDF Abhaya model; $\overline{W}_k$, is mean waiting time for a packet of stream/priority k; $\overline{W}^i_0$ is Mean time delay experienced by an arrival from stream i, from the packets already in progress; $D_{k,i}$ is the difference in the deadline offsets of streams i and k; $D_{i,k}$ is the difference in the deadline offsets of streams k and i; N is the number of independent streams through which requests arrive at the system following a Poisson process; and ρ_k is the system load due to queue k packets. The other additional parameter m stands for the number of indentical servers in an M/G/m queue.

We make the following assumptions: In our system, 4 sources, 2 routers and 10 destination mobile nodes are the three main components. A router can send the packet to the destination mobile nodes via wireless Ad Hoc networks. The system has two (02) identical servers.

3.3 Performance of the Adopted Abhaya EDF Model

We first look at the performance of the Adopted Abhaya EDF model under the M/M/m queueing system. Our goal here is to show the weakness of the Adopted

Abhaya EDF in terms of penalizing low priority class packets in favor of higher priority packets. Due to limited space, we only show delay performances of the Adopted Abhaya EDF for four priority classes. We present more results of the Adopted Abhaya EDF performance when we compare it with the Improved Adopted Abhaya EDF in Sect. 5.

Figure 1 shows the waiting time as function of total load. We observe that: (i) $P1$ packets have a better performance overall among the all compared priority packets making the Adopted Abhaya EDF model to penalize low priority packet. (ii) waiting time for $P3$ and $P4$ packets increases uniformly with increasing load. (iii) waiting time for $P1$ and $P2$ packets increases uniformly with increasing load up to the 0.6 network load, beyond this load it drops up to 0.75 network load; and again it gradually increases till the end.

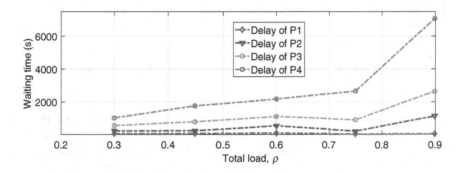

Fig. 1. Waiting time as a function of total load

4   Improving the Adopted Abhaya EDF Model

We indicate the following improvements in the Adopted Abhaya EDF model. (i) The component $\sum_{k=i+1}^{N} \rho_k max(0, \overline{W}_k - D_{k,i})$ is removed to avoid excessive waiting time for low priority packets. (ii) The component $\sum_{k=1}^{i-1} \rho_k min(\overline{W}_i(Adp), D_{i,k})$ is changed to $\sum_{i=2}^{N-1} \rho_i min(\overline{W}_i(imp), D_{i+1,i})$. It is these modifications that are responsible for shortening the waiting times for the low priority packets. We present the Improved Adopted Abhaya EDF model in Algorithm 3. In the Improved Adopted EDF Abhaya model, traffic consists of N number of independent queues that are classified by the scheduler into priority queues. Each queue is identified by $i, i = 1, 2, ..N$ and is associated with a different deadline. Packets from the same queue get assigned a constant deadline offset. Scheduling of packets among different queues uses IEDF and requests from the same queue are serviced in a First-Come First-Served basis. We consider the scenario of four priority queues where $N = 4$ i.e., $P1$-high, $P2$-medium, $P3$-normal and $P4$-low. Packets from $P1$ are assumed to have shorter deadlines than packets from $P2$, $P3$ and $P4$. In a typical priority based system, higher

input : Consider a non-preemptive M/G/m queue
output: Mean waiting time for any queue i

For all incoming jobs classify into Priority Queues;
Assign a deadline;
for $i = 1 \leftarrow N$ **do**
    for $j = i + 1 \leftarrow N$ **do**
       $D_{i,j} = d_j - d_i;$
    end
    Compute the;
    Service times;
    Second moments;
    System loads;
    Waiting Probability of a request;
    Mean mean residual service time;
    Mean delay experienced by a new arrival after removal of excessive delay
    componets;
    Mean waiting time;
end

Algorithm 3. The Improved Adopted EDF Abhaya model

priority packets are always serviced ahead of lower priority packets, since the priority is determined by the absolute deadline in the system under consideration. Since packets from $P1$ have higher priority over $P2, P3$ and $P4$ packets, under a high arrival rate of $P1$ packets; $P2, P3$ and $P4$ packets are served after $P1$. For the case of four priority queues $N = 4$, we have four view points of the average delay of a tagged packet in a specific queue after delay. (i) The average delay of $P1$ packets. The tagged $P1$ packet will experience the following delays: $P1$ packets found in the queue will be serviced before the tagged packet, in this case $\overline{N}_{1,1} = \lambda_1 \overline{W}_1$. Where λ_1 is the arrival rate of $P1$ queue packets, and $\overline{W}_1$ is the mean waiting time for $P1$ queue packet. $P1$ packets from stream 1 arriving at the system after the tagged request will be served later i.e., $M_{1,1} = 0$. Therefore, the *average waiting time*, $\overline{W}_1$ for a tagged packet in $P1$ queue is given as;

$$\overline{W}_1 = \overline{W}_0 + \rho_1 \overline{W}_1 \tag{3}$$

(ii) The average delay of $P2$ packets. The following are the delays experienced by the tagged $P2$ packets; delay due to $P1$ packets found in the queue when the tagged packet arrives, these packets will experience delay given by; $N_{1,2} = \lambda_1 \overline{W}_1$. Delay due to $P2$ packets found in queue $N_{2,2} = \lambda_2 \overline{W}_2$. Where λ_2 is the arrival rate of $P2$ queue packets, and $\overline{W}_2$ is the mean waiting time for $P2$ queue packet. Once the tagged packet arrives at the system, it will not wait for a portion of $P1$ packets to be served before it. These packets will have deadlines earlier than the tagged packet. Because packets from $P1$ that arrive after the tagged packet, they will be served after the tagged packet. Therefore $M_{1,2} = 0$, and the delay experienced by the tagged packet can be expressed by;

$\overline{W}_2 = \overline{W}_0 + \overline{X}_1\lambda_1\overline{W}_1 + \overline{X}_2\lambda_2\overline{W}_2$. The *average waiting time*, $\overline{W}_2$ for a tagged packet in $P2$ queue is given as;

$$\overline{W}_2 = \overline{W}_0 + \rho_1\overline{W}_1 + \rho_2\overline{W}_2 \tag{4}$$

(iii) The average delay of $P3$ packet. The following are the delays experienced by the tagged $P3$ packet: delay due to $P1$ packets in queue $N_{1,3} = \lambda_1\overline{W}_1$; $P2$ packets in queue $N_{2,3} = \lambda_2\overline{W}_2$; and $P2$ packets in queue $N_{3,3} = \lambda_3\overline{W}_3$. Where λ_3 is the arrival rate of $P3$ queue packets, and $\overline{W}_3$ is the mean waiting time for $P3$ queue packet. Given the waiting time of $P3$, the tagged packet may be in the queue for a time period less than $D_{3,2}$ given that $W_3 < D_{3,2}$. The delay can be estimated as $M_{2,3} = \lambda_2 min(\overline{W}_3, D_{3,2})$.
$\overline{W}_3 = \overline{W}_0 + \rho_1\overline{W}_1 + \rho_2\overline{W}_2 + \rho_3\overline{W}_3 + \overline{X}_2\lambda_2 min(\overline{W}_3, D_{3,2})$. $D_{3,2}$ is the difference in the deadline offsets of streams 3 and 2. The *average waiting time*, $\overline{W}_3$ for a tagged packet in $P3$ queue is given as;

$$\overline{W}_3 = \overline{W}_0 + \rho_1\overline{W}_1 + \rho_2\overline{W}_2 + \rho_3\overline{W}_3 + \rho_2 min(\overline{W}_3, D_{3,2}) \tag{5}$$

(iv) The average delay of $P4$ packet. The following are the delays experienced by the tagged $P4$ packet: delay due to $P1$ packets in queue $N_{1,4} = \lambda_1\overline{W}_1$; delay due to $P2$ packets in queue $N_{2,4} = \lambda_2\overline{W}_2$; delay due to $P3$ packets in queue $N_{3,4} = \lambda_3\overline{W}_3$; and delay due to $P4$ packets in queue $N_{4,4} = \lambda_4\overline{W}_4$. Where λ_4 is the arrival rate of $P4$ queue packets, and $\overline{W}_4$ is the mean waiting time for $P4$ queue packet. Given the waiting time of stream 4, the tagged packet may be in the queue for a time period less than $D_{4,3}$ given that $W_4 < D_{3,2}$ and less than $D_{4,3}$ given that $W_4 < D_{4,3}$. The delay can be estimated as $M_{2,3} = \lambda_2 min(\overline{W}_3, D_{3,2})$ and $M_{3,4} = \lambda_3 min(\overline{W}_4, D_{4,3})$. $D_{4,3}$ is the difference in the deadline offsets of streams 4 and 3. $\overline{W}_4 = \overline{W}_3 + \rho_4\overline{W}_4 + \overline{X}_3\lambda_3 min(\overline{W}_4, D_{4,3})$.

The *average waiting time*, $\overline{W}_4$ for a tagged packet in $P4$ queue is given as;

$$\overline{W}_4 = \overline{W}_0 + \rho_1\overline{W}_1 + \rho_2\overline{W}_2 + \rho_3\overline{W}_3 + \rho_4\overline{W}_4 + \rho_2 min(\overline{W}_3, D_{3,2}) + \rho_3 min(\overline{W}_4, D_{4,3}) \tag{6}$$

Given the scheduling discipline considered, the mean waiting times must satisfy the conservation law for M/G/m queues [15, 16]. Because of the m servers;

$$\sum_{k=1}^{i} \rho_k W_k = \frac{\sigma_i \overline{W}^i{}_0}{m(1 - \sigma_i)} \tag{7}$$

Note: $\sigma_i = \sum_{k=1}^{i} \rho_k$. Substituting Eq. (7) into Eqs. (3), (4), (5) and (6), become Eqs. (8), (9), (10), (11) respectively.

The *average waiting time*, $\overline{W}_1$ for a tagged packet in $P1$ queue is:

$$\overline{W}_1 = \frac{\overline{W}^1{}_0}{m(1 - \sigma_1)} \tag{8}$$

The *average waiting time*, $\overline{W}_2$ for a tagged packet in $P2$ queue is:

$$\overline{W}_2 = \frac{\overline{W}^2{}_0}{m(1 - \sigma_2)} \tag{9}$$

The *average waiting time*, $\overline{W}_3$ for a tagged packet in $P3$ queue is:

$$\overline{W}_3 = \frac{\overline{W^3}_0}{m(1 - \sigma_3)} + \rho_2 min(\overline{W}_3, D_{3,2}) \tag{10}$$

And the *average waiting time*, $\overline{W}_4$ for a tagged packet in $P4$ queue is:

$$\overline{W}_4 = \frac{\overline{W^4}_0}{1 - \sigma_4} + \rho_2 min(\overline{W}_3, D_{3,2}) + \rho_3 min(\overline{W}_4, D_{4,3}) \tag{11}$$

The generic equation for the *average waiting time*, $\overline{W}_i(imp)$ for the IEDF for P_i queue is given by;

$$\overline{W}_i(imp) = \frac{\overline{W^i}_0}{m(1 - \sigma_i)} + \sum_{i=2}^{N-1} \rho_i min(\overline{W}_i(imp), D_{i+1,i}) \tag{12}$$

5   Results and Discussions

The intention of this Section is to experiment the IEDF and benchmark it against the adopted Abhaya EDF model in Sect. 3.2. The evaluation of the models was carried out using analytical methods. The main metrics measured are average waiting time. We implemented EDF models in Matlab to evaluate the performance.

5.1   The Analytical Results

The waiting times of the four priority queues were computed for both models using an iterative process at system loads, $\rho = 0.3, 0.45, 0.6, 0.75$ and 0.9. Table 1 shows the estimated waiting times the four priority queues for the Adopted and Improved EDF models. We assumed the same parameters for deadlines, deadline differences, service times and second moments for various system loads.

Table 1. Waiting times for Adopted and Improved Abhaya EDF models-four priority queues

Load	AEDF P1	AEDF P2	AEDF P3	AEDF P4	IEDF P1	IEDF P2	IEDF P3	IEDF P4
0.30	51.335	225.843	549.792	1019.489	51.335	207.775	500.911	876.030
0.45	64.232	232.496	788.239	1758.080	64.232	205.624	672.913	1354.04
0.60	91.612	535.430	1107.482	2171.020	91.612	431.022	816.768	1299.689
0.75	29.225	212.829	902.871	2661.403	29.225	170.263	663.700	1392.291
0.90	36.283	1127.756	2639.266	7067.499	36.283	258.811	1175.739	4324.818

5.2   Discussions of the Results

Figure 2 is a graphic representation of the waiting time against total load for four priority queues of the EDF and IEDF models. Results obtained show that: (i) the highest priority $P1$ packets had the lowest waiting times at all loads for the Adopted Abhaya EDF and Improved Adopted Abhaya EDF models. Packets that arrive are serviced on first come first serve basis with minimal delay. This validates the claim that in multi-server Queuing Systems when the average service rate is more than average arrival rate then there are no or minimal delays. (ii) the waiting time for $P2$, $P3$ and $P4$ packets increases with increasing total load in both the Adopted and Improved Adopted Abhaya EDF models. This confirms fact that in multi-server Queuing Systems increasing total load, and when the number of packets in the system is more than or equal to the number of servers then all servers will be busy resulting into increasing longer waiting times. (iii) At any instant the waiting time for $P4$ is significantly higher than $P3$, $P2$ and $P1$ packets in the Adopted Abhaya EDF model; We further note that the Improved Adopted Abhaya EDF model provides bigger relative improvements in waiting times for $P4$, $P3$ and $P2$ packets. This validates the authors two claims that (a) by EDF favoring higher priority packets ends up increasing the waiting times of lower priority packets. (b) low-priority queue packet starvation is avoided by the IEDF model. (iv) at higher system loads, IEDF model provides higher improvements in waiting times for packets compared to EDF. High system loads are associated with high arrival rates resulting into long delays for lower priority class packets.

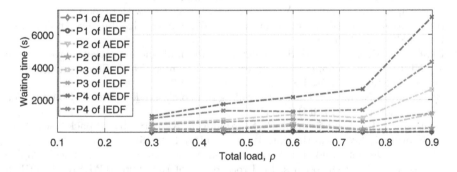

Fig. 2. Waiting time as a function of total load

6   Conclusion and Future Research

We developed a novel IEDF scheduling scheme that reduces the average waiting time of the priority queue packets. We compared average waiting times of four priority queues i.e, $P1$-high, $P2$-medium, $P3$-normal and $P4$-low at various system loads for the IEDF and AEDF models. From the results obtained, the IEDF shortens the waiting times of packets in all queues as compared to AEDF. In future research a new algorithm should be developed that will minimize relative performance gaps, study starvation trends and effects of selective preemption based on remaining processing time of lower queue packets.

References

1. Kuo, W., Chu, S.: Energy efficiency optimization for mobile ad-hoc networks. IEEE Open Access J. **4**, 928–940 (2016)
2. Chen, W., Guan, Q., Jiang, S., Guan, Q., Huang, T.: Joint QoS provisioning and congestion control for multihop wireless networks. EURASIP J. Wirel. Commun. Network. **2016** (2016)
3. Malik, S., Ahmad, S., Ullah, I., Park, D.H., Kim, D.: An adaptive emergency first intelligent scheduling algorithm for efficient task management and scheduling in hybrid of hard real-time and soft real-time embedded IoT systems. Sustainability **11**(8), 2192 (2019)
4. Abhaya, V., Tari, Z., Zeephongsekul, P., Zomaya, A.Y.: Performance analysis of EDF scheduling in a multi-priority preemptive M/G/1 queue. IEEE Trans. Parallel Distrib. Syst. **25**(8), 2149–2158 (2014)
5. Abhaya, G.: Towards achieving execution time predictability in web services middleware. Ph.D. dissertation, School of Computer Science and Information Technology, College of Science, Engineering, and Health, RMIT University, Melbourne, Victoria (2012)
6. Liu, C., Layland, J.W.: Scheduling algorithms for multiprogramming in a hard-real-time environment. J. ACM **20**(1), 46–61 (1973)
7. Rath, M., Pati, B., Pattanayak, B.K.: Cross layer based QoS platform for multimedia transmission in MANET. In: Proceedings of the 11th International Conference on Intelligent Systems and Control (ISCO), January 2017
8. Kargahi, M., Movaghar, A.: A two-class M/M/1 system with preemptive non real-time jobs and prioritized real-time jobs under earliest-deadline-first policy. Sci. Iran. **15**(2), 252–265 (2008)
9. Dehbi, Y., Mikou, N.: Priority assignment for multimedia packet scheduling in MANET. In: Proceedings of the International Conference on Signal Image Technology and Internet Based Systems, November 2008
10. Barhoun, R., Namir, A.: Packet scheduling of two classes flow. Int. J. Comput. Sci. Inf. Technol. (IJCSIT) **3**(4) (2011)
11. Arunkumar, B., Avudaiammal, R., Swarnalatha, A.: QoS - based packet scheduler for hybrid wireless networks. Int. J. Netw. (IJN) **1** (2015)
12. Chen, K., Decreusefond, L.: An approximate analysis of waiting time in multi-classes M/G/1/./EDF queues. In: Proceedings of the 1996 ACM SIGMETRICS International Conference on Measurement and Modeling of Com, Las Vegas, NY,USA (1996)
13. Charles, A., Bensraj, R.: Enhanced weighted fair-queuing technique for improving the QoS in MANET. Int. J. Adv. Eng. Technol. **7** (2016)
14. Kumar, V.: Improving quality of service in mobile ad-hoc networks (MANETs) using adaptive broadcast scheduling algorithm with dynamic source routing protocol. J. Comput. Theor. Nanosci. **14**(9), 4370–4376 (2017)
15. Bolch, G., Greiner, S., Meer, H.D., Trivedi, K.S.: Queueing Networks and Markov Chains: Modeling and Performance Evaluation with Computer Science Applications. Wiley-Blackwell, Hoboken (2006)
16. Kleinrock, L.: Queueing Systems Volume 2: Computer Applications (1976)

Joint Collaborative Task Offloading for Cost-Efficient Applications in Edge Computing

Chaochen Ma[1]([⊠]), Zhida Qin[2], Xiaoying Gan[2,3], and Luoyi Fu[2]

[1] SJTU ParisTech Elite Institute of Technology, Shanghai Jiao Tong University,
Shanghai 200030, China
machaochen1995@sjtu.edu.cn
[2] Department of Electronics Engineering, Shanghai Jiao Tong University,
Shanghai 200030, China
[3] National Mobile Communications Research Laboratory, Southeast University,
Nanjing 210096, China

Abstract. Edge computing is a new network model providing low-latency service with low bandwidth cost for the users by nearby edge servers. Due to the limited computational capacity of edge servers and devices, some edge servers need to offload some tasks to other servers in the edge network. Although offloading task to other edge servers may improve the service quality, the offloading process will be charged by the operator. In this paper, the goal is to determine the task offloading decisions of all the edge servers in the network. A model is designed with different types of cost in edge computing, where the overall cost of the system reflects the performance of the network. We formulate a cost minimization problem which is NP-hard. To solve the NP-hard problem, we propose a Joint Collaborative Task Offloading algorithm by adopting the optimization process in nearby edge servers. In our algorithm, an edge server can only offload its tasks to other edge servers within a neighborhood range. Based on the real-world data set, an adequate range is determined for the edge computing network. In cases of different density of tasks, the evaluations demonstrate that our algorithm has a good performance in term of overall cost, which outperforms an algorithm without considering the influence of neighborhood range.

Keywords: Edge computing · Task offloading · Quality of service · Cost-efficiency

1 Introduction

With the continuous development of technologies such as the Internet of Things, mobile Internet, and big data, in recent years, a surge of network applications is witnessed. The numbers of websites and mobile applications grow rapidly, and different smart terminals are available online anytime, anywhere. According to

© ICST Institute for Computer Sciences, Social Informatics and Telecommunications Engineering 2020
Published by Springer Nature Switzerland AG 2020. All Rights Reserved
H. Gao et al. (Eds.): ChinaCom 2019, LNICST 312, pp. 77–90, 2020.
https://doi.org/10.1007/978-3-030-41114-5_7

an in-depth market report published by Cisco, by 2022, 59.7% of the population on earth will be the user of the internet, the average devices and connections per person will be 3.6, and the average traffic per person per month will be 49.8 GB [1].

To satisfy the demand driven by the sustained and rapid traffic growth, more requirements have been put forward for the data storage and processing technology. Edge computing has been proven an efficient method to meet the increasing demands. Due to the drawbacks of traditional cloud computing, such as insufficient bandwidth, lack of mobility support and location awareness, high transmission delay, cloud data centers have been incapable to efficiently and timely process massive data generated by edge devices. Therefore, edge computing has emerged as a new data processing model without the drawbacks of cloud computing. By extending computation power from the cloud data center to the edge of the network, the local data streams will be processed by nearby edge servers rather than transported to the remote cloud data centers, the transmission delay and bandwidth cost will be greatly reduced, which satisfies quality-of-service requirements of users. Due to the above advantages, edge computing has been adopted in different fields such as augmented reality, virtual reality, video image analysis and smart traffic system.

A lot of work has been done in task offloading of edge computing network. Some research work concentrates on the incentive mechanism, energy consumption, service of quality in resource allocation and task offloading of edge computing. Chen et al. study coalition formation algorithm based on the coalition game theory, the incentive mechanism and social trust network in edge computing [2]. Li et al. focus on the placement of edge servers for reducing the overall energy consumption [3]. Lyu et al. presents a new fully distributed optimization of fog computing to minimize the time-average cost in a large-scale network [4]. Pasteris et al. propose a deterministic approximation algorithm to solve the reward maximization problem in a mobile edge computing network [5]. Pu et al. focus on minimizing the time-average energy consumption for task executions of all users in device-to-device fogging [6]. Xiao et al. investigate a task offloading problem which aims to maximize quality-of-experience of users under the given power efficiency [7].

Some research work focuses on the algorithms that optimize the system performance by task offloading under certain constraints in edge network. Wang et al. propose an online algorithm that optimally solves an edge cloud resource allocation problem with arbitrary user mobility over time, and an algorithm for an offline case of social virtual reality applications in edge computing [8,9]. Hou et al. propose a tractable online algorithm that configures edge-clouds dynamically solely based on past system history [10]. Xu et al. develop an online algorithm based on Lyapunov optimization and Gibbs sampling for the problem of dynamic service caching in dense cellular networks of mobile edge computing [11]. Zhou et al. concentrate on the proactive cost management problem by deciding the server provisioning ahead of time, based on prediction of the upcoming workload [12]. Sundar et al. design an algorithm to solve the problem with a completion deadline allocated to each individual task by greedily optimizing the scheduling of each task subject to its time allowance [13]. To the best of our knowledge, few researchers consider energy consumption, quality of service, cost of communication simultaneously, and the influence of neighborhood range in task offloading process of edge computing has not been taken into account by the algorithm researchers.

In this paper, we focus on the joint collaborative task offloading decision problem in edge computing. As edge computing and storage capabilities continue to increase, computing tasks are processed on the edge side, which decrease the distance between computing devices and users. Due to the constrained resource of edge devices, we should note that it is difficult for an edge device to support latency-sensitive applications with vast computation amount alone. Therefore, to improve the quality of service of an edge computing network, a natural idea is offloading some of the tasks of edge nodes with high computation load to other edge nodes with fewer tasks to be processed. To find out the best task offloading decision, we are faced up with following challenges: Firstly, an edge server is usually equipped with limited storage and computation capacity compared with cloud computing center. Thus an edge server should not be too crowded with computational tasks. Secondly, the edge servers will update the state of other edge servers and the data of tasks placed on the servers, the regular exchange of a large number of controlling messages may cause the congestion of the network. Thirdly, while shipping the tasks from the task-crowded edge server to other servers may improve the quality of service, the communication between edge servers will generate extra costs. The tradeoff between the quality of service and the communication cost must be carefully considered in order to obtain a better cost efficiency.

To cope with the above challenges, firstly, we model the system with four types of cost, including energy cost, placement cost, computation cost and communication cost. With these four types of cost, a lot of performance measure in reality can be represented. Then, we formulate a cost minimization problem which is NP-hard. The overall cost can evaluate the performance of network after task offloading. The solution designed for the problem is Joint Collaborative Task Offloading algorithm. We optimize each edge server by deciding which of its tasks would be offloaded to which of the other edge servers in its neighbourhood range. The above optimization process will continue until the overall cost converge. The algorithm has following advantages: (1) Each server can only offload its tasks to a small set of nearby servers. Without massive calculation, the optimization for each edge server is fast. (2) For the fact that each edge server only needs to know the task information of the nodes in its neighbourhood range, less controlling message to update the network state is needed. (3) Finally, we evaluate the algorithm performance by carrying out experiment in the large-scale network and find out a better performance compared to a typical optimization algorithm.

2 System Model

The structure of an edge computing system is illustrated in Fig. 1. The computation tasks will firstly generated by users. Each user transmits the task to the nearest edge server with computation and storage capacity. Considering the fact that some edge servers have received too many tasks from users, some of the tasks on the edge server would be offloaded to other edge servers in order to improve the service of quality with high cost-efficiency.

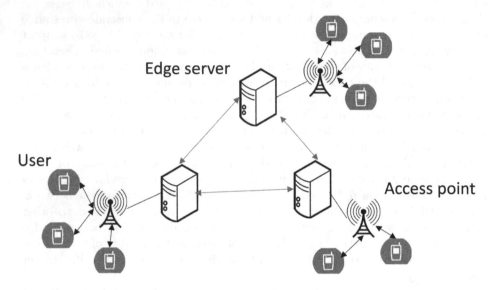

Fig. 1. Example of a wireless application in edge computing network. Users can connect to the edge computing network through the nearest access point.

In a large-scale network, we consider a set of m edge servers in the network. The set is denoted by $S = \{s_1, s_2, ..., s_m\}$. The servers are geographically dispersed in the city, in proximity to the devices of users. Each edge server contains a wireless access point which allows the connection between users and edge server. The capacity for the storage of the data generated from the tasks of users in every edge server is sufficient. The edge servers are connected through local-area-network or a metropolitan-area-network. The distance between two edge servers p, q dispersed in the network is denoted by $d(s_p, s_q)$.

In the network, we consider an application serve a set of n users with the edge servers. The set of users is denoted as $U = \{u_1, u_2, ..., u_n\}$. Each user can get access to the nearest edge server through the access point, and uploads its task to the edge network. Every computational task generated by a user is not separable, and thus it can only be processed by one single edge server. To identify in which edge server the task uploaded by the server is temporarily placed, we define binary variables $b_{i,j} \in \{0, 1\}$ for all $i \in U, j \in S$. If the task of user i is placed in server j, $b_{i,j} = 1$, else $b_{i,j} = 0$.

2.1 Edge Network Cost Model

To evaluate multiple performance measures of the network, we define four types of cost: energy cost, placement cost, computation cost and communication cost.

Energy Cost. In energy cost, we concentrate on the energy consumed by edge servers. For each edge server, its energy consumption can be divided into two parts. The first part is the energy cost to keep the edge server activated. This part of energy is static due to the maintenance of server in the activation state. The second part of energy cost is generated by the processing of the tasks placed on edge servers. For each edge server, the energy to deal with the computational tasks is proportional to the number of tasks placed in the server. We use α_i to denote the energy cost to keep edge server $i \in S$ activated, and efficiency factor β_i is denoted as the ratio of between the energy cost of processing a computational task and the workload offloaded on edge server i. The number of tasks placed in server i is defined as x_i. The total energy cost in the edge computing network is given by:

$$E_e = \sum_{i \in S, x_i > 0} \alpha_i + \sum_{i \in S} \beta_i x_i \tag{1}$$

Placement Cost. Placement cost is generated due to the communication between edge server and users. After the creation of task on a use's device, the task will be uploaded to the nearest edge server through wireless access point. The cost of placing the task of an user $n \in U$ in its nearest edge server $m \in S$ is denoted as $l_n(s_m)$ which varies due to the different locations of user. The placement cost to upload all the tasks from users to edge servers is denoted as:

$$E_p = \sum_{n \in U} l_n(s_m) \tag{2}$$

Computation Cost. Computation cost is associated to the congestion of the task placed on edge servers. As an edge server is designed with limited computational resources and large-scale parallel processing can be difficult, when the number of tasks places in an edge server increases, the computational cost increases which reflects a worse quality of service. For each server $i \in S$, its computation cost is denoted as $\gamma_i(x_i)^2 + \delta_i x_i$. x_i is the number of tasks in server i. γ_i and δ_i are parameters. We assume that in worst case, server i deal with the tasks with only one CPU, and each task needs time t to be processed. The first task needs t to be finished; the second task needs $2t$; the n-th task needs nt. We can evaluate the overall quality of service by summing up the above quadratic terms, thus $\gamma_i(x_i)^2 + \delta_i x_i$ is reasonable to represent its computation cost. If the server has multiple CPUs, γ_i and δ_i should be adjusted. The generalization of the model can be realized through altering for different types of applications or different edge servers. As a result, the total computational cost of the network is denoted as:

$$E_c = \sum_{i \in S} \gamma_i(x_i)^2 + \delta_i x_i \tag{3}$$

Communication Cost. The edge servers are connected with each other by local-area-network or metropolitan-area-network. The transmission of data between edge servers would be charged by the edge network operator considering the amount of data which has been transferred. We denote the communication fee charged by the operator for the transmission of per unit of data from server i to server k as ϵ_{ik}. The parameter ϵ_{ik}, can be approximated as the distance between two edge servers in the network. The communication cost can be divided into two parts. The first part is the communication cost to transport the task generated by user n from edge server u to edge server v, denoted as the $k(d(s_u, s_v)C_n)$ where k is the price parameter decided by the operator and C_n is the amount of data of the task of user n. The second part represent the communication cost when we forward the result of task n processed by edge server v back to edge server u, which can be denoted as $k(d(s_u, s_v)C_n\theta_n)$, where θ_n represents the data size change rate after task initialized from user n has been computed. If multiple task is shipped between two edge servers, we should multiply the cost by $\eta_{u,v}$, which is denoted as the number of task transferred from edge server u to edge server v. The communication cost of the edge network can be computed by:

$$
E_{com} = k\left(\sum_{n\in U}\sum_{u,v\in S} d(s_u, s_v)C_n\eta_{u,v}\right.
$$
$$
\left. + \sum_{n\in U}\sum_{u,v\in S} d(s_v, s_u)C_n\theta_n\eta_{u,v}\right) \tag{4}
$$

2.2 Problem Formulation

The overall cost of the edge computing system is the sum of above four types of cost, denoted as:

$$
E = E_e + E_p + E_c + E_{com} \tag{5}
$$

The task offloading decision problem in the edge network system can be formulated as a cost minimization problem with several constraints:

$$
\min E \tag{6}
$$

$$
\text{s.t. } b_{i,j} \in \{0,1\} \quad \forall i \in U, j \in S \tag{7}
$$

$$
\sum_{j\in S} b_{i,j} = 1 \quad \forall i \in U \tag{8}
$$

$$
\sum_{v\in S} \eta_{u,v} \leq x_u \quad \forall u \in S \tag{9}
$$

In some circumstances, we can alternate the parameters of each type of cost to adjust the weights of different cost so that the cost model can be designed for achieving different trade-off goals or adapting new specifications of the edge networks and applications. For example, if the system attaches great importance to the quality of service, the parameters of computation cost γ_i and δ_i can be increased to meet the demands. For the constraints in the cost minimization problem, Eq. (8) means that a task can only be placed on one edge server, Eq. (9) means that the number of tasks transferred from edge server u to edge server p would not exceed the number of tasks placed on server u. For the simplicity, constraint of the storage capacity of edge servers has not been taken into considered, and each task generated by users need the same time span to be computed by a server.

The above cost minimization problem can be found as NP-hard by converting the problem into the Simple Plant Location Problem (SPLP) which has been known as NP-hard [14]. The placement cost and the energy cost to activate the servers can be treated as the facility establishment cost in SPLP. The energy cost of task processing can represent the operating cost of SPLP. The communication cost and computation cost can be regarded as the transportation cost in SPLP. Thus, the cost minimization problem is NP-hard.

3   Algorithm Design

To solve the above task offloading decision problem, the general idea is to realize the overall cost minimization by continuous optimization process in each edge server. We find out the task offloading decision with the maximum cost decrease for a certain server, and continue the procedure for other servers in the edge network. This optimization process will be iterated until the overall cost does not decrease after an iteration. Following this idea, we propose a Joint Collab-

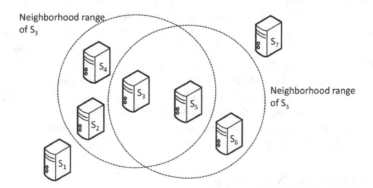

Fig. 2. An example of the neighborhood range of different edge servers in an edge computing network.

orative Task Offloading (JCTO) algorithm. The pseudo-code of JCTO is listed in Algorithm 1.

In the JCTO algorithm, a neighbourhood range is defined as the maximum range between two edge servers that one server is allowed to offload its tasks to another edge server. For the guaranty of bidirectional communication, the neighbourhood range is considered as the same for all servers in a single edge network. As is illustrated in Fig. 2, seven edge servers $S_1, S_2, ..., S_7$ are geographically distributed in an edge network. S_2, S_4, S_5 are within the neighborhood range of S_3, and S_3, S_6 are in the neighborhood range of S_5. A task originally placed at S_3 cannot be shipped directly to S_6, as S_6 is not in the neighborhood range of S_3. Multi-hop transmission is available in the network. For instance, a task placed at S_3 can be firstly shipped to S_5 then to S_6. The range is designed to restrict the tasks to be offloaded to other edge servers too far away, so that the communication cost generated by task offloading process can be reduced. In practice, neighborhood range should be decided by the size of the network and the density of edge servers.

The optimization process for the network is performed in the sequence of edge servers. For each edge server, it is allowed to offload the task to its neighborhood servers in its optimization process. We apply the last in first out regulation for the tasks in an edge server to be offloaded. For a task x placed in edge server j, where $b_{x,j} = 1$, the change of cost if task x is shipped to a neighborhood server k of edge server j is denoted as:

$$\Delta E_{x,j,k} = \Delta E_{\Delta b_{x,j}} + \Delta E_{\Delta b_{x,k}} + \Delta E_{com,x,j,k} \tag{10}$$

Intuitively, $\Delta b_{x,j}$ is a variable with respect to the alternation of $b_{x,j}$, where $\Delta b_{x,j} = -1, \Delta b_{x,j} = 1$ in case x is shipped from server j to server k. The first and second terms of Eq. (10) represent respectively the change of computation cost and energy cost of server j and k after offloading task x. The third term represents the communication cost incurred by the transmission of task x from server j to k. The above calculation of Eq. (10) will be done for all the edge servers within the neighborhood range of server j, and the neighbor server with a minimum cost $\Delta E_{x,j,k_1}$ would be found, meaning that the placement of task x is decided to be offloaded to server k_1 if $\Delta E_{x,j,k_1} < 0$. The process continue for the task in server j until the minimum cost change is superior to 0 which means any task offloading originated from server j can not decrease the overall cost of the network. After the optimization of server j is finished, the optimization process of next edge server would be carried out. We will traverse all the servers during the optimization process in one iteration, and the process does not stop until the overall cost converges after several times of iterations.

4 Performance Evaluation

4.1 Dataset and Settings

We obtain a dataset of the metro stations in Beijing from the map. It contains the longitude and latitude of each metro station of a total 337 stations which are

---

Algorithm 1. Joint Collaborative Task Offloading Algorithm

1: Initialize $E, b_{i,j}$ for all $i \in U, j \in S$
2: Initialize $E_{min} = E$
3: **while** $True$ **do**
4:     **for all** server $j \in S$ **do**
5:         **for all** task x in task sequence of edge server j **do**
6:             Calculate $\Delta E_{x,j,k_1}, \Delta E_{x,j,k_2}..\Delta E_{x,j,k_y}$, where $k_1, k_2..k_y$ are neighbor servers of server j;
7:             $\Delta Cost = \min\{0, \Delta E_{x,j,k_1}, \Delta E_{x,j,k_2}..\Delta E_{x,j,k_y}\}$;
8:             **if** $\Delta Cost < 0$ **then**
9:                 $E = E + \Delta Cost$, update $b_{x,j}$ for all $j \in S$;
10:            **else**
11:                **Break**;
12:            **end if**
13:        **end for**
14:    **end for**
15:    Compare E and E_{min} ;
16:    **if** $E_{min} = E$ **then**
17:        **Break**
18:    **end if**
19: **end while**
20: Output total cost E_{min} after the optimization

---

regarded as the locations where edge servers are placed. The user is distributed randomly in proximity of edge servers. Every user generates one task. For each edge server, the number of users in its proximity is randomly distributed in $[0, z]$ where z is the max number of users initialized near each server which represents the initial maximum number of task in an edge server, and z can be altered to adjust the total number of tasks in the edge network. In energy cost, the energy of activation and the efficiency factor for computation follow normal distribution. For the placement cost, the cost is calculated by the extent of proximity of randomly generated users. For the computation cost, by assuming that every edge server in the edge network has the same computation capacity for simplicity, the parameters are set as the same for all edge servers. For the communication cost, the amount of data of task n follows normal distribution. The data size change rate is set as 0.5. The price parameter k is set with 3 levels which will be evaluated in the experiment.

4.2   Results

Firstly, we study the influence of altering neighborhood range which is a vital parameter in the JCTO algorithm. The performance of the algorithm is evaluated by the cost minimized ratio, which represents the ratio between the overall cost after optimization and the initial overall cost. A smaller ratio means a better performance of the algorithm. In Fig. 3, it is shown that with the increase of the total number of tasks, the edge network becomes more congested and it is much

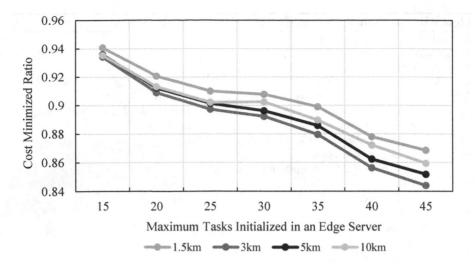

Fig. 3. Cost minimized ratio of JCTO algorithm with different neighborhood ranges.

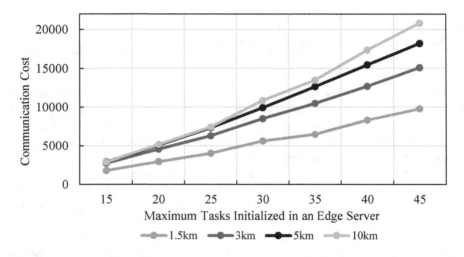

Fig. 4. Communication cost of JCTO algorithm with different neighborhood ranges.

more beneficial to offload the tasks from a crowded edge server to other servers for the reduction of the computation cost. Comparing the performances when the neighborhood range of each edge server is set as 1.5 km, 3 km, 5 km and 10 km, it is found that the neighborhood range of 3 km has the best performance. This is because: (1) When the neighborhood range is too small, such as 1.5 km, the number of neighbor servers for a certain edge server where it can directly place its tasks is small. It will be difficult to find an adequate server to offload the task from the source server for the reduction of overall cost. (2) As is shown in Fig. 4, the communication cost of the network will increase if the total number of tasks increase, and it is obvious as more tasks will be offloaded to other servers in the optimization process. The communication cost will also increase when the neighborhood range increases as a task is allowed to be shipped to further edge servers. In our experiment, while the neighborhood range is set as 5 km, 10 km, the communication cost is much higher than the case of 3 km. Thus, it results in a better overall cost minimization performance when the range is set as 3 km. In short, the setting of neighborhood range is crucial for a good performance of Joint Collaborative Task Offloading Algorithm. The range should be carefully decided in case of different datasets.

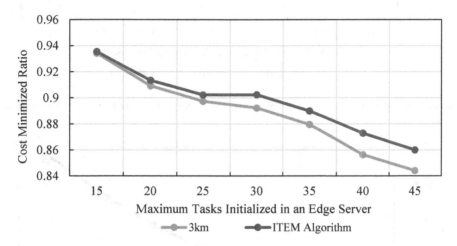

Fig. 5. Comparison between JCTO algorithm with neighborhood range set as 3 km and an optimization algorithm ITEM.

In Fig. 5, we make a comparison between Joint Collaborative Task Offloading Algorithm and another optimization algorithm: Iterative Expansion Moves algorithm (ITEM) [7]. In each iteration of ITEM algorithm, for the edge server i being optimized all the tasks placed in other edge servers are allowed to be placed in server i. By solving a minimum cut problem formed by the cost in the edge network, a set of tasks would be found and be offloaded to server i with a maximum cost decrease for the network and then continue to the next server until the overall cost converges. However, ITEM has not considered the influence of neighbourhood range. By comparison, we find out that the JCTO algorithm with the neighbor range set as 3 km has a better performance than ITEM. The reason is that the tasks throughout the network can be shipped to an edge server in the optimization process which results in a bigger communication cost compared to JCTO. Besides, ITEM needs to update regularly task informational in the whole network for each server, while JCTO only needs the information in a small neighbor range for an edge server. Thus, compared to ITEM, JCTO requires less control message with a better optimization speed.

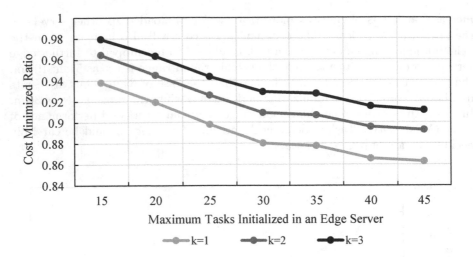

Fig. 6. Comparison of different price parameter k for communication cost in term of cost minimized ratio.

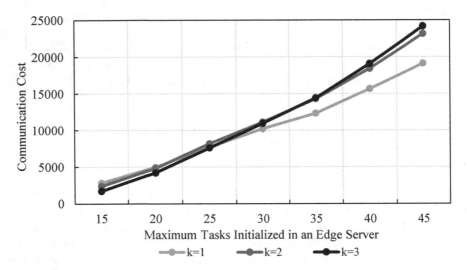

Fig. 7. Comparison of different price parameter k for communication cost in term of communication cost.

Communication cost is the fee charged by the operator for the transmission of data between edge servers. For the operator, its goal is to maximize its income, that is the communication cost. We alter the price parameter k of communication cost which is originally set as 1 to determine its influence while the neighborhood range set as 5 km. As is shown in Fig. 6, with the increase of k, the cost ratio increases because of the rise of communication cost. For the communication cost, as is illustrated in Fig. 7, when the maximum tasks initialized in a server z is set as 15 or 20, we obtain the maximum communication cost with $k = 1$. However, $k = 2$ is proved to be a better choice when z equals to 25, 30, and $k = 3$ is the optimal solution for the case when $z = 35, 40, 45$. This is because: when the total number of task is small, it is not congested in the edge servers. An edge server prefers to handle the tasks by itself if the price for the transmission of data is high. Thus, setting a high price parameter is not beneficial. By contrary, when it is extremely congested in the servers, although the communication price is high, it is profitable by offloading the tasks to other edge servers to reduce the computation cost and improve the quality of service. Thus, for an operator, setting a price parameter such as $k = 3$ will result in a greater communication cost when it is extremely congested. In short, operator should decide the price parameter k dynamically according to the density of tasks and users in order to maximize its income incurred by the data transmission between edge servers.

5   Conclusion

In this paper, we study the task offloading decision problem in an edge computing network. We characterize the major challenges and convert the task offloading problem to a cost minimization problem. To solve the problem which is found to be NP-hard, an algorithm JCTO is proposed with the concept of the optimization of edge servers based on the neighborhood range. We evaluate the algorithm and the influence of different parameters by extensive experiments. Compared to the ITEM optimization algorithm, JCTO has a better performance in term of the cost minimized ratio after the optimization, which can be widely adopted for the edge computing networks with computational capacity constraint of edge servers.

Acknowledgement. This paper was partly supported by National Key RD Program of China Grant (No. 2018YFB2100302, No. 2017YFB1003000), NSFC Grant (No. 61671478, No. 61672342, No. 61532012, No. 61602303), the Science&Technology Innovation Program of Shanghai Grant (No. 17511105103, No. 18510761200) and the open research fund of National Mobile Communications Research Laboratory, Southeast University under Grant (No. 2018D06).

References

1. Cisco Visual Networking Index: Global Mobile Data Traffic Forecast Update, 2017–2022 White Paper. Technical report (2019)
2. Chen, L., Xu, J.: Socially trusted collaborative edge computing in ultra dense networks. In: Proceedings of the Second ACM/IEEE Symposium on Edge Computing, p. 9. ACM (2017)
3. Li, Y., Wang, S.: An energy-aware edge server placement algorithm in mobile edge computing. In: 2018 IEEE International Conference on Edge Computing (EDGE), pp. 66–73. IEEE (2018)
4. Lyu, X., Ren, C., Ni, W., Tian, H., Liu, R.P.: Distributed optimization of collaborative regions in large-scale in homogeneous fog computing. IEEE J. Sel. Areas Commun. **36**(3), 574–586 (2018)

5. Pasteris, S., Wang, S., Herbster, M., He, T.: Service placement with provable guarantees in heterogeneous edge computing systems. In: IEEE INFOCOM 2019-IEEE Conference on Computer Communications, pp. 514–522. IEEE (2019)

6. Pu, L., Chen, X., Xu, J., Fu, X.: D2D fogging: an energy-efficient and incentive-aware task offloading framework via network-assisted D2D collaboration. IEEE J. Sel. Areas Commun. **34**(12), 3887–3901 (2016)

7. Xiao, Y., Krunz, M.: QoE and power efficiency tradeoff for fog computing networks with fog node cooperation. In: IEEE INFOCOM 2017-IEEE Conference on Computer Communications, pp. 1–9. IEEE (2017)

8. Wang, L., Jiao, L., He, T., Li, J., Mühlhäuser, M.: Service entity placement for social virtual reality applications in edge computing. In: IEEE INFOCOM 2018-IEEE Conference on Computer Communications, pp. 468–476. IEEE (2018)

9. Wang, L., Jiao, L., Li, J., Mühlhäuser, M.: Online resource allocation for arbitrary user mobility in distributed edge clouds. In: 2017 IEEE 37th International Conference on Distributed Computing Systems (ICDCS), pp. 1281–1290. IEEE (2017)

10. Hou, I., Zhao, T., Wang, S., Chan, K., et al.: Asymptotically optimal algorithm for online reconfiguration of edge-clouds. In: Proceedings of the 17th ACM International Symposium on Mobile Ad Hoc Networking and Computing, pp. 291–300. ACM (2016)

11. Xu, J., Chen, L., Zhou, P.: Joint service caching and task offloading for mobile edge computing in dense networks. In: IEEE INFOCOM 2018-IEEE Conference on Computer Communications, pp. 207–215. IEEE (2018)

12. Zhou, Z., Chen, X., Wu, W., Wu, D., Zhang, J.: Predictive online server provisioning for cost-efficient IoT data streaming across collaborative edges. In: Proceedings of the Twentieth ACM International Symposium on Mobile Ad Hoc Networking and Computing, pp. 321–330. ACM (2019)

13. Sundar, S., Liang, B.: Offloading dependent tasks with communication delay and deadline constraint. In: IEEE INFOCOM 2018-IEEE Conference on Computer Communications, pp. 37–45. IEEE (2018)

14. Krarup, J., Pruzen, P.M.: The simple plant location problem: survey and synthesis. Eur. J. Oper. Res. **12**, 36–81 (1983)

Energy-Efficient Coded Caching and Resource Allocation for Smart Grid-Supported HetNets

Fangfang Yin[✉], Junyi Lyu, Danpu Liu, Zhilong Zhang, and Minyin Zeng

Beijing Laboratory of Advanced Information Network,
Beijing Key Laboratory of Network System Architecture and Convergence,
Beijing University of Posts and Telecommunications, Beijing 100876, China
{yinff,lvjunyi,dpliu,zhangzhilong,zengmy}@bupt.edu.cn

Abstract. Compared with uncoded caching, coded caching (CC) that exploits accumulated cache size and distributes fractions of a file in different base stations (BSs), can significantly reduce delays and backhaul transmissions. Small base stations (SBSs) with both cache and energy harvesting (EH) ability have attracted extensive attention in recent years. Moreover, renewable energy (RE) also called green energy can be shared between SBSs via the Smart Grid (SG). This paper investigates CC, resource allocation (RA) and energy cooperation (EC) in cache-enabled energy harvesting (EH) heterogeneous networks (HetNets). We formulate the joint optimization problem, aims at minimizing the conventional grid energy consumption while satisfying quality of service (QoS) requirements of users. Simulation results demonstrate the considerable reduction in conventional grid energy consumption compared with other benchmarks.

Keywords: Coded caching · Matching · Energy cooperation · Smart grid · Resource allocation

1   Introduction

With the development of intelligent terminals and new applications, we have witnessed explosive data tsunami for entertainment and socializing. And can foreknow, the mobile data traffic is expected to achieve up to 100 exabytes in 2023, and over 75% of this traffic is expected to be stepped from high bandwidth-demanding video services [1]. Notably, a large number of repeated deliveries for popular videos would bring pressure over backhaul links and cause huge resource wastes. Caching is viewed as one of the promising approaches to relieve the backhaul traffic congestion by offloading the data from service providers to BSs even to users [2]. Additionally, CC can effectively reduce latency and power consumption of wireless systems [3].

The latest analysis shows that, the weighted carbon footprint of the Internet is estimated to be about 320 Mtons of in 2020 [4]. And in particular, mobile

© ICST Institute for Computer Sciences, Social Informatics and Telecommunications Engineering 2020
Published by Springer Nature Switzerland AG 2020. All Rights Reserved
H. Gao et al. (Eds.): ChinaCom 2019, LNICST 312, pp. 91–101, 2020.
https://doi.org/10.1007/978-3-030-41114-5_8

communication infrastructures contribute over 50% of the emission, while the BSs are estimated to be responsible for 60%–80% of the total energy cost [4]. The future fifth generation (5G) networks are expected to be more energy-saving and environmental friendly. BSs powered by RE (e.g., solar panels and wind turbines) is an attractive alternative to lessen energy consumption and environmental problems. To effectively utilize the unevenly RE over geographically distributed BSs, a novel EC framework based on an aggregator of SG is developed [5]. In other words, the energy sharing between BSs can be realized by the SG at the expense of service fee.

Existing works have paid attention to CC enabled HetNets [6–8]. Authors in [6] proposed a mobility and popularity-aware CC scheme for a HetNet, comprising macro and small-cell base stations, i.e., MBS and SBSs, where only the latter are capable to cache contents. In [7], a joint CC and RA problem is designed based on backhaul limited small cell networks, where the long-term average backhaul load is minimized. For the given CC strategy, we jointly considered the user association (UA) and RA strategies to reduce the energy cost in [8]. In addition, EC in SG-supported scenarios has been studied in [9–11]. M. Sheng *et al.* [9] considered RA and EC among BSs with EH capability. Authors in [10,11] formulated the joint UA and power allocation (PA) schemes in EC enabled HetNets.

The design of CC, RA and EC strategies mainly depends on the interdependent and interactive relations with each other. The CC strategy decides the location and quantity of cached videos. Then, based on those, the RA strategy determine how to transport the cached videos to users. More narrowly, the RA strategy decides how to send the cached video content, by determining the transmission parameters, such as the UA, bandwidth allocation (BA), PA etc, which affect the CC strategy as well [2]. Furthermore, both CC and RA strategy determine the real-time energy level of each BS, i.e, extra and insufficient RE, which affects the EC between BSs.

Motivated by the issues mentioned above, we build a systematic energy model which captures the key components of maximum-distance separable (MDS) coded cache and SG enabled HetNets. The contributions of this paper can be summarized as follows.

- We analytically formulate a joint CC, UA, BA and EC problem to reduce the conventional energy consumption under the constraints of limited storage capacities and bandwidth resources at SBSs as well as the QoS of users.
- The original complex problem can be decomposed into three lower level problems: CC and content delivery (CD) problems which are able to be solved by convex optimization and matching game, respectively. While the third problem, the EC between SBSs. The solutions of the three problems are then combined to solve the original problem, iteratively.
- Simulation results indicate considerable reduction in energy consumption thanks to the proposed optimization algorithm.

The remainder of this paper is organized as follows. In Sect. 2, we describe the system model. Then, the mixed integer optimization problem is formulated, and the problem solution is presented in Sect. 3. The simulation results are given in Sect. 4 and the whole paper is concluded in Sect. 5.

2   System Model and Problem Formulation

We consider the downlink cache and SG enabled HetNets as depicted in Fig. 1, in which a single MBS acts as the control plane (C-plane) serving U users. Moreover, K SBSs connect to the MBS via wireless backhaul links. Let $\mathcal{K}$ denote the set of the SBSs that are randomly distributed in the MBS coverage area, while $\mathcal{U}$ denotes the set of users. Due to the limited cache capacity of each SBS, if the requested video is not recovered from associated SBSs, the missing portion of the requested video has to be fetched from the MBS via backhaul links. In addition, SBSs are assumed locally deployed with solar panels and/or wind turbines for EH from the environment and equipped with smart meters to enable their EC through the aggregator in SG. In addition, SBSs deployed with solar panels and/or wind turbines for EH also equipped with smart meters to implement EC through the aggregator in SG. Meanwhile, the MBS draws energy from the conventional grid.

2.1   Coded Caching Model

The library contains N files with equal size of B bits and is denoted by $\mathcal{F} \triangleq \{F_1, F_2, ..., F_N\}$. The popularity for the file $F_j (1 \leq j \leq N)$ is denoted as p_j, satisfying $0 \leq p_j \leq 1$ and $\sum_{j=1}^{N} p_j = 1$. We suppose the content popularity follows Zipf distribution with a shape parameter α, i.e., $p_j = \frac{j^{-\alpha}}{\sum_{j=1}^{N} j^{-\alpha}}$. Without loss of generality, the files are sorted by popularity such that $p_j \geq p_{j+1}$.

The similar MDS coded caching strategy as [3] is considered in this paper. Thus, due to the property of MDS CC, each user can be served by multiple hybrid energy-powered SBSs. A video content can be retrieved when B parity bits are collected in any order, from any associated SBSs. Different from our previous work [8] that only considered the given MDS caching state, based on which the RA is jointly optimized, we introduce the optimization of CC strategy in this paper.

2.2   Transmission Model

Since the users are assumed to be static in the transmission period, it is reasonable to treat the interference as noise [12]. For user u associated with SBS k, the received signal-to-interference-plus-noise ratio (SINR) of SBS k towards user u can be expressed by [12]

$$SINR_{ku} = \frac{P_{ku}g_{ku}}{\sigma_0^2} \tag{1}$$

where σ_0^2 is the Gaussian noise and interference [12]. P_{ku} and g_{ku} denote, respectively, the transmission power and channel gain from the SBS k to user u.

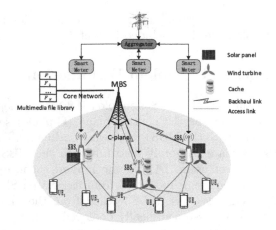

Fig. 1. System model of smart grid cache-enabled HetNets.

Then, the achievable download rate from SBS k to user u is given by

$$R_{ku} = W_{ku}\log_2(1 + \frac{P_{ku}g_{ku}}{\sigma_0^2}) \tag{2}$$

where W_{ku} represents the allocated bandwidth resource between the SBS k and user u.

Thus, given the R_{ku}, the transmission power from SBS k to user u can be calculated by

$$P_{ku} = \left(2^{R_{ku}/W_{ku}} - 1\right)\frac{\sigma_0^2}{g_{ku}} \tag{3}$$

2.3 Power Consumption Model

For simplicity, since we are optimizing for a single time slot, the time (t) will be dropped from our formulation [13]. In addition, we do not consider the energy storage. During each transmission time slot, the total power consumption mainly consists of content caching power, transmission power, backhaul transport power and RE trades. We consider the energy consumption as follows:

(1) *Caching Power Consumption:* The cache power consumption of each SBS can be expressed as

$$P_k^{ca} = w_k^{ca}B\sum_{j \in N} q_{jk} \tag{4}$$

where w_k^{ca} represents the power efficiency computed in watt per bit, and q_{jk} denotes the cache fraction of each file cached at each SBS.

(2) *Transmission Power Consumption:* Assume the UA indicator between user u and SBS k as x_{ku}, if the user u is associated with the SBS k, $x_{ku} = 1$; and

0, otherwise. Thus, the transmission power of the SBS k can be written as

$$P_k^{tr} = \sum_{u \in \mathcal{U}} P_{ku} x_{ku} \tag{5}$$

(3) *Renewable Energy:* In our model, each SBS draws energy from both the grid and RE sources. The energy harvested by SBS k from RE sources is E_k. The energy transferred from SBS k to SBS k' is $\delta_{kk'}$, and the energy transfer efficiency factor between SBSs is $\beta_{kk'}$ ($0 \leq \beta_{kk'} \leq 1$), here, $(1 - \beta_{kk'})$ represents the percentage of energy loss during the energy transmission process. Thus, we denote the RE of each SBS as

$$P_k^{re} = E_k + \beta_{k'k} \sum_{k' \in \mathcal{K}, k' \neq k} \delta_{k'k} - \sum_{k' \in \mathcal{K}, k' \neq k} \delta_{kk'} \tag{6}$$

Then, the conventional grid power consumption of each SBS can be calculated by

$$P_k^{grid} = \left[P_k^{ca} + P_k^{tr} - P_k^{re} \right]^+ \tag{7}$$

where $(\cdot)^+ = \max(\cdot, 0)$. Based on the analysis above, the grid power consumption of all SBSs can be expressed as

$$P_{SBS}^{grid} = \sum_{k \in \mathcal{K}} \left[P_k^{ca} + P_k^{tr} - P_k^{re} \right]^+ \tag{8}$$

(4) *Backhaul Power Consumption:* The backhaul power consumption from the MBS to SBSs can be calculated by

$$P_{MBS}^{grid} = e_{MBS} \sum_{u \in U} \sum_{j \in N} p_j R_0 [1 - \sum_{k \in \mathcal{K}} q_{jk} x_{ku}]^+ \tag{9}$$

where $[1 - \sum_{k \in \mathcal{K}} q_{jk} x_{ku}]^+$ denotes the missing portion of the file F_j requested by user u should be fetched from the MBS via backhaul links. e_{MBS} (J/bit) is the backhaul energy consumption per bit transmitted, R_0 denotes the minimum rate requirement of each user for requesting the file,

Denote by P_{total} the total grid power consumption, which is given by

$$P_{total} = P_{SBS}^{grid} + P_{MBS}^{grid} \tag{10}$$

2.4   Problem Formulation

We investigate the conventional grid energy consumption problem by jointly considering CC, UA, BA, and EC, which is formulated as

$$\mathcal{P}: \min_{q_{jk}, x_{ku}, W_{ku}, \delta_{k'k}} P_{total} \tag{11}$$

$$\text{s.t.} \quad \sum_{k \in \mathcal{K}} R_{ku} = R_0, \forall u \in \mathcal{U} \tag{11a}$$

$$\sum_{u \in \mathcal{U}} W_{ku} x_{ku} \le W_k^{\max}, \forall k \in \mathcal{K} \tag{11b}$$

$$\sum_{k \in \mathcal{K}} x_{ku} \le s_u, \forall u \in \mathcal{U} \tag{11c}$$

$$W_{ku} \ge 0, P_{ku} \ge 0, \forall (k, u) \in \mathcal{K} \times \mathcal{U} \tag{11d}$$

$$x_{ku} \in \{0, 1\}, \forall (k, u) \in \mathcal{K} \times \mathcal{U} \tag{11e}$$

$$B \sum_{j \in N} q_{jk} \le C_k^{\max}, \forall k \in \mathcal{K} \tag{11f}$$

$$0 \le q_{jk} \le 1, \forall j, k \tag{11g}$$

$$P_k^{ca} + P_k^{tr} \le P_k^{grid} + P_k^{re}, \forall k \in \mathcal{K} \tag{11h}$$

$$\delta_{k'k} \ge 0, P_k^{grid} \ge 0, \forall k, k' \in \mathcal{K} \tag{11i}$$

where constraint (11a) guarantees the rate requirement R_0 for each user. (11b) limit the maximum bandwidth for each SBS. (11c) states that each user is allowed to be served by s_u SBSs. The constraint (11d) ensures the non-negativity on radio wireless variables. (11e) limits the association indicators x_{ku} binary. (11f) and (11g) limit the cache capacity and fraction of the requested file F_j at each SBS k. (11h) is the energy consumption constraint of SBS k, (11i) keeps the transferred RE and consumed grid energy non-negativity. The discrete nature of x_{ku} and the continuous nature of W_{ku}, q_{jk} and $\delta_{k'k}$, lead the problem (11) to a non-convex problem, which is generally NP-hard.

3   Problem Solution

In this section, we focus on solving the problem $\mathcal{P}$ distributively by employing some decomposition methods, i.e., we split the original problem $\mathcal{P}$ into three problems. The first problem CC, aims at caching a feasible portion of the requested file to serve all users. The second RA problem, consists (i) deciding which users should be served by which SBSs, (ii) assigning a feasible bandwidth to serve all users while meeting their QoS requirements. While the third problem, the EC between SBSs. The solution of the three problems are then combined to solve the original problem $\mathcal{P}$.

3.1   Coded Caching Problem

For any given variables x_{ku}, W_{ku} and $\delta_{k'k}$, the problem $\mathcal{P}$ can be simplified to decide the fraction of each file to be cached at SBSs, aims at minimizing the cache power (4) and backhaul power consumption (9). Thus, in this case, the optimizing problem $\mathcal{P}$ is transformed into the following CC problem:

$$\mathcal{P}_C : \quad \min_{q_{jk}} \sum_{k \in \mathcal{K}} P_k^{ca} + P_{MBS}^{grid} \tag{12}$$

$$\text{s.t. } (11f)(11g) \tag{12a}$$

Since both terms in Eq. (12) are convex function of q_{jk}, their sum is a convex function as well. In addition that, the constraints in (11f) and (11g) are linear, hence $\mathcal{P}_{\mathcal{C}}$ is a typical convex optimization problem. Thus, the CC problem can be solved by available software packages such as CVX [16].

3.2   Resource Allocation Problem

In this subsection, given the CC fraction q_{jk}, we focus on the RA optimization to jointly reduce the transmission power and backhaul power for SBSs and the MBS.

$$\mathcal{P}_{\mathcal{R}}: \quad \min_{x_{ku}, W_{ku}} \sum_{k \in \mathcal{K}} P_k^{tr} + P_{MBS}^{grid} \tag{13}$$

$$\text{s.t. } (11a)(11b)(11c)(11d)(11e) \tag{13a}$$

To solve $\mathcal{P}_{\mathcal{R}}$, we propose an efficient scheme which divides the optimization task into multiple subproblems in a distributed manner, followed by a centralized UA strategy to further reduce the transmission power consumption, i.e., once the UA indicators x_{ku} are fixed, the problem $\mathcal{P}_{\mathcal{R}}$ can be decomposed into K independent subproblems, which also are the convex problems and can be solved by the interior method. In addition, we resort to VSU-based matching algorithm of our previous work [8] to solve the UA problem. Finally, the alternative iteration optimization algorithm (JCUBA) [15] is applied to jointly optimize CC, and RA. Due to the limited space and the complex problem $\mathcal{P}$, we omit the joint optimization of CC and RA in this paper.

3.3   Energy Cooperation Problem

After obtaining the solution of problems $\mathcal{P}_{\mathcal{C}}$ and $\mathcal{P}_{\mathcal{R}}$, the original problem $\mathcal{P}$ can be calculated by solving the following linear programming (LP)

$$\mathcal{P}_{\mathcal{LP}}: \quad \min_{\delta_{k'k}, P_{SBS}^{grid}} P_{total} \tag{14}$$

$$\text{s.t. } (11h)(11i) \tag{14a}$$

Here, the corresponding $\mathcal{P}_{\mathcal{LP}}$ can be solved by the CVX [16]. And the EC is realised by the aggregator of SG, which can aggregate all distributed RE information of SBSs. Finally, the solution of problem $\mathcal{P}$ can be iteratively updated, which is shown in Algorithm 1.

Algorithm 1. Joint CC, RA and EC algorithm (AES)

1: **if** $t = 0$

2:   Initialize P_k^{tr}, P_k^{ca}, $\delta_{k'k}$, E_k, $\forall k$

3: **else**

4: Given the variables x_{ku} and W_{ku}, determine q_{jk} under $(\mathbf{P}, \mathbf{E}, \delta)$ via CVX;

5: Given the cache fraction q_{jk} and the corresponding $(\mathbf{P}, \mathbf{E}, \delta)$, update x_{ku} and W_{ku} by the aid of VSU-based matching [8] and bisection method;

6: Based on the updated variables q_{jk}, x_{ku} and W_{ku}, update P_k^{tr}, P_k^{ca}, P_k^{grid}, and $\delta_{k'k}$ by CVX;

7: **if** convergence

8: Obtain multidimensional resource allocation policies x_{ku}^*, W_{ku}^*, q_{jk}^* and $\delta_{k'k}^*$, the minimum conventional grid power consumption value is achieved.

9:   **break**

10: **else**

11:   $t \leftarrow t + 1$

12: **end if**

13:**end if**

---

4   Simulation Results

In this section, we compare the proposed AES algorithm with conventional benchmarks in MATLAB. One MBS is located at the center, and SBSs are evenly distributed on the circumference of MBS with the radius $r = 100$ m. Users are randomly distributed in the MBS coverage area. The basic simulation parameters are the same as in [8]. In addition, we assume each SBS has the same cache capacity $C_k^{\max}$ and $P_k^{\max} = 40$ dBm. As the distribution of harvested RE at the location is scenario-dependent, we assume it being uniformly distributed followed by [10]. In the following, we compare the performance of the proposed AES algorithm with two other schemes: sequential waterfilling algorithm (SWF) [9] and non-energy cooperation (NEC).

Figure 2(a) shows the total grid energy consumption versus the number of users. We set the minimum rate requirement of each user $R_0 = 15$ Mbps, and $\beta_{kk'}$ randomly generated in $[0.7, 0.9]$. As shown in Fig. 2(a), with the increasing number of users, the conventional grid energy consumption increases. The reason is that, with the growing number in users, the bandwidth resource allocates to each user decreases, each hybrid energy-powered SBS will carry more traffic. In other words, the RE enabled SBSs need to increase its transmission power to meet the QoS requirements of all users. Based on the above analysis, the transmission power consumption of each SBS greatly increases, which contributes to the total grid energy consumption. However, the proposed AES still achieves better energy saving performance than the SWF and NEC baselines. No doubt that the NEC algorithm which does not apply the EC between SBSs obtain the most grid energy consumption of all. The SWF algorithm which explores the two-hop energy flows, also consumes more grid energy consumption than the proposed AES algorithm due to the more energy loss during the EC.

Figure 2(b) depicts total grid power consumption versus the minimum rate requirement of users with $|\mathcal{U}| = 60$. The higher rate requirements the users require, the more grid energy consumes in the network. The reason can be concluded by the Shannon formula easily, i.e., considering feasible bandwidth allocation resource, high data rate require higher transmission energy of BSs. Fortunately, as shown in Fig. 2(b), for any given minimum rate requirement, the proposed AES algorithm outperforms the benchmarks along with joint CC and RA. The main reasons are: Firstly, the joint CC, UA and BA degrades each SBS's energy consumption, i.e., less power demand is required by all the users. The efficacy of the joint CC and RA algorithm has been verified in [15], which will not present in this paper again. Secondly, the EC of the proposed AES algorithm effectively balances the RE sharing among SBSs and thereby greatly reduces the unnecessary RE waste. In summary, both the effective EC approach (i.e., energy supply) and low energy demand jointly contribute to the lowest energy consumption of the proposed AES algorithm.

Figure 2(c) shows the total grid energy consumption versus the energy transfer efficiency factor when $R0 = 10$ Mbps and $|\mathcal{U}| = 60$. And the uniform distribution of the energy transfer efficiency factor is discussed. As Fig. 2(c) shows, when the factor $\beta_{kk'}$ varies from 0.95 to 0.55, the larger $\beta_{kk'}$ is, the smaller grid energy consumes. And, for arbitrary $\beta_{kk'}$, the grid power consumption of the proposed AES algorithm always lower than SWF. This is understandable: On the one hand, during the EC period, the smaller energy transfer efficiency factor leads more energy loss. On the other, the SWF algorithm consumes more grid energy due to the two hop RE transfer mechanism. In nutshell, the energy loss of the SWF algorithm is more than the that of the proposed AES algorithm.

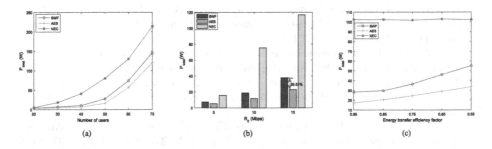

(a)   (b)   (c)

Fig. 2. Comparison on power consumption: (a) Total grid power consumption vs. number of users (b) Total grid power consumption vs. R_0. (c) Total grid power consumption v.s. β.

5   Conclusion

In this paper, we study the joint coded caching, resource allocation and energy cooperation problem in cache and Smart Grid enabled HetNets, aiming to minimize the conventional grid energy consumption. Firstly, we decompose the original problem into three lower level problems, i.e., coded caching, resource allocation and energy cooperation. Secondly, we propose a low-complexity alternative optimization algorithm to solve the coded caching, user association, bandwidth allocation distributedly and iteratively. Finally, via the aggregator of Smart Grid, a centralised energy cooperation algorithm is provided to realise energy sharing among SBSs. Simulation results confirmed the effectiveness of the proposed joint optimization algorithm.

Acknowledgment. This work is supported by the National Natural Science Foundation of China under Grant No.61971069, 61801051, the Beijing Natural Science Foundation under Grant No. L172032, the Key R&D Program Projects in Shanxi Province under Grant No. 2019ZDLGY07-10 and the Open Project of Information Security Laboratory of National Defense Scientific Research and Test under Grant No. 2016XXAQ09.

References

1. Zhang, X., et al.: Energy-efficient caching for scalable videos in heterogeneous networks. IEEE J. Sel. Areas Commun. **36**(8), 1802–1815 (2018)
2. Li, L., Zhao, G., Blum, R.S.: A survey of caching techniques in cellular networks: research issues and challenges in content placement and delivery strategies. IEEE Commun. Surv. Tutor. **20**(3), 1710–1732 (2018)
3. Gabry, F., Bioglio, V., Land, I.: On energy-efficient edge caching in heterogeneous networks. IEEE J. Sel. Areas Commun. **34**(12), 3288–3298 (2016)
4. Wu, Y., et al.: Green-oriented traffic offloading through dual connectivity in future heterogeneous small cell networks. IEEE Commun. Mag. **56**(5), 140–147 (2018)
5. Rahbar, K., Chai, C.C., Zhang, R.: Energy cooperation optimization in microgrids with renewable energy integration. IEEE Trans. Smart Grid **9**(2), 1482–1493 (2018)
6. Ozfatura, E.: Mobility and popularity-aware coded small-cell caching. IEEE Commun. Lett. **22**(2), 288–291 (2018)
7. Liao, J., et al.: Coding, multicast, and cooperation for cache-enabled heterogeneous small cell networks. IEEE Trans. Wireless Commun. **16**(10), 6838–6853 (2017)
8. Yin, F., Wang, A., Liu, D., Zhang, Z.: Energy-aware joint user association and resource allocation for coded cache-enabled HetNets. IEEE Access **7**, 94128–94142 (2019)
9. Sheng, M., et al.: Intelligent energy and traffic coordination for green cellular networks with hybrid energy supply. IEEE Trans. Veh. Technol. **66**(2), 1631–1646 (2017)
10. Xu, B., et al.: Resource allocation in energy-cooperation enabled two-tier NOMA HetNets toward green 5G. IEEE J. Sel. Areas Commun. **35**(12), 2758–2770 (2017)
11. Xu, B., et al.: Resource allocation for wireless virtualized hetnet with caching and hybrid energy supply. In: IEEE WCNC, pp. 1–6, April 2018
12. Guo, F., Zhang, H., Li, X., Ji, H., Leung, V.C.M.: Joint optimization of caching and association in energy-harvesting-powered small-cell networks. IEEE Trans. Veh. Technol. **67**(7), 6469–6480 (2018)
13. Rahbar, K., Chai, C.C., Zhang, R.: Energy cooperation optimization in microgrids with renewable energy integration. IEEE Trans. Smart Grid **9**, 1482–1493 (2018)

14. Younis, A.: Bandwidth and energy aware resource allocation for cloud radio access networks. IEEE Trans. Wireless Commun. $17(10)$, 6487–6500 (2018)
15. Yin, F., et al.: Coded caching for energy efficient HetNets with bandwidth allocation and user association. In: IEEE VTC-Fall, pp. 1–6 (2019)
16. CVX Research Inc.: CVX: Matlab software for disciplined convex programming, version 3.0 beta (2015). http://cvxr.com/cvx

Task-Aware Joint Computation Offloading for UAV-Enabled Mobile Edge Computing Systems

Junshi Hu[✉], Heli Zhang, Xi Li, and Hong Ji

Key Laboratory of Universal Wireless Communications, Ministry of Education,
Beijing University of Posts and Telecommunications,
Beijing, People's Republic of China
{hujunshi,zhangheli,lixi,jihong}@bupt.edu.cn

Abstract. With the emergence of diverse computation-intensive mobile applications (such as virtual reality), demands for data processing from users are rapidly increasing in mobile edge computing (MEC). However, existing mobile edge servers (MES) are susceptible to propagation delays and loss and fail to provide timely and efficient services. Facing this problem, we focus on applying unmanned aerial vehicles (UAVs) equipped with computing resources to provide mobile edge computing offload services for users. UAV as an MES can guarantee low propagation delay and high reliability due to its maneuverability and short-distance line-of-sight communications. In this paper, we study a joint computing offloading problem consideration of user equipments, ground base stations and aerial UAVs. The system provides two offloading methods. The first offloading method is the air-offloading, where a user equipment can offload computing tasks to UAV-enabled MEC servers. The second offloading method is ground-offloading, where a user equipment can offload computing tasks to existing MESs. The task-aware optimization offloading scheme is proposed and it selects local execution or an offloading method based on the latency and energy constraints. Simulation results show that our proposed offloading selection scheme outperforms benchmark schemes. The results demonstrate that the proposed schemes improve quality of service (QoS) and have low task block rate under latency and energy constraints.

Keywords: UAV · Offloading selection · Air-offloading · Ground-offloading · Latency · Energy · MEC

1 Introduction

With recent development of technology and the decline in manufacturing costs, unmanned aerial vehicles (UAVs) have received growing interests in a wide range of applications such as post-disaster estimation, cargo delivery, search and rescue, as well as aerial photography [1]. In future mobile communications, with the

© ICST Institute for Computer Sciences, Social Informatics and Telecommunications Engineering 2020
Published by Springer Nature Switzerland AG 2020. All Rights Reserved
H. Gao et al. (Eds.): ChinaCom 2019, LNICST 312, pp. 102–116, 2020.
https://doi.org/10.1007/978-3-030-41114-5_9

emergence of diverse computation-intensive and latency-critical mobile applications (e.g. video calls, virtual reality, and online game pervasive), the existing mobile edge servers (MES) are difficult to provide satisfactory quality of experience (QoE). UAV-enabled mobile edge computing, which is close to smart mobile devices (SMDs) and possesses stronger and more reliable line-of-sight (LoS), is undoubtedly one of the most critical applications to address the above problem.

Due to the limited battery and low computation capability, it is challenging for mobile devices to execute computation-intensive and latency-sensitive applications [2]. Fortunately, the emergence of MEC technology is promising to address this problem. Mobile users can offload computing tasks to edge networks with enormous computing resources to reduce application latency and save energy. In UAV-enabled networks, UAVs as mobile edge servers are capable of providing timely and efficient services, they provide seamless wireless coverage and ubiquitous computing offload services owing to their high maneuverability and low cost deployment. Meanwhile, flexible connectivity reduces the traffic load at the fixed cloud servers [3]. Therefore, the UAV equipped with a MEC server offers promising advantages compared to the conventional ground cellular network with fixed BSs. The UAV equipped with an MEC server offers promising advantages compared to the conventional ground cellular network with fixed BSs.

Recently, UAV-Enabled MEC provide UEs with mobile edge offload services, which have received extensive attention on the academic community. The work in [4] proposed a deep reinforce learning (DRL)-based scheme to maximize the throughput of offloading tasks offloading with limited UAV energy, and optimized objective function formulated by a semi-Markov decision process (SMDP). The work in [5] proposed a novel penalty dual decomposition (PDD) based algorithm to minimize the sum of the maximum delay among all the mobile users by combining UAV flight Trajectory optimization. The authors use local computing and partial offloading scheme, which each user offloads some tasks to the UAV, and the rest of the tasks are executed locally. In [6], the authors studied an UAV-enabled wireless powered MEC system, and proposed the sequential convex optimization (SCA) techniques to the power minimization problem. The authors formulated a non-convex optimization equation according to constraints on energy harvesting causality and the number of calculated bits. In [7], the authors considered that an unmanned aerial vehicle as edge servers to provide data processing services to the Internet of things devices (IoTDs). The paper minimizes the energy consumption of UAVs subject to the quality service requirement of IoT and the limited computing resource at UAVs. However, the above research only considers UAV-enabled MEC, they ignore ground cellular network with fixed BSs and latency- and energy-awareness for different offload tasks, which will result in loss in UAV-enabled networks performance. Therefore, these aspects will be incorporated into our work of task-aware joint offloading scheme in an MEC system with air-offloading and ground-offloading.

In this paper, we propose a task-aware MEC based on a joint computation offloading scheme, which including air-offloading and ground-offloading. Users can select to offload different computing tasks to edge servers collocated at base stations or UAV-enabled mobile edge servers or local computing according to available computing and energy resources. The proposed scheme employs the greedy based algorithm to select the best execution location for the current task. Our optimization objective is to minimize the energy consumption of the UE and the UAV under the conditions that satisfy the different latency constraints of each task. Furthermore, the proposed scheme reduces the probability of task blocking and the average delay of handling computing tasks in the system. This scheme is designed for applications, such as images, videos and so on, which requires critical computational latency and computing resources. The obtained results show that our scheme improves quality of servers (QoS) of MEC and extends the operational lifetime of the UE and the UAV to some extent.

The remainder of our work is organized as follows. Section 2 gives the system model and proposed optimization problem. In Sect. 3, the solution to joint offload optimization is presented. Simulation results and discussions are given in Sect. 4. Finally, the conclusions are drawn in Sect. 5.

2 System Model and Problem Formulation

In this section, we introduce the system model and formulate the joint computation offloading optimization problem.

2.1 System Model

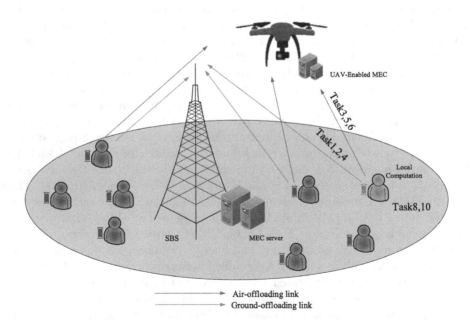

Fig. 1. The system model for task-aware joint computing offloading

As shown in Fig. 1, a joint computing offloading system is considered, which consists of the UAV-enabled MEC system and the ground MEC system. The UAV equipped with MEC servers or ground station connected to cloud servers provide computing offload services for M users. In this paper, the binary offloading paradigm is applied [8]. Each user can select to offload computing tasks to the UAV-enabled MEC server through air offloading or to ground base stations through ground offloading or execute locally. We apply the orthogonal frequency division multiple access (OFDMA) protocol to ensure that all users can offload their tasks to the UAV or the ground base station. Each UE is allowed to occupy one of sub-channels and the sub-channels are not reused, therefore, co-channel interference is ignored. Similar to [9–11], the energy consumption and delay for transmitting the computed results of the UAV and the ground base station are ignored. This paper considers a multitasking joint offloading problem for one user. For one UE, there are multiple different application tasks generated, task m is described by three terms d_m, c_m, t_m^{max}, where d_m is total size of input data of a task in bits, which includes program codes, input files, etc., c_m is the number of CPU cycles required to computing the task offloaded, and t_m^{max} is maximum allowable latency of a task.

2.2   Local Computing

If the task is executed at the UE locally, the execution time is denoted as:

$$t_m^L = \frac{c_m}{f^L}, \tag{1}$$

where f^L is local computing speed of UE in number of CPU cycles per second, and the local energy consumption is denoted as:

$$E_m^L = P_m^L t_m^L, \tag{2}$$

where P_m^L is local power consumption for the CPU to execute tasks.

2.3   Ground Mobile Edge Computing

For ground offloading, the goal of this paper is to minimize the energy consumption of mobile devices within the QoS latency time, so we ignore the energy consumption of the SBS. Energy consumption of ground offloading is the energy consumed at UE for offloading the task to the SBS through the wireless channel. Energy consumption of transmitting task m to the SBS is given by

$$E_m^{T_{SBS}} = P_m^T t_m^{UE-SBS}, \tag{3}$$

where P_m^T is data transmission power of the UE, and t_m^{UE-SBS} represents the transmission time of the wireless link, which is denoted as

$$t_m^{UE-SBS} = \frac{d_m}{R_{UE-SBS}}, \tag{4}$$

where R_{UE-SBS} is the data transmission rate of the UE to the SBS, and it can be calculated as

$$R_{UE-SBS} = W_{UE-SBS} \log_2(1 + \frac{P_m^T G_{UE-SBS}}{\sigma^2}), \tag{5}$$

where W_{UE-SBS} denotes the transmission sub-channel of the UE to the SBS, G_{UE-SBS} denotes the channel gain between the UE and the SBS, and σ^2 denotes the noise power at the SBS receiver. The time of the SBS executing task m is expressed as

$$t_m^{SBS} = \frac{c_m}{f^{SBS}}, \tag{6}$$

where f^{SBS} denotes SBS computing speed in number of CPU cycles per second.

2.4   UAV-Enabled Mobile Edge Computing

Without loss of generality, we adopt a three-dimensional (3D) Euclidean coordinate. Each user is fixed at the ground and the location is represented as l, where $l = [x,y]$, the UAV flies at a fixed altitude A_{UAV} during the period when the UAV communicates with the user and the horizontal plane coordinate of the UAV is $\hat{l} = [x_{UAV}, y_{UAV}]$. A LoS model is applied between the UAV and the user. During the finite time, the channel is unchanged. The channel power gain is given as

$$H_{UE-UAV} = \beta_0 D_{UE-UAV}^{-2} = \frac{\beta_0}{A_{UAV}^2 + ||\hat{l} - l||^2}, \tag{7}$$

where β_0 is the channel power gain at a reference distance $d_0 = 1m$. Then, the transmission rate of the UE to the UAV is expressed as

$$R_{UE-UAV} = W_{UE-UAV} \log_2(1 + \frac{P_m^T H_{UE-UAV}}{\hat{\sigma}^2}), \tag{8}$$

where W_{UE-UAV} denotes the transmission sub-channel of the UE to the UAV, H_{UE-UAV} denotes the channel gain between the UE and the UAV, and $\hat{\sigma}^2$ denotes the noise power at the UAV receiver. The time and the energy consumption for offloading the task m of the UE to the UAV are given by

$$t_m^{UE-UAV} = \frac{d_m}{R_{UE-UAV}} \tag{9}$$

and

$$E_m^{T_{UAV}} = P_m^T t_m^{UE-UAV}. \tag{10}$$

The time and energy consumption of the UAV executing task m are expressed as

$$t_m^{UAV} = \frac{c_m}{f^{UAV}}, \tag{11}$$

where f^{UAV} denotes UAV computing speed in number of CPU cycles per second and

$$E_m^{E_{UAV}} = P_m^{UAV} t_m^{UAV}, \tag{12}$$

where P_m^{UAV} is the UAV power consumption for the CPU to execute tasks. In this paper, for deployed UAVs, we ignore the energy consumption at the UAV due to flight.

2.5   Problem Formulation

In this paper, we focus on the energy consumption of UEs and UAVs in the joint offloading selection scheme. Therefore, the optimal problem can be formulated as minimizing the energy consumption of UEs and UAVs with satisfying the delay tolerance for given tasks, and the available resource constraints. For the $task_m$ which is described by three terms (d_m, c_m, t_m^{max}), optimization equation is given by

$$\min_{\omega,\eta}(\omega E_m^{loc} + \eta E_m^{uav})$$

$$\begin{aligned}
\text{s.t. } & C1 : t_m \leq t_m^{max}, \quad m = 1, 2, ..., M \\
& C2 : \omega > \eta \quad \forall task_m, m = 1, 2, ..., M \\
& C3 : \omega + \eta = 1 \quad \forall task_m, m = 1, 2, ..., M \\
& C4 : 0 < \omega < 1 \quad \forall task_m, m = 1, 2, ..., M \\
& C5 : 0 < \eta < 1 \quad \forall task_m, m = 1, 2, ..., M \\
& C6 : E_m^{loc_{re}} \geq E_{th}^{loc} \quad \forall task_m, m = 1, 2, ..., M \\
& C7 : E_m^{uav_{re}} \geq E_{th}^{uav} \quad \forall task_m, m = 1, 2, ..., M
\end{aligned} \tag{13}$$

Among all the constraints, $C1$ is to enforce the hard deadline of the task tolerance delay, $C2$, $C3$, $C4$, $C5$ are to ensure that UE energy optimization priority is higher than UAV energy optimization, $C6$ is to ensure that the UE has energy remaining after executing the $task_m$, $C7$ is to ensure that the UAV has energy remaining after executing the $task_m$.

3   Solution to the Joint Offloading Optimization Problem

In this section, we first decompose the optimization in (13) into the offloading selection subproblem, which can be converted to an optimal matching problem based on the latency and energy limits of each specific task and solved using the greedy based offload selection algorithm.

For a specific task, the UE broadcasts a request message to all surrounding UAVs and SBSs. As shown in Table 1, the request message contains two main fields, respectively, the location field and the task information field. The location field indicates the current location of the UE. The task information field contains three terms of the offloaded task d_m, c_m, t_m^{max}. As shown in Table 2, all nearby UAVs and SBSs receive the discovery message broadcasted by the UE, and send a response message to the UE. The response message contains three main fields, respectively, the location field, offloading decision, and execution details. The location field in respond message indicates the location of the current task,

Table 1. Request message

Request message	
Identification	Task specification
Location	Type | Size

Table 2. Response message

Response message		
Identification	Offloading decision	Execution details
Location	One/Zero	Execution time | Energy consumption

offloading decision indicates whether the task can be offloaded according to the energy limit of the UAV or SBS and the delay limit of the task, execution details contain time and energy consumption required to execute the task offloaded.

For the offloading selection subproblem, a specific task can be executed in three location including local, the UAV base station and the SBS in this paper. The UE reasonably selects the location where the task is offloaded based on the response message. In (13), The energy consumption of task offloading to the local, the UAV, and the SBS is described as follows:

$$\hat{E}_{loc} = E_m^L$$
$$\hat{E}_{uav} = \omega E_m^{T_{UAV}} + \eta E_m^{E_{UAV}} \tag{14}$$
$$\hat{E}_{sbs} = E_m^{T_{SBS}}$$
$$\text{s.t.} \quad C2, C3, C4, C5$$

(a) *The Task Is Executed Locally:* Upon generating a task, the UE broadcasts the request message to seek a suitable execution location based on task energy consumption and QoS latency requirement. The UE executes offloading selection according to received response message. The task is executed locally as described below:

$$\min_{\omega, \eta}(\omega E_m^{loc} + \eta E_m^{uav}) = \hat{E}_{loc}$$

$$\text{s.t.} \quad C3, C4, C5$$
$$C1 : t_m^L \leq t_m^{max}$$
$$C2 : \omega = 1, \eta = 0 \tag{15}$$
$$C6 : E_{loc} - E_m^L \geq E_{th}^{loc}$$
$$C8 : \hat{E}_{loc} < \hat{E}_{sbs} \quad (if \ t_m^{UE-SBS} + t_m^{SBS} \leq t_m^{max})$$
$$C9 : \hat{E}_{loc} < \hat{E}_{uav} \quad (if \ t_m^{UE-UAV} + t_m^{UAV} \leq t_m^{max}).$$

Within the required QoS latency, if the local calculations have the lowest energy consumption and after the task is completed, the remaining energy resources of the UE are greater than the threshold energy of the UE, which is presented in $C6$, the task is executed by the UE.

(b) *The Task Is Executed at The SBS*: The UE determines whether to offload the task by comparing local execution time with maximum tolerance delay t_m^{max} and the remaining energy of the UE $E_m^{loc_{re}}$ with the threshold of energy of the UE E_{th}^{loc}.

$$D_{T-offload} = I(t_m^L, t_m^{max}) = \begin{cases} 0 \ IF(t_m^L \leq t_m^{max}) \\ 1 \ IF(t_m^L > t_m^{max}) \end{cases}$$

$$D_{E-offload} = I(E_m^{loc_{re}}, E_{th}^{loc}) = \begin{cases} 0 \ IF(E_m^{loc_{re}} \geq E_{th}^{loc}) \\ 1 \ IF(E_m^{loc_{re}} < E_{th}^{loc}). \end{cases} \tag{16}$$

When the time decision and the energy decision are both positive, the task is executed locally, otherwise the task is offloaded. The task is executed at the SBS as described below:

$$\min_{\omega,\eta}(\omega E_m^{loc} + \eta E_m^{uav}) = \hat{E}_{sbs}$$

$$\text{s.t.} \quad C3, C4, C5$$

$$C1 : t_m^{UE-SBS} + t_m^{SBS} \leq t_m^{max}$$

$$C2 : \omega = 1, \eta = 0 \tag{17}$$

$$C6 : E_{loc} - E_m^{T_{SBS}} \geq E_{th}^{loc}$$

$$C10 : \hat{E}_{sbs} < \hat{E}_{uav} \quad (if \ t_m^{UE-UAV} + t_m^{UAV} \leq t_m^{max}).$$

When the QoS latency requirement of the task is guaranteed for offloading to the SBS, if the energy consumption is the lowest, and after the task offloading is completed, the remaining energy resources of the UE are greater than the threshold energy of the UE, the task is executed at the SBS.

(c) *The Task Is Executed at The UAV*: For computation-intensive and latency-sensitive tasks, the UE can not guarantee the Qos and select to offload the task [12]. Compared to offload to the SBS, UAV-enabled MEC provides higher bandwidth and more stable communication link, which can ensure more critical QoS latency requirement of the task. The task is executed at the UAV as described below: executed at the SBS as described below:

$$\min_{\omega,\eta}(\omega E_m^{loc} + \eta E_m^{uav}) = \hat{E}_{uav}$$

$$\text{s.t.}\quad C2, C3, C4, C5$$

$$C1 : t_m^{UE-UAV} + t_m^{UAV} \leq t_m^{max} \tag{18}$$

$$C6 : E_{loc} - E_m^{T_{UAV}} \geq E_{th}^{loc}$$

$$C7 : E_{uav} - E_m^{E_{UAV}} \geq E_{th}^{uav}$$

$$C11 : \hat{E}_{uav} < \hat{E}_{sbs} \quad (if \ t_m^{UE-SBS} + t_m^{SBS} \leq t_m^{max}).$$

When the QoS latency requirement of the task is guaranteed for offloading to the UAV, if the remaining energy of the UE and the UAV are greater than the threshold energy after the task is completed and the energy consumption is the lowest, the task is executed at the UAV.

The detail steps of a task-aware joint computation offloading scheme are described in Algorithm 1.

4   Simulation Results and Discussions

In this section, we examine the performance of the task-aware joint computation offloading scheme based on ground offloading and air offloading. For comparison, we also simulate the following typical scheme: (1) just consider that tasks are processed locally at the UE, which is denoted as scheme(1); (2) consider local execution and the ground-offloading without air-offloading, which is denoted as scheme (2); (3) consider local execution and the air-offloading without ground-offloading, which is denoted as scheme (3); the joint computation offloading scheme proposed in this paper is denoted as scheme (4).

In this simulation, Tables 3 and 4 respectively indicate the size of the considered tasks, a certain value of maximum allowable latency for each task. The computation capability of the UE, the SBS and the UAV are 2.2 GHz, 5 GHz, 4 GHz respectively [13]. UAV is assumed to fly at a fixed altitude A = 80 m. Most other parameters used in the simulation are summarized in Table 5.

Figure 2 illustrates optimal execution location of each task for different applications based on the proposed scheme. The result shows that for computation-intensive or latency-sensitive computing tasks, the UE cannot meet its requirements. And the computing tasks are offloaded to the UAV or UE by air-offloading and ground-offloading according to the delay and energy consumption of each computing task. If there is no air-offloading or ground-offloading, a lot of tasks will be blocked.

Algorithm 1. The Latency-aware and Energy-aware MEC Based on a Joint Computation Offloading Scheme

1: **Initialization:**
   a)Set f^L, f^{UAV}, $\{P_m^L, P_m^T, P_m^{UAV}\}$, $m \in M$, ω, η, β_0, A_{UAV}, W_{UE-SBS}, E_{loc}, E_{uav}, E_{th}^{loc}, E_{th}^{uav}
   b)Calculate G_{UE-SBS}, H_{UE-UAV}
   c)Initialize three terms (d_m, c_m, t_m^{max}) of $task_m$, $m \in M$, according to different applications;
2: **for** $m = 1, \cdots, M$ **do**
3:    Calculate t_m^L, E_m^L, t_m^{UE-SBS}, t_m^{SBS}, E_m^{TSBS}, t_m^{UE-UAV}, t_m^{UAV}, E_m^{EUAV}, E_m^{TUAV}
4:    **if** $t_m^L \le t_m^{max}$ & $E_{loc} - E_m^L \ge E_{th}^{loc}$ **then**
5:      **if** $t_m^{UE-SBS} + t_m^{SBS} \le t_m^{max}$ & $E_{loc} - E_m^{TSBS} \ge E_{th}^{loc}$ **then**
6:        **if** $t_m^{UE-UAV} + t_m^{UAV} \le t_m^{max}$ & $E_{loc} - E_m^{TUAV} \ge E_{th}^{loc}$ & $E_{uav} - E_m^{EUAV} \ge E_{th}^{uav}$ **then**
7:          Compare the size of $\hat{E}_{loc}, \hat{E}_{uav}, \hat{E}_{sbs}$
8:          Select the optimal offloading location with the lowest energy consumption in line 7
9:        **else**
10:          Compare the size of $\hat{E}_{loc}, \hat{E}_{sbs}$
11:          Select the optimal offloading location with the lowest energy consumption in line 10
12:        **end if**
13:      **else if** $t_m^{UE-UAV} + t_m^{UAV} \le t_m^{max}$ & $E_{loc} - E_m^{TUAV} \ge E_{th}^{loc}$ & $E_{uav} - E_m^{EUAV} \ge E_{th}^{uav}$ **then**
14:        Compare the size of $\hat{E}_{loc}, \hat{E}_{uav}$
15:        Select the optimal offloading location with the lowest energy consumption in line 14
16:      **else**
17:        E=$\hat{E}_{loc}$
18:        The task offloads to local
19:      **end if**
20:    **else if** $t_m^{UE-SBS} + t_m^{SBS} \le t_m^{max}$ & $E_{loc} - E_m^{TSBS} \ge E_{th}^{loc}$ **then**
21:      **if** $t_m^{UE-UAV} + t_m^{UAV} \le t_m^{max}$ & $E_{loc} - E_m^{TUAV} \ge E_{th}^{loc}$ & $E_{uav} - E_m^{EUAV} \ge E_{th}^{uav}$ **then**
22:        Compare the size of $\hat{E}_{uav}, \hat{E}_{sbs}$
23:        Select the optimal offloading location with the lowest energy consumption in line 22
24:      **else**
25:        E=$\hat{E}_{sbs}$
26:        The task offloads to the SBS
27:      **end if**
28:    **else if** $t_m^{UE-UAV} + t_m^{UAV} \le t_m^{max}$ & $E_{loc} - E_m^{TUAV} \ge E_{th}^{loc}$ & $E_{uav} - E_m^{EUAV} \ge E_{th}^{uav}$ **then**
29:      E=$\hat{E}_{uav}$
30:      The task offloads to the UAV
31:    **else**
32:      The task is blocked
33:    **end if**
34: **end for**
35: Output: the location where the task is offloaded and average energy consumption and latency for tasks execution

Figure 3 illustrate the blocking rate and average latency of handling for each scheme. And we can find that the proposed scheme can achieve the lowest blocking rate and average delay compared other schemes. In Fig. 3, we can find that the number of blocked tasks is reduced consideration of ground-offloading besides the local computing or air-offloading besides the local computing, but there

Table 3. The size of different tasks

Task	Task(1)	Task(2)	Task(3)	Task(4)	Task(5)
d_m(KB)	100	270	320	370	600
Task	Task(6)	Task(7)	Task(8)	Task(9)	Task(10)
d_m(KB)	780	850	900	910	1000

Table 4. QoS latency for different tasks

Task	Task(1)	Task(2)	Task(3)	Task(4)	Task(5)
t_m^{max}(ms)	440	520	260	420	490
Task	Task(6)	Task(7)	Task(8)	Task(9)	Task(10)
t_m^{max}(ms)	500	470	560	600	200

Table 5. Simulation parameters

Parameters	Values
Sub-channel bandwidth W_{UE-SBS}	2.5 MHz
Sub-channel bandwidth W_{UE-UAV}	4 MHz
Processing power for P_m^L, P_m^{UAV}	[1,5, 0.8] W
Tx power	24 dBm
Bandwidth	20 MHz
Small cell path loss (in dB)	$147.4 + 43.3 log_{10}(R)$
UAV channel power gain β_0	-50 dB
Computing capability for f^L, f^{SBS}, f^{UAV}	[2.2, 5, 4] GHz
Height of UAVs	80 m
Noise power spectral density (PSD)	-174 dBm/Hz
Threshold level of energy of UE E_{th}^{loc}	0.2 WH
Threshold level of energy of UE E_{th}^{uav}	1 WH

are still some blocked tasks. The proposed scheme in this paper joint ground-offloading and air-offloading achieves the best performance. Meanwhile, it can be observed that the proposed scheme can achieve the lowest average latency based on latency-awareness and energy-awareness of tasks. Each task is offloaded to the best execution location to meet QoS latency requirement.

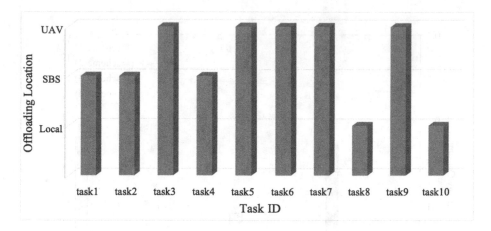

Fig. 2. Offloading location of each task.

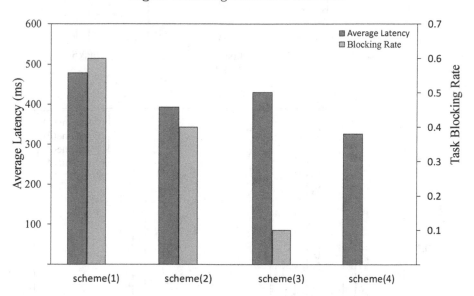

Fig. 3. Blocking rate and average latency of tasks handling for different schemes of each task.

Figure 4 shows energy consumption of each task for different schemes. And we can find that the proposed scheme can minimize the energy consumption while satisfying the QoS latency. The calculation task blocking rate even dropped to 0%. It prolongs the lifetime of the UAV and the UE while improving the performance of UAV-enabled mobile edge computing systems.

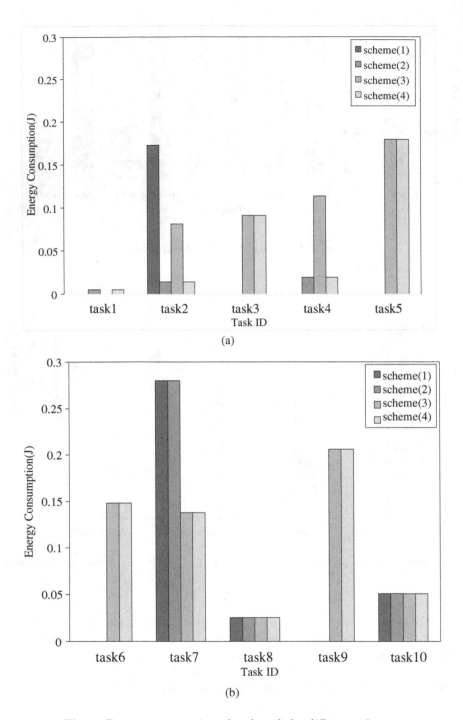

Fig. 4. Energy consumption of each task for different schemes.

5 Conclusion

In this paper, we focus on a latency-aware and energy-aware mobile edge computing for time critical applications based on a joint computation offloading scheme. The proposed scheme decides the location of task execution based on the available resources and the required QoS constraints. For different tasks with different QoS latency constraints and resource requirement, they are decided to execute locally or offload to UAV-enabled MEC servers by air-offloading method or offload to the SBS with conventional MESs by ground-offloading method. The simulation results demonstrate that our scheme achieves higher efficiency in terms of latency and blocking probability. Meanwhile, the proposed scheme minimizes the energy consumption of UEs and UAVs under the conditions that satisfy the different delay limits of each task.

Acknowledgement. This work is jointly supported by National Natural Science Foundation of China (Grant No. 61671088), and the National Natural Science Foundation of China (Grant No. 61771070).

References

1. Gupta, L., Jain, R., Vaszkun, G.: Survey of important issues in UAV communication networks. IEEE Commun. Surv. Tutor. **18**(2), 1123–1152 (2016). Secondquarter
2. Fan, L., Yan, W., Chen, X., Chen, Z., Shi, Q.: An energy efficient design for UAV communication with mobile edge computing. China Commun. **16**(1), 26–36 (2019)
3. Ruan, L., et al.: Energy-efficient multi-UAV coverage deployment in UAV networks: a game-theoretic framework. China Commun. **15**(10), 194–209 (2018)
4. Li, J., Liu, Q., Wu, P., Shu, F., Jin, S.: Task offloading for UAV-based mobile edge computing via deep reinforcement learning. In: 2018 IEEE/CIC International Conference on Communications in China (ICCC), pp. 798–802, August 2018
5. Hu, Q., Cai, Y., Yu, G., Qin, Z., Zhao, M., Li, G.Y.: Joint offloading and trajectory design for UAV-enabled mobile edge computing systems. IEEE Internet Things J. **6**(2), 1879–1892 (2019)
6. Zhou, F., Wu, Y., Sun, H., Chu, Z.: UAV-enabled mobile edge computing: offloading optimization and trajectory design. In: 2018 IEEE International Conference on Communications (ICC), pp. 1–6, May 2018
7. Sharma, V., You, I., Jayakody, D.N.K., Reina, D.G., Choo, K.R.: Neural-blockchain based ultra-reliable caching for edge-enabled UAV networks. IEEE Trans. Ind. Inform. **15**, 5723–5736 (2019)
8. Du, Y., Wang, K., Yang, K., Zhang, G.: Energy-efficient resource allocation in UAV based MEC system for IoT devices. In: 2018 IEEE Global Communications Conference (GLOBECOM), pp. 1–6, December 2018
9. Zhou, F., Wu, Y., Hu, R.Q., Qian, Y.: Computation rate maximization in UAV-enabled wireless-powered mobile-edge computing systems. IEEE J. Sel. Areas Commun. **36**(9), 1927–1941 (2018)
10. Bai, T., Wang, J., Ren, Y., Hanzo, L.: Energy-efficient computation offloading for secure UAV-edge-computing systems. IEEE Trans. Veh. Technol. **68**, 6074–6087 (2019)

11. Zhang, J., et al.: Stochastic computation offloading and trajectory scheduling for UAV-assisted mobile edge computing. IEEE Internet Things J. **6**(2), 3688–3699 (2019)
12. Qian, Y., Wang, F., Li, J., Shi, L., Cai, K., Shu, F.: User association and path planning for UAV-aided mobile edge computing with energy restriction. IEEE Wirel. Commun. Lett. **8**, 1312–1315 (2019)
13. Khuwaja, A.A., Chen, Y., Zhao, N., Alouini, M., Dobbins, P.: A survey of channel modeling for UAV communications. IEEE Commun. Surv. Tutor. **20**(4), 2804–2821 (2018). Fourthquarter

Burst Traffic Awareness WRR Scheduling Algorithm in Wide Area Network for Smart Grid

Xin Tan[1], Xiaohui Li[1(✉)] (iD), Zhenxing Liu[1], and Yuemin Ding[2] (iD)

[1] School of information Science and Engineering,
Wuhan University of Science and Technology, Wuhan 430081, China
lixiaohui@wust.edu.cn
[2] School of Computer Science and Engineering, Tianjin University of Technology,
Tianjin 300384, China

Abstract. Smart grid achieves optimal management of the entire power system operation by constant monitoring and rapid demand response (DR) for power supply-demand balance. Constantly monitoring the system state realized by Wide Area Measurement Systems (WAMS) provides a global view of the power grid. With a global view of the grid, Wide Area Control (WAC) generated DR command to improve the stability of power systems. When the regular monitoring data flow and the sudden DR data coexist, the suddenness of the demand response may result in delay or loss of the data packet due to uneven resource allocation when the network communication resources are limited, thereby affecting the accuracy of the power system state estimation. To solve this problem, this paper proposes a burst traffic perception weighted round robin algorithm (BTAWRR). The proposed algorithm defines the weight of the cyclic scheduling according to the periodicity of the monitoring data and the suddenness of the demand response. Then it adopts the iterative cyclic scheduling to adjust the transmission of data packets in time by adaptively sensing the changes of the traffic flow. The simulation results show that the proposed algorithm can effectively reduce the scheduling delay and packet loss rate when the two data coexist, and improve the throughput, which is beneficial to ensure the stability of the smart grid.

Keywords: Burst traffic · Scheduling algorithm · Weight · Monitoring data · Demand response

1 Introduction

Smart Grid achieves optimal management of the entire power system operation by collecting, integrating, analyzing, and mining data obtained by real-time monitoring of the key equipment in different parts of power grid such as generation,

Supported in part by the National Natural Science Foundation of China under Grant 61702369.

H. Gao et al. (Eds.): ChinaCom 2019, LNICST 312, pp. 117–128, 2020.
https://doi.org/10.1007/978-3-030-41114-5_10

transmission, distribution, and power consumption [1]. With its rapid development, a huge number of monitoring data and DR data are transmitted and exchanged in order to ensure the stability and efficiency of its operation. Monitoring data comes from WAMS, which implements real-time high-rate acquisition of main monitoring data for grid operation by arranging GPS-based Phased Measurement Units (PMUs) at key measurement points in the power grid. DR data comes from the control commands which are used to change the power consumption of an electric customer to better match the demand for power with the supply. Monitoring data traffic is generally periodic. DR traffic is generally burst traffic. Two kinds of data traffic are required to transmit to the primary station system in power grid. Therefore, the efficiency, integrity and low latency of data transmission for two coexisting data traffic are an important guarantee for the stability of power grid [2,3].

There are many scholars who have studied data preprocessing of PMU in recent years. The focus of their study is to ensure the completeness and efficiency of power grid monitoring data transmission [4]. A new approach to the application of compressed sampling techniques in the field of power system synchronous phasor measurement is proposed in [5]. Multi-scale compression processing for PMU is proposed in [6]. There are also many scholars who have studied DR command data transmission. The focus of their study is to ensure the rapid and reliable response of the changes in state of power grid. A multicast tree construction method considering both load power and communication delay is introduced, which is called multicast routing algorithm based on DR capability constraint in [7]. A DR energy management scheme for industrial facilities based on the state task network (STN) and mixed integer linear programming (MILP) is proposed in [8]. However, it is rarely noted that monitoring data and DR data usually coexist in the communication networks in power grid. The burst of DR leads to the sudden change of the traffic flow in smart grid. When the network bandwidth is limited, the sudden change of the traffic will cause the data packet transmission to be late, which leads to the loss of data and ultimately affects the stability of the system [9,10].

Aiming at the above problem, this paper proposes a kind of Burst Traffic Awareness Weighted Round Robin (BTAWRR) algorithm, which takes the periodicity of PMU data traffic and the burst traffic of DR command into account. The proposed algorithm adopts the iterative cyclic scheduling to adjust the transmission of data packets in time by adaptively sensing the changes of the traffic flow. The goal of the proposed algorithm is to reduce latency and packet loss due to sudden changes in traffic, and increase throughput. By analyzing the BTAWRR algorithm and WRR algorithm, the results show that the BTAWRR algorithm is superior to the WRR algorithm in terms of average delay, packet loss rate and throughput.

The rest of paper is organized as follows: Sect. 2 describes the WAMS structure. Section 3 introduces the algorithm we propose. Section 4 gives the results and analysis of the simulation and final conclusions are drawn in Sect. 5.

2   WAMS Structure

Smart grid could provide wider view of the grid through WAMS. The WAMS structure is shown in Fig. 1. The basic components of WAMs are PMUs, Phasor Data Concentrator (PDCs), and the associated wide area network (WAN) [11,12]. PMUs can measure high resolution measurements of voltage, phase angle, frequency and current phasors from different parts of the power grid and export these measurements to a PDC [13]. The global positioning system (GPS) is used to synchronize the phasor measurements to a common time base. The most important function of a PDC is to collect the phasor measurements from a set of PMUs and align the measurements according to their GPS time stamp. The main stations collects measurements from different PDC pools, time-aligns them, and sends them to the control center for state estimation, dynamic monitoring, and transient stability analysis of the power system. The power demand response is that when the power consumption of an electric customer doesn't match the demand for power with the supply, the control centers need to send DR commands to the supply side and customer side in order to make them match. Therefore, PMU monitoring data and DR commands coexist in WAN. If their transmission in WAN was to experience abnormal delays or packet losses, some measurements or DR commands can be lost. Such cases will affect the stability of the entire power grid.

As can be seen from Fig. 1, multiple PDCs transmit the aggregated PMU data to the primary station through the WAN. There is a need to exchange PMU data and DR data between the primary stations. In the future, with the continuous development of smart grids and the constant changes in demand, DR commands from WAC may produce burst traffic flow. If the traffic flow in power grid suddenly increases, the insufficient allocation of network communication resources will cause an increase in delay and a large amount of packet loss. If the traffic flow in the power grid suddenly decreases, excessive allocation of network communication resources will result in waste of resources, while other PMUs will have lower throughput due to insufficient resource allocation. The lack of PMU measurement value will lead to the accuracy of the main station's estimation of the power system state, which is not conducive to the related protection, detection and control of the power grid, thus affecting the stability of the power grid.

In order to solve the above problem, a scheduling algorithm running on the primary station system are introduced in this paper. By adaptively sensing the burst traffic, the proposed algorithm can dynamically allocate network communication resources to the PMU in a balanced manner, which reduces the delay and packet loss rate of PMU data and DR data transmission.

3   BTAWRR Algorithm

Among many classic scheduling algorithms, the performance of WRR algorithm on scheduling real-time and packet loss rate is relatively good. The WRR algorithm assigns a weight to each queue and sets the associated weight counter.

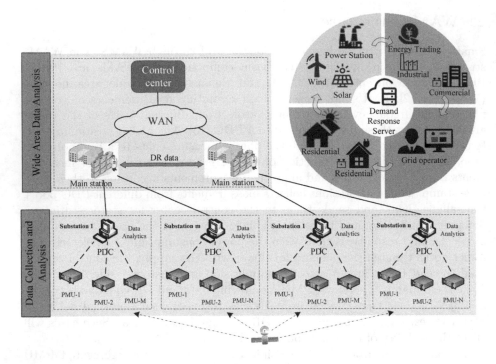

Fig. 1. WAMS structure.

Before scheduling, the weight is assigned to corresponding counters, which specify the number of packets transmitted in the corresponding queue in one round. If a queue sends a packet, the queue weight counter is decremented by one. Continue to send packets until the counter reaches zero or the queue is empty. Finally, all queue counters are reset to their weight values.

When WRR is introduced in the WAMS to allocate network communication resources in a reasonable and balanced manner, there are three characteristics of WAMS that need to be considered: (1) PMU sampling frequency; (2) PMU data packet size; (3) The variance of the normal distribution DR_traffic.

3.1   Weighted Design

Figure 2 shows two rounds of scheduling of three PMU queues (named PMU_q_2, PMU_q_3 and PMU_q_4) and one DR queue (named DR_q_1) where the weight of each queue is 3. Figure 2(a) indicates the first round of scheduling, and Fig. 2(b) indicates the second round of scheduling. The dotted box indicates the packets that are scheduled to be sent out of the queue, and the solid line box indicates the remaining packets in the queue. Figure 2(a) shows the situation after the queue has passed the first round of scheduling. It can be seen from the picture that there are fewer data packets in q_1, and the allocated resources are not used up. At this time, there are 1, 2 packets of q_3 and q_4, respectively, which are not transmitted. Figure 2(b) shows the results of the queue after the second round of scheduling, we can see that q_1 suddenly increased, at this time due to insufficient allocation of resources, there are still 3 packets stranded, and q_4 has a packet loss in the second round due to more stranded packets in the first round. As the DR queue service flow changes continuously, more resources are wasted and packets are lost if the weight in WRR is not changed.

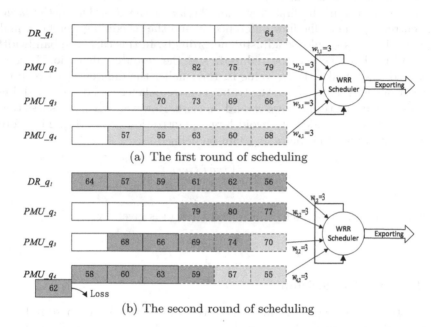

(a) The first round of scheduling

(b) The second round of scheduling

Fig. 2. Example of WRR algorithm.

In order to solve the above problem, it is necessary to redefine the weight in combination with the sampling frequency and the packet size of the PMU data, and the variance of the normal distribution DR traffic. There are two main steps in this weight calculation:

1. Multiple queue traffic flows are normalized
   The mean square error of the current plurality of queue traffic flows is determined according to the current round of queue traffic flow size. This step can decide the traffic flow dispersion of all the queues. Assume that at round k, the traffic of queue i is $traffic_{i,k}$, where $1 \leq i \leq n$ with n queue. $\langle traffic_k \rangle$ is the mean from round k,

$$\langle traffic_k \rangle = \frac{1}{n} \sum_{i=1}^{n} traffic_{i,k} \tag{1}$$

the standard deviation at round k (β_k) are determined as:

$$\beta_k = \sqrt{\frac{1}{n}\sum_{i=1}^{n}(traffic_{i,k} - \langle traffic_k \rangle)^2} \qquad (2)$$

2. Determine the new weight $w_{i,k}$
   It can be seen from the first step that the larger the β_k value is, the larger the current queue traffic flow difference is, and the scheduling weight of multiple traffic flows should be adjusted accordingly. In this case, the bandwidth division module needs to be reduced, and the resource allocation is more balanced; the smaller the β_k value is, the smaller the difference between the current queue traffic flows is, the traffic is more balanced, and the scheduling weight of multiple traffic flows should be close. However, when β_k is less than 1, it is necessary to add 1 to avoid large quantization errors [17]. Therefore, the weight adjustment factor $\omega_{i,k}$ can be defined as:

$$\omega_{i,k} = \left\lceil \frac{traffic_{i,k}}{\beta_k + 1} \right\rceil \qquad (3)$$

The current weight of queue i in round k $(w_{i,k})$ is given by:

$$w_{i,k} = \omega_{i,k} W_i \qquad (4)$$

3.2   BTAWRR Algorithm

Based on the above weight design, the BTAWRR algorithm is proposed in Fig. 3. When establishing the WAM model, the number of queues n is defined, which corresponds with the number of PMUs and DR controls flows. The length of all the queues (the maximum number of packets in the queue) is assumed as the same, and is defined l. The number of packets of queue i in the kth round scheduling is $q_{i,k}$. The weight of $q_{i,k}$ is $w_{i,k}$, and its weight counter is $WC_{i,k}$, which specifies the number of packets transmitted in queue i of the kth round scheduling. For the convenience of performance observation, the maximum number of scheduling rounds is assumed as k_{max}.

Once the queues get scheduled in each scheduling round, the proposed algorithm first computes the weight for each queue using Eq. 4 according to the current flow traffic and sets weight counter for each queue. If a queue sends a data packet, the queue weight counter is decremented by 1. The algorithm continues to send packets until the weight counter reaches zero or the queue is empty. Then the next queue gets scheduled and repeats the above process until all the queues are scheduled in current round.

Due to the iterative calculation of Eq. 4, the proposed algorithm can calculate the weight as the DR traffic changes. Therefore, BTAWRR algorithm can adaptively perceive the DR traffic change, and adjust the weight in the each scheduling round according to the traffic flow in the current queue in time.

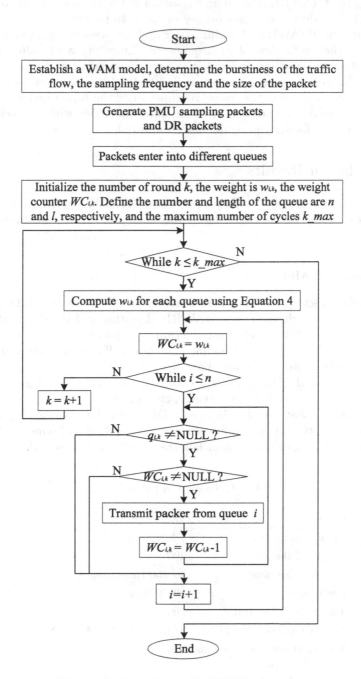

Fig. 3. The flow chart of BTAWRR algorithm.

By running the BTAWRR scheduling algorithm at the primary station of Fig. 1, it is possible to reduce the queuing delay of the data packets.

Applying the BTAWRR algorithm to Fig. 2 for scheduling, it can be calculated that the traffic flow of each queue in Figure (a) is 64, 236, 278, and 293, respectively. According to Eq. 4, the current round of each queue can be obtained. The weights that follow are 3, 9, 12, and 12, so no packets are stuck in the first round. Because the queue is empty after the first scheduling round, the second scheduling round of packets can enter the queue without packet loss. The transmission efficiency is significantly improved.

4   Simulation Results

In this section, we analyze the impact of the BTAWRR algorithm on the efficiency, integrity and timeliness of data transmission in smart grid through simulations.

4.1   Simulation Model

The transmission scheduling model on main stations are developed and simulated on MATLAB. The performance of BTAWRR algorithm and WRR algorithm are compared in terms of delay relative reduction rate, packet loss rate and relative increase rate of throughput. We assume that DR traffic is normally distributed and the simulation parameters are shown in Table 1.

The variance of the DR traffic is a scalar that describes the degree of burst traffic flow. The smaller the variance value, the smaller the degree of burst traffic flow, which means that the distribution of DR traffic data is relatively concentrated. The larger the variance value, the greater the degree of burst traffic flow, which means that the distribution of DR traffic data is relatively discrete.

Table 1. Simulation parameter

Parameter	Value
Number of queues	1 DR, 99 PMU
Length of the queue	200
Sampling frequency	50 150 times/round
Packet size	60 80 byte
The mean of DR_traffic	100
The variance of DR_traffic	2/4/6/8/10/12/14/16/18/20
Maximum number of rounds	100

4.2   Simulation Result Analysis

Figure 4 shows the delay reduction rate of the BTAWRR algorithm relative to the WRR algorithm. The scheduling delay of the BTAWRR algorithm is reduced by about 95% compared to the WRR algorithm. In the case of the same DR traffic burst, the weight of the BTAWRR is determined by the current queue service flow, so the network communication resources can be more effectively utilized, which results in timely data packet transmission. Accordingly, the scheduling delay of the BTAWRR algorithm for the data packet is less than that of the WRR algorithm scheduling.

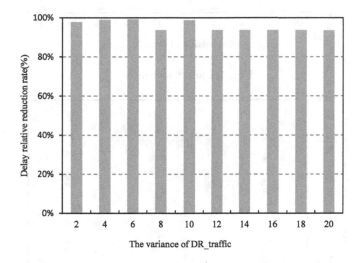

Fig. 4. Delay relative reduction rate.

Figure 5 shows a comparison of packet loss rates for the two scheduling algorithms. As the variance of DR traffic increases, the DR traffic flow changes a lot. The packet loss rate of the two algorithms does not change significantly, so the scheduling is stable for both two algorithm. However, the packet loss rate of the BTAWRR algorithm is lower than that of the WRR algorithm. Since the BTAWRR can adaptively sense the DR traffic changes and adjust the weight in each round, the BTAWRR algorithm schedules packets among the queues in a more balanced way and the possibility of queue overflow is also reduced.

Figure 6 shows the throughput increase rate of the BTAWRR algorithm relative to the WRR algorithm. The throughput of the BTAWRR scheduling algorithm is increased by about 230% compared to the throughput scheduled by the WRR algorithm. In the case of the same DR traffic burst, the total throughput of the BTAWRR algorithm is more than that of the WRR algorithm because the BTAWRR algorithm transmits more data packets than the WRR algorithm in each scheduling round.

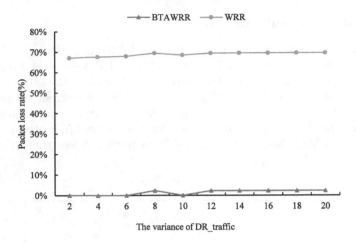

Fig. 5. Packet loss rate.

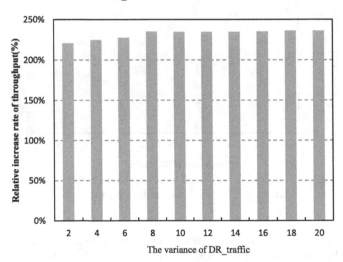

Fig. 6. Relative increase rate of throughput.

5   Conclusions

This paper proposes a kind of BTAWRR algorithm to solve the problem that network communication resources may be unevenly distributed when DR burst traffic occurs. The proposed algorithm used the periodicity of PMU data traffic as well as the burst traffic of demand response to define the weight of the cyclic scheduling, so that the scheduled data packets are efficiently transmitted. Due to the iterative calculation of weight, the algorithm can adaptively sense burst traffic changes and adjust packet transmission in time. The simulation results show that the proposed algorithm can increase the throughput of the data packet and reduce the scheduling delay and packet loss rate. The BTAWRR algorithm can be applied to the transmission of data packets for the main station in smart grid to ensure the efficiency, integrity and timely data transmission. It is conducive to the stability of the smart grid.

References

1. Fang, X., Misra, S., Xue, G.L., Yang, D.J.: Smart grid—the new and improved power grid: a survey. IEEE Commun. Surv. Tutor. **14**(4), 944–980 (2011)
2. Xu, S.K., Xie, X.R., Xin, Y.Z.: Present application situation and development tendency of synchronous phasor measurement technology based wide area measurement system. Power Syst. Technol. **29**(2), 44–49 (2005)
3. Mahmud, A.S.M.A., Sant, P.: Real-time price savings through price suggestions for the smart grid demand response model. In: 5th International Istanbul Smart Grid and Cities Congress and Fair (ICSG), Turkey, pp. 65–69 (2017)
4. Dasgupta, S., Paramasivam, M., Vaidya, U., Ajjarapu, V.: Real-time monitoring of short-term voltage stability using PMU data. IEEE Trans. Power Syst. **28**(4), 3702–3711 (2013)
5. Aravind, M.N., Anju, L.S., Sunitha, R.: Application of compressed sampling to overcome big data issues in synchrophasors. In: 6th International Conference on Power Systems (ICPS), New Delhi, India, pp. 1–5 (2016)
6. Lee, G., Shin, Y.J.: Multiscale PMU data compression based on wide-area event detection. In: 2017 IEEE International Conference on Smart Grid Communications (SmartGridComm), Dresden, Germany, pp. 437–442 (2017)
7. Long, D., Li, X.H., Ding, Y.M.: Multicast routing of power grid based on demand response constraints. J. Comput. Appl. **38**(4), 1102–1105 (2018)
8. Ding, Y.M., Hong, S.H., Li, X.H.: A demand response energy management scheme for industrial facilities in smart grid. IEEE Trans. Ind. Inform. **10**(4), 2257–2269 (2014)
9. Meliopoulos, A.P.S., Cokkinides, G.J., Wasynczuk, O.: PMU data characterization and application to stability monitoring. In: 2006 IEEE PES Power Systems Conference and Exposition, pp. 151–158. IEEE, Atlanta (2016)
10. Chenine, M., Nordstrom, L.: Investigation of communication delays and data incompleteness in multi-PMU wide area monitoring and control systems. In: 2009 International Conference on Electric Power and Energy Conversion Systems (EPECS), Sharjah, United Arab Emirates, pp. 1–6. IEEE (2009)
11. Rehtanz, C., Beland, J., Benmouyal, G.: Wide area monitoring and control for transmission capability enhancement. CIGRE Technical Brochure, 330 (2007)
12. Ju, P.: Power System Wide Area Measurement Technology. China Machine Press, Beijing (2008)
13. Zivanovic, R., Cairns, C.: Implementation of PMU technology in state estimation: an overview. In: Proceedings of IEEE. AFRICON 1996, Stellenbosch, South Africa, pp. 1006–1011. IEEE (1996)
14. Pan, D., Yang, Y.: FIFO-based multicast scheduling algorithm for virtual output queued packet switches. IEEE Trans. Comput. **54**(10), 1283–1297 (2005)
15. Hahne, E.L., Gallager, R.G.: Round robin scheduling for fair flow control in data communication networks. Massachusetts Institute of Technology, 86 (1986)

16. Katevenis, M., Sidiropoulos, S., Courcoubetis, C.: Weighted round-robin cell multi-plexing in a general-purpose ATM switch chip. IEEE J. Sel. Areas Commun. **9**(8), 1265–1279 (1991)
17. Ito, Y., Tasaka, S., Ishibashi, Y.: Variably weighted round robin queueing for core IP routers. In: Conference Proceedings of the IEEE International Performance, Computing, and Communications Conference, Phoenix, AZ, USA, pp. 159–166. IEEE (2002)

Joint Task Offloading, CNN Layer Scheduling and Resource Allocation in Cooperative Computing System

Xia Song[✉], Rong Chai, and Qianbin Chen

Key Lab of Mobile Communication Technology,
Chongqing University of Posts and Telecommunications, Chongqing 400065, China
2360321633@qq.com, {chairong,chenqb}@cqupt.edu.cn

Abstract. In this paper, we consider a cooperative computing system which consists of a number of mobile edge computing (MEC) servers deployed with convolutional neural network (CNN) model, a remote mobile cloud computing (MCC) server deployed with CNN model and a number of mobile devices (MDs). We assume that each MD has a computation task and is allowed to offload its task to one MEC server where the CNN model with various layers is applied to conduct task execution, and one MEC server can accept multiple tasks of MDs. To enable the cooperative between the MEC servers and the MCC server, we assume that the task of MD which has been processed partially by the CNN model of the MEC server will be sent to CNN model of the MCC server for further processing. We study the joint task offloading, CNN layer scheduling and resource allocation problem. By stressing the importance of task execution latency, the joint optimization problem is formulated as an overall task latency minimization problem. As the original optimization problem is NP hard, which cannot be solved conveniently, we transform it into three subproblems, i.e., CNN layer scheduling subproblem, task offloading subproblem and resource allocation subproblem, and solve the three subproblems by means of extensive search algorithm, reformulation-linearization-technique (RLT) and Lagrangian dual method, respectively. Numerical results demonstrate the effectiveness of the proposed algorithm.

Keywords: Cooperative computing · MEC server · MCC server · CNN layer scheduling · Task offloading

1 Introduction

The rapid development of mobile Internet and smart devices promotes the emergence of new applications such as interactive gaming, virtual reality, augment reality, etc. However, the intensive computing requirements of these emerging applications pose great challenges to the computation and process capability of

H. Gao et al. (Eds.): ChinaCom 2019, LNICST 312, pp. 129–142, 2020.
https://doi.org/10.1007/978-3-030-41114-5_11

mobile devices (MDs). While mobile cloud computing (MCC) can be applied to address these challenges, it suffers from long latency and low efficiency for transmitting and processing huge amounts of data collected from MDs [1]. To overcome the drawback of MCC, the concept of mobile edge computing (MEC) is proposed [2]. By deploying high performance MEC servers at the network edge in a distributed manner, MDs are allowed to offload their computation task to the MEC servers, which then execute the task on behalf of the MDs. Therefore, the task execution cost of the MDs especially in terms of task execution latency and energy consumption can be reduced significantly.

While acting as an efficient manner for task execution, the MEC servers may be subject to relatively limited computational capability especially compared to the remote MCC servers. Hence, cooperative computing system which enables the cooperative between remote MCC servers and MEC servers in task execution will be highly desired as it may enhance the performance of task execution and achieve the efficient resource utilization of the network. To further facilitate efficient task execution of the cooperative computing system, convolutional neural network (CNN) models can be applied at the MEC servers [3]. As a typical CNN model is composed of multiple tiers with each tier having various data processing capability, it is possible to process the task of MDs with a number of CNN layers, then transmit the reduced intermediate data to the MCC server to complete the task execution [4].

In recent years, the problem of task offloading has received considerable attentions [5–10]. To minimize the system-wide computation overheads, the authors in [5] formulate the task offloading problem as an offloading game and demonstrate the existence of Nash equilibrium point. Task offloading problem in MEC system was considered in [7,8], the weighted sum of the energy consumption and task execution delay was formulated and optimized in [7] and the maximum task execution latency of all the MDs was minimized in [8].

Joint task offloading and resource allocation problem was addressed in [6,9]. The authors in [6] defined an offloading priority function that depends on the local computing energy of the MDs and the channel gain between the MDs and the MEC servers. Based on the offloading priority of the MDs, a joint offloading decision and resource allocation strategy is designed to achieve the minimum weighted sum of the energy consumption. In [9], the problem of joint task offloading and resource allocation in an MEC system with multiple MDs was formulated as energy consumption minimization problem. To solve the formulated optimization problem, the authors further decoupled the original optimization problem into two problems, i.e., the resource allocation problem and the task offloading problem, and solved the two problems respectively by using the Lagrange method and the Hungarian method.

The aforementioned researches mainly address the problem of task offloading in MEC system, however, the cooperative between MCC schemes and MEC schemes has not been studied extensively. The authors in [10] considered the task offloading problem in a cooperative computing system serving one MD at certain time period, and proposed a greedy algorithm to maximize the number of tasks which can be offloaded to the system successfully. The authors in [10] failed to consider the resource sharing at the computing server, thus may result in inefficient resource utilization and highly limited task offloading performance. Furthermore, the task execution time failed to be stressed, thus, may lead to relatively long task execution time, which is undesired, especially for delay-sensitive MD tasks.

In this paper, we consider a cooperative computing system which allows the cooperative between the MEC servers and the MCC server in task execution. Assuming that the task execution at each MEC server is conducted by a CNN model with multiple layer, we study the joint task offloading, CNN layer scheduling and resource allocation problem. The joint optimization problem is formulated as an overall task latency minimization problem. As the original optimization problem is NP hard, which cannot be solved conveniently, we transform it into three subproblems, i.e., CNN layer scheduling subproblem, task offloading subproblem and resource allocation subproblem, and solve the three subproblems by means of extensive search algorithm, reformulation-linearization-technique (RLT) and Lagrangian dual method, respectively.

2   System Model

In this paper, we consider a cooperative computing system which consists of N MEC servers, an MCC server and M MDs. Suppose each MEC server is deployed with a CNN model which is composed of one input layer, one output layer and a number of hidden layers. We assume that each MD has a single task which can be offloaded to one MEC server and the task execution at the MEC server is conducted by the CNN model. More specifically, the input data of MD task will be processed by the input layer and various hidden layers or/and output layer, and then is sent out at one particular hidden layer or the output layer of the CNN model. We further assume that the cooperative between the MEC servers and the MCC server in task execution is allowed, i.e., the MD task which has been processed partially by the CNN model will be sent to the MCC server for further processing. Figure 1 shows the system model considered in this paper.

Let MD_m denote the mth MD and $T = \{T_1, ..., T_M\}$ denote the set of MD tasks, where T_m denotes the task of MD_m, $1 \leq m \leq M$. T_m can be characterized by a 3-tuple $\langle S_m, R_m^{\min}, D_m^{\max} \rangle$, where S_m denotes the size of input data of T_m, $R_m^{\min}$ and $D_m^{\max}$ denote the minimum transmission rate and the maximum tolerable task execution latency of T_m, respectively. We denote $E = \{E_1, ..., E_N\}$ as the set of MEC servers, where E_n denotes the nth MEC server, $1 \leq n \leq N$. Let F_n denote the computation capability of E_n, B_n denote the bandwidth of the wireless link between E_n and the MDs, and C_n denote the capacity of the fronthaul link between E_n and the MCC server.

To improve the resource utilization of the MEC servers, we assume that multiple MDs are allowed to offload their task to one MEC server. However, in this case, the resource sharing between multiple MD tasks has to be considered. In particular, the bandwidth resource and computation resource of the MEC servers and the capacity of the fronthaul link between the MEC servers and the MCC server should be allocated to various MD tasks.

We further denote r_n^k as the ratio of the intermediate data size generated at the kth CNN layer of E_n to the input data size of MD tasks and denote p_n^k as the computational overhead of a unit of input data at the kth CNN layer of E_n, $1 \leq n \leq N$, $1 \leq k \leq K$, where K denotes the total number of the layers in the CNN models employed at the MEC servers.

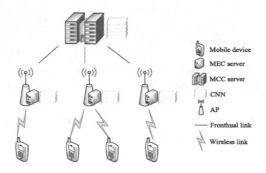

Fig. 1. System model

3 Optimization Problem Formulation

In this section, we examine the overall task latency in the considered cooperative computing system and formulate the joint task offloading, CNN layer scheduling and resource allocation problem as overall task latency minimization problem.

3.1 Objective Function

Stressing the performance of task execution in the cooperative computing system, we define overall task latency D as

$$D = \sum_{m=1}^{M} \sum_{n=1}^{N} x_{mn} D_{mn} \tag{1}$$

where D_{mn} denotes the task execution latency of T_m which is offloaded to E_n, x_{mn} denotes the task offloading variable of T_m. That is, if T_m is offloaded to E_n, $x_{mn} = 1$, otherwise, $x_{mn} = 0$. Jointly considering the time required to transmit MD tasks to the MEC servers and the MCC server, as well as the processing time at both servers, we formulate D_{mn} as

$$D_{mn} = D_{mn}^{\text{t}} + D_{mn}^{\text{p}} + D_{mn}^{\text{tc}} + D_{mn}^{\text{pc}} \tag{2}$$

where D_{mn}^{t} denotes the transmission latency required to offload T_m to E_n, D_{mn}^{p} denotes the task execution latency of T_m at E_n, D_{mn}^{tc} denotes the transmission latency of T_m when being transmitted from E_n to the MCC server, D_{mn}^{pc} denotes the task executing latency of T_m at the MCC server.

D_{mn}^{t} in (2) can be formulated as

$$D_{mn}^{t} = \frac{S_m}{R_{mn}} \tag{3}$$

where R_{mn} denotes the achievable data rate of T_m when being transmitted to E_n, which can be expressed as

$$R_{mn} = \alpha_{mn} r_{mn} \tag{4}$$

where $\alpha_{mn} \in [0, 1]$ denotes the fraction of the bandwidth resource allocated to T_m from E_n, r_{mn} denotes the data rate of T_m when being transmitted to E_n with the total bandwidth resource of E_n, i.e.,

$$r_{mn} = B_n \log_2 \left(1 + \frac{P_m g_{mn}}{\sigma^2} \right) \tag{5}$$

where P_m denotes the transmission power of MD_m when transmitting T_m to E_n, g_{mn} and σ^2 denote respectively the channel gain and the noise power of the link between MD_m and E_n.

D_{mn}^{p} in (2) can be calculated as

$$D_{mn}^{p} = \sum_{k=1}^{K} \delta_{mn}^{k} p_n^{k} \frac{S_m}{\beta_{mn} F_n} \tag{6}$$

where δ_{mn}^{k} denotes CNN layer scheduling variable. If the first k layers of the CNN model is scheduled to process T_m at E_n, $\delta_{mn}^{k} = 1$, otherwise, $\delta_{mn}^{k} = 1$, $\beta_{mn} \in [0, 1]$ denotes the fraction of the computation capability allocated to T_m at E_n.

D_{mn}^{tc} in (2) can be calculated as

$$D_{mn}^{tc} = \sum_{k=1}^{K} \delta_{mn}^{k} r_n^{k} \frac{S_m}{\lambda_{mn} C_n} \tag{7}$$

where $\lambda_{mn} \in [0, 1]$ denotes the fraction of the fronthaul capacity allocated to T_m when E_n transmits the intermediate data of T_m to the MCC server.

In this paper, we assume that the MCC server has relatively high computation capability, thus the latency term D_{mn}^{pc} in (2) is negligible.

3.2   Optimization Constraints

To design the optimal joint task offloading, CNN layer scheduling and resource allocation strategy which minimizes the overall task latency of the system, we should consider a number of constraints.

CNN Layer Scheduling Constraint. In this paper, we assume that at the MEC servers, one or multiple layer of the CNN model is assigned for executing one MD task, thus, we can express the CNN layer scheduling constraints as

$$C1: \delta_{mn}^k \in \{0,1\}, \tag{8}$$

$$C2: \sum_{k=1}^{K} \delta_{mn}^k \le 1. \tag{9}$$

Task Offloading Constraint. We assume that each task can be offloaded to at most one MEC server, hence, the constraints can be

$$C3: x_{mn} \in \{0,1\}, \tag{10}$$

$$C4: \sum_{n=1}^{N} x_{mn} = 1, 1 \le m \le M. \tag{11}$$

Resource Allocation Constraints. In the case that one MEC server executes multiple MD tasks, the resource allocation constraints should be satisfied, which can be expressed as

$$C5: \alpha_{mn}, \beta_{mn}, \lambda_{mn} \in [0,1], \tag{12}$$

$$C6: \sum_{m=1}^{M} \alpha_{mn} \le 1, \tag{13}$$

$$C7: \sum_{m=1}^{M} \beta_{mn} \le 1, \tag{14}$$

$$C8: \sum_{m=1}^{M} \lambda_{mn} \le 1. \tag{15}$$

Data Rate and Latency Requirements. Stressing the task offloading requirement, we assume that the link between MD_m and E_n should meet a minimum transmission rate constraint when T_m is offloaded to one MEC server, i.e.,

$$C9: \sum_{n=1}^{N} x_{mn} R_{mn} \ge R_m^{\min}, 1 \le m \le M. \tag{16}$$

As the task execution latency of T_m should meet a tolerable maximum latency requirement, we can express the task execution latency constraint as

$$C10: \sum_{n=1}^{N} x_{mn} D_{mn} \le D_m^{\max}. \tag{17}$$

3.3 Optimization Problem

Considering the aforementioned objective function and optimization constraints, we formulate the overall task latency minimization-based joint task offloading, CNN layer scheduling and resource allocation problem as

$$\min_{x_{mn}, \delta^k_{mn}, \alpha_{mn}, \beta_{mn}, \lambda_{mn}} D$$

$$\text{s.t.} \quad C1 - C10. \tag{18}$$

Through solving above optimization problem, we can obtain the joint task offloading, CNN layer scheduling and resource allocation strategies.

4 Solution of the Optimization Problem

The formulated optimization problem is a non-convex mixed integer programming problem which is NP-hard and cannot be solved conveniently. In this section, we decompose the formulated optimization problem into three subproblems, i.e., CNN layer scheduling subproblem, task offloading subproblem and resource allocation subproblem, and solve the three sub-problems successively to obtain the joint task offloading, CNN layer scheduling and resource allocation strategies.

4.1 CNN Layer Scheduling Subproblem

In this subsection, we first assume that task offloading strategy is given, e.g., $x_{mn} = 1$, and no resource sharing among tasks is required, i.e., $\alpha_{mn} = 1$, $\beta_{mn} = 1$, $\lambda_{mn} = 1$. Substituting α_{mn}, β_{mn}, λ_{mn} into (2)–(7), we may rewrite D_{mn} as

$$D^0_{mn} = \frac{S_m}{r_{mn}} + \sum_{k=1}^{K} \delta^k_{mn}\left(p^k_n \frac{S_m}{F_n} + r^k_n \frac{S_m}{C_n}\right). \tag{19}$$

As the only optimization variable contained in D^0_{mn} is the CNN layer scheduling variable, denoted by δ^k_{mn}, we may design the optimal CNN layer scheduling strategy by minimizing D^0_{mn}. Hence, the optimization problem formulated in (18) is now reduced to the CNN layer scheduling subproblem, which is formulated as

$$\min_{\delta^k_{mn}} D^0_{mn}$$

$$\text{s.t. C1, C2, C10 in (18).} \tag{20}$$

Since the above optimization problem is a simple one-variable optimization problem, we may solve it based on extensive search algorithm and obtain the optimal CNN layer scheduling strategy, denotd by $\delta^{k,*}_{mn}$.

4.2 Task Offloading Subproblem

Substituting $\delta_{mn}^{k,*}$ into the optimization problem formulated in (18), we can observe that the optimization problem is now a joint task offloading and resource allocation problem, and the objective function D can be rewritten as D^0, i.e.,

$$D^0 = \sum_{m=1}^{M} \sum_{n=1}^{N} x_{mn} \left(\frac{\hat{D}_{mn}^{t}}{\alpha_{mn}} + \frac{\hat{D}_{mn}^{p}}{\beta_{mn}} + \frac{\hat{D}_{mn}^{tc}}{\lambda_{mn}} \right) \tag{21}$$

where $\hat{D}_{mn}^{t} = \frac{S_m}{r_{mn}}$, $\hat{D}_{mn}^{p} = \sum_{k=1}^{K} \delta_{mn}^{k,*} \frac{p_n^k S_m}{F_n}$, $\hat{D}_{mn}^{tc} = \sum_{k=1}^{K} \delta_{mn}^{k,*} \frac{r_n^k S_m}{C_n}$.

It can be observed that the objective function D^0 is a mixed discrete and second order function of the optimization variables x_{mn}, α_{mn}, β_{mn} and λ_{mn}, which is notoriously difficult to solve. To address the difficulties, we apply variable transformation, discrete variable relaxation method and the RLT to reformulate the problem.

To tackle the problem of fraction optimization, we first define $\iota_{mn} = \frac{1}{\alpha_{mn}+\varepsilon_b}$, $\nu_{mn} = \frac{1}{\beta_{mn}+\varepsilon_c}$, and $\emptyset_{mn} = \frac{1}{\lambda_{mn}+\varepsilon_f}$ where ε_b, ε_c and ε_f are microscales introduced to avoid divide-by-zero error, then we can rewrite the optimization problem in (18) as follows.

$$\min_{\substack{x_{mn} \\ \iota_{mn},\nu_{mn},\emptyset_{mn}}} \sum_{m=1}^{M} \sum_{n=1}^{N} x_{mn}(\iota_{mn}\hat{D}_{mn}^{t} + \nu_{mn}\hat{D}_{mn}^{p} + \emptyset_{mn}\hat{D}_{mn}^{tc})$$

$$\text{s.t.} \quad \text{C3}, \text{C4}, \text{C9}, \text{C10 in (18)}$$

$$\text{C11}: \sum_{m=1}^{M} \frac{1}{\iota_{mn}} \leq 1 + M\varepsilon_b, \iota_{mn} \in \left[\frac{1}{1+\varepsilon_b}, \frac{1}{\varepsilon_b} \right]$$

$$\text{C12}: \sum_{m=1}^{M} \frac{1}{\nu_{mn}} \leq 1 + M\varepsilon_c, \nu_{mn} \in \left[\frac{1}{1+\varepsilon_c}, \frac{1}{\varepsilon_c} \right]$$

$$\text{C13}: \sum_{m=1}^{M} \frac{1}{\emptyset_{mn}} \leq 1 + M\varepsilon_f, \emptyset_{mn} \in \left[\frac{1}{1+\varepsilon_f}, \frac{1}{\varepsilon_f} \right]. \tag{22}$$

Problem (22) is still a non-convex problem because of the discrete variable x_{mn} and the second order form of the optimization variables. We now employ discrete variable relaxation method to convert $x_{mn} \in \{0,1\}$ to $0 \leq x_{mn} \leq 1$, then we adopt the RLT to linearize the objective function and constraints in (22). To linearize the second order terms $x_{mn}\iota_{mn}$, $x_{mn}\nu_{mn}$ and $x_{mn}\emptyset_{mn}$, we define $\varphi_{mn} = x_{mn}\iota_{mn}$, $\varsigma_{mn} = x_{mn}\nu_{mn}$ and $\vartheta_{mn} = x_{mn}\emptyset_{mn}$. Considering the constraints on x_{mn}, ι_{mn}, ν_{mn} and $\emptyset_{mn}$, we can obtain respectively the RLT bound-factor product constraints for φ_{mn}, ς_{mn} and ϑ_{mn} as

$$\Xi_{mn}^{\varphi} = \begin{cases} \varphi_{mn} - \frac{1}{1+\varepsilon_b}x_{mn} \geq 0 \\ \iota_{mn} - \frac{1}{1+\varepsilon_b} - \varphi_{mn} + \frac{1}{1+\varepsilon_b}x_{mn} \geq 0 \\ \frac{1}{\varepsilon_b}x_{mn} - \varphi_{mn} \geq 0 \\ \frac{1}{\varepsilon_b} - \iota_{mn} - \frac{1}{\varepsilon_b}x_{mn} + \varphi_{mn} \geq 0 \end{cases} \tag{23}$$

$$\Xi^{\varsigma}_{mn} = \begin{cases} \varsigma_{mn} - \frac{1}{1+\varepsilon_c}x_{mn} \geq 0 \\ \nu_{mn} - \frac{1}{1+\varepsilon_c} - \varsigma_{mn} + \frac{1}{1+\varepsilon_c}x_{mn} \geq 0 \\ \frac{1}{\varepsilon_c}x_{mn} - \varsigma_{mn} \geq 0 \\ \frac{1}{\varepsilon_c} - \nu_{mn} - \frac{1}{\varepsilon_c}x_{mn} + \varsigma_{mn} \geq 0 \end{cases} \tag{24}$$

$$\Xi^{\vartheta}_{mn} = \begin{cases} \vartheta_{mn} - \frac{1}{1+\varepsilon_f}x_{mn} \geq 0 \\ \emptyset_{mn} - \frac{1}{1+\varepsilon_f} - \vartheta_{mn} + \frac{1}{1+\varepsilon_f}x_{mn} \geq 0 \\ \frac{1}{\varepsilon_f}x_{mn} - \vartheta_{mn} \geq 0 \\ \frac{1}{\varepsilon_f} - \emptyset_{mn} - \frac{1}{\varepsilon_f}x_{mn} + \vartheta_{mn} \geq 0 \end{cases} \tag{25}$$

After substituting φ_{mn}, ς_{mn} and ϑ_{mn} into (22), we obtain a convex optimization problem:

$$\min_{\substack{x_{mn} \\ \iota_{mn},\nu_{mn},\emptyset_{mn} \\ \varphi_{mn},\varsigma_{mn},\vartheta_{mn}}} \sum_{m=1}^{M}\sum_{n=1}^{N}(\varphi_{mn}\hat{D}^{t}_{mn} + \varsigma_{mn}\hat{D}^{p}_{mn} + \vartheta_{mn}\hat{D}^{tc}_{mn})$$

$$\begin{aligned} \text{s.t.} \quad & C4, C9, C10 \text{ in } (18) \\ & C11-C13 \text{ in } (22) \\ & C14 : 0 \leq x_{mn} \leq 1 \\ & C15 : \varphi_{mn} \in \Xi^{\varphi}_{mn} \\ & C16 : \varsigma_{mn} \in \Xi^{\varsigma}_{mn} \\ & C17 : \vartheta_{mn} \in \Xi^{\vartheta}_{mn} \end{aligned} \tag{26}$$

Problem (26) is now a convex optimization problem, therefore it can be solved efficiently in polynomial time using standard software such as CVX, MOSEK, etc. Let $\left\{\hat{x}_{mn},\ \hat{\iota}_{mn},\ \hat{\nu}_{mn},\ \hat{\emptyset}_{mn},\ \hat{\varphi}_{mn},\ \hat{\varsigma}_{mn},\ \hat{\vartheta}_{mn}\right\}$ denote the optimal solution of (26). As $\hat{x}_{mn}$ is a continuous approximation of x_{mn}, to obtain the binary task offloading strategy x^{*}_{mn} of (18), we define

$$\begin{cases} x^{*}_{mn} = 1, & \hat{x}_{mn} \geq 0.5 \\ x^{*}_{mn} = 0, & \hat{x}_{mn} < 0.5. \end{cases} \tag{27}$$

4.3   Resource Allocation Subproblem

While the optimal resource allocation strategy denoted by $\hat{\alpha}_{mn}$, $\hat{\beta}_{mn}$ and $\hat{\lambda}_{mn}$ can be obtained from $\hat{\iota}_{mn}$, $\hat{\nu}_{mn}$, $\hat{\emptyset}_{mn}$, the suboptimality may occur due to the approximation of x_{mn}. In this paper, given the task offloading strategy x^{*}_{mn}, we further formulate the resource allocation subproblem and calculate the optimal resource allocation strategy by means of Lagrange dual method.

Based on the obtained task offloading strategy x^{*}_{mn}, we calculate the number of tasks being offloaded to individual MEC servers. In the case that $\sum_{m=1}^{M} x^{*}_{mn} \geq 1$ for any E_n, i.e., more than one task is offloaded to E_n, resource sharing occurs at E_n and the optimal resource allocation strategy should be designed. Let $\Phi_n = \{T_m | x_{mn}^* = 1\}$ denote the set of MD tasks which are offloaded to E_n.

We denote $\bar{D}_{mn}$ as the task latency when T_m is offloaded to E_n, i.e., $x_{mn}^* = 1$, we obtain

$$\bar{D}_{mn} = \frac{S_m}{R_{mn}} + \sum_{k=1}^{K} \delta_{mn}^{k,*} \left(\frac{p_n^k S_m}{\beta_{mn} F_n} + \frac{r_n^k S_m}{\lambda_{mn} C_n} \right). \tag{28}$$

The resource allocation subproblem can be formulated as

$$\min_{\alpha_{mn}, \beta_{mn}, \lambda_{mn}} \sum_{T_m \in \Phi_n} \bar{D}_{mn}$$

$$\text{s.t.} \quad C5 - C10. \tag{29}$$

It can be proved that the optimization problem formulated in (29) is a convex problem which can be solved by using the Lagrange dual method. The corresponding Lagrange function can be expressed as

$$L\left(\alpha_{mn}, \beta_{mn}, \lambda_{mn}, \eta_{mn}, \mu_{mn}, \gamma_{mn}, \theta_{mn}, \omega_{mn}, \varepsilon, \tau, \psi\right)$$

$$= \sum_{T_m \in \Phi_n} \bar{D}_{mn} + \sum_{T_m \in \Phi_n} \eta_{mn} \left(\bar{D}_{mn} - D_m^{\max}\right)$$

$$+ \sum_{T_m \in \Phi_n} \mu_{mn} \left(R_m^{\min} - R_{mn}\right) + \sum_{T_m \in \Phi_n} \gamma_{mn} \left(\alpha_{mn} - 1\right)$$

$$+ \sum_{T_m \in \Phi_n} \theta_{mn} \left(\beta_{mn} - 1\right) + \sum_{T_m \in \Phi_n} \omega_{mn} \left(\lambda_{mn} - 1\right)$$

$$+ \varepsilon \left(\sum_{T_m \in \Phi_n} \alpha_{mn} - 1\right) + \tau \left(\sum_{T_m \in \Phi_T^n} \beta_{mn} - 1\right)$$

$$+ \psi \left(\sum_{T_m \in \Phi_n} \lambda_{mn} - 1\right) \tag{30}$$

where $\eta_{mn}, \mu_{mn}, \gamma_{mn}, \theta_{mn}, \omega_{mn}, \varepsilon, \tau, \psi$ are Lagrange multipliers. The Lagrange dual problem is formulated as

$$\max_{\substack{\eta_{mn}, \mu_{mn} \\ \gamma_{mn}, \theta_{mn}, \omega_{mn} \\ \varepsilon, \tau, \psi}} \quad \min_{\alpha_{mn}, \beta_{mn}, \lambda_{mn}} \quad L$$

$$\text{s.t.} \quad \eta_{mn}, \mu_{mn}, \gamma_{mn}, \theta_{mn}, \omega_{mn}, \varepsilon, \tau, \psi \geq 0. \tag{31}$$

For a given set of Lagrange multipliers, the optimal resource allocation strategy can be obtained as

$$\alpha_{mn}^* = \left[\sqrt{\frac{(1 + \eta_{mn}) S_m}{(\gamma_{mn} + \varepsilon - \mu_{mn}) r_{mn}}} \right]^+, \tag{32}$$

$$\beta_{mn}^* = \left[\sqrt{\frac{(1 + \eta_{mn}) S_m p_n^k}{(\theta_{mn} + \tau) F_n}} \right]^+, \tag{33}$$

$$\lambda_{mn}^* = \left[\sqrt{\frac{(1 + \eta_{mn})S_m r_n^k}{(\omega_{mn} + \psi)\, C_n}} \right]^+ \tag{34}$$

where $[x]^+ = \max\{x, 0\}$.

Replacing α_{mn}, β_{mn} and λ_{mn} by α_{mn}^*, β_{mn}^* and λ_{mn}^* respectively in D_{mn}, we will be able to obtain the optimal task latency of T_m at E_n when sharing bandwidth, computation and fronthual resource of E_n with other tasks.

5   Simulation Results

In this section, we evaluate the performance of the proposed algorithm by simulations. In the simulation, we consider a rectangular region with the size being $100\,\text{m} \times 100\,\text{m}$ where the MEC servers and the MDs are randomly located. The number of MEC servers is set as 2, 3, 4, respectively and the number of tasks is set from 25 to 35, the total number of CNN layers is set as $K = 5$ in the simulation. Other simulation parameters employed in the simulations, unless otherwise mentioned, are summarized in Table 1. The simulation results are averaged over 1000 independent experiments.

Table 1. Simulation parameter

Parameters	Value
Input data size (S_m)	$[1, 10]$Mb
Transmission power of MD_m (P_m)	$0.6\,\text{W}$
Noise power (σ^2)	$-110\,\text{dBm}$
Channel path loss model	$128.1 + 27\log(d)\text{dB}$
Bandwidth of E_n (B_n)	$10\,\text{MHz}$
Computation capability of E_n (F_n)	$\{600, 800\}\text{GHz}$
Fronthaul capacity of E_n (C_n)	$100\,\text{Mbps}$
Reduction ratio (r_n^k)	$[0.4, 0.2, 0.16, 0.128, 0.1152]$
Computational overhead of unit data (p_n^k)	$[0.5, 1.1, 1.8, 2.84, 3.992]\text{GHz/M}$

In Fig. 2, we examine the performance of our proposed algorithm, the RLT algorithm without the Lagrangian dual method (RLT-0), the algorithm proposed in [9], the average resource allocation (ARA) algorithm, which allocates the resource of the MEC servers equally to the associated MDs and a benchmark algorithm, i.e., the minimum distance based task offloading (MDO) algorithm, which allows the MDs to select the nearest MEC server to offload their tasks.

The overall task latency obtained from different algorithms is shown in Fig. 2. From the figure, we can observe that while the overall task latency increases as the number of tasks of MDs increases for all the considered algorithms, our proposed algorithm offers the minimum overall task latency compared with other algorithms. This is mainly benefited from the joint optimization of task offloading, CNN layer scheduling and resource allocation, and the combination of RLT and Lagrange dual method.

In Fig. 3, we plot the overall task latency versus the number of tasks obtained from our proposed algorithm and the one proposed in [9]. Different number of MEC servers, i.e., $N = 2, 3, 4$ is considered in the simulation. From the figure, we can see that lower overall task latency can be achieved with the increased number of the MEC servers. Comparing the results obtained from our proposed algorithm and the one proposed in [9], we can see that our proposed algorithm offers lower overall task latency. The reason is that our proposed algorithm aims to minimize the overall task latency while the authors in [9] tend to minimize the energy consumption required for task execution, hence may result in longer task latency.

In Fig. 4, we examine the overall task latency versus the available bandwidth of the MEC servers. The number of MEC servers and tasks are set as 2 and 30, respectively in the simulation. It can be seen from the figure that the overall task latency decreases as the bandwidth of the MEC servers increases. Comparing the results obtained from the proposed algorithm and the algorithm proposed in [9], we can see that the proposed algorithm offers better performance.

In Fig. 5, we compare the simulation results of our proposed algorithm with two baseline algorithms which employ different task offloading schemes and no cooperative computing is applied. For baseline algorithm 1, we assume that tasks can only be offloaded to the MEC servers and no MCC server is available. For baseline algorithm 2, we assume that no MEC servers are deployed and tasks can only be offloaded to the MCC server. From Fig. 5, we can observe that our proposed algorithm outperforms the two baseline algorithms demonstrating the performance benefits by conducting cooperative computing between the MEC servers and the MCC server.

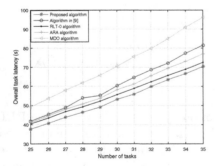

Fig. 2. Overall task latency versus number of tasks (different algorithms).

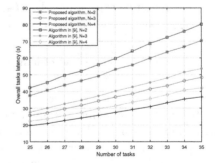

Fig. 3. Overall task latency versus number of tasks (different number of MEC servers).

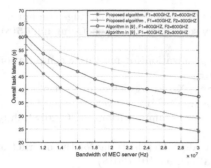 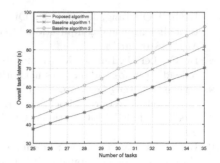

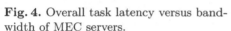

Fig. 4. Overall task latency versus bandwidth of MEC servers.

Fig. 5. Overall task latency versus number of tasks (different task offloading schemes).

6 Conclusions

In this paper, we consider a cooperative computing system and formulate the joint task offloading, CNN layer scheduling and resource allocation as an optimization problem which minimizes overall task latency. As the formulated optimization problem is NP-hard, we decompose the original optimization problem into CNN layer scheduling subproblem, task offloading subproblem and resource allocation subproblem, and solve the three subproblems based on extensive search algorithm, the RLT and Lagrangian dual method, respectively. Numerical results demonstrate the proposed algorithm outperforms previously proposed algorithms and the baseline algorithms which fail to apply cooperative computing schemes.

References

1. Fu, X., Secci, S., Huang, D., Jana, R.: Mobile cloud computing. IEEE Commun. Mag. **53**, 61–62 (2015)
2. Mao, Y., You, C., Zhang, J., Huang, K., Letaief, K.B.: A survey on mobile edge computing: the communication perspective. IEEE Commun. Surv. Tutor. **19**(4), 2322–2358 (2017)
3. Yaseen, M.U., Anjum, A., Antonopoulos, N.: Modeling and analysis of a deep learning pipeline for cloud based video analytics. In: Proceedings of the Fourth IEEE/ACM International Conference on Big Data Computing Applications and Technologies, pp. 121–130 (2017)
4. Li, L., Ota, K., Dong, M.: Eyes in the dark: distributed scene understanding for disaster management. IEEE Trans. Parallel Distrib. Syst. (2017). https://doi.org/10.1109/TPDS.2017.2740294
5. Chen, X., Lei, J., Li, W., Fu, X.: Efficient multi-user computation offloading for mobile edge cloud computing. IEEE/ACM Trans. Netw. **24**(5), 2795–2808 (2016)
6. You, C., Huang, K., Chae, H., Kim, B.H.: Energy-efficient resource allocation for mobile edge computation offloading. IEEE Trans. Wirel. Commun. **16**(3), 1397–1411 (2017)

7. Dinh, T.Q., Tang, J., La, Q.D., Quek, Q.S.: Offloading in mobile edge computing: task allocation and computational frequency scaling. IEEE Trans. Commun. **65**(8), 4798–4810 (2017)
8. Li, Q., Lei, J., Lin, J.: Min-max latency optimization for multiuser computation offloading in fog-radio access networks (2018)
9. Cheng, K., Teng, Y., Sun, W., Liu, A., Wang, X.: Energy-efficient joint offloading and wireless resource allocation strategy in multi-MEC server systems. In: Proceedings of IEEE International Conference on Communications (ICC 2018), July 2018
10. Li, H., Ota, K., Dong, M.: Learning IoT in edge: deep learning for the internet of things with edge computing. IEEE Netw. **32**(1), 96–101 (2018)

A Resource Scheduling Algorithm with High Task Request Acceptance Rate for Multi-platform Avionics System

Kui Li[1](✉), Qing Zhou[1], Guonan Cui[2], and Liang Liu[2]

[1] National Key Laboratory of Science and Technology on Avionics Integration,
China Aeronautical Radio Electronics Research Institute, Shanghai 200233, China
Likuiavic19@163.com
[2] College of Computer Science and Technology,
Nanjing University of Aeronautics and Astronautics, Nanjing 211016, China

Abstract. At present, Multi-platform Avionics System (MPA) has been widely used. The existing adaptive scheduling algorithm based on Sliding-Scheduled Tenant (SST) simulates and verifies the resource management and task scheduling of MPA, and analyzes the task requirements of MPA. However, due to the shortcomings of SST algorithm in considering energy consumption and other aspects, it reduces the task acceptance rate, and does not consider the limitations of sensors and priorities, which makes al algorithm unable to meet the requirements of avionics system. This paper proposes a method of system resource selection, which considers the energy consumption, sensor and priority limit, so as to improve the acceptance rate of tasks, improve the acceptance rate of high priority, and get a scheduling algorithm with high acceptance rate of tasks. Finally, through the comprehensive analysis of the experimental results and experimental results in different scenes, it is shown that the algorithm proposed in this paper outperforms the existing algorithm in terms of the acceptance rate.

Keywords: Multi-platform Avionics System · Resource modeling · Resource scheduling

1 Introduction

Multi-platform Avionics System (MPA) is a brand-new Avionics System Architecture, it is a new architecture after Integrated Modular Avionics (IMA) [1–3] and Distributed Integrated Modular Avionics (DIMA) [4, 17]. For MPA, scheduling algorithm plays an important role in coordinating avionics resources under different platforms. At present, the research on the scheduling algorithm of multi-platform avionics resources is still in its infancy, and the domestic and foreign research results on this aspect are limited. In the distributed integrated modular avionics system, functions are no longer tied to hardware, and devices are no longer centralized, but connected to multiple devices on the aircraft by the network. Multi-platform avionics system also manages the avionics resources of

© ICST Institute for Computer Sciences, Social Informatics and Telecommunications Engineering 2020
Published by Springer Nature Switzerland AG 2020. All Rights Reserved
H. Gao et al. (Eds.): ChinaCom 2019, LNICST 312, pp. 143–166, 2020.
https://doi.org/10.1007/978-3-030-41114-5_12

each aircraft. Therefore, the realization of aircraft function becomes a request problem to existing hardware resources. Functional application software issues the application of hardware resources according to its requirements on hardware resources (such as CPU, memory, sensor, etc.), and the multi-platform avionics system responds to the application based on the existing resources of each device, ensuring that the functional application software can complete its tasks on the appropriate equipment. There are many types of research on the algorithm of resource scheduling in the field of cloud computing. In the multi-platform avionics system, network communication, computing resource allocation and module cooperative work are the main considerations. In addition, the avionics system focuses on the reliability and stability of the system and emphasizes on the performance. Therefore, the domestic and foreign research status mainly focuses on the research on the service quality (QoS) demand of cloud application in the field of cloud computing [5].

Literature [6, 7] considers the constraints of network communication. In literature [6], the author proposed a generalized resource allocation method, which can allocate resources according to resource request constraints under different cloud architectures in the case of real-time request arrival and departure. This is an online algorithm where the allocation is done without any knowledge of the resource request that will arrive in the future. The algorithm considers constraint information such as data center location and network delay, and the resource allocation method accepts future resource requests as much as possible. In the literature [7], the author studies the dynamic online social network environment cost optimization problem on multiple geographically distributed clouds over a continuous period of time. However, their consideration of network communication basically only stays on the delay, without paying attention to the impact of network bandwidth on performance. In literature [8] considers the network routing problem of data center, and proposed a joint optimization scheme to optimize virtual machine placement and network routing, and described a parallel method to divide the data center network into parallel processing clusters. In order to find the effective traffic path, a multi-path routing algorithm is proposed to reduce the energy consumption of the data center network while ensuring the service quality. In literature [9], the author proposed a new request model. In addition to providing the user's resource requirements, the request can also specify the user's required duration and other information. In literature [27], an SST adaptive scheduling algorithm (sliding scheduled tenant) is proposed, which can be used to solve the task scheduling and resource management of avionics system by dividing it into long task request and short task request, and rearranging it in the way of alternating long task and short task.

Although SST adaptive scheduling algorithm accords with some characteristics of avionics system, it can't be directly transplanted to distributed avionics system. This is because in addition to the requirements of robust zoning, the distributed avionics system also has the following characteristics: function and sensor Association, different task priority, different network communication protocols and scheduling focus on acceptance rate. In this paper, a scheduling algorithm is designed aims at the defects that SST algorithm reduces the task acceptance rate due to considering energy consumption and does not consider the limitation of sensors and priorities. It improves the selection of system resources and improves the high priority acceptance rate, so as to obtain a scheduling algorithm with high task acceptance rate.

In Sect. 2 introduces the related work and background knowledge; Sect. 3 introduces the existing problems of the algorithm, puts forward the idea and advantages of distributed avionics resource scheduling algorithm, and gives the detailed design of the algorithm; In Sect. 4 carries out the experimental analysis of the proposed algorithm and Sect. 5 is the conclusion.

2   Related Work

2.1   Avionics System Resources Model

In this paper, we abstract the avionics system resource model into a weighted directed graph $G(V, E)$, where V represents the set of nodes in the network and E represents the set of links. In G, node $v \in V$ is denoted by switch or computer; directed edges $\langle o, p \rangle \in E$ expression links between node o and p, whose bandwidth is denoted by the symbol $B\_<o, p>$.

The sets of computers and sets of switches are denoted by S and W respectively. The set of sensors owned by the computer in s is represented by the symbol P_s. The set of cabinet switches is represented by the symbol R, the set of convergence switches is represented by the symbol Ag, and the set of core switches is represented by the symbol Co, all of which are subsets of set W. The computing power of computer hardware is abstracted by literature [22], that is, standard capacity units are used to describe it. The resource capacity of computer v for S is described by the number of CPU and represented by the symbol C_v. Scheduling adopts the method of matching resources, which is not only easy to be popularized, but also helpful to consider the allocation of network and time resources without loss of generality. According to the demand of different resources, this paper defines the size five different instances of the resources to support resource heterogeneity; while symbol Ψ denotes the collection resource instances.

2.2   Task Request Model

The task request model represents a set of related functions (as shown in Fig. 1), that the flight formation needs to complete at a given time. The implementation of a function in a task request may involve some of the same sub-functions, we define the resource requirements for the sub-functions as a dynamic partition. Therefore, this article combines the task model with the Application's resource abstraction diagram (i.e. TAG [19], Tenant Application Graph) to represent the resource abstraction of the task through the Application. The resource abstraction diagram represents the functional module structure of the task as well as the communication mode between the functional modules. Each node in the figure corresponds to a functional module, and each directed edge corresponds to the bandwidth requirement required for a dynamic partition to communicate with related functional modules. Functional modules represent the type and number of dynamic partitions associated with them, while directed edges represent the exit and entry bandwidth requirements between any subset of dynamic partitions in the dynamic partition and any other related functional modules. Resource requirements for dynamic partitioning can be calculated by measuring [24] or by the processing power and workload of dynamic partitioning [23].

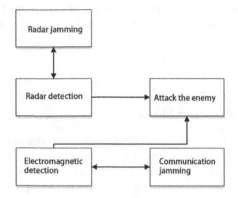

Fig. 1. Function relationship diagram

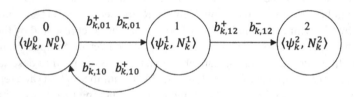

Fig. 2. Resource abstraction diagram

To facilitate the implementation of time partitioning, time is divided into uniform time slots represented by T, A task request k is represented by $\left(B_k, t_k^A, d_k, \left[w_k^S, w_k^E\right], p_k\right)$, B_k is the resource abstract graph, t_k^A represents the time when the task request arrives, d_k represents the time when the task runs, $\left[w_k^S, w_k^E\right]$ represents the time interval when the task runs t_k^A, $w_k^S, w_k^E \in T$, and p_k represents the priority of the task request. w_k^L represents the latest start time of task request k, which is calculated by $w_k^E - d_k$ According to the above Settings, the possible start time of the task is $\Delta_k = \left\{w_k^S, \ldots, w_k^E\right\}$.

Resource abstract graph B_k is represented by (H_k, I_k), where H_k is a set of functional modules, each defined based on the type and number of dynamic partitions, and I_k is a set with edge between functional modules, each specifying the bandwidth requirements between corresponding modules. For a function module $\eta \in H_k$, it is associated with $\left\langle \psi_k^\eta, N_k^\eta, P_k^\eta \right\rangle$, including $\psi_k^\eta \in \Psi$ said the type of dynamic partitioning (CPU cores), eta said the number of dynamic partitioning, eta said need a collection of sensors. N_k^η represents the number of dynamic partitions, and P_k^η represents the set of sensors required. While a directed edge $\iota \in I_k$ is associated with $\left\langle b_{k,\iota}^+, b_{k,\iota}^- \right\rangle$, where $b_{k,\iota}^+$ and $b_{k,\iota}^-$ specify the exit and entrance bandwidth requirements of each dynamic partition of its source and destination function modules respectively. The directed edge represents the bandwidth requirement for any dynamic partition in a functional module to communicate with any dynamic partition subset in another functional module, rather than the bandwidth requirement for separate dynamic partitioning to dynamic partitioning. As can be seen from Fig. 2, each dynamic partition in function module 1 needs bandwidth $b_{k,12}^{+}$ to send information to any dynamic partition subset in function module 2, while each dynamic partition in function module 2 needs bandwidth $b_{k,12}^{-}$ to receive information of any dynamic partition subset in function module 1. Use $b_{k,12}^{-}$ and $b_{k,12}^{-}$ to represent the total exit and total entrance bandwidth requirements for each dynamic partition of module $\eta \in H_k$. For example, $\beta_{k,1}^{+} = b_{k,12}^{+} + b_{k,10}^{+}$ in Fig. 2. In this case, the exits and entrances of each edge are associated with the bandwidth requirement rather than a single edge corresponding to a separate bandwidth requirement, because the number of dynamic partitions in a task may vary depending on the functional module. When the number of dynamic partitions of the two functional modules involved in a task is different, this app-roach ensures that the results of the bandwidth used between the two functional modules are consistent. Take Fig. 2 as an example, for directed edge $\iota = \langle \eta_1, \eta_2 \rangle$, the required bandwidth is $N_k^{\eta_1} b_{k,\iota}^{+} = N_k^{\eta_2} b_{k,\iota}^{-}$.

2.3 SST Adaptive Scheduling Algorithm

The research of Dalvandi et al. In the field of cloud computing puts forward an SST (Sliding Scheduled Tenant) adaptive scheduling algorithm [9] to solve the problem of resource scheduling in the field of cloud computing.

For each SST problem, the acceptance rate is maximized (equivalent, the rejection rate is minimized) while the total power consumption is kept as low as possible. The objective function can be expressed as follows:

$$\text{Minimize}: \quad C^{Raj} + C^{Acc} \tag{1}$$

C^{Raj} is the total rejection cost, and C^{Acc} is the total power consumed by all powered-on components due to the accepted requests. Considering c as the cost per rejected request, the value of C^{Raj} is determined by:

$$C^{Raj} = c * \left(K - \sum_{k \in K} z_k \right) \tag{2}$$

where the term $K - \sum_{k \in K} z_k$) determines the total number of rejected requests, and the value of C^{Acc} is determined by:

$$Cacc = \left(\sum_{t \in T, v \in V} P_v^0 X_v^t + \sum_{t \in T, v \in V} P_v^* Y_{v,p}^t + \sum_{t \in T, v \in V} P_v^* f_{i,v}^{k,t} \right) \tag{3}$$

where the X_v^t is if node $v \in V$ is active in timeslot $t \in T$, the $Y_{o,p}^t$ is if link $\langle o, p \rangle \in E$ is active in timeslot $t \in T$, and the $f_{i,v}^{k,t}$ is if source-VM/destination-VM of request $k \in K$ is placed on server $v \in V$ in timeslot t.

3 Efficient Scheduling Algorithm for Multi-platform Avionics System

Based on the above system modeling, our concern is that in a certain time interval, the avionics system resource model received a series of task request models, and how the avionics system should place the task function modules to accept as many tasks as possible. In addition, since the task request model contains the concept of priority, the avionics system should satisfy the request of high priority task first. In literature [27], the problems studied by Dalvandi et al. [9] in the field of cloud computing are somewhat similar to the problems discussed in this paper. In the previous section, Dalvandi et al. Analyzed the problem of SAPR (sliding scheduled application placement and routing), that is, SST (sliding scheduled tenant) adaptive scheduling algorithm [9]. Since the scheduling algorithm does not take into account the problems of sensors and priority in avionics system, and the energy consumption is reduced to a certain extent, this paper proposes an algorithm with high task acceptance rate as the target, and gives priority to ensuring resource allocation of high-priority tasks.

3.1 The Ideas of Algorithm

According to the analysis in the above section, the existing SST adaptive scheduling algorithm needs to be improved from four aspects: sensor, priority, bandwidth allocation and improved acceptance rate, so as to be applied in the application field of multi-platform avionics system. Specific improvements will be described next.

On the sensor aspect, the original algorithm did not consider the condition of sensor, but the resource model and task request model of the avionics system constructed by us all have sensors. In task assignment, each functional module of the task should be assigned to a computer whose computing resources and sensors can meet the task requirements to meet the requirements of avionics system.

In terms of priority, the task request model presented in this paper includes priority. When resources are allocated, resource requests for high-priority tasks are first met, followed by lower-priority tasks.

In terms of bandwidth allocation, the AFDX standard separates the sending and receiving channels. The output bandwidth of a functional module is different from the bandwidth used by the input bandwidth. In the calculation, they should be considered separately. For example, if there is a dynamic partition ψ that wants to put on the computer $s \in S$ (the computer s is connected to the switch $v \in W$, and the output bandwidth of the dynamic partition ψ is B), it is to determine whether $B_{\langle s,v \rangle}$ is greater than B, rather than treating the input/output bandwidth as a whole.

In avionics system, it is its goal to reduce the number of rejection tasks as much as possible, that is, to complete the tasks with limited resources as much as possible. In order to improve the acceptance rate, the following three factors were considered:

(1) Sensor: in the task sequencing, arrange in ascending order according to the tightness, and rank in descending order according to the number of types of sensor. This is expected to give priority to tasks with large sensor requirements.

(2) Priority: since the task is dynamically arriving in the avionics system, a high-priority task may be received when the low-priority task accepted by the avionics system has allocated resources in a certain period of time but has not started to execute. Therefore, after the high-priority task arrives, try first to allocate on the existing resource graph. When the allocation fails, the resources of the unexecuted low-priority tasks that have been accepted are released, tried again to allocate the tasks, and again allocated resources for the low-priority tasks that have just been released, so as to guarantee the resources of high-priority tasks and increase the high priority.

(3) Dynamic partition placement: dynamic partition placement becomes more flexible when energy saving is not a limitation. The system does not need a switch that prioritizes the lowest power cost to place the requested partition. Multiple dynamic partitions of a functional module can also be placed on different computers, because the avionics system does not have to worry about the energy consumption caused by the operation of the computer.

3.2 Algorithm Targets and Constraints

Based on the above analysis, the scheduling algorithm considers a multi-platform avionics system and a set of task requests dynamically arriving. The scheduling algorithm selects the appropriate start time in the time window specified by the request, and allocates the resources of the multi-platform avionics system to the task request to meet the computing resources and network resources of the task request, and the time of resource allocation is equal to the time of the request. The purpose of the scheduling algorithm is to accept as many requests as possible. The problem is described as a MILP optimization problem using multiple commodity flow expressions. Table 1 is a description of the variables to be used next.

Table 1. Variable declaration

Variable name	Variable meaning
$f_{k,\eta}^{t,v}$	Indicate how many dynamic partitions are placed on $v \in S$ for the function module $\eta \in H_k$ in request $k \in K$ on slot $t \in T$
$l_{s,r}^{t,k,\iota}$	Indicates whether the side $\iota \in I_k$ in request $k \in K$ uses link $\langle s, r \rangle \in E$ on slot $t \in T$
z_k	Indicates whether the system accepts request for $k \in K$
τ_k^t	Indicate whether the time slot $t \in T$ is the start time of request $t \in T$
$\pi_{k,r}^{\eta}$	Indicates whether the dynamic partition of function module $\eta \in H_k$ in request $k \in K$ is placed on cabinet switch $r \in R$

The multi-platform avionics system aims to maximize the acceptance rate of task requests and make full use of all resources in the system. In other words, the multi-platform avionics system should minimize the total number of rejected requests.

Therefore, the objective function is as follows:

$$\text{Minimize}: \quad C^{Rej} \qquad (4)$$

In the formula: C^{Rej} is the total number of rejected requests, whose value is defined as $|K| - \sum_{k \in K} z_k$.

As this problem is a common problem of scheduling, dynamic partition placement and routing, it is a multi-commodity flow problem, which must satisfy the following constraints: link traffic restriction, link demand restriction, and dynamic partition placement restriction. Link traffic limits ensure that the total flow through each link does not exceed the link's capacity. It is defined

$$\left. \begin{array}{l} B_{o,p} \geq \sum_{k \in K} \sum_{\eta \in H_k} \beta_{k,\eta}^{+} f_{k,\eta}^{t,o} \; if \; o \in S \\ B_{o,p} \geq \sum_{k \in K} \sum_{\eta \in H_k} \beta_{k,\eta}^{-} f_{k,\eta}^{t,p} \; if \; p \in S \\ B_{o,p} \geq \sum_{k \in K} \sum_{\iota \in I_k} \bar{b}_{k,\iota} l_{o,p}^{t,k,\iota} \; otherwise \end{array} \right\} \forall \langle o, p \rangle \in E, \; \forall t \in T \qquad (5)$$

In the formula: $\bar{b}_{k,\iota}$ is the total bandwidth demand of edge $\iota \in I_k$, and $\beta_{k,\eta}^{+}$ and $\beta_{k,\eta}^{-}$ are the output bandwidth and input bandwidth of dynamic partition of functional η module dedication respectively. The first two conditions of formula (5) ensure that the total output bandwidth and input bandwidth of the dynamic partition on the computer do not exceed the link capacity, and the latter condition guarantees that the link flow between switches is sufficient.

The link requirement constraint is represented by formulas (6), (7), (8) and (9). Suppose src(ι) and dst(ι) represent the source function module and target function module of side $\iota \in I_k$ respectively. Given that S_r is the set of all the computers under the cabinet switch r, formula (6) means that if the computer $s \in S_r$ is running a dynamic partition of the functional module src(ι) (or dst(ι)), then the boroughs must be through the link $\langle s, r \rangle$ (or $\langle s, r \rangle$), that is, $l_{s,r}^{t,k,\iota}$ (or $l_{r,s}^{t,k,\iota}$) is 1. Formula (7) indicates that if there is no dynamic partition of functional modules on the computer s, that is, $f_{k,\text{src}(\iota)}^{t,s}$ (or $f_{k,\text{dst}(\iota)}^{t,s}$) is 0, the side will not pass the link $\langle s, r \rangle$ (or $\langle r, s \rangle$).

$$\left. \begin{array}{l} N_k^{\text{src}(\iota)} l_{s,r}^{t,k,\iota} \geq f_{k,\text{src}(\iota)}^{t,s} \\ N_k^{\text{dst}(\iota)} l_{s,r}^{t,k,\iota} \geq f_{k,\text{dst}(\iota)}^{t,s} \end{array} \right\} \forall t \in T, \forall \iota \in I_k, \forall k \in K, \forall r \in R, \forall s \in S_r. \qquad (6)$$

$$\left. \begin{array}{l} l_{s,r}^{t,k,\iota} \leq f_{k,\text{src}(\iota)}^{t,s} \\ l_{s,r}^{t,k,\iota} \leq f_{k,\text{dst}(\iota)}^{t,s} \end{array} \right\} \forall t \in T, \forall \iota \in I_k, \forall k \in K, \forall r \in R, \forall s \in S_r \qquad (7)$$

Formula (8) is used to ensure that when the source dynamic partition and target dynamic partition are placed under the same cabinet switch, the flow of side $\iota \in I_k$ will only be transmitted in the cabinet switch, and will not reach the convergence switch or core switch. When the dynamic partition of src(ι) and dst(ι) is under the same cabinet switch, there exists equation $\pi_{k,r}^{\text{src}(\iota)} = \pi_{k,r}^{\text{dst}(\iota)} = 1$. At this time, the flow of side $\iota \in I_k$ does not go through the link connected by cabinet switch and aggregation switch. Formula (9) ensures that when the source dynamic partition and target dynamic partition are placed under different cabinet switches, the flow is connected through the link between cabinet switch and convergence switch.

$$
\left.\begin{aligned}
\sum_{p \in W:\langle r,p\rangle \in E} l_{r,p}^{t,k,\iota} &\leq \left(\pi_{k,r}^{\mathrm{src}(\iota)} - \pi_{k,r}^{\mathrm{dst}(\iota)} + 1\right)/2 \\
\sum_{p \in W:\langle p,r\rangle \in E} l_{p,r}^{t,k,\iota} &\leq \left(\pi_{k,r}^{\mathrm{dst}(\iota)} - \pi_{k,r}^{\mathrm{src}(\iota)} + 1\right)/2
\end{aligned}\right\} \forall t \in T, \forall \iota \in I_k, \forall k \in K, \forall r \in R
$$

$$(8)$$

$$
\left.\begin{aligned}
\sum_{p \in W:\langle r,p\rangle \in E} l_{r,p}^{t,k,\iota} &\geq \pi_{k,r}^{\mathrm{src}(\iota)} - \pi_{k,r}^{\mathrm{dst}(\iota)} \\
\sum_{p \in W:\langle p,r\rangle \in E} l_{p,r}^{t,k,\iota} &\geq \pi_{k,r}^{\mathrm{dst}(\iota)} - \pi_{k,r}^{\mathrm{src}(\iota)}
\end{aligned}\right\} \forall t \in T, \forall \iota \in I_k, \forall k \in K, \forall r \in R \quad (9)
$$

The constraint conditions of dynamic partition placement are formula (10), (11), (12), (13) and (14). Formula (10) ensures that the dynamic partition only USES the time of its request and that the rejected dynamic partition does not use resources in any time slot. For more efficient use of network resources, formula (11) ensures that each dynamic partition is placed on only one computer. Formula (12) ensures that the dynamic partition does not move during the time it is requested. Formula (13) ensures that the total resources used by the dynamic partition on the computer shall not exceed the total resources of the computer. Formula (14) ensures that the sensor of the computer can meet the requirements of dynamic partitioning.

$$
\sum_{s \in S} f_{k,\eta}^{t,s} = \sum_{j=0}^{d_k-1} \tau_k^{t-j} N_k^{\eta}, \forall \eta \in H_k, \forall k \in K, \forall t \in T \tag{10}
$$

$$
\sum_{r \in R} \pi_{k,r}^{\eta} = z_k, \forall k \in K, \forall t \in T \tag{11}
$$

$$
d_k f_{k,\eta}^{t,s} \leq \sum_{j=1-d_k}^{d_k-1} f_{k,\eta}^{t+j,s}, \forall \eta \in H_k, \forall k \in K, \forall t \in T, \forall s \in S \tag{12}
$$

$$
\sum_{k \in K} \sum_{\eta \in H_k} \psi_k^{\eta} f_{k,\eta}^{t,s} \leq C_s, \forall t \in T, \forall s \in S \tag{13}
$$

$$
\bigcup_{k \in K} \bigcup_{\eta \in H_k} P_k^{\eta} \subseteq P_s, \forall t \in T, \forall s \in S \tag{14}
$$

3.3 The Design of Algorithm

(1) Sorting module

Sorting module input is to be processed, a priority task request collection and an adaptive threshold, the priority is used to show which priority task module will handle the request, and the adaptive threshold is the time slot to receive all of the request the average duration of task, task request for divided into long task request and short tasks. As shown by Function Sequencing, the module first wants to process priority task requests into the set $K_{t,p}$ (see line 1). If the priority has a task request to be processed, the module will sort the task request set (see lines 2–12), otherwise it will not operate and return an empty set directly (see lines 13–15). When the module sorts the task request set, it will divide the set K_{long} into the long task request set K_{long} and the short task request set K_{short} (see lines 2–8), and then the module will calculate the tightness a_k of the priority task request. Compactness a_k is given by the ratio of the duration of the task request to the length of the time window, that is, $a_k = d_k/(w_k^E - w_k^S)$. The sorting module will arrange all the long task requests and short task requests in descending order of compactness, because the possibility of rejecting the request increases with the increase of compactness. In order to increase the acceptance rate of the system, this paper will give priority to the task with high sensor demand. Therefore, when the density a_k is the same, the sensor types are sorted in descending order (see line 10). The validity of the consideration of the sensor will be verified in the experimental section. After the task is sorted, the module sorts the task request by alternating the long task request with the short task request, and puts the result into the set $K_{sequence}$ (see line 11). The final output of the module is the processed collection $K_{sequence}$

Function Sequencing (K_t, Priority, Threshold)

    Input: K_t, Priority, Threshold;

  1: Traversing set K_t puts task requests with priority Priority into set $K_{t,p}$

  2: if set $K_{t,p}$ isn't null then

  3:    for $k \in K_{t,p}$ do

  4:      if $d_k \geq$ Threshold then

  5:        Put task k into the long task request set K_{long}

  6:      else

  7:        Put task k into the long task request set K_{short}

  8:      end if

  9:    end for

10:    Arrange sets K_{long} and K_{short} in descending order according to the a_k of the task and. the number of sensors

11:    Set $K_{sequence}$ is generated in the order of long tasks and short tasks alternation

12:    return $K_{sequence}$

13: else

14:    return null

15: end if

---

(2) **Time to choose**

The time selection module defines candidate start times based on the type of each request, the required duration, and the specified time window. As shown by Function Candidate, for a short task request, its Candidate start time is considered as Δ_k, and its element is every possible start time for the task request (see lines 3–4). This is because short task requests need to start as early as possible to increase task acceptance and to ensure the full utilization of resources in the near future. On the other hand, for long task requests, it will traverse all time slots in Δ_k and find the time slots with the minimum standard deviation of the minimum average number of active requests for its subsequent time slots as the start time of long task requests (see lines 6–14). This is because long task requests need to be placed as evenly over the time slot as possible to improve resource utilization.

Function Candidate ($K_{sequence}$, Threshold)

Input: $K_{sequence}$, Threshold;

1: if set $K_{sequence}$ isn't null then
2:     for $k \in K_{sequence}$ do
3:         if $d_k <$ threshold then
4:             The candidate start time set for task k is set to Δ_k
5:         else
6:             $\mu = \infty$, $\sigma = \infty$
7:             for $i \in \Delta_k$ do
8:                 μ_i is the average number of tasks on slot $[i, d_k + i)$
9:                 σ_i is the standard deviation number of tasks on slot $[i, d_k + i)$
10:                 if $\mu_i < \mu \,||\, (\mu_i = \mu$ && $\sigma_i < \sigma)$ then
11:                     The candidate start time set of task k is set to $\{i\}$
12:                     $\mu = \mu_i$; $\sigma = \sigma_i$;
13:                 end if
14:             end for
15:         end if
16:     end for
17: end if

---

(3) Resource allocation module

The main tasks of the resource allocation module are two. One is to obtain the system available resource information according to the start time and duration; The second is to allocate resources reasonably to the task to make the system's task acceptance rate as high as possible.

The function to obtain the system's available resource information is performed by function Aggregator (t, d_k). Where t is the assumed starting time of the task and d_k is the number of time slots required for the task to run. This function returns a multi-platform avionics system resource model to represent the resource state of multi-platform avionics system in d_k slots starting from time slot t. This function combines the sequence of the given multi-platform avionics system resource model to create a weighted directed graph $G^*(V^*, E^*)$. This weighted directed graph G^* is formally consistent with the multi-platform avionics system resource model, which is used to represent the available resource information of all avionics system resource models in different time slots during the duration of task request.

Function Aggregator (t, d_k)

Input: t, d_k;

1: According to t, d_k gets set $G_{deal} = \{G_t, G_{t+1}, ..., G_{t+d_k-1}\}$;
2: Generate a resource map G^* of unallocated resources
3: for $G \in G_{deal}$ do
4:     for $element \in G$ do
5:         if The value of $element$ is less than the value of $element$ in the corresponding.
                resource graph G^* then
6:             Modify the value of $element$ of resource graph G^* as the value of $element$ of.
                G
7:         end if
8:     end for
9: end for
10: return G^*

It is assumed that the weighted directed graph $G_t(V_t, E_t)$ represents the state of an avionics system belonging to time gap t. As shown in the Function Aggregator, when given t and k, A Function can obtain A sequence $\{G_t, G_{t+1}, \ldots, G_{t+d_k-1}\}$, represented by the set G_{deal}. The module USES set G_{deal} to construct a new weighted directed graph G^*. The set of nodes of this graph is the intersection of all weighted directed graphs in the sequence, and the set of links is consistent with the node. And in figure G^*, the resource capacity of nodes and links takes the smallest remaining capacity in all weighted directed graphs (see lines 3–9).

The function of assigning system resources to tasks is performed by function App_Place_Route(G^*, B_k), where G^* is the weighted directed graph of available resources obtained by function Aggregator, and B_k is the resource graph of task request (set H_k containing functional modules and set I_k with directional edges between functional modules). This function is used to place the functional modules of a task and determine the communication path between the modules. By finding a set of computers and communication paths with sufficient resources, the function places the request to the lowest layer possible in the avionics system, that is, if the task can be completed by the computer under the cabinet switch, the aggregation switch is not used. The lowest-level priority is to increase the likelihood of using shorter paths while maximizing higher bandwidth availability. For the given request k and the weighted directed graph G^* provided by the resource allocation module, App_Place_Route checks the availability of the multi-platform avionics system in bottom-up order (i.e. first the cabinet switch, then the convergence switch, and finally the order of the core switch) until the resource is allocated or the request is rejected after all layers are checked.

A key function in the App_Place_Route function is map_switch(v, η), which is used to check the feasibility of placing the function module of the task request under a switch where v represents the switch and η represents the function module. For the given switch v and function module η, map_switch function checks all the computers under switch v to allocate all the computing resources and bandwidth resources required by the dynamic partition in the function module η. Unlike SST adaptive scheduling algorithm, which takes energy consumption into account, the emphasis here is to make full use of resources to improve system utilization.

Function map_switch (v, η)

Input : v, η;
1: According to the switch, get the set S of all the computers under the switch
2: for $c \in S$ do
3:     if *The sensor of c can meet the requirement of dynamic partition* then
4:         Cnt represents the number of dynamic partitions that computer c can place
5:         $Cnt = \min(N, \lfloor C_v/\psi_k^\eta \rfloor, \lfloor B_{c,r}/\beta_{k,\eta}^+ \rfloor, \lfloor B_{r,c}/\beta_{k,\eta}^- \rfloor)$
6:         if $Cnt > 0$ then
7:             $N = N - Cnt$;
8:             How are the resources allocated using Mapping
9:             if $N == 0$ then
10:                 return Mapping
11:             end if
12:         end if
13:     end if
14: end for
15: return null

Function App_Place_Route first tries to use the computer of the cabinet switch to complete all function modules of the task request, that is, to judge whether the remaining resources of the computer and network bandwidth under a cabinet switch can meet the requirements of all function modules of the task. The function App_Place_Route USES the function map_switch(v, η) to check the feasibility of placing the function module of the task request under the cabinet switch. If the cabinet switch does not have enough resources to place all the functional modules of the task request, it continues to check the availability of all resources under the aggregation switch of the avionics system. If it cannot find an aggregate switch with sufficient capacity, check the last layer of the core switch.

Function App_Place_Route (G^*, B_k)

Input: G^*, B_k;

1: A set Place is generated to store resource allocation information, and a temporary variable $G=G^*$ is created. The sets of cabinet switches, convergence switches and core switches in g are R, Ag and Co respectively

2 : for $v \in R$ do

3 :   for $\eta \in H_k$

4 :   Call map_switch(v, η) to determine whether function module η can be completed on v

5:       if Mapping != null then

6:          Add Mapping in Place and update G

7:       else

8:          break

9:       end if

10:    end for

11:    If H_k all modules can be placed, update G^* and return to Place

12: end for

13 : $G=G^*$

14 : for $v \in Ag$ do

15:    Similar to set R

16: end for

17 : $G=G^*$

17 : for $v \in Co$ do

18:    Similar to set R

19: end for

20: return null

If it is judged that the resources under the avionics system can meet the task demand, function App_Place_Route will save the resource allocation information into the task allocation list, so as to apply the resource according to the allocation information when the start time comes. In addition, the function updates the resource allocation information to all the relevant avionics system resource model sequences, so that the following tasks can get the correct resource surplus through the function Aggregator.

When the resources under the core switch cannot meet the task request, the SST adaptive scheduling algorithm will reject the request directly. However, as mentioned above, we hope to increase the acceptance rate of high-priority tasks, so the resource release module is added.

(4) **Resource release**

The role of the resource release module is to release resources requested by unexecuted low-priority tasks, thereby increasing the acceptance rate of high-priority tasks. The module gets the priority information of task allocation below the priority of the task request to be assigned from the task allocation list, and then releases the resources in the resource model sequence of all related resources in the avionics system according to the allocation information and task duration obtained. The released low-priority tasks are placed in the set of tasks to be processed so that they can be re-placed when the priority task is processed. The resource release module then calls the resource allocation module again to determine the availability of system resources after the release of low-priority task resources. If the freed system resource can meet the task requirement, the task request is accepted. If the released system resources are still unable to meet the task requirements, the task is rejected.

(5) **Time complexity analysis**

By analyzing the worst case of each module, the worst time complexity of the algorithm can be obtained. Due to the different processing methods of long task request and short task request, we consider them separately. For the long task request, the time selection module needs to traverse the candidate start time Δ_k and calculate the average task number of d_k gaps to get a start time, whose time complexity is $O(d_k|\Delta_k|)$; The candidate start time of short task request is set k directly, and its time complexity can be ignored. For the resource allocation module and the resource release module, the number of times the task request calls them is different. The long task request calls only once, while the short task request calls O times.

The time complexity of the resource allocation module is determined by functions Aggregator and App_Place_Route. The function Aggregator needs to take the intersection of the system resource model of d_k time slots of the task request, so its time complexity is $O(d_k|G|)$, and $|G|$ is the sum of node number $|V|$ and edge number $|E|$. The time complexity of map_switch, a key function in the function App_Place_Route, is $O(|S_r|)$, where S represents the set of all computers. This is because the worst thing about map_switch is that it tries to put a portion of the dynamic partition on all the computers in the system. The function App_Place_Route calls the map_switch function $O(|W||H_k|)$ times to ensure that all functional modules for task requests are tried under all switches, where $|W|$ is the number of switches and $|H_k|$ is the number of functional modules. Therefore, the time complexity of function App_Place_Route is $O(|W||H_k||S_r|)$. Therefore, the time complexity of the resource allocation module is $O(d_k|G| + |W||H_k||S_r|)$.

The resource release module needs to release all resources that are lower priority than the current task request and are executed, and try again to allocate them. The time complexity of the resource that releases a task request k is $O(d_k|G|)$, so the time complexity of the resource release module is $O(Cd_k|G|)$, and C is the number of tasks that need to be released.

To sum up, the time complexity of long task request is $O(d_k|\Delta_k| + Cd_k|G| + 2|W||H_k||S_r|)$, while that of short task request is $O(|\Delta_k|(Cd_k|G| + 2|W||H_k||S_r|))$, which can be completed in polynomial time.

4 Experiment and Analysis

4.1 Experimental Parameters

(1) Multi-platform avionics system resources

This paper considers a multi-layered topology consisting of a core switch and five aircraft. The five aircraft are one AWACS, two e-jets and two fighters. As shown in Table 2, the AWACS is used to search and monitor air or sea targets. It needs to complete radar reconnaissance and electromagnetic reconnaissance. Therefore, the AWACS has radar reconnaissance sensors and electromagnetic reconnaissance sensors. They are used to disable the warning, communication, and radar systems, requiring radar jammers and electromagnetic jammers to complete the mission. Fighter planes are used to fight for control of the air, to protect the safety of flight formation, need infrared reconnaissance sensors and missile launchers. In addition to sensor differences, the five aircraft share the same computing resources. Each aircraft has a convergence switch connected to three cabinet switches. Each cabinet switch has four computers. Each computer has eight computing resources, or 8-core CPU. The link bandwidth of the computer and cabinet switch is set at 0.1 Gbps, while the link bandwidth of the cabinet switch and convergence switch and the link bandwidth of the convergence switch and core switch are set at 1 Gbps.

Table 2. Functions of all aircraft models

Models	Function
AWACS	Radar reconnaissance, electromagnetic reconnaissance
Electronic fighter	Radar interference, electromagnetic interference
Fighters	Infrared reconnaissance, missile strike

(2) Task request

According to the research on flow characteristics between switches in literature [26] and [27], it can be known that flow distribution includes exponential and lognormal distribution, etc. In the multi-platform avionics system, the allocation of resources by time period is a key point. In this paper, the algorithm will be evaluated in different flow distribution modes to ensure the comprehensiveness of the experiment.

All task requests in the experiment were randomly generated. It is assumed that the distribution of the time interval between the arrival of the task request satisfies the weibull distribution, while the duration of the request follows a lognormal distribution. The tightness of A task, that is, the ratio of the duration of the task request to the length of the time window, is randomly selected from set $A = \{0.1, 0.2, \ldots, 0.9\}$. The time window of the task request is obtained according to the duration and tightness of the task request. A task request has three functional modules, and a functional module contains three dynamic partitions. Under each functional module, the number of computing resources and sensor type of dynamic partition are the same. A dynamic partitioning request of computing resources in the resource instance set Ψ randomly selected, and corresponding to a random sensor types, and each dynamic partitioning of bandwidth demand are set to 25 Mbps. Resources collection instance Ψ defines five different instances of the resources to support the heterogeneity of resources. These five resource instances consume one to five computer resource units.

The main influencing conditions of the experiment are as follows:

(1) Flow volatility. Flow fluctuation is defined as the degree of change of request duration, and its flow fluctuation is related to the standard deviation of lognormal distribution followed by duration. The specific quantization method is shown in Table 3.

Table 3. Flow volatility quantification table

Degree of flow fluctuation	The standard deviation of a lognormal distribution
High	1.00
Middle	0.75
Low	0.50

Unexpected request. Request suddenness is defined as the degree of burst that represents the arrival of task request. Its suddenness is related to the shape parameters of weibull distribution followed by the time interval between the arrivals of task request. The specific quantization method is shown in Table 4.

Table 4. Sudden request quantization table

Request suddenness	Weibull distribution shape parameters
Nonsudden	1.00
Half a sudden	0.75
Sudden	0.50

By modifying the above conditions, the experiment can set different scenes. According to the scenario design in literature [9], the following four different scenarios are considered in this paper:

(1) High flow fluctuation and unexpected arrival of request: in this scenario, the standard deviation of lognormal distribution followed by the change degree of request duration was set to 1.00, and the shape parameter of distribution followed by the degree of request arrival burst was set to 0.5. The effectiveness of the scheduling algorithm is evaluated by comparing the influence of one or more factors of sensor, priority and placement on the acceptance rate of the multi-platform avionics system.

(2) Low flow volatility and unexpected arrival of requests: the difference between this scenario and scenario one is that the flow volatility is changed from high volatility to low volatility, that is, the standard deviation of lognormal distribution followed by the change degree of request duration is set to 0.50.

(3) High traffic fluctuation and non-abrupt arrival of request: this scenario assumes that the arrival of task request is non-emergent, so the distribution shape parameter followed by the degree of request arrival in scenario 1 is set as 1.00.

(4) Impact of request suddenness: in this scenario, the impact of request suddenness on the scheduling algorithm is mainly discussed. As the previous experiment shows that tasks with priority and partition placement have a better acceptance rate, the analysis will be carried out around the scheduling algorithm.

4.2 Analysis of Experimental Results

In order to guarantee the reliability of the experimental results, this paper each algorithm under each scenario are sent 10000 times the task request set, ensures that the duration of the request of the experimental data and meet the sudden request they follow the mode of distribution, and use in CloudSim simulation platform to realize the algorithm simulation program finished the results of data collection work, here are the experimental results and results of each scenario analysis.

(1) **High flow volatility and unexpected arrival of requests**

Figure 3 shows the acceptance of all task requests by multi-platform avionics system after the scheduling algorithm takes different influencing factors into account in the case of high flow fluctuation and unexpected arrival of request. The horizontal axis represents the average number of task requests per unit time slot and the vertical axis represents the acceptance rate of multi-platform avionics system.

As can be seen from the figure above, although under low load (that is, the average number of task requests is low), the task request acceptance rate of the multi-platform avionics system is close to 100%, but with the increase of load, the task request acceptance rate of the system will gradually decline.

According to Fig. 3, the reception rate of all scheduling algorithms that take partition placement into consideration is much higher than those that do not take this factor into account. This is because after receiving the task request without considering the scheduling algorithm of partition placement, the dynamic partition of each functional module is required to be completed on the computer under the same cabinet switch, which will lead to the improvement of the computing capacity requirements of cabinet switch

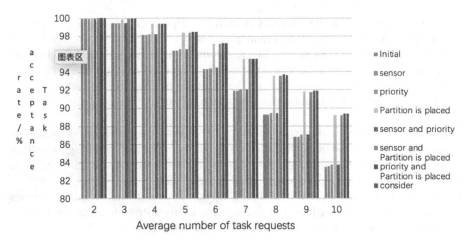

Fig. 3. The overall task acceptance rate under scenario

and reduce the task acceptance rate. The scheduling algorithm considering partition placement can place the dynamic partition of functional modules on different cabinet switches. When a cabinet switch cannot meet the needs of a functional module, it will accept part of the dynamic partition under the functional module, make full use of the existing resources, and reduce the resource requirements of the functional module for subsequent cabinet switches.

In addition, it can be seen that the priority scheduling algorithm can slightly improve the acceptance rate of the system, while the influence of sensors on the acceptance rate of the system is not obvious. The reason why the influence of sensors on the system acceptance rate is not obvious may be that the sensor demand in the experiment is generated randomly, while the model of task request is relatively fixed, resulting in no significant change in the requirement of the number of sensors. The reason why the prioritized scheduling algorithm can slightly improve the system acceptance rate may be that the release of low-priority task request resources might release a long task request, resulting in the system accepting shorter task requests.

Figure 4 shows the acceptance rate of high-priority tasks with priority scheduling algorithm and no priority scheduling algorithm. According to the data shown in Fig. 3, it can be seen that the acceptance rate of the priority scheduling algorithm is not lower than the original scheduling algorithm, and there is a small improvement. However, Fig. 4 shows that the scheduling algorithm considering priority has a certain degree of improvement in the acceptance of high-priority tasks, and the scheduling algorithm considering priority has a higher acceptance rate for high-priority tasks than the scheduling algorithm considering only partition placement.

To sum up, in the case of high traffic fluctuation and unexpected arrival of requests, the scheduling algorithm of priority and partition placement and the scheduling algorithm of all three considered have higher task request acceptance rate and can accept more high-priority task requests.

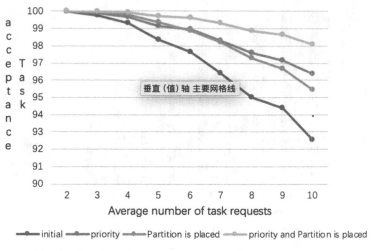

Fig. 4. The high priority task acceptance rate in the scenario

(2) Low flow fluctuation and unexpected arrival of request

Figure 5 shows the acceptance of all task requests by multi-platform avionics system after the scheduling algorithm takes different influencing factors into account in the case of low flow fluctuation and unexpected arrival of request. Similar to the results of scenario 1, the acceptance rate of all scheduling algorithms that take partition placement into account is much higher than those that do not take this factor into account. And those that take priority into account have a certain degree of improvement in acceptance rate. However, the sensor scheduling algorithm has a negative effect on the task acceptance rate. Figure 6 shows the acceptance rate of high-priority tasks with priority scheduling algorithm and no priority scheduling algorithm. It can be seen that the priority scheduling algorithm still improves the acceptance of high-priority tasks to some extent.

Therefore, in the case of low traffic fluctuation and unexpected arrival of requests, the scheduling algorithm of priority and partition placement has higher task request acceptance rate and can accept more high-priority task requests.

Compared with scenario 1, the acceptance rate of task request is reduced to some extent, which is because low flow fluctuation makes the duration of task increase and the overall system resources are insufficient. However, as the change is not large, the factors of flow fluctuation will not be analyzed afterwards.

(3) High traffic fluctuation and request non-unexpected arrival

Figure 7 shows the acceptance of all task requests by multi-platform avionics system after considering different influencing factors in the case of high flow fluctuation and non-unexpected arrival of request. Similar to the results of scenario 1, the acceptance rate of all scheduling algorithms that take partition placement into account is much higher than those that do not take this factor into account. Figure 8 shows the acceptance rate of high-priority tasks with priority scheduling algorithm and no priority scheduling algorithm.

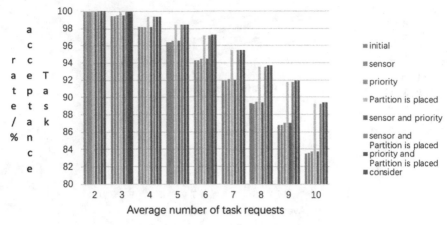

Fig. 5. The overall task acceptance rate under scenario 2

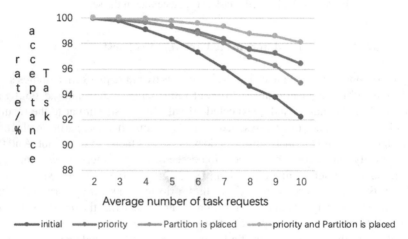

Fig. 6. High priority task acceptance rate under scenario 2

It can be seen that the priority scheduling algorithm still improves the acceptance of high-priority tasks to some extent.

However, compared with scenario 1, the arrival of non-suddenness of request reduces the performance of all scheduling algorithms significantly. This is because the arrival of sudden request, the available time slots are relatively sufficient, while the continuous arrival of non-suddenness of request, and the time gaps are relatively saturated and cannot accept more tasks. In the case of low overall acceptance rate, the priority scheduling algorithm can still guarantee the acceptance rate of high-priority task requests (20% higher than the overall acceptance rate).

Therefore, in the case of high traffic fluctuation and non-unexpected arrival of requests, priority and partition placement scheduling algorithms have higher task request acceptance rate and can accept more high-priority task requests.

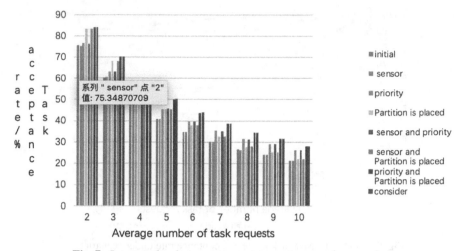

Fig. 7. Integrated task request acceptance rate sensor in scenario 3

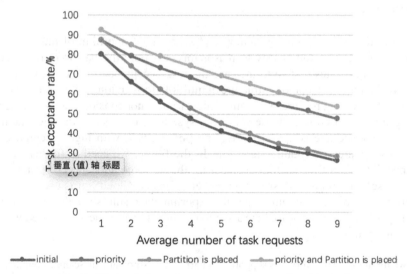

Fig. 8. High priority task acceptance rate a under scenario 3

(4) Sudden impact of request

Figure 9 shows the acceptance of all task requests by multi-platform avionics system with different request suddenness after the scheduling algorithm considers priority and partition placement in the case of low flow fluctuation. The acceptance rate of the system decreases with the sudden decrease of request. As shown in scenario 3, as request suddenness increases, the available time slots begin to saturate and shift to sufficient, and thus the high abrupt task acceptance rate is significantly higher than other situations.

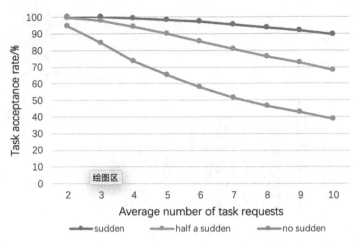

Fig. 9. Comprehensive task request acceptance rate under scenario 4

5 Conclusions

This paper studies the modeling method and scheduling algorithm of multi-platform avionics resource, and solves how to reasonably schedule the hardware resource on multi-platform avionics system to increase the task acceptance rate. First, we use the multi-layer hierarchical topology structure of multiplatform avionics resource modeling, in view of the existing resource scheduling algorithm is not considering the problem of sensor, priority restrictions, choose way from system resources and improve the high-priority acceptance rate is optimized, and proposes a task with high acceptance rate of avionics resource scheduling algorithm. In the future, we need to further improve this scheduling algorithm, such as considering the resource allocation of primary and secondary sensors, priority in special cases, etc. Finally, CloudSim is used to build a simulation experiment environment, and the experimental results show that the algorithm in this paper has greatly improved the acceptance rate of task request compared with the original algorithm.

Acknowledgments. This work was supported in part by the Aeronautical Science Foundation of China under Grant 20165515001.

References

1. Watkins, C.B., Walter, R.: Transitioning from federated avionics architectures to integrated modular avionics. In: IEEE/AIAA 26th Digital Avionics Systems Conference, DASC 2007, pp. 2.A.1-1–2.A.1-10. IEEE (2007)
2. Zaruba, R.: Air/ground data communication radios for future ATM. In: IEEE 2015 IEEE/AIAA 34th Digital Avionics Systems Conference (DASC), Prague, Czech Republic, 13 September 2015–17 September 2015 (2015)
3. Digital avionics systems conference (2012)

4. Halle, M., Thielecke, F.: Next generation IMA configuration engineering-from architecture to application. In: 2015 IEEE/AIAA 34th Digital Avionics Systems Conference (DASC), pp. 6B2-1–6B2-13. IEEE (2015)
5. Zhang, X., Yang, J., Sun, X., Wu, J.: Survey of geo-distributed cloud research progress. J. Softw. **29**(7), 2116–2132 (2018)
6. Hao, F., Kodialam, M., Lakshman, T.V., et al.: Online allocation of virtual machines in a distributed cloud. IEEE/ACM Trans. Netw. **25**(1), 238–249 (2017)
7. Jiao, L., Li, J., Xu, T., et al.: Optimizing cost for online social networks on geo-distributed clouds. IEEE/ACM Trans. Netw. (TON) **24**(1), 99–112 (2016)
8. Jin, H., Cheocherngngarn, T., Levy, D., et al.: Joint host-network optimization for energy-efficient data center networking. In: 2013 IEEE 27th International Symposium on Parallel & Distributed Processing (IPDPS), pp. 623–634. IEEE (2013)
9. Dalvandi, A., Gurusamy, M., Chua, K.C.: Application scheduling, placement, and routing for power efficiency in cloud data centers. IEEE Trans. Parallel Distrib. Syst. **28**(4), 947–960 (2017)
10. Calheiros, R.N., Ranjan, R., Beloglazov, A., et al.: CloudSim: a toolkit for modeling and simulation of cloud computing environments and evaluation of resource provisioning algorithms. Softw. Pract. Exp. **41**(1), 23–50 (2011)
11. ARINC653-1: Avionics Application Software Standard Interface. ARINC Annapolis, Maryland (2003)
12. Rushby, J.: Partitioning in avionics architectures: requirements, mechanisms, and assurance. SRI International Menlo Park CA Computer Science Lab (2000)
13. DO-178B: Software Considerations in Airborne Systems and Equipment Certification. RTCA (1992)
14. DO-248B: Final Annual Report For Clarification Of DO-178B "Software Considerations in Airborne Systems and Equipment Certification". RTCA (2001)
15. Carmel-Veilleux, T.: Adaptation multicoeur d'un noyau de partitionnement robuste vers l'architecture PowerPC. École de technologie supérieure (2011)
16. Beaulieu, S.: Analyse du déterminisme et de la fiabilité du protocole PCI express dans un contexte de certification avionique. École de technologie supérieure (2012)
17. Feng, F.: Research on validity evaluation technology of avionics system with DIMA architecture. Nanjing University of Aeronautics and Astronautics (2014)
18. Barnhart, C., Cohn, A.: Airline schedule planning: accomplishments and opportunities. Manuf. Serv. Oper. Manag. **6**(1), 3–22 (2004)
19. Meisen, M.: Optimizing long-haul transportation considering alternative transportation routes within a parcel distribution network. In: Sebastian, H.J., Kaminsky, P., Müller, T. (eds.) Quantitative Approaches in Logistics and Supply Chain Management. Lecture Notes in Logistics, pp. 129–147. Springer, Cham (2015). https://doi.org/10.1007/978-3-319-12856-6_6
20. Crainic, T.G., Gendreau, M., Farvolden, J.M.: A simplex-based tabu search method for capacitated network design. INFORMS J. Comput. **12**(3), 223–236 (2000)
21. Knauth, T., Fetzer, C.: Energy-aware scheduling for infrastructure clouds. In: 2012 IEEE 4th International Conference on Cloud Computing Technology and Science (CloudCom), pp. 58–65. IEEE (2012)
22. Lee, J., Lee, M., Popa, L., et al.: CloudMirror: application-aware bandwidth reservations in the cloud. In: HotCloud (2013)
23. Hajjat, M., Sun, X., Sung, Y.W.E., et al.: Cloudward bound: planning for beneficial migration of enterprise applications to the cloud. ACM SIGCOMM Comput. Commun. Rev. **40**(4), 243–254 (2010)
24. Hou, C., Zhang, F., Lin, W., et al.: A hop-by-hop energy efficient distributed routing scheme. ACM Sigmetrics Perform. Eval. Rev. **41**(3), 101–106 (2014)

25. Benson, T., Akella, A., Maltz, D.A.: Network traffic characteristics of data centers in the wild. In: Proceedings of the 10th ACM SIGCOMM Conference on Internet Measurement, pp. 267–280. ACM (2010)
26. Benson, T., Anand, A., Akella, A., et al.: Understanding data center traffic characteristics. In: Proceedings of the 1st ACM workshop on Research on Enterprise Networking, pp. 65–72. ACM (2009)
27. Dalvandi, A., Gurusamy, M., Chua, K.C.: Power-efficient and predictable data centers with sliding scheduled tenant requests. In: IEEE International Conference on Cloud Computing Technology & Science (2014)

DPTM: A UAV Message Transmission Path Optimization Method Under Dynamic Programming

Pingyu Deng[1(✉)], Qing Zhou[1], Kui Li[1], and Feifei Zhu[2]

[1] National Key Laboratory of Science and Technology on Avionics Integration, China Aeronautical Radio Electronics Research Institute, Shanghai 200233, China
dengpingyuavic@163.com

[2] College of Computer Science and Technology, Nanjing University of Aeronautics and Astronautics, 29 Jiangjun Avenue, Nanjing 210016, China

Abstract. In the process of missions, how to transmit messages to the destination node quickly is a crucial issue for UAVs. Some existing methods show bad effects such as low delivery ratio, long delay, large average hop count, and high ping-pong effect ratio, thus this paper proposes a new algorithm. By considering the position of all UAVs at each moment, UAVs can obtain optimal message transmission, thus get the optimal path for the message to reach the destination node. After doing simulation experiments with the existing algorithms as DTNgeo, DTNclose and DTNload, the DPTM algorithm is superior to those in terms of delivery ratio, delay, hop count and ping-pong effect ratio.

Keywords: Dynamic programming · UAV · DTN · Ping-pong effect

1 Introduction

UAVs are the hotspot of a new round of scientific and technological revolution and industrial revolution in the world, and their industrial development is related to national interests. For many tasks that require drones, many UAVs are often required to work together to complete the task [1]. At this time, according to the characteristics of UAV networks, how to use routing strategies to quickly transmit messages to the ground station becomes an important technical problem [2].

UAVs establish high-throughput links through wireless transmission to form a temporary, multi-hop regional connection, which is a mobile ad hoc network [3]. However, due to the high-speed continuous movement of the drone, the network topology of drones changes frequently. When traditional MANET routing methods were used in UAVs, a series of problems occurred, such as low delivery rate and long delay, greatly affecting network performance [4].

Therefore, it is necessary to put forward higher requirements for UAV network routing strategy and conduct relevant researches in a targeted manner. At present, many scenes using UAVs are based on task-driven [5], and artificially plan the trajectory of

© ICST Institute for Computer Sciences, Social Informatics and Telecommunications Engineering 2020
Published by Springer Nature Switzerland AG 2020. All Rights Reserved
H. Gao et al. (Eds.): ChinaCom 2019, LNICST 312, pp. 167–176, 2020.
https://doi.org/10.1007/978-3-030-41114-5_13

the drone in advance. The drones can only move according to the planned trajectory [6]. Many existing methods [7, 8] only consider the current position status of UAVs, but not fully consider the current task-driven nature of UAVs, which makes it difficult to find the optimal transmission object.

In view of the above problems, this paper proposed a UAV message transmission path optimization method under dynamic programming (DPTM) based on the characteristics of task-driven. By globally considering positions of all UAVs at each moment, the method obtains the optimal object of message transmission at each moment, and then obtains the optimal path of messages to the destination node, reducing ping-pong effect ratio and delay. In addition, since the method avoids many unnecessary transmissions of messages, more messages can reach the ground station, thereby achieving the purpose of improving the delivery rate of the message transmission.

2 Related Work

In view of the frequent changes of network topology of UAVs, many researchers have studied it. The routing methods mainly include:

(1) *Traditional mobile ad-hoc network (MANET) routing algorithms.* The traditional routing protocol OLSR is applied in the network of two micro-aircrafts and ground stations in [9]. The results show that traditional routing protocols can't cope with rapidly changing topologies [10]. The main reason is that the UAV moves extremely fast, establishment and breakdown of the communication link is extremely frequent, which causes the network topology to change extremely fast [11]. The traditional mobile ad-hoc routing protocol does not have a certain time to converge, so the transmission efficiency is low [12].

(2) *DTN routing algorithms.* Since messages are allowed to be stored and carried, another methods are based on DTN network. DTN routing algorithms are suitable for intermittent connection [9]. Pure DTN routing methods such as Epidemic Routing [13] often use a multi-copy mechanism. Although the Spray and Wait [14] limits the number of copies, it still makes the nodes in the network carry many unnecessary information. This type of methods is generally applicable to limited flooding of mobile nodes and network in a long-term disconnected state, but can cause unnecessary loss for long-time connected networks such as the UAV network [15, 16].

(3) *Geographic routing algorithms.* Another idea is to transmit messages in a direction closer to the target node based on geographic routing [17]. In [18], DTNgeo is proposed, which is combined with geographic routing and DTN algorithm. DTNgeo forwards one message to a neighbor node that is closer to the destination in space. If there is no neighbor node closer to the ground station, the message will be carried. However, DTNgeo only considers the current position of drones, which is easy to cause messages to be transmitted back and forth and experiments show that the ping-pong effect ratio is very large. In addition, DTNclose and DTNload are proposed. These two algorithms predict the future time position after a short time according to the current motion state of UAVs [17], and forward messages

to the neighbor node that is closer to the destination node in the future, to achieve the purpose of reaching the ground station as soon as possible [19]. These two heuristic algorithms only consider position information of the next moment, but do not consider the position of the future time as much as possible. The path of one message from source to destination node may still not be the optimal transmission path. The experimental result shows that ping-pong effect ratio still large, and there is still room for optimization in delay.

3 Time Consumption Model for UAVs' Message Transmission

Based on characteristics of UAVs for message transmission, the mathematical model for the time consumption of UAVs' message transmission is as follows:

$$minT = (x, t) \tag{1}$$

Where x represents UAV's ID, and $x \in [1, N]$ (N is the number of UAVs performing the task), in particular, we define the ID of the ground station as 0; t represents a certain moment; F indicates the time at which the message carried on one drone numbered x reaches the ground station at current time t.

In particular, when the message arrives at the ground station, process of message transmission ends, whereby a special value of Eq. (1) can be obtained:

$$F(0, t) = t \tag{2}$$

In addition, during mission, even if some messages cannot be transmitted to the ground station in the form of multiple hops, UAVs will fly back to the ground station at the end of mission to bring messages back. So the moment that one message arrives at the ground station at the latest is the end of the mission, it can be deduced that:

$$F_{max}(x, t) = Final \tag{3}$$

The choice of the next nod for transmission at time t only consider the chronological order of the message to reach the ground station, and selects the UAV with the earliest time to the ground at time t as the next object. From this we can get:

$$F(x, t) = min\left\{ F(x, t + 1), \min_{y \in \{neighbours\}} F(y, t) \right\} \tag{4}$$

Where $\{neighbours\}$ is the set of neighbor nodes of the drone numbered x at time t, $\forall y$, if $d(x, y) < Range$, $put\ y\ into\ \{neighbours\}$, $F(x, t + 1)$ is the time of messages carried by the node x to reach the ground station at time $t + 1$, and $\min_{y \in \{neighbours\}} \{F(y, t)\}$ is the earliest time of messages carried by neighbor nodes to reach the ground station at time t. Then compare the value of the function F, and select the node with the smallest value as the transmission object at time t.

Therefore, the transmission object of drones at each moment can be obtained, and the transmission object selected according to this algorithm can effectively avoid ping-pong effect, so that messages can reach the ground station as soon as possible, thereby obtaining a short delay.

4 DPTM

Based on the time consumption model of UAVs' message transmission in Sect. 3, this section introduces a UAV message transmission path optimization method under dynamic programming—DPTM. We firstly introduce several variables their meanings used in DPTM, as shown in Table 1:

Table 1. Meaning table of variables

Variable	Value
t	Current moment
f	A short time interval
T	All moments divided by f for time interval
N	The number of UAVs performing the task
i	One UAV numbered i $(i \in [1, N])$
Final	End moment of mission
{neighbours}	Set of neighbor nodes of UAV numbered x at current time t
F(N,T)	Recording all moments when all UAVs carry message at the moment to the ground station. ∃x∈N, F(x,t) indicates the time when UAV numbered x carries the message at time t to the ground station earliest
location(N,T)	Position of all UAVs at each moment, ∃x∈N, location(x,t) indicates the position of UAV numbered x at time t
next(N,T)	Recording transfer objects of all UAVs at each moment,∃x∈N, next(x,t) indicates the transfer object of UAV numbered x at time t
d(N,N)	Recording all distances between all UAVs

For calculating message transmission object $next(i, T)$ at any moment of any UAV, the specific steps of DPTM are as follows:

Step 1: Define a state function, obtain and the state transition equation the boundary conditions of the state transition equation.

From the time consumption model of UAVs' message transmission in the previous section, the state function of UAV numbered i at the time t can be obtained as F(i, t); from the formula (4), the state transition equation of UAV numbered i can be obtained as follows:

$$F(i, t) = min\{F(i, t + 1), \min_{j \in \xi i} F(j, t)\} \tag{5}$$

Where ξ_i is the set of neighbor nodes of UAV numbered i at time t.

In addition, according to formula (2) (3), the boundary conditions of the state transition equation of UAV numbered i can be obtained as follows:

$$F(0, t) = t \tag{6}$$

$$F_{max}(i, t) = Final \tag{7}$$

Step 2: Collect the position of all UAVs at each moment.

Since trajectories of UAVs are planned by the ground station, the ground station can get all position of all drones at each moment and get the location(N, T).

Step 3: Calculate distance between UAV numbered i and any other UAV, and obtain the neighbor nodes that can communicate with i at time t.

Calculate the distance $d(i, j)$ between UAV numbered i and any other UAV numbered j at time t, and record the distance to $d(N, N)$. if $d(i, j) \leq$ *Range*, then put j into ξ_i, where ξ_i is the set of neighbor nodes of i at time t.

Step 4: According to the state transition Eq. (5), the next hop at current moment is obtained until all the moments update, and the optimal message transmission object of one drone at each moment is obtained.

According to the formula (5) (6) (7), firstly compare the value of function F at the current moment t and the next moment $t + 1$, if $F(i, t + 1) < F(i, t)$, then F(i, t) = F(i, t + 1), next(i, t + 1) = next(i, t). Then compare the value of function F of i with its neighbor nodes, and send messages to the neighbor node with the smallest value of function F. $\forall j \in \zeta_i$, if $F(j, t) < F(i, t)$, then F(i, t) = F(j, t)and next(i, t) = j.

After updating F(N, T) and next(N, T), let t = t + 1 and judge if it has reached Final time. If t < Final, then repeat steps 3 and 4, otherwise end the operation.

Over time, DPTM finally converges to get message transmission object of all UAVs at each moment next(N, T). When one UAV need to transmit messages to the next hop obtained by DPTM, it need to judge if they can communicate with each other. If it cannot at current moment, it will carry until it can communicate with it (Table 2).

Table 2. DPTM algorithm

DPTM Algorithm
1: **Input:** location(N,T)
2: **Output:** next(N,T)
3: **Inital:**
4: t=0;   //current moment
5: Next (N,T)= -1;
6: F (N,T) =Final;
7: **Procedure DPTM:**
8: F(0,t)=t
9: Repeat
10:   t=t+1
11:   If F(x,t)>F(x,t+1) then
12:      F(x,t)=F(x,t+1)
13:      Next(x,t)=next(x,t+1)
14:   For j ∈ {neighbours} do
15:      If F(x,t)>F(j,t) then
16:         F(x,t)=F(j,t)
17:         Next(x,t)=j
18: Until t=Final

5   Simulation Results

5.1   Simulation Setup

This article uses ONE to implement DTNgeo, DTNclose, DTNload and DPTM. The simulation scenario is a typical task-driven scenario– search and rescue. In order to find the target person and rescue him as soon as possible, the ground station pre-plans the trajectory of each drone. UAV collects message such as pictures and videos and quickly transmits them back to the ground station. The simulation experiment borrows the most cases of the number of drones in [18], as shown in Fig. 1.

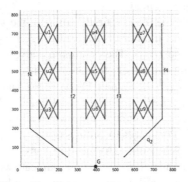

Fig. 1. Simulation experiment scene graph

Where G is the ground station; u1-9 are searching UAVs and are responsible to search and collect information, and can also serve as relays for transmission; f1-4 are ferry UAVs and act only as relays to help the search UAVs transmit. The search trajectory is shown in the figure. UAVs cooperate with each other to transmit information to the ground station G as soon as possible. Then ground station puts together the topography of entire search in area and finds location of the target person.

Table 3. The table of experimental parameters

Parameter	Value
Test area	800 * 800 m
The number of grounds	1
The number of UAVs (searching/ferry)	13 (9/4)
Mission time	8 min
Speed	4.5 m/s
Range	200 m
Size of each message	1.4 kb
The number of messages per second	5
f	0.1/0.2/0.5/1/2/4

In addition, the specific parameter settings during the experiment are shown in Table 3.

5.2 Discussion of Results

Experiments were carried out for different time intervals F. According to the data of ONE simulation experiments, we set the delivery rate, delay, hop count and ping-pong effect ratio as evaluation indexes to compare DPTM with DTNgeo, DTNclose and DTNload.

(1) **Comparison of delivery rate of different algorithms in different interval experiments**
    The results in Fig. 2 show that the delivery rate of these four algorithms are all very high during the experimental time. Compared with other algorithms, DPTM slightly increases the delivery rate to about 90%. Since DPTM can obtain the optimal transmission path of messages, many unnecessary transmissions in other algorithm are avoided, so that more messages can reach the ground station.

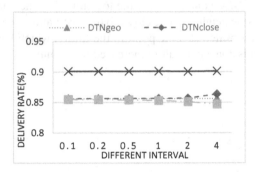

Fig. 2. Comparison of delivery rate between DPTM and DTNgeo, DTNclose, DTNload

(2) **Comparison of delay of different algorithms in different interval experiments**
    The results in Fig. 3 show that DPTM reduces delay to about 40 s at different interval compared to other three algorithms. The reason is that DPTM obtains the optimal path of messages to the ground station according to the position information of all the drones at each moment. DTNgeo only considers the location information at current time. DTNclose and DTNload only consider the location of the next moment. So message transmission object of these three algorithms is optimal for current network topology, but not for the changing UAV network. The optimal object at a certain moment is likely to be not optimal for the whole process, so DTNgeo, DTNclose and DTNload cause long delay.

(3) **Comparison of hop count of different algorithms in different interval experiments**
    The results in Fig. 4 show that DPTM reduces hop count to less than 4.8 at different interval compared to other three algorithms. The reason is that DPTM plans the optimal transmission path in advance according to the position information of all drones at each moment, so that drones can remember the transmission object at

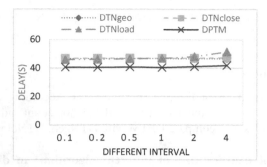

Fig. 3. Comparison of delay between DPTM and DTNgeo, DTNclose, DTNload

each moment. If the communication link between current node and the next hop can be established, messages will be transmitted, otherwise messages will be carried. The unnecessary round-trip transmission of messages is reduced, resulting in smaller hop count. DTNgeo only considers the location information of current time. DTNclose and DTNload only consider the location of the next moment. Messages are transmitted to the neighbor node closet to the destination, so many messages are likely to be re-transmitted at some point in the future, which leads to unnecessary ping-pong transmission and result in increased hop count.

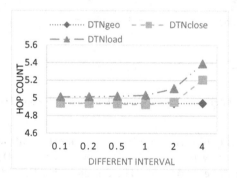

Fig. 4. Comparison of hop count between DPTM and DTNgeo, DTNclose, DTNload

(4) **Comparison of ping-pong effect ratio of different algorithms in different interval experiments**

The results in Fig. 5 show that DPTM can significantly reduce the ping-pong effect ratio to less than 5%. According to theoretical analysis of DPTM, the algorithm can find the optimal transmission path and completely eliminate the ping-pong effect ratio. However, in the actual execution of the mission, speed of messages transmission is fast, but it also spends time. Therefore, for some situations where the connection time is extremely short and the load is too heavy, some drones may not be able to transmit all messages to the planned next hop as a whole. It causes some messages to miss the optimal object, thus result in a small proportion of ping-pong effect. Even so, DPTM significantly reduces the ping-pong effect ratio and reduces the time delay.

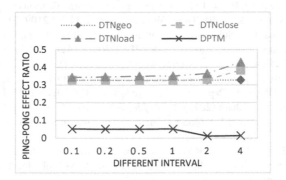

Fig. 5. Comparison of ping-pong ratio between DPTM and DTNgeo, DTNclose, DTNload.

6 Conclusion

This paper proposed a UAV message transmission path optimization method under dynamic programming named DPTM. By globally considering positions of all UAVs at each moment, DPTM obtains the optimal object of message transmission at each moment, and then obtains the optimal path of messages to the destination node, to reduce ping-pong effect ratio and delay. Comparing DPTM with DTNgeo, DTNclose and DTNload through simulation experiments, the results show that DPTM slightly improves the message delivery ratio. In terms of delay, DPTM has a reduction of nearly 6%. In terms of hop count, DPTM reduces it to 4.8 or less, and the result can reduce the waste of energy used by drones for messages' transmission. In terms of ping-pong effect ratio, DPTM significantly reduce it down to 5%, so that drones will waste less energy for useless transmission and use as much energy as possible to perform tasks.

Since many applications of UAVs, such as the scenario search and rescue mentioned in this paper at present are planned in advance, the UAVs only need to move according to the pre-planned trajectory of the ground station, so DPTM is of great significance in the current unmanned unit communication.

References

1. Canis, B.: Unmanned Aircraft Systems (UAS): commercial outlook for a new industry. In: Congressional Research Service Reports. Library of Congress. Congressional Research Service (2015)
2. Zhou, Y., Cheng, N., Lu, N., et al.: Multi-UAV-aided networks: aerial-ground cooperative vehicular networking architecture. IEEE Veh. Technol. Mag. **10**(4), 36–44 (2015)
3. Guvenc, I., Saad, W., Bennis, M., et al.: Wireless communications, networking, and positioning with unmanned aerial vehicles [Guest Editorial]. IEEE Commun. Mag. **54**(5), 24–25 (2016)

4. Grodi, R., Rawat, D.B., Bajracharya, C., et al.: Performance evaluation of Unmanned Aerial Vehicle ad hoc networks. Southeastcon, pp. 1–4 (2015)
5. Anantapalli, M.K., Li, W.: Multipath multihop routing analysis in mobile ad hoc networks. Wirel. Netw. **16**(1), 79–94 (2010)
6. Wu, Q., Zeng, Y., Zhang, R., et al.: Joint trajectory and communication design for multi-UAV enabled wireless networks. IEEE Trans. Wirel. Commun. **17**(3), 2109–2121 (2018)
7. Hausman, K., Preiss, J.A., Sukhatme, G.S., et al.: Observability-aware trajectory optimization for self-calibration with application to UAVs. IEEE Robot. Autom. **2**(3), 1770–1777 (2017)
8. Harounabadi, M., Puschmann, A., Artemenko, O., Mitschele-Thiel, A.: TAG: trajectory aware geographical routing in cognitive radio ad hoc networks with UAV nodes. In: Mitton, N., Kantarci, M.E., Gallais, A., Papavassiliou, S. (eds.) ADHOCNETS 2015. LNICST, vol. 155, pp. 111–122. Springer, Cham (2015). https://doi.org/10.1007/978-3-319-25067-0_9
9. Badis, H., Agha, K.A.: QOLSR, QoS routing for ad hoc wireless networks using OLSR. Eur. Trans. Telecommun. **16**(5), 427–442 (2010)
10. Asadpour, M., Egli, S., Hummel, K.A., Giustiniano, D.: Routing in a fleet of micro aerial vehicles: first experimental insights. In: Proceedings of 3rd ACM MobiHoc Workshop Airborne Networks and Communication, pp. 9–10 (2014)
11. Bekmezci, I., Sahingoz, O.K., Temel, Ş., et al.: Flying ad-hoc networks (FANETs). Ad Hoc Netw. **11**(3), 1254–1270 (2013)
12. Cetinkaya, E.K., Rohrer, J.P., Jabbar, A., et al.: Protocols for highly-dynamic airborne networks. In: ACM/IEEE International Conference on Mobile Computing and Networking, pp. 411–414 (2012)
13. Vahdat, A., Becker, D.: Epidemic Routing for Partially-Connected Ad Hoc Networks. Master Thesis (2000)
14. Li, J., Guan, J., Xu, C., et al.: Adaptive multiple spray and wait routing algorithm. J. Chin. Comput. Syst. **36**(10), 2275–2278 (2015)
15. Lu, F., Li, J., Song, Y., et al.: Location position and message delivery ratio based controlled epidemic routing for DTNs. J. Chin. Comput. Syst. **39**(5), 918–923 (2018)
16. Caini, C., Cruickshank, H.S., Farrell, S., et al.: Delay- and disruption-tolerant networking (DTN): an alternative solution for future satellite networking applications. Proc. IEEE **99**(11), 1980–1997 (2011)
17. Shirani, R., St-Hilaire, M., Kunz, T., et al.: Quadratic estimation of success probability of greedy geographic forwarding in unmanned aeronautical ad-hoc networks. In: Vehicular Technology Conference, pp. 1–5. IEEE (2012)
18. Asadpour, M., Hummel, K.A., Giustiniano, D., et al.: Route or carry: motion-driven packet forwarding in micro aerial vehicle networks. IEEE Trans. Mobile Comput. **16**(3), 843–856 (2017)
19. Muzaffar, R., Yanmaz, E.: Trajectory-aware Ad hoc routing protocol for micro aerial vehicle networks. In: IMAV 2014: International Micro Air Vehicle Conference and Competition 2014, Delft, The Netherlands, 12–15 August 2014. Delft University of Technology, pp. 301–315 (2014)

Antenna, Microwave and Cellular Communication

Orbital Angular Momentum Microwave Generated by Free Electron Beam

Pengfei Xu and Chao Zhang[⊠]

Labs of Avionics, School of Aerospace Engineering, Tsinghua University,
Beijing 100084, People's Republic of China
zhangchao@mail.tsinghua.edu.cn

Abstract. Based on the theory of classical electrodynamics and quantum mechanics, we quantitatively deduce microwave carrying Orbital Angular Momentum (OAM) radiated from the moving free electron beams on different closed-curved trajectories. It shows that the non-relativistic free electrons can also transit quantized OAM to the microwave in addition to the relativistic cyclotron electrons in the magnetic field. This work indicates the effective way to construct the antennas to generate high OAM modes of the microwave by multi-electron radiation.

Keywords: Orbital Angular Momentum (OAM) · Free electron · Microwave · Magnetic field

1 Introduction

Electro-Magnetic (EM) wave has angular momentum, which can be considered as a fundamental physical quantity and a new degree of freedom in both classical and quantum electrodynamics [1,2]. Moreover, the angular momentum can be divided into Spin Angular Momentum (SAM) and Orbital Angular Momentum (OAM). Unlike the linear momentum or SAM related to the polarization [3], OAM is the result of the spatial spiral distribution of electric field strength and phase, which is expected to be one of the candidate technologies for Beyond 5th Generation (B5G) and 6th Generation (6G) mobile communications because of its rotational degrees of freedom. Hence, the signals with different OAMs in the same carrier frequency are mutually orthogonal and propagate independently. This phenomenon can provide the benefits of the transmission with a very high spectrum efficiency [4]. A photon at optical frequency with OAM was originally discussed by Allen *et al.* with respect to a specific mode of EM wave called the Laguerre-Gaussian mode [5]. While in radio beams, Thidé *et al.* proposed to use antenna arrays for generating and detecting EM wave carrying both SAM

This work has been supported by National Natural Science Foundation of China with project number 61731011.

© ICST Institute for Computer Sciences, Social Informatics and Telecommunications Engineering 2020
Published by Springer Nature Switzerland AG 2020. All Rights Reserved
H. Gao et al. (Eds.): ChinaCom 2019, LNICST 312, pp. 179–192, 2020.
https://doi.org/10.1007/978-3-030-41114-5_14

and OAM called Bessel-Gaussian mode [6]. Since then, in addition to using the Uniform Circular Antenna (UCA) method to generate OAM wave at radio frequency [6,7]. Many studies are also considering the use of electron beams to generate OAM waves. In 2015, Asner *et al.* showed that a single electron that makes a relativistic cyclotron motion in a magnetic field can radiate EM waves, and the radiated EM wave energy has discrete properties [8]. Besides, Sawant *et al.* demonstrated through simulation and experiment that the use of relativistic electron beams in the gyrotron can generate microwaves carrying high-order OAM in 2017 [9].

According to the radiation mode, the OAM beam can be divided into the statistical state beam and the quantum state beam. The former has an equivalent spiral wave front and the single photon is a plane wave photon, while the latter is that each photon constituting the EM wave is a vortex photon and their wave fronts form a spiral wave front. The spatial phase modulation methods such as a Spiral Phase Plate (SPP) and a UCA belong to the statistical beam generation method. In contrast, the way in which vortex photons are directly radiated by electrons with quantized OAM belongs to the quantum beam generation method. The difference between the methods is whether the OAM of the EM wave is mapped to the gyrotron electron OAM. From the perspective of quantum mechanics, quantized EM wave is composed of photons in the form of harmonic oscillators [1], and the quantum state of a photon can be described by a multipole expansion of EM wave with a well-defined value of the energy ($\hbar\omega$, where $\hbar$ and ω denote reduced Planck constant and the angular frequency of the EM wave), parity (odd or even) and the total angular momentum (polarization or spin, and OAM), given by the corresponding quantum eigenvalue $l(l+1)\hbar$ and OAM in a fixed direction (say z-axis normally and l is an integer denoting OAM mode number), given by the eigenvalue $l\hbar$ [10]. When the frequency is constant, the even parity photon that does not carry OAM is called the electric dipole photon, while the odd parity photon that does not carry OAM is called the magnetic dipole photon. In addition, photons carrying $l\hbar$ OAM are called $2^{(|l|+1)}$-pole photons. For instance, photons with OAM of $\hbar$ are called quadrupole photons. Because photons are the medium of electron transfer interaction, the OAM of photons can also be naturally obtained by the OAM of electrons. However, for a single dipole antenna (electrons can only vibrate in one direction in the antenna and carry no angular momentum), the EM wave radiation carrying a high order OAM are unlikely to occur because the angular momentum L selection rule for dipole approximation radiation is $\Delta L = 0, \pm 1$ [11]. In order to directly radiate microwave carrying OAM, it is necessary to construct electrical multipole radiation and change the selection rule. Therefore, there are two ways to modify the selection rule: (1) single relativistic electron radiation [8]; (2) multi-electron radiation [1].

For the first method, the single relativistic electron can produce pure OAM photons, but the cost is high, generally requiring at least the speed of the electron to reach half the speed of light. In 2017, Katoh *et al.* theoretically showed that a single free electron in circular motion will radiate the EM wave with OAM [12]. When the speed of the electron is relativistic, the radiation field contains harmonic components and the photons of l-th harmonic carry $l\hbar$ total angular momentum including $\pm\hbar$ SAM and $(l \mp 1)\hbar$ OAM. So it is theoretically and experimentally proved that a single electron can emit pure twisted photons rather than a beam carrying OAM [12,13]. However, there is only transmitter in the aforementioned method. In other words, there lacks corresponding receiver. The relativistic electron means that the speed of free electron approaches the speed of light, which is difficult for popularization and application in practice.

For the second method, the model of non-relativistic free electrons continuously circling in different closed-curved trajectories are proposed in this paper. In addition, we theoretically demonstrate the EM wave with OAM can be emitted from classical electrodynamics and quantum mechanics theory. Furthermore, the corresponding receiver is designed and the motion of the free electron is theoretically demonstrated to move in different trajectories, which can be utilized for OAM demultiplexing.

2 Preliminary Knowledge

The EM wave with OAM has a helical wave front, an azimuthal term $e^{il\phi}$, and an OAM of $l\hbar$ per photon, where ϕ is the azimuthal angle. Moreover, the microwave OAM signals propagating along the z-axis can be expressed in the cylindrical coordinate (r, θ, ϕ) as

$$\mathbf{U}_{kl}(r, \phi, \theta) = \boldsymbol{\varepsilon} \frac{A_l e^{-i(\omega_0 t + \phi_l)}}{r} J_l(k_\perp r \sin\theta) e^{-i(k_\| z + l\phi)}, \tag{1}$$

where $J_l(\cdot)$ denotes Bessel function of the order l, $\boldsymbol{\varepsilon}$ denotes the polarization vector, θ denotes the pitch angle, $\perp$ and $\|$ stand for the transverse and propagation vector component, and satisfy the wave number relationship $k^2 = k_\perp^2 + k_\|^2$. $A_l e^{-i(\omega_0 t + \phi_l)}$ is the modulated signal in the traditional main channel, where A_l and ϕ_l are the amplitude and phase of the signal respectively. According to Eq. (1), it can be easily seen that different OAM signals are orthogonal to each other, i.e., $\mathbf{U}_{kl}\mathbf{U}_{k'l'} = \delta_{kk'}\delta_{ll'}$, where δ is Dirac function, which means that signals with different OAM mode numbers at the same frequency can transmit in the channel without interference. In addition, the OAM mode is a new freedom of EM wave, and it can be combined with the digital modulation of conventional EM wave to improve transmission performance.

According to Refs. [14–16], OAM-based microwave transmission systems can enjoy the benefit of the mode division multiplexing for short-range communications. The emerging physical layer solution for such short-range line-of-sight wireless communication provides a relatively low detection complexity and high spectral efficiency. Moreover, it can be used for the OAM transmission system through the partial phase plane index modulation receiving method. Usually, OAM can add new degrees of freedom to the traditional wireless microwave transmission systems. An OAM-based Multiple Input Multiple-Output (MIMO) transmission system was proposed in Ref. [17]. When the transmission distance is greater than a certain distance, the capacity of OAM-MIMO is larger than that of the traditional MIMO. The expression of OAM-MIMO transmission capacity can be written as

$$C = \log_2 \det \left[\mathbf{I}_N + \frac{P}{\sigma^2 N_{\mathrm{OAM}}} \mathbf{H}_{\mathrm{OAM}} \mathbf{H}_{\mathrm{OAM}}^{\mathrm{H}} \right], \tag{2}$$

where $\mathbf{H}_{\mathrm{OAM}} \in \mathbb{C}^{M \times N}$ is the OAM channel matrix, $\mathbf{I}_N$ is the $N \times N$ unit matrix, $(\cdot)^{\mathrm{H}}$ is the conjugate transition operation, $\det[\cdot]$ represents the determinant of a square matrix, P is the total transmission power, N_{OAM} denotes the number of OAM modes, and σ^2 is the variance of the Gaussian white noise [14]. OAM as a new dimension can also be combined with the modulation and coding methods, expand European space and improve communication performance, such as with the Low-Density Parity-Check (LDPC) coding [18].

The angular momentum $\mathbf{J}$ including SAM $\mathbf{S}$ and OAM $\mathbf{L}$ of the EM wave $(\mathbf{E}, \mathbf{B})$ in vacuum can be expressed as

$$\mathbf{J} = \mathbf{S} + \mathbf{L} = \frac{1}{\mu_0 c^2} \int_V \mathbf{r} \times (\mathbf{E} \times \mathbf{B}) \mathrm{d}V = \frac{1}{4\pi c} \int_V [(\mathbf{E} \times \mathbf{A}) + \mathbf{E} \cdot (\mathbf{r} \times -i\nabla \cdot \mathbf{A})] \mathrm{d}V, \tag{3}$$

where μ_0, c, $\mathbf{r}$, $\mathbf{A}$, ∇ and V denote the permeability in vacuum, the speed of light, the field location vector, the vector potential, the Laplace operator and the integrated full volume. The first term of Eq. (3) denotes the SAM of the EM wave, which is well known as the photon spin and polarization. The second term of Eq. (3) contains the total OAM operator $\mathbf{r} \times -i\nabla$ item, which is consistent with the OAM operator in quantum mechanics $\mathcal{L} = \mathbf{r} \times \mathbf{p} = \mathbf{r} \times -i\hbar\nabla$, where $\mathbf{p}$ is the momentum operator.

While the angular momentum is the basic property of the field and matter, except that the photons constituting the microwave can have angular momentum, the EM wave radiated by the electrons can also have the angular momentum. The whole radiation process satisfies the angular momentum conservation and the selection rule. Hence, electrons carrying angular momentum can radiate microwaves that carry both SAM and OAM.

3   System Model

As shown in Fig. 1, a non-relativistic electron rotates around the z-axis at an angular velocity ω in the Cartesian coordinate system, and its velocity is $\mathbf{v}$. The dotted line indicates the conceptual trajectory of the moving electron with different OAM. The acceleration of the electron can be expressed as $a_0 = |\dot{\mathbf{v}}|$. According to Ref. [19], the expression of the radiation produced by the motion of the electronic acceleration can be described by Liénard-Wiechert field and the second order term $o\left(1/r^2\right)$ called generalized Coulomb field is ignored:

$$\mathbf{E}_e(\mathbf{r}, t) = \frac{q}{4\pi\varepsilon_0 c^2} \frac{\mathbf{e}_r \times (\mathbf{e}_r \times \dot{\mathbf{v}})}{r'} \approx \frac{q}{4\pi\varepsilon_0 c^2 r} (\mathbf{e}_r \cdot \dot{\mathbf{v}}) \cdot \mathbf{e}_r - \dot{\mathbf{v}}, \tag{4}$$

$$\mathbf{B}_e(\mathbf{r}, t) = \mathbf{e}_r \times \mathbf{E}_e/c, \tag{5}$$

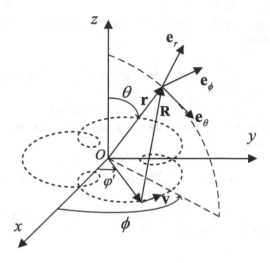

Fig. 1. A non-relativistic electron rotates around the z-axis.

where $\mathbf{r}'\left(t'\right) = \mathbf{r} - \mathbf{r}_0\left(t'\right)$, $r' = \left|\mathbf{r}'\left(t'\right)\right| \approx r$, $\mathbf{e}_r = \mathbf{r}/r$, which is the unit vector between the observation point and the position of the electron at the retarded time, $\mathbf{r}_0$ denotes the position vector of the electron, $t' = t - \left|\mathbf{r} - \mathbf{r}'\right|/c$ is the retarded time, q denotes the charge of the electron, and ϵ_0 denotes the permittivity of vacuum. In addition, $\mathbf{E}_e$ and $\mathbf{B}_e$ are the EM radiation from the single electron to the observer at $\mathbf{r}$.

In order to calculate $\mathbf{E}_e$ and $\mathbf{B}_e$, the expression of $\mathbf{e}_r$, $\mathbf{r}_0$ and $\dot{\mathbf{v}}$ can be obtained from the geometric relationship in the spherical coordinate system of Fig. 1 as follows:

$$\mathbf{e}_r = \left\{\sin\theta\cos\phi\,\mathbf{n}_x + \sin\theta\sin\phi\,\mathbf{n}_y + \cos\theta\,\mathbf{n}_z\right\}, \tag{6}$$

$$\mathbf{r}_0\left(t\right) = r_0\left\{\cos\omega t\,e^{il\varphi(t)}\mathbf{n}_x + \sin\omega t\,e^{il\varphi(t)}\mathbf{n}_y\right\}, \tag{7}$$

$$\dot{\mathbf{v}}\left(t\right) \approx a_0\left\{-\cos\omega t\,e^{il\varphi(t)}\mathbf{n}_x - \sin\omega t\,e^{il\varphi(t)}\mathbf{n}_y\right\}, \tag{8}$$

where $\mathbf{n}_x$, $\mathbf{n}_y$ and $\mathbf{n}_z$ are unit vectors of x, y, and z axes, r_0 denotes the constant relavent to the positional parameters and $\varphi(t)$ denotes the phase of the electron. By substituting Eqs. (6) and (8) into Eq. (4), we can calculate the specific expression of the electric field in the Cartesian coordinate system:

$$\begin{cases} E_{ex} = \dfrac{E_e}{r}e^{il\varphi(t)}\left[-\sin^2\theta\sin\phi\sin\left(\omega t - \phi\right) + \cos^2\theta\cos\omega t\right] \\[2mm] E_{ey} = \dfrac{E_e}{r}e^{il\varphi(t)}\left[+\sin^2\theta\cos\phi\sin\left(\omega t - \phi\right) + \cos^2\theta\sin\omega t\right] \\[2mm] E_{ez} = \dfrac{E_e}{r}e^{il\varphi(t)}\left[-\sin\theta\cos\theta\cos\left(\omega t - \phi\right)\right] \\[2mm] E_e = \dfrac{qa_0}{4\pi\varepsilon_0 c^2} \end{cases} \tag{9}$$

The instantaneous energy flow resulting from the Liénard-Wiechert field is given by the Poynting vector

$$\mathbf{S} = \frac{q^2 a_0^2}{16\pi^2 \varepsilon_0 c^3 r^2} \left[\cos^2\theta + \sin^2\theta \sin^2\left(\omega t - \phi\right) \right] \mathbf{e}_r. \tag{10}$$

When $\omega t = \phi$, setting the angle between the acceleration and the radiation direction as Θ, the energy radiated into per solid angle Ω during each cycle of the rotating electron is

$$\frac{dP}{d\Omega} = r^2 \mathbf{S} \cdot \mathbf{e}_r = \frac{q^2 a_0^2}{16\pi^2 \varepsilon_0 c^3} \cos^2\theta = \frac{q^2 a_0^2}{16\pi^2 \varepsilon_0 c^3} \sin^2\Theta. \tag{11}$$

Integrating Eq. (11) over the all solid angles, we get the non-relativistic electron generalization of Larmor's formula:

$$P = \int_0^{2\pi} \int_0^{\pi} \frac{q^2 a_0^2}{16\pi^2 \varepsilon_0 c^3} \sin^2\Theta \sin\Theta d\Theta d\phi = \frac{q^2 a_0^2}{6\pi \varepsilon_0 c^3}. \tag{12}$$

Now considering that the total radiation field produced by an electron in one cycle, the expression of the radiation fields at any time generated by the electron is Eq. (9), but their phases are different from each other. Therefore, the total electric field expression after coherent superposition is

$$\mathbf{E}_{\text{total}} = \sum \mathbf{E}_e e^{ikR} e^{-i\omega(t - \mathbf{e}_r \cdot \mathbf{R}/c)}$$

$$\approx e^{i(kr - \omega t + l\phi)} \int_0^{2\pi} |\mathbf{E}_e| e^{il(\varphi - \phi)} e^{i\beta \sin\theta \cos(\varphi - \phi)} d\varphi', \tag{13}$$

where k denotes the wave number, $\mathbf{R}$ denotes the vector from the electron to the observer, $R = |\mathbf{R}|$, $\omega\mathbf{e}_r \cdot \mathbf{R}/c \approx \beta \sin\theta \cos(\varphi - \phi)$, $\varphi' = \omega t$ and $\beta = v/c$ denotes the ratio of the speed of the electron to c. When $l = 0$ and $\varphi = \varphi'$, the integral of Eq. (13) can be obtained as follows:

$$\begin{cases} E_x = \dfrac{E_e J_l \left(\beta \sin\theta\right) \cos^2\theta \pi e^{i(kr - \omega t + l\phi)}}{r} \left(ie^{i\phi} + \dfrac{i}{e^{i\phi}}\right) \\[2ex] E_y = \dfrac{E_e J_l \left(\beta \sin\theta\right) \cos^2\theta \pi e^{i(kr - \omega t + l\phi)}}{r} \left(e^{i\phi} + \dfrac{1}{e^{i\phi}}\right) \\[2ex] E_z = \dfrac{E_e J_l \left(\beta \sin\theta\right) \sin\theta \cos\theta \pi e^{i(kr - \omega t + l\phi)}}{r} \left(i - \dfrac{1}{i}\right) \end{cases} \tag{14}$$

According to Eqs. (9) and (14), the coherent radiation of the electric field does not affect the total angular momentum including SAM and OAM. It can be seen that SAM is +1 and OAM is l, because $\mathbf{E}_{\text{total}}$ contains the $e^{il\phi}$ item and the phase difference between E_x and E_y is 90°. In addition, the total angular momentum along the z-axis remains unchanged while propagating. When $l \geq 1$, the trajectory of the electron is not a perfect circle, so it is difficult to get the integral expression of Eq. (13). However, the phase of $\mathbf{E}_{\text{total}}$ can be proven to be $\exp\left[i\left(kr - \omega t + l\phi + c_l\right)\right]$ by computer numerical integration, where c_l denotes a constant associated with l. Through the OAM operator in the cylindrical coordinate system $\mathcal{L}_z = -i\hbar\partial/\partial\phi$, the OAM of each photon in the EM wave can be calculated as $l\hbar$.

Overall, when the electrons are moving on different trajectories, whose acceleration expression contains the space related item $e^{il\varphi(t)}$ with different OAM mode numbers l, the EM wave radiated by the electron carries both SAM and OAM. In other words, electron beams rotating around the z-axis can radiate vortex microwave carrying OAM, which leads to that OAM transits from the free electrons to the microwave and the total angular momentum remains conserved.

When each electron of the electron beam moves on a corresponding different trajectory, each electron generates a radiation field around it, and when the electric fields generated by the electron beams are superposed on each other, EM wave of different OAMs can be generated. Moreover, as the number of OAM modes increases, the center hole of the electric field also increases. In summary, by utilizing the two-dimensional motion characteristics of electrons and the superposition characteristics of electron-radiating electric fields, it is possible to theoretically generate OAM microwaves of arbitrary modes, which can greatly expand the radiation freedom of conventional dipole antennas.

Table 1. Microwave radiation parameters

Parameter	Value	Dimension
Electron density ρ	1×10^{10}	cm^{-3}
Speed of electron v	1×10^7	m/s
Electron Beam current I	1.0	mA
Acceleration of electron a_0	2.199×10^{18}	m/s^2
Microwave frequency f	35.0	GHz
Speed of light c	3×10^8	m/s
Charge of electron q	1.6×10^{-19}	C
Permittivity of vacuum ϵ_0	8.854×10^{-12}	F/m
Planck constant h	6.626×10^{-34}	J·s

To calculate the radiated power, an optional parameter list is shown in Table 1 when the frequency of photons carrying OAM radiated by the non-relativistic free electron is in the microwave band. Obviously, the radiated power of a single free electron is $P_e = 2.754 \times 10^{-17}$ W according to Eq. (12), and the average number of photons radiated by a single electron per unit time can be calculated as $N_p = P_e/(hf)$. Of course, the average number is about 1.188×10^6 s^{-1} for microwave photons, which is much smaller than one photon. When the electron density in the free space or the electron beam current increases, the radiation power increases. To calculate the radiation field generated by the free electron beam, an electron beam or a single electron can be considered as the equivalent current, using the full space-time Fourier transform of the current density of the single point charge:

$$\mathbf{J}(\mathbf{r}, t) = q\dot{\mathbf{r}}_0(t)\,\delta\left[\mathbf{r} - \mathbf{r}_0(t)\right], \tag{15}$$

where $\dot{\mathbf{r}}_0(t)$ denotes the velocity of the charge and $\delta\left[\mathbf{r} - \mathbf{r}_0(t)\right]$ denotes the spatial unit impulse function [20]. The expression of the velocity is:

$$\dot{\mathbf{r}}_0(t) = d\left\{\sin\omega_0 t\mathbf{n}_x + \cos\omega_0 t\mathbf{n}_y + 0\mathbf{n}_z\right\}, \tag{16}$$

where d denotes a constant. According to [20], the full space-time Fourier transform of the current density can be expressed as follows:

$$\mathbf{J}(\mathbf{k}, \omega) = \int q\dot{\mathbf{r}}_0(t)\, e^{-i\mathbf{k}\cdot\mathbf{r}_0} e^{i\omega t} dt, \tag{17}$$

By substituting Eq. (16) into Eq. (17), the frequency domain expression of the current density can be described as:

$$|\mathbf{J}(\mathbf{k}, \omega)| = \frac{\sqrt{2}q\omega_0 d}{2} J_0\left(kd\cos\alpha\right)\left[\delta\left(\omega - \omega_0\right) + \delta\left(\omega + \omega_0\right)\right], \tag{18}$$

where α is the angle between $\mathbf{v}$ and $\mathbf{k}$. According to Eq. (18), a conclusion can be drawn that there is a radiation field only if $k = \omega_0/c$. Moreover, the current density can be substituted into Maxwell's equations to solve the radiation field:

$$\mathbf{E}(\mathbf{k}, \omega) = \frac{-i\omega\mu_0 \mathbf{n} \times [\mathbf{n} \times \mathbf{J}(\mathbf{k}, \omega)]}{k^2 - (\omega^2/c^2)}, \tag{19}$$

where $\mathbf{n} = \mathbf{k}/k$, μ_0 denotes the permeability of vacuum. That is to say, the calculation result and expression form are equivalent to Eq. (4). When the quantity of electrons contained in the electron beam is N, The total radiation field of the electron beam can be expressed as $\sum_{n=1}^{N} \mathbf{E}(\mathbf{k}, \omega)\varphi_n$, where φ_n denotes the phase of each electron radiation field.

On the other hand, the reason why electrons rotating around the z-axis can radiate high-order OAM microwaves is that electrons also carry the quantized angular momentum in addition to the classical angular momentum $\mathbf{L} = \mathbf{r} \times (m_e\mathbf{v})$. It is well known that there are two solutions to the Schrödinger equation for quantum mechanics. One is the time-independent solution, the other is the time-dependent solution, which can be regarded as the linear superposition of the time-independent solutions. The reason why rotating electrons carry the quantized OAM is that the wave function of the electron is a standing wave function along the tangential direction of the closed trajectory, which is a solution of the time-independent Schrödinger equation.

Assuming that the circumference of the electron's motion is L, its wave function $\psi(x)$ satisfies the following conditions:

$$-\frac{\hbar^2}{2m}\frac{\mathrm{d}^2\psi}{\mathrm{d}x^2} + V(x)\psi = E\psi,\tag{20}$$

$$\psi\left[x + L/(|l|+1)\right] = \psi(x),\tag{21}$$

where m, $V(x)$ and E denote the mass, the potential function and the energy of the electron, respectively. Besides, it is self-evident that $V(x)$ does not change with time and is always zero. The influence of EM wave generated by electrons on themselves is ignored. For example, an electron is making circular motion at the uniform velocity in a constant magnetic field and there is not any force in the direction of movement of the electron. Therefore, the general solution of the electron wave function is $\psi(x) = Ae^{ikx} + Be^{-ikx}$, where $k = \sqrt{2mE}/\hbar$, A and B are both undetermined coefficients of the solution. Furthermore, we can get a series of solutions of the time-independent Schrödinger equation:

$$\psi(x) = A\exp\left[\frac{\pm i2n(|l|+1)\pi x}{L}\right]\ (n = 1,2,3,\cdots).\tag{22}$$

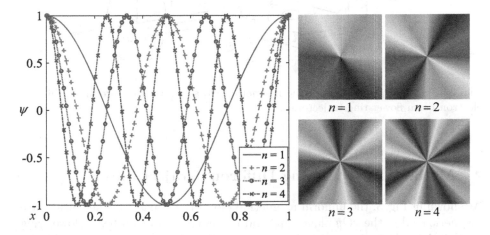

Fig. 2. Normalized ring standing wave function and quantum angular momentum formed by rotating lectrons.

Moreover, it is easy to know that $A = 1/\sqrt{L}$ from the normalization condition of the wave function $\int |\Psi(x,t)|^2\mathrm{d}x = 1$. It can be seen from Eq. (22) clearly that all solutions of the time-independent Schrödinger equation form standing waves of length L and are orthogonal to each other with the ring phase from 0 to $2n\pi$. In the polar coordinate system, the expression of Eq. (22) is $A\exp(in\varphi + in|l|\varphi)$ according to $x \approx \varphi/(2\pi)$. As shown in Fig. 2, when the wave functions of the electron are in states with different n and $l = 1$, the electron forms a standing wave with an integer multiple of n in the direction of electron motion. At the same time, the electron forms a spiral phase in the two-dimensional plane and has a quantization angular momentum $(n + |l|)\hbar$ along the z-axis.

Finally, the expression of the energy eigenvalue is:

$$E_n = \frac{\hbar^2}{2m}\left(\frac{2\pi n + 2\pi n\,|l|}{L}\right)^2 = \frac{2\pi^2(n + n\,|l|)^2\hbar^2}{mL^2}. \tag{23}$$

Besides, ψ_1 has the lowest energy, which is called the ground state, and the energy of the other excited states is proportional to the increasing of $(n + n\,|l|)^2$. When electrons radiate microwaves, there will be quantized angular momentum transitions in addition to the energy transitions from the electron to the microwave beam.

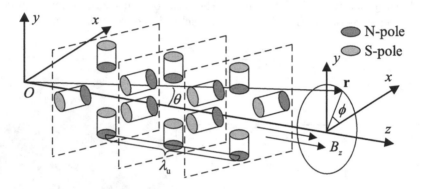

Fig. 3. The conceptual figure of the magnetic field structure that produces different electron beam flower ring trajectories.

4   Method of Generating Different Trajectories

As shown in Fig. 3, the uniform magnetic field of the z-axis and the spiral wave magnetic field in the xOy plane can produce different electron beam flower ring trajectories, which causes the electrons to radiate EM wave carrying OAM. It is assumed that the electron moves along the z-axis at the initial moment from the origin of the coordinate. The direction of the spatial undulating magnetic field is along the x-axis and the y-axis. The vertical components of the magnetic induction B_x and B_y are both the sine function related to the space, and the free electron initially moves along the z-axis. Moreover, the space period of the N-pole and S-pole magnet arrays is λ_u, and the number of the pole pairs is M. Hence, the expression of the magnetic field generated by the magnet arrays is

$$\mathbf{B} = \left\{B_0 \cos\left(\frac{2\pi z}{\lambda_u}\right), B_0 \sin\left(\frac{2\pi z}{\lambda_u}\right), B_z\right\}, \tag{24}$$

where B_0 is the maximum value of the sinusoidal magnetic field along the x-axis and y-axis. The magnetic field Lorentz force causes the free electrons to acquire acceleration and generate radiation, and it can be observed that the EM field generated by free electrons is along the positive direction of the z-axis. Since free electrons make a uniform circular motion in the uniform magnetic field of the z-axis, we consider the uniaxial undulating magnetic field firstly. Assuming $B_z = 0$, the equation of motion of moving electrons in the Cartesian coordinate system from Newton's second law can be written as follows:

$$\begin{cases} m\dot{v}_x = -qv_zB_0\sin\dfrac{2\pi z}{\lambda_u} \\[2mm] m\dot{v}_y = -qv_zB_0\cos\dfrac{2\pi z}{\lambda_u} \\[2mm] m\dot{v}_z = qv_xB_0\sin\dfrac{2\pi z}{\lambda_u} + qv_yB_0\cos\dfrac{2\pi z}{\lambda_u} \\[2mm] v_0^2 = v_x^2 + v_y^2 + v_z^2 \\[2mm] \dot{v}_x = \dfrac{dv_x}{dz}\cdot\dfrac{dz}{dt} = v_z\dfrac{dv_x}{dz}, \dot{v}_y = \dfrac{dv_y}{dz}\cdot\dfrac{dz}{dt} = v_z\dfrac{dv_y}{dz} \end{cases} \tag{25}$$

where v_*, $\dot{v}_*$ and v_0 denote the speed, acceleration of the electron at $*$-axis and the initial speed of the electron respectively. According to Eq. (25), the expression of the electron velocity can be solved as

$$\begin{cases} v_x = K_yv_0\cos\omega_0 t \\[2mm] v_y = K_xv_0\sin\omega_0 t \\[2mm] v_z = v_0\left[1 - \left(K_x^2 + K_y^2\right)/4 + \left(K_x^2 - K_y^2\right)/4\right]\cos 2\omega_0 t \\[2mm] K_x = K_y = K = \dfrac{q\lambda_uB_0}{2\pi mv_0} \end{cases} \tag{26}$$

where $\omega_0 \approx 2\pi v_0/\lambda_u$ denotes the angular frequency of radiated EM field, K_x and K_y denote the deflection parameters of the x-axis and y-axis. In addition, the average electron speed of the z-axis is $\bar{v}_z = v_0\left(1 - K^2/2\right)$, and the acceleration of the electron cyclotron motion is $a_0 \approx qB_0v_0/m = \omega_0^2R$, which means constructing a virtual magnetic field B_0 along the z-axis and R is the electron cyclotron radius in the virtual magnetic field. When there is only the spiral wave magnetic field in the xOy plane, the electrons are rotated by a spiral magnetic field that periodically changes in the horizontal and vertical directions, and a circular motion that rotates around the central axis of the magnetic field can generate circularly polarized EM wave.

Since the wavelength of the radiated EM wave is much larger than the radius of the electronic spiral motion along the z-axis, the number of magnets M is large, and the observation point is along the z-axis direction, and the angular momentum along the z-axis is invariant by the Lorentz transformation. The electron can be regarded as a circular motion and the distance of the z-axis movement can be ignored. When $B_z = lB_0$ and l take different integer values, the electrons can circulate around the z-axis in a double-center rotation mode and construct different flower ring trajectories projected on the xOy plane, which can radiate EM wave with different OAM modes.

Specifically, we can refer to the method mentioned in Ref. [9] to make the electrons with the whirling motion in the waveguide. The waveguide adopts the rotating TE_{mn} mode, and the OAM wave is radiated into the free space. The circularly polarized EM wave expression in the waveguide is as follows:

$$\begin{cases} E_r = -E_0 m J_m \left(kr \sin \theta \right) \exp \left[i \left(kz + m\phi - \omega t \right) \right] / \left(kr \sin \theta \right) \\ E_\theta = E_0 J'_m \left(kr \sin \theta \right) \exp \left[i \left(kz + m\phi - \omega t \right) \right] \\ B_r = E_0 k \cos \theta J'_m \left(kr \sin \theta \right) \exp \left[i \left(kz + m\phi - \omega t \right) \right] / \omega \\ B_\theta = -E_0 k \cos \theta m J_m \left(kr \sin \theta \right) \exp \left[i \left(kz + m\phi - \omega t \right) \right] / \left(kr\omega \sin \theta \right) \\ B_z = E_0 k \sin \theta J_m \left(kr \sin \theta \right) \exp \left[i \left(kz + m\phi - \omega t \right) \right] / \omega \end{cases} \quad (27)$$

where $J'_m (*)$ denotes the derivative of m-order first type Bessel function, m and n denote two quantum numbers indicating that the circular waveguides are independent of each other. It can be seen from the formula that the operating frequency ω of the waveguide is determined by the waveguide size and the quantum number. The total angular momentum of the waveguide operating mode is $m\hbar$, where the SAM is $\hbar$, and the OAM is $(m - 1)\hbar$. Therefore, the circular waveguide is a good medium for transmitting the high order OAM wave. Moreover, the OAM radiation and reception can be accomplished by means of a circular waveguide and two-dimensionally moving free electrons.

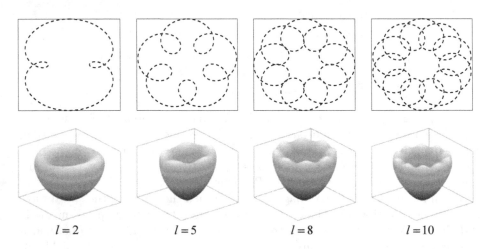

$l = 2$ $l = 5$ $l = 8$ $l = 10$

Fig. 4. Electron beams with different flower ring trajectories radiating the microwave with different OAM modes.

5   Example

As shown in Fig. 4, when each electron of the electron beam moves on a same trajectory, each electron generates a radiation field. When the electric fields generated by the electron beams are superposed on each other, EM wave of different OAM modes can be generated. In summary, by utilizing the two-dimensional motion characteristics of electrons and the superposition characteristics of multielectron radiation fields, it is possible to theoretically generate OAM microwaves of arbitrary modes, which can greatly expand the radiation freedom of antennas. On the contrary, it is also possible to use rotating electrons to detect OAM of a radiated EM field. Since OAM microwaves can directly transfer angular momentum to free electrons rather than the bound electrons of the antenna in the free space, which provides a method for directly detecting electric field strength and OAM for OAM microwave applications.

6   Discussion

By constructing an elaborately designed magnetic field structure, the electrons at the transmitting end have a bi-center rotation acceleration, and the electrons can rotate around the z-axis with different trajectories to radiate EM waves with different high-order OAMs. In order to receive the multiplexed OAM wave generated by the cyclotron electron, UCA can be used to demultiplex the OAM wave. However, the EM wave angular momentum that is mapped to two-dimensional moving electron beam angular momentum proposed in the paper provides a possible solution for directly detecting OAM wave.

Compared with the traditional OAM-MIMO system with the UCA or the SPP method [6,15,17], the proposed method in this paper can change the problem that the single antenna can not directly radiate the OAM wave. Specifically, the use of a helical magnetic field and electrons in the free space, as well as a waveguide system that conforms to the OAM mode for the OAM wave transmission can take advantage of OAM as a new dimension, not just as an additional degree of freedom of the MIMO system.

7   Conclusion

In this paper, we propose a new method for generating microwave beams carrying OAM with non-relativistic multi-electron flower ring trajectories and we can use the spiral wave magnetic field and the uniform magnetic field to generate different trajectories, which provides a new theoretical solution for existing microwave OAM applications. In the future, we may use superconducting quantum circuits or electron tubes to generate microwave beams carrying OAM experimentally. Furthermore, our work may be important for future mobile communications such as B5G and 6G.

References

1. Cohen-Tannoudji, C., Dupont-Roc, J., Grynberg, G.: Introduction to Quantum Electrodynamics. Wiley, Hoboken (1989)

2. Jackson, J.D.: Classical Electrodynamics. Wiley, New York (1999)
3. Beth, R.A.: Mechanical detection and measurement of the angular momentum of light. Phys. Rev. **50**, 115–125 (1936)
4. Zhang, C., Ma, L.: Millimetre wave with rotational orbital angular momentum. Sci. Rep. **6**, 31921 (2016)
5. Allen, L., Beijersbergen, M., Spreeuw, R., Woerdman, J.P.: Orbital angular momentum of light and transformation of Laguerre Gaussian laser modes. Phys. Rev. A **45**, 8185–8189 (1992)
6. Thidé, B., et al.: Utilization of photon orbital angular momentum in the low-frequency radio domain. Phys. Rev. Lett. **99**, 087701 (2007)
7. Chen, R., Xu, H., Moretti, M., Li, J.: Beam steering for the misalignment in UCA-based oam communication systems. IEEE Wirel. Commun. Lett. **7**(4), 582–585 (2018)
8. Asner, D.M., et al.: Single-electron detection and spectroscopy via relativistic cyclotron radiation. Phys. Rev. Lett. **114**, 162501 (2015)
9. Sawant, A., Choe, M.S., Thumm, M., Choi, E.: Orbital angular momentum (OAM) of rotating modes driven by electrons in electron cyclotron masers. Sci. Rep. **7**, 3372 (2017)
10. Molina, T., Torres, J.P., Torner, L.: Twisted photons. Nat. Phys. **3**, 305 (2007)
11. Bronzan, J.B., Low, F.E.: Selection rule for bosons. Phys. Rev. Lett. **12**, 522–523 (1964)
12. Katoh, M., et al.: Angular momentum of twisted radiation from an electron in spiral motion. Phys. Rev. Lett. **118**, 094801 (2017)
13. Katoh, M., et al.: Helical phase structure of radiation from an electron in circular motion. Sci. Rep. **7**, 6130 (2017)
14. Goldsmith, A.: Wireless Communications. Cambridge Univ. Press, Cambridge (2005)
15. Basar, E.: Orbital angular momentum with index modulation. IEEE Trans. Wirel. Commun. **17**(3), 2029–2037 (2018)
16. Zhang, C., Zhao, Y.: Orbital angular momentum nondegenerate index mapping for long distance transmission. IEEE Trans. Wirel. Commun. **18**, 5027–5036 (2019)
17. Wang, L., Ge, X., Zi, R., Wang, C.: Capacity analysis of orbital angular momentum wireless channels. IEEE Access **5**, 23069–23077 (2017)
18. Sun, B., Wang, G., Yang, W., Zheng, L.: Joint LDPC and physical layer network coding for two-way relay channels with different frequency offsets. In: 2015 10th International Conference on Communications and Networking in China (China-Com), pp. 692–696, August 2015
19. Elder, F.R., Gurewitsch, A.M., Langmuir, R.V., Pollock, H.C.: Radiation from electrons in a synchrotron. Phys. Rev. **71**, 829–830 (1947)
20. Boyer, T.H.: Diamagnetism of a free particle in classical electron theory with classical electromagnetic zero-point radiation. Phys. Rev. A **21**, 66–72 (1980)

MmWave-NOMA-Based Semi-persistent Scheduling for Enhanced V2X Services

Fanwei Shi[✉], Bicheng Wang, Ruoqi Shi, Jian Tang, and Jianling Hu

School of Electronic and Information Engineering, Soochow University, Suzhou, China
fwshi@qq.com, jlhu@suda.edu.cn

Abstract. This paper investigates the semi-persistent scheduling (SPS) strategy for enhanced vehicle-to-everything (eV2X) services, which aims to meet the low latency and high reliability (LLHR) demands. To increase available spectrum and improve resource utilization, millimeter wave (mmWave) and non-orthogonal multiple access (NOMA) are considered. We first formulate the optimization problem of scheduling and resource allocation to minimize the SPS period. To solve this problem, the LLHR power control algorithm is proposed to provide evaluation indicators for user scheduling. Then, the beam division and user clustering algorithm is designed to reduce the complexity of the matching between users and resource blocks. After that, the matching problem with peer effects is solved by the proposed union-based matching algorithm. Complexity analysis is presented, and simulation results show that the scheduling period of eV2X systems can be improved by the proposed SPS strategy compared with the conventional mmWave SPS schemes.

Keywords: NOMA · mmWave · eV2X · Hybrid precoding · Semi-persistent scheduling

1 Introduction

Intelligent transport system (ITS) has been one of the highly concerned transmission systems, since it can provide security, transport efficiency and energy conservation [1]. To meet the requirements of the fifth generation (5G) ITS, the 3rd generation partnership project (3GPP) has proposed the enhanced vehicle-to-everything (eV2X) networks [2], which contains two interfaces [3], i.e. PC5 interface for sidelink (SL) and Uu interface for downlink/uplink (DL/UL). A typical type of eV2X services, e.g. advanced driving, is called time-triggered service, since it has obvious periodicity. Semi-persistent scheduling (SPS) has been proven to be better for time-triggered services than dynamic scheduling (DS), since it can reduce the signaling overhead [4]. However, eV2X networks also require a higher data rate, e.g. Gbps, than before [5].

To handle this challenge, millimeter waves (mmWave), e.g. 30 GHz and 63 GHz [6], are considered for eV2X networks. The shorter wavelengths facilitate the deployment of large-scale antenna system, which can improve the beamforming gain [7]. Typically, to achieve a balance between radio frequency (RF)

© ICST Institute for Computer Sciences, Social Informatics and Telecommunications Engineering 2020
Published by Springer Nature Switzerland AG 2020. All Rights Reserved
H. Gao et al. (Eds.): ChinaCom 2019, LNICST 312, pp. 193–206, 2020.
https://doi.org/10.1007/978-3-030-41114-5_15

chain overhead and transmission performance, hybrid precoding is proposed for mmWave systems [8]. Many advantages do the mmWave V2X systems have, but they also suffer from several drawbacks. For instance, the Doppler effect causes carrier frequency offset (CFO) in V2X systems.

Benefit from the non-orthogonal nature in frequency domain, power-domain non-orthogonal multiple access (NOMA) has been considered to solve the problem of CFO and frequent handovers of mmWave cells caused by vehicle mobility [9,10]. Moreover, the pairing-based NOMA can achieve the spectral efficiency about 30% higher than orthogonal multiple access (OMA) with a given bandwidth [11], which facilitates the transmission of large packets. Specifically, [12] designed a joint precoding and dynamic power control schemes for mmWave-NOMA systems with lens antenna arrays; [13] and [14] investigated the user selection and power allocation scheme for mmWave-NOMA networks. However, the above solutions [12–14] are designed to maximize system throughput for conventional cellular networks. Different from them, the key performance indicator (KPI) of eV2X systems is considered to be latency [3]. Therefore, the low latency and high reliability (LLHR) eV2X networks need a novel design of mmWave-NOMA schemes.

Specifically, we design a mmWave-NOMA-based SPS scheme for DL. The existing researches like [15] were also directed at DL. Note that eV2X systems prefer to utilize the least number of RBs to serve all VUEs in coverage under the constraints of quality of service (QoS), which is different from the event-triggered services in conventional cellular systems. This view was also reflected in [16], where a centralized SPS strategy is designed for machine-type communications (MTC) to minimize the system bandwidth. Specially, for eV2X system, the minimization of SPS period is more flexible and reasonable, since the users have a uniform constraint of latency and realiability [3].

The rest of the paper is organized as follows. In Sect. 2, the system model is described and the SPS problem is formulated. In Sect. 3, the SPS strategy is designed and analyzed. Specifically, the LLHR power control (LLHR-PC) algorithm, the beam division and VUE clustering (BD&VC) algorithm, and union-based VUE-RB matching algorithm is proposed respectively. Finally, simulation results are presented in Sect. 4 and conclusions are drawn in Sect. 5.

2   System Model and Problem Formulation

2.1   Scenario Description

Figure 1 shows the considered mmWave-NOMA-based cellular eV2X system, where base station (BS) is equipped with M_{BS} transmit antennas and G_{BS} RF chains. Each VUE is equipped with single antenna. Each RF chain is connected to all antennas to form a fully connected structure [8].

The VUE set of the n-th cluster in the g-th beam is expressed as $\mathcal{N}_{g,n}$, which contains no more than two VUEs $V_{g,n}^i$, $i = 1, 2$ [18]. $|\mathcal{N}_{g,n}|$ represents the number of elements in the set $\mathcal{N}_{g,n}$. Hence, $|\mathcal{N}_{g,n}| \leq 2$ and $\mathcal{N}_{g,n} \cap \mathcal{N}_{g',n'} = \phi$ for $|g - g'| + |n - n'| \neq 0$. An adaptive NOMA/OMA clustering is considered

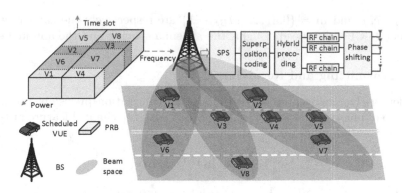

Fig. 1. System model of Cellular V2X transmission.

in this system, since one beam may have an odd number of VUEs. Specifically, NOMA is adopted when $|\mathcal{N}_{g,n}| = 2$, while OMA is adopted when $|\mathcal{N}_{g,n}| = 1$. Without loss of generality, assume that the channel gain of $V_{g,n}^1$ is stronger than $V_{g,n}^2$. The cluster set of the g-th beam is expressed as $\mathcal{N}_g$, which satisfies $|\mathcal{N}_g| = \lceil (\sum_n |\mathcal{N}_{g,n}|)/2 \rceil$. Hence, the number of VUEs and the number of clusters are respectively $U = \sum_{g=1}^{G_D} \sum_{n=1}^{|\mathcal{N}_g|} |\mathcal{N}_{g,n}|$ and $|\mathcal{N}| = \sum_{g=1}^{G_D} |\mathcal{N}_g|$, where G_D is the number of formed beams, $G_D \leq G_{BS}$.

Particularly, the bandwidth of each RB is defined as the DL aggregate system bandwidth ω, and the width of time slot is τ_{RB}. One SPS period requires K time slots to finish the transmission of packets under the QoS constraints, i.e., the SPS period is $K\tau_{RB}$.

2.2 Channel Model

We adopt the channel model widely used in mmWave systems [12–15]. The channel vector of $V_{g,n}^i$ is

$$\mathbf{h}_{g,n}^i = \sqrt{M_{BS}} \sum_{l=1}^{L} \beta_{g,n,l}^i \mathbf{a}\left(\phi_{g,n}^i\right), \tag{1}$$

where L is the number of paths from BS to each VUE. $\beta_{g,n,l}^i$ is the complex Gaussian gain of $V_{g,n}^i$ in the l-th path, and $\beta_{g,n,l}^i \sim \mathcal{CN}(0, \ell_{g,n,l}^i)$. $\ell_{g,n,l}^i$ is the average path loss from BS to $V_{g,n}^i$. Considering the mobility of VUEs, we have $\ell_{g,n,l}^i = |\mathbf{d}_{g,n}^i + \mathbf{v}_{g,n}^i t_w|^{-\eta_l}$, where $\mathbf{d}_{g,n}^i$ and $\mathbf{v}_{g,n}^i$ are the displacement vector and relative velocity between BS and $V_{g,n}^i$, respectively. t_w is the waiting interval, and the maximum can be $t_w = K\tau_{RB}$. η_l is the path loss exponent of the l-th path.

$\mathbf{a}(\phi_{g,n}^i)$ represents the array steering vector, and $\phi_{g,n}^i$ represents the azimuth angle of departure (AoD). Particularly, the uniform linear array (ULA) is adopted, and $\mathbf{a}(\phi_{g,n}^i)$ can be expressed as

$$\mathbf{a}(\phi_{g,n}^i) = M_{BS}^{-\frac{1}{2}} [e^{\frac{j2\pi \mathbf{m} f_c d \sin(\phi_{g,n}^i)}{c}}]^T, \tag{2}$$

where f_c, c, d and $\mathbf{m} = \{0, 1, \ldots, M_{BS} - 1\}$ are respectively the carrier center frequency (CCF), the speed of light, the antenna spacing and the antenna set.

2.3 Transmitting and Receiving

Considering the analog precoder with B bits quantization precision, the minimum step of phase shifter is $2^{1-B}\pi$. Combined with the channel feature of ULA, the analog precoding vector $\mathbf{w}_g^a$ satisfies

$$\mathbf{w}_g^a \in \mathcal{W}^a = \left[\mathbf{a}\left(2^{1-B}\pi\mathbf{b}\right)\right], \tag{3}$$

where $\mathbf{b} = \{0, 1, \ldots, 2^B - 1\}$ represent phase shift set, and $\mathbf{w}_g^a$ is the analog precoding vector of the g-th beam. Hence, the analog precoding matrix can be expressed as

$$\mathbf{W}^a = \left[\mathbf{w}_1^a, \mathbf{w}_2^a, \ldots, \mathbf{w}_{G_D}^a\right]. \tag{4}$$

Then, the digital precoding vector $\mathbf{w}_{g,n}^i$ of $V_{g,n}^i$ is calculated. The adopted zero-forcing digital precoding scheme is given by

$$\tilde{\mathbf{W}}^d = (\mathbf{W}^a)^H \mathbf{H}\left(\mathbf{H}^H \mathbf{W}^a (\mathbf{W}^a)^H \mathbf{H}\right)^{-1}, \tag{5}$$

where the channel matrix is $\mathbf{H} = [\mathbf{h}_{1,1}^1, \ldots, \mathbf{h}_{2,1}^1, \ldots]$, containing the channel vectors of all VUEs. The digital precoding matrix is $\tilde{\mathbf{W}}^d = [\tilde{\mathbf{w}}_{1,1}^1, \ldots, \tilde{\mathbf{w}}_{2,1}^1, \ldots]$. After normalization, $\mathbf{w}_{g,n}^i$ can be expressed as

$$\mathbf{w}_{g,n}^i = \tilde{\mathbf{w}}_{g,n}^i / \left\|\tilde{\mathbf{w}}_{g,n}^i\right\|. \tag{6}$$

To facilitate the expression of signal, we define a scheduling indicator $\theta_{g,n}^k$ for the VUEs in $\mathcal{N}_{g,n}$, where

$$\theta_{g,n}^k = \begin{cases} 1, & \text{if } \mathcal{N}_{g,n} \text{ is scheduled in the k - th PRB,} \\ 0, & \text{otherwise.} \end{cases} \tag{7}$$

Then, the received signal of $V_{g,n}^i$ in the k-th RB can be expressed as

$$y_{g,n}^{i(k)} = \sqrt{P_t}\bar{\mathbf{h}}_{g,n}^i \sum_{x=1}^{G_D} \sum_{y=1}^{|\mathcal{N}_x|} \sum_{z=1}^{|\mathcal{N}_{x,y}|} \mathbf{w}_{x,y}^z \sqrt{\theta_{x,y}^k \alpha_{x,y}^z} x_{x,y}^z + v_{g,n}^i, \tag{8}$$

where $\bar{\mathbf{h}}_{g,n}^i = (\mathbf{h}_{g,n}^i)^H \mathbf{W}^a$. P_t represents the transmit power, and $v_{g,n}^i$ represents the additive noise with a power spectral density of σ_v. $\alpha_{g,n}^i$ is the power allocation factor, which satisfies

$$\sum_{g=1}^{G_D} \sum_{n=1}^{|\mathcal{N}_g|} \sum_{i=1}^{|\mathcal{N}_{g,n}|} \theta_{g,n}^k \alpha_{g,n}^i \leq 1, \tag{9}$$

where $k \in \{1, 2, \ldots K\}$. Minimum mean square error - successive interference cancellation (MMSE-SIC) is adopted to decode the received signal [11], where the mean square error (MSE) is given by

$$e_{g,n}^i = E[||\rho_{g,n}^i y_{g,n}^{i(k)} - \theta_{g,n}^k x_{g,n}^i||^2]. \tag{10}$$

$\rho_{g,n}^i$ represents the channel equalization coefficient (CEC) of $V_{g,n}^i$, and we assume $E\left[||x_{g,n}^i||^2\right] = 1$.

2.4   SPS Problem Formulation

The spectral efficiency for $V_{g,n}^i$ to transmit a packet of $L_{g,n}^i$ bytes is given by

$$\bar{R}_{g,n}^i = 8 \ln 2 \cdot \frac{L_{g,n}^i}{\tau_{RB}\omega}, \tag{11}$$

where nature unit is utilized as the unit of data to simplify calculations, and thus, the unit of $\bar{R}_{g,n}^i$ is $nats/(s \cdot Hz)$.

According to (8), the signal to interference plus noise ratio (SINR) of $V_{g,n}^i$ can be expressed as

$$\gamma_{g,n}^i = \frac{||\bar{\mathbf{h}}_{g,n}^i \mathbf{w}_{g,n}^i||^2 \theta_{g,n}^k \alpha_{g,n}^i P_{BS}}{P_t \sum\limits_{x \neq g} \sum\limits_{y=1}^{|\mathcal{N}_x|} \sum\limits_{z=1}^{|\mathcal{N}_{g,n}|} ||\bar{\mathbf{h}}_{g,n}^i \mathbf{w}_{x,y}^z||^2 \theta_{x,y}^k \alpha_{x,y}^z + \xi_{g,n}^i + \sigma_v^2}, \tag{12}$$

where $\xi_{g,n}^i$ represents the intra-beam interference. Since the clusters in the same beam cannot be multiplexed in the same RB, $\xi_{g,n}^i$ is also the intra-cluster interference, where

$$\xi_{g,n}^i = \begin{cases} P_t ||\bar{\mathbf{h}}_{g,n}^{(1)} \mathbf{w}_{g,n}^i||^2 \theta_{g,n}^k \alpha_{g,n}^{(1)}, & \text{if } |\mathcal{N}_{g,n}| = 2, \ i = 2, \\ 0, & \text{otherwise.} \end{cases} \tag{13}$$

Then, the achievable spectral efficiency of $V_{g,n}^i$ is

$$R_{g,n}^i = \ln(1 + \gamma_{g,n}^i). \tag{14}$$

Since latency is the goal of optimization, the QoS constraints are mostly concerned with reliability. In this paper, PRR is utilized to describe reliability [6], which is given by

$$\delta_{g,n}^i = (1 + e^{-\mu(R_{g,n}^i - \bar{R}_{g,n}^i)})^{-1} \geq \delta_{th}, \tag{15}$$

where μ is the slope parameter [1], and δ_{th} represents the threshold of reliability in one SPS period.

Based on the above model, the time-frequency resource allocation and power control problem of the BS in one SPS period can then be formulated as,

$$\min_{\{\theta_{g,n}^k\}, \{\alpha_{g,n}^i\}} K\tau_{RB}, \tag{16}$$

s.t. (9), (15),

$$\alpha_{g,n}^i \geq 0, \forall 1 \leq g \leq G_D, 1 \leq n \leq |\mathcal{N}_g|, 1 \leq i \leq |\mathcal{N}_{g,n}|, \tag{16a}$$

$$\sum_{k=1}^{K} \theta_{g,n}^k = 1, \forall 1 \leq g \leq G_D, 1 \leq n \leq |\mathcal{N}_g|, \tag{16b}$$

$$\sum_{n=1}^{|\mathcal{N}_g|} \theta_{g,n}^k \leq 1, \forall 1 \leq g \leq G_D, 1 \leq k \leq K. \tag{16c}$$

The constraints of transmit power and QoS are described in constraints (9), (16a) and (15). Constraint (16b) represents that each cluster in each beam is scheduled once and only once in one SPS period, and thus, $\sum_{g=1}^{G_D} \sum_{n=1}^{|\mathcal{N}_g|} \sum_{k=1}^{K} \theta_{g,n}^k = |\mathcal{N}|$. The constraint (16c) represents that no more than one VUE in the same beam is scheduled in the same time slot.

As is shown in problem (16), the multiplexing in power domain and spatial domain increases the complexity. Hence, we split problem (16) into a power control process and a VUE-RB matching process, and design an iterative algorithm to solve the joint optimization problem of $\{\theta_{g,n}^k\}$ and $\{\alpha_{g,n}^i\}$.

3   MmWave-NOMA-Based SPS Strategy

3.1   Optimal LLHR Power Control

The premise of performing power control is that we have known the VUE-RB matching result, i.e., $\{\theta_{g,n}^k\}$ is determined. Hence, a temporary period $K_{T_{RB}}$ is also known. For the k-th time slot, this sub-problem can be described as

$$\max_{\{\alpha_{g,n}^i\}} \min_{\{g,n,i\} \in \Gamma_k} \delta_{g,n}^i, \tag{17}$$

$$s.t. \alpha_{g,n}^i \geq 0, \tag{17a}$$

$$\sum_{g=1}^{G_D} \sum_{n=1}^{|\mathcal{N}_g|} \sum_{i=1}^{|\mathcal{N}_{g,n}|} \theta_{g,n}^k \alpha_{g,n}^i \leq 1, \tag{17b}$$

where $\Gamma_k = \{g, n, i | \theta_{g,n}^k = 1, V_{g,n}^i \in \mathcal{N}_{g,n}\}$ represents the VUE set scheduled in the k-th time slot. The power constraint in the k-th time slot is shown in (17a) and (17b). Additionally, if the result $\{\alpha_{g,n}^i\}$ satisfies constraint (15), it can be one of the feasible solutions to problem (16), and thus, we can try to schedule another cluster in the k-th time slot to shorten SPS period, until constrain (15) cannot be satisfied.

According to (10), a MSE is generated when the received signal of $V_{g,n}^i$ is decoded by MMSE-SIC, which can be expressed as

$$e_{g,n}^i = |\rho_{g,n}^i \sqrt{P_t \theta_{g,n}^k \alpha_{g,n}^i} \bar{\mathbf{h}}_{g,n}^i \mathbf{w}_{g,n}^i - \theta_{g,n}^k|^2 + |\rho_{g,n}^i|^2 \varsigma_{g,n}^i, \tag{18}$$

where $\varsigma_{g,n}^i$ contains the intra-beam interference, the inter-beam interference and the additive noise. $\varsigma_{g,n}^i$ is formulated as

$$\varsigma_{g,n}^i = P_t \sum_{x \neq g}^{|\mathcal{N}_x|} \sum_{y=1} \theta_{x,y}^k \sum_{z=1}^{|\mathcal{N}_{g,n}|} ||\bar{\mathbf{h}}_{g,n}^i \mathbf{w}_{x,y}^z||^2 \alpha_{x,y}^z + \xi_{g,n}^i + \sigma_v^2. \tag{19}$$

By deriving $e_{g,n}^i$ with respect to $\rho_{g,n}^i$, we can get the optimal CEC when the minimum MSE is obtained,

$$\rho_{g,n}^i = 1 - \varsigma_{g,n}^i (\sqrt{P_t \theta_{g,n}^k \alpha_{g,n}^i} \bar{\mathbf{h}}_{g,n}^i \mathbf{w}_{g,n}^i + \varsigma_{g,n}^i)^{-1}. \tag{20}$$

At this point, the MSE can be formulated as

$$E_{g,n}^i = \min_{\rho_{g,n}^i} e_{g,n}^i = \varsigma_{g,n}^i (\sqrt{P_t \theta_{g,n}^k \alpha_{g,n}^i} \bar{\mathbf{h}}_{g,n}^i \mathbf{w}_{g,n}^i + \varsigma_{g,n}^i)^{-1}. \tag{21}$$

According to (21) and (14), $R_{g,n}^i = -\min_{\rho_{g,n}^i} \ln e_{g,n}^i$. Substituting it into the objective function of problem (17), we have

$$\delta_{g,n}^i = \max_{\rho_{g,n}^i} \frac{1}{1 + e^{\mu \bar{R}_{g,n}^i} (e_{g,n}^i)^\mu}. \tag{22}$$

However, the objective function of problem (17) is still non-convex with respect to $\{\alpha_{g,n}^i\}$. Hence, we then convert it into a convex problem. According to (22) and (15), we have

$$\max_{\rho_{g,n}^i} \frac{1}{1 + e^{\mu \bar{R}_{g,n}^i} (e_{g,n}^i)^\mu} \geq \delta_{th}, \tag{23}$$

Note that according to (20), the optimal CEC can be uniquely determined by $\{\alpha_{g,n}^i\}$ after $\{\theta_{g,n}^k\}$ is given. Therefore, constraint (15) can be formulated as

$$\varsigma_{g,n}^i - [e^{-\mu \bar{R}_{g,n}^i} (\tilde{\delta}_{th}^{-1} - 1)]^{\frac{1}{\mu}} (\sqrt{P_t \theta_{g,n}^k \alpha_{g,n}^i} \bar{\mathbf{h}}_{g,n}^i \mathbf{w}_{g,n}^i + \varsigma_{g,n}^i) \leq 0, \tag{24}$$

where $\tilde{\delta}_{th}$ is the PRR threshold of the current round in LLHR-PC algorithm. Then, problem (17) can be transferred into the following form,

$$\min_{\{\alpha_{g,n}^i\}} \sum_{g=1}^{G_D} \sum_{n=1}^{|\mathcal{N}_g|} \sum_{i=1}^{|\mathcal{N}_{g,n}|} \theta_{g,n}^k \alpha_{g,n}^i, \tag{25}$$

$$s.t.(17a), (24).$$

In the proposed LLHR-PC algorithm shown in Algorithm 1, the optimal power allocation $\{\alpha_{g,n}^i\}$ is calculated for the k-th time slot. If the solution to problem (25) cannot satisfy constraint (17b) when $\tilde{\delta}_{th} = \delta_{th}$, the current matching $\{\theta_{g,n}^k\}$ is proven to be infeasible. Otherwise, we have $\tilde{\delta}_{th} \in [\delta_{th}, 1)$. In each round, a temporary PRR threshold $\tilde{\delta}_{th}$, is utilized to calculate $\{\alpha_{g,n}^i\}$, until the search space of $\tilde{\delta}_{th}$ is limited to ε_δ.

Algorithm 1. Proposed LLHR-PC Algorithm

Require: $\{\theta_{g,n}^k\}$ of the k-th time slot.
Ensure: $\{\alpha_{g,n}^i\}$, δ_{LB}.
 1: Init. $\delta_{LB} = \delta_{th}$, $\delta_{UB} = 1$, $\tilde{\delta}_{th} = \delta_{LB}$;
 2: Solve problem (25);
 3: **if** $\sum_{g=1}^{G_D} \sum_{n=1}^{|\mathcal{N}_g|} \sum_{i=1}^{|\mathcal{N}_{g,n}|} \theta_{g,n}^k \alpha_{g,n}^i > 1$ or (25) is infeasible **then**
 4:    $\{\theta_{g,n}^k\}$ is infeasible;
 5: **else**
 6:    **while** $\delta_{UB} - \delta_{LB} \geq \varepsilon_\delta$ **do**
 7:       $\tilde{\delta}_{th} = (\delta_{DB} + \delta_{UB})/2$ and solve problem (25);
 8:       **if** $\sum_{g=1}^{G_D} \sum_{n=1}^{|\mathcal{N}_g|} \sum_{i=1}^{|\mathcal{N}_{g,n}|} \theta_{g,n}^k \alpha_{g,n}^i \leq 1$ **then**
 9:          $\delta_{LB} = \tilde{\delta}_{th}$ and record $\{\alpha_{g,n}^i\}$;
10:       **else**
11:          $\delta_{UB} = \tilde{\delta}_{th}$;

3.2 Union-Based VUE-RB Matching

The following matching problem is formed and analyzed to calculate both $\{\theta_{g,n}^k\}$ and $\{\alpha_{g,n}^i\}$. Use two disjoint sets of V and F to respectively represent U VUEs and K RBs in an eV2X system, where $V = \{v_1, v_2, \ldots, v_U\}$, $F = \{f_1, f_2, \ldots, f_K\}$. The matching problem with respect to V and F can be described as follows.

Definition 1. A matching Ψ is a mapping from the set $V \cup F$ to the set $V \cup F$, where (1) $\Psi(v_i) \in F \cup \{v_i\}$; (2) $\Psi(f_k) \subset V \cup \{f_k\}$; (3) $\Psi(v_u) = f_k \Leftrightarrow v_u \in \Psi(f_k)$;

Condition (1) implies that each VUE is scheduled in no more than one RB, i.e., $|\Psi(v_i)| = 1$ and $|\Psi(v_i) \cap F| \leq 1$, while condition (2) implies that each RB can serve several VUEs. Condition (3) indicates that the mapping between v_k and f_k is symmetrical. Specially, $\Psi(j) = \{j\}$ happens when there is no other matching for element j. Note that if $\exists j \in V \cup F$ such that $\Psi(j) = \{j\}$, the current matching Ψ will be infeasible.

When $\Psi(v_u) = \Psi\left(v_u'\right) = f_k$ and $v_u, v_u' \in V$, the co-channel interference will occur between v_u and v_u'. Since the co-channel interference can be intra-beam or inter-beam, Ψ suffers from more complex peer effects compared with the existing matching problem [4]. Hence, the preference $\mathcal{R}$ is formed to helps players search for other players by interesting.

Definition 2. For two sets of VUEs $V^i, V^j \subseteq V$, $\mathcal{R}\left(V^i f_k V^j\right)$ represents that f_k prefers V^i than V^j, while for two sets of RBs $f_i, f_j \in F$, $\mathcal{R}\left(f_i v_u f_j\right)$ represents that v_u prefers f_i than f_j, which can be formulated as

$$\mathcal{R}\left(V^i f_k V^j\right) \Leftrightarrow \tilde{\delta}_{th}\left(f_k, V^i\right) > \tilde{\delta}_{th}\left(f_k, V^j\right), \tag{26}$$

$$\mathcal{R}\left(f_i v_u f_j\right) \Leftrightarrow \min\{\tilde{\delta}_{th}(f_i, \Psi(f_i) \cup v_u), \tilde{\delta}_{th}(f_j, \Psi(f_j)\}$$
$$> \min\{\tilde{\delta}_{th}(f_i, \Psi(f_i)), \tilde{\delta}_{th}(f_j, \Psi(f_j) \cup v_u\}$$

(27)

Note that the preference is transitive, and thus, a preference list can be formed by (26) and (27). A feasible Ψ should satisfies that for $\forall v_u \in V$ and $\forall f_k \in F$, $\mathcal{R}\left(\Psi\left(f_k\right) f_k \{f_k\}\right)$ and $\mathcal{R}\left(\Psi\left(v_u\right) v_u \{v_u\}\right)$ are always established. Additionally, if v_u and v'_u are in the same beam, v'_u can replace the position of v_u in the RB. Such a relationship is called alternative.

Algorithm 2. Proposed BD&VC Algorithm

Require: $\mathcal{W}^a$; VUE set V; $\mathbf{h}_u$, $u \in \{1, 2, \ldots, U\}$.
Ensure: Cluster set $\mathcal{N}$; G_D; $\mathbf{W}^a$; $\{\mathbf{w}^i_{g,n}\}$.
1: Init. VUE set in each beam $\Gamma = \{\Gamma_1, \Gamma_2, \ldots, \Gamma_{G_{BS}}\}$, where $\Gamma_x = \varnothing$ for $x \in \{1, 2, \ldots, G_{BS}\}$; $\mathbf{W}^a = \varnothing$;
2: **for all** $u \in U$ **do**
3: $\quad g = \arg \max\limits_{x \in G_{BS}} \left\{ \frac{\|\mathbf{h}_u^H \mathbf{w}_x^a\|}{\|\mathbf{h}_u\| \|\mathbf{w}_x^a\|} \right\}$; $\Gamma_g = \Gamma_g \cup v_u$;
4: $\mathbf{G} = \{x | \Gamma_x \neq \varnothing, 1 \leq x \leq G_{BS}\}$;
5: $G_D = |\mathbf{G}|$ and $\mathbf{W}_a = \bigcup\limits_{g \in \mathbf{G}} \mathbf{w}_g^a$;
6: **for all** $g \in \mathbf{G}$ **do**
7: $\quad \mathrm{H} = \left\{ \|\mathbf{h}_x^H \mathbf{W}_g^a\|^2 | v_x \in \Gamma_g \right\}$;
8: $\quad [\sim, \Lambda] = sort(\mathbf{H}, 'descend')$;
9: $\quad$ **if** $|\Gamma_g|$ is odd **then**
10: $\qquad V^1_{g,i} = \Lambda\left(i\right)$, $V^2_{g,i} = \Lambda[i + \frac{|\Gamma_g| - 1}{2}]$ for $1 \leq i \leq \frac{|\Gamma_g| - 1}{2}$;
11: $\qquad V^1_{g, \frac{|\Gamma_g| + 1}{2}} = \Lambda\left(|\Gamma_g|\right)$;
12: $\quad$ **else**
13: $\qquad V^1_{g,i} = \Lambda\left(i\right)$, $V^2_{g,i} = \Lambda[\frac{i + |\Gamma_g|}{2}]$ for $1 \leq i \leq \frac{|\Gamma_g|}{2}$;
14: $\quad$ Calculate $\mathbf{w}^i_{g,n}$ according to (6);

Based on the above discussion, the union-based VUE-RB matching algorithm is proposed, including clustering phase and matching phase. In Algorithm 2, BD&VC algorithm is proposed for clustering phase, where each VUE is sequentially allocated to the optimal analog beam according to channel correlation. Specially, $\mathbf{w}_g^a$ may not be matched with VUEs. Considering the overhead of the digital precoder, such $\mathbf{w}_g^a$ is deleted by $\mathbf{w}_g^a$ to decrease G_D. The quantization precision of the analog precoder is set as $B = \lfloor \log_2(G_{BS}) \rfloor$ to ensure that $G_D \leq G_{BS}$ can always be satisfied [17]. Then, to make the VUEs in the same NOMA cluster have a certain difference of channel gain [18], VUEs is sorted according to path loss.

Remark 1. BD&VC algorithm has the polynomial complexity. Specifically, the maximum complexity is $\mathcal{O}\left(G_{BS}U\right)$ from step 2 to 3, while the maximum complexity is $\mathcal{O}(\sum\limits_{g=1}^{G_{BS}} |\Gamma_g| \log |\Gamma_g|) \leq \mathcal{O}\left(G_{BS}U \log U\right)$ from step 6 to 14.

Cluster-RB matching has compatible definitions and properties with VUE-RB matching. Specifically, for Ψ, the VUE set $V = \{v_1, v_2, \ldots, v_U\}$ can be represented by the cluster set $\mathcal{N} = \{\mathcal{N}_{1,1}, \mathcal{N}_{1,2}, \ldots, \mathcal{N}_{g,n}, \ldots, \mathcal{N}_{G_D, |\mathcal{N}_{G_D}|}\}$.

Algorithm 3 describes the propsosed matching algorithm. In clustering phase, a series of minimal unions are formed by BD&VC algorithm, where the prior knowledge for matching, i.e. alternative and preference, is obtained. In matching phase, the largest stable unions in each RB are formed. Specifically, considering constraint (16c) and the multiplexing ability, a suitable cluster $\mathcal{N}_{g,n}$ is selected. Then, alternative and preference are utilized for f_k to update $\Psi(f_k)$, until $(f_k, \Psi(f_k))$ cannot be blocked by any cluster. At this point, $\Psi(f_k)$ is regarded as the current largest stable union of f_k. Finally, the matching phase terminates when all VUEs are scheduled.

Algorithm 3. Union-based VUE-RB Matching Algorithm

Require: The input in **Algorithm 2**; threshold δ_{th}.
Ensure: SPS period $K\tau_{RB}$; $\{\theta_{g,n}^k\}$; $\{\alpha_{g,n}^i\}$.
 1: Init. $\Psi = \varnothing$; $k = 0$;
 2: Run BD&VC algorithm;
 3: **repeat**
 4:     $c = 1$ and $k = k + 1$;
 5:     $g = \arg \max\limits_{l \in G_D} (|\mathcal{N}| - \sum\limits_{i=1}^{k} \sum\limits_{j=1}^{|N_l|} \theta_{l,j}^i)$;
 6:     $n = \arg \max\limits_{j \in |\mathcal{N}_g|} \|\mathbf{h}_{g,j}^1\|^2$;
 7:     $\Psi(f_k) = \Psi(f_k) \cup \mathcal{N}_{g,n}$ and $\Psi(\mathcal{N}_{g,n}) = f_k$;
 8:     **repeat**
 9:         Form $\mathcal{R}$ for $\{\mathcal{N}_{g,n} | \Psi(\mathcal{N}_{g,n}) == \mathcal{N}_{g,n}, \mathcal{N}_{g,n} \in \mathcal{N}\}$ to find the most preferred $\mathcal{N}_{g',n'}$ for $(f_k, \Psi(f_k))$;
10:         **if** $\delta_{th}(f_k, \Psi(f_k) \cup \{\mathcal{N}_{g',n'}\}) < \delta_{th}$ or problem (26) is infeasible **then**
11:             $c = 0$;
12:         **else**
13:             $\Psi(f_k) = \Psi(f_k) \cup \mathcal{N}_{g',n'}$ and $\Psi(\mathcal{N}_{g',n'}) = f_k$;
14:             Update $\{\theta_{g,n}^k\}$, then record $\{\alpha_{g,n}^i\}$ and $\tilde{\delta}_{th}$ for f_k;
15:     **until** $c == 0$
16:     **if** $k > 1$ **then**
17:         $[\sim, ind] = \min \left\{ \tilde{\delta}_{th}^1, \tilde{\delta}_{th}^2, \ldots, \tilde{\delta}_{th}^{k-1} \right\}$;
18:         Find the alternative-pair set $\{(\mathcal{N}_{g,n}, \mathcal{N}_{g,n'})\}$, where $\mathcal{N}_{g,n} \in \Psi(f_k)$, $\mathcal{N}_{g,n'} \in \Psi(f_{ind})$, $ind < k$;
19:         Judge for alternative pairs according to (28);
20: **until** $\forall v_u \in V, \Psi(v_u) \neq \{v_u\}$

3.3   Performance Analysis

In Algorithm 3, the number of proposals for unscheduled clusters is $N_1^k \leq \frac{1}{2}[(|N| - \sum_{i=1}^{k-1} |\Psi(f_i)|)^2 + |N| - \sum_{i=1}^{k-1} |\Psi(f_i)|] \leq \frac{|N|^2 + |N|}{2}$, while the number of proposals for scheduled clusters is $N_2^k \leq |\Psi(f_k)| \leq |\mathcal{N}|$. Hence, the upper bound of proposals for f_k can be expressed as

$$N_1^k + N_2^k \leq \max_{n=1,2,\ldots,|\mathcal{N}|} \{\frac{1}{2}(|\mathcal{N}| - n)^2 + \frac{1}{2}(|\mathcal{N}| - n) + n\}$$
$$\leq \frac{1}{2}|\mathcal{N}|^2 - \frac{1}{2}|\mathcal{N}| + 1. \tag{28}$$

For each proposal, $\mathcal{R}$ is formed by LLHR-PC algorithm, where the binary search is utilized. Hence, the number of searches to initiate a proposal is

$$|\mathcal{N}|(1 + \log\frac{1 - \delta_{th}}{\varepsilon_\delta}) \leq U(1 + \log\frac{1 - \delta_{th}}{\varepsilon_\delta}). \tag{29}$$

Combining with the complexity of BD&VC algorithm, the complexity of Union-based VUE-RB Matching Algorithm is

$$\mathcal{O}(G_{BS}U \log U) + \mathcal{O}(|\mathcal{N}|(1 + \log\frac{1 - \delta_{th}}{\varepsilon_\delta})K \sum_{k=1}^{K}(N_1^k + N_2^k))$$
$$= \mathcal{O}(U \log U) + \mathcal{O}(|\mathcal{N}|^3). \tag{30}$$

4   Simulation Results

The performance in terms of SPS period of the mmWave-NOMA-based SPS strategy proposed in this paper is evaluated by simulations. For comparison, we consider the following five typical schemes to respectively show the performance of resource allocation, multiplexing, precoding: (1) "Greedy VUE-RB Matching", where LLHR-PC and BD&VC are also utilized, while VUEs and RBs are matched greedily until all VUEs can meet the QoS constraints in one SPS period [4]; (2) "Hybrid Precoding (HP) OMA", where the scheduling strategy is similar to the proposed scheme, but all VUEs are orthogonal in power domain.; (3) "Fully Analog Precoding (FAP) NOMA" [14], where only (4) is utilized for precoding; (4) "Strong user (SU) based HP NOMA" [17,18], where the HP scheme is similar to the proposed one, while the digital precoding vectors are calculated according to the normalized channel vectors of SU; (5) "Weak user (WU) based HP NOMA", where the digital precoding vectors are calculated according to the normalized channel vectors of WU.

Specifically, the simulation parameters are described as follows. CCF is set as $f_c = 63\,\text{GHz}$, and the aggregated system bandwidth is $\omega = 1\,\text{GHz}$ [6]. For the transmitting process, $P_t = 43\,\text{dBm}$, $\sigma_v = -174\,\text{dbm/Hz}$, $M_{BS} = 64$ and $G_{BS} = 16$. For $V_{g,n}^i$, the channel vector is generated by (1), where we assume the number of paths is $L = 3$, including the line-of-sight (LoS) path with the path loss exponent $\eta_1 = 4$ and the non-line-of-sight (NLoS) paths with $\eta_2 = \eta_3 = 5$. PRR is calculated by (15), where we assume: the slope parameter $\mu = 8$, the size of packets $L_{g,n}^i = 1200$ bytes, short time slot $\tau_{RB} = 1/14\,\text{ms}$ [19]. Moreover, the road configuration for unban grid discussed in this paper is presented in

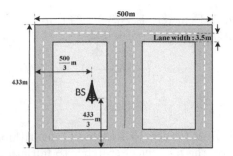

Fig. 2. Road configuration for urban grid.

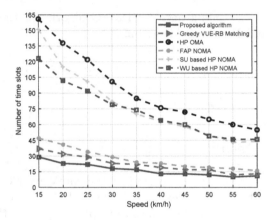

Fig. 3. Number of time slots in one SPS period against speed of vehicles.

Fig. 2 according to 3GPP eV2X systems defined in [6], where the car distance is $|\mathbf{v}_{g,n}^i| \times 2.5\,\mathrm{s}$ [4].

Figure 3 shows number of time slots in one SPS period against speed of vehicles from 15 km/h to 60 km/h. The packet of $v_{g,n}^i$ is successfully received only when $\delta_{g,n}^i \geq 99\%$. The density of VUE decreases when the speed increases, and thus, there are fewer clusters, leading to a shortening of SPS period. Moreover, it is intuitive that the proposed strategy works better than other five schemes, especially in a dense network.

Figure 4 shows SPS period, i.e. $K\tau_{RB}$, against PRR threshold from 80% to 99.999%, where the speed is 30 km/h. The SPS period increases as threshold increases. For "Greedy VUE-RB Matching" and "FAP NOMA" as well as the proposed algorithm, the systems can achieve a very short period when threshold is low. However, the period of "FAP NOMA" increases rapidly as threshold increases, since its space division multiplexing ability is limited. Additionally, the proposed algorithm always outperforms "Greedy VUE-RB Matching", since the properties of preference are utilized.

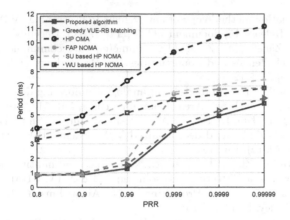

Fig. 4. SPS period against PRR threshold.

5 Conclusions

In this paper, we studied the SPS strategy in mmWave-NOMA-based eV2X systems, including hybrid precoding, user scheduling and resource allocation. The VUE-RB matching problem with peer effects was solved by the proposed union-based two-phase matching algorithm. Specifically, in clustering phase, BD&VC algorithm was designed to reduce the matching complexity; in matching phase, LLHR-PC algorithm was proposed to provide evaluation indicators for scheduling. Simulation results showed that the scheduling period of eV2X systems can be improved by the proposed SPS strategy compared with the conventional mmWave SPS schemes.

Acknowledgment. This work was supported by the Postgraduate Research & Practice Innovation Program of Jiangsu Province under grant number SJKY19_2285.

References

1. Di, B., Song, L., Li, Y., Li, G.Y.: Non-orthogonal multiple access for high-reliable and low-latency V2X communications in 5G systems. IEEE J. Sel. Areas Commun. **35**(10), 2383–2397 (2017)
2. Study on enhancement of 3GPP Support for 5G V2X Services, Release 16, document 3GPP TR 22.886, December 2018
3. Study on NR Vehicle-to-Everything (V2X), Release 16, document 3GPP TR 38.885, March 2019
4. Wang, P., Di, B., Zhang, H., Bian, K., Song, L.: Cellular V2X communications in unlicensed spectrum: harmonious coexistence With VANET in 5G systems. IEEE Trans. Wireless Commun. **17**(8), 5212–5224 (2018)
5. Asadi, A., Müller, S., Sim, G.H., Klein, A., Hollick, M.: FML: fast machine learning for 5G mmWave vehicular communications. In: Proceedings of IEEE INFOCOM, Honolulu, HI, pp. 1961–1969 (2018)

6. Study on evaluation methodology of new vehicle-to-everything (V2X) use cases for LTE and NR, Release 15, document 3GPP, TR 37.885, December 2018

7. Giordani, M., Zanella, A., Zorzi, M.: Millimeter wave communication in vehicular networks: challenges and opportunities. In: Proceedings of IEEE MOCAST, Thessaloniki, pp. 1–6 (2017)

8. Sohrabi, F., Yu, W.: Hybrid digital and analog beamforming design for large-scale antenna arrays. IEEE J. Sel. Areas Commun. **10**(3), 501–513 (2016)

9. Zhang, D., Liu, Y., Dai, L., Bashir, A.K., Nallanathan, A., Shim, B.: Performance analysis of FD-NOMA-based decentralized V2X systems. IEEE Trans. Commun. **67**, 5024–5036 (2019). (in press)

10. Qian, L.P., Wu, Y., Zhou, H., Shen, X.: Non-orthogonal multiple access vehicular small cell networks: architecture and solution. IEEE Netw. **31**(4), 15–21 (2017)

11. Luo, F.L., Zhang, C.J.: Signal Processing for 5G: Algorithms and Implementations, pp. 143–166. Wiley, London (2016)

12. Wang, B., Dai, L., Gao, X., Hanzo, L.: Beamspace MIMO-NOMA for millimeter-wave communications using lens antenna arrays. In: Proceedings of IEEE VTC-Fall, Toronto, ON, pp. 1–5 (2017)

13. Wei, Z., Zhao, L., Guo, J., Ng, D.W.K., Yuan, J.: A multi-beam NOMA framework for hybrid mmWave systems. In: Proceedings of IEEE ICC, Kansas City, MO, pp. 1–7 (2018)

14. Cui, J., Liu, Y., Ding, Z., Fan, P., Nallanathan, A.: User selection and power allocation for mmWave-NOMA networks. In: Proceedings IEEE GLOBECOM, Singapore, pp. 1–6 (2017)

15. Wang, B., Dai, L., Wang, Z., Ge, N., Zhou, S.: Spectrum and energy-efficient beamspace MIMO-NOMA for millimeter-wave communications using lens antenna array. IEEE J. Sel. Areas Commun. **35**(10), 2370–2382 (2017)

16. Karadag, G., Gul, R., Sadi, Y., Coleri Ergen, S.: QoS-constrained semi-persistent scheduling of machine-type communications in cellular networks. IEEE Trans. Wireless Commun. **18**(5), 2737–2750 (2019)

17. Dai, L., Wang, B., Peng, M., Chen, S.: Hybrid precoding-based millimeter-wave massive MIMO-NOMA with simultaneous wireless information and power transfer. IEEE J. Sel. Areas Commun. **37**(1), 131–141 (2019)

18. Alsaba, Y., Leow, C.Y., Abdul Rahim, S.K.: Full-duplex cooperative non-orthogonal multiple access with beamforming and energy harvesting. IEEE Access **6**, 19726–19738 (2018)

19. Lee, K., Kim, J., Park, Y., Wang, H., Hong, D.: Latency of cellular-based V2X: perspectives on TTI-proportional latency and TTI-independent latency. IEEE Access **5**, 15800–15809 (2017)

Underwater Acoustic Channel Estimation Based on Signal Cancellation

Junkai Liu[1,2]([⊠]) [iD], Yangze Dong[1] [iD], Gangqiang Zhang[1] [iD], and Junqing Zhang[1] [iD]

[1] National Key Laboratory of Science and Technology on Underwater Acoustic Antagonizing, Shanghai 201108, China
Junkai_LIU726@163.com
[2] Zhejiang University, Zhoushan 316021, China

Abstract. Aiming at the requirement of underwater information security transmission, the security of encryption key generation and distribution in underwater acoustic communication is concerned. Key generation technology based on underwater acoustic channel (UAC) estimation can improve the security and real-time generation of encryption keys. In this paper, the idea of estimating the multipath structure of UAC is to retrieve the arrival signal by acquiring the parameters of larger energy Eigen-ray from real arrival signal, and to eliminate the arrival signal of larger energy Eigen-ray path from the real signal through signal cancellation, so as to eliminate the influence of side lobes of larger energy signal to arrival signals of other Eigen-ray path, to improve the estimation performance of multipath structure in underwater acoustic channel. The simulation and experimental results show that the improved algorithm can estimate the multipath structure of underwater acoustic channel more accurately and provide support for the subsequent underwater information security transmission.

Keywords: Underwater acoustic channel · Matched filtering · Parameters inversion · Signal cancellation · Channel correction

1 Introduction

Ocean channel is a time-varying and space-varying random channel, which can be regarded as a time-varying random filter to transform the signal waveform. If the observation or processing time is not too long, the acoustic channel can be described by a time-invariant filter. Match filter (MF) is the most basic detection algorithm based on matched filtering. MF is the optimal detector under Gaussian white noise, and is one of the classical underwater acoustic signal detection algorithms. Matched filters are also commonly used in underwater acoustic channel estimation.

Author's Brief Introduction: Liu Junkai (1990-), Baoding City, Hebei Province, Research Direction: Underwater Acoustic Communication and Network.
Project Funding: Laboratory fund of Key Laboratory of Ocean Observation Imaging Testbed of Zhejiang Province (201801); Basic Research and Frontier Technological Projects of Strong Foundation Engineering for National Defense Basic Scientific Research (19-0391).

H. Gao et al. (Eds.): ChinaCom 2019, LNICST 312, pp. 207–219, 2020.
https://doi.org/10.1007/978-3-030-41114-5_16

In non-stationary environment, the optimal decision threshold of MF will fluctuate with the change of signal-to-noise ratio, which seriously affects the detection performance of MF. In order to solve this problem, Conte and Lops in 1995 normalized the matched output using the received data and obtained the normalized matched filter. At the same time, the covariance matrix of background noise was obtained using the auxiliary data without targets. Then the matrix was substituted into MF to obtain the adaptive normalized matched filter [1]. In 2002, Abraham first introduced the cumulative sum detection algorithm PT into underwater acoustic signal processing, and then adaptively accumulated the square output value of the normalized matcher to detect. PT algorithm takes full account of the multipath effect of the channel and shows good detection performance [2]. Yin Jingwei of Harbin University of Engineering has studied the underwater acoustic channel estimation based on FRFT. Without Doppler frequency offset, the accuracy of the matched filtering algorithm is higher [3]. Li Jun of Dalian Naval Ship College adopts matched filtering technology to estimate the time delay structure of underwater acoustic multipath channel, and the estimation effect of single-frequency pulse and frequency modulation pulse signal is compared [4, 5]. But the above method does not solve the problem of underwater acoustic channel structure estimation when the time delay between channels is smaller than the pulse width. Chen Xing et al., Chengdu Institute of Information Engineering, proposed a clean algorithm based on matched filter to improve the range resolution of multi-target recognition. The simulation results are effective [6], but the correction of the estimated target strength and time delay estimation error is not considered.

In view of the above problems, this paper introduces signal cancellation algorithm into the field of underwater acoustic channel multipath structure estimation, improves the time delay resolution of underwater acoustic channel multipath structure estimation, and proposes an error compensation algorithm for underwater acoustic channel multipath structure estimation to correct the estimated underwater acoustic channel multipath structure. The simulation and experimental results show that the proposed algorithm can improve the time delay resolution of underwater acoustic channel multipath structure estimation. The proposed channel estimation algorithm can estimate the multipath structure of underwater acoustic channel more accurately.

2 Channel Estimation Principle Based on Matched Filter

MF is an optimal linear filter. Its criterion is that the output signal-to-noise ratio (SNR) is the largest, and it is often used in communication, detection and other systems [7, 8]. When the input signal of a linear time invariant filter is a known signal and the noise is an additive stationary noise, the matched filter can maximize the output power signal-to-noise ratio under a certain input power signal-to-noise ratio, which is a filter matching the input signal.

For the input signal s(t), the impulse response function of the matched filter is:

$$h(t) = ks * (t_0 - t) \tag{1}$$

Among them, k is an arbitrary constant.

Formula (1) shows that the impulse response of the matched filter is the mirror of input signal s(t), but there is only one delay time t_0.

Suppose there are p eigen rays, the underwater acoustic multipath channel is considered to have p path. The impulse response of underwater acoustic multipath channel can be obtained as follows:

$$h(t) = \sum_{i=1}^{P} a_i p(t - \tau_i) \tag{2}$$

If the transmitting signal is s(t), the received signal after propagation through underwater acoustic channel is as follows:

$$x(t) = s(t) * h(t) = a_1 s(t - \tau_1) + \ldots + a_i s(t - \tau_i) \tag{3}$$

The estimation of underwater acoustic channel multipath structure is to obtain a_i and τ_i, which can be estimated by matched filtering.

Figure 1 is schematic block diagram of matched filtering.

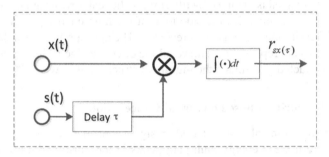

Fig. 1. Schematic block diagram of matched filtering

If the noise of the marine environment is n(t), the actual received signal is $x_i(t) = x(t) + n(t)$, s(t) is local copied signal, and the output of the matched filter is:

$$r_{x_1 t}(\tau) = \int_{-\infty}^{\infty} [x(t) + n(t)]s(t - \tau)dt = r_{xs}(\tau) + r_{ns}(\tau) \tag{4}$$

If the noise n(t) is not correlated with the signal s(t) and the mean value of the noise is zero, then there is $r_{x_1 t}(\tau) = r_{xs}(\tau)$, the output signal modulus $|r_{x_1 t}(\tau)|$ of matched filter will form a series of peaks in the corresponding correlation domain, and the corresponding peak position of each multipath signal will be delayed τ_i relative to the direct sound. The estimation of multipath structure of UAC can be realized by extracting the larger peak parameters among $|r_{x_1 t}(\tau)|$.

3 Improved Channel Estimation Algorithms Based on Signal Cancellation

3.1 Zero-Setting Algorithm for Peak Region

Zero-setting algorithm for peak region represents the signal zero-setting process within a certain width of the peak value in the process of extracting underwater acoustic channel structure after LFM matched filtering. When the LFM signal is received, the received LFM signal is processed with the local copy LFM signal to obtain the matched filtering signal after pulse compression; the peak value and location information of the maximum energy peak are extracted, and the data in the pulse width of LFM after matched filtering around the peak value is set to zero; the peak threshold and the number of routes are set. Two parameters are used to search the output of the matched filter, and the estimation of the multipath structure of UAC is obtained.

3.2 Signal Cancellation Algorithms

Signal cancellation algorithm is a recursive idea. Firstly, the received LFM signal is processed by matched filtering to obtain the matched filtering signal after pulse compression. Then, the matched filtering signal is processed to detect the parameters such as amplitude and time at the maximum peak value, and the arrival time-domain form of the signal is inverted by the obtained maximum energy signal parameters, and matched. The ideal matched filter signal is obtained by filtering. In the real arrival signal, the estimated high energy signal is eliminated, the side lobe of the high energy peak is eliminated, and the weak intensity multipath peak is revealed. The appropriate threshold is set, and the above two steps are repeated to achieve all the effective eigenvalues. The parameter information is extracted to estimate the multipath structure of UAC.

3.3 Improved Algorithm Based on Signal Cancellation

The peak area zero-setting algorithm based on signal cancellation does not consider the masking problem of weak energy multipath peaks in the pulse width range of strong energy multipath peaks, but removes the arrival signal of strong energy sound lines through the method of zero-setting in the pulse width range, which is easy to cause the loss or distortion of multipath structure of underwater acoustic channel; signal cancellation algorithm considers the masking problem of weak energy multipath peaks in the pulse width range of strong energy multipath peaks, and eliminates the arrival signal of strong energy sound lines by inversion signal cancellation method, which has no effect on weak energy peaks. However, the algorithm does not consider that when the peak interval is less than the pulse width, the adjacent pulses have both the peak value and the location of the estimated peak. It has a certain impact on the accuracy of underwater acoustic channel multipath structure estimation.

Therefore, based on the signal cancellation algorithm, this paper proposes an error compensation algorithm for underwater acoustic channel multipath structure estimation, which fine-tunes the estimated multipath delay and amplitude of underwater acoustic channel, and then matches the corrected results with the underwater acoustic multipath channel obtained by matched filtering to determine the optimal corrected value. Finally, more accurate information of multipath structure parameters of underwater acoustic channel is obtained.

The implementation process of the proposed algorithm is as follows:

(1) The received LFM signal is processed by matched filtering to obtain the matched filtering signal after pulse compression.

(2) The signal after matched filtering is processed to detect parameters such as amplitude and time at the maximum peak.

(3) The time-domain form of arrival of the signal is retrieved by using the parameters of the maximum energy signal, and the retrieved signal is removed from the received signal by using the signal cancellation algorithm.

(4) In the signal arrived in real environment, the estimated high energy signal is eliminated, and the sidelobe of the high energy correlation peak is eliminated, while the weak energy peaks by other paths are revealed.

(5) Setting appropriate threshold and repeating (2)-(4) so as to extract the parameter information of all effective eigenvalues and obtain the estimation of the multipath structure of underwater acoustic channel.

(6) To obtain the multi-path structure of underwater acoustic channel, the local signal of underwater acoustic channel is reconstructed by traversing the preset amplitude and time-delay transformations, and the optimal solution is found by matching the actual impulse response signal of underwater acoustic channel in the corresponding region.

4   An Improved Algorithm Model Based on Signal Cancellation

The underwater acoustic channel estimation algorithm proposed in this paper is based on signal cancellation. Firstly, the impulse response of UAC is obtained by matched filtering algorithm. Then, the impulse response of UAC is estimated by signal cancellation algorithm. Finally, the obtained UAC multipath structure is modified.

Figure 2 shows the flow chart of the improved algorithm based on signal cancellation.

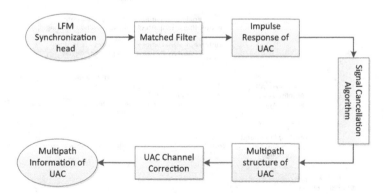

Fig. 2. Flow chart of improved algorithm based on signal cancellation

Figure 3 is flow chart of signal cancellation algorithm.

Because the expression of each eigen-ray's arrival signal in impulse response of UAC after matched filtering is influenced by the adjacent eigen-ray's arrival signal, the correlation waveform of high-energy eigen-ray's arrival signal has greater influence on

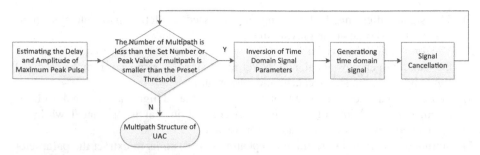

Fig. 3. Flow chart of signal cancellation algorithm

the correlation waveform of low-energy eigen-ray's arrival signal, so it can be eliminated by processing larger peak multipath first.

Figure 4 is flow chart of underwater acoustic multipath correction algorithm.

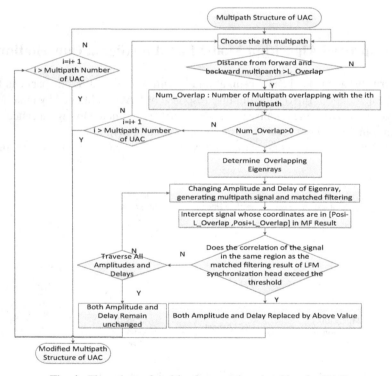

Fig. 4. Flow chart of multipath correction algorithm for UAC

In the correction stage of underwater acoustic channel, because the error of the amplitude and delay of some multipath is mainly affected by noise and the arrival signal of the two eigenvalues that close to it, the improved algorithm calculating the space between the estimated eigen ray with two other eigen rays that close to it to judge whether the two eigen rays have overlapping areas with the estimated eigen ray. The predict impulse response signal of underwater acoustic channel is reconstructed by traversing the preset amplitude and time-delay transformations, and matched with the actual impulse response signal of underwater acoustic channel in the corresponding region to find the optimal amplitudes and delay times.

5   Simulation of Multipath Structure Estimation for UAC

Table 1 shows LFM simulation signal parameters.

Table 1. Summary of LFM simulation signal parameters

Parameters	Bandwidth/kHz	Duration/s
Value	5	1, 0.5, 0.05

Table 2 shows the simulation channel multipath parameters.

Table 2. Summary of multipath parameters of underwater acoustic channel

UAC		Eigen rays					
		1	2	3	4	5	6
A	Amplitude	3.58	2.40	1.70	1.38	0.95	−0.2
	Time delay/ms	1.50	2.30	6.20	8.00	5.05	5.0
B	Amplitude	3.80	2.40	1.70	1.35	0.88	−0.2
	Time delay/ms	0.40	2.80	7.80	8.40	5.10	2.0

There are two groups of underwater acoustic multipath channels, all of multipath delay intervals of the first group data are larger than pulse width of LFM signal after matched filtering, and the multipath delay intervals of the second group data has one eigen rays smaller than t pulse width of LFM signal after matched filtering; the noise is Gauss white noise; the Monte Carlo statistical method is used to analyze underwater acoustic signals. The statistics of channel amplitude estimation error, underwater acoustic channel delay estimation error and underwater acoustic channel multipath number error are carried out; the number of statistics is 100.

Figure 5 is schematic diagram of the transmission signal.

The synchronization signal in Fig. 5 is used to synchronize the received signal; the detected signal is LFM signal with different time lengths (each group of LFM signals has the same time duration); after synchronization, the LFM detection signal in the data segment is used to estimate the multipath structure of UAC. The number, amplitude and time delay of the multipath sound lines are used as statistics of the performance of UAC multipath structure estimation.

		Data Segement1		Data Segement2
Synchronization Signal(LFM)	Space	Detection Signal(LFM)	Space	Detection Signal(LFM)

Fig. 5. Composition diagram of transmission signal

Figure 6 is a comparison of the performance of zero-setting algorithm, signal cancellation algorithm and the proposed algorithm for underwater acoustic channel estimation when all of the multipath delay intervals are larger than the matched output pulse width of LFM signal after matched filtering.

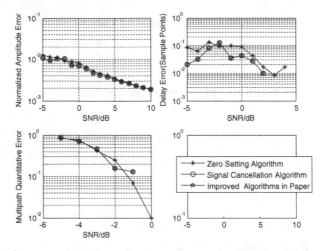

Fig. 6. Performance comparison of underwater acoustic channel estimation algorithm

From Fig. 7, it can be seen that when all of multipath delay intervals of UAC are greater than pulse width of LFM signal after matched filtering, the performance of zero-setting algorithm is similar to that of the proposed algorithm by comparing the amplitude error, delay error and multipath number error of UAC estimation.

Figure 7 shows the performance comparison of zero-setting algorithm, signal cancellation algorithm and the underwater acoustic channel estimation algorithm proposed in this paper when one of multipath delay intervals is less than pulse width of LFM signal after matched filtering.

From Fig. 7, we can see that when one of multipath delay intervals of UAC is less than pulse width of LFM signal after matched filtering, the performance of the proposed algorithm is better than that of zero-setting algorithm; the estimation results are more accurate compared with the signal cancellation algorithm.

Figure 8 is the performance of underwater acoustic channel estimation for LFM signals with different duration.

From Fig. 8, it can be seen that the performance of UAC multipath structure estimation increases with the increase of SNR when the duration of LFM signal is constant, and

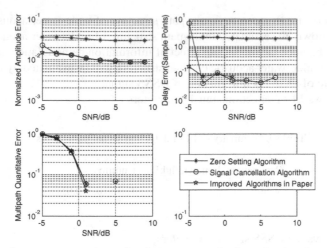

Fig. 7. Performance comparison of underwater acoustic channel estimation algorithms

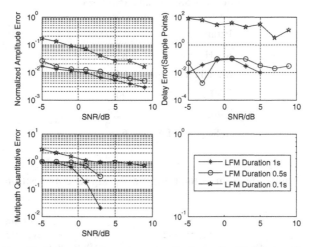

Fig. 8. The relationship between underwater acoustic channel estimation performance and signal duration

the performance of underwater acoustic channel multipath structure estimation increases with the increase of the time of LFM signal when the SNR is constant.

6 Data Analysis of Lake Test

In order to test the actual performance of the improved algorithm based on signal cancelling, channel-free estimation algorithm, zero-setting algorithm, signal cancellation algorithm and the algorithm proposed in this paper are used to process the lake test data. Among them, channel-free estimation algorithm means that no channel equalization processing of received signal directly carries out despread and demodulation operations for information recovery. Because the multi-path structure of underwater acoustic channel on Lake is unknown, the estimated multi-path structure of underwater acoustic channel will be used to balance the multi-path effect of information demodulation, and the estimation effect of underwater acoustic channel structure will be evaluated by transmitting the bit error rate of recovery information of DSSS signal.

Table 3 shows LFM detection signal parameters.

Table 3. Summary of LFM detection signal parameters

Parameters	Bandwidth/kHz	Duration/s
Value	5	1, 0.5, 0.1, 0.05

Table 4 shows the DSSS signal parameters.

Table 4. DSSS signal parameters

Parameters	Value
fc/kHz	8
Modulation Style	BPSK
fs/kHz	96
Ts/ms	12.6
m Sequence Length	63

Figure 9 is schematic diagram of the transmission signal composition.

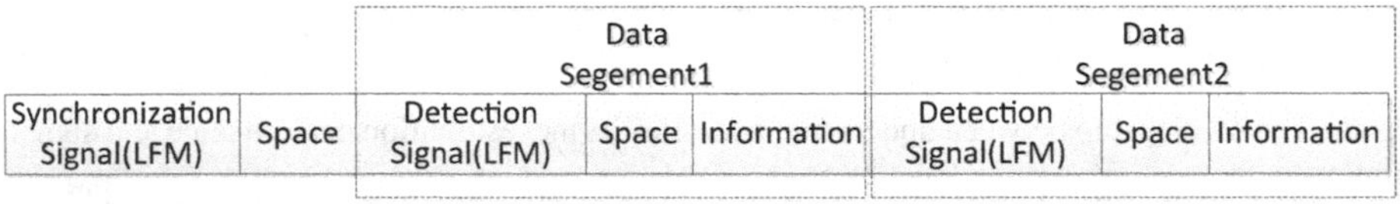

		Data Segment1			Data Segment2		
Synchronization Signal(LFM)	Space	Detection Signal(LFM)	Space	Information	Detection Signal(LFM)	Space	Information

Fig. 9. Composition diagram of transmission signal

The synchronization signal in Fig. 9 is used to synchronize the transmitted signal; the detected signal is LFM signal with different duration (each group of LFM signals has the same duration); the information segment is DSSS modulated information, which consist of 6 segments that has 420 bits.

Test conditions: the water depth is 20 m, the transducer is placed 3 m underwater and the hydrophone is placed 3 m underwater, they are 50 m apart.

Figure 10 is received underwater acoustic signals.

By synchronizing the received signals in Fig. 10, each data segment is extracted. The LFM detection signal in the data segment is used to estimate the multipath structure of

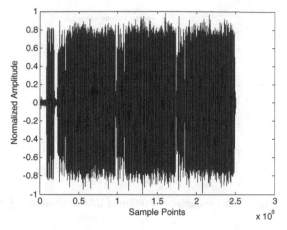

Fig. 10. Received underwater acoustic signals

UAC, and the estimated underwater acoustic channel structure is used to equalize the information in the data segment. Finally, the transmitted information is recovered and the bit error rate (BER) is calculated.

Figure 11 is correlation comparison of channel estimation results for different algorithms.

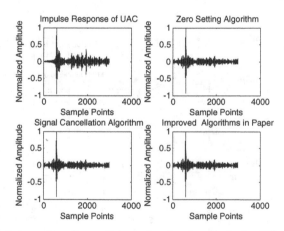

Fig. 11. Correlation comparisons of channel estimation results for different algorithms

Figure 11 shows that when the channel estimation results are used to equalize the underwater acoustic channel influence of LFM synchronization head, the peak value of the correlation results is sharper and its energy is more concentrated. But it is difficult to draw a conclusion from the correlation results of zero-setting algorithm, signal cancellation algorithm and the proposed algorithm in this paper.

Figure 12 is comparisons of the performance of underwater acoustic channel structure estimation with different UAC estimation algorithms.

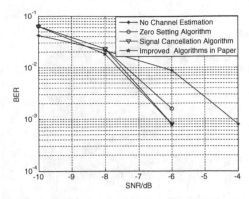

Fig. 12. Performance comparison of different UAC estimation algorithms

The performance comparison of different underwater acoustic channel structure estimates with LFM duration of 0.5 s is shown in Fig. 12. Figure 12 shows that when the SNR condition is good (the SNR in the figure is greater than −8 dB), the BER is higher without channel estimation, and the performance of cancellation algorithm is slightly better than that of zero-setting algorithm; the performance of the proposed algorithm in the paper is the best.

Figure 13 shows the influence of LFM duration for the structure estimation performance of UAC.

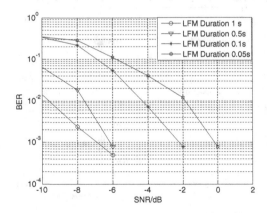

Fig. 13. Effect of different LFM durations on estimation performance

Figure 13 shows that the estimation performance of the proposed underwater acoustic channel structure estimation algorithm improves with the increase of LFM signal duration.

7 Conclusions

The performance of zero-setting algorithm is better on the premise that there is only one eigen ray in the pulse width of LFM signal after matched filtering. In the actual underwater acoustic environment, there will be overlapping results of multiple eigen ray signals, so the estimation results are not ideal. The performance of signal cancellation algorithm is better than the zero-setting algorithm. However, it does not consider the influence of adjacent eigen rays on the estimation, so the accuracy of channel multipath structure estimation decreases. The channel estimation algorithm proposed in this paper uses the principle of signal cancellation to remove the energy multipath signal, eliminating the masking effect of the side lobe of the high energy multipath signal for the low energy multipath signal, and improving the performance of low energy multipath signal. Then, we improve the estimation accuracy of multipath structure of UAC by modifying the multipath structure of UAC. The simulation and experimental results show the effectiveness of the improved algorithm proposed in this paper. Because the above research does not consider the computational complexity in practical application, we will further optimize the above modified algorithm in the later stage in order to achieve the goal of real-time channel estimation.

References

1. Conte, E., Lops, M., Ricci, G.: Asymptotically optimum radar detection in compound Gaussian clutter. Trans. Aerosp. Electron. Syst. **31**(2), 617–625 (1995)
2. Abraham, D.A., Willett, P.K.: Active sonar detection in shallow water using the page test. IEEE J. Ocean. Eng. **27**(1), 35–46 (2002)
3. Yin, J.: Principle of Underwater Acoustic Communication and Signal Processing Technology. National Defense Industry Press, Beijing (2011)
4. Wang, K., Li, J.: Underwater acoustic channel estimate based on matched filtering. Tech. Acoust. **30**(4), 10–12 (2011)
5. Zhang, L., Wu, X.: On cross correlation based discrete time delay estimation. In: ICASSP 2005, vol. 7, pp. 981–984 (2005)
6. Chen, X., Du, Y.: A new algorithm based on matched filter pulse compression. Commun. Technol. **46**(4), 133–135 (2013)
7. Liang, H., Zhang, X.: Signal Detection and Estimation. Northwest Polytechnic University Press, Xi'an (2011)
8. Liu, J., Dong, Y., Zhang, G.: Key generation technology based on underwater acoustic channel estimation in covert communication. J. Appl. Acoust. **38**(4), 681–687 (2019)

A Novel Spectrum Correlation Based Energy Detection for Wideband Spectrum Sensing

Bo Lan[✉][iD], Tao Peng, PeiLiang Zuo, and Wenbo Wang

Wireless Signal Processing and Networks Laboratory (WSPN),
Key Laboratory of Universal Wireless Communications, Ministry of Education,
Beijing University of Posts and Telecommunications, Beijing, China
{lanboxianren,pengtao,zplzpl88,wbwang}@bupt.edu.cn

Abstract. With the rapid development of wireless communications technology, the problem of scarcity of spectrum resources is becoming serious. Cognitive radio (CR) which is an effective technology to improve the utilization of spectrum resources is getting more and more attention. Spectrum sensing is a key technology in cognitive radio. Wideband spectrum sensing (WBSS) can help secondary users (SUs) find more spectrum holes. However, for the traditional energy detection (ED) algorithm, when the signal-to-noise ratio (SNR) of the primary user (PU) is low, the detection performance is extremely poor owing to the single frequency point detection method. Therefore, the concept of spectrum correlation is proposed. Spectrum correlation algorithm uses the detection window to realize joint detection of multiple frequency points which can improve performance. This paper focuses on how to make the best of spectrum correlation to ensure the detection performance for low SNR signals. We propose an adaptive detection window (ADW) method, whose detection window is adaptively selected based on the estimated SNR of signal. The method can be directly used for wideband spectrum sensing when the approximate position of each signal and its estimated SNR are known. In this context, to show the robustness of the ADW method, a simulation of the sensitivity of the ADW method to the SNR estimation error is performed. Meanwhile, simulations of methods comparison demonstrate that the proposed ADW method outperforms the commonly used iterative energy detection method, frequency correlation methods and histogram-based segmentation method by far.

Keywords: Cognitive radio (CR) · Wideband spectrum sensing (WBSS) · Energy detection (ED) · Spectrum correlation · Detection window

This work is supported in part by the National Natural Science Foundation of China (No. 61631004) and the National Science and Technology Major Project of China under Grant 2016ZX03001017.

H. Gao et al. (Eds.): ChinaCom 2019, LNICST 312, pp. 220–234, 2020.
https://doi.org/10.1007/978-3-030-41114-5_17

1   Introduction

With the development of wireless communications technology, The fixed allocation of spectrum resources seems to be unable to meet the growing spectrum demand. However, many surveys indicate that most of the spectrum resources are not fully utilized [1]. Cognitive radio (CR) [2] is considered to be a promising technology to improve spectrum utilization. To ensure that secondary users (SUs) use shared spectrum without interfering with primary users (PUs), spectrum sensing is essential for CR [3]. Through spectrum sensing, SUs can seize the available opportunities of shared spectrum. Especially when the shared spectrum is idle, they can use spectrum resources for transmission. Once the PUs occupy the spectrum again, they can also give up the channel resources in time to avoid affecting the transmission quality of the PUs.

Many methods are proposed for the narrowband spectrum sensing (NBSS) [4], such as energy detection (ED) [5], matched filtering and cyclostationary feature detection. Although the latter two methods have better detection performance, ED is more widely used because it does not require any prior information of PU signals and has lower computational complexity. However, NBSS can only detect one channel at a time. Even though a larger spectrum sensing range can be obtained by a sequential sweep-tune fashion [6], it takes longer to perceive the wideband spectrum. Therefore, it is more appropriate to directly use wideband spectrum sensing (WBSS) for multi-channel detection. Due to the advantages of ED, it can also be used for WBSS. However, when the signal power is particularly low, its detection performance is poor.

In order to detect multiple signals with different bandwidths and SNRs in the spectrum, some ED-based WBSS method is proposed. In [7], a multi-band joint detection algorithm is proposed to optimize the decision thresholds of each subband. But the adopted detection method is also based on the single frequency point, the detection results for low SNR signals are still not satisfactory. In order to locate the boundary between sub-bands, [8] proposed a histogram-based segmentation method. However the distinction between noise and low SNR signal is not obvious. Detection window is a tool used by the spectrum correlation algorithm to detect signals, [9] first used the fixed detection window to detect the signal. The final performance improvement is limited due to the underutilization of spectrum correlation. In this paper, the histogram segmentation method, traditional iterative energy detection and spectrum correlation are used as the comparison methods.

This paper focuses on the full-utiliazation of spectrum correlation in wideband spectrum sensing. Specifically, the theoretical relationship between detection window and detection performance is acquired. The corresponding detection window can be selected according to the estimated SNR of the signal to guarantee performance rather than fixed. We propose an adaptive detection window (ADW) method, the detection window can be adaptively utilized for detecting the signals in wideband provided that the approximate position of the signals and the estimated SNR are known. The method has a theoretical minimum detectable bandwidth at each SNR. For signals with a certain SNR, the method can detect the signal having a bandwidth greater than the corresponding minimum detectable bandwidth.

The structure of the paper is as follows. We first briefly introduce the wideband sampling model and the single frequency point detection mode in Sect. 2. Then we detail the frequency correlation in Sect. 3. In Sect. 4, the performance of the proposed method is simulated and compared with the previously mentioned method. Finally, conclusions are given in Sect. 5.

2 Preliminary

2.1 Wideband Sampling Model

The sampling frequency of the signal in the time domain is f which is higher than the Nyquist rate. N represents the number of points per sampling, and N_t denotes the total number of sampling times. As shown in Fig. 1, N sampled signal is converted into the signal in frequency domain by Fast Fourier Transform (NFFT). $Y(k)$ is the kth frequency value of the sampled signal after FFT, then

$$
\begin{aligned}
Y(k) &= \frac{1}{\sqrt{N}} \sum_{n=0}^{N-1} y(n) \cdot e^{-j\frac{2\pi}{N} \cdot kn} \\
&= \frac{1}{\sqrt{N}} \sum_{n=0}^{N-1} y(n) \cdot \cos(\frac{2\pi kn}{N}) - j\frac{1}{\sqrt{N}} \sum_{n=0}^{N-1} y(n) \cdot \sin(\frac{2\pi kn}{N}) \\
&= Y_{real} + jY_{imag}
\end{aligned}
\tag{1}
$$

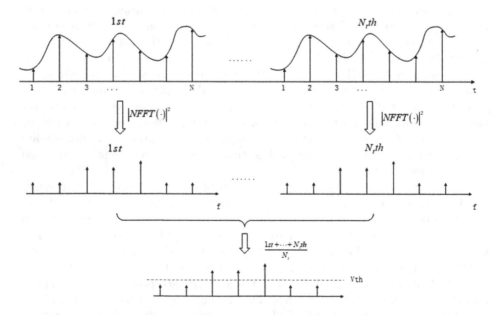

Fig. 1. The sampling process of the signal in the time domain

The energy of the signal in frequency domain obtained by each sampling is averaged to obtain the average power of each frequency point. The average statistic is T, which is obtained according to the signal sampling model:

$$T = \frac{1}{N_t} \cdot \sum_{N_t} |Y(k)|^2 \tag{2}$$

According to the sampled signal model, the sampling result can be defined as a binary hypothesis model: H_0 means that the frequency point is idle, and H_1 means that the frequency point is occupied. $\sigma_{s,i}^2$ represents the power of i-th signal frequency point and σ_w^2 represents the power of white Gaussian noise.

When H_0 is true, $|Y(k)|^2$ obeys the exponential distribution of the parameter $1/\sigma_w^2$. When H_1 is true, $|Y(k)|^2$ obeys the exponential distribution of the parameter $1/(\sigma_s^2 + \sigma_w^2)$, According to the central limit theorem, when N_t is large, T obeys the following Gaussian distribution [9]:

$$H_0 : T - Normal(\sigma_w^2, \; \sigma_w^4/N_t)$$

$$H_1 : T - Normal((\sigma_s^2 + \sigma_w^2), \; (\sigma_s^2 + \sigma_w^2)^2 / N_t) \tag{3}$$

2.2 Single Frequency Point Detection Model

In the traditional energy detection algorithm, after the statistic T is obtained, a power threshold V_{th} needs to be designed [10]. The frequency point above the threshold is the signal frequency point, and lower than the threshold is the noise frequency point. The selection of the threshold value will directly affect the detection performance of the energy detection algorithm. If the threshold value is too high, some signal frequency points will be missed and the detection ratio will be reduced. If the threshold is too low, some noise frequency points will be misjudged as signal frequency points, which will increase the false alarm ratio. In practical applications, two decision criteria are obtained according to the energy detection performance index: constant detection rate criterion (CDR) and constant false-alarm rate criterion (CFAR) [11]. [12] proposed a double-threshold based energy detection (DTED) for the cooperative spectrum sensing (CSS). A common feature of these methods is that the judgment of a single frequency point depends only on its own power.

In the single frequency point detection model, $P_{d,single}$ indicates the probability that the signal frequency point is judged correctly (i.e the probability that the frequency point power exceeds the threshold V_{th} when H_1 is true). Where $Q(x) = \int_x^\infty \frac{1}{\sqrt{2\pi}} e^{\frac{t^2}{2}} dt$

$$P_{d,single} = \{T > V_{th}|H_1\} = Q\left(\frac{V_{th} - (\sigma_s^2 + \sigma_w^2)}{(\sigma_s^2 + \sigma_w^2)/\sqrt{N_t}}\right) \tag{4}$$

$P_{f,single}$ denotes the probability that the noise frequency point is judged wrong (i.e the probability that the frequency point is below V_{th} the threshold when H_0 is true).

$$P_{f,\text{single}} = \{T > V_{th}|H_0\} = Q\left(\frac{V_{th} - \sigma_w^2}{\sigma_w^2/\sqrt{N_t}}\right) \tag{5}$$

Suppose the threshold V_{th} is noise power (i.e. $V_{th} = \sigma_w^2$), the theoretical value of P_d will be given in the following table.

As can be seen from Table 1, the value of $P_{d,single}$ has been on a steady decline with the decreasing SNR. The results can explain the reason why the traditional energy detection algorithm using single frequency point detection has the poor detection performance for low SNR signals.

Table 1. The theoretical value of $P_{d,single}$

SNR (dB)	$P_{d,single}$
−19	56.98%
−18	58.73%
−17	60.90%
−16	63.55%
−15	66.77%
−14	70.59%
−13	75.01%
−12	79.94%
−11	85.10%
−10	90.07%
−9	94.31%
−8	97.35%

3   Research on Spectrum Correlation

This section first introduces the concept of spectrum correlation, and then gives the theoretical relationship between detection window and detection performance, finally puts forward the ADW method which adopts adaptive detection window according to the SNRs to detect signal.

3.1   Spectrum Correlation

The spectrum correlation algorithm mainly uses the correlation between adjacent signal frequency points for joint detection. If there is a signal in the spectrum, since the signal has the certain bandwidth, the frequency point near the signal point is also a signal point, then the probability that the adjacent frequency point is higher than the noise power will exceed 50%. The noise frequency points are independent and identically distributed. Thus, there is no correlation between adjacent noise points.

For a single frequency point, the probability that the point is higher than the estimated noise is $P_{s,T>\hat{\sigma}_w^2}$ [13], and the noise frequency point higher than the estimated noise is $P_{w,T>\hat{\sigma}_w^2}$.

$$P_{s,T>\hat{\sigma}_w^2} = H_1 : P(T > \hat{\sigma}_w^2) = Q(\frac{\hat{\sigma}_w^2 - (\sigma_s^2 + \sigma_w^2)}{(\sigma_s^2 + \sigma_w^2)/\sqrt{Nt}})$$

$$= Q((\frac{\mu}{1+r} - 1) * \sqrt{Nt}) \tag{6}$$

$$P_{w,T>\hat{\sigma}_w^2} = H_0 : P(T > \hat{\sigma}_w^2) = Q(\frac{\hat{\sigma}_w^2 - \sigma_w^2}{\sigma_w^2/\sqrt{Nt}})$$

$$= Q((\mu - 1) * \sqrt{Nt}) \tag{7}$$

$\hat{\sigma}_w^2$ is the estimated noise power, $\gamma = \sigma_s^2/\sigma_w^2$ is the SNR of the signal, $\mu = \hat{\sigma}_w^2/\sigma_w^2$ is the ratio of the estimated noise power value to the actual noise value.

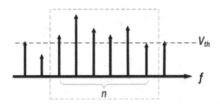

Fig. 2. Multi frequency point joint detection model (Color figure online)

In the spectrum correlation algorithm, we will refer to the window containing multiple frequency points as the detection window (the red dotted line area of Fig. 2), assuming the window size is n (i.e there are n frequency points in the detection window). If at least n_1 frequency points of the n frequency points are higher than the noise power, then we think that the frequency points in the window are the signal frequency points, otherwise they are noise frequency points. $\rho = n_1/n$ is the correlation rate. n and ρ are the most important factors in the subsequent process. P_d is the probability that the signal frequency points are determined as signal points and P_f is the probability that noise frequency points are determined as a signal point. $P_{s,T>\hat{\sigma}_w^2}$, $P_{w,T>\hat{\sigma}_w^2}$ can be simply expressed as P_s, P_w.

$$P_d = \sum_{k=n\cdot\rho}^{n} C_n^k \cdot p_s{}^k \cdot (1-p_s)^{n-k} \tag{8}$$

$$P_f = \sum_{k=n\cdot\rho}^{n} C_n^k \cdot p_w{}^k \cdot (1-p_w)^{n-k} = (\sum_{k=n_1}^{n} C_n^k) \cdot 0.5^n \tag{9}$$

Assume the noise estimation is accurate (i.e. $\mu = 1$), and the sampling times N_t is 200, $n = 200$, $\rho = 0.65$. Table 2 gives the theoretical value of P_d.

Table 2. The theoretical value of P_d and $P_{d,single}$

SNR (dB)	P_d	$P_{d,single}$
−19	1.26%	56.98%
−18	4.10%	58.73%
−17	13.18%	60.90%
−16	36.47%	63.55%
−15	72.94%	66.77%
−14	93.64%	70.59%
−13	99.94%	75.01%
−12	100.00%	79.94%
−11	100.00%	85.10%
−10	100.00%	90.07%
−9	100.00%	94.31%
−8	100.00%	97.35%

It can be concluded from the results that the joint detection P_d outperforms the single frequency point detection $P_{d,single}$ when SNR is above −14dB. If single frequency point detection gets into trouble, joint detection using the correlation of signal frequency points is the method that can effectively improve performance.

From the above description of spectrum correlation, the detection window is the most important parameter to reflect the correlation. The window size n represents the number of signal frequencies participating in the joint detection, and the correlation ratio ρ indicates the decision threshold. Although the existing method using detection window utilizes the spectrum correlation of the signal, the research on the spectrum correlation is insufficient. The selection of window parameters lacks theoretical basis and the window parameters are fixed at different SNRs. As shown in Table 2, once the SNR is too low, the detection performance will drop dramatically. The theoretical lowest detectable SNR and minimum detectable bandwidth of the signal cannot be calculated by theoretical formula. In order to further improve the detection performance, it's necessary to study the effect of the detection window on performance. The next section will discuss how to choose the best detection window and give the specific detection process.

3.2 Adaptive Detection Window

To ensure the optimal detection performance, we define the following formula, P_{dset} and P_{fset} are the preset performance requirements.

$$Target : P_d > P_{dset} \, and \, P_{fset} < P_f \tag{10}$$

Since P_s is related to γ and P_d is affected by P_s, the higher the SNR of the signal, the value of P_s is larger. When the window parameters (i.e. n and ρ), and other conditions (e.g. bandwidth) are the same under signals with different SNRs, the detection performance of the high SNR will be better than the performance of low SNR. When the fixed detection window are used, there is a certain threshold, if the SNR is higher than the threshold, the performance can achieve (10), but if the SNR is lower than the threshold, the performance cannot meet (10). In order to make different SNR signals satisfy (10), different detection window can be set at different SNRs. Since n indicates that n frequency points are participated in the detection process, if the number of frequency points of the signal itself is less than n, the detection performance will decrease, so we will try to make n small enough to make more signals meet the requirements of bandwidth.

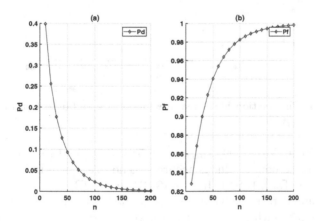

Fig. 3. The relationship between window size and detection ratio (a) $\rho > P_s$ (b)$\rho < P_d$

When the SNR is fixed, if $\rho > P_s$, as shown in Fig. 3(a), P_d is inversely related to n and the maximum value does not exceed 0.5. If $\rho < P_w$, as shown in Fig. 3(b), P_f is positively correlated with n and the minimum value is not less than 0.5. Therefore the correlation ratio should satisfy $P_w < \rho < P_s$.

When $P_w < \rho < P_s$, as shown in Fig. 4, n is positively correlated with P_d and negatively correlated with P_f. So the larger n is, the more values of ρ can satisfied (10). The selection process of the minimum detection window at a specific SNR can be divided into the following five steps:

- *Step 1*, Initialize n and n_1 to 1;
- *Step 2*, By gradually increasing n_1, the corresponding p_d and p_f can be obtained. when the formula (10) is satisfied, it will jump to step 5. If (10) is not reached until $n_1 > n$, step 3 will be executed;
- *Step 3*, Let $n = n + 1$, $n_1 = 1$;
- *Step 4*, Gradually increase n_1. when (10) is met, skip to step 5. If (10) is not reached until $n_1 > n$, it will return to step 3;
- *Step 5*, The current n and $\rho = n_1/n$ are the parameters of the detection window under the SNR.

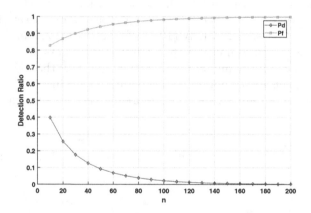

Fig. 4. The relationship between window size and detection ratio

Let $N = 5000$, $N_t = 200$, $P_{dset} = 99.5\%$, $P_{fset} = 0.1\%$ and assume that the estimated noise power value is accurate. The size of window and correlation ratio are given in Table 1, SNR from -19 dB to -8 dB.

The minimum detectable bandwidth is defined as the bandwidth of the signal when its passband width is equal to the size of detection window. In other words, the minimum detectable bandwidth is different under different SNR. Therefore, in this improved method we can know the lowest detectable SNR and the minimum detectable bandwidth, and for low SNR signals, the detection performance can also satisfy (10).

The specific process of the ADW method is as follows.

Table 3. Selected detection window parameters

SNR (dB)	n	ρ	SNR (dB)	n	ρ
-19	1647	53.8%	-18.5	1309	54.3%
-18	1045	54.8%	-17.5	839	55.4%
-17	667	56.0%	-16.5	537	56.7%
-16	427	57.5%	-15.5	347	58.3%
-15	279	59.3%	-14.5	221	60.2%
-14	181	61.5%	-13.5	144	62.6%
-13	119	64.2%	-12.5	95	65.3%
-12	81	66.7%	-11.5	66	68.2%
-11	54	70.4%	-10.5	43	72.1%
-10	38	73.7%	-9.5	33	75.8%
-9	27	77.8%	-8.5	24	79.2%
-8	21	81.0%	-7.5	18	83.4%

- Obtain the estimated noise power, the approximate position and the estimated SNR of the signal by using methods such as edge judgement;
- Adopt corresponding detection window parameters based on estimated SNR;
- Slide the detection window from left to right at the approximate position of the signal. When the ratio of the frequency points above the estimated noise power to the total points in the detection window is higher than ρ, the frequency points in the window are determined as the signal frequency points.

4   Simulation and Discussion

In the end of Sect. 3.1, the theoretical probability that a single signal frequency point power exceed the noise power $P_{d,single}$ is lower than the probability of joint detection P_d. The following simulations are used to verify whether the above theory is accurate. Use the detection window parameters obtained in Method 1 to obtain P_d (Tables 4 and 5).

Table 4. Simulation parameters

Parameter	Value
Total bandwidth	50 MHz
Sampling duration d_t	0.01 s
Sampling times N_t	200
Sampling points per time N	5000
Frequency resolution	10 KHz
Preset signal detection ratio P_{dset}	99.5%
Preset false alarm ratio P_{fset}	0.1%

Table 5. Detection methods

Methods	Detailed description
Method 1	Adaptive detection window in Sect. 3.2 in this paper
Method 2	The detection window is fixed of the frequency correlation method in [9]
Method 3	The iterative detection algorithm given in [7]
Method 4	The histogram-based segmentation method proposed in [8]

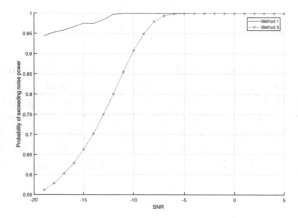

Fig. 5. Probability of exceeding noise power

The simulation result (Fig. 5) confirms that the probability that the frequency point is higher than the noise power can be greatly improved when the correlation of the signal is utilized. Then, we will detect the entire signal. The bandwidth of the signal to be detected is 25 MHz, the modulation method is Direct Sequence Spread Spectrum (DSSS), and the root raised cosine filter with a roll-off factor of 0.22 is used. Other parameters related to adaptive detection window(ADW) are given in Table 2. Comparison algorithms are common detection methods in simulation, and their detailed introduction is shown in Table 3. Use these methods to detect the passband of the signal.

The detection ratio indicates the proportion of the signal frequency points determined as signal points by the detection methods to the total signal frequency points. As can be seen from Fig. 6, Method 1 has the highest ratio of signal detection for different SNR signals, and the detection ratio is both above 96%. The signal detection ratio of Method 4 fluctuates with the change of

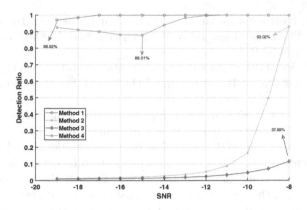

Fig. 6. Detection ratio of the signal passband

SNR, but in general, the performance of Method 4 is only worse than Method 1 and obviously better than Method 2 and 3. When the SNR of the signal is −19 dB −10 dB, the detection ratios of Method 2 and 3 are basically close to 0. As the SNR of signals increases, the detection ratio becomes larger, and the improvement of Method 2 is larger than that of Method 3. When the SNR ratio of the signal is −8 dB, the detection ratio of the Method 2 has reached 93%, which is close to the detection performance of the Method 1 and 4.

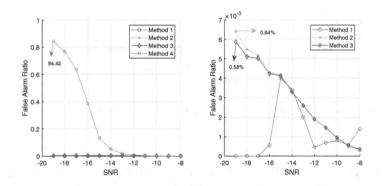

Fig. 7. False alarm ratio of the noise stopband

Then use these methods to detect the stopband, and the results are shown in Fig. 7. The false alarm ratio denotes the proportion of the frequency points in the stopband are determined as signal frequency points by the detection methods to the total noise signal frequency points. It can be seen that the false alarm ratio of Method 4 gradually increases with the decrease of SNR, and the highest is 84.4%. The false alarm ratio of the other three methods has been very low, basically less than 1%. The false alarm ratio of Method 1 fluctuates with the change of SNR, reaching a maximum of 0.4%, but it has been the lowest of the four methods. The false alarm ratio of Method 2 and Method 3 is positively correlated with the SNR.

Since the choice of detection window parameters is related to the SNR, when there is an error in the SNR estimation of the signal, the detection ratio of the signal using the detection window is as follows:

The coordinate axis SNR in Fig. 8 represents the actual SNR of the signal. The SNR Error is the estimated SNR of the signal minus the actual SNR. We can conclude that as the SNR error value becomes smaller, the detection ratio of the signal gradually increases. The simulation results are consistent with the conclusions mentioned at the beginning of 3.2. Even if the estimated error of SNR reaches 1.5 dB, the detection ratio of most signals is higher than 95%, and the worst can also be higher than 90%. The reason why the detection ratio with SNR error of −1.5 dB is much higher than that with +1.5 dB, and even higher than that with no error (0 dB) is that the detection window parameters used are for the lower SNR When the SNR error becomes lower.

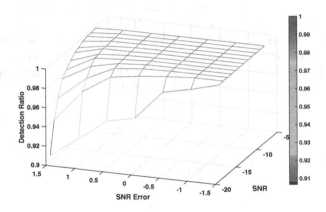

Fig. 8. The influence of the SNR estimation error on the detection ratio of signal passband

The detection ratio of Method 2 and 3 is positively correlated with the SNR. The false alarm ratio is negatively correlated with the SNR. Although the detection performance (comprehensive consideration of detection ratio and false alarm ratio) improved with the increase of the SNR, it is still not well. Even though the detection ratio of Method 4 has been relatively high, the false alarm ratio is very high at low SNR, reaching 84%. The detection ratio of method 1 is always above 95%, and the false alarm ratio is the lowest among the four methods. The detection performance is the best of the four methods.

5   Conclusion

Since the traditional energy detection adopts the single frequency point detection mode, the detection performance of the low SNR signal is poor. Spectrum correlation algorithm using multi frequency point joint detection is a promising improvement scheme. However, the detection window parameters used in the existing methods are fixed and have no theoretical support. This paper fully considers the influence of the detection window on the performance, and then proposes the ADW method. The commonly used wideband spectrum detection method is used to compare the detection performance with the proposed method. Simulation results in several aspects show that the performance of the method is better than the comparison method when the approximate position and the estimated SNR of the signal are known. The method can detect the signals with low SNR in the spectrum with high probability at a low false alarm ratio.

References

1. Facilitating Opportunities for Flexible, Efficient, and Reliable Spe ctrum Use Employing Cognitive Radio Technologies, FCC 03–322. Federal Commun. Commission, Washington, DC, USA, December 2003
2. Haykin, S.: Cognitive radio: brain-empowered wireless communications. IEEE J. Sel. Areas Commun. **23**(2), 201–220 (2005)
3. Mitola, J., Maguire, G.Q.: Cognitive radio: making software radios more personal. IEEE Pers. Commun. **6**(4), 13–18 (1999)
4. Yucek, T., Arslan, H.: A survey of spectrum sensing algorithms for cognitive radio applications. IEEE Commun. Surv. Tutor. **11**(1), 116–130 (2009)
5. Mariani, A., Giorgetti, A., Chiani, M.: Effects of noise power estimation on energy detection for cognitive radio applications. IEEE Trans. Commun. **59**(12), 3410–3420 (2011)
6. Hwang, J., Chang, W., Hu, P.: A sub-nyquist wideband spectrum sensing scheme using aliased spectral edge detection and database matching. In: 2015 International Conference on Wireless Communications and Signal Processing (WCSP), Nanjing, pp. 1–5 (2015)
7. Quan, Z., Cui, S., Sayed, A.H., Poor, H.V.: Optimal multiband joint detection for spectrum sensing in cognitive radio networks. IEEE Trans. Signal Process. **57**(3), 1128–1140 (2009)
8. Bao, D., De Vito, L., Rapuano, S.: A histogram-based segmentation method for wideband spectrum sensing in cognitive radios. IEEE Trans. Instrum. Meas. **62**(7), 1900–1908 (2013)
9. Yuan, L., Ren, F., Xing, L., Peng, T., Wang, W.: Wideband spectrum sensing algorithm based on frequency correlation. In: 2013 15th IEEE International Conference on Communication Technology, Guilin, pp. 211–217 (2013)
10. Gahane, L., Sharma, P.K., Varshney, N., Tsiftsis, T.A., Kumar, P.: An improved energy detector for mobile cognitive users over generalized fading channels. IEEE Trans. Commun. **66**(2), 534–545 (2018)
11. Ziyang, L., Tao, P.: Energy detection about broadband signal without priori information of interference system. J. Beijing Univ. Posts Telecommun. **35**(5), 31–35 (2012)

12. Bhowmick, A., Chandra, A., Roy, S.D., Kundu, S.: Double threshold-based cooperative spectrum sensing for a cognitive radio network with improved energy detectors. IET Commun. **9**(18), 2216–2226 (2015)
13. Wang, X., Peng, T., Wang, W.: Low-SNR energy detection based on relevance in power density spectrum. In: Liang, Q., Mu, J., Wang, W., Zhang, B. (eds.) Proceedings of the 2015 International Conference on Communications, Signal Processing, and Systems. LNEE, vol. 386, pp. 283–291. Springer, Heidelberg (2016). https://doi.org/10.1007/978-3-662-49831-6_29

Spread Spectrum Audio Watermark Based on Non-uniform Quantization

MeiJun Ning⑩, Tao Peng$^{(\boxtimes)}$, YueQing Xu, and QingYi Quan

Wireless Signal Processing and Networks Laboratory (WSPN),
Key Laboratory of Universal Wireless Communications, Ministry of Education,
Beijing University of Posts and Telecommunications, Beijing, China
{ningmeijun,pengtao,xuyueqing10952,qyquan}@bupt.edu.cn

Abstract. Audio watermarking is an information hiding technology which is widely used in copyright protection and information security. This paper proposes a novel audio watermarking scheme based on spread spectrum and non-uniform quantization. The watermarks are embedded by modifying the quantization coefficients. The proposed algorithm utilizes the characteristics of non-uniform quantization to adopt different quantized signal-to-noise ratios for the low-frequency and high-frequency parts of the audio signal, thus improving the robustness of the technology while ensuring the sound quality is not damaged. Compared with the existing audio watermarking methods, the proposed scheme is especially robust against additive white Gaussian noise (AWGN). Experimental analysis shows that the proposed method provides high audio quality and excellent capability to withstand various noise attacks particularly in AWGN.

Keywords: Audio watermarking · Non-uniform quantization · Robustness

1 Introduction

In recent years, due to the rapid development of the Internet, digital multimedia data can be easily distributed to all over the world. But this has brought about a critical issue for copyright protection. In that context, the audio watermarking technology was proposed. Audio watermarking technology uses audio as a carrier to embed information. The human ear cannot distinguish the difference between the original audio and the watermark audio, hence the copyright information which can be used to verify the original author can be hidden in the audio. Moreover, the audio watermarking technology plays an important role not only in copyright protection, but in other fields, such as content authentication, information security, broadcast monitoring and secret communication.

This work is supported in part by the National Natural Science Foundation of China (No. 61631004) and the National Science and Technology Major Project of China under Grant 2016ZX03001017.

H. Gao et al. (Eds.): ChinaCom 2019, LNICST 312, pp. 235–245, 2020.
https://doi.org/10.1007/978-3-030-41114-5_18

Generally speaking, the audio watermark technology should satisfy three requirements:

- Robustness: The embedded watermarks ought to tolerant different types of attacks such as MP3 compression, requantization, amplitude compression and AWGN, etc.
- Imperceptibility: The embedded watermarks should not affect the quality of the original signal.
- Payload: The amount of watermark that can be embedded into the host audio signal.

However, these three requirements are contradictory, for instance, in order to improve the robustness, the origial signals will make greater changes, which will bring about lower imperceptibility. Consequently, there is a trade-off bewteen these requirements.

The audio watermarking technique can be classified into two types: time domain technique and frequency domain technique. The time domain technique including LSB hiding [1] and echo hiding [2] embeds information in the time domian. Although it's easy to implement, it has the weakness of low robustness. Thus, the frequency domain technique has attracted the attention of many scholars. The frequency domain methods hide the messages into the audio signals which have been converted to frequency domain. The general transform methods are Discrete Fourier Transform (DFT), Discrete Cosine Transform (DCT) and Discrete Wavlet Transform (DWT). Chen et al. [3] proposed a method to modify the low-frequency efficients in DWT, this algorithm is robust against common signal processing attacks including compression and time scale modification, but has a weak robustness to amplitude scaling, cropping. Li et al. [4] presented a spread spectrum audio watermarking based on perceptual characteristic aware which has good robustness and imperceptibility, while the scheme's payload is low. Similarly, Erfani et al. [5] put forward an audio watermarking technique rely on a perceptual kernel representation of audio signals (spikegram), it owns outstanding performance in resisting audio processing attacks but achieves worst payload. With a superior payload, Kaur et al. [6] proposed a blind audio water-marked algorithm based on SVD, while this algorithm has poor property in robustness. Garlapati et al. [7] brought forward a enhanced spread spectrum audio watermark, it's proved that it has high payload but without the proof of robustness agagin the AWGN attack. Identically, Gupta et al. [8] proposed an efficient audio watermarking scheme based on lifting wavelet transform (LWT) and quantization. Aparna et al. [9] adopted Modified Discrete Fourier Transform (MDCT) in the proposed algorithm, but they didn't verify the capability against noise attack including AWGN. Proposed by Wang et al. [10], the scheme with MDCT could resist the common attacks, it achieved excellent performance in MP3 compression and recompression attacks but had a weak property in com-bating with AWGN. Sakai et al. [11] presented a develped watermark algorithm to withstand the band-pass filtering attacks. However, in wireless communica-tion, the AWGN noise is more common and serious, so this paper proposes an advanced watermark scheme based on MDCT to resist the noise attacks. This strategy not only can combat with AWGN attack, but also can endure other attacks.

The remaining of the paper is organized as follows. Section 2 discusses the preliminary in the audio watermark. In Sect. 3 the noval method for audio watermarking is proposed and Sect. 4 shows the experimental results. Finally, Sect. 5 concludes the paper.

2   Preliminary

Due to high compression ratio and brilliant tone quality, MPEG Audio Layer III (MP3) is a popular compression format. MP3 encoder's procedure of processing audio mainly includes the following parts: MDCT, the psychoacoustic model II, the bit allocation, quantization and bitstream formatting. The proposed method mainly takes use of MDCT, psychoacoustic model II and the process of quantization.

2.1   MDCT in MP3 Encoding

During the MP3 encoding, MDCT is used to convert the time domain signal into frequency domain. The encoder divides audio signals into frames. Every frame is composed of two granules and frame's length is 1152. After MDCT, one granule signal is divided into 32 subbands and each subband has 18 frequency lines.

MDCT is a linear orthogonal overlap transform. MDCT can effectively overcome the edge effect in DCT without reducing the coding performance, thus effectively removing the periodic noise generated by edge effects. The mathematical expression for MDCT is given.

$$X(i) = \sum_{k=0}^{N-1} Z(k) cos[\frac{(2k+1+\frac{N}{2})(2i+1)\pi}{2N}] \tag{1}$$

where $Z(k)$ is the result of multiplying audio signals and window function [12], $i = 0, 1, ..., \frac{N}{2} - 1$, $N = 12$ or 36.

2.2   Quantization in MP3 Encoding

The MP3 encoder adopts a non-uniform quantizer. The non-uniform quantizer determines the quantization interval based on different intervals of the signal. That means the encoder performs different processing on signals of different frequencies. MP3 exploits the characteristic of non-uniform quantization to ameliorate the sound quality. The quantitative calculation formula is

$$q_i = \lfloor (\frac{|x_i|}{\sqrt[4]{2}^{step}})^{3/4} - 0.0946 \rfloor \tag{2}$$

where x_i is the result after MDCT. q_i is quantitative result, and *step* is the quantization stepsize calculated by:

$$step = 8.0 * ln(k) \tag{3}$$

$$k = \frac{e^{\frac{1}{N}(\sum_{i=0}^{575} ln x_i{}^2)}}{\frac{1}{N}\sum_{i=0}^{575} x_i{}^2} \tag{4}$$

2.3 The Psychoacoustic in MP3 Encoding

The MP3 encoder has a high compression ratio and good sound quality, which is attributed to the use of psychoacoustic model. The psychoacoustic model simulates the human ear hearing which has masking effect. The model calculates the maximum quantization error of each subband with masking thresholds obtained by masking effect.

The encoder adopts psychoacoustic model II, the model II imitates the frequency of the human ear to 19 kHz. In the calculation process, psychoacoustic model II divide the frequency band in higher precision. For example, with the sampling rate of 44.1 kHz, the audio signal's frequency band is split into more regions to calculate the masking thresholds and then mapping regions to 21 scalefactor bands.

3 The Proposed Audio Watermark Scheme

3.1 Spread Spectrum Audio Watermark

In the spread spectrum audio watermark system, the watermarked signal is expressed as

$$\mathbf{s} = \mathbf{x} + b * p * \mathbf{u} \tag{5}$$

where $\mathbf{x}$ is the vector of host signal, $b = \{\pm 1\}$ is the watermark message, $\mathbf{u}$ is a PN sequence and p is the embedding strength calculated by psychoacoustic model II, the value of p is a trade-off between robustness and imperceptibility.

In the procedure of decoding, the signal can be expressed as

$$\mathbf{y} = \mathbf{s} + \mathbf{n} \tag{6}$$

where $\mathbf{n}$ represents the noise. According to the Eq. (6), the watermark can be extracted by calculating the correlation between the signal and PN sequence which is used in encoding process. The correlation can be calculated as follows

$$
\begin{aligned}
r &= <\mathbf{y}, \mathbf{u}> \\
&= <\mathbf{s} + \mathbf{n}, \mathbf{u}> \\
&= <\mathbf{x} + b * p * \mathbf{u} + \mathbf{n}, \mathbf{u}> \\
&= <\mathbf{x}, \mathbf{u}> + <\mathbf{n}, \mathbf{u}> + b * p
\end{aligned}
\tag{7}
$$

In the proposed scheme, $\mathbf{x}$ is uncorrelated with PN sequence $\mathbf{u}$ and the result of $<\mathbf{n}, \mathbf{u}>$ is approximately equal to zero. Therefore, the watermark is decoded by $sign(r)$.

3.2   Watermark Embedding Algorithm

This paper aims at a watermarking algorithm that performs well focused on imperceptibility and robustness. To improve robustness, watermark should be embedded with maximum possible energy lean against the human auditory system. In the process of original MP3 quantizing, the watermark parameters just need to be less than the threshold calculated by psychoacoustic model II. That causes most of the watermark coefficients are too small compared with the masking threshold. While, the MP3 encoder's non-uniform quantizer uses different quantization intervals for the low and high frequency portions of the audio signal, this is benefit for the sound quality of the audio. Hence, this scheme learns from the MP3 encoder's quantizer, and modified the watermarking parameters in the encoding process.

The following details the embedding steps.

Step1. The original audio signals are processed by MP3 encoder and they are segmented into non-overlapping frames, with a frame size of 1152 samples. Then, the encoder generates the signal-masking-ratio (SMR) from the original signal through the psychoacoustic model II.

Step2. The audio signals are tranformed from time domain to frequency domain by MDCT.

Step3. Implement non-uniform quantization and inverse non-uniform quantization to adjust the stepsize.

The calculation formula are as follows:

$$q_i = \lfloor |x_i|^{3/4} * 2^{(k-210)*-0.1875} - 0.0946 \rfloor \tag{8}$$

where x_i represents a MDCT value in a frame, k is the stepsize, q_i is the outcome of non-uniform quantization.

$$p_i = (q_{i+1}^{4/3} - q_i^{4/3})/4/(2^{(k-210)*-0.1875} - 0.0946) \tag{9}$$

where p_i is the result of inverse non-uniform quantization, n is the num of spectral values in one scalefactor band.

Step4. Calculate the quantization noise (xr) as watermark parameters. Then, compare xr with SMR, back to step3 and adjust k until we find the most suitable xr, which is closest but does not exceed the SMR.

$$xr = \sum_{i=1}^{n} p_i * p_i \tag{10}$$

Step5. After regulating the stepsize, the encoder redoes quantization and inverse quantization. The calculation results of inverse quantization are watermarking parameters. Therefore, the embed equation is

$$s_i = |x_i| + p_i * u_i * b \tag{11}$$

where u_i is a PN sequence and $b = \{\pm 1\}$ represent the watermark message.

Step6. Apply inverse MDCT to restore audio signal.

3.3 Watermark Extraction Algorithm

In the extraction process, the algorithm is a blind watermark extraction algorithm which can extract watermark without original audio signal. For watermark extraction, the correlation coefficients can be used to recover watermark with the known PN sequence $\mathbf{u}$. Due to the embedded strategy, the decoder calculates the correlation coefficients by substract the values in the first granule and the second granule.

The following illustrates the extraction steps in detail.

Step1. The MP3 decoder read the audio signals and divides the signals into frames which length is 1152. Then, the decoder finds the first frame that contains watermark.

Step2. The decoder does MDCT to transform audio signals from time domain to frequency domain.

Step3. The algorithm calculates the correlation coefficients.

$$r_i = r_{i2} - r_{i1}$$
$$= <x_{i2} - x_{i1}, \mathbf{u}> + <\Delta n, \mathbf{u}> - p * 2b \tag{12}$$

where $\Delta n = n_{i2} - n_{i1}$ is a new random noise. Considering stationary signal in short time, where x_{i2} is approximately equal to x_{i1} and n_{i2} is approximately equal to n_{i1}, that means

$$<x_{i2} - x_{i1}, \mathbf{u}> \approx 0 \tag{13}$$

Step4. Sum r_i for a hard detection value.

$$\hat{r} = \sum r_i \tag{14}$$

$$b = sign(\hat{r}) \tag{15}$$

if $b > 0$, the watermark message is decoded as 1, if $b < 0$, the watermark message is decoded as -1.

4 Experimental Result and Evalutions

The sample audio files used in this experiment are sampled at 44.1kHz. The algorithm uses LAME which is a MP3 encoder and decoder with the version of 3.70 which open source codes are changed to add the proposed algorithm. The paper evaluates the performance in the following three aspects.

4.1 Imperceptibility Test

For imperceptibility evaluations, the objective difference grade (ODG) are universally adopted to measure the watermarked audio quality.

Table 1. Objective difference grade

ODG	Quality	Impairment
0	Excellent	Imperceptible
−1	Good	Perceptible but not annoying
−2	Fair	Slightly annoying
−3	Poor	Annoying
−4	Bad	Very annoying

The ODG is calculated by using perceived audio quality (PEAQ) which is an international standard, ITU-R BS.1387 [15]. Discription for ODG are listed in Table 1.

The paper uses different types of audio to verify the performance of the proposed algorithm, such as pop music, rock music and jazz music. The ODG values of the three types of audio are −0.736, −0.594 and −0.979, respectively. The results show that the proposed scheme has good imperceptible for different genres of audios.

4.2 Robustness Test

To analyze the proposed algorithm against robustness for different attacks such as additive white Gaussian noise (AWGN), the scheme used decoding accuracy. The experiment used SNR to measure embedding strength in order to compare robustness under the same conditions.

The SNR is defined as

$$SNR = 10 * log \frac{\sum_i x_i^2}{\sum_i (s_i - x_i)^2} \tag{16}$$

where x_i is the original audio signal and s_i is the watermarked audio signal.

To analysis the performance of the proposed scheme, the paper did another set of experiments using the method of Improved Spread Spectrum (ISS) [13]. ISS's core method is based on spread spectrum, it improved basic spread spectrum audio watermark by utilizing a linear function. In order to compare the performance of the two methods under the same conditions, the paper modified the payload of the ISS. Under the premise of similar SNR and same payload, the paper tested the performance of the two methods under the same AWGN attack. The SNR of the ISS is 10.3 and the proposed algorithm is 10.1. The experimental results presented in Fig. 1.

In the precondition of same SNR and same payload, the results show that the proposed algorithm has good capability to withstand the AWGN attack.

For a more comprehensive verification of the performance of the proposed method, the paper attemped five different types of attacks.

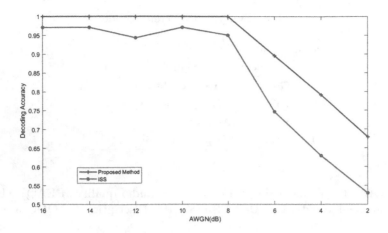

Fig. 1. Decoding accuracy of the two methods.

- Re-sampling: The original signal is sampled at 44.1 kHz, and then it is re-sampled at 22.05 kHz, and the audio is restored back by sampling again at 44.1 kHz.
- Echo addition: An echo signal is added to the watermarked audio signal.
- Amplify: The watermarked signal's amplitude is scaled up with factor of 0.5 and 1.5.
- Low-Pass Filtering: The signal is cutted off with frequency of 9 kHz.
- Re-quantization: The 16-bit watermarked audio signal is re-quantized down to 8 bits/sample and then back to 16 bits/sample.

Table 2. Decoding accuracy

Type of attack	Decoding accuracy
Re-sampling	100%
Echo	100%
Amplify-0.5	100%
Amplify-1.5	100%
Low-pass	100%
Re-quantization	100%

Table 2 are robustness results of different type of noise attack. As shown in the table, the presented scheme's ability to resist other type of attacks is excellent.

4.3   Payload Test

The payload is defined as the number of watermark bits embedded each second of the host signal. The audio's sample rate is 44.1 kHz, hence

$$Payload = \frac{44100}{1152} * 3 \approx 114(bps) \tag{17}$$

Audio Watermark in AM (AWAM) [14] is a blind audio watermark algorithm, it employed FFT and psychoacoustics model, and its innovation is every frame has a shift step to make the watermark more perceptually indistinguishable. The payload of reference is 43 bps. Figure 2 shows the performance of the proposed scheme and AWAM.

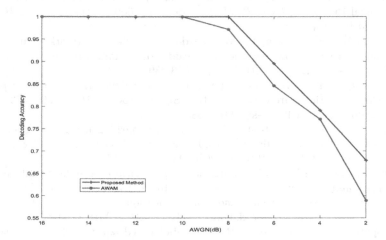

Fig. 2. Decoding accuracy of the two methods.

From the outcomes obtained by Fig. 2, the proposed method's decoding accuracy is only little better than AWAM, but the payload of the advanced method is bigger than AWAM.

The above conclusions show that the proposed algorithm has higher payload and better performance against various attacks compared to earlier audio watermarking schemes. The scheme balances the three conflict requirements including imperceptibility, robustness and payload.

5   Conclusions

This paper presented a spread spectrum audio watermarking method based on MDCT and non-uniform quantization. Watermark embedding is performed by taking advantage of the property of non-uniform quantization and the process of MP3 encoding. Watermark extraction is carried out by using the same PN sequence used for embedding process. The paper simulated AWGN as noise attack in communication and simulated other attacks as digital attack. The experimental results show that the proposed algorithm has excellent capability to withstand the noise attack durning communication.

References

1. Bamatraf, A., Ibrahim, R., Salleh, M.N.B.M.: Digital watermarking algorithm using LSB. In: 2010 International Conference on Computer Applications and Industrial Electronics, Kuala Lumpur, pp. 155–159 (2010). https://doi.org/10.1109/ICCAIE.2010.5735066
2. Wei, F.S., Qi, D.: Audio watermarking of stereo signals based on echo-hiding method. In: 2009 7th International Conference on Information, Communications and Signal Processing (ICICS), Macau, pp. 1–4 (2009). https://doi.org/10.1109/ICICS.2009.5397487
3. Chen, S., Hsu, C., Huang, H.: Wavelet-domain audio watermarking using optimal modification on low-frequency amplitude. IET Signal Process. **9**(2), 166–176 (2015). https://doi.org/10.1049/iet-spr.2013.0399
4. Li, R., Xu, S., Yang, H.: Spread spectrum audio watermarking based on perceptual characteristic aware extraction. IET Signal Process. **10**(3), 266–273 (2016). https://doi.org/10.1049/iet-spr.2014.0388
5. Erfani, Y., Pichevar, R., Rouat, J.: Audio watermarking using spikegram and a two-dictionary approach. IEEE Trans. Inf. Forensics Secur. **12**(4), 840–852 (2017). https://doi.org/10.1109/TIFS.2016.2636094
6. Kaur, A., Dutta, M.K.: A blind watermarking algorithm for audio signals in multi-resolution and singular value decomposition. In: 2018 4th International Conference on Computational Intelligence and Communication Technology (CICT), Ghaziabad, pp. 1–5 (2018). https://doi.org/10.1109/CIACT.2018.8480367
7. Garlapati, B.M., Chalamala, S.R.: A symbol based watermarking approach for spread spectrum audio watermarking methods. In: 2016 7th International Conference on Intelligent Systems, Modelling and Simulation (ISMS), Bangkok, pp. 180–184 (2016). https://doi.org/10.1109/ISMS.2016.31
8. Gupta, A.K., Agarwal, A., Singh, A., Vimal, D., Kumar, D.: Blind audio watermarking using adaptive quantization and lifting wavelet transform. In: 2018 5th International Conference on Signal Processing and Integrated Networks (SPIN), Noida, pp. 556–559 (2018). https://doi.org/10.1109/SPIN.2018.8474250
9. Aparna, S., Baiju, P.S.: Audio watermarking technique using modified discrete cosine transform. In: 2016 International Conference on Communication Systems and Networks (ComNet), Thiruvananthapuram, pp. 227–230 (2016). https://doi.org/10.1109/CSN.2016.7824019
10. Wang, K., Li, C., Tian, L.: Audio zero watermarking for MP3 based on low frequency energy. In: 2017 6th International Conference on Informatics, Electronics and Vision and 2017 7th International Symposium in Computational Medical and Health Technology (ICIEV-ISCMHT), Himeji, pp. 1–5 (2017). https://doi.org/10.1109/ICIEV.2017.8338599
11. Sakai, H., Iwaki, M.: Audio watermarking method based on phase-shifting having robustness against band-pass filtering attacks. 2018 IEEE 7th Global Conference on Consumer Electronics (GCCE), Nara, pp. 343–346 (2018). https://doi.org/10.1109/GCCE.2018.8574765

12. ISO/IEC 11172–3: Coding of moving pictures and associated audio for digital storage media at up to about 1,5 Mbit/s Part 3: Audio (1993)
13. Zhang, P., Xu, S., Yang, H.: Robust and transparent audio watermarking based on improved spread spectrum and psychoacoustic masking. In: 2012 IEEE International Conference on Information Science and Technology, Hubei, pp. 640–643 (2012). https://doi.org/10.1109/ICIST.2012.6221723
14. Li, M., Lei, Y., Zhang, X., Liu, J., Yan, Y.: Authentication and quality monitoring based on audio watermark for analog AM shortwave broadcasting. In: Third International Conference on Intelligent Information Hiding and Multimedia Signal Processing (IIH-MSP 2007), Kaohsiung, pp. 263–266 (2007). https://doi.org/10.1109/IIHMSP.2007.4457701
15. Method for objective measurements of perceived audio quality (PEAQ): International Telecommunication Union. ITU-R. BS. 1387 (1998)

DBS: Delay Based Hierarchical Downlink Scheduling for Real-Time Stream in Cellular Networks

Wenjin Fan[✉], Yu Liu, and Yumei Wang

School of Information and Communication Engineering,
Beijing University of Posts and Telecommunications, Beijing 100876, China
{wjfan,liuy,ymwang}@bupt.edu.cn

Abstract. With the rapid development of cellular networks, demand for real-time stream is increasing dramatically. How to guarantee better quality-of-service (QoS) of real-time stream services under limited resources becomes an increasingly important issue. This paper proposes a delay based hierarchical downlink scheduling (DBS) algorithm for real-time stream in cellular networks. The hierarchical scheduler is divided into two levels. The upper level scheduler offers a prediction of the number of data bits that each real-time stream needs to guarantee the QoS. The lower level scheduler classifies all real-time streams into grade A, B and C according to Head of Line Delay and allocates resources to streams according to their different grades. The simulation results show that our algorithm performs better than other real-time schedulers, such as frame level scheduler (FLS), Modified Largest Weight Delay First (M-LWDF), EXP/PF and EXP-LOG in the aspects of delay and throughput.

Keywords: Downlink schedule · Resource allocation · Stream classify · Cellular network

1 Introduction

The transmission of real-time stream, especially video content, over wireless communications is becoming a major contributor to future Internet application traffic. With the increasing demand for real-time stream, better quality-of-service (QoS) perceived by users will become increasingly important [1].

Such improvement of QoS performance can be achieved with developing up-layer functionality, such as radio resource allocation, and lower-layer functionality, including Orthogonal Frequency-division Multiple Access (OFDMA), Modulation and Coding Schemes (MCSs) and Hybrid Automatic Repeat Request (HARQ), etc. Radio resource allocation is one of most important issue in the above factors. To meet the needs of as many requesters as possible, resources should be allocated with proper scheduling policies. For example, 5G performance goals include to achieve higher data rate, reduced latency, and higher system spectrum efficiency [2], etc. To achieve these targets, in 5G

© ICST Institute for Computer Sciences, Social Informatics and Telecommunications Engineering 2020
Published by Springer Nature Switzerland AG 2020. All Rights Reserved
H. Gao et al. (Eds.): ChinaCom 2019, LNICST 312, pp. 246–257, 2020.
https://doi.org/10.1007/978-3-030-41114-5_19

networks a lot of lower-layer functionality, such as New Radio Frequencies, Massive MIMO, Edge Computing and Small Cell are developed. More importantly, the scheduling algorithm in the high-level functionality should also be improved to achieve better QoS with lower latency and lower packet loss rate [3].

The Media Access Control (MAC) layer carries out the allocation of wireless resources. However, due to the complex and changeable wireless environment and various QoS needs of stream, effective resource allocation is extremely challenging. Some algorithms [3–9] for real-time stream consider different network parameters and achieve real-time stream optimization. More details will be discussed in the next section.

This paper proposes a delay based hierarchical downlink scheduling (DBS) algorithm for real-time stream in cellular networks. The upper level scheduler is the same as that in FLS [5] to offer a predicted number of data that each real-time stream needs to ensure the QoS. Then, the lower level scheduler classifies all real-time streams into grade A, B and C according to $D_{HOL,i}$ (Head of line packet delay), and allocates resources to streams by their different grades. TTI-level delay characteristics are sufficiently applied through the classification to improve Packet Loss Rate (PLR) and throughput.

The remainder of this paper consists of several sections. In Sect. 2, related work is depicted. In Sect. 3, the proposed algorithm is concretely presented. Section 4 describes simulation scenario parameters and discusses the results. Finally, concluding observations are drawn in Sect. 5.

2   Scheduling Policies

In cellular networks, large performance gains can be achieved by properly allocating the number of frequency resources to users at each TTI 5. Due to the high demand of real-time stream for QoS, many QoS-aware scheduling algorithms have been proposed. Related meaning of expressions in these algorithms are shown in Table 1.

Table 1. Notations used in scheduling algorithms.

Expression	Meaning
RB	Resource block
$w_{i,j}$	The priority of the i-th user on the j-th RB
$r_{i,j}$	Attainable data rate
$\overline{R}_i$	The approximated regular precedent data rate
$D_{HOL,i}$	Head of line packet delay
δ_i	Delay threshold
τ_i	Acceptable packet loss rate
c_j^i	Spectral efficiency for the i-th user over the j-th RB
N	The number of real-time streams
$u_i(k)$	Data to be transmitted during the kth frame

2.1 M-LWDF [6]

The Modified Largest Weighted Delay First (M-LWDF) algorithm not only takes account of the channel quality and fairness, but also provides guarantee for real-time services from the perspective of delay and packet loss rate. The metric is defined as

$$w_{i,j}^{M\text{-}LWDF} = \alpha_i \cdot D_{HOL,i} \cdot \frac{r_{i,j}}{\overline{R_i}} \tag{1}$$

where α_i is further elaborated in (2). α_i weights the metric so that the streams with most urgent requirements are preferred for allocation.

$$\alpha_i = -\frac{\log \delta_i}{\tau_i} \tag{2}$$

In particular, attainable data rate $r_{i,j}$ for each User Equipment (UE) is evaluated by the link adaptation module according to feedbacks on channel quality. In general, the better channel condition is, the larger $r_{i,j}$ UE will have with higher priority. $\overline{R_i}$ is the approximated regular precedent data rate of i-th flow. As shown in Eq. (1), $\overline{R_i}$ is used to restrict users with large traffic and maintain fairness. For example, a high rate user may be constantly allocated with more resources in the past. But with the growth of $\overline{R_i}$, its priority will be reduced. The role of $D_{HOL,i}$ is to increase the priority of packets with longer waiting time in line.

As a whole, M-LWDF guarantees a good balance among spectrum efficiency, fairness and QoS provisioning.

2.2 EXP/PF [7]

It is also important to know that the metric of Proportional Fairness (PF) 4 is computed as the attainable data rate over the average data rate. The Exponential Proportional Fairness (EXP/PF) algorithm adds an exponential term based on the PF algorithm to increase the priority of the real-time stream. As its name states, EXP/PF considers both the characteristics of PF and of an exponential function of the end-to-end delay. The metric is described as

$$w_{i,j}^{EXP/PF} = exp(\frac{\alpha_i \cdot D_{HOL,i} - X}{1 + \sqrt{X}}) \cdot \frac{r_{i,j}}{\overline{R_i}} \tag{3}$$

where α_i is similarly defined as in (2), and

$$X = \frac{1}{N} \cdot \sum_{i=1}^{N} \alpha_i \cdot D_{HOL,i} \tag{4}$$

2.3 EXP-Rule and LOG-Rule [8]

EXP-rule and LOG-rule are very similar. They can quickly increase the priority of real-time flows approaching the delay threshold. In addition, priority formula considers the overall situation of the network by using the sum of all user delays. As their names indicate, the main difference between the two algorithms is that one uses the log function and the other uses the exponential function as the main part of the priority formula.

$$w_{i,j}^{EXP\text{-}rule} = b_i \cdot exp(\frac{a_i \cdot D_{HOL,i}}{c+\sqrt{1/N \cdot \Sigma D_{HOL,i}}}) \cdot z_j^i \tag{5}$$

$$w_{i,j}^{LOG\text{-}rule} = b_i \cdot log(c + a_i \cdot D_{HOL,i}) \cdot z_j^i \tag{6}$$

where a_i, b_i and c are defined in (7) and (8) respectively.

$$\begin{cases} b_i = 1/E[z_j^i] \\ c = 1.1 \cdot a_i = 5/0.99\tau_i \end{cases} \tag{7}$$

$$\begin{cases} a_i \epsilon E[5/0.99\tau_i, 10/0.99\tau_i] \\ b_i = 1/E[z_j^i] \\ c = 1 \end{cases} \tag{8}$$

2.4 Delay-Prioritized Scheduler (DPS) [9]

DPS utilizes each user's packet delay information and its instantaneous downlink channel conditions for scheduling. Firstly, DPS orders candidate flows to the remaining time before the deadline expires. Once the user with the highest urgency is selected, the resource allocation step is performed in order to transmit the head of line packet (i.e. the most delayed one). A new iteration is then run on the remaining flows in the list until all RBs are assigned.

2.5 Frame Level Scheduler (FLS) [5]

The FLS algorithm consists of two layers. The upper level of the scheduler first estimates the amount of data that guarantees the QoS requirements of each real-time stream on the LTE radio frame (10 sub-frames). Then the lower level of the scheduler assigns resources to each real-time stream mainly according to the channel quality at each Transmission Time Interval (TTI) (1 ms). The better the channel quality, the higher the priority of resource allocation, and each stream stops resource allocation when the transmission completes the amount of data within the LTE frame. Once there is a surplus, lower level of scheduler allocates resources for the remaining non-real-time streams.

2.6 Other Real-Time Scheduling Algorithms

In [10], a delay-based weighted proportional fairness algorithm (DBWPF) is proposed, which considers weighted average delay of each user in addition to the trade-off between throughput and throughput fairness. The algorithm can improve delay fairness and implementation rate fairness. In [11], a delay–based and QoS–aware scheduling algorithm (DQAS) weights the delay priority of each queue by analyzing the queue buffer of each user stream. This weight is the decision basis for flow scheduling. This algorithm can effectively achieve the balance between experiment and system throughput during heavy loads.

3   Problem Presentation and DBS Algorithm

3.1   Problem Presentation

Although algorithms mentioned in Sect. 2 have good performance for real-time streaming, there is still the possibility of further improvement. The reasons are as follows:

(1)   Inadequate use of delay

For real-time streams, the delays and the PLR are closely related. In general, if the packet in the buffer of eNodeB exceeds the delay threshold, then it will be dropped. Similarly, if an overdue packet is already sent, then it will also be dropped by its receiver (i.e. UE) and resource will be wasted. Thus, PLR will increase. Consequently, the real-time flow near the delay threshold has a larger probability of packet dropping, and PLR will increase when the delay increases [12].

In M-LWDF, EXP/PF and other algorithms, metrics become larger with the increasing of delay. But for some streams approaching to the delay threshold, owing to different channel conditions and historical transmission rate, the metrics may be lower. In this way, the priority of these streams cannot be guaranteed, and PLR due to timeout will increase.

Although in FLS algorithm, the upper level scheduling algorithm can calculate the amount of data that the real-time stream needs to transmit with larger scale (10 TTIs), the lower level assigns RBs to each user directly by the channel condition in each TTI. The lack of consideration for delay in the TTI scale could reduce throughput and increase PLR of real-time streams. The TTI-level delay characteristic reflects the relationship between delay of each flow and the time delay threshold, and it is indirectly related to packet loss. For example, there are two flows (flow A and flow B) in the lower level of scheduler. The delay of flow A is larger than flow B and close to the delay threshold. If the channel condition of flow A is slightly poor, flow A will probably lose packets due to timeout, which will affect the overall QoS satisfaction. Promisingly, the attribute of delay can be used at a more detailed scale to improve Packet Loss Rate (PLR) and throughput.

(2)   Lack of competition

DPS algorithm assigns RBs depending on each flow's packet delay information and downlink channel conditions. If there are two streams with similar delays, DPS will allocate RBs to the flow with higher delay. But for real-time flow with slightly less delay and much better channel quality, this allocation method is not fair and has lower system efficiency. Therefore, it is more reasonable that the flows with near delay get the RBs through intra grade competition depending on channel quality.

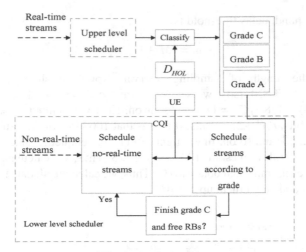

Fig. 1. DBS algorithm

3.2 Upper Level Scheduler

As shown in Fig. 1, the upper level scheduler is only valid for real-time stream. FLS algorithm [5] is exploited as the upper level scheduler. FLS algorithm estimates the amount of data that guarantees the QoS requirements of each real-time stream on the LTE frame. The authors of FLS suppose that packets of each real-time stream waiting for transmission are stored in a queue. Specifically, let $q_i(k)$ indicate the length of i th queue; $d_i(k)$ is the amount of newly filled data to i th queue; $u_i(k)$ is the amount of date corresponding to the flow's QoS requirements during the k th frame. The connection among the above values can be established by the following equation:

$$q_i(k+1) - q_i(k) = d_i(k) - u_i(k) \tag{9}$$

where $0 \le q_i(k) \le q_{max}$, $u_i(k) \ge 0$, $d_i(k) \ge 0$ and q_{max} presents the maximum length of queue q_i. To compute $u_i(k)$, FLS designs the following control method:

$$u_i(k) = h_i(k) * q_i(k) \tag{10}$$

where the "$*$" indicates the discrete-time convolution and $h_i(k)$ represents pulse response.

According to the derivation of (9) and (10) in [9], we can get $u_i(k)$ as follows:

$$u_i(k) = q_i(k) + \sum_{n=2}^{M_i} c_i(n)[q_i(k-n+1) - q_i(k-n+2) - q_i(k-n+1)] \tag{11}$$

where M_i indicates the width of the pulse-response, $c_i(n)$ represent a coefficient constrained by (12).

$$\begin{cases} 0 \le c_i(n) \le 1, \forall n \\ c_i(n) \ge c_i(n+1), n \ge 1 \text{ with } c_i(n) \in \mathbb{R} \end{cases} \tag{12}$$

On the other hand, delay threshold is

$$\delta_i = (M_i+1)T_f \tag{13}$$

where T_f is the length of sampling interval. Now, we show an example in Fig. 2 to illustrate FLS. Firstly, we set $M_i = 9$ and $c_i(0) = 0$, $c_i(1) = 1$, $c_i(2) = 1/2$, $c_i(3) = 1/4, c_i(4) = 1/8, c_i(5) = 1/16$ and soon on. Then, we set inputs $d_i(k) = 2000$ bits, $d_i(k+1) = 1000$ bits, $d_i(k+2) = 0$ bits. It means that 1000 bits of data submitted to the queue in the frame k and so on. In the light of (11), the enqueued data over kth, (k + 1)th, ..., and (k + 9)th frames are 1000, 500, ..., 3. Thus, we calculate all data need transported over each frame and obtain $u_i(k)$. Thus, we calculate all data that each frame need to transport and count them up as $u_i(k)$.

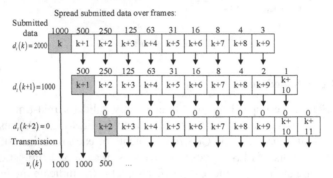

Fig. 2. Example of FLS

3.3 Lower Level Scheduler

We propose DBS algorithm (as shown in Fig. 1) that combines the upper level scheduler of FLS algorithm and a new lower level scheduler. Specifically, when a stream needs scheduling, we should judge whether it is a real-time stream. If yes, the upper estimates the amount of data that guarantees the QoS requirements of each real-time stream on the LTE frame. This also means that once the flow is satisfied with the amount of data required, it will not be allocated resources within the entire LTE frame. Figure 3 shows the flow chart of the DBS algorithm.

Then, all real-time streams are classified into grade A, B and C according to D_{HOL}. The real-time flow approaching the delay threshold has larger probability of packet dropping. We first determine that the interval near the delay threshold is [90%* δ_i, δ_i) and classify all real-time flows in this interval as grade A. These streams will have the highest priority for resources allocation and slightly lower PLR than before.

On the other hand, we should strive to reduce the possibility of streams being classified as grade A due to still larger PRL. The residual streams with small delay have little PLR or being dividing into grade A. Therefore, for real-time flows with medium delay performance and good delay performance, we divide them into grade B and C and with interval [50%* δ_i, 90%* δ_i) and (0, 50%* δ_i) respectively as shown in (14). Thus, each

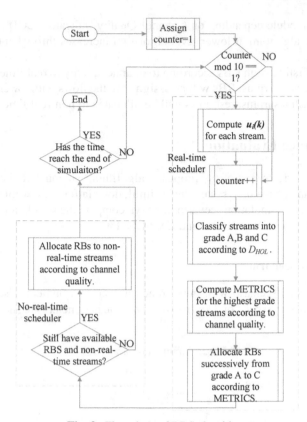

Fig. 3. Flowchart of DBS algorithm

real-time stream will be mapped to a unique grade.

$$grade(D_{HOL,i}) = \begin{cases} A & 90\% \cdot \delta_i \leq D_{HOL,i} < \delta_i \\ B & 50\% \cdot \delta_i \leq D_{HOL,i} < 90\% \cdot \delta_i \\ C & 0 < D_{HOL,i} < 50\% \cdot \delta_i \end{cases} \quad (14)$$

This classification method can make full use of delay in the TTI scale on the basis of FLS and guarantee the priority of the flows close to the threshold. Moreover, intra grade competition depending on channel quality can further improve throughput and reduce packet loss rate. The above classification strategy is determined by a large number of simulations, but it could be further improved.

After categorizing, we can allocate resources strictly according to the grades by Maximum Throughput (MT) algorithm [13] as (15).

$$w_{i,j}^{MT} = r_{i,j} \quad (15)$$

MT allocates the RBs only depending on the attainable data rate $r_{i,j}$. The larger $r_{i,j}$, the higher priority $r_{i,j}$ UE has. Attainable data rate $r_{i,j}$ for each UE is computed by the link adaptation module depending on Channel Quality Indicator (CQI) from UE. The adoption of MT algorithm at lower level algorithm increases throughput and reduces PLR.

Briefly, we firstly assign RBs according to channel quality to real-time streams with grade A. If there is a surplus, RBs will be assigned to the flows with lower grade. In the end, if there is still a surplus, resources will be allocated to non-real-time flows.

4 Performance Evaluation

To evaluate the performance of the proposed algorithm, we conduct simulations with LTE-Sim [14], an open-source system level simulation platform for whole LTE system. Firstly, we introduce simulation scenario; then we compare the simulation results of our DBS to those of M-LWDF, EXP/PF and EXP-LOG.

4.1 Simulation Scenario

We use a single cell scenario with interference as our environment. Users move in a random direction at the speed of 3 km/h. More specific parameters are shown in Table 2.

Table 2. Simulation parameters

Parameter	Value
Simulation duration	40 s
Physical detail	Carrier Frequency: 2 GHz Downlink Bandwidth: 5 MHz Number of RBs: 25
Link adaptation	Modulation Scheme: QPSK, 16QAM, 64QAM Target BLER: 10^{-1}
Cell layout	Radius: 1 km Number of UE: [10, 30]
UE mobility	Mobility model: Random Walk; UE speed: 3 km/h
Traffic model	Real-time flow type: H.264 440 kbps; best effort flow: infinite buffer

4.2 Performance Metrics

We mainly evaluate performance of the DBS algorithm based on PLR and system throughput.

The PLR and system throughput are given as follow:

$$\text{PLR} = \frac{\sum_{i=1}^{K} \sum_{t=1}^{T} pdiscard_i(t)}{\sum_{i=1}^{K} \sum_{t=1}^{T} psize_i(t)} \tag{16}$$

$$\text{system\_throughput} = \frac{1}{T} \sum_{i=1}^{K} \sum_{t=1}^{T} \text{ptransmit}_i(t) \tag{17}$$

where $pdiscard_i(t)$, $psize_i(t)$ and $ptransmit_i(t)$ represent the size of all dropped packets, the size of all packets arriving into the working eNodeB buffer and total size of transmitted packets of user i at time t 9.

4.3 Results and Discussion

We evaluate the performance of DBS, FLS, M-LWDF, EXP/PF and EXP-LOG by changing the number of UEs and the delay threshold of real-time flows.

As shown in Fig. 4(a) and (b), we set the number of users in the system from 10 to 30. We can observe that average PLR and average throughput increase with the number of UEs owing to higher network load. Throughputs of algorithms other than DBS and FLS are different. Because they do not distinguish between real-time flows and non-real-time flows as DBS. Figure 4(a) shows that DBS has lower PLR than FLS. Especially when the number of users is between 12 and 22, the advantage of PLR is more evident. On the whole, the average value of PLR of DBS is 1.54% lower than that of algorithm FLS. The effect is obvious.

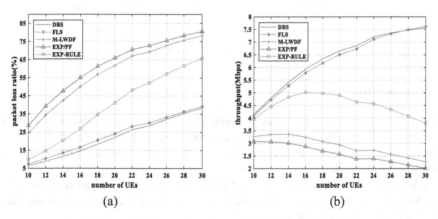

Fig. 4. (a). Video packet loss ratio (b). Video throughput

Figure 4(b) shows that the throughput of DBS is larger than FLS except for 28 UEs. Because when the number of users is too high, the load is extremely large. A large part of packets cannot be sent in time. That is to say, most packets have a large delay. Therefore, in this scenario the DBS is not as good as that of FLS. In addition, EXP-RULE as an upgrade of EXP/PF has a higher degree of emphasis on delay. Therefore, the performance of EXP-RULE is better than M-LWDF and EXP/PF. The two figures clearly show that DBS can improve throughput and reduce packet loss rate.

In Fig. 5(a) and (b), the curves of PLR and throughput under different delay thresholds are shown when the number of UE is 10. It is noteworthy that due to the limitation of FLS algorithm, simulation involves only four delay thresholds. Plainly, a larger value of delay threshold implies a lower PLR due to a less number of packets violating the deadline. The trend of throughput is similar to PLR curve. Figure 5(a) clearly indicates that PLR of DBS is slightly lower than that of FLS and far smaller than that of EXP-RULE and other algorithms. But when the threshold is the minimum, the PLR of DBS is nearly the same as that of FLS. On the whole, the advantages of DBS under different delay thresholds are much conspicuous. Figure 5(b) compares the performance of throughput. It shows that DBS can enhance video throughput on the basis of FLS. This is due to the improvement of PLR.

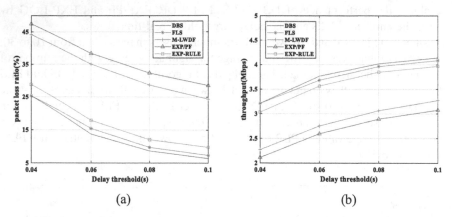

(a)   (b)

Fig. 5. (a). Video packet loss ratio for 10 UEs (b). Video throughput for 10 UEs

5   Conclusion

In this paper, we propose a delay based hierarchical downlink scheduling algorithm for real-time stream in cellular networks. Upper level scheduler offers a prediction of the number of data that each real-time stream needs to ensure the QoS. After classifying all real-time streams into grade A, B and C according to their D_{HOL}, the lower level scheduler allocates resource to streams by their different grades. The results of simulation have obviously shown that DBS algorithm improves the performance of FLS algorithm in terms of delay and throughput.

Acknowledgment. This work has been sponsored by National Engineering Laboratory for Next Generation Internet Technologies open fund project, Research on network traffic prediction technology based on spatiotemporal deep learning model, National Science Foundation of China (No. 61201149) and Huawei Research Fund (grant No. YBN2016110032). The authors would also like to thank the reviewers for their constructive comments.

References

1. Wang, Y.C., Hsieh, S.Y.: Service-differentiated downlink flow scheduling to support QoS in long term evolution. Comput. Netw. **94**, 344–359 (2016)

2. Krasilov, E., Krasilov, A., Malyshev, A.: Radio resource and traffic management for ultra-reliable low latency communications. In: Proceedings of IEEE WCNC (2018)
3. Shafi, M., et al.: 5G: a tutorial overview of standards trials challenges deployment and practice. IEEE J. Sel. Areas Commun. **35**(6), 1201–1221 (2017)
4. Girici, T., Zhu, C., Agre, J.R., Ephremides, A.: Proportional fair scheduling algorithm in OFDMA-based wireless systems with QoS constraints. J. Commun. Netw. **12**(1), 30–42 (2010)
5. Piro, G., et al.: Two-level downlink scheduling for real-time multimedia services in LTE networks. IEEE Trans. Multimedia **13**(5), 1052–1065 (2011)
6. Ramli, H., Basukala, R., Sandrasegaran, K., Patachaianand, R.: Performance of well-known packet scheduling algorithms in the downlink 3GPP LTE system. In: Proceedings of MICC, pp. 815–820 (2009)
7. Basukala, R., Ramli, H.M., Sandrasegaran, K.: Performance analysis of EXP/PF and M-LWDF in downlink 3GPP LTE system. In: Proceedings of AH – ICI (2009)
8. Sadiq, B., Baek, S.J., de Veciana, G.: Delay-optimal opportunistic scheduling and approximations: the Log rule. IEEE Trans. Netw. **19**(2), 406–418 (2011)
9. Sandrasegaran, K., Ramli, H.A.M., Basukala, R.: Delay-prioritized scheduling (DPS) for real time-traffic in 3GPP LTE system. In: Proceedings of IEEE WCNC, pp. 18–21 (2010)
10. Liu, S., Zhang, C., Zhou, Y., Zhang, Y.: Delay-based weighted proportional fair algorithm for LTE downlink packet scheduling. Wireless Pers. Commun. **82**(3), 1955–1965 (2015)
11. Madi, N.K., Hanapi, Z.M., Othman, M., Subramaniam, S.K.: Delay-based and QoS-aware packet scheduling for RT and NRT multimedia services in LTE downlink systems. EURASIP J. Wirel. Commun. Netw. **2018**, 180 (2018)
12. Hendaoui, S., Zangar, N., Tabbane, S.: Downlink scheduling for real time application over LTE-A network: delay aware scheduling. In: Proceedings of COMNET, pp. 4–7 (2015)
13. Kela, P., et al.: Dynamic packet scheduling performance in UTRA long term evolution downlink. In: Proceedings of ISWPC (2008)
14. Piro, G., Grieco, L., Boggia, G., Capozzi, F., Camarda, P.: Simulating LTE cellular systems: an open-source framework. IEEE Trans. Veh. Technol. **60**(2), 498–513 (2011)

Combination of Multiple PBCH Blocks in 5G NR Systems

Fang Wang[✉], Hang Long, and Wenxi He

Wireless Signal Processing and Network Lab,
Key Laboratory of Universal Wireless Communication, Ministry of Education,
Beijing University of Posts and Telecommunications,
Beijing, China
buptwfang@163.com

Abstract. Physical broadcast channel (PBCH) in 5G new radio (NR) systems transmits system informations required for the user equipment (UE) to access the cell. In the long term evolution (LTE) system, multiple PBCHs are usually combined to improve demodulation performances in the case of poor channel conditions. However, in 5G NR systems, the payload of PBCH includes the system frame number and the payloads of multiple frames are not exactly consistent. Hence, it is impossible to adopt the same combination approach as that in LTE. In this paper, there proposes a method to solve the problem of combining multiple PBCH blocks in 5G NR systems. The main idea is to convert log likelihood ratios (LLRs) of all transmitted PBCH blocks into that of the first block and accumulate all LLRs at the receiving end. Then, an improved combination algorithm is considered to reduce the complexity. The simulation results show that the proposed combination algorithm can correctly combine multiple PBCH blocks. Besides, the improved combination algorithm with sort can also reduce the complexity.

Keywords: New radio · Physical broadcast channel · Combination

1 Introduction

For the user equipment (UE), efficient decoding of physical broadcast channel (PBCH) is of great importance, even for UEs in low signal conditions. Right decoding of PBCH can help to improve the device performance in terms of faster cell selection and lower power consumption [1]. So in low signal conditions, it is necessary to combine PBCH blocks to improve demodulation performances. In long term evolution (LTE), the content of continuous frames mapping is the same [2], PBCH blocks in the 40 ms can be soft combined and decoded [3]. That

Supported by China Unicom Network Technology Research Institute and project 61302088 which was supported by National Natural Science Foundation of China.

H. Gao et al. (Eds.): ChinaCom 2019, LNICST 312, pp. 258–268, 2020.
https://doi.org/10.1007/978-3-030-41114-5_20

is, log likelihood ratios (LLRs) of multiple transmissions can be added at the receiving end.

In 5G new radio (NR) systems, SS/PBCH block (SSB) is always transmitted at the interval of 80 ms [4]. In the 80 ms, the maximum number of retransmissions depends on the SSB reception periodicity. For initial cell selection, a UE may assume that half frames with SSBs occur with a periodicity of 2 frames [5]. So this paper mainly takes the periodicity of 20 ms as an example. When the channel condition is poor, there needs to combine multiple PBCH blocks. The master information block (MIB) generated by the higher layer does not change within 80 ms. But the composition of PBCH includes system frame number (SFN), the payloads of multiple frames are different. In the existing combination solutions, such as equal gain combining and maximum ratio combining [6], the combination can only be performed in the case where the same data is transmitted multiple times. Therefore, soft-combination cannot be performed directly as in LTE.

For solving the above problem, there are already some studies. Ref. [7] proposes a Polar code design that explicitly transmits the time information on PBCH. The time-index-associated transformation is applied on information bit vector. The transformation is that multiplying the information bit vector by a constant matrix $\mathbf{T_u}$ according to SSB index. In Ref. [8], Sequans Communications proposes a scrambling design for SFN indication. At the receiving end, as for different blocks, use different scrambling sequences to descramble and then accumulate LLR from different blocks. After traversing all the scrambling sequence possibilities, choose the maximal power among the accumulated LLRs. But with the advancement of the 3GPP protocol, Polar code and scrambling [4] are finally determined. Under the premise of not changing the coding design and scrambling, the above methods are no longer applicable. So a novel and effective combination approach is needed.

In this paper, we propose an algorithm to combine multiple PBCH blocks. Due to the operations such as the cyclic redundancy check (CRC) and polar coding are linear, the LLRs sequence of multiple PBCH blocks all can be converted into that of the first block, and then LLRs of all PBCH blocks can be accumulated. When UEs initially access the cell, they can not know the SFN. So the SFN needs to be assumed during the combination process and there needs to traverse multiple SFN assumptions. Then, an improved combination algorithm is proposed to reduce the complexity of combination. In this paper, the sum of absolute values of the LLR sequences is used as the sort criterion. The larger the sum of absolute values is, the more reliable the SFN hypothesis is considered. The simulation results show that the improved combination method proposed in this paper can correctly combine multiple PBCH blocks and reduce the complexity.

The remainder of this paper is organized as follows. Section 2 mainly describes the system model, and Sect. 3 elaborates the algorithm of combination. Section 4 introduces the main process of the receiver, including combination process and sorting algorithm. Section 5 shows the simulation results and analyzes the performance of the proposed algorithm by comparison. And finally Sect. 6 concludes this paper.

Notations: $\oplus$ is used to denote the XOR operator. The j-th entry of a matrix $\mathbf{X}$ is denoted as $\mathbf{X}(j)$. And $\mathbb{N}^{m \times n}$ denotes a set of natural number with m rows and n columns.

2   System Model

The payload in 5G NR PBCH denoted as $\mathbf{x} \in \mathbb{N}^{1 \times 32}$ consists of MIB and some time-dependent bits, where the size of MIB is 24. The 24 bits of MIB denoted as $\mathbf{x}(0), \mathbf{x}(1), \ldots, \mathbf{x}(23)$, are the same in the 80 ms period, i.e., TTI. Then, an 8-bit time-dependent PBCH payload bit is added, where $\mathbf{x}(24), \mathbf{x}(25), \mathbf{x}(26), \mathbf{x}(27)$ are the least significant bits of the SFN, $\mathbf{x}(28)$ refers to the half radio frame bit and this bit will not change in the TTI. As for $\mathbf{x}(29), \mathbf{x}(30), \mathbf{x}(31)$, when the number of SSBs in a half radio frame is larger than 64, they mean the indexes of SSB [2]. They has not been determined when the number of SSB is smaller than 64, so it is assumed that these three bits are random and do not change during the TTI. An example of the payload composition under 4 GHz carrier frequency is illustrated in Fig. 1.

Information bit 24bit	LSBs of the SFN 4bit	Half frame bit 1bit	MSB of subcarrier offset 1bit	Reserved bits 2bit	CRC 24bit

Fig. 1. The composition of the payload in 5G NR PBCH.

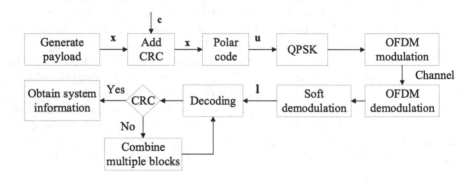

Fig. 2. The general process of PBCH

The general process of PBCH is shown in Fig. 2. In Fig. 2, the algorithm of combining multiple blocks is described in detail in Sect. 3. According to the agreements of 3GPP, the initial cell selection takes 20 ms as the SSB transmission period [5], so this paper mainly simulates the case of sending PBCH four times at most in the TTI. According to Fig. 1, the different parts in multiple PBCH payloads are the middle two bits between the four least significant bits of SFN, that is $\mathbf{x}(25), \mathbf{x}(26)$. There sets that when $\mathbf{x}(25), \mathbf{x}(26)$ changes from 00 to 11, correspondingly, i changes from 0 to 3 and multiple payload sequences of retransmission are denoted as $\mathbf{x}_i$. Then, we can get that,

$$
\begin{aligned}
\mathbf{x}_i &= \mathbf{x}_0 \oplus \mathbf{d}_i, \\
i &= 1 \sim 3,
\end{aligned}
\tag{1}
$$

where $\mathbf{d}_i = [0, 0, 0 \ldots 0, 0]_{1\times 32}$, and $[\mathbf{d}_i(25), \mathbf{d}_i(26)] = [\mathbf{x}_i(25), \mathbf{x}_i(26)]$ are part of the SFN, i.e., $\mathbf{d}_i$ is a difference sequence which represents the difference between payloads.

In Fig. 2, the CRC sequence of $\mathbf{x}$ is $\mathbf{c}$. 3GPP specifies that the parity bits of PBCH are generated by [4], CRC is linear and CRC code matrix is set as $\mathbf{C}$. So the CRC sequence $\mathbf{c}$ can be calculated as

$$
\mathbf{c} = \mathbf{x}\mathbf{C},
\tag{2}
$$

Correspondingly, the sequence after CRC added of $\mathbf{x}$ is denoted as $\tilde{\mathbf{x}}$. In 5G NR systems, PBCH uses Polar code at the transmitting end, and the generator matrix of Polar code is set as $\mathbf{G_N}$. As shown in Fig. 2, the sequence after Polar encoding is denoted as $\mathbf{u}$. And the output sequence of soft demodulation of $\mathbf{u}$ is $\mathbf{l}$.

3   Algorithm of Combination

In this section, it is theoretically analyzed why multiple PBCH blocks can be combined when their payloads are different. Firstly, according to (2), CRC output sequences $\mathbf{c}_i$ of $\mathbf{x}_i$ are caluculated as

$$
\begin{aligned}
\mathbf{c}_{\mathbf{d}_i} &= \mathbf{d}_i\mathbf{C}, \\
\mathbf{c}_0 &= \mathbf{x}_0\mathbf{C},
\end{aligned}
\tag{3}
$$

$$
\begin{aligned}
\mathbf{c}_i = \mathbf{x}_i\mathbf{C} &= (\mathbf{x}_0 \oplus \mathbf{d}_i)\,\mathbf{C} \\
&= (\mathbf{x}_0\mathbf{C}) \oplus (\mathbf{d}_i\mathbf{C}) \\
&= \mathbf{c}_0 \oplus \mathbf{c}_{\mathbf{d}_i},
\end{aligned}
\tag{4}
$$

where $i = 1$–3 and $\mathbf{c}_{\mathbf{d}_i}$ is the output bit sequence to CRC of $\mathbf{d}_i$. Then the output after encoding of $\mathbf{x}_i$ can be obtained as

$$
\begin{aligned}
\mathbf{u}_i = [\mathbf{x}_i, \mathbf{c}_i]\,\mathbf{G_N} &= [\mathbf{x}_0 \oplus \mathbf{d}_i, \mathbf{c}_0 \oplus \mathbf{c}_{\mathbf{d}_i}]\,\mathbf{G_N} \\
&= ([\mathbf{x}_0, \mathbf{c}_0] \oplus [\mathbf{d}_i, \mathbf{c}_{\mathbf{d}_i}])\,\mathbf{G_N} \\
&= ([\mathbf{x}_0, \mathbf{c}_0]\,\mathbf{G_N}) \oplus ([\mathbf{d}_i, \mathbf{c}_{\mathbf{d}_i}]\,\mathbf{G_N}),
\end{aligned}
\tag{5}
$$

Set $\mathbf{f}_i = [\mathbf{d}_i, \mathbf{c}_{\mathbf{d}_i}]\,\mathbf{G_N}$, then

$$\mathbf{u_i} = \mathbf{u_0} \oplus \mathbf{f_i}. \tag{6}$$

So when the SFN changes, the relationship between LLRs with different SFNs can be deduced. At the receiving end, $\mathbf{l_i}$ can be given as

$$\mathbf{l_0}(j) = \log\left(\frac{P(\mathbf{y}|\mathbf{u_0}(j)=1)}{P(\mathbf{y}|\mathbf{u_0}(j)=0)}\right),$$
$$j = 0, 1, ..., J-1, \tag{7}$$

where J is the length of the sequence $\mathbf{l_i}$. Then,

$$\mathbf{l_i}(j) = \log\left(\frac{P\left(\mathbf{y}|\mathbf{u_i}(j)=1\right)}{P\left(\mathbf{y}|\mathbf{u_i}(j)=0\right)}\right) = \log\left(\frac{P\left(\mathbf{y}|\mathbf{u_0}(j)\oplus\mathbf{f_i}(j)=1\right)}{P\left(\mathbf{y}|\mathbf{u_0}(j)\oplus\mathbf{f_i}(j)=0\right)}\right). \tag{8}$$

So we can get that

$$\begin{aligned}\mathbf{f_i}(j)=0 &\rightarrow \mathbf{l_i}(j)=\mathbf{l_0}(j)\\ \mathbf{f_i}(j)=1 &\rightarrow \mathbf{l_i}(j)=-\mathbf{l_0}(j)\end{aligned}. \tag{9}$$

The relationship between $\mathbf{l_0}$ and $\mathbf{l_i}$ can be concluded that,

$$\mathbf{l_i}(j) = \mathbf{l_0}(j)\cdot(-1)^{\mathbf{f_i}(j)}. \tag{10}$$

From (10), when the payloads of multiple PBCH transmissions are different in SFN, LLRs of $\mathbf{x_i}, i = 1, 2, 3$, can be reversed after soft demodulation to LLRs of $\mathbf{x_0}$. And then accumulate LLRs to combine multiple PBCH blocks. Therefore, difference sequences, i.e., $\mathbf{f_i}$ can be stored at the transmitting end. When the SFN is 11, i.e., $i = 3$, $\mathbf{f_3}$ can be obtained as

$$\begin{aligned}\mathbf{f_3} &= [\mathbf{d_3}, \mathbf{c_{d_3}}]\,\mathbf{G_N} = [\mathbf{d_1}\oplus\mathbf{d_2}, \mathbf{c_{d_1}}\oplus\mathbf{c_{d_2}}]\,\mathbf{G_N}\\ &= [\mathbf{d_1}, \mathbf{c_{d_1}}]\,\mathbf{G_N} \oplus [\mathbf{d_2}, \mathbf{c_{d_2}}]\,\mathbf{G_N}\\ &= \mathbf{f_1} \oplus \mathbf{f_2}.\end{aligned} \tag{11}$$

Therefore, in order to reduce the number of stored difference sequences, there only holds the difference sequences $\mathbf{f_1}$ and $\mathbf{f_2}$. So when combination is needed, LLRs of $\mathbf{x_i}$ are converted into LLRs of $\mathbf{x_0}$. For example, when combining two PBCH blocks, the payload sequences are denoted as $\mathbf{x_0}$ and $\mathbf{x_1}$ respectively. At this time, only $\mathbf{l_1}$, LLRs of $\mathbf{x_1}$, need to be reversed, according to the difference sequence $\mathbf{f_1}$. According to (10), when $\mathbf{f_1}(j)$ is 1, reverse $\mathbf{l_1}(j)$, or $\mathbf{l_1}(j)$ stay the same otherwise. Then accumulate $\mathbf{l_0}$ and $\mathbf{l_1}$. Finally, decode the accumulated LLRs sequence.

Considering the initial cell selection assumption, UEs do not know the SFN, so various assumptions are made on the SFN at the receiving end during the combination process. Compared with the same payloads that can be combined directly, the complexity of proposed combination method is higher. And if there are more PBCH blocks to combine, there are more than assumptions, which makes the complexity even higher. So multiple SFN assumptions should be sorted and then choose the most reliable assumption to traverse first.

4 Receiver Process of PBCH in 5G NR Systems

The main process of the receiving end includes orthogonal frequency division multiplexing (OFDM) demodulation, channel estimation, channel equalization, soft demodulation, de-rate matching, and channel decoding, etc. If retransmission is required, it needs to be combined before soft demodulation. As described in Sect. 3, the main idea of combination in this paper is that, at the transmitting end, the changes in the multiple encoded sequences are recorded through the difference sequences, i.e., f_1 and f_2. Then reverse LLRs of received SSBs according to f_1, f_2 and the current SFN hypothesis.

4.1 Specific Steps for Combination

This subsection mainly describes the specific steps of combination at the receiving end.

Step 1: Firstly, receive first SSB and keep the LLRs. If CRC is passed, obtain the system information. Then repeat Step 1.

Step 2: Otherwise, receive second SSB after 20 ms. When SFN of the first received SSB is 00, 01, 10 or 11 respectively, combine according to the detailed process in Fig. 3. Four hypotheses are elaborated below.

- Hypothesis 1 (SFN of first received SSB is 00): Reverse the LLRs of the second SSB according to f_1.
- Hypothesis 2 (SFN of first received SSB is 01): the LLRs of the two SSBs need to be reversed according to f_1 and f_2. And the two LLRs sequences after the reversal accumulate.
- Hypothesis 3 (SFN of first received SSB is 10): As is described in Hypothesis 2, the LLRs of the two blocks should be reversed.
- Hypothesis 4 (SFN of first received SSB is 11): At this time, SFN of the second SSB is 00. Obviously, they are in the different TTI. So payloads of the two SSBs are not only different in SFN. It is assumed that the two SSBs cannot be combined. In this case, only decode the second SSB.

The detailed process of Step 2 is shown in Fig. 3. Where SFN_SSB1 refers to SFN of the first SSB and then SFN of the next SSB adds one in turn. LLRs_SSB1 and LLRs_SSB2 refer to the received LLRs after soft demodulation of the first SSB and second SSB. Partial reversal in Fig. 3 means reversing the LLRs sequences by f_1 and f_2. LLR combination means accumulating the LLRs sequence after the reversion.

Step 3: If four hypotheses of Step 2 fail to pass, receive the third SSB after 20 ms. As shown in Step 2, there are also four SFN hypotheses. Combine three blocks respectively under four SFN hypotheses.

Step 4: If Step 3 cannot pass CRC, it is necessary to receive the fourth SSB after 20 ms. If one of the four hypotheses passes, the system information can be obtained. Otherwise, go to the Step 5.

Step 5: Drop the first SSB, receive the next SSB after 20 ms. Return to Step 4, and combine the last four SSBs.

4.2 Multiple SFN Hypotheses Sorting

In this paper, the times of traversing SFN hypotheses are taken as the measure of complexity. As can be seen from the above descriptions, in terms of complexity, it may be higher than combining same payloads with existing algorithms. According to this paper, it is necessary to make assumptions about SFN at the receiving end. Due to the maximum number of retransmissions in this paper is 4, there are up to 4 hypothetical situations at a time. However, there may be up to eight hypotheses under 5G NR PBCH in the TTI. This complexity may be a bit unacceptable. To reduce complexity, it is necessary to look for an indicator to characterize the reliability of each hypothesis. Then the four hypotheses can be sorted based on their reliability and a more reliable hypothesis can be traversed first to reduce the numbers of traversal.

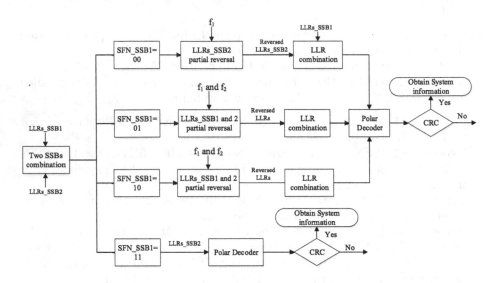

Fig. 3. Specific method of combining two SSBs

In Ref. [9], the author expounds the relationship between LLR and an estimation of the bit error rate (BER). From the author's description and theoretical deduction, the larger the absolute value of LLR is, the smaller the BER. And in Ref. [9], the author employs the calculated BER metric to perform a prediction on the reliability of the transmission. So in our paper, the reliability of the hypotheses is characterized with the sum of absolute values of the reversed LLR sequences. There are K hypotheses, numbered 1 to K. For hypothesis k, the reliability is calculated as shown in (12),

$$\mathbf{s}(k) = \sum_{j=0}^{J-1} \mathbf{l}(j),$$

$$k = 1, ...K,$$ (12)

$$k = \arg\max\{\mathbf{s}(k)\}.$$

From (12), it is assumed that the larger $\mathbf{s}(k)$ is, the hypothesis k more reliable. In the cases where combination cannot be performed, it is considered to give a weight to the sum of absolute values of the LLRs sequence, so that they can also participate in sort. Simulations are performed to determine the weight value, so that the complexity can be minimized. In this paper, the combination of two PBCH blocks are used as an example. Since it is unable to distinguish Hypothesis 1 and 3 in Sect. 4 through the combined LLRs, Hypothesis 3 is always put after Hypothesis 1 during the sorting.

5   Simulation Results and Analysis

In this section, simulations are performed for comparison and analysis, including the combination performance and complexity of combination process. There mainly simulates the performance of ideal and linear minimum mean square error (LMMSE) channel estimation. Simulation parameters are shown in the Table 1.

Table 1. Simulation parameters of the PBCH [10].

Simulation parameters	Values
Antenna configuration	1Tx*4Rx
Bandwidth	20 MHz
Carrier frequency	4 GHz
Velocity	3 km/h
Cell ID	1
DCI	32 + 24(CRC) = 56bit
Encoding method	Polar
Channel estimation method	LMMSE/ ideal
Code rate	56/(24*9*2*2)
Channel model	CDL-C [11] 300 ns

In this part, the Signal to Noise Ratio (SNR) at 1% Block Error Ratio (BLER) is taken as a performance metric [10], and the performance gain between combination and without combination are compared. Besides, the performance of combining multiple PBCH blocks by the algorithm proposed in this paper and that of combining the same payloads are analysed. The simulation results are

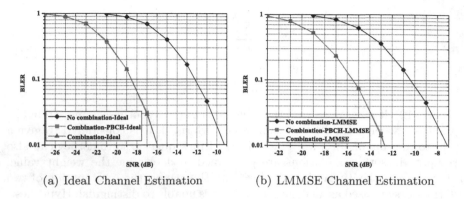

(a) Ideal Channel Estimation   (b) LMMSE Channel Estimation

Fig. 4. Simulation results with CDL-C 300 ns

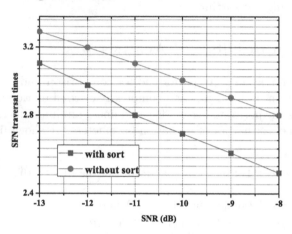

Fig. 5. Complexity with sort

shown below. Where no combination represents the performance of transmission only once within 20 ms, Combination denotes combining the same PBCHs and Combination-PBCH denotes combining multiple PBCH blocks in 5G NR systems.

Firstly the result of ideal channel estimation is shown as Fig. 4(a). As can be seen from Fig. 4(a), compared with the same PBCHs retransmitted four times, the performance of combining different PBCH blocks in 5G NR systems by proposed algorithm is the same on the whole. And when retransmitting up to 4 times, the performance gain is about 6.8 dB compared with no retransmission. Then, the performance with LMMSE channel estimation is presented in Fig. 4(b). In the case of real channel estimation, the SNR gain is about 5.6 dB. At this time, the channel estimation is considered to be not accurate, resulting in insufficient gain compared with ideal channel estimation.

In the combination process, the complexity is also statistically analyzed. The following is mainly the analysis on the process of combining two SSBs. The complexity is compared between the improved combination algorithm with sort and the combination algorithm without sort. Without sort refers to traversing in the order of SFN Hypothesis 1, 2, 3, 4 in Sect. 4. According to the simulation results, it is found that with the improved combination algorithm with sort, there is no effect on performance, e.g., BLER. Moreover, the average times of traversing SFN hypothesis decreases. From Fig. 5, it is seen that complexity decreases as the SNR increases. And even the SNR is higher, the complexity can also reduce up to 10%.

6   Conclusion

In order to solve the combination problem of PBCH in 5G NR systems, an algorithm is proposed in this paper. Although the payloads of multiple PBCH blocks in the 5G NR system are different, the difference only lies in two bits of the SFN, and it also shows the continuity. So we can use the proposed algorithm to convert LLRs of all transmitted PBCH blocks, and then accumulate them. The simulation results show that the algorithm in this paper can bring reasonable gains in BLER, compared with combining the same PBCHs.

In addition, in the proposed combination algorithm, the complexity is relatively high due to the need of making multiple assumptions about the SFN. Hence, an improved combination algorithm is proposed to reduce the complexity. The absolute value of LLRs after the combination is mainly used to determine the reliability of the SFN hypotheses. These hypotheses can be sorted based on their reliability. The simulation results indicate that the complexity can be reduced by about 10% in the case of combining two SSBs. The improved combination algorithm proposed in this paper plays a certain role in reducing the complexity, but there is room for improvement.

References

1. Annamalai, P., Das, S.K., Bapat, J., Das, D.: Coverage enhancement of PBCH using reduced search Viterbi for MTC in LTE-advanced networks. In: 2015 13th International Symposium on Modeling and Optimization in Mobile, Ad Hoc, and Wireless Networks (WiOpt), Mumbai, India, pp. 110–114 (2015)
2. Chen, F., Chen, B.: Research and DSP on eNodeB of PBCH in LTE system. In: 2013 International Conference on Computational and Information Sciences, Shiyang, China, pp. 1471–1474 (2013)
3. Han, S., Xiong, G., Khoryaev, A.: Transmission of physical broadcast channel (PBCH) contents (2016). (US patent)
4. 3GPP TS 38.212: 3rd Generation Partnership Project, Technical Specification Group Radio Access Network, NR, Multiplexing and channel coding, Release 15 (2018)
5. 3GPP TS 38.213: 3rd Generation Partnership Project, Technical Specification Group Radio Access Network, NR, Physical layer procedures for control, Release 15 (2018)

6. Nakamura, A., Itami, M.: A study on LLR calculation scheme under mobile reception of OFDM. In: 2018 IEEE International Conference on Consumer Electronics (ICCE), Las Vegas, NV, USA, pp. 1–2 (2018)
7. R1-1718373: Polar code for PBCH and soft combining. Huawei, HiSilicon, 3GPP TSG RAN WG1 Meeting # 90bis, Prague, Czech Republic, October 2017
8. R1-1717728: Scrambling sequence design for PBCH. Sequans Communications, 3GPP TSG RAN WG1 Meeting # 90bis, Prague, Czech Republic, October 2017
9. Goektepe, B., Faehse, S., Thiele, L., Schierl, T., Hellge, C.: Subcode-based early HARQ for 5G. In: 2018 IEEE International Conference on Communications Workshops, ICC Workshops, Kansas City, MO, USA, pp. 1–6 (2018)
10. R4-1810407: Discussion on NR PBCH demodulation requirements. CMCC, 3GPP TSG-RAN WG4 Meeting # 88, Gothenburg, Sweden, August 2018
11. 3GPP TR 38.901: 3rd Generation Partnership Project, Technical Specification Group Radio Access Network, Study on channel model for frequencies from 0.5 to 100 GHz, Release 15 (2018)

A Channel Threshold Based Multiple Access Protocol for Airborne Tactical Networks

Bo Zheng[1,2(✉)], Yong Li[1], Wei Cheng[1], and Wei-Lun Liu[2]

[1] College of Electronics and Information, Northwestern Polytechnical University,
Xi'an 710129, China
zbkgd@163.com
[2] Information and Navigation Institute, Air Force Engineering University, Xi'an 710077, China

Abstract. Airborne Tactical Network is a promising and special mobile Ad hoc network, connecting the ground stations and all kinds of flying combat aircrafts on battlefield through tactical data links. Designing a low delay, large capacity, high flexibility, strong scalability, and multi-priority traffic differentiated medium access control (MAC) protocol is a great challenge in the researches and applications of ATNs. In order to overcome the disadvantages in IEEE 802.11 Distributed Coordination Function (DCF) and Time Division Multiple Access (TDMA) protocols, we present a channel threshold based multiple access (CTMA) protocol for ATNs in this paper. The CTMA protocol is a novel random contention type of MAC protocols, and it can differentiate multiple priority services, and utilize multi-channel resource based on channel awareness. We intensively describe the channel occupancy statistic mechanism, multi-queueing and scheduling mechanism of multi-priority services, and channel threshold based admission control mechanism involved in the protocol. We further derive the channel threshold of each priority service, the expressions of the successful transmission probability and mean delay mathematically. Simulation results show that the CTMA protocol can differentiate services for different priorities in ATNs according to the real-time channel state, and provide effective QoS guarantee for transmissions of various information.

Keywords: Airborne Tactical Network · Medium access control protocol · Channel threshold · Priority differentiation · Multi-channel · Admission control

1 Introduction

In order to meet the requirement of Network Centric Warfare, the U.S. Air Force is engaging in developing Airborne Tactical Network (ATN) in recent years. ATN is a new type of wireless network, connecting the ground stations and all kinds of flying combat aircrafts on battlefield through tactical data links [1–5]. In essence, ATN is a special kind of Mobile Ad hoc Network (MANET), with the characteristics of great flexibility, high dynamics, rapid self-organizing, large capacity, good robustness and reliability. It can improve the capability of cooperative operation for combat aircrafts, and has become one of the most important developing trends of military aeronautical communication

© ICST Institute for Computer Sciences, Social Informatics and Telecommunications Engineering 2020
Published by Springer Nature Switzerland AG 2020. All Rights Reserved
H. Gao et al. (Eds.): ChinaCom 2019, LNICST 312, pp. 269–282, 2020.
https://doi.org/10.1007/978-3-030-41114-5_21

networks. In ATNs, such as TTNT (Tactical Targeting Network Technology) [6], JALN (Joint Aerial Layered Network) [7], BACN (Battlefield Airborne Communication Node) [8], QNT (Quint Networking Technology) [9], etc., the capabilities of quick finding and accurate attack against the ground and aerial targets with strong mobility, i.e., time-sensitive target, is regarded as one of the key technologies. Medium Access Control (MAC) protocol mainly solves the problem of sharing the wireless channel resources between nodes in ATNs efficiently, and is the main factor influencing the information transmission delay. In ATNs, there exist the issues of long transmission delay and unstable channel, etc., influencing on the real-time and reliability of information transmissions drastically. Thus, these issues put forward a higher requirement for MAC protocol than the traditional MANETs.

The existing MAC protocols in ATNs mainly contain IEEE 802.11 Distributed Coordination Function (DCF) protocol [10–14], and Time Division Multiple Access (TDMA) protocol [15–19]. The IEEE 802.11 DCF adopts RTS/CTS frames to reserve channel resources in order to avoid collisions. The RTS/CTS handshaking mechanism is not quite suitable for the delay-sensitive aeronautical communications, due to the large transmission delay of interactive information in long communication range. As a fixed allocation MAC protocol, TDMA has the advantages of high throughput and large capacity. However, it needs to pre-assign time-slots for each user, and the transmission delay is seriously influenced by user number. Thus, it is also not applicable to the delay-sensitive ATN. A MAC protocol based on burst communication and asynchronous frequency hopping is proposed for ATNs in [20]. However, it cannot differentiate multiple services.

The MAC protocol in ATN should meet the following requirements: (1) transmission delay for the high priority traffic is very low; (2) the first time packet delivery success rate reaches 99%; (3) different Classes of Service (CoS) is supported; (4) large number of users can be contained. Therefore, it is necessary to design a novel MAC protocol with low delay, large capacity, high flexibility, strong scalability, and multi-priority traffic differentiated for ATNs.

In our previous work, we have presented a priority differentiated and multi-channel (PDM) MAC protocol in [21] and a channel busy recognition mechanism combined with auto regressive forecasting in [22] for ATNs. The PDM protocol in [21] addressed the multi-priority services differentiation through an adaptive jitter mechanism. For different priority packets, time to access to channels is controlled by the adaptive jitter mechanism. The channel busy recognition mechanism in [22] can be an important module in PDM protocol.

In order to guarantee the co-transmissions of traffic of multiple priorities and meet the strict QoS requirement of delay-sensitive information transmissions in ATNs, some effective mechanisms, such as multiple priority differentiation and channel awareness, should also be adopted in the MAC protocol. Therefore, we are motivated to propose a novel Channel Threshold based Multiple Access (CTMA) MAC protocol in this paper. Based on the real-time channel occupancy awareness, the protocol can differentiate multiple priority traffic, and provide effective QoS guarantee for information transmissions. The protocol employs a simple and effective channel occupancy statistic mechanism. It introduces a multi-queueing and scheduling strategy for multi-priority traffic. It also adopts a novel channel threshold based admission control mechanism to control the access of packets with different priority services to multi-channel.

The proposed MAC protocol has the following attractive advantages: (1) It can support multiple service classes. (2) It can guarantee the extremely low delay and extremely high successful transmission ratio for the highest priority service. (3) It involves a novel adaptive backoff algorithm for multiple service types. (4) It controls the access of packets (except the highest priority service) to channel according to the busy degree of the channel.

The reminder of the paper is organized as follows. Section 2 presents the CTMA protocol for ATNs, describes the its main components in detail, and models it theoretically. Section 3 derives the mathematical expressions of some key metrics of the protocol. In Sect. 4, we conduct simulations to show the protocol performance and verify the mathematical derivations. Finally, we conclude our work in Sect. 5.

2 Protocol Description

2.1 General Description of CTMA Protocol

The CTMA protocol proposed in this paper is a distributed random contention MAC protocol. It includes 4 components, namely the channel occupancy statistic mechanism, multi-queuing and scheduling mechanism, channel threshold admission control mechanism, and multi-priority adaptive backoff mechanism, as shown in Fig. 1.

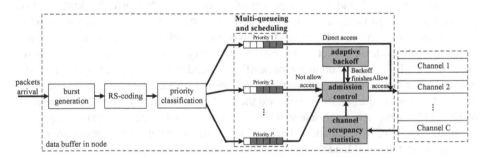

Fig. 1. Main components of the CTMA protocol.

(1) Burst generation module. In order to improve the reliability of packet transmission in wireless channel, the CTMA protocol employs the burst communication, i.e., each packet is split into short bursts to be transmitted in channel. Therefore, each packet arrived from the upper layer is firstly split into a bunch of bursts with equal length.

(2) RS-Turbo coding module. After burst generation, each burst is coded with RS-Turbo to have a fault-tolerant ability [23].

(3) Priority classification module. In this module, each burst is classified according to their priority.

(4) Multi-queueing and scheduling module. In the buffer of each node, packets of each priority wait in an individual queue. And each priority maintains a First-In-First-Out (FIFO) queue. The arrived bursts will be discarded when the node buffer is full.

(5) Channel occupancy statistic module. This module records the number of bursts transmitted during a period of time in each channel in order to calculate the channel occupancy rate and provide reference to the subsequent admission control module.

(6) Channel threshold based admission control module. This module judges whether a burst can be accessed to channel immediately. If the channel occupancy rate is higher than the channel access threshold of the burst's priority, it cannot be transmitted immediately and the backoff mechanism will be started. If the channel occupancy rate is lower than its channel threshold, it will be accessed to channel.

(7) Adaptive backoff module. This module adopts a multi-priority backoff algorithm based on channel busy-idle sensing, and the contention window can be adaptively and dynamically adjusted with the occupancy of channel in real time. In this paper, for ease of analysis, we adopt a simplified backoff algorithm with a fixed contention window for all priority services. The multi-priority adaptive backoff mechanism for ATNs is described and analyzed in detail in [24].

The node state transition in CTMA protocol is shown in Fig. 2. All nodes in the network work on the basis of the following state transition scheme. (1) In the state "initialization/idle", if the node receives a packet from the upper layer, the packet will be inserted into the corresponding priority queue. (2) When the packet is in head of the queue, the next state "send the head packet of the queue" or "adaptive backoff" will be judged according to the current channel occupancy state and the channel threshold of its priority. If the current channel load is lower than its channel threshold, it can enter the state "send the head packet of the queue"; otherwise, it will enter the state "adaptive backoff". (3) In the state "adaptive backoff" or "send the head packet of the queue", when new packets arrive, if the corresponding priority queue is not full, the packets will be insert into the queue, otherwise discard the packets. (4) After the state "send the head packet of the queue", the next state will be chosen in "send the head packet of the queue", "initialization/idle", and "adaptive backoff" according to whether all queues are empty and the current channel load.

2.2 Channel Occupancy Statistic Mechanism

For a fully connected network, all nodes can record the number of bursts received in the whole network during a period of time. As illustrated in Fig. 3, the current time is t_0, and the size of the statistic window is T_s. The number of bursts during $[t_0 - T_s, t_0]$ can be used to approximately represent the channel occupancy at t_0.

Define G_{total} as the number of bursts accessed to all channels. Since all nodes can record the number of bursts sensed in each channel, G_{total} can be obtained according to the total number of bursts sensed in all channel. Thus it is calculated as

$$G_{total} = \sum_{c=1}^{C} G_c, \qquad (1)$$

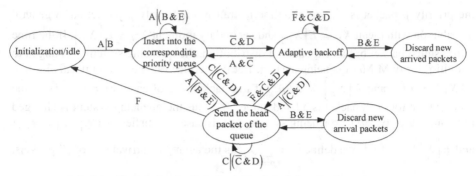

A: Packets with priority 1 arrive; B: Packets with priority 2, 3, ···, P arrive;
C: The queue of priority 1 has packets; $\overline{C}$: The queue of priority 1 has no packets;
D: The channel load is lower than the channel threshold of the priority service;
$\overline{D}$: The channel load is equal to or higher than the channel threshold of the priority service;
E: The queue is full; $\overline{E}$: The queue is not full;
F: All queues are empty; $\overline{F}$: Not all queues are empty.

Fig. 2. Node state transition in CTMA protocol.

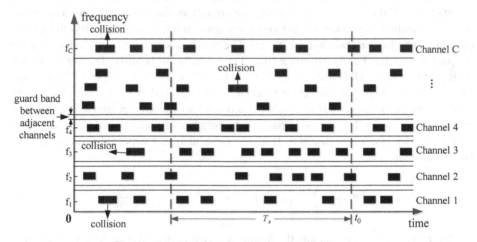

Fig. 3. Time and frequency state of multi-channel.

where G_c denotes the number of bursts sensed in channel c.

Define η as the mean channel occupancy rate, meaning the mean ratio of the total channel transmission time of all bursts received in T_s. So η can be calculated as

$$\eta = \frac{G_{total}}{C} \cdot \frac{T_{packet}}{T_s}. \tag{2}$$

2.3 Multi-priority Multi-queuing and Scheduling Mechanism

The priority of services in the network is denoted by p, where $p = 1, 2, \cdots, P$. $p = 1$ denotes the highest priority, and $p = P$ denotes the lowest priority. The arrival rate of the priority p packet is λ_p, and the time to transmit a priority p packet has a general distribution with mean $\bar{X}_p = E[X_p]$ and secondary moment $\overline{X_p^2} = E[X_p^2]$. If the time to transmit a packet has an exponential distribution, the queueing system is changed to a multi-priority M/M/1 queueing system. Let the service rate be μ, and it satisfies that $E[X_p] = 1/\mu$ and $E[X_p^2] = 2/\mu^2$. If the packet size of each priority is fixed, the service time for each packet is a fixed value, and thus the queueing system is changed to a multi-priority M/D/1 queueing system. In this case, it satisfies that $E[X_p] = 1/\mu$ and $E[X_p^2] = 1/\mu^2$. We define $\lambda = \sum_{p=1}^{P} \lambda_p$ as the aggregate arrival rate of all packets, $\rho_p = \lambda_p E[X_p]$ as the utilization of the server by the priority p packets, and $\sigma_k = \sum_{p=1}^{k} \rho_p$ as the utilization of the server by the priority 1 to k packets. Let W_p be the waiting time of priority p packets, and let T_p denote the total time that a priority p packet spends in the system, namely the sojourn time.

Due to the backoff mechanism, before the service for a priority p ($p > 1$) packet, the node needs to judge whether it can be served immediately according to the current channel state. If it does not satisfy the service condition, the server will start a vacation. After the vacation, the node needs to judge once again. If it still does not satisfy the service condition, another vacation will be started. The process is repeated until the service for the packet is started. For the priority p ($p > 1$) packet, the probability of server's vacation is denoted as P_p^{vac}. Obviously, it satisfies that $P_2^{vac} < P_3^{vac} < \cdots < P_P^{vac}$. For any priority p ($p > 1$) packet, the server's vacations are denoted as $V_1, V_2, \cdots, V_m$, where V_i is an independent and uniformly distributed random variable on interval $[0, W]$ with mean $\frac{W}{2}$. For a priority p ($p > 1$) packet, the number of times of server's vacation is represented by m_p, where $m_p = 0, 1, 2, \cdots$. Obviously, the expected value of m_p can be expressed as

$$E[m_p] = \sum_{i=0}^{\infty} i \left(P_p^{vac} \right)^i \left(1 - P_p^{vac} \right) = \frac{P_p^{vac}}{1 - P_p^{vac}}. \tag{3}$$

Every priority service adopts the nonpreemptive policy. That is to say, if a higher priority packet arrives when a lower priority packet is being transmitted, the arriving higher priority packet will wait until the lower priority packet's transmission is completed. Thus, any packet that enters for transmission will complete the transmission without interruption.

According to the multi-priority queueing theory, without considering the server's vacations, the mean waiting time of the priority 1 packet is given by

$$E[W_1] = \frac{E[R_{pac}]}{1 - \rho_1}, \tag{4}$$

where $E[R_{pac}]$ is the expected residual service time for all priority packets. From renewal theory we know that

$$E[R_{pac}] = \frac{1}{2} \sum_{p=1}^{P} \lambda_p E[X_p^2]. \tag{5}$$

For the highest priority packets, the server's vacations could not influence the service for them obviously. Thus, the mean waiting time of the priority 1 packet is invariable, i.e.,

$$E[W_1] = \frac{\sum_{p=1}^{P} \lambda_p E[X_p^2]}{2(1 - \rho_1)}. \tag{6}$$

The waiting time of the priority 2 packet contains the residual service time of the packet receiving service when it arrives, the time to serve the priority 1 packets which are in queue, the service time and backoff time of the priority 2 packets which are in queue, the time to serve those priority 1 packets who arrive while the tagged priority 2 packet is waiting to be served, and the backoff time of the tagged priority 2 packet. Thus, its mean waiting time is

$$\begin{aligned} E[W_2] = {} & E[L_1]E[X_1] + E[L_2]E[X_2] + \lambda_1 E[W_2]E[X_1] \\ & + E[L_2]E[m_2]E[V] + E[m_2]E[V] + E[R_{pac}] \end{aligned}, \tag{7}$$

where $E[L_1]$ and $E[L_2]$ respectively represents the expected number of priority 1 packet and priority 2 packet waiting in queue when the tagged priority 2 packet arrives. From Little's formula we have $E[L_1] = \lambda_1 E[W_1]$ and $E[L_2] = \lambda_2 E[W_2]$. This gives that

$$E[W_2] = \frac{\rho_1 E[W_1] + E[R_{pac}] + E[m_2]E[V]}{1 - \rho_1 - \rho_2 - \lambda_2 E[m_2]E[V]}. \tag{8}$$

According to (2) and (6), we can obtain that

$$E[W_2] = \frac{2E[R_{pac}] + W(1 - \rho_1)E[m_2]}{(1 - \rho_1)(2 - 2\rho_1 - 2\rho_2 - W\lambda_2 E[m_2])}. \tag{9}$$

Following the same approach used for the priority 2 packet, for a priority 3 packet, we have that

$$E[W_3] = \frac{2(1 - \rho_1)E[W_2] + W(E[m_3] - E[m_2])}{2 - 2(\rho_1 + \rho_2 + \rho_3) - W\lambda_3 E[m_3]}. \tag{10}$$

By continuing in the same way, we can obtain the mean waiting time of a priority p ($p \geq 3$) packet as

$$E[W_p] = \frac{2(1 - \rho_1 - \cdots - \rho_{p-2})E[W_{p-1}] + W(E[m_p] - E[m_{p-1}])}{2 - 2(\rho_1 + \cdots + \rho_p) - W\lambda_p E[m_p]}. \tag{11}$$

The mean sojourn time of a priority p packet is

$$E[T_p] = E[W_p] + E[X_p].$$ (12)

The mean sojourn time of all priority classes is

$$E[T] = \frac{\sum_{p=1}^{P} \lambda_p E[T_p]}{\sum_{p=1}^{P} \lambda_p}.$$ (13)

The mean queue length of priority p is

$$N_Q^k = \lambda_k E[W_k].$$ (14)

2.4 Channel Threshold Based Admission Control Mechanism

In the channel threshold based admission control mechanism, the key problem is to acquire the optimal channel threshold for each priority service (except the highest priority service).

Let λ_c^{in} denote the burst access rate in channel c, and k denote the number of burst transmitted in channel c during the unit time σ. According to the Poisson Equation, the probability that k bursts are transmitted in channel c during σ is

$$P_c^{in}(k) = \frac{e^{-\lambda_c^{in}} \left(-\lambda_c^{in}\right)^k}{k!}.$$ (15)

According to the principle of CTMA protocol, if G_c is lower than the channel threshold T_p^{ch} of the priority $p(p > 1)$ service, the bursts of priority $p(p > 1)$ can be accessed to channel c. Thus, the probability that the burst can be accessed to channel c is

$$p_p^c = P\left\{G_{\alpha-pre}^m < T_p^{ch}\right\} = \sum_{k=0}^{T_p^{ch}} P_c^{in}(k).$$ (16)

Therefore, the probability that the burst of priority $p(p > 1)$ chooses channel c to be accessed is

$$p_r^p = p_p^c \cdot C_{C-1}^S \prod_{r \in G(r,S)} \left(p_p^c\right)^S \frac{1}{S+1} \cdot \prod_{r \in G(r,C-1-S)} \left(1 - p_p^c\right)^r, \quad S \in [1, C-1],$$ (17)

where $G(r, S)$ indicates the set of S channels (not including channel r) to which the burst can be accessed, and $G(r, M-1-S)$ indicates the set of $M-1-S$ channels (not including channel r) to which the burst cannot be accessed.

Hence, the access rate of burst with priority 1 to channel c is $\frac{1}{\lambda_1^{-1}+E[T_1]} \cdot \frac{1}{C}$, and the access rate of burst with priority $p(p > 1)$ to channel c is

$$\lambda_c^{in} = \frac{1}{\lambda_1^{-1} + E[T_1]} \cdot \frac{1}{C} + \sum_{p=2}^{P} \frac{p_p^{in}}{\lambda_p^{-1} + E[T_p]}, \tag{18}$$

According to (15) to (18), λ_c^{in} and p_r^p can obtained. Here p_p^{in} is defined as the probability that bursts of priority p can be accessed to channel, and it is easy to acquire that

$$p_p^{in} = \sum_{r=1}^{C} p_r^p. \tag{19}$$

Assume that the time intervals of bursts obey exponential distribution with parameter λ_c^{in} in a single channel, so the probability density function of time interval on arbitrary channel is deduced as

$$f(t) = \lambda_c^{in} \cdot e^{-\lambda_c^{in}t}. \tag{20}$$

Define P_{bur_suc} as the burst successful transmission probability, and it can be calculated as

$$P_{bur\_suc} = e^{-2\lambda_c^{in}T_{burst}}. \tag{21}$$

Define P_{pac_suc} as packet successful transmission probability. According to RS-Turbo theory, only if M_{burst} bursts are successfully received, the original packet can be recovered by receiving terminals. According to the permutation and combination theory, the packet successful transmission probability can be calculated as

$$P_{pac\_suc} = \sum_{k=M_{burst}}^{N_{burst}} C_{N_{burst}}^{k} \cdot \left(P_{bur\_suc}\right)^k \cdot \left(1 - P_{bur\_suc}\right)^{N_{burst}-k}. \tag{22}$$

T_{max}^{ch} is defined as the maximum access rate of the whole network. Different thresholds for other priority services are set to guarantee the requirement of the highest priority service. Suppose the ratio of packet arrival rate of priority $1, 2, \cdots, P$ is $k_1 : k_2 : \cdots : k_P$, and thus T_p^{ch} can be calculated as

$$T_p^{ch} \left(\frac{\sum_{r=1}^{p} k_r}{\sum_{r=1}^{P} k_r} \right) = T_{max}^{ch}. \tag{23}$$

3 Performance Analysis

3.1 Successful Transmission Probability of Each Priority

Let P_{suc}^p be the packet successful transmission probability of priority p. It can be easily acquired that

$$P_{suc}^p = p_p^{in} \cdot P_{pac\_suc}. \tag{24}$$

3.2 Mean Delay of Each Priority

Let $E[T_D^p]$ be the mean delay of priority p, defined as the during from a packet entering the buffer of sender to the receiver. $E[T_D^p]$ is composed of the mean sojourn time and the propagation delay of the packet with priority p. As discussed in Sect. 2.3, for the packet with priority 1, the mean sojourn time $E[T_1]$ only contains the mean queuing time and the transmission delay. For the packet with priority $p(p > 1)$, the mean sojourn time $E[T_p]$ contains the mean queuing time, mean backoff time and the transmission delay.

Define $E[T_{pro}]$ as the packet propagation delay, and its value is related to the communication distance. Let L' be the maximum communication distance in a single hop, and c is the speed of light. So $E[T_{pro}]$ can be calculated as

$$E[T_{pro}] = \frac{L'}{2c}. \tag{25}$$

Therefore, T_D^p can be expressed as

$$E[T_D^p] = E[T_p] + E[T_{pro}]. \tag{26}$$

4 Simulations

In this section, we will verify the performance of CTMA protocol through simulations in OMNeT++. The simulations are based on the following assumptions:

(1) All nodes are randomly distributed among the scenario in the beginning, and make uniform linear motions with the speed of 300 m/s and random directions in simulations. A fully connected ATN is formed by all nodes.
(2) Every node has a sending pathway and multiple receiving pathways as many as the channels. The receiving pathways are not blocked when packet are sending.
(3) The traffic in the network has 4 priorities. The arrival of packets obeys the Poisson distribution. All packets of any priority are of the same length and data transmission rate, and packets of the same priority are of the same packet arrival rate.
(4) When bursts are accessed to channels, the channel is chosen randomly among all channels.

Table 1. Simulation parameters.

Parameter	Value	Parameter	Value
Number of nodes	50	Number of channels	10
Data transmission rate on each channel	2 Mbit/s	Packet length	600 bits
Number of bursts that a packet is divided into (N_{burst})	30	Ratio of packet arrival rates of different priority (from high to low)	1:2:4:6
Minimum bursts needed to be recovery a packet (M_{burst})	15	Node communication range	250 km
Scenario size	600×600 km^2	Node speed	300 m/s

In simulations, the lower limit of the successful transmission probability for priority 1, 2, 3 is set as 99%, 80% and 60%, respectively. Hence, according to the mathematical model, the channel threshold T_2^{ch}, T_3^{ch} and T_4^{ch} can be obtained. The detailed simulation parameters are shown in Table 1.

Firstly, we will show the comparison of theoretical results and the simulation results in the CTMA protocol. The effects of traffic loads on network performance of each priority in CTMA protocol is shown in Fig. 4. The theoretical results match well with the simulation results on the whole, which indicates the correctness of the mathematical model. As is depicted in Fig. 4, the performance of different priorities has a great difference, because of their different channel threshold. In light load condition, each priority has high successful transmission probability and low delay. However, in heavy load condition, the performance of low priority becomes worse with the increase of load, while that of the highest priority almost keeps stable. Furthermore, the mean delay for each priority tends to reach their life cycle under heavy load.

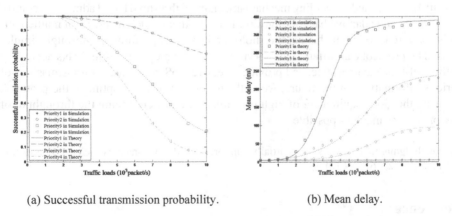

(a) Successful transmission probability.   (b) Mean delay.

Fig. 4. Network performance of each priority in CTMA protocol.

In the following, we will compare the performance of CTMA protocol with that of the PDM protocol proposed in [21]. The simulation results are shown in Fig. 5, containing the successful transmission probability and the mean delay. As is depicted in Fig. 5(a), the successful transmission probability of the highest priority in CTMA protocol can maintain at 99% all the time with increase of the channel load, but that of PDM protocol can only reach 95%. As is shown in Fig. 5(b), the mean delay of the highest priority in CTMA protocol can maintain at 2 ms with increase of the channel load, but that of PDM protocol is about 7 ms.

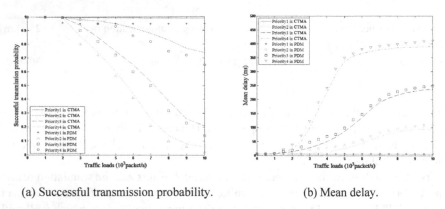

(a) Successful transmission probability.   (b) Mean delay.

Fig. 5. Comparison of network performance between CTMA and PDM protocol.

5 Conclusions

In this paper, we propose a novel multi-priority differentiated, multi-channel and distributed random contention MAC protocol based on channel awareness for ATNs. This protocol contains four main parts, i.e., channel occupancy statistic mechanism, multi-priority queueing and scheduling mechanism, channel threshold based admission control mechanism, and adaptive backoff algorithm. We further model the protocol mathematically, acquire its optimal channel threshold, and show its performance through simulations. The protocol can differentiate services for different priorities in ATNs according to the real-time channel state, and provide effective QoS guarantee for transmissions of various information. In the future, we will further improve and optimize the protocol, ensuring the QoS requirement of high priority, as well as enhancing the throughput of low priority as much as possible.

Acknowledgment. This work was partially supported by the Aeronautical Science Foundation of China (No. 20161996010).

References

1. Cheng, B.N., Block, F.J., Hamilton, B.R., et al.: Design considerations for next-generation airborne tactical networks. IEEE Commun. Mag. **52**(5), 138–145 (2014)

2. Hu, L., Hu, F., Kumar, S.: Moth- and ant-inspired routing in hierarchical airborne networks with multi-beam antennas. IEEE Trans. Mob. Comput. **18**(4), 910–922 (2019)
3. Amin, R., Ripplinger, D., Mehta, D., et al.: Design considerations in applying disruption tolerant networking to tactical edge networks. IEEE Commun. Mag. **53**(10), 32–38 (2015)
4. Cao, X., Yang, P., Alzenad, M., et al.: Airborne communication networks: a survey. IEEE J. Sel. Areas Commun. **36**(9), 1907–1926 (2018)
5. Sklivanitis, G., Gannon, A., Tountas, K., et al.: Airborne cognitive networking: design, development, and deployment. IEEE Access **6**, 47217–47239 (2018)
6. Herder, J.C., Stevens, J.A.: Method and architecture for TTNT symbol rate scaling modes. USA Patent, 7839900 B1 (2010)
7. Wang, J., Shake, T., Deutsch, P., et al.: Topology management algorithms for large-scale aerial high capacity directional networks. In: Military Communications Conference (MILCOM), Baltimore, MD, USA, pp. 1–6. IEEE (2016)
8. Burns, K., Smith, K.: Battlefield Airborne Communications Node (BACN) realizing the vision of the Aerial Layered Network (ALN). AIAA, San Diego, California, USA, pp. 1–20 (2016)
9. Ramanujan, R.S., Burnett, B., Trent, B.A., et al.: Hybrid autonomous network and router for communication between heterogeneous subnets. USA Patent, 0257081 A1 (2015)
10. Alshbatat, A.I., Dong, L.: Adaptive MAC protocol for UAV communication networks using directional antennas. In: International Conference on Networking, Sensing and Control (ICNSC), Chicago, IL, USA, pp. 598–603. IEEE (2010)
11. Cheng, B., Ci, L., Yang, M., et al.: DA-MAC: a duty-cycled, directional adaptive MAC protocol for airborne mobile sensor network. In: 4th International Conference on Digital Manufacturing and Automation (ICDMA), Qingdao, China, pp. 389–392. IEEE (2013)
12. Li, J., Zhou, Y.F., Lamout, L., et al.: Packet delay in UAV wireless networks under non-saturated traffic and channel fading conditions. Wireless Pers. Commun. **72**(2), 1105–1123 (2013)
13. Temel, S., Bekmezci, I.: LODMAC: location oriented directional MAC protocol for FANETs. Comput. Netw. **83**(3), 76–84 (2015)
14. Ho, D.T., Grtli, E.I., Shimamoto, S., et al.: Optimal relay path selection and cooperative communication protocol for a swarm of UAVs. In: GLOBECOM Workshop, Atlanta, CA, USA, pp. 1585–1590. IEEE (2012)
15. Li, J., Gong, E., Sun, Z., et al.: An interference-based distributed TDMA scheduling algorithm for aeronautical ad hoc networks. In: International Conference on Cyber-Enabled Distributed Computing and Knowledge Discovery (CyberC), Beijing, China, pp. 453–460. IEEE (2013)
16. Jang, H., Kim, E., Lee, J.J., et al.: Location-based TDMA MAC for reliable aeronautical communications. IEEE Trans. Aerosp. Electron. Syst. **48**(2), 1848–1854 (2012)
17. Ripplinger, D., Tam, A.N., Szeto, K.: Scheduling vs. random access in frequency hopped airborne networks. In: Military Communications Conference, Orlando, FL, USA, pp. 1–6. IEEE (2012)
18. Hu, F., Li, X., Bentley, E., et al.: Intelligent multi-beam transmissions for mission-oriented airborne networks. IEEE Trans. Aerosp. Electron. Syst. **55**(2), 619–630 (2019)
19. Li, X., Hu, F., Qi, J., et al.: Systematic medium access control in hierarchical airborne networks with multi-beam and single-beam antennas. IEEE Trans. Aerosp. Electron. Syst. **55**(2), 706–717 (2019)
20. Tang, J.H., Wang, Y.Q., Dong, S.F., et al.: A feedback-retransmission based asynchronous frequency hopping MAC protocol for military aeronautical ad hoc networks. Chin. J. Aeronaut. **31**(5), 1130–1140 (2018)
21. Xu, D., Zhang, H., Zheng, B., et al.: A priority differentiated and multi-channel MAC protocol for airborne networks. In: 8th International Conference on Communication Software and Networks (ICCSN), Beijing, China, pp. 64–70. IEEE (2016)

22. Fang, Z., Zheng, B., Zhao, W., et al.: A novel statistical multi-channel busy recognition mechanism in the MAC layer for airborne tactical networks. IEEE Access **5**, 19662–19667 (2017)
23. Borui, Z., Hu, Z.L., Xing, K.F.: Performance of RS-Turbo concatenated code in AOS. In: 11th International Conference on Electronic Measurement & Instruments (ICEMI), Harbin, China, pp. 983–987. IEEE (2013)
24. Zheng, B., Zhang, H.Y., Zhuo, K., et al.: A multi-priority service differentiated and adaptive backoff mechanism over IEEE 802.11 DCF for wireless mobile networks. KSII Trans. Internet Inf. Syst. **11**(7), 3446–3464 (2017)

Multi-service Routing with Guaranteed Load Balancing for LEO Satellite Networks

Cui-Qin Dai[1][(✉)], Guangyan Liao[1], P. Takis Mathiopoulos[2], and Qianbin Chen[3]

[1] School of Communication and Information Engineering, Chongqing University of Posts and Telecommunications, Chongqing, China
daicq@cqupt.edu.cn, liaogy.cqupt@qq.com
[2] Department of Informatics and Telecommunications, National and Kapodestrian University of Athens, Athens, Greece
mathio@di.uoa.gr
[3] Chongqing Key Lab of Mobile Communication Technology, Chongqing University of Posts and Telecommunications, Chongqing, China
chenqb@cqupt.edu.cn

Abstract. Low Earth Orbit (LEO) Satellite Networks (SN) offers communication services with low delay, low overhead, and flexible networking. As service types and traffic demands increase, the multi-service routing algorithms play an important role in ensuring users' Quality of Service (QoS) requirements in LEO-SN. However, the multi-service routing algorithm only considers the link QoS information, ignoring the uneven distribution of ground users, causing satellite link or node congestion, increasing the packet transmission delay, and packet loss rate. In order to solve the above problems, we propose a Multi-Service Routing with Guaranteed Load Balancing (MSR-GLB) algorithm which balances the network load while satisfying multi-service QoS requirements. Firstly, the Geographic Location Information Factors (GLIF) are defined to balance the network load by scheduling the ISLs with lower loads. Then, the optimization objective function is constructed by considering delay, remaining bandwidth, packet loss rate, and GLIF in order to characterize the routing problems caused by multi-service and load balancing. Following this, we propose an MSR-GLB algorithm that includes the state transition rule and the pheromone update rule. Among them, the state transition rule is based on QoS information and link GLIF, and the pheromone update rule has the characteristics of positive and negative feedback mechanism. The simulation results show that the MSR-GLB algorithm can well meet the QoS requirements of different services, balance the network load compared to Cross-layer design and Ant-colony optimization based Load-balancing routing algorithm in LEO Satellite Network (CAL-LSN) and Multi-service On-demand Routing (MOR) algorithm.

Keywords: LEO satellite network · Routing · Multi-service · Load balancing

1 Introduction

As an indispensable part of future communications, Low Earth Orbit Satellite Networks (LEO-SN) offer high-speed and reliable data transmission with wider coverage, higher

H. Gao et al. (Eds.): ChinaCom 2019, LNICST 312, pp. 283–298, 2020.
https://doi.org/10.1007/978-3-030-41114-5_22

bandwidth, lower delay, and cost-efficient networking capabilities [1]. As the capacity of Inter-Satellite Links (ISLs) increases coupled with the great enhancement of on-board signal processing capabilities of LEO-SN, routing plays an important role to fulfil the requirements of high-speed, low-delay and reliable transmission for spatial information [2].

For dynamic SN, the traditional routing algorithms can be broadly divided in accordance to the topology control methods as follows: (i) Virtual topology routing [3]; (ii) Virtual node routing [4]; and (iii) Footprint-based routing [5]. Among these three categories, virtual topology routing has become more popular as it requires lower on-board processing capability and supports wider orbit type characteristics, e.g. see [6, 7]. The algorithms described in [6, 7] deal with the Quality of Service (QoS) of a single service and have proposed optimal routing paths. However, the LEO-SCN service types have been diversified because of its rapid development, and the different service types require different QoS requirements. In a consequence, various optimization researches for multi-service routing algorithms have been published in the past, including [8–11]. In [8], a Multi-service On-demand Routing (MOR) protocol, which adopts different routing modes for different service types to improve network efficiency while ensuring different service QoS, has been proposed. In [9, 10], the services were classified according to the QoS requirements of various services, and then corresponding routing algorithms are designed for different services. In order to solve the problem of service quality requirements for different services and unbalanced link resource utilization, a multi-service routing algorithm based on multi-objective decision-making for LEO satellite network was proposed in [11]. However, under high traffic loads, some ISLs in these algorithms may become heavily loaded even congested while others remain in underutilized condition.

Another commonly encountered problem with LEO-SN is that of Load Balancing (LB) which typically occurs because of the uneven distribution of ground users. In the past there have been several attempts to include the LB into the design of the routing algorithms, e.g. see [12–14]. For example, Song et al. in [12] have proposed a Traffic-Light-based intelligent Routing strategy (TLR). A Cross-layer design and Ant-colony optimization based Load-balancing routing algorithm in LEO Satellite Network (CAL-LSN), which uses multi-objective optimization model to achieve load balancing, and can meet the requirement of video transmission, was introduced in [13]. In [14], a hybrid global-local load routing scheme was proposed by taking advantage of the predictive nature of Internet of Things (IoT) traffic distribution as well as the position of the LEO satellites. It should be emphasized that all these load balancing routing algorithms are designed to optimize the QoS of a single service, i.e. they don't consider the fact that different services usually have different QoS requirements.

From the previous literature review, it is evident that no generic approach exists which can deal effectively with multi-service and load-balancing routing problems encountered in LEO-SCN supporting multiple services and high traffic. In order to fill this gap, in this paper, we address such problems by providing a solution to the following question: How should the network load be balanced while satisfying multi-service QoS requirements in LEO-SCN? In particular, a Multi-Service Routing with Guaranteed Load Balancing (MSR-GLB) algorithm was proposed by taking into account the influence of factors such as delay, residual bandwidth, packet loss rate and geographic location information factor (GLIF) on path selection. Firstly, the GLIF was defined by analyzing the traffic demand distributions of satellites covering terrestrial users to show the relative traffic load of the ISLs. Secondly, the routing problem is formulated as a multi-constrained QoS optimization objective function by considering link QoS information and GLIF. Finally, the state transition rule was improved to obtain an optimal transmission path that satisfies the QoS requirements of different services and balances the network load, and the pheromone updating rule was optimized by positive feedback and negative feedback mechanism.

The remainder of this paper is organized as follows. Section 2 presents the system model, which is composed of the system network model and GLIF. Section 3 introduces problem formulation. Section 4 introduces the MSR-GLB algorithm proposed in this paper. This is following by the performance evaluation results and discussion in Sect. 5. And Sect. 6 concludes this paper.

2 System Model

In this section, the satellite network model will be first presented. Then, we have defined GLIF. The load status of the inter-satellite link is predicted by the value of GLIF.

2.1 Satellite Network

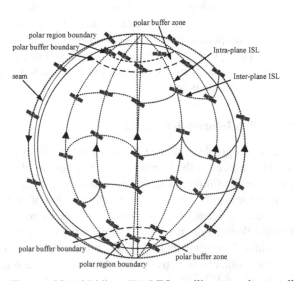

Fig. 1. The considered Iridium-like LEO satellite network constellation.

As illustrated in Fig. 1, we consider a LEO Iridium-like constellation, which consists of six planes with an inclination of having 11 satellites distributed in every plane [15]. For the operation of this satellite network, each satellite has four ISLs: two IntrA-Plane (IAP)

ISLs and two IntEr-Plane (IEP) ISLs, expect for the satellites along the counter-rotating seam only have three active ISLs, because the cross-seam ISLs, namely links between satellites in counter-rotating orbits, are not used due to link acquisition and special antenna steering requirement. The IAP ISLs connect adjacent satellites within the same plane, while IEP ISLs link connects adjacent satellites across neighboring orbits. The IAP ISLs is maintained all times as the same orbital operation rule is followed and the nodes are relatively stationary, and is expressed as Eq. (1).

$$L_a = \sqrt{2}R\sqrt{1 - \cos(\frac{2\pi}{M})} \tag{1}$$

where M is the number of satellites each plane and R is the radius of the earth.

The IEP ISLs lengths vary over time with the satellite movement, and the on-off state switching of IEP links is carried out because the satellite trajectory operates differently. When the satellite moves toward the Polar Regions, the IEP ISLs become shorter, as in Eq. (2).

$$L_e = \sqrt{2}R\sqrt{1 - \cos(2\pi \frac{1}{2N})} \cos(\text{lat}) \tag{2}$$

where N is the number of planes and lat represents for the latitude difference at which the IEP ISLs.

The high-speed motion of the satellite network has resulted in the change of the network topology, but it has periodicity and predictability. In a certain time range, it considered that the network topology is fixed. For the LEO satellite network, the virtual topology strategy [16] makes the entire topology in a relatively static state, namely, a complete satellite system operation cycle T divided into n definite time slice, it is $[t_0 = 0, t_1], [t_1, t_2], \cdots, [t_{n-1}, t_n = T]$. And each time segment has the following characteristics: The network topology is invariable, and the network topology changes and link switching occurs only at time point $t_0, t_1, \cdots, t_n$.

2.2 Geographic Location Information Factor

Due to the differences in geography, climate and economic development, the population distribution is relatively uneven, so the number of users accessing the satellite network varies. According to the level of traffic load, the satellite coverage surface is divided into hotspot and non-hotspot zones [17]. According to the distribution of the world population and their telecommunication needs, three hotspots were set up, namely Eastern Asia, North America, Europe-Western Asia. Figure 2 depicts the division strategy of these hotspot zones while Table 1 presents their central latitudes. In order to avoid satellite network congestion, the traffic can be actively dispersed, that is, the traffic of high-load ISLs is dispersed to low-load ISLs for transmission. Consequently, we can define the Geographic Location Information Factor (GLIF) to estimate the ISLs load status. The GLIF can be expressed as a function related to the geographic location of the satellite. The higher the GLIF value is, the traffic load on the satellite inter-satellite link is greater. Following the type of satellite links, the GLIF is divided into IAP-GLIF and IEP-GLIF. The relevant equation is shown in Eqs. (3) and (4).

(1) IntrA-Plane Geographic Location Information Factor (IAP-GLIF)

$$\lambda_{\text{u-intra}} = \begin{cases} \exp(2lat_u / \pi), & -\pi/2 \le lat_u \le lat_c \\ \exp(-2(lat_u - 2lat_c)/\pi), & lat_c \le lat_u \le \pi/2 \end{cases} \tag{3}$$

where lat_u denotes the latitude of the satellite node u. Here, $lat_c (0 < lat_c < \pi/2)$ denotes the latitude of the central area of hotspot zones within the Northern Hemisphere. Hereinafter, lat_c is called as central latitude.

(2) IntEr-Plane Geographic Location Information Factor (IEP-GLIF)

$$\lambda_{\text{u-inter}} = \begin{cases} \exp(-2(lat_u + 2lat_T)/\pi), & -\pi/2 \le lat_u < -lat_T \\ \exp(lat_u / \pi), & -lat_T \le lat_u < lat_c \\ \exp(-2(lat_u - 2lat_c)/\pi), & lat_c \le lat_u < lat_T \\ \exp(2(lat_u + 2lat_c - 2lat_T)/\pi), & lat_T \le lat_u \le \pi/2 \end{cases} \tag{4}$$

where lat_T denotes the threshold latitude.

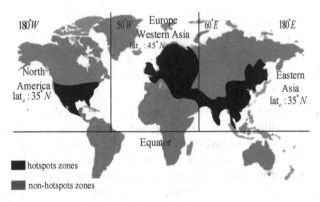

Fig. 2. Division of hotspot zones.

Table 1. Parameters for the division.

Name	Coverage area	Central latitude
Eastern Asia	$60°E{-}180°E$	$35°N$
North America	$50°W{-}180°W$	$35°N$
Europe-Western Asia	$50°W{-}60°E$	$45°N$

3 Problem Formulation

With the rapid development of LEO satellite networks, the types of services are also developing and changing differently day by day. According to the QoS requirements of diverse services such as data, voice and video, the services are divided into three types [18]: Class A is the delay-sensitive service, such as command voice with high latency requirements; Class B is the bandwidth-sensitive service, such as the terrestrial observing service. Class C is the packet loss rate of sensitive service. The packet transmission of their path requires low latency, high residual bandwidth, and low packet loss rate, respectively.

When the satellite nodes in the network are moving in its orbit, the service types are changing accordingly. However, the different service types have different requirements for QoS, and the optimization for a certain QoS parameter cannot satisfy the user's needs. Meanwhile, due to the rapid growth of satellite communication service demand and the uneven distribution of satellite coverage services demand on the ground, the path of routing calculation is easy to select the link of the hotspot zones, which leads to link and node congestion. Therefore, in order to meet the diversified service requirements and balance the network load, the optimization function is proposed, as in Eq. (5).

$$
\min F = \sum_{e(i,j) \in P_{SD}} \lambda_{ij} \left(w_1 \left(d_{ij} / D_{\max} \right) + w_2 \left(C_{\min} / c_{ij} \right) + w_3 \left(l_{ij} / L_{\max} \right) \right)
$$

$$
s.t. \quad d_{P_{SD}} = \sum_{e(i,j) \in P_{SD}} d_{ij} \leq D_{\max}
$$

$$
c_{P_{SD}} = \min_{e(i,j) \in P_{SD}} \{ c_{ij} \} \geq C_{\min} \tag{5}
$$

$$
l_{P_{SD}} = \left(1 - \prod_{e(i,j) \in P_{SD}} (1 - l_{ij}) \right) \leq L_{\max}
$$

where $\lambda_{ij}(t)$ represents the GLIF of link $e(i, j)$; P_{SD} represents the path from the source satellite S to the destination satellite D; $e(i, j)$ is the link between satellite nodes i and j; d_{ij} represents the delay of the link $e(i, j)$; c_{ij} denotes the remaining bandwidth of the link $e(i, j)$; l_{ij} is the packet loss rate of the link $e(i, j)$ and $w_k \in [0, 1](k = 1, 2, 3)$ is the weighting factors of the link QoS attribute, i.e., the delay, residual bandwidth, and packet loss rate, for the link $e(i, j)$, which can be evaluated by the eigenvector method [11]. $d_{P_{SD}}$, $c_{P_{SD}}$, and $l_{P_{SD}}$ represent the delay, remaining bandwidth, and packet loss rate of the path P_{SD}, respectively. $D_{\max}$, $C_{\min}$, and $L_{\max}$ represent the QoS attribute constraint values of the ideal path P_{SD} such as delay, residual bandwidth, and packet loss rate, respectively. The relevant QoS attribute definitions are as follows:

Delay: It is the sum of the propagation delay and queuing delay of the data packet, and is expressed as Eq. (6).

$$
d_{ij} = d_p(i, j) + d_q(i, j) \tag{6}
$$

where, $d_p(i, j)$ and $d_q(i, j)$ are the propagation delay and queuing delay of the link $e(i, j)$. The relevant equation is shown in Eqs. (7) and (8).

$$
d_p(i, j) = \frac{L(i, j)}{c_p} \tag{7}
$$

where $L(i, j)$ is the length of the inter-satellite link $e(i, j)$, and c_p is the speed of light.

$$
d_q(i, j) = \frac{N_q(i, j) \times L_\alpha}{C} \tag{8}
$$

where $N_q(i, j)$ is the number of packets in the buffer of $e(i, j)$. L_α is the average length of packets. C is the total link capacity of the link.

The delay is the additive parameter, that is, the total delay of the path P_{SD} is equal to the sum of the delay of each link in the path P_{SD}.

Remaining bandwidth: The remaining bandwidth is the total bandwidth of the link minus the link bandwidth used by the transport packet. As shown in Eq. (9).

$$c_{ij} = C - c_{used}(i, j) \tag{9}$$

where C is the total link capacity of the link $e(i, j)$. $c_{used}(i, j)$ is the bandwidth used by the link $e(i, j)$.

The remaining bandwidth is a concave parameter, where the remaining bandwidth of each link in the path P_{SD} is compared, and the minimum value is taken as the residual bandwidth value of the path P_{SD}.

Packet loss rate: The packet loss rate is the ratio of the number of lost packets to the all transmitted data packets per unit time. It is a multiplicative parameter, and is expressed as Eq. (10).

$$l_{ij} = \frac{N_{\text{lost}}(i, j)}{N_{all\_send}(i, j)} \tag{10}$$

where, $N_{\text{lost}}(i, j)$ is the lost packet in link $e(i, j)$ and $N_{all\_send}(i, j)$ is the total data packet sent by link $e(i, j)$ per unit time.

4 The MSR-GLB Algorithm

In this section, we firstly introduce the MSR-GLB algorithm, and then introduce two important processes in the MSR-GLB algorithm, namely state transition rules and pheromone update rules. To solve this problem, we introduced an Ant Colony Optimization (ACO)[1]. In the pathfinding process, they behave very similarly, that is, the satellite node selects the path according to the link QoS information and GLIF, and the ants select the path according to the link pheromone. In addition, ACO has the characteristics of positive feedback mechanism, strong robustness, distributed computing and low complexity, which can find a better solution for solving multi-constrained optimization problems [20, 21]. Therefore, it is feasible to apply the ACO algorithm to the satellite network to solve the multi-service problem and load problem in this paper.

4.1 Algorithm Presentation

The MSR-GLB algorithm is an intelligent bionic algorithm based on ACO. In the pathfinding process, the MSR-GLB performs the next hop node selection depending on

---

[1] The ACO algorithm was proposed by the famous Italian scholar Dorigo [19] in 1991. The algorithm simulates that ants will leave a pheromone on the path when they are foraging. The concentration of the pheromone is inversely proportional to the path length and will volatilize as time passed. More specifically, the shorter path owns such more pheromone that it attracts a larger number of ants going along itself. After a period, the shortest path will always be selected.

the link pheromone, QoS status information, and GLIF. In addition, MSR-GLB updates the pheromone of the link through positive and negative feedback mechanisms, so that the ant colony quickly converges the optimal path. When the source satellite S makes a routing request of sending a message to the destination satellite D, the corresponding MSR-GLB algorithm steps are listed in the following. The MSR-GLB algorithm flow chart is shown in Fig. 3. We also have the corresponding pseudo-code in Algorithm 1.

Step 1: The satellite network topology $G(V, E)^t$ is obtained under the determined current satellite cycle time slot t and then the searching is started based on the network topology.

Step 2: Determine the type of service and initialize the network parameters: QoS parameters of links in the network, limit values of multi-constraint QoS conditions, initial pheromone concentration $\tau(0)$, volatilization coefficient ρ, pheromone factor α, QoS status factor β, GLIF factor r, pheromone punishment coefficient c, ant number m, maximum cycle number NC_{max}, etc.

Step 3: Obtaining any pair of source-destination node pairs (S, D), and setting the number of cycles nc to 0.

Step 4: The ant searches for the path from the source node S.

Step 5: Initialize and update the current node: The source node initializes the current node and the next hop node updates the current node, and the current node is added to the tabu table.

Step 6: The ant determines whether the *allowed* of the current node is empty or not. If it is empty, the pathfinding fails and process to step 9. Otherwise, it executes the next step.

Step 7: The ant selects the next hop node according to the state transition rule (11), and adds the selected node to the tabu table.

Step 8: The ant judges whether the next hop node is the destination node or not and if it is destination node then the path search succeeds and process to step 9, otherwise it returns to step 5.

Step 9: Whether all ants complete the pathfinding. If it is fulfilled, the pheromone is updated according to the pheromone updating rule (13) and the number of cycles is $nc = nc + 1$, otherwise goes back to the step 4.

Step 10: If the nc reaches to the maximum number of cycles NC_{max}, the output is the optimal solution of the corresponding transmission path otherwise it goes back to the step 4.

Algorithm 1 MSR-GLB algorithm

Input: The network topology $G(V,E)^t$, the number of satellite nodes n, the type of service, the limit values of multi-constraint QoS conditions, initial pheromone concentration $\tau(o)$, volatilization coef cient ρ, pheromone factor α, QoS status factor β, GLIF factor r, pheromone punishment co-ef cient c, ant number m, maximum cycle number NC_{max}, source node S, destination node D.

Output: The best solution corresponding to the transmission path

1: Initialization: $currentnode = S$, $cyclenumber = 1$,
2: **for** $i = 1, 2, ..., n$ **do**
3:     Set $allowed(i) = 1$
4: **end for**
5: **while** $cyclenumber <= NC_{max}$ **do**
6:     **for** $i = 1, 2, ..., m$ **do**
7:         **while** $currentnode \neq D$ **do**
8:             **for** each node j in the neighbor list of current node **do**
9:                 **if** $allowed(j) == 1$ **then**
10:                     Choose the next hop x with the state transition rule
11:                     Set $allowed(x) = 0$
12:                 **end if**
13:             **end for**
14:             $currentnode = x$
15:         **end while**
16:     **end for**
17:     **for** each link **do**
18:         Update the pheromone value
19:     **end for**
20: **end while**

4.2 State Transition Rule

When the ant k reaches the satellite node i, the next hop satellite node j is selected according to the pseudo-random scale rule. The next hop node selection rule is expressed as Eq. (11).

$$
j = \begin{cases} \arg \max_{j \in allowed_k} \left\{ \tau_{ij}^{\alpha}(t)\eta_{ij}^{\beta}(t)\xi_{ij}^{r}(t) \right\}, & q \leq q_0 \\ J & , \quad q > q_0 \end{cases}
\tag{11}
$$

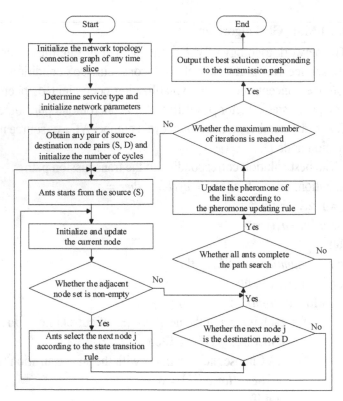

Fig. 3. Flow chart of MSR-GLB algorithm.

where $allowed_k = \{V(i, :) - tabu_k\}$ represents the set of satellite nodes that the ant k next hop can select, and the ant adds the node to the tabu table $tabu_k$ every time a node passes. $\tau_{ij}(t)$ represents the pheromone concentration of the link $e(i, j)$ at time t, and will be over time volatile. $\eta_{ij}(t) = 1/\omega_{ij}(t)$, $\omega_{ij}(t) = w_1(d_{ij}/D_{\max}) + w_2(C_{\min}/c_{ij}) + w_3(l_{ij}/L_{\max})$ represents the QoS status value of the link $e(i, j)$ at time t. $\xi_{ij}(t) = 1/\lambda_{ij}(t)$. α, β, and r reflect the relative importance of pheromones concentration, QoS status value, and GLIF of the link $e(i, j)$ during the path finding process. $q \sim U(0, 1)$, and $q_0 \in [0, 1]$ is a parameter which determines the relative importance of exploitation versus exploration: the ant k samples a random number $0 \le q \le 1$. If $q \le q_0$ then the best next hop node, according to (11) is chosen, otherwise a next hop node is chosen according to (12). J is a random variable selected according to the probability distribution, as in Eq. (12).

$$
p_{ij}^k(t) = \begin{cases} \dfrac{\tau_{ij}^{\alpha}(t)\eta_{ij}^{\beta}(t)\xi_{ij}^{r}(t)}{\displaystyle\sum_{s \in allowed_k} \tau_{is}^{\alpha}(t)\eta_{is}^{\beta}(t)\xi_{is}^{r}(t)} & , j \in allowed_k \\[4mm] 0 & , \text{elsewhere} \end{cases} \tag{12}
$$

4.3 Pheromone Updating Rule

After completing one iteration, all ants have used positive and negative feedback mechanisms to update the pheromone on the path. The pheromone concentration on the corresponding link increases when the ant finds the path successfully, otherwise the concentration decreases. The pheromone updating rule is expressed as Eq. (13).

$$\tau_{ij}(t+1) = (1-\rho)\tau_{ij}(t) + \Delta\tau_{ij}^{s}(t) + \Delta\tau_{ij}^{f}(t) \tag{13}$$

where $\rho \in (0,1)$ is the pheromone volatilization coefficient. $\Delta\tau_{ij}^{s}(t)$ represents the pheromone increment on the link $e(i,j)$ of all ants reaching the destination node success at time t, $\Delta\tau_{ij}^{f}(t)$ represents the pheromone reduction on the link $e(i,j)$ of all ants reaching the destination node failure at time t. The relevant equation is shown in Eqs. (14), (15), (16) and (17).

$$\Delta\tau_{ij}^{s}(t) = \sum_{k=1}^{m} a_{ij}^{k}\eta_{ij}^{k}(t)\xi_{ij}^{k}(t) + a_{ij}^{M}\eta_{ij}^{M}(t)\xi_{ij}^{M}(t), ij \in path \tag{14}$$

$$a_{ij}^{k} = \begin{cases} 1, (flag==success \,\&\,\&ij \in path^{k}) \\ 0, (flag==failure \,\&\,\&ij \in path^{k}) \end{cases} \tag{15}$$

where $path$ represents the path set of all ants, i.e. $path = \{path^{1}, path^{2}, \cdots, path^{m}\}$. a_{ij}^{k} indicates whether ant k increases the link $e(i,j)$ pheromone concentration. M is the ant corresponding to the minimum QoS status value of the current iteration. $\sum_{ij \in path} \omega_{ij}^{nc,k}$ is the QoS status value of the current iteration ant k. $flag$ indicates whether the ant k has successfully reached the destination node. If it reaches the destination node successfully, the value of $flag$ is $success$; otherwise, it is $failure$.

$$\Delta\tau_{ij}^{f}(t) = c\sum_{k=1}^{m} b_{ij}^{k}\eta_{ij}^{k}(t)\xi_{ij}^{k}(t), ij \in path \tag{16}$$

$$b_{ij}^{k} = \begin{cases} 0, (flag = success \,\&\,\&ij \in path^{k}) \\ -1, (flag = failure \,\&\,\&ij \in path^{k}) \end{cases} \tag{17}$$

where $c \in [0,1]$ is the pheromone punishment coefficient, and b_{ij}^{k} indicates whether ant k decreases the pheromone concentration on the link $e(i,j)$.

5 Performance Evaluation Results and Discussion

5.1 Simulation Platform

An Iridium-like constellation system is built using the Satellite Tool Kit (STK). The specific parameters are shown in Table 2. Other simulation parameters are set to: number of ants $m = 40$, number of iterations $NC_{max} = 50$, $\alpha = 2$, $\beta = 4$, $r = 2$, $c = 0.1$,

$\rho = 0.3$, $\tau(0) = 50$, $q_0 = 0.1$, $lat_T = 70°$, $lat_c = 45°$. In the simulation, the inter-satellite link bandwidth is 10 Mbit/s, and each output Link is allocated a 4 MB buffer with an average packet size of 500 B. Five pairs of source-destination nodes are randomly selected; the simulation time is 100 min, and the number of node requests increases with time.

When the delay sensitive service, the bandwidth sensitive service, and the packet loss rate sensitive service are simultaneously present in the network, and the source node and the destination node are the same, the transmission efficiency of the three types of services is shown in Table 3. The relative importance of each QoS attribute calculated by the eigenvector method is shown in Table 4.

Table 2. Iridium-like constellation system parameter.

Parameters	Value
Orbit height	780 km
Number of orbital planes	6
Number of satellites in orbit	11
Track inclination	$86.4°$
Polar buffer boundary latitude	$60°$
Polar region boundary latitude Threshold	$70°$

Table 3. Service transmission efficiency parameters.

Services type	Delay (ms)	Average bandwidth (Mbit/s)	Packet loss rate (%)
Delay Sensitive Services	83.6	3	0.06
Bandwidth Sensitive Services	98.7	4	0.08
Packet Loss Rate Sensitive Services	91.2	2	0.03

Table 4. Relative importance.

Services type	Relative importance
Delay Sensitive Services	(0.55 0.24 0.21)
Bandwidth Sensitive Services	(0.25 0.54 0.21)
Packet Loss Rate Sensitive Services	(0.26 0.20 0.54)

5.2   Results and Analysis

The MSR-GLB algorithm is compared with CAL-LSN and MOR to evaluate network performance such as end-to-end delay, packet loss rate, throughput, and traffic distribution index.

As shown in Fig. 4, with the increase of simulation time, the end-to-end delay of MSR-GLB algorithm is lower than CAL-LSN and MOR. Because the CAL-LSN algorithm guarantees reliable transmission of data packets, selects the minimum hop path, and does not consider the delay. The MOR algorithm designs different routing algorithms for different services, considers the delay of the link for delay-sensitive and best-effort services, and considers the bandwidth and number of paths for the bandwidth-sensitive service. When the network load is aggravated, the algorithm is prone to link congestion, resulting in increased delay. The MSR-GLB algorithm considers the delay of the link for different services, and the delay has different weights in different services.

As shown in Fig. 5, as the simulation time increases, the packet loss rate of the three routing algorithms increases, but the packet loss rate of the MSR-GLB algorithm is lower than CAL-LSN and MOR. The CAL-LSN algorithm selects the link with a relatively small error rate when selecting the path, but does not support multiple QoS. Although the MOR algorithm designs different routing algorithms for different services, it does not consider the packet loss rate information of the link. However, when the MSR-GLB algorithm performs path selection for the service, regardless of the service, the packet loss information of the link is considered, and the path transmission of the lower packet loss information is selected.

As shown in Fig. 6, the throughput of the three algorithms increases with the simulation time increases, and the performance of the MSR-GLB algorithm throughput is advantageous. The CAL-LSN algorithm considers the remaining bandwidth of the link when selecting the path but does not consider the packet loss rate of the link. The MOR algorithm uses different routing algorithms for different service types, but does not consider the load state of the link. When the network load is large, MOR and CAL-LSN packet loss is more serious. Nevertheless, the MSR-GLB algorithm considers not only the remaining bandwidth of the link and the packet loss rate when selecting paths for different services but also the geographic location information factor of the network.

As shown in Fig. 7, as the simulation time increases, the traffic distribution index of the three algorithms increase, but the MSR-GLB algorithm is better than the other two algorithms. The CAL-LSN algorithm ensures reliable transmission of data packets and selects the path with low delay and high residual bandwidth without, but cannot satisfy the QoS. The MOR algorithm of different services to select suitable paths for different services, but does not consider the link load. When the network load is large, some links may be congested, and some links are relatively idle. However, the MSR-GLB algorithm considers the load of the network when selecting paths for different services and selects links with relatively small traffic demand for data packet transmission.

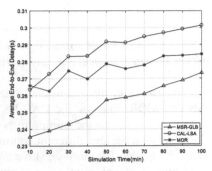

Fig. 4. Average end-to-end delay.

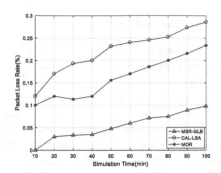

Fig. 5. Packet loss rate.

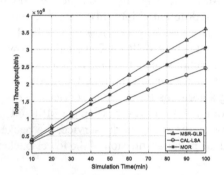

Fig. 6. Throughput.

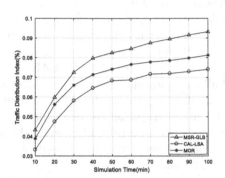

Fig. 7. Traffic distribution index.

6 Conclusion

In this paper, a multi-service routing with guaranteed load balancing (MSR-GLB) algorithm is proposed to meet the differentiated service QoS requirements and balance the network load. Firstly, an Iridium-like LEO network model is constructed with the virtual topology method, and the GLIF is modeled as a function related to the geographic location of the satellite to predict the ISLs traffic load. Secondly, an optimization objective function was formulated based on link QoS information and GLIF in order to describe the multi-service and load routing problems in an Iridium-like LEO satellite network. Thirdly, the state transition rule with QoS information and link GLIF is defined to identify the next-hop node. Meanwhile, the link pheromone updating rule with positive and negative feedback mechanism is presented to improve the search-ability and convergence speed of the MSR-GLB algorithm, and finally, the optimal QoS path of the current service is obtained. Finally, the simulation results show that the MSR-GLB algorithm has obvious advantages in terms of delay, throughput, and packet loss rate and traffic distribution index under the condition of heavy load in the satellite network comparing with MOR and CAL-LSN.

Acknowledgment. This work was jointly supported by the National Natural Science Foundation in China (61601075), the Natural Science Foundation Project of CQUPT (A2019-40).

References

1. Radhakrishnan, R., Edmonson, W.W., Afghah, F., Rodriguez-Osorio, R.M., Pinto, F., Burleigh, S.C.: Survey of inter-satellite communication for small satellite systems: physical layer to network layer view. IEEE Commun. Surv. Tutorials **18**(4), 2442–2473 (2016)
2. Choi, J.P., Chang, S., Chan, V.W.S.: Cross-layer routing and scheduling for onboard processing satellites with phased array antenna. IEEE Trans. Wireless Commun. **16**(1), 180–192 (2017)
3. Werner, M.: A dynamic routing concept for ATM-based satellite personal communication networks. IEEE J. Sel. Areas Commun. **15**(8), 1636–1648 (1997)
4. Mauger, R., Rosenberg, C.: QoS guarantees for multimedia services on a TDMA-based satellite network. IEEE Commun. Mag. **35**(7), 56–65 (1997)
5. Hashimoto, Y., Sarikaya, B.: Design of IP-based routing in a LEO satellite network. In: Third International Workshop on Satellite-based Information Services, pp. 81–88 (1998)
6. Tan, H., Zhu, L.L.: A novel routing algorithm based on virtual topology snapshot in LEO satellite networks. In: IEEE 17th International Conference on Computational Science and Engineering, pp. 357–361 (2014)
7. Liu, Y., Zhu, L.: A suboptimal routing algorithm for massive LEO satellite networks. In: International Symposium on Networks, Computers and Communications (ISNCC), pp. 1–5 (2018)
8. Karapantazis, S., Papapetrou, E., Pavlidou, F.-N.: Multiservice on-demand routing in LEO satellite networks. In: IEEE Transactions on Wireless Communications, vol. 8, no. 1, pp. 107–112 (2009)
9. Jiang, W., Zong, P.: QoS routing algorithm based on traffic classification in LEO satellite networks. In: Eighth International Conference on Wireless and Optical Communications Networks, pp. 1–5 (2011)
10. Jiang, W., Zong, P.: A mew constellation network multi-service QoS routing algorithm. J. Jiangsu Univ. (Nat. Sci. Ed.) **34**(4), 428–434 (2013)
11. Yang, L., Sun, J., Pan, C.: LEO multi-service routing algorithm based on multi-objective decision making. J. Commun. **37**(10), 25–32 (2016)
12. Song, G., Chao, M., Yang, B., Zheng, Y.: TLR: a traffic-light-based intelligent routing strategy for NGEO satellite IP networks. IEEE Trans. Wireless Commun. **13**(6), 3380–3393 (2014)
13. Wang, H., Zhang, Q., Xin, X., Tao, Y., Liu, N.: Cross-layer design and ant-colony optimization based routing algorithm for low earth orbit satellite networks. China Commun. **10**(10), 37–46 (2013)
14. Liu, Z., Li, J., Wang, Y., Li, X., Chen, S.: HGL: a hybrid global-local load balancing routing scheme for the Internet of Things through satellite networks. Int. J. Distrib. Sens. Netw. **13**(3) (2017)
15. Maine, K., Devieux, C., Swan, P.: Overview of IRIDIUM satellite network. In: WESCON 1995, p. 483 (1995)
16. Wood, L., Clerget, A., Andrikopoulos, I., Pavlou, G., Dabbous, W.: IP routing issues in satellite constellation networks. Int. J. Satell. Commun. **19**(1), 69–92 (2001)
17. Rao, Y., et al.: Agent-based multi-service routing for polar-orbit LEO broadband satellite networks. Ad Hoc Netw. **13**(1), 575–597 (2014)
18. Dai, Z.: Research on QoS routing under service classification system. Nanjing University of Posts and Telecommunications (2013)
19. Dorigo, M., Maniezzo, V., Colorni, A.: Ant system: optimization by a colony of cooperating agents. IEEE Trans. Syst. Man Cybern. Part B (Cybern.) **26**(1), 29–41 (1996)

20. Mouhcine, E., Khalifa, M., Mohamed, Y.: Route optimization for school bus scheduling problem based on a distributed ant colony system algorithm. In: 2017 Intelligent Systems and Computer Vision (ISCV), pp. 1–8 (2017)
21. Wen, G., et al.: Cross-layer design based ant colony optimization for routing and wavelength assignment in an optical satellite network. In: 2016 15th International Conference on Optical Communications and Networks (ICOCN), pp. 1–3 (2016)

Wireless Communications and Networking

Mode Identification of OAM with Compressive Sensing in the Secondary Frequency Domain

Jin Li and Chao Zhang[✉]

Labs of Avionics, School of Aerospace Engineering,
Tsinghua University, Beijing 100084, People's Republic of China
zhangchao@mail.tsinghua.edu.cn

Abstract. The Electro-Magnetic (EM) waves with Orbital Angular Momentum (OAM) can achieve high spectral efficiency by multiplexing different OAM modes. Different modes are mapped to the frequency shifts in the secondary frequency domain at the receiving end, in order to effectively identify the OAM modes received in partial phase plane. The traditional method requires high-speed acquisition equipment in the process of receiving Radio Frequency (RF) signals directly and its hardware cost is high. Even if analog devices are used for down-conversion to Intermediate Frequency (IF) sampling, the IF bandwidth limits the transmission rate. However, Compressive Sensing (CS) can break the Nyquist restriction by random observation, and is expected to realize the detection and identification of different OAM modes at a lower sampling rate, so that the cost is low. Therefore, this paper proposes an OAM mode identification method based on CS. At the same time, the random sampling is carried out based on the existing hardware device, i.e. Analog-to-Information Converter (AIC), to realize the OAM modes identification with the low sampling rate. The simulation results verify the correctness and effectiveness of the method.

Keywords: Orbital Angular Momentum · Secondary frequency domain · Compressive Sensing · Analog-to-Information Converter · OAM multiplexing · Mode detection and identification

1 Introduction

Orbital Angular Momentum (OAM), as an intrinsic characteristic of electromagnetic wave, is considered as the new dimension of wireless transmission, especially in future mobile communications. Because of the orthogonality between different OAM modes, they can be multiplexed to obtain the higher spectral efficiency

---

This work is supported by National Natural Science Foundation of China with project number 61731011.

H. Gao et al. (Eds.): ChinaCom 2019, LNICST 312, pp. 301–315, 2020.
https://doi.org/10.1007/978-3-030-41114-5_23

and transmission rate, which makes OAM become an important development direction of Beyond 5th Generation (B5G) and 6th Generation (6G) mobile communications in the future. Besides, OAM can not only increase the capacity by multiplexing, but also improve the transmission performance by Index Modulation (IM) [1]. However, the inverted cone beams and the spiral phase distribution result in the non-zero beam divergent angle. When propagating in free space, the divergence of the non-zero beam angle leads to the increase of the circular energy ring radius in the transverse plane, which makes it difficult for all-phase plane receiving in a long-distance transmission [2]. Therefore, it is necessary to consider partial phase plane reception.

For the partial phase plane receiving method [3], when multiplexing electromagnetic waves with different non-degenerate OAM modes, one-to-one frequency shift can be mapped to the secondary frequency domain by Virtual Rotating Antenna (VRA) [2,4], thus realizing the accurate identification of OAM modes. In Dec. 2016, the 27.5 km electromagnetic wave OAM transmission experiment was successfully completed [5,6]. In Apr. 2018, the same research team also completed a 172 km long ground-to-air transmission experiment from Beijing to Xiong An New Area in the north of Hebei Province, China [7]. However, in the future B5G and 6G high-capacity transmission even with Terahertz, due to the limited sampling rate of our existing hardware devices, it is difficult to meet our transmission rate requirements, or even if high sampling rate can be achieved, the cost is huge. Therefore, how to reduce the sampling rate to identify the OAM mode has become a problem.

The Compressive Sensing (CS) as a new sampling theory [8,9], exploits the sparse characteristics of the signal and uses random sampling to obtain discrete samples of the signal under the condition of the far less than Nyquist sampling rate, and then recovers the signal perfectly through the non-linear reconstruction algorithm [10]. Recently, CS theory has been applied to the detection of Generalized Space Shift Keying (GSSK) symbols in the uncertain Multiple-Input Multiple-Output (MIMO) systems with better performance [11], such as Orthogonal Matching Pursuit (OMP) [12] and the Basis Pursuit (BP) [13]. In addition, in the wake of the related research of the Analog-to-Information Converter (AIC) with Limited Random Sequence (LRS) modulation [14], the required sampling rate may be further reduced.

In this paper, the CS is applied to nondegenerate OAM multiplexing transmissions. Using AIC with LRS modulation as detector through random sampling [14], the low sampling rate with CS can be used to accurately identify OAM modes in the secondary frequency domain, and then high-speed transmission will be achieved. Notably, the method proposed in this paper is able to effectively solve the major problems, i.e., (1) When sampling Radio Frequency (RF) signals directly, the sampling rate is very high, and the hardware equipment is very expensive; (2) Besides, if analog devices are used to down convert the RF signals received by antennas and sample them at Intermediate Frequency (IF), the phase error and attenuation will be caused, which seriously affects our identification of OAM modes. Simultaneously, the sampling rate of the employed data acquisition card limits the data rate of the high-speed transmission.

2   Preliminary Knowledge

In the previous work, it was proposed that the VRA interpolation could be used to detect OAM through the method of the partial phase plane receiving [5]. Processing the signals received by antennas with VRA interpolation will cause the frequency shift in the corresponding transform domain. In this transform domain, different index sets will bring different combinations of OAM modes, different combinations of OAM modes will produce different frequency shifts, but only one spectrum line will be formed. Because it has the same dimension as the traditional frequency domain, we name the transform domain as the secondary frequency domain [4]. Usually, the first frequency domain refers to the traditional frequency domain.

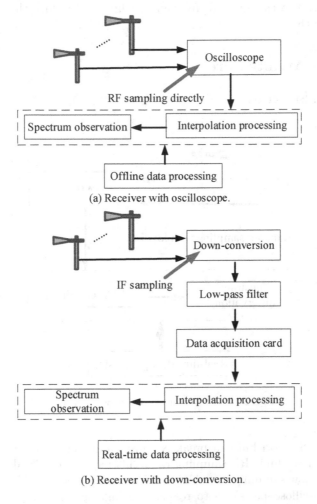

(a) Receiver with oscilloscope.

(b) Receiver with down-conversion.

Fig. 1. The comparison of receiver structures based on RF and IF sampling.

In this process, the multiple combinations of different nondegenerate OAM will be converted into the same frequency signal but different frequency shift combinations, which realizes the demodulation and identification of multiplexed OAM modes. Based on VRA, there are two commonly used receiver structures based on RF and IF sampling, as shown in Fig. 1. Specifically, in Fig. 1(a), RF signals are over-sampled directly by the high-speed sampling oscilloscope at the receiving end, and then different OAM modes are converted into the frequency shifts by VRA, which can be used for offline detection of OAM modes. This method has high cost because of the high sampling rate requirements.

In contrast, in Fig. 1(b), the RF signal obtained by the receiver is down-converted to IF with the frequency shifts in the secondary frequency domain. Then, the low-rate data acquisition card is used to identify the real-time OAM modes. However, due to the hardware limitation of the low sampling rate, this method will lead to the lower IF frequency, which will reduce the data carried by IF bandwidth.

3 System Architecture

3.1 System Structure

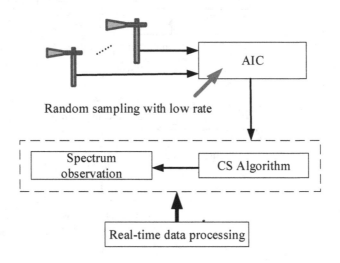

Fig. 2. The receiver structure with AIC.

As we know, CS algorithm can break Nyquist sampling theorem. Because the hardware resources limit RF sampling rate, this paper uses CS algorithm combined with the low sampling rate AIC to effectively replace the high-speed sampling of the oscilloscope, so as to realize the high-speed and accurate identification of OAM modes. Specifically, the RF signals received by antennas are

sampled randomly by AIC, and the spectral line mapped to OAM mode is separated and recovered in the secondary frequency domain by CS, which greatly
improves the data transmission rate and avoids the cost of the high-speed sampling device. Figure 2 illustrates the receiver with AIC.

3.2   Analog-to-Information Converter

In this subsection, we review a promising symbol detector for random sampling.
AIC with LRS modulation is used at the receiving end, and the structure of AIC
with LRS modulation is shown in Fig. 3. It consists of limited random sequence,
integrator and low-power Analog-to-Digital Converter (ADC). The AIC differs
from the traditional ADC because it can sample the signal randomly. The LRS
elements are composed of 1 and 0. The sampler completes the physical process
of random sampling well by mixing the sequence of "0" and "1" and integrating
the mixed signal. The sequence in length N and consists of M frames, and each
frame is in length L. The elements are composed of $N - 1$ "0" and only one "1",
and the location of 1 is random [14].

The input signal $s(t)$ and the signal $p(t)$ generated by periodic transmission
of a finite length random sequence are mixed and the results of mixing are
fed into the integrator, where the period of the integrator is the reciprocal of
the average sampling rate of the random sampler, and then the integrator is
connected to the traditional low-power ADC sampler. The sampling period is
also T. In the process of sampling, the random sampling of the analog signal can
be realized only by synchronizing the integrator and ADC with the finite length
sequence generator. The output $s(n)$ is a discrete signal, which will be sent to
the successive real-time data processing module for recovery with CS algorithm.

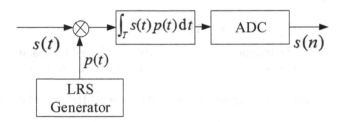

Fig. 3. The structure of AIC with LRS modulation.

3.3   Compressive Sensing Algorithm

The CS technology breaks through the limitation of uniform sampling rate in
the traditional Nyquist sampling theorem. For sparse signals, random sampling
is used to restore the complete signal with sampling data much less than Nyquist
sampling rate [10].

It is precise because AIC random sampling at the receiver can meet the
requirement of CS, so that CS algorithm can be used to identify the OAM

modes utilizing the known sparsity. Furthermore, the known sparsity is 1. For CS, greedy algorithms mainly used are Matching Pursuit (MP) algorithm and Orthogonal Matching Pursuit (OMP) algorithm at present.

Specifically, when the measurement matrix is not easy to obtain or unknown, MP algorithm can use greedy iteration algorithm to construct matching dictionary and obtain sparse vectors. Compared with MP algorithm, the improvement of OMP algorithm is that it can accelerate the convergence speed of the algorithm by Schmidt orthogonalization of the columns selected in each iteration. For OAM modes identification, the measurement matrix is known and the real-time demodulation needs to be guaranteed. Thereby, OMP algorithm is considered and employed in this paper [15].

4   Mathematical Model

As mentioned above, assuming that N data symbols are transmitted, then $\mathbf{x}$ can be expressed as the symbol vector of the transmitter

$$\mathbf{x} = [x_0, x_1, ..., x_{N-1}]^{\mathrm{T}}. \tag{1}$$

If the l-th OAM mode needs to be generated, the phase shifting vector $\mathbf{W}$ of the each element in Uniform Circular Array (UCA) composed of N arrays can be denoted as

$$\mathbf{W} = [1, e^{j\frac{2\pi l}{N}}, ..., e^{j\frac{2\pi l(N-1)}{N}}]^{\mathrm{T}}, \tag{2}$$

where $j = \sqrt{-1}$ is the imaginary unit.

Therefore, the received signal $\mathbf{s}$ with M elements at the antenna array can be expressed as

$$\mathbf{s} = \mathbf{HWx} + \mathbf{N}, \tag{3}$$

where $\mathbf{N}$ represents the independent identically distributed Gaussian white noise vector, $\mathbf{H}$ is the channel matrix from the transmitter to the receiver in free space [16, 18].

According to Fig. 3, the signal through AIC with LRS modulation denoted as follows

$$\mathbf{s}(n) = \int_T \mathbf{s}(t)\mathbf{p}(t)\mathrm{d}t. \tag{4}$$

It is well known that the recover process of OMP is to reconstruct the P-dimensional original signal $\mathbf{z}(t)$ from the known Q-dimensional measurement signal $\mathbf{s}(n)$ and the measurement matrix $\mathbf{\Phi}$. Assuming that the length of signal $\mathbf{z}(t)$ is P, it is sparse under a projection array $\mathbf{\Psi}$, $\mathbf{\Psi} \in P \times P$, only K elements are greater than the threshold ϵ, where K is far less than P, the measured value can be obtained by observing the signal $\mathbf{z}(t)$ on a basis $\mathbf{\Phi}$, $\mathbf{\Phi} \in Q \times P$, then we can get

$$\mathbf{s} = \mathbf{\Phi z} = \mathbf{\Phi\Psi f} = \mathbf{\Theta f}, \tag{5}$$

where, $\Theta = \Phi\Psi$, Θ is the sparse representation of the signal, $\mathbf{z}(t)$ is based on projection and $\mathbf{f}$ is the spectrum in the secondary frequency domain. The dimension Q of the measured value in the above Eq. (5) is less than the dimension P of the signal. There are infinite solutions to the equation. It needs exhaustive time to search the correct result. However, this problem can be solved by the minimum norm problem. Usually, the minimum norm problem can be transformed into the following Eq. (6) [19]:

$$\hat{\mathbf{z}} = \min \|\mathbf{z}\|_0 \qquad \text{s.t. } \mathbf{s} = \Phi\mathbf{z}, \tag{6}$$

where, $\|\|_0$ denotes the zero norm for the vector, that is, the number of non-zero elements in the vector. When considering noise or error, Eq. (6) can be rewritten as

$$\hat{\mathbf{z}} = \min \|\mathbf{z}\|_0 \qquad \text{s.t. } \|\mathbf{s} - \Phi\mathbf{z}\|_2 \leq \varepsilon, \tag{7}$$

in which ε is a decimal positive number representing the threshold.

Since LRS sequence can satisfy the random sampling requirement of OMP algorithm, OMP algorithm is considered to recover the spectral line in the secondary frequency domain according to the signal after AIC with LRS. Thus, according to [5], the measurement matrix Φ can be defined as

$$\Phi = \mathbf{w}^T = \mathbf{P}^T\mathbf{R}^{-T}, \tag{8}$$

where $\mathbf{w}$ is matrix of the weighting coefficient for the received signal after AIC, $(\cdot)^T$ denotes the transpose of matrix, $\mathbf{P}$ is the cross-correlation matrix between the received signal and the interpolated signal, and $\mathbf{R}$ is the autocorrelation matrix of the received signal.

5   Performance Evaluation

According to the description in Sects. 3 and 4, an example is proposed to confirm the correctness of the proposed method. Additionally, in order to further analyze the efficiency, we compare the identification probability, the Bit Error Rate (BER) performance and the capacities in three cases, i.e., the cases of RF sampling directly, IF sampling and OMP with AIC.

5.1   Example

The main simulation parameters are listed in Table 1 and results are all conducted with MATLAB R2016a programming platform. Assuming that the separated OAM Mode 1 and OAM Mode 2 are respectively generated for index keying transmission at the transmitter, and the 100 MHz IF signal is up-converted to 10 GHz RF, fed to the UCA composed of 16 array elements, then received by two antennas placed at the receiving energy ring through the partial phase plane method at the receiver. The receiver will restore spectral lines according to the index set of the different OAM combinations. Figure 4 illustrates the signals received by Antenna 1 and Antenna 2 for OAM Mode 1, and Fig. 5 shows the signals received by Antenna 1 and Antenna 2 for Mode 2.

Table 1. Simulation parameters.

Parameters	Value
Carrier frequency f	10 GHz
Modulation scheme	QPSK
Signal length	128
Beam divergence angle	2°
Transmission distance	100 m
UCA radius	9 cm
Element number in UCA	16
Receiver ring radius	3.49 m
Receiver antennas space	1 m
OAM modes	1, 2
Sampling rate	1.25 GHz

The limited random sequence $\mathbf{p}(t)$ designed is shown in Fig. 6. The length of the signal is 128, and consists of 16 frames, each frame is in length 8. Then, the measurement signals utilized by CS for OAM Mode 1 after AIC with LRS can be shown in Fig. 7, and the measurement signals used by CS for OAM Mode 2 after AIC with LRS can be shown in Fig. 8. Both low-rate measurement signals will be applied to recover the spectrum line in the secondary frequency domain.

According to the known sparsity of 1 and the measurement signals, the reconstruction is carried out by combining OMP algorithm. Finally, the recovered signal can be converted to a spectral line in the secondary frequency domain, so that separated Mode 1 and Mode 2 are respectively converted to frequency shift in the secondary frequency domain. As shown in Fig. 9, the index of the different OAM mode will be obtained based on the different frequency shift.

As we all know, if the Nyquist sampling is used, two sampling points at least are required for each signal period, so for this example, there are at least 26 sampling points. However, 16 sampling points have been used to realize the low-rate sampling of 10 GHz RF signal and reconstruct the spectrum line in the secondary frequency domain, so that OAM mode identification is achieved. Thus, the method of AIC with CS proposed in this paper has been verified.

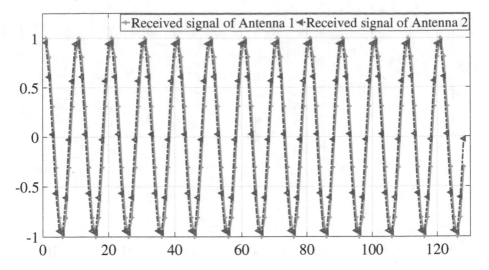

Fig. 4. Typical received signals of Antenna 1 and 2 for Mode 1.

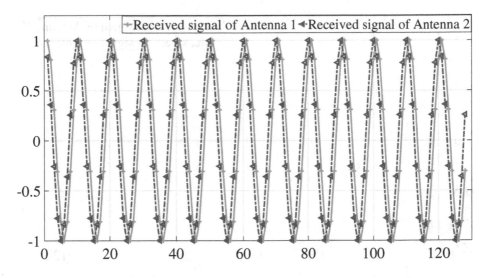

Fig. 5. Typical received signals of Antenna 1 and 2 for Mode 2.

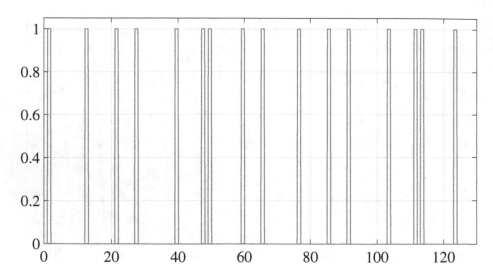

Fig. 6. Typical figure of the limited random sequence $\mathbf{p}(t)$.

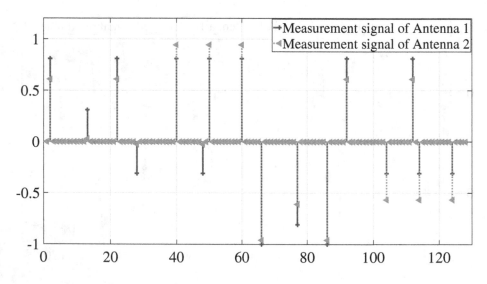

Fig. 7. Typical measurement signals used by CS for Mode 1 after AIC.

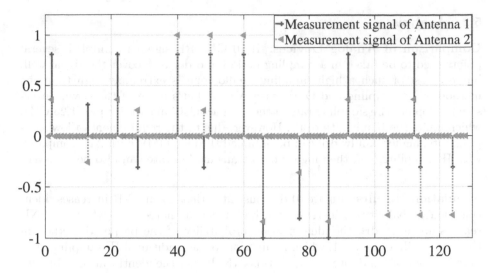

Fig. 8. Typical measurement signals used by CS for Mode 2 after AIC.

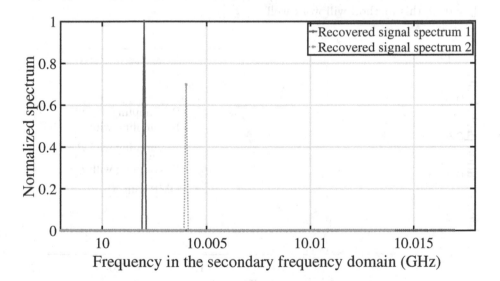

Fig. 9. The spectrum in the secondary frequency domain.

5.2   Analysis

Comparison of Analog Devices. If 10 GHz RF signal is sampled, several points need to be taken in a sampling period in order to recover the signal well, but the cost of such a high sampling oscilloscope is extremely high than the method of IF sampling and OMP with AIC. What's more, if the downconversion is adopted, the sampling rate of the data acquisition card is up to 1.25 GHz, which limits the bandwidth of IF. However, due to the requirement of low sampling rate, higher bandwidth can be obtained through OMP with AIC compared with IF sampling, and then higher data transmission rate can also be achieved.

Simulation Results. Figure 10 demonstrates that when SNR increases, identification probability P_I increases quickly. It can be noted that when the SNR reaches about 19 dB, the identification probability of the proposed method in this paper will approach 1, which is superior to the traditional IF sampling. The lower the out-of-band interference ratio is, the higher the identification probability of OAM is. Besides, if the out-of-band interference ratio is as low as 0.001, the identification probability of IF sampling is very close to that of RF sampling and OMP with AIC. Especially, when P_I is greater than the threshold probability $P_0 = 0.89$, this method will work well.

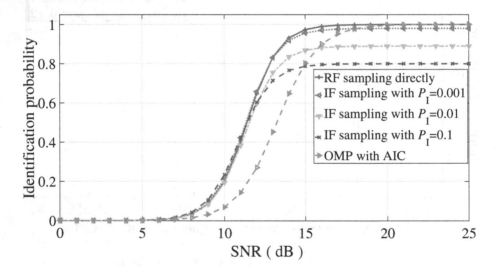

Fig. 10. Identification probability varys with SNR.

According to the identification probability P_I, the P_{BER} can be obtained as

$$P_{BER} = 1 - P_I. \tag{9}$$

Therefore, the BER performance simulation is shown in Fig. 11, the highest BER performance of IF sampling can be found under certain SNR, and the BER performance of OMP with AIC is fairly better than IF sampling.

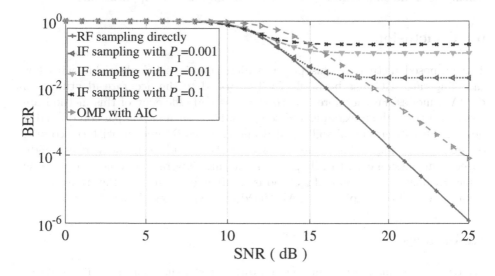

Fig. 11. The BER performance simulation results vary with SNR.

For a communication system, the transmission capacity is also a extremely important evaluation index. Consequently, Fig. 12 illustrates the capacity curve as BER changes according to the Shannon formula and BER curve, the capacity curve of OMP with AIC is close to the RF sampling directly.

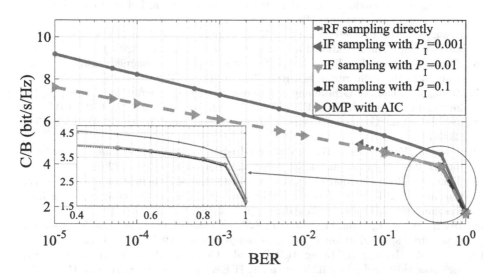

Fig. 12. The transmission capacity simulation comparison.

Overall, OMP with AIC is able to be used for random sampling at a fairly low sampling rate, which is of great benefit to replace the high-speed sampling scheme. However, the sampling equipment with AIC increases the difficulty. Then, the trade-off should be considered in the practical application.

6 Conclusion

The proposed method in this paper, which combines CS algorithm with low sampling rate AIC, has been effectively applied to the accurate identification of OAM modes. Furthermore, the correctness and efficiency of this method are confirmed through an example and some analysis, such as comparison of analog devices, identification probability, BER and capacity. Moreover, with the coming of next generation mobile communications (B5G and 6G), the wireless high-speed transmission even to 1 Tbps with low sampling rate becomes a promising topic. Evidently, the proposed method is significant to promote the transmission capacity with low sampling rate AIC hardware equipment in the future.

References

1. Basar, E.: Orbital angular momentum with index modulation. IEEE Trans. Wirel. Commun. **17**(3), 2029–2037 (2018)
2. Zhang, C., Ma, L.: Millimetre wave with rotational orbital angular momentum. Sci. Rep. **6**, 31921 (2016)
3. Zhang, W., Zheng, S., Chen, Y., et al.: Orbital angular momentum-based communications with partial arc sampling receiving. IEEE Commun. Lett. **20**(7), 1–1 (2016)
4. Zhao, Y., Jiang, J., Jiang, X., et al.: Orbital angular momentum multiplexing with non-degenerate modes in secondary frequency domain. In: IEEE MTT-S International Wireless Symposium (IWS), Chengdu, pp. 1–4 (2018)
5. Zhang, C., Ma, L.: Detecting the orbital angular momentum of electro-magnetic waves using virtual rotational antenna. Sci. Rep. **7**(1), 4585 (2017)
6. Zhang, C., Chen, D., Jiang, X.: RCS diversity of electromagnetic wave carrying orbital angular momentum. Sci. Rep. **7**(1), 15412 (2017)
7. Zhang, C., Zhao, Y.: Orbital angular momentum nondegenerate index mapping for long distance transmission. IEEE Trans. Wirel. Commun. **29**(2), 7672 (2019)
8. Donoho, D.L.: Compressed sensing. IEEE Trans. Inf. Theory **52**(4), 1289–1306 (2006)
9. Ding, W., Yang, F., Dai, W., et al.: Time-frequency joint sparse channel estimation for MIMO-OFDM systems. IEEE Commun. Lett. **19**(1), 58–61 (2014)
10. Jiang, J., Chen, C.: Analysis in theory and technology application of compressive sensing. In: 2014 Sixth International Conference on Intelligent Human-Machine Systems and Cybernetics, Hangzhou, pp. 184–187 (2014)
11. He, L., Wang, J., Ding, W., Song, J.: ℓ_∞ Minimization based symbol detection for generalized space shift keying. IEEE Commun. Lett. **19**(7), 1109–1112 (2015)
12. Yu, C.M., Hsieh, S.H., Liang, H.W., et al.: Compressed sensing detector design for space shift keying in MIMO systems. IEEE Commun. Lett. **16**(10), 1556–1559 (2012)

13. Liu, W., Wang, N., Jin, M., Xu, H.: Denoising detection for the generalized spatial modulation system using sparse property. IEEE Commun. Lett. **18**(1), 22–25 (2014)
14. Zhang, C., Wu, Z., Xiao, J.: Adaptive analog-to-information converter with limited random sequence modulation. In: 2011 International Conference on Wireless Communications and Signal Processing (WCSP), Nanjing, pp. 1–5 (2011)
15. Tropp, J.A., Gilbert, A.C.: Signal recovery from random measurements via orthogonal matching pursuit. IEEE Trans. Inf. Theory **53**(12), 4655–4666 (2007)
16. Jackson, J.D.: Classical Electrodynamics. Wiley, New York (1999)
17. Zhang, W., Zheng, S., Hui, X., et al.: Mode division multiplexing communication using microwave orbital angular momentum: an experimental study. IEEE Trans. Wirel. Commun. **16**(2), 1308–1318 (2017)
18. Jiang, X., Zhao, Y., Jiang, X., Zhang, C.: Capacity evaluation on the long-distance orbital angular momentum non-orthogonal transmission. In: IEEE MTT-S International Wireless Symposium (IWS), Chengdu, pp. 1–4 (2018)
19. Li, H., Zhang, Q., Cui, A., et al.: Minimization of fraction function penalty in compressed sensing. IEEE Trans. Neural Netw. Learn. Syst. 1–12 (2017)

Improved Incremental Freezing HARQ Schemes Using Polar Codes over Degraded Compound Channels

Tianze Hu[1], Lei Xie[1,2(✉)], Huifang Chen[1,3], Hongda Duan[1], and Kuang Wang[1,2]

[1] College of Information Science and Electronic Engineering, Zhejiang University, Hangzhou 310027, China
{21631077,xiel,chenhf,wangk}@zju.edu.cn
[2] Zhejiang Provincial Key Laboratory of Information Processing, Communication and Networking, Hangzhou 310027, China
[3] Zhoushan Ocean Research Center, Zhoushan 316021, China

Abstract. The error propagation problem in incremental freezing (IF) hybrid automatic repeat request (HARQ) scheme using Polar codes is studied. We propose two IF HARQ schemes using polar codes, namely the cyclic redundancy check (CRC)-aided IF HARQ scheme and the cumulative-path-metrics-based IF HARQ scheme. In the CRC-aided IF HARQ scheme, several CRC bits are added to each transmitted block. Using these CRC bits, the proposed IF HARQ scheme and the Chase Combining HARQ scheme can be combined to achieve a better error correction performance in the cost of a larger decoding delay. In the cumulative-path-metrics-based IF HARQ scheme, the successive joint decoder maintains multiple possible paths simultaneously, and the cumulative path metrics is used to represent the reliability of each surviving path in the decoding process. Moreover, a modified path splitting reduced successive cancellation list (SCL) decoding algorithm is presented to reduce the computational complexity and the memory requirement of cumulative-path-metrics-based IF HARQ scheme. Simulation results show that, using the Polar code constructed under long block length and high block error rate, the CRC-aided IF HARQ scheme has a higher system throughput. With the Polar code constructed under short block length and low block error rate, the cumulative-path-metrics-based IF HARQ scheme has a higher system throughput. In both situations, the system block error rate of the CRC-aided IF HARQ scheme performs well.

Keywords: Degraded compound channel · Polar codes · Incremental freezing HARQ scheme · Path splitting reduced SCL decoding algorithm

This work was partly supported by the Science and Technology Department of Zhejiang Province (No. LGG18F010005, No. 2018R52046), and National Natural Science Foundation of China (No. 61671410).

H. Gao et al. (Eds.): ChinaCom 2019, LNICST 312, pp. 316–330, 2020.
https://doi.org/10.1007/978-3-030-41114-5_24

1 Introduction

Polar codes are one of capacity-achieving linear block codes first proposed in [1]. In order to construct polar codes, it is necessary to acquire the reliability of each polarized channel. Given the code length, the transmission rate and the signal-to-noise ratio (SNR) of channel, a variety of algorithms can be used to calculate the construction of polar codes effectively. However, in many communication scenarios, the channel state is time-varying and unknown by the transmitter. Hence, how to construct polar codes under such situation is an open problem.

The most conservative transmission strategy is to develop a code structure with a fixed rate in the worst possible channel, but this strategy results in a low transmission efficiency. For another transmission scheme, the transmitter continues to transmit the encoded bits until the receiver can decode them correctly. However, this transmission scheme requires the receiver to send a feedback (ACK/NACK) to indicate whether the decoding is successful or not although the condition can be satisfied easily in most communication scenarios. The transmission strategy with feedback is known as hybrid automatic repeat request (HARQ) which can resolve the error problem caused by the mismatch between the channel state and the code construction.

Recently, some HARQ schemes using polar codes have been proposed. In [2], a chase combining (CC) HARQ scheme using polar code is presented, where each retransmission code block is identical to the original one. The receiver combines the soft information of current received block with all the previous decoding-failed blocks using the maximum ratio combination (MRC) rule, and tries to decode the code block again. Hence, the CC HARQ scheme achieves a diversity gain. In [3], an incremental redundancy (IR) HARQ scheme using polar code is proposed, where each retransmission code block contains different information compared with the CC HARQ scheme. For a set of information bits, multiple sets of coded bits are generated. The retransmission uses a different set of coded bits with different redundancy versions generated by puncturing the encoder output. Hence, with each retransmission, the receiver obtains the extra information. In [4], an incremental freezing (IF) HARQ scheme using polar code is proposed, where the retransmitted bits are the information bits with a lower reliability in previous incorrect decoding blocks. The IF HARQ scheme is proved to be capacity-achieving over a class of channels with degradation relationship which also named as the degraded compound channels.

However, the IF HARQ scheme proposed in [4] adopts a successive joint decoding structure, which results in the problem of error propagation. At the receiver, some information bits in previous received code block are used as the frozen bits in subsequent received blocks' decoding process. Hence, if the decoding result of previous received block is incorrect, all the decoding results of subsequent received blocks should be wrong, which leads to the performance degradation of error correction.

To mitigate the error propagation, we propose two improved IF HARQ schemes using polar codes, the cyclic redundancy check (CRC)-aided IF HARQ scheme and the cumulative-path-metrics-based IF HARQ scheme.

The idea of the CRC-aided IF HARQ scheme is straightforward. Several CRC bits are added to each retransmitted block as well as the original transmitted block. With the help of these CRC bits, the IF HARQ scheme can be combined with the CC HARQ scheme to achieve a good error correction performance. The receiver has the information that whether the current transmitted block is decoded correctly or not using the CRC bits. If the decoding result is incorrect, the receiver sends a feedback to the transmitter for requesting a re-transmission until the decoding successes or the retransmission time exceeds the upper limit. Hence, the performance degradation caused by the decoding error propagation problem is mitigated. However, the CRC-aided IF HARQ scheme has a larger decoding delay, and the additional CRC bits in each retransmission block reduces the system throughput.

In the cumulative-path-metrics-based IF HARQ scheme, referring to the idea of the successive cancellation list (SCL) decoding algorithm, we introduce the cumulative path metrics to represent the reliability of each surviving path in the decoding process. The successive joint decoder maintains multiple possible decoding paths at the same time to eliminate the error propagation. To reduce the calculation complexity and space complexity, a path splitting reduced SCL decoding algorithm is used in the proposed cumulative-path-metrics-based IF HARQ scheme.

2 Preliminaries

In this section, we briefly introduce the polar code, channel model and the IF HARQ scheme using polar codes.

2.1 Polar Code

Let $\mathbf{X} = \{0, 1\}$ and $\mathbf{Y} = \{0, 1\}$. $W : \mathbf{X} \rightarrow \mathbf{Y}$ denotes a binary-input discrete memoryless channel (B-DMC). The basic channel transform of polar code creates two polarized channels with different capacities as

$$W_2^{(0)}\left(y_0^1|u_0\right) = \frac{1}{2}\sum_{u_1} W(y_0|u_0 \oplus u_1)W(y_1|u_1) \Bigg\} = (W, W)^-, \tag{1}$$

$$W_2^{(1)}\left(y_0^1, u_0|u_1\right) = \frac{1}{2}W(y_0|u_0 \oplus u_1)W(y_1|u_1) = (W, W)^+. \tag{2}$$

where u_0^1 is the input vector uniformly distributed over $\mathbf{X}^2$, and y_0^1 is the corresponding channel output.

For a block of bits, the construction of polar code lays on the polarization effect of matrix $\mathbf{G}_2 = \begin{bmatrix} 1 & 0 \\ 1 & 1 \end{bmatrix}$. Let $\mathbf{G}_2^{\otimes n}$ denote the nth Kronecker power of $\mathbf{G}_2$. For a block of $N = 2^n$ bits, U_0^{N-1}, applying the transform $\mathbf{G}_2^{\otimes n}$ to get the encoded block, $X_0^{N-1} = U_0^{N-1}\mathbf{G}_2^{\otimes n}$, and transmitting each bit through independent copies of B-DMC, W.

Applying the chain rule to mutual information between input U_0^{N-1} and output Y_0^{N-1}, we have

$$I\left(U_0^{N-1}; Y_0^{N-1}\right) = \sum_{i=0}^{N-1} I\left(U_i; Y_0^{N-1}|U_0^{i-1}\right) = \sum_0^{N-1} I\left(U_i; Y_0^{N-1}, U_0^{i-1}\right). \tag{3}$$

An important property of polar code is that, except for a negligible fraction, the terms in the right summation of (3) either approach to 0 (bad channel) or 1 (good channel) as n increases. Moreover, the fraction of those terms approaching to 1 converges the symmetric mutual information, $I(W)$. This phenomenon is the channel polarization.

The recursive expressions of polarization channel are

$$W_N^{(2i)} = \left(W_{N/2}^{(i)}, W_{N/2}^{(i)}\right)^-, \tag{4}$$

$$W_N^{(2i+1)} = \left(W_{N/2}^{(i)}, W_{N/2}^{(i)}\right)^+. \tag{5}$$

2.2 Channel Model

Let $\mathbf{W}_c$ denote a compound channel, which is a set of S sub-channels, $\mathbf{W}_c = \{W_1, W_2, \ldots, W_S\}$. This work aims at the flat-fading channel environment, which means each symbol in one block will transmit through the same channel state. The channel state information (CSI) and channel distribution information (CDI) are unknown to the transmitter. The knowledge it only has is the set of channels to which the channel belongs. Every round of transmission (including the original transmitted block and retransmitted blocks) happens on one of sub-channels, W_i. On the other hand, the CSI is known at the receiver. In the real applications, this assumption is correct in most cases since the receiver can use pilot symbols to estimate the channel state.

Let $I(\mathbf{W}_c)$ denote the compound capacity of $\mathbf{W}_c$, which is the rate that can be reliably transmitted irrespective of used channel. The compound capacity is defined as [5]

$$I(\mathbf{W}_c) = \max_P \inf_{W_i \in \mathbf{W}_c} I_P(W_i), \tag{6}$$

where $I_P(W_i)$ denotes the mutual information between the input and output of W_i with the input distribution P.

The compound capacity of $\mathbf{W}_c$ can be smaller than the infimum of the capacity of individual channels in $\mathbf{W}_c$, because the capacity achieving distribution for the individual channels might be different. If W_i is a symmetric channel, the compound capacity equals to the infimum of individual capacities. If channels in $\mathbf{W}_c$ are degraded, the infimum is obtained by the worst channel, and then the compound capacity equals to the capacity of the worst channel.

2.3 IF HARQ Scheme

Given two channels $Q : \mathbf{X} \rightarrow \mathbf{Z}$ and $W : \mathbf{X} \rightarrow \mathbf{Y}$, we say that Q is degraded with respect to W if there exists a channel $V : \mathbf{Y} \rightarrow \mathbf{Z}$ such that for all $z \in \mathbf{Z}$ and $x \in \mathbf{X}$,

$$Q(z|x) = \sum_{y \in \mathbf{Y}} W(y|x) V(z|y). \tag{7}$$

Let $Q \preccurlyeq W$ denote that Q is degraded with respect to W. It is proved in [6] that the channel polarization preserves degradedness. That is, if $Q \preccurlyeq W$, we have $Q^+ \preccurlyeq W^+$ and $Q^- \preccurlyeq W^-$. According to the recursive expressions (4) and (5), we have $Q_N^{(i)} \preccurlyeq W_N^{(i)}$, which means that the good polarization channel indices set $\mathbf{A}_Q$ for channel Q must be a subset of the good polarization channel indices $\mathbf{A}_W$ for channel W in the polarization process. This is called as the nesting property of polar codes, which leads to the development of the IF HARQ scheme.

For the compound channel $\mathbf{W}_c$, we assume that all the sub-channels are B-DMCs and have a degradation relationship. That is, $W_S \preccurlyeq W_{S-1} \preccurlyeq \ldots \preccurlyeq W_1$. According to the nesting property, we have $\mathbf{A}_{W_s} \subseteq \mathbf{A}_{W_{s-1}} \subseteq \cdots \subseteq \mathbf{A}_{W_1}$. At the transmitter, let $\mathbf{S}_k$ denote the kth transmitted block, polar code construction $PC_{W_i}\left(N, K_{W_i}, \mathbf{A}_{W_i}, u_{\mathbf{A}_{W_i}^c}\right)$ on each sub-channel is calculated offline before the transmission starts, where N denotes the code length, K_{W_i} denotes the length of information bits for sub-channel W_i, $u_{\mathbf{A}_{W_i}^c}$ denotes the frozen bits for sub-channel W_i.

We greedily use the PC_{W_1} to encode the first transmission information bits and get $\mathbf{S}_1$, send it to the receiver, and wait for the feedback. If an ACK is received, the transmitter knows that all the transmitted bits are decoded correctly, and it prepares for the next transmission. However, if a NACK is received, which means a decoding error has happened at the receiver or the receiver cannot decode the information, the transmitter will reduce the transmission rate and transmit some information bits with a lower reliability from the previous transmitted blocks. Generally speaking, if k NACK feedbacks have been received, which means the previous k blocks are not decoded correctly or cannot be decoded, the transmitter will choose the information bits at the polarization channel indices of $\mathbf{A}_{W_k} - \mathbf{A}_{W_{k+1}}$ from previous k transmitted blocks, $\mathbf{S}_1$, $\mathbf{S}_2$, ..., $\mathbf{S}_k$, and use $PC_{W_{k+1}}$ to encode the retransmitted bits. The number of the $(k+1)^{\text{th}}$ retransmitted bits is $k\left|\mathbf{A}_{W_k} - \mathbf{A}_{W_{k+1}}\right|$. We can put $\left|\mathbf{A}_{W_{k+1}}\right| - k\left|\mathbf{A}_{W_k} - \mathbf{A}_{W_{k+1}}\right|$ new information bits into the block and get $\mathbf{S}_{k+1}$.

Let $\mathbf{R}_k$ denote the kth received block at the receiver. When $\mathbf{R}_k$ is received, the receiver decides whether to decode it according to the real channel state W_r. If $W_r \preccurlyeq W_k$, the transmission rate $R = I(W_k) > I(W_r)$. Referring to the Shannon theorem, the block $\mathbf{R}_k$ cannot be decoded, and then the receiver sends a NACK. If $W_r \succcurlyeq W_k$, the receiver needs to decode all the information bits from $\mathbf{R}_1, \mathbf{R}_2, ..., \mathbf{R}_k$ blocks, which is a successive joint decoding structure. Since block $\mathbf{S}_i$ contains some information bits with a lower reliability in $\mathbf{S}_1, \mathbf{S}_2, ..., \mathbf{S}_{i-1}$ blocks, we can take the decoding result of $\mathbf{R}_i$ as the side information of frozen bits and put it into the decoding process of $\mathbf{R}_{i-1}, \mathbf{R}_{i-2}, ..., \mathbf{R}_1$, which leads to a lower successive joint decoding rate. It is proved in [4] that the IF HARQ scheme using polar code is capacity-achieving over the degraded compound channel owing to the nesting property.

3   Proposed IF HARQ Schemes Using Polar Codes

Since the IF HARQ scheme adopts a successive joint decoding structure, the problem of error propagation takes place. As the block error rate on polar code PC_{W_i} is e_i, the system block error rate should be $e_s = 1 - \prod\limits_{i=1}^{k} (1 - e_i)$.

3.1 CRC-Aided IF HARQ Scheme Using Polar Code

To mitigate the error propagation problem of the IF HARQ scheme using polar code, a straightforward method is to add the extra CRC bits in the original transmission block and retransmission block(s). Using these CRC bits, the decoder can know the block is decoded correctly or not. Moreover, with CRC bits, the IF HARQ scheme and the CC HARQ scheme can be combined to achieve a better error correction performance.

In order to combine the CC HARQ scheme, we extend the NACK message to IF NACK and CC NACK.

If receiving an IF NACK message, the transmitter knows the previous transmission rate exceeds the channel capacity, and the receiver cannot decode the received block. Thus, the transmitter reduces the transmission rate, and sends some redundant information bits with a lower reliability in the previous transmitted blocks, as the IF HARQ scheme in the Subsect. 2.3.

If the transmitter receives a CC NACK message, it means that the previous transmission rate is smaller than the channel capacity. A successive joint decoding process is executed at the receiver, but a decoding error occurred in one of received blocks. Thus, the transmitter retransmits the corresponding block according to the index information carried in the CC NACK message.

At the receiver, the condition of whether sending ACK message or IF NACK message is the same as the IF HARQ scheme. It is assumed that the receiver has received k blocks. If $W_r \succcurlyeq W_k$, the receiver should decode all the information bits from $\mathbf{R}_1, \mathbf{R}_2, ..., \mathbf{R}_k$ blocks. In the successive joint decoding structure, if block $\mathbf{R}_i$ fails to decode, the receiver sends a CC NACK message including the index of $\mathbf{R}_i$, i.

Hence, a better error correction performance can be achieved at the price of a higher decoding delay, and a slight reduction system throughput.

It is analyzed in [7] that the computation complexity of the SCL decoding algorithm is $O(LN\log N)$, and the space complexity is $O(LN)$. Hence, the computation complexity of the CRC-aided IF HARQ scheme is $O(kLN\log N)$, and the space complexity is $O(kLN)$.

3.2 Cumulative-Path-Metrics-Based IF HARQ Scheme Using Polar Code

As we know, the successive joint decoding structure is similar to the SC decoding algorithm. For the SC decoding algorithm, the decoding results of all the previous bits $\hat{u}_1^{i-1}$ are needed to decode the current bit $\hat{u}_i$. For the successive joint decoding structure of IF HARQ scheme, if the receiver has received k blocks, the decoding results of $\mathbf{R}_{i+1}$, $\mathbf{R}_{i+2}, ..., \mathbf{R}_k$ are needed to decode $\mathbf{R}_i$ block.

For the SCL decoding algorithm, several SC decoders operate in parallel and maintain multiple possible decoding paths at the same time to improve the block error correction performance. Referring to the idea of the SCL decoding algorithm, the successive joint decoder can also maintain multiple possible paths at the same time to improve the error correction performance.

In the successive joint decoding structure, the decoding results of received blocks are needed to form a decoding path. As the path metrics in the SCL algorithm, we introduce the cumulative path metrics to indicate the reliability of a decoding path. Let $\hat{\mathbf{c}}_i$ denote the SCL decoding results of block $\mathbf{R}_i$, and the list size of $\hat{\mathbf{c}}_i$ is L. Let $\hat{\mathbf{c}}_{i,l}$ be one of the decoding results in list, $1 \leqslant l \leqslant I$. Let $\mathbf{p}_i$ be the decoding path set in successive joint decoding structure after $\mathbf{R}_i$ is decoded, the cardinality of $\mathbf{p}_i$ is M, $M \leqslant L$. Each decoding path $\mathbf{p}_{i,m}$ contains the decoding results of $\mathbf{R}_i$, $\mathbf{R}_{i+1}$, ..., $\mathbf{R}_k$. That is,

$$\mathbf{p}_{i,m} = \left\{ \hat{\mathbf{c}}_{i,l_{i,m}}, \hat{\mathbf{c}}_{i+1,l_{i+1,m}}, \ldots, \hat{\mathbf{c}}_{k,l_{k,m}} \right\}, \ 1 \leqslant m \leqslant M, \tag{8}$$

where $l_{i,m}$ means that for different decoding path and block, the decoding result chosen by the SCL decoder may be different.

Let $\mathrm{pm}_{i,l}$ be the path metrics of decoding result $\hat{\mathbf{c}}_{i,l}$, $\mathbf{PM}_i$ is the cumulative path metrics set after $\mathbf{R}_i$ is decoded, the cardinality of set $\mathbf{PM}_i$ is M. We have

$$\mathbf{PM}_{i,m} = \sum_{j=i}^{k} \mathrm{pm}_{j,l_{j,m}}, \ 1 \leqslant m \leqslant M. \tag{9}$$

Let $\mathbf{D}_i$ denote the decoding output of $\mathbf{R}_i$ including the decoding path and the cumulative path metrics of this path. That is,

$$\mathbf{D}_i = \left\{ (\mathbf{p}_{i,1}, \mathbf{PM}_{i,1}), (\mathbf{p}_{i,2}, \mathbf{PM}_{i,2}), \ldots, (\mathbf{p}_{i,M}, \mathbf{PM}_{i,M}) \right\}. \tag{10}$$

Let $\mathbf{B}_i$ be the decoding buffer for block $\mathbf{R}_i$, and its size is ML.

Without CRC bits in retransmission block, the decoders in successive joint decoding structure do not output a decoding result but maintain M possible paths to participate in the subsequent decoding process. Based on this idea, we propose the cumulative-path-metrics-based IF HARQ scheme using polar code. The logic at transmitter is the same as the IF HARQ scheme using polar code. The decoding algorithm at the receiver is summarized in Algorithm 1 as follows.

Algorithm 1: The decoding algorithm of cumulative-path-metrics-based IF HARQ scheme using polar code

Input: the received block **R**, the channel state W_r, the maximum retransmission time T.
Output: feedback = union {ACK, NACK}.
Decoding Procedure
(1)   Calculate polar code construction PC_{W_i} on each sub-channel offline. Let **RB** denote the receiver buffer, c be the received block number. $c = 0$.
(2)   **while true**
(3)   Wait for the block to arrive. Receive the block, $c = c + 1$.
(4)   **if** $c > T + 1$
(5)   Maximum retransmission time is exceeded. Current received block is the first block of a new round transmission. Empty **RB** and set $c = 1$.
(6)   **end if**
(7)   Set **RB**[c] = **R**, received block goes into the buffer and waits to be decoded.
(8)   **if** $W_r \preccurlyeq W_c$
(9)   feedback = NACK.
(10)   **else**
(11)   Initialize $\mathbf{D}_{c+1} = \underbrace{\{(\varnothing, 0), \dots, (\varnothing, 0)\}}_{M \text{ pairs}}$, the decoding paths are initialized as empty, the cumulative path metrics of each decoding path is initialized to be 0.
(12)   **for** $i = c : 1$
(13)   **for** $m = 1 : M$
(14)   Choose the decoding path $\mathbf{D}_{i+1}[m]$, select correspond information bits in $\mathbf{p}_{i+1,m}$ and set them as frozen bits for **RB**[i] block. Decode **RB**[i] block.
(15)   **for** $l = 1 : L$
(16) $\mathbf{curPath} = \mathbf{p}_{i+1,m} \cup \{\hat{\mathbf{c}}_{i,l}\}.$
(17) $curPM = \mathbf{PM}_{i+1,m} + pm_{i,l}.$
(18) $\mathbf{B}_i[m][l] = (\mathbf{curPath}, curPM).$
(19)   **end for**
(20)   **end for**
(21)   If $i = 1$, choose the path with the smallest cumulative path metrics from $\mathbf{B}_i$ as the decoding result, feedback = ACK. Otherwise, choose M paths with small cumulative path metrics as the decoding results of **RB**[i] block, and $\mathbf{D}_i = \{(\mathbf{p}_{i,1}, \mathbf{PM}_{i,1}), \dots, (\mathbf{p}_{i,M}, \mathbf{PM}_{i,M})\}.$
(22)   **end for**
(23)   **end if**
(24) **end while**

As shown in the Algorithm 1, the performance degradation is mitigated by maintaining multiple decoding paths through the successive joint decoding structure.

The computation complexity of cumulative-path-metrics-based IF HARQ scheme using polar code is $O(kMLN\log N)$, and the space complexity is $O(kMLN)$. Hence, the cumulative-path-metrics-based IF HARQ scheme is too complex to use.

3.3 Modified Path Splitting Reduced SCL Algorithm

To reduce the complexity of the cumulative-path-metrics-based IF HARQ scheme, the system should adaptively adjust the number of maintained paths according to the decoding likelihood ratio, and only maintain those paths with a higher reliability.

In the SCL decoding algorithm, each path will split into two after one information bit is decoded. When the decoding confidence of an information bit is high enough, the path does not need to split. Although the hard decision according to the likelihood ratio is used, the error correction performance of the decoder will not degrade too much. In [8], a rule for controlling the path splitting in the SCL decoding algorithm is proposed.

Let $P_e(u_i)$ denote the decoding error rate of information bit u_i. We have

$$
\begin{aligned}
P_e(u_i) &= P\left(\hat{u}_i = u_i \oplus 1\right) \\
&= \sum_{u_1^{i=1} \in \mathbf{x}} \sum_{y_1^N \in \mathbf{Y}} P\left((1 - 2u_i)L(u_i) < 0 | \hat{u}_1^{i-1} = u_1^{i-1}, u_i, y_1^N\right)
\end{aligned}
\tag{11}
$$

Therefore, $1 - P_e(u_i)$ can be used as a criterion to determine whether the path is split or not. The value of $P_e(u_i)$ can be estimated by Monte-Carlo simulation or Gaussian approximation algorithm [9]. The rule of path splitting is defined as

$$
\hat{u}_i =
\begin{cases}
0, & L_l(u_i) > \log \frac{1 - P_e(u_i)}{P_e(u_i)}, \\
1, & L_l(u_i) < -\log \frac{1 - P_e(u_i)}{P_e(u_i)}, \\
\text{split, otherwise,}
\end{cases}
\tag{12}
$$

where $L_l(u_i)$ denotes the decoding log-likelihood ratio of u_i in the lth path.

The splitting features of the correct decoding path and wrong decoding path are studied in [8] as following:

(i) If all the decoding results of previous information bits $\hat{u}_1^{i-1}$ are correct, after decoding u_i, this path tends not to split and be retained by the decoder.

(ii) For any error decoding path reached at u_i, it tends to split at $\{i + 1, i + 2, \ldots, N\}$ indices.

We modify the path splitting reduced SCL algorithm in [8], where a threshold for the number of continuous splits to remove the paths be more possible wrong is introduced. The modified algorithm is summarized in Algorithm 2 as following.

Algorithm 2: Modified path splitting reduced SCL algorithm

Decoding Procedure

(1) Decode the first bit u_1 of the block. Initialize continuous non-splitting counter $\omega_l[i] = 0$, continuous splitting counter $\theta_l[i] = 0$.

(2) For the lth decoding path and current decoding bit u_i, if u_i is a frozen bit, set $\hat{u}_i = u_i$. If u_i is an information bit, and the rule of path splitting is not satisfied, directly using hard decision according to the likelihood ratio to decode bit u_i, update the counter, $\omega_l[i] = \omega_l[i-1] + 1$, $\theta_l[i] = 0$; Otherwise, split the current path l into two paths l' and l'', set $\omega_{l'}[i] = \omega_{l''}[i] = 0$, $\theta_{l'}[i] = \theta_{l''}[i] = \theta_l[i-1] + 1$.

(3) If the number of surviving paths exceeds the upper limit L, delete those paths with continuous non-splitting counter less than a threshold value ω. If there is no such path, delete those paths with continuous splitting counter greater than another threshold value θ. If the continuous splitting counter of all the surviving paths are greater than θ or less than θ, choose L paths with the highest reliability according to the path metrics.

(4) Decode the next bit. If $i < N$, set $i = i + 1$, go to step (2). Otherwise, the surviving paths are the decoding results.

Combining the modified path splitting reduced SCL algorithm to the successive joint decoding structure, not only the computation complexity of each decoding process can be reduced, but also the error decoding paths of previous decoded block can be filtered according to the path splitting feature.

For the cumulative-path-metrics-based IF HARQ scheme, if the receiver has decoded block $\mathbf{R}_i$ using the modified path splitting reduced SCL algorithm to get p possible decoding paths, the decoding process for next block $\mathbf{R}_{i-1}$ is performed by the decoder. If the number of surviving paths exceeds the upper limit pL, those paths with continuous non-splitting counter less than a threshold value ω are removed. If there is no path with continuous non-splitting counter less than a threshold value ω, those paths with continuous splitting counter greater than another threshold value θ are deleted. If the continuous splitting counter of all the surviving paths are greater than θ or less than θ, pL paths with the highest reliability according to the path metrics are selected.

After the last bit is decoded and the number of surviving paths exceeds M, M paths with small cumulative path metrics are chosen as the decoding results of $\mathbf{R}_{i-1}$.

In the best condition, the decoding confidence of each bit is very high, the path splitting reduced SCL algorithm turns to the SC decoding algorithm. Hence, the computation complexity is $O(kN\log N)$, and the space complexity is $O(kN)$.

In the worst condition, each path splits after the decoding of information bits, the path splitting reduced SCL algorithm degenerates to the SCL decoding algorithm. Hence, the computation complexity is $O(kMLN\log N)$, and the space complexity is $O(kMLN)$.

4   Simulation Results

Figure 1 shows the comparison of the error correction performance of the SCL algorithm, the CRC-aided SCL algorithm, the path splitting reduced SCL algorithm and the modified path splitting reduced SCL algorithm in terms of the block error rate, where $N = 256$, $K = 128$, $L = 8$, the generator polynomial of CRC bits is $g(D) = D^{24} + D^{23} + D^6 + D^5 + D + 1$. From Fig. 1, we observe that given the set value of continuous non-splitting time threshold ω, as continuous splitting time threshold θ gets larger, the block error rate of modified path splitting reduced SCL algorithm decreases, and finally converges to the performance of path splitting reduced SCL algorithm.

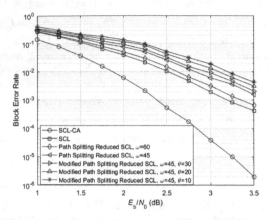

Fig. 1. The error correction performance of different decoding algorithms.

Figure 2 shows the comparison of the average number of surviving paths after each bit is decoded in the SCL algorithm, the path splitting reduced SCL algorithm and the modified path splitting reduced SCL algorithm, where $N = 256$, $K = 128$, $L = 8$, and $E_b/N_0 = 2$ dB. The area between each curve and x axis denotes the computation complexity and space complexity of each algorithm. From Fig. 2, we observe that as the continuous splitting time threshold θ goes smaller, the average number of surviving paths decreases. Hence, the computation complexity and space complexity reduce.

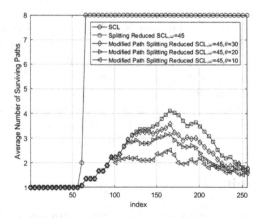

Fig. 2. The complexity of different decoding algorithms.

Two performance metrics are considered for a HARQ scheme, the system throughput and the block error rate. The throughput is the ratio of the expected number of information bits be decoded correctly and the expected number of all the bits be transmitted. For the IF HARQ scheme, if the receiver decodes the information bits out of k blocks, $\mathbf{R}_k$, $\mathbf{R}_{k-1}$, ..., $\mathbf{R}_1$, the system throughput can be calculated as

$$
\begin{aligned}
\eta_t &= \frac{\sum\limits_{i=1}^{k} |\mathcal{A}_{W_i}| - (i-1)|\mathcal{A}_{W_{i-1}} - \mathcal{A}_{W_i}|}{kN} \\
&= \frac{\sum\limits_{i=1}^{k} |\mathcal{A}_{w_i}| - (i-1)(|\mathcal{A}_{w_{i-1}}| - |\mathcal{A}_{w_i}|)}{kN} \\
&= \frac{k|\mathcal{A}_{w_{k+1}}|}{kN} = \frac{|\mathcal{A}_{w_k}|}{N},
\end{aligned}
\tag{13}
$$

which is capacity-achieving.

Figures 3 and 4 show the comparison of the system throughput and the block error rate of the CC HARQ scheme, the IF HARQ scheme, the CRC-aided IF HARQ scheme and the cumulative-path-metrics-based IF HARQ scheme, where the simulations are performed over degraded compound channel $\mathbf{W}_c = \{W_1, W_2, \ldots W_7\}$, the sub-channels are binary input additive white Gaussian noise (BIAWGN), $L = 8$, and polar code is constructed under given block error rate and code length, e_b and N.

For the CC HARQ scheme and the IF HARQ scheme, the maximum retransmission time is 6. For the CRC-aided IF HARQ scheme, the generator polynomial of CRC is $g(D) = D^{24} + D^{23} + D^6 + D^5 + D + 1$, the maximum retransmission time for incremental freezing bits is 6, and the maximum retransmission time for CC bits is 1. For the cumulative-path-metrics-based IF HARQ scheme, the maximum retransmission time is 6, $M = 8$, $\omega = 60$, and $\theta = 40$.

The transmission rate of polar codes over sub-channels is listed in Table 1. Here, the SNR is calculated by $E_b/N_0 = 1/(2C_{\text{BIAWGN}}\sigma^2)$. Hence, the real SNR for polar encoded blocks should be lower than the calculated value.

Table 1. The transmission rate of polar codes

SNR (dB)	$e_b = 0.01, N = 1024$	$e_b = 0.1, N = 4096$
W_7: 0.5	0.4229	0.4878
W_6: 1.0	0.5166	0.5815
W_5: 1.5	0.5977	0.6614
W_4: 2.0	0.6729	0.7312
W_3: 2.5	0.7344	0.7878
W_2: 3.0	0.7969	0.8428
W_1: 3.5	0.8467	0.8862

From Figs. 3 and 4, we observe that the CC HARQ scheme does not apply to degraded compound channel, the system throughput is lower than that of the IF HARQ scheme, and it has the discontinuous feature. This is because the retransmission blocks in the CC HARQ scheme is the same as the original transmission block. That is, after the kth retransmission, the system throughput is $\frac{|A_{W_1}|}{(k+1)N}$. The advantages of the CC HARQ are simple design and low retransmission times.

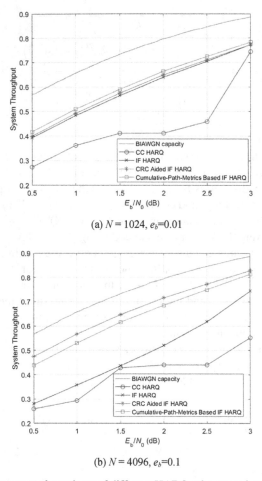

(a) $N = 1024$, $e_b = 0.01$

(b) $N = 4096$, $e_b = 0.1$

Fig. 3. The system throughput of different HARQ schemes using polar codes.

The IF HARQ scheme performs better than the CC HARQ using polar codes construction in a low the block error rate, e_b. However, the performance of the IF HARQ scheme degrades as the block error rate goes larger, which is caused by error propagation.

For the CRC-aided IF HARQ scheme, the performance in terms of the error correction performs the best. It works well under polar code with long block length and high block error rate. This is because the error propagation problem is resolved by adding

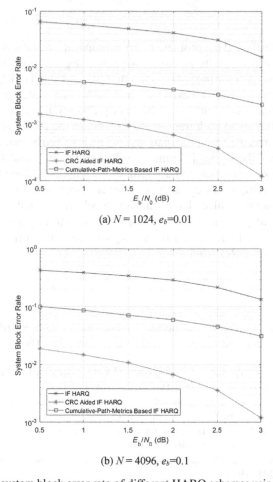

(a) $N = 1024$, e_b=0.01

(b) $N = 4096$, e_b=0.1

Fig. 4. The system block error rate of different HARQ schemes using polar codes.

extra CRC bits. However, under polar code with short block length and low block error rate, the reduction of system throughput caused by CRC bits appended in each transmission block cannot be negligible. Moreover, the CRC-aided IF HARQ scheme has a large decoding delay.

For the cumulative-path-metrics-based IF HARQ scheme, the error propagation problem is resolved by maintaining several decoding paths among the successive joint decoding structure. This HARQ scheme performs well under polar code with short block length and low block error rate. Under polar code with long block length and high block error rate, the gap of the error correction between the path splitting reduced SCL algorithm and the CA-SCL algorithm becomes larger. Hence, the system throughput of cumulative-path-metrics-based IF HARQ scheme is lower than that of CRC-aided IF HARQ scheme.

5   Conclusions

In this paper, we investigated the problem of error propagation in the IF HARQ scheme using polar codes, which results in the performance degradation. We proposed two improved IF HARQ schemes using polar codes, the CRC-aided IF HARQ scheme and the cumulative-path-metrics-based IF HARQ scheme. In the CRC-aided IF HARQ scheme, the CC HARQ scheme is combined, and the error propagation problem is mitigated by appending extra CRC bits to each transmission block. In the cumulative-path-metrics-based IF HARQ scheme, the error propagation problem is solved by maintaining multiple decoding paths among the successive joint decoding structure. Simulation results show that, for the polar code constructed under long block length and high block error rate, the CRC-aided IF HARQ scheme achieves a higher system throughput. For the polar code constructed under short block length and low block error rate, the cumulative-path-metrics-based IF HARQ scheme obtains a higher system throughput. In addition, the system block error rate of CRC-aided IF HARQ scheme outperforms the cumulative-path-metrics-based IF HARQ scheme.

References

1. Arikan, E.: Channel polarization: a method for constructing capacity-achieving codes for symmetric binary-input memoryless channels. IEEE Trans. Inf. Theory **55**(7), 3051–3073 (2009)
2. Chen, K., Niu, K., He, Z., Lin, J.: Polar coded HARQ scheme with chase combining. In: Proceedings of IEEE WCNC, Istanbul, Turkey, pp. 474–479, April 2014
3. Saber, H., Marsland, I.: An incremental redundancy hybrid ARQ scheme via puncturing and extending of polar codes. IEEE Trans. Commun. **63**(11), 3964–3973 (2015)
4. Li, B., Tse, D., Chen, K., Shen, H.: Capacity-achieving rateless polar codes. In: Proceedings of IEEE ISIT, Barcelona, Spain, pp. 46–50 (2016)
5. Blackwell, D., Breiman, L., Thomasian, A.J.: The capacity of a class of channels. Ann. Math. Stat. **3**(4), 1229–1241 (1959)
6. Tal, I., Vardy, A.: How to construct polar codes. IEEE Trans. Inf. Theory **59**(10), 6562–6582 (2013)
7. Tal, I., Vardy, A.: List decoding of polar codes. IEEE Trans. Inf. Theory **61**(5), 2213–2226 (2015)
8. Zhang, Z., Zhang, L., Wang, X., Zhong, C., Poor, H.V.: A split-reduced successive cancellation list decoder for polar codes. IEEE J. Sel. Areas Commun. **34**(2), 292–302 (2016)
9. Trifonov, P.: Efficient design and decoding of polar codes. IEEE Trans. Commun. **60**(11), 3221–3227 (2012)

Maximum Ergodic Capacity of Intelligent Reflecting Surface Assisted MIMO Wireless Communication System

Chang Guo[1,3] , Zhufei Lu[2] , Zhe Guo[3] , Feng Yang[1(✉)] ,
and Lianghui Ding[1]

[1] Department of Electronic Engineering,
Shanghai Jiao Tong University, Shanghai, China
{13122152125,yangfeng,lhding}@sjtu.edu.cn
[2] Yichang Testing Institute of Technology Research, Hubei, China
flypeter@126.com
[3] CETC Key Laboratory of Data Link Technology and Shanghai Microwave
Research Institute, Shanghai, China
guozhe@foxmail.com

Abstract. Intelligent reflecting surface (IRS) is currently adopted by massive multiple-input multiple-output (MIMO) systems as a new expansion scheme. It effectively copes with the increasing cost and energy consumption. In this paper, we concentrate on an IRS-assisted MIMO system, in which the base station, IRS and user are all equipped with multiple antennas. We first give the upper bound of the ergodic capacity of the system. Then we maximize this upper bound and obtain the sub-optimal phase shifts of IRS by applying semi-definite relax and Gaussian random methods. Numerical results shows the advantage of the proposed solution and the performance increase brought by multiple antennas.

Keywords: Intelligent reflecting surface · Massive multiple-input multiple-output · Ergodic capacity · Semi-definite relax

1 Introduction

Massive multiple-input multiple-output (MIMO) is an essential and widely used technology in the fifth-generation (5G) communication system [12]. As the number of antennas increases, more spatial degrees of freedom can be used to greatly improve the performance of the communication system [13]. However, the increasing number of antennas also has an impact on the energy consumption, the overall system complexity as well as the hardware cost [1,13]. Therefore, energy efficiency and hardware cost need to be addressed in future constructions of wireless networks [15].

This paper is supported in part by NSFC China (61771309, 61671301, 61420106008, 61521062), Shanghai Key Laboratory Funding (STCSM18DZ1200102) and CETC Key Laboratory of Data Link Technology Foundation (CLDL-20162306).

H. Gao et al. (Eds.): ChinaCom 2019, LNICST 312, pp. 331–343, 2020.
https://doi.org/10.1007/978-3-030-41114-5_25

Intelligent reflecting surface (IRS), also known as large intelligent surface (LIS), has been introduced to massive MIMO systems as a new expansion scheme [7]. Specifically, IRS can be treated as a reflection plane composed of a set of passive components, such as varactor diodes [11] and devices with special materials [2,8]. Owing to the different electromagnetic and material properties of the components, the elements of IRS can be controlled by signals to generate different electromagnetic responses, making it possible to adjust the phase shifts of the reflected signals.

The IRS-assisted system has large advantages of cost and energy consumption. In addition, IRS is convenient to introduce to the current massive MIMO systems because it can be easily placed on or removed from various surfaces [14]. By adjusting the phase shifts of the IRS, the signals reflected by IRS can be an effective link supplement for the system, thus achieving signal power enhancement or interference signals suppression.

Currently, researches have been conducted on the deployment of IRS in actual scenarios and joint beamforming design. The work led by Xin showed that the use of IRS can achieve higher spectral space efficiency without any addition payload of the hardware and software at the user by developing an experimental test platform [17]. The research led by Wu studied an IRS-enhanced point-to-point multiple-input single-output (MISO) wireless system by jointly optimizing active transmit beamforming at the base station (BS) and passive reflected beamforming at the IRS [16]. Han obtained a closed form solution of the optimal phase shifts of a MISO system by introducing a strict approximation of ergodic capacity of IRS-assisted large-scale antenna systems [6]. In the work of Huang, the transmission power and IRS reflection phase shifts are designed with the aim of maximizing the achievable rate. Under the same energy consumption, the system throughput increases a lot compared to the system without IRS [10].

Previous researches also focuses on other aspects such as energy efficiency and physical layer security. Huang's work maximized energy and spectral efficiency, which has large advantages comparing to traditional amplified and forward (AF) relay [9]. The IRS-assisted system also contributes to physical layer security of wireless communication systems [3,18], which maximized the safe reception rate. The introduction of IRS brought more degrees of freedom to solve the problem of secure transmission in special scenarios.

Existing works mainly focus on the beamforming problem of the IRS-assisted system with multi-antenna at the BS and IRS, without considering multi-antenna at the user. In reality, the application of multiple antennas at the user helps increase the system capacity significantly. In this paper, we consider an IRS-assisted communication system that the BS, IRS and user all have multiple antennas. We analyze the upper bound of the ergodic capacity and formulate a problem of maximizing this upper bound. Considering the problem is not convex and hard to solve, we transform it into a convex semi-definite programming (SDP) problem by using semi-definite relax (SDR) method. The SDP problem can be easily solved by the optimization methods such as interior point method. Gaussian random method is used to decompose the optimal phase shifts of IRS from the optimal solution. Through numerical simulation, we prove the advantages of the proposed solution and the result shows additional gains provided by multi-antenna system.

The rest of this paper is organized as follows, in Sect. 2, the system model is given, which consists of the channel model and the ergodic capacity. In Sect. 3, we analyze the upper bound of ergodic capacity and obtain the optimal solution by solving the problem of maximizing the the upper bound of ergodic capacity. In Sect. 4, we verify the analysis by numerical simulation. Finally, conclusion is drawn in Sect. 5.

Notations: Vectors and matrices are denoted by bold lowercase and uppercase letters, respectively. For a vector $\mathbf{v}$, diag$(\mathbf{v})$ represents a diagonal matrix consists of corresponding element of $\mathbf{v}$. arg$(\mathbf{v})$ represents the phase vector of $\mathbf{v}$. For a matrix $\mathbf{V}$, $\mathbf{V} \in \mathbb{C}^{m \times n}$ represents that the row and column of $\mathbf{V}$ are m and n. $\mathbf{V} \succeq 0$ represents $\mathbf{V}$ is a semi-definite matrix. $\mathbf{V}^H$, rank$(\mathbf{V})$, rvec$(\mathbf{V})$, $\mathbf{V}^i$ and $\mathbf{V}_{ij}$ denote the conjugate transpose, rank, row vectorization, the i-th column and the (i,j)-th element of a general matrix $\mathbf{V}$, respectively. det$(\mathbf{S})$, tr$(\mathbf{S})$ and $\mathbf{S}^{-1}$ denote the determinant, trace and inverse of a square matrix $\mathbf{S}$, respectively. $\mathbf{I}_K$ denotes K-order unit matrix, $\mathbb{E}\{\cdot\}$ denotes the statistical expectation, and $\mathcal{CN}(\mu, \sigma^2)$ denotes circular symmetric complex Gaussian distribution with mean μ and variance σ^2.

2   System Model

As shown in Fig. 1, we consider an IRS-assisted downlink MIMO wireless communication system, which consists of a base station (BS) equipped with M ($M = M_r \times M_c$) antennas and a user equipped with L ($L = L_r \times L_c$) antennas. There is an IRS assisting to transmit information between the BS and the user, which equipped by N ($N = N_r \times N_c$) reconfigurable reflection elements. Each element can apply different reflect phase shifts through a controller that connected to the BS.

We model the multiple antennas as a uniform rectangular array (URA). The wavelength of transmission signals is λ and the distance of adjacent antennas is d. Then the response of a URA with K ($K = K_r \times K_c$, K_r and K_c denote the row and column) elements can be denoted by $\mathbf{A}(x^{(h)}, x^{(v)}, K_r, K_c) \triangleq$ $\left(e^{j\phi(x^{(h)}, x^{(v)}, m, n)}\right)_{m=1,\cdots,K_r, n=1,\cdots,K_c} \in \mathbb{C}^{K_r \times K_c}$, where $\phi(x^{(h)}, x^{(v)}, m, n)$ represents the phase difference between the (m,n)-th element and the $(1, 1)$-st element of the IRS, denoted by

$$\phi(x^{(h)}, x^{(v)}, m, n) \triangleq 2\pi \frac{d}{\lambda} \sin x^{(v)} \left((m-1) \cos x^{(h)} + (n-1) \sin x^{(h)}\right), \quad (1)$$

where $x^{(h)}$ and $x^{(v)}$ represent the horizontal and vertical angle of departure or arrival (AoD or AoA) of transmission signals, respectively. Denote the response of the URA as a vector, i.e, $\mathbf{a}(x^{(h)}, x^{(v)}, K_r, K_c) \triangleq$ rvec$(\mathbf{A}(x^{(h)}, x^{(v)}, K_r, K_c))$ $\in \mathbb{C}^{1 \times K}$.

334   C. Guo et al.

Generally, the IRS is installed on the wall of high buildings. Considering scattering is often rich, the channel from the BS to the IRS and the channel from the IRS to the user can be modeled in Rician fading, denoted by $\mathbf{H}_{bi} \in \mathbb{C}^{M \times N}$ and $\mathbf{H}_{iu} \in \mathbb{C}^{N \times L}$, i.e.,

$$\mathbf{H}_{bi} = \sqrt{\alpha_{bi}} \left(\sqrt{\frac{\mathcal{K}_{bi}}{\mathcal{K}_{bi}+1}} \bar{\mathbf{H}}_{bi} + \sqrt{\frac{1}{\mathcal{K}_{bi}+1}} \tilde{\mathbf{H}}_{bi} \right), \tag{2}$$

$$\mathbf{H}_{iu} = \sqrt{\alpha_{iu}} \left(\sqrt{\frac{\mathcal{K}_{iu}}{\mathcal{K}_{iu}+1}} \bar{\mathbf{H}}_{iu} + \sqrt{\frac{1}{\mathcal{K}_{iu}+1}} \tilde{\mathbf{H}}_{iu} \right), \tag{3}$$

where $\mathcal{K}_{bi}$, $\mathcal{K}_{iu}$ denote the Rice factors, α_{bi}, α_{iu} denote the distance-dependent path losses, $\tilde{\mathbf{H}}_{bi}$, $\tilde{\mathbf{H}}_{iu}$ denote the non-line-of-sight (NLoS) components and each element of them follows $\mathcal{CN}(0,1)$, $\bar{\mathbf{H}}_{bi}$, $\bar{\mathbf{H}}_{iu}$ denote the line-of-sight (LoS) components, which can be expressed as

$$\bar{\mathbf{H}}_{bi} = \mathbf{a}^H \big(\gamma_{bi}^{(h)}, \gamma_{bi}^{(v)}, M_r, M_c \big) \mathbf{a} \big(\delta_{bi}^{(h)}, \delta_{bi}^{(v)}, N_r, N_c \big), \tag{4}$$

$$\bar{\mathbf{H}}_{iu} = \mathbf{a}^H \big(\gamma_{iu}^{(h)}, \gamma_{iu}^{(v)}, N_r, N_c \big) \mathbf{a} \big(\delta_{iu}^{(h)}, \delta_{iu}^{(v)}, L_r, L_c \big), \tag{5}$$

where $\gamma_{bi}^{(h)}$, $\gamma_{bi}^{(v)}$ denote the horizontal AoD and vertical AoD from the BS, $\delta_{bi}^{(h)}$, $\delta_{bi}^{(v)}$ denote the horizontal AoA and vertical AoA to the IRS, $\gamma_{iu}^{(h)}$ and $\gamma_{iu}^{(v)}$ denote the horizontal AoD and vertical AoD from the IRS, $\delta_{iu}^{(h)}$ and $\delta_{iu}^{(v)}$ denote the horizontal AoA and vertical AoA to the user.

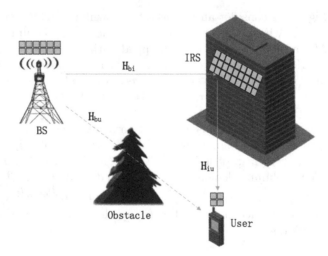

Fig. 1. System model

In addition, owing to the distance from the BS to the user is always far, the LoS may be blocked by obstacles. Thus, the channel between them is modeled in Rayleigh fading, denoted by $\mathbf{H}_{bu} \in \mathbb{C}^{M \times L}$, i.e.,

$$\mathbf{H}_{bu} = \sqrt{\alpha_{bu}}\tilde{\mathbf{H}}_{bi}, \tag{6}$$

where α_{bu} denotes the distance-dependent path loss, $\tilde{\mathbf{H}}_{bi}$ denotes the NLoS components and each element of $\tilde{\mathbf{H}}_{bi}$ follows $\mathcal{CN}(0,1)$.

Let $\boldsymbol{\Theta} = (\theta_{m,n})_{m=1,\cdots,N_r,n=1,\cdots,N_c} \in \mathbb{C}^{N_r \times N_c}$, where $\theta_{m,n}$ denotes the phase shift of the (m,n)-th element of the IRS. Define $\boldsymbol{\Phi} \triangleq \mathrm{diag}(\mathrm{rvec}(e^{j\boldsymbol{\Theta}})) \in \mathbb{C}^{N \times N}$. Thus, the equivalent channel, denoted by $\mathbf{H}(\boldsymbol{\Phi}) \in \mathbb{C}^{M \times L}$, can be expressed as

$$\mathbf{H}(\boldsymbol{\Phi}) = \mathbf{H}_{bi}\boldsymbol{\Phi}\mathbf{H}_{iu} + \mathbf{H}_{bu}. \tag{7}$$

For a given MIMO channel, the capacity is given by [4]. Therefore, the ergodic capacity of the IRS-assisted system can be expressed as

$$C(\boldsymbol{\Phi}) = \mathbb{E}\left\{\log_2 \det\left(\mathbf{I}_L + \rho \mathbf{H}^H(\boldsymbol{\Phi})\mathbf{H}(\boldsymbol{\Phi})\right)\right\}, \tag{8}$$

where $\rho = \frac{SNR}{M}$ and SNR denotes the average signal-to-noise ratio (SNR).

3 Ergodic Capacity Analysis and Optimization

In this section, we analyze the ergodic capacity of the system at first. Then we formulate an optimization problem based on the ergodic capacity and give the solution.

3.1 Ergodic Capacity Analysis

By applying Jensen Inequality, the upper bound of ergodic capacity of the IRS-assisted system is given by the following theorem.

Theorem 1.

$$\begin{aligned}
C(\boldsymbol{\Phi}) &\leqslant \log_2 \det(\rho\beta_1 \bar{\mathbf{H}}_{iu}^H \boldsymbol{\Phi}^H \bar{\mathbf{H}}_{bi}^H \bar{\mathbf{H}}_{bi} \boldsymbol{\Phi} \bar{\mathbf{H}}_{iu} \\
&\quad + \rho\beta_2 M \bar{\mathbf{H}}_{iu}^H \bar{\mathbf{H}}_{iu} + (1 + \rho(\beta_3 MN + \beta_4 M))\mathbf{I}_L),
\end{aligned} \tag{9}$$

where

$$\beta_1 = \frac{\alpha_{bi}\alpha_{iu}\mathcal{K}_{bi}\mathcal{K}_{iu}}{(\mathcal{K}_{bi}+1)(\mathcal{K}_{iu}+1)}, \qquad \beta_3 = \frac{\alpha_{bi}\alpha_{iu}}{\mathcal{K}_{iu}+1},$$
$$\beta_2 = \frac{\alpha_{bi}\alpha_{iu}\mathcal{K}_{iu}}{(\mathcal{K}_{bi}+1)(\mathcal{K}_{iu}+1)}, \qquad \beta_4 = \alpha_{bu}. \tag{10}$$

Proof. Owing to $\mathbf{I}_L + \rho\mathbf{H}^H(\boldsymbol{\Phi})\mathbf{H}(\boldsymbol{\Phi})$ is a positive definite matrix, the function $\log_2 \det\left(\mathbf{I}_L + \rho\mathbf{H}^H(\boldsymbol{\Phi})\mathbf{H}(\boldsymbol{\Phi})\right)$ is concave. According to the Jensen Inequality, we obtain

$$C(\boldsymbol{\Phi}) \leqslant \log_2 \det\left(\mathbb{E}\left\{\mathbf{I}_L + \rho\mathbf{H}^H(\boldsymbol{\Phi})\mathbf{H}(\boldsymbol{\Phi})\right\}\right). \tag{11}$$

Here, $\mathbb{E}\left\{\mathbf{H}^H(\boldsymbol{\Phi})\mathbf{H}(\boldsymbol{\Phi})\right\}$ can be decomposed by

$$
\begin{aligned}
&\mathbb{E}\left\{\mathbf{H}^H(\boldsymbol{\Phi})\mathbf{H}(\boldsymbol{\Phi})\right\} \\
=&\mathbb{E}\left\{\mathbf{H}_{iu}^H\boldsymbol{\Phi}^H\mathbf{H}_{bi}^H\mathbf{H}_{bi}\boldsymbol{\Phi}\mathbf{H}_{iu}\right\} + \mathbb{E}\left\{\mathbf{H}_{bu}^H\mathbf{H}_{bu}\right\} \\
+&\mathbb{E}\left\{\mathbf{H}_{iu}^H\boldsymbol{\Phi}^H\mathbf{H}_{bi}^H\mathbf{H}_{bu}\right\} + \mathbb{E}\left\{\mathbf{H}_{bu}^H\mathbf{H}_{bi}\boldsymbol{\Phi}\mathbf{H}_{iu}\right\} \\
=&\mathbb{E}\left\{\mathbf{H}_{iu}^H\boldsymbol{\Phi}^H\mathbf{H}_{bi}^H\mathbf{H}_{bi}\boldsymbol{\Phi}\mathbf{H}_{iu}\right\} + \beta_4 M\mathbf{I}_L.
\end{aligned}
\tag{12}
$$

And

$$
\begin{aligned}
&\mathbb{E}\left\{\mathbf{H}_{iu}^H\boldsymbol{\Phi}^H\mathbf{H}_{bi}^H\mathbf{H}_{bi}\boldsymbol{\Phi}\mathbf{H}_{iu}\right\} \\
=&\beta_1\mathbb{E}\big\{\underbrace{\bar{\mathbf{H}}_{iu}^H\boldsymbol{\Phi}^H\bar{\mathbf{H}}_{bi}^H\bar{\mathbf{H}}_{bi}\boldsymbol{\Phi}\bar{\mathbf{H}}_{iu}}_{\mathbf{Z}_1}\big\} + \beta_2\mathbb{E}\big\{\underbrace{\bar{\mathbf{H}}_{iu}^H\boldsymbol{\Phi}^H\tilde{\mathbf{H}}_{bi}^H\tilde{\mathbf{H}}_{bi}\boldsymbol{\Phi}\bar{\mathbf{H}}_{iu}}_{\mathbf{Z}_2}\big\} \\
+&\frac{\alpha_{bi}\alpha_{iu}\mathcal{K}_{bi}}{(\mathcal{K}_{bi}+1)(\mathcal{K}_{iu}+1)}\mathbb{E}\big\{\underbrace{\tilde{\mathbf{H}}_{iu}^H\boldsymbol{\Phi}^H\bar{\mathbf{H}}_{bi}^H\bar{\mathbf{H}}_{bi}\boldsymbol{\Phi}\tilde{\mathbf{H}}_{iu}}_{\mathbf{Z}_3}\big\} \\
+&\frac{\alpha_{bi}\alpha_{iu}}{(\mathcal{K}_{bi}+1)(\mathcal{K}_{iu}+1)}\mathbb{E}\big\{\underbrace{\tilde{\mathbf{H}}_{iu}^H\boldsymbol{\Phi}^H\tilde{\mathbf{H}}_{bi}^H\tilde{\mathbf{H}}_{bi}\boldsymbol{\Phi}\tilde{\mathbf{H}}_{iu}}_{\mathbf{Z}_4}\big\},
\end{aligned}
\tag{13}
$$

where

$$
\mathbb{E}\left\{\mathbf{Z}_1\right\} = \bar{\mathbf{H}}_{iu}^H\boldsymbol{\Phi}^H\bar{\mathbf{H}}_{bi}^H\bar{\mathbf{H}}_{bi}\boldsymbol{\Phi}\bar{\mathbf{H}}_{iu},
\tag{14}
$$

$$
\mathbb{E}\left\{\mathbf{Z}_2\right\} = \bar{\mathbf{H}}_{iu}^H\boldsymbol{\Phi}^H\mathbb{E}\{\tilde{\mathbf{H}}_{bi}^H\tilde{\mathbf{H}}_{bi}\}\boldsymbol{\Phi}\bar{\mathbf{H}}_{iu} = M\bar{\mathbf{H}}_{iu}^H\bar{\mathbf{H}}_{iu},
\tag{15}
$$

$$
\mathbb{E}\left\{\mathbf{Z}_3\right\} = MN\mathbf{I}_L,
\tag{16}
$$

$$
\mathbb{E}\left\{\mathbf{Z}_4\right\} = \mathbb{E}\{\tilde{\mathbf{H}}_{iu}^H\boldsymbol{\Phi}^H\mathbb{E}\{\tilde{\mathbf{H}}_{bi}^H\tilde{\mathbf{H}}_{bi}\}\boldsymbol{\Phi}\tilde{\mathbf{H}}_{iu}\} = MN\mathbf{I}_L.
\tag{17}
$$

Here, (16) holds is owing to each non-diagonal element of $\mathbf{Z}_3$ exists Gaussian variables with zero mean. In the end, substituting the results of each part into the original formula, we obtain the final result.

Theorem 1 indicates that the upper bound of ergodic capacity is just related to the matrix $\bar{\mathbf{H}}_{iu}^H\boldsymbol{\Phi}^H\bar{\mathbf{H}}_{bi}^H\bar{\mathbf{H}}_{bi}\boldsymbol{\Phi}\bar{\mathbf{H}}_{iu}$. When applying suitable phase shifts of the IRS, the upper bound of ergodic capacity is also influenced by the distance-dependent path losses and Rician factors.

3.2   Problem Formulation

In this subsection, in order to obtain the optimal phase shifts of the IRS, we formulate an optimization problem (P1) which maximizes the upper bound of ergodic capacity. It is expressed as

$$
\begin{aligned}
(P1): \quad &\max_{\boldsymbol{\Phi}} \ \log_2\det(\rho\beta_1\bar{\mathbf{H}}_{iu}^H\boldsymbol{\Phi}^H\bar{\mathbf{H}}_{bi}^H\bar{\mathbf{H}}_{bi}\boldsymbol{\Phi}\bar{\mathbf{H}}_{iu} \\
&\qquad + \rho\beta_2 M\bar{\mathbf{H}}_{iu}^H\bar{\mathbf{H}}_{iu} + (1+\rho(\beta_3 MN + \beta_4 M))\mathbf{I}_L) \\
&s.t. \ \theta_{m,n} \in [0,2\pi), m = 1,\cdots,N_r, n = 1,\cdots,N_c.
\end{aligned}
\tag{18}
$$

The function $\log_2 \det(\mathbf{A})$ is concave when $\mathbf{A}$ is a positive definite matrix, and the matrix in the object function is positive definite. However, the object function is not concave with respect to $\boldsymbol{\Phi}$. In addition, the constraint of (P1) is equivalent to $|\boldsymbol{\Phi}_{m,n}| = 1$, which is not convex. Thus, it's not easy to obtain an great solution of this problem.

3.3 Solution

In this subsection, we apply SDR to transport (P1) into a convex problem to solve. At first, we introduce a matrix variable $\mathbf{Y} = \bar{\mathbf{H}}_{iu}^H \boldsymbol{\Phi}^H \bar{\mathbf{H}}_{bi}^H \bar{\mathbf{H}}_{bi} \boldsymbol{\Phi} \bar{\mathbf{H}}_{iu}$. Secondly, we denote $\bar{\mathbf{H}}_{iu}$ as a block matrix $\bar{\mathbf{H}}_{iu} = [\bar{\mathbf{H}}_{iu}^1, \ldots, \bar{\mathbf{H}}_{iu}^L]$. Thirdly, we define $\mathbf{R}_j \triangleq \bar{\mathbf{H}}_{bi} \mathrm{diag}(\bar{\mathbf{H}}_{iu}^j) \in \mathbb{C}^{M \times N}$ and $\mathbf{w} \triangleq \mathrm{rvec}(e^{j\Theta}) \in \mathbb{C}^{1 \times N}$. Thus, we obtain

$$\bar{\mathbf{H}}_{bi} \boldsymbol{\Phi} \bar{\mathbf{H}}_{iu} = \begin{bmatrix} \mathbf{R}_1 \mathbf{w}^H & \mathbf{R}_2 \mathbf{w}^H & \cdots & \mathbf{R}_L \mathbf{w}^H \end{bmatrix}, \tag{19}$$

and

$$\mathbf{Y} = \begin{bmatrix} \mathbf{w} \mathbf{R}_1^H \mathbf{R}_1 \mathbf{w}^H & \mathbf{w} \mathbf{R}_1^H \mathbf{R}_2 \mathbf{w}^H & \cdots & \mathbf{w} \mathbf{R}_1^H \mathbf{R}_L \mathbf{w}^H \\ \mathbf{w} \mathbf{R}_2^H \mathbf{R}_1 \mathbf{w}^H & \mathbf{w} \mathbf{R}_2^H \mathbf{R}_2 \mathbf{w}^H & \cdots & \mathbf{w} \mathbf{R}_2^H \mathbf{R}_L \mathbf{w}^H \\ \vdots & \vdots & \ddots & \vdots \\ \mathbf{w} \mathbf{R}_L^H \mathbf{R}_1 \mathbf{w}^H & \mathbf{w} \mathbf{R}_L^H \mathbf{R}_2 \mathbf{w}^H & \cdots & \mathbf{w} \mathbf{R}_L^H \mathbf{R}_L \mathbf{w}^H \end{bmatrix}. \tag{20}$$

At last, we introduce an hermitian semi-definite matrix $\mathbf{W} = \mathbf{w}^H \mathbf{w} \in \mathbb{C}^{N \times N}$, which satisfies $\mathrm{rank}(\mathbf{W}) = 1$ and $\mathbf{W}_{ii} = 1, i = 1, \cdots, N$. Thus,

$$\begin{aligned} \mathbf{Y}_{ij} &= \mathrm{tr}(\mathbf{w} \mathbf{R}_i^H \mathbf{R}_j \mathbf{w}^H) = \mathrm{tr}(\mathbf{R}_i^H \mathbf{R}_j \mathbf{w}^H \mathbf{w}) \\ &= \mathrm{tr}(\mathbf{R}_i^H \mathbf{R}_j \mathbf{W}), \ i, j = 1, \cdots, L. \end{aligned} \tag{21}$$

In summary, we relax the constraint $\mathrm{rank}(\mathbf{W}) = 1$ and transport (P1) into the following problem (P2)

$$\begin{aligned} (P2): \quad \max_{\mathbf{W}, \mathbf{Y}} \ & \log_2 \det(\rho \beta_1 \mathbf{Y} + \rho \beta_2 M \bar{\mathbf{H}}_{iu}^H \bar{\mathbf{H}}_{iu} \\ & + (1 + \rho(\beta_3 MN + \beta_4 M)) \mathbf{I}_L) \\ s.t. \ \mathbf{Y} = & \begin{bmatrix} \mathrm{tr}(\mathbf{R}_1^H \mathbf{R}_1 \mathbf{W}) & \cdots & \mathrm{tr}(\mathbf{R}_1^H \mathbf{R}_L \mathbf{W}) \\ \vdots & \ddots & \vdots \\ \mathrm{tr}(\mathbf{R}_L^H \mathbf{R}_1 \mathbf{W}) & \cdots & \mathrm{tr}(\mathbf{R}_L^H \mathbf{R}_L \mathbf{W}) \end{bmatrix}, \\ & \mathbf{W} \succeq 0, \\ & \mathbf{W}_{ii} = 1, i = 1, \cdots, L. \end{aligned} \tag{22}$$

The problem (P2) is a convex semi-definite program (SDP) problem, we can obtain the optimal solution easily by some convex optimization toolboxes such as CVX [5]. By solving (P2), the optimal solution is about $\mathbf{W}$, then we decompose the optimal $\mathbf{w}$ from the optimal $\mathbf{W}$.

Actually, it is easy to obtain the optimal $\mathbf{w}$ when the optimal $\mathbf{W}$ satisfies $\mathrm{rank}(\mathbf{W}) = 1$. If $\mathrm{rank}(\mathbf{W}) \neq 1$, the optimal solution of problem (P2) is just an upper bound of the original problem. At this situation, we can obtain the sub-optimal solution by Gaussian random method. At first, the eigenvalue decomposition of $\mathbf{W}$ can be denoted as $\mathbf{W} = \mathbf{U\Sigma U}^H$, where $\mathbf{\Sigma} \in \mathbb{C}^{N \times N}$ is a diagonal matrix consists of the eigenvalues of $\mathbf{W}$ and $\mathbf{U} \in \mathbb{C}^{N \times N}$ is composed of the corresponding eigenvectors. Secondly, by generating a random vector $\mathbf{r} \in \mathbb{C}^{1 \times N}$ whose elements follow $\mathcal{CN}(0, 1)$, we obtain a sub-optimal solution $\mathbf{w} = \mathbf{r\Sigma}^{\frac{1}{2}}\mathbf{U}^H$. At last, we can choose the best solution by repeating the previous step for a certain number of times. The process of obtaining the optimal $\mathbf{w}$ is show in Algorithm 1.

Algorithm 1. optimal $\mathbf{w}$

---

initialization set system parameters

1: obtain the optimal $\mathbf{W}$ by solving Problem (P2)
2: **if** rank$(\mathbf{W}) = 1$ **then**
3:     decomposition: $\mathbf{W} = \mathbf{w}^H\mathbf{w}$
4: **if** rank$(\mathbf{W}) \neq 1$ **then**
5:     eigenvalue decomposition: $\mathbf{W} = \mathbf{U\Sigma U}^H$
6:     **repeat**
7:         generate a Gaussian random vector $\mathbf{r}$
8:         obtain a sub-optimal solution: $\mathbf{w} = \mathbf{r\Sigma}^{\frac{1}{2}}\mathbf{U}^H$
9:     **until** a certain number of times
10:    choose a $\mathbf{w}$ satisfies that the value of Problem (P1) is the biggest

return w

---

4   Numerical Result

In this section, the numerical results are given to verify the above theoretical derivation and show the performance of the solution we proposed.

At first, we build an geometric model to describe the positional relationship of the BS, IRS and user in the system, which is shown in Fig. 2. The antennas of the BS and IRS are placed on the high buildings, and the distance between them is denoted by d_{bi}. The user is on the ground, and the distances to the BS are denoted by d_x and d_y, respectively. Thus, the distances from the BS and IRS to the user are denoted by $d_{bu} = \sqrt{d_x^2 + d_y^2}$ and $d_{iu} = \sqrt{(d_{bi} - d_x)^2 + d_y^2}$, respectively.

In addition, the distance-dependent path loss is given by

$$\alpha = \alpha_0 \left(\frac{d}{d_0}\right)^{-\eta}, \tag{23}$$

where η denotes the fading factor and α_0 denotes the relative power at the distance of d_0. Thus, the corresponding power at the distance of d is α. In the simulation, the main parameters are set in Table 1.

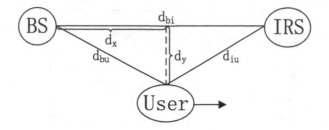

Fig. 2. Simulation model

Table 1. Simulation parameters.

BS antennas ($M_r \times M_c$)	4×8	IRS elements ($N_r \times N_c$)	8×8
Rician factor ($\mathcal{K}_{bi}$)	1	Rician factor ($\mathcal{K}_{iu}$)	1
Vertical AoD ($\delta_{bi}^{(v)}$)	$90°$	Vertical AoA ($\gamma_{bi}^{(v)}$)	$90°$
Vertical AoD ($\delta_{iu}^{(v)}$)	$45°$	Vertical AoA ($\gamma_{iu}^{(v)}$)	$45°$
Horizontal AoD ($\delta_{bi}^{(h)}$)	$90°$	Horizontal AoA ($\gamma_{bi}^{(h)}$)	$90°$
Horizontal AoD ($\delta_{iu}^{(h)}$)	$\arccos \frac{d_y}{d_{iu}}$	Horizontal AoA ($\gamma_{iu}^{(h)}$)	$\arcsin \frac{d_y}{d_{iu}}$
Distance (d_{bi})	$100\,\mathrm{m}$	Distance (d_y)	$20\,\mathrm{m}$
Path loss (α_0)	$-10\,\mathrm{dB}$	Distance (d_0)	$100\,\mathrm{m}$
Fading factor (η)	2	SNR	$20\,\mathrm{dB}$

4.1 Ergodic Capacity

In this subsection, We apply the optimal solution to compare the upper bound of ergodic capacity of the system with 1000000 times Monte Carlo results. The result is shown in Fig. 3, d_x changes with the user's movement in the horizontal direction. Thus, the distance-dependent path loss changes accordingly.

We set $L = 1(1 \times 1)$, $L = 2(1 \times 2)$ and $L = 3(1 \times 3)$ respectively to show the gap. When $L = 1$, the two curves are very close. And the gap enlarges as the number of user's antennas L increases. It is worth noticing that the gap stays unchanged as d_x varies. Thus, we can obtain better solution by optimizing the upper bound of the ergodic capacity of the system.

4.2 Optimal Solution

In this subsection, we set a few groups of phase shifts to compare with each other and verify the advantage of our proposed solution. The results are shown in Figs. 4 and 5, we consider two situations where $L = 2(1 \times 2)$ and $L = 3(1 \times 3)$. The performances of applying random phase shifts and optimal phase shifts are shown. Here the results of applying random phase shifts are obtained by choosing the best performance of 10000 types results with different random phase shifts. In addition, the performance without IRS is also shown as a baseline.

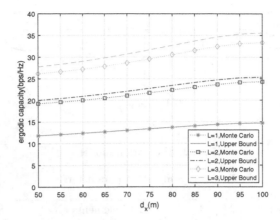

Fig. 3. Upper bound of ergodic capacity and Monte Carlo results

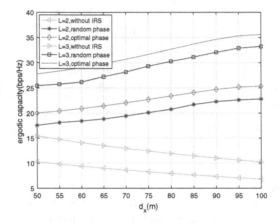

Fig. 4. Performance of optimal solution with d_x

From Figs. 4 and 5, we see that the performance of the IRS-assisted system is significantly better than the system without IRS. The 10000 results with random phase shifts can not achieve the performance of applying optimal phase shifts. The ergodic capacity decreases with the increase of d_x, due to that the power attenuation intensifies as the distance between the BS and the user grows. On the contrary, the ergodic capacity of the IRS-assisted system increases, due to that IRS provides more signal energy gains. Besides, the gap between random phase shifts and optimal phase shifts enlarges as N increases, indicating that applying optimal phase shifts is significant when N is relatively large.

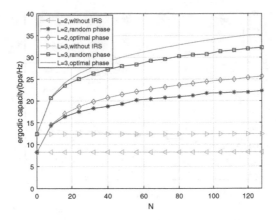

Fig. 5. Performance of optimal solution with N

4.3 Performance of Multiple Receive Antennas

In this subsection, we show the performance gains provided by multiple antennas. We apply the optimal phase shifts of IRS and compare the performance with different receive antennas.

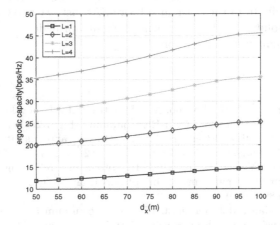

Fig. 6. Performance of multiple receive antennas with d_x

The result is shown in Figs. 6 and 7, we set $L = 1(1 \times 1)$, $L = 2(1 \times 2)$, $L = 3(1 \times 3)$ and $L = 4(2 \times 2)$, respectively. It is obviously that the ergodic capacity grows a lot as the receive antennas L increases. Therefore, applying multi-antenna at the user helps improve the signal quality of the IRS-assisted system. In addition, with the increase of N, the performance advantages of system are more significant.

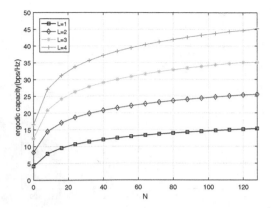

Fig. 7. Performance of multiple receive antennas with N

5   Conclusion

In this paper, we analyze the ergodic capacity of the IRS-assisted MIMO wireless communication system. We give the upper bound of ergodic capacity and maximize it to obtain the optimal phase shifts of IRS. We apply SDR method to transform the original problem into a convex SDP problem and solve it by CVX. By applying Gaussian random method, we decompose the optimal or suboptimal phase shifts from the optimal solution. At last, we show the advantages of our proposed solution and the performance gains provided by multiple antennas through the numerical simulation.

References

1. Boccardi, F., Heath, R.W., Lozano, A., Marzetta, T.L., Popovski, P.: Five disruptive technology directions for 5G. IEEE Commun. Mag. **52**(2), 74–80 (2014)
2. Carrasco, E., Perruisseau-Carrier, J.: Reflectarray antenna at terahertz using graphene. IEEE Antennas Wirel. Propag. Lett. **12**(3), 253–256 (2013)
3. Chen, J., Liang, Y.C., Pei, Y., Guo, H.: Intelligent reflecting surface: a programmable wireless environment for physical layer security. arXiv preprint arXiv:1905.03689 (2019)
4. Foschini, G.J., Gans, M.J.: On limits of wireless communications in a fading environment when using multiple antennas. Wirel. Pers. Commun. **6**(3), 311–335 (1998)
5. Grant, M., Boyd, S., Ye, Y.: CVX: Matlab software for disciplined convex programming (2008)
6. Han, Y., Tang, W., Jin, S., Wen, C.K., Ma, X.: Large intelligent surface-assisted wireless communication exploiting statistical CSI (2018)
7. Hu, S., Rusek, F., Edfors, O.: Beyond massive MIMO: the potential of data transmission with large intelligent surfaces. IEEE Trans. Sig. Process. **66**(10), 2746–2758 (2018)
8. Hu, W., et al.: Design and measurement of reconfigurable millimeter wave reflectarray cells with nematic liquid crystal. IEEE Trans. Antennas Propag. **56**(10), 3112–3117 (2008)

9. Huang, C., Zappone, A., Alexandropoulos, G.C., Debbah, M., Yuen, C.: Large intelligent surfaces for energy efficiency in wireless communication (2018)
10. Huang, C., Zappone, A., Debbah, M., Yuen, C.: Achievable rate maximization by passive intelligent mirrors (2018)
11. Hum, S.V., Perruisseaucarrier, J.: Reconfigurable reflectarrays and array lenses for dynamic antenna beam control: a review. IEEE Trans. Antennas Propag. **62**(1), 183–198 (2014)
12. Larsson, E.G., Edfors, O., Tufvesson, F., Marzetta, T.L.: Massive mimo for next generation wireless systems. IEEE Commun. Mag. **52**(2), 186–195 (2014)
13. Lu, L., Li, G.Y., Swindlehurst, A.L., Ashikhmin, A., Zhang, R.: An overview of massive MIMO: benefits and challenges. IEEE J. Sel.d Top. Sig. Process. **8**(5), 742–758 (2014)
14. Subrt, L., Pechac, P.: Intelligent walls as autonomous parts of smart indoor environments. IET Commun. **6**(8), 1004–1010 (2012)
15. Wu, Q., Li, G.Y., Chen, W., Ng, D.W.K., Schober, R.: An overview of sustainable green 5G networks. IEEE Wirel. Commun. **24**(4), 72–80 (2017)
16. Wu, Q., Zhang, R.: Intelligent reflecting surface enhanced wireless network: joint active and passive beamforming design (2018)
17. Xin, T., Zhi, S., Jornet, J.M., Pados, D.: Increasing indoor spectrum sharing capacity using smart reflect-array. Mathematics (2015)
18. Yu, X., Xu, D., Schober, R.: Enabling secure wireless communications via intelligent reflecting surfaces. arXiv preprint arXiv:1904.09573 (2019)

Trajectory Optimization for UAV Assisted Fog-RAN Network

Qi Qin[1](✉), Erwu Liu[1], and Rui Wang[1,2]

[1] School of Electronics and Information Engineering,
Tongji University, Shanghai, China
{qinqi,ruiwang}@tongji.edu.cn, erwu.liu@ieee.org
[2] Shanghai Institute of Intelligent Science and Technology,
Tongji University, Shanghai, China

Abstract. In this paper, we study an unmanned aerial vehicle (UAV) assisted Fog-RAN network where an UAV perform as mobile remote radio head (RRH) to help base station forwards signals to the multiple users in the downlink transmissions, and a dedicated ground station (GS) acts as baseband unit (BBU) pool. To achieve fairness among users, we minimize the maximum transmission delay for all terrestrial users in downlink communication by jointly optimizing the user scheduling and the UAVs trajectory. Since the formulation problem is an integer non-convex optimization problem, we propose an effective iterative algorithm to find efficient solutions by using Majorize Minimization (MM) algorithm. We also confirm the convergence of our proposed algorithm. Numerical results indicate that the proposed algorithm can significantly reduces transmission delay compared to circular trajectories and fixed base station solutions.

Keywords: UAV communications · Delay minimization · Trajectory design

1 Introduction

With high mobility ability, unmanned aerial vehicle (UAV) wireless communication can fully exploit this potential to more efficiently communicate with terrestrial users. The communication assistance of UAV can significantly reduce the delay between the core network and the ground user comparing with traditional small-cell technology [1]. A large amount of research work has been devoted to studies of UAV-assisted communication. Among them, most researchers focused on optimizing the transmit power and trajectory of the UAV to improve the performance. For example, the authors in [2] describe an UAV wireless network in which a UAV is used to act as airborne mobile base stations to serve some users on the ground, and the objective is to maximize throughput of all ground users by jointly optimizing the UAV trajectories and user scheduling. Wireless communication using UAVs has become an attractive technology for many applications

© ICST Institute for Computer Sciences, Social Informatics and Telecommunications Engineering 2020
Published by Springer Nature Switzerland AG 2020. All Rights Reserved
H. Gao et al. (Eds.): ChinaCom 2019, LNICST 312, pp. 344–355, 2020.
https://doi.org/10.1007/978-3-030-41114-5_26

in the future wireless systems. However, the limited durability of drones greatly hampers the practical implementation of drone communications. To overcome the limited durability of UAVs, the authors in [3] propose a new UAV communication solution that address durability issues by using active caching at the user. Besides, the uplink transmission energy of the ground terminal and propulsion energy of the UAV trade-off via trajectory design is considered in [4]. Regarding the backhaul link between the UAV and the core network, the researchers mainly optimize the UAV antenna transmit power and core network layout to achieve UAV backhaul performance optimization. Unmanned aerial vehicles (UAVs) are considered as wireless access points for services in commercial operating networks. The author models the drone in [5], which operates at a certain height on the ground to provide wireless service in the coverage area covered by its directional antenna, while the drone uses the existing ground base station network performs wireless backhaul. The formula for successfully establishing the probability of a backhaul and the expected data rate on the backhaul link are derived in [6].

The previous studies show the performance optimization of the UAV communication network. However, most of them focus on the communication between the user and the UAV. In the upcoming 5G, Fog-RAN network architecture has become one of promising solutions to reduce the transmission delay by introducing edge computing and edge caching. In this study, we intend to combine the advantages of UAV assisted communication and Fog-RAN by proposing a UAV assisted Fog-RAN network [7]. Specifically, we assume that an UAV are deployed as mobile remote radio head (RRH) to provide wireless connectivity, and a dedicated ground station (GS) acts as baseband unit (BBU) pool. Our aim is to improve the performance of this communication network by optimizing the UAV's trajectory.

In specific, in the considered UAV assisted Fog-RAN network, we assume that an UAV are deployed as RRH to provide wireless connectivity, and a dedicated GS acts as BBU pool as mentioned in [5]. Compared to previous research, this paper firstly considers deploying UAV in Fog-RAN network. To achieve fairness among users, we minimize the maximum transmission delay by optimizing the multiuser communication scheduling, the UAVs trajectory at GS. This optimization problem has not been studied in the previous literature according to the author's knowledge. As the problem is the non-convex optimization problem, we propose an the efficient iterative algorithm to solve it. In particular, we apply the block coordinate descent method to divide the problem into two sub-questions. The UAV trajectory optimization problem with fixed user scheduling is hard to solve due to its non-convexity. Therefore, we apply the Majorize-Minimization algorithm [8] to replace the concave part of the objective function with its first-order Taylor expansion. Through multiple iterations, the solution that is closer to the optimal solution of the objective function can be obtained. By relaxing the binary variables for multiuser communication schedule into continuous variables, the user scheduling problem with fixed UAV trajectory becomes an linear programming (LP) problem. Through formula derivation, we also confirm the convergence of our proposed algorithm. Numerical results demonstrate that the proposed algorithm is able to significantly reduces transmission delay compared to circular trajectories and fixed base station solutions.

The rest of this article is explained below. Section 2 introduces the drone communication model and problem description. In Sect. 3, by using block coordinate descent method and Majorize-Minimization (MM) algorithm, we propose an iterative algorithm based on UAV delay optimization. In Sect. 4, the convergence performance of the proposed algorithm is verified. Section 5 presents the performance of the newly proposed algorithm can be proved based on numerical results. In the end, we summarize the article in Sect. 6.

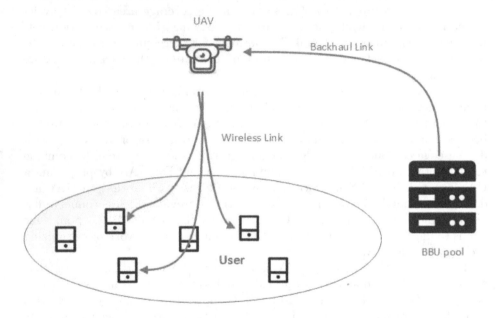

Fig. 1. An UAV assisted Fog-RAN network.

2 System Model and Problem Formulation

2.1 System Model

As shown in Fig. 1, the considered UAV assisted Fog-RAN network consists of the UAV deployed as mobile RRH to serve a set of K ground users (GUs), and GS acts as BBU pool. The level position of GU k is denoted as $w_k \in \mathbb{R}^{2 \times 1}, k \in K$. The level position of GS is denoted as $w_S \in \mathbb{R}^{2 \times 1}$ and the dedicated GS height is h. Assume that all UAVs share the common frequency band for each successive period of duration $T > 0$ s. All drones are flying at a fixed ground level for H and the level location of UAV at instant t is denoted by $q(t) = [x(t), y(t)]^T \in \mathbb{R}^{2 \times 1}$ with $0 \leq t \leq T$. For convenience of explanation, the period T is discretized into N equal time slots with each be $\tau = \frac{T}{N}$. We assume that the UAV needs to return to its initial position at the end of each period T. The trajectories of the UAV are also limited by the maximum speed. In total, the UAV trajectories need to meet the following constraints

$$q[1] = q[N], \forall m, \tag{1}$$

$$\|q[n+1] - q[n]\|^2 \leq V_m^2 \tau^2, \quad n = 1, \ldots, N-1. \tag{2}$$

The distance from the UAV to user k in time slot n is

$$d_k[n] = \sqrt{\|q[n] - w_k\|^2 + H^2}. \tag{3}$$

The distance from the UAV to GS in time slot n can be expressed as

$$d[n] = \sqrt{\|q[n] - w_S\|^2 + (H - h)^2}. \tag{4}$$

We assume that the small-scale fading of the links from the UAV to the ground users follows Rayleigh fading. Then, the signal to noise ratio (SNR) of the link between the UAV to user k during slot n can be expressed as

$$r_k[n] = \frac{P_u g_k[n] A_0 d_k[n]^{-\alpha_u}}{N_0}, \tag{5}$$

where P_u denotes the UAV transmit power, N_0 is the noise power, $g_k[n]$ corresponds to the small-scale fading and $g_k[n] \sim exp(1)$, A_0 is a constant, and α_u is path loss exponent. We suppose that each user is served by at most one UAV per time slot. We use a binary variable $\alpha_k[n] \in \{0, 1\}$, to indicate the fact whether the UAV serves user k in time slot n. This yields the following constraints, $\alpha_{k,m}[n] \leq 1, \forall k, \sum_{k=1}^{K} \alpha_k[n] \leq 1$ and $\alpha_k[n] \in \{0, 1\}, \forall k$. We mainly aim to improve the transmission reliability, and the transmission reliability is the probability that the signal receiver's SNR is greater than or equal to the preset SNR threshold β. The successful transmission probability of the UAV and the user k during slot n is given by

$$P_k[n]^s = Pr\left\{ g_k[n] \geq \frac{\beta_u N_0}{P_u A_0 d_k[n]^{-\alpha_u}} \right\}$$
$$= \exp\left(-\frac{\beta_u N_0}{P_u A_0 d_k[n]^{-\alpha_u}} \right). \tag{6}$$

The same procedure may be easily adapted to obtain the successful transmission probability of the GS and the UAV communication given by

$$P[n]^s = Pr\left\{ g[n] \geq \frac{\beta_S N_0}{P_S A_0 d[n]^{-\alpha_S}} \right\}$$
$$= \exp\left(-\frac{\beta_S N_0}{P_S A_0 d[n]^{-\alpha_S}} \right). \tag{7}$$

We assume the size of each of the I files is X bit. Suppose each file is divided into $Y = X/R_p$ packets, where R_p represents the packet size (in bits). We also assume that random linear code [9] is used for each file and a file can be recovered from any $Y_p = (1 + \varepsilon)Y$ coded packets, where $\varepsilon \ll 1$ is the coding overhead. GU k should at least receive the Y encoded packet successfully if it wants to recover the file. We define T_{f_i} as the time required for packet transmission so that on average Y packets are received by GU k during slot n. Otherwise, the UAV can retrieve file f_i from the GS with each transmitted packet having success probability $P[n]^s$ (transmission duration of one packet is t_p). In conclude, file f_i costs time of required packet transmission between the UAV and the GU k during slot n is given by

$$T_{f_i} = \frac{Y}{P_k[n]^s}t_p + \frac{Y}{P_k[n]^s P[n]^s}t_p. \tag{8}$$

We define T_k as the average time required for serving one file request for the GU k, which is given by

$$T_k = \frac{1}{N}\sum_{i=1}^{I} a_i \sum_{n=1}^{N} \alpha_k[n](\frac{Y}{P_k[n]^s}t_p + \frac{Y}{P_k[n]^s P[n]^s}t_p), \forall k. \tag{9}$$

2.2 Problem Formulation

By assuming that the locations of the GUS and the dedicated GS are known, the optimization problem is formulated as

$$\min_{q,\alpha} \ \max_{k \in K} T_k$$
$$s.t. \quad \alpha_k[n] = 1, \forall k \tag{10a}$$
$$\sum_{k=1}^{K} \alpha_k[n] = 1 \tag{10b}$$
$$\alpha_k \in (0,1), \forall k \tag{10c}$$
$$\|q[n+1] - q[n]\|^2 \le V_m^2 \tau^2, \ n = 1, ..., N-1 \tag{10d}$$
$$q[1] = q[N]. \tag{10e}$$

3 Proposed Solution

The formulated problem is divided into two sub-questions. The UAV trajectory optimization problem with fixed user scheduling is hard to solve due to its non-convexity. Therefore, we apply the Majorize-Minimization algorithm [8] to replace the concave part of the objective function with its first-order Taylor expansion. Through multiple iterations, the solution that is closer to the optimal solution of the objective function can be obtained. By relaxing the binary variables for multiuser communication schedule into continuous variables, the user scheduling problem with fixed UAV trajectory becomes an LP problem.

3.1 UAV Trajectory Optimization

Define μ is $\max_{k \in K} T_k$, for given user scheduling, the UAV trajectory of problem can be expressed as

$$\min_{\mu, q[n]} \mu$$

$$\|q[n+1] - q[n]\|^2 \le V_m^2 \tau^2, n = 1,.., N-1 \tag{11a}$$

$$q[1] = q[N] \tag{11b}$$

$$T_k \le \mu. \forall k. \tag{11c}$$

Note that due to the non-convex constraints (11c) respect to $q[n]$, the problem (11) is not a convex minimization problem. In general, there is no efficient way to obtain the optimal solution. To tackle the non-convexity of (11c), the Majorize-Minimization algorithm can be applied. Under the given conditions, the original function is approximated as a more manageable function. Specifically, define $q^r[n]$ as the UAV trajectory in the r-th iteration. According to prior knowledge, any convex function is globally delimited by its first-order Taylor expansion at any point. Based on this, we get the following lower bound of $T_k[n]$ in r iterations

$$T_k[n] = \frac{Y}{P_k[n]^s P[n]^s} t_p$$
$$\ge A_k^r[n](q[n] - q[n]^r) + B_k[n] = \hat{T}_k[n], \tag{12}$$

where $A_k^r[n]$ and $B_k^r[n]$ are constants which can be written as

$$A_k^r[n] = Y \exp \left(\frac{\beta_u N_0}{P_u A_0 d_k^r[n]^{-\alpha_u}} + \frac{\beta_S N_0}{P_S A_0\, d^r[n]^{-\alpha_S}} \right) t_p$$
$$\left(\frac{2\beta_u N_0 (q^r[n] - w_k)^T}{P_u A_0} + \frac{2\beta_S N_0 (q^r[n] - w_0)^T}{P_S A_0} \right). \forall k, n, \tag{13}$$

$$B_k^r[n] = Y \exp \left(\frac{\beta_u N_0}{P_u A_0 d_k^r[n]^{-\alpha_u}} + \frac{\beta_S N_0}{P_S A_0 d^r[n]^{-\alpha_S}} \right) t_p. \forall k, n. \tag{14}$$

To this end, T_k in constraints (11c) are transformed into

$$T_k = \frac{1}{N} \sum_{i=1}^{I} a_i \sum_{n=1}^{N} \alpha_k[n] [\frac{Y}{P_k[n]^s} t_p + T_k[n]] \le \mu. \forall k. \tag{15}$$

Problem (11) is converted to the following question

$$\min_{\mu, q[n]} \mu$$

$$\|q[n+1] - q[n]\|^2 \le V_m^2 \tau^2, n = 1,.., N-1 \tag{16a}$$

$$q[1] = q[N] \tag{16b}$$

$$\frac{1}{N} \sum_{i=1}^{I} a_i \sum_{n=1}^{N} \alpha_k[n] [\frac{Y}{P_k[n]^s} t_p + \hat{T}_k[n]] \le \mu. \forall k. \tag{16c}$$

Since the right side of the constraint (16c) is convex for $q^r[n]$, (16c) becomes convex constraint. Furthermore, (16a) are convex quadratic constraints and (16b) is a linear constraint. Therefore, the problem (16) is a convex problem that can be solved by CVX.

3.2 User Scheduling Optimization

For a given drone trajectory, the user-scheduled optimization variables are binary. We relax the binary variables in (10d) as continuous variables, the user scheduling of problem (10) can be solved by optimizing the following issues

$$\min_{\mu,\alpha_k[n]} \quad \mu$$

$$s.t. \qquad T_k \leq \mu. \forall k \tag{17a}$$

$$\sum_{k=1}^{K} \alpha_k[n] = 1, \forall n \tag{17b}$$

$$0 \leq \alpha_k[n] \leq 1, \forall k, n. \tag{17c}$$

Since the problem (17) is a standard LP, existing optimization tools can effectively solve this problem. With the obtained continuous-value solution, the binary solution needs to be refactored. Here, we simply assume $\alpha_k[n] = [\alpha_k[n]] = 0$ if $0 < \alpha_k[n] < 0.5$. Otherwise, $\alpha_k[n] = [\alpha_k[n]] = 1$.

4 Convergence Analysis

Based on the solutions obtained from the previous two problems, we propose a global iterative algorithm for the problem (10) by applying the block coordinate descent method. Then, by solving problems (17), and (11) respectively, while keeping the other variable blocks fixed, the UAV trajectory, and user scheduling are alternately optimized. In summary, we obtain Algorithm 1 by combining the solutions of three subproblems. When given user scheduling, the algorithm of UAV trajectory problem are summarized in Algorithm 2. We next demonstrate the convergence of Algorithm 1. In step 4 of Algorithm 1, we obtain the optimal solution for (17) for a given $q^r[n]$. The problem follows that

$$\mu \{\alpha_k^{r+1}[n], q^r[n]\} \geq \mu \{\alpha_k^r[n], q^r[n]\}. \tag{18}$$

For given $q^r[n]$, $\alpha_k^{r+1}[n]$ in step 5 of Algorithm 1, we obtain the approximately optimal solution for (11) and we have

$$\mu\{\alpha_k^{r+1}[n], q^r[n]\} \overset{(a)}{=} \mu^t\{\alpha_k^{r+1}[n], q^r[n]\}$$

$$\overset{b)}{\geq} \mu^t\{\alpha_k^{r+1}[n], q^{r+1}[n]\} \tag{19}$$

$$\overset{(c)}{\geq} \mu\{\alpha_k^{r+1}[n], q^{r+1}[n]\},$$

Where equation (a) holds because the first-order Taylor in (12) expands at the given point $q^r[n]$. This means that problem (16) has the same target value as the problem (11). Equation (b) holds, because we obtained the optimal solution for (16) in step 6 of Algorithm 1. Equation (c) holds, because the optimal value calculated in the problem (16) is the upper bound of the problem (11). In summary, we obtain

$$\mu\{\alpha_k^r[n],\, q^r[n]\} \geq \mu\{\alpha_{k,}^{r+1}[n],\, q^{r+1}[n]\}. \tag{20}$$

Equation (20) indicates that the objective value of the problem (10) after each iteration of Algorithm 1 is non-increasing. On the other hand, the objective function must have a lower bound, for example 0. Therefore, we claim that Algorithm 1 converges to at least the local optimal solution.

Algorithm 1: Block coordinate descent algorithm for problem (10)

Input   : The objective value μ^{r+1};
Output: The optimal solution as $\{q^r, \alpha^r\}$;
1 Initialize $b_n^0[i]$ and $q^0[n]$. Let $r = 0$;
2 Set the convergence threshold δ_1;
3 **repeat**
4   Optimize problem (17) for given $q^r[n]$, and the solution is expressed as $\alpha_k^{r+1}[n]$;
5   Optimize problem (11) for given $\{q^r[n], \alpha_k^{r+1}[n]\}$ and the solution is expressed as $q^{r+1}[n]$;
6   Update $r = r + 1$;
7 **until** $|\mu^{r+1} - \mu^r| < \delta_1$;

---

5   Simulation Results

In the following, we present some simulations to verify the effectiveness of the algorithm in this work. The basic simulation parameters are listed in Table 1. We

---

Algorithm 2: Majorization-Minimization Algorithm for problem (11)

Input   : The objective value $(\mu^r)^{i+1}$;
Output: The optimal trajectory as $q^r[n]$;
1 Solve problem (11), initialize the UAV trajectory $(q^r[n])^0$;
2 Set the SNR requirements β;
3 Set the convergence limit δ_2;
4 **repeat**
5   Solve problem (11), and denote the optimal solution as $(q^r[n])^{i+1}$;
6 **until** $|(\mu^r)^{i+1} - (\mu^r)^i| < \delta_2$;

Table 1. Simulation parameters

Parameter	Value	Description
Y	100	Coded packets of each of the I files
H	100 m	UAV flight altitude
h	50 m	GS height
V_m	50 m/s	The maximum UAV speed
P_u	0.5 W	The UAV transmit power
P_S	5 W	The GS transmit power
t_p	1 ms	Transmission duration of one packet
β_u, β_S	3 dB	SNR threshold
A_0	−15 dB	Path loss constant
N_0	−50 dBm	Noise power
α_u, α_S	3 dB	Path loss exponent

consider a set of 6 GU and a dedicated GS wireless systems. They are randomly and evenly distributed in a 2D area of $1.5 \times 1.5 \, \text{km}^2$. Figure 2 shows the optimized trajectory of Algorithm 1 solved at different times T. According to the trajectory diagram Fig. 2, as the cycle T increases, the drone uses its maneuverability to modify its trajectory to bring it closer to GUS. When $T = 210$ s, the UAV remains stationary for a period of time at the apex of the trajectory, flying at maximum speed between the vertices of the trajectory. When $T = 30$ and 90 s, the UAVs fly at maximum speed V_m so as to be as close as possible to each user in each period T to obtain higher communication quality.

In Fig. 3, we show that Algorithm 1 can finally converge when $T = 90$s. According to Fig. 3, the minimized maximum delay of the proposed algorithm is rapidly reduced as the number of iterations increases. After about 20 iterations, the algorithm finally converges. In Fig. 4, we consider the scenario of using single UAVs; (1) Static UAV, where each UAV is placed in the geometric center of the ground users position and GS position; (2) Simple circular trajectory, With the geometric center position of the user and GS position as the center; (3) Optimized trajectory, obtained by Algorithm 1. Compared the performance of three different scenarios in Fig. 4, the benefits of the proposed trajectory are fully demonstrated. For optimized trajectories with large periods T, the UAV can provide higher quality communication for the ground users, and the transmission delay will be smaller.

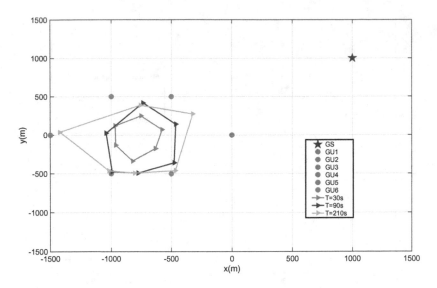

Fig. 2. The optimized trajectory of Algorithm 1 solved at different times T.

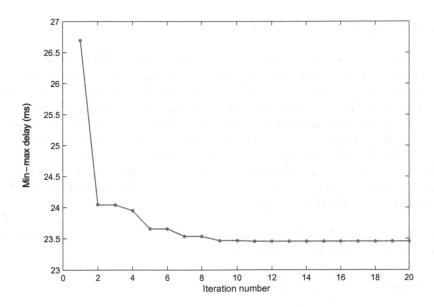

Fig. 3. Convergence performance of the Algorithm 1.

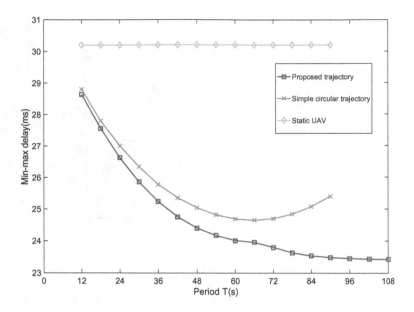

Fig. 4. Min-max delay with different trajectory designs as a function of period T.

6   Conclusions

Reducing transmission delay is one of the main challenges in UAV-enabled communication research. To achieve fairness among users, we minimize the maximum delay by jointly optimizing the UAVs trajectory and communication scheduling. The simulation results show that the algorithm can significantly reduce the total transmission delay of multi-UAV networks. We found a fundamental tradeoff between the total transmission delay of multi-UAV communication network model and the UAV flight period T. In the future work, we consider the scenario of using a single UAV, and designing a new scheme caching at the UAV. We aim to improve the performance of this communication network by optimizing the UAVs trajectory and caching design.

Acknowledgement. This work was supported by the National Science Foundation China under Grant 61571330 and Grant 61771345.

References

1. Wu, Q., Li, G., Chen, W., Ng, D.W.K.: Energy-efficient small cell with spectrum-power trading. IEEE J. Sel. Areas Commun. **PP**(99), 1 (2016)
2. Wu, Q., Yong, Z., Zhang, R.: Joint trajectory and communication design for UAV-enabled multiple access (2017)
3. Xu, X., Zeng, Y., Guan, Y., Zhang, R.: Overcoming endurance issue: UAV-enabled communications with proactive caching. IEEE J. Sel. Areas Commun. **PP**(99), 1 (2017)

4. Yang, D., Wu, Q., Zeng, Y., Zhang, R.: Energy trade-off in ground-to-UAV communication via trajectory design. IEEE Trans. Veh. Technol. **PP**(99), 1 (2017)
5. Galkin, B., Kibilda, J., Dasilva, L.A.: A stochastic geometry model of backhaul and user coverage in urban UAV networks (2017)
6. Galkin, B., Kibilda, J., DaSilva, L.A.: Backhaul for low-altitude UAVs in urban environments (2017)
7. Zhang, H., Qiu, Y., Chu, X., Long, K., Leung, V.C.M.: Fog radio access networks: mobility management, interference mitigation, and resource optimization. IEEE Wirel. Commun. **24**(6), 120–127 (2017)
8. Yan, D., Wang, R., Liu, E., Hou, Q.: ADMM-based robust beamforming design for downlink cloud radio access networks. IEEE Access **6**, 27912–27922 (2018)
9. Byers, J.W., Luby, M., Mitzenmacher, M., Rege, A.: A digital fountain approach to reliable distribution of bulk data. ACM SIGCOMM Comput. Commun. Rev. **28**, 56–67 (1998)

A Design of D2D-Clustering Algorithm for Group D2D Communication

Ruoqi Shi$^{(\boxtimes)}$, Bicheng Wang, Fanwei Shi, Dongming Piao, and Jianling Hu

School of Electronic and Information Engineering,
Soochow University, Suzhou, China
rqshi7@stu.suda.edu.cn, jlhu@suda.edu.cn

Abstract. Due to the characteristics of low latency and proximity discovery, D2D communication is considered to have an inherent advantage in supporting Internet-of-Vehicles (IoV) service. In this paper, considering that vehicular users can detect neighbor nodes in adjacent areas which are able to maintain high reliable communication with themselves, a novel design of D2D-Clustering algorithm is proposed in order to improve the QoS of users. The algorithm uses undirected graph to describe the neighborhood relationship between users. And the undirected graph is continuously simplified by multi-round traversal of vehicular users until user clustering is completed. Simulation results prove the validity of the proposed algorithm, pointing out that it helps reduce the energy consumption of the whole system.

Keywords: Internet-of-Vehicles · D2D communication · Clustering · Neighbor detection · Undirected graph

1 Introduction

Intelligent Transportation System (ITS) provides support for various kinds of applications for IoV, making modern transportation much more efficient [1]. However, with the massive access of intelligent devices, mobile communication traffic is increasing rapidly, which brings huge burden to cellular network. 3GPP proposed Device-to-Device (D2D) communication technology in LTE Release 12. Due to the way of short-distance direct communication, D2D Technology has less energy consumption and lower transmission latency, solving the contradiction between throughput and reliability in traditional cellular network. It has been considered as a promising candidate technology to support vehicle-to-everything (V2X) services. D2D based V2X enables vehicles to quickly exchange information with adjacent vehicles, pedestrians, road-side units [2], etc. It is an excellent solution to improve the quality of service for IoV users.

In many scenarios, base stations need to continuously broadcast the same or similar content due to the common interests from a large number of users, such as a crowded concert or stadium. These services generate a rather steady load at the physical layer. In other words, base stations will need to send small-scale

© ICST Institute for Computer Sciences, Social Informatics and Telecommunications Engineering 2020
Published by Springer Nature Switzerland AG 2020. All Rights Reserved
H. Gao et al. (Eds.): ChinaCom 2019, LNICST 312, pp. 356–367, 2020.
https://doi.org/10.1007/978-3-030-41114-5_27

data packets to most of the users in the cell periodically. The same is true for many V2X services, such as road condition update service and traffic accident broadcasting. Beacons which are used to mark specific events need to be periodically transmitted in a reliable way [3]. Thus, it is very important to design a good multicast scheme for this kind of service. In [4], the author put forward the concept of D2D multicast communication. Through D2D multicast communication, user can share information data to its multiple neighbors using the proximity relationship of user equipment's location. Therefore, the introduction of D2D multicast technology helps expand the coverage of multicast services and share common content between users, reducing the load of base stations.

For the scenarios with periodic transmission opportunities at the physical layer, a persistent resource scheduling scheme LDRAS is proposed in [3]. LDRAS divided each cell sector into several spatially disjoint regions, where in which region a fixed but different set of RBs is preserved for D2D users and cellular users (C-UE). The resource scheduling is mainly dependent on the current location of users. Besides, in order to limit the interference of D2D transmission to conventional cellular users, C-UE region must be far enough separated from D2D region when they share the same set of RBs.

Considering that mobile devices with interest in the same content in the network can be grouped into a cluster under the existing system framework, the introduction of D2D clustering is a great promotion to improve system performance. In [5], Peng et al. proposed a cooperative communication scheme, in which base station and D2D transmitters were in charge of two-round broadcasting, respectively. Thus, the QoS of mobile video service of cell-edge users can be improved. The researches in [4] and [6] focused on how to determine whether user devices should work under D2D multicast communication mode or cellular communication mode, and the mode switching conditions. In [7], Koskela et al. derived the mathematical solution equation for assigning optimal communication mode for devices by introducing the concept of clustering with mode switching. It was pointed out that the system performance in the optimal communication mode is related to degree of separation of cluster members. On the other hand, the researches in [8] and [9] focused on D2D user clustering algorithm. A D2D multicast cluster head selection strategy was presented in [8], which can improve the system throughput and reduce the transmission delay. In [9], Zhu et al. proposed a multicast clustering algorithm for multi-hop communication by introducing cluster head node selection criteria and cluster member reassignment mechanism, efficient intra-group content sharing is achieved and transmission latency is reduced. In [10], a heuristic framework for clustering LTE-D2D devices for group D2D communication was presented. The channel states between users and the residual energy of nodes were mainly considered. However, cluster member assigning mechanism was rather complex.

Many features have been taken into consideration in those researches above, such as multi-hop, multi-mode, buffer-aided and multi-round-cooperation. However, there are still few user clustering schemes serving for efficient D2D multicast communication. Moreover, these existing clustering schemes in related researches do not make full use of the neighborhood relationship between cell users. The principle of opportunism is not followed in the selection of cluster heads. Inspired by the above issues, a novel Undirected Graph Simplification based Clustering (UGSC) algorithm for group D2D communication is proposed in this paper. Channel condition between users is considered as the most critical factor for clustering. After neighbor discovery, user equipments (UEs) update the list of its strong neighbor nodes (SNN) to the evolved Node B (eNB), which controls the D2D clustering. The proposed algorithm creatively uses an undirected graph to describe the neighborhood relationship between user devices in a cell. The undirected graph is continuously simplified in an iterative manner. Finally, D2D clustering of all user devices is completed to serve the subsequent D2D multicast communication.

The rest of this paper is organized as follows. In Sect. 2, the scenario description and neighbor detection mechanism are given. In Sect. 3, we present the basic principles and procedures of the UGSC algorithm. Simulation results and analysis are provided in Sect. 4. Finally, conclusions are drawn in Sect. 5.

2   System Model

2.1   Scenario Description

We consider a single-cell scenario as shown in Fig. 1, where there are M vehicular-user equipments (V-UEs) running V2V applications. Each V-UE is equipped with one antenna. U_i denotes the ith V-UE. h_{ij} represents the channel coefficient between U_i and U_j. Besides, We use P_B and P_u to denote the transmitting power of eNB and V-UEs respectively. So, the Signal-Interference-Noise-Ratio (SINR) for the transmission between U_i and U_j is calculated as:

$$\gamma_{ij} = \frac{P_u |h_{ij}|^2}{\sigma_n^2}, \ \forall i,j \in \{1,2,\ldots M\} \tag{1}$$

Where σ_n^2 is the variance of the channel noise.

2.2   Detection of Strong Neighbor Nodes

Each UE can execute neighbor node discovery algorithm to finding out other UEs near itself [11]. Specifically speaking, U_i performs channel estimation based on the discovery beacon (reference signal) sent by the surrounding nodes and calculate the SINR of the reference signal. If the SINR is higher than a given threshold, the UE which sent that beacon will be considered as a strong neighbor node to U_i. Then U_i will add it to its own list of strong neighbors $\mathbf{SNN}_i$ and reply with an acknowledgment beacon.

After the strong neighbor node detection process is finished, the neighbor lists will be reported to eNB using the granted Physical Uplink Shared Channel (PUSCH) [12,13]. One RB is always preserved for updating the table of Strong-Neighbor-Node $\mathbf{SNN}_i$. Clearly, eNB can also obtain the channel state information of all UEs at the same time, which is preserved as $\mathbf{TAB}_{SINR}$. Under the

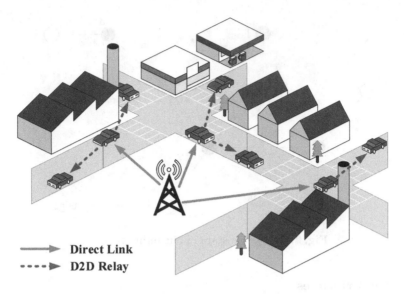

Fig. 1. Urban vehicular network scenario

assumption of channel reciprocity, the eNB will consider two V-UEs as strong neighbors if they are in each other's neighborhood list. Note that, such an updating process does not need to be performed very frequently in order to reduce signaling overhead in the system. The eNB can perform information uploading over large time scale cycles (e.g., hundreds of milliseconds) according to specific V2V application service types.

3   UGSC Algorithm

Clustering and the following resource scheduling is controlled by eNB. Firstly, a few cluster heads (CHs) and their corresponding cluster members are selected by eNB according to **SNN** and **TAB**$_{SINR}$. Then, the eNB allocates time-frequency resources to each cluster for the subsequent information exchange inside each cluster. The key point of this paper is to design a reasonable and fast D2D-Clustering algorithm, reducing the complexity of the algorithm and the energy consumption of whole system.

Consider the neighborhood relationship between V-UEs in a cell as an undirected graph. Clearly, each vertex represents a V-UE. The edge between two vertices represents that the corresponding V-UEs are strong neighbor to each other. The key idea of the UGSC Algorithm is to simplify the undirected graph in multi-round iterations according to the distribution of edges between different vertices. Here are the basic principles and procedures of the UGSC Algorithm.

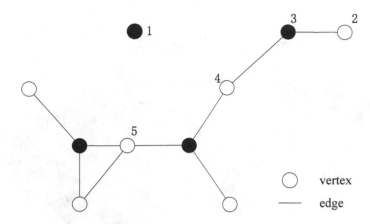

Fig. 2. A possible state in clustering process

3.1   Basic Principles

- If there is no edge connected to one specific node (like Node **No. 1** in Fig. 2), this node will be labeled as an isolated vertex. It means that there is no proximity between this V-UE and other V-UEs in the cell. The eNB must regard this kind of node as an individual cluster, the CH of which is the node itself. The eNB will communicate with it directly.
- If there is only one edge connected to one specific node (like Node **No. 2** in Fig. 2), this node will be considered as a terminal vertex. It means that there exists only one strong neighbor node (like **Node No. 3** in Fig. 2) to this V-UE. In this situation, the eNB must regard the connected neighbor node as a CH, while this terminal node becomes a member of the cluster. The eNB will communicate with this terminal node at the assistance of the corresponding CH.
- If there are more than one edges connected to one specific node (like **Node No. 4** and **No. 5** in Fig. 2), this node will be considered as a multi-joined vertex. The eNB can not determine that whether this node should be regarded as a CH node or an ordinary cluster member immediately. In this situation, we should firstly turn to its strong neighbor nodes, checking that whether anyone of them has been regarded as a CH or not.

In other words, due to the existence of multi-joined vertices, it is not enough to complete the whole clustering process through only one-round traversal of all V-UEs in the cell. Thus, we propose an iterative algorithm for cyclic traversal. In each round of iteration, V-UEs that were assigned to a specific cluster will be removed from the list. By doing so, irrelevant vertices and edges in complex undirected graph are gradually deleted until the assignment of all V-UEs is finished.

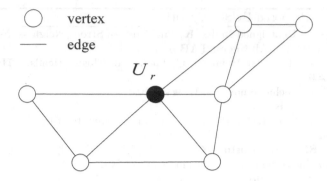

Fig. 3. The Impasse-Break mechanism

3.2 Procedure

The procedure of UGSC Algorithm is shown in Algorithm 1.

As shown in Step 2–6 in Algorithm 1, in each round of traversal, we find out the set of all unreachable nodes K_0 from the set of unassigned nodes K firstly. Clearly, each node in K_0 will be assigned to an individual cluster by the eNB. After this step of assignment, those mentioned nodes must be deleted from K and **SNN**.

Then, as shown in Step 7–15 in Algorithm 1, we find out the set of all single-connection nodes K_1 from K. The single strong neighbor node of these nodes in K_1 will be assigned as CHs, while nodes in K_1 become members of corresponding clusters. Note that, the neighbor list of the aforementioned selected CH may contain more strong neighbor nodes except that single-connection one. For example, **Node No. 2** in Fig. 2 is a single-connection node. If we assign **Node No. 3** as a CH, we have to pay attention that the neighbor list of **Node No. 3** contains not only **Node No. 2** but also other nodes. These nodes may already be assigned as a cluster member or may be in an uncertain state. At this time, we should add nodes in uncertain state to a pending-node set **PN**. Once the traversal of K_1 is finished, we should start the traversal of **PN**, in which we find the most suitable (the best channel condition) CH for each node in **PN** and make them a cluster member of their most suitable CH. Similarly, after this step of assignment, those mentioned nodes which have been assigned as a cluster member must be deleted from K and **SNN**. The process is repeated until K becomes an empty set, meaning that assignment of all V-UEs is finished.

It is worthy to mention that the continuous deletion of UE in the table of Strong Neighbor Node **SNN** and set of unassigned nodes K, is exactly the process of continuous simplification of the complex undirected graph corresponding to cell network. The whole process may turn into a special state, which is like what can be seen in Fig. 3. In this situation, K is not an empty set. However, there is no unreachable node or single-connection node in K. We propose an Impasse-Break mechanism that an unassigned node U_r is randomly selected as the CH of a new cluster. All of the strong neighbor nodes of U_r are assigned

---

Algorithm 1. Proposed UGSC Algorithm

Input: The Set of Unassigned Nodes, **K**; The Table of Strong Neighbor Nodes, **SNN**; The Table of CSI of All Nodes, **TAB**$_{SINR}$;

Output: The Set of Cluster Members, **C**; The Set of Cluster Heads, **CH**;

1: **while K** $\neq \emptyset$ **do**
2:     Find all unreachable nodes in **K** as set $\mathbf{K_0}$;
3:     **for** each $U_i \in \mathbf{K_0}$ **do**
4:         Update **C, CH, K** with U_i; //New cluster consists of U_i
5:     **end for**
6:     Update **SNN** with existing **K**;
7:     Find all single-connection nodes in **K** as set $\mathbf{K_1}$;
8:     **for** each $U_i \in \mathbf{K_1}$ **do**
9:         Update **C, CH, K** with U_i ans SNN_i; //New cluster consists of U_i and SNN_i.
10:         **PN** = **PN** $\cap$ **SNN**$_{SNN_i}$; //Gather all neighbor nodes of SNN_i
11:     **end for**
12:     **for** each $V_i \in$ **PN do**
13:         Update **C, K** with V_i; //join in the best CH
14:     **end for**
15:     Update **SNN** with existing **K**;
16:     **if** $\mathbf{K_0} = \emptyset$ and $\mathbf{K_1} = \emptyset$ **then**
17:         Randomly select $U_r \in$ **K** as a new CH, remove U_r from **K**;
18:         Update **C, CH, K** with U_r;
19:         Update **SNN** with existing **K**;
20:     **end if**
21: **end while**
22: **for** each ordinary cluster member U_i **do**
23:     Update **C, CH** with Reassignment of U_i; //join in the best CH
24: **end for**
25: **return C, CH**;

---

as the ordinary members of the cluster. Similarly, after this step of assignment, those mentioned nodes must be deleted from **K** and **SNN**. Then, we start a new round of traversal. In the scenario where multiple UEs are adjacent to each other but separated from the majority of other cell users, the proposed Impasse-Break mechanism effectively avoids the clustering algorithm entering a dead-cycle state. The Impasse-Break mechanism is shown in Step 16–20 in Algorithm 1.

Finally, due to the Impasse-Break mechanism, new CH is randomly selected by eNB. So, it is possible that some V-UEs are not with their optimal choice of CH (there may exist CH with better channel condition) when assignment of all V-UEs is finished. In this situation, a reassignment step is needed. We check every ordinary cluster member whether its CH is the optimal choice of CH (the best channel condition). If it isn't, then this node joins in the cluster corresponding to its optimal choice of CH. Reassignment Mechanism is shown in Step 22–24 in Algorithm 1.

4   Simulation Results

In this section, we provide Monte-Carlo simulations to evaluate the performance of the proposed algorithm.

4.1   Road Configuration and Channel Model

At first, road configuration for simulation is shown in Fig. 4. We set two Manhattan grids so the size of simulation area is 433 m × 500 m. There are 2 lanes in each direction of every street. For V-UE drop modeling, we assume all V-UEs in the same lane have the same speed. The distance between two V-UEs in the same lane obeys exponential distribution, while the average inter-vehicle distance is 2 sec × the speed of V-UE [14].

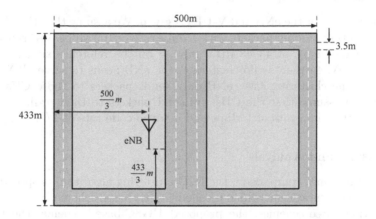

Fig. 4. Road configuration for simulation

Then, we use the channel model of V2V link for the urban grid scenario from [15]. Furthermore, we set the shadowing standard deviations as 3 dB and 4 dB for LOS(NLOSv) state and NLOS state. The probability of V2V links being LOS(NLOSv) or NLOS state is determined by transmission distance and whether the path is blocked by buildings or vehicles. The pathloss calculation for LOS and NLOSv link is:

$$PL = 38.77 + 16.7 \log_{10}(d) + 18.2 \log_{10}(f_c), \quad LOSLink \tag{2}$$

$$PL = 36.85 + 30 \log_{10}(d) + 18.9 \log_{10}(f_c), \quad NLOSLink \tag{3}$$

Where d denotes the Euclidean distance between transmitter and receiver in meters, while f_c denotes the carrier center frequency.

Simulation parameters are summarized in Table 1.

Table 1. Simulation parameters

Parameter	Value
Carrier center frequency	2 GHz
System bandwidth	10 MHz
Transmitting power of V-UE	23 dBm
Transmitting power of eNB	43–48 dBm [16]
Noise spectral density	−165 dBm/Hz
V-UE SINR threshold	20 dB [17]
Speed of V-UEs	60 km/h
Data packet size	1 KB

4.2   Simulation Setup

Simulation setup for the eNB and V-UEs is given. We assume that the eNB is an LTE base station sending packets with a data rate of 100 Mbps. Its transmitting power is in the range of 43–48 dBm relying on the reference signals received from V-UEs. When there is no clustering, the eNB needs to serve all V-UEs in cell. As for the clustering case, eNB only sends packets to those CHs. In the following, we assume that the CHs will send packets to their ordinary cluster members with a data rate of 1 Mbps and a turbo code rate of 1/3.

4.3   Results and Analysis

For the performance comparison, the D2D-clustering algorithm proposed in [10] is used as a baseline scheme, which is called CCRE-based scheme. So, we compare the following three schemes: the proposed UGSC-based scheme, the baseline CCRE-based scheme and the traditional non-clustering scheme.

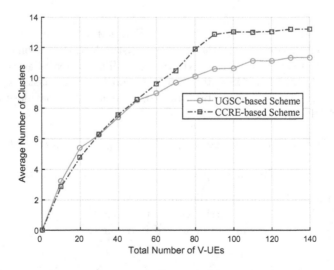

Fig. 5. Average number of clusters vs. number of V-UEs

(1) Validity and Efficiency. As illustrated in Fig. 5, the clustering efficiencies of UGSC-based and CCRE-based schemes are compared as shown in Fig. 5. It can be seen from Fig. 5 that with the increase of the number of V-UEs, the increasing trend of average number of clusters in UGSC-based scheme is similar to that in CCRE-based scheme. In details, the average number of clusters will not increase endlessly, but reach an asymptotic value in both schemes.

Obviously, each V-UE has a greater probability to detect Strong-Neighbor-Nodes around it due to the increasing number of V-UEs. Therefore, they have more opportunities to form a common cluster for efficient content sharing when vehicles are densely distributed, while additional new clusters become unnecessary. Thus, simulation results prove the validity of the UGSC Algorithm. Furthermore, it can be observed that the asymptotic value of number of clusters in UGSC-based scheme is smaller than that in CCRE-based scheme. It means that UGSC-based scheme is more effective than CCRE-based one especially in the case of dense traffic.

(2) Energy Consumption. Figure 6 illustrates the total energy consumption of these three schemes. As can be seen in Fig. 6, the energy consumption increases in all schemes, while with clustering the system can achieve an energy-saving gain. Besides, the performance of UGSC-based scheme is similar to that of CCRE scheme when the number of V-UEs is small. However, with the increase of the number of V-UEs, UGSC-based scheme has less energy consumption.

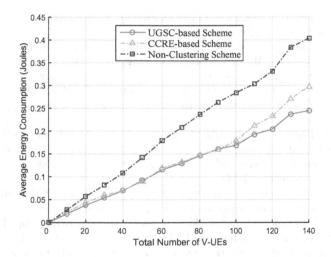

Fig. 6. Average energy consumption vs. number of V-UEs

Furthermore, the gap between energy consumption in three schemes is also gradually widening. Note that, the energy saving of eNB transmission is achieved at the cost of increasing energy consumption of CHs in UGSC-based scheme.

Therefore, with the increasing number of V-UEs, the benefits resulting from clustering become more and more obvious. The energy-saving efficiency is getting higher, respectively. This also proves the validity of the UGSC Algorithm from another point of view.

5   Conclusions

In this paper, we studied the clustering algorithm for group D2D communication in LTE-V2V systems. The Strong-Neighbor-Node detection was carried out on every V-UE in order to provide channel state information of itself to eNB. In the proposed UGSC Algorithm, neighborhood relationship between V-UEs in a cell was considered as an undirected graph. By taking the current unassigned users as the object of traversal, the undirected graph was continuously simplified in an iterative manner. Simulation results proved the validity of the clustering algorithm, pointing out that it is of a promotion on energy saving of the whole system. In the future work, we plan to consider whether to introduce more clustering criteria, including moving state prediction for V-UE, etc.

Acknowledgment. This work was supported by the Postgraduate Research & Practice Innovation Program of Jiangsu Province under grant number SJKY19_2285.

References

1. George, D., Demestichas, P.: Intelligent transportation systems. IEEE Veh. Technol. Mag. **5**(1), 77–84 (2010)
2. Araniti, G., Campolo, C., Condoluci, M., Iera, A., Molinaro, A.: LTE for vehicular networking: a survey. IEEE Veh. Technol. Mag. **51**(5), 148–157 (2015)
3. Botsov, M., Klügel, M., Kellerer, W., Fertl, P.: Location dependent resource allocation for mobile device-to-device communications. In: IEEE Wireless Communications and Networking Conference (WCNC), Istanbul, Turkey, pp. 1679–1684 (2014)
4. Seppälä, J., Koskela, T., Chen, T., Hakola, S.: Network controlled device-to-device (D2D) and cluster multicast concept for LTE and LTE-A networks. In: IEEE Wireless Communications and Networking Conference (WCNC), Cancun, Quintana Roo, pp. 986–991 (2011)
5. Peng, X., Liu, J., Wuyu, L., Wang, P., Kai, C., Zhang, S.: D2D communications based scarcity-aware two-stage multicast for video streaming. In: 23rd Asia-Pacific Conference on Communications (APCC), Perth, WA, Australia, pp. 1–6 (2017)
6. Hakola, S., Chen, T., Lehtomaki, J., Koskela, T.: Device-to-device (D2D) communication in cellular network - analysis of optimum and practical performance in interference limited system. Submitted to IEEE Wireless Communications and Networking Conference (WCNC) (2010)
7. Koskela, T., Hakola, S., Chen, T., Lehtomaki, J.: Clustering concept using device-to-device communication in cellular system. In: IEEE Wireless Communications and Networking Conference (WCNC), Sydney, Australia, pp. 1–6 (2010)

8. Ren, F., Wang, X., Wang, D., Zhang, Y., Lan, Y.: Joint social, energy and transfer rate cluster head selection strategy for D2D multicast communication. In: International Conference on Information Systems and Computer Aided Education (ICISCAE), Changchun, China, pp. 146–151 (2018)
9. Zhu, Y., Qin, X., Zhang, P.: An efficient multicast clustering scheme for D2D assisted offloading in cellular networks. In: IEEE/CIC International Conference on Communications in China (ICCC), Beijing, China, pp. 480–484 (2018)
10. Doumiati, S., Artail, H., Kabalan, K.: A framework for clustering LTE devices for implementing group D2D communication and multicast capability. In: 8th International Conference on Information and Communication Systems (ICICS), Irbid, pp. 216–221 (2017)
11. Naslcheraghi, M., Marandi, L., Ghorashi, S.A.: A novel device-to-device discovery scheme for underlay cellular networks. In: Iranian Conference on Electrical Engineering (ICEE), Tehran, pp. 2106–2110 (2017)
12. Zou, K.J., et al.: Proximity discovery for device-to-device communications over a cellular network. IEEE Commun. Mag. **52**(6), 98–107 (2014)
13. Hajiaghayi, M., Wijting, C., Ribeiro, C., Hajiaghayi, M.T.: Efficient and practical resource block allocation for LTE-based D2D network via graph coloring. Wirel. Netw. **20**(4), 611–624 (2013)
14. 3GPP TR 36.885: Technical Specification Group Radio Access Network; Study on LTE-based V2X Services, June 2016
15. 3GPP TR 37.885: Technical Specification Group Radio Access Network; Study on evaluation methodology of new Vehicle-to-Everything (V2X) use cases for LTE and NR, June 2019
16. 3GPP TR 36.843: Study on LTE Device to Device Proximity Services, Radio Aspects (Release 12), v.12.0.1, March 2014
17. Patent application title: Transmission of Device-to-Device sounding reference signals using macrocell communication resources

Cluster and Time Slot Based Cross-Layer Protocol for Ad Hoc Network

Yifan Qiu[1], Xiandeng He[1(✉)], Qingcai Wang[1], Heping Yao[2], and Nan Chen[1]

[1] State Key Laboratory of Integrated Service Networks, Xidian University, Xi'an, Shaanxi, China
xdhe@mail.xidian.edu.cn
[2] Dalian Haoyang Technology Development Ltd., Dalian, Liaoning, China

Abstract. Due to its good extendibility and robustness, Ad hoc network has been widely used in various aspects. However, its performance is restricted by the mobility, limited bandwidth and centerless architecture. In order to improve the performance of Ad hoc network, this paper proposes a cross-layer Hexagonal Clustering, Position and Time slot based (HCPT) protocol, in which clusters and time slots are divided according to the geographical location. And furthermore, an effective algorithm to find routes through the geographical locations of cluster heads is proposed, which can greatly reduce message collisions and reduce network overhead. By doing simulations in the Network Simulator 2 (NS2) software, we found that the HCPT protocol shows better performance in network topology discovery compared with the Optimized Link State Routing (OLSR) protocol. Simulation results also show that the proposed scheme outperforms the standard OLSR and the improved OLSR algorithm, which is proposed by N. Harrag, in terms of routing overhead and packet delivery ratio.

Keywords: Ad hoc network · Hybrid MAC access · Clustering · Cross-layer protocol · Location-based

1 Introduction

Ad hoc network is a kind of temporary self-organizing network system based on multi-hop routing. There is no need for fixed infrastructure support in wireless Ad hoc network. All nodes are equal, and each node has the ability of wireless communication and the basic routing function [1]. Compared with centralized control networks, wireless Ad hoc network has the characteristics of dynamic network topology, strong invulnerability and self-healing [2]. For the disadvantages of limited energy and bandwidth, as well as poor security, wireless Ad hoc network still has many challenges to be solved [3]. As two core technologies of

---

Supported by the Key Research and Development Program of Shaanxi Province (Grant No. 2019ZDLGY09-02).

H. Gao et al. (Eds.): ChinaCom 2019, LNICST 312, pp. 368–384, 2020.
https://doi.org/10.1007/978-3-030-41114-5_28

Ad hoc network, the channel intervention mechanism of Medium Access Control (MAC) layer and the routing technology of network layer, still have many problems, which restrict its application.

Traditional MAC protocols for wireless networks are basically designed for Wireless Local Area Networks (WLAN). When they are applied to Ad hoc network, common problems such as long access delay and unfair resource allocation come into being. In order to improve the utilization of the Ad hoc network, a lot of work has been done. In [4], a new back-off scheme in the saturated network scenario is proposed. This scheme does not attempt to adjust the back-off window, but makes small modifications during the back-off freezing process to determine the optimal configuration. In [5], time slot occupancy tables for nodes in the two-hop range are built to achieve Time Division Multiple Access (TDMA) dynamic allocation by monitoring the periodic broadcast control messages. Therefore, the throughput is improved and the delay is reduced. Although contention based protocols are simple, flexible, robust to node mobility and independent of a central entity, conflicts may not be completely avoided. Meanwhile the TDMA based MAC protocol needs to know the entire topology of the network in order to provide scheduling that allows each node to access the channel, which causes the scalability problem [6].

The routing protocol is the most important support for multi-hop communication between nodes. The performance of the routing protocol directly affects the network implementation and overall performance. Optimized Link State Routing (OLSR) is a typical proactive routing protocol, which regularly produces and updates routing information to other nodes in the network. In OLSR, the hello messages are used to exchange neighbor node information, and the Topology Control (TC) messages are used to broadcast the integrated messages to the entire network. OLSR uses Multipoint Relay (MPR) mechanism, where only selected MPR nodes can forward TC messages to each node in the network [7]. In order to get the information of the whole network more quickly, some research has been done. [8] proposes an adaptive modification of the transmission interval of hello messages to improve the efficiency of neighbor node discovery and the performance of the whole network. In [9], the influence of the transmission interval of the hello messages and the TC messages during the network topology discovery is studied. Thereby, the purpose of fully perceiving the network topology change while minimizing the routing overhead caused by the beacon messages can be achieved. However, a large number of message collisions and message flooding during topology discovery remain unresolved in the above articles.

Compared with traditional topology-based routing protocols, location-based routing protocols use node location to guide the direction of packet forwarding. One of the most widely used routing protocols based on location information is Greedy Perimeter Stateless Routing (GPSR) which has effective relay node selection strategies to choose the relay node [10]. GPSR uses active update method to distribute location information through periodic beacon messages [10]. However, in order to obtain high-precision real-time location updates, it will bring more routing overhead [11]. In [12], a simple and efficient update algorithm based on dynamic fuzzy logic controller and mobility prediction is proposed. It can improve the accuracy of node location information in the case of less beacon traffic and achieve the purpose of saving network overhead. But this algorithm, like GPSR, needs to know the geographic location of the destination node in advance through the location service protocol. [13] gives a location based localized broadcast algorithm, which jointly uses distance based deferring and angle based deferring to encourage nodes with higher contributions to retransmit first. In this way, the broadcast redundancy can be reduced during achieving guaranteed packet delivery. However, when this broadcast mechanism is used, there is a certain probability that the time spent on route establishment will increase.

Since the traditional hierarchical optimization methods do not significantly improve the network performance, it is necessary to use available information across layers, that is, to exchange information directly between layers to perform subsequent operations [14]. [15] proposes a cross-layer scheme, which is based on the Adhoc On-demand Distance Vector (AODV) routing of the network layer and the distributed scheduling protocol of the MAC layer. In [15], the route layer uses the link resource to select the best route, and by adding bandwidth allocation into the routing messages, the resource allocation is accomplished during the establishment of the route.

In order to further improve the performance of Ad hoc network, this paper proposes a Hexagonal Clustering, Position and Time slot based (HCPT) protocol for Very High Frequency (VHF) maritime communication scenario. In this communication scenario, the channel is dominated by Rician fading channel, and the communication range is mainly limited by the distance between sender and receiver. Moreover, because geographic location information can be easily obtained through Geographic Information System (GIS), cluster management can be carried out by geographical location. In HCPT, clusters and time slots are divided according to geographic location, and information in the cluster is forwarded through the cluster heads. On this basis, an effective algorithm to find routes through the geographical locations of cluster heads is proposed. Simulation results show that HCPT can effectively reduce network routing overhead and improve packet delivery rate.

The paper is organized as follows. Section 2 presents the system model. Then, the cross-layer protocol is designed in Sect. 3. Simulation results and analyses are provided in Sect. 4. Finally, conclusions are made in Sect. 5.

2   System Model

2.1   Assumption

In the HCPT protocol, we assume that each node obtains its own geographic location information through GIS and keeps the clocks synchronized. And there is no fixed central node in any cluster.

2.2   Geographic Location Based Clustering

Although the planar Ad hoc network is simple in structure, when the network scale expands, the routing overhead also increases, which causes the problem of poor expansibility. Layered Ad hoc is more suitable for large-scale networks than planar Ad hoc. A hierarchical Ad hoc network has a cluster head in each area which manages the nodes in the cluster and communicates with other cluster heads. Therefore, routing overhead is reduced and the network is easy to be managed [16].

By using hexagonal clustering structure to closely spread the network, each cluster has the same structure and the same coverage area. In this way, clusters can completely cover the entire network area [17,18].

In HCPT protocol, hexagonal clustering is also adopted. The entire network area is divided into multiple hexagons by corresponding algorithm based on location information. Through this clustering method, nodes can clearly know the clusters to which they belong with the help of their geographic location information. In addition, the hexagon cluster is further divided into 6 equilateral triangles and marked from 1 to 6 in Fig. 1. Each index corresponds to a time slot. By this way, the nodes with different indexes but within a cluster can avoid communication collision. Moreover, the nodes with the same index but in different clusters can send hello messages at the same time, which achieving the effect of space division multiplexing.

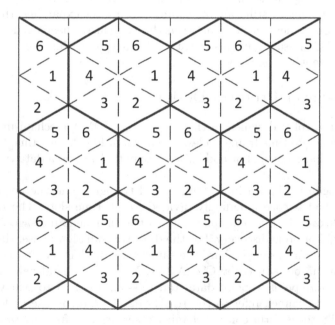

Fig. 1. Network scenario divided with hexagon

2.3 Communication Range

In this paper, the radius of a hexagon is R and the communication radius is set to $3/2R$. In order to enable TC messages generated by cluster heads to be broadcast to neighboring clusters successfully, we need to expand the communication range between cluster heads. The communication radius can be extended by reducing the communication bandwidth according to the free space loss model [19] and the reception sensitivity formula [20], which are shown in (1) and (2), respectively.

$$L_{bf} = 32.4 + 20\log f + 20\log d \tag{1}$$

The relationship between free space loss (L_{bf}) and frequency (f) and distance (d) is shown in (1), where L_{bf} in dB, f in MHz and d in km.

$$S_i(dbm) = -174 + 10\log B + NF + (S/N)_o \tag{2}$$

The relationship between receiver sensitivity (S_i) and thermal noise (NF), bandwidth (B), and output signal-to-noise ratio of the receiver ($(S/N)_o$) is shown in (2), when phase noise is not considered in a non-spread spectrum system. In the above formula, B is in Hz.

$$P_t - L_{bf} = S_i(dbm) \tag{3}$$

In (3), P_t represents the transmit power. By combining (1), (2) and (3), it can be concluded that when d is need to be doubled, we can only reduce B by four times to make the equation tenable. In the extreme case that two neighbor cluster heads still cannot communicate after expanding the scope of communication, a member node between the two cluster heads is designated to forward the TC messages. In this way, the information within the cluster can be extended to the whole network.

3 Cross-Layer Protocol Design

When the protocol is designed in this paper, the TDMA mechanism is used to divide the time into time frame cycles. As shown in Fig. 2, each time frame cycle is T which includes a neighbor node discovery period T_1 and a data transmission period T_2.

The hexagon is divided into 6 equilateral triangles, and the neighbor node discovery period is correspondingly divided into 6 time slots. The nodes with different indexes take different time slots to transmit hello messages, which are used for neighbor node discovery. For the data transmission phase, the TC messages and the data messages share the same wireless channel, and communication collision can be reduced by CSMA/CA. Meanwhile, handshake mechanism is required before point-to-point data transmission. In order to achieve effective wireless shared channel, refer to the IEEE 802.11 protocol, the node first uses the RTS/CTS to perform control channel reservation. After the reservation is successful, data transmission can be carried out, and the reliability of the network can be ensured through the DATA/ACK process. The flow chart for each node is shown in Fig. 3.

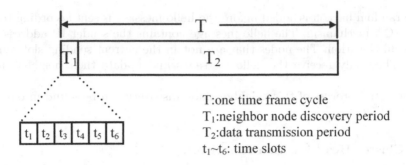

T: one time frame cycle
T_1: neighbor node discovery period
T_2: data transmission period
$t_1 \sim t_6$: time slots

Fig. 2. TDMA frame allocation

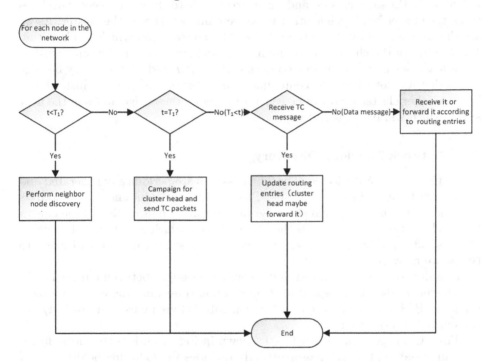

Fig. 3. The flow chart for each node in a cycle

3.1 Neighbor Node Discovery

Neighbor nodes of a node refer to nodes within the communication range of the node. In the phase of neighbor node discovery, the nodes send hello messages according to the time frame corresponding to their geographic location. The hello messages are generated and sent only during the discovery phase of the neighboring node. There is no re-transmission mechanism. If it is not sent within the specified neighbor discovery time, discard will be happen. In order to reduce communication collisions when multiple nodes send messages at the same time slot, a random backoff is added before the hello message is sent according to the CSMA/CA mechanism. The hello message contains the sender IP address and geographic location. The nodes that are not in the current sending slot remain silent. They only receive the hello messages and update their neighbor node tables.

The detail process of this neighbor node discovery can be found in our previous work [21].

3.2   Cluster Head Election Algorithm

After six time slots, each node locally compares its own location with that of its neighbors in the same cluster, and the nearest node to the cluster center declares to be the cluster head. While other nodes remain members in the cluster. As we set the communication range to be $3/2R$, the cluster head which locals within $1/2R$ radius of the cluster can communicate with any node in the same cluster. For a few cases where there are no nodes within $1/2R$ radius, there may be edge nodes that are not within the communication range of the selected cluster head. Then another cluster head will be generated among these edge nodes in the next stage, which will be explained later.

3.3   Network Topology Discovery

When the clusters are selected, The TC messages are periodically generated and broadcast through the cluster heads. The TC message contains the IP address of all nodes in the cluster and the geographic location information of the cluster head. The cluster head forwards the TC messages, which are produced by other clusters, after receiving them, so that the TC messages can be broadcasted to the entire network.

In order to facilitate sending and receiving messages between cluster heads, the cluster heads use low speed for transmission to expand the communication range. In HCPT protocol, the transmission rate between cluster heads is $1/4$ of the normal transmission rate.

The TC message frame structure is shown in Fig. 4. Besides the intra-cluster node information, the TC message mainly includes the following fields:

Type: Used to indicate the message type, such as TC message, 8-bit storage.

Packet length: Used to indicate the total length of the packet, in bytes, 8-bit storage.

Seq (Message Sequence Number): Used to identify the old and new messages to ensure that the message will not be forwarded twice by the same node. Each time there is a new message, the sequence number is increased by 1, 8-bit storage.

Vtime: Used to indicate the effective time of the message, 8-bit storage.

TTL: Used to indicate the maximum number of hops that the message will be sent. The TTL must be decremented by 1 before the message is forwarded. When a node receives a message with a TTL equal to 0 or 1, the message cannot be forwarded under any circumstances. The flood radius can be limited by setting this field.

Type	Packet length	Seq	Vtime
TTL	Hop count	Reserved	
Source node(cluster head) IP address			
Source node(cluster head) geographic location information			
IP address of node 1 in the cluster			
IP address of node 2 in the cluster			
......			

Fig. 4. TC message frame structure

Hop count: Initialized to 0. This field contains the number of hops the message has reached and is incremented by 1 before the message is forwarded.

After receiving the TC message in the cluster, if the member node finds that the node information in the cluster of the TC message does not contain itself, that means that the node is an edge node. Among all edge nodes in the cluster, the nearest edge node to the cluster center will become a new cluster head. The information of its neighbor nodes in this cluster, which is not included in the received TC message, is packaged and broadcast to the whole network through the new generated TC message. The whole process of cluster head election is detailed in Table 1 and Algorithm 1.

The TC messages are forwarded and flooded between cluster heads. After the cluster heads receive all the topology information sent by other cluster heads in the network, the topology information of the entire network can be obtained. The non-cluster head nodes of the whole network only receive the TC messages, process the data without forwarding, and use the update information to acquire the state of the current network. The process flow of TC messages is shown in Fig. 5. After completing topology discovery and real-time update, all nodes know the geographic location and information of the cluster heads of the whole network, and know in which cluster the other nodes are. In this way, it is not necessary to know the geographic location of all nodes in the entire network, so the size of the TC messages is reduced, which reduces the overhead of topology discovery and maintenance.

3.4 Route Establishment

During the process of neighbor node discovery, each node knows the geographic location of its neighbor nodes through the exchange of the hello messages. Then through the broadcasting of the TC messages, the specific location of the cluster head and the information of which cluster the nodes belong to are obtained.

After obtaining the above geographic location information, how to select the next hop more effectively is an important part of routing discovery. In HCPT, a packet forwarding strategy based on cluster head location information is designed. When there is a data transmission request, the node searches

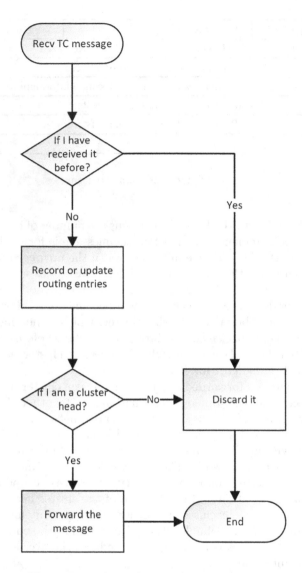

Fig. 5. Processing after receiving TC messages

Table 1. Major parameters of cluster head election algorithm

Parameters	Explanation
$own\_distance\_to\_center$	Distance from the node to the cluster center
own_ID	Node's own ID number
nb_sum	The total number of neighbor nodes in this cluster
$nb\_distance\_to\_center[i]$	Distance from neighbor node i to cluster center
$nb\_ID[i]$	The ID number of neighbor node i in the Cluster
$min\_distance\_to\_center$	The shortest distance from node in the cluster to the cluster center
$cluster\_ID$	Cluster head ID number calculated by the node

Algorithm 1. Cluster Head Election Algorithm
___
1: After neighbor node discovery, each node in the network starts cluster head algorithm;
2: $min\_distance\_to\_center = own\_distance\_to\_center$;
3: $cluster\_ID = own\_ID$;
4: **for** each $i \in [1, nb\_sum]$ **do**
5:     **if** $nb\_distance\_to\_center[i] < min\_distance\_to\_center$ **then**
6:         $min\_distance\_to\_center = nb\_distance\_to\_center[i]$;
7:         $cluster\_ID = nb\_ID[i]$;
8:     **end if**
9: **end for**
10: **if** $cluster\_ID == own\_ID$ **then**
11:     //It shows that the node is a cluster head;
12:     Send TC messages;
13: **else**
14:     **if** receive TC message from node j of own cluster **then**
15:         **if** $j == cluster\_ID$ **then**
16:             Become an ordinary member of the cluster;
17:         **else**
18:             //It shows that the node is an edge node;
19:             **if** The node is nearest to the cluster center in the edge nodes **then**
20:                 Become a new cluster head in edge nodes and send TC messages;
21:             **else**
22:                 Become an ordinary member of the cluster;
23:             **end if**
24:         **end if**
25:     **else**
26:         //TC packets from other clusters are not processed in this function;
27:     **end if**
28: **end if**
___

the cluster head location of the destination node, and then combines the greedy principle to select the neighbor node closest to this cluster head as the next hop. For the last-hop node, if the destination node happens to be the neighbor node of the current node, the data can be sent directly to the destination node without forwarding through the cluster head of the destination node.

The greedy routing transmission process in the HCPT is shown in Fig. 6. The source node is S, the destination node is D, and the node H is the cluster head of the cluster where the destination node D is located. The dotted circles in the graph represent the maximum data communication coverage of the center node of the circle. All the nodes in the circle are the candidates of the next hop for the center node.

As shown in Fig. 6, node S will uses greedy forwarding strategy to select the node M, which is nearest to H, as its next hop relay node. When the data packet is forwarded to M, M also selects the neighbor node N, which is closest to H, to forward the data packet according to the greedy principle. After successfully receiving the data packet, N searches its neighbor node list and finds that the

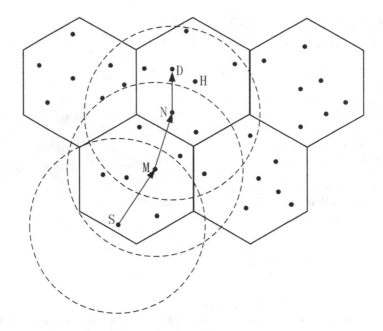

Fig. 6. Example of greedy forwarding

destination node D is reachable. Then the packet is directly transmitted to the node D.

When the distance from the neighbor node to the destination node is farther than the distance from the current node to the destination node, and the current node to the destination node is unreachable, greedy forwarding is no longer applicable. At this point, the peripheral forwarding mode is triggered to search for new routes along the perimeter of the void area using the right-hand rule [22].

After bypassing the void area, the routing policy will automatically switch back to the greedy forwarding mode again. This forwarding will continue until the packet is successfully sent to the destination node. If the nodes are evenly distributed and tightly connected, the void area is hardly to occur. In the network scenario where the nodes are sparse, the peripheral forwarding mode is used to solve the problem. Therefore, this can adapt to the dynamic changes of the communication network.

In HCPT, by selecting the neighbor node closest to the cluster head of the destination node as the relay node, data packets are forwarded hop-by-hop, which can make the hop count of selected path to be the shortest one. Therefore, a smaller end-to-end delay can be obtained. Moreover, since the nodes only need to maintain the information of their neighboring nodes and the specific locations of all cluster heads, the performance will not be degraded due to the frequent breakage of the link. Thus, the routing overhead and the time for establishing the route in the network are reduced.

4   Simulation Results and Analysis

The Network Simulator 2 (NS2) software is used for network simulations. When the simulation runs, the node discovery for the whole network is conducted first, followed by data transmission. This section first gives the efficiency of network topology discovery of HCPT, and then gives the overall network performance of HCPT.

4.1   Topology Discovery Efficiency

In order to obtain the performance of network topology discovery of HCPT, we selected the proactive routing OLSR for comparison. The simulated network environment of OLSR and HCPT is the same, and we take the topology discovery every two seconds, which means the time frame cycle $T = 2$ s.

The following is the simulation scenario: 20 nodes are randomly distributed within a square of 500 m × 500 m, the wireless transmission distance D_t is 250 m, the neighbor node discovery period T_1 is 60 ms, the radius of hexagonal cellular is set to 166.7 m, and the unlisted parameters are set to the default value in NS2.

Figure 7 shows the ratio of node discovery in HCPT and OLSR. As can be seen from the figure, within the first 2 s, the HCPT can discover 89% of nodes while OLSR can only discover 19% of nodes. And the HCPT can discover all nodes in about 2.2 s, but OLSR needs about 5.2 s. This is because in HCPT protocol, as shown in Figs. 1 and 2, the neighbor discovery is divided into 6 time slots by location, and the hello messages are sent in specific time slots, which greatly improves the transmission success rate of the hello messages. After that, the cluster heads send and forward the TC messages so that the node information is broadcast to the whole network quickly.

In OLSR protocol, hello messages and TC messages are generated simultaneously at the beginning of each time frame cycle. At the beginning, for the information collected by the MPRs is insufficient, the information sent by the TC messages is less effective, the rate of node discovery is slow. Later, when the MPRs have collected enough node information, the rate of node discovery begins to improve. When the new cycle arrives, the packages of the previous cycle may still have not been sent, so the rising phase of the OLSR curve will be postponed accordingly.

In summary, compared to OLSR, the HCPT can discover the entire network topology more efficiently.

4.2   Overall Network Performance

In this section, we compare the overall performance of the cross-layer HCPT protocol with that of the standard OLSR and the newly improved OLSR algorithm [8]. The simulations run for 100 s and apply Constant Bit Rate (CBR) sources which send packets with the length of 512 bytes every 100 ms. The moving speed of nodes is changed from 1 m/s to 6 m/s, MAC layer is applied by

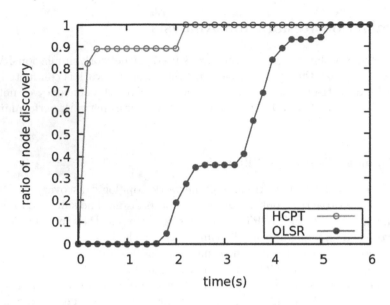

Fig. 7. Ratio of node discovery in the whole network

IEEE 802.11, and other simulation parameters are the same as the section A. The following performance metrics are evaluated.

Packet Delivery Ratio (PDR): The ratio of number of data packets successfully delivered to the destination to the number of data packets generated by the sources.

Average End-to-End Delay (AEED): The ratio of the sum of transmission packet delays to the number of successfully received packets.

Network Routing Load (NRL): The ratio of the total number of routing packets transmitted to the total number of data packets delivered.

The routing overhead of HCPT, OLSR, and the improved OLSR algorithm proposed by N. Harrag are giving in Fig. 8. We can see from Fig. 8 that The NRL of HCPT proposed in this paper and the improved OLSR algorithm proposed by N. Harrag are greatly improved compared with that of the traditional OLSR. The performance of HCPT is even slightly better than that of N. Harrag's algorithm. His scheme is to control the overhead by adaptively changing the transmission interval of hello messages, while HCPT in this paper is to reduce the overhead by reducing the number of TC messages and the size of TC messages at the same time. This is because the TC messages are generated and forwarded by the cluster heads in HCPT, while in OLSR the TC messages are generated and forwarded by MPRs. In a same network, the number of cluster heads is much smaller than that of MPRs. Meanwhile, The TC message only contains the IP address of all nodes in the cluster and the geographic location information of the cluster head, which reduces the size of the message.

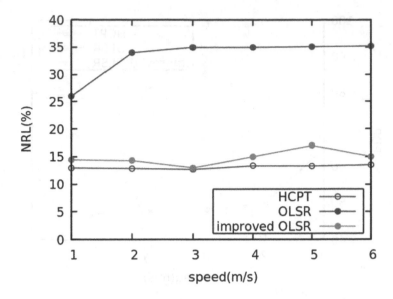

Fig. 8. NRL vs. speed

Figure 9 presents the relationship between the PDR and the speed. From Fig. 9, we can see that the PDR of HCPT is much superior to the traditional OLSR and the improved OLSR. HCPT can maintain a high level of PDR when the node moves at a slower speed. As the speed of node movement increases, although the PDR of HCPT has decreased, it still maintains a great advantage compared with the other two protocols. This excellent performance should owe to the time slot mechanism during the neighbor node discovery period and the TC messages only broadcasting within cluster heads in HCPT. By the time slot mechanism, the collisions between the hello messages are avoided as much as possible. Moreover, the network topology discovery based on the cluster head mechanism has smaller routing overhead, and the greedy principle forwarding mechanism based on the geographic location assistance can more effectively select the next relay node to transmit the data packet. However, in such a dense network scenario, the other two algorithms suffer from a large number of packet loss due to collisions between nodes, which leads to a decrease in the efficiency of network topology discovery, and results in a large number of packet losses.

Figure 10 shows the AEED vs. speed. In Fig. 10, the delay of HCPT is slightly larger than that of the other two protocols, but this is due to the high delivery rate. Because high delivery rate means more data links are successfully established. For the other two protocols, when there is a data transmission request between two distant nodes, the link establishment may not be successful, and the links successfully established in the network are almost shorter links, which bring a smaller average delay. For the HCPT protocol, when the moving speed increases, the topology changes faster, so the information of the neighbor node

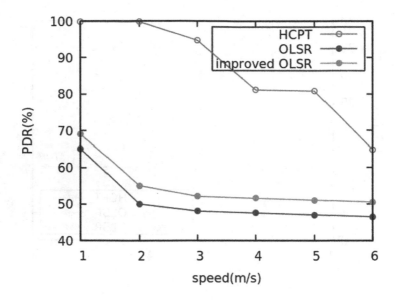

Fig. 9. PDR vs. speed

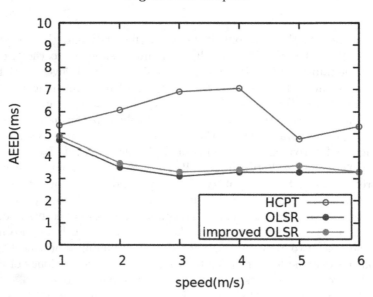

Fig. 10. AEED vs. speed

stored may not be updated in time. This will also lead to the unsuccessful establishment of part of the long link, so the average delay decreases as the moving
speed increases from 4 m/s to 5 m/s.

5   Conclusion

In this paper, we propose a clustered cross-layer protocol named HCPT based on hexagonal clustering and time slot. By simplifying the content of the TC messages and forwarding the TC messages using the cluster heads, the network overhead is reduced, and the network topology discovery rate is improved. Compared with the topology discovery of proactive routing OLSR, HCPT can discover the whole network topology more effectively. Compared with the overall performance of standard OLSR and the improved OLSR algorithm proposed by N. Harrag, the HCPT has smaller network routing load and higher packet delivery ratio.

References

1. Vinay, S., Honnalli, S.B., Varaprasad, G.: Multipath source routing protocol for mobile adhoc networks with performance effective analysis. In: 2018 Second International Conference on Inventive Communication and Computational Technologies (ICICCT), Coimbatore, pp. 41–44 (2018). https://doi.org/10.1109/ICICCT.2018.8473258
2. Sultana, J., Ahmed, T.: Securing AOMDV protocol in mobile adhoc network with elliptic curve cryptography. In: 2017 International Conference on Electrical, Computer and Communication Engineering (ECCE), Cox's Bazar, pp. 539–543 (2017). https://doi.org/10.1109/ECACE.2017.7912964
3. Gadekar, S., Kadam, S.: Secure optimized link state routing (OLSR) protocol against node isolation attack. In: 2017 IEEE International Conference on Power, Control, Signals and Instrumentation Engineering (ICPCSI), Chennai, pp. 684–687 (2017). https://doi.org/10.1109/ICPCSI.2017.8391800
4. Karaca, M., Bastani, S., Landfeldt, B.: Modifying backoff freezing mechanism to optimize dense IEEE 802.11 networks. IEEE Trans. Veh. Technol. **66**, 9470–9482 (2017). https://doi.org/10.1109/TVT.2017.2705343
5. Lin, C., Cai, X., Su, Y., Ni, P., Shi, H.: A dynamic slot assignment algorithm of TDMA for the distribution class protocol using node neighborhood information. In: 2017 11th IEEE International Conference on Anti-counterfeiting, Security, and Identification (ASID), Xiamen, pp. 138–141 (2017). https://doi.org/10.1109/ICASID.2017.8285760
6. Naguib, A., Saad, W., Shokair, M.: Remaining energy aware ML-CSMA/TDMA hybrid MAC protocol for LTE-M2M wireless network. In: 2019 International Conference on Innovative Trends in Computer Engineering (ITCE), Aswan, Egypt, pp. 322–327 (2019). https://doi.org/10.1109/ITCE.2019.8646538
7. Chbib, F., Khalil, A., Fahs, W., Chbib, R., Raad, A.: Improvement of OLSR protocol by using bacis up MPR and routing table mechanisms. In: 2018 International Arab Conference on Information Technology (ACIT), Werdanye, Lebanon, pp. 1–6 (2018). https://doi.org/10.1109/ACIT.2018.8672716
8. Harrag, N., Refoufi, A., Harrag, A.: Neighbor discovery using novel DE-based adaptive hello messaging scheme improving OLSR routing protocol performances. In: 2017 6th International Conference on Systems and Control (ICSC), Batna, pp. 308-312 (2017). https://doi.org/10.1109/ICoSC.2017.7958731

9. Jiang, Y., Mi, Z., Wang, H., Wang, X., Zhao, N.: The experiment and performance analysis of multi-node UAV ad hoc network based on swarm tactics. In: 2018 10th International Conference on Wireless Communications and Signal Processing (WCSP), Hangzhou, pp. 1–6 (2018). https://doi.org/10.1109/WCSP.2018.8555914

10. Liu, K., Niu, K.: A hybrid relay node selection strategy for VANET routing. In: 2017 IEEE/CIC International Conference on Communications in China (ICCC), Qingdao, pp. 1–6 (2017). https://doi.org/10.1109/ICCChina.2017.8330400

11. Zhang, L., Guo, J.: A vector-based improved geographic information routing protocol. In: 2017 7th IEEE International Conference on Electronics Information and Emergency Communication (ICEIEC), Macau, pp. 421–424 (2017). https://doi.org/10.1109/ICEIEC.2017.8076596

12. Al-shugran, M.A., Shqier, M.M.A., Jaradat, G.M.: Adaptive dynamic update for greedy routing protocol using fuzzy logic controller and mobility prediction. In: 2018 IEEE International Conference on Electro/Information Technology (EIT), Rochester, MI, pp. 0852–0857 (2018). https://doi.org/10.1109/EIT.2018.8500126

13. Qin, X., Wang, T., Zhang, B.: An efficient location based localized broadcasting algorithm for wireless ad hoc and sensor networks. In: 2018 10th International Conference on Wireless Communications and Signal Processing (WCSP), Hangzhou, pp. 1–6 (2018). https://doi.org/10.1109/WCSP.2018.8555530

14. Savalkar, V.A.: Link prediction for identifying link failure using cross layer approach. In: 2018 2nd International Conference on Inventive Systems and Control (ICISC), Coimbatore, pp. 1120–1129 (2018). https://doi.org/10.1109/ICISC.2018.8398978

15. Peng, J., Niu, H., Huang, W., Yin, X., Jiang, Y.: Cross layer design and optimization for multi-hop ad hoc networks. In: IEEE 2nd Advanced Information Technology, Electronic and Automation Control Conference (IAEAC). Chongqing, pp. 1678–1682 (2017). https://doi.org/10.1109/IAEAC.2017.8054300

16. Kanthimathi, S., Jhansi Rani, P.: Defending against packet dropping attacks in wireless adhoc networks using cluster based trust entropy. In: 2018 International Conference on Advances in Computing, Communications and Informatics (ICACCI), Bangalore, pp. 2447–2452 (2018). https://doi.org/10.1109/ICACCI.2018.8554751

17. Liu, D., Zhou, Q., Zhang, Z., Liu, B.: Cluster-based energy-efficient transmission using a new hybrid compressed sensing in WSN. In: 2016 IEEE Conference on Computer Communications Workshops (INFOCOM WKSHPS), San Francisco, CA, 2016, pp. 372–376 (2016). https://doi.org/10.1109/INFOCOMW.2016.7562104

18. Sharma, S., Choudhary, H.: Optimal deployment of mobile sensors nodes using signal strength equalization. In: 2018 IEEE International Students' Conference on Electrical, Electronics and Computer Science (SCEECS), Bhopal, pp. 1–6 (2018). https://doi.org/10.1109/SCEECS.2018.8546990

19. IEEE802.11n, Standard for information technology. Part 11: Wireless LAN Medium Access Control (MAC) and Physical Layer (PHY) - Amendment: Enhancements for Higher Throughput (2009)

20. Lee, J.S., Miller, L.E.: CDMA Systems Engineering Handbook (1998)

21. Wang, Q., He, X., Chen, N.: A cross-layer neighbor discovery algorithm in ad hoc networks based on hexagonal clustering and GPS. In: 6th Annual 2018 International Conference on Geo-Spatial Knowledge and Intelligence (2019). https://doi.org/10.1088/1755-1315/234/1/012050

22. Yang, X., Li, M., Qian, Z., Di, T.: Improvement of GPSR protocol in vehicular ad hoc network. IEEE Access **6**, 39515–39524 (2018). https://doi.org/10.1109/ACCESS.2018.2853112

A Cluster-Based Small Cell On/Off Scheme for Energy Efficiency Optimization in Ultra-Dense Networks

Cui-Qin Dai[1][(✉)], Biao Fu[1], and Qianbin Chen[2]

[1] School of Communication and Information Engineering,
Chongqing University of Posts and Telecommunications, Chongqing, China
daicq@cqupt.edu.cn, fub_b@qq.com
[2] Chongqing Key Lab of Mobile Communication Technology,
Chongqing University of Posts and Telecommunications, Chongqing, China
chenqb@cqupt.edu.cn

Abstract. Ultra-Dense Networks (UDN) can greatly meet the demand for explosively growing data traffic via deploying small cells (SCs) densely. However, the SCs densification causes higher energy consumption and more severe inter-cell interference (ICI). The SC on/off control is one of the effective ways to solve above problems, but the challenge is to maintain network coverage while avoiding degradation of the quality of service (QoS) of user equipment (UEs). In this paper, we formulate energy efficiency (EE) optimization problem in stochastic geometry-based network and take into consideration the QoS of UEs and ICI to maximize the EE. The solution is obtained by dividing the problem into SCs clustering and intra-cluster SC on/off control. We first use an improved K-means clustering algorithm to divide the dense SCs into disjoint clusters according to the distance and density of SCs. Then, within each cluster, selecting a SC as the cluster head (CH) is responsible for performing SC on/off operations under taking minimum rate of UEs and ICI as constraints. In addition, a heuristic search algorithm (HSA) is proposed for the intra-cluster SC on/off control. Simulation results demonstrate that the proposed scheme can effectively improve the network energy efficiency and suppress interference.

Keywords: UDN · Small cell on/off · Clustering · Energy efficiency

1 Introduction

With the proliferation of smart mobile devices and the development of real-time video streaming applications, a tremendous pressure on cellular networks has been put by the increasing capacity demands and explosive data traffic in the past decade [1, 2]. As a feasible solution, Ultra-Dense Networks (UDN) are envisioned to deal with the significantly increasing network capacity and data traffic problem via densifying communications infrastructure, viz., intensive deployment of the low-cost and low-power small cells (SCs) in hotspots (e.g., stadiums, airports, train stations, etc.) [3].

© ICST Institute for Computer Sciences, Social Informatics and Telecommunications Engineering 2020
Published by Springer Nature Switzerland AG 2020. All Rights Reserved
H. Gao et al. (Eds.): ChinaCom 2019, LNICST 312, pp. 385–401, 2020.
https://doi.org/10.1007/978-3-030-41114-5_29

In UDN, the density of SCs is significantly increased. On one hand, this shortens the communication distance between the user equipment (UEs) and the base station to improve signal quality. On the other hand, this can spatially reuse the spectrum to increase capacity. However, with the densification of SCs, some problems in UDN arise such as redundant SCs energy consumption [4], the severe mutual interference between SCs [5] and limited backhaul capacity [6]. Among them, improving the energy efficiency (EE) of UDN by reducing energy consumption and interference has become the focus of research. Study in [7] has shown that the operation of SCs accounts for 60%–80% total energy consumption of network. As a result, all the SCs in the network remain open will waste a lot of energy as well as resulting in EE reduction. Moreover, the performance regimes in dense small cellular networks will gradually transition from noise-limited to dense interference-limited [8], which may further degrade the EE of UDN.

As an effective approach, SC on/off scheme (also known as SC sleep control) is used to save energy and promote EE [9]. It can turn off some specific SCs and traffic load of the sleeping SCs can transfer to neighbor SCs, which has shown that SC on/off mechanisms have great potential by reducing SCs' static power consumption [10]. However, when some SCs enter the sleep state, the average number of connections of active SCs will increase, which reduces the bandwidth obtained by the UEs and affects the QoS [11]. Therefore, many existing literatures have been devoted to studying the feasibility of SC on/off operation under QoS constraints. In [12], a random sleeping policy and a strategic sleeping policy based on multilevel sleep modes in heterogeneous cellular network were proposed to optimize EE. A strategic SCs sleeping mechanism according to the traffic demand was proposed in [13] to achieve energy saving, in which UEs associated with SCs in sleep close to the macro base station coverage area would be handed over to the macro-cell. Enhanced small inter-cell interference coordination was used to avoid QoS degradation. In [14] proposed a distributed SC on/off scheme that regularly checking the traffic load level and making sleep decisions under the constraints of QoS.

In addition, the number of possible the SC on/off combination grows exponentially with the number of SCs. So, some researches have focused on reducing the computational complexity of SC on/off operations [15–19]. The clustering approach was considered in [15, 16] to reduce the complexity of SC on/off. In [15], the locally coupled SCs was first grouped into clusters based on location and traffic load, and then the on/off algorithm was performed by local information in the cluster, wherein the SC with low traffic load was selected as the cluster head (CH). Another example is [16]. The difference is that it formed all SCs into a graph and then cut it into clusters. In [17], network-impact was introduced to decide to turn off SCs that minimize the increase in their neighbor load, in which SCs got turned on/off one by one. The author of [18] solved the energy-saving problem of SC on/off in two steps. It first adjusted the transmission power of active SCs and then introduced a state transition graph to reduce the switching cost incurred by the on/off. A single Q-Learning based probabilistic policy was proposed in [19] to obtain the optimal on/off switch policy, but this approach needs a long time for exploration, so as to get the optimal pattern. While these interesting efforts can effectively reduce complexity and power consumption, they lack the consideration of inter-cell interference (ICI) during SC on/off operations.

Therefore, we propose a cluster-based small cell on/off scheme in this paper to improve EE and mitigate ICI for UDN with low complexity. First of all, considering the increased network size of the UDN leads to more irregular coverage, we introduce stochastic geometry [20, 21] to capture the more realistic location distribution of the SCs and UEs. Then, a modified K-means clustering algorithm is proposed based on the distribution location of SCs. It can dynamically adjust the size of SCs clusters according to the density of SCs. After forming SCs clusters, one SC, in each cluster, is elected as a cluster CH and performs SC on/off scheme in its cluster to facilitate the reduction of signaling interactions. Finally, a heuristic search algorithm (HSA) is proposed for the intra-cluster SC on/off phase, which can be turned off without sacrificing the QoS requirements of UEs. The main contributions of this paper can be summarized as follows:

(1) *Proposed a modified clustering algorithm in UDN:* We divide UDN into disjoint sub-area, which can classify NP-hard problem into many manageable sub-problems. Although performing SC on/off in each sub-area is still NP-hard, it can reduce the search space. Moreover, it can adaptively form clusters according to the location distribution of SCs to simplify the topology of the UDN.
(2) *Reduced the complexity of SC on/off with HSA:* Based on the clustering results, each CH performs SC on/off scheme with QoS requirements of UEs and the interference constraints between SCs. The HSA is proposed to avoid the exponential complexity associated with obtaining the optimal SC on/off combination by exhaustive search. Furthermore, we also analyze the complexity of our scheme.

The remainder of this paper is organized as follows. Section 2 introduces the system model and gives the detailed problem formulation. In Sect. 3, we propose a SC on/off scheme based on clustering and theoretically analyze the complexity of our scheme. This is follow by the simulation experiments and performance analysis in Sect. 4. Section 5 concludes this paper with a summary. Also, the key notations and nomenclature used in the paper are listed in Table 1.

Table 1. List of key notations and nomenclature

Symbol	Explanation
UDN	Ultra-Dense Networks
PPP	Poisson Point Process
CH	Cluster Head
QoS	Quality of Service
Ψ_b	The set of SCs
Ψ_u	The set of UEs
ρ_{b_m}	The load of SC b_m
c_l	The l-th SC cluster
U_{c_l}	The set of UEs in cluster c_l
ε_{b_m}	The set of neighborhoods of SC b_m
γ_{b_m}	The density of SC b_m

2 System Model and Problem Formulation

2.1 System Model

We consider an UDN which are distributed according to a homogeneous PPP in a finite two-dimensional plane $\Re^2$. Specifically, we use a homogeneous PPP with the density of λ_b to simulate the location distribution of SCs in the network and denoted by the set $\Psi_b = \{b_1, b_2, \cdots, b_m\}$. Similarly, the location distribution randomly of single-antenna UEs are modeled as a homogeneous PPP $\Psi_u = \{u_1, u_2, \cdots, u_n\}$ with the density of λ_u. Each UE is connected with SCs according to the closest distances while all other SCs act as interferers, thus the coverage areas of SCs comprise a Voronoi tessellation on the plane [21]. Due to the independent distribution of SCs and UEs and the coverage area of each SC, some SCs may have no users, which is called void cell [22]. Figure 1 shows an example of such a network.

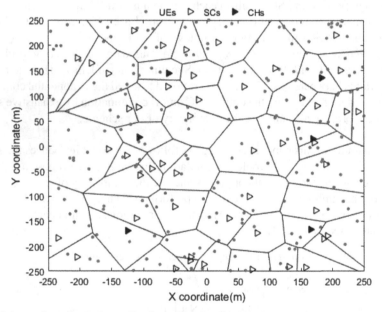

Fig. 1. A layout based on Poisson distributed small cells (SCs), user equipment (UEs) and cluster heads (CHs) on a 500 m * 500 m plane, with cell boundaries corresponding to a Voronoi tessellation.

To reduce energy consumption and co-tier interference in the UDN, each SC can be switched between working and sleeping. We use the set $X = \{x_{b_m}, \forall b_m \in \Psi_b\}$ to indicate the two different status of all SCs, where the binary variable $x_{b_m} = \{0, 1\}$, which is 0 if sleep mode and 1 if active mode. Assume all SCs transmit at a fixed power P_{tx}, then, the received signal strength of UE u_n from SC b_m is determined by:

$$S^r_{b_m, u_n} = x_{b_m} P_{tx} h_{b_m, u_n} d^{-\alpha}_{b_m, u_n} \tag{1}$$

where, h_{b_m, u_n} is an exponential random variable with mean 1 incorporating the effect of Rayleigh fading, d_{b_m, u_n} is the distance between the UE u_n and the SC b_m, and α is the path loss factor of SCs, generally $\alpha > 2$[20]. Then, the downlink Signal to Interference plus Noise Ratio (SINR) of UE u_n associated with SC b_m can be defined as in [18] as:

$$SINR_{b_m,u_n} = \frac{S^r_{b_m,u_n}}{\sum_{b_i \in \psi_b \setminus \{b_m\}} S^r_{b_i,u_n} + \sigma^2} \tag{2}$$

where σ^2 is the noise power. According to the Shannon capacity, the achievable data rate of UE u_n associating with SC b_m is given by:

$$R_{b_m,u_n} = y_{b_m,u_n} W_{RB} \log_2(1 + SINR_{b_m,u_n}) \tag{3}$$

where y_{b_m,u_n} indicates the number of resource block (RB) required to meet the QoS of the UE u_n associated with SC b_m, W_{RB} represents the bandwidth per RB. Therefore, the number of RB required for the SC b_m to meet the minimum rate requirement of the UE u_n can be written as:

$$y_{b_m,u_n} = \left\lceil \frac{R_{\min}}{W_{RB} \log_2(1 + SINR_{b_m,u_n})} \right\rceil \tag{4}$$

Therefore, the SC should assign a certain amount of resources according to UEs' service rate for guarantee the QoS. Thus, the load of the SC b_m can defined as the fraction of serving UEs resources to total resources:

$$\rho_{b_m} = \frac{\sum_{u_j \in \zeta_{b_m}} y_{b_m,u_j}}{RB^{total}_{b_m}} \tag{5}$$

where ζ_{b_m} represents the set of UEs associated with the SC b_m.

2.2 Problem Formulation

When no UEs are associated with the SC, the SC will enter sleep mode to save energy [22]. Not only that, our scheme will close the empty SC and then close the SCs with light load and heavy interference. Therefore, we discuss the problem of turn off those SCs to achieve more energy savings while ensuring the QoS of UEs. That is to find the best combination of SC on/off to maximize the EE, the EE maximization problem is computed as:

$$\max_{x,y} \left(\frac{\sum_{m=1}^{|\Psi_b|} x_{b_m} \sum_{u_j \in \zeta_{b_m}} R_{b_m,u_j}}{P_{total}} \right) \tag{6}$$

where P_{total} is the total power consumption of the entire network. The energy consumption of SCs are usually composed of power amplifiers, radio frequency circuit, power supplies and other power components according to the power consumption model descriptions in [14] and [18]. We divide the SCs power consumption P_{b_m} into dynamic power $P^{dy}_{b_m}$ and static power $P^{st}_{b_m}$, the total power consumption P_{total} can be calculated as:

$$P_{total} = \sum_{m=1}^{|\Psi_b|} P_{b_m} = \sum_{m=1}^{|\Psi_b|} P^{dy}_{b_m} + \sum_{m=1}^{|\Psi_b|} P^{st}_{b_m} \tag{7}$$

where the static power consumption includes fixed power consumption P_{fix} when SC is on and sleeping power consumption P_{off} when it is off. The dynamic power consumption consists of transmission power consumption and switching power consumption P^{sw}. Then, the power consumption and the power of each part of SC b_m can be expressed as:

$$P_{b_m}^{dy} = P_{b_m}^{sw} + x_{b_m} \partial_{b_m} \rho_{b_m} P_{tx} \tag{8}$$

$$P_{b_m}^{st} = x_{b_m} P_{fix} + (1 - x_{b_m}) P_{off} \tag{9}$$

$$P_{b_m} = x_{b_m}(P_{fix} + \partial_{b_m} \rho_{b_m} P_{tx}) + (1 - x_{b_m}) P_{off} + P_{b_m}^{sw} \tag{10}$$

where ∂_{b_m} is the power amplifier efficiency. P_{fix} and P_{off} respectively indicate the fixed power consumption when SC is turned on and off. $P_{b_m}^{sw}$ is the switching power consumption that can be regarded as the signal processing of the UEs when the SCs perform the switching operation [18]. Since the SC switching operation needs to ensure the QoS for each UE, the switching power consumption can be expressed a linear:

$$P_{b_m}^{sw} = (1 - x_{b_m})|\zeta_{b_m}|P_o \tag{11}$$

where P_o is the power consumption that handles each UE re-associate to other SCs. Since given that the number of RB is a ceil integer and assume that the QoS can be maintained as long as the minimum throughput by each UE can be satisfied, we roughly consider the whole network throughput as a constant value and minimize network energy consumption and the number of required RBs while meeting users' the minimum demanded data rate to solve (6). The mathematical expression that minimizes problem η can be written as:

$$
\begin{aligned}
&\min \sum_{b_m \in \Psi_b} \sum_{u_n \in \Psi_n} \left(\mu_b P_{b_m} + \phi_b y_{b_m, u_n} k_{b_m, u_n} \right) \\
&s.t.\ \text{C1}: \sum_{b_m \in \Psi_b} k_{b_m, u_n} = 1,\ \forall u_n \in \Psi_u \\
&\text{C2}: \sum_{u_n \in \Psi_u} k_{b_m, u_n} \cdot y_{b_m, u_n} \leq RB_{b_m}^{total},\ \forall b_m \in \Psi_b \\
&\text{C3}: k_{b_m, u_n} \cdot R_{b_m, u_n} \geq R_{\min},\ \forall u_n \in \Psi_u \\
&\text{C4}: k_{b_m, u_n} = \{0, 1\},\ \forall b_m \in \Psi_b, \forall u_n \in \Psi_u \\
&\text{C5}: x_{b_m} = \{0, 1\},\ \forall b_m \in \Psi_b
\end{aligned}
\tag{12}
$$

where k_{b_m, u_n} is an indicator of the associated status. If UE u_n is served by SC b_m, there is $k_{b_m, u_n} = 1$, otherwise $k_{b_m, u_n} = 0$. μ_b and ϕ_b are the weight parameters that indicate the impact of energy consumption and RB on the problem. Constraint C1 determines that each UE can only be associated with one SC. Constraint C2 indicates that the UEs connected to the SC should not exceed the capacity of the SC. Constraint C3 ensures QoS for each UE. Note that the objective that minimize energy consumption and reduce the number of required RBs by selecting SCs among all the SCs to be turned on or off is a combination problem, which requires extremely high computational complexity in exhaustive combinational search for the optimal solution.

3 The Cluster-Based Small Cell On/Off Scheme

3.1 Overview

Network-level coordination in the UDN to determine the best SC on/off combination to address problem (12) is usually NP-hard and is nearly impossible to solve with a central controller for global optimization [4]. This solution in a fully centralized manner not only leads to excessive complexity, but the control overhead can be very large [9].

To address this problem, we split the whole UDN into multiple parts. The SC is selected in each part as the CH to act as the controller, and the CH asynchronously performs on/off control with reasonable overhead within the cluster. Specifically, we propose a cluster-based SC on/off scheme in UDN, which consists of SCs clustering and intra-cluster SC on/off control.

The overall procedure of the proposed scheme is shown in Fig. 2, which is divided into the following main steps:

Step 1: Calculate the location information of SCs to determine their density.
Step 2: Perform K-means clustering after performing max-min distance clustering.

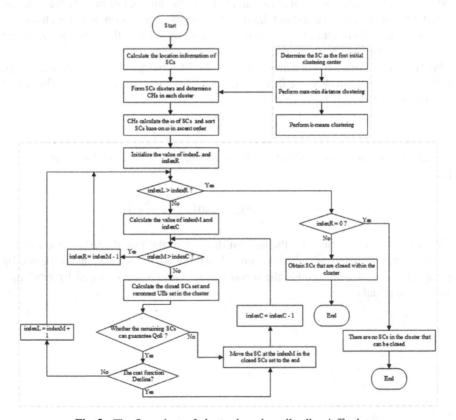

Fig. 2. The flow chart of cluster-based small cell on/off scheme

Step 3: An active SC closest to the final clustering center is selected as a CH in each cluster.

Step 4: CH collects coordination information within the cluster.

Step 5: Execute HSA.

In the following sub-sections, we describe the two phases of the proposed scheme. Specifically, steps 1 to 3 are the SC clustering and are described in detail in Sect. 3.2. Step 4 and 5 are the intra-cluster SC on/off control and are given in Sect. 3.3.

3.2 SCs Clustering

In general, the distance and density between SCs mirror their ability of collaborate and interference intensity. If several SCs that are far from each other form a cluster, the performance of the cluster cell on/off coordinated transmission is significantly reduced. Therefore, SCs that are close to each other preferentially form a cluster, and dense SCs are formed into different clusters by combining max-min distance clustering and K-means clustering algorithm. However, the traditional K-means clustering algorithm usually randomly selects the initial clustering center and the number of clusters needs to be preset, which leads to local optimum [15]. So, the number of pre-set clusters and the initial cluster centers are first obtained by the modified max-min distance clustering algorithm. Then, the output of the max-min distance is used as the initial value of the K-means clustering to obtain the final SCs cluster and CHs.

Firstly, we calculate the distance between the SCs before clustering to determine density of SCs, and the distance denoted by $d = [d_{b_m,b_i}, \forall b_m, b_i \in \Psi_b]$. The set of neighborhoods of the SC b_m is given by:

$$\varepsilon_{b_m} = \left\{ b_i \in \Psi_b \big| d_{b_m,b_i} \leq d_{th} \right\} \tag{13}$$

where d_{th} is the threshold of distance. In addition, the density of the SC b_m can be calculated as:

$$\gamma_{b_m} = \sum_{b_k \in \varepsilon_{b_m}} |\varepsilon_{b_m}| \cdot \exp\left(\frac{-d_{b_m,b_k}}{(0.5d_{th})^2} \right) \tag{14}$$

We then choose the SC with the highest density as the initial cluster center of the max-min distance clustering, which ensures that there is at least one cluster formed by a group of dense SCs and avoids the inconsistent cluster results caused by randomly selecting the initial center.

Algorithm 1 SCs Clustering Algorithm

Input: θ, Ψ_b, $d_{b_m,b_i}, \forall b_m, b_i \in \Psi_b$

Output: $C = \{c_1, c_2, ..., c_l\}$

  1: Initialization: $D = \emptyset$, $Z = \emptyset$,

  2: Calculate the density γ of each SC by Equation (14)

  3: Find SC $b_m^* = \arg\max \gamma$ as the rst clustering center,
     $z_1 \leftarrow b_m^*$, $\forall b_m \in \Psi_b$

  4: Find SC $b_i^* = \underset{i=1,...,m}{\arg\max} \, d_{b_m^*,b_i}$, $z_2 \leftarrow b_i^*$, $D_{th} \leftarrow d_{b_m^*,b_i^*}$

  5: $D = \{d_{z_1,b_i}, i = 1, ..., m\}$, $l = 2$

  6: **while** true **do**

  7:     $D_{z_l,b_p} = \{d_{z_l,b_p}, p = 1, ..., m\}$,

  8:     $D \leftarrow D \cup \{D_{z_l,b_p}\}$

  9:     $D_{th} \leftarrow \underset{b_p^*}{\max}\{\min D\}$

10:     **if** $D_{th} > \theta \times d_{b_m^*,b_i^*}$ **then**

11:         $l = l + 1, z_l \leftarrow b_p^*$

12:     **else**

13:         **break**

14:     **end if**

15: **end while**

16: Using $Z = \{z_1, ..., z_l\}$ and l as the initial value of
     K-means clustering to get the nal cluster $C = \{c_1, c_2, ..., c_l\}$

Finally, the cluster center and number obtained by the max-min distance algorithm are taken as the initial value of the K-means algorithm to obtain the final SCs clusters formed by set of SCs and denoted by $C = \{c_1, c_2, \cdots, c_l\}$. The specific SCs clustering process is in Algorithm 1. Based on the clustering results, the CH within each cluster is responsible for SC on/off to facilitate the reduction of network state information and signaling interactions. Then we select the active SC closest to the clustering center as the CH.

3.3 Intra-cluster SC On/Off Control

After obtaining clusters of SCs according to Algorithm 1, the objective function of (12) can be divided into sub-problems corresponding to all clusters of SCs. That is, reducing the energy consumption and RBs of the entire network is approximately equal to minimizing the energy consumption and RB of each cluster. Then, the optimization problem η can be rewritten as:

$$\sum_{c_l=1}^{|C|} \min \sum_{b_m \in c_l} \sum_{u_n \in \Psi_n} \left(\mu_b P_{b_m} + \phi_b y_{b_m, u_n} k_{b_m, u_n} \right)$$

$$s.t. \, C1: \sum_{b_m \in \Psi_b} k_{b_m, u_n} = 1, \forall u_n \in \Psi_u$$

$$C2: \sum_{u_n \in \Psi_u} k_{b_m, u_n} \cdot y_{b_m, u_n} \le RB_{b_m}^{total}, \forall b_m \in \Psi_b$$

$$C3: k_{b_m, u_n} \cdot R_{b_m, u_n} \ge R_{\min}, \forall u_n \in \Psi_u \tag{15}$$

$$C4: k_{b_m, u_n} = \{0, 1\}, \forall b_m \in \Psi_b, \forall u_n \in \Psi_n$$

$$C5: x_{b_m} = \{0, 1\}, \forall b_m \in \Psi_b$$

$$C6: \bigcup_{l=1}^{|C|} c_l = \Psi_b \quad C7: \bigcap_{l=1}^{|C|} c_l = \emptyset$$

constraints C6 and C7 indicate that the SCs set in the entire UDN is divided into a number of SCs clusters and each SC can only be located in one cluster so as not to intersect, respectively.

For a given the set of SCs clusters, since there are only a few SCs per cluster, it becomes feasible to obtain the optimal on/off combination for each cluster by exhaustive search. However, this solution still has high search complexity, and we propose a heuristic search algorithm to solve the optimization problem.

In the cluster c_l, the SC b_m is able to close only if each of its UE can be served by other SCs in the same cluster. However, turning off the SCs with fewer service UEs will save more power consumption under the condition that the same number of SCs can be closed. On one hand, this avoids generating more switching power that is proportional to the number of service UEs. On the other hand, this avoids turning off the SCs with lots of UEs. Then, the additional dynamic power generated if the SC b_m is turned off is:

$$\omega_{b_m} = P_{sw_{b_m}} + \sum_{b_p \in C_l \setminus \{b_m\}} \partial \rho_{b_m \to b_p} P_{tx} \tag{16}$$

where $\rho_{b_m \to b_p}$ is the load transferred to SC b_p when the SC b_m is switched off in the cluster. The actual load change of each SC is unknown before the shutdown occurs, so we approximately estimate the transferred load. It is assumed that the load transferred is related to the initial load of the SC b_m and its service UEs' interference which suffered from SC b_p. The interference of SC b_m suffered from the SC b_p can be expressed as $I_{b_m, b_p} = |\zeta_{b_m}| P_{tx} G_{b_m, b_p}$, where G_{b_m, b_p} is the channel gain between SC b_m and b_p[23]. Furthermore, it may become useful signals for its users when the SC b_m is turned off. Thus, the relation can be given as:

$$\rho_{b_m \to b_p} = \rho_{b_m} \beta_{b_m, b_p} \mu \tag{17}$$

where $\beta_{b_m, b_p} = 1/I_{b_m, b_p}$, $\mu = 1/\sum_{b_j \in c_l \setminus \{b_p\}} \beta_{b_m, b_j}$. We are acknowledged that a SC with less additional dynamic power generated, has a higher probability to be closed off. The specific HSA in intra-cluster SC on/off control is shown in Algorithm 2.

Algorithm 2 Heuristic Search Algorithm

Input: c_l, U_{c_l}

Output: The set c_l^{off} of SCs turned off in cluster

1: Initialization: $indexL = 1$, $indexR = |c_l|$,

2: calculate the value ω of each SC in cluster c_l and sort them in ascending order as $c_l^* = \{b_1, ..., b_p\}$,

3: **while** $indexL <= indexR$ **do**

4:     $indexM = \lfloor \frac{indexL + indexR}{2} \rfloor$; $indexC = |c_l|$

5:     **while** $indexC >= indexM$ **do**

6:         $c_l^{off} \leftarrow$ SCs at 1 to $indexM$ in set c_l^*

7:         $U_{c_l}^{off} \leftarrow$ UEs associated with SCs in set c_l^{off}

8:         **if** all UE $\in U_{c_l}^{off}$ can be served by the remaining SCs $\in c_l^{on} = c_l^* \setminus c_l^{off}$ and the η decrease **then**

9:             $indexL = indexM + 1$

10:            **break**

11:        **else**

12:            Move the SC at the $indexM$ in set c_l^* to the end; $indexC = indexC - 1$

13:        **end if**

14:    **end while**

15:    If $indexM$ is greater than $indexC$ then $indexR$ equals $indexM$ minus 1

16: **end while**

17: **if** $indexR$ is equal to zero **then**

18:    **return** $c_l^{off} \leftarrow \emptyset$

19: **else**

20:    **return** $c_l^{off} \leftarrow$ SCs at 1 to $\lfloor \frac{indexL + indexR}{2} \rfloor$ in set c_l^*

21: **end if**

3.4 Computational Complexity Analysis

In this part, we analyze the complexity of the two stages of clustering and intra-cluster SC on/off in the proposed scheme. Assume that there are M SCs and L clusters are formed. Firstly, the max-min distance clustering algorithm needs to compare the distance between the existing cluster center node and other nodes to iteratively generate a new cluster center, thus the complexity of max-min distance can be calculated as $O(ML)$. Then the complexity of K-means clustering algorithm is $O(dMLt)$, $d = 2$ represents the two dimensional coordinate of SCs, and t is number of iterations of K-means algorithm. Finally, the time complexity of the first stage clustering is:

$$T_{clustering} = O(ML) + O(dMLt) \tag{18}$$

For the second stage of SC on/off operation, we assume that each SC serves P UEs. There are 2^M combinations if we get the optimal on/off combination by exhaustively searching each SC, and each UE will re-associate in $M - 1$ SCs when the SC is off. The exhaustively searching algorithm time complexity is:

$$T_{optimal} = O(2^M PM) \tag{19}$$

In our proposed scheme, the SCs in each cluster are sorted in ascending order according to Eq. 16, and then closed by using the modified binary search. Assume that each cluster c_l contains S SCs. The complexity of binary search is $O(\log_2 S)$. The complexity of reconnecting the UEs to the remaining SCs at total search step is $PS[S/2(S - S/2) + S/2^2(S - S/2^2) + \cdots + S/2^r(S - S/2^r)]$, which can be rewritten as $O(S^3 P)$, $r = \log_2 S$ indicates the number of searches. Therefore, the complexity of second stage is $O(S^3 P \log_2 S)$. As a result, the complexity of our proposed scheme is:

$$T_{proposed} = \max(O(dMLt), O(S^3 PL \log_2 S)) \tag{20}$$

It is worth noting that although SCs clustering increases computational complexity, they reduce the complexity of performing SC on/off in UND. Generally $M >> L$ and $M >> S$, thus the time complexity of our scheme is much lower than the optimal exhaustive search approach as the number of SCs increases.

4   Simulation Results

4.1   Parameters Settings

In order to simulate the performance of the proposed cluster-based SC on/off scheme, we consider a downlink scenario of ultra-dense network. It is composed of many SCs

Table 2. Major simulation parameters

Parameters	Value
Carrier frequency	2 GHz
Bandwidth	20 MHz
Total number of RBs per SC	100
Transmit power	30 dBm
Density of SCs	0.0002–0.002 SCs/m^2
Fixed power consumption	106 W [14]
Sleep power consumption	10 W[14]
P_o	30 dBm [18]
Traffic model	Full buffer
Path loss factor α	4 [21]
White noise power	−174 dBm/Hz
Minimum required rate per User	1 Mbps

and UEs randomly distributed within an area size of 500 m × 500 m. In this scenario, we set the density of users distributed in the area to 0.002 UE/m², while the density of SCs continues to increase to the same density as UEs. The major parameters used for the simulation are listed in Table 2.

4.2 Result Analysis

We compare the other three schemes to evaluate the performance gain of the proposed scheme. The first is none SC on/off scheme [20] that all SCs are always on and there is no optimization method in the network, which is the benchmark compared with other scheme. The random SC on/off is the second scheme [12], which randomly choose to close a certain proportion of SCs in the network and switch users to the remaining SCs. If the closed SC has UEs, these users will switch to adjacent active SCs. The last one is void SC on/off scheme [22]: a SC will be turned on when it has at least one user to serve, otherwise it will be turned off.

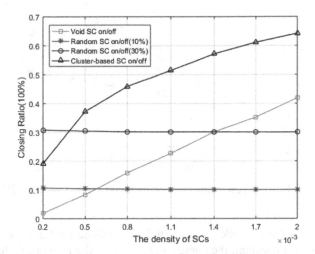

Fig. 3. The closing ratio under different densities of SCs

In Fig. 3, we compare the closing ratio of different SC on/off schemes under different distribution densities of SCs. It can be observed that the random SC on/off scheme always turns off a certain proportion of SCs regardless of the increase in the density of SCs. However, the proportion of SCs that are idle in the system is higher than about 30% as the density of SCs continues to increase, which results in the closing rate of the void SC on/off scheme will be higher than that of random SC on/off scheme. The closing ratio of cluster-based SC on/off scheme is always about 20% higher than that of the void SC on/off scheme with the increase of the density of SCs, that is, more SCs will be turned off to achieve higher power efficiency.

Figure 4 illustrates the total power consumption of all SCs in the network as the density of SCs increases. As can be seen from the figure, the network with the on/off scheme will save the power consumption of the SC. When the density of SCs is low, the total power consumption of SCs realized by the four on/off schemes is almost equal. This is because a large amount of switching power consumption at this time replaces the energy saved by the SCs shutdown. That is to say, there are fewer SCs turned off when the density is low, but more users need to switch, leading to an increase in switching power consumption. However, as the density of the SCs increase, the number of SCs that are closed by the corresponding on/off scheme increases, so that power consumption is significantly reduced. When the density of SCs increases to the same density as the user, the total power consumption of SCs that achieved by the void SC on/off scheme will be reduced by about 38%, while 58% of the total power consumption can be saved through cluster-based SC on/off scheme.

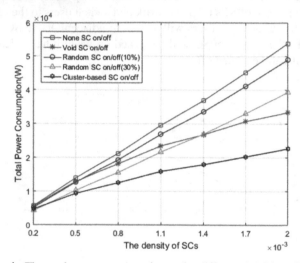

Fig. 4. The total power consumption under different densities of SCs

Figure 5 shows the network energy efficiency defined by Eq. 6. When the total throughput is almost constant, the energy efficiency of the network is determined by the total energy consumption. It can be seen from Figs. 2 and 3 that the total power consumption of the network is proportional to the number of SCs opened, and the impact of switching power consumption on the total power consumption will decrease as the density of SCs increases. Our proposed will close more SCs as the density of SCs increases, thus having better energy efficient than other on/off schemes.

Figure 6 implies the cumulative distribution function of SINR values of UEs in the case where the SCs and the user density are the same. As shown in the figure, the random on/off scheme does not improve SINR or even worse because it turns off SCs without guaranteeing the QoS of UEs. Both void SC on/off scheme and our scheme can suppress some interference, but our scheme can close more SCs and reduce more interference under the premise of guaranteeing the QoS of UEs, thus showing a better SINR of UEs than void SC on/off scheme.

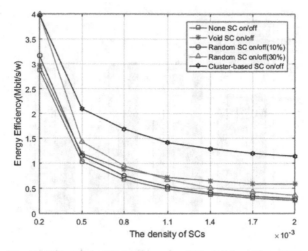

Fig. 5. The energy efficiency under different densities of SCs

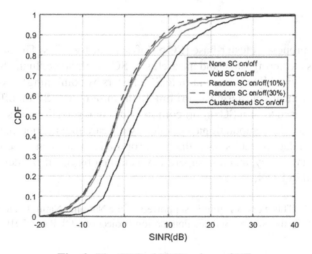

Fig. 6. The CDF of SINR values of UEs

The relationship between the SCs density and the RB cost of each on/off scheme is depicted in Fig. 7. It can be seen that there is no significant difference in the RB cost of none SC on/off scheme and random SC on/off scheme because their SINR levels are almost the same. Since closing some SCs can improve channel conditions, choosing to turn off the appropriate SCs can reduce the RB cost. Compared to the benchmark, our proposed scheme can reduce RB cost by about 50% when densities of UEs and SCs are the same.

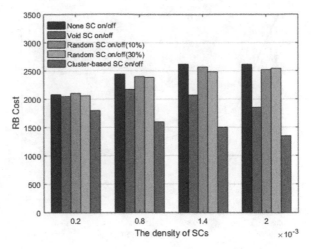

Fig. 7. The RB cost under different densities of SCs

5   Conclusions

In this paper, we propose a cluster-based SC on/off scheme for UDN. This scheme has two stages, viz., SCs clustering stage and intra-cluster SC on/off stage. In the SCs clustering stage, we firstly divide all SCs into multiple SC clusters by combining max-min distance clustering with K-means clustering algorithm. In the intra-cluster SC on/off stage, a HSA algorithm is proposed to turn SC on/off combo issues into selection questions, which is beneficial to reduce the computational complexity of searching the optimal combination of SC on/off. Simulation results show that the proposed scheme can effectively improve network energy efficiency, and this superiority is more obvious if the density of SCs is further increased in UDN.

Acknowledgment. This work was jointly supported by the National Natural Science Foundation in China (61601075), the Natural Science Foundation Project of CQUPT (A2019-40).

References

1. Teng, Y., Liu, M., Yu, F.R., Leung, V.C.M., Song, M., Zhang, Y.: Resource allocation for ultra-dense networks: a survey, some research issues and challenges. IEEE Commun. Surv. Tutor. **21**(3), 2134–2168 (2019)
2. Wu, Y., Qian, L.P., Zheng, J., Zhou, H., Shen, X.S.: Green-oriented traffic offloading through dual connectivity in future heterogeneous small cell networks. IEEE Commun. Mag. **56**(5), 140–147 (2018)
3. Kamel, M., Hamouda, W., Youssef, A.: Ultra-dense networks: a survey. IEEE Commun. Surv. Tutor. **18**(4), 2522–2545 (2016)
4. Mollahasani, S., Onur, E.: Density-aware, energy-and spectrum-efficient small cell scheduling. IEEE Access **7**, 65852–65869 (2019)

5. Cao, J., Peng, T., Qi, Z., Duan, R., Yuan, Y., Wang, W.: Interference management in ultradense networks: a user-centric coalition formation game approach. IEEE Trans. Veh. Technol. **67**(6), 5188–5202 (2018)
6. Zhuang, H., Chen, J., Wu, D.O.: Joint access and backhaul resource management for ultra-dense networks. In: IEEE International Conference on Communications (ICC), Paris, pp. 1–6 (2017)
7. Son, K., Kim, H., Yi, Y., Krishnamachari, B.: Base station operation and user association mechanisms for energy-delay tradeoffs in green cellular networks. IEEE J. Sel. Areas Commun. **29**(8), 1525–1536 (2011)
8. Yang, B., Mao, G., Ding, M., Ge, X., Tao, X.: Dense small cell networks: from noise-limited to dense interference-limited. IEEE Trans. Veh. Technol. **67**(5), 4262–4277 (2018)
9. Feng, M., Mao, S., Jiang, T.: Base station ON-OFF switching in 5G wireless networks: approaches and challenges. IEEE Wirel. Commun. **24**(4), 46–54 (2017)
10. Kim, J., Lee, H., Chong, S.: Traffic-aware energy-saving base station sleeping and clustering in cooperative networks. IEEE Trans. Wireless Commun. **17**(2), 1173–1186 (2018)
11. Pei, L., Huilin, J., Zhiwen, P., Xiaohu, Y.: Energy-delay tradeoff in ultra-dense networks considering bs sleeping and cell association. IEEE Trans. Veh. Technol. **67**(1), 734–751 (2018)
12. Liu, C., Natarajan, B., Xia, H.: Small cell base station sleep strategies for energy efficiency. IEEE Trans. Veh. Technol. **65**(3), 1652–1661 (2016)
13. Tao, R., Zhang, J., Chu, X.: An energy saving small cell sleeping mechanism with cell expansion in heterogeneous networks. In: 2016 IEEE 83rd Vehicular Technology Conference (VTC Spring), Nanjing, pp. 1–5 (2016)
14. Wang, Q., Zheng, J.: A distributed base station On/Off Control Mechanism for energy efficiency of small cell networks. In: 2015 IEEE International Conference on Communications (ICC), London, pp. 3317–3322 (2015)
15. Samarakoon, S., Bennis, M., Saad, W., Latva-aho, M.: Dynamic clustering and on/off strategies for wireless small cell networks. IEEE Trans. Wireless Commun. **15**(3), 2164–2178 (2016)
16. Ye, Y., Zhang, H., Xiong, X., Liu, Y.: Dynamic min-cut clustering for energy savings in ultra-dense networks. In: 2015 IEEE 82nd Vehicular Technology Conference (VTC 2015-Fall), Boston, MA, pp. 1–5 (2015)
17. Oh, E., Son, K., Krishnamachari, B.: Dynamic base station switching-on/off strategies for green cellular networks. IEEE Trans. Wireless Commun. **12**(5), 2126–2136 (2013)
18. Yu, N., Miao, Y., Mu, L., Du, H., Huang, H., Jia, X.: Minimizing energy cost by dynamic switching ON/OFF base stations in cellular networks. IEEE Trans. Wireless Commun. **15**(11), 7457–7469 (2016)
19. Gan, X., et al.: Energy efficient switch policy for small cells. Commun. China **12**(1), 78–88 (2015)
20. Peng, J., Hong, P., Xue, K.: Stochastic analysis of optimal base station energy saving in cellular networks with sleep mode. IEEE Commun. Lett. **18**(4), 612–615 (2014)
21. Andrews, J.G., Baccelli, F., Ganti, R.K.: A tractable approach to coverage and rate in cellular networks. IEEE Trans. Commun. **59**(11), 3122–3134 (2011)
22. Peng, C., Wang, L., Liu, C.: Optimal base station deployment for small cell networks with energy-efficient power control. In: 2015 IEEE International Conference on Communications (ICC), London, pp. 1863–1868 (2015)
23. Tung, L., Wang, L., Chen, K.: An interference-aware small cell on/off mechanism in hyper dense small cell networks. In: 2017 International Conference on Computing, Networking and Communications (ICNC), Santa Clara, CA, pp. 767–771 (2017)

A DASH-Based Peer-to-Peer VoD Streaming Scheme

Pingshan Liu[1,2], Yaqing Fan[2(✉)], Kai Huang[2], and Guimin Huang[2]

[1] Business School, Guilin University of Electronic Technology, Guilin, China
ps.liu@foxmail.com
[2] Guangxi Key Laboratory of Trusted Software, Guilin University of Electronic Technology,
Guilin, China
fan.yaq@foxmail.com

Abstract. For peer-to-peer (P2P) video-on-demand (VoD) streaming, this paper proposes a new P2P VoD scheme based on Dynamic Adaptive Streaming over HTTP (DASH), called P2P-DASH VoD scheme. The scheme takes advantage of both the scalability and low cost properties of P2P technology and the dynamic self-adaptation of DASH. In the proposed scheme, a multi-overlay architecture is constructed, and a DASH streaming rate control approach is proposed. The multi-overlay architecture integrates the power-law ring overlay structure and the Fibonacci ring overlay structure. Peers can search the target video segments based on the power-law ring overlay structure or the Fibonacci ring overlay structure according to the search distance. The integrated overlay structure can reduce the jump latency caused by VCR operations and improve the smoothness of playback. Furthermore, the DASH streaming rate control approach is proposed to combine DASH in P2P VoD Streaming. The DASH streaming rate control approach considers four adaptive factors (on-time arrival rate of segment, peer's available buffer length, current overlay available bandwidth and current overlay upload bandwidth utilization). Through simulations, we demonstrate that the proposed P2P-DASH VoD scheme has short jump latency, high playback fluency and the satisfaction of users.

Keywords: Peer-to-peer · Video-on-demand · Dynamic Adaptive Streaming over HTTP (DASH) · Overlay · Streaming rate control · Video streaming

1 Introduction

With the promotion and popularization of Internet in contemporary society, the number of Internet users is increasing. As one of the main applications of Internet, network video has a huge user base. According to data provided by *Baidu.com*, as of December 2018, China had 829 million Internet users and 612 million video users. Video users accounted for 73.9% of the total number of Internet users. The huge number of video users will incur huge network bandwidth costs when watching network video. In addition, they place higher demands on viewing quality, including fluency and clarity. Therefore, improving the users' viewing quality while reducing the network bandwidth costs has become a hot

© ICST Institute for Computer Sciences, Social Informatics and Telecommunications Engineering 2020
Published by Springer Nature Switzerland AG 2020. All Rights Reserved
H. Gao et al. (Eds.): ChinaCom 2019, LNICST 312, pp. 402–416, 2020.
https://doi.org/10.1007/978-3-030-41114-5_30

spot of current research. P2P video on demand (VoD) technology can effectively deal with this problem.

Video on demand (VoD) is popular because it can deliver video content to users based on user requirements. Therefore, the research in this paper is for VoD. In VoD, P2P technology is widely used to provide VoD services due to its high scalability and low deployment cost [1–3]. On the other hand, DASH is widely used in VoD streaming and live streaming because it provides users with the best video quality based on current network conditions [4, 8]. These studies also show that DASH can effectively improve the viewing quality of users. In addition, DASH is based on the standard HTTP protocol and defines a mechanism suitable for real-time transmission of video data based on the HTTP protocol. Therefore, DASH effectively ensures real-time transmission of video data. Besides, most firewalls allow HTTP protocol penetration by default, that is, the HTTP protocol has strong applicability to the network. So, DASH has strong network adaptability and is easy to deploy. Therefore, building P2P VoD system based on DASH can adapt to existing networks, greatly reducing deployment costs and providing users with a better experience.

In this paper, we propose a new P2P-DASH VoD scheme for peer-to-peer VoD streaming, which combines the advantages of DASH technology and P2P technology. The scheme takes advantage of the high scalability and low cost of P2P technology and the dynamic adaptability of DASH. The scheme guarantees low deployment cost, short jump latency, high playback fluency and satisfaction of users. First, we propose a new multi-layer overlay structure which consists of a power-law ring overlay structure and Fibonacci ring overlay structure. The integrated overlay structure is used to reduce the jump latency caused by VCR operations and improve playback fluency. It can also handle the high dynamic features and asynchronous features of VoD service. High dynamic feature means that client peers can join/leave at any time and can drag playback point at any time. Asynchronous feature means that users watching the same video can watch different parts of the video. Final, a DASH streaming rate control approach is proposed. Through the rate control approach, users can adaptively choose their best watching experiences and obtain the best satisfaction of users.

2   Related Work

The research on P2P VoD streaming mainly includes [5–7]. Ganapathi et al. [5] propose the hierarchical prefetching technology based on popularity. First, the method estimates the popularity of each video by proxies. Then, the proxies cache the popular videos and distributes the videos to the desired peers. This method can effectively solve the problem that P2P system is difficult to provide constant download and playback services due to frequent VCR operations. In order to improve the quality of video playback and reduce the consumption of cloud bandwidth, the authors of [6] propose an incentive scheme based on adaptive bitrate streaming method. In this scheme, the quality of the video received by a user depends on the user's contribution to the upload bandwidth of the P2P network. The authors of [7] study the buffer-map exchange problem in a pull-based P2P VoD streaming system. They propose an adaptive mechanism to reduce overhead. The mechanism sends the buffer-maps based on playing position of peers. Experiments show that this method effectively reduces the bandwidth overhead of buffer-map exchange in P2P VoD streaming systems.

Most of the research on P2P-DASH focuses on the construction of P2P-DASH system, and proposes a new DASH rate control approach when constructing the system. The authors of [9] propose a DASH rate control method. Before downloading video segments, the method estimates the throughput of peers based on the changes in network throughput. Peers select streaming rate based on the estimated throughput and playback buffer occupancy. The authors of [11] propose a block-based rate adaptation method. The method considers both the difference in bandwidth and the video time of the feedback buffer. Experiments show that this method effectively solves the problem that the video rate switching on multiple servers is not smooth due to different bandwidth. A DASH method based on machine learning is proposed by the authors of [12]. The approach enables customers to understand the environment in an unsupervised way to help clients adapt to the changing network environment. The method eliminates redundant adaptive work similar to network signatures and reduces the complexity of running time. Other studies have focused on live streaming. Such as the research work of [10] is a DASH rate control algorithm for live streaming. A decentralized rate control scheme is proposed by the authors of [10]. Peers independently performed the rate control algorithm to select the appropriate streaming rate. Based on paper [10], the authors of [13] made a more detailed study and explanation of the work of [10]. They add the description of system parameter selection and perform the same simulation experiment as [10], and reach the same conclusion.

Different from previous work, the research of P2P-DASH in this paper is aimed at VoD streaming. We propose a new P2P-DASH VoD scheme. This paper investigates the method of constructing an overlay structure in a VoD stream to reduce the playback delay caused by VCR operations in the VoD stream. On the other hand, this paper studies a new DASH streaming rate control approach for streaming rate conversion in video transmission to maximize the satisfaction of users.

3   System Overview and Overlay Structure Construction

3.1   System Overview

In this paper, only VoD streaming is studied. We consider the construction and maintenance of P2P overlay structure under the condition of AVC video coding. First, a multi-layer overlay structure is constructed according to different DASH representations (i.e., streaming rates). Each DASH representation corresponds to an overlay. In AVC coding, peers with different streaming rates do not have the ability to share video segments. The P2P overlay structure in our system is mesh-based. The overlay structure consists of power-law ring overlay structures and Fibonacci ring overlay structures. The peers are organized into Fibonacci ring overlay structures and power-law ring overlay structures based on distance between peers. Based on search distance, peers decide in which ring structure to find target video segments. This integrated overlay structure effectively shortens the jump latency and effectively handles the dynamic and asynchronous nature of VoD services.

Then, a DASH streaming rate control approach is proposed to control the streaming rate in VoD. Based on the situation of overlay, the DASH streaming rate control approach selects the best streaming rate for peers. When peers switch their streaming rate, they will migrate from one overlay to another. In order to maximize the viewing quality and ensure the good performance of P2P overlay structure, DASH streaming rate control approach considers four adaptive factors. The four adaptive factors including the on-time arrival rate of segment AR, available buffer length $W_{availiable}$, current overlay available bandwidth μ, and current overlay upload bandwidth utilization η. The adaptive factors determine whether peers can switch streaming rate (i.e., migrating their overlay).

3.2 Overlay Structure Construction

The overlay structure of this system is a multi-layer mesh-based structure. Peers in the system are organized in a comprehensive structure of Fibonacci ring and power-law ring. The number of overlays in the system is the same as the number of DASH representations of video. Each DASH representation (i.e., streaming rate) corresponds to an overlay. Our system structure consists of a streaming server, a tracker, and many peers. The system structure is shown in Fig. 1. The streaming server distributes different DASH representations to the corresponding overlay. In the system, we use $rate$ represent DASH representation, $rate_j$ is streaming rate in $overlay_j$. $overlay_j$ represents the jth overlay and $1 \leq j \leq max$. The maximum streaming rate and overlay are represented as $rate_{max}$ and $overlay_{max}$, respectively. Each peer belongs to an overlay at a time. Each peer provides its cached video segments to other peers. The streaming server divides a video into multiple segments. Each segment contains a certain number of video encoding frames. From previous research [14], it can be concluded that the larger the video segment, the better the user experience. Since the DASH video segments are small (generally 2 s or 10 s), this paper divides a certain number of video segments into a video group. In the system, the tracker saves peers' information, including the upload bandwidth, ID and streaming video resources. Besides, the tracker organize the peers into clusters. When a new peer i joins the overlay structure, it first notifies the tracker. Then, the tracker selects some neighbor peers for peer i based on its playing position. Each peer stores its own ID information and the video being played. Each peer joins the system based on its playing position.

When constructing the overlay structure, the distance between peers (d_{peer}) is calculated based on the playing position. For example, the playing position of peer i and peer n is cur_i and cur_n. The distance from peer n to peer i (d_{peer}^n) is calculated as $d_{peer}^n = cur_n - cur_i$. Then, according to d_{peer}, the neighbor peers are organized into the Fibonacci ring overlay and the power-law ring overlay. Final, when a peer searches for the target video segment, the peer first calculates the search distance (d_{search}). d_{search} is the interval between the current playing position of a peer and the position of target video segments. We use tar_i for the target segment position of peer i. Then, the search distance (d_{search}^i) equals $tar_i - cur_i$. According to d_{search}, peers decide to search for the target segment in Fibonacci ring overlay or power-law ring overlay.

The authors of papers [15] and [16] show that Fibonacci ring overlay structure supports short-range search and power-law ring overlay structure supports remote search. Specifically, when d_{search} is small, a peer searches for target segment in its Fibonacci

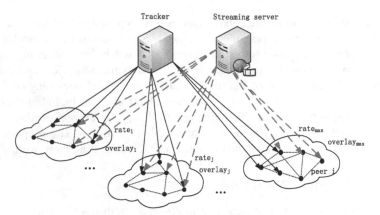

Fig. 1. System architecture

ring overlay structure. Instead, a peer will find the target segment in its power-law ring overlay structure when d_{search} is large. In this way, the jump latency of our system is short. The critical distance which determine a peer search a target segment in Fibonacci ring overlay or power-law ring overlay is called $d_{critical}$. Through experiments, it can be concluded that when $d_{critical}$ is equal to 8, the jump latency is short and the search speed of the whole system is the fastest. That is, when $d_{critical}$ less than or equal to 8, peers look for target segments in their Fibonacci ring overlay. Otherwise, when $d_{critical}$ is greater than 8, peers look for target segments in their power-law ring overlay.

According to the pseudo-code of Algorithm 1, the steps for a peer to search for a target segment are as follows. First, calculate the distance d_{peer} of peers in the system. According to d_{peer}, the peers are organized into the Fibonacci ring overlay and the power-law ring overlay. Then, calculate d^i_{search} of peer i sending a request. If $d^i_{search} \le d_{critical}$, the peer i looks for the target segment in its Fibonacci ring overlay. If $d^i_{search} > d_{critical}$, the peer i looks for the target segment in its power-law ring overlay. If the required segment of peer i is found, then the information of the neighbor peer that cached the desired segment is returned. Peer i sends a request to the neighbor peer to get the target segment. If there is no required segment in the neighbor ring of peer i, then peer i sends the request to its nearest neighbor peer. The neighbor peer finds the target segment according to the above rules, until the target segment is fond or TTL becomes to 0.

	Algorithm 1
1	**for** each peer i and its neighbor peer n in the system **do**
	compute the distance $d^n_{peer} = cur_n - cur_i$
2	// d^n_{peer} is the distance between peer i and peer n , cur_n and cur_i are playing position of peer n and peer i
3	organize peer n into Fibonacci ring overlay, according to the d^n_{peer}
4	organize peer n into power-law ring overlay, according to the d^n_{peer}
5	**end for**
6	**for** peer i and its neighbor peers **do**
7	compute the search distance $d^t_{search} = tar_i - cur_i$ // d^t_{search} is the search distance, tar_i is the target segment position of peer i
8	**if** $d^t_{search} \leq d_{critical}$ **then** // $d_{critical}$ is the critical distance
9	peer i look for target segment in the Fibonacci ring overlay
10	**if** the target segment of peer i is found in its Fibonacci ring overlay **then**
11	peer i sends a request to the neighbor peer to get the target segment
12	**else** peer i sends the request to its nearest neighbor peer **continue**
13	**end if**
14	**else** Peer i look for target segment in the power-law ring overlay
15	**if** the target segment of peer i is found in its power-law ring overlay **then**
16	peer i sends a request to the neighbor peer to get the target segment
17	**else** peer i sends the request to its nearest neighbor peer **continue**
18	**end if**
19	**end if**
20	**while** TTL=0 **break**
21	**end for**

4 DASH Streaming Rate Control Approach

DASH streaming rate control approach is used to handle streaming rate conversion during video playback. In our approach, when a peer starts playing a video, it first requests video segments with the lowest streaming rate to quickly play the video and reduce the startup delay. During playback, a peer will attempt to request video segments with higher streaming rate or video segments with lower streaming rate. The streaming rate conversion of a peer is the conversion process of a peer from one overlay to another. Our streaming rate control approach restricts that a peer exclusively moves from its current overlay to an adjacent overlay. Therefore, the approach avoids the large fluctuations of video quality caused by large switching range.

In the traditional DASH client-server scenario, only the peer's buffer status and the peer's upload bandwidth utilization are considered when switching streaming rate.

Unlike the traditional DASH client-server scenario, in the P2P-DASH scheme, each peer is a client and a server. Each peer obtains video from other peers and provides cached video to other peers. Therefore, when a peer switch its streaming rate, a peer autonomously executes the streaming rate control approach. The approach considers not only the performance of a peer itself, but also the performance of the whole overlay structure.

The DASH streaming rate control approach proposed in this paper considers four adaptive factors. They comprehensive indicator peers switch their streaming rate. The factors including on-time arrival rate of segment AR, peer's available buffer length $W_{available}$, current overlay available bandwidth μ and current overlay upload bandwidth utilization η. The following four adaptive factors are introduced separately.

(1) The on-time arrival rate of segment

AR_i is the on-time arrival rate of segment of peer i, which is defined as: in the period τ, the ratio between the number of video segments that meet the playback deadline and the total number of segments that peer i should receive. The calculation formula of AR_i is

$$AR_i = \frac{S_{ontime}^i}{S_{total}^i} \tag{1}$$

In the formula (1), S_{ontime}^i is the number of video segments that meet the playback deadline of peer i. S_{total}^i is the total number of video segments that peer i should receive.

(2) The peer's available buffer length

$W_{availiable}^i$ is the available buffer length of peer i, which is defined as: the interval between the total buffer size of a peer (the sliding window size) and the buffer size already used by the peer. The calculation formula of $W_{availiable}^i$ is

$$W_{availiable}^i = W - W_{used}^i \tag{2}$$

In the formula (2), W is the total buffer size of peer i. W_{used}^i is the buffer size already used by peer i. W_{used}^i is calculated as

$$W_{used}^i = \frac{S_w + S_k}{b_i} \tag{3}$$

In the formula (3), S_w is the size of the segments waiting to be sent in the buffer. S_k is the size of segment k that peer i is requesting. b_i is the upload bandwidth of peer i.

(3) The current overlay available bandwidth

According to the paper [17], the current overlay available bandwidth of overlay j at time t is defined as:

$$\mu_j(t) = \frac{b_{server}^j + \sum_{i \in Q_j(t)} b_i}{q \cdot rate_j} \tag{4}$$

In the formula (4), b^j_{server} is the upload bandwidth provided by the streaming server for overlay j to transmit segments with streaming rate $rate_j$ at time t. b_i is the upload bandwidth of peer i. $Q_j(t)$ is the set of active peers in overlay j at time t. q is the number of peers in set $Q_j(t)$. $rate_j$ is the streaming rate of overlay j.

(4) The current overlay upload bandwidth utilization

The current overlay upload bandwidth utilization of overlay j at time t is defined as:

$$\eta_j(t) = \frac{U^j_{server} + \sum_{i \in Q_j(t)} U_i}{q \cdot rate_j} \tag{5}$$

In the formula (5), U^j_{server} is the server's upload bandwidth utilization of overlay j at time t. U_i is the upload bandwidth utilization of peer i.

The adaptive factors $\mu_j(t)$ and $\eta_j(t)$ are used to judge the overall performance of current overlay structure. $\mu_j(t)$ indicates whether the available bandwidth of the network can support peers switch to an overlay with higher streaming rate at time t. When $\mu_j(t) \geq 1$, it means that the performance of current network is good. At this time, the upload bandwidth of the network ensures that the target video segment is sent to the requesting peer. $\mu_j(t) < 1$ is the opposite. $\eta_j(t)$ is a deeper judgment index for global network performance. $\eta_j(t)$ represents the effective upload bandwidth utilization of peers on overlay j. If new peers join to the overlay structure, the value of $\eta_j(t)$ will significantly decrease. This is because the new peers do not contribute upload bandwidth immediately. In our DASH streaming rate control approach, a peer switches to DASH representation with higher streaming rate, call a peer switches upward. When a peer switches upward, our approach comprehensively consider four adaptive factors. These four adaptive factors jointly determine whether a peer can successfully switch upward. When a peer switches downward, only the indexes of itself (AR and $W_{availiable}$) are considered.

According to the pseudo-code of Algorithm 2, the steps of our DASH streaming rate control approach are as follows. We assume that r^i_{target} is the target streaming rate of peer i. In each period τ, when $raet_j < r^i_{target}$, it means peer i is not satisfied with the current streaming rate. Then, peer i expects to switch upward. If $AR_i > AR_{thres}$ and $W^i_{availiable} > W_{thres}$, it means that the peer has the ability to switch to overlay with a higher streaming rate. AR_{thres} is the threshold of the on-time arrival rate. W_{thres} is the threshold of the available buffer length of a peer. Then, the approach judge the current overlay performance. If $\mu_j < 1$ and $b_i \geq rate_j$, it means that the current overlay state cannot guarantee the peer to switch an overlay with higher streaming rate successfully. So the peer remains in the current overlay j. Otherwise, the state of the target overlay is judged. If $b_i > rate_{j+1}$, peer i switch to overlay $j + 1$. If $\mu_{j+1} > 1$ and $\eta_{j+1} > \eta_{thres}$, peer i switch to overlay $j + 1$. η_{thres} is the threshold of the overlay upload bandwidth utilization. If $AR_i < AR_{thres}$ and $W^i_{availiable} < W_{thres}$, it indicates that the peer cannot guarantee normal playback at the current streaming rate and needs to move to overlay $j - 1$ with lower streaming rate.

Algorithm 2
1   **for** peer i in the network in every period τ **do**
2   **if** $(rate_j < r^i_{target})$ **and** $((AR_i > AR_{thres})$ **and** $(W^i_{availiable} > W_{thres}))$ //Determine the current global network performance
3   **if** $(\mu_j < 1)$ **and** $(b_i \geq rate_j)$ **then**
4   Peer i remains at overlay j
5   **else** // Determine the target overlay status
6   **if** $(b_i > rate_{j+1})$ **or** $((\mu_{j+1} > 1)$ **and** $(\eta_{j+1} > \eta_{thres}))$ **then**
7   peer i switch to overlay $j+1$
8   **end if**
9   **end if**
10   **else**
11   **if** $(AR_i < AR_{thres})$ **and** $(W^i_{availiable} < W_{thres})$ **then**
12   peer i switch to overlay $j-1$
13   **else**
14   peer i remains at overlay j
15   **end if**
16   **end if**
17   **end for**

5 Performance Evaluation

In this section, we demonstrate the performance of P2P-DASH VoD scheme through simulation. First, we introduce the simulation steps and evaluation indicators. Then, the performance of P2P-DASH VoD scheme is represented by graphs.

5.1 Simulation Setup

We implement an event-driven simulator based on the Peersim simulation platform to evaluate the performance of the P2P-DASH VoD scheme. We build a multi-overlay system where each cluster transmits the same video at a different streaming rate. First, we set different upload and download capabilities for the peers in the system by referring to the paper [10]. The specific settings of peers are shown in Table 1. The number of peers we consider in our experiment is 2000. In the experiment, a network with four overlays is considered. The streaming rates corresponding to the four overlays are 700 kbit/s, 1500 kbit/s, 2500 kbit/s and 3500 kbit/s respectively. We consider the case where peers download the high streaming rate as high as possible within the capacity of their download bandwidth. In order to simulate the real network status, the system randomly selects 1% of active peers to join or leave the system. To illustrate the P2P characteristics of our system, our system allocates a small amount of streaming server upload bandwidth for each overlay. The streaming server upload bandwidth is set to four times the streaming rate of each overlay, i.e., $b_{server}^j = 4r_j$. In order to compare with the P2P-DASH scheme proposed in paper [10], some parameter values of our system are consistent with those in the paper [10]. The sliding window is set to 20 s, $\eta_{thres}=$ 0.8, $AR_{thres}= 0.55$, $W_{thres}= 14$ s. Final, we ran our P2P-DASH VoD scheme on the simulation platform and implemented the DASH-P2P scheme in the same way.

Table. 1. The parameter distribution of peers

Peers	Class 1	Class 2	Class 3	Class 4
Upload capacity (kbit/s)	704	1024	1500	10000
Download capacity (kbit/s)	2048	8192	10000	50000
% of peers	20	21	42	17

In the simulation, we first test the jump latency of our scheme and compare it with the Fibonacci ring overlay structure and the power-law ring overlay structure. Then, in order to illustrate the playback fluency brought by our scheme, we test three indicators and compare them with the P2P-DASH method. The three indicators including the PMF of hops, the average playback delay and the on-time arrival rate of segments. The number of hops tested is the hop generated by the peer switching streaming rate when our system does not generate VCR operations. We use improvements in these three indicators to illustrate the improvements in playback fluency. Final, we test the satisfaction of users and compare it to the DASH method.

5.2 Simulation Result

(1) Jump latency

The jump latency is defined as the average number of message hops per peer. In the experiment, we record the number of jumping peers and the number of message hops generated by each peer. Then, we calculate the average number of message hops for each peer. Based on the data provided by the paper [15], we assume that the probability of peers generating a jump operation during playback is 30%. The author of [18] show that 80% of the VRC operations generated by the user while watching the video are close-range drags, and 20% are long-distance drags. So, in our experiments, it is assumed that 80% of jump operations are close jumps and 20% are long jumps. We compare the jump latency of power-law ring overlay structure, Fibonacci ring overlay structure and our integrated overlay structure under different peers. As can be seen from Fig. 2, the jump latency of our integrated overlay structure is shorter than that of power-law ring overlay structure and Fibonacci ring overlay structure. This shows that our integrated overlay structure can effectively reduce the jump delay then the other two structures.

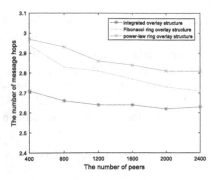

Fig. 2. Jump latency

(2) The PMF of hops

The Probability Mass Function (PMF) of hops represents the probability of the number of peer hops when the peers convert streaming rate. In this part, we test the number of peer hops in target overlay 2 and target overlay 4 when our system do not generate VCR operations. We draw the PMF graph of the number of peer hops. From Fig. 3, we can clearly see that the number of hops in our P2P-DASH VoD scheme is significantly less than the P2P-DASH scheme. As can be clearly seen from Fig. 3, when the target overlay is 2, the number of peer hops are mostly 1 with a probability of 0.861. This is because, in our scheme the new peer is first allowed to request the video segment with lowest streaming rate. So, most peers need to switch from overlay 1 to overlay 2 when the target overlay is 2. When the target overlay is 4, the number of peer hops are mostly 3 with a probability of 0.623. The small number of peer hops indicate that our scheme is very efficient for video segment searches.

(3) Average playback delay

The average playback delay is defined as the interval between a peer make a request of a video segment and the peer receiving the video segment. In Fig. 4, we test the average playback delay in the four overlays. As can be seen from Fig. 4, our P2P-DASH VoD scheme can guarantee a lower playback delay and is much lower than the P2P-DASH scheme. The playback delay in overlay 1 is the lowest, while the playback delay in other overlays is higher. This is because the higher streaming rate of video segments require longer transmission times. However, since our streaming rate control approach strictly limits the transition of peers from the lower rate representation to the higher rate representation, there is little difference in the average playback delay for the peers in overlay 2, 3 and 4. As can be seen from Fig. 4, the minimum values of the average playback delay of P2P-DASH VoD scheme and P2P-DASH scheme are 5 s and 12 s respectively. The maximum values of the average playback delay of P2P-DASH VoD scheme and P2P-DASH scheme are 26 s and 35 s, respectively.

(4) The on-time arrival rate

The on-time arrival rate is the ratio between the number of video segments that meet the playback deadline and the total number of segments that peer i should receive, as defined in part 4. In Fig. 5, we test the on-time arrival rate for each overlay in the

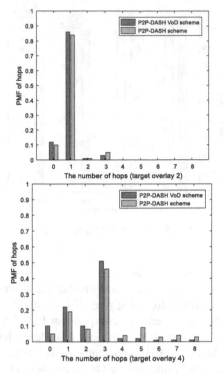

Fig. 3. The PMF of hops in target overlay 2 and target overlay 4

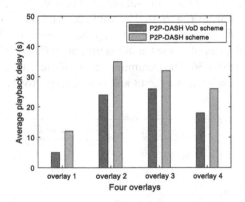

Fig. 4. The average playback delay

system. As is apparent from Fig. 5, the on-time arrival rate of our P2P-DASH VoD scheme is higher than the P2P-DASH scheme, especially in overlay 2 and overlay 3. The on-time arrival rate for the four overlays in our scheme are 0.980, 0.957, 0.945 and 0.916 respectively. The on-time arrival rate for the four overlays in the P2P-DASH scheme are 0.974, 0.934, 0.887 and 0.921 respectively. This shows that our scheme can effectively send target video segments to the required peers.

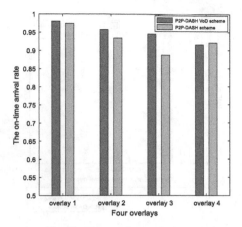

Fig. 5. The on-time arrival rate

(5) The global system satisfaction of users

The global system satisfaction indicates whether the streaming rate received by peers can meet the required streaming rate. This evaluation indicator was used in the paper [10]. In the experiment, we compare our P2P-DASH VoD scheme with the P2P-DASH scheme. First, the scenario we consider is that the target video segment of peers is the highest DASH representation within their download capability. However, the upload bandwidth provided by peers themselves is limited. The total upload bandwidth in the network is relatively small due to the upload bandwidth of the peers. In Fig. 6, we show the satisfaction of users for five consecutive periods. As can be seen from Fig. 6, in the same scenario, the satisfaction of users of our P2P-DASH VoD scheme is significantly better than the P2P-DASH scheme. The satisfaction of users of our scheme reaches up to 0.660, while the P2P-DASH scheme reaches up to 0.636. The minimum values of user satisfaction of our scheme and the P2P-DASH scheme are 0.648 and 0.619, respectively. In addition, we can

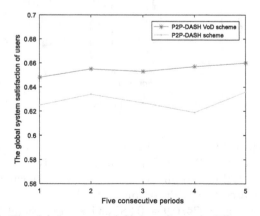

Fig. 6. The global system satisfaction of users in different periods

see that the global system satisfaction of users of our scheme is more stable than the P2P-DASH scheme.

6 Conclusions

For peer-to-peer VoD streaming, this paper proposed a new P2P-DASH VoD scheme, which takes advantage of the dynamic adaptive characteristic of DASH and the low cost characteristic of P2P. First, the P2P overlay structure of the P2P-DASH VoD scheme adopts the combination of the power-law ring overlay structure and the Fibonacci ring overlay structure. The overlay structure can effectively reduce the jump latency caused by VCR operations in VoD service. Then, in terms of streaming rate control, we proposed a DASH streaming rate control approach. Each peer in our system performs a streaming rate control approach to control its streaming rate change (switching overlay). Peers moves from one overlay to another based on four adaptive factors. So our streaming rate control approach can cope with the streaming rate conversion generated during playback and improve the user's viewing quality. The effectiveness of the P2P-DASH VoD scheme is verified by simulations. The simulation experiments show that the P2P-DASH VoD scheme can effectively reduce jump latency, improve playback fluency and the satisfaction of users.

Acknowledgement. The research was supported by the National Natural Science Foundation (No. 61762029, No. 61662012, No. U1811264), Guangxi Natural Science Foundation (No. 2016GXNSFAA380011), Guangxi Key Laboratory of Trusted Software (No. kx201726), and the Foundation of Key Laboratory of Cognitive Radio and Information Processing, Ministry of Education (No. CRKL150105).

References

1. Rohmer, T., Nakib, A., Nafaa, A.: Priori knowledge guided approach for optimal peer selection in P2P VoD systems. IEEE Trans. Netw. Serv. Manage. **11**(3), 350–362 (2014)
2. Faiqurahman, M., Kistijantoro, A.I.: Implementation of modified probabilistic caching schema on Bittorrent protocol for video on demand content. In: International Seminar on Intelligent Technology and Its Applications (ISITIA), Surabaya, Indonesia, pp. 357–362 (2015)
3. Huang, G., Yu, T.: An upload bandwidth allocation algorithm in data scheduling of P2P VoD system. In: Babu, S.P., Wenzheng, L. (eds.) 5th IEEE International Conference on Software Engineering and Service Science (ICSESS), Beijing, People's Republic of China, pp. 435–438 (2014)
4. Li, B., Wang, Z., Zhu, W.: Two decades of internet video streaming: a retrospective view. ACM Trans. Multimedia Comput. Commun. Appl. **9S**(331), 1551–6857 (2013)
5. Ganapathi, S., Varadharajan, V.: Popularity based hierarchical prefetching technique for P2P video-on-demand. Multimedia Tools Appl. **77**(12), 15913–15928 (2018)
6. Huang, G., Gao, Y., Kong, L.: An incentive scheme based on bitrate adaptation for cloud-assisted P2P video-on-demand streaming systems. In: 3rd IEEE International Conference on Cloud Computing and Big Data Analysis (ICCCBDA), Chengdu, People's Republic of China, pp. 404–408 (2018)

7. Sheshjavani, A.G., Akbari, B.: An adaptive buffer-map exchange mechanism for pull-based peer-to-peer video-on-demand streaming systems. Multimedia Tools Appl. **76**(5), 7535–7561 (2017)
8. De Cicco, L., Caldaralo, V., Palmisano, V.: ELASTIC: a client-side controller for dynamic adaptive streaming over HTTP (DASH). In: 20th International Packet Video Workshop (PV), San Jose, CA, pp. 978–986. Cisco (2013)
9. Rahman, W.U., Chung, K.: A novel adaptive logic for dynamic adaptive streaming over HTTP. J. Vis. Commun. Image Represent. **49**, 433–446 (2017)
10. Natali, L., Merani, M.L.: A novel rate control scheme for adaptive video streaming in P2P overlays. In: IEEE Global Telecommunications Conference (GLOBECOM), San Diego, CA, pp. 1–7 (2015)
11. Zhou, C., Lin, C.W., Zhang, X.: A control-theoretic approach to rate adaption for DASH over multiple content distribution servers. IEEE Trans. Circuits Syst. Video Technol. **24**(4), 1–6 (2014)
12. Bhat, A.R., Bhadu, S.K.: Machine learning based rate adaptation in DASH to improve quality of experience. In: IEEE International Conference on Smart Technologies and Management for Computing, Communication, Controls, Energy and Materials (ICSTM), Chennai, India, pp. 82–89 (2017)
13. Natali, L., Merani, M.L.: Adaptive streaming in P2P live video systems: a distributed rate control approach. ACM Trans. Multimedia Comput. Commun. Appl. **12**(463), 1–46 (2016)
14. Sideris, A., Markakis, E., Zotos, N.: MPEG-DASH users' QoE: the segment duration effect. In: Seventh International Workshop on Quality of Multimedia Experience (QoMEX), Pylos Nestoras, pp. 1–6 (2015)
15. Liu, P.S., Huang, G.M., Cheng, J.F.: Fibonacci ring overlay structure with distributed chunk storage for P2P VoD streaming. In: International Conference on Computational Science (ICCS), Omaha, NE, vol. 3, pp. 1354–1362 (2012)
16. Cheng, B., Jin, H., Liao, X.: RINDY: a ring based overlay network for peer-to-peer on-demand streaming. In: Ma, J., Jin, H., Yang, L.T., Tsai, J.J.-P. (eds.) UIC 2006. LNCS, vol. 4159, pp. 1048–1058. Springer, Heidelberg (2006). https://doi.org/10.1007/11833529_106
17. Wu, D.L., Liu, C., Keith, Y.R.: View-upload decoupling: a redesign of multi-channel P2P video system. In: IEEE INFOCOM Conference 2009, Rio de Janeiro, Brazil, pp. 2726–2730 (2009)
18. Huang, Y., Fu, T.Z., Chiu, D.-M.: Challenges, design and analysis of a large-scale P2P-VoD system. In: Proceedings of the ACM SIGCOMM 2008 Conference on Data Communication, New York, NY, USA, pp. 375–388 (2008)

A Generic Polynomial-Time Cell Association Scheme in Ultra-Dense Cellular Networks

Chao Fang[1], Lusheng Wang[1(✉)], Hai Lin[2], and Min Peng[1]

[1] Anhui Province Key Laboratory of Industry Safety and Emergency Technology,
School of Computer Science and Information Engineering,
Hefei University of Technology, Hefei, China
wanglusheng@hfut.edu.cn
[2] Key Laboratory of Aerospace Information Security and Trusted Computing,
Ministry of Education, School of Cyber Science and Engineering,
Wuhan University, Wuhan, China

Abstract. Cell association in heterogeneous cellular networks is a significant research issue, but existing schemes mainly optimize a single objective and could not solve such a problem with a generic utility function in polynomial time. This paper proposes a cell association scheme for generic optimization objectives with polynomial-time complexity, which employs a virtual base station method to transform it into a 2-dimensional assignment problem solved by Hungarian algorithm. Based on this scheme, a framework for the tradeoff among multiple optimization objectives is designed. This framework jointly considers spectral efficiency and load balancing, designs a weight factor to adjust their impacts on the optimization, and uses an experience pool to store the relationship between performance demands and corresponding weight factor values. For an instantaneous cell association decision in a given network scenario, the association results are obtained as soon as the corresponding factor value is taken from the pool and the Hungarian algorithm is called for the matching. Compared with existing schemes, our proposal achieves a better tradeoff between system capacity and UE fairness with an extremely low time cost.

Keywords: Heterogeneous cellular networks · Cell association · 2-dimensional assignment problem · Hungarian algorithm · Fairness

1 Introduction

To solve problems caused by the increment of traffic load and the lack of wireless resource, cellular networks evolve toward heterogeneity integrating femtocells with traditional macrocells, called heterogeneous cellular networks (HCNs) [1]. The deployment of femtocells brings in an augmentation of the system capacity thanks to the small-scale reuse of resource [2], but the association problem

H. Gao et al. (Eds.): ChinaCom 2019, LNICST 312, pp. 417–432, 2020.
https://doi.org/10.1007/978-3-030-41114-5_31

between all the base stations (BSs) and user equipments (UEs) becomes more and more complex when the densification of BSs increases. Therefore, it becomes a critical issue to find a fast cell association scheme in HCNs, which should achieve a good tradeoff between multiple performance metrics.

In the literature, there are many studies on cell association in HCNs. Some of them just considered a traditional performance metric, such as signal-to-interference-plus-noise ratio (SINR), so that an association strategy with high system capacity could be quickly obtained [3]. However, due to the difference of transmission powers between a femtocell and a macrocell, too many UEs tended to access the macro one, making the traditional SINR-based scheme unsuitable for HCNs. To find a suitable solution for HCNs, cell association and scheduling were jointly optimized in [4], which transformed it into a distributed convex optimization and used an alternating direction method of multipliers to solve it. This algorithm associated more UEs to underloaded femtocells to improve load balancing and the throughput on cell edges. [5] proposed a cell association scheme based on UE behavior awareness, which obtained the association result based on UEs' instantaneous states (such as their deployment and mobility features) and cells' characteristics, so that the scheme could dynamically approach the network's maximum throughput.

There are some other studies on the optimization methods of cell association. [6] considered the problem with the proportional-fair utility function and transformed it into a convex optimization by relaxing the binary variables representing the associations into continuous variables between 0 and 1, which was then solved by the Lagrange duality method. [7] jointly optimized cell association and power control to maximize the system total utility and minimize the power consumption. The problem was modeled as a mixed integer convex optimization by an annealing-based coalition game and the primal decomposition theory. [8] proposed a cell association scheme based on online Q-learning, which continuously learned UE behaviors and the dynamic UE environment, so that load balancing was improved under the premise of guaranteeing UE quality of service (QoS). [9] proposed a deep Q-learning based scheme, which achieved an optimal association under the premise of guaranteeing the downlink UE QoS.

None of the above schemes is polynomial, but some existing studies transform cell association into an assignment problem that is solvable in polynomial time. [10] considered a virtual base station (VBS) idea to transform the problem into the association between UEs and VBSs, where one BS was mapped into a number of VBSs, hence becoming a 2-dimensional assignment problem. UEs wanted to maximize their own profits and BSs wanted load balancing, so a Nash bargaining game was used to model the conflicts between UEs and BSs. [11] jointly optimized the cell association problem with BS dormancy and considered a utility function obeying proportional fairness. On the one hand, the cell association subproblem was transformed into a 2-dimensional assignment problem and solved by Hungarian algorithm. On the other hand, a low-complex algorithm based on a successive approximation method was proposed for joint optimization. [12] jointly considered cell association and almost blank subframe (ABS) ratio as a combinatorial optimization problem. For a given ABS ratio,

Hungarian algorithm was used to match UEs and VBSs, and finally a strategy corresponding to a relatively small ABS ratio but a large number of associated UEs was obtained.

In summary, existing cell association schemes mainly optimize a single performance metric and most of them are not polynomial. Some polynomial-time schemes only work for proportional-fair utility functions. Therefore, this paper proposes a generic polynomial-time scheme and uses it as the core of a cell association framework that optimizes multiple performance metrics with a tradeoff. In details, a VBS method is employed to transform cell association into a 2-dimensional assignment problem between UEs and VBSs. Then, a weighting factor is used to adjust the impacts of spectral efficiency and load balancing. We store the relationship between achieved performance and corresponding factor values in an experience pool. Once an association decision is required, an association result is obtained by running Hungarian algorithm on a virtual weight matrix that is calculated based on the corresponding factor taken from the experience pool. The advantages of the proposal are threefold: its complexity is polynomial, its objective function could be generic, and it achieves a better tradeoff among multiple performance metrics.

The remainder of this paper is organized as follows. Section 2 provides the system model. Section 3 describes the proposed scheme and the framework. Section 4 shows the simulation results. In the end, the paper is concluded in Sect. 5.

2   System Model

We consider a circular region covered by a macrocell and a number of femtocells. The BS of the former is in the center and the BSs of the latter are deployed in the circle obeying a certain distribution, as shown in Fig. 1. $\mathbf{BS} = \{BS_j | j = 1, \ldots, N\}$ is used to denote all of them, where N is the total number of BSs in the whole region. UEs in the area are represented by $\mathbf{UE} = \{UE_i | i = 1, \ldots, M\}$, where M is the total number.

The scheme in this paper is designed to be generic for a series of utility functions and for different levels of fairness, as explained at the end of Sect. 3.1, but to simplify the description of the proposal and to make it easy to follow, we model the problem here as the maximization of the system capacity, given by

$$\max_{x_{ij}} \sum_{j \in \mathbf{BS}} \sum_{i \in \mathbf{UE}} x_{ij} C_{ij} \tag{1}$$

$$s.t. \sum_{j \in \mathbf{BS}} x_{ij} = 1 \ \forall i \in \mathbf{UE} \tag{1a}$$

$$x_{ij} = \{0, 1\} \ \forall i \in \mathbf{UE}, j \in \mathbf{BS} \tag{1b}$$

where $C_{ij} = B \cdot s_{ij} / \sum_{i \in \mathbf{UE}} x_{ij}$ is the capacity of the link between UE_i and BS_j, B is the total bandwidth that a BS possesses in the system. x_{ij} represents the association between UE_i and BS_j, i.e., $x_{ij} = 1$ if it is associated and 0 otherwise,

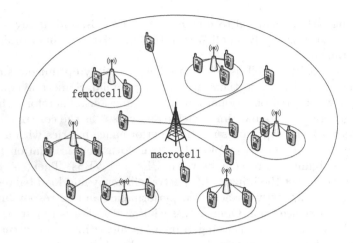

Fig. 1. System model.

so $\sum_{i\in\mathbf{UE}} x_{ij}$ represents the total number of UEs associating with BS_j. (1b) indicates that one UE can only associate with a single BS. s_{ij} represents the spectral efficiency of UE_i associating with BS_j which can be written as

$$s_{ij} = \log_2\left(1 + \frac{Pr_{ij}}{I_j + N_0}\right) \tag{2}$$

where N_0 is the variance of the additive white Gaussian noise (AWGN). Pr_{ij} is the reception power for the link between UE_i and BS_j, and it is calculated by

$$Pr_{ij} = Pt_j - PL_{ij} \tag{3}$$

where Pt_j is the transmission power for the link between UE_i and BS_j, and PL_{ij} is the link's pathloss. I_j represents the total interference from the other cells

$$I_j = \sum_{\beta\in\mathbf{BS}/j} Ir_j\left(\beta\right) \tag{4}$$

where $Ir_j\left(\beta\right)$ represents the interference from cell β to BS_j. Note that, the calculation of $Ir_j\left(\beta\right)$ is different for uplink and downlink, so the values in the formed weighting matrix are different, as well as the association results, but it does not affect much of the proposal in this paper. Meanwhile, we do not combine uplink and downlink for an integrated decision, because traffic loads of uplink and downlink may go through different BSs in HCNs.

3   Proposed Scheme and Framework

3.1   Proposed Generic Polynomial-Time Scheme

The system capacity maximization problem modeled by (1) is a typical one-to-multiple assignment problem. To the best of our knowledge, it cannot be solved in polynomial time if the utility function is not in a proportional-fair form [10,11]. We employ the VBS concept in [11] and try to find a heuristic method to transform the problem with generic utility functions to a 2-dimensional assignment problem, so that it can be solved in polynomial time by a traditional method, called Hungarian algorithm.

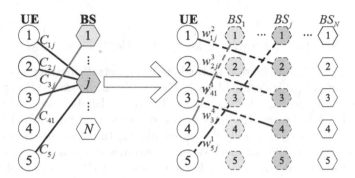

(a) Associations between UEs and BSs   (b) Associations between UEs and VBSs

Fig. 2. An example of VBS method.

The VBS method maps each BS into M VBSs and each VBS can only be associated with one single UE. In this way, we may transform the one-to-multiple assignment problem between UEs and BSs into a 2-dimensional assignment problem between UEs and VBSs, as shown in Fig. 2. Lines in Fig. 2a represent the associations between UEs and BSs, and symbols marked on the lines denote these links' capacities. Similarly, spotted lines in Fig. 2b represent the associations between UEs and VBSs, and symbols marked on the spotted lines denote the utilities of these associations, i.e., w_{ij}^l denotes the utility obtained by associating UE_i with the lth VBS of BS_j.

To make sure the objective function of the transformed problem is equivalent to the original in (1), the total capacities of the UEs associated with each BS should equal to the summation of the utilities of these UEs associated with VBSs (Condition 1). Taking Fig. 2 as an example, we should have $C_{1j} + C_{2j} + C_{3j} + C_{5j} = w_{1j}^2 + w_{2j}^3 + w_{3j}^4 + w_{5j}^1$ and $C_{41} = w_{41}^1$. In the meantime, since the method used to solve the transformed association problem is the Hungarian algorithm which chooses in priority the VSB providing a larger utility for each UE, w_{ij}^l should be monotonously decreasing with the increasing of l (Condition 2). Finally, w_{ij}^l is used to calculate the input matrix of the Hungarian algorithm, so each w_{ij}^l for any i, j, and l should be known before an association result is obtained. In other words, w_{ij}^l should not be related to other UEs' features, such as their capacities and their associated VBSs, because you do not know if they are associated with the same BS during the Hungarian algorithm. Therefore, w_{ij}^l should be an expression only related to UE_i, BS_j, and the VBS index l (Condition 3).

To design an expression of w_{ij}^l that fits for all the above conditions simultaneously is a mission impossible, otherwise problem (1) should have been already precisely transformed into a 2-dimensional assignment problem and solved. Inspired by the design of w_{ij}^l for the problem with a proportional-fair objective function in [11], we relax Condition 1 by giving the summation of w_{ij}^l a range that may contain the total capacity of these UEs, so a heuristic design is obtained as

$$w_{ij}^l = \begin{cases} s_{ij} & l = 1 \\ s_{ij} + k \times [(l-1)\log(l-1) - l\log(l)] & 2 \leq l \leq M \end{cases} \quad (5)$$

where $k \in [0, +\infty)$ is a weighting factor between spectral efficiency and fairness. When $k = 0$, w_{ij}^l in (5) is decided by s_{ij}. Thus, UEs all choose the BSs providing them the highest spectral efficiencies, leading to load imbalance and poor UE fairness. When k increases, the importance of the second part in (5) increases and the impact from s_{ij} gradually decreases, making the difference between associating with different BSs smaller. When k becomes quite large, w_{ij}^l is mainly decided by the second part in (5). Even though the UEs may be distributed asymmetrically, they tend to be averagely assigned to the BSs, making UE fairness varies without caring about their locations. In a word, $k = 0$ and $k = +\infty$ are two extremes representing the considerations of only spectral efficiency and of only averaging the number of UEs among the BSs, so there must be a k that achieves a good tradeoff between the two objectives. Based on the VBS method and the designed w_{ij}^l in (5), problem (1) is transformed into a 2-dimensional assignment problem as follows:

$$\max_{x_{ij}^l} \sum_{j \in \mathbf{BS}} \sum_{i \in \mathbf{UE}} \sum_{l=1}^{M} x_{ij}^l w_{ij}^l \quad (6)$$

$$s.t. \sum_{j \in \mathbf{BS}} \sum_{l=1}^{M} x_{ij}^l = 1 \; \forall i \in \mathbf{UE} \quad (6a)$$

$$\sum_{i \in \mathbf{UE}} x_{ij}^l \leq 1 \; \forall j \in \mathbf{BS}, 1 \leq l \leq M \quad (6b)$$

$$x_{ij}^l \in \{0, 1\} \; \forall i \in \mathbf{UE}, \forall j \in \mathbf{BS}, 1 \leq l \leq M \quad (6c)$$

where x_{ij}^l represents the association between UE_i and the lth VBS of BS_j, i.e., $x_{ij}^l = 1$ if it is associated and 0 otherwise. (6a) guarantees that each UE only associates with one single VBS, (6b) guarantees that each VBS is only associated with one UE. In the meantime, note that (1) is also a utility function integrating the two objectives, so there is probably a k making (6) almost equivalent to (1).

Based on the above analysis and design, problem (1) is heuristically transformed into a 2-dimensional assignment problem. Then, Hungarian algorithm is employed to solve it with the following key steps:

(a) for each BS, the utility between each of its VBS and each UE is calculated, and an M-by-M utility matrix is obtained. For the N BSs, we obtain N M-by-M utility matrices and joint them as an M-by-MN long square matrix $\mathbf{W}$. Denoting its entry on the ith row and the yth column as $W(i, y)$, it can be represented by $W(i, y) = w_{ij}^l$, where $j = y$ ceil M, $l = y$ mod M.

(b) we use the Hungarian algorithm on $\mathbf{W}$ to obtain the associations between UEs and VBSs, which can be simply transformed back to the associations between UEs and BSs.

Note that, although (1) is modeled as a capacity maximization problem, the proposed scheme is generic for utility functions with a form of $\sum_{i \in \mathbf{UE}} x_{ij} f(\cdot)$, as well as different fairness levels integrated on it. The function is a summation of the utilities of all the UEs, $\{x_{ij} | i \in \mathbf{UE}, j \in \mathbf{BS}\}$ are the binary variables representing the associations, and $f(\cdot)$ should be a utility function integrating the concept that the resource of a BS is averagely divided by all its associated UEs. All kinds of utility functions obeying these conditions can be solved by our proposal. Meanwhile, the effect of the weighting factor $k \in [0, +\infty)$ integrated in our scheme similarly corresponds to the effect of $\alpha \in [0, +\infty)$ in the well-known α-fairness concept, so our scheme could equivalently solve the utility functions integrating different levels of fairness by taking a corresponding k value. In summary, our scheme is generic for all kinds of utility functions obeying the above conditions and different levels of fairness.

3.2 Usage of the Proposed Scheme in a Two-Stage Framework

The above subsection is described in a theoretical way, but the usage of such a method for cell association in a real network should be explained and one key problem must be further considered, i.e., the process to obtain a suitable k is too slow for an instantaneous cell association decision. Therefore, a cell association framework is proposed in this subsection, which uses the above theoretical method as the core and achieves a tradeoff among multiple performance metrics. This framework divides the cell association process into two stages: one preprocessed experimental stage, as shown by the left part of Fig. 3, to obtain an experience pool containing a number of representative k values and corresponding performance metric values, and one trigger-based instantaneous decision stage, as shown by the right part of Fig. 3, to quickly reach an appropriate association result.

The experimental stage may be run in a centralized manner by a macro BS or in a distributed manner by a number of cloud computers. In details, it first deploys BSs and UEs to form a similar network as the real scenario, and each BS is mapped to M VBSs. For each k value, it then obtains the long square utility matrix $\mathbf{W}$ by (5) and calls Hungarian algorithm to reach an association result. Finally, the performance in terms of various metrics for this association is calculated. After a large number of simulation rounds are completed, the average performance metric values for each k are calculated and stored into the experience pool which is actually a table containing the k values and their corresponding performance metric values. Since this pool is decided by

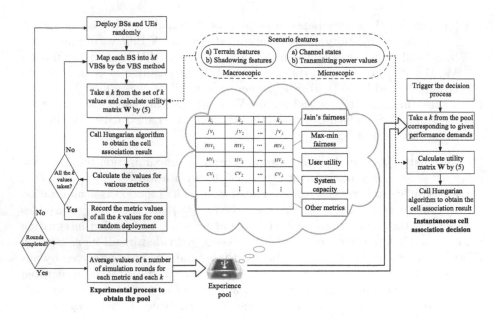

Fig. 3. A two-stage framework using the proposed cell association scheme.

the macroscopic features of the scenario, it is updated only when the scenario encounters an obvious change.

After the pool is obtained, it is ready for usage during an instantaneous cell association decision. The decision stage may be triggered periodically or by some obvious changes, such as the movement of some representative UEs, but the triggering issue is out of the scope of this study. Once the decision process is triggered, a k value corresponding to the demanded performance is taken from the experience pool. Then, (5) is used to calculate the long square utility matrix $\mathbf{W}$ and Hungarian algorithm is used to reach an association result for this instantaneous decision. Note that, the receiving power values of useful signals and interferences for the calculation of $\mathbf{W}$ in the experimental process is different from those values in the decision process. For the former, the useful signals and interferences are calculated based on the channel model and the randomly deployed BSs and UEs in the simulation. For the latter, they are calculated based on the real values evaluated by channel estimation in the network, i.e., the microscopic features of the scenario shown by Fig. 3.

4 Performance Evaluation

In our simulations, BSs and UEs are distributed within a circular region with a radius of 25 m. For the sake of limited space, only downlink channel features are used for the calculation of utility matrices, and the channel is modeled by the close-in free space reference distance model with frequency-dependent path loss exponent for 5G scenarios [13]:

$$PL(f, d)[\text{dBm}] = 20 \log_{10} \left(\frac{4\pi f}{c} \right)$$

$$+ 10n \left[1 + b \left(\frac{f - f_0}{f_0} \right) \right] \log_{10} \left(\frac{d}{1m} \right) + X_\sigma \tag{7}$$

where f is the carrier frequency, n is the path loss exponent, b is a slope parameter, X_σ represents the shadowing, and f_0 is the reference frequency. Detailed parameter values are listed in Table 1.

Table 1. Simulation parameters.

Parameter	Value
Circular region radius	25 m
Femtocell transmission power	21 dBm
Macrocell transmission power	30 dBm
Femtocell bandwidth	6 MHz
Macrocell bandwidth	20 MHz
Variance of AWGN	-174 dBm/Hz
Carrier frequency	3.5 GHz
Path loss exponent	2.59
Slope parameter	0.01
Shadowing	7.4 dBm
Reference frequency	39.5 GHz

4.1 Simulations of the Preprocessed Experimental Stage

In this subsection, the preprocessed experimental stage in the framework is simulated. According to our experience, k in (5) should take representative values to form an appropriate experience pool, but here we take values $\{0, 0.05, 0.1, 0.3, 0.5, 0.7, 0.9, 1, 1.2, 1.4, 1.6, 1.8, 2, 4, 6, 8, 10, 20, 30, 35, 40\}$ so that the changes of the curves are clearly demonstrated. For each k, performances should be averaged by a large number of simulation rounds, such as 500 in our simulation. We simulate two scenarios, one heterogeneous network scenario and one homogeneous network scenario. At the beginning of 5G network construction, femtocells cannot be densely deployed and macrocells should be still used as a main bearer for traffic loads, forming an uncrowded heterogeneous network. Therefore, the simulated heterogeneous network is composed of 1 macro BS in the center (the big red triangle), 2 femtocells (the small black triangles), and 15 uniformly-distributed UEs. The 2 femtocells' locations may be random and changeable during the 500 simulation rounds, as shown in Fig. 4a or fixed on the right corner as shown in Fig. 4b.

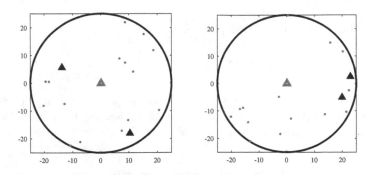

(a) Femtocell random deployment. (b) Femtocell special deployment.

Fig. 4. BS deployments in the heterogeneous network scenario.

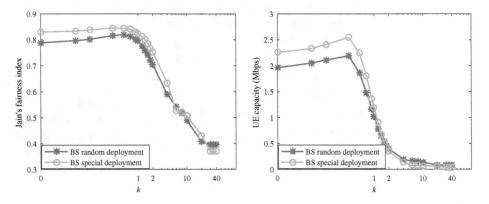

Fig. 5. UE fairness for heterogeneous net- **Fig. 6.** Minimum UE capacity for hetero-
work scenario. geneous network scenario.

Figure 5 shows the Jain's fairness values of the two types of BS deployments. Along with the increase of k, the trends of UE fairness curves generally increase at first and then decrease. As explained in Subsect. 3.1, it is not difficult to understand that $k = 0$ and $k = +\infty$ are two extremes resulting in low fairness, so there must be a a k in the middle corresponding to the maximum Jain's fairness. Seen from Fig. 5, the k should be both around [0.3, 0.5] for the two types of deployments of the simulated heterogeneous network scenario. Figure 6 shows the minimum UE capacity of all the UEs. We find that, the trends of the curves are similar to those of fairness, and the best k for this performance metric should be also around 0.3.

The system utilities obtained by (5) are shown in Fig. 7. Since the part multiplied on k is negative in (5), the curves always decrease with the increase of k. Figure 8 shows the system capacities of the two types of deployments. We can see that, the curves gradually increase with the increase of k. Since bandwidth

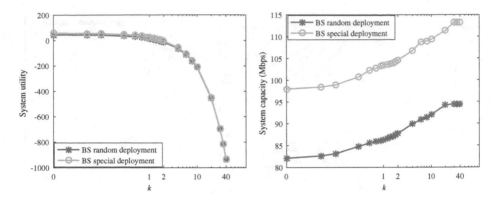

Fig. 7. System utility for heterogeneous network scenario.

Fig. 8. System capacity for heterogeneous network scenario.

and transmission power of the macrocell are both much larger than those of femtocells, most of the UEs tend to choose the macrocell when $k = 0$, which can be easily understood by checking (5). This is actually inbeneficial to the system capacity due to the fact that too many UEs share the bandwidth of the macrocell. When k increases, some UEs gradually change to choose the femtocells, improving the system capacity until the association becomes average among the three BSs.

The simulated homogeneous network scenario is shown by Fig. 9, where 10 femtocells and 80 UEs are deployed in the circular region, and two types of deployments are considered, i.e., random deployment and special deployment with 5 femtocells on the right corner. This scenario may represent the case when 5G network is fully constructed, so femtocells are dense enough to afford all the traffic loads and macrocells are free for network management only.

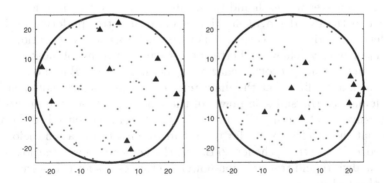

(a) Femtocell random deployment.   (b) Femtocell special deployment.

Fig. 9. BS deployments in the homogeneous network scenario.

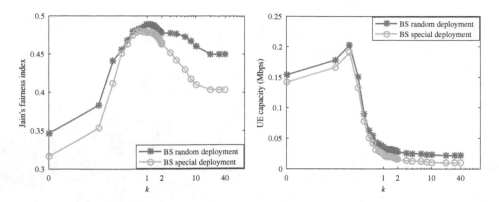

Fig. 10. UE fairness for homogeneous network scenario.

Fig. 11. Minimum UE capacity for homogeneous network scenario.

Generally speaking, UE fairness, minimum UE capacity, system utility, and capacity of the homogeneous scenario have similar trends as the heterogeneous one, as shown in Figs. 10, 11, 12, and 13, but there are also some differences. One is the Jain's fairness values when k is relatively small. For the heterogeneous scenario, most UEs tend to choose the macro BS when k is small as explained above. Meanwhile, we note that the simulation area is within a 25-meter circle, so the UEs are all relatively close to the macro BS with small path loss values. Now that these UEs share the bandwidth of the macro BS averagely and their path loss values are all small, they tend to obtain similar capacities, leading to large Jain's fairness. By contrast, UEs in the homogeneous scenario tend to choose different femtocells and the transmission power of femto BSs is relatively small, so they tend to obtain obviously different capacities, leading to small Jain's fairness, as shown in Fig. 10. Also note that for different scenarios, the k values corresponding to the maximum Jain's fairness could be different, and for the homogeneous scenario it should be around $k = 1$ as shown in Fig. 10.

The one of the two deployments that leads to a better performance is also quite different for the two scenarios. For the heterogeneous scenario, special deployment obviously achieves a better performance in terms of most evaluated metrics, while the homogeneous scenario is generally inverse. Based on our massive experiments, we find that the main reason for this phenomenon is still the bandwidth and the transmission power of the macro BS. Since the macro BS is quite aggressive for attracting UEs to associate, it seems beneficial to the whole system to put the two femto BSs far from it in the small simulation region, such as on the edge. By contrast, the femto BSs in the homogeneous scenario are with the same bandwidth and transmission power, so the results for this scenario does not show this feature.

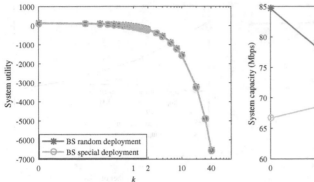

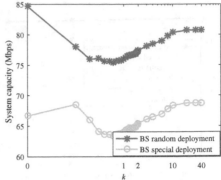

Fig. 12. System utility for homogeneous network scenario.

Fig. 13. System capacity for homogeneous network scenario.

4.2 Simulations of Cell Association Decision and Comparisons with Other Schemes

This subsection simulates the cell association decision stage in the framework and evaluates the performance of the final association results. A k value should be taken from the experience pool, so that multiple performance metrics could be comprehensively considered by a tradeoff or a quite high performance for a certain metric is reached as an objective performance for comparison. To compare with our scheme, we select the max SINR scheme in [3], the simulated annealing based scheme in [7], and the Q-learning based scheme in [8] for the following simulations. Besides, the heterogeneous network scenario with randomly deployed femtocells in Subsect. 4.1 is selected due to the fact that existing related works mainly consider heterogeneous networks. Based on the simulation results in Subsect. 4.1, we select $k = 0.3$ in our scheme for the comparisons with the other schemes. This k value emphasizes UE fairness and the capacity of the worst UE due to the fact that compared schemes generally consider system capacity more than fairness.

Figure 14 shows the Jain's fairness values of various schemes. The proposed scheme achieves a high UE fairness. $k = 0.3$ in the simulation corresponds to a very high UE fairness already demonstrated by Fig. 5, and here we also find that the proposed scheme can get higher UE fairness when optimizing UE fairness alone in this figure. Figure 15 shows the minimum UE capacities (max-min fairness) of various schemes. Similar to UE fairness, our scheme also achieves a very good result. Note that, our scheme is better than Q-learning scheme and Max-SINR scheme in terms of UE fairness and minimum UE capacity.

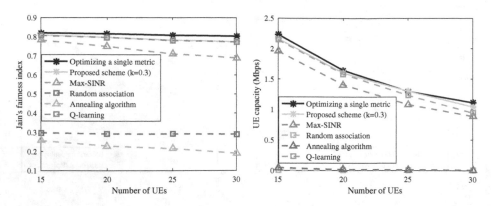

Fig. 14. UE fairness values of various schemes.

Fig. 15. Minimum UE capacities of various schemes.

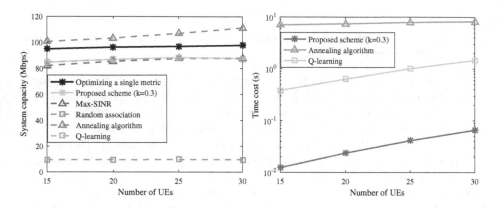

Fig. 16. System capacities of various schemes.

Fig. 17. Time costs of various schemes.

Figure 16 shows the system capacities of various schemes. Simulated annealing takes a quite long time to search for a near-optimal solution, so its achieved system capacity is obviously better than the others. Q-learning based scheme and our proposed scheme both achieve relatively high system capacity. Note that, we set $k = 0.3$ that is a value corresponding to high fairness, but the achieved system capacity is still quite competitive in the simulated schemes. If a different k is set for optimizing system capacity only, our scheme achieves an obviously better system capacity, as shown by the curve "Optimizing a single metric".

Figure 17 shows the time costs of three schemes. Simulated annealing based scheme is undoubtedly slow, and the proposed scheme is obviously faster than the Q-learning based scheme. The reason is that, Q-learning requires too many iterations before finding a good solution, but our scheme requires only solving a 2-dimensional assignment problem with polynomial-time complexity.

5   Conclusion

This paper studied the cell association problem in heterogeneous cellular networks and a generic polynomial-time scheme was proposed. On the one hand, the scheme employed the VBS method to transform heuristically the problem into a form that was solvable in polynomial time. On the other hand, the scheme achieved a tradeoff among multiple performance metrics by a two-stage framework. An experience pool containing a series of k values and corresponding performance metric values was used to link the two stages. Simulation results showed that the proposed scheme achieved a better tradeoff between spectral efficiency and UE fairness with an extremely low time cost. For the sake of limited space, this paper only simulated the case using downlink channel features for the calculation of the utility matrix, and simulations of the case using uplink channel features will be a future work.

Acknowledgements. This work was funded by the Fundamental Research Funds for the Central Universities of China under grant no. PA2019GDQT0012.

References

1. Liu, D., et al.: User association in 5G networks: a survey and an outlook. IEEE Commun. Surv. Tutor. **18**(2), 1018–1044 (2016)
2. Andrews, J., Claussen, H., Dohler, M., Rangan, S., Reed, M.: Femtocell: past, present, and future. IEEE J. Sel. Areas Commun. **30**(3), 497–508 (2012)
3. Andrews, J., Singh, S., Ye, Q., Lin, X., Dhillon, H.: An overview of load balancing in HetNets: old myths and open problems. IEEE Wirel. Commun. **21**(2), 18–25 (2014)
4. Ge, X., Li, X., Jin, H., Cheng, J., Leung, V.: Joint user association and user scheduling for load balancing in heterogeneous networks. IEEE Trans. Wirel. Commun. **17**(5), 3211–3225 (2018)
5. Sun, Y., Feng, G., Qin, S., Sun, S.: Cell association with user behavior awareness in heterogeneous cellular networks. IEEE Trans. Veh. Technol. **67**(5), 4589–4601 (2018)
6. Shen, K., Yu, W.: Distributed pricing-based user association for downlink heterogeneous cellular networks. IEEE J. Sel. Areas Commun. **32**(6), 1100–1113 (2014)
7. Qian, L., Wu, Y., Zhou, H., Shen, X.: Joint uplink base station association and power control for small-cell networks with non-orthogonal multiple access. IEEE Trans. Wirel. Commun. **16**(9), 5567–5582 (2017)
8. Li, Z., Wang, C., Jiang, C.: User association for load balancing in vehicular networks: an online reinforcement learning approach. IEEE Trans. Intell. Transp. Syst. **18**(8), 2217–2228 (2017)
9. Zhao, N., Liang, Y., Niyato, D., Pei, Y., Wu, M., Jiang, Y.: Deep reinforcement learning for user association and resource allocation in heterogeneous cellular networks. IEEE Trans. Wirel. Commun. (in press)
10. Wang, W., Wu, X., Xie, L., Lu, S.: Femto-matching: efficient traffic offloading in heterogeneous cellular networks. In: IEEE INFOCOM, pp. 325–333. IEEE, Hong Kong (2015)

11. Prasad, N., Arslan, M., Rangarajan, S.: Exploiting cell dormancy and load balancing in LTE HetNets: optimizing the proportional fairness utility. IEEE Trans. Commun. **62**(10), 3706–3722 (2014)
12. Mishra, S., Rangineni, S., Murthy, C.: Exploiting an optimal user association strategy for interference management in HetNets. IEEE Commun. Lett. **18**(10), 1799–1802 (2014)
13. 5GCM. http://www.5gworkshops.com/5GCM.html

Deep Q Network for Wiretap Channel Model with Energy Harvesting

Zhaohui Li$^{(\boxtimes)}$ and Weijia Lei

School of Communication and Information Engineering, Chongqing University of Posts and
Telecommunications, Chongqing, China
lizhaohui40@foxmail.com

Abstract. An energy harvesting wiretap channel model is considered in which
the sender is an energy harvesting node. It is assumed that at each time slot only
information about the current state of the sending node is available. In order to find
an effective power allocation strategy to maximize secrecy rate, we put forward
a deep Q network (DQN) scheme. First, we analyze the constraints of the system
and the issue of maximizing the secrecy rate. Next, the power allocation problem
is formulated as a Markov Decision Process (MDP) with unknown transition
probabilities. In order to solve the continuous state space problem that traditional
Q learning algorithms cannot handle, we apply neural networks to approximate
the value function. Finally, an online joint resource power allocation algorithm
based on DQN is presented. Simulation results show that the proposed algorithm
can effectively improve the secrecy rate of the model.

Keywords: Energy harvesting · Deep Q network · Online power allocation ·
Secrecy rate

1 Introduction

With the rapid development of communication industry, the demand for energy supply in
communication networks is increasing. Huge energy consumption inevitably produces
large amounts of greenhouse gases. Looking for new green energy and using energy
reasonably and efficiently has become one of the key issues in the development of
communications industry. Energy harvesting node collects energy from environment for
information transmission. theoretically, it can work continuously and permanently [1].
Due to the randomness and intermittency of energy harvesting, energy management and
power allocation are problems that such nodes need to solve [2].

The energy management model of energy harvesting communication system can
be divided into offline management model and online management model according to
whether the node knows the information of energy arrival and channel state in advance.
The offline management model assumes that data arrival, harvested energy, and channel
state of the energy harvesting process are known at the beginning of the communication.
Although this assumption inconsistent with reality, it provides a theoretical performance
upper bound of energy harvesting communication system. [3–5] studied offline energy

H. Gao et al. (Eds.): ChinaCom 2019, LNICST 312, pp. 433–444, 2020.
https://doi.org/10.1007/978-3-030-41114-5_32

management strategies in different scenarios. [3] studied the optimal offline power allocation strategy for point-to-point energy harvesting communication systems. The transmitter is equipped with an energy harvesting device. A power allocation scheme for maximizing system throughput is given for the single-hop model of direct transmission and the double-hop model forwarded by the relay node. In [4], the energy arrival is known in advance, and the algorithm that finds the optimal transmission policy with respect to the short-term throughput and the minimum transmission completion time is given. In [5], the non-convex power control optimization problem is transformed into a convex optimization problem, and an effective offline algorithm is given. Unlike the specific information of data arrival, harvested energy, and channel state are known in the offline management model, only the statistical information is known of the online management model. [6, 7] researched online energy management strategies. In [6], the issue of dynamical adaptation of transmission rate with regards to the energy arrival process is discussed. In order to optimize system performance, a low complexity transmission power allocation scheme is proposed. In [7], a cooperative communication system consisting of a source node, destination node and relay node with energy harvesting is considered. The optimal joint link selection and power allocation policies for minimizing the average outage probability were obtained through dynamic programming algorithms.

In practical scenario, the system has no prior knowledge about the environment. Therefore, the offline energy management framework is not applicable. These statistics are actually difficult to obtain, so online energy control strategies based on statistical information is also greatly limited. Reinforcement learning is an adaptive online learning that requires no prior knowledge. The agent learns to maximize the reward in the constant interaction with environment. [8, 9] studied the energy control problem in communication systems using reinforcement learning to solve the problem without environmental prior knowledge. In [8], a point-to-point communication system in which the sending node is energy harvesting node is considered. The optimal power control problem is formulated as a reinforcement learning problem. Then, the effects of the parameters of each algorithm are discussed. In [9], a MIMO wireless communication link in which the nodes are equipped with energy harvesters and rechargeable batteries that are continuously charging from a renewable energy source is studied. And a learning approach in order to find the most efficient transmission policy for data communication that maximizes throughput is proposed. It is assumed that the state space is finite, and the channel coefficients are discrete values in [8, 9], but the actual situation is not the case. [10] proposed the DQN algorithm, which uses neural networks to solve the continuous state space problem that cannot be solved in the traditional reinforcement learning algorithm.

The security threat to wireless communication is more serious than wire communication because of its broadcast characteristics and openness. With the development of computing technology, traditional encryption technology has a risk of failure. The security of information transmission from the physical layer came into being. In 1975, Wyner proposed the wiretap channel model [11], which defined secrecy capacity to evaluate the performance of the system's secure transmission. Wyner's research shows that when legal channel is superior to wiretap channel, theoretically secure communication between legitimate users is possible even without any encryption measures. [12] introduces the basic theory of physical layer security and outlines the latest work and future challenges of physical layer security technology. In [13], the secure communication of energy harvesting Gaussian wiretap channel based on save-then-transmit protocol is studied. Under the condition of limited energy harvested, an optimization algorithm targeting secrecy rate is proposed.

In this paper, an online power allocation algorithm is studied to maximize secrecy rate. And an energy harvesting wiretap channel model composed of three single antenna nodes is considered. Different from [8] and [9], channel coefficients, battery capacity, and harvested energy in the model are all consecutive values. Therefore, the sending node has infinite-state in our model. To solve this problem, we present an online power allocation algorithm based on DQN.

2 System Model

In this paper, the physical layer security transmission problem under the energy harvesting wiretap channel model consisting of three single antenna nodes is considered. As shown in Fig. 1, the sending node contains an energy harvesting device and a rechargeable battery. The energy harvesting device collects energy from the environment and uses it for sending data to destination node B. During transmission, the energy harvested by the sending node changes randomly, so does the wireless channel. In our scenario, node A has no prior knowledge of energy harvested and channel state. In order to maximize the long-term average secrecy rate, the sending node dynamically adjusts the transmission power according to the instantaneous channel state and energy harvested.

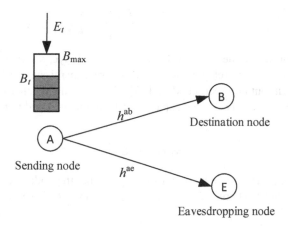

Fig. 1. System model

It is assumed that an amount of energy E_t Joule (J) is harvested at time slot t, and the maximum energy can be harvested is E_{max} J. The harvested energy is stored in a rechargeable battery with maximum capacity B_{max} J. There is no energy loss while charging or discharging from the battery. Additionally, the current state of the battery termed B_t J, the transmission power of node A is P_t Watt (W), the channel coefficients of the sending node to the destination node and the sending node to the eavesdropping node are h_t^{ab} and h_t^{ae} respectively. The transmission power should be less than the maximum discharging power P_{max} of the battery. Therefore, the constraint in Eq. (1) must be considered.

$$0 \leq P_t \leq P_{max} \tag{1}$$

At the same time, the transmission power can be allocated only after the harvested energy has been stored in the battery. As a result, causal constraint

$$\tau \cdot P_t \leq B_t \, \forall t = 1, 2, \ldots, T \tag{2}$$

should be satisfied. Where τ is the duration of one time slot. At the beginning of the next time slot, the battery level is

$$B_{t+1} = \min(B_t - \tau \cdot P_t + E_t, B_{max}) \tag{3}$$

It is assumed that the channel coefficients keep invariant in one time slot. The noise of the legal channel and the wiretap channel is assumed to be independent and identically distributed (i.i.d.) zero mean additive white Gaussian noise with variances σ_b^2 and σ_e^2 respectively. Consequently, the channel capacity of the legal channel and the wiretap channel are

$$C_t^b = \log_2\left(1 + \frac{P_t |h_t^{ab}|^2}{\sigma_b^2}\right) \tag{4}$$

and

$$C_t^e = \log_2\left(1 + \frac{P_t |h_t^{ae}|^2}{\sigma_e^2}\right) \tag{5}$$

respectively. According to the relevant theory of physical layer security, when the legal channel is superior to the wiretap channel, the secure transmission of information can be realized even without any secret coding [12]. The system's reachable secrecy rate is defined as the difference between the capacity of legal channel and wiretap channel, as follows.

$$R_{s_t} = \left[C_t^b - C_t^e\right]^+ \tag{6}$$

Where $[a]^+ = \max\{0, a\}$. It can be seen from Eq. (6) that the node A can send message only when $|h_t^{ab}| > |h_t^{ae}|$. Therefore, the transmission power P_t is set to 0 when $|h_t^{ae}| \geq |h_t^{ab}|$.

To sum up, the goal of power allocation is to maximize the long-term average secrecy rate within the constraints of energy harvesting and battery characteristics, i.e.

$$\max_{\{P_t\}} \lim_{T \to \infty} E\left[\sum_{t=1}^{T} R_{s_t}\right]$$
$$\text{s.t.} \quad \text{a)} \ 0 \leq P_t \leq P_{max} \tag{7}$$
$$\text{b)} \ \tau \cdot P_t \leq B_t$$
$$\text{c)} \ P_t = 0, |h_t^{ae}| \geq |h_t^{ab}|$$

3 Reinforcement Learning

3.1 Q Learning

Reinforcement learning [14] is a kind of machine learning that reflects the interaction between agent and environment with states, actions and rewards. The Agent constantly improves strategies in interaction with the environment to maximize the benefits. Reinforcement learning is often modeled as an MDP of quintuples (S, A, T, R, γ). Where S is a set of environmental states. A is a set of actions. T represents the state transition function. R is the reward function. And $\gamma \in [0, 1]$ is the discount factor used to calculate the accumulated reward.

For an MDP, the ultimate goal of reinforcement learning is to find the optimal policy for completing the task. A policy π is a mapping from a given state to the action, i.e. $a_t = \pi(s_t)$. For a given policy π, the accumulated reward is defined as

$$G_t^\pi = R_t + \gamma R_{t+1} + \gamma^2 R_{t+2} + \cdots = \sum_{k=0}^{\infty} \gamma^k R_{t+k} \tag{8}$$

In the formula, R_t is the reward obtained at time slot t. Since the sequence of actions in the same state may be different, the accumulated reward for a certain state is not a specific value, but an expected value. We can define a state-action value function to represent the expected value of the accumulated reward for a given strategy, as follows.

$$Q(s_t, a_t) = E_\pi \{ G_t^\pi | s = s_t, a = a_t \} \tag{9}$$

where E is the mathematical expectation of the strategy. According to the Bellman equation, the accumulated reward is calculated as

$$Q(s_t, a_t) = E_\pi \{ R_t + \gamma Q(s_{t+1}, a_{t+1}) | s = s_t, a = a_t \} \tag{10}$$

During the learning process, the agent continuously optimizes policy π and finally reaches the optimal policy π^*. The essence of reinforcement learning is to find the best Q function for each state-action pair

$$Q*(s_t, a_t) = E_\pi \left\{ R_t + \gamma \max_{a_{t+1}} Q(s_{t+1}, a_{t+1}) | s = s_t, a = a_t \right\} \tag{11}$$

Q learning [15] is a reinforcement learning algorithm based on Q function estimation, also known as Temporal Difference (TD) learning algorithm. The rules for updating the Q function are as follows.

$$Q(s_t, a_t) \leftarrow Q(s_t, a_t) + \alpha \left[R_t + \gamma \max_{a_{t+1}} Q(s_{t+1}, a_{t+1}) - Q(s_t, a_t) \right] \tag{12}$$

Where $\alpha \in [0, 1]$ is the learning rate and $R_t + \gamma \max_{a_{t+1}} Q(s_{t+1}, a_{t+1})$ is TD target (estimate of the target value function).

3.2 Deep Q Network

The Q learning algorithm finds the optimal policy by establishing and updating a Q value table. Q learning works well when the state space is small. However, when the state space and the action space are large or continuous, the value function cannot be represented by a table. To solve this problem, an approximation method can be used to estimate $Q(s_t, a_t)$, i.e.

$$Q(s_t, a_t) \approx \tilde{Q}(s_t, a_t; \theta) \tag{13}$$

Where θ is parameter for Approximating the state-action value function. The approximation of value functions can be divided into linear approximation and nonlinear approximation. The use of neural network to approximation value function is a common nonlinear approximation method. The function approximation is a process of supervised learning. The goal of training is

$$\arg\min_{\theta} \left(Q(s_t, a_t) - \tilde{Q}(s_t, a_t; \theta) \right)^2 \tag{14}$$

When training neural networks, the training data is required to be independent. But the data obtained at each time slot in reinforcement learning is ordered. Training directly with these data may lead to instability of the neural network. DQN adopts a double neural network with the same structure but different parameters to solve the problem of unstable training caused by the correlation between samples. One for calculating the value function with parameter θ, the other is used to calculate the TD target with parameter θ^{TD}. The parameter θ is updated in every step of learning, while the parameter θ^{TD} is updated every fixed step. Besides, DQN set a reply memory to store sample data for each time slot, randomly extracts data from the memory for learning, which breaks the correlation between experiences and improves the training efficiency of the neural network.

DQN is an algorithm based on Q-learning. During the learning process, the parameters of the neural network are updated by the gradient descent method. Therefore, Eq. (12) is changed into

$$\theta_{t+1} = \theta_t + \alpha \left[R_t + \gamma \max_{a_{t+1}} Q\left(s_{t+1}, a_{t+1}; \theta^{TD} \right) - Q(s_t, a_t; \theta_t) \right] \nabla Q(s_t, a_t; \theta_t) \tag{15}$$

Where $R_t + \gamma \max_{a_{t+1}} Q\left(s_{t+1}, a_{t+1}; \theta^{TD} \right)$ is TD target.

4 Power Allocation Algorithm Based on DQN

In this section, an online power allocation algorithm based on DQN is designed to maximize the secrecy rate of the model shown in Fig. 1. At time slot t, node A selects the transmission power P_t based on the information of the current battery level, the harvested energy, and the channel coefficients.

4.1 Problem Formulation

Define the following key elements to map the problems to the Q learning model.

(1) **State space:** At time slot t, the system state includes battery level B_t, harvested energy E_t, channel coefficients h_t^{ab} and h_t^{ae}, i.e. $s_t = \left(B_t, E_t, h_t^{ab}, h_t^{ae}\right)$.

(2) **Action space:** The action space is a set of transmission power that the sending node can select. In our model, the action set A is a set of values from 0 to P_{max} by step size δ. Since the transmission power selectable by the sending node is limited by the current battery level and the maximum discharge power of the battery, the action set A_t is set to

$$A_t = \left\{0, \delta, 2\delta, \ldots, \hat{P}_{max}\right\} \tag{16}$$

where $\hat{P}_{max} = \begin{cases} P_{max}, & B_t/\tau > P_{max} \\ B_t/\tau, & B_t/\tau \leq P_{max} \end{cases}$.

(3) **Reward function:** In this paper, the reward function is improved to the sum of the immediate reward r_t and penalty functions g_t, as follows.

$$R_t = r_t + \beta g_t \tag{17}$$

where $\beta \in [0, 1]$ is a positive real number used to weigh the additional function. The immediate reward is the corresponding benefit when the sending node selects the transmission power P_t, as show in Eq. (18).

$$r_t = \begin{cases} \log_2\left(1 + \frac{P_t|h_t^{ab}|^2}{\sigma_b^2}\right) - \log_2\left(1 + \frac{P_t|h_t^{ae}|^2}{\sigma_e^2}\right), & |h_t^{ab}| > |h_t^{ae}| \\ 0, & |h_t^{ab}| \leq |h_t^{ae}| \end{cases} \tag{18}$$

Since the limitation of battery level, overflow situations must be avoided. Set an additional function

$$g_t = \begin{cases} -1, & B_{t+1} > B_{max} \\ 0, & B_{t+1} \leq B_{max} \end{cases} \tag{19}$$

to punish the actions that cause the battery overflow.

4.2 Exploration and Exploitation

In the process of reinforcement learning, there are two choices: exploration and exploitation. Exploration tries different actions and exploitation selects the currently optimal action. Exploration is aggressive behavior that has the opportunity to discover higher-return actions, but may also adopt actions with lower returns. Exploitation is a conservative behavior, which takes action with the highest current return. In DQN, the ε-greedy strategy is used to trade off between exploration and exploitation, as follows.

$$a_t = \begin{cases} a_{random}, & \text{Probability } \varepsilon \\ \arg\max_{a_t} Q(s_t, a_t), & \text{Probability } 1 - \varepsilon \end{cases} \tag{20}$$

where ε $(0 \le \varepsilon \le 1)$ is a parameter for the compromise of exploration and exploitation. a_{random} represents randomly selected actions. In the early stages of training, the agent explores experience to store in replay memory. As the training progresses, more exploitation is chosen to obtain a higher reward, so the ε gradually decreases. One way to control ε as follows.

$$\varepsilon = \begin{cases} 1, & t \le T_1 \\ 1 - (t - T_1)/T_2, & T_1 < t \le T_1 + T_2 \\ 0, & T_1 + T_2 < t \end{cases} \tag{21}$$

where T_1 is the duration of the exploration phase only, and T_2 is the duration of exploration and exploitation phase. The sending node selects the action of the maximum output Q value of the neural network in the current state When $\varepsilon = 0$. To validate the performance of the proposed algorithm, the duration of $\varepsilon = 0$ is set to T_3.

4.3 Proposed Algorithm

As mentioned before, DQN has a replay memory D with a capacity of N to store the sample data of each time slot. The agent randomly extracts M sample data from the memory to learn. And update the parameters θ to θ^{TD} every C step. The online power allocation algorithm based on DQN is shown in Algorithm 1.

Algorithm 1 DQN-based online joint resource power allocation algorithm

---

Initialize:

    neural network parameter update steps C, replay memory D to capacity N, the Q network with random parameters θ, the target Q network with random parameters θ^{TD}

1. Observe the initial observation
2. **For** $t \le T_1 + T_2 + T_3$ **do**
3.   Select the transmit power P_t by (20)
4.   Get corresponding reward from (17)
5.   Observe the next state s_{t+1}
6.   Store (s_t, P_t, R_t, s_{t+1}) in replay memory
7.   **If** $t > T_1$ **then**
8.   Sample random M of (s_i, P_i, R_i, s_{i+1}) from D and calculate TD target y_i
9. $y_i \begin{cases} R_i, & i = T_1 + T_2 + T_3 \\ R_i + \gamma \max_{a_{i+1}} Q\left(s_{i+1}, P_{i+1}; \theta^{\text{TD}}\right), & i \ne T_1 + T_2 + T_3 \end{cases}$
10.   perform a gradient descent step on $\left(y_i - Q(s_i, P_i; \theta)\right)^2$ with respect to the network parameter θ
11.   Every C step reset $\theta^{\text{TD}} = \theta$
12.   **End if**
13. $s_t \leftarrow s_{t+1}$
14. **End for**

---

5 Simulation Results

In this section, numerical results for the evaluation of the proposed algorithm on improving the system security rate are presented. For the simulations, the length of the time slot $\tau = 1$ s. The energy harvested by node A at each time slot follows a uniform distribution between $[0, E_{max}]$. It is assumed that the channel coefficients h_t^{ab} and h_t^{ae} are taken from i.i.d. Rayleigh fading process with zero mean and unit variance, and keep invariant within a time slot. The noise variance is set to $\sigma_b^2 = \sigma_e^2 = 1W$. The initial battery power is 0 J. The maximum discharge power $P_{max} = 5$ W. The step size δ of the action set is set to $0.04\, P_{max}$. In addition, Table 1 provides some relevant parameters used in the simulations.

For comparison, we compare it with greedy policy and random policy. Greedy policy allocations the maximum power available for every time slot that satisfies the communication condition, i.e.

$$P_t = \begin{cases} \min\left(\frac{B_t}{\tau}, P_{max}\right), & |h_t^{ab}| > |h_t^{ae}| \\ 0, & |h_t^{ab}| \le |h_t^{ae}| \end{cases} \tag{22}$$

Table 1. Related simulation parameters

Parameter	Value	Meaning
M	32	Sample size each step
N	20000	Memory size
C	200	Update frequency of TD target neural network
γ	0.9	Discount factor
α	0.01	Learning rate
β	0.5	The arguments used to weigh additional function
T1	2000	Exploration phase
T2	48000	Exploration-exploitation phase
T3	10000	Exploitation phase

The greedy policy maximizes current reward without considering the impact of current decisions on the future. Random policy randomly selects the transmission power within the maximum available power range in the time slot that satisfies $|h_t^{ab}| \ge |h_t^{ae}|$.

In Fig. 2, we compare the performance of the proposed algorithm with greedy policy and random policy. The time average secrecy rate is the average of the secrecy rate of each time slot from the beginning of the simulation to the current time. In this case, the battery capacity is set as $B_{max} = 15$ J, and the maximum energy of collection $E_{max} = 1$ J. Results show that the performance of the proposed algorithm is significantly better than the other two algorithms.

Figure 3 shows the curve of the average security rate changing with the maximum E_{max} of collected energy. In the simulation, $B_{max} = 12E_{max}$. It can be seen from the

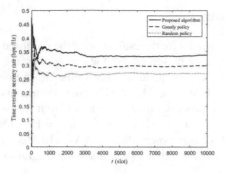

Fig. 2. Time average secrecy rate versus time

figure that the average secrecy rate of all algorithms increases as the E_{max} increases. This is because, with the harvested energy increases, the more energy the transmission node can use to transmit data, the higher the transmission rate will be.

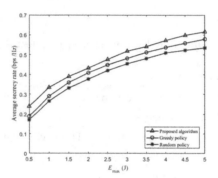

Fig. 3. Average secrecy rate versus E_{max}

Figure 4 shows the effect of the battery buffer size on the performance for $E_{max} = 1$ J. It can be seen that the performance of the proposed algorithm is close to greedy policy when $B_{max} < 5$ J. The reason for this is that when the battery capacity is low, it is easy to overflow. In order to avoid this situation, it is reasonable to choose a larger transmission power, so the performance of the proposed algorithm is similar to greedy algorithm. Additionally, the secrecy rate of all algorithms saturates when $B_{max} > 11$ J. Because the battery has sufficient capacity to buffer the harvested energy for energy dispatching.

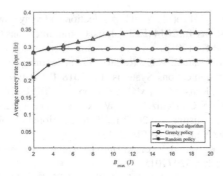

Fig. 4. Average secrecy rate versus B_{max}

6   Conclusion

Based on reinforcement learning, we have studied the maximum secrecy rate of energy harvesting wiretap channel model. The model includes a sending node equipped with energy harvesters, a destination node, and an eavesdropping node. It is assumed that at each time slot only information about the current state of the sending node is available, i.e., battery level, harvested energy, channel state. We analyze the problem of maximizing secrecy rate and model the power allocation problem as an MDP. In order to solve the formulated problem, we use neural networks to estimate the value function. In the end, an online power allocation algorithm based on DQN to improve the secrecy rate is proposed. Simulation results show that the proposed algorithm can effectively optimize energy efficiency.

Acknowledgement. This paper is sponsored by the National Nature Science Foundation of China (61971080, 61471076); Chongqing Basic Research and Frontier Exploration Project (cstc2018jcyjAX0432, cstc2017jcyjAX0204); The Key Project of Science and Technology Research of Chongqing Education Commission (KJZD-K201800603).

References

1. Ku, M., Li, W., Chen, Y., et al.: Advances in energy harvesting communications: past, present, and future challenges. IEEE Commun. Surv. Tutor. **18**(2), 1384–1412 (2016)
2. Ulukus, S., Yener, A., Erkip, E., et al.: Energy harvesting wireless communications: a review of recent advances. IEEE J. Sel. Areas Commun. **33**(3), 360–381 (2015)
3. He, Y., Cheng, X., Peng, W., et al.: A survey of energy harvesting communications: models and offline optimal policies. IEEE Commun. Mag. **53**(6), 79–85 (2015)
4. Tutuncuoglu, K., Yener, A.: Optimum transmission policies for battery limited energy harvesting nodes. IEEE Trans. Wireless Commun. **11**(3), 1180–1189 (2012)
5. Zhou, Q., Yang, Z., Liu, N., et al.: Energy-efficient data transmission with non-FIFO packets with processing cost. IEEE Access **5**, 5158–5170 (2017)
6. Koirala, R., Severi, S., Parajuli, J., et al.: Transmission power optimization for energy harvesting wireless nodes. In: 2015 49th Asilomar Conference on Signals, Systems and Computers, Pacific Grove, CA, USA, pp. 823–827. IEEE (2015)

7. Mao, Y., Zhang, J., Song, S.H., et al.: Joint link selection and relay power allocation for energy harvesting relaying systems. In: 2014 IEEE Global Communications Conference, Austin, TX, USA, pp. 2568–2573. IEEE (2014)
8. Masadeh, A., Wang, Z., Kamal, A.E.: Reinforcement learning exploration algorithms for energy harvesting communications Systems. In: 2018 IEEE International Conference on Communications (ICC), Kansas City, MO, USA, pp. 1–6. IEEE (2018)
9. Ayatollahi, H., Tapparello, C., Heinzelman, W.: Reinforcement learning in MIMO wireless networks with energy harvesting. In: 2017 IEEE International Conference on Communications (ICC), Paris, France, pp. 1–6. IEEE (2017)
10. Volodymyr, M., Koray, K., David, S., et al.: Human-level control through deep reinforcement learning. Nature **518**(7540), 529 (2015)
11. Wyner, A.D.: The wire-tap channel. Bell Syst. Tech. J. **54**(8), 1355–1387 (1975)
12. Chen, X., Ng, D.W.K., Gerstacker, W.H., et al.: A survey on multiple-antenna techniques for physical layer security. IEEE Commun. Surv. Tutor. **19**(2), 1027–1053 (2017)
13. Xie, X., Zhang, X., Lei, W.: Optimization of secrecy rate for energy harvesting Gaussian wiretap channel. J. Electron. Inf. Technol. **37**(11), 2678–2684 (2015)
14. Jiang, C., Zhang, H., Ren, Y., et al.: Machine learning paradigms for next-generation wireless networks. IEEE Wirel. Commun. **24**(2), 98–105 (2017)
15. Sutton, R.S., Barto, A.G.: Reinforcement Learning: An Introduction. MIT Press, Cambridge (2018)

Building Gateway Interconnected Heterogeneous ZigBee and WiFi Network Based on Software Defined Radio

Shuhao Wang, Yonggang Li[✉], Chunqiang Ming, and Zhizhong Zhang

School of Communication and Information Engineering, Chongqing University of Posts and Telecommunications, Chongqing 400065, China
lyg@cqupt.edu.cn

Abstract. The ZigBee Alliance Lab proposes the concept of ZigBee-WiFi network. ZigBee-WiFi network has a broad development space when combined with the advantages of ZigBee and WiFi. However, since ZigBee and WiFi are heterogeneous in various aspects, it is necessary to find a way to interconnect the two networks. The traditional approach is to design dedicated hardware. Since the physical layer functions and part of MAC layer functions in the hardware are fixed, this method cannot adapt to the new physical layer and signal processing algorithms. Software Defined Radio (SDR) is an emerging and flexible method of transferring signal processing components from dedicated hardware to a combination of software and general purpose processors. In this paper, we use SDR in conjunction with the Universal Software Radio Peripheral (USRP) to build a flexible and universal ZigBee-WiFi gateway for interconnecting heterogeneous ZigBee and WiFi networks. The gateway has the ability to simultaneously receive and demodulate ZigBee packets, create and transmit WiFi data frames. A comprehensive performance test confirmed that the built gateway can well interconnect heterogeneous ZigBee and WiFi networks. And the built gateway provides a reference prototype for the interconnection research of heterogeneous networks.

Keywords: Software Defined Radio · ZigBee-WiFi gateway · Heterogeneous network · USRP

1 Introduction

ZigBee is an open wireless standard designed to provide the foundation for the Internet of Things (IoT) by enabling items to work together. ZigBee is often chosen as the technology to connect things because of its network flexibility, interoperability and low power consumption [1]. WiFi functions as a bridge between network base stations and a large number of portable terminal devices. However, ZigBee and WiFi are heterogeneous in various aspects. WiFi and ZigBee have different transmit power, asynchronous time slots and incompatible physical layers. ZigBee devices and WiFi devices cannot communicate directly, so it is necessary to find a way to connect these two heterogeneous networks.

H. Gao et al. (Eds.): ChinaCom 2019, LNICST 312, pp. 445–456, 2020.
https://doi.org/10.1007/978-3-030-41114-5_33

For this limitation, The traditional approach is to design dedicated hardware based on heterogeneous networks. The physical layer function and some MAC layer functions are integrated in the hardware circuit. In [2], The author designed the interface between ZigBee and the WiFi communication standard. In order to realize the conversion of ZigBee protocol data and WiFi protocol data frames. Smart Home Automation communicates through a dedicated processor. It sends commands to the ZigBee coordinator and the devices connected to the WiFi network [3]. This approach lacks flexibility. It cannot cope with new physical layers and signal processing algorithms. But software defined radios overcome this drawback.

Software Defined Radio (SDR) is a type of radio communication system where some or all signal processing components are implemented in software and executed on a General Purpose Processor (GPP) [4]. GNU Radio is an open source software framework for efficient deployment of SDR applications [5], which is used in conjunction with Universal Software Radio Peripheral (USRP). For the new protocol standard IEEE 802.11p, the IEEE 802.11p transceiver is implemented with GNU Radio and USRP [6]. IPTS algorithm in OFDM system is improved to reduce computational complexity based on GNU Radio platform [7]. In [8], the authors use the advantages of GNU Radio and the USRP platform to verify the performance of unsampled WiFi in decoding performance and energy efficiency. The POLYPHONY prototype can be implemented via GNU Radio and deployed to a 16-node enterprise network [9].

In this paper, we use a flexible way to interconnect heterogeneous networks. SDR is used to build a universal gateway to interconnect heterogeneous ZigBee and WiFi networks. We implement the ZigBee-WiFi gateway based on GNU Radio and exe-cute it on the USRP N210. The gateway first receives and demodulates ZigBee packets. An IEEE 802.11 data frame is then created based on the extracted data payload. Finally, the physical layer is modulated and transmitted using OFDM technology. Through three experiments, it was confirmed that the gateway has good performance. The built gateway can well interconnect ZigBee and WiFi networks. The rest of the paper is organized as follows. In Sect. 2 we introduce the GNU Radio framework and the ZigBee-WiFi gateway implementation over GNU Radio. The gateway test platform is established in Sect. 3. Performance measures and numerical results, as well as discussion, are given in Sect. 4. Finally, we conclude this paper in Sect. 5.

2   System Design

2.1   GNU Radio and Flow Graph Construction

GNU Radio is an open source software framework for rapid deployment of SDR applications. We implement the ZigBee-WiFi gateway based on GNU Radio and execute it on the USRP N210. The gateway is capable of interconnecting heterogeneous ZigBee and WiFi networks. The ZigBee-WiFi gateway flow graph is shown in Fig. 1. The development languages used by GNU Radio are Python and C. Signal processing blocks in GNU Radio are generally written in C, such as the block IIR Filter, FFT.

The gateway flow graph can be divided into two parts in Fig. 1. The left part of the block diagram represents the ZigBee packet reception, and the other side represents the creation of the WiFi data frame. In GNU Radio companion, a set of signal processing

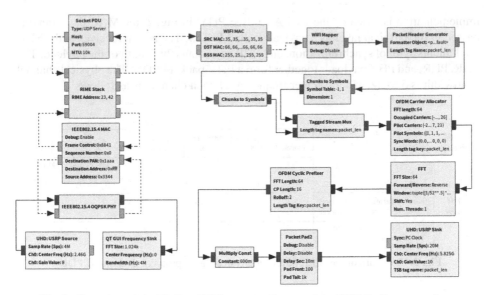

Fig. 1. Overview of the ZigBee-WiFi gateway flow graph in GNU Radio companion

blocks are connected in a specified order to generate a gateway flow graph. Python generates scripts based on flow graph to create a complete signal processing flow. The USRP is the hardware peripheral of GNU Radio. GNU Radio calls the USRP through the UHD block, and the two combined to build a radio communication system. The USRP consists of RF daughter boards, antennas, ADCs, DACs, FPGAs, etc., to receive and transmit radio signals.

There are two ways to transfer GNU Radio data, namely Stream tagging and Message passing. The tag stream is synchronized with the data stream and is used to store metadata and control information. GNU Radio typically sends and receives packets based on packets, introducing asynchronous messaging. In Fig. 1, the blue port and the solid line connection indicate synchronous transmission, and the gray port and dashed line connection indicate asynchronous transmission.

2.2 ZigBee Packet Reception

In Fig. 1, the left portion of the block diagram of the gateway flow graph represents the ZigBee packet reception. In the receive and demodulation process of the data packet, the direction of data information flows first from the UHD USRP Source block to the OQPSK PHY. The physical layer demodulates the physical layer protocol data unit (PPDU), and the extracted payload is delivered to the MAC block. The MAC layer parses the MAC layer data frame and passes the payload to the upper RIME Stack. Finally, the RIME Stack block parses and restores the valid data payload in the ZigBee packet. The following briefly describes the functions of each block in receiving ZigBee packets.

The physical layer in Fig. 1 is encapsulated in a hierarchical block. It contains a complete flow graph that hides the details of signal processing. The OQPSK PHY block implementation is based on the UCLA ZigBee PHY. In Fig. 2, the MAC data frame is passed to the physical layer as a payload, called PSDU. The action receiver of the SHR implements symbol synchronization, and PHR represents the length of the payload. The SHR, PHR, and PHY payloads together form a PHY packet PPDU. The physical channel bandwidth is 5 MHz, and the center frequency of each channel is as follows

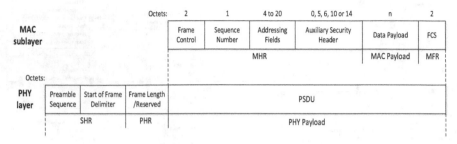

Fig. 2. Structure of the IEEE 802.15.4 physical layer protocol data unit (PPDU)

$$f_c = 2405 + 5(k - 11) 11 \le k \le 26 \tag{1}$$

The physical layer uses OQPSK modulation and demodulation technology. The general OQPSK modulation signal is expressed as

$$s(t) = \sqrt{p} c_1(t) \cos[\omega_0 t + \theta_d(t)] + \sqrt{p} c_2(t) \sin[\omega_0 t + \theta_d(t)] \tag{2}$$

where $\theta_d(t)$ represents data phase modulation, $c_1(t)$ and $c_2(t)$ represent mutually independent orthogonal spread codes.

The USRP source block is connected to the hardware USRP to transmit the received data frame information to the OQPSK PHY block. When the OQPSK PHY block demodulates the physical layer data frame, the OQPSK signal in the complex baseband can be expressed as

$$s(k) = \sqrt{E_b} e^{j(\omega(k)kT_s + \theta_0)} \left[\sum_i a_i g(kT_s - iT) + j \sum_i b_i g(kT_s - iT) + j \right] \tag{3}$$

where E_b represents the average bit energy, T is the symbol period, T_S is the signal sampling period, and g represents the impulse response of the pulse filter. a_i and b_i represent orthogonal modulation I and Q channel respectively. The OQPSK PHY block parses the PPDU and extracts the payload to the MAC layer.

The MAC block can receive the data packet from the upper layer as the data payload, and add the frame header MHR and the frame tail MFR to form a complete MPDU. When receiving data from the following physical layer, the MAC layer removes the header of the MPDU. Then check the CRC in the end of the frame, and if it is correct, extract the payload to the upper layer. Currently, the MAC layer in Fig. 1 has basic encapsulation framing and parsing capabilities. The Rime stack is a lightweight network stack for WSN with low power consumption and simple implementation [10]. The Rime stack in Fig. 1 is only a stack of frame transmission and frame reception. It is equivalent to the network layer in a layered architecture. It adds header information to the upper layer data packets, enabling broadcast communication, unicast communication, and reliable unicast communication. The address of the rime stack is configured in GNU Radio companion. In terms of frame reception, it parses data from the MAC layer and extracts the payload.

2.3 WiFi Data Frame Transmission

The right side of the block diagram in Fig. 1 represents the generation of an IEEE 802.11 data frame PPDU. The physical layer of IEEE 802.11a uses OFDM technology and operates in the 5 GHz band. It can support channel bandwidths of 20 MHz, 10 MHz, and 5 MHz. OFDM is a special multi-carrier modulation technique that modulates serial data streams in parallel on multiple orthogonal subcarriers.

The functions of block are described below. The WiFi MAC block generates a MAC data frame based on the payload of the ZigBee packet, which will serve as the data payload for the physical layer. The WiFi Mapper creates the rate and service fields of the PLCP header of the physical layer frame PPDU. Next, the Packet Header Generator block is used to generate the header of the physical layer frame PPDU, which consists of a PLCP Header and a PLCP Preamble. The next block Chunks to Symbols modulates the signal. The OFDM Carrier Allocator block acts to create OFDM symbols, meaning that the incoming complex streams are allocated to different data subcarriers. An OFDM symbol has a plurality of orthogonal subcarriers, the starting time is t_s, and the OFDM symbol at time t can be expressed as

$$
s(t) = \begin{cases} \mathrm{Re}\left\{ \sum_{i=0}^{N-1} d_i rect(t - t_s - \frac{T}{2}) \exp[j2\pi f_i(t - t_s)] \right\} & t_s \leq t \leq t_s + T \\ 0 & t < t_s \wedge t > t_s + T \end{cases} \tag{4}
$$

where T is an OFDM symbol period, N represents the number of subcarriers, d_i is modulation data on a corresponding subcarrier, and f_i is a frequency of a corresponding subcarrier. Since each subcarrier contains an integer number of periods in the OFDM symbol period, and the number of adjacent subcarrier periods differs by 1, the subcarriers are orthogonal.

$$
\frac{1}{T} \int_0^T \exp(j\omega_n t) \times \exp(-j\omega_m t) dt = \begin{cases} 1 & m = n \\ 0 & m \neq n \end{cases} \tag{5}
$$

For the integral operation of the corresponding subcarriers in Eq. (4), within the time interval T, the following equation can be derived

$$
\begin{aligned}
\hat{d_j} &= \frac{1}{T} \int_{t_s}^{t_s+T} \exp\left(-j2\pi \frac{j}{T}(t - t_s)\right) \sum_{i=0}^{N-1} d_i \exp\left(j2\pi \frac{j}{T}(t - t_s)\right) d_t \\
&= \sum_{i=0}^{N-1} d_i \int_{t_s}^{t_s+T} \exp\left(j2\pi \frac{i-j}{T}(t - t_s)\right) d_i = d_j
\end{aligned} \tag{6}
$$

Obtained by Eq. (6), coherent demodulation of the j-subcarrier can obtain the expected symbol d_j. Since the other subcarriers are integrated in the integration interval, the result is zero. Based on the orthogonal characteristics of subcarriers, the modulation of OFDM can be obtained by IDFT operation to obtain a discretized time domain signal, and the sampling rate of s(t) is set to T/N

$$s_k = s(kT/N) = \sum_{i=0}^{N-1} d_i \exp j\left(\frac{2\pi ik}{N}\right) 0 \le k \le N-1 \tag{7}$$

The FFT block uses IFFF operations to convert frequency domain data into time domain data, which is more efficient and faster than IDFT. In addition, the OFDM Cyclic Prefixer block adds a cyclic prefix to the OFDM symbol. In order to solve the Inter Symbol interference (ISI) caused by the multipath delay of the wireless channel transmission. The last block, the USRP Sink block, uses the hardware USRP to convert IEEE 802.11 data frames into analog signals and move them to the intermediate frequency. The radio board is transmitted at a frequency of 5.825 GHz.

3 Experimental Environment Construction

The ZigBee-WiFi gateway flow graph has been built in GNU Radio companion, and then the flow graph needs to be executed to measure the performance of the ZigBee-WiFi gateway. The USRP acts as a hardware peripheral for the ZigBee-WiFi gateway flow graph, and the two are combined to implement the corresponding functions of the ZigBee-WiFi gateway. Currently the gateway is unidirectional. It receives and demodulates the ZigBee packet, then extracts the payload and encapsulates it to form a WiFi data frame for transmission. The gateway cannot receive and demodulate WiFi packets and then generate ZigBee packets. The test scenario is shown in Fig. 3.

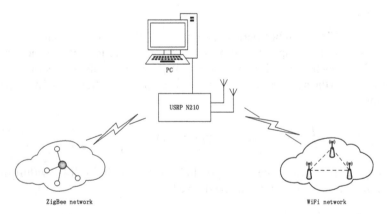

Fig. 3. ZigBee-WiFi gateway performance test scenario

The ZigBee device selects the TelosB node, and the USRP N210 daughter board UBX-40 acts as the RF front end. It has a full-duplex transceiver with tunable frequencies from 10 MHz to 6 GHz. Therefore, the USRP can simultaneously receive ZigBee packets and send WiFi data frames. Table 1 shows the important components of the experimental test.

Table 1. The important components of the experimental test.

Component	Detailed information
ZigBee node	Type TelosB
USRP	Type N210
Daughterboard	UBX-40
GNU Radio	Version 3.7.10
UHD	Version 3.10.1
Operating system	Ubuntu 16.04
CPU	I5-7500 3.4 GHz
Memory	8 G

We present details of the important components of the experimental scenario in Table 1. In order to simplify the test, there is one node device in each of the ZigBee network and the WiFi network. According to the literature [11], a USRP N210 is configured as a WiFi receiver in the WiFi network to conveniently view the received data frames. Below we conducted three experiments to measure the performance of the built ZigBee-WiFi gateway. The first experimental test gateway receives and demodulates ZigBee packets. The second experiment simulates the reception rate of the WiFi packet when the gateway sends the WiFi data frame through the channel containing the noise. The third experimental test gateway receives and demodulates the ZigBee data packet and then transmits the WiFi data frame in the real scene.

4   Performance Measures and Numerical Results

The performance of the ZigBee-WiFi gateway is mainly reflected in two aspects, one is to receive and demodulate ZigBee data packets. On the other hand, the ability to create IEEE 802.11 (WiFi) data frames and transmit. Next, The first experiment tests that the gateway receives ZigBee packets. We set the ZigBee node TelosB to operate at 2.46 GHz and select 22 channels. The transmitted ZigBee packet sizes are 28 bytes, 48 bytes, 68 bytes, and 88 bytes, respectively. The sending interval is 250 ms, and the number of packets is increased from 80 to 560. The receiving gain of the USRP is set to a minimum of 0 dB. The experimental results are shown in Fig. 4.

The ZigBee nodes can only communicate on the same channel, so the USRP also works at 2.46 GHz. In the gateway flow graph, we connect the wireshark block to the output port of the OQPSK PHY block. And then the file sink block connect to the output port of the wireshark block. The file sink block generates a PCAP format file to view the number of received ZigBee packets. In Fig. 4, As the size of the packet increases, the reception rate decreases to some extent. When 480 ZigBee packets are transmitted, the reception rate of the 28-byte packet and the 88-byte packet is 98.9% and 93.3%, respectively. When the USRP receive gain is increased to 6 dB, the gateway's receive rate for the 88 Byte ZigBee packet can reaches 100%. This can indicate that the gateway has good ability to receive and demodulate ZigBee packets.

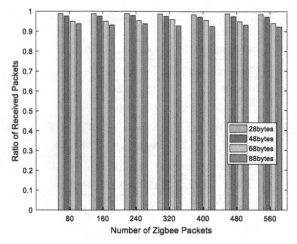

Fig. 4. ZigBee packet reception rate of gateways under different packet sizes

The second test simulates the gateway flow graph in GNU Radio companion. First, the flow graph will create WiFi data frame, then transmit through the channel containing noise, and finally measure the WiFi packet reception rate. We compare the WiFi packet reception rate under different modulation mode when the channel contains Gaussian noise and uniform noise respectively. The simulation results are shown in Figs. 5 and 6.

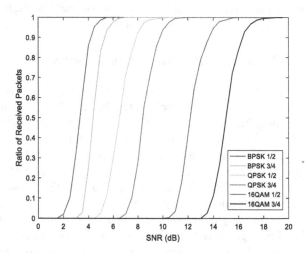

Fig. 5. Simulation of WiFi packet reception rate over the channel containing Gaussian noise

In the simulation, the created WiFi data frame length is 114 bytes. The operating frequency of the WiFi is set to 5.825 GHz and the bandwidth is 20 MHz. In addition, SNR starts from 0 dB and increases by 0.5 dB each time until 20 dB. The gateway generates 100 WiFi data frames each time and then transmits them through a channel containing noise. The WiFi packet reception rate is obtained by checking the number of

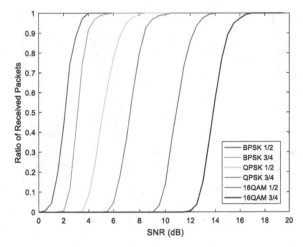

Fig. 6. Simulation of WiFi packet reception rate over the channel containing uniform noise

the received WiFi packets. In Fig. 5, the WiFi packet is transmitted through a channel model containing Gaussian noise. For any modulation mode, the packet reception rate increases as the SNR increases.

The simulation curves in Figs. 5 and 6 are reasonable because the higher order modulation mode 16QAM requires a higher SNR than QPSK and BPSK. For the same modulation scheme, such as QPSK, a higher SNR is required in a Gaussian noise channel than in a uniform noise channel to achieve the same WiFi packet reception rate.

The third experiment tests that the performance of ZigBee-WiFi gateway in the real scene. The purpose of this test is to view the real-time signal processing capabilities of the ZigBee-WiFi gateway and the transmission of WiFi data frames in the actual scene. The ZigBee packets is sent by the TelosB node. And the other USRP acts as the WiFi receiver which receives the WiFi data frame transmitted by the ZigBee-WiFi gateway. The experimental results are shown in Figs. 7 and 8. In this experiment, the size of the ZigBee packet sent is 88 bytes. The transmission interval is 250 ms. The ZigBee-WiFi gateway receives and demodulates the ZigBee packets, and then extracts the payload to generate IEEE 802.11 data frame with a length of 114 Bytes.

In Fig. 7, the USRP acts as the WiFi receiver, but it cannot record SNR values. The SNR is calculated to be equivalent to the difference between the transmit gain of the gateway and the receive gain of the WiFi receiver. The symbol S in BPSK-1/2-S in Fig. 7 represents the Gaussian channel simulation scenario of Fig. 5, and R in BPSK-1/2-R represents the actual scene. The dashed curve in Fig. 7 is also the Gaussian channel scene simulation result in Fig. 5. The results are reasonable in the sense that a higher SNR is required in the actual scenario to achieve the same receiving rate. In addition, the WiFi packet reception rate can reach 1 as the SNR increases. The experimental results in the actual scene are not much different from the simulation results. This shows that the built ZigBee-WiFi gateway has good ability to create IEEE 802.11 data frames and transmit them. Due to other WiFi device interference in the actual environment and oscillator drift in hardware USRP, the curve in the actual scene is not smooth and has some differences

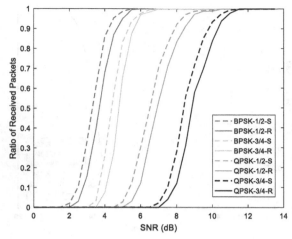

Fig. 7. Compare WiFi packet reception rate when ZigBee-WiFi gateway transmits WiFi data frame in simulated scene and real scene

from the simulation results in Fig. 7. It is more likely that nonlinearities in the amplifier may slightly interfere with the signal, resulting in packet errors.

It shows the runtime proportion of individual blocks when the ZigBee-WiFi gateway is executed in Fig. 8. The runtime proportion of all blocks is added up to a total of 1. The block runtime is measured with the help of gr-perf-monitorx in GNU Radio [12]. The five red bars indicate the runtime of the IEEE 802.15.4 OQPSK PHY internal block when the gateway demodulates the ZigBee packet. The three blue block probes work in conjunction with the tool gr-perf-monitorx to measure the block runtime. The cyan bar represents the runtime of the block that creates the WiFi data frame, and the OFDM Carrier Allocator block accounts for 74.14%. Due to the high computational complexity of the block, it is the core block for creating WiFi data frames. In Fig. 8, the various

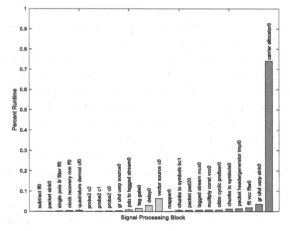

Fig. 8. Runtime proportion of individual signal processing blocks

signal processing modules of the gateway operate normally. Combined with Fig. 7, it can be concluded that the gateway has better real-time signal processing capability under actual scenarios.

5 Conclusion

In this paper, we use SDR combined with USRP to build a flexible and universal ZigBee-WiFi gateway which interconnects heterogeneous ZigBee and WiFi network. A comprehensive performance measurement of the gateway is performed. The first experiment tests that the gateway receives ZigBee packets, and the result shows that the gateway has good ability to receive and demodulate data packets. The second and third experiments are respectively tested in the simulation scenario and the actual scenario, comparing the receiving rate of the WiFi packet when the ZigBee-WiFi gateway transmits the WiFi packet. The results are reasonable in the sense that a higher SNR is required in the actual scenario to achieve the same receiving rate. Combined with the above three experimental results, it shows that the ZigBee-WiFi gateway has good ability to receive and demodulate the ZigBee packets and then extract the payload to generate IEEE 802.11 data frame. It proves that the built gateway can well interconnect heterogeneous ZigBee and WiFi networks.

References

1. Davoli, L., Belli, L., Cilfone, A., Ferrari, G.: From micro to macro IoT: challenges and solutions in the integration of IEEE 802.15.4/802.11 and sub-GHz technologies. IEEE Internet Things J. **5**(2), 784–793 (2017)
2. Nugroho, E., Sahroni, A.: ZigBee and wifi network interface on wireless sensor networks. In: 2014 Makassar International Conference on Electrical Engineering and Informatics (MICEEI), pp. 54–58. IEEE (2014)
3. Vivek, G.V., Sunil, M.P.: Enabling IOT services using WIFI-ZigBee gateway for a home automation system. In: 2015 IEEE International Conference on Research in Computational Intelligence and Communication Networks (ICRCICN), pp. 77–80. IEEE (2015)
4. Arcos, G., Ferreri, R., Richart, M., Ezzatti, P., Grampín, E.: Accelerating an IEEE 802.11 a/g/p transceiver in GNU radio. In: Proceedings of the 9th Latin America Networking Conference, pp. 13–19. ACM (2016)
5. Robert, M., Sun, Y., Goodwin, T., Turner, H., Reed, J.H., White, J.: Software frameworks for SDR. Proc. IEEE **103**, 452–475 (2015)
6. Bloessl, B., Segata, M., Sommer, C., Dressler, F.: Performance assessment of IEEE 802.11 p with an open source SDR-based prototype. IEEE Trans. Mob. Comput. **17**(5), 1162–1175 (2017)
7. Ming, A., Xiaosong, Z.: Improved IPTS algorithm in OFDM system based on GNU radio. In: 2018 10th International Conference on Communication Software and Networks (ICCSN), pp. 352–356. IEEE (2018)
8. Wang, W., Chen, Y., Wang, L., Zhang, Q.: From rateless to sampleless: Wi-Fi connectivity made energy efficient. In: IEEE INFOCOM 2016-The 35th Annual IEEE International Conference on Computer Communications, pp. 1–9. IEEE (2016)
9. Yang, P., Yan, Y., Li, X.Y., Zhang, Y.: POLYPHONY: scheduling-free cooperative signal recovery in enterprise wireless networks. IEEE Trans. Mob. Comput. **16**(9), 2599–2610 (2016)

10. Dunkels, A., Österlind, F., He, Z.: An adaptive communication architecture for wireless sensor networks. In: Proceedings of the 5th International Conference on Embedded Networked Sensor Systems, pp. 335–349. ACM (2007)
11. Bloessl, B., Segata, M., Sommer, C., Dressler, F.: An IEEE 802.11 a/g/p OFDM receiver for GNU radio. In: Proceedings of the Second Workshop on Software Radio Implementation Forum, pp. 9–16. ACM (2013)
12. Rondeau, T.W., O'Shea, T., Goergen, N.: Inspecting GNU radio applications with control-port and performance counters. In: Proceedings of the Second Workshop on Software Radio Implementation Forum, pp. 65–70. ACM (2013)

A Cross-Layer Protocol for Mobile Ad Hoc Network Based on Hexagonal Clustering and Hybrid MAC Access Approach

Longchao Wang[1], Xiandeng He[1(✉)], Qingcai Wang[1], Heping Yao[2], and Yifan Qiu[1]

[1] State Key Laboratory of Integrated Service Networks, Xidian University, Xi'an, Shaanxi, China
xdhe@mail.xidian.edu.cn
[2] Dalian Haoyang Technology Development Ltd., Dalian, Liaoning, China

Abstract. Due to its flexible and convenient networking, Ad hoc networks have been used in more and more scenarios. But, the features of mobility, constantly changing topologies and centerless architecture limit its applications. In order to improve the performance of Ad hoc, this paper proposes a cross-layer protocol for mobile Ad hoc network based on Hexagonal Clustering and Hybrid MAC Access (HCHMA) approach. Through the clustering algorithm, cluster heads are selected to form a backbone network for route discovery and establishment. And the MAC layer uses two different access mechanisms to ensure efficient transmission of routing packets and data packets. Benefiting from the above approaches, network overhead is greatly reduced and the throughput is improved. By doing simulations in the network simulator 2 (NS2) software, the HCHMA protocol shows better packet delivery rate, higher throughput and lower end-to-end delay compared with the Ad hoc On-demand Distance Vector Routing (AODV) protocol and the Optimized Link State Routing (OLSR) protocol.

Keywords: Ad hoc network · Hybrid MAC access · Clustering · Cross-layer protocol · Location-based

1 Introduction

Mobile ad hoc networks (MANETs) have attracted increasing attention in recent years due to the capacity in support of multi-hop communications, infrastructure- independent network topology, self-management and easy-deployment. In terms of applications, MANETs have been widely used in the civil and military area to provide ad hoc based communication capacity in support

Supported by the Key Research and Development Program of Shaanxi Province (Grant No. 2019ZDLGY09-02).

H. Gao et al. (Eds.): ChinaCom 2019, LNICST 312, pp. 457–470, 2020.
https://doi.org/10.1007/978-3-030-41114-5_34

of emergency evacuation in the natural disaster or mission-based operations in battlefield [1]. As for its self-management, ad hoc networks need well-organized distributed algorithms to determine network organization, link scheduling, and routing [2]. As two core technologies of Ad hoc network, the channel intervention mechanism of medium access control (MAC) layer and the routing technology of network layer, still have many problems and need more efficient, stable and robust algorithm.

MAC protocol plays an important role in MANETs to provide efficient data transmission service. In order to improve the utilization of the Ad hoc network, a lot of work has been done. In [3], the authors propose a dynamic TDMA protocol based on node neighborhood information (TDMA-NNI) which at different packet send rates. The delay, throughput, and packet loss rate have been improved. How- ever, it has high requirements for the efficient transmission of messages from neighbor nodes. In [4], a hybrid channel access strategy with CSMA/CA and Self-Organized Time Division Multiple Access (SOTDMA) is implemented to improve the application performance of MANETs. To ensure stability and trans- mission efficiency of MANETs, CSMA/CA and SOTDMA are considered to switch according throughput rate of network automatically or manually. In order to further improve network throughput, the time synchronization is specially designed for SOTDMA, and a new power control scheme of multi-hop communication is proposed to increase the stability of hybrid channel access. However, switching requires more signaling frames to collect information, wastes a certain amount of bandwidth, and even requires manual switching.

Routing is a significant issue in Mobile Ad hoc Networks. There are two classifications of routing protocols in MANETs: 1. Table driven routing protocols; 2. Reactive or on-demand routing protocols. Many routing protocols are proposed in MANETs like AODV, DSR and OLSR [5]. Many scholars are also doing further research on routing protocols. In [6], the authors proposed an AODV based routing algorithm "Q-AODV" by controlling the broadcast storm and reducing the total number of RREQ relayed during the route discovery process. It improves QoS parameters, namely average jitter, throughput and average end to end delay. However, it does not perform particularly well on sparse networks. To mitigate the problem caused by route fractures, [7] presents a new routing algorithm. It stores all the available paths. Therefore, whenever the link between the nodes gets break, it can immediately replace with the new route. However, the backup route is not real-time and the protocol is insensitive to changes in network topology.

In traditional methods, most researchers conclude the problems faced by ad-hoc a routing problem and only solve it in the network by considering routing cost, such as delay, congestion metric and distance. And the others only consider the dynamic changes of the spectrum in the MAC layer [8]. Due to the dynamic changes of network nodes, limited bandwidth and unpredictable channel conditions, the traditional hierarchical optimization method is not enough to improve the performance of Ad hoc network. In order to further improve the network quality of Ad hoc, it is necessary to use available information across layers, that is, to exchange information directly between layers to perform subsequent operations [9]. [10] is based on the cross layer design of AODV protocol, and let the routing layer interact with MAC layer to obtain the link quality information. In addition to considering the path hop count, the link information is also used as the basis when selecting the route.

To apply ad hoc in fishery communication system, this paper proposes a cross-layer protocol based on Hexagonal Clustering and Hybrid MAC Access (HCHMA) approach, which combines the MAC layer and the network routing layer together. The HCHMA protocol divides the time slots according to the geographic location in the neighborhood discovery phase and adopts CSMA/CA mechanism in the data transmission phase. The cluster heads are selected after the ends of neighbor node discovery phase. It establish routing by transmitting route request (RREQ) messages and route reply (RREP) messages only between cluster heads. Therefore, routing overhead and delay can be optimized.

The paper is organized as follows. Section 2 presents the system model. Then, we design the cross-layer protocol in Sect. 3. Simulation results and analyses are provided in Sect. 4. Finally, conclusions are made in Sect. 5.

2 System Model

2.1 Geographic Location Based Clustering

In the HCHMA protocol, we assume that each node obtains its own geographic location information through geographic information system (GIS) and keeps the clocks synchronized. And there is no fixed central node in any cluster.

The proposed protocol adopts hexagonal clustering. As shown in Fig. 1, the entire network area is divided into multiple hexagons by corresponding algorithm based on location information. There are no empty nodes or overlapping areas between clusters. Through this clustering method, nodes can clearly know the clusters to which they belong according to their geographic location information. Based on these advantages, regular hexagon clustering method has been widely studied and applied.

In Fig. 1, a hexagon cluster is further divided into 6 equilateral triangles and marked from 1 to 6. Each index corresponds to a time slot. By this way, the nodes in the same cluster with different indexs can avoid communication collision, while the nodes in different clusters with the same index can implement space division multiplexing.

2.2 Communication Range

In this paper, the radius of a hexagon is R and the communication radius of member nodes is set to $3/2R$. By reduce the communication rate, the communication radius are increased and the neighbor cluster header can communicate with each other directly.

$$L_{bf} = 32.4 + 20 \log f + 20 \log d \tag{1}$$

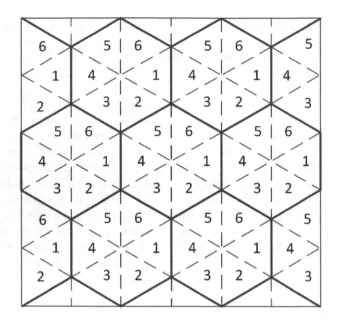

Fig. 1. Network scenario divided with hexagon

Equation (1) describes the relationship between free space loss (L_{bf}) and frequency (f) and transmission distance (d), where L_{bf} in dB, f in MHz and d in km [11].

$$S_i(dbm) = -174 + 10 \log B + NF + (S/N)_o \qquad (2)$$

Equation (2) describes the relationship between receiver sensitivity (S_i)and thermal noise (NF), bandwidth (B), and output signal-to-noise ratio of the receiver ($(S/N)_o$) when phase noise is not considered in a non-spread spectrum system. The unit of B is Hz [12].

$$P_t - L_{bf} = S_i(dbm) \qquad (3)$$

In (3), P_t represents the transmit power. By combining (1), (2) and (3), it can be concluded that when d is need to be doubled, we can only reduce B by four times to make the equation tenable. In the common modulation modes such as MASK, MPSK, and MQAM, B is approximately proportional to the data transmission rate. Therefore, in HCHMA protocol, the transmission rate between cluster heads is 1/4 of the normal transmissions.

3   Cross-Layer Protocol Design

In the proposed protocol, the TDMA mechanism is used to divide the time into time frame cycles. As shown in Fig. 2, each time frame cycle is T which includes a neighbor node discovery period T_1 and a data transmission period T_2.

The hexagon is divided into 6 equilateral triangles, and the neighbor node discovery period is correspondingly divided into 6 time slots. During the neighbor node discovery period, the nodes with different indexes take different time slots to transmit hello messages and the nodes with same index share same time slots by CSMA/CA mechanism. The nodes with the same index but in different clusters can send hello messages at the same time. The time slots are divided by geographical locations, and the total number of nodes competing for channels at the same time is relatively reduced. Therefore, in this way, the probability of the message collision occurrence is reduced, channel utilization is improved, and hello messages can be transmitted more efficiently.

During the data transmission period, route messages and the data messages share the same time slots by CSMA/CA mechanism. However, in order to make the routing messages have higher priority, the fixed backoff of the routing messages is smaller than the data packets in the random backoff algorithm of the MAC layer. Meanwhile, Handshake mechanism is required before point-to-point data transmission. In order to achieve effective wireless shared channel, refer to the IEEE 802.11 protocol, the node first uses the RTS/CTS to perform control channel reservation, and the data transmission can be performed after the reservation is successful. The data is transmitted through the DATA/ACK process to ensure the reliability of the network. The detail process of the route establishment will be given later.

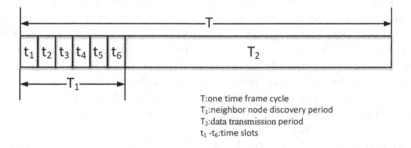

T:one time frame cycle
T_1:neighbor node discovery period
T_2:data transmission period
t_1 -t_6:time slots

Fig. 2. TDMA frame allocation

3.1 Neighbor Node Discovery

Neighbor nodes of a node refer to nodes within the communication range of the node. During neighbor node discovery period, the nodes send hello messages according to the time frame corresponding to their geographic location. The hello messages are generated and sent only during the discovery period of the neighboring node. There is no re-transmission mechanism. If it is not sent within the specified neighbor discovery time, discard will happen. In order to reduce collisions occurred when more than one node send messages at the same time slot, a random backoff is added before the hello message is sent according to the

CSMA/CA mechanism. The hello message contains the sender IP address and geographic location information. The nodes that are not in the current sending slot are silent to receive the hello messages and updates their neighbor node tables.

The detail process of this neighbor node discovery can be found in our previous work [13].

3.2   Cluster Head Election Algorithm

After six time slots, each node locally compares its own location with that of its neighbors in the same cluster, and the nearest node to the cluster center declares to be the cluster head while the other nodes remain members in the cluster. As we set the communication range to be $3/2R$, the cluster head which locals within $1/2R$ radius of the cluster can communicate with any node in the same cluster. For a few cases where there are no nodes within $1/2R$ radius, some edge nodes are not within the communication range of the selected cluster head node. Another cluster head will be selected among these edge nodes, which will be explained later.

After the election of the cluster head, the nodes which are elected to a cluster head periodically generated the cluster hello message sending to the cluster heads of the neighboring cluster. Same as the hello message, there is no re-transmission mechanism and a random backoff is added before the hello message is sent. The hello message contains the IP address and geographic location of the neighbor nodes of the cluster head. In order to facilitate sending and receiving messages between cluster heads in its cluster, the cluster heads use low speed for transmission to expand the communication range. The propagation range of the routing messages generated by the cluster head is 3R, and all nodes in the hexagonal cluster can receive and parse them. The edge nodes mentioned in the previous paragraph are verifying that they are not in the cluster by parsing these packages. Among these edge nodes, the node closest to the center of the cluster becomes a new cluster head.

After this process, the cluster head node obtains the IP address and geographical location of the nodes in the neighbor cluster. The distance between the nodes in its own cluster and those in the neighbor clusters is calculated through the obtained geographical location. By comparing the result with the communication radius, we can calculate whether there is a connection between our own cluster and the neighboring cluster, which is used for route discovery and establishment.

3.3   Network Topology Discovery

When a node has a data packet to send, it first detects whether there is a route from itself to the destination node. If there is a route, it will forward the data to the next hop node. If there is no route, it needs to find the route. The node sends a RREQ message to the cluster head, and the message is unicast. After receiving the RREQ from the node in its own cluster, the cluster head broadcasts the RREQ to the neighbor cluster heads. Similarly, in order to facilitate sending and receiving messages between cluster heads, the cluster heads use low speed for transmission to expand the communication range.

The RREQ message format is given in Fig. 3. As is shown in Fig. 3, besides the intra-cluster node information, the RREQ packet mainly includes the following fields:

Type	Hop_Count	Cluster_ID_Line	Cluster_ID_Column
RREQ_Broadcast_ID			
Source Cluster Head IP Address			
Source Node IP Address			
Source Node Sequence Number			
Desination Node IP Address			
Desination Node Sequence Number			
Message Valid Time			

Fig. 3. RREQ message frame structure

Type: Used to indicate the message type, such as TC message, 8-bit storage.

Hop_count: Used to record the number of hops that the RREQ message propagates, 8-bit storage.

Cluster_ID_Line and Cluster_ID_Column: Used to indicate source cluster ID, 16-bit storage.

RREQ_Broadcast_ID: Used to record the ID of RREQ message and prevent retransmission, 32-bit storage.

Sequence Number: Used to indicate the latest serial number of the node and to update route, 32-bit storage.

When the member node receives the RREQ message, it simply discards the message without any processing. When the cluster head receives the RREQ message, the following steps are performed:

Step 1: If such a RREQ has been received before, the node silently discards the newly received RREQ and the process ends. Otherwise, the next step is performed.

Step 2: If the nodes in own cluster does not connect with nodes in the neighbor cluster whose cluster head sent this message, the node silently discards the newly received RREQ and the process ends. Otherwise, the next step is performed.

Step 3: The cluster head records the inter-cluster routing to the RREQ message source cluster head node and perform the next step.

Step 4: If the destination node found by RREQ is in this cluster, it produces the RREP message. Otherwise,the message is forwarded and the process ends.

Let's use the example in Fig. 4 to illustrate the proposed routing discovery process. The source node S sends an RREQ message to its cluster head node 2. After receiving the message, node 2 starts flooding the message among the neighbor cluster heads. After the cluster head node 4 receives it, because the node 3 in its own cluster and the node 1 in the cluster of node 2 are in communication range, node 4 records the route to cluster head 2 which generates the RREQ message, and then forwards the RREQ message. Conversely, since the nodes in the cluster can not connected to the nodes in the cluster of node 2, node 9 discards the RREQ message, as well as the node 10. After receiving the RREQ message, node 7 starts to send a route reply because the destination node D is in its cluster.

By passing RREQ packets between cluster heads (backbone network) to reduced the number of RREP message forwardings, the routing overhead is reduced.

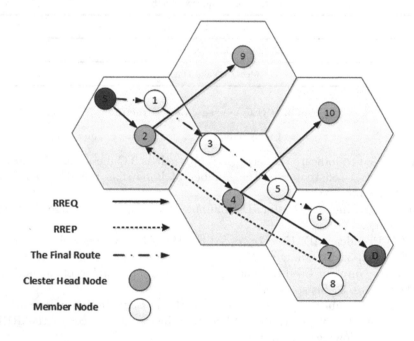

Fig. 4. Route discovery and route establishment

3.4   Route Establishment

The cluster head where the destination node is located responds to the received RREQ message by generating a RREP message. The RREP message is broadcast to the next hop, in the opposite direction of the RREP message propagation path. Similarly, the propagation range of RREP message generated by the cluster head is twice that of member nodes.

The format of the package is given in Fig. 5.

Type	Reserved	Hop_Count	Node_Num_In_Route
Next Cluster Head IP Address			
The IP Address of the Last Node of Last Cluster in Route			
The IP Address of the Node of This Cluster in Route[1]			
The IP Address of the Node of This Cluster in Route[2]			
....			
The IP Address of the Node of This Cluster in Route[Node_Num_In_Route]			
The Geographic Location Information of the last Node of This Cluster in Route			
Desination Node Sequence Number			
Desination Node IP Address			
Source Node IP Address			
Message Valid Time			

Fig. 5. RREP message frame structure

Node_Num_In_Route: The number of nodes in the routing link calculated by the cluster head in this cluster, 8-bit storage.

To establish a route, the destination node is selected as the first node participating in the route. The cluster head is responsible for selecting and assigning which nodes within the cluster to participate in route establishment. We set the initial value of i to 1. The process of a cluster head to select cluster members in this routing link is given by follow steps:

Step 1: The cluster head select the node that can connect with the last node that has participated in the routing, as candidate nodes. The nodes participating in the routing that are selected by the cluster head one by one from the destination node to the source node. Then from these candidate nodes, select the node nearest to the geographic center of the next cluster which cluster head the RREP message will send to. The IP address of this node will be recorded in *The IP Address of the Node of This Cluster in Route*[i] in the RREP packet. Then the value of i is incremented by one. And this selected node will become the latest node that has participated in the routing.

Step 2: This cluster head determines if this selected node is connected to any of the nodes in the next cluster. Yes, perform step 3. No, go back to step 1.

Step 3: Information of nodes in the cluster selected to participate in route establishment is packed by the cluster head and broadcast to the next cluster head.

When a member node receives a RREP message, it first detects whether the message is sent by its cluster head. If not, discard the package directly. If so, it further detects whether it is in the routing link calculated by the cluster head. In other words, it is determined whether its IP address is the same as *The IP Address of the Node of This Cluster in Route[i]* in the RREP message. If not, discard the package. If so, this node records the next hop to destination node is *The IP Address of the Node of This Cluster in Route[i − 1]*. If $i = 1$, the next hop is *The IP Address of the Last Node of Last Cluster in Route*. The member nodes analyze the RREP message sent by the cluster heads, and the route is established hop by hop.

After the cluster header node receives the RREP message, it detects whether it is the next hop of the message. If not, discard the package directly. If so, select the nodes participating in the routing as described above, pack the information of the selected nodes in its cluster, and forward the packet.

Similarly, Let's use the example in Fig. 4 to illustrate this process. After receiving the RREQ message, node 7 begins to generate a RREP message. First, the nodes 6 and 8 will be found in the cluster that have connections with the destination node D. Then, by comparing the distances between the two nodes and the central geographic location of the cluster where the node 4 is located, the node 6 is selected as the previous hop node of the destination node. Since node 5 can be connected to node 6 of the cluster in which node 4 is located, there is no need to select other nodes in this cluster to participate in routing. Then, node 7 broadcasts a RREP message to the cluster head node 4. After receiving the broadcasted RREP message, nodes 7 makes a route to the destination node by parsing the packet. After receiving the RREP packet, the cluster head node 4 first selects a node 5 that is connected to the node 6. However node 5 can not connect with the nodes of the cluster where the node 2 is located. Therefore, another node need to be selected. Then, the node 3 is selected because it is connected to the node 5 and has a connection with the node of the cluster where the node 2 is located. The cluster head node 4 records the selected nodes into the RREP message and broadcasts it out. Similarly, nodes 3 and 5 use the information in the broadcast packet to make a route to the destination node. In this way, the route labeled in Fig. 4 is finally made.

Because of the existence of cluster heads, a backbone network is formed in the whole network. The direct communication between cluster heads is used to establish routes, which effectively reduces the flooding of routing messages. In addition, GPS is used to calculate routing, which effectively reduces the amount of data required to establish routing interactions and reduces routing overhead.

4   Simulation Results and Analysis

NS-2 is used to visualize the ns simulations and trace packet data. The trace file contains topology information like nodes, links, queues, node connectivity and packet trace information. In the simulation, 60 nodes are randomly distributed within a square of $1000\,\text{m} \times 1000\,\text{m}$. The wireless transmission distance D_t is

250 m, the carrier sensing range D_r is 550 m, the radius of hexagonal cellular is set to 166.7 m, the channel bandwidth is 1 Mbps, the neighbor node discovery period T1 of HCHMA is 60 ms, and the time frame cycle T of HCHMA is 2 s. The simulations run for 100 s and apply Constant Bit Rate (CBR) sources where the packet generated rate is from 50 to 300 kbps. The max moving speed of nodes is 1 m/s. The unlisted parameters are set to the default value in NS2. We selected traditional proactive routing OLSR and traditional passive routing AODV for comparison, in which MAC layer are applied by IEEE 802.11. We will compare the performance of these three protocols from the average end-to-end delay (AEED), packet loss rate and throughput. The results are given by the averages of 20 times simulations.

Figure 6 presents the relationship between the AEED and the data generation rate. The AEED is caused by two reasons: one is the waiting time before the route established at the routing layer, the other is the waiting time for the access channel and collision retransmission at the MAC layer. The HCHMA protocol uses the backbone network formed by the cluster head to establish routes, which reduces the number of flooding of routing messages, reduces the time required to establish routes, and reduces AEED.

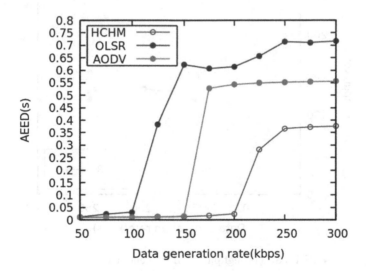

Fig. 6. AEED vs. data generation rate

Figure 7 presents the relationship between the packet loss rate and the data generation rate. As can be seen from the figure, our protocol outperforms the other two protocols in terms of packet loss rate performance. This is because we use different channel access algorithms to ensure the effective transmission of neighboring node detection messages and routing messages, and improve the success rate of route establishment.

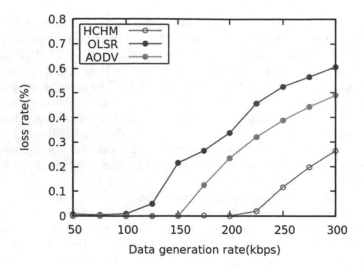

Fig. 7. Packet Loss rate vs. data generation rate

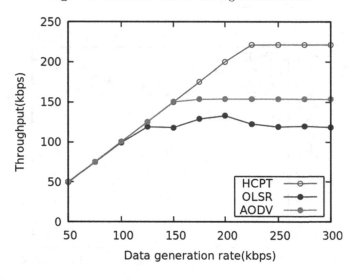

Fig. 8. Throughput vs. data generation rate

Figure 8 shows the throughput vs. the data generation rate. As the rate of data generation increases, each protocol reaches its own throughput maximum and remains the same. As we can see from the figure, The throughput of our protocol is higher than the other two protocols. We have better AAED and packet loss rates because of the advantages described above, so we have higher throughput accordingly.

5 Conclusion

In this paper, we propose a cross-layer protocol named HCHMA. The protocol guarantees the effective transmission of different types of messages through different MAC layer algorithms and forms the backbone network by using the cluster head generated by the clustering algorithm, which effectively improves the probability of successful route establishment and reduces the average end-to-end delay. Compared with the traditional AODV and OLSR protocols, the HCHMA protocol has lower latency and packet loss rate and higher throughput.

References

1. Xu, H., Zhao, Y., Zhang, L., Wang, J.: A bio-inspired gateway selection scheme for hybrid mobile ad hoc networks. IEEE Access **7**, 61997–62010 (2019). https://doi.org/10.1109/ACCESS.2019.2916189
2. Agarkhed, J., Ainapure, A., Kulkarni, A.: Performance issues of routing protocols in ad hoc networks. In: 2017 International Conference on Current Trends in Computer, Electrical, Electronics and Communication (CTCEEC), Mysore, pp. 1178–1181 (2017). https://doi.org/10.1109/CTCEEC.2017.8455087
3. Lin, C., Cai, X., Su, Y., Ni, P., Shi, H.: A dynamic slot assignment algorithm of TDMA for the distribution class protocol using node neighborhood information. In: 2017 11th IEEE International Conference on Anti-counterfeiting, Security, and Identification (ASID), Xiamen, pp. 138–141 (2017). https://doi.org/10.1109/ICASID.2017.8285760
4. Fu, Y., Ding, Z.: Hybrid channel access with CSMA/CA and SOTDMA to improve the performance of MANET. In: 2017 IEEE 17th International Conference on Communication Technology (ICCT), Chengdu, pp. 793–799 (2017). https://doi.org/10.1109/ICCT.2017.8359746
5. Sureshbhai, T.H., Mahajan, M., Rai, M.K.: An investigational analysis of DSDV, AODV and DSR Routing Protocols in mobile ad hoc networks. In: 2018 International Conference on Intelligent Circuits and Systems (ICICS), Phagwara, pp. 281–285 (2018). https://doi.org/10.1109/ICICS.2018.00064
6. Dogra, A.K.: Q-AODV: a flood control ad-hoc on demand distance vector routing protocol. In: 2018 First International Conference on Secure Cyber Computing and Communication (ICSCCC), Jalandhar, India, pp. 294–299 (2018). https://doi.org/10.1109/ICSCCC.2018.8703220
7. Sruthy, S., Geetha, G.: AODV based backup routing for optimized performance in mobile ad-hoc networks. In: 2017 International Conference on Computing Methodologies and Communication (ICCMC), Erode, pp. 684–688 (2017). https://doi.org/10.1109/ICCMC.2017.8282553
8. Warrier, M.M., Kumar, A.: Energy efficient routing in wireless sensor networks: a survey. In: 2016 International Conference on Wireless Communications, Signal Processing and Networking (WiSPNET), Chennai, pp. 1987–1992 (2016). https://doi.org/10.1109/WiSPNET.2016.7566490
9. Savalkar, V.A.: Link prediction for identifying link failure using cross layer approach. In: 2018 2nd International Conference on Inventive Systems and Control (ICISC), Coimbatore, pp. 1120–1129 (2018). https://doi.org/10.1109/ICISC.2018.8398978

10. Zuo, J., Dong, C., Ng, S.X., Yang, L., Hanzo, L.: Cross-layer aided energy-efficient routing design for ad hoc networks. IEEE Commun. Surv. Tutor. **17**(3), 1214–1238 (2015). https://doi.org/10.1109/COMST.2015.2395378. Thirdquarter
11. IEEE802.11n, Standard for information technology. Part 11: Wireless LAN Medium Access Control (MAC) and Physical Layer (PHY) - Amendment: Enhancements for Higher Throughput (2009)
12. Lee, J.S., Miller, L.E.: CDMA Systems Engineering Handbook. Artech House Inc., Boston (1998)
13. Wang, Q., He, X., Chen, N.: A cross-layer neighbor discovery algorithm in ad hoc networks based on hexagonal clustering and GPS. In: 6th Annual 2018 International Conference on Geo-Spatial Knowledge and Intelligence (2019). https://doi.org/10.1088/1755-1315/234/1/012050

On SDN Controllers Placement Problem in Wide Area Networks

Firas Fawzy Zobary[1,2]([✉]) and ChunLin Li[1]

[1] School of Computer Science and Technology, Wuhan University of Technology, Wuhan, People's Republic of China
firas_zobary@hotmail.com
[2] Faculty of Information Engineering, Damascus University, Damascus, Syrian Arab Republic

Abstract. Software Defined Networking (SDN) is a new paradigm where the forward plan is decoupled from the control plan. The controller is a central program that tells the switches and routers how to react to the incoming flows and different network changes. The placement of the controllers considering different metrics becomes a challenge in SDN WAN. In this paper, we study the controller placement problem in terms of propagation delay and load balancing. An extended K-means algorithm is introduced to partition the network into several subnetworks and place the controllers in nodes that minimize the network delay. Then a load balance index is calculated to check the effectiveness of the load balancing considering a metric β as the load difference between controllers. The result analysis shows that a trade off should be done between the delay and load balancing depending on the priority of the network and no optimal case can be found that minimize both of the metrics at the same time.

Keywords: Software Defined Network · Controller placement · Propagation delay · Load balancing

1 Introduction

Even with their widespread adoption, traditional IP networks are still complex, very hard to manage, and start to show their limitations. Software Defined networking (SDN) is the new paradigm for managing the programmability of the networks. The idea behind SDN is to decouple the control plane from the data/forwarding plane (network devices). The control plane is presented as a central program called "Controller" which will tell the forwarding plane how to respond to different incoming network flows and changing network conditions. For Local Area Networks (LANs) like datacenters, a single controller will be enough and the performance will be well. The challenge will arise when we apply SDN to Wide Area Networks (WANs) where the delay between nodes can be high and the coverage area is large. Multiple controllers should be applied to cover the whole WAN. Network devices and the communications between controllers themselves should be studied carefully. Where to put the controllers is a very important question in this case as different controller placements will affect the delay and the behavior of

© ICST Institute for Computer Sciences, Social Informatics and Telecommunications Engineering 2020
Published by Springer Nature Switzerland AG 2020. All Rights Reserved
H. Gao et al. (Eds.): ChinaCom 2019, LNICST 312, pp. 471–479, 2020.
https://doi.org/10.1007/978-3-030-41114-5_35

the whole network. In this paper, we will focus on SDN WAN controller placement in terms of delay and load balancing. The main goal is to partition the network into several subnetworks each is managed by one controller, and to find the best location to place that controller taking into consideration to minimize the delay and maximize the load balance for the controllers. The contribution of this paper is as follows:

1. An Extended K-means algorithm is proposed to partition the network.
2. In addition to the delay, we tried to balance the load of controllers by reassigning the switches between the controllers depending on the difference of loads between each pair of controllers.

The rest of paper is organized as Sect. 2 will brief the related work. In Sect. 3 we formulate the problem. Section 4 explains the Extended K-means algorithm and the load balancing algorithm. The performance evaluation and results analysing are described in Sect. 5. Finally, Sect. 6 summarizes the conclusion and future work.

2   Related Work

Controller placement problem (CPP) is always been as a critical issue when it comes to large sized SDN as many controllers are introduced and their development is increasing such as Kandoo [1] and Hyperflow [2]. Heller et al. [3] firstly proposed a solution in terms of propagation latency, but focusing only on delay may lead to imbalanced controller distribution. This work was the most cited work for controller placement problem. Their work considered the average latency and worst case latency. A step forward was done by Yao et al. [4] as they take into consideration not only the delay but also the load balancing. Their proposed algorithm named Capacitated Controller Placement Problem (CCPP) reduced the number of controllers required to remove the overload as well as reducing the load on the heaviest controller.

Mamushiane et al. [5] asked a question about how many controllers are needed and where should they go given an SDN topology. They proposed three algorithms to address the controller placement problem, but first they mentioned only the metric of latency. However, their algorithms are accurate but are exhaustive and don't work well in the presence of time constraints.

In [6], the authors studied the controller placement problem in WAN network.

Their goal was to partition the network into several small subnetworks by using spectral clustering algorithm. They used the propagation delay between nodes as weights for edges, and according to that delay the nodes that have low weighted edges creates the small subnetworks while the links with high weights will be used to connect the subnetworks together.

An algorithm named K^*-means was used by Qi et al. [7] to merge clusters that are connected with the shortest edge. Kuang et al. [8] used the same previous algorithm to merge the clusters until the number reaches k, but they imbedded it in a hierarchical K-means algorithm to solve controller placement problem. In [9] Sahoo et al. have considered CPP as a multi-objective combinatorial optimization problem and solved it using two population-based meta-heuristic techniques. They investigated the problem in terms of three metrics: controller to switch latency, inter-controller latency and multi-path between the switch and controller. Their proposed scheme improves the survivability of the control path in case of a link failure, but they didn't mention the load balancing of the network. In [10] Hu et al. proposed a greedy algorithm to study the reliability in placement problem. Lu et al. [11] used a hierarchical approach to find better initial centers by treating the clustering problem as a weighted clustering problem. K-centers is the most well-known algorithm that have been used in controller placement problem [3, 12] and this problem is introduced as an NP-Hard [4].

3 Problem Formulation

In this section, we describe and then formulate the controller placement and network partition problems in terms of network delay and load balancing. The network topology is denoted as an undirected graph $G = (V, E)$, where V is the set of nodes, and E is the set of edges between nodes. Each edge between two nodes has a weight $w \in W$, where W is the set of weights which refers to the delay w_{ij} as the time delay between node i and node j. The time delay is calculated by the distance between the two nodes divided by speed of light $2 * 10^8$ m/s.

$$w_{ij}(millisecond) = \frac{distance_{i,j}(meter)}{2 * 10^8 \left(\frac{meter}{second}\right)} * 1000 \tag{1}$$

The shortest path distance between two nodes $(u, v \in V)$ is denoted by $d(u, v)$. The network is divided into k subnetworks and we define a set C contains the controller places c_i, where $i \in k$.

Each one of the subnetworks can be referred to as an SDN network and will contain nodes and edges between them as $SDN_i(V_i, E_i)$ with only one controller manages it. We define a binary variable x_{vc} equals to 1 if the node v is connected to the controller c, otherwise it equals to 0. These SDNs should follow the following rules and constraints:

$$\cup_{i=1}^k SDN_i = SDN \quad \cup_{i=1}^k V_i = V \quad \cup_{i=1}^k E_i = E \tag{2}$$

$$SDN_i \cap SDN_j = \emptyset \, where \, i, j \in k \tag{3}$$

$$\sum_{c=1}^V x_{vc} = 1 \, \forall v \in V \tag{4}$$

Equation (2) indicates that the total number of subnetworks will shape the whole big network. Equation (3) ensures that each node, edge belongs to only one subnetwork. Equation (4) refers to a constraint guaranteed that every node is connected to one and only one controller.

For load balancing, we assume the number of switches the controller manages as the load of that controller $L(c_i)$. We will define a metric β as the maximum difference between the loads of each two clusters. The constraint is as follows:

$$|L(c_i) - L(c_j)| \leq \beta \quad \forall i, j \tag{5}$$

4 An Extended K-means Algorithm

For partition problems, K-means was widely used and it's an effective and fast method to do that [13, 14]. We proposed an extended K-means to partition the network in terms of time delay and load balancing. The initial nodes where the controllers are placed will be called 'centres' and the updated centres after applying the algorithm are called 'centroids'.

First, we will explain the standard K-means which is used for clustering the network. This algorithm should follow main steps as follows: (1) randomly select k points from the data set and assign each point to be as a center for a cluster, where one cluster has one and only one center, (2) each data point is assigned to its nearest cluster based on the Euclidean distance to the center of that cluster; (3) update the centers of each cluster; (4) repeat step 2 and 3 until there are no changes in clusters' centers.

Although K-means is widely used for most clustering problems, it has many drawbacks when it is applied for network topology partitioning. First, if we choose random centers we will not guarantee the minimum time delay between the node and its centroid. Second, the algorithm doesn't ensure that the updated centroids will be chosen from the nodes in the topology as the centroids must be chosen from ($v \in V$) to be sure there is a real connection between the centroid and the nodes in that cluster because K-means choose the mean between the two nodes. Third, by applying the Euclidean distance we will not ensure that the link between the centroid and the node is physically exists.

For these reasons we proposed an extended K-means as explained in Algorithm 1 in order to adjust the previous drawbacks in standard K-means. The major steps in this algorithm are related to the initializing the centers, distributing the nodes to clusters and updating the centroids. The randomly initializing the centers as presented in standard K-means is not used in our algorithm and be replaced by another process for initializing the clusters' centers. In fact, initializing the centers in K-means was widely studied and many solutions were proposed to make this process more effective as in [15, 16]. We will use the initializing method proposed in [16] as it is an efficient technique and it reduces the complexity of computational and achieves a better local minimum. In Step 2, the nodes will be distributed to the clusters depends on their shortest path distance to the centers. In Step 3, the updating process of the centers will depend on the nodes inside the cluster.

Algorithm 1: Extended K-means

Algorithm 1: Extended K-means
Step 1: choose the first node randomly as a center.
    Step 2: distribute nodes to clusters, each node ($v \in V$) to one cluster as following:

$$if\ d(v, c_i) < d(v, c_j) then\ v \in cluster_i \quad \forall j \in \{1, 2, ..., k\}$$

    Step 3: for each $cluster_i$, calculate the sum of shortest path distances to every node in the cluster. The node that has the minimum sum will be chosen as the new center for $cluster_i$.

$$if \sum_n d(v, v_n) = minimum\ then\ c_i^* = v \quad \forall n \in size(cluster_i),$$

$$(v, v_n \in cluster_i), \quad i = 1..k$$

    Step 4: repeat steps 2, 3 until the centers are not updated anymore.
    Step 5: choose the node which has the largest shortest path distance from the previous centroid from step 4 to be the next initial center.
    Step 6: repeat step 2, 3, 4 until the network is partitioned into k clusters.

Algorithm 2: Load Balancing

Step 1: Check $|L(c_i) - L(c_j)|$ $\forall i, j$
    Step 2: If $|L(c_i) - L(c_j)| \geq \beta$ then reassign the nodes between $cluster_i$ and $cluster_j$.
    Step 3: repeat step 1 and step 2 until the load is balanced.

The main idea about Algorithm 2 is to balance the load depending on the difference between the clusters loads. As we mention before, we assume the number of nodes that controller c_i manages as the cluster load. The algorithm compares the load of each two clusters and reassigns the nodes between clusters depending on the constraint β. The reassigning procedure is done by removing nodes from the cluster that has more nodes and assign it to the cluster that has fewer nodes. This process will be repeated until the load of all clusters is balanced.

5 Performance Evaluation

5.1 Experimental Setup

In this section we evaluate Algorithms 1, 2 in terms of network delay and load balancing with different numbers of clusters. The network topology on which we deploy the algorithms is Internet2 OS3E topology [17] and the simulation is done by using Matlab R2018a, 2.50 GHz Intel Core i5 CPU, 4.00 GB of RAM and Windows 7 operating system. The topology has 34 nodes and 42 edges between them. The weight of the edge is the delay between the two nodes.

For network delay we calculate the time delay of each cluster depending on the shortest path distance between each node and the controller it mapped to as in Eq. 5, and then we take the average of them to find the delay of the whole network as in Eq. 6.

$$delay(cluster_i) = \frac{1}{N_i} \sum d(v, c_i) \tag{6}$$

$$delay(Netwrok) = \frac{1}{k} \sum_{i=1}^{k} delay(cluster_i) \tag{7}$$

Where N_i is the number of nodes in $cluster_i$ and k is the number of clusters. For load balancing effectiveness we use the standard deviation as a balance index, the smaller the value the better the balance of the load is. The balance index is as follows:

$$Balance\ Index = \sqrt{\frac{1}{k} \sum_{i=1}^{k} (N_i - \frac{N}{K})^2} \tag{8}$$

where N is the number of switches in the whole topology.

5.2 Results Analysis

The simulation is applied on the topology shown in Fig. 1 as the number of controllers is different for every simulation, and we also change the value of β for load balancing results.

The number of controllers k will vary from 1 to 5. When $k = 1$, it doesn't matter which node will be selected as initial center as the algorithm will choose node 16 as the center every time because it always has the minimum sum of shortest path distances to every other node in the cluster, and the next initial center is node 32 because this node has the largest shortest path distance to the node 16, but as the network has only one controller so the load on that controller will be the maximum and the nodes can't be reassigned so the results can be omitted. For $k = 2$, even the initial centers are nodes 16, 32 but the final centroids will be chosen as nodes 16 and 31 because they are the nodes which have the minimum sum of the shortest path to every node in the clusters they belong to. The node that has the largest shortest path distance to node 31 is node 9, so the initial centers will be nodes 16, 31 and 9 but the centroids will be 16, 31 and 10. When $k = 4$ the centroids are nodes 16, 28, 10 and 33; and for $k = 5$ the centroids are nodes 8, 28, 10, 33 and 22.

After the network is partitioned for each k, the network delay and balance index are calculated with different β, and the results are as shown in the Fig. 2.

Figure 2 shows that as β increases, the network delay decreases and the network become less balanced as balance index increases. For $k = 2$, the 32 switches are divided into {24, 8} in the beginning with network delay 7.06 ms and balance index 8. As β increases, the delay decreases slowly and balance index increases. The switches are divide into {16, 16} when $\beta = 1$ with optimal load balancing but maximum delay, {17, 15} when $\beta = 2, 3$, {18, 14} when $\beta = 4, 5$ and {19, 13} when $\beta = 6$. When $k = 3$, the 31 switches are divided into {13, 8, 10} when network is unbalanced, {11, 10, 10} when $\beta = 1, 2$, {12, 9, 10} when $\beta = 3, 4$, and the network is back to the original state when $\beta = 5, 6$. When $k = 4$, the 30 switches are divided into {7, 8, 8, 7} when $\beta = 1$,

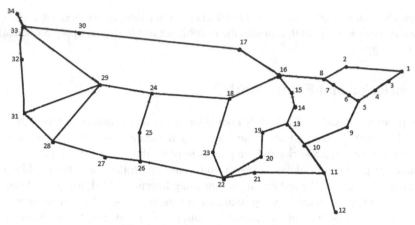

Fig. 1. Topology of Internet2 OS3E

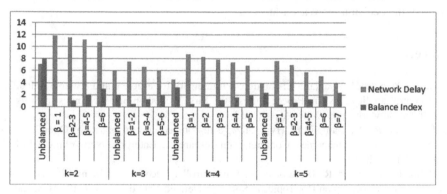

Fig. 2. Network delay and balance index for different k and β

$\{8, 7, 8, 7\}$ when $\beta = 2$, $\{8, 7, 9, 6\}$ when $\beta = 3$, $\{9, 7, 9, 5\}$ when $\beta = 4$, $\{10, 6, 9, 5\}$ when $\beta = 5$ and $\{10, 6, 10, 4\}$ when $\beta = 6, 7$. When $k = 5$, the 29 switches are divided into $\{6, 6, 6, 5, 6\}$ when $\beta = 1$, $\{7, 5, 6, 5, 6\}$ when $\beta = 2, 3$, $\{8, 5, 6, 4, 6\}$ when $\beta = 4, 5$, $\{9, 4, 6, 4, 6\}$ when $\beta = 6$ and $\{10, 4, 6, 3, 6\}$ when $\beta = 7$.

In most cases, the network delay is decreasing slowly except when $k = 5$. For $k = 2$, the delay is decreasing from 11.85 when $\beta = 1$ to 10.74 when $\beta = 6$, and when $k = 3$ it is decreasing from 7.5 when $\beta = 1, 2$ to 6.04 when $\beta = 5, 6$ and when $k = 4$ the delay is 8.7 when $\beta = 1$ and 6.04 when $\beta = 6, 7$. But when $k = 5$ we can see that the delay is 7.6 when $\beta = 1$ and 3.9 when $\beta = 7$. The balance index is increasing almost in the same manner. From Fig. 2, the minimum network delay will happen when $k = 5$ in case of unbalanced case or $\beta = 7$ as it is 3.9 ms, and the balance index is 2.4 with switches divided into $\{10, 4, 6, 3, 6\}$.

From the above discussion, we can say that there is no optimal case for the network to be in minimum delay and maximum load balancing. A trade-off should be made between the two metrics and the decision should be made according to our priority. However, other metrics can be studied and affect the decision. For example, the best network delay we have is when k = 5, but that makes the cost higher as we should apply 5 controllers in the topology.

6 Conclusion and Future Work

In this paper we introduced the SDN controller placement problem in terms of delay and load balancing. We first apply an Extended K-means algorithm to partition the WAN into several subnetworks and the goal is to place the controllers in positions that minimize the propagation delay between nodes and controllers, and then balance the loads of the controllers. We test our algorithm using Internet2 OS3E topology. From the results we can say that there is no optimal case for the network to be in minimum delay and maximum load balancing. A trade-off should be done between the two metrics and the decision should be made according to our priority. However, other metrics such as resilience, reliability and energy saving can be addressed in the future studies so that can affect the decision more accurately.

References

1. Hassas Yeganeh, S., Ganjali, Y.: Kandoo: a framework for efficient and scalable offloading of control applications. In: Proceedings of the First Workshop on Hot Topics in Software Defined Networks, pp. 19–24. ACM (2012)
2. Tootoonchian, A., Ganjali, Y.: HyperFlow: a distributed control plane for OpenFlow. In: Internet Network Management Conference on Research on Enterprise Networking. USENIX Association (2010)
3. Heller, B., Sherwood, R., McKeown, N.: The controller placement problem. In: Proceedings of the First Workshop on Hot Topics in Software Defined Networks, pp. 7–12. ACM (2012)
4. Yao, G., Bi, J., Li, Y., Guo, L.: On the capacitated controller placement problem in software defined networks. IEEE Commun. Lett. 18(8), 1339–1342 (2014)
5. Mamushiane, L., Mwangama, J., Lysko, A.A.: Given a SDN topology, how many controllers are needed and where should they go? In: 2018 IEEE Conference on Network Function Virtualization and Software Defined Networks (NFV-SDN), pp. 1–6. IEEE (2018)
6. Xiao, P., Qu, W., Qi, H., Li, Z., Xu, Y.: The SDN controller placement problem for WAN. In: 2014 IEEE/CIC International Conference on Communications in China (ICCC), pp. 220–224. IEEE (2014)
7. Qi, J., Yu, Y., Wang, L., Liu, J.: K*-means: an effective and efficient K-means clustering algorithm. In: IEEE International Conferences on Big Data and Cloud Computing (BDCloud), Social Computing and Networking (SocialCom), Sustainable Computing and Communications (SustainCom) (BDCloud-SocialCom-SustainCom), pp. 242–249. IEEE (2016)
8. Kuang, H., Qiu, Y., Li, R., Liu, X.: A hierarchical K-means algorithm for controller placement in SDN-based WAN architecture. In: 2018 10th International Conference on Measuring Technology and Mechatronics Automation (ICMTMA), pp. 263–267. IEEE (2018)
9. Sahoo, K.S., Puthal, D., Obaidat, M.S., Sarkar, A., Mishra, S.K., Sahoo, B.: On the placement of controllers in software-defined-WAN using meta-heuristic approach. J. Syst. Softw. 145, 180–194 (2018)

10. Hu, Y.N., Wang, W.D., Gong, X.Y., Que, X.R., Cheng, S.D.: On the placement of controllers in software-defined networks. J. China Univ. Posts Telecommun. **19**, 92–171 (2012)
11. Lu, J.F., Tang, J.B., Tang, Z.M., Yang, J.Y.: Hierarchical initialization approach for K-means clustering. Pattern Recognit. Lett. **29**(6), 787–795 (2008)
12. Jimenez, Y., Cervelló-Pastor, C., García, A.J.: On the controller placement for designing a distributed SDN control layer. In: IFIP Networking Conference, pp. 1–9. IEEE (2014)
13. Al-Mohair, H.K., Saleh, J.M., Suandi, S.A.: Hybrid human skin detection using neural network and K-means clustering technique. Appl. Soft Comput. **33**, 337–347 (2015)
14. López Del Alamo, C., Calla, R., Arnaldo, L., Fuentes Pérez, L.J.: Parallelization of the algorithm K-means applied in image segmentation. Int. J. Comput. Appl. **88**(17) (2014)
15. Celebi, M.E., Kingravi, H.A., Vela, P.A.: A comparative study of efficient initialization methods for the K-means clustering algorithm. Expert Syst. Appl. **40**(1), 200–210 (2013)
16. Katsavounidis, I., Kuo, C.C.J., Zhang, Z.: A new initialization technique for generalized Lloyd iteration. IEEE Signal Process. Lett. **1**(10), 144–146 (1994)
17. Internet2 Open science, scholarship and services exchange. http://www.internet2.edu/network/ose/. Accessed 22 Mar 2019

Network and Information Security

Performance Analysis of Consensus-Based Distributed System Under False Data Injection Attacks

Xiaoyan Zheng[1], Lei Xie[1,2], Huifang Chen[1,3(✉)], and Chao Song[1]

[1] College of Information Science and Electronic Engineering,
Zhejiang University, Hangzhou 310027, China
{21631151,xiel,chenhf,songchao31097}@zju.edu.cn
[2] Zhejiang Provincial Key Laboratory of Information Processing,
Communication and Networking, Hangzhou 310027, China
[3] Zhoushan Ocean Research Center, Zhoushan 316021, China

Abstract. This paper investigates the security problem of consensus-based distributed system under false data injection attacks (FDIAs). Since the injected false data will spread to the whole network through data exchange between neighbor nodes, and result in continuing effect on the system performance, it is significant to study the impact of the attack. In this paper, we consider two attack models according to the property of the injection data, the deterministic attack and the stochastic attack. Then, the necessary and sufficient condition for the convergence of distributed system under the attack are derived, and the attack feature making the system unable to converge is provided. Moreover, the convergence result under resource-limited attack is deviated. On the other hand, the statistical properties of the convergence performance under zero-mean and non-zero-mean stochastic attacks are analyzed, respectively. Simulation results illustrate the effects caused by FDIAs on the convergence performance of distributed system.

Keywords: Consensus-based distributed system · False data injection attack (FDIA) · Performance analysis · Convergence

1 Introduction

Recently, the consensus-based distributed system has been received wide attention with the widespread use of wireless networks [1]. For a distributed system, each node is treated equally, and the load of each communication link is almost balanced. The distributed structure can reduce communication load, computation burden and energy consumption compared to the traditional centralized structure [2, 3]. Furthermore, the distributed structure is flexible for dynamical network topologies [4, 5].

This work was partly supported by National Natural Science Foundation of China (No. 61671410, No. 61471318) and Zhejiang Provincial Natural Science Foundation of China (No. LGG18F010005, No. 2018R52046).

However, due to the open characteristic of the distributed system, it is vulnerable to malicious attacks [6]. The false data injection attack (FDIA) is one of typical attacks for the distributed system, which injects false data into the unprotected procedure during information exchange process, intending to degrade the performance and threat the security of the distributed system.

In recent years, researchers have been beginning to pay attention to the impact of random or artificial injected false data on the system performance. In [7], the necessary and sufficient condition to guarantee the convergence of distributed system under bounded noise is proved, and the closed expression of the relationship between the noise bound and the consensus accuracy is derived. In [8], the expression of weighted least-squared error of nodes when the distributed system reaches the steady state under noise is deduced. In [9], the author further explored the influence of noise on performance of distributed system under different topologies on the basis of [8], and indicated that the error caused by noise is related to the depth of the graph. In [10] and [11], authors analyzed the effects of zero-mean random noise and non-zero-mean random noise on the convergence performance of the broadcast-based consensus algorithm, and derived the upper and lower performance bounds under noise interference. In [12], the stability of the distributed detection system under the interference of two kinds of energy limited signals is discussed for the resilient consensus problem.

In this paper, we study the security problem of the consensus-based distributed system and analyze the impact of FDIA on the system performance. Two types of FDIAs, the deterministic attack and the stochastic attack, are considered in the fusion phase of distributed system. The effect of the deterministic attack and the stochastic attack on the convergence performance of distributed system is analyzed in detail. For the distributed system under different FDIAs, some interesting theoretical results are derived. Finally, the theoretical results are verified by simulations.

The rest of the paper is organized as follows. Section 2 describes the system model. Section 3 analyzes the impact of the FDIA on the performance of distributed system. Section 4 gives simulation results and discussions. Finally, the paper is concluded in Sect. 5.

Notations: Boldfaced capital and lower-case letters represent matrices and vectors, respectively. $\mathbf{I}_n$ denotes the identity matrix of dimension $n \times n$. $\mathbf{1}_n$ denotes the n-column vector with all elements to be 1. $\mathcal{N}(\mu, \sigma^2)$ denotes the normal distribution with mean μ and variance σ^2. Besides, det($\cdot$) denotes the determinant operation. diag($\cdot$) denotes the creation operation of the diagonal matrix with supplied elements.

2 System Model

2.1 Network Model

Considering a distributed network consisting of N sensor nodes, where the topology structure is connected, and communication links are steady. The network is described by an undirected graph $\mathcal{G} = (v, \varepsilon)$, where $\mathcal{V}$ represents the set of nodes in the network, and $\mathcal{V} = \{v_1, v_2, \ldots, v_N\}$, ε represents the set of edges in the network, and $\varepsilon \subseteq \mathcal{V} \times \mathcal{V}$. If $(v_i, v_j) \in \varepsilon$, node i and node j are adjacent and they can exchange information with each other. Hence, the neighboring set of node i is defined as $\mathcal{N}_i = \{v_j \in \mathcal{V} \cap (v_i, v_j) \in \varepsilon\}$.

The characteristics of a network can be expressed using a set of matrices. Adjacent matrix $\mathbf{A}$ denotes the neighborhood relationship. If node i and node j are adjacent, the corresponding entry in $\mathbf{A}$ is $a_{ij} = 1$; otherwise, $a_{ij} = 0$. Degree matrix $\mathbf{D}$ is a diagonal matrix whose diagonal element d_i is the sum of neighbors of node i, $d_i = |\mathcal{N}_i|$ and $\mathbf{D} = \mathrm{diag}(d_1, d_2, \ldots, d_N)$. Laplacian matrix $\mathbf{L}$ is defined as $\mathbf{L} = \mathbf{D} - \mathbf{A}$. That is, the element is $l_{ij} = d_{ij}$ if $i = j$; otherwise, $l_{ij} = -a_{ij}$.

2.2 Attack Model

It is assumed that there exists malicious attacker(s) in the distributed network. In order to degrade the performance of the distributed system, an attacker captures part of unprotected sensor node(s) and makes them be malicious node(s). Malicious sensor nodes will launch the FDIA to degrade the system performance.

The operation of the distributed system over the network includes three phases: local measurement, distributed fusion and distributed inference (detection, classification and estimation). In this work, we focus on the FDIA in the distributed fusion phase.

As the FDIA is launched by malicious node(s), the false data are added to the state update step in the distributed system. Let $\mathcal{V}_a$ be the set of malicious sensor nodes, and $\mathcal{V}_a \subseteq \mathcal{V}$. Let $\mathcal{V}_s$ be the set of normal sensor nodes, and $\mathcal{V}_s = \mathcal{V} \backslash \mathcal{V}_a$.

In the fusion phase, each sensor node exchanges information with its one-hop neighboring nodes. The local state of the target will be updated until the whole network reaches a consensus if there is no attack. When malicious nodes launch the attack, the state update process can be denoted as

$$x_i(k+1) = x_i(k) + \frac{\varepsilon}{w_i} \sum_{j \in \mathcal{N}_i} \left[x_j(k) - x_i(k) \right] + u_i(k), \qquad (1)$$

where $x_i(k)$ is the state of the target at sensor node i at the kth iteration, ε is the iteration step, and w_i is the weight coefficient at sensor node i. In order to ensure the convergence of the algorithm, the iteration step needs to satisfy $0 < \varepsilon < \min(w_i/d_i)$. The injection data $u_i(k) = 0$ if node i is normal; otherwise, $u_i(k) \neq 0$ if node i is malicious.

For convenience, the update process in (1) can also be represented in the form of matrix as:

$$\mathbf{x}(k+1) = \mathbf{W}\mathbf{x}(k) + \mathbf{u}(k), \qquad (2)$$

where $\mathbf{x}(k)$ is the state vector, and $\mathbf{x}(k) = [x_1(k), x_2(k), \ldots, x_N(k)]^T$, $\mathbf{W}$ is the weight matrix, and $\mathbf{W} = \mathbf{I}_N - \varepsilon \, \mathrm{diag}(1/w_1, 1/w_2, \ldots, 1/w_N)\mathbf{L}$.

Let the weight coefficient vector be $\mathbf{w}^T = [w_1, w_2, \ldots, w_N]^T$. Thus, $\mathbf{W} = \mathbf{I}_N - \varepsilon \, \mathrm{diag}(\mathbf{1}_N/\mathbf{w}^T)\mathbf{L}$. We assume that the weight matrix $\mathbf{W}$ is invariant.

FDIA can be divided into two categories based on the injected data of the attacker, the deterministic attack and the stochastic attack. For the deterministic attack, the injected data of the attacker is a deterministic variable. And in the stochastic attack, the injected data of the attacker is a random variable.

3 Performance Analysis of Distributed System Under FDIAs

In this section, we analyze the effect of different FDIAs on the performance of the distributed system.

3.1 Performance Metrics

We introduce the definition of the convergence and consensus of the distributed system.

Definition 1: For the distributed system $\mathbf{x}(k + 1) = \mathbf{W}\mathbf{x}(k)$ with any initial state $\mathbf{x}(0)$, $\exists \mathbf{x}^* \in \mathbb{R}^N$, if $\lim_{k\to\infty} \mathbf{x}(k) = \mathbf{x}^*$, the system is convergent.

Definition 2: For the distributed system $\mathbf{x}(k + 1) = \mathbf{W}\mathbf{x}(k)$ with any initial state $\mathbf{x}(0)$, $\exists x^* \in \mathbb{R}$, if $\lim_{k\to\infty} \mathbf{x}(k) = x^*\mathbf{1}_N$, i.e., $\lim_{k\to\infty} x_i(k) = x^*$, the system is consensus.

Lemma 1: For the consensus-based distributed system $\mathbf{x}(k + 1) = \mathbf{W}\mathbf{x}(k)$, the convergence is equivalent to the consensus.

Proof: 1. If the distributed system is consensus, i.e., when $k \to \infty, \mathbf{x}(k) \to x^*\mathbf{1}_N$, where $x^*\mathbf{1}_N$ is a constant vector. Hence, the system is convergent according to the Definition 1.
2. If the distributed system is convergent, i.e., when $k \to \infty, \mathbf{x}(k) \to \mathbf{x}^*$, where $\mathbf{x}^*$ is a constant vector. Since $\lim_{k\to\infty} \mathbf{x}(k+1) = \lim_{k\to\infty} \mathbf{W}\mathbf{x}(k) = \mathbf{W}\mathbf{x}^* = \mathbf{x}^*$, and according to the definition of weight matrix $\mathbf{W}$, $\mathbf{W}\mathbf{x}^* - \mathbf{x}^* = \varepsilon \, \text{diag}(\mathbf{1}_N/\mathbf{w})\mathbf{L}\mathbf{x}^* = \mathbf{0}, \mathbf{L}\mathbf{x}^* = \mathbf{0}$, $(\mathbf{x}^*)^T\mathbf{L}\mathbf{x}^* = \sum_{i=1}^N \sum_{j=1}^N (x_i^* - x_j^*)^2 = 0$ for any $\mathbf{x}^*$. That is, $x_i^* = x_j^*, \forall i, j \in \mathcal{V}$, i.e., $\mathbf{x}^* = x^*\mathbf{1}_N$. Hence, the system is consensus.   ∎

3.2 Under Deterministic Attack

The attack may make the distributed system unable to reach consensus or converge to a wrong result.

First, we derivate the necessary and sufficient condition for the convergence of the distributed system.

Theorem 1: The necessary condition for the convergence of the distributed system is that $\lim_{k\to\infty} \mathbf{u}(k) = \mathbf{0}$.

Proof: Assume that the convergent state of nodes is constant x^*, the state vector is $\mathbf{x}^* = x^*\mathbf{1}_N$. When $k \to \infty, \lim_{k\to\infty} \mathbf{x}(k + 1) = \lim_{k\to\infty} (\mathbf{W}\mathbf{x}(k) + \mathbf{u}(k))$.

Since $\lim_{k\to\infty} \mathbf{x}(k + 1) = \lim_{k\to\infty} \mathbf{x}(k) = x^*\mathbf{1}_N$ and the weight matrix is a stochastic matrix, $\mathbf{W}\mathbf{1}_N = \mathbf{1}_N, x^*\mathbf{1}_N = \mathbf{W}x^*\mathbf{1}_N + \lim_{k\to\infty} \mathbf{u}(k) = x^*\mathbf{1}_N + \lim_{k\to\infty} \mathbf{u}(k), \lim_{k\to\infty} \mathbf{u}(k) = \mathbf{0}$.   ∎

Theorem 2: The sufficient condition for the convergence of the distributed consensus system is that $\lim_{k \to \infty} \sum_{\tau=0}^{k} ||\mathbf{u}(\tau)|| = C$, where $C \in \mathbb{R}$.

Proof: According to Perron-Frobenius Theorem, $\lim_{k \to \infty} \mathbf{W}^k = \mathbf{1}_N \boldsymbol{\pi}^T$, where $\boldsymbol{\pi}^T = (\mathbf{w}^T \mathbf{1}_N)^{-1} \mathbf{w}^T$. When $k \to \infty$,

$$\lim_{k \to \infty} \mathbf{x}(k+1) = \lim_{k \to \infty} \mathbf{W}^{k+1} \mathbf{x}(0) + \lim_{k \to \infty} \sum_{\tau=0}^{k} \mathbf{W}^{k-\tau} \mathbf{u}(\tau)$$

$$= \mathbf{1}_N \boldsymbol{\pi}^T \mathbf{x}(0) + \lim_{k \to \infty} \sum_{\tau=0}^{k} \mathbf{W}^{k-\tau} \mathbf{u}(\tau). \tag{3}$$

Using the properties of norms, we have

$$\lim_{k \to \infty} ||\mathbf{x}(k+1)|| = \left\| \mathbf{1}_N \boldsymbol{\pi}^T \mathbf{x}(0) + \lim_{k \to \infty} \sum_{\tau=0}^{k} \mathbf{W}^{k-\tau} \mathbf{u}(\tau) \right\|$$

$$\leq \left\| \mathbf{1}_N \boldsymbol{\pi}^T \mathbf{x}(0) \right\| + \lim_{k \to \infty} \sum_{\tau=0}^{k} \left\| \mathbf{W}^{k-\tau} \mathbf{u}(\tau) \right\|. \tag{4}$$

Since $\lim_{k \to \infty} \sum_{\tau=0}^{k} ||\mathbf{u}(\tau)|| = C$, $\lim_{k \to \infty} \sum_{\tau=0}^{k} \mathbf{u}(\tau) = \mathbf{c}$, where $\mathbf{c} \in \mathbb{R}^N$, and $\lim_{k \to \infty} \mathbf{u}(k) = \mathbf{0}$. According to Cauchy criterion, $\forall \varepsilon > 0, \exists M > 0, ||\mathbf{u}(\tau)|| < \varepsilon$ when $\tau > M$; $\forall \upsilon > 0, \exists N > 0, ||\mathbf{W}^\tau - \mathbf{1}_N \boldsymbol{\pi}^T|| < \upsilon$, when $\tau > N$. Therefore, $||\mathbf{W}^\tau|| < \tau + ||\mathbf{1}_N \boldsymbol{\pi}^T||$. Since $k - N >> M$ when $k \to \infty$, $||\mathbf{u}(k - N)||, \ldots, ||\mathbf{u}(k)|| < \varepsilon$. Hence,

$$\lim_{k \to \infty} \left\| \sum_{\tau=0}^{k} \mathbf{W}^{k-\tau} \mathbf{u}(\tau) \right\| \leq \lim_{k \to \infty} \left(\left\| \mathbf{W}^k \right\| ||\mathbf{u}(0)|| + \ldots + \left\| \mathbf{W}^{N+1} \right\| ||\mathbf{u}(k - N - 1)|| \right.$$

$$\left. + \left\| \mathbf{W}^N \right\| ||\mathbf{u}(k - N)|| + \ldots + ||\mathbf{u}(k)|| \right)$$

$$< \left(\upsilon + \left\| \mathbf{1}_N \boldsymbol{\pi}^T \right\| \right) C + \varepsilon \sum_{\tau=0}^{N} ||\mathbf{W}||^\tau$$

Moreover, norm and spectral radius of matrix satisfy that $||\mathbf{W}|| \geq \rho(\mathbf{W}) = 1$. When $||\mathbf{W}|| = 1, \varepsilon \sum_{\tau=0}^{N} ||\mathbf{W}^\tau|| < \varepsilon N$. When $||\mathbf{W}|| > 1, \varepsilon \sum_{\tau=0}^{N} ||\mathbf{W}^\tau|| = \varepsilon (1 - ||\mathbf{W}||^{N+1})(1 - ||\mathbf{W}||)^{-1}$. Hence, Eq. (4) is convergent.

Therefore, when the attack vector satisfies $\lim_{k \to \infty} \sum_{\tau=0}^{k} ||\mathbf{u}(k)|| = C$, the norm of state vector is convergent, i.e., the states of all nodes converge. ∎

In Theorems 1 and 2, the necessary condition and sufficient condition to convergent for the distributed system under FDIA are proved, respectively. Therefore, the attack strategy making the network unable converge should have

$$\lim_{k \to \infty} \sum_{\tau=0}^{k} ||\mathbf{u}(\tau)|| = \infty. \tag{5}$$

That is, when the series of vectors are not converge, the system cannot reach consensus although the iteration step increases.

From (2), we find that the impact of FDIA on the performance of distributed system is continuous. That is, once the attacker launches the attack (although the attack subsequently stops), the injected false data will spread to the surrounding nodes during nodes exchange information. The false data injected by the attacker will remain in the convergence result. Hence, it is necessary to analyze the deviation between the wrong convergence result and the normal convergence result under the FDIA.

Theorem 3: When the attack vector series converge, $\lim_{k\to\infty} \sum_{\tau=0}^{k} \mathbf{u}(\tau) = \mathbf{c}$ and $\mathbf{c} \in \mathbb{R}^N$, the convergence result of nodes is

$$\lim_{k\to\infty} \mathbf{x}(k) = \mathbf{1}_N \boldsymbol{\pi}^T(\mathbf{x}(0) + \mathbf{c}). \tag{6}$$

Proof: According to (2), the convergence result of state vector under FDIA is

$$\lim_{k\to\infty} \mathbf{x}(k+1) = \mathbf{1}_N \boldsymbol{\pi}^T \mathbf{x}(0) + \lim_{k\to\infty} \sum_{\tau=0}^{k} \mathbf{W}^{k-\tau} \mathbf{u}(\tau).$$

As $\boldsymbol{\pi}^T \mathbf{W} = \boldsymbol{\pi}^T$, $\boldsymbol{\pi}^T \mathbf{W}^k = \boldsymbol{\pi}^T \mathbf{W}^{k-1} = \dots = \boldsymbol{\pi}^T \mathbf{W} = \boldsymbol{\pi}^T$. And then,

$$\boldsymbol{\pi}^T \lim_{k\to\infty} \sum_{\tau=0}^{k} \mathbf{W}^{k-\tau} \mathbf{u}(\tau) = \lim_{k\to\infty} \boldsymbol{\pi}^T \mathbf{W}^k \mathbf{u}(0) + \dots + \boldsymbol{\pi}^T \mathbf{W} \mathbf{u}(k-1) + \boldsymbol{\pi}^T \mathbf{u}(k)$$

$$= \lim_{k\to\infty} \boldsymbol{\pi}^T [\mathbf{u}(0) + \dots + \mathbf{u}(k-1) + \mathbf{u}(k)] = \boldsymbol{\pi}^T \mathbf{c}$$

As $\mathbf{b} = \lim_{k\to\infty} \sum_{\tau=0}^{k} \mathbf{W}^{k-\tau} \mathbf{u}(\tau)$, $\boldsymbol{\pi}^T \mathbf{b} = \boldsymbol{\pi}^T \mathbf{c}$. When $\lim_{k\to\infty} \sum_{\tau=0}^{k} \mathbf{u}(\tau) = \mathbf{c}$, the states of nodes are convergent. Thus, $b_i = b_j, \forall i, j \in V$. If $\mathbf{b} = b\mathbf{1}_N, b\boldsymbol{\pi}^T \mathbf{1}_N = \boldsymbol{\pi}^T \mathbf{c}$, *i.e.*, $b = \boldsymbol{\pi}^T \mathbf{c}$. Therefore, we have

$$\lim_{k\to\infty} \sum_{\tau=0}^{k} \mathbf{W}^{k-\tau} \mathbf{u}(\tau) = \mathbf{1}_N \boldsymbol{\pi}^T \mathbf{c}. \tag{7}$$

From (7), one finds that the series of injected attack vector will directly affect the convergence result of the distributed system. ∎

Lemma 2: If and only if the weighted average of attack vector series converges to zero, $\lim_{k\to\infty} \boldsymbol{\pi}^T \sum_{\tau=0}^{k} \mathbf{u}(\tau) = 0$, the convergence result will be the weighted average of initial states of nodes.

3.3 Under Stochastic Attack

When the injection attack vector is random, we consider the case of Gaussian random variable. That is, the malicious node i injects false data $u_i(k)$ at step k, $u_i(k) \sim \mathcal{N}(\mu_i, \sigma 2i)$, and the attack vector satisfies $\mathbf{u}(k) \sim \mathcal{N}(\boldsymbol{\mu}, \boldsymbol{\Sigma})$.

To facilitate the subsequent derivation, we introduce the nature of normalized weighted average matrix, $\mathbf{Q} = \mathbf{1}_N \boldsymbol{\pi}^T$, and its relationship with the weight matrix $\mathbf{W}$.

Property 1: The normalized weighted average matrix $\mathbf{Q}$ has the following properties:

(1) $\mathbf{Q} = \lim_{k \to \infty} \mathbf{W}^k$;
(2) $\mathbf{QW} = \mathbf{Q}$;
(3) $\mathbf{WQ} = \mathbf{Q}$;
(4) $\mathbf{Q}^2 = \mathbf{Q}$;
(5) $(\mathbf{W} - \mathbf{Q})^k = \mathbf{W}^k - \mathbf{Q}$;
(6) $(\mathbf{W} - \mathbf{Q})^k (\mathbf{I}_N - \mathbf{Q}) = \mathbf{W}^k - \mathbf{Q}$;
(7) $\rho(\mathbf{W} - \mathbf{Q}) < 1$.

Since the injected attack vector is random, the state vector under its influence is also random. In the view of the statistical characteristics, we analyze the impact of the stochastic attack on the performance of distributed system.

The divergence vector of current nodes' state is defined as

$$\delta(k) = \mathbf{x}(k) - \mathbf{Qx}(k), \tag{8}$$

which can be used to measure the convergence performance of distributed system. The system state converges as the divergence is zero. The larger the divergence vector, the more obvious the divergence of distributed system.

Lemma 3: The divergence vector $\delta(k)$ satisfies the recursive relationship as

$$\delta(k + 1) = (\mathbf{W} - \mathbf{Q})\delta(k) + (\mathbf{I}_N - \mathbf{Q})\mathbf{u}(k). \tag{9}$$

Proof: According to the definition of $\delta(k)$ and the properties of matrix $\mathbf{Q}$, we have

$$\begin{aligned}
\delta(k + 1) &= \mathbf{x}(k + 1) - \mathbf{Qx}(k + 1) = \mathbf{Wx}(k) + \mathbf{u}(k) - \mathbf{QWx}(k) - \mathbf{Qu}(k) \\
&= (\mathbf{W} - \mathbf{Q})\mathbf{x}(k) + (\mathbf{I}_N - \mathbf{Q})\mathbf{u}(k).
\end{aligned}$$

While $(\mathbf{W} - \mathbf{Q})\mathbf{Qx}(k) = (\mathbf{WQ} - \mathbf{Q}^2)\mathbf{x}(k) = 0$,

$$\begin{aligned}
\delta(k + 1) &= (\mathbf{W} - \mathbf{Q})\mathbf{x}(k) - (\mathbf{W} - \mathbf{Q})\mathbf{Qx}(k) + (\mathbf{I}_N - \mathbf{Q})\mathbf{u}(k) \\
&= (\mathbf{W} - \mathbf{Q})(\mathbf{x}(k) - \mathbf{Qx}(k)) + (\mathbf{I}_N - \mathbf{Q})\mathbf{u}(k) \\
&= (\mathbf{W} - \mathbf{Q})\delta(k) + (\mathbf{I}_N - \mathbf{Q})\mathbf{u}(k). \qquad \blacksquare
\end{aligned}$$

First, we analyze the mean of divergence vector, $E[\delta(k)]$ or $\bar{\delta}(k)$.
Using the recursive relationship in (9), we have

$$\delta(k + 1) = (\mathbf{W} - \mathbf{Q})^{k+1}\delta(0) + \sum_{\tau=0}^{k} (\mathbf{W} - \mathbf{Q})^{\tau}(\mathbf{I}_N - \mathbf{Q})\mathbf{u}(k - \tau). \tag{10}$$

Since $\delta(0) = \mathbf{x}(0) - \mathbf{Qx}(0) = (\mathbf{I}_N - \mathbf{Q})\mathbf{x}(0)$,

$$\delta(k + 1) = (\mathbf{W} - \mathbf{Q})^{k+1}(\mathbf{I}_N - \mathbf{Q})\mathbf{x}(0) + \sum_{\tau=0}^{k} (\mathbf{W} - \mathbf{Q})^{\tau}(\mathbf{I}_N - \mathbf{Q})\mathbf{u}(k - \tau). \tag{11}$$

Since the mean of attack vector is $E[\mathbf{u}(k)] = \bar{\mathbf{u}}$, $k \in N$, taking expectation and limitation on both sides of (11), we get

$$\lim_{k\to\infty} E[\delta(k+1)] = \lim_{k\to\infty} \sum_{\tau=0}^{k} (\mathbf{W} - \mathbf{Q})^{\tau}(\mathbf{I}_N - \mathbf{Q})\bar{\mathbf{u}}. \tag{12}$$

As $\rho(\mathbf{W} - \mathbf{Q}) < 1$, the series is convergent and $\lim_{k\to\infty} \sum_{\tau=0}^{k} (\mathbf{W} - \mathbf{Q})^{\tau} = [\mathbf{I}_N - (\mathbf{W} - \mathbf{Q})]^{-1}$. Hence, the mean of divergence vector is convergent, and the convergence result is

$$\lim_{k\to\infty} E[\delta(k)] = [\mathbf{I}_N - (\mathbf{W} - \mathbf{Q})]^{-1}(\mathbf{I}_N - \mathbf{Q})\bar{\mathbf{u}}. \tag{13}$$

From (2), we find that, as the number of iterations increases, the mean of the divergence will converge, and the convergence result is related to the mean of attack vector. If the mean of attack vector is non-zero, the mean of divergence is also non-zero, which means that the state of nodes cannot converge.

Second, we analyze the covariance of divergence, $\Phi(k)$.

Suppose that $\delta(k)$ is independent of $\mathbf{u}(k)$ and the covariance of $\mathbf{u}(k)$ is Σ, the covariance can be further simplified as

$$\Phi(k+1) = (\mathbf{W} - \mathbf{Q})\Phi(k)(\mathbf{W} - \mathbf{Q})^{\mathrm{T}} + (\mathbf{I}_N - \mathbf{Q})\Sigma(\mathbf{I}_N - \mathbf{Q})^{\mathrm{T}}. \tag{14}$$

Then,

$$\Phi(k+1) = (\mathbf{W} - \mathbf{Q})^{k+1}\Phi(0)[(\mathbf{W} - \mathbf{Q})^{\mathrm{T}}]^{k+1}$$
$$+ \sum_{\tau=0}^{k} (\mathbf{W} - \mathbf{Q})^{\tau}(\mathbf{I}_N - \mathbf{Q})\Sigma(\mathbf{I}_N - \mathbf{Q})^{\mathrm{T}}[(\mathbf{W} - \mathbf{Q})^{\mathrm{T}}]^{\tau}. \tag{15}$$

Since $\delta(0) = \mathbf{x}(0) - \mathbf{Q}\mathbf{x}(0) = \bar{\delta}(0)$ and $\Phi(0) = 0$,

$$\lim_{k\to\infty} \Phi(k+1) = \lim_{k\to\infty} \sum_{\tau=0}^{k} (\mathbf{W} - \mathbf{Q})^{\tau}(\mathbf{I}_N - \mathbf{Q})\Sigma(\mathbf{I}_N - \mathbf{Q})^{\mathrm{T}}[(\mathbf{W} - \mathbf{Q})^{\mathrm{T}}]^{\tau}. \tag{16}$$

As $\rho(\mathbf{W} - \mathbf{Q}) < 1$, the series is convergent, $\lim_{k\to\infty} \sum_{\tau=0}^{k} (\mathbf{W} - \mathbf{Q})^{\tau}$ and $\lim_{k\to\infty} \sum_{\tau=0}^{k} [(\mathbf{W} - \mathbf{Q})^{\mathrm{T}}]^{\tau}$ are convergent. Hence, the covariance of divergence vector is also convergent. Moreover,

$$\lim_{k\to\infty} (\mathbf{W} - \mathbf{Q})\Phi(k+1)(\mathbf{W} - \mathbf{Q})^{\mathrm{T}} = \lim_{k\to\infty} \Phi(k+1) - (\mathbf{I}_N - \mathbf{Q})\Sigma(\mathbf{I}_N - \mathbf{Q})^{\mathrm{T}}.$$

Suppose that the convergence result is $\mathbf{X} = \lim_{k\to\infty} \Phi(k)$, $\mathbf{F} = \mathbf{W} - \mathbf{Q}$, and $\mathbf{G} = (\mathbf{I}_N - \mathbf{Q})\Sigma(\mathbf{I}_N - \mathbf{Q})^{\mathrm{T}}$. That is,

$$\mathbf{X} - \mathbf{F}\mathbf{X}\mathbf{F}^{\mathrm{T}} = \mathbf{G}. \tag{17}$$

The formula of (17) is a discrete Lyapunov equation. To resolve the equation, the Kronecker product, vectorization function and Matricization function will be used.

Theorem 4: For $m \times n$ dimension matrix $\mathbf{A}$, $n \times p$ dimension matrix $\mathbf{B}$, $p \times q$ dimension matrix $\mathbf{B}$,

$$\text{vec}(\mathbf{ABC}) = (\mathbf{C}^T \otimes \mathbf{A})\text{vec}(\mathbf{B}).$$

For convenience, we vectorize both sides of matrix equation $\mathbf{X} - \mathbf{FXF}^T = \mathbf{G}$. According to Theorem 4, we have $(\mathbf{I}_{N^2} - \mathbf{F} \otimes \mathbf{F})\text{vec}(\mathbf{X}) = \text{vec}(\mathbf{G})$. Since $\det(\mathbf{I}_{N^2} - \mathbf{F} \otimes \mathbf{F}) \neq 0$, $\text{vec}(\mathbf{X}) = (\mathbf{I}_{N^2} - \mathbf{F} \otimes \mathbf{F})^{-1}\text{vec}(\mathbf{G})$. Using the matricization function, we get the convergence result of covariance matrix as

$$\lim_{k \to \infty} \mathbf{\Phi}(k) = \text{unvec}_{N,N}\{[\mathbf{I}_{N^2} - (\mathbf{W} - \mathbf{Q}) \otimes (\mathbf{W} - \mathbf{Q})]^{-1}$$
$$*\text{vec}[(\mathbf{I}_N - \mathbf{Q})\mathbf{\Sigma}(\mathbf{I}_N - \mathbf{Q})^T]\}. \tag{18}$$

According to the steady-state expression of the covariance matrix of divergence vector, we find that when the covariance matrix of attack vector is zero, the covariance of divergence is also zero. When the covariance matrix of attack vector is non-zero, the covariance of divergence is also non-zero. It means that the deviation will fluctuate around its mean. The larger the covariance of attack vector, the more dramatic the fluctuation.

Furthermore, to analyze the impact of stochastic attack on the system convergence results, the deviation vector is defined as $\varphi(k) = \mathbf{x}(k) - \mathbf{Qx}(0)$, which represents the deviation from the state of the kth step and the weighted average result of the initial state.

Lemma 4: The deviation vector $\varphi(k)$ satisfies the recursive relation as

$$\varphi(k + 1) = \mathbf{W}\varphi(k) + \mathbf{u}(k). \tag{19}$$

Proof: According to the definition of $\varphi(k)$ and the property of matrix $\mathbf{Q}$, we have

$$\varphi(k + 1) = \mathbf{x}(k + 1) - \mathbf{Qx}(0) = \mathbf{Wx}(k) + \mathbf{u}(k) - \mathbf{WQx}(0)$$
$$= \mathbf{W}[\mathbf{x}(k) - \mathbf{Qx}(0)] + \mathbf{u}(k) = \mathbf{W}\varphi(k) + \mathbf{u}(k). \qquad \blacksquare$$

First, we calculate the mean of the deviation vector, $E[\varphi(k)]$ or $\overline{\varphi}(k)$.
Using the recursive relation,

$$\varphi(k + 1) = \mathbf{W}^{k+1}\varphi(0) + \sum_{\tau=0}^{k} \mathbf{W}^\tau \mathbf{u}(k - \tau). \tag{20}$$

Since $\varphi(0) = \mathbf{x}(0) - \mathbf{Qx}(0)$,

$$\varphi(k + 1) = (\mathbf{W}^{k+1} - \mathbf{Q})\mathbf{x}(0) + \sum_{\tau=0}^{k} \mathbf{W}^\tau \mathbf{u}(k - \tau). \tag{21}$$

Calculating the expectation both sides of (21), we have

$$\lim_{k \to \infty} E[\varphi(k + 1)] = \lim_{k \to \infty} \sum_{\tau=0}^{k} \mathbf{W}^\tau \bar{\mathbf{u}}. \tag{22}$$

As $\rho(\mathbf{W}) = 1$, the matrix series $\sum_{\tau=0}^{k} \mathbf{W}^{\tau}$ is not convergent. Thus, only when the mean of injected attack vector is zero, the mean of deviation is convergent to zero. Moreover, the state of nodes converges to the convergence result without attacks; otherwise, the state of nodes cannot converge.

Second, we calculate the covariance of deviation vector, $\mathbf{\Psi}(k)$.

Suppose that $\boldsymbol{\varphi}(k)$ is independent to $\mathbf{u}(k)$, and the covariance of $\mathbf{u}(k)$ is $\boldsymbol{\Sigma}$,

$$\mathbf{\Psi}(k + 1) = \mathbf{W}\mathbf{\Psi}(k)\mathbf{W}^{T} + \boldsymbol{\Sigma}. \tag{23}$$

According to recursive relation, we have

$$\mathbf{\Psi}(k + 1) = \mathbf{W}^{k+1}\mathbf{\Psi}(0)(\mathbf{W}^{T})^{k+1} + \sum_{\tau=0}^{k} \mathbf{W}^{\tau}\boldsymbol{\Sigma}(\mathbf{W}^{T})^{\tau}. \tag{24}$$

Since $\boldsymbol{\varphi}(0) = \mathbf{x}(0) - \mathbf{Q}\mathbf{x}(0) = \overline{\boldsymbol{\varphi}}(0)$ and $\mathbf{\Psi}(0) = 0$,

$$\lim_{k\to\infty} \mathbf{\Psi}(k + 1) = \lim_{k\to\infty} \sum_{\tau=0}^{k} \mathbf{W}^{\tau}\boldsymbol{\Sigma}(\mathbf{W}^{T})^{\tau}. \tag{25}$$

As $\rho(\mathbf{W}) = 1$, the matrix series $\sum_{\tau=0}^{k} \mathbf{W}^{\tau}\boldsymbol{\Sigma}(\mathbf{W}^{T})^{\tau}$ is not convergent When $\boldsymbol{\Sigma} \neq \mathbf{0}$. Thus, the range of deviation between the node state and the true convergence result is always changing, and the range of deviation is increasing. The series converges to zero when $\boldsymbol{\Sigma} = \mathbf{0}$, which means that the deviation between the node state and the true convergence result is fixed.

4   Simulation Results and Discussions

The impact of FDIA on the system convergence are simulated. Suppose that there are 10 nodes in the network, among which there are several malicious nodes.

Considering a network with 10 nodes, as shown in Fig. 1, among which several nodes are malicious. It is assumed that the communication channel is error-free. The initial state of nodes is randomly set as $\mathbf{x}(0) = [18.13, 19.90, 24.34, 18.50, 23.72, 12.65, 7.33, 21.04, 21.32, 13.96]^{T}$. The weight coefficient of all nodes is 0.1. Thus, the theoretical convergent value is the weighted average of initial state is 18.09.

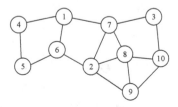

Fig. 1. Network model.

4.1 Under Deterministic Attack

Figure 2 shows the convergence performance of distributed system under deterministic attack. In the figures, the solid line denotes the state of each node, the dash line indicates the state of malicious node, and the orange horizontal dotted line indicates the theoretical convergence result.

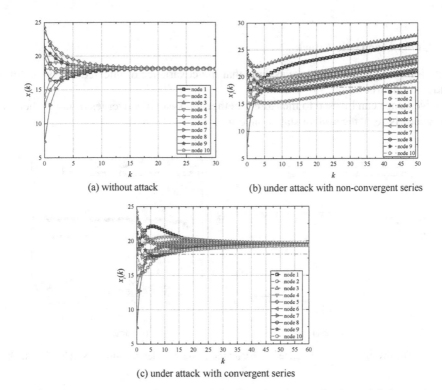

(a) without attack

(b) under attack with non-convergent series

(c) under attack with convergent series

Fig. 2. The convergence performance of distributed system under deterministic attack.

Figure 2(a) shows the convergence performance of distributed system without attack. From Fig. 2(a), we observe that the state of nodes gradually converges as the number of iterations increases. After iterating 18 times, the state of each node converges to the desired weighted average of 18.09.

Figure 2(b) shows the convergence performance of distributed system under attack, where the attack series is not convergent, nodes 1, 2 and 3 are malicious, and the injected false vector is $\mathbf{m}(k) = \begin{bmatrix} 3 \times 0.8^k, -2 \times 0.5^k, 0.6^k \end{bmatrix}^{\mathrm{T}}$, $k \in \mathrm{N}$. From Fig. 2(b), we observe that when the distributed system encounters the attack with non-convergent series, the system state cannot converge although the number of iterations increases. Hence, Fig. 2(b) verifies that the attack with non-convergent series will make the system state unable to converge.

Figure 2(c) shows the convergence performance of distributed system under attack, where the attack series is convergent, nodes 1, 2 and 3 are malicious, and the injected false vector is $\mathbf{m}(k) = [1, -1, 1]^T, k \in N$. From Fig. 2(c), we observe that when the distributed system encounters the attack with convergent series, the system state will reach convergence as the number of iterations increases. The convergence result is about 19.44, which is different from the expected convergence result without attack, 18.09. That is, the convergent attack will cause the system state to converge to a wrong result, and the convergence result deviation equals to the weighted average of attack vector series.

4.2 Under Stochastic Attack

In the following simulations, we assume that the covariance of injected attack vector is an identity matrix.

Divergence can be used to measure whether the system converges or not. When the divergence is zero, the system state converges.

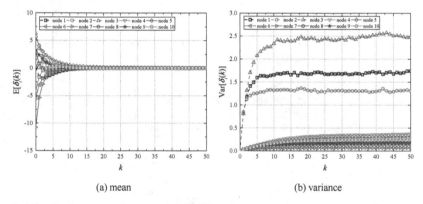

(a) mean   (b) variance

Fig. 3. The divergence performance of distributed system under zero-mean stochastic attack.

Figure 3 shows the divergence performance of distributed system under zero-mean stochastic attack, where Fig. 3(a) and (b) gives the mean and variance of divergence, respectively. From Fig. 3(a), we observe that the divergence tends to zero as the number of iterations increases, which means that the node state converges. Moreover, from Fig. 3(b), we observe that the variance of divergence first increases, and then stabilizes as the number of iterations increases. This indicates that the fluctuation of divergence at each node gradually stabilizes as the number of iterations increases.

Figure 4 shows the divergence performance of distributed system under non-zero-mean stochastic attack, where Fig. 4(a) and (b) gives the mean and variance of divergence, respectively. From Fig. 4(a) and (b), we observe that as the number of iterations increases, the mean of divergence at each node converges to a non-zero value, and the variance of divergence also converges. Moreover, the mean of divergence at each node converges different value, which means the node state cannot converge. According to the theoretical results, the divergence convergent value is $[-2.57, 3.43, 15.32, -9.43, -10.28, -5.14, 2.85, 1.22, 0.81, 3.78]^T$, which is the same as simulation result.

When the deviation equals to zero, the system state converges to the true result. The deviation can be used to measure how convergence result deviates from the true result.

Figure 5 shows the deviation performance of distributed system under non-zero-mean stochastic attack, where Fig. 5(a) and (b) gives the mean and variance of deviation, respectively. From Fig. 5(a), we observe that the mean of deviation tends to zero as the number of iterations increases, which means that the node state converges to the true value. Thus, the theoretical analysis is verified. However, from Fig. 5(b), we observe that the variance of deviation increases as the number of iterations increases. The results in Fig. 5(b) indicate that the internal fluctuation increases gradually although the node state converges to the true result as expected.

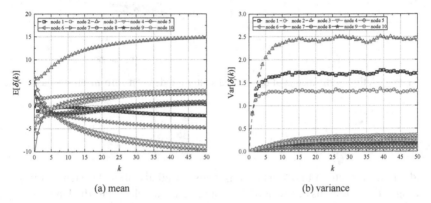

(a) mean   (b) variance

Fig. 4. The divergence performance of distributed system under non-zero-mean stochastic attack.

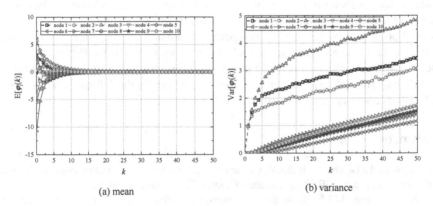

(a) mean   (b) variance

Fig. 5. The deviation performance of distributed system under zero-mean stochastic attack.

Figure 6 shows the deviation performance of distributed system under non-zero-mean stochastic attack, where Fig. 6(a) and (b) gives the mean and variance of divergence, respectively. From Figs. 6(a) and (b), we observe that the mean and variance of deviation at each node do not converge as the number of iterations increases. The results in Fig. 6

indicate that the node state gradually deviates from the true result under the interference of non-zero mean stochastic attack. Hence, the theoretical analysis is verified.

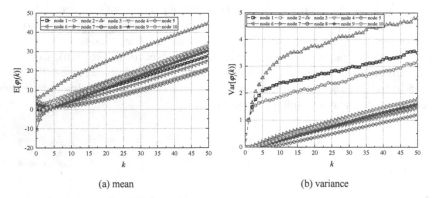

(a) mean   (b) variance

Fig. 6. The deviation performance of distributed system under non-zero-mean stochastic attack.

5   Conclusions

We studied the problem of FDIA in the consensus-based distributed system in this paper. According to the malicious behavior of the attacker, the attack is classified into two types, deterministic attack and stochastic attack. The impact of the FDIA on the performance of distributed system is emphatically analyzed. Under the deterministic attack, we first addressed the necessary and sufficient condition for the system convergence, and derived the attack characteristics making the network unable to converge. Moreover, the convergence result with limited attack resources is deduced. On the other hand, we analyzed the statistical properties of the convergence performance and convergence result at nodes under zero-mean and non-zero-mean stochastic attacks, respectively. Finally, the effects of deterministic attack and stochastic attack on the performance of distributed system are verified by simulation results. In the future, we will study the defense strategy against FDIA in the consensus-based distributed system.

References

1. Pasqualetti, F., Bicchi, A., Bullo, F.: Consensus computation in unreliable networks: a system theoretic approach. IEEE Trans. Autom. Control **57**(1), 90–104 (2012)
2. Kar, S., Moura, J.M.F.: Consensus + innovations distributed inference over networks: cooperation and sensing in networked systems. IEEE Signal Process. Mag. **30**(3), 99–109 (2013)
3. Zhang, W., Wang, Z., Guo, Y., Liu, H., Chen, Y., Mitola III, J.: Distributed cooperative spectrum sensing based on weighted average consensus. In: Proceedings of IEEE GLOBECOM, Houston, TX, USA, pp. 1–6 (2011)
4. Olfati-Saber, R., Murray, R.M.: Consensus problems in networks of agents with switching topology and time-delays. IEEE Trans. Autom. Control **49**(9), 1520–1533 (2004)

5. Kailkhura, B., Brahma, S., Varshney, P.K.: Data falsification attacks on consensus-based detection systems. IEEE Trans. Signal Inf. Process. Netw. **3**(1), 145–158 (2017)
6. Yan, Q., Li, M., Jiang, T., Lou, W., Hou, Y.T.: Vulnerability and protection for distributed consensus-based spectrum sensing in cognitive radio networks. In: Proceedings of IEEE INFOCOM, Orlando, FL, USA, pp. 900–908 (2012)
7. He, J., Zhou, M., Cheng, P., Shi, L., Chen, J.: Consensus under bounded noise in discrete network systems: an algorithm with fast convergence and high accuracy. IEEE Trans Cybern. **46**(12), 2874–2884 (2016)
8. Jadbabaie, A., Olshevsky, A.: On performance of consensus protocols subject to noise: role of hitting times and network structure. In: Proceedings of 2016 IEEE CDC, Las Vegas, NV, pp. 179–184 (2016)
9. Jadbabaie, A., Olshevsky, A.: Scaling laws for consensus protocols subject to noise. IEEE Trans. Autom. Control **64**(4), 1389–1402 (2019)
10. Aysal, T.C., Barner, K.E.: Convergence of consensus models with stochastic disturbances. IEEE Trans. Inf. Theory **56**(8), 4101–4113 (2010)
11. Yang, Y., Blum, R.S.: Broadcast-based consensus with non-zero-mean stochastic perturbations. IEEE Trans. Inf. Theory **59**(6), 3971–3989 (2013)
12. Meng, D., Moore, K.L.: Studies on resilient control through multiagent consensus networks subject to disturbances. IEEE Trans Cybern. **44**(11), 2050–2064 (2014)

Trajectory Clustering Based Oceanic Anomaly Detection Using Argo Profile Floats

Wen-Yu Cai[1], Zi-Qiang Liu[1], and Mei-Yan Zhang[2]($\boxtimes$)

[1] College of Electronics and Information, Hangzhou Dianzi University, Hangzhou, China
[2] School of Electrical Engineering, Zhejiang University of Water Resources and Electric Power, Hangzhou, China
`dreampp2000@163.com`

Abstract. The observation data of Argo profile floats are very crucial for long-term climate change and natural variability, which reflect three-dimensional distribution of temperature and salinity in the sea. In order to solve the anomalies in the profile caused by uncertainties factors, this paper proposes a novel anomaly detection method for Argo profile floats using an improved trajectory clustering method to discriminate normal and abnormal. The proposed algorithm partitions Argo data into a set of line segments, and then clusters line segments to get rid of noisy data, finally recovers the line segments to the raw data accordingly. As a result, the proposed oceanic anomaly detection method subtly converts the sequence data into line segments for anomaly detection, which considers both positional relationship and trend of data source. Extensive experiments on real dataset from Argo floats verify that our method has better results under different conditions compared to existing methods such as LOF and DBSCAN.

Keywords: Anomaly detection · Trajectory clustering · Oceanic observation data · Argo profile floats

1 Introduction

With the increasingly concerned about global change and its regional impacts, practical oceanic observation data are becoming more and more crucial. To combat historical lack of data, an innovative project named Argo was taken by scientists to greatly improve the collection of observations inside the ocean through increased sampling of old and new quantities and increased coverage in terms of time and area. Argo is a global array of 3,800 free-drifting profiling floats that measure the temperature and salinity of the upper 2000 m of the ocean. The Argo project allows a long-term continuous monitoring of the temperature, salinity, and velocity of the upper ocean, with all data being relayed and made publicly available within hours after collection [1]. However, the observation data of Argo profile floats are very valuable, which reflect the three-dimensional distribution of temperature and salinity of the sea and offer a database.

The data acquisition period of Argo profile floats is generally 10 days. They dive to a depth of 1000 m and drift for 9 days, and then descend to 2,000 m. The conductivity,

H. Gao et al. (Eds.): ChinaCom 2019, LNICST 312, pp. 498–508, 2020.
https://doi.org/10.1007/978-3-030-41114-5_37

temperature, depth (CTD) sensors are assembled on the Argo floats to record the ocean profile during the ascent. They transmit the collected profile to the satellite when back to sea surface. Due to the limited battery carried, Argo floats have a typical life cycle of 4–5 years. The positional uncertainty caused by the free-drifting of the floats makes maintenance and calibration very difficult. Argo profile floats work in the sea for a long time and the positional uncertainty caused by the free-drifting of the floats makes maintenance and calibration very difficult. Since local sensory data of Argo floats are prone to occur exceptions when sensors encounter a water mass abrupt layer or data transmission failure occurs. Moreover, sensors equipped in the floats are vulnerable by marine organisms or pollutants when it has been working for a long time, as a result the entire profile collected by underwater sensors may shift.

These anomalous data will affect some of the relevant research conducted by scientific researchers if they cannot be effectively identified. One of the most prominent being is the deviation of data from the adjacent data would not in the normal range. Several abnormal data detection methods in the marine field have been proposed. In order to guarantee the quality of data, Yusheng et al. [2] use a sliding window and improved AutoRegressive Integrated Moving Average model to detect and fill up the missing or suspect data. This simple method works well for continuously observed data, but it has some defects for non-continuous data. Andreas et al. [3] propose a robust and fast anomaly detection framework consists of cluster based auto associative kernel regression and sequential probability ratio test, which reconstructs the data and perform residual analysis to determine whether it is abnormal. Yosuke et al. [4] propose a new method for error detection in Argo observation data using conditional random field to realize an automatic QC (Quality Control) with high accuracy equal to human experts, but it has to consider the surrounding labels when assigns QC labels. Besides, a series of test methods for CTD data including location test, speed test, spike test, stuck value test, density inversion and etc. have been applied [5]. Furthermore, Jae-Gil et al. [6] propose a trajectory clustering method, which divides the complete trajectory into multiple line segments and then clusters the line segments to obtain a similar line segment set. Since it has many good features, we are devoting to improving and applying this idea to the filed of oceanic anomaly detection in this paper.

The rest of the paper is organized as follows. Section 2 presents our trajectory clustering based anomaly detection algorithm. Experiments and results are carried out in Sect. 3. Section 4 concludes this paper.

2 Trajectory Clustering Based Anomaly Detection

In this paper, we propose the clustering and restore framework to detect anomaly of Argo data. The proposed method consists of three main phases. Firstly, the characteristic data in the original data of Argo profile floats are extracted in the pre-processing phase. Afterwards, in the clustering phase, an improved Line Segment Clustering algorithm is used to cluster the line segments which are composed of adjacent two characteristic data. The line segments with the classification labels are reconstructed to the original data in the restore phase, and the raw data corresponding to noise segments will be determined as abnormal data.

2.1 Pre-processing Module

The Argo profile floats spread all over the world, and the profiles of different regions and time are quite different. Therefore, the adjacent similar profiles in time and space are selected as the basic dataset $T = \{TR_1, TR_2, ..., TR_{numtra}\}$, where num_{tra} is total number of profiles, and we treat each profile as a single trajectory and each data as a data point. A trajectory consists of many sequential data points denoted as $TR_i = \{p_1, p_2, ..., p_j ..., p_{leni}\}$, where the point p_j is three-dimensional data, $p_j = \{Pressure_j, Sensor\text{-}Data_j, Global\text{-}Index_j\}$. The first two dimensions of data are pressure value and sensory data using for segmentation and clustering. The global-index indicates the order for data point p_j in the basic dataset, used only in the restore section.

It is necessary to scale the points before partitioning and clustering sections, because the value difference in scale of different sensor is not the same, e.g., the pressure range is generally between 0–2000 dbar, but the salinity in range 2 to 41 PSU. Data can be normalized using Min-Max feature scaling according to the standard variation range of the data, and it can avoid the abnormal extremes effectively. The normalized formula is defined as Eq. (1). It is well known that the pressure range of Argo profile floats is between 0 to 2000 dbar, so we set X_{min} to 0 and X_{max} to 2000 when normalizing pressure data. The variation range of sensory data is not fixed, and it varies with the sea area. First, we find the maximal and the minimal sensory data in each trajectory TR_i, then calculate the difference between them to get the variation range V_{ri}. The median value from the V is chosen as the standard range M_r, $V = \{V_{r1}, V_{r2}, ..., V_{rnumtra}\}$. Finally, the median value is calculated from all sensory data in the dataset T as M_d, so X_{min} is $M_d\text{-}M_r/2$ and X_{max} is $M_d + M_r/2$.

$$Z_i = \frac{X_i - X_{\min}}{X_{\max} - X_{\min}} \times 10 \tag{1}$$

Herein, the data characteristic points in each trajectory are extracted after normalizing raw dataset. The line segment consists of adjacent characteristic points that not only represent all data points, but also reflect the trend of these points, so as to reduce the number of data and operation consumption in the clustering process. The method of Approximate Trajectory Partitioning [6] is applied to find characteristic points in the data trajectory.

This proposed algorithm mainly uses the Minimum Description Length (MDL) principle to find the optimal trade-off between precision and simplicity. The input of this algorithm is a trajectory $TR_i = \{p_1, p_2, ..., p_j, ..., p_{leni}\}$, and the output is a set of characteristic points $CP_i = \{p_{c1}, p_{c2}, ..., p_{lenci}\}$. Two adjacent characteristic points in the set constitute a sub-trajectory (or line segment) $L_i = \{p_{ci}, p_{ci+1}\}$. Moreover, the trajectory and the line segment set can be represented by $TRL_i = \{L_1, L_2, ..., L_{lenci-1}\}$ and $\mathcal{D} = \{TRL_1, TRL_2, ..., TRL_{numtra}\}$ respectively.

2.2 Clustering Module

In this module, we propose a line segment clustering algorithm with noise interference, which is derived from Line Segment Clustering algorithm [6]. In line segment clustering process, we try compare two line segments instead of two data points, so the distance definition between two line segments is crucial to performance. The process consists of three main parts: perpendicular distance ($d_\perp$), parallel distance ($d_{//}$), and angle distance (d_θ). Let $L_i = \{s_i, e_i\}$, $L_j = \{s_j, e_j\}$, where L_i is longer than L_j, p_s and p_e are the projections of points s_j and e_j on line segment L_i, which are illustrated in Fig. 1.

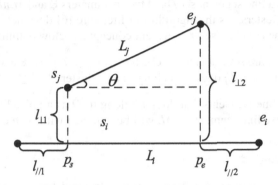

Fig. 1. The distance between two line segments.

Definition 1: The perpendicular distance between L_i and L_j is defined as Eq. (2). $l_{\perp 1}$ denotes the distance from point s_j to line L_i, which is the Euclidean distance from s_j to p_s, $l_{\perp 2}$ is that between e_j and p_e.

$$d_\perp = \frac{l_{\perp 1}^2 + l_{\perp 2}^2}{l_{\perp 1} + l_{\perp 2}} \tag{2}$$

Definition 2: The parallel distance between L_i and L_j is defined as Eq. (3). $l_{//1}$ is the minimum of the Euclidean distance between point p_s to s_i or e_i. $l_{//2}$ is the minimum of the Euclidean distance between point p_e to s_i or e_i.

$$d_{//} = \text{MIN}(l_{//1}, l_{//2}) \tag{3}$$

Definition 3: The angle distance between L_i and L_j is defined as Eq. (4). $\|L_i\|$ is the length of L_i, and θ is the angle between L_i and L_j. In the literature [6], the angle distance is defined as $\|L_j\| \times \sin\theta$, but we notice it is difficult to detect the angular abnormal line segment because the long abnormal line segment will be affected by the short line segment, even if the angle difference is large. $\|L_j\|$ is small, the angle distance is also small. Hence we improve the definition as follows.

$$d_\theta = \begin{cases} \|L_i\| \times \sin\theta & 0° \leq \theta \leq 90° \\ \|L_i\| & 90° \leq \theta \leq 180° \end{cases} \tag{4}$$

Definition 4: The total distance between the two line segments is defined as Eq. (5), w denotes the weighting value, and usually all of the weights are taken as 1.

$$\text{dist}(L_i, L_j) = w_\theta{}' \cdot d_\theta(L_i, L_j) + w_{//} \cdot d_{//}(L_i, L_j) + w_\perp \cdot d_\perp(L_i, L_j) \qquad (5)$$

Up to now, we can discuss our trajectory anomaly detection algorithm. The proposed algorithm requires a line segment set D and two parameters $\mathcal{E}$ and $MinLns$, then we can get a set of O of clusters. As the algorithm in literature [6] does not define noise line segments, we define novel noise line segment concept as below definition.

Definition 5: There are several clusters $C_1, C_2, \ldots C_k \subseteq D$ w.r.t. $\mathcal{E}$ and $MinLns$. A line segment $L_j \in D$ is noise if L_j does not belong to any cluster C_i, $1 \leq i \leq k$.

We regard the line segments that do not belong to O as a noise line segment after clustering, so a noise line segment set AL will be obtained with such operations.

2.3 Restore Module

The objective of this process is to restore from clustered line segments to raw data points so as to distinguish which points are normal or abnormal. Each line segment $L_i = \{p_{ci}, p_{ci+1}\}$ consists of two characteristic points, and the line segment can represent all the points between the two characteristic points. These two points are not necessarily adjacent in the basic dataset T, so we need Global-Index to indicate the position of the characteristic point in the basic dataset T. The raw points corresponding to the noise line segment set AL are marked as abnormal points. Due to the sensor drift phenomenon after being used for a long time, there may be a few entire profile anomalies in Argos. Hence, we need to check all of the trajectories, the entire anomalous trajectory is defined as Definition 6.

Definition 6: The points set of an anomalous trajectory are defined by $TRn_i = \{p \in TR_i|,$ p denotes an abnormal point$\}$. $|TRn_i|$ denotes the number of points in TRn_i. The entire trajectory is abnormal if it satisfies Eq. (6), where S denotes a parameter given by a user.

$$\frac{|TRn_i|}{|TR_i|} \geq S \qquad (6)$$

Usually, we regard a trajectory containing more than 70% of the erroneous points as an abnormal trajectory, i.e., the points contained therein are all abnormal points. So here we set S to 0.7. The total process of abnormal detection algorithm is illustrated in Fig. 2.

3 Experiments

In this section, we evaluate the proposed method using real dataset and compare it with other well-known approaches in the field of anomaly detection.

Algorithm Abnormal Detection based on Line Segment Clustering

Input: A set of trajectories $T=\{TR_1, TR_2, ..., TR_{numtra}\}$
Output: A set of abnormal $Ap=\{p_1, p_2,..., p_{numAp}\}$
Algorithm:
  /*Pre-processing Phase*/
01: for each TR in T do
02:   $V_r = \max(TR._{Sensor\_Data}) - \min(TR._{Sensor\_Data})$
03:   $V = V \cup V_r$
04: end
05: $M_r = \text{media}(V)$
06: $M_d = \text{media}(T._{Sensor\_Data.})$
07: for each p in T do
08:   $p._{Pressure} = p._{Pressure} * 10 / 2000$
09:   $p._{Sensor\_Data} = (p._{Sensor\_Data} - M_d + M_r / 2) * 10 / M_r$
     normalize the $p._{Pressure}$ and $p._{Sensor-Data}$;
10: end
11: for each TR in T do
12:   Execute Approximate Trajectory Partitioning;
     Get a set L of line segments;
13: end
  /*Clustering Phase*/
14: Execute Line Segment Clustering for D;
   Get a set of O of clusters as the result;
15: for each L in D do
16:   if $L \notin O$
17:     $AL = AL \cup L$
18:   end
19: end
  /*Restore Phase*/
20: for each L in AL do
21:   Mark the raw points in T as abnormal points according to the range
     between the $p_{c\cdot Global\text{-}Index}$ And $p_{c+1\cdot Global\text{-}Index}$ in L as the result;
22: end
23: for each TR in T do
24:   if $|TRn| / |TR| \geq S$
25:     $Ap = Ap \cup TR$
     TR is an abnormal trajectory;
26:   else
27:     $Ap = Ap \cup TRn$
28:   end
29: end

Fig. 2. Abnormal Detection Algorithm based on Line Segment Clustering.

3.1 Experimental Setting

The experimental data are derived from the Argo dataset in Argo China [7]. We randomly choose the profile data from January to March 2017 with longitude from 25 to 28 and latitude from 32.5 to 35.5. There are 224 profiles consisting of 69,499 points, and the salinity data is selected as the sensor data. Our experiments are conducted on Intel i5

3.0 GHz PC with 4 G Byte of main memory, and the simulation software is Matlab on Windows7 OS.

In order to investigate the validity of the proposed method, the unsupervised methods DBSCAN [8] and LOF [9] are used for comparisons. We use these three methods to calculate the same dataset, and compare the calculated predicted value with the real one. Four metrics are introduced to compare the difference between predicted value and real value. True Positive (*TP*) denotes the number of real abnormal points that are correctly identified as the abnormal points, False Negative (*FN*) denotes the number of real abnormal points that are not recognized, False Positive (*FP*) denotes the number of real normal points that are predicted as the abnormal points, and True Negative (*TN*) denotes the number of real normal points that prediction correct.

The FPR (false positive rate) metric indicates the ratio of number of normal points identified by the error to the number of all normal points, which is defined as,

$$\mathrm{FPR} = \frac{FP}{FP + TN} \tag{7}$$

The TPR (true positive rate) metric represents the ratio of points correctly identified as abnormal with real abnormal points, which is defined as,

$$\mathrm{TPR} = \frac{TP}{TP + FN} \tag{8}$$

3.2 Simulation Results

In order to determine the influence of parameters ε (Eps) and *MinLns* on the final results, we compare results with different values. First, we fix the value *MinLns*, and then we calculate the corresponding prediction accuracy by taking different ε value, finally we change *MinLns* value sequentially to obtain multiple curves. The results are illustrated in Fig. 3.

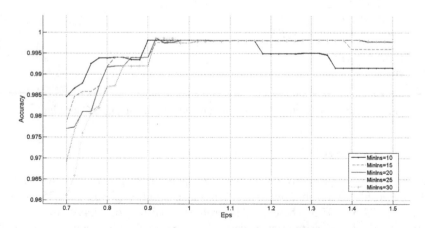

Fig. 3. Prediction accuracy with different *MinLns* and Eps.

When *MinLns* is at 10, the accuracy increases first and then decreases with increase-ment of ε. But the curve gradually becomes stable as the value of *MinLns* increases. When ε is between 1 and 1.16, the accuracy of different *MinLns* values is same approx-imately, so herein we set *MinLns* and ε to 20 and 1.1 respectively. In order to compare ROC (Receiver Operating Characteristic) curves of different methods, we set *MinLns* to 20 and change the value of ε to figure ROC curves. Figure 4 illustrates the compari-son of ROC curves for LOF, DBSCAN and our proposed method. The area AUC (Area Under Curve) under the ROC curve of LOF, DBSCAN and proposed method are 0.8924, 0.9424 and 0.9783, respectively. As larger the AUC value is, the better the performance of classifier. Therefore, the proposed method has better performance than the other two methods.

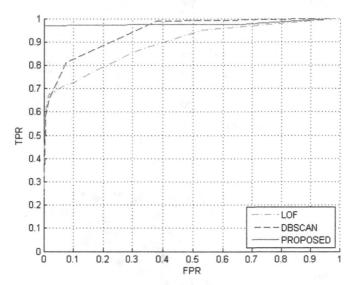

Fig. 4. ROC curve for DBSCAN, LOF and proposed method.

The highest accuracy of the results of LOF and DBSCAN methods are compared in Fig. 5, where green '+' are *TP* points, magenta 'o' are *FN* points, red '+' are *FP* points, and blue 'o' are *TN* points.

There are some anomaly profiles such as entire anomaly profiles and local anomaly profiles in the dataset. In Fig. 5(a), the LOF method can detect some abnormal data points but cannot identify the entire abnormal profile, e.g., there are 162 normal data points are recognized as erroneous points. The DBSCAN method can only detect 220 abnormal data points in Fig. 5(b), which is lower than that of LOF method, but the number of normal data points recognized as errors is only 29. Both of the above methods are directly processed with raw data points, so they are easily affected by the local density of data points. Moreover, change trend of data points has not been considered together.

Our results are better than that of two methods because it not only can identify the entire profile anomaly, but also detect some local anomaly profile hidden in raw dataset according to the change trend of data points so as to improve detection accuracy.

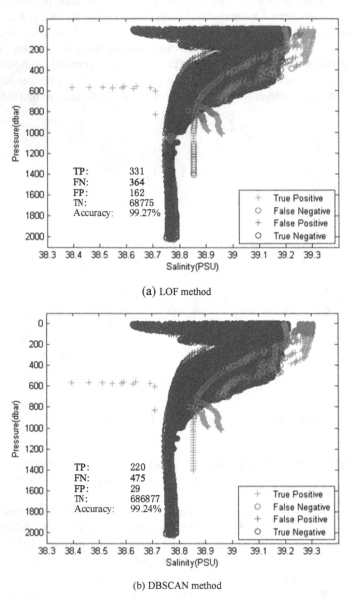

(a) LOF method

(b) DBSCAN method

Fig. 5. Detection results comparison (Color figure online)

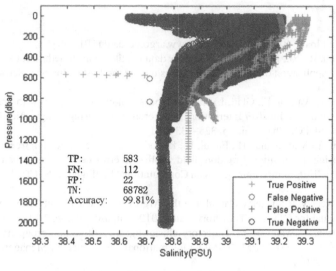

(c) Proposed method

Fig. 5. (*continued*)

4 Conclusion

To solve the anomalies in the profile which caused by uncertainties factors, we propose an improved trajectory clustering method to discriminate Argo data' normal and abnormal. We take the trend of data points into account, and data points with the same trend are regarded as a line segment, so it can detect the abnormal points hidden in total raw dataset very well. Compared with LOF and DBSCAN methods, the proposed algorithm has better performance in terms of detection accuracy. However, it is not particularly effective for some of the mutation points, because these points are not used as characteristic points in the partitioning step and are replaced by other normal line segments. In our future works, we will apply different trajectory partition methods to improve detection accuracy. Moreover, more practical data will be used to measure our methods.

Acknowledgment. The authors would like to thank the anonymous reviewers for their helpful and constructive comments that greatly contributed to improving the final version of the paper. These data were collected and made freely available by the International Argo Program and the national initiatives that contribute to it (http://www.argo.net). This research has been partially supported by National Natural Science Foundation of China (No. 61871163 and No. 61801431), Zhejiang Public Welfare Technology Research Project (No. LGF20F010005) and Key Research and Development Program of Hainan Province (ZDYF2017006). Natural Science Foundation of Zhejiang Province (No. LY18F030006) and Open funding of Zhejiang Provincial Key Lab of Equipment Electronics.

References

1. Argo Profile Floats, 10 June 2019. http://www.argo.ucsd.edu [BL/OL]
2. Zhou, Y., Qin, R., Xu, H., Sadiq, S., Yu, Y.: A data quality control method for seafloor observatories: the application of observed time series data in the East China Sea. Sensors **18**, 2628 (2018)
3. Brandsæter, A., Vanem, E., Glad, I.K.: Cluster based anomaly detection with applications in the maritime industry. In: 2017 International Conference on Sensing, Diagnostics, Prognostics, and Control (SDPC), Shanghai, pp. 328–333 (2017)
4. Kamikawaji, Y., Matsuyama, H., Fukui, K., Hosoda, S., Ono, S.: Decision tree-based feature function design in conditional random field applied to error detection of ocean observation data. In: 2016 IEEE Symposium Series on Computational Intelligence (SSCI), Athens, pp. 1–8 (2016)
5. Wong, A., Keeley, R.: Thierry Carval and the Argo Data Management Team. Argo Quality Control Manual for CTD and Trajectory Data (2019). http://dx.doi.org/10.13155/33951
6. Lee, J.G., Han, J., Wang, K.Y.: Trajectory clustering: a partition-and-group framework. In: Proceedings of the 2007 ACM SIGMOD International Conference on Management of Data, pp. 593–604 (2007)
7. Argo Data 10 June 2019. ftp://ftp.argo.org.cn/pub/ARGO/global/core/ [BL/OL]
8. Ester, M., Kriegel, H.P., Sander, J., Xu, X.: A density-based algorithm for discovering clusters in large spatial databases with noise. KDD **96**, 226–231 (1996)
9. Breunig, M.M., Kriegel, H.-P., Ng, R.T., Sander, J.: LOF: identifying density-based local outliers. In: Proceedings of the SIGMOD Conference, pp. 93–104 (2000)

DICOM-Fuzzer: Research on DICOM Vulnerability Mining Based on Fuzzing Technology

Zhiqiang Wang[1,2,3], Quanqi Li[1], Qian Liu[1], Biao Liu[1(✉)], Jianyi Zhang[1(✉)], Tao Yang[3], and Qixu Liu[4]

[1] Beijing Electronic Science and Technology Institute, Beijing, China
{wangzq,liubiao}@besti.edu.cn, liquanqi_China@163.com,
qianniu_1@163.com, nese@163.com
[2] State Information Center, Beijing, China
[3] Key Lab of Information Network Security, Ministry of Public Security,
Shanghai, China
[4] Key Laboratory of Network Assessment Technology,
Institute of Information Engineering, Chinese Academy of Sciences, Beijing, China
liuqixu@iie.ac.cn

Abstract. In recent years, the medical equipment and related information systems show the characteristics of mobility, networking, intelligence. At the same time, security incidents caused by medical equipment emerge in an endless stream, which brings a huge threat to the information security of users and causes serious harm. Most medical devices use open source protocol library, which brings great security risks to the digitalization and informatization of medical devices. Therefore, in the face of growing security threats and challenges, it is urgent to study the security of medical equipment. In this paper, the vulnerability mining of DICOM was studied, the most commonly used communication standard for high-performance medical devices, and a vulnerability mining model based on Fuzzing technology was proposed. This model constructed a vulnerability mining environment by simulating PACS system, and implemented a prototype system DICOM-Fuzzer. The system includes initialization, test case generation and other modules, which can complete large-scale automatic testing and exception monitoring. Then, three different versions of the open source library were selected to test the 1000 test cases generated respectively. It was found that when the received file data was greater than 7080 lines, the overflow would occur, resulting in the denial of service of the system. Finally, the security suggestions and repair measures were put forward, and the future research was described.

Keywords: DICOM · Fuzzing · PACS · DCMTK

1 Introduction

With the development of cloud computing, Internet of things, and mobile Internet, medical equipment and related information systems show intelligent, mobile,

H. Gao et al. (Eds.): ChinaCom 2019, LNICST 312, pp. 509–524, 2020.
https://doi.org/10.1007/978-3-030-41114-5_38

networked and other characteristics. Due to the lack of safety awareness of medical equipment manufacturers in the research and development process, the digitization and informatization of medical equipment have huge safety risks.

DICOM (Digital Imaging and Communications in Medicine) is an international standard for medical imaging and related information (ISO 12052). It is the basis of all medical imaging technologies, and it defines medical image formats that can be used for data exchange to meet clinical needs in quality. Conceptually, DICOM mainly includes two aspects: communication and service for medical image. That is to say, DICOM can be understood as a format standard for medical digital image communication. DICOM is widely used in radiological medicine, including cardiovascular imaging and radiological diagnostic equipment (X-ray, CT, MRI, ultrasound, etc.). The DICOM protocol solves the problem of how to associate the information of patients with medical images. However, since DICOM did not involve communication security at the beginning of its design, a large number of security threats and hidden dangers have been introduced into the digitization and informatization process of medical equipment. Since 2008, the medical equipment has exposed a lot of security vulnerabilities and attack events, such as remote attacks on heart pacemakers, insulin pumps, bluetooth defibrillator, X-ray machine, and so on, which have caused serious injury and huge losses to patients. Therefore, facing the growing security threats and challenges, there is an urgent need to conduct research on the security of medical devices.

This paper mainly focuses on the research of vulnerability mining for DICOM, the most commonly used communication standard for high-performance medical equipment. This paper proposes a DICOM vulnerability mining model based on Fuzzing technology, which constructs a DICOM vulnerability mining environment by simulating PACS (Picture Archiving and Communication Systems) system, and constructs test cases by combining strategies based on generation, variation and artificial construction. On this basis, a prototype system DICOM-Fuzzer is implemented, which can complete large-scale automatic test and abnormal monitoring. Finally, a kind of DoS (Denial of Service) vulnerability is found through the test of DICOM parsing library DCMTK, which proves the effectiveness of the model and tool.

The innovations and contributions of this paper are as follows:

(1) A DICOM vulnerability mining model based on Fuzzing technology is proposed for the first time, which combines three strategies to realize test case construction and can improve the efficiency of test case construction.
(2) The prototype system DICOM-Fuzzer implemented in this paper can realize the automatic test of PACS system and greatly improve the test efficiency.
(3) We found the DoS vulnerability of DICOM parsing library DCMTK, which will affect all medical devices using the open source library in a relatively large scope.

The other chapters of this paper are organized as follows: Sect. 2 introduces relevant work; Sect. 3 introduces the architecture of the model. Section 4 introduces the implementation of DICOM-Fuzzer tool. Section 5 introduces the experimental results and analysis. Section 6 introduces the conclusion and future research direction.

2   Related Work

Through the investigation of the research status of DICOM medical protocol, the specific analysis is as follows:

Farhadi et al. investigated the protection of Iran's domestic PACS [11,15], and evaluated the security control of PACS. After analysis by SPSS software, they found that PACS did not record the transmission path, nor use digital signatures or watermarks to protect medical images. This paper evaluates the protection of Iran's medical imaging information system as a whole, and analyzes the information security requirements of the medical imaging information system [5].

Gutierrez-martinez et al. proposed a business model for ISO/IEC 27002:2013 standard and security and privacy standards to improve the information security management level of large-scale PACS, aiming at the lack of effective management mechanism in medical institutions. The method associated with this pattern can be used to monitor the data flow in PACS, thus facilitating the detection of unauthorized access to images and other abnormal activities [6].

Tim Elrod et al. conducted vulnerability mining research on two PACS's protocols DICOM, Health Level 7(HL7) [1,2,4,7,14], and electronic medical information recording system. They used Fuzzing technology and penetration technology to find several security vulnerabilities, including the use of Web browser to enable medical staff to automatically distribute drugs using the dispensing cabinet made by Omnicell, and the use of "forced browsing" attacks giving unauthorized users unauthorized access to the control of a hospital medicine dispenser operated by Integris Heath [10].

Anirudh Duggal conducted attack and defense technology research for HL7 2.X protocol, he mainly used the Fuzzing technology to test HL7 protocol stack, discovering the man-in-the-middle attack, message source and size not validated, denial of service attacks and other security threats, and proposed some security suggestions and threat elimination measures, such as message size verification, enforcing two-way TLS connection, content input filtering, adding the checksum [1].

Codenomicon company issued unknown vulnerability management guidelines for medical equipment, putting forward using the Fuzzing testing technology based on generating to structure test cases, and to detect unknown security vulnerabilities. This guide mainly introduces the testing process of "Analyzing Attack Surface", "Reducing Risk" and "Generating-based Fuzzing". Finally, it recommends safety recommendations for testing and validation for medical equipment manufacturers. Among them, Fuzzing technology [3,9,12,17–22] is an effective flaw injection vulnerability mining method, with a certain degree of randomness and blindness. This guide does not propose a solution to this problem [13].

3   System Architecture and Design

This chapter mainly introduces the system architecture and the design of three core modules: test case construction module, DICOM test module and exception monitoring module.

3.1   System Architecture

The system architecture consists of six modules, including system initialization module, test case construction module, DICOM protocol test module, exception monitoring module, exception verification module and log output module. The core architecture of the system is shown in Fig. 1.

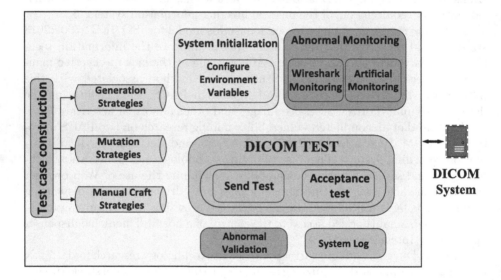

Fig. 1. DICOM vulnerability mining system architecture.

The system initialization module is responsible for configuring the environment required for operation, setting up the open source library DCMTK of DICOM protocol, uninstalling irrelevant object files, and installing object files to be tested. The test case construction module uses three types: generation-based construction, mutation-based construction and manual construction to construct the test case package. The DICOM test module sends the constructed DICOM packet file to the DICOM system to be tested for test. The anomaly monitoring module catches and monitors the test process and analyzes the feedback data concretely. Exception validation module is to re-verify the monitored exception to confirm the existence and availability of the exception. The log output module records the abnormal information that may be generated during the test.

Among them, test case construction module, DICOM test module and exception monitoring module are the core parts of the system, which are described in detail in the following chapters.

3.2 Test Case Construction

Construction Strategy. The construction strategy adopts the test case construction method based on Fuzzing technology. Fuzzing technology is an automated software testing technology. It is one of the important means of vulnerability mining by inputting a large amount of abnormal data to the tested target and monitoring its anomalies to find vulnerabilities. Test case construction strategies are divided into automatic random construction based on generation, analysis construction based on variation, and manual construction, which are described in detail as follows.

Automated Random Construction Based on Generation. This construction strategy adopts the idea of Fuzzing test to construct random DICOM data packet as input, and uses random function to arbitrarily change any value of this data packet, or modifies any bit of this binary DICOM data packet by cyclic modification. This generation strategy can allow the computer to construct a large number of random data packets, which has the advantages of low cost, high degree of automation, and can explore many unexpected vulnerabilities. However, most deformed data packets constructed by this method are invalid and will be abandoned by the equipment to be tested, leading to low efficiency of the final test process.

Analysis Construction Based on Mutation. This strategy based on mutation analysis is more purposeful and targeted than random construction. According to existing vulnerability analysis, most vulnerabilities are prone to appear on the boundary value. For example, normally required input type is int, while the maximum value defined by int can be input when testing. Applying this idea to the construction of packets, it is speculated that setting a byte in the DICOM packet as the boundary value may lead to triggering vulnerability.

Artificial Structure. Artificial construction is to construct test cases purposefully and pertinently through the constructor's understanding of protocol and other contents. Based on experience, the author guesses the place where the vulnerability may be triggered, and sets the numerical value manually. For example, there is a string "DICM" with a length of four bytes in the header file Header of DICOM packet. Changing the string to a value that is not the string "DICM" to observe whether the modified packet can trigger the vulnerability.

After the test case construction is completed, it is verified by sending it to the test program. This is done by constructing the fuzzer. Figure 2 shows the general testing process of the fuzzer.

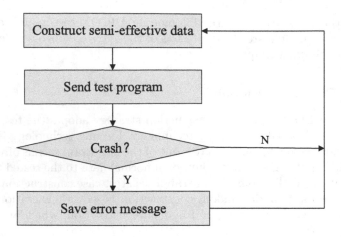

Fig. 2. General testing process for Fuzzer.

Vulnerability Analysis. A DICOM file generally consists of a DICOM file header and a DICOM data set. Introduction to the file, consisting of 128 bytes. DICOM prefix, which can be used to determine whether the file is a DICOM file based on whether the 4-byte string equals "DICM".

The main component of a DICOM file is a data set. Including:

(1) Tag: an ordered pair of 16-bit unsigned integers, with the first 8 bits representing the group number and the last 8 bits representing the element number.
(2) Value representation: indicating the data type in the data element.
(3) Value length: an unsigned 16-bit or 32-bit integer representing the length of the data field.
(4) Data domain: the data type of the value that exists in this field is determined by the value representation of this data element, and its storage length is even bytes.

Analyzing the file structure in Fig. 3, and paying attention to the parts of "value length" and "value range". It can be seen that the ultra-long value length and the transmission of odd bytes of data may lead to buffer overflow and other anomalies:

Extra Long Value Length. When implementing the DICOM protocol, programmers may assume that an unsigned integer with a value length of 16 or 32 bits in the DICOM file structure is sufficient to meet the usage requirements. This approach is not rigorous and scientific, and may cause some unexpected consequences. Therefore, the future vulnerability mining can start from this aspect.

Odd Data Field. As mentioned above, the data type of the value stored in the data domain is determined by the value of the data representation, and its

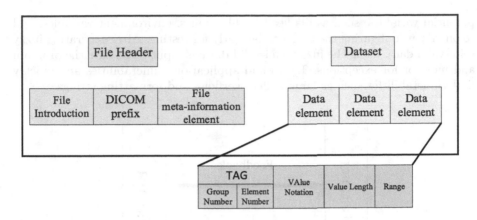

Fig. 3. DICOM file structure diagram.

storage length is an even number of bytes. If the data stored in data domain is odd in the process of data transmission, whether the DICOM protocol still can correctly handle the situation is one of the areas that the tester concern and needs to test.

3.3 DICOM Test

PACS is a system applied in the hospital imaging department, the main task is to digitally store everyday of all kinds of medical images (including the MRI, CT, ultrasound, X-ray machines, infrared instrument, the microscopic instrument equipment) through various interfaces (analog, DICOM, network), when needed, it can be used quickly under certain authorization back to use, adding a few auxiliary diagnosis and management functions. Because of the numerous interface categories of medical imaging devices and the large amount of data generated every day, how to transfer data between various imaging devices and how to organize the storage of data are crucial to the system.

The benefits brought to hospitals by PACS are obvious, including the following aspects: (1) reduction of material cost. (2) reduction of management costs. (3) improve work efficiency. (4) improve the medical level of hospitals. (5) provide resources accumulation for hospitals. (6) make full use of our hospital resources and other hospital resources.

The relationship between the test case and the PACS system is shown in Fig. 4. The purpose of fuzziness testing is to test whether various network protocols or related applications have security vulnerabilities. Fuzzing testing is a well-known black box technology for application security testing [16]. The principle is to send test data in a specific format to the target through the Socket API and monitor the abnormities in the target [8,16]. The testing process can be roughly divided into five steps [16]. First, identifying the target to be tested and getting more details about the target. Second, determining the input and potential variables, such as file headers, file names, environment variables, and so on. Then configuring the target to be ready for testing. After generating fuzzy semi-valid data, using the fuzzy semi-valid data as input to execute the program and monitor for exceptions. Try to find application vulnerabilities and quickly find vulnerabilities such as large buffer overflows and formatting strings.

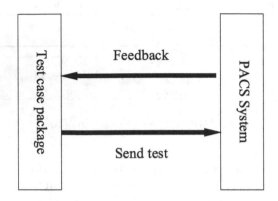

Fig. 4. Test structure diagram.

Fuzzy half valid data is for some applications, most of the data is valid, when testing, the application will first consider it to be valid data, but because of the rest of the invalid data, so there is a high probability of compiling or executing exceptions when a program processes data. Such exceptions include access cross-border, data overflow and so on, which eventually lead to application crash, delay, and so on. Figure 5 shows the general testing process for Fuzzing.

3.4 Abnormal Monitoring

In this paper, the abnormal monitoring mainly adopts two means, including Wireshark monitoring and manual monitoring.

Wireshark Monitoring. Wireshark is the world's foremost and widely-used network protocol analyzer. It lets you see what's happening on your network at a microscopic level and is the de facto (and often de jure) standard across many commercial and non-profit enterprises, government agencies, and educational institutions.

Wireshark has a rich feature set which includes the following:

- Deep inspection of hundreds of protocols, with more being added all the time.
- Live capture and offline analysis.
- Standard three-pane packet browser, etc.

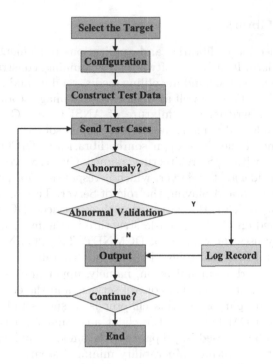

Fig. 5. Flow chart of test program.

In this article, you can use Wireshark to monitor the vulnerability mining system under test. In the running environment of vulnerability mining system, after opening Wireshark, you can easily select the information you want to capture, which can help analyze the cause of this exception by analyzing and reading the captured packet data. Wireshark can select the Npcap Loopback Adapter interface to capture various protocol packages, and then select DICOM protocol in the capture filter to capture the DICOM protocol packages, and conduct the required exception analysis through manual analysis.

Artificial Monitoring. Manual monitoring means that security personnel conduct penetration testing on the protocol according to their experience and monitor possible abnormal results. Due to the participation of human beings, the identification and reliability of manual monitoring are relatively high. However, its disadvantage is that it is purely manual monitoring, which cannot find loopholes thoroughly and requires the participation of engineers with rich experience.

4   Experiment

In this paper, different versions of DCMTK open source library are selected to conduct DICOM vulnerability mining test, and methods such as test case construction, fuzzy test and exception monitoring are introduced.

4.1 DCMTK Library

DCMTK is a collection of libraries and applications implementing large parts the DICOM standard. It includes software for examining, constructing and converting DICOM image files, handling offline media, sending and receiving images over a network connection, as well as demonstrative image storage and worklist servers. DCMTK is written in a mixture of ANSI C and C++. It comes in complete source code and is made available as "open source" software.

DCMTK is one of the three open source libraries of DICOM, which is an open source library with C/S architecture, namely Client/Server structure. SCP (Service Class Provider) is the Server, which is responsible for providing various services for image data and playing the role of Server. The SCU (Service Class User) is the Client, which is the party using these services. DCMTK is an open source library based on C++. Its basic structure is a number of packages, and this article mainly uses the content of DCMNET. The DCMNET package is a network library and available tools. This module contains all function sets to realize DICOM network communication, namely, upper finite state machine of DICOM, the element of association control service, and the element of DICOM message service. The purpose of this chapter is to successfully build a server that can receive DICOM files from the client and simulate a DICOM running environment. DCMTK is used to prepare for the smooth implementation of the design scheme of the following vulnerability mining system.

In order to verify the effectiveness of the Fuzzing technology-based DICOM protocol security analysis method proposed in this paper, it is tested and analyzed for DCMTK3.5.3, DCMTK3.5.4, DCMTK3.6.0–DICOM open source protocol library.

4.2 DCMTK Test

This system runs under a virtual machine configured with Intel(R) Core(TM) i7-8750h dual processor of 2.20 GHz and 2.21 GHz, memory of 2 GB, and the system version is WIN7.

In this paper, three different versions of DCMTK3.5.3, DCMTK3.5.4 and DCMTK3.6.0 of DICOM open source protocol library DCMTK were selected for comparison test, and 1000 test cases were respectively used to perform Fuzzing test on the above three different versions of open source libraries.

The test is based on the analysis of the DICOM protocol. Besides, it also includes basic programming language knowledge such as reading and writing files, loops, sockets, random number and so on. In the specific Fuzzing, the writing of the data packet sending and receiving test program mainly uses Socket to send data. Through Socket, a computer can accept the data of other computers and send data to other computers.

sockaddr_in sockAddr;
memset(&sockAddr, 0, sizeof(sockAddr)); // Each byte is padded with zero
sockAddr.sin_family = PF_INET; // IPv4 address
sockAddr.sin_addr.s_addr = inet_addr("127.0.0.1"); // IP address
sockAddr.sin_port = htons(1234); //Port

The Fuzzing test of the DICOM open source protocol library DCMTK3.5.3 is shown in the Figs. 6 and 7.

```
C:\New Folder\dcmtk-3.5.3\dcmnet\apps\Release>storescp.exe -dhl --aetitle TESTAE
X -od "C:\UC" -v -uf 104
Association Received
```

Fig. 6. DCMTK3.5.3 SCP receiving test.

```
C:\Users\Li>cd C:\New Folder\dcmtk-3.5.3\dcmnet\apps\Release
C:\dcmtk-3.5.3\dcmnet\apps\Release>storescu.exe 127.0.0.1 104 02.dcm
C:\dcmtk-3.5.3\dcmnet\apps\Release>
Press any key to continue
```

Fig. 7. DCMTK3.5.3 SCU send test.

As shown in Figs. 6 and 7, the test environment runs successfully. Figure 6 is the server-side SCP, and Fig. 7 is the client-side SCU. It can be seen that the SCU successfully sends DICOM files (02.dcm) to SCP, and the SCP receives them successfully. The port selected by SCU is 104, and the IP address selected is 127.0.0.1.

The Fuzzing test of the DICOM open source protocol library DCMTK3.5.4 is shown in the Figs. 8 and 9.

```
C:\New Folder\dcmtk-3.5.4\dcmnet\apps\Release>storescp exe -dhl --aetitle TESTAE
X -od "C:\UC" -v -uf 104
Association Received
Association Acknowledged (Max Send PDU: 16372)
Received c-store RQ MsgID: 1
  AffectedSOPClassUID: =SecondaryCap tur eImageS tor age
  AffectedSOPInstanceUID: 1.3.6.1.4.1.25403.17170403807.3304.20100205032740.1
  Priority: 2
  Data Set: Present
RECU:.....
Association Release
```

Fig. 8. DCMTK3.5.4 SCP receiving test.

The Fuzzing test of the DICOM open source protocol library DCMTK3.6.0 is shown in the Figs. 10 and 11.

We use the program to automatically generate a large number of DICOM file test cases, as shown in Fig. 12:

```
C:\Users\Li>cd C:\New Folder\dcmtk-3.5.4\dcmnet\apps\Release
C:\New Folder\dcmtk-3.5.4\dcmnet\apps\Release>storescu.exe 127.0.0.1 104 02.dcm
C:\New Folder\dcmtk-3.5.4\dcmnet\apps\Release>
```

Fig. 9. DCMTK3.5.4 SCU send test.

```
C:\dcmtk-3.6.0\dcmnet\apps\Release>storescp.exe -dhl --aetitle TESTAEX -od "C:\U
C" -v -uf 104
Association Received
```

Fig. 10. DCMTK3.6.0 SCP receiving test.

```
C:\Users\Li>cd C:\New Folder\dcmtk-3.6.0\dcmnet\apps\Release
C:\dcmtk-3.6.0\dcmnet\apps\Release>storescu.exe 127.0.0.1 104 02.dcm
C:\dcmtk-3.6.0\dcmnet\apps\Release>
Press any key to continue
```

Fig. 11. DCMTK3.6.0 SCU send test.

24.dcm	2019/6/13 20:19	DCM 文件	5 KB
25.dcm	2019/6/13 20:19	DCM 文件	4 KB
26.dcm	2019/6/13 20:19	DCM 文件	3 KB
27.dcm	2019/6/13 20:19	DCM 文件	5 KB
28.dcm	2019/6/13 20:19	DCM 文件	1 KB
29.dcm	2019/6/13 20:19	DCM 文件	2 KB
30.dcm	2019/6/13 20:19	DCM 文件	2 KB

Fig. 12. Generate test cases of DICOM type.

5   Results and Analysis

The code for the Fuzzing test was successfully run, compiled, and executed on the server side. Automated testing after the server successfully receives the file.

After a large number of test cases are constructed and the system is repeatedly tested for a long time. A large number of data packets were generated, with valid input and many invalid input. One of the typical data packets was selected for testing.

An exception was found during the Fuzzing test of the DICOM open source protocol library DCMTK3.5.4.

As shown in Fig. 13, the system exception is caught in the process of fuzzy test of DCMTK3.5.4. The file of fuzzy test has been successfully sent to the server side of DCMTK3.5.4. After that, it can be found that the originally opened server side automatically stops working, the system crashes causing anomalies, and SCP stops working. This test resulted in a system crash caused by the bug. During the test run, Wireshark software was used to record and monitor packages.

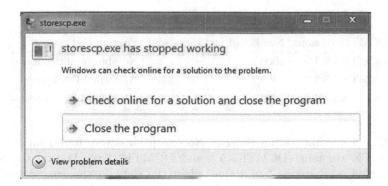

Fig. 13. Abnormal test results of DCMTK3.5.4.

Through packet capture analysis, it can be seen that the DICOM file has been transferred, that is to say, the DICOM file has been sent from the client to the server side, and then the server side crashes, so it is preliminarily determined that the problem is caused by the constructed test case.

lo.	Time	Source	Destination	Protocol	Length	Info
141	-27.356083	127.0.0.1	127.0.0.1	DICOM	1476	A-ASSOCIATE ...
146	-27.348802	127.0.0.1	127.0.0.1	DICOM	2378	A-ASSOCIATE ...
150	-27.343212	127.0.0.1	127.0.0.1	DICOM	380	P-DATA, C-ST...
166	-27.057909	127.0.0.1	127.0.0.1	DICOM	708	P-DATA, X-Ra...
181	-27.056773	127.0.0.1	127.0.0.1	DICOM	708	P-DATA, X-Ra...
196	-27.056449	127.0.0.1	127.0.0.1	DICOM	708	P-DATA, X-Ra...
211	-27.056137	127.0.0.1	127.0.0.1	DICOM	708	P-DATA, X-Ra...
226	-27.055832	127.0.0.1	127.0.0.1	DICOM	708	P-DATA, X-Ra...
241	-27.055525	127.0.0.1	127.0.0.1	DICOM	708	P-DATA, X-Ra...
256	-27.055228	127.0.0.1	127.0.0.1	DICOM	708	P-DATA, X-Ra...

Fig. 14. Wireshark interface.

Starting the server and client of DCMTK3.5.4, opening Wireshark, selecting the required monitoring interface, and running the command "storescu.exe 127.0.0.1 104 test1" on the client. As shown in Fig. 14, the monitoring data of the system is obtained. In addition, regular expressions can be modified to further filter specific error messages, as shown in Fig. 15.

After the Fuzzing test were performed on DCMTK3.5.3 and DCMTK3.6.0, no PACS system exception were found after the test data were sent (no vulnerability were found). The summary of the experimental results is shown in the Table 1.

The experiment is the first to design vulnerability mining framework and the test of Fuzzing for DICOM protocol. This experiment verified the vulnerability mining framework proposed in Sect. 3.1. A total of three different versions of DCMTK were selected for Fuzzing testing, and comparisons were also made during the testing process. Among them, abnormalities were found during the

Table 1. Test results of three different versions of DCMTK.

DCMTK versions	Number of test cases sent	Fuzzing test results
DCMTK3.5.3	1000	No abnormalities found
DCMTK3.5.4	1000	Abnormalities found
DCMTK3.6.0	1000	No abnormalities found

DCMTK3.5.4 version testing process. No exceptions were found for the other two DCMTK versions (DCMTK3.5.3 and DCMTK3.6.0). During the test of DCMTK3.5.4, and it was found that when the data in the constructed data package was larger than 8070 rows, the system would crash, and the reasons for the system crash were preliminarily analyzed as the large DICOM data package and data overflow. It is recommended that developers check the length of data capacity when developing software. Avoid the harm such as denial of service, attack, process crash and outage of PACS system caused by vulnerability.

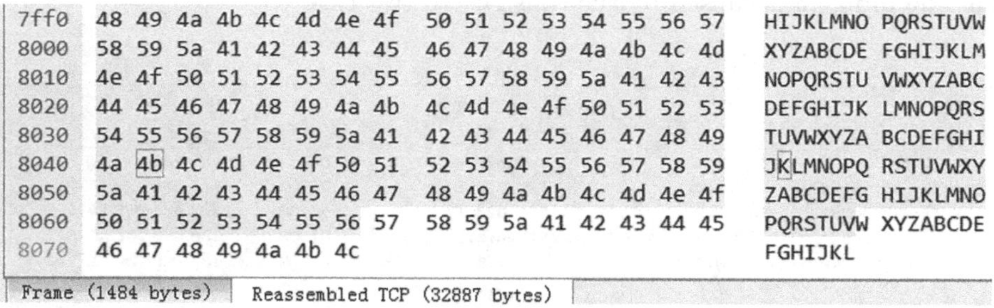

```
7ff0   48 49 4a 4b 4c 4d 4e 4f   50 51 52 53 54 55 56 57   HIJKLMNO PQRSTUVW
8000   58 59 5a 41 42 43 44 45   46 47 48 49 4a 4b 4c 4d   XYZABCDE FGHIJKLM
8010   4e 4f 50 51 52 53 54 55   56 57 58 59 5a 41 42 43   NOPQRSTU VWXYZABC
8020   44 45 46 47 48 49 4a 4b   4c 4d 4e 4f 50 51 52 53   DEFGHIJK LMNOPQRS
8030   54 55 56 57 58 59 5a 41   42 43 44 45 46 47 48 49   TUVWXYZA BCDEFGHI
8040   4a 4b 4c 4d 4e 4f 50 51   52 53 54 55 56 57 58 59   JKLMNOPQ RSTUVWXY
8050   5a 41 42 43 44 45 46 47   48 49 4a 4b 4c 4d 4e 4f   ZABCDEFG HIJKLMNO
8060   50 51 52 53 54 55 56 57   58 59 5a 41 42 43 44 45   PQRSTUVW XYZABCDE
8070   46 47 48 49 4a 4b 4c                                FGHIJKL
```
Frame (1484 bytes)   Reassembled TCP (32887 bytes)

Fig. 15. Test case that caused storescp to crash.

6   Conclusion

DICOM is an international standard for medical images and related information (ISO 12052). DICOM solves the problem of how to associate patient information with medical images. Therefore, DICOM is widely used in radiation medicine, including cardiovascular imaging and diagnostic equipment. However, since DICOM did not involve communication security at the beginning of design, a large number of security threats and hidden dangers were introduced in the process of digitalization and informatization of medical equipment. In this paper, we studied the vulnerability mining of DICOM open source database, and proposed the framework of vulnerability mining for DICOM for the first time. We used the generated and manually constructed strategies to construct test cases, and built a security test system of DCMTK open source database, simulated the transmission process using DICOM protocol, and Fuzzing test different versions of the DCMTK open source database. The purpose of Fuzzing testing is to test whether various network protocols or related applications have security vulnerabilities. Fuzzing testing is a well-known black box technology for security testing. Fuzzing technology is a kind of automatic software testing technology. It is one of the important means of vulnerability mining by inputting a large number of abnormal data to the tested object and monitoring its abnormalities. Secondly, through manual monitoring and Wireshark monitoring, the whole test process was monitored for exceptions. A total of three different versions of the DCMTK open source library were selected for Fuzzing test, and a comparison was made during the test. Among them, during the testing of the DCMTK3.5.4 version, the vulnerability caused by the constructed packet overflow was found. No exceptions were found for the other two DCMTK versions (DCMTK3.5.3 and DCMTK3.6.0). The overall test effect is satisfactory. The designed vulnerability mining system based on Fuzzing technology can dig out the vulnerabilities of DICOM protocol or the logic or design vulnerabilities existing in the system when using DICOM protocol to some extent. At last, some suggestions on development and repair are proposed to software developers, and it is hoped that the experimental results can provide references for the safe development and utilization of medical imaging applications.

In general, the overall framework of this paper and the method of exploiting vulnerabilities by using Fuzzing technology are beneficial attempts to exploit vulnerabilities of DCIOM protocol. Especially in the current situation of the increasingly severe security situation in the form of network security, especially in the medical field, the results of vulnerability mining of DICOM protocol can provide references for medical device developers, and to some extent reduce the possible security risks of DICOM protocol. Currently, Artificial Intelligence (AI) technology is developing rapidly, and work efficiency is greatly improved in the process of generating and using large data, especially the application effect of generated adversarial network in large data is gratifying. Next, we will continue to perfect and improve the experimental methods, furthermore, the test case construction, screening and testing are optimized and reformed in combination with the generated adversarial network. By combining the static vulnerability mining and artificial intelligence to improve the efficiency of vulnerability mining as the future research direction, and the security vulnerabilities in DICOM protocol will be further explored in the future.

Acknowledgments. This research was financially supported by the National Key Research and Development Plan (2018YFB1004101), Key Lab of Information Network Security, Ministry of Public Security (C19614), Special fund on education and teaching reform of Besti (jy201805), the Fundamental Research Funds for the Central Universities (328201804, 328201910), key laboratory of network assessment technology of Institute of Information Engineering, Chinese Academy of Sciences.

References

1. Duggal, A.: Hl7 2.x security. In: The 8th Annual HITB Security Conference (2017)

2. Blazona, B., Koncar, M.: Hl7 and DICOM based integration of radiology departments with healthcare enterprise information systems. Int. J. Med. Inform. **76**, S425–S432 (2007)
3. Chen, Y., Wang, Z.: Progress in fuzzy testing. Comput. Appl. Softw. **28**(7), 291–293 (2011)
4. Dolin, R.H., et al.: Hl7 clinical document architecture, release 2. J. Am. Med. Inform. Assoc. **13**(1), 30–39 (2006)
5. Farhadi, A., Ahmadi, M.: The information security needs in radiological information systems–an insight on state hospitals of Iran, 2012. J. Digit. Imaging **26**(6), 1040–1044 (2013)
6. Gutiérrez-Martínez, J., Núñez-Gaona, M.A., Aguirre-Meneses, H.: Business model for the security of a large-scale PACS, compliance with ISO/27002: 2013 standard. J. Digit. Imaging **28**(4), 481–491 (2015)
7. Hasman, A., et al.: Hl7 RIM: an incoherent standard. In: Ubiquity: Technologies for Better Health in Aging Societies, Proceedings of Mie 2006, vol. 124, p. 133 (2006)
8. Liu, Q., Zhang, Y.: TFTP vulnerability mining technology based on fuzzing. Comput. Eng. **33**(20), 142–144 (2007)
9. Luo, Y.: Design and implementation of network security vulnerability scanning system. Ph.D. thesis, National University of Defense Science and Technology, Chang-Sha (2007)
10. Elrod, T., Morris, S.: I'm not a doctor but i play one on your network (2011)
11. Nagy, P., Bowers, G., Reiner, B.I., Siegel, E.L.: Defining the pacs profession: an initial survey of skills, training, and capabilities for PACS administrators. J. Digit. Imaging **18**(4), 252–259 (2005)
12. Pianykh, O.S.: Digital Imaging and Communications in Medicine (DICOM): A Practical Introduction and Survival Guide. Springer, Heidelberg (2009)
13. US Food and Drug Administration: Content of premarket submissions for management of cybersecurity in medical devices: draft guidance for industry and food and drug administration staff (2013). Accessed 1 May 2014
14. Vossberg, M., Tolxdorff, T., Krefting, D.: DICOM image communication in globus-based medical grids. IEEE Trans. Inf. Technol. Biomed. **12**(2), 145–153 (2008)
15. Wiese, M., Beck, K., Tschöpel, E., Reindl, P., Carl, P.: PACS-picture archiving and communication system. Der Urologe B **39**(3), 237–244 (1999)
16. Xu, Y.: Research and implementation of fuzzing test technology for streaming media protocol. Ph.D. thesis, Beijing University of Posts and Telecommunications (2009)
17. Zhang, B., Zhang, Y., Xu, Y.: Exploring network protocol vulnerabilities based on fuzzy testing. J. Tsinghua Univ.: Nat. Sci. Ed. **S2**, 2113–2118 (2009)
18. Zhang, G., Shi, X., Li, R., Ren, J.: Fuzzy test optimization scheme for NFC protocol. Hebei Ind. Sci. Technol. **34**(3), 155–161 (2017)
19. Zhang, X., He, Y.: Overview of software testing methods. Sci-tech horizon (4), 35–37 (2012)
20. Zhang, Y., Wang, Z., Liu, Q., Lou, J., Yao, D.: Research progress and development trend of near-field communication technology security. J. Comput. Sci. **39**(6), 1190–1207 (2016)
21. Zhuang, T.: The Application of Computer in Biomedicine. Science Press, Beijing (2000)
22. Zou, Q., et al.: From automation to intelligence: advances in software vulnerability mining technology (2018)

Secure Communication with a Proactive Eavesdropper Under Perfect CSI and CDI

Qun Li and Ding Xu[✉]

Nanjing University of Posts and Telecommunications, Nanjing, China
xuding@ieee.org

Abstract. This paper studies physical layer security of a three node multicarrier network with a source node, a destination node and a full-duplex proactive eavesdropper who sends jamming signals for improving its eavesdropping performance. The problem of transmit power allocation for minimizing the average secrecy outage probability on all subcarriers is investigated under the assumptions that the channel state information (CSI) related to the eavesdropper is perfectly known and only channel distribution information (CDI) is known. Algorithms are proposed for the optimization problem and are shown to greatly outperform the benchmark algorithms.

Keywords: Physical layer security · Proactive eavesdropper · Secrecy outage probability · Channel distribution information

1 Introduction

Physical layer security is a promising technology that can achieve perfect secure communication from the aspect of information theory [1–4]. In physical layer security, the eavesdroppers can be passive or proactive. Specially, passive eavesdroppers only receive legitimate communication signals, while proactive eavesdroppers not only receive legitimate communication signals but also send jamming signals to interfere with the legitimate communication for improving the eavesdropping performance. This paper focuses on proactive eavesdroppers.

Secure communication with proactive eavesdroppers has been researched a lot in literature. The work in [5] modeled the interaction between the proactive eavesdropper and the legitimate user as a Stackelberg game, where the eavesdropper acted as a leader and the legitimate user acted as a follower to minimize power consumption with the minimum secrecy rate constraint. The work in [6] maximized the secrecy rate at the legitimate user's side and the wiretap rate at the eavesdropper's side. The work in [7] proposed to adopt cooperative relays to improve the secrecy rate of the legitimate user with attacks from the proactive eavesdroppers. The work in [8] modeled the interaction between the proactive eavesdropper and the legitimate user as a non-cooperative game. The work in [9] proposed to let the legitimate user send jamming signals to interfere with the proactive eavesdropper and derived the expression for the hybrid outage

© ICST Institute for Computer Sciences, Social Informatics and Telecommunications Engineering 2020
Published by Springer Nature Switzerland AG 2020. All Rights Reserved
H. Gao et al. (Eds.): ChinaCom 2019, LNICST 312, pp. 525–536, 2020.
https://doi.org/10.1007/978-3-030-41114-5_39

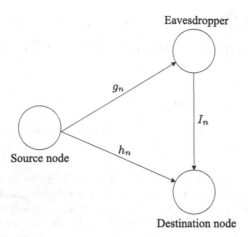

Fig. 1. System model.

probability. The work in [10] proposed to let the legitimate receiver transmit jamming signals using a subset of the antennas and maximized the secrecy rate by optimizing the antenna allocation. Although the work in [5–10] has investigated various problems with proactive eavesdroppers, secrecy outage probability was seldom minimized by optimizing resource allocation with imperfect channel state information (CSI).

This paper investigates secure communication of a three node multicarrier network with a source node, a destination node, and a full-duplex proactive eavesdropper. The eavesdropper keeps sending jamming signals for improving its eavesdropping performance. The source node aims to minimize the average secrecy outage probability on all subcarriers by optimizing the transmit power allocation. Two scenarios are considered. The first scenario assumes perfect CSI and the second scenario assumes only channel distribution information (CDI) on the channels related to the eavesdropper is available. For both scenarios, we propose algorithms to solve the optimization problems. It is shown that the proposed algorithms can achieve much lower average secrecy outage probability than the benchmark algorithms.

The rest of the paper is organized as follows. Section 2 presents the system model and formulates the problem. Section 3 investigates the perfect CSI scenario and Sect. 4 investigates the CDI scenario. Section 5 verifies the proposed algorithm by simulations. Section 6 concludes the paper.

2   System Model

As shown in Fig. 1, a three-node network consisting of a source node, a destination node and an eavesdropper, is considered. Both the source node and the destination node are assumed to be half-duplex, while the eavesdropper is assumed to be full-duplex. The spectrum is assumed to be divided into N sub-carriers, and the channel gains on subcarrier n from the source node to the destination node, from the source node to the eavesdropper, and from the eaves-dropper to the destination node are denoted as h_n, g_n and I_n, respectively. It is assumed that the source node knows the perfect CSI on h_n. For the CSI on g_n and I_n, two scenarios are considered. The first scenario assumes that g_n and I_n are perfectly known. The second scenario assumes that only CDI on g_n and I_n is available. Specially, the channels from the source node to the eavesdropper and from the eavesdropper to the destination node follow Rayleigh fading with unit mean, i.e., the probability density functions of g_n and I_n are respectively as $f_{g_n}(g_n) = e^{-g_n}$ and $f_{I_n}(I_n) = e^{-I_n}$.

Let p_n denote the transmit power of the source node on subcarrier n and q denote the fixed transmit power of the eavesdropper on all subcarriers. Note that $\{p_n\}$ is restricted by the total transmit constraint, as well as the peak transmit power constraint. Specifically, the total transmit power constraint is written as

$$\sum_{n=1}^{N} p_n \leq P_{max}, \tag{1}$$

where P_{max} is the total transmit power limit. The peak transmit power con-straint is written as

$$p_n \leq P_{pk}, n = 1, \ldots, N. \tag{2}$$

The achievable communication rate of the source-destination pair on subcar-rier n is written as

$$r_{0,n} = \log_2\left(1 + \frac{p_n h_n}{\sigma^2 + qI_n}\right), \tag{3}$$

where σ^2 denotes the noise power. The achievable eavesdropping rate of the eavesdropper on subcarrier n is written as

$$r_{1,n} = \log_2\left(1 + \frac{p_n g_n}{\sigma^2}\right). \tag{4}$$

The secrecy rate of the source-destination pair on subcarrier n is defined as $(r_{0,n} - r_{1,n})^+$ [11], where $(.)^+ = \max(0, .)$. The secrecy outage probability on subcarrier n is then defined as $\Pr\{(r_{0,n} - r_{1,n})^+ < R\}$, where R is the target secrecy rate.

We aim to minimize the average secrecy outage probability of the source-destination pair on all subcarriers by optimizing the transmit power $\{p_n\}$ as given by

$$(P1) : \min_{\{p_n\}} \frac{1}{N} \sum_{n=1}^{N} \Pr\{(r_{0,n} - r_{1,n})^+ < R\} \tag{5}$$

$$\text{s.t.} \sum_{n=1}^{N} p_n \leq P_{max}, \tag{6}$$

$$0 \leq p_n \leq P_{pk}, n = 1, \ldots, N. \tag{7}$$

3   Perfect CSI Scenario

In this section, we investigate P1 under the scenario of perfect CSI on g_n and I_n. To solve P1, we define

$$X_n = \begin{cases} 1, & r_{0,n} - r_{1,n} < R, \\ 0, & r_{0,n} - r_{1,n} \geq R. \end{cases} \tag{8}$$

Then, P1 is reformulated as

$$(\text{P1.1}) : \min_{\{p_n\}} \frac{1}{N} \sum_{n=1}^{N} \mathbb{E}\{X_n\} \tag{9}$$

$$\text{s.t.} \sum_{n=1}^{N} p_n \leq P_{max}, \tag{10}$$

$$0 \leq p_n \leq P_{pk}, n = 1, \ldots, N, \tag{11}$$

where $\mathbb{E}\{.\}$ denotes the expectation. P1.1 can be decomposed into subproblems, one for each channel fading state as

$$(\text{P1.2}) : \min_{\{p_n\}} \frac{1}{N} \sum_{n=1}^{N} X_n \tag{12}$$

$$\text{s.t.} \sum_{n=1}^{N} p_n \leq P_{max}, \tag{13}$$

$$0 \leq p_n \leq P_{pk}, n = 1, \ldots, N. \tag{14}$$

We solve P1.2 using the Lagrange duality method [12,13]. The Lagrangian of P1.2 is written as

$$L(\lambda, \{p_n\}) = \frac{1}{N} \sum_{n=1}^{N} X_n + \lambda \left(\sum_{n=1}^{N} p_n - P_{max} \right), \tag{15}$$

where λ is the non-negative dual variable associated with the constraint in (13). The Lagrange dual function is then defined as

$$G(\lambda) = \min_{\{p_n\}} L(\lambda, \{p_n\}) \tag{16}$$

$$\text{s.t. } 0 \leq p_n \leq P_{pk}, n = 1, \ldots, N. \tag{17}$$

The problem in (16) can be decomposed into N subproblems, as given by

$$(\text{P1.3}) : \min_{p_n} \frac{1}{N} X_n + \lambda p_n \tag{18}$$

$$\text{s.t. } 0 \leq p_n \leq P_{pk}, \tag{19}$$

for $i = 1, \ldots, N$. Let $f(p_n) = r_{0,n} - r_{1,n}$. Then, the inequality $f(p_n) < R$ is equivalent to $p_n < y_n$, where

$$y_n = \frac{2^R - 1}{\frac{h_n}{\sigma^2 + qI_n} - \frac{2^R g_n}{\sigma^2}}. \tag{20}$$

Theorem 1. The optimal solution of P1.3, p_n^*, is given by

$$p_n^* = \begin{cases} y_n, & 0 \leq y_n \leq P_{pk}, \frac{1}{N} \geq \lambda y_n, \\ 0, & \text{otherwise.} \end{cases} \tag{21}$$

Proof. The value of p_n^* is discussed in the following two cases:

Case 1: $y_n < 0$. In this case, $\frac{1}{N} X_n + \lambda p_n$ is equal to λp_n in the interval $[0, P_{pk}]$. Thus, it is easy to obtain $p_n^* = 0$.

Case 2: $0 \leq y_n \leq P_{pk}$. In this case, $\frac{1}{N} X_n + \lambda p_n$ is equal to $\frac{1}{N} + \lambda p_n$ in the interval $[0, y_n)$ and is equal to λp_n in the interval $[y, P_{pk}]$. Thus, the minimum of $\frac{1}{N} X_n + \lambda p_n$ is achieved at $p_n = 0$ or $p_n = y_n$ depending on the objective function values achieved at $p_n = 0$ and $p_n = y_n$, i.e.

$$p_n^* = \begin{cases} 0, & \frac{1}{N} < \lambda y_n, \\ y_n, & \frac{1}{N} \geq \lambda y_n. \end{cases} \tag{22}$$

Case 3: $y_n > P_{pk}$. In this case, $\frac{1}{N} X_n + \lambda p_n$ is equal to $\frac{1}{N} + \lambda p_n$ in the interval $[0, P_{pk}]$. Thus, it is easy to obtain $p_n^* = 0$.
Based on the above discussions, p_n^* is given by

$$p_n^* = \begin{cases} y_n, & 0 \leq y_n \leq P_{pk}, \frac{1}{N} \geq \lambda y_n, \\ 0, & \text{otherwise.} \end{cases} \tag{23}$$

This completes the proof.   ∎
Then, the dual problem is defined as

$$\max_{\lambda \geq 0} G(\lambda), \tag{24}$$

which can be solved efficiently with the bisection method.
The algorithm to solve P1 with perfect CSI is summarized in Algorithm 1.

4   CDI Scenario

In this section, we investigate P1 under the scenario of CDI on g_n and I_n. By inserting $f_{g_n}(g_n) = e^{-g_n}$ and $f_{I_n}(I_n) = e^{-I_n}$ into $\Pr\{(r_{0,n} - r_{1,n})^+ < R\}$, we have

---

Algorithm 1. Proposed algorithm to solve P1 with perfect CSI.

1: Initialize: λ_{min}, λ_{max}.
2: **repeat**
3:    $\lambda = \frac{\lambda_{min}+\lambda_{max}}{2}$.
4:    $p_n^* = \begin{cases} y_n, & 0 \leq y_n \leq P_{pk}, \frac{1}{N} \geq \lambda y_n, \\ 0, & \text{otherwise.} \end{cases}$, $n = 1, \ldots, N$.
5:    **if** $\sum_{n=1}^{N} p_n^* > P_{max}$ **then**
6:        $\lambda_{min} = \lambda$.
7:    **else**
8:        $\lambda_{max} = \lambda$.
9:    **end if**
10: **until** λ converges to a desired accuracy.

$$\Pr\{(r_{0,n} - r_{1,n})^+ < R\}$$
$$= \Pr\left\{\log_2\left(1 + \frac{p_n h_n}{\sigma^2 + qI_n}\right) - \log_2\left(1 + \frac{p_n g_n}{\sigma^2}\right) < R\right\}$$
$$= \Pr\left\{g_n > \frac{\sigma^2}{p_n}\left(\frac{1}{2^R}\left(1 + \frac{p_n h_n}{\sigma^2 + qI_n}\right) - 1\right)\right\}. \tag{25}$$

The Lagrangian of P1 is then written as

$$L(\lambda, \{p_n\})$$
$$= \frac{1}{N}\sum_{n=1}^{N}\Pr\left\{g_n > \frac{\sigma^2}{p_n}\left(\frac{1}{2^R}\left(1 + \frac{p_n h_n}{\sigma^2 + qI_n}\right) - 1\right)\right\}$$
$$+ \lambda\left(\sum_{n=1}^{N} p_n - P_{max}\right), \tag{26}$$

where λ is the non-negative dual variable associated with the constraint in (13). The Lagrange dual function is defined as

$$G(\lambda) = \min_{\{p_n\}} L(\lambda, \{p_n\}) \tag{27}$$
$$\text{s.t. } 0 \leq p_n \leq P_{pk}, n = 1, \ldots, N, \tag{28}$$

which can be decoupled into N subproblems, as given by

$$(\text{P1.4}): \min_{p_n} \frac{1}{N}\Pr\left\{g_n > \frac{\sigma^2}{p_n}\left(\frac{1}{2^R}\left(1 + \frac{p_n h_n}{\sigma^2 + qI_n}\right) - 1\right)\right\}$$
$$+ \lambda p_n \tag{29}$$
$$\text{s.t. } 0 \leq p_n \leq P_{pk}, \tag{30}$$

for $i = 1, \ldots, N$. P1.4 can be decomposed into two subproblems as given by

$$(\text{P1.4.1}): \min_{p_n} \frac{1}{N} \Pr\left\{ g_n > \frac{\sigma^2}{p_n}\left(\frac{1}{2^R}\left(1 + \frac{p_n h_n}{\sigma^2 + qI_n}\right) - 1\right)\right\}$$

$$+ \lambda p_n \tag{31}$$

$$\text{s.t. } 0 \leq p_n \leq P_{pk}, \tag{32}$$

$$\frac{p_n h_n}{2^R - 1} \leq \sigma^2, \tag{33}$$

and

$$(\text{P1.4.2}): \min_{p_n} \frac{1}{N} \Pr\left\{ g_n > \frac{\sigma^2}{p_n}\left(\frac{1}{2^R}\left(1 + \frac{p_n h_n}{\sigma^2 + qI_n}\right) - 1\right)\right\}$$

$$+ \lambda p_n \tag{34}$$

$$\text{s.t. } 0 \leq p_n \leq P_{pk}, \tag{35}$$

$$\frac{p_n h_n}{2^R - 1} \geq \sigma^2. \tag{36}$$

The solution of P1.4 is the solution of the problem with lower objective function value. Since $\frac{\sigma^2}{p_n}\left(\frac{1}{2^R}\left(1 + \frac{p_n h_n}{\sigma^2 + qI_n}\right) - 1\right)$ must be small than zero when $\frac{p_n h_n}{2^R - 1} \leq \sigma^2$, P1.4.1 can be rewritten as

$$\min_{p_n} \frac{1}{N} + \lambda p_n \tag{37}$$

$$\text{s.t. } 0 \leq p_n \leq P_{pk}, \tag{38}$$

$$\frac{p_n h_n}{2^R - 1} \leq \sigma^2. \tag{39}$$

It is easy to verify that the optimal solution of the above problem is $p_n = 0$ and the optimal objective function value is $\frac{1}{N}$. As for P1.4.2, when $\frac{p_n h_n}{2^R - 1} \geq \sigma^2$, the probability $\Pr\left\{ g_n > \frac{\sigma^2}{p_n}\left(\frac{1}{2^R}\left(1 + \frac{p_n h_n}{\sigma^2 + qI_n}\right) - 1\right)\right\}$ can be rewritten as given by

$$\Pr\left\{ g_n > \frac{\sigma^2}{p_n}\left(\frac{1}{2^R}\left(1 + \frac{p_n h_n}{\sigma^2 + qI_n}\right) - 1\right)\right\}$$

$$= \Pr\left\{ g_n > \frac{\sigma^2}{p_n}\left(\frac{1}{2^R}\left(1 + \frac{p_n h_n}{\sigma^2 + qI_n}\right) - 1\right)\Bigg| I_n \leq \frac{1}{q}\left(\frac{p_n h_n}{2^R - 1} - \sigma^2\right)\right\}$$

$$+ \Pr\left\{ g_n > \frac{\sigma^2}{p_n}\left(\frac{1}{2^R}\left(1 + \frac{p_n h_n}{\sigma^2 + qI_n}\right) - 1\right)\Bigg| I_n \geq \frac{1}{q}\left(\frac{p_n h_n}{2^R - 1} - \sigma^2\right)\right\}$$

$$= \int_0^{\frac{1}{q}\left(\frac{p_n h_n}{2^R - 1} - \sigma^2\right)} e^{-I_n} dI_n \int_{\frac{\sigma^2}{p_n}\left(\frac{1}{2^R}\left(1 + \frac{p_n h_n}{\sigma^2 + qI_n}\right) - 1\right)}^{\infty} e^{-g_n} dg_n$$

$$+ \int_{\frac{1}{q}\left(\frac{p_n h_n}{2^R - 1} - \sigma^2\right)}^{\infty} e^{-I_n} dI_n \int_0^{\infty} e^{-g_n} dg_n$$

$$= e^{\frac{\sigma^2}{p_n}\left(1 - \frac{1}{2^R}\right)} \int_0^{\frac{1}{q}\left(\frac{p_n h_n}{2^R - 1} - \sigma^2\right)} e^{-I_n - \frac{\sigma^2 h_n}{2^R(\sigma^2 + qI_n)}} dI_n + e^{-\frac{1}{q}\left(\frac{p_n h_n}{2^R - 1} - \sigma^2\right)}. \tag{40}$$

Algorithm 2. Proposed algorithm to solve P1 with CDI.

1: Initialize: λ_{min}, λ_{max}.
2: **repeat**
3:    $\lambda = \frac{\lambda_{min} + \lambda_{max}}{2}$.
4:    **for** $i = 1$ to N **do**
5:        **if** $\frac{\sigma^2(2^R-1)}{h_n} > P_{pk}$ **then**
6:            Set $p_n = 0$.
7:        **else**
8:            Obtain p_n by solving the problem in (41) using a one-dimensional exhaustive search over $\left[\frac{\sigma^2(2^R-1)}{h_n}, P_{pk}\right]$.
9:            **if** the optimal objective function value in (41) is larger than $\frac{1}{N}$ **then**
10:                Set $p_n = 0$.
11:            **end if**
12:        **end if**
13:    **end for**
14:    **if** $\sum_{n=1}^{N} p_n^* > P_{max}$ **then**
15:        $\lambda_{min} = \lambda$.
16:    **else**
17:        $\lambda_{max} = \lambda$.
18:    **end if**
19: **until** λ converges to a desired accuracy.

Therefore, P1.4.2 can be rewritten as

$$\min_{p_n} \frac{1}{N} e^{\frac{\sigma^2}{p_n}\left(1-\frac{1}{2^R}\right)} \int_0^{\frac{1}{q}\left(\frac{p_n h_n}{2^R-1}-\sigma^2\right)} e^{-I_n - \frac{\sigma^2 h_n}{2^R(\sigma^2 + qI_n)}} dI_n$$

$$+ \frac{1}{N} e^{-\frac{1}{q}\left(\frac{p_n h_n}{2^R-1}-\sigma^2\right)} + \lambda p_n \tag{41}$$

$$\text{s.t.} \quad \frac{\sigma^2(2^R-1)}{h_n} \le p_n \le P_{pk}. \tag{42}$$

The above problem is infeasible if $\frac{\sigma^2(2^R-1)}{h_n} > P_{pk}$. If the above problem is feasible, the optimal solution can be obtained by a one-dimensional exhaustive search of p_n over the interval $\left[\frac{\sigma^2(2^R-1)}{h_n}, P_{pk}\right]$.

Finally, the value of λ can be obtained by the bisection method. The algorithm to solve P1 with CDI is summarized in Algorithm 2.

5   Simulation Results

The parameters of simulation are set as follows. The channel from the source node to the destination node is assumed to following Rayleigh fading with mean 5. Unless otherwise specified, we set $\sigma^2 = 1$, $N = 8$, $P_{max} = 1.5$ Watt, $P_{pk} = 0.5$ Watt, $q = 0.5$ Watt and $R = 0.3$ bps/Hz. For the purpose of comparison, we propose one benchmark algorithm named as the equal-power allocation algorithm which equally allocates the transmit power, and one benchmark algorithm

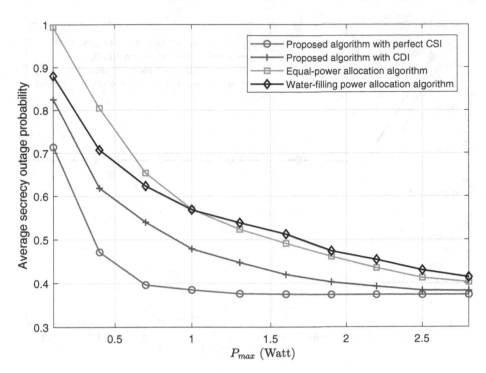

Fig. 2. Average secrecy outage probability achieved by different algorithms versus P_{max}.

named as the water-filling power allocation algorithm which allocates the transmit power following the water-filling style.

Figure 2 plots the average secrecy outage probability achieved by different algorithms versus P_{max}. It is seen that the average secrecy outage probability decreases as P_{max} increases until saturates to a certain level. It is also seen that the average secrecy outage probability achieved by the proposed algorithm with perfect CSI is the lowest, while the average secrecy outage probability achieved by the proposed algorithm with CDI is higher than the proposed algorithm with perfect CSI. This indicates that only knowing CDI degrades the secrecy performance compared to perfect CSI. Besides, it is seen that both the proposed algorithm with perfect CSI and the algorithm with CDI achieve lower average secrecy outage probability than the other two benchmark algorithms. It is also seen that the average secrecy outage probabilities achieved by different algorithms are very close when P_{max} is large.

Figure 3 plots the average secrecy outage probability achieved by different algorithms versus P_{pk}. It is seen that the average secrecy outage probability decreases as P_{pk} increases until saturates to a certain level. It is also seen that the average secrecy outage probability achieved by both the proposed algorithm with perfect CSI and the proposed algorithm with CDI is much lower than

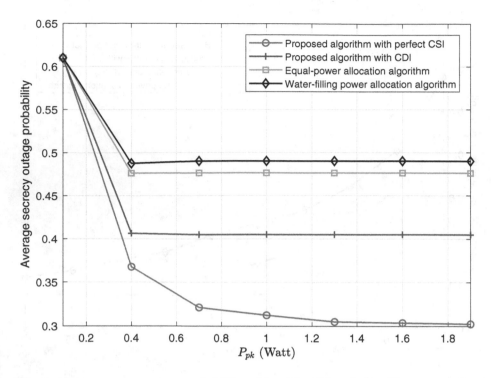

Fig. 3. Average secrecy outage probability achieved by different algorithms versus P_{pk}.

the other two algorithms, especially when P_{pk} is large. Besides, it is seen that the average secrecy outage probability achieved by the proposed algorithm with perfect CSI is much lower than the proposed algorithm with CDI, especially when P_{pk} is large. It is also seen that the average secrecy outage probabilities achieved by different algorithms are very close when P_{pk} is small.

Figure 4 plots the average secrecy outage probability achieved by different algorithms versus q. It is seen that the average secrecy outage probability increases as q increases. This is as expected since lower secrecy rate is achieved with higher interference from the eavesdropper. It is also seen that the average secrecy outage probability achieved by the proposed algorithm with perfect CSI is the lowest while the average secrecy outage probability achieved by the proposed algorithm with CDI is the second lowest among the four algorithms. Besides, it is seen that the performance gap between the proposed algorithm with perfect CSI and the proposed algorithm with CDI is almost independent of q.

Figure 5 plots the average secrecy outage probability achieved by different algorithms versus R. It is seen that the average secrecy outage probability increases as R increases. It is also seen that the proposed algorithms outperform the water-filling power allocation benchmark algorithm, especially when

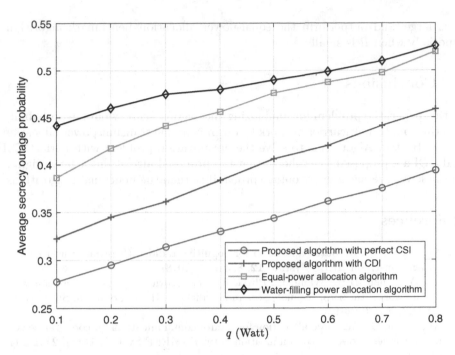

Fig. 4. Average secrecy outage probability achieved by different algorithms versus q.

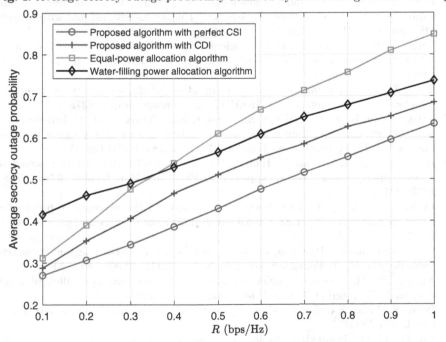

Fig. 5. Average secrecy outage probability achieved by different algorithms versus R.

R is large, and outperform the equal-power allocation benchmark algorithm, especially when R is small.

6   Conclusions

In this paper, the problem for minimizing the average secrecy outage probability of a three node multicarrier network by optimizing the transmit power allocation is investigated. Algorithms to solve the optimization problem with perfect CSI and CDI are proposed. It is shown that the proposed algorithms achieve significantly lower average secrecy outage probability than the benchmark algorithms.

References

1. Xu, D., Li, Q.: Resource allocation for cognitive radio with primary user secrecy outage constraint. IEEE Syst. J. **12**, 893–904 (2018)
2. Liu, Y., Chen, H.H., Wang, L.: Physical layer security for next generation wireless networks: theories, technologies, and challenges. IEEE Commun. Surv. Tutor. **19**(1), 347–376 (2017)
3. Xu, D., Li, Q.: Resource allocation for secure communications in cooperative cognitive wireless powered communication networks. IEEE Syst. J. **13**(3), 2431–2442 (2019)
4. Zhang, H., Xing, H., Cheng, J., Nallanathan, A., Leung, V.C.: Secure resource allocation for ofdma two-way relay wireless sensor networks without and with cooperative jamming. IEEE Trans. Ind. Inf. **12**(5), 1714–1725 (2015)
5. Tang, X., Ren, P., Han, Z.: Power-efficient secure transmission against full-duplex active eavesdropper: a game-theoretic framework. IEEE Access **5**, 24632–24645 (2017)
6. Tang, X., Ren, P., Wang, Y., Han, Z.: Combating full-duplex active eavesdropper: a hierarchical game perspective. IEEE Trans. Commun. **65**(3), 1379–1395 (2017)
7. Fang, H., Xu, L., Zou, Y., Wang, X., Choo, K.K.R.: Three-stage stackelberg game for defending against full-duplex active eavesdropping attacks in cooperative communication. IEEE Trans. Veh. Technol. **67**(11), 10788–10799 (2018)
8. Huang, W., Chen, W., Bai, B., Han, Z.: Wiretap channel with full-duplex proactive eavesdropper: a game theoretic approach. IEEE Trans. Veh. Technol. **67**(8), 7658–7663 (2018)
9. Liu, C., Lee, J., Quek, T.Q.: Secure transmission in the presence of full-duplex active eavesdropper. In: IEEE Global Communications Conference, pp. 1–6. IEEE (2017)
10. Li, L., Petropulu, A.P., Chen, Z.: Mimo secret communications against an active eavesdropper. IEEE Trans. Inf. Forensics Secur. **12**(10), 2387–2401 (2017)
11. Xu, D., Zhu, H.: Secure transmission for SWIPT IoT systems with full-duplex IoT devices. IEEE Internet Things J. **6**(6), 10915–10933 (2019)
12. Boyd, S., Vandenberghe, L.: Convex Optimization. Cambridge University Press, Cambridge (2004)
13. Xu, D., Li, Q.: Improving physical-layer security for primary users in cognitive radio networks. IET Commun. **11**(15), 2303–2310 (2017)

GNSS Spoofing Detection Using Moving Variance of Signal Quality Monitoring Metrics and Signal Power

Lixuan Li, Chao Sun[✉], Hongbo Zhao, Hua Sun, and Wenquan Feng

Beihang University, Beijing 100191, China
sunchao@buaa.edu.cn

Abstract. Spoofing represents a significant threat to the integrity of applications relying on Global Navigation Satellite System (GNSS). A spoofer transmits counterfeit satellite signals to deceive the operation of a receiver. As multipath and spoofing signals have similar signal structures, Signal Quality Monitoring (SQM) techniques, originally designed for multipath detection, were identified to be useful for spoofing detection. Recently, a moving variance (MV) based SQM method was developed to improve the performance of raw SQM metrics. However, the main problem with implementing the MV-based SQM technique is differentiating the spoofing attack from multipath. This work presents a two-dimensional detection method using carrier power and moving variance to improve detection performance. Besides, false alarms caused by multipath are avoided by the two-dimensional threshold. A dataset called Texas Spoofing Test Battery and a multipath scenario from Osaka were employed to evaluate the performance of the proposed algorithm.

Keywords: Moving variance · Carrier power · Spoofing · Signal quality monitoring

1 Introduction

Global Navigation Satellite System (GNSS) provides accurate positioning and timing services and is therefore used widely in various fields including civil aviation, mapping, maritime, military reconnaissance and finance. Despite the advantages of continuous and real-time working, GNSS is vulnerable to intentional as well as other types of interference due to its low signal power, and poor channel conditions.

Spoofing, studied in this work, represents one of the intentional interferences mentioned above and involves transmitting counterfeit satellite signals to deceive the target receiver into obtaining the wrong position results. It is worth mentioning that this kind of attack is often hidden and difficult to perceive. Therefore, in recent years, with the recognition of the danger of spoofing attacks, some researches have focused on their detection.

H. Gao et al. (Eds.): ChinaCom 2019, LNICST 312, pp. 537–548, 2020.
https://doi.org/10.1007/978-3-030-41114-5_40

The similarity between the complex correlation functions of counterfeit and multipath signals which sees them both delayed with varying phases of the authentic signal (also LOS in terms of multipath vocabulary), has attracted the attention of several research groups [1–3]. These groups have suggested that signal quality monitoring (SQM) techniques designed for multipath signals can also be used for the detection of spoofing. These SQM techniques consist in metrics computed from correlator outputs with their performances studied for multipath, as well as spoofing detection [2–5]. On this basis, Ali Pirsiavash et al. proposed a two-dimensional SQM method. However, the performance of the metrics proposed by these technologies is purely dedicated to detecting fraudulent signals and lacks the ability to distinguish the effects when there is an existence of multipath signals. On the other hand, power and carrier-to-noise ratio have also been used to detect spoofing signals [6]. In addition, Kyle D. Wesson et al. proposed power and distortion monitoring methods [7].

Recently, a SQM method using moving variance has been proposed and behaves superior in the detection of the onset of a frequency unlocked spoofing attack [8], which still lacks discussion of multipath conditions. To improve the detection performance of the moving variance method, we additionally use carrier power for two-dimensional observation. On the basis of this, the work further proposes a time threshold detection technique to help distinguish spoofing from possible multipath signals while detecting these attacks.

2 Spoofing Pattern

Spoofer aims at all the visible satellite signals of the target receiver and tracks each one to obtain the navigation and timing data corresponding to the authentic signal, Fig. 1b (1), so that it is able to generate counterfeit signals with the same code delay and Doppler shift as the legitimate signals.

Subsequently, the authentic satellite and broadcast spoofing signals simultaneously arrive at the receiver antenna, indicating the beginning of a spoofing attack.

To ensure the success of the spoofing attack, the two kinds of signals' complex correlation functions have to be aligned and the power of the generated signal must initially be at a low level.

However, spoofer slowly increases the power until it exceeds the authentic one, Fig. 1b (2). As a result, the receiver starts tracking fake signals the next moment, which means that the spoofer gains control of the tracking loop. After that, the tracking loop is further guided till it is removed from the legitimate signal, Fig. 1b (3).

In this way, spoofing attacks can be covertly carried out while the victim still be-lieves that the obtained position and timing information is derived from authentic signals.

Two different kinds of spoofing attacks are to be distinguished:

- named Matched-Power spoofing attack [1] in this paper they are sophisticated attacks where the spoofer attempts to closely match the power of the authentic signals.
- named Overpowered spoofing attack [1] in this paper they are sophisticated at-tacks where the spoofer eclipses the power of the authentic signals.

Once the spoofing signal is broadcast, Fig. 1b (2), the receiver obtains a mixed signal comprising authentic and counterfeit signals.

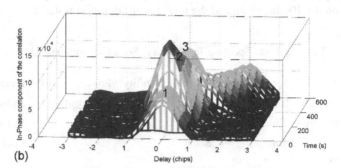

Fig. 1. In Phase component of a signal complex correlation function under no-spoofing circumstances (a) and assuming a spoofing attack (b).

The total received signal presented in Fig. 2 comprises a Line of Sight GPS signal, a spoofing component; some multipath components and additive noise which we assumed to be additive white Gaussian noise in this study.

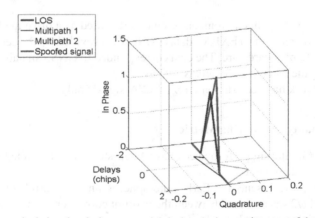

Fig. 2. The theoretical signals admixture model during the interaction step of the spoofing attack [2].

3 Signal Generation and Detection Metrics

3.1 Scenario

The Radio navigation Laboratory at the University of Texas provided a dataset of scenarios collections, known as the Texas Spoofing Test Battery (TEXBAT), for the analysis of the performance of the metrics with regard to spoofing detection. In addition, signals tracking is implemented by a GPS software receiver.

Under the assumption of no spoofing attacks, TEXBAT includes records of both static and dynamic GPS signals, with the same records being presented in Table 1 in six different spoofing scenarios. In all the scenarios, the spoofing attack begins approximately on the 100th second and the total record duration is 420 s.

Table 1. Texas Spoofing Test Battery: Scenarios Summary [1].

Scenario description	Spoofing type	Platform mobility	Power adv.(dB)	Frequency lock
1: Static switch	N/A	Static	Unlocked	Unlocked
2: Static overpowered	Time	Static	10	Unlocked
3: Static matched-power	Time	Static	1.3	Locked
4: Static matched-power	Position	Static	0.4	Locked
5: Dynamic overpowered	Time	Dynamic	9.9	Unlocked
6: Dynamic matched-power	Position	Dynamic	0.8	Locked

In addition, a multipath environment scenario recorded as a drive in Osaka, Japan, was used to supplement the TEXBAT datasets. It was provided by the set of examples available on the LabSat hardware. The data corresponded to GNSS signals and was post processed using the receiver software, NordNav.

Hence, the work had been run on GPS L1 C/A signals only.

3.2 Signal Quality Monitoring Metric

Signal Quality Monitoring performances have been studied and detailed in [3]. Their formulas are presented below.

In this paper, δ represents the Early-Late spacing and the correlator spacing was called the actual $\delta/2$ spacing used between the prompt correlator and the Late and Early ones, respectively ahead and behind.

Delta. The Delta Metric $\Delta_{\delta(t)}$ is defined as [2].

$$\Delta_{\delta(t)} = \frac{I_{E,\delta(t)} - I_{L,\delta(t)}}{2 * I_P} \tag{1}$$

Ratio. The Ratio Metric $RT_{\delta(t)}$ is defined as [2].

$$RT_{\delta(t)} = \frac{I_{E,\delta(t)} + I_{L,\delta(t)}}{2 * I_P} \tag{2}$$

Early Late Phase. The Early-Late Phase Metric $ELP_{\delta(t)}$ is defined as [2].

$$ELP_{\delta(t)} = tan^{-1}\left(\frac{Q_{L,\delta(t)}}{I_{L,\delta(t)}}\right) - tan^{-1}\left(\frac{Q_{E,\delta(t)}}{I_{E,\delta(t)}}\right) \tag{3}$$

Magnitude Difference Metric. The Magnitude Difference Metric $MD_{\delta(t)}$ is defined as [2].

$$MD_{\delta(t)} = \frac{|x_{E,\delta(t)}| - |x_{L,\delta(t)}|}{2 * |x_P|} \tag{4}$$

3.3   Metric Responses to Spoofing and Multipath

Figure 3 shows the typical profile of metric responses to a spoofing attack. There is a progressive rising and declivity of the metric values during the second step with the interactions of authentic and counterfeit signals occurring between the 180th and the 280th seconds. For the first and third steps, when the authentic signal or the counterfeit signal is tracked, before the 150th second and after 280th seconds respectively in Fig. 3, the values keep a steady behavior overall.

Significant metric variations occurred at the second stage, making the SQM-based spoofing detection method feasible. These metric fluctuations were due to the variations of the correlator outputs caused by the distortion of the mixed signals' correlation function.

However, it is worth noting that large variations were observed for the Matched-Power spoofing attack while weaker ones occurred for the Overpowered attack because the interaction during the latter scenario is less than that in the former.

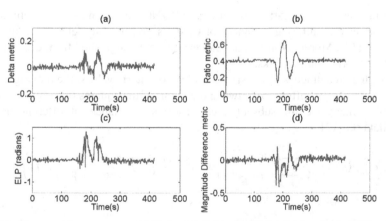

Fig. 3. The four metric responses: (a) Delta (b) Ratio (c) ELP (d) Magnitude Difference to a Matched-Power spoofing scenario: scenario 6 from TEXBAT and computed with a 0.56 chip correlator spacing.

Different from spoofing, metric responses to multipath have random peaks, as shown in Fig. 4. Nonetheless, the metric values vary within the same amplitude range in both conditions, which may lead to false alarms when using the method of a threshold on metric values to detect spoofing.

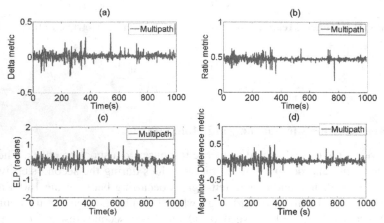

Fig. 4. The four metric responses: (a) Delta (b) Ratio (c) ELP (d) Magnitude Difference, in a multipath environment corresponding to a drive in Osaka and processed with a 0.56 chip correlator spacing.

4 Detection Process Using Moving Variance

4.1 Moving Variance Definition and Distribution

Considering the change in carrier-to-noise ratio (C/N0) during an attack, a method called moving variance monitoring variances of C/N0 is proposed to detect spoofing in the second step [12]. Moreover, multipath can easily be distinguished from deception as a result of its short duration peaks.

Through a predefined window sizing a subset of metric values, the moving variance formula evaluates the difference between the mean of the squares of the subset and the square of the mean over this subset to create a series of variances of different subsets of the full data set [12].

$$\sigma_{MV}^2(n) = \frac{1}{W} \sum_{i=(n-1)*W+1}^{n+W} x(i)^2 - \left(\frac{1}{W} \sum_{i=(n-1)*W+1}^{n+W} x(i) \right)^2 \tag{5}$$

where,

$x(i)$ is the value of the i-th sample in the data,
W the length of one subset,
n the number of subsets of size W in the data.

In order to further improve the detection performance, carrier power was additionally used for two-dimensional observation and is calculated by the given formula.

$$Pd = 10 * \log\left(\sqrt{2\left(\overline{\|R(x)\|^2}\right)^2 - \overline{\|R(x)\|^4}}\right) \tag{6}$$

and,

$$R(x) = I_p(x) + i * Q_p(x) \tag{7}$$

where, $I_p(x)$ and $Q_p(x)$ are the xth prompt correlator output of in-phase (I) and quadrature(Q) branch, respectively.

4.2 Thresholds Determination

Threshold in Time. To exclusively detect spoofing without multipath peaks, the moving variance curve needs to be evaluated in terms of its width as well as its height by a double threshold method. If the moving variance exceeds the predefined threshold during a certain amount of time defined as a threshold in time, a spoofing attack alert will then be triggered.

Threshold on Moving Variance Value. It has been studied to achieve a typical detection method for the establishment of a threshold over a set of data [13, 14] and more rigorous techniques for establishing a threshold on SQM metrics have also been studied [15].

Then, we can come to the conclusion that to get a threshold, the moving variance distribution has to be estimated with regards to a clear data (the considered signal neither affected by spoofing nor multipath). However, such estimations are not suitable with real time computation, as long as the distribution is dependent on the window size, the number of samples of correlator's outputs and the receiver's sampling frequency.

Therefore, the hypothesis was assumed that the moving variance of a clear signal without the effects of spoofing or multipath can be distributed through a Gaussian distribution and the threshold computed from this signal can then be used for the basic statistical detection method [3].

For each PRN and SQM metric, the threshold Th is computed as [3].

$$Th = m* + m_{exp} \times \sigma \tag{8}$$

where,

$m*$: The long term mean value of the clear signal moving variance,
m_{exp}: The expansion factor related to the probability of a false alarm by Table 2 under the hypothesis of a Gaussian distribution,
σ: The standard deviation of the clear signal moving variance.

Table 2. False alarm rate with regard to the expansion factor for a Gaussian distribution [14].

Expansion factor m_{exp}	1	2	3	4	5	6
Monitor threshold	1σ	2σ	3σ	4σ	5σ	6σ
False alarm rate	0.3173	0.0455	0.0027	6.35E-5	5.73E-7	1.97E-9

4.3 Algorithm Performance

Comparing Fig. 6 with Fig. 5, it can be seen that the moving variance helps gathering groups of low values in two stages when only authentic or counterfeit signals are tracked. In addition, it enlightens the values taken during the interaction phase as extra ones, which leads to a more available and observable threshold.

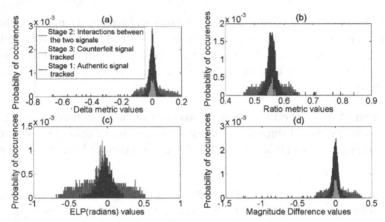

Fig. 5. Distribution of the raw metric values during the different steps of a spoofing attack in Scenario 2 from TEXBAT at 0.01 s average (a) Delta (b) Ratio (c) ELP (d) Magnitude Difference.

As shown in Fig. 7, a distinguished difference exists between the distribution in the presence of spoofing and that of the clean signal condition. The counterfeit signal has a higher power and a wider distribution of moving variance, while the authentic signal is low at both levels.

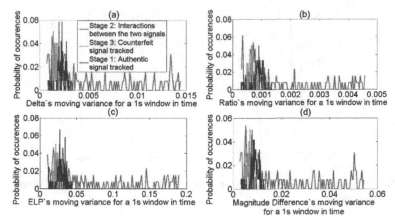

Fig. 6. Distribution of the moving variance values for a 1 s time-window during the different steps of a spoofing attack in Scenario 2 from TEXBAT (a) Delta (b) Ratio (c) ELP (d) Magnitude Difference.

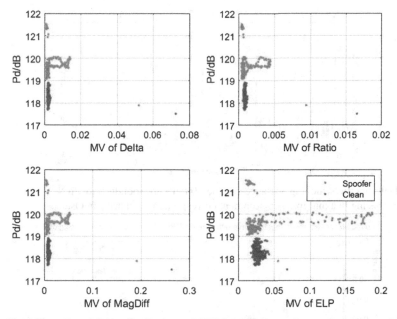

Fig. 7. Two-dimensional joint distribution of SQM metrics' moving variance for a 1 s time-window and carrier power in Scenario 2 from TEXBAT and no-spoofing scenario.

To compare the differences in the two scenarios, the gravity center of the distribution is displayed in Fig. 8 with the lines representing the distance; upper endpoints in spoofing condition and lower ones in no-spoofing. It is worth noting that the ELP metric has the longest distance, which means it is easier to establish a detection threshold. In addition, according to the formula, only the ELP value is uncorrelated with the carrier power.

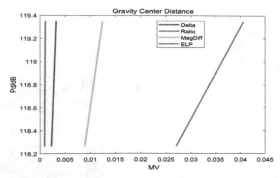

Fig. 8. Gravity center distance of two-dimensional joint distribution in Scenario 2 from TEXBAT and no-spoofing scenario.

As mentioned above, due to the short duration peaks of multipath, the moving variance values in multipath environments display a distribution as random peaks, Fig. 9, while they last for a longer time under spoofing conditions, Fig. 10.

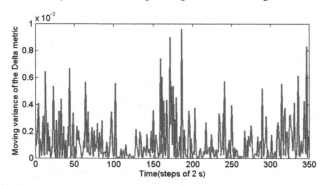

Fig. 9. Delta metric's moving variance for the signal corresponding to PRN 17 for a 0.5625 correlator spacing in a multipath environment corresponding to a drive in Osaka.

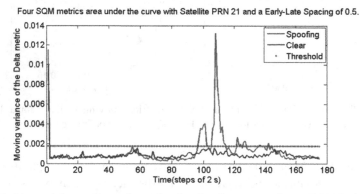

Fig. 10. Delta metric's moving variance for the signal corresponding to PRN 21 in scenario 6 from TEXBAT and its established threshold (detailed in next chapter) computed with $m_{exp} = 3$ with a 0.5 correlator spacing.

5 Conclusion

Four metrics for monitoring were adopted and their performance was compared between traditional SQM and moving variance methods. Then, a method of two-dimensional observation involving moving variance and carrier power was proposed to improve the detection performance. As a result, a distinguished difference exists between the distribution in the presence of spoofing and that of the clean signal condition, in which ELP's moving variance and the carrier power is the best combination without correlation. At last, this work verifies the feasibility of using threshold in time to distinguish spoof from multipath signals through the comparison of peak durations.

Acknowledgement. We would like to thank all those who have helped the work. First of all, we extend our sincere gratitude to the committee of Chinacom 2019 - 14th EAI International Conference on Communications and Networking in China for providing the opportunity and support. High tribute shall be paid to Joon Wayn Cheong Andrew G. Dempster and Laure Demicheli from The University of New South Wales whose profound knowledge greatly promoted this work. Finally, we are also indebted to William's team for correct language expression.

References

1. Humphreys, T.E., Bhatti, J.A., Shepard, D.P., Wesson, K.D.: The texas spoofing test batte. In: Proceedings of the ION GNSS Meeting (2012)
2. Wesson, K.D., Shepard, D.P., Bhatti, J.A., Humphreys, T.E.: An evaluation of the vestigial signal defense for civil GPS anti-spoofing. In: Proceedings of the ION GNSS Meeting (2011)
3. Demicheli L. Cetin, E., Thompson, R.J., Dempster, A.G.: Assessment of Signal Quality Monitoring (SQM) metrics performances. In: Dissertation, UNSW
4. Phelts, R.E.: Multicorrelator techniques for robust mitigation of threats to GPS signal quality. In: Doctoral dissertation, Stanford University (2001)
5. Manfredini, E.G., Dovis, F., Motella, B.: Validation of a signal quality monitoring technique over a set of spoofed scenarios. In: 2014 7th ESA Workshop on Satellite Navigation Technologies and European Workshop on GNSS Signals and Signal Processing (NAVITEC), pp. 1–7 (2014)
6. Jahromi, A.J., Broumandan, A., Nielsen, J., Lachapelle, G.: GPS spoofer countermeasure effectiveness based on signal strength, noise power, and C/N0 measurements. Int. J. Satell. Commun. Network. **30**, 181–191 (2012)
7. Wesson, K.D., Gross, J.N., Humphreys, T.E., Evans, B.L.: GNSS signal authentication via power and distortion monitoring. In: Draft of Article in IEEE Transactions on Aerospace and Electronic Systems, vol. X, No. X, Month 201X
8. Sun, Chao, et al.: Moving variance-based signal quality monitoring method for spoofing detection. GPS Solutions **22**(3), 1–13 (2018)
9. Cetin, E., Thompson, R.J., Dempster, A.G.: Analysis of receiver observables to spoofing attacks using software receivers. In: Seminar, UNSW
10. Broumandan, A., Jafarnia-Jahromi, A., Dehghanian, V., Nielsen, J., Lachapelle, G.: GNSS spoofing detection in handheld receivers based on signal spatial correlation. In: 2012 IEEE/ION Position Location and Navigation Symposium (PLANS), pp. 479–487 (2012)
11. Ali, K., Manfredini, E. G., Dovis, F.: Vestigial signal defense through signal quality monitoring techniques based on joint use of two metrics. In: 2014 IEEE/ION Position, Location and Navigation Symposium-PLANS 2014, pp. 1240–1247 (2014)

12. Jovanovic, A., Botteron, C., Fariné, P.A.: Multi-test detection and protection algorithm against spoofing attacks on GNSS receivers. In: 2014 IEEE/ION Position, Location and Navigation Symposium-PLANS 2014, pp. 1258–1271 (2014)
13. Tawk, Y., et al.: A new movement recognition technique for flight mode detection. Int. J. Veh. Technol. (2013)
14. Irsigler, M., Hein, G.: Development of a real time multipath monitor based on multi-correlator observations. In: Proceedings of the ION-GNSS (2005)
15. Brocard, P., Thevenon, P., Julien, O., Salos, D., Mabilleau, M.: Measurement quality assessment in urban environments using correlation function distortion metrics. In: ENAC, Egis France

Towards a Complete View of the SSL/TLS Service Ports in the Wild

Peipei Fu[1,2]([⊠]), Mingxin Cui[1,2], and Zhenzhen Li[1,2]

[1] Institute of Information Engineering, Chinese Academy of Sciences, Beijing, China
{fupeipei,cuimingxin,lizhenzhen}@iie.ac.cn
[2] School of Cyber Security, University of Chinese Academy of Sciences,
Beijing, China

Abstract. With the emergence of service port obfuscation and abuse, malicious services can hide their communication behaviors in large-scale normal SSL/TLS traffic easily. Therefore, it is of great significance to get the complete view of SSL/TLS service ports and understand the potential threat of SSL/TLS usage. In this paper, we conduct a comprehensive analysis of the SSL/TLS service port by carrying out a large-scale passive measurement based on two ISP-level networks with a total bandwidth of up to 100 Gbps for over one year. Specifically, we first investigate the overall SSL/TLS service port view and uncover that the actual usage of port is in a state of confusion. At the same time, through in-depth analysis of specific well-known ports which are used by SSL/TLS, it is revealed that the well-known ports could be exploited by malicious SSL/TLS services easily. Then, we dig into some specific certificates to explore their ports behavior and discover that the self-signed certificates and EV certificates are in sorry state. Meanwhile, we uncover practices that may be exploited by malicious services, and reveal the potential threats or vulnerabilities in SSL/TLS service ports. We believe that the work will be beneficial to both SSL/TLS and web security in the future.

Keywords: SSL/TLS · Security · Service port · Certificate · Measurement

1 Introduction

Nowadays, more and more network encrypted services use the SSL/TLS protocol to protect their communications. However, with the widespread of the protocol, malicious services are increasingly using non-standard SSL/TLS service ports to launch and hide their communications. And, the free certificates have become an easy disguise for attackers. According to the February 2018 Zscaler SSL Threat Report [1], the threats from SSL have increased by 30% in 6 months. Therefore, how to strengthen the network management and guarantee the network security is becoming one of the most concerns to network users.

In general, SSL/TLS service use port 443 (HTTPS) to transfer communication data. However, some malicious services may communicate with well-known

© ICST Institute for Computer Sciences, Social Informatics and Telecommunications Engineering 2020
Published by Springer Nature Switzerland AG 2020. All Rights Reserved
H. Gao et al. (Eds.): ChinaCom 2019, LNICST 312, pp. 549–563, 2020.
https://doi.org/10.1007/978-3-030-41114-5_41

or commonly used ports to bypass firewalls or network detection systems and blend with normal network activity to avoid more detailed inspection or detection. X.509 certificate [2], which is known as public key certificate, is general entity that SSL/TLS protocol authentication relies. But they can be easily obtained for free in some cases recently. Cyber criminals and hackers have got interested in the PKI environment and the digital certificates in order to conduct illicit activities such as cyber espionage, sabotage or malware diffusion [3]. Therefore, it is of great significance to understand the real world SSL/TLS usage, especially in security.

The research on SSL/TLS security has never been stopped. However, there are few works only focused on the analysis of SSL/TLS service ports to reach our scale. This paper explores the SSL/TLS service usage by thoroughly analyzing SSL/TLS service ports, which is rarely comprehensively studied in this way in other measurement studies [10–12]. Our study is conducted on what is, to the best of our knowledge, the largest-scale passive measurement of SSL/TLS service ports usage in the wild. We elaborate the measurement work at two ISP level networks, namely China Education and Research Network and China Science and Technology Network, which have a total of over 100 Gbps of bandwidth and about 20 million users. Between January 2018 and February 2019, we extract all certificates and statistical information appearing in the SSL/TLS sessions at both gateways.

In summary, we make the following contributions:

- **SSL/TLS service ports:** By analyzing the service ports used by SSL/TLS thoroughly, we get the complete view of SSL/TLS service ports and reveal that the SSL/TLS services are on all available TCP ports, which is a sad finding. It uncovers that the actual usage of the SSL/TLS port is in a state of confusion.
- **Well-known ports:** Through in-depth analysis of the specific well-known ports, it is found that the well-known ports could be exploited by some normal services (such as Tor) and malicious services easily, leading to serious port abuse situation. Meanwhile, we find the cloud service, which allows for multiple services running over on it, also incline to use well-known ports and provide a novel channel and reasonable platform for the malicious services to hide their behaviors.
- **Specific certificates' ports:** The service ports analysis on some specific certificates are performed to reveal the SSL/TLS services usage in the wild. Through the port behavior analysis of free certificates, the performance of Let's Encrypt certificates are better than self-signed certificates, as less than 1% Let's Encrypt [6] certificates use non-standard SSL/TLS ports, but almost 33% to self-signed certificates. From the analysis of DV, OV, EV certificates, it is revealed that EV certificates are the worst in port performance, which is beyond our expectations.

Meanwhile, the anomalies we noticed during the analysis are discussed. Lastly, based on the measurement, it reveals the current status of SSL/TLS services ports usage in the wild, and represents how the measurement results can be used to improve SSL services usage security. We believe that the results and findings will no doubt benefit SSL/TLS security researches in future.

The rest of the paper is organized as follows. Section 2 presents the related work. Section 3 briefly elaborates on the passive framework and Sect. 4 shows the datasets of our work. The measurement and investigation of SSL/TLS service ports is presented in Sect. 5 and the related security risks are also analyzed deeply. Finally, Sect. 6 concludes the paper.

2   Related Work

The research on SSL/TLS has always been active and long term in the field of network security. Our work is different from previous work in the method we used, the size of our datasets, and the focus of our research.

At present, there are many studies focus on SSL/TLS malicious behavior detection [4,5,7]. Almishari et al. [4] presented a novel technique to detect web-fraud domains that utilize HTTPS based on 13 characteristics from the digital certificate. Dong [5] exploited six machine learning methods to classify phishing sites using HTTPS. And, Anderson et al. [7] provided a comprehensive study of malware's use of TLS by observing the unencrypted TLS handshake messages. Unlike these work to detect the malicious services, the broad goal of our paper is to understand what kinds of loopholes or insecure factors of SSL/TLS service port could be exploited by malicious services.

Measurement is one of the most direct and effective way to know the practice of the SSL/TLS usage. Akhawe et al. [8] presented a large-scale measurement study of common TLS warnings. Chung et al. [9] took another look at the SSL certificate ecosystem, focusing on the invalid certificates measurement. However, our work has different emphasis and we focus on the service port and certificate to reveal the overall status quo of the SSL/TLS services in the wild.

There have been several previous works to measure the SSL/TLS and its certificate ecosystem [10–12]. Levillain et al. [10] assessed the quality of HTTPS servers in the wild through a year SSL measurement. Holz et al. [11] presented a comprehensive analysis of X.509 certificates from active and passive measurement and Durumeric et al. [12] conducted a large-scale active measurement study of X.509 certificates ecosystem, and uncover practices that may put the security of the ecosystem at risk. Both active and passive measuring techniques are exploited to explore different aspects of SSL/TLS. Active measurement is easy to carry out with low cost, but they only collect data through probing the specific ports or IPs. And existed typical passive measurements are done in 10 Gbps bandwidth environments at universities or research institutions, such as in [11]. In contrast, in this paper, we try to make up the weakness of active scanning by carrying out a large-scale passive measurement to 100 Gbps networks.

3   Passive Measurement Framework

Passive monitor is usually installed at the existing network vantage points to capture network traffic and monitor network nodes in a passive manner,

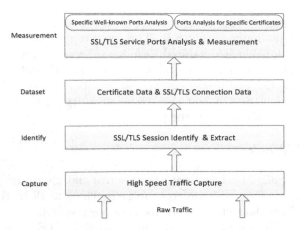

Fig. 1. Passive measurement framework.

without injecting any probing packets to a network. We adopt the passive measurement method to obtain X509 certificates and monitor all SSL/TLS flows through China Education and Research Network (CERNET) and China Science and Technology Network. The gateway link bandwidths of the two ISPs are 61,440 Mbps and 47,104 Mbps, respectively, with a total of over 100 Gbps bandwidth and a total of 17 million IPv4 addresses and about 30 million users. In order to achieve the high speed of passive monitoring on the link, we need to improve the configuration of hardware devices and adjust our monitoring strategy for complete flow monitoring and information data transmission on the entire link.

The passive measurement framework of our work is shown in Fig. 1. First, we adopt our high speed capture module to capture the raw traffic. Then we identify the SSL/TLS session and monitor all SSL/TLS flows to obtain SSL certificates and session statistical information. Third, we begin to accumulate the data set, including the certificate data and the connection data. Section 4 describes the data set thoroughly. Finally, based on our passive datasets, the measurement and analysis of the SSL/TLS service ports are investigated, which contains specific well-known ports analysis and the ports analysis of specific certificates.

However, the problem of privacy and ethical issues is very important in passive measurements. In our work, we limit our range of observations and focus on the SSL/TLS handshake phase for the extract of the certificate. And, our institution formulates strict access control policies. Using typical IP address anonymization technology to hide the personally identifiable information. At the same time, only specific people can access and analyze the data, and they are subject to strict restrictions and training. What's more, our work is not attempting to compromise normal network traffic and explore user's privacy information.

4   Data Description

This section mainly describes the datasets we used in the paper. Firstly, we present the datasets collected by our passive framework and then illustrates the malicious services datasets used in our work.

Passive Datasets. Based on our passive measurement framework, we get two kinds of datasets, the SSL/TLS certificate datasets and the SSL/TLS connection datasets.

As we all know, a X.509 certificate mainly includes the attributes: version, serial number, signature, issuer, validity, subject, information on the public key of the subject. We extract all the certificate information when it is identified to accumulate our certificate datasets. Meanwhile, we generate a hash value of the entire certificate in order to uniquely identify a certificate.

Meanwhile, each SSL/TLS connection information is recorded to create our connection datasets. The datasets mainly include the following information: server IP, server port, number of packets, number of bytes, and hash of the certificate. Through the hash of the certificate, we can associate each connection information with the certificate information.

Finally, we complete the accumulation of the two kinds of datasets : SSL/TLS certificate datasets and connection datasets. From January 2018 to February 2019, we finally collect and parse 102,553,231 unique certificates totally. And the corresponding connection information are stored in time.

Malicious Service Dataset. The malicious SSL/TLS services datasets of the SSL Blacklist (SSLBL) [13] are mainly used in our study. The SHA1 fingerprints and IP addresses of known malicious SSL certificates are revealed in SSLBL, which is very useful for our research. It mainly provides the SHA1 fingerprints, Subject, Issuer, Server IP, Server Port, Listing reason and time. We use these certificates as our original source to analyze the certificate collected in our work. Then we collect all the malicious certificate information listed in SSLBL up to February 28, 2019 to help our analysis.

5   Measurement and Investigation

This section aims to describe the overall results of our analysis and measurement. Section 5.1 presents the analysis result of the server port usage of the SSL services. And two special kinds of certificates of SSL services are shown in Sect. 5.3.

5.1   Overall SSL/TLS Service Port Analysis

HTTPs (port 443) is the most widely used for secure communication on the Internet, which is encrypted by SSL/TLS. Except HTTPs protocol, there are

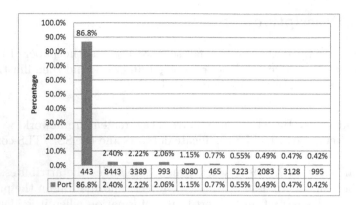

Fig. 2. The top 10 port distribution of SSL/TLS services.

some other protocols based on SSL/TLS protocol, such as IMAPs (port 993), POP3s (port 995), and so on. Generally, except for the ports which are used by the protocols over SSL/TLS, other ports should not be used by SSL/TLS service. However, based on our analysis, we detect that 65536 different server ports running on SSL/TLS protocol, which means that all available ports have been used to run SSL/TLS. The top 10 server ports are shown in Fig. 2.

As the lowest numbered 1024 port numbers are called the well-known port numbers, which is registered to identify the specific network services officially, such as port 80 is allocated for HTTP service, and port 53 is allocated for DNS service. However, based on the results, it finds that all well-known ports are appeared in SSL/TLS server ports. This is a sad finding. According to the result, the percentage of well-konwn ports reaches 90.45%. There is no doubt that port 443 is the highest and reaches to 86.8%. However, except for the protocol over SSL/TLS, all other well-known ports are used by SSL/TLS service now, which lead to the abuse or confusion of the server ports. In this way, the SSL/TLS service can hide their traffic to escape detection.

We then study the certificates' server port in SSLBL, and discover that 80% malicious services listed in SSL Blacklist use port 443, and about 20% servers that provide malicious services on non-typical SSL/TLS ports. The blacklisted malicious services used almost 450 port numbers, and there is 32 well-known ports among them. Port 4443, 80, and 447 are mostly used. According to the analysis results, we can conclude that malicious services or attackers are more inclined to use well-known ports to escape the detection of firewall.

From the measurement and analysis, we reveal the overall status quo of the SSL/TLS services ports usage in the wild. The actual usage of the SSL/TLS service ports is in a state of confusion, and all available ports are covered. All well-known ports appear in SSL/TLS service ports, such as the most commonly used ports: 80 (HTTP), 53 (DNS), et al. It is a sad finding for the SSL/TLS service ports usage.

5.2   Specific Well-Known Ports Analysis

We are curious about the SSL/TLS services running on these well-known ports. In our paper, we select two kinds of typical well-known ports, 80 and 53, to analyze their security risk.

Port 80 Analysis. It is well known that port 80 is allocated for HTTP service, namely the web service, which is one of the most commonly used network service by users. Therefore, we extract corresponding certificates separately according to our datasets. After a coarse-grained analysis, we find that most connections running over port 80 are confirmed to be connected with SAMSUNG service. More than 86% connections are protected by two certificates, whose Subject CN are "*.push.samsungosp.com" and "*.bigdata.ssp.samsung.com", which may indicate the message push and data uploading services of SAMSUNG smart devices.

However, the more commonly used a port is, the easier it can be exploited by malicious services. Combing with the malicious certificates' server IP and server Port listed in SSLBL, we find two types of "bad" SSL certificates run over port 80 from our passive measurement, and the certificate information is listed in Table 1. They use "localhost" or "localhost.localdomain" as their Common Names, in order to hide their real malicious services.

Meanwhile, in our analysis, we find some cloud certificates are hosted on port 80. The subject CN "sni77007.cloudflaressl.com" is selected to analyze the cloud certificate, which is used by URL "https://www.us-proxy.org/". According to our active analysis, it reveals that this certificate supports 69 domains, which are presented in Fig. 3. We visit these domain names for active verification and verify that these domains are really using the same CloudFlare certificate. These domains are located in the Subject Alternative Name (SAN) [2] field in a certificate. SAN is an extension to X.509 that allows various values (including IP address, DNS names and so on) to be associated with a security certificate using a subjectAltName field. An SSL/TLS certificate that uses an SAN field can extend the domain name that this certificate supports so that a certificate can support the resolution of multiple different domain names. Therefore, it reveals that the cloud certificates could be shared by different kinds of SSL/TLS services.

Currently, there are many cloud computing providers, like Amazon ec2, Microsoft Azure, Cloudflare and so on. With the development of cloud services, more and more SSL/TLS encrypted network services are hosted on these legal cloud platforms. Therefore, when a user visits a website on the cloud, the certificate provided by the server during the SSL/TLS handshake is not the certificate of the website, but the certificate provided by the cloud service provider. Even though the malicious services host on the cloud services, we can not identify them easily as they use the legal cloud resources. That is to say, only according to the cloud certificate Common Names, we can't get the real services under the cloud certificates, only know which cloud service provider it belongs to. According to

Fig. 3. The SAN field of us proxy.

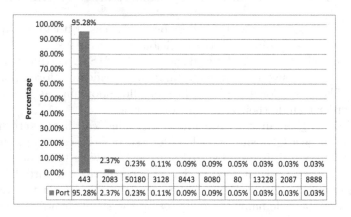

Fig. 4. The top 10 port distribution of CloudFlare certificate.

the Malwarebytes blog in [15], the cloudflare SSL certificates are abused in phishing scam and the original certificate was issued to "sni67342.cloudflaressl.com" (Cloudflare). In the situation, many malicious applications could host their services on various cloud platforms and use the legal "shell" of the cloud platform to hide their behaviors.

Since cloud certificates provide an efficient way for malicious services, we want to know which ports can be used by cloud certificates. We focus on the analysis of CloudFlare certificates and the port distribution is shown in Fig. 4. We detect almost 22268 different ports used by CloudFlare certificates based on our passive measurement. Among them, there are 71 well-known ports and port 80 is the most frequently used by CloudFlare certificates.

Therefore, according to our measurement, some SSL/TLS services running on port 80 may be a kind of normal application, like message push and data uploading services of SAMSUNG. While, the port also can be exploited by malicious services (like Gootkit C&C) and cloud certificate which could provide a new channel for malicious service also incline to use well-known ports. They hide their true service behavior through this way.

Table 1. The malicious certificate information based on Port 80.

Subject common names	Subject organization	Subject email	Malicious service
localhost	My company Ltd.	NULL	Gootkit C&C
localhost.localdomain	SomeOrganization	root@localhost. localdomain	Gootkit C&C

Port 53 Analysis. Port 53 is allocated for DNS service, which is an important network service used for domain name resolution. Therefore, we want to know why this port is also used by SSL/TLS. The certificates of port 53 (typically for DNS) are extracted and analyzed. From the analysis of the Common Names, we find that there are about 87.56% of certificates whose subject CNs are in the style of "www.*.net" (e.g.,www.3hbgd654dfpl.net), and the issuer CNs are in the style of "www.*.com" (e.g.,www.5hbdf654dcvh.com). At the same time, it also found that port 23, port 20 and port 21 etc, all have this kind of certificate Common Names and the percentage are relatively high (shown in Table 2).

Table 2. The percentage of "www.*.net" certificate on some well-known ports.

Port	Typical port usage	Percentage
53	Domain Name System (DNS)	87.56%
23	Telnet protocol	61.94%
20	File Transfer Protocol (FTP) data transfer	99.00%
21	File Transfer Protocol (FTP) control	91.78%
110	Post Office Protocol, version 3 (POP3)	88.10%

We analyze the kind of certificates in detail and extract the middle field of the subject Common Names to analyze. For instance, the middle field is "abc" in "www.abc.net". We find that the middle field is generated randomly and the length of the middle field is from 8 to 20 at large. According to the properties of the Tor certificates described in [14], both the issuer and the subject of the certificates use random Common Names consisting of the components www., a random 8 to 20 letter base-32 encoded domain name, and a .com or .net ending. Therefore, we can get that these kinds of certificates are used by Tor, which is the most popular anonymous service system to keep users' identity and location private communicating.

Therefore, from the analysis results, we conclude that many well-known ports are exploited by SSL services, like Tor. Although Tor services aim to protect the

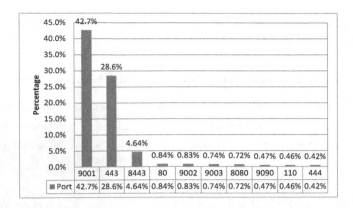

Fig. 5. The top 10 port distribution of Tor.

private and security of users, it is also not advisable to randomly occupy well-known ports to communicate. Meanwhile, we can not get whether it is a kind of normal Tor behavior. Therefore, we conduct an analysis of Tor services in the following. Tor certificates are selected through pattern recognition of the certificate Common Names. We explore the port distribution of the Tor service and the top 10 ports used by Tor service are shown in Fig. 5.

We detect almost 6707 different ports used by Tor based on our passive measurement. Among them, there are 88 well-known ports. The most usually used port number of the Tor network is 9001, which is unofficial default port of Tor network. Based on the measurement, as a kind of special and typical SSL encrypted service, Tor makes use of diverse ports to serve their users.

According to the usage status of the Tor, we can infer that one SSL/TLS service can select different ports to serve its users. This phenomenon will seriously affect the normal use of network ports, resulting in the actual use of ports in a chaotic state.

From the measurement and analysis of the specific well-known service ports, we reveal some status quo of the SSL/TLS services ports usage in the wild, which is shown in the following.

1. Using well-known service ports to escape is a common trick of malicious applications, like port 80 is commonly used by malicious services.
2. Some SSL/TLS encrypted services exploit different ports to serve their communications, like Tor, leading to serious port abuse situation.

From our analysis results, we can understand the security implications of service ports. SSL/TLS services whether malicious or benign all can switch their server ports or abuse well-known ports to escape detection or hide their behaviors. The port flux of the SSL services and the abuse of well-known ports will bring a great challenge to the security and management of network ports.

5.3   Port Analysis for Specific Certificates

SSL/TLS services are relying on the underlying X.509 certificate infrastructure for authentication. There are a few different ways for us to obtain SSL/TLS certificates, and depending on the budget, audience, and a few other factors, we could choose between a commercial certificate, a new automated and free certificate, self-signed certificates, and so on. According to the method of obtaining the free certificate, we focus on the self-signed certificate which is generated by using the OpenSSL library, and the certificate which is signed by Let's Encrypt CA. Meanwhile, according to the validation method, SSL/TLS certificates can be divided into three kinds: Domain Validation (DV) certificates, Organization Validation (OV) certificates, and Extended Validation (EV) certificates. Therefore, this section begins to explore the port behavior of these different kinds of certificates.

Free Certificates. Using SSL/TLS Certificates issued from a trusted Certificate Authority eliminates scary browser security warnings, protecting customer trust, as well as encouraging safe Internet behavior. However, with the development of SSL/TLS certificate, different kinds of free certificates appeared. In this section, we aim to analyze the port distribution of free certificate, which contains the self-signed certificate and the certificate which is signed by Let's Encrypt CA.

Many organizations are tempted to use free SSL Certificates instead of those issued and verified by a trusted Certificate Authority mainly because of the price difference. Unlike CA issued certificates, self-signed certificates are free of charge, are signed by themselves rather than by a trusted certificate authority and can be made with the openssl command that ships with the OpenSSL library. Let's Encrypt(a free, automated, and open certificate authority) started issuing free certificates to the public in December 2015, aiming to promote the popularization of SSL/TLS encryption services on the Internet with a free and automated certificate issuing process.

Therefore, according to the certificate characteristic, we extract the self-signed certificates and the Let's Encrypt certificates from our datasets. The certificate quantity and the server ports number are shown in Table 3. From the results, it finds that although the number of self-signed certificates is not as large as the number of Let's Encrypt certificates, the number of ports for self-signed certificates is almost twice the number of Let's Encrypt certificate. It reveals the number of server ports used by the self-signed certificate is very dispersed.

Table 3. The free certificates.

Type	Server ports number	Well-known ports number	Certificate quantity
Self-signed certificate	62401	902	21.43%
Let's encrypt certificate	31780	489	32.88%

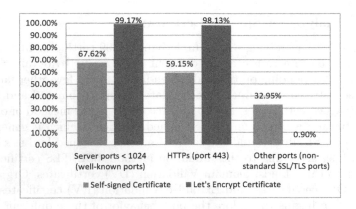

Fig. 6. The port distribution of free certificate.

Then, the port distribution of the two kinds of free certificates have been analyzed. The percentage of port 443, well-known ports and the non-standard SSL/TLS ports (which exclude all ports based on the SSL/TLS protocol) are shown in Fig. 6. According to the comparison of the two kinds of free certificates, we discover that almost 33% self-signed certificates use non-standard SSL/TLS ports, but less than 1% to Let's Encrypt certificates. And 98.13% Let's Encrypt certificates use port 443. Therefore, we can get that the port usage of self-signed certificates is relatively random and chaotic, and the port use status quo of Let's Encrypt certificates is relatively good now.

For reasons of economy, convenience, and anonymity, self-signed certificates are widely used in actual network environments. However, in the malicious certificate data set SSLBL, more than 95% of the certificates are self-signed certificates, which indicates that malicious SSL/TLS service incline to use self-signed certificates. Meanwhile, the port behavior of self-signed certificates further confirms the insecurity of self-signed certificates, as the malicious service could use the non-standard SSL/TLS ports to hide their traffic, which will bring great difficult to identify malicious behavior.

Table 4. The DV, OV, EV certificates.

Type	Server ports number	Well-known ports number	Certificate quantity
DV certificate	62875	429	8.73%
OV certificate	64389	269	0.97%
EV certificate	63029	252	0.56%

DV, EV, OV Certificates. Although all SSL/TLS certificates are used to protect and validate the communication data, an effective way to categorize them is by validation method. Therefore, in this section, we focus on the analysis of DV certificates, OV certificates and EV certificates.

DV (Domain validation) certificates are the most common type of SSL/TLS certificate, and only verify domain ownership. OV (Organization validation) certificates require the validation of actual business, and provide more trust than DV certificates. EV (Extended validation) certificates provide the maximum amount of trust to visitors. Different network services often choose to apply for different certification types under the condition of security and cost.

We extract the three types of certificates based on the issuer information. We determine that the certificate belongs to an EV certificate, an OV certificate, or a DV certificate based on the "Extended Validation", "Organization Validation", and "Domain Validation" contained in its issuer field. Although this method leaves out some certificates, it ensures maximum accuracy. The certificate quantity and the server ports number are shown in Table 4. The result reveals that there is not much difference in the number of server ports in the three types of certificates, but there are more DV certificates than other certificates, which is in line with our expectations as DV certificate is issued quickly and at a low price. And in the well-konwn ports, port 80 and port 25 is used most by the three types of certificates.

According to the strictness of validation method, the EV certificate is the most expensive, secure and credible among the three certificates, and it should have a better performance on port usage. However, from the port distribution result of DV, OV, EV certificates which is shown in Fig. 7, EV certificates are the worst in port performance, almost 50% EV certificates use non-standard SSL/TLS ports, which is beyond our expectations. Through the analysis of the subject information of EV certificates who use non-standard SSL/TLS ports, most of the certificates are used by Apple service, like "secure.store.apple.com", "setsupport.apple.com", "itunes.apple.com" and so on. The phenomenon indicates that some large service company incline to use EV certificates to protect their communication, but not use standard SSL/TLS ports. Although such service may be normal service, it still causes confusion in the use of ports.

In this work, the measurement and analysis of SSL/TLS service ports usage in the wild is completed. In order to strengthen the network security management, we conclude some recommendations. In terms of service port, network manager should not ignore the use of well-known ports, as some malicious services incline to use well-known ports to evade auditing. In terms of SSL/TLS certificate, it is particularly necessary to strengthen the management of the port usage of various certificates to prevent malicious exploitation, especially self-signed certificates and EV certificates. Meanwhile, network manager should strengthen the management of cloud services platform to prevent exploitation by malicious services.

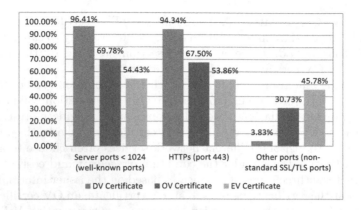

Fig. 7. The port distribution of DV, EV, OV certificate.

6   Conclusion

In this work, we have successfully completed the in-depth measurement study of the SSL/TLS service ports by performing passive measurement on 100 Gbps network over one year. Our study investigates the SSL/TLS service ports and shows the complete view of the SSL/TLS services port usage in the wild. We find that all available TCP ports are used by SSL/TLS services, and some services whether malicious or benign could switch their service ports or abuse well-known ports to hide their behaviors. By analyzing the service ports of different kinds of free certificates, we find that Let's Encrypt certificates perform better in port usage than the self-signed certificates. Among DV, OV, and EV certificates, EV certificates have the worst performance on the port behavior, which exceeded our expectations. Meanwhile, the potential threats in SSL/TLS service ports usage are presented and the implications of our results are discussed. We believe our analysis will provide direction information for future decisions of SSL/TLS service ports usage.

Acknowledgments. This work is supported by The National Key Research and Development Program of China (No. 2016QY05X1000 and No. 2016YFB0801200) and The National Natural Science Foundation of China (No. U1636217) and Key research and Development Program for Guangdong Province under grant No. 2019B010137003.

References

1. February 2018 Zscaler SSL Threat Report. https://www.zscaler.com/blogs/research/february-2018-zscaler-ssl-threat-report
2. Cooper, D., et al.: Internet X.509 Public Key Infrastructure Certificate and Certificate Revocation List (CRL) Profile (IETF RFC5280) (2008). http://www.ietf.org/rfc/rfc5280.txt
3. How Cybercrime Exploits Digital Certificates. http://resources.infosecinstitute.com/cybercrime-exploits-digital-certificates/

4. Almishari, M., et al.: Harvesting SSL certificate data to identify web-fraud. Int. J. Netw. Secur. **14**(6), 324–338 (2012)
5. Dong, Z., et al.: Beyond the lock icon: real-time detection of phishing websites using public key certificates. In: Electronic Crime Research (2015)
6. Let's Encrypt. https://letsencrypt.org/
7. Anderson, B., et al.: Deciphering malware's use of TLS (without decryption). J. Comput. Virol. Hacking Tech. **14**, 1–17 (2016)
8. Akhawe, D., Amann, B., et al.: Here's My Cert, So Trust Me, Maybe? Understanding TLS Errors on the Web, pp. 59–70. ACM, New York (2013)
9. Chung, T., Liu, Y., Choffnes, D., et al.: Measuring and applying invalid SSL certificates: the silent majority. In: Proceedings of the 2016 Internet Measurement Conference, pp. 527–541. ACM (2016)
10. Levillain, O., et al.: One year of SSL internet measurement. In: Computer Security Applications Conference, NY, USA, pp. 11–20 (2012)
11. Holz, R., et al.: The SSL landscape: a thorough analysis of the x. 509 PKI using active and passive measurements. In: ACM SIGCOMM Conference on Internet Measurement, Toronto, Ontario, Canada, pp. 427–444 (2011)
12. Durumeric, Z., Kasten, J., et al.: Analysis of the HTTPS certificate ecosystem. In: Proceedings of the 2013 Conference on Internet Measurement Conference, Barcelona, Spain, pp. 291–304. ACM (2013)
13. SSL Blacklist. https://sslbl.abuse.ch/
14. Amann, J., Sommer, R.: Exploring tor's activity through long-term passive TLS traffic measurement. In: Karagiannis, T., Dimitropoulos, X. (eds.) PAM 2016. LNCS, vol. 9631, pp. 3–15. Springer, Cham (2016). https://doi.org/10.1007/978-3-319-30505-9_1
15. Free SSL certificate from CloudFlare abused in phishing scam. https://blog.malwarebytes.com/threat-analysis/2014/12/free-ssl-certificate-from-cloudflare-abused-in-phishing-scam/

Secrecy Precoder Design for k-User MIMO Interference Channels

Bing Fang[1]($\boxtimes$) and Wei Shao[2]

[1] Army Command College of PLA, Nanjing, China
bingfang_ch@163.com
[2] Army Engineering University of PLA, Nanjing, China
swlxssz@126.com

Abstract. In this paper, we have studied the secrecy precoder design problem for a k-user multiple-input multiple-output (MIMO) interference channel (IFC), where an external eavesdropper intends to wiretap one of the legitimate wireless links. By adopting the "maxmin" fairness criteria, we define the secure precoding problem as an achievable secrecy-rate maximization problem, which is inherent nonconvex and pretty hard to deal with. To tackle the inherent complexity, we recast the original nonconvex problem into a difference-of-convex (DC) programming problem through a series of equivalent transformations. Based on these endeavors, a coordinated iterative precoding algorithm is designed to solve the achievable secrecy rate maximization problem within the framework of successive convex approximation (SCA) method. The basic idea of the proposed SCA method consists in recasting the DC-programming problem into a series of convexified subproblems, where the nonconvex parts of it are linearized to their first-order Taylor expansion. Moreover, in order to ensure the convergence of the proposed iterative algorithm, a regularization method based on the proximal point idea is also employed. Numerical simulations further show that our algorithm can achieve a satisfactory performance on the premise of ensuring convergence.

Keywords: MIMO precoding · Interference channel · Physical layer security · Successive convex approximation

1 Introduction

From a mathematical point of view, many real communication scenarios can be modeled as the interference channels (IFCs), where multiple uncoordinated communication links share the same radio spectrum at the same time. With multiple-input multiple-output (MIMO) having become a key technology for the

This work was supported by the State Key Laboratory of Complex Electromagnetic Environment Effects on Electronics and Information System (CEMEE) Open Foundation of China (grant CEMEE2019Z0202B) and the Jiangsu Provincial Natural Science Foundation of China (grant BK20160080).

H. Gao et al. (Eds.): ChinaCom 2019, LNICST 312, pp. 564–575, 2020.
https://doi.org/10.1007/978-3-030-41114-5_42

fifth-generation mobile networks, i.e., 5G, the researches concerned on MIMO IFCs have gained considerable attention, refer to [1–4] and their references. On the other hand, there are also extensive interests in utilizing the extra benefits, i.e, the spatial degree-of-freedom (DoF), provided by MIMO technology to enhance the secrecy capabilities of pervasive wireless communication [5–7]. Naturally, it has become a critical issue to model and analyze physical layer security (PLS) performance for the MIMO IFCs [8,9].

In this work, we center on the design problem of secure precoding for a k-user MIMO IFC, where an external eavesdropper aims to wiretap one of the k legitimate wireless links. Here, we assume that the k legitimate transmitters simultaneously transmit independent messages to their corresponding receivers, while attempting to remain confidential to the external eavesdropper. In this setup, it is further assumed that all the transmitters, the receivers and the external eavesdropper are equipped with multiple antennas. Hence, our problem setup naturally constitutes a MIMO interference wiretap channel. By adopting the "maxmin" fairness criteria, the secrecy precoder design problem is defined as an achievable secrecy rate maximization problem, which subjects to individual transmit power budget allocated for each transmitter. However, the proposed problem is non-smooth and nonconvex and pretty hard to deal with.

To tackle the inherent complexity, we first resort to the epigraph optimization technique and equivalently relax the formulated problem to a smooth problem. Then, we recast the original nonconvex problem into a DC programming problem by a series of equivalent mathematical transformations. Based on these endeavors, a coordinated iterative precoding algorithm is designed to solve the achievable secrecy rate maximization problem within the framework of successive convex approximation (SCA) method [10,11]. The basic idea of the proposed SCA method is recasting the DC-programming problem into a sequence of convexified subproblems, where the nonconvex parts of it are linearized to their first-order Taylor expansion. Moreover, in order to ensure the convergence of the proposed iterative algorithm, a regularization method based on the proximal point thought is also employed here. Numerical simulations further show that our algorithm can achieve a satisfactory performance on the premise of ensuring convergence.

Notations: Bold uppercase letters denote matrices and bold lowercase letters denote vectors; $\mathbb{C}^{m \times n}$ defines the space of all $m \times n$ complex matrices; $\boldsymbol{A} \succeq 0$ means that the matrix $\boldsymbol{A}$ is positive semidefinite; Hermitian transpose of matrix $\boldsymbol{A}$ is represented as $\boldsymbol{A}^H$; inverse of matrix $\boldsymbol{A}$ is represented as $\boldsymbol{A}^{-1}$; determinant of matrix $\boldsymbol{A}$ is denoted as $|\boldsymbol{A}|$; trace of matrix $\boldsymbol{A}$ is denoted as $\mathrm{Tr}(\boldsymbol{A})$; and $\log(\cdot)$ denotes the natural logarithm.

2　System Model and Problem Formulation

This work studies the design problem of secure precoding for a k-user MIMO IFC. The system considered here is composed of k legitimate wireless links (Alice-to-Bob) and an external eavesdropper (Eve). As presented in Fig. 1, Alice, Bob, and Eve are all mounted with multiple antennas. We assume that each transmitter (Alice) aims to communicate confidential messages with its corresponding receiver (Bob), respectively, in the presence of an external eavesdropper (Eve), and further assume that Bob i only interests in the message sent by Alice i. However, Eve may have a general interest to wiretap the message transmitted by every one of the k transmitters. It is further assumed that all transmitters have N_t antennas, all receivers have N_r antennas, and Eve is enabled with N_e antennas.

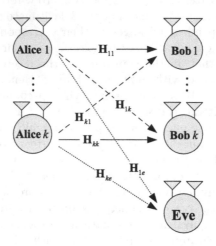

Fig. 1. System model of a k-user MIMO interference wiretap channel.

Here, it is assumed that a quasi-static frequency-flat fading communication environment for all wireless transmit links. The vector-valued signal received by Bob i is given as

$$\boldsymbol{y}_i = \sum_{j=1}^{k} \boldsymbol{H}_{ji}\boldsymbol{x}_j + \boldsymbol{n}_i, \forall i \in \mathcal{K}, \tag{1}$$

where $\boldsymbol{x}_j \in \mathbb{C}^{N_t \times 1}$ is the signal vector transmitted by Alice j, $\boldsymbol{H}_{ji} \in \mathbb{C}^{N_r \times N_t}$ denotes the complex channel matrix from Alice j to Bob i, $\boldsymbol{n}_i \in \mathbb{C}^{N_r \times 1}$ is additive Gaussian noise vector received by Bob i, and the user set $\mathcal{K}$ is defined as $\mathcal{K} = \{1, 2, \cdots, k\}$.

Then, the achievable data rate of the ith legitimate wireless link can be given in the following formula

$$R_i^b(\boldsymbol{Q}) = \log \left| \boldsymbol{I} + \boldsymbol{H}_{ii}^H \boldsymbol{Z}_i^{-1} \boldsymbol{H}_{ii} \boldsymbol{Q}_i \right|, \forall i \in \mathcal{K}, \tag{2}$$

where $\boldsymbol{Q}_i$ is the transmit covariance matrix, i.e., the precoding matrix, of Alice i, and $\boldsymbol{Q}$ denotes the profile of precoding matrix of all transmitters, which is framed as $\boldsymbol{Q} = \{\boldsymbol{Q}_i\}_{i=1}^k$. $\boldsymbol{Z}_i$ is the covariance matrix of the additive noise plus all interference received by Bob i, which is defined in the following formula

$$\boldsymbol{Z}_i = \sum_{j \neq i}^k \boldsymbol{H}_{ji} \boldsymbol{Q}_j \boldsymbol{H}_{ji}^H + \boldsymbol{N}_i, \forall i \in \mathcal{K}, \tag{3}$$

where $\boldsymbol{N}_i$ is the covariance matrix of additive noise vector received by Bob i.

On the other hand, the vector-valued signal received by Eve can be written in the following formula

$$\boldsymbol{y}_e = \sum_{j=1}^k \boldsymbol{H}_{je} \boldsymbol{x}_j + \boldsymbol{n}_e, \tag{4}$$

where $\boldsymbol{x}_j \in \mathbb{C}^{N_t \times 1}$ is the signal vector transmitted by Alice j, $\boldsymbol{H}_{je} \in \mathbb{C}^{N_e \times N_t}$ denotes the complex channel matrix from Alice j to Eve, and $\boldsymbol{n}_e \in \mathbb{C}^{N_e \times 1}$ is additive Gaussian noise vector received by Eve.

Then, the achievable data rate of the ith Alice-to-Eve wiretap link can be given as

$$R_i^e(\boldsymbol{Q}) = \log \left| \boldsymbol{I} + \boldsymbol{H}_{ie}^H \boldsymbol{N}_e^{-1} \boldsymbol{H}_{ie} \boldsymbol{Q}_i \right|, \forall i \in \mathcal{K}, \tag{5}$$

where $\boldsymbol{N}_e$ is the covariance matrix of the additive noise vector received by Eve. Note that, we consider a worst-case scenario here, that the external eavesdropper can remove all multiuser interference by using the successive interference cancelation (SIC) technique.

Therefore, the achievable secrecy data rate of the ith legitimate wireless link can be given as

$$R_i^s(\boldsymbol{Q}) = [R_i^b(\boldsymbol{Q}) - R_i^e(\boldsymbol{Q})]^+, \tag{6}$$

where $[\cdot]^+$ denotes the Euclidean projection onto $\mathbb{R}^+$. With the "maxmin" fairness criteria being adopted, the achievable secrecy rate maximization problem for the proposed MIMO IFC system can be formally formulated as

$$(\text{P1}): \max_{\boldsymbol{Q}} \min_i R_i^s(\boldsymbol{Q})$$
$$\text{s.t. } \text{Tr}(\boldsymbol{Q}_i) \leq \text{P}_i, \boldsymbol{Q}_i \succeq 0, \forall i \in \mathcal{K}, \tag{7}$$

where P_i denotes the maximum transmit power budget allocated for Alice i.

Note that, problem (P1) is non-smooth and of notoriously nonconvex complexity, which is pretty hard to solve directly. As shown in the next section, such a problem can be reformulated as a DC programming problem, through some equivalent mathematical transformation, which can be iteratively solved by employing the famous SCA method.

3   Coordinated Iterative Precoding Algorithm

In this section, a coordinated iterative precoding algorithm is designed within the framework of the SCA method. Moreover, a regularization method based on the proximal point idea is also pursued to ensure the convergence of the proposed algorithm.

3.1   Algorithm Design

By introducing a slack variable, i.e., $t > 0$, problem (P1) can be equivalently reformulated as the following epigraph optimization problem [12]

$$(P2): \max_{Q,t} t$$

$$s.t.\ R_i^b(Q) - R_i^e(Q) \geq t, t > 0, \tag{8}$$

$$\text{Tr}(Q_i) \leq P_i, Q_i \succeq 0, \forall i \in \mathcal{K}.$$

Note that, problem (P2) is exactly equivalent to problem (P1), the difference between (P1) and (P2) is only in the mathematical form. However, this simple transformation from (P1) to (P2) changes problem (P2) into a smooth problem and opens the way for further mathematical transformation.

To proceed, we further define the following two auxiliary functions

$$\phi_i(Q) = \log \left| H_{ii} Q_i H_{ii}^H + Z_i \right|,$$
$$\varphi_i(Q) = \log \left| I + H_{ie}^H N_e^{-1} H_{ie} Q_i \right| + \log |Z_i|. \tag{9}$$

Note that, $\phi_i(Q)$ and $\varphi_i(Q)$ are both concave with respect to Q. Then, problem (P2) can be equivalently reformulated in the following optimization problem

$$(P3): \max_{Q,t} t$$

$$s.t.\ \phi_i(Q) - \varphi_i(Q) \geq t, t > 0, \forall i \in \mathcal{K}, \tag{10}$$

$$\text{Tr}(Q_i) \leq P_i, Q_i \succeq 0, \forall i \in \mathcal{K}.$$

Thus, we have formulated a DC programming problem. And, the difficult in solving problem (P3) lies in the constraints $\phi_i(Q) - \varphi_i(Q) \geq t, t > 0, \forall i \in \mathcal{K}$.

According to the formula proposed in [13], the first-order differential of the concave function $\varphi_i(Q), \forall i \in \mathcal{K}$ can be calculated as

$$d\varphi_i(Q) = \sum_{j \neq i}^{k} \text{Tr}(H_{ji}^H Z_i^{-1} H_{ji} dQ_j) + \text{Tr}(H_{ie}^H R_{ie}^{-1} H_{ie} dQ_i). \tag{11}$$

Here, the intermediate parameter matrix R_{ie} is defined in the following formula

$$R_{ie} = H_{ie} Q_i H_{ie}^H + N_e, \tag{12}$$

where N_e is the covariance matrix of additive noise vector received by Eve.

Then, with a given point Q^v which is feasible to problem (P3), the concave function $\varphi_i(Q), \forall i \in \mathcal{K}$ can be locally linearized to

$$\varphi_i(Q) \cong \varphi_i(Q^v) + \sum_{j=1}^{k} \text{Tr}[D_{ij}(Q_j - Q_j^v)] \triangleq \overline{\varphi}_i(Q), \tag{13}$$

Algorithm 1. Iterative precoding algorithm for solving problem (P1).

1: initially set k, $\boldsymbol{H}_i$, P_i, $\forall k \in \mathcal{K}$, $\boldsymbol{H}_e$, $\boldsymbol{Q}^v$, and $v = 0$.

2: **repeat**

3:     compute $\boldsymbol{R}_e$ and $\boldsymbol{Z}_i, \forall i \in \mathcal{K}$ with $\boldsymbol{Q}^v$ according to formulae (12) and (3).

4:     compute $\boldsymbol{D}_{ij}(\boldsymbol{Q}^v)$, $\forall i, j \in \mathcal{K}$ according to formula (14).

5:     compute $\boldsymbol{Q}$ by solving problem (P4) with CVX solver

6:     update $v = v + 1$, and $\boldsymbol{Q}^v = \boldsymbol{Q}$.

7:     compute $R(\boldsymbol{Q}^v) = \min_i R_i^s(\boldsymbol{Q}^v)$, $\forall i \in \mathcal{K}$.

8: **until** the termination criteria are satisfied.

9: **return** $\boldsymbol{Q}^v$ and $R(\boldsymbol{Q}^v)$.

---

which is further denoted as $\overline{\varphi}_i(\boldsymbol{Q})$. Here, the intermediate parameter matrix $\boldsymbol{D}_{ij}$ can be computed as

$$
\boldsymbol{D}_{ij} = \begin{cases} \boldsymbol{H}_{ie}^H \boldsymbol{R}_{ie}^{-1} \boldsymbol{H}_{ie}, & \text{if } j = i, \\ \boldsymbol{H}_{ji}^H \boldsymbol{Z}_i^{-1} \boldsymbol{H}_{ji}, & \text{if } j \neq i, \end{cases} \tag{14}
$$

where the process parameter matrices $\boldsymbol{R}_e$ and $\boldsymbol{Z}_i, \forall i \in \mathcal{K}$ are all computed with $\boldsymbol{Q}^v$. Note that, the function $\overline{\varphi}_i(\boldsymbol{Q}), \forall i \in \mathcal{K}$ is a linear approximation of the concave function $\varphi_i(\boldsymbol{Q}), \forall i \in \mathcal{K}$. Thus, we always have the following inequality

$$
\varphi_i(\boldsymbol{Q}) \leqslant \overline{\varphi}_i(\boldsymbol{Q}), \forall i \in \mathcal{K}, \tag{15}
$$

due to the concavity of the function $\varphi_i(\boldsymbol{Q}), \forall i \in \mathcal{K}$.

Therefore, with the given point $\boldsymbol{Q}^v$, problem (P3) can be locally convexified to the following optimization problem

$$
\text{(P4)}: \quad \max_{\boldsymbol{Q}, t} t
$$

$$
\text{s.t. } \phi_i(\boldsymbol{Q}) - \overline{\varphi}_i(\boldsymbol{Q}) \geq t, t > 0, \forall i \in \mathcal{K}, \tag{16}
$$

$$
\mathrm{Tr}(\boldsymbol{Q}_i) \leq \mathrm{P}_i, \boldsymbol{Q}_i \succeq 0, \forall i \in \mathcal{K}.
$$

Note that, problem (P4) is convex and can be solved by a standard convex programming algorithm in polynomial time, e.g., with CVX solver [14]. Thus, a coordinated iterative precoding algorithm, proposed as *Algorithm 1*, can be framed based on the following dynamic: with a feasible solution $\boldsymbol{Q}^v$ obtained in the vth iteration, the next feasible solution $\boldsymbol{Q}^{v+1}$ can be obtained by solving problem (P4) in the $(v + 1)$th iteration. Obviously, *Algorithm 1* is designed in a centralized fashion, and practical implement of it needs deep cooperation between all legitimate transmitters, which is the reason that it being named as "*coordinated iterative precoding algorithm*".

3.2   Convergence Analysis

Because problem (P1) is inherent nonconvex, the convergence property of *Algorithm 1* with local Linearization has to be analytically established, which is elaborated in the following theorem.

Theorem 1. *Suppose that problem (P4) is strictly convex with respect to $\boldsymbol{Q}$, then, starts from any feasible solution $\boldsymbol{Q}^v$, the running of* Algorithm 1 *must converge to a feasible solution to problem (P1) by solving problem (P4) in an iterative way.*

Proof. According to the concavity of auxiliary function $\varphi_i(\boldsymbol{Q}), \forall i \in \mathcal{K}$, the following inequality

$$\varphi_i(\boldsymbol{Q}) \leqslant \overline{\varphi}_i(\boldsymbol{Q}), \forall i \in \mathcal{K} \tag{17}$$

always holds. It is thus concluded that the following constraint condition of problem (P4) is always stricter than that of problem (P3)

$$\phi_i(\boldsymbol{Q}) - \overline{\varphi}_i(\boldsymbol{Q}) \geq t, \forall i \in \mathcal{K}. \tag{18}$$

Thus, we can draw a conclusion that any feasible solution of problem (P4) must be a feasible solution of problem (P3), because problem (P3) is exactly equivalent to problem (P1).

Let $\widetilde{R}_i^s(\boldsymbol{Q}|\boldsymbol{Q}^v)$ denote the objective function of problem (P4), which is the concave surrogate of $R_i^s(\boldsymbol{Q})$, i.e., the objective function of problem (P1). Then, consider the update dynamic of *Algorithm 1*

$$\boldsymbol{Q}^{v+1} = \arg\max_{\boldsymbol{Q}} \min_i \widetilde{R}_i^s(\boldsymbol{Q}|\boldsymbol{Q}^v). \tag{19}$$

Then, we can come to a conclusion that the following inequality always holds

$$\min_i \widetilde{R}_i^s(\boldsymbol{Q}^{v+1}) \geq \min_i R_i^s(\boldsymbol{Q}^v). \tag{20}$$

Note that, the above inequality results from the strict convexity of problem (P4), which is the preconditions of this theorem.

On the other hand, we can also have the following inequality according to the inequality in formula (17)

$$\min_i R_i^s(\boldsymbol{Q}^{v+1}) \geq \min_i \widetilde{R}_i^s(\boldsymbol{Q}^{v+1}). \tag{21}$$

Then, we can have the following inequality relationship by combining the formulae (20) and (21)

$$\min_i R_i^s(\boldsymbol{Q}^{v+1}) \geq \min_i R_i^s(\boldsymbol{Q}^v), \tag{22}$$

which means that the sequence $R(\boldsymbol{Q}^v)$ obtained by employing *Algorithm 1* is always monotonically non-decreasing.

Under limited transmit power constraints, we can come to a conclusion that the sequence $R(\boldsymbol{Q}^v)$ is always upper bounded, i.e.,

$$R(\boldsymbol{Q}^v) \leq \min_i R_i^s(\boldsymbol{Q}^*), \tag{23}$$

where $R(\boldsymbol{Q}^*)$ is the maximum value obtained under given transmit power budgets. Therefore, the convergence property of *Algorithm 1* is guaranteed, because a monotonically non-decreasing sequence that is upper bounded always converges.

Meanwhile, we can also draw a conclusion that there must exist a limit point of sequence $\boldsymbol{Q}^v$, which is generated by running *Algorithm 1*. Moreover, the limit point must constitute a stationary point of problem (P4). Because the stationary point of problem (P4) is also a maxima of problem (P1), the limit point of sequence $\boldsymbol{Q}^v$ must form a feasible solution to problem (P1).

Hence, it can be concluded that *Algorithm 1* will always converge to a feasible solution to problem (P1) under the precondition that problem (P4) is strictly convex over $\boldsymbol{Q}$.

According to Theorem 1, we can draw a conclusion that the convergence of *Algorithm 1* is centered on the precondition that problem (P4) is strict convex. However, such a precondition isn't always met, especially when some of the wireless channels of above-mentioned MIMO IFC systems are rank deficit. Therefore, we will resort to a regularization method in the next subsection, which is based on the proximal point thought, to ensure the strict convexity of problem (P4) and thus ensure the convergence of *Algorithm 1*.

3.3   Regularized Iterative Precoding Algorithm

The regularization method based on the proximal point thought consists in utilizing a quadratic term to penalize the constraints condition of problem (P4), and thus guarantee the strict convexity of it. Mathematically, the above idea can be formally written as the following convex problem

$$(\text{P5}): \ \max_{Q,t} \ t$$
$$s.t. \ \phi_i(\boldsymbol{Q}) - \widetilde{\varphi}_i(\boldsymbol{Q}) \geq t, t > 0, \forall i \in \mathcal{K}, \tag{24}$$
$$\text{Tr}(\boldsymbol{Q}_i) \leq \text{P}_i, \boldsymbol{Q}_i \succeq 0, \forall i \in \mathcal{K},$$

where the surrogate function $\widetilde{\varphi}_i(\boldsymbol{Q})$ is introduced by using the quadratic regularization term. Specifically, the modified function is given as

$$\widetilde{\varphi}_i(\boldsymbol{Q}) = \overline{\varphi}_i(\boldsymbol{Q}) + \tau \|\boldsymbol{Q} - \boldsymbol{Q}^v\|_F^2, \tag{25}$$

where $\tau > 0$ is a small number used to constrain $\boldsymbol{Q}$ keeping "close" to $\boldsymbol{Q}^v$. The strict convexity of problem (P5) is thus guaranteed, because the Frobenius norm is always strict convex. Moreover, the strict convexity is obtained requiring no special restrictions on the proposed MIMO IFC system.

The regularized iterative precoding algorithm based on the idea of proximal point can also be presented in the framework of *Algorithm 1*, only problem (P4) being replaced with problem (P5). However, the regularized iterative precoding algorithm is hereafter named as *Algorithm 1*(P) to avoid some ambiguity. The convergence property of the resultant *Algorithm 1*(P) will be analyzed in the following theorem.

Theorem 2. *Because the strict convexity of problem (P5) is ensured by the regularization term,* Algorithm 1 *(P) must converge to a feasible solution to problem (P1) by solving problem (P5) in an iterative way.*

Proof. Because problem (P5) is strict convex by adding a regularization term composed of Frobenius norm, the precondition of Theorem 1 is thus guaranteed. Then, according to analysis process of *Algorithm 1*, which is detailed in Theorem 1, we can draw a conclusion that the convergence property of *Algorithm 1*(P) is guaranteed.

Suppose that the sequence Q^v is generated by running *Algorithm 1*(P). Then, we can draw a conclusion from the analysis presented in Theorem 1, that the limit point of Q^v must be a stationary point of problem (P5). Meanwhile, we also have

$$\lim_{v \to \infty} ||Q^{v+1} - Q^v||_F^2 = 0, \tag{26}$$

which means that the limit point of sequence Q^v also constitutes a stationary point of problem (P4), sine regularization term is approaching to zero when Q^v approaching to the limit point. Thus, the limit point of sequence Q^v, which is generated by running *Algorithm 1*(P), must be a feasible solution to problem (P1).

Therefore, we can draw a conclusion that *Algorithm 1*(P) must converge to a feasible solution to problem (P1).

According to Theorem 2, we can come to a conclusion that *Algorithm 1*(P) always converges to a feasible solution to problem (P1) with guaranteed convergence. However, a possibly slower convergence rate is the price to pay for the guaranteed convergence, which is common to the regularization method and will be further demonstrated by numerical simulations in the next section.

4   Numerical Simulations

In this section, the proposed algorithm is intensively investigated via numerical simulations.

The simulation condition is assumed that there are $k = 3$ Alice-to-Bob wireless links, and the transmit power budget of all transmitters are set to be equal, i.e.,

$$P_i = P, \forall i \in \mathcal{K}.$$

The elements of the channel matrices $\mathbf{H}_{ij}, \forall i, j \in \mathcal{K}$ are all set to be i.i.d. ZMC-SCG random variables. And, the variances of these matrices' elements are further set to be

$$\sigma_{ij}^2 = 1, \text{if } i = j,$$
$$\sigma_{ij}^2 = 0.25, \text{other.}$$

The elements of the channel matrices $\mathbf{H}_{ie}, \forall i \in \mathcal{K}$ are also set to be i.i.d. ZMC-SCG random variable, and the variances of these matrices' elements are given as

$$\sigma_{ie}^2 = 0.25, \forall i \in \mathcal{K}.$$

Moreover, the element of the additive noise $\mathbf{n}_i, \forall i \in \mathcal{K}$ and $\mathbf{n}_e$ are all set to be i.i.d. ZMCSCG random variables with unit variance.

The convergence property of *Algorithm 1*(P) is presented in Fig. 2, and the simulation result is obtained by setting P = 1 and $N_t = N_r = N_e = 2$. This figure shows that *Algorithm 1*(P) converges quite quickly, e.g., in no more than 6 iterations, to a common solution under different τ. It is also shown that the convergence rate is slightly slower when τ becomes larger, which is the price to pay for the ensuring convergence as detailed in Theorem 2.

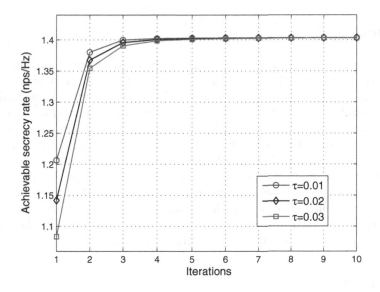

Fig. 2. The convergence property of *Algorithm 1*(P) under different τ.

The achievable secrecy rate achieved with *Algorithm 1*(P) is demonstrated in Fig. 3, which is achieved by setting $\tau = 0.01$ and $N_t = N_r = 2$. This figure shows that the achievable secrecy rate of the proposed MIMO IFC system increases with Alice's transmit power budget in a nonlinear way, and the performance is dramatically decreased when the power of Eve becomes stronger, i.e., when N_e becomes larger.

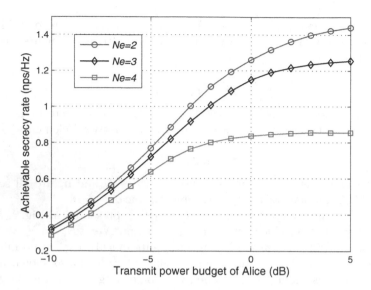

Fig. 3. The achievable secrecy rate versus Alice's transmit power budget P.

5 Conclusion

In this paper, we have studied the design problem of secure precoding for a k-user MIMO interference channel. By adopting the "maxmin" fairness criteria, the secure precoding problem is defined as an achievable secrecy rate maximization problem, which is nonconvex and non-smooth in nature. To tackle the inherent complexity, we recast the formulated problem into a DC programming problem by a series of equivalent mathematical transformations. Using the successive convex approximation method as a corner stone, a coordinated iterative precoding algorithm is developed by solving a sequence of convexified subproblems. In order to ensure the accuracy convergence of the proposed iterative algorithm, a regularization method based on the proximal point thought is also pursued. Numerical results further show that our algorithm can converge quickly to a feasible solution on the premise of ensuring convergence.

References

1. Razavi, S.M.: Beamformer design for MIMO interference broadcast channels with semidefinite programming. IEEE Trans. Signal Process. **66**(17), 4504–4515 (2018)
2. Jing, X., Mo, L., Liu, H., Zhang, C.: Linear space-time interference alignment for K-user MIMO interference channels. IEEE Access **6**, 3085–3095 (2018)
3. Shang, X., Poor, H.V.: Noisy-interference sum-rate capacity for vector Gaussian interference channels. IEEE Trans. Inf. Theory **59**(1), 132–153 (2013)
4. Larsson, E.G., Jorswieck, E.A.: Competition versus cooperation on the MISO interference channel. IEEE J. Sel. Areas Commun. **26**(7), 1059–1069 (2008)

5. Fan, Y., Wang, X., Liao, X.: On the secure degrees of freedom for two-user MIMO interference channel with a cooperative jammer. IEEE Trans. Commun. **67**(8), 5390–5402 (2019)
6. Siyari, P., Krunz, M., Nguyen, D.N.: Power games for secure communications in single-stream MIMO interference networks. IEEE Trans. Wireless Commun. **17**(9), 5759–5773 (2018)
7. Mukherjee, A., Fakoorian, S.A.A., Huang, J., Swindlehurst, A.L.: Principles of physical layer security in multiuser wireless networks: a survey. IEEE Commun. Surv. Tutor. **16**(3), 1550–1573 (2014)
8. Oggier, F., Hassibi, B.: The secrecy capacity of the MIMO wiretap channel. IEEE Trans. Inf. Theory **57**(8), 4961–4972 (2011)
9. Li, Q., Hong, M., Wai, H.-T., Liu, Y.-F., Ma, W.-K., Luo, Z.-Q.: Transmit solutions for MIMO wiretap channels using alternating optimization. IEEE J. Sel. Areas Commun. **31**(9), 2704–2717 (2013)
10. Zhang, Y., DallAnese, E., Giannakis, G.B.: Distributed optimal beamformers for cognitive radios robust to channel uncertainties. IEEE Trans. Signal Process. **60**(12), 6495–6508 (2012)
11. Alvarado, A., Scutari, G., Pang, J.-S.: A new decomposition method for multiuser DC-programming and its applications. IEEE Trans. Signal Process. **62**(11), 2984–2998 (2014)
12. Boyd, S., Vandenberghe, L.: Convex Optimization. Cambridge University Press, Cambridge (2004)
13. Zhang, X.: Matrix Analysis and Applications. Tsinghua University Press, Beijing (2004)
14. CVX Research, Inc. CVX: Matlab software for disciplined convex programming, version 2.0, April 2011. http://cvxr.com/cvx

Communication QoS, Reliability and Modeling

Wireless Channel Pattern Recognition Using k-Nearest Neighbor Algorithm for High-Speed Railway

Lei Xiong[1(✉)], Huayu Li[1], Zhengyu Zhang[1], Bo Ai[1], and Pei Tang[2]

[1] State Key Laboratory of Rail Traffic Control and Safety,
Beijing Jiaotong University, Beijing 100044, China
lxiong@bjtu.edu.cn

[2] China Railway Siyuan Survey and Design Group Co., Ltd., Wuhan 430063, Hubei, China

Abstract. Channel is important for the wireless communication system. The channel in high-speed railway is rapid time-variation and non-stationary. This papers discusses the channel characteristic in open space scenario, and defines 4 patterns. Furthermore a channel pattern recognition algorithm is proposed using k-nearest neighbor method. Simulation results show that the proposed method performs well with high accuracy and robust.

Keywords: Channel · Pattern recognition · k-nearest neighbor (kNN) · High-speed railway

1 Introduction

In recent years, the high-speed railway achieves good development, especially in China. By the end of 2018, China has the longest high speed railway network in the world over 29, 000 km, accounting for about two-thirds of the world's high-speed railway tracks in commercial service. Millions of passengers travel by high-speed railway every day, and the demand of high network capacity and reliable communication services has been growing rapidly. Thus, high-speed railway scenarios are the most important scenarios for wireless communication system, such as LTE and fifth generation (5G) communication systems, and dedicated wireless communication system, such as GSM-R and LTE-R [1–4].

Channel is of vital importance for a communication system. In high-speed railway, users have usually experienced that the throughput declines rapidly and the quality of transmission deteriorates seriously, which have become urgent problems to be solved. The reliable knowledge of the wireless channel characteristic is the foundation of the design and optimization of wireless communication system [5]. Due to the significance of this topic, channel characteristic in the high-speed railway have attracted more and more attention.

The wireless communication in high-speed railway has the unique channel characteristic, as shown below:

(1) Due to the large Doppler shift is caused by high speed moving, and the channel state is rapidly time-varying [6–8].

(2) Due to the switch of the propagation condition, the channel doesn't satisfy the stationary assumption any more, which means the channel parameters vary with time, thus it cannot improve estimation accuracy of channel parameter with time average [9, 10].

(3) The moving direction and velocity of the train don't change rapidly, thus the wireless channel has obvious pattern characteristic, and can be predicted in a certain extent.

According to the characteristic mentioned above, the channel pattern recognition method based on the k-nearest neighbor (kNN) algorithm is proposed in the paper for the open space scenario. By the channel pattern recognition, we can make the channel prediction in further.

The remainder of the paper is organized as follows. Section 2 introduces the 3GPP high speed train (HST) channel model and discuss the patterns of Doppler shift. Section 3 discusses the kNN algorithm for channel patterns recognition. The simulation results are shown in Sect. 4. Finally, we draw some conclusions in Sect. 5.

2 Wireless Channel in High-Speed Railway

For the high-speed railway, 3GPP RAN4 have defined 4 scenarios, including scenario 1 (open space SFN), scenario 2 (tunnel), scenario 3 (relay in open space) and scenario 4 (traditional public network scenario), shown as Table 1 [11, 12].

Table 1. Summary of high-speed railway scenarios.

Scenarios	Cell diameter	Hop
1: Open space SFN	2 km−3 km	1 hop
2d: Tunnel SFN	1 km	1 hop
2e: Tunnel multi-antenna	–	1 hop
2f: Tunnel SFN CPE	2 km	1 hop
2g: Tunnel: Leaky cable to UE	–	1 hop
4: Public network	3 km	1 hop
2a: Tunnel SFN- RP; RP –UE with leaky cable	6 km	2 hops
2b: Tunnel: RRH with different id- RP; RP –UE with leaky cable	3 km	2 hops
2c: Leaky cable in tunnel- RP; RP –UE with leaky cable	1.5 km	2 hops
3: Open space eNB- RP; RP –UE with leaky cable	5 km	2 hops

Many channel models have been proposed for each scenario. For example, single-tap and two-tap HST channel model has been approved by 3GPP for open space scenario, and Ricean channel model for the tunnel with leaky cable scenario. In this paper, we focus on the open space scenario. The single-tap HST channel model is defined as below [13].

Due to the high speed moving of the train, the Doppler shift has severely impact on the performance of communication system. Thus, only the Doppler shift of the signal from the nearest Remote Radio Head (RRH) is considered in the single-tap channel model. The Doppler shift is calculated as:

$$f_d(t) = f\frac{v}{c}\cos\theta(t) \tag{1}$$

where f is carrier frequency, v is the velocity of the train, c is light speed, θ is the angle between the LoS path and moving direction, and

$$\cos(\theta(t)) = \begin{cases} \frac{0.5D_s - vt}{\sqrt{D_{min}^2 + (0.5Ds - vt)^2}}, 0 < t \le \frac{D_s}{v} \\ \frac{-1.5D_s + vt}{\sqrt{D_{min}^2 + (-1.5D_s + vt)^2}}, \frac{D_s}{v} < t \le \frac{2D_s}{v} \\ \cos\theta(t \bmod (\frac{2D_s}{v})), t > \frac{2D_s}{v} \end{cases} \tag{2}$$

where D_s is the distance between two neighbor RRHs, D_{min} is RRH railway track distance, shown as Fig. 1.

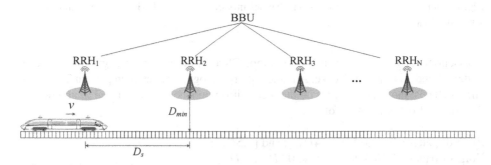

Fig. 1. Single-tap HST channel model

As shown in the Fig. 2, there are 4 variation patterns of the Doppler shift. In the pattern 1, the Doppler shift keeps almost constant positive value; In the pattern 2, the Doppler shift hops from negative value to positive value (the change rate of Doppler shift up to 2000 Hz/s); In the pattern 3, the Doppler shift keeps almost constant negative value; In the pattern 4, the Doppler shift hops from negative value to positive value.

The patterns are very important in the channel parameters estimation. For example, in the pattern 1 and 3, the receiver can take the time average to reduce measurement error of Doppler shift, but in the pattern 2 and 4, it doesn't work. Thus, the pattern recognition

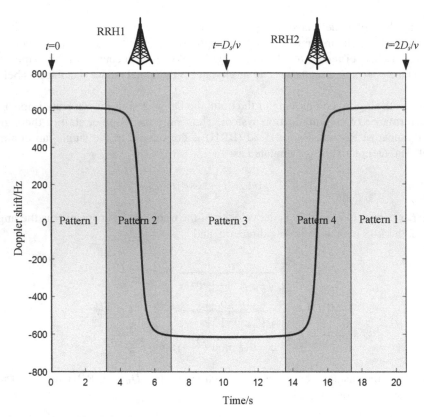

Fig. 2. Doppler shift of single-tap HST channel model ($f = 1890$ MHz, $v = 350$ km/h, $D_s = 1000$ m, $D_{min} = 30$ m)

is essential for the Doppler shift estimation. Clearly, the pattern recognition between pattern 1 and 3 is a piece of cake. And the pattern recognition between pattern 2 and 4 is similar. Thus, the paper focuses on the recognition between pattern 1 and 2, and define the zones of pattern 1–4 as follow:

Zone of pattern 1: $[0, 0.5D_s - 4D_{min})$ and $[1.5D_s + 4D_{min}, 2.0D_s]$
Zone of pattern 2: $[0.5D_s - 4D_{min}, 0.5D_s + 4D_{min})$
Zone of pattern 3: $[0.5D_s + 4D_{min}, 1.5D_s - 4D_{min})$
Zone of pattern 4: $[1.5D_s - 4D_{min}, 1.5D_s + 4D_{min})$

3   Pattern Recognition Based on KNN Algorithm

Pattern recognition is an important topic and widely used in many areas such as speech and character recognition, medical diagnosis, remote sensing, and etc. KNN is one of the most popular classification algorithms in pattern recognition, machine learning, and data mining, which assume that data which are close together based upon some metrics, such as Euclidean distance, more likely belong to the same category. Thus KNN searches for the group of K objects in the closest training data (similar) to objects in new data or data testing [14–16].

(1) Training data set

In the KNN algorithm, suppose that a training data set $\{(\bar{X}_i, p_i)\}$ with M elements, where each element consists of an object vector $\bar{X}_i$ with its classification label p_i, where $p_i = -1$ and $+1$ corresponding to the pattern 1 and pattern 2.

The training data set is generated as Eqs. (1) and (2). The parameter f is known to the receiver, and D_s only changes the cycle of the Doppler shift instead of the pattern recognition. And the v and D_{min} will be set according to the rail, shown as Table 2. The Each object vector $\bar{X}_i$ consist of L continuously Doppler shift measurement values with measurement interval Δt.

Table 2. The parameters of the training set.

Parameter	Value
f(MHz)	1890
v(km/h)	40, 60, 80, 100, 120, 160, 200, 250, 300, 350
D_{min}(m)	20, 30, 40, 50
D_s(m)	1000
Δt (ms)	10

(2) The distance between test vector and training vector

We also have a test set $\{(\bar{Y}_j, p'_j)\}$, $j = 1 \ldots N$ of N test vector $\bar{Y}_j$ with unknown pattern label p'_j. Our goal is to calculate the Euclidean distance between the test vector $\bar{Y}_j$ and the training vector $\bar{X}_i$.

Generally the Euclidean distance formula is used to define the distance between the training data and testing data. However, the test vector may be shorter than the training vector, the modified Euclidean distance with sliding is applied,

$$d(\bar{X}_i, \bar{Y}_j) = \min_{\tau} \sqrt{\sum_{n=1}^{L} (x_{i,n+\tau} - y_{j,n})^2} \tag{3}$$

where $x_{i,n}$ and $y_{j,n}$ are the elements of $\bar{X}_i$ and $\bar{Y}_j$.

(3) **Pattern recognition**

Find the K closest vectors of the training set, namely $\bar{X}'_i$, and adopt the distance-weighted criterion

$$C_j = \sum_K \frac{1}{d\left(\bar{X}'_i, \bar{Y}_j\right)} p_i \qquad (4)$$

Thus, the label p'_j of the test vector $\bar{Y}_j$ is determined by

$$p'_j = \begin{cases} 1 & if\ C_j \geq 0 \\ -1 & if\ C_j < 0 \end{cases} \qquad (5)$$

Now, we have achieved the pattern recognition for the test vector.

4 Simulation Results

To evaluate the performance of proposed pattern recognition algorithm, we conduct several experiments with the simulation parameters shown in Table 3. And we assume the error of Doppler shift measurement is the Gaussian distribution with zero mean and standard deviation σ_{fd}.

Table 3. Simulation parameter.

Parameter	Value
Frequency f (MHz)	1890
v (km/h)	350
Number of the testing data N	10000
Doppler Measurement interval Δt (ms)	10
K	3, 4, 5, 6
σ_{fd}(Hz)	0, 10, 20, 40, 70, 100
L	20, 30, 40, 50, 70
D_{min}(s)	30, 60, 70, 80, 90, 100

The recognition error rate with K is shown as Fig. 3. We can see the recognition error rate varies with the K. When $K = 3$ and 4, the recognition error rate of pattern 1 is higher, whereas the recognition error rate of pattern 2 is higher when $K = 5$ and 6. Furthermore, there is a smaller gap between the recognition error rate of pattern 1 and pattern 2 when $K = 3$. Thus, the K is set to be 3 in the following simulation.

The recognition error rate with various σ_{fd} is shown as Fig. 4. We can see the recognition error rate is approximated to 0 when σ_{fd} is no more than 40 Hz, and increases with σ_{fd}, in which the recognition error rate of pattern 1 increases faster than pattern 2.

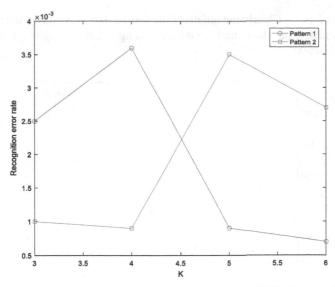

Fig. 3. The recognition error rate with K ($L = 50$, $\sigma_{fd} = 70$ Hz, $D_{min} = 30$ m).

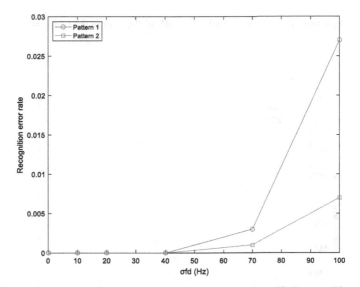

Fig. 4. The recognition error rate with various σ_{fd} ($L = 50$, $D_{min} = 30$ m).

For example, when $\sigma_{fd} = 70$ Hz the recognition error rate of pattern 1 is 0.25%, but the recognition error rate of pattern 2 is only 0.1%. Since the σ_{fd} of LTE system is below 40 Hz in practice, the presented algorithm will work very well.

As shown in Fig. 5, the recognition error rate is close to zero when L is greater than 50. And the recognition error rate increase with the decease of the L. For example the recognition error rate of pattern 1 is 8.3, and the recognition error rate of pattern 2 is

0.1% when the L is 30. Clearly the length of the testing data L is higher, the recognition error rate is smaller, but the complex and processing delay are higher. Thus, the L is recommended as 50.

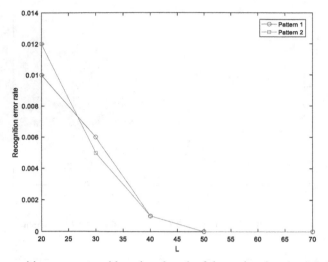

Fig. 5. The recognition error rate with various length of the testing data ($\sigma_{fd} = 40$ Hz, $D_{min} = 30$ m).

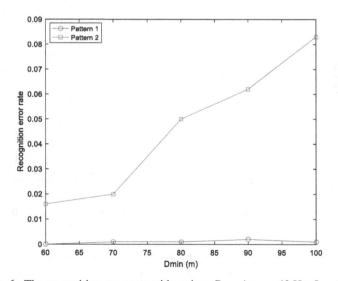

Fig. 6. The recognition error rate with various D_{min} ($\sigma_{fd} = 40$ Hz, $L = 50$).

In the rail, the D_{min} is usually 20–50 m, and the training set is generated in this range. However, the D_{min} may be greater than 50 m in some case. The recognition error rate is shown as Fig. 6 for such a case. It can be seen, the recognition error rate of pattern 1 increase faster than that of pattern 1. For example, when $D_{min} = 100$ m, the recognition error rate of pattern 1 is 0.3%, but the recognition error rate of pattern 2 is 8.3%. It shown the algorithm requires further optimization for the high D_{min}.

5 Conclusion

The channel pattern recognition is crucial to the communication system. In the paper, we discuss the channel pattern in the open space scenario, and propose a channel pattern recognition method based on the KNN algorithm for channel pattern recognition. The simulation results show the pattern recognition method has high accuracy and robustness, can satisfy the demand of the receiver in high speed rail.

Acknowledgments. This work was supported the Fundamental Research Funds for the Central Universities (2018JBM079).

References

1. Zhou, Y., Pan, Z., Hu, J., Shi, J., Mo, X.: Broadband wireless communications on high speed trains. In: Proceedings of the WOCC, pp. 1–6 (2011)
2. Chen, C., Li, C.: Review of high speed rail communication systems. Comput. Technol. Appl. **46**, 24–26 (2010)
3. Wang, C.-X., et al.: Cellular architecture and key technologies for 5G wireless communication networks. IEEE Commun. Mag. **52**(2), 122–130 (2014)
4. Gonzalez-Plaza, A., et al.: 5G communications in high speed and metropolitan railways. In: 11th European Conference on Antennas and Propagation (EUCAP 2017), pp. 658–660. IEEE, Paris (2017)
5. Guan, K., et al.: Towards realistic high-speed train channels at 5G millimeter-wave band—Part I: paradigm, significance analysis, and scenario reconstruction. IEEE Trans. Veh. Technol. **67**(10), 9112–9128 (2018)
6. Zhou, Y., Wang, J., Sawahashi, M.: Downlink transmission of broadband OFCDM systems Part II: effect of doppler shift. IEEE Trans. Commun. **54**(6), 1097–1108 (2006)
7. Hui, B., et al.: Efficient Doppler mitigation for high-speed railway communications. In: 18th International Conference on Advanced Communication Technology (ICACT 2016), pp. 634–638. IEEE, Paris (2016)
8. Wang, S., et al.: Doppler shift and coherence time of 5G vehicular channels at 3.5 GHz. In 2018 IEEE International Symposium on Antennas and Propagation & USNC/URSI National Radio Science Meeting (AP-S 2018), pp. 2005–2006. IEEE, Boston (2018)
9. Ghazal, A., et al.: A generic non-stationary MIMO channel model for different high-speed train scenarios. In: Symposium on Wireless Communications Systems of the International Conference on Communications in China (ICCC 2015), pp. 1–3. IEEE/CIC, Shenzhen (2015)
10. Wang, C.-X., Ghazal, A., Ai, B., Liu, Y., Fan, P.: Channel measurements and models for high-speed train communication systems: a survey. IEEE Commun. Surv. Tutor. **18**(2), 974–987 (2016)
11. Huawei, HiSilicon: UE demodulation performance evaluation under the new scenarios (R4-152601), pp. 1–3. 3GPP, Fukuoka, Japan (2015)

12. Huawei, HiSilicon: Scenario Summary (R4-153904). pp. 1–4. 3GPP, Fukuoka, Japan (2015)
13. Samsung: Discussion on High speed train scenarios (R4-152277). pp. 1–2. 3GPP, Rio de Janeiro, Brazil (2015)
14. Zhang, S.: Nearest neighbor selection for iteratively KNN imputation. J. Syst. Softw. **85**(11), 2541–2552 (2012)
15. Zhang, S., Li, X., Zong, M., Zhu, X., Wang, R.: Efficient kNN classification with different numbers of nearest neighbors. IEEE Trans. Neural Netw. Learn. Syst. **29**(5), 1774–1885 (2018)
16. Cui, L., Zhu, H., Zhang, L., Luan, R.: Improved k nearest neighbors transductive confidence machine for pattern recognition. In: International Conference on Computer Design and Applications (ICCDA 2010), pp. 172–175. IEEE, Qinhuangdao (2010)

Price-Based Power Control in NOMA Based Cognitive Radio Networks Using Stackelberg Game

Zhengqiang Wang[1](✉), Hongjia Zhang[1], Zifu Fan[2], Xiaoyu Wan[2], and Xiaoxia Yang[1]

[1] School of Communication and Information Engineering, Chongqing University of Posts and Telecommunications, Chongqing, People's Republic of China
wangzq@cqupt.edu.cn
[2] Next Generation Networks, Chongqing University of Posts and Telecommunications, Chongqing, People's Republic of China

Abstract. This paper studies the price-based power control strategies for non-orthogonal multiple access (NOMA) based cognitive radio networks. The primary user (PU) profits from the secondary users (SUs) by pricing the interference power made by them. Then, SUs cooperate to maximize their total revenue at the base station (BS) with successive interference cancellation (SIC) while considering their payoff to the primary user. The pricing and power control strategies between the PU and SUs are modeled as a Stackelberg game. The closed-form expression of the optimal price for the non-uniform pricing scheme is given. The computational complexity of the proposed uniform-pricing algorithm is only linear with respect to the number of SNs. Simulation results are presented to verify the effectiveness of our proposed pricing algorithm.

Keywords: Non-orthogonal multiple access · Cognitive radio network · Successive interference cancellation · Stackelberg game

1 Introduction

With the rapid development of wireless communications and the growing shortage of spectrum resources, cognitive radio has been proposed to improve spectrum and energy efficiency by sharing the spectrum of primary users (PUs) with secondary users (SUs) in future network [1–3]. Besides, non-orthogonal multiple access (NOMA) technology is another promising technique to improve spectrum efficiency and support the great traffic volume in the fifth generation (5G) Network [4–6]. In the underlay based CR network, SUs can access the spectrum

This work was partially supported by the National Natural Science Foundation of P. R. China (No. 61701064), Basic Research and Frontier Exploration Project of Chongqing (cstc2019jcyj-msxmX0264) and the China Scholarship Council (file No. 201808500024).

owned by PUs if the interference power (IP) from the SUs to the PU's receiver under interference temperature power (ITP) limit. Furthermore, the NOMA technique can be used in underly CR networks to improve the system performance of SUs because the interference power from weak SU can be canceled at the based station.

There are many studies focus on CR-NOMA system [7–11]. In [7], the authors proposed cooperative relaying strategies to address inter-network and intra-network interference in cognitive NOMA system. Liu *et al.* in [8] studied the large-scale underlay CR-NOMA system with two different power constraints to characterize the performance. In [9], Liang *et al.* studied the spectrum sharing in an underlay CR-NOMA system, and presented a non-transferable utility (NTU) coalition formation game between the cognitive users (CUs) and the PU. Moreover, some studies are also concerned with resource allocation of underlay CR-NOMA system [10,11]. For instance, Song *et al.* in [10] considered NOMA-based cognitive radio network with SWIPT, joint power allocation and sensing time optimizing algorithm based on dichotomy method is proposed to maximize the system throughput. Considering a cognitive multiple-input single-output NOMA with SWIPT, Mao *et al.* in [11] proposed a penalty function-based algorithm to minimize system power consumption.

Price-based power control of CR networks was investigated in [12–17]. By using the non-cooperative game with pricing scheme, the authors in [12] proposed a payment-based power control scheme to ensure the fairness of power control among SUs in CR networks. Considering the system efficiency and user-fairness issues, Yang *et al.* in [13] investigated cooperative Nash bargaining power-control game (NBPCG) model based on distributed power control and gave a signal-to-interference-plus-noise ratio (SINR)-based utility function. In [14], Yu *et al.* studied the pricing-based power control problems in CR networks, and they considered the competition as a non-cooperative game between SUs, and model the pricing problem as a non-convex optimization problem. Using a Stackelberg game to model the competitive behavior in [15], BS can maximize its revenue by pricing and SUs can profit by controlling its transmit power. In order to gain more revenue for a general case based CR networks system model compared with [15], the authors in [16] proposed a novel algorithm to find the optimal price for the PU and SUs. In [17], considering the quality of service (QoS) of the SUs, the authors proposed an optimal pricing algorithm for the interaction between the PU and the SUs. Wang *et al.* in [18] proposed a novel price-based power allocation algorithm based on the Stackelberg game to improve the revenue of BS and the sum rate of the users. In [19], the authors proposed a branch and bound based price-based power control algorithm to solve the non-convex revenue maximization problem for CR networks.

In this paper, we model the pricing strategy between PU and SUs as a Stackelberg game under the ITP model. First, PU plays a leader who prices the SUs to control the interference power made by SUs under the ITP limit. Then, the PU will select a suitable price to gain higher revenue from SUs. Simultaneously, SUs will choose an optimal power to maximize their total revenue at BS. Finally, we use Stackelberg game with non-uniform pricing (N-UP) scheme and uniform pricing (UP) scheme to model the strategy between them.

The rest of this paper is organized as follows. In Sect. 2, we present the system model for NOMA system based cognitive radio networks. Section 3 introduces the optimal price for two pricing schemes, and a distributed algorithm is proposed for UP scheme. In Sect. 4, the performance of the proposed two pricing schemes are evaluated by simulations. Finally, conclusions are stated in Sect. 5.

2   System Model

Considering the NOMA based CR networks comprised of one base station (BS), n SUs and one PU as shown in Fig. 1. The SUs transmit the signal to BS with NOMA technology and SIC is employed at BS. The channel coefficient of SU i to BS and PU link is denoted by $h_i(i = 1, \ldots, n)$ and $h_{i0}(i = 1, \ldots, n)$, respectively. At first, the PU charges each SU with a proportional price according to its interference power $p_i(i = 1, \ldots, n)$, and p_i needs satisfy $\sum_{i=1}^{n} h_{j0}p_i \leq T$, where T is the maximal interference power of PU. Then, SUs will pay PU to access the spectrum, and they will form a group to maximize the total utility.

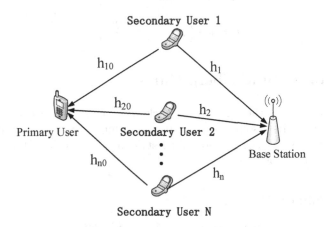

Fig. 1. System model.

We model the strategy between SUs and PU as a Stackelberg game. PU plays the leader that chooses a price for each SU to maximize its total revenue under ITP limit. Then, SUs can be viewed as the followers to obtain the best power for optimal revenue while considering their payoff to PU. Let u denotes the PU's revenue, and the optimization problem of PU can be written as

$$\text{maximize } u\left(c_1, \cdots, c_n\right) = \sum_{i=1}^{n} c_i h_{i0} p_i$$

$$\text{subject to } p_i \geq 0, \quad \sum_{j=1}^{n} h_{j0} p_j \leq T, \tag{1}$$

where p_i is interference power of the i-th SU under the given price of c_i, and T denotes the maximal interference power at PU.

Let $\tilde{u}$ denotes the utility of the ith SU, and it contains two parts: wR is the income from the total rate achieved at BS when SUs transmit the given power $p_i (i = 1, \ldots, n)$, and $\sum_{i=1}^{n} c_i h_{i0} p_i$ is the payment to the PU. So the revenue optimization problem of ith SU can be expressed as

$$\text{maximize } \tilde{u}\left(p_1, \cdots, p_n\right) = wR - \sum_{i=1}^{n} c_i h_{i0} p_i$$

$$\text{subject to } 0 \leq p_i \leq p_i^{max}, \tag{2}$$

where w is the preference of SUs for the gain of unit rate. c_i is the price of ith user per unit of interference power. Let the SINR of PU to BS link is n_0, thus the sum rate of SUs R can be written as:

$$R = \log\left(1 + \frac{\sum_{i}^{n} h_i p_i}{n_0}\right). \tag{3}$$

3   Solution to Stackelberg Game

In this section, we give the solution to Stackelberg game under the N-UP scheme and UP scheme. First, some lemmas are introduced to solve the above game. And the lemmas show the relationship between p_i and $c_i (i = 1, \ldots, n)$ for the lower-level problem for SUs.

3.1   Non-uniform Pricing

Lemma 1. *Given a fixed price $c_i(i = 1, \ldots, n)$, let $P = (p_1, \ldots, p_n)$ be the optimal transmit power of problem (2). For all $i \in \{1, \cdots, n\}$, there exists a set of Lagrange multiplier $\lambda_1, \cdots, \lambda_n$, and $\mu_1, \cdots, \mu_n$, which satisfy the following equations:*

$$\frac{wh_i}{n_0 + \sum_{i=1}^{n} h_i p_i} - c_i h_{i0} + \mu_i - \lambda_i = 0,$$

$$\mu_i p_i = 0,$$

$$\lambda_i(p_i^{max} - p_i) = 0,$$

$$\lambda_i \geq 0, \mu_i \geq 0, (i = 1, \ldots, n). \tag{4}$$

Proof: Let $L(p, \lambda, \mu) = w\log\left(1 + \frac{\sum_i^n h_i p_i}{n_0}\right) - \sum_{i=1}^n c_i h_{i0} p_i + \sum_{i=1}^n \mu_i p_i + \sum_{i=1}^n \lambda_i(p_i^{max} - p_i)$, then by using Karush-Kuhn-Tucker (KKT) conditions [20], we can obtain

$$\frac{\partial L(p, \lambda, \mu)}{\partial p_i} = 0,$$

$$\mu_i p_i = 0, \tag{5}$$

$$\lambda_i(p_i^{max} - p_i) = 0,$$

$$\lambda_i \geq 0, \mu_i \geq 0, (i = 1, \ldots, n).$$

Then, substituting $L(p, \lambda, \mu)$ into the first equation of (5), the proof of the Lemma 1 is completed.

Next, multiplying p_i in the first equations of (4), we can get

$$\frac{wh_i p_i}{n_0 + \sum_{i=1}^n h_i p_i} - c_i h_{i0} p_i + \mu_i p_i - \lambda_i p_i$$

$$= \frac{wh_i p_i}{n_0 + \sum_{i=1}^n h_i p_i} - c_i h_{i0} p_i - \lambda_i p_i^{max} = 0 \tag{6}$$

so the revenue of PU from SU i can be written as:

$$c_i h_{i0} p_i = \frac{wh_i p_i}{n_0 + \sum_{i=1}^n h_i p_i} - \lambda_i p_i^{max}, \tag{7}$$

However, PU wants to choose a price $c_i (i = 1, \cdots, n)$ to maximize the total revenue u, that means $\lambda_i = 0$, $(i = 1, \cdots, n)$. Then, put (7) to (4), we can get following lemma:

Lemma 2. *When PU gets the maximal utility with the optimal price, the optimal transmit power for each SU can be obtained by solving the following problem:*

$$\text{maximize} \quad u(p_1, \cdots, p_n) = \sum_{i=1}^n c_i h_{i0} p_i = \frac{w\sum_{i=1}^n h_i p_i}{n_0 + \sum_{i=1}^n h_i p_i} \tag{8}$$

$$\text{subject to} \quad 0 \leq p_i \leq p_i^{max}, \quad \sum_{j=1}^n h_{j0} p_j \leq T.$$

Because (8) is increased with $\sum\limits_{i=1}^{n} h_i p_i$, it can be equivalent to the following optimization problem:

$$\text{maximize } \bar{u}(p_1, \cdots, p_n) = \sum_{i=1}^{n} h_i p_i$$
$$\text{subject to } 0 \le p_i \le p_i^{max}, \ \sum_{j=1}^{n} h_{j0} p_j \le T. \tag{9}$$

Theorem 1. *Sorting the index number of SUs in descending order by h_i/h_{i0}, the optimal transmit power p_i of the ith SU is given by:*

$$p_i = \begin{cases} p_i^{max}, \ if \ \sum\limits_{j=1}^{i} h_{j0} p_j^{max} \le T, \\ T - \sum\limits_{j=1}^{i-1} h_{i0} p_i^{max}, \ if \ \sum\limits_{j=1}^{i-1} h_{j0} p_j < T \le \sum\limits_{j=1}^{i} h_{j0} p_j, \\ 0, \ else. \end{cases} \tag{10}$$

Proof: We prove the theorem with different case of active constraint. First, we consider the case of the ITP constraint is satisfied under the maximum transmit power. That means $\sum\limits_{i=1}^{n} h_{i0} p_i^{max} \le T$, then the problem (9) is equal to maximize the linear combination of each SU's transmit power with the weighting factor h_i under the power constraint of p_i^{max}. Since the object function is increasing with p_i, then the optimal power is $p_i = p_i^{max}$. Next, we consider the case that $\sum\limits_{i=1}^{n} h_{i0} p_i^{max} > T$ is valid. Since $\bar{u}$ increases with p_i, we have $\sum\limits_{i=1}^{n} h_{i0} \tilde{p}_i = T$ at the optimal power $\tilde{p} = (\tilde{p}_1, \ldots, \tilde{p}_n)$. It means the ITL constraint is an active constraint. Moreover, as the object function is a linear function, the optimal power must exist at the extreme point of the constraint. So the optimal power must have an expression as (10). Furthermore, if the index number of two SU is not sorted in descending order by h_i/h_{i0}, we can change their power to optimize the objection function. From the above discussion, we have completed the proof of Theorem 1.

From Theorem 1 and the relationship between the optimal price and power in Lemma 1, we give the optimal price for PU as follows:

Theorem 2. *Let p_i be the expression as (10), then the optimal price c_i that PU charge for the ith SU can be written as*

$$c_i = \frac{w h_i}{h_{i0} \left(n_0 + \sum\limits_{j=1}^{n} h_j p_j \right)}. \tag{11}$$

From Theorems 1 and 2, the SU has a better effective channel gain h_i/h_{i0}, it will have more opportunities to transmit. The optimal price for each SU is proportional to $\frac{h_i}{h_{i0}}$, which means the SU who has a better effective channel gain $\frac{h_i}{h_{i0}}$ will pay a higher price than others. Since PU charges a better SU with a higher price, the profit of PU will be higher. If the interference power is an active constraint, then the interference power to the PU will be equal to the ITP at the optimal price. The utility of PU is bounded by the effective channel gain of SU. If the effective channel gain is larger, PU will get more benefit. This is because the SU with the larger effective channel gain will prefer to pay the PU to access the spectrum. Moreover, if the $p_i^{max} \geq T/h_{i0}$, then the optimal price of the PU just allowed one SU who have the largest $\frac{h_i}{h_{i0}}$ to transmit with the power T/h_{i0}.

Since the optimal prices is expressed as a closed-form, PU can set them if it has all the channel information of the CR networks. Assuming that the user is indexed by the descending order of h_i/h_{i0}, PU can get the optimal price even if it doesn't know the channel information between the SUs and the BS by following distributed algorithm:

(1) PU chooses a uniform price c_0 large enough for all SU which can admit only one SU and the interference power is less than T.

(2) While the interference power is less than T, PU decreases the price c_0 until the new SU is admit or the interference power is equal to T, set the pricing for the $1 - th$ SU by $c_1 = c_0$. If the former admit user i decreases its power, PU reduces the maximal price c_i to let the power of user i to be p_i^{max}

(3) Repeated (2) for the new SU until interference power is equal to T or all the SUs are admitted to transmit with their maximum power.

The proposed algorithm above is easy to implement in a distributed way. Moreover, the algorithm can find the optimal price for each SU as described by the following Lemma.

Lemma 3. *The distributed algorithm will be converged to the optimal price.*

Proof: Without of loss generality, we index the number of SUs such that $h_1/h_{10} > h_2/h_{20} > \ldots > h_n/h_{n0}$. From the distributed algorithm, all SUs will sequentially access the spectrum of PU with a uniform price c_0. As the price c_0 decreases, the SUs will admit in the spectrum in ascending order. PU decreases c_0 until ITL will meet with equal. Then, PU increases c_i for those admitted users if the power of those users are unchanged. We only need to prove that the utility of PU is decreasing function of the price c_i when the power used by the $i - th$ SU is less than its maximal power. Case one: $\sum_i^n h_{i0}p_i^{max} > T$. First, all SUs decrease to such that the interference power at the primary user is T. Set the price large enough for those not admission user and not admit them. The PU increases the price c_i for the user i if the power of user i remains unchanged. Case two: $\sum_i^n h_{i0}p_i^{max} \leq T$. Then all the users are admitted to access the spectrum of the PU, the price c_i updates as the case one.

Since the N-UP needs PU to measure each SUs interference power, this will be complex at the PU's receiver. Then we consider the UP case that the PU charges the total interference power from SUs by using the same price.

3.2 Uniform Pricing

In this section, PU sets a uniform interference power price $c = c_i, (i = 1, \cdots, n)$ for SUs. Thus, the optimal transmit power control strategy for SUs is denoted as:

$$\text{maximize } \tilde{u}(p_1, \cdots, p_n) = w\log\left(1 + \frac{\sum_i^n h_i p_i}{n_0}\right) - c\sum_{i=1}^n h_{i0} p_i \tag{12}$$

$$\text{subject to } 0 \le p_i \le p_i^{max}.$$

And the PUs revenue optimization problem is:

$$\text{maximize } u(c) = c\sum_{i=1}^n h_{i0} p_i$$

$$\text{subject to } \sum_{i=1}^n h_{i0} p_i \le T. \tag{13}$$

Theorem 3. *Assuming that the ratio of channel coefficient between $SUs - BS$ link and $SUs - PU$ link denotes as $h_i/h_{i0}, (i = 1, \cdots, n)$ and the ratio order is decreasing as $h_1/h_{10} > h_2/h_{20} > \ldots > h_n/h_{n0}$. Given a uniform price c, the optimal transmit power from (12) can be expressed as:*

$$p_i = \max\left\{\min\{p_i^{max}, w/(ch_{i0}) - \sum_{j=1}^{i-1} h_j p_j^{max}/h_i - n_0/h_i\}, 0\right\}. \tag{14}$$

Before proving Theorem 3, we first give Lemma 4 to show the optimal power for each SU with uniform price c.

Lemma 4: *Assuming that $h_1/h_{10} > h_2/h_{20} > \ldots > h_n/h_{n0}$ and let $p^* = (p_1^*, \ldots, p_n^*)$ be the optimal solution of (13) for a fixed price $c > 0$. If $p_i^* < p_i^{max}$, then $p_j^* = 0$ $(j = i + 1, \ldots, n)$.*

Proof: We prove it by using the contradiction method. Let $p^* = (p_1^*, \ldots, p_n^*)$ be the optimal solution of (13). If $p_i^* < p_i^{max}$, there exists $j > i$ such that $p_j^* > 0$. And the following must be satisfied.

$$\frac{\partial u}{\partial p_i}(p_1, \ldots, p_n)|_{p_i=p_i^*} = \frac{wh_i}{n_0 + \sum_{i=1}^n h_i p_i^*} - ch_{i0} = 0 \tag{15}$$

and

$$\frac{\partial u}{\partial p_j}(p_1, \ldots, p_n)|_{p_j=p_j^*} = \frac{wh_j}{n_0 + \sum_{i=1}^n h_i p_i^*} - ch_{j0} \ge 0. \tag{16}$$

From (15), $\frac{1}{n_0 + \sum_{i=1}^n h_i p_i^*} = \frac{ch_{i0}}{wh_i}$ is obtained, then substituting it into (16), we get

$$\frac{ch_{i0}h_j}{h_i} - ch_{j0} \ge 0,$$

that means $\frac{h_i}{h_{i0}} \le \frac{h_j}{h_{j0}}$.

We can see that the above process contradicts the fact that $\frac{h_i}{h_{i0}} > \frac{h_j}{h_{j0}} \, (j > i)$. Thus, the proof is completed.

Lemma 4 shows that for the optimal solution to (13), if $\frac{h_i}{h_{i0}} > \frac{h_j}{h_{j0}}$, the user j can't transmit when user i transmit power is less than its maximum power.

Let $p^* = (p_1^*, \ldots, p_n^*)$ be the optimal solution of (13). Next, we prove Theorem 3 by considering different value of c.

Let $\overrightarrow{0} = (0, \ldots, 0)$, and $\overrightarrow{p_i^{max}} = (p_1^{max}, \ldots, p_i^{max}, \ldots, 0)$, that means the elements of $\overrightarrow{p_i^{max}}$ is zero while $j \geq i$,

Case 1: $c \geq \frac{wh_1}{n_0 h_{10}}$, $\frac{\partial u}{\partial p_i}(p_1, \ldots, p_n) = \frac{wh_i}{n_0 + \sum_{i=1}^{n} h_i p_i} - ch_{i0} \leq 0$, so the optimal power is $p^* = (p_1^*, \ldots, p_n^*) = (0, \ldots, 0)$.

Case 2: $\frac{wh_1}{(n_0 + h_1 p_1^{max})h_{10}} \leq c < \frac{wh_1}{n_0 h_{10}}$,

$$\frac{\partial u}{\partial p_1}(p_1, \ldots, p_n)\Big|_{p=\overrightarrow{0}} = \frac{wh_1}{n_0} - ch_{10} > 0, \tag{17}$$

$$\frac{\partial u}{\partial p_1}(p_1, \ldots, p_n)\Big|_{p=\overrightarrow{p_1^{max}}} = \frac{wh_1}{n_0 + h_1 p_1^{max}} - ch_{10} \leq 0, \tag{18}$$

From (17), (18) and Lemma 4, we know when $\frac{wh_1}{(n_0 h_{10} + h_1 p_1^{max})} \leq c < \frac{wh_1}{n_0 h_{10}}$, only p_1 is not zero. From

$$\frac{\partial u}{\partial p_1}(p_1, \ldots, p_n)\Big|_{(p_1, 0, \ldots, 0)} = \frac{wh_i}{n_0 + h_1 p_1} - ch_{i0} = 0, \tag{19}$$

then p_1 is obtained as follows:

$$p_1 = \frac{w}{ch_{10}} - \frac{n_0}{h_{10}}, \tag{20}$$

So if $c \in \left(\frac{wh_1}{(n_0 + h_1 p_1^{max})h_{10}}, \frac{wh_1}{n_0 h_{10}} \right)$, the optimal solution is

$$p_1^* = \frac{1}{h_1}\left(\frac{wh_1}{ch_{10}} - n_0 \right) = \frac{w}{ch_{10}} - \frac{n_0}{h_{10}}, p_i^* = 0 \, (i = 2, \ldots, n).$$

Case 3: $\frac{wh_2}{h_{20}(n_0 + h_1 p_1^{max})} \leq c \leq \frac{wh_1}{(n_0 + h_1 p_1^{max})h_{10}}$

$$\frac{\partial u}{\partial p_1}(p_1, \ldots, p_n)\Big|_{p=\overrightarrow{p_1^{max}}} = \frac{wh_1}{n_0 + h_1 p_1^{max}} - ch_{10} \geq 0, \tag{21}$$

$$\frac{\partial u}{\partial p_2}(p_1, \ldots, p_n)\Big|_{p=\overrightarrow{p_1^{max}}} = \frac{wh_2}{n_0 + h_1 p_1^{max}} - ch_{20} \leq 0, \tag{22}$$

From (21), (22) and Lemma 4, the optimal solution is

$$p_1^* = p_1^{max}, p_i^* = 0 \, (i = 2, \ldots, n),$$

when $c \in \left[\frac{wh_2}{h_{20}(n_0 + h_1 p_1^{max})}, \frac{wh_1}{(n_0 + h_1 p_1^{max})h_{10}} \right]$,

Using the same argument, when $c \in \left(\frac{wh_i}{h_{i0}\left(n_0 + \sum_{j=1}^{i} h_j p_j^{\max}\right)}, \right.$ $\left. \frac{wh_i}{h_{i0}\left(n_0 + \sum_{j=1}^{i-1} h_j p_j^{\max}\right)} \right)$ $(i = 2, \ldots, n)$, For $j = 1, \ldots, i-1$

$$\frac{\partial u}{\partial p_j}(p_1, \ldots, p_n)\Big|_{p=\overrightarrow{p_j^{max}}} = \frac{wh_j}{n_0 + \sum_{k=1}^{j} h_k p_k^{max}} - ch_{j0} > 0, \qquad (23)$$

$$\frac{\partial u}{\partial p_i}(p_1, \ldots, p_n)\Big|_{p=\overrightarrow{p_i^{max}}} = \frac{wh_j}{n_0 + \sum_{k=1}^{i} h_k p_k^{max}} - ch_{i0} \leq 0, \qquad (24)$$

From (23), (24) and Lemma 4, then the optimal solution is $p_1^* = p_1^{\max}, \ldots, p_{i-1}^* = p_{i-1}^{\max}$, $p_i^* = \frac{w}{ch_{i0}} - \frac{\left(n_0 + \sum_{j=1}^{i-1} h_j p_j^{\max}\right)}{h_i}$, $p_j^* = 0 \,(j = i+1, \ldots, n)$, when $c \in \left(\frac{wh_i}{h_{i0}\left(n_0 + \sum_{j=1}^{i} h_j p_j^{\max}\right)}, \frac{wh_i}{h_{i0}\left(n_0 + \sum_{j=1}^{i-1} h_j p_j^{\max}\right)} \right)$ $(i = 2, \ldots, n)$.

when $c \in \left(\frac{wh_i}{h_{i0}\left(n_0 + \sum_{j=1}^{i-1} h_j p_j^{\max}\right)}, \frac{wh_{i-1}}{h_{i-1 0}\left(n_0 + \sum_{j=1}^{i-1} h_j p_j^{\max}\right)} \right)$ $(i = 2, \ldots, n)$, For $j = 1, \ldots, i-1$, we have

$$\frac{\partial u}{\partial p_j}(p_1, \ldots, p_n)\Big|_{p=\overrightarrow{p_j^{max}}} = \frac{wh_j}{n_0 + \sum_{k=1}^{j} h_k p_k^{max}} - ch_{j0} > 0, \qquad (25)$$

$$\frac{\partial u}{\partial p_i}(p_1, \ldots, p_n)\Big|_{p=\overrightarrow{p_{i-1}^{max}}} = \frac{wh_i}{n_0 + \sum_{k=1}^{i-1} h_k p_k^{max}} - ch_{i0} < 0, \qquad (26)$$

from (25), (26) and Lemma 4, then the optimal solution is $p^* = (p_1^{max}, \ldots, p_{i-1}^{max}, 0, \ldots, 0)$, when $c \in \left(\frac{wh_i}{h_{i0}\left(n_0 + \sum_{j=1}^{i-1} h_j p_j^{\max}\right)}, \frac{wh_{i-1}}{h_{i-1 0}\left(n_0 + \sum_{j=1}^{i-1} h_j p_j^{\max}\right)} \right)$ $(i = 2, \ldots, n)$, when $c \leq \frac{wh_n}{h_{n0}(n_0 + \sum_{i=1}^{n} h_i p_i^{max})}$,

$$\frac{\partial u}{\partial p_i}(p_1, \ldots, p_n)\Big|_{p=\overrightarrow{p_n^{max}}} = \frac{wh_i}{n_0 + \sum_{k=1}^{n} h_k p_k^{max}} - ch_{i0} \geq 0, \qquad (27)$$

From (27), then the optimal solution is $p^* = (p_1^{max}, \ldots, p_n^{max})$, when $c \leq \frac{wh_n}{h_{n0}(n_0 + \sum_{i=1}^{n} h_i p_i^{max})}$.

From the above discussion, the optimal solution p^* for a fixed price c can be concluded as:

$$p^* = \begin{cases} (0, \cdots, 0), & \text{if } c \geq \frac{wh_1}{h_{10}n_0}, \\ (w - \frac{ch_{10}n_0}{h_1}, 0, \ldots, 0), & \text{if } \frac{wh_1}{h_{10}n_0} \geq c \geq \frac{wh_1}{h_{10}(n_0 + h_1 p_1^{max})}, \\ (p_1^{max}, 0, \ldots, 0), & \text{if } \frac{wh_1}{h_{10}(n_0 + h_1 p_1^{max})} \geq c \geq \frac{wh_2}{h_{20}(n_0 + h_1 p_1^{max})}, \\ (p_1^{max}, \ldots, p_{i-1}^{max}, 0, \ldots, 0), & \text{if } \frac{wh_{i-1}}{h_{i-1 0}(n_0 + \sum_{j=1}^{i-1} h_j p_j^{max})} > c \geq \frac{wh_i}{h_{i0}(n_0 + \sum_{j=1}^{i-1} h_j p_j^{max})}, \\ (p_1^{max}, \cdots, p_{i-1}^{max}, p_i^*, 0, \cdots, 0), & \text{if } \frac{wh_i}{h_{i0}(n_0 + \sum_{j=1}^{i-1} h_j p_j^{max})} > c \geq \frac{wh_i}{h_{i0}(n_0 + \sum_{j=1}^{i} h_j p_j^{max})}, \\ (p_1^{max}, \ldots, p_n^{max}), & \text{if } \frac{wh_n}{h_{n0}(n_0 + \sum_{i=1}^{n} h_i p_i^{max})} \geq c, \end{cases} \qquad (28)$$

where $p_i^* = c\sum\limits_{j=1}^{i-1} h_{j0}p_j^{\max} + w - \dfrac{ch_{i0}\sum\limits_{j=1}^{i-1} h_j p_j^{\max}}{h_i}$. Because the expression (14) in

Theorem 3 is equivalent to (28), the proof of Theorem 3 is completed.

Theorem 3 shows that when the price $c \in \left[\dfrac{wh_i}{h_{i0}(n+\sum\limits_{j=1}^{i-1} h_j p_j^{\max})},\right.$

$\left.\dfrac{wh_i}{h_{i0}(n_0+\sum\limits_{j=1}^{i} h_j p_j^{\max})}\right]$, user $j(j < i-1)$ will use the maximal power p_j^{max}, user

i will use power $\dfrac{w}{ch_{i0}} - \dfrac{\sum_{j=1}^{i-1} h_j p_j^{\max}}{h_j} - \dfrac{n_0}{h_j}$, and other users' power will be zero.
Therefore, at most one user's power less than the maximal power while others
will transmit signal with maximal power or not transmit for a fixed price c.

Substitute the optimal power given by (14) and $c_i = c$ into (1), the optimization problem for the PU can be rewritten as:

$$\text{maximize } u(c) = c\sum_{i=1}^{n} h_{i0}p_i$$

$$\text{subject to } p_i \geq 0, \quad \sum_{j=1}^{n} h_{j0}p_j \leq T, \tag{29}$$

where $p_i = \max\left\{\min\{p_i^{\max}, w/(ch_{i0}) - \sum\limits_{j=1}^{i-1} h_j p_j^{\max}/h_i - n_0/h_i\}, 0\right\}$.

We give the optimal solution to (29) and consider two different cases under the constraint of interference temperature limit:

Case One: $\sum\limits_{i=1}^{n} h_{i0}p_i^{max} \leq T$, which means that the PU can tolerate the interference of all SUs with the maximum transmit power. When the price $c \in [b_i, a_i]$, $u(c)$ can be reduced to

$$u(c) = \begin{cases} 0, & \text{if } c \geq \frac{wh_1}{h_{10}n_0}, \\ w - \frac{ch_{10}n_0}{h_1}, & \text{if } \frac{wh_1}{h_{10}n_0} \geq c \geq \frac{wh_1}{h_{10}(n_0+p_1^{max})}, \\ ch_{10}p_1^{max}, & \text{if } \frac{wh_1}{h_{10}(n_0+p_1^{max})} \geq c \geq \frac{wh_2}{h_{20}(n_0+p_1^{max})}, \\ c\sum\limits_{j=1}^{i-1} h_{j0}p_j^{max} + w - \frac{ch_{i0}\sum\limits_{j=1}^{i-1} h_j p_j^{max}}{h_i}, & \text{if } b_i > c \geq a_i, \\ c\sum\limits_{j=1}^{i-1} h_{j0}p_j^{max}, & \text{if } a_i > c \geq b_{i+1}, \\ c\sum\limits_{j=1}^{n} h_{i0}p_i^{max}, & \text{if } \frac{wh_n}{h_{n0}(n_0+\sum_{i=1}^{n} h_i p_i^{max})} \geq c, \end{cases}$$

where $a_i = \dfrac{wh_i}{h_{i0}(n_0 + \sum\limits_{j=1}^{i} h_j p_j^{max})}$, $b_i = \dfrac{wh_i}{h_{i0}(n_0 + \sum\limits_{j=1}^{i-1} h_j p_j^{max})}$ $(i = 1, \cdots, n)$. $u(c)$ is a

piecewise linear function and $u(a_i) > u(b_{i+1})$, so the optimal price c^* can be written as:

$$c^* = \underset{a \in \{a_1, \ldots, a_n\}}{\arg\max} \ u(a) \tag{30}$$

Case Two: When $\sum\limits_{j=1}^{n} h_{i0} p_i^{max} > T$, there must exist $k \in (1, \cdots, n)$ such that

$$\sum_i^{k-1} h_i p_i^{max} < T, \tag{31}$$

and

$$\sum_i^{k} h_i p_i^{max} \geq T, \tag{32}$$

Using Lemma 4, only the first k users can be admitted to transmit when the interference power constraint is satisfied. From (12), the power of each user deceases with c, there exists a maximal c_{max} such that the transmit power of the user will be $p_{max} = (p_1^{max}, \cdots, p_{k-1}^{max}, (T - \sum_i^{k} p_i^{max})/h_{k0}, 0, \cdots, 0)$.

$$c_{max} = \frac{wh_k}{h_{k0}(n_0 + \sum_i^{k-1} h_i p_i^{max}) + h_k(T - \sum_i^{k} p_i^{max})} \tag{33}$$

Since the $u(c)$ is piecewise linear function in $[c_{max}, \infty)$, using the same argument as case one, the optimal price c^* can be written as:

$$c^* = \underset{a \in \{a_1, \ldots, a_{k-1}, c_{max}\}}{\arg\max} \ u(a) \tag{34}$$

From (30) and (34), the optimal price for PU is given. It can be seen that the complexity to find the optimal price is at most $O(n)$, where n is the number of SUs.

We give the closed-form optimal price for the N-UP scheme and propose the best power control strategies for CR networks to admit one user access the spectrum if the transmit power of each user is large enough. Then, the simulations compare the influence of N-UP and UP scheme on the performance of PU and SUs in the next section.

4   Simulation Results

In this section, we evaluate the performance of the proposed pricing scheme. The channel gains of all links experience Rayleigh fading with the variance of 1. We set $w = 1$, $T = 1$, $p_i^{max} = 10$, $\forall i$, the variance of the noise is 1. The channel gain h and h_0 is randomly generated 10^4 times in our simulations. Figures 2 and 3 show the utility of PU and SUs versus the number of SUs. It can be seen that

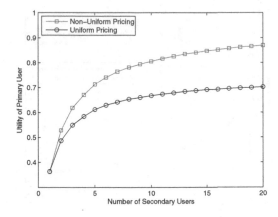

Fig. 2. Utility of primary user versus the number of secondary users.

the utilities of PU and SUs increases with the number of SUs. This is because the probability of the channel gains of SUs is better when the number of SUs is larger. Therefore, SUs need to pay more for PU in order to gain more profit.

Figure 4 shows the interference power of PU versus the number of SUs. We can see that the interference power under the N-UP scheme is larger than UP scheme when the number of SUs is more than one. Moreover, the interference power of PU under the N-UP scheme increases as the number of SUs first, then they meet the interference power when the number of SUs is more than five. However, the interference power of PU under the UP scheme decreases as the number of SUs increases. The difference between these two schemes is that the interference power limit is always attained for N-UP scheme when the maximal interference power made by SUs is larger than the interference power limit. For

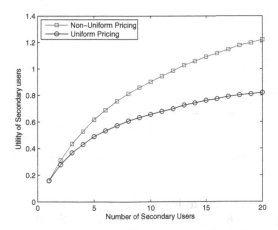

Fig. 3. Utility of secondary users versus the number of secondary users.

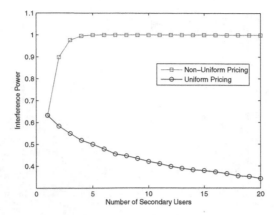

Fig. 4. Total interference power versus the number of secondary users.

UP scheme, when the utility of PU is determined by the channel gain of SUs other than the interference power limit, so the interference power limit is not meet as equality at the optimal price.

Figure 5 shows the sum rate of SUs versus the number of SUs. The sum rate under both UP and N-UP scheme increases as the number of SUs increases. This is because the N-UP scheme also allows SUs to transmit more power than UP scheme, which can be seen from Fig. 6.

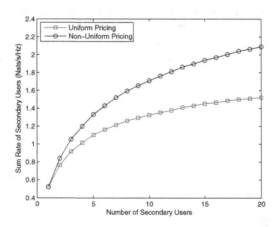

Fig. 5. Sum rate of secondary users versus the number of secondary users.

Figures 7 and 8 shows the utility of the PU and SUs versus the ITP when $p_i^{max} = 10$ dB and $n = 8$ is given in the CR networks. We can see the utility of SU of two schemes increases with ITP. While ITP is less than -5 dB, two schemes have the same utility. This is because the optimal two pricing scheme

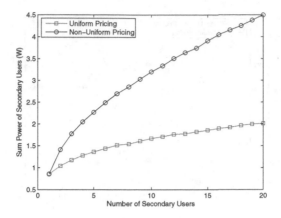

Fig. 6. Sum power of secondary users versus the number of secondary users.

allows only one user has the best channel condition to access the spectrum. As ITP increases from −5 dB to 30 dB, the utility of PU under N-UP scheme is larger than UP scheme. The reason is that N-UP scheme allows more SUs to access the spectrum. And the utilities of SUs of two schemes begin to saturate when ITP reaches 20 dB.

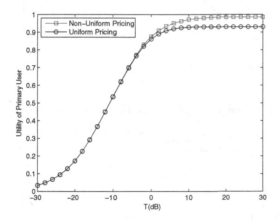

Fig. 7. Utility of primary user versus the interference temperature power.

Figure 9 shows the interference power versus ITP. The interference power of two schemes are the same when ITP is less than −5 dB, because the optimal price for two schemes are the same when ITP is small. As ITP increases from −5 dB to 30 dB, the interference power of N-UP scheme is larger than NU scheme. This is because the N-UP scheme always allows more users to transmit at their maximal power until the interference power constraint is satisfied.

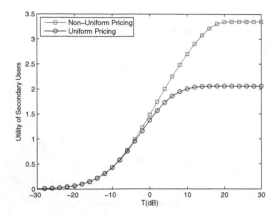

Fig. 8. Utility of secondary users versus the interference temperature power.

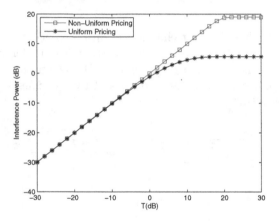

Fig. 9. Interference power versus the interference temperature power.

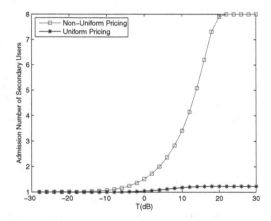

Fig. 10. Admission number of secondary users versus the interference temperature power.

Figure 10 shows the average admission SUs versus the ITP. When the ITP is less than −5 dB, both schemes admit one user. As the ITP increases from −5 dB to 30 dB, the admission number of SUs of N-UP scheme increases, that means all SUs will be allowed to access the spectrum when the ITP is large. However, the admission number of SUs of UP scheme is less than two even the ITP is large enough. This is because the interference power is always not equal to ITL at the optimal price for uniform scheme.

5 Conclusion

In this paper, we consider the price-based power control problem for CR-NOMA networks which contains one base station (BS), multiple SUs and one PU, and SIC is employed at receiver. We first model the pricing and power control strategies between PU and SUs as a Stackelberg game based on the interference temperature power. Then, PU plays a leader in the game and chooses a price for SUs in order to obtain maximum revenue under ITP limit. Moreover, SUs act as followers to select the optimal power while considering their payoff to PU. Furthermore, the non-uniform pricing scheme and uniform pricing scheme are proposed to evaluate the revenue of PU and SUs. Simulation results compare the different performance indexes of two schemes.

References

1. Hong, X., Wang, J., Wang, C., Shi, J.: Cognitive radio in 5G: a perspective on energy-spectral efficiency trade-off. IEEE Commun. Mag. 52(7), 46–53 (2014)
2. Liang, Y., Zeng, Y., et al.: Sensing-throughput tradeoff for cognitive radio networks. IEEE Trans. Wirel. Commun. 7(4), 1326–1337 (2008)
3. Hasegawa, M., Hirai, H., et al.: Optimization for centralized and decentralized cognitive radio networks. Proc. IEEE 102(4), 574–584 (2014)
4. Islam, S.M.R., Avazov, N., Dobre, O.A., Kwak, K.: Power-domain non-orthogonal multiple access (NOMA) in 5G systems: potentials and challenges. IEEE Commun. Surv. Tutor. 19(2), 721–742 (2017)
5. Higuchi, K., Benjebbou, A.: Non-orthogonal multiple access (NOMA) with successive interference cancellation for future radio access. IEICE Trans. Commun. 98(3), 403–414 (2015)
6. Ding, Z., et al.: Application of non-orthogonal multiple access in LTE and 5G networks. IEEE Commun. Mag. 55(2), 185–191 (2017)
7. Lv, L., Chen, J., Ni, Q., Ding, Z., Jiang, H.: Cognitive non-orthogonal multiple access with cooperative relaying: a new wireless frontier for 5G spectrum sharing. IEEE Commun. Mag. 56(4), 188–195 (2018)
8. Liu, Y., Ding, Z., Elkashlan, M., Yuan, J.: Nonorthogonal multiple access in large-scale underlay cognitive radio networks. IEEE Trans. Veh. Technol. 65(12), 10152–10157 (2016)
9. Liang, W., Li, L., Shi, J., Fang, F., Ding, Z.: Cooperative game aided spectrum sharing in underlay cognitive radio networks employing NOMA schemes. In: Proceedings 2018 IEEE Globecom Workshops (GC Wkshps), Abu Dhabi, pp. 1–6 (2018)

10. Song, Z., Wang, X., Liu, Y., Zhang, Z.: Joint spectrum resource allocation in NOMA-based cognitive radio network with SWIPT. IEEE Access **7**, 89594–89603 (2019)
11. Mao, S., Leng, S., Hu, J., Yang, K.: Power minimization resource allocation for underlay MISO-NOMA SWIPT systems. IEEE Access **7**, 17247–17255 (2019)
12. Xie, X., Yang, H., Vasilakos, A.V., He, L.: Fair power control using game theory with pricing scheme in cognitive radio networks. J. Commun. Netw **16**(2), 183–192 (2014)
13. Yang, C., Li, J., Tian, Z.: Optimal power control for cognitive radio networks under coupled interference constraints: a cooperative game-theoretic perspective. IEEE Trans. Veh. Technol. **59**(4), 1696–1706 (2010)
14. Yu, H., Gao, L., Li, Z., Wang, X., Hossain, E.: Pricing for uplink power control in cognitive radio networks. IEEE Trans. Veh. Technol. **59**(4), 1769–1778 (2010)
15. Wang, Z., Jiang, L., He, C.: A novel price-based power control algorithm in cognitive radio networks. IEEE Commun. Lett. **17**(1), 43–46 (2013)
16. Wang, Z., Jiang, L., He, C.: Optimal price-based power control algorithm in cognitive radio networks. IEEE Trans. Wirel. Commun. **13**(11), 5909–5920 (2014)
17. Kang, X., Zhang, R., Motani, M.: Price-based resource allocation for spectrum-sharing femtocell networks: a stackelberg game approach. IEEE J. Sel. Areas Commun. **30**(3), 538–549 (2012)
18. Wang, Z., Wen, C., Fan, Z., Wan, X.: A novel price-based power allocation algorithm in non-orthogonal multiple access networks. IEEE Wirel. Commun. **7**(2), 230–233 (2018)
19. Wang, Z., Xiao, W., Wan, X., Fan, Z.: Price-based power control algorithm in cognitive radio networks via branch and bound. IEICE Trans. Inf. Syst. **102**(3), 505–511 (2019)
20. Luo, Z.-Q., Yu, W.: An introduction to convex optimization for communications and signal processing. IEEE J. Sel. Areas Commun. **24**(8), 1426–1438 (2006)

Deep Learning Based Single-Channel Blind Separation of Co-frequency Modulated Signals

Chen Chen[1,3] , Zhufei Lu[2] , Zhe Guo[3] , Feng Yang[1](✉) ,
and Lianghui Ding[1]

[1] Department of Electronic Engineering, Shanghai Jiao Tong University,
Shanghai, China
{chenchensjtu,yangfeng,lhding}@sjtu.edu.cn
[2] Yichang Testing Institute of Technology Research, Yichang 443003, China
flypeter@126.com
[3] Shanghai Microwave Research Institute and CETC Key Laboratory of
Data Link Technology, Shanghai 200063, China
guozhe@foxmail.com

Abstract. This paper presents our results in deep learning (DL) based single-channel blind separation (SCBS). Here, we propose a bidirectional recurrent neural network (BRNN) based separation method which can recover information bits directly from co-frequency modulated signals after end-to-end learning. Aiming at the real-time processing, a strategy of block processing is proposed, solving high error rate at the beginning and end of each block of data. Compared with the conventional PSP method, the proposed DL separation method achieves better BER performance in linear case and nonlinear distortion case with lower computational complexity. Simulation results further demonstrate the generalization ability and robustness of the proposed approach in terms of mismatching amplitude ratios.

Keywords: Single-channel blind separation (SCBS) · Deep learning (DL) · Bidirectional recurrent neural network (BRNN)

1 Introduction

Single-channel blind separation (SCBS) of co-frequency overlapping signals is vital in blind signal processing and widely applied in paired carrier multiple access (PCMA) noncooperative communication. Since the two signals completely overlap in the time-frequency domain and are similar in power, conventional multi-user detection algorithms such as successive interference cancellation (SIC) is difficult to apply to SCBS.

This paper is supported in part by NSFC China (61771309, 61671301, 61420106008, 61521062), Shanghai Key Laboratory Funding (STCSM18DZ1200102) and CETC Key Laboratory of Data Link Technology Foundation (CLDL-20162306).

H. Gao et al. (Eds.): ChinaCom 2019, LNICST 312, pp. 607–618, 2020.
https://doi.org/10.1007/978-3-030-41114-5_45

During the last two decades, several approaches have been utilized for two signals with distinct symbol rates, different amplitudes, and different roll-off factors. Further, particle filter (PF) [10] and per-survivor processing (PSP) [11] algorithm were investigated for realistic scenarios. Although the performance of these algorithms is superior, their applications are limited due to the high complexity. PSP is a maximum likelihood sequence estimate (MLSE) based algorithm that requires traversal search for possible symbols, of which the modulation order and channel memory length cause an exponential increase in time complexity. Thus, it is not practical to implement PSP in the scenario with channel of large memory length. Currently, researches mainly focus on the complexity reduction and the joint separation and decoding algorithms.

In recent years, deep learning (DL) has shown its overwhelming privilege in computer vision, speech recognition and natural language processing. Based on artificial neural network (ANN) theory, DL is essentially a general function approximation with the ability to learn from large data set. DL has also shown great promise in complex scenarios of physical layer communication [7] such as channel decoding [1], channel modeling [12], signal detection [3,6] and end-to-end communication system [2]. SCBS can be modeled as a joint detection problem of two signals. Recurrent neural network (RNN) is appropriate for learning sequences and has achieved excellent performance in single-signal detection [3] because it can make full use of the correlation between symbols. However, it has not been well investigated in overlapped signal detection. Therefore, we conduct research on DL based SCBS.

In this article, we introduce a DL approach for SCBS, and a novel bidirectional recurrent neural network (BRNN) based separation network, called SepNet, is proposed. Its computational complexity does not increase exponentially with the channel memory length. Considering the inter-symbol correlation (such as ISI) caused by the memory channel, the search for symbols is avoided, which greatly reduces the computational complexity and thus achieves a compromise between performance and complexity. Our contributions in this paper are as follows. First, a separation network based on BGRU is designed. Then, aiming at the real-time processing of continuous received signals, a strategy of block processing is proposed, and high error rate at the beginning and the end of each block of data is solved. Finally, the performance and robustness of the algorithm are verified. Simulation results show that the proposed method performs better than the PSP algorithm with lower complexity.

The rest of this paper is structured as follows. In the next section, we describe the system architecture and signal model for single-channel received mixtures of two modulated signals. Section 3 shows the architecture of the proposed SepNet and training details. In Sect. 4, the simulation results and interpretations are presented and conclusions are drawn in Sect. 5.

2   System Architecture and Signal Model

2.1   System Architecture

The architecture of co-frequency modulated signals with DL based SCBS is illustrated in Fig. 1. The baseband system is similar to the conventional ones. At the transmitter, the source signals are first modulated from bit streams to symbol sequences. Second, the symbol sequences are upsampled and then passed through the pulse shaping filters to limit their bandwidth and reduce inter-symbol interference (ISI). After that, two source signals are transmitted through the channel with noise and hardware impairments such as nonlinear distortion. Then, at the receiver, overlapping signals pass the matched filter and are downsampled.

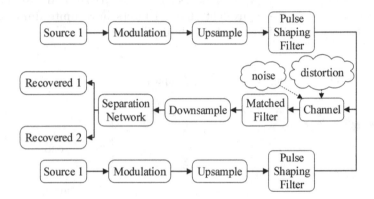

Fig. 1. The system architecture of DL based SCBS.

The SepNet should be trained with the labeled data to learn separation. After training stage, it takes the single-channel received data consisting of two overlapping signals as input, and then directly outputs two raw bit streams.

2.2   Signal Model

The received mixed signal model is described as follow. The baseband-equivalent single-channel received signal, which consists of two MPSK or MQAM signals, can be expressed as

$$y(t) = h_1 e^{j(\Delta\omega_1 t + \theta_1)} x_1(t) + h_2 e^{j(\Delta\omega_2 t + \theta_2)} x_2(t) + v(t), \tag{1}$$

where h_i denotes the amplitude of two modulated signals, $\Delta\omega_i$, θ_i, and $v(t)$ represent the carrier frequency offset, the initial phases, and additive white Gaussian noise (AWGN), respectively. The source signals $x_i(t)$ are defined as

$$x_i(t) = \sum_{n=-\infty}^{n=\infty} s_n^{(i)} g_i(t - nT + \tau_i), \tag{2}$$

where $s_n^{(i)}$ is nth symbol of two transmitted signals, which are independent and identically distributed (i.i.d.) random sequences; $g_i(t)$ is the pulse response of equivalent channel filters, which consist of shaping filters, channel filters and matched filters; T is the symbol period; $0 < \tau_i < T$ are the relative time delays between the two received modulated signals and the local clock reference.

Sampling the signals at symbol rate $1/T$, (1)–(2) can be rewritten respectively as

$$y_k = h_1 e^{j(\Delta\omega_1 kT + \theta_1)} x_k^{(1)} + h_2 e^{j(\Delta\omega_2 kT + \theta_2)} x_k^{(2)} + v_k, \tag{3}$$

$$x_k^{(i)} = \sum_{n=1-L_1}^{L_2} s_{k+n}^{(i)} g_i(-nT + \tau_k^{(i)}), \tag{4}$$

where $y_k = y(kT)$, $x_k^{(i)} = x_i(kT)$, $v_k = v(kT)$, $\tau_k^{(i)} = \tau_i(kT)$, and assuming that the pulse responses of the equivalent channel filters have finite duration from $(1 - L_1)T$ to L_2T, $k = 0, 1..., K - 1$ in a limited time.

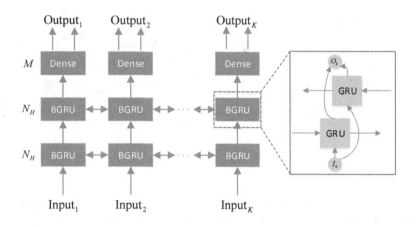

Fig. 2. The architecture of SepNet.

3   Separation Using Deep Learning

This section presents the SepNet for SCBS, and analyzes the motivation and necessity of the network structure design, while training details are specified afterwards.

3.1   Network Architecture

SCBS of co-frequency modulated signals is to detect the symbol sequences $s_{1:K}^{(i)} = \{s_1^{(i)}, s_2^{(i)}, ..., s_K^{(i)}\}$ from the set of received sampled points $y_{1:K} = \{y_1, y_2, ..., y_K\}$.

Symbol sequences detection can be treated as a classification problem in deep learning for each of the symbols $s_k^{(i)}$. For the sake of simplicity, QPSK is taken as an example, and other modulation methods can be analogized. A QPSK modulated symbol can be expressed as

$$s_k^{(i)} = \frac{1}{\sqrt{2}}(2b_{k,1}^{(i)} - 1) + j\frac{1}{\sqrt{2}}(2b_{k,2}^{(i)} - 1), \tag{5}$$

where $b_{k,1}^{(i)}$ and $b_{k,2}^{(i)}$ denote two bits of a symbol.

To make full use of the information between symbols, we intend to design the SepNet using BRNN architectures. It ensures that in the estimation of a symbol, future signal observations are taken into account, which overcomes the limitations of RNN.

Long Short-Term Memory (LSTM) and Gated Recurrent Unit (GRU) are the most widely utilized unit structures in RNN, for solving long-term dependencies. GRU simplifies the structure of LSTM, making it easier to train and converge. In this work, we adopt the bidirectional GRU (BGRU) as the basic cell in the SepNet.

Figure 2 shows the structure of this network. It has two layers of BGRU, followed by a fully connected output layer. The BGRU is a combination of two GRUs. One of the GRUs is used for forward propagation and the other is used for backward propagation. At each time step, the output of two GRUs are concatenated as an output of the BGRU.

The activation function of the output layer is sigmoid $f_{Si}(a) = \frac{1}{1+e^{-a}}$ to force the output neurons to be in between zero and one, which can be interpreted as the probability of transmitting a bit equals one.

The amount of input node is 2 when the received signal is not oversampled. The number of hidden unit of BGRU is N_H, which is a hyper-parameter that can be adjusted. The amount of output node M depends on the modulation mode (e.g., for QPSK, the output number is 4 for 2 bits of two raw symbols).

The input of the SepNet is a noisy version of complex sequence of received signal, $y_1, y_2, ..., y_K$. At every time step, the real and imaginary part of a sampled symbol are concatenated as the input to the network:

$$\text{Input}_k = \begin{bmatrix} \text{Re}(y_k) \\ \text{Im}(y_k) \end{bmatrix}, \tag{6}$$

The output is the concatenated estimated information bits $\hat{b}_{k,m}^{(i)}$ of two source signals:

$$\text{Output}_k = \begin{bmatrix} \hat{b}_{k,1}^{(1)} \\ \hat{b}_{k,2}^{(1)} \\ \hat{b}_{k,1}^{(2)} \\ \hat{b}_{k,2}^{(2)} \end{bmatrix} = \begin{bmatrix} \Pr(b_{k,1}^{(1)} = 1 | y_{1:K}, \Theta) \\ \Pr(b_{k,2}^{(1)} = 1 | y_{1:K}, \Theta) \\ \Pr(b_{k,1}^{(2)} = 1 | y_{1:K}, \Theta) \\ \Pr(b_{k,2}^{(2)} = 1 | y_{1:K}, \Theta) \end{bmatrix}, \tag{7}$$

where Θ denotes the parameters in the SepNet, including weights and biases.

The decision bit $\tilde{b}_{k,m}^{(i)}$ is decided to be 0 or 1 according to whether $\hat{b}_{k,m}^{(i)}$ is greater than 0.5:

$$\tilde{b}_{k,m}^{(i)} = \begin{cases} 0 & 0 \le \hat{b}_{k,m}^{(i)} < 0.5 \\ 1 & 0.5 < \hat{b}_{k,m}^{(i)} \le 1 \end{cases} \tag{8}$$

and then bit error rate (BER) is calculated as a measurement of separation performance:

$$P_e = \frac{1}{4N} \sum_i \Pr(b_{k,m}^{(i)} \ne \tilde{b}_{k,m}^{(i)}), \tag{9}$$

In addition, the maximum time step of the network is fixed to $K_{max} = 80$ for the following reasons: First, the data stream arriving at the receiver is of arbitrary length and must be divided into blocks for real-time processing. Second, too many time steps will cause gradient disappearance, making it difficult to train the network.

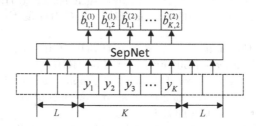

Fig. 3. Block processing method for received signal sequence.

However, since some of the information is not in this block, a large number of detection errors may occur for the symbol at the beginning and end of a block of data. To solve this problem, we divide the data stream into blocks and add L symbols to the beginning and end of each block of data as input to the network, as illustrated in Fig. 3, thereby improving the overall performance.

Algorithm 1. Proposed scheme

Input: Received signal sequence $y_{1:N} = \{y_1, y_2, ..., y_N\}$.
1: Divide the received overlapped signal sequence $y_{1:N}$ into $\lfloor \frac{N}{K} \rfloor$ blocks, each block $y_{jK:(j+1)K}$ contains K symbols.
2: **for** $j = 1 : \lfloor \frac{N}{K} \rfloor$ **do**
3:     Add L symbols to the beginning and the end of each block to form a new block $y_{jK-L:(j+1)K+L}$.
4:     Feed the new block $y_{jK-L:(j+1)K+L}$ to the SepNet and get the estimated sequences $\hat{b}_{jK:(j+1)K,m}^{(1)}$, $\hat{b}_{jK:(j+1)K,m}^{(2)}$.
5:     By (8), we get the raw data bit sequences $\tilde{b}_{jK:(j+1)K,m}^{(1)}$ and $\tilde{b}_{jK:(j+1)K,m}^{(2)}$.
6: **end for**
Output: Reconsturcted raw data bit sequences $\tilde{b}_{1:N,m}^{(1)}$ and $\tilde{b}_{1:N,m}^{(2)}$.

The scheme of the proposed DL based separation is summarized in Algorithm 1.

3.2 Training Details

The goal of training stage is to minimize the distance between the detected symbols $\hat{s}_k^{(i)}$ and raw transmitted symbols $s_k^{(i)}$. Actually, as the output of our network is information bits, the objective function, or loss function is not related to the raw symbols $s_k^{(i)}$ but related to the transmitted data bits.

According to [4], there is a binary cross-entropy (CE) loss function suitable for this work, which is defined as

$$L_{CE} = \sum_{i,m,k} [b_{k,m}^{(i)} \log(\hat{b}_{k,m}^{(i)}) + (1 - b_{k,m}^{(i)}) \log(1 - \hat{b}_{k,m}^{(i)})], \tag{10}$$

where $\hat{b}_{k,m}^{(i)} \in [0,1]$ and $b_{k,m}^{(i)} \in \{0,1\}$ denote the output of the SepNet and the raw transmitted bit respectively, with k representing the symbol index and m being the mth bit in a symbol. It shows that in RNN, the loss function is defined as the sum of loss functions in all time steps.

The parameters Θ in the SepNet can be updated using the stochastic gradient descent (SGD) method:

$$\Theta \leftarrow \Theta - \alpha \frac{\partial L_{CE}}{\partial \Theta}, \tag{11}$$

where α is the learning rate, with initial values of 0.001 and decreases as the epochs increase. The gradient $\frac{\partial L_{CE}}{\partial \Theta}$ can be calculated by the use of back propagation through time (BPTT) approach [5].

Furthermore, a good initialization method is helpful for the convergence of the network and avoiding the gradient explosion and disappearance. Therefore, the Xavier method is adopted to initialize the network weights. To accelerate the training process and ease the gradient diffusion, batch normalization operation is added after the two BGRU unit layers.

4   Simulation Results

The target of our simulation is to demonstrate the performance of the DL methods for SCBS of co-frequency overlapping signals performs better than the conventional PSP method, and the model has the generalization ability to adapt to the amplitude shaking. For the sake of simplicity, we counted BER of two signals together instead of counting separately to characterize the performance of the different methods. In our simulation, root raised cosine filter was adopted as the shaping filter and matched filter. Its roll-off factor was set to be 0.35.

Labeled data is generated by simulation. For training set, According to (3)–(4)–(5), 8,000,000 symbols of received overlapped signal y_k and four corresponding raw data bits $b_{k,1}^{(1)}$, $b_{k,1}^{(2)}$, $b_{k,2}^{(1)}$, $b_{k,2}^{(2)}$ are randomly generated. The amount of

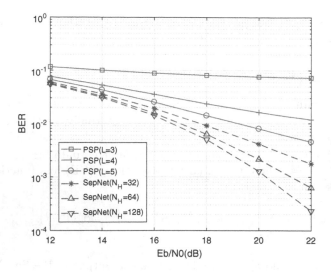

Fig. 4. BER of PSP and SepNet under the linear case.

testing set is $\frac{1}{10}$ of the training set, with other configurations remaining the same.

At first, we compare the BER performance of the conventional PSP method and the proposed SepNet method both in the linear case and the nonlinear case. Besides, we evaluate the BER performance of SepNet for different amplitude ratio, confirming the generalization ability of SepNet by its robustness in the mismatching amplitude ratio. Moreover, the effect of oversampling, training noise and the computational complexity is also discussed.

4.1   SepNet and PSP

Linear Case. The SepNet method is compared with the conventional PSP method for SCBS under the linear case, where the system is not affected by nonlinearity. In this case, we fix $\tau_1 = 0.4T$, $\tau_2 = 0.6T$, and $\Delta\omega_1 = \Delta\omega_2 = 0$, $\theta_1 = \theta_2 = 0$, $h_1 = h_2 = 1$, $L_1 = L_2 = 6$.

We compare the two algorithms at $L = 3, 4, 5$ and $N_H = 32, 64, 128$. As illustrated in Fig. 4 and Table 1, the performance of SepNet exceeds the PSP and the complexity is reduced. Compared with PSP ($L = 5$), SepNet ($N_H = 32$) has a performance gain of about 1 dB, while the computational complexity is only 0.058% of the former. As N_H increases, the separation performance of SepNet increases. It is because the network has a more powerful representation ability when the number of hidden unit increases. When the estimated L in the PSP is smaller than the actual channel memory length $L = L_1 + L_2 = 12$, the correlation between symbols is insufficient. Therefore, although the FLOPs of PSP ($L = 5$) is sufficiently high, the performance is still not ideal.

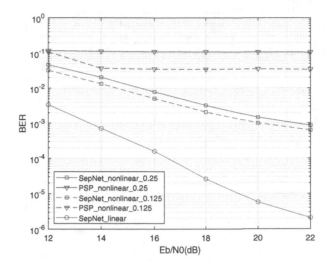

Fig. 5. BER of PSP and SepNet under the nonlinear case.

Nonlinear Case. To demonstrate the flexibility of separation network adaptable to non-ideal factors, nonlinear distortion is appended to the simulations. As indicated in [9], assuming that there are nonlinear amplifiers in the communication system, and the amplitude-to-amplitude (AM-AM) distortion is described by a third-order nonlinear function $f(x) = x - \beta_3|x|^2x$, where $\beta_3 = 0.25$ for travelling wave tube amplifiers (TWTA) and $\beta_3 = 0.125$ for solid-state amplifiers (SSA).

We compare the BER performance of the SepNet method and the PSP method under the nonlinear distortion. In this case, $\theta_1 = 0.2$, $\theta_2 = 0.5$, while other parameters are consistent with the setup of linear case. As shown in Fig. 5, the SepNet method significantly outperform the PSP method under the nonlinear distortion, which can be explained as nonlinear activation in the neural network introduces nonlinearity so as to realize nonlinear separation.

4.2 Performance Evaluation

Effect of Different Amplitude Ratios and Mismatching Robustness. Assuming that two signals overlapping in different amplitude ratios h_2/h_1 with other parameters are the same, correspondingly, the network is trained at different amplitude ratios. It can be seen in Fig. 6 that as the amplitude ratio decreases, the separation performance of the two signals is improved.

BER with amplitude ratio mismatching between training stage and testing stage is also illustrated in Fig. 6. The results are obtained by training the network under the amplitude ratio of $h_2/h_1 = 0.6$ while testing it under $h_2/h_1 = 0.8$ and $h_2/h_1 = 0.9$. The robustness of the SepNet, as indicated by the BER performance under the mismatched condition is close to that of matched condition, suggests that it has the generalization ability to avoid amplitude shaking.

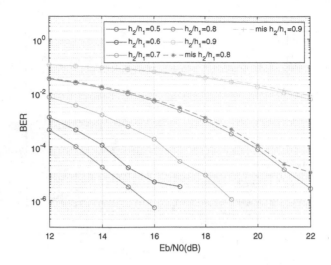

Fig. 6. BER of different amplitude ratios and amplitude ratios mismatching. Where mis $h_2/h_1 = 0.8$ and mis $h_2/h_1 = 0.9$ represent the performance of SepNet trained at the amplitude ratio of 0.6 whereas tested at 0.8, 0.9, respectively.

Effect of Oversampling and Training Noise. To investigate the effect of oversampling and training noise, we train and test the network under the same setup of the linear case except for oversampling and different training noise. It can be seen in Fig. 7 that the performance of two networks trained under AWGN ($E_b/N_0 = 12$ dB) is better than that of no AWGN added to the training stage. According to [6], adding noise can make more training examples lie at the decision boundary to make full use of it. It shows that training with noise strengthens the generalization ability of the network and reduces the over-fitting of the training data, which improves the performance of separation.

In actual communication, the bandwidth of the modulated signal is larger than the symbol rate since the shaping filter is used. Therefore, when the complex signal is sampled at the symbol rate, the Nyquist sampling theorem is not satisfied, resulting in information loss. In other words, the oversampling method can compensate for the information loss caused by symbol rate sampling. Compared with the original network, the input of the network that processes the oversampled signal becomes p times the original input, that is, the number of input nodes becomes $2p$. As observed in Fig. 7, for the network trained under AWGN, the oversampled signal outperforms the signal without oversampled. However, for the network trained without AWGN, the performance of oversampled signal is worse than the signal without oversampled. This is because the input features of the oversampled signal are more complicated, but no AWGN is added, which makes the network difficult to converge.

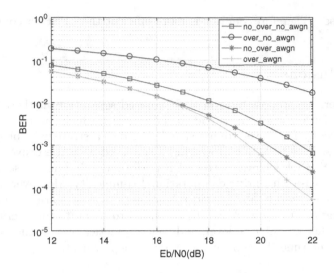

Fig. 7. BER of whether oversampled and whether added AWGN: (a) oversampled and not oversampled case marked as "_over" and "no_over" (b) added AWGN and not added AWGN case denoted as "_awgn" and "no_awgn".

Table 1. Computational complexities of SepNet and PSP

	Conditions	FLOPs
PSP	$L = 3$	106496
	$L = 4$	2228224
	$L = 5$	44040192
SepNet	$N_H = 32$	25344
	$N_H = 64$	99840
	$N_H = 128$	396288

4.3 Complexity Analysis

In Table 1, we compare the computational complexities of SepNet and PSP [2] in terms of the amount of floating-point multiplication-adds (FLOPs) to separate one QPSK symbol. Let M be the modulation level (eg. for QPSK, $M = 4$), and recall that L is the channel memory length. I_j and O_j denote the dimension of input and output of jth layer in SepNet, respectively.

The FLOPs of PSP can be expressed as $(8L + 2)M^{2L}$ for the number of states in trellis is $M^{2(L-1)}$ and each state has M^2 branches, while each branch metric needs $8L + 2$ real multiplication-adds [8]. For SepNet, the number of FLOPs is $\sum_j 6((I_j + O_j)O_j + O_j)$ as jth layer in BGRU has $6((I_j + O_j)O_j + O_j)$ network parameters and each parameter needs a real multiplication-adds [4]. It shows that FLOPs of PSP increase exponentially with L, whereas FLOPs of SepNet can be flexibly set. Therefore, SepNet is more efficient than PSP in computational complexity.

5   Conclusions

In this paper, we propose a novel BRNN based separation method SepNet for SCBS. The SepNet works in an end-to-end manner, which can recover information bits directly from overlapping signal. Besides, a strategy of block processing is proposed for real-time processing. Compared with the conventional PSP method, the SepNet achieves better BER performance in linear case and nonlinear distortion case with lower computational complexity. Moreover, the SepNet shows its generalization ability and robustness in the scenario of mismatching amplitude ratio. Future work can be extended to separate the overlapping signals with higher modulation level, and collect practical communication data to retrain and fine-tune the SepNet for practical deployment.

References

1. Cammerer, S., Hoydis, J., Brink, S.T.: On deep learning-based channel decoding (2017)
2. Dörner, S., Cammerer, S., Hoydis, J., ten Brink, S.: Deep learning based communication over the air. IEEE J. Sel. Top. Signal Process. **12**(1), 132–143 (2017)
3. Farsad, N., Goldsmith, A.: Neural network detection of data sequences in communication systems. IEEE Trans. Signal Process. **66**(21), 5663–5678 (2018)
4. Goodfellow, I., Bengio, Y., Courville, A.: Deep Learning. MIT Press, Cambridge (2016)
5. Jaeger, H.: Tutorial on Training Recurrent Neural Networks, Covering BPPT, RTRL, EKF and the "Echo State Network" Approach, vol. 5. GMD-Forschungszentrum Informationstechnik, Bonn (2002)
6. Kim, H., Jiang, Y., Rana, R., Kannan, S., Oh, S., Viswanath, P.: Communication algorithms via deep learning. arXiv preprint arXiv:1805.09317 (2018)
7. Qin, Z., Ye, H., Li, G.Y., Juang, B.H.F.: Deep learning in physical layer communications. IEEE Wirel. Commun. **26**(2), 93–99 (2019)
8. Raheli, R., Polydoros, A., Tzou, C.K.: Per-survivor processing: a general approach to MLSE in uncertain environments. IEEE Trans. Commun. **43**(2/3/4), 354–364 (1995)
9. Schenk, T.: RF Imperfections in High-Rate Wireless Systems: Impact and Digital Compensation. Springer, Dordrecht (2008). https://doi.org/10.1007/978-1-4020-6903-1
10. Tu, S., Chen, S., Hui, Z., Jian, W.: Particle filtering based single-channel blind separation of co-frequency MPSK signals. In: International Symposium on Intelligent Signal Processing & Communication Systems (2008)
11. Tu, S., Hui, Z., Na, G.: Single-channel blind separation of two QPSK signals using per-survivor processing. In: IEEE Asia Pacific Conference on Circuits & Systems (2009)
12. Ye, H., Li, G.Y., Juang, B.H.F.: Power of deep learning for channel estimation and signal detection in OFDM systems. IEEE Wirel. Commun. Lett. **7**(1), 114–117 (2018)

Personalized QoS Improvement in User-Centered Heterogeneous V2X Communication Networks

Mo Zhou[1] , Chuan Xu[1(✉)] , Guofeng Zhao[1] ,
and Syed Mushhad Mustuzhar Gilani[2]

[1] School of Communication and Information Engineering,
Chongqing University of Posts and Telecommunications, Chongqing, China
343442977@qq.com, {xuchuan,zhaogf}@cqupt.edu.cn
[2] Institute of Information Technology, PMAS-Arid Agriculture University,
Rawalpindi, Pakistan
mushhad@uaar.edu.pk

Abstract. With the rapid increasing personalized demand of C-V2X (cellular V2X) and vehicular ad hoc networks (VANET), the hybrid application of the two vehicular communications on unlicensed spectrum is becoming a trend. However, due to channel conflicts, the coexistence issue will lead to a serious drop in QoS of vehicular users. It is a challenge to allocate the wireless resource to ensure comprehensive user experience. In this paper, in order to satisfy the personalized QoS of different users while guarantee fair coexistence, we propose a conflict mitigation scheme through user association and time allocation to jointly optimize the delay and throughput, then formulate the multi-objective optimization into a mixed integer nonlinear programming (MINLP). To solve the NP-hard problem and obtain the Pareto optimal solution efficiently, we propose a PSO-based joint optimization of delay-throughput algorithm (DT-PSO). Simulation results show that our scheme outperforms existing approaches.

Keywords: Cellular V2X · VANET · Joint optimization

1 Introduction

In recent years, with the explosive growth of vehicular communication data, limited licensed spectrum is gradually difficult to meet the demand of 5G vehicular network communication. It is a trend to extend C-V2X (Cellular V2X) to unlicensed spectrum and integrate it with vehicular ad hoc network (VANET). However, due to channel collision, when C-V2X is extended to unauthorized spectrum, the quality of service (QoS) of VANET users will decrease dramatically. Therefore, it is necessary to improve the QoS of each heterogeneous network user while ensuring fair coexistence. Previous works have attempted to improve the

© ICST Institute for Computer Sciences, Social Informatics and Telecommunications Engineering 2020
Published by Springer Nature Switzerland AG 2020. All Rights Reserved
H. Gao et al. (Eds.): ChinaCom 2019, LNICST 312, pp. 619–630, 2020.
https://doi.org/10.1007/978-3-030-41114-5_46

user's QoS through the following aspects: improve the active user number [1], improve the throughput [2,3], and reduce the delay [4]. In fact, both delay and throughput will seriously affect the vehicle users' QoS [5]. When user transmit safe-related messages, low delay is required, while non-security-related messages require a large amount of bandwidth and can tolerate high latency. Obviously, appropriate wireless resource allocation to jointly optimize throughput and delay can improve the comprehensive heterogeneous network performance.

In literature, several existing works have studied the problem in traditional network. In work [6], the joint optimization of energy saving and interference in WLAN is studied. In work [7], authors propose a resource allocation method to optimize the throughput and spectrum efficiency of LTE-U and Wi-Fi heterogeneous networks, but ignore the personalized QoS of different users. In work [8], the author studies the joint optimization of throughput and delay in LTE and Wi-Fi heterogeneous networks. However, unlike traditional networks, the rapid movement of vehicles will seriously affect the communication quality of vehicles, it is necessary to take the speed of vehicles into account. In addition, the joint optimization process is usually very complex which is intolerable in time-delay-sensitive vehicular network.

In this paper, our goal is to mitigate channel conflicts through user scheduling and transmission time allocation, and to increase the throughput and latency of each vehicle user while ensuring fair coexistence. Since these two indicators usually conflict with each other, we model the throughput and delay of C-V2X and VANET respectively, and formulate the problem as a multi-objective Mixed Integer Non-Linear Programming (MINLP). In addition, to further enhance the user experience, we also optimize the slot jitter in TDMA cellular network. In order to solve the NP-hard problem of discrete and continuous variables, we propose a joint delay and throughput PSO-based optimization algorithm (MOPSO) to obtain the Pareto balance solution. Simulation results demonstrate that our scheme is effective, and the QoE of different user can be improved.

2   System Model

A heterogeneous network scenario is considered which consists of $i \in N_{va} = \{1, 2, \cdots, N_V\}$ VANET users and $j \in \mathbf{N}_{cel} = \{1, 2, \cdots, N_L\}$ C-V2X users, in total of $N_{sum} = N_V + N_L$ vehicular users coexist with each other, as shown in Fig. 1. The cellular BS can work on both licensed and unlicensed spectrum, while VANET work on 2.4–5 GHz unlicensed spectrum. The bandwidth of the unlicensed spectrum is divided into C subchannels denoted by $\Phi = \{1, 2, \ldots, C\}$, and the transmission time is divided into $\Gamma = \{1, 2, \cdots, T\}$ subframes. Here the Super-BS is introduced [7], which integrates the functions of AP, and the controller inside can implement time allocation and user scheduling. The software defined network (SDN) technology is also employed in the heterogeneous network, because the Super-BS needs to know the information of each vehicular user (including channel status information, speed, service requirement, etc.) to make decisions.

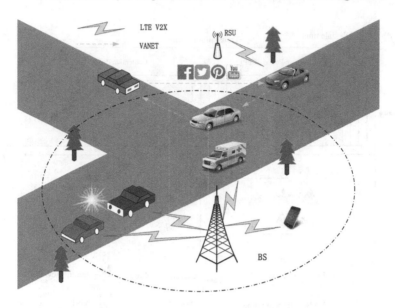

Fig. 1. Heterogeneous coexistence system of C-V2X and VANET

As shown in Fig. 2, the basic transmission period T is divided into two durations: αT content free period (CFP) for C-V2X users, and $(1-\alpha)T$ content period (CP) for VANET users. In the vehicular communication, safe-related services require stable delay response and only need low data rates, and C-V2X network just has these features. On the contrary, entertainment services typically have a large amount of data and can tolerate higher delay, VANET just meets these needs, so we classify the vehicular users into emergency users N_e and no-emergency users N_{ne}, easy to provide them with personalized services by supporting an appropriate access network.

2.1 Throughput of VANET and C-V2X

VANET: The considered VANET is a V2V communication network which based on 802.11p protocol, users need to compete for transmission channel with each other due to Carrier Sense Multiple Access with Collision Avoidance (CSMA/CA) mechanism, the competitive and transmission process can be described as a two-dimensional discrete Markov Chain [3]. In the stochastic process, we define the backoff count state $b(t) = m$, $m \in [0, 2^n CW_{\min}]$, and backoff step state $s(t) = n$, $n \in [0, m']$. m' is the max backoff step, and $2^n CW_{\min}$ is the compete window value after n_{th} fail transmission. Then the stationary distribution can be expressed as: $b_{n,m} = \lim\limits_{t \to \infty} P\{s(t) = n, b(t) = m\}$,

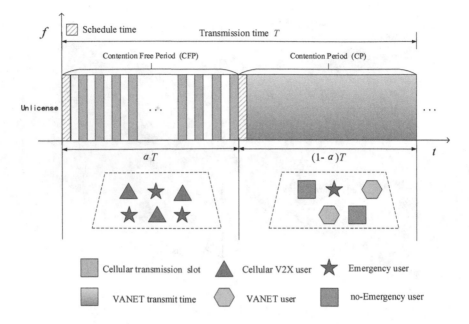

Fig. 2. Transmission time divide scheme

$n \in [0, m'], m \in [0, 2^n CW_{\min}]$, and the relationship between $b_{0,0}$ and p_c can be obtained:

$$b_{0,0} = \frac{2 \cdot (1 - 2p_c) \cdot (1 - p_c)}{(1 - 2p_c) \cdot (CW + 1) + CW \cdot p_c \cdot \left[1 - (2p_c)^{m'}\right]}, \tag{1}$$

Where p_c is the collision probability of a user in a considered slot time. Due to CSMA/CA mechanism, user can transmit data when backoff time is equal to 0, τ is used to denote the independent transmit probability:

$$\tau = \sum_{n=0}^{m'} b_{n,0} = \frac{b_{0,0}}{1 - p_c} = \frac{2 \cdot (1 - 2p_c)}{(1 - 2p_c) \cdot (CW + 1) + CW \cdot p_c \cdot \left[1 - (2p_c)^{m'}\right]}, \tag{2}$$

Then the collision probability p_c is the probability that more than two users transmit which can be calculated as:

$$p_c = 1 - (1 - \tau)^{N_V - 1}, \tag{3}$$

N_V is the number of VANET users. The probability that at least one user transmits in a slot time is:

$$p_{tr} = 1 - (1 - \tau)^{N_V}, \tag{4}$$

Thus the successful transmission probability $p_{suc}(i)$ equals to the probability that only user i transmits and the other $N_V - 1$ users keep silent:

$$p_{suc}(i) = \frac{C_{N_V}^1 \cdot \tau \cdot (1 - \tau)^{N_V - 1}}{p_{tr}}, \tag{5}$$

Since there are three situations in a transmission process: idle, success, collision, and the possibilities of them can be expressed as $1 - p_{tr}$, $p_{tr}p_{suc}$, $p_{tr}(1 - p_{suc})$ respectively, we can obtain the normalized throughput of the VANET network:

$$R_V(i) = \frac{p_{tr} \cdot p_{suc}(i) \cdot E[l]}{E[s]}. \tag{6}$$

Where $E[l]$ represents the packet size, and the length of a time slot can be calculated as:

$$E[s] = (1 - p_{tr})\sigma + p_{tr}p_{suc}T_s + p_{tr}(1 - p_{suc})T_c. \tag{7}$$

Where T_s, T_c and σ respectively represent the average time of successful transmission, collision transmission and empty duration.

C-V2X: Since VANET is a communication between vehicles, the relative speed difference is not significant and the transmission range of VANET is not large, so there is no need to consider the impact of vehicles speed in VANET. But in C-V2X communication, the dynamic change of distance between vehicle and BS will have a great impact on transmission, so we take the speed information of V2X users into account to estimate the channel quality.

A subchannel can only be allocated to one user at the same time, we introduce an indicator $\beta_j^{c,t}$ to denote whether V2X user j utilize the subchannel c in the subframe t :

$$\beta_j^{c,t} = \begin{cases} 1, & \text{if subchannel } c \text{ is allocated to } j, \\ 0, & \text{otherwise.} \end{cases} \tag{8}$$

The propagation path-loss process can be described by Rayleigh fading, we assume BS transmits with a fixed power P^B, and the received signal power of user j is: $P_j^v = P^B \cdot |h_j|^2$. The speed of user j is denoted by $\mathbf{v}_j$, it varies with the different dense vehicle scenes and follows the Normal Distribution $\mathbf{v}_j \sim N(v_0, \sigma^2)$, thus the distance change of the user j in Δt can be expressed as $\Delta d = \mathbf{v}_j \cdot \Delta t$, then the channel gain can be calculated as:

$$|h_j|^2 = G_0 \cdot |d_j + \Delta d|^{-\partial} \cdot |h_0|^2, \tag{9}$$

Where the G_0 is the power gain factor caused by amplifier and antenna, Δt represents the time duration from the moment last data transmission was completed to the moment next data transmission is ready. d_j is the distance factor between BS and user j, ∂ is the path-loss exponent, and $h_0 \sim CN(0,1)$ is a complex Gaussian variable representing the Rayleigh fading. Thus the SINR of the V2X LTE user j could be calculated as:

$$\gamma_j^{c,t} = \frac{\beta_j^{c,t} \cdot P^B \cdot |h_j|^2}{\sigma^2 + \sum_{k=1}^{N_v} \beta_k^{c,t} \cdot P_k^v \cdot |g_k|^2}, \tag{10}$$

P_k^v is the transmission power of other users, $g_j(k)$ is the interference of user j caused by other k users [1]. Consequently, the achievable data rate of V2X LTE user j can be calculated as:

$$R_L^{c,t}(j) = B_0 \cdot g_0 \cdot \log_2 \left[1 + \gamma_j^{c,t} \right]. \tag{11}$$

Where B_0 represents the allocated bandwidth for each user, and the g_0 represents the throughput attenuation due to the framing (header, CRC, and cyclic prefix) and signaling overheads.

2.2   Delay of VANET and C-V2X

VANET: As above mention, T_s, T_c and σ respectively represent the average time of successful transmission, collision transmission and empty duration. Since the heterogenous network is controlled by the Hyper-BS, the hidden terminal problem can be avoided.

Packet Drop Delay: If the transmission process of user i reaches the retry limit, the packet will be dropped. According to [10], the packet drop probability is $p_{drop} = p_c^{m+1}$, and the average time slots required for a packet to experience $m + 1$ collision is:

$$E\left[T_{drop}\right] = \sum_{n=0}^{m} \frac{CW_n + 1}{2} = \frac{CW \cdot (2^{m'+1} - 1) + (m' + 1)}{2}, \tag{12}$$

Thus, the average time to drop a packet in a subframe can be calculated as:

$$E\left[D_{drop}\right] = E\left[T_{drop}\right] \cdot E\left[s\right], \tag{13}$$

Success Packet Delay: Similar to the analysis of packet drop delay, we use $E\left[T_{suc}\right]$ to denote the average time slots required for a successful transmission which can be calculated as:

$$E\left[T_{suc}\right] = \sum_{n=0}^{m} \left[\frac{(p' - p^{m'+1}) \cdot \frac{CW_n + 1}{2}}{1 - p^{m+1}} \right], \tag{14}$$

The successful transmission average delay is defined as the time interval from the time the packet is ready to be transmitted to the time the acknowledgement is received, which is given by:

$$E\left[D_{suc}\right] = E\left[T_{suc}\right] \cdot E\left[s\right]. \tag{15}$$

From what has been discussed above, the average delay of VANET user i can be expressed as:

$$E\left[D_V(i)\right] = \begin{cases} E\left[D_{suc}\right], & m < m', \\ E\left[D_{drop}\right], & others. \end{cases} \tag{16}$$

C-V2X: In cellular communication, 3GPP specified that GBR resource type like real-time video or vehicle safety services should control the latency under 50 ms. According to [5], in the UL/DL-based V2X with no-relay mode, the latency for message transmission from BS to user can be expressed as:

$$D_L(j) = (L - RRC) + (L - UL) + (L - NW) + (L - DL). \tag{17}$$

Where the $L - RRC$ is the connection time duration required to change the RRC state, $L - UL$ and $L - DL$ are the time required for the eNB to send the message to the destination through uplink and downlink, and the $L - NW$ denote the configuration latency and processing latency respectively.

Considering TDMA is widely adopted in cellular network, delay can be effectively reduced by an appropriate slot allocation, in order to further enhance the reliability of delay-sensitive V2X network, especially the safe-related messages, the slot jitter of C-V2X must be strictly controlled.

We assume the waiting queue length of user j is Q_j, which follows the normal distribution, then the number of slots n_j which user j require is:

$$n_j = \frac{Q_j}{R_L^{c,t}(j) \cdot l}, \tag{18}$$

where l is the length of a slot, since there are total S slots in a considered transmission frame T, thus the ideal uniform interval between slots can be expressed as:

$$U = \frac{S}{\sum_{1}^{j} n_j}, \tag{19}$$

Users send their queue length information to BS, then controller implement the time slot allocation $D = \{d_1, d_2, \ldots, d_j\}$, here d_j is the allocated interval between user j slot and user $j + 1$. The closer actual allocated slot interval d_j is to the ideal interval U, the smaller jitter is. Then the slot jitter can be described as the variance of d_j and U:

$$Var(j) = \sum_{1}^{j} \left[\frac{(d_j - U)^2}{\sum_{1}^{j} n_j} \right]. \tag{20}$$

3 Problem Formulation

In a periodic transmission time T, we describe the throughput by user's achievable data rate, and describe the system delay by average user delay, both of them are related to the number of users and time divide ratio. We aim to maximize the throughput and minimize the delay and jitter of total network, while simultaneously satisfying the different QoS requirements. Therefore, the joint optimization problem can be formulated as follows:

$$
\max_{\alpha, N_L} \left\{ \alpha \cdot \left[\sum_{t=1}^{T} \sum_{c=1}^{C} \sum_{j=1}^{N_L} R_L^{c,t}(j) - \sum_{t=1}^{T} \left(\sum_{j=1}^{N_L} \frac{D_L(j)}{N_L} + Var(j) \right) \right] \right\}
$$
$$
+ \left\{ (1-\alpha) \cdot \left[\sum_{t=1}^{T} \sum_{i=1}^{N_V} R_V(i) - \sum_{t=1}^{T} \sum_{i=1}^{N_V} \frac{E[D_V(i)]}{N_V} \right] \right\}. \tag{21}
$$

$$
\text{s.t.} \quad 0 \le \alpha \le 1, \tag{22}
$$
$$
\sum_{1}^{N_L} \beta_j^{c,t} \le 1, \ k \in [1, K], \ 1 \le t \le T, \tag{23}
$$
$$
\gamma_j^{c,t} \ge \gamma_{th}, \ k \in [1, K], \ 1 \le t \le T, \tag{24}
$$
$$
P_j^v \le P_{\max}, \tag{25}
$$
$$
D_L(j) \le D_e^{\max}, \tag{26}
$$
$$
R_V \ge R_{ne}^{\min}, \tag{27}
$$
$$
M \le N_e, \tag{28}
$$
$$
N \ge N_{ne}. \tag{29}
$$

In above, constraint (22) limits the ratio parameter α within 0 and 1; constraint (23) show that one subchannel can only be allocated to one C-V2X user ; constraint (24) and (25) shows the SINR threshold and the max transmit power; (26) and (27) show the maximum delay emergency users can tolerate, and $R_{ne}^{\min}$ is the minimum data rate requirement of non-emergency users; constraint (28) and (29) show that the C-V2X network could off-load some emergency users to VANET if the VANET system have very few users, to get lower delay. This is a mixed integer non-linear programming (MINLP), it is difficult to solve these problems in polynomial time. We will describe how to address the problem in next section.

4 Proposed Method

In this section, we propose a delay-throughput joint optimization algorithm (DT-PSO).

The stated mixed integer non-linear programming (21) have two objectives to optimize, which are usually conflicting with each other and difficult to solve at the same time. So we introduce the Mixed Discrete Multi-Objective Particle Swarm

---

Algorithm 1. PSO based Delay-Throughput Joint Optimizaion Algorithm

---

Require: Max generation: $maxgen$;
    Swarm size: pop;
    Learning factors: C_1, C_2;
Ensure: Pareto front solutions
 1: Initialization: v, p, P_{best}, G_{best}, w, t.
 2: **while** $(t < \text{max}gen)$ **do**
 3:   **for** $i = 1, 2, \ldots, pop$ **do**
 4:      Calculate fitness $F(x_i)$;
 5:      **if** $F(x_i(t)) \leq F(x_i(t+1))$ **then**
 6:         Update local $P_{best} = x_i(t+1)$
 7:      **end if**
 8:      **if** $F(G_{best}(t)) \leq F(P_{best}(t+1))$ **then**
 9:         Update global $G_{best}(t+1) = P_{best}(t+1)$
10:      **end if**
11:      **for** each particle **do**
12:         Velocity evaluation $v_i(t+1)$;
13:         Position eveluation $p_i(t+1)$;
14:      **end for**
15:      $t++$;
16:   **end for**
17: **end while**

Optimization (MDMO-PSO) algorithm [9], and modify it to solve complex multi-objective problems with mixed-discrete design variables. For simplicity, (21) can be reformulated as follow:

$$\min_{\alpha, N_L, d_j} \left\{ \alpha \cdot \left[\sum_{t=1}^{T} \left(\sum_{j=1}^{N_L} \frac{D_L(j)}{N_L} + Var(j) \right) - \sum_{t=1}^{T} \sum_{c=1}^{C} \sum_{j=1}^{N_L} R_L^{c,t}(j) \right] \right\}$$
$$\min_{\alpha, N_L} \left\{ (1-\alpha) \cdot \left[\sum_{t=1}^{T} \sum_{i=1}^{N_V} \frac{E[D_V(i)]}{N_V} - \sum_{t=1}^{T} \sum_{i=1}^{N_V} R_V(i) \right] \right\}. \tag{30}$$

The two polynomials in (30) are denoted by objective1 and objective2. The DT-PSO is presented in Algorithm 1. With the fixed max generation $maxgen$, swarm size pop, and inertia weigh ω, firstly, we initialize the position p, velocity v, local best position P_{best} and global best position G_{best}. Then, calculate the fitness of each particle, and the current fitness value $F(x)$ is obtained. Secondly, compare the fitness value of each particle $F(x_i(t))$ with the neighbor, if the current fitness value is better, then update the local leader P_{best}, otherwise, remain unchanged. Thirdly, select the best local solution P_{best} as the global best solution G_{best}. Fourthly, update the velocity and position, according to $v_i(t+1) = \omega v_i(t) + r_1 C_1 [P_{best_i(t)} - x_i(t)] + r_2 C_2 [G_{best_i(t)} - x_i(t)] +$
$r_3 \theta_{c,i} [x_i(t) - G_{best_i(t)}]$ and $x_i(t+1) = \begin{cases} 1, rand[0,1] < \frac{1}{1+\exp(-v_i(t+1))} \\ 0, \qquad otherwise \end{cases}$.
Lastly, if iteration t reaches the $maxgen$ or G_{best} is stable, we obtain the Pareto optimal solution. Furthermore, since the PSO has the defect of premature particle clustering, we improve the original diversity preservation mechanism by

changing the velocity update equation $r_3\theta_{c,i}\left[x_i(t) - G_{best_i(t)}\right]$ to avoid that, which is the diversity preservation item.

5   Simulation Result

We set the Hyper-BS transmits with fixed power $P^B = 43\,\text{dBm}$, and power gain factor $G = -31.5\,\text{dB}$. The user's receiving power threshold is $P_{th}^v = -75\,\text{dBm}$, and SINR threshold is $\gamma_{th} = 0\,\text{dB}$. The subchannel bandwidth is $B_0 = 15\,\text{kHz}$, number of subframes in each frame is 12. For safety's sake, the maximum delay that a emergency vehicle user can tolerance is $D_e^{\max} = 50\,\text{ms}$, and the minimum data rate required for non-emergency user is $R_{ne}^{\min} = 5\,\text{Mbit/s}$. The speed of vehicle range is 10–60 km/h, in urban scene, the average speed can be set as $v_0 = 40\,\text{km/h}$.

As shown in Fig. 3, since the two objectives in (30) are conflict with each other and cannot be optimized at the same time, we get the Pareto optimal solutions by using proposed algorithm, then the curve of Pareto front can be obtained according to these Pareto optimal sets. The green, red and blue markers show the ideal point, and extreme points respectively.

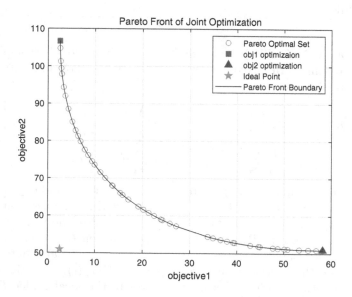

Fig. 3. The pareto front of joint optimization. (Color figure online)

Figures 4 and 5 shows the performance evaluation of the proposed DT-PSO. We can observe that, the average delay of emergency users increase as the number of users increases because of channel collision, while the throughput of no-emergency users decreases as the number of users increases due to growing signaling occupation. Compared with single optimization [3] and RAS algorithm

[6], in our scheme, the emergency users have lower average delay under the condition of same throughput, while the no-emergency users have higher data rate under the condition of same delay. And in Fig. 5 we can observe that emergency users have smaller jitter in our scheme when compare to other approaches.

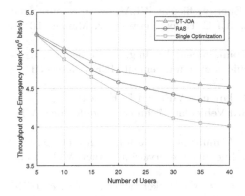
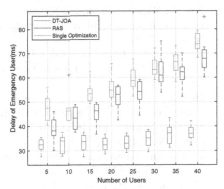

Fig. 4. Throughput of non-emergency users.

Fig. 5. Delay of emergency users.

6 Conclusion

In this paper, we investigate the coexistence problem of the heterogeneous vehicular network include C-V2X and VANET. To meet the QoS of different users, we jointly optimize the overall delay and throughput by user scheduling and time allocation, then formulate the problem into a mixed integer non-linear programming (MINLP). To solve the stated problem, we propose a delay-throughput joint optimization algorithm (DT-PSO) to get the Pareto optimal solution efficiently. Simulation results show that the proposed scheme outperforms existing approaches both in delay and throughput.

References

1. Wang, P., et al.: Cellular V2X communications in unlicensed spectrum: harmonious coexistence with VANET in 5G systems. IEEE Trans. Wirel. Commun. **17**(8), 5212–5224 (2018)
2. Wu, W., Kong, L., Xue, T.: Resource allocation algorithm for V2X communications based on SCMA. In: Liang, Q., Mu, J., Jia, M., Wang, W., Feng, X., Zhang, B. (eds.) CSPS 2017. LNEE, vol. 463, pp. 1997–2004. Springer, Singapore (2019). https://doi.org/10.1007/978-981-10-6571-2_243
3. Wei, Q., et al.: Wireless resource management in LTE-U driven heterogeneous V2X communication networks. IEEE Trans. Veh. Technol. **67**(8), 7508–7522 (2018)

4. Peng, H., et al.: Performance analysis of IEEE 802.11p DCF for multiplatooning communications with autonomous vehicles. IEEE Trans. Veh. Technol. **66**(3), 2485–2498 (2017)
5. Lee, K., Kim, J., Park, Y., Wang, H., Hong, D.: Latency of cellular-based V2X: perspectives on TTI-proportional latency and TTI-independent latency. IEEE Access **5**, 15800–15809 (2017)
6. Xu, C., Wang, J., Zhu, Z., Niyato, D.: Energy-efficient WLANs with resource and re-association scheduling optimization. IEEE Trans. Netw. Serv. Manag. **16**(2), 563–577 (2019)
7. Chen, Q., Yu, G., Elmaghraby, H.M., Hamalainen, J., Ding, Z.: Embedding LTE-U within Wi-Fi bands for spectrum efficiency improvement. IEEE Netw. **31**(2), 72–79 (2017)
8. He, K., Yu, G.: Genetic algorithm for balancing WiFi and LTE coexistence in the unlicensed spectrum. In: 2016 IEEE 83rd Vehicular Technology Conference (VTC Spring), Nanjing, pp. 1–5 (2016)
9. Tong, W., Chowdhury, S., Messac, A.: A multi-objective mixed-discrete particle swarm optimization with multi-domain diversity preservation. Struct. Multidiscip. Optim. **53**(3), 471–488 (2016)
10. Chatzimisios, P., Boucouvalas, A.C., Vitsas, V.: Packet delay analysis of IEEE 802.11 MAC protocol. Electron. Lett. **39**(18), 1358–1359 (2003)
11. Feng, M., Guomin, L., Wenrong, G.: Heterogeneous network resource allocation optimization based on improved bat algorithm. In: 2018 International Conference on Sensor Networks and Signal Processing (SNSP), Xi'an, China, pp. 55–59 (2018)
12. Martin-Sacristan, D., et al.: Low-latency V2X communication through localized MBMS with local V2X servers coordination. In: 2018 IEEE International Symposium on Broadband Multimedia Systems and Broadcasting (BMSB), Valencia, pp. 1–8 (2018)
13. Li, X., Ma, L., Shankaran, R., Xu, Y., Orgun, M.: Joint power control and resource allocation mode selection for safety-related V2X communication. IEEE Trans. Veh. Technol. **68**(8), 7970–7986 (2019)

A Lightweight Interference Measurement Algorithm for Wireless Sensor Networks

Bo Zeng[1,3(✉)], Gege Zhang[2], Zhixue Zhang[3], and Shanshan Li[3]

[1] School of Information Technology, Luoyang Normal Univerisity, Luoyang, China
hn@163.com
[2] Department of Automation, Shanghai Jiao Tong University, Minhang, China
ggzhang@sjtu.edu.cn
[3] School of Information Engineering, Henan University of Science and Technology,
Luoyang, China
{zhangzx,lss}@haust.edu.cn

Abstract. The most applications of wireless sensor network have stringent requirements for communication performance. To meet applications requirements, it is crucial to measure the wireless interference between nodes, which is the major factor that reduces the performance of wireless sensor networks (WSNs). However, the key problem of accurately measuring wireless interference is that the node cannot predict the neighbor node information after the network is deployed, and thus cannot establish the correspondence between the wireless interference strength and the neighbor node. To tackle this problem, this paper presents a lightweight interference measurement algorithm for WSNs. The algorithm divides the interference measurement process into three phases. The first two phases are used to gather all two-hop neighbor information by exchanging between nodes. In the third phase, each node performs interference measurements and builds the relationship of wireless interference between nodes. The experimental results show that our proposed approaches can obtain accurate inter-node wireless interference strength with low energy and communication overhead.

1 Introduction

Wireless sensor networks have been widely used in transportation, agriculture, construction, military and other fields. Most wireless sensor network applications impose strict requirements on communication performance. In general, wireless sensor nodes are interconnected by wireless links and self-organized to form an interconnected network. Due to the broadcastability of the wireless channel, the data transmission of the node will cause significant wireless interference to its neighboring nodes, then affecting the data transmission of its neighbor nodes, thereby reducing the network transmission efficiency and increasing the data transmission delay. For wireless sensor network applications, accurate measurement of wireless interference between nodes is the key to improve communication

H. Gao et al. (Eds.): ChinaCom 2019, LNICST 312, pp. 631–641, 2020.
https://doi.org/10.1007/978-3-030-41114-5_47

performance. Due to the limited communication and computing power of wire-less sensor nodes, it is challenging to achieve accurate measurement of wireless interference of nodes with lower energy and communication overhead.

Early research on wireless interference focused on modeling the relation-ship between wireless interference and packet reception ratio(PRR). Usually, the paper studies the wireless interference between several nodes and constructs wireless interference model, such as SINR-PRR [1–3]. By using these research results, the scheduling of node data transmission can be realized, thereby improv-ing the communication performance of link scheduling, media access control, and routing protocols [3–5]. Since the wireless interference model constructed based on the small-scale sensor test network, the wireless interference model can effec-tively improve the communication performance in a network environment similar to the experiment. However, when extended to large-scale sensor networks, the node's wireless interference environment is very complex, and the link status between nodes is time-varying. The adaptability of wireless interference models cannot be effectively guaranteed. Therefore, the run-time measurement of wire-less interference is one of the feasible solutions to solve the wireless interference model's adaptability to the network environment.

Based on the TDMA protocol, the paper combines the node ID with the time slot allocation by using the unique ID of the node in the network. Each node has a unique time slot, which ensures that the wireless interference of the node can be accurately measured and recorded. The algorithm divides the interfer-ence measurement process into three phases. The first two phases complete the information collection of the two-hop neighbor nodes through the information exchange of neighbor nodes. Each node broadcasts in its own time slot in the third phase, and the neighbor nodes complete the measurement of the wireless interference strength by monitoring the wireless channel. After all nodes com-plete the broadcast, each node can accurately construct a wireless interference matrix based on the result of interference measurement. Based on this, more reliable node transmission activity scheduling and network performance opti-mization can be realized.

2   Related Work

Since Gupta and Kumar [6] proposed an accurate interference model for wireless networks, there are many works were carried out for researching the behavior of interference in wireless networks. In this section, we review these related work.

Zhao's work [7] showed that the communication links are often lossy and asymmetric. In [8], the author proposed a calculation model to compute inter-ference levels in wireless multi-hop ad-hoc networks. The object of the model is to calculate the expected value of carrier to interference ratio (C/I) and evalu-ate performance of mobile wireless ad-hoc networks. The relationship of wireless interference and path reception ratio is referred in [9]. The author show that the average signal to noise and interference ratio (SINR) either remains constant , or decays when the number of interferers scales to infinity in the network. In order to understand the role of interference on the overall performance of wireless networks, Razak et al. [10] show that the number of scenarios of two-flow interaction is very larger when relax the assumption that the wireless interference range is equal to the receipting range.

Unlike the previous works, some works study the interference by examples. Subbu et al. [11] examines the impact of collocated 802.15.4 devices on each other by observing the effect of interfering device on the desired device in terms of packet error rate (PER). The author want to understand how and when 802.15.4 may impact each others performance. In [12], the author experimentally investigate the effects of WLAN and realistic RF interference on packet delivery performance in body area networks (BANs). Rahul et al. [13] propose a approach to detecting and mitigation interference occurs in two different ZigBee networks. When interference happened, the protocol leverages collaboration between interfering networks to determine which network should switch to a different channel. Interference also can be used to discovery wireless LAN, and a interesting approach is described in [14].

3   Interference Measurement Algorithm

Consider a homogeneous sensor network that is composed of a single base station (BS) and N sensors are randomly distributed in a monitoring area. We use $S = s_1, s_2, \ldots, s_n$ to denote the set of sensors. Each node has the same initial energy. For node i and node j, the communication is reliable iff the distance $d_{ij} \leq d_o$, otherwise there is only wireless interference between two nodes. d_o was defined in [15]. For simplicity, we only considers wireless inteference measurements within two hops.

The problem to be solved in this paper is described as follows: In a given wireless sensor network, for any node i in the network, it is assumed that the set of one-hop and two-hop neighbor set are represented by L_1 and L_2, respectively. The interference measurement algorithm can be used to accurately measure the two-way wireless interference strength between the node and any of the node in $L_1 \cup L_2$, while the algorithm has lower time and energy overhead.

The paper designs a TDMA-based interference measurement algorithm. Each node is assigned a unique time slot, and the ID of the node is the time slot assigned to the node, and the ID is begin with 1. The node transmits data only when its time slot arrives, otherwise it switchs to the listening state. In order to ensure that the proposed algorithm can be executed correctly, clock synchronization is necessary between nodes. Many efficient clock synchronization mechanisms can be combined with our algorithm, such as TPSN [16]. For the sake of discussion, this article assumes that all nodes have completed clock synchronization. The algorithm consists of three phases: the first phase is used to complete the information collection of the one-hop neighbor node and the partial two-hop neighbor node; the second phase is executed to improve the information of the two-hop neighbor node; finally, the node interference measurement is finished in the third phase, and each node can construct a local interference matrix after completing the interference measurement.

The first stage: one-hop neighbor node information collection. Since the ID number of each node in the network is unique, the time slot $slot_i$ assigned to the node i can calculate using Eq. 1.

$$slot_i = (s_{id} - 1) * t_{slot} + t_{init} \tag{1}$$

where $slot_i$ represents the ID of the node i, t_{slot} represents the length of the time slot, and t_{init} represents the start time of the first phase. Note that in order to ensure that our algorithm can perform normally, the setting of t_{init} should take into account the time of network deployment.

After completing the slot calculation, each node broadcasts the node's neighbor information N_{info} to its one-hop range in its time slot. The node will then stay in the listening state for the remaining time slots of this phase to receive neighbor information broadcast by its neighbor nodes. The generation and update process of the one-hop neighbor information table is shown in Fig. 1.

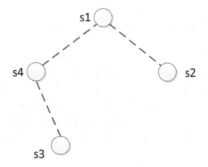

Fig. 1. The network topology of our illusration

The dashed line between nodes is just to indicate the neighbor relationship. It can be concluded that the one-hop and two-hop neighbor relationships of node s1 can be represented by the set: $L_1 = (s2, s4)$ and $L_2 = (s3)$, respectively. According to time slot arrangement method, the time slots of the nodes $s1$, $s2$, $s3$, and $s4$ are $slot_1$, $slot_2$, $slot_3$, and $slot_4$, respectively. Therefore, node $s1$ will first broadcast its neighbor information N_{info}. The N_{info} contains $s1$'s slot information and the partial one-hop neighbor time slot information that it has collected so far. At this time, the neighbor information N_{info} of $s1$ is shown in Table 1.

Since there is no radio interference and is located within the effective communication range of the node $s1$, the neighbor nodes $s2$, $s4$ can correctly receive the neighbor information of the node $s1$ and construct its own neighbor information table. The neighbor information tables of nodes $s2$ and $s4$ are shown in Tables 2 and 3, respectively.

Table 1. The $s1$'s neighbor information

s_{id}	$s1$
t_{slot}	1
hop	0

Table 2. The $s2$'s neighbor information

s_{id}	$s1$	$s2$
t_{slot}	1	2
hop	1	0

Table 3. The $s4$'s neighbor information

s_{id}	$s1$	$s4$
t_{slot}	1	4
hop	1	0

Next, the node $s2$ broadcasts its neighbor information in the time slot 2. For the same reason, the node $s1$ will be able to correctly receive the neighbor information of $s2$, and after updating based on the the neighbor information of $s2$, the neighbor information of s1 is as shown in the Table 4.

Table 4. The updated $s1$'s neighbor information

s_{id}	$s1$	$s2$
t_{slot}	1	2
hop	0	1

According to the time slot arrangement, the node $s3$ broadcasts its neighbor information during the time slot 3, the node $s4$ receives the neighbor information of $s3$, and after updating based on this information, the neighbor information of $s4$ is shown in Table 5.

Table 5. The updated $s4$'s neighbor information

s_{id}	$s1$	$s3$	$s4$
t_{slot}	1	2	4
hop	1	1	0

Finally, $s4$ broadcasts its neighbor information in time slot 4. The nodes $s1$ and $s3$ receive the neighbor information of s4 and update according to it. The updated neighbor information of $s1$ and $s4$ are Tables 6 and 7, respectively.

Table 6. The updated $s1$'s neighbor information

s_{id}	$s1$	$s2$	$s3$	$s4$
t_{slot}	1	2	3	4
hop	0	1	2	1

Table 7. The updated $s3$'s neighbor information

s_{id}	$s1$	$s3$	$s4$
t_{slot}	1	3	4
hop	2	0	1

In the first phase, the node collects some two-hop neighbor information, such as nodes $s1$ and $s3$. However, since $s1$ finished the neighbor information broadcast before $s2$ and $s4$, $s2$ and $s4$ cannot successfully collect the two-hop neighbor information related to $s1$. In order to solve this problem, the algorithm will execute the second phase to improve the two-hop neighbor information of all nodes.

In the first phase, each node uses only one time slot, so the duration of the first phase is $N * t_{slot}$.

The second stage: the exchange and update of two-hop neighbor information. This phase is mainly used to improve the two-hop neighbor information of all nodes. In order to ensure the smooth progress of the second phase, we have $t_{init} = N * t_{slot} + t_{gap}$, where t_{gap} is mainly used to ensure that the second phase can start correctly. Therefore, in the second phase, the time slot of the node is calculated using Eq. 2.

$$slot_t = (s_{id} - 1) * t_{slot} + N * t_{slot} + t_{gap} \qquad (2)$$

Each node broadcasts neighbor information according to the allocated time slot. After the second phase is executed, all nodes can obtain complete one-hop and two-hop neighbor information. For example, nodes $s2$, $s4$ will receive the neighbor information broadcast by node $s1$ in time slot 1. After the neighbor information table is updated, the neighbor information of the nodes $s2$ and $s4$ are shown in Tables 8 and 9.

In this phase, since each node occupies one time slot, the duration of this phase is $N * t_{slot}$.

The third phase: the node performs interference measurement and constructs a local interference matrix. The node will listen to the wireless channel according

Table 8. The updated $s2$'s neighbor information

s_{id}	$s1$	$s2$	$s4$
t_{slot}	1	2	4
hop	1	0	2

Table 9. The updated $s4$'s neighbor information

s_{id}	$s1$	$s2$	$s3$	$s4$
t_{slot}	1	2	3	4
hop	1	2	1	0

to its neighbor information to measure the wireless interference strength related to the neighbor node, and then switch into sleep model until the active time slot of neighbor node arrives. In the third phase, the initial time of the node slot is $t_{init} = 2 * N * t_{slot} + t_{gap}$, and the slot of each node is set by equation (3).

$$slot_t = (s_{id} - 1) * t_{slot} + 2 * N * t_{slot} + t_{gap} \qquad (3)$$

After the interference measurement is completed, each node will construct an interference matrix as shown in Table 10 (for example, 50 nodes are randomly deployed in a 100 m × 100 m area. The wireless signal propagation model is Two Ray model).

Table 10. A node's interference matrix (db)

s_{id}	$s6$	$s8$	$s15$	13
Strength	−23.5	−23.1	−26.5	−13.6
hop	2	2	2	1

4   Numerical Results

We evaluate our interference measurement algorithm by simulation examples with random network has different diameter and the amount of nodes. The energy model we used is described in [15]. The energy model is expressed as follows:

$$E_{Tx}(P_l, d) = P_l E_e + P_l \varepsilon_{fs} d^2$$
$$E_{Rx}(P_l, d) = P_l E_e \qquad (4)$$

where P_l denotes the size of packet, the default value is 1000 bits. E_e denotes the energy consumed by the circuit when transmitting and receiving data, the

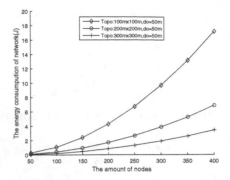

Fig. 2. The network energy consumption vs the amount of nodes

default value is 50 nJ/bit. ε_{fs} is the power loss factor, the default value is 0.0013 $(\mathrm{pJ/bit})/m^4$. d denotes the communication distance between two nodes, and $d \leq d_o$.

Figure 2 shows the relationship between network energy consumption and the number of nodes. In all experiments, the node effective communication distance d_o is set to 50 m. It can be seen from the figure that when the network has the same number of nodes, changing the network coverage (from 100 m × 100 m to 300×300 m) will reduce the total energy consumption of the interference measurement, which means that distributing the nodes in a wider area will reduce the node density, thus Reduce interference measurement energy consumption. For the same reason, for the same network topology, for example, 100 m × 100 m, changing the number of nodes significantly increases the energy consumption of the interference measurement.

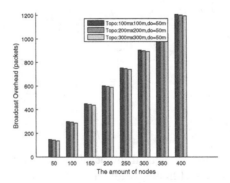

Fig. 3. The communication overhead vs the amount of nodes

Figure 3 shows the relationship between the number of nodes and communication overhead. The effective communication distance d_o is set to 50 m. It can be seen from the figure that as the number of nodes increases, the number of packets that need to be broadcasted to complete the interference measurement also increases significantly, and the total number of packets is basically three times the number of nodes. This is basically in line with the theoretical results of the interference measurement algorithm in this paper.

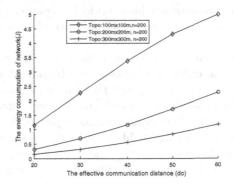

Fig. 4. The energy consumption vs effective communication distance

Figure 4 shows the relationship between communication distance *do* and network energy consumption. It can be concluded that the increase of the effective communication distance of the node will increase the number of neighbor nodes, thereby significantly increasing the energy consumption. For a network with a high node density, for example, deploying 400 nodes in a 100 m × 100 m area, the energy consumption is significantly higher than that of the other two scales, and the energy consumption is nearly five times different. This shows that the interference measurement algorithm is not suitable for networks with high node density.

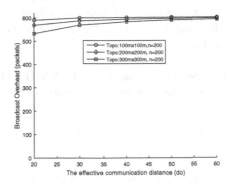

Fig. 5. Communication overhead vs effective communication distance

Figure 5 shows the relationship between effective communication distance and network communication overhead. It can be concluded from the figure that for networks of different network sizes, when the communication distance of nodes increases, the difference in broadcast overhead of the algorithm will gradually become smaller. The reason is that the increase of the communication distance of the node will lead to an increase in the number of neighbor nodes, and more neighbor information can be obtained by the broadcast of the node, so that the node can obtain complete neighbor node information, and the node that broadcasts in the second stage is reduced. Then, the broadcast overhead of the network is reduced.

It is worth noting that, as shown in Figs. 4 and 5, under the same communication distance, the difference between the broadcast overheads of different networks is gradually decreasing, and the difference in energy consumption is significantly increased, which indicates that the large energy consumption is consumption during the interference measurement phase. As the communication distance increases, the number of neighbor nodes of the node increases, and the number of times the node needs to detect the interference strength will increase significantly, resulting in an increase in node energy consumption.

5   Conclusion

The paper proposes a lightweight interference measurement algorithm. The algorithm divides the interference measurement process into three phases. The first two phases realize the information exchange and collection of the two-hop neighbor nodes by letting the nodes schedule the broadcasts according to the time slots, and provide complete neighbor node information for the third-stage interference measurement. In the third phase, each node broadcasts an interference measurement packet in its own time slot, and monitors the wireless signal strength in the neighbor node time slot, and completes the measurement and acquisition of the neighbor node interference strength. The accurate measurement results provided by the algorithm can be used for network transmission activity scheduling of nodes, which can achieve reliable concurrency of data transmission activities between nodes, thereby improving network efficiency and reducing transmission delay.

Acknowledgment. This research was funded by CERNET Innovation Project (No. NGII20160517,NGII20180313). Scientific and technological project in Henan Province (No. 172102210255).

References

1. Chang, X., et al.: Accuracy-aware interference modeling and measurement in wireless sensor networks. IEEE Trans. Mob. Comput. **15**, 278–291 (2016)
2. Son, D., Krishnamachari, B., Heidemann, J.S.: Experimental study of concurrent transmission in wireless sensor networks. In: International Conference on Embedded Networked Sensor Systems (2006)

3. Maheshwari, R., Jain, S., Das, S.R.: A measurement study of interference modeling and scheduling in low-power wireless networks. In: Acm Conference on Embedded Network Sensor Systems (2008)
4. Staniec, K., Debita, G.: Interference mitigation in WSN by means of directional antennas and duty cycle control. Wirel. Commun. Mob. Comput. **12**(16), 1481–1492 (2012)
5. Ahmed, N., Kanhere, S.S., Jha, S.: Mitigating the effect of interference in wireless sensor networks. In: IEEE Conference on Local Computer Networks (2010)
6. Gupta, P., Kumar, P.: The capacity of wireless networks. IEEE Trans. Inf. Theor. **46**(2), 388–404 (2000)
7. Zhao, J., Govindan, R.: Understanding packet delivery performance in dense wireless sensor networks. In: Proceedings of the 1st International Conference on Embedded Networked Sensor Systems, pp. 1–13 (2004)
8. Hekmat, R., Van Mieghem, P.: Interference in wireless multi-hop ad-hoc networks and its effect on network capacity. Wirel. Netw. **10**, 389–399 (2004)
9. Moraes, R., Arajo, F.: Modeling interference in wireless ad hoc networks. In: 15th International Symposium on Modeling, Analysis, and Simulation of Computer and Telecommunication Systems, MASCOTS 2007 , October 2007, pp. 54–59 (2007)
10. Razak, S., Kolar, V., Abu-Ghazaleh, N.B.: Modeling and analysis of two-flow interactions in wireless networks. Ad Hoc Netw. **8**(6), 564–581 (2010)
11. Subbu, K., Howitt, I.: Empirical study of IEEE 802.15.4 mutual interference issues. In: Proceedings 2007 SoutheastCon, pp. 191–195. IEEE, March 2007
12. Hauer, J.-H., Handziski, V., Wolisz, A.: Experimental study of the impact of WLAN interference on IEEE 802.15.4 body area networks. In: Roedig, U., Sreenan, C.J. (eds.) EWSN 2009. LNCS, vol. 5432, pp. 17–32. Springer, Heidelberg (2009). https://doi.org/10.1007/978-3-642-00224-3_2
13. Shah, R.C., Nachman, L.: Interference detection and mitigation in IEEE 802.15.4 networks. In: International Conference on Information Processingin Sensor Networks, pp. 553–554 (2008)
14. Zhou, R., Xiong, Y., Xing, G., Sun, L., Ma, J.: ZiFi: wireless LAN discovery via zigBee interference signatures. In: Proceedings of the Sixteenth Annual International Conference on Mobile computing and networking, ser. MobiCom 2010, pp. 49–60. ACM, New York (2010)
15. Heinzelman, W., Chandrakasan, A., Balakrishnan, H.: An application-specific protocol architecture for wireless microsensor networks. IEEE Trans. Wirel. Commun. **1**(4), 660–670 (2002)
16. Ganeriwawal, S., et al.: Timing-sync protocol for sensor networks. In: Proceedings of Sensor Sysrem (2003)

Dynamic Network Change Detection via Dynamic Network Representation Learning

Hao Feng, Yan Liu$^{(\boxtimes)}$, Ziqiao Zhou, and Jing Chen

China State Key Laboratory of Mathematical Engineering and Advanced Computing,
Zhengzhou, China
hycka@sohu.com, ms_liuyan@aliyun.com, 897777143@qq.com,
15138721829@163.com

Abstract. The structure of the network in the real world is very complex, as the dynamic network structure evolves in time dimension, how to detect network changes accurately and further locate abnormal nodes is a research hotspot. Most current feature learning methods are difficult to capture a variety of network connectivity patterns, and have a high time complexity. In order to overcome this limitation, we introduce the network embedding method into the field of network change detection, we find that node-based egonet can better reflect the connectivity patterns of the node, so a dynamic network embedding model Egonet2Vec is proposed, which is based on extracting the connectivity patterns of the node-based egonets. After the dynamic network representation learning, we use a dynamic network change detection strategy to detect network change time points and locate abnormal nodes. We apply our method to real dynamic network datasets to demonstrate the validity of this method.

Keywords: Network representation learning · Social network · Egonet

1 Introduction

Dynamic network refers to the network that changes with time. Such as social networks, communication networks, and topological networks are common dynamic networks, which widely exist in real life. Taking social networks as an example, with the widespread use of various network services such as Twitter, Facebook on the Internet, people widely communicate and transmit information through networks. Therefore, a huge social network is formed in the virtual network space, in which the nodes of the network represent each individual, and the edges represents the connection between people, and the network changes over time. Usually, the structural features of the network maintain a stable state, which changes slightly over time. When an anomalous event occurs, the structure of the network and related nodes often change dramatically. By detecting the structural changes of dynamic network, the occurrence of anomalous events can

H. Gao et al. (Eds.): ChinaCom 2019, LNICST 312, pp. 642–658, 2020.
https://doi.org/10.1007/978-3-030-41114-5_48

be detected, and then the abnormal nodes can be located. However, in the face of large-scale and complex network data, traditional dynamic network detection methods are often difficult to extract network structural features comprehensively, thus affecting the effect of dynamic network detection.

Network representation learning has caused the widespread research upsurge in recent years, the basic idea is to extract the structural features of the network and transform the nodes into vector representations through the neural network model. The vector should reflect the structural features of the original network as much as possible. However, most of the existing network representation learning methods can not be directly applied to dynamic networks. We find that the neighborhood structure features of the nodes are basically stable at ordinary times, and will also change drastically when anomalous events occur. Based on this, we propose a dynamic network representation learning method based on extracting the neighborhood structural features of the nodes, which can be directly applied to dynamic networks. Then a dynamic network change detection strategy is carried out by this embedding method. The contributions of this paper are listed as follows:

(1) We propose the Egonet2Vec (Egonet to vector) model, an dynamic network representation learning method that computes the vector representations of nodes by extracting the node-based structural features.
(2) Based on the Egonet2Vec model, a dynamic network anomaly detection method is designed. The anomalous time points and the abnormal node set under the anomalous time points are located by calculating similarity of the nodes and time slice networks.
(3) Experiment verification on real dynamic network datasets, in Enron email dataset and AS links dataset, our method has achieved good results, can identify most abnormal time points and locate the abnormal nodes.

The rest of the paper is organized as follows: In the next section, we comprehensively analyze and discuss the related work. Problem definitions is described in Sect. 3. Section 4 introduces the dynamic network change detection method. Section 5 verifies the experimental results of the anomaly detection algorithm. Section 6 summarizes the contributions and forecasts the next research direction.

2   Related Work

In the field of dynamic network anomaly detection, Michele et al. [1] proposed NetSimile method, which extracts the node-based structural features, calculates network similarity at different time slice network through feature aggregation, finally identifies abnormal time points by similarity changes. Volodymyr et al. [2] proposed a dynamic network anomaly detection algorithm based on Hopfield neural network. This method first filters the non-anomalous nodes in the dynamic network, and then uses Hopfield neural network to locate the abnormal node set and the abnormal time points. Yu et al. [3] proposed NetWalk method, which is a network embedding method based on autoencoder neural network.

After obtaining the vector representations of each node, k-means clustering is performed according to the vector representations of each node. For the newly joined nodes, the degree of anomaly of those nodes is judged by calculating the distance from the nearest class in k-means clustering. The farther the distance is, the more abnormal the node is. Sun et al. [4] divides the nodes in the network into source nodes and target nodes, and performs community partitioning based on entropy (minimum coding length) in the source nodes and the target nodes, respectively. Finally nodes with large difference in entropy are marked as abnormal nodes.

In the field of network representation learning, Inspired by the word2vec model, Perozzi et al. [5] proposed the DeepWalk method, which introduced the deep learning technique to the field of graph representation for the first time. This algorithm uses random walks to generate a sequence of nodes similar to sentences in the document, and finally get vector representations of each node. Introducing two hyper parameters(p and q) to control the depth and width of the random walks, the node2vec [8] follows the DeepWalk algorithm and improves the generation of random walk paths. The LINE [9] method obtains the final vector representations by probabilistic modeling of all first-order and second-order proximity of nodes, and minimizing the probability distribution and the empirical distribution distance. The Subgraph2Vec [10] constructs the rooted subgraph of each node as the target word whose neighbor nodes and their rooted subgraphs are regarded as the context, and finally calls the word2vec model to learn the vector representation of the subgraph. The Graph2Vec [11] method, proposed based on the Subgraph2Vec algorithm, also uses the rooted subgraph as the target word. The neighbor nodes and their rooted subgraphs are used as context of those target words, the doc2vec [6] model is used to directly obtain the vector representation of the whole graph. The GE-FSG [12] method first mines frequent subgraphs on the graph dataset, and identifies frequent subgraphs by serial number. If a subgraph appears in the graph, the subgraph number is added to the context of the graph, so that each graph in the dataset maintains a context consisting of frequent subgraphs. Then calling the doc2vec model for training, this algorithm finally gets the vector representations of each graph in the graph dataset.

However, most of the existing network embedding methods learn the representation vectors for nodes in a static manner, which are not suitable for dynamic network embedding. At the same time, the traditional anomaly detection methods have the problem of high computational cost. Based on this, we propose a new representation learning model for dynamic networks, and develop a dynamic network anomaly detection method based on this model.

3   Problem Descriptions

3.1   Related Conceptions

Definition 1 *(Dynamic Network). Unlike static networks, dynamic networks change over time. A dynamic network containing n time slices is represented* as $G = \{G_1, G_2, ..., G_t, G_{t+1}, ..., G_n\}$, where the t th time slice network is $G_t = (V_t, E_t)$. V_t is the set of vertices in the network, and E_t is the edge set representing the relationship between the vertices. $G_t = (V_t, E_t, W_t)$ when the network is a weighted network and W_t is the weights set.

Definition 2 *(Network Embedding). Given a network $G = (V, E)$, the purpose of network embedding is to learn a mapping function to map each node in the network to a low-dimensional vector: $v_i \rightarrow y_i \in R^d$, $d \ll |V|$. The algorithm finally gets the low-dimensional dense vector representations of network nodes, which is very effective when dealing with large scale complex networks.*

3.2 Problem Descriptions

In this paper, dynamic network change refers to the abnormal changes in the process of network evolution. Doing dynamic network change detection needs to solve three problems: dynamic network model construction, network embedding model construction and design detection strategy.

Dynamic network modeling: At present, the method widely used in dynamic network modeling is the time slice partitioning method, which needs to choose the appropriate time slice size to divide the network. Too long time slice setting may make the important change information of the network hidden in the time slice window, and too short time slice may lead to little information contained in a time slice network.

Network representation learning: Existing network representation learning models such as Line, node2vec, etc. can only perform representation learning on each time slice network, and the obtained vector representations of the same node in different time slice networks cannot compare similarities directly. At the same time, the structural information of nodes can not be extracted comprehensively based on random walk. Therefore, a new network representation learning method is needed, which can extract the node's structural features comprehensively and obtain the vector representations of each node in different time slice networks. At the same time, not only the similarity between nodes in the same time slice network, but also the similarity between nodes in different time slice networks can also be compared.

Detection strategy: After obtaining the vector representation of the nodes, in order to detect the overall change of the current time slice network, we need to aggregate the vector representations of each node as the vector representation of the entire time slice network, and calculate the similarity between adjacent time slice networks. By setting the network similarity threshold, if recently arrived network's similarity exceeds the threshold, we can judge that the current network has changed.

In summary, network representation learning is the core of our dynamic network change detection method, and how to extract node based structural features is the focus of the network representation learning method.

4   Dynamic Network Change Detection Model

4.1   Related Conceptions

Definition 3 *(Label Graph). The Label Graph is a graph with node labels and edge labels, which is described as: $G = (V, E, L)$, where V and E are the set of vertices and edges in the graph, and L is the label mapping function of edges and nodes.*

Definition 4 *(Subgraph). Given a label graph $S = (V_S, E_S, L_S)$, for any $V_S \subseteq V$, $E_S \subseteq E$, if and only if $L_S(v) = L(v)$ is true for each $v \in V_S$, and $L_S(u, v) = L(u, v)$ is true for each $(u, v) \in E_S$, the graph S is called the subgraph of the graph G.*

Definition 5 *(DFS Edge (depth-first search edge)). An edge can be presented by a 5-tuple $(from, to, vlb_i, elb, vlb_j)$, where from and to are the ordinal number of nodes (v_i, v_j) in depth-first search, vlb_i and vlb_j are the labels of v_i and v_j, and elb is the label of edge between them.*

Definition 6 *(DFS Code). DFS Code [17] is a combination of a series of DFS Edges. The DFS Code of an n-edge graph is $\{DFSEdge_1, DFSEdge_2, ..., DFSEdge_n\}$.*

Definition 7 *(DFS Lexicographic Order). In order to compare the size relationship between DFS Edges , we define the priority of elements in 5-tuple $(frm, to, vlb_i, elb, vlb_j)$ decreases in turn. We determine the relationship of size between DFS Edges by comparing the lexicographic order of each element in turn.*

Definition 8 *(Minimum DFS Code). A graph can be represented by different DFS Codes. According to DFS Lexicographic Order, the minimum one is called minimum DFS Code. A graph has only one minimum DFS Code representation, the minimum DFS Code is used to uniquely identify a graph.*

Definition 9 *(N-edge Subgraphs). Given a graph $G = (V, E, L)$, SS, a collection of all sub-graph of graph G. For each subgraph $S \in SS$, $S = (V_S, E_S, L_S)$, if the number of edges in graph S is not greater than N, $|E_S| \leq N$, $N \in R$, then graph S is called a N-edge subgraph of G, the collection of all N-edge subgraphs is called N-edge Subgraphs.*

Definition 10 *(Egonet). Node-based egonet refers to a node-centered self-graph, which consists of all the nodes connected to it and the edges between them.*

4.2   Egonet2Vec Network Representation Learning Method

N-Edge Subgraphs Extraction. Egonet2Vec dynamic network representation learning algorithm aims to learn the vector representations of each node in all time slice networks. To do this, we need to construct structural feature set for each node. Then based on the current popular doc2vec models, the structural

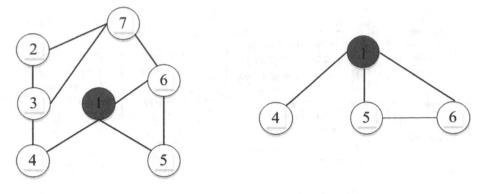

Fig. 1. The generation of node-based egonet

feature set of the single node is regarded as a document, and the substructure in the feature set is regarded as a word in the document. Finally, based on the above model, we can obtain the vector representations of each node in all time slice networks.

The construction of egonet is shown in Fig. 1, the egonet of node 1 is constructed. If we construct egonets for all nodes in a graph, then the original graph structure can be restored by combining the egonets of the nodes. In general, node-based egonet is more focused on the neighborhood structural features of individual nodes. Therefore, we choose the node-based egonet as the basis for network representation learning. Then the following question is how to extract substructures from the graph-based egonet as the structural feature set of the node. The types of substructures can be divided into nodes, subgraphs, paths, etc., simply using nodes for representation learning is not a good solution, because it ignores graph structure features. Paths can reflect the link relationship of nodes in the graph, but using paths for representation learning also ignores some complex graph structures. As an ordered collection of nodes and edges in a graph, subgraphs can reflect almost all structural features of the graph. Therefore, we choose the subgraph as the basic unit for network representation learning. We extract all the N-edge Subgraphs as the structural feature set of each node by traversing the corresponding egonet, the subgraph is uniquely identified by the minimum DFSCode. The maximum number of edges in a subgraph N is set to 3 in the experiment, which can ensure sufficient number of subgraphs and can be completed in a short time. The overall framework of the algorithm is shown in Fig. 2.

We named the N-edge Subgraphs extraction algorithm as StructureExtract, then perform StructureExtract sequentially for each node-based egonet in per time slice network. Algorithm 1 outlines the pseudo-code of the algorithm. In Algorithm 1 line 2, we begin by generating the initial 1-edge subgraphs. Subsequently, in Algorithm 1 line 4–7, for each initial subgraph we perform N-edge Subgraphs extraction, the SubgraphMining function in line 6 is a subgraph mining function shown in Algorithm 2. Algorithm 2 mainly performs subgraph

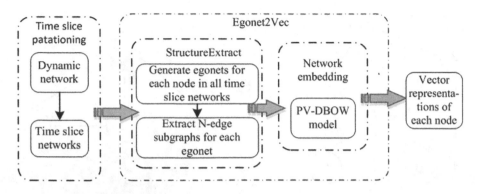

Fig. 2. The framework of Egonet2vec

mining and stops extension after reaching the specified threshold N. In Algorithm 2 line 2–4, when extending a subgraph, we should first determine whether the current subgraph is minimum DFS Code, in Algorithm 2 line 5–11, we extend the subgraph with its children by calling the SubgraphMining function recursively.

Algorithm 1. The StructureExtract algorithm

Require: G: Egonet to be extracted, $G = (V, E, L)$
Require: N: Maximum number of edges in a subgraph
Ensure: S: All extracted subgraphs
1: /*Extract 1-edge graphs from graph G*/
2: sort E in DFS lexicographic order
3: $S \leftarrow \{\}$
4: **for all** edge e such that $e \in E$ **do**
5:     initialize s with e
6:     SubgraphMining(G, S, s, N)
7: **end for**
8: **return** S

Learning Embeddings of Each Node. We use the Distributed Bag of Words version of Paragraph Vector (PV-DBOW) model, as shown in Fig. 3, an extended model of skip-gram model belonging to doc2vec, to learn the representations of each node. Ignoring the input context, this model directly predicts random words of the document in the training process. Specifically, the node-based egonet is considered as a document, and the subgraph is regarded as a single word. Given a group of node-based egonets GS, for each egonet G_i in GS, its subgraph set is $c(G_i) = \{sg_1, sg_2, ..., sg_n\}$. Finally, our goal is maximizing the following formula:

$$\sum_{j=1}^{n} \log pr(sg_j|d_i) \tag{1}$$

Algorithm 2. The SubgraphMining algorithm

Require: G: Egonet to be extracted, $G = (V, E, L)$
Require: N: Maximum number of edges in a subgraph
Require: S: All extracted subgraphs
Require: s: DFS Code of a subgraph
 1: /* Check if s is the smallest DFS Code */
 2: **if** $s \neq \min(s)$ **then**
 3:     return
 4: **end if**
 5: $S \leftarrow S \cup \{s\}$
 6: /* extend subgraph s */
 7: generate all s potential children with one edge growth
 8: $S \leftarrow E$
 9: **for all** c such that $c \in s$' children **do**
10:     SubgraphMining(G, S, s, N)
11: **end for**

$sg_j \in c(G_i)$, sg_j is a subgraph of graph G_i.

$$Pr(sg_j | G_i) = \frac{\exp(sg_j.G_i)}{\sum_{i=1}^{V} \exp(sg_i.G_i)} \qquad (2)$$

where sg_j is the vector representation of the subgraph, and v is the number of all substructures. In order to optimize the calculation, a negative sampling technique can be used to construct a new objective function. Furthermore, maximizing the likelihood of positive samples and minimizing the likelihood of negative samples can improve the computational efficiency.

After learning the vector representations of the nodes in all time slice networks, if the neighborhood structural features of the nodes are similar, then the vector representations of them are close too.

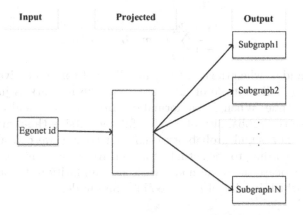

Fig. 3. PV-DBOW model

4.3   Dynamic Network Anomaly Detection Strategy

The nodes in the network are denoted as $G = \{v_1, v_2, \cdots, v_m\}$, m is the number of nodes in the network. After obtaining the vector representations of each node in all time slice networks, for the t th time slice network, the vector representation of the nodes in the network is $G_t = \{v^t{}_1, v^t{}_2, \cdots, v^t{}_m\}$, $v^t{}_i \in R^d$, $i \in [1, m]$, d is the dimension of the vector representation. For each node, we compute the similarity between the vector representations in the current time slice network and the adjacent time slice network. For the t th time slice network, we need to compute the similarity between the vector representations in the t th time slice network and t-1 th time slice network. The similarities of each node in the t th time slice network is represented as $sim(G_{t-1}, G_t) = \{sim(v^{t-1}{}_1, v^t{}_1), sim(v^{t-1}{}_2, v^t{}_2), ..., sim(v^{t-1}{}_m, v^t{}_m)\}$, in which the similarity measure of each node we use cosine similarity:

$$sim(v_i^{t-1}, v_i^t) = \frac{v_i^{t-1} \bullet v_i^t}{||v_i^{t-1}|| \times ||v_i^t||} \tag{3}$$

By taking the mean of the similarity of all nodes in the current time slice network as the similarity of the time slice network, the similarity of the entire dynamic network $GS = \{G_1, G_2, \cdots, G_t, G_{t+1}, \cdots, G_n\}$ is recorded as $\{sim(G_1, G_2), sim(G_2, G_3) \cdots, sim(G_{n-1}, G_n)\}$, The distribution of $sim(G_{t-1}, G_t)$ in the steady state of the network is recorded as f, where n is the number of dynamic network time slices.

$$sim(G_{t-1}, G_t) = \frac{\sum\limits_{i=1}^{m} sim(v_i^{t-1}, v_i^t)}{m} \tag{4}$$

Then we calculate the mean and variance of the distribution f:

$$\mu = \frac{1}{n-1} \sum_{t=2}^{n} sim(G_{t-1}, G_t) \tag{5}$$

$$\sigma^2 = \frac{1}{n-1} \sum_{t=2}^{n} (sim(G_{t-1}, G_t) - \mu)^2 \tag{6}$$

Given a threshold α, when the new t th time slice network G_t arrives, if the value of $sim(G_{t-1}, G_t)$ falls outside of $[\mu - \alpha, \mu + \alpha]$, the network is judged to have changed at this time. When f is a normal distribution, we usually set $\alpha = 2\sigma$ or $\alpha = 3\sigma$, because the probability of a value falling outside the region is only 5% or 0.3%, which is a small probability event. Of course, we can also determine the value of α according to the actual situation. After determining the abnormal time points, we locate the set of nodes with low similarity in the abnormal time slice network, which is a set of possible abnormal nodes.

5   Experiment

We evaluate our method on the Enron email dataset and the AS links dataset. The Enron email dataset is derived from Enron employees' email folders, is a directed weighted network dataset. The AS links dataset belongs to undirected weightless network dataset, which is a collection of snapshots composed of all AS belonging to a certain country or a region over a period of time.

5.1   Enron Email Dataset

Enron's email data set is Enron's (formerly one of the world's largest integrated gas and power companies, and is the number one natural gas and power wholesaler in North America) senior executives of the email. It has been publicly available by the US Federal Energy Regulatory Commission and is currently available online. We use the processed version form [13], the dataset retains only 184 communications data between Enron senior executives.

Data Preprocessing. We extract the email address and the sending time of the sender and receiver in the email record to build the mail network. A node in the network represents a communicating member, and if member a sends a message to member b, an edge is added between a and b. The time slice size is set to one week (7 days) and the messaging records for 728 days from 2000/1/4 to 2001/12/30 are divided into 104 time slices.

In Enron email network, the employees are regarded as nodes in the network, and the number of communications between nodes in each time slice network is taken as the weights of edges. Since edge weights cannot be directly applied to the subgraph mining, we use the equal frequency grouping method to map different weights of the same edge in different time slice networks, and use the label of the group instead of the weight as the label of the edge. In the experiment, we set the number of groups to 3, that is, the labels of the edges are grade1, grade2, grade3. Then node-based egonets for each node in all time slice networks are constructed after the edge label is determined. In the stage of N-edge Subgraphs extraction in each egonet, because the number of communications between nodes is inclusion relationship, that is, if A and B are connected twice, then they must be connected once. So, the high-grade label on the edge contains the lower-grade label, i.e. grade2 contains grade1 and grade3 contains grade2, grade1. As shown in Fig. 4, graph A is the original graph, graph B is the graph with new edge labels after equal frequency grouping of edge weights in different time slice networks, and graph C is the actual graph to be extracted in the N-edge Subgraphs extraction stage.

Experimental Results of Enron Email Dataset. Figure 5 shows the variation of $sim(G_{t-1}, G_t)$ over time. The calculated parameters of the distribution f of $sim(G_{t-1}, G_t)$ under Enron stability are $\mu = 0.89$, $\sigma = 0.05$, we set $a = 2\sigma$, and the interval of $\mu \pm \alpha$ is $[0.79 - 0.99]$. The potential abnormal time points we

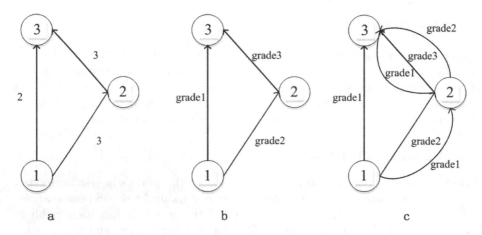

Fig. 4. The process of edge weight conversion

obtained were 95, 93, 92, 73, 94, and 96. The Enron's important events occurring at the above time points are shown in Table 1. From Table 1, we can find that most of the potential abnormal time points mentioned above have important incidents happened in Enron. Among them, Enron's email network fluctuated the most in the 95th time slice network. While Enron's third quarter loss is announced in 94th time slice network, this event opened the prelude of Enron's bankruptcy and was an important turning point for Enron. The 92nd and 93rd time slice network occurred before the turning point of Enron's bankruptcy, although there was no important event occurs, they could be regarded as early warnings of abnormal events in Enron.

Table 1. Enron's important events

2001/5/22, 73	John Mintz sends a memorandum to Jeffrey Skilling (CEO for a few months) for his sign-off on LJM paperwork
2001/10/16, 94	Enron announced that they had restated their financial statements for the years 1997 to 2000 to correct accounting irregularities
2001/10/22, 95	The Securities and Exchange Commission conducted a survey of potential conflicts of interest between Enron and its directors and their special partner-ships
2001/10/24-25, 95	Jeff McMahon takes over as CFO. Email to all employees states that all the pertinent documents should be preserved
2001/11/1, 96	The mortgage company Enron assets, access to J. P Morgan and Salomon Smith Barney's 1 billion US dollars credit line secured, but Merrill Lynch and Standard & Poor's still on Enron again lowered the rating
2001/12/2, 100	Enron filed for bankruptcy in New York and simultaneously sued Dynegy for breach of contract

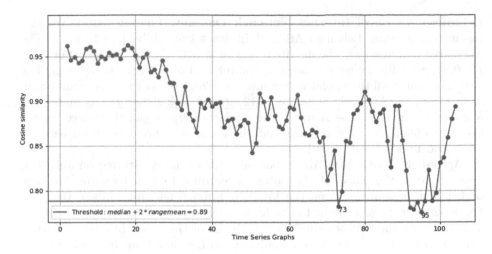

Fig. 5. The test results of Enron email dataset

Table 2. Statistical information of Lebanon and Venezuela

Country	Start time	End time	Number of snapshots
Lebanon	2012/7/3 00:00	2012/7/6 22:00	48
Venezuela	2019/3/1 02:00	2019/3/8 22:00	95

5.2 As Links Dataset

At a specific time t, the AS-level Internet of a country refers to a snapshot of all AS directly connected to the AS belongs to the country. The snapshot can intuitively display the status of the Internet connection in that country at a specific time. For a period of time, many AS links snapshots constitute a dynamic network, which can reflect the evolution of network connectivity. Usually, the normal changes of AS-level Internet network reflect the gradual evolution of the network scale and topology. However, the dramatic changes in AS-level Internet are usually caused by network anomalies, such as router misconfiguration, physical link failures, and network attacks, etc., those can lead to dramatic changes in the structure of AS-level Internet.

In this paper, Lebanon and Venezuela's AS-level Internet networks are selected for experimental verification. By analyzing the public routing data of the Route Views project [14], the AS-level Internet networks of the corresponding countries can be obtained. Route Views project samples global AS-level routes every two hours. Therefore, the interval between adjacent network snapshots in the dynamic network is also 2 h, and the accuracy of the change detection is also 2 h. Statistical information on the AS-level Internet networks of Lebanon and Venezuela is shown in Table 2.

Lebanese AS-Level Internet Network Dataset. Figure 6 reflects the test results of detecting Lebanese AS-level Internet from July 3 to 6, 2012. The calculated parameters of the distribution f of $sim(G_{t-1}, G_t)$ under stability are $\mu = 0.98$, $\sigma = 0.04$, we set $a = 3\sigma$, and the interval of $\mu \pm \alpha$ is $[0.87 - 1.1]$. The potential abnormal time point we obtained was 2012-07-04 18:00. As can be seen from Fig. 6, at 18 o'clock on July 4, 2012, its network structure has undergone a major change. Because Route Views project samples global AS-level routes every two hours, so we can judge that the anomalous event occurred between 16:00 and 18:00 on July 4, 2012.

According to BGPMon [15], Lebanese internet outage started on July 4th, 16:16 (UTC), the cause of the outage according to the Telecoms Ministry in Lebanon is a fiber cut on the IMEWE Submarine cable. Liban Teleccom (AS42020), the largest Internet provider in Lebanon, has been seriously affected. Table 3 shows the network similarity statistics of the seven Internet providers with the greatest changes (lowest similarity) in Lebanon from 16:00 to 18:00 on July 4, 2012. As shown in Table 3, AS42020 has the greatest change between 16:00–18:00, and the similarity with the previous time slice network is only 0.41. Table 4 shows the edge numbers of the seven Internet providers mentioned above in time slice networks from 14 to 20 o'clock on July 4. It can be seen from the table that the connectivity of the Lebanese Internet providers at 16:00 to 18:00 has changed a lot.

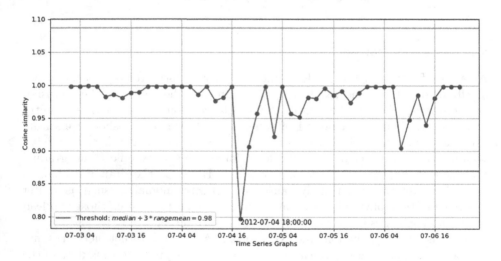

Fig. 6. The test results of Lebanese AS-level Internet network

Venezuelan AS-Level Internet Network Dataset. Figure 7 shows the test results of the Venezuelan AS-level internet network from March 1 to 9, 2019. The calculated parameters of the distribution f of $sim(G_{t-1}, G_t)$ under stability are $\mu = 0.99$, $\sigma = 0.004$, we set $a = 3\sigma$, and the interval of $\mu \pm \alpha$ is $[0.98 - 1.0]$. The

Table 3. Partial Lebanese Internet providers' similarity test results

Internet provider	14:00–16:00	16:00–18:00	18:00–20:00
AS42020	1.00	0.41	0.95
AS34370	1.00	0.47	0.47
AS31126	1.00	0.49	0.67
AS41211	1.00	0.55	1.00
AS39010	1.00	0.55	1.00
AS39275	1.00	0.64	1.00
AS9051	1.00	0.64	0.46

Table 4. Statistics of partial Lebanese Internet providers

Internet provider	14:00–16:00	16:00–18:00	18:00–20:00
AS42020	19	6	7
AS34370	1	1	1
AS31126	9	10	11
AS41211	1	1	1
AS39010	11	5	5
AS39275	1	1	1
AS9051	14	0	14

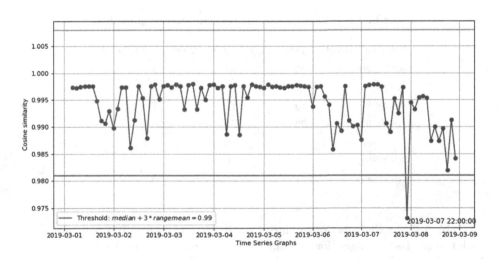

Fig. 7. The test results of Venezuelan AS-level Internet network

potential abnormal time point we obtained was 2019-03-07 22:00. As shown in Fig. 7, at 22:00 on March 7, 2019, its network structure has undergone a major change, so we can judge that the anomalous event occurred between 20:00 and 22:00 on March 7, 2019 (UTC).

Local time in Venezuela is 4 h later than the standard time, and the time between 20:00 and 22:00 UTC corresponds to Venezuela's local time between 16:00 and 18:00. According to CNN [16] reported on March 9, 2019, Venezuela suffered a power outage crisis in most areas on the evening of March 7, and many areas were still in darkness until March 8. Venezuelan local media reported that 15 of the country's 23 states had blackouts.

Table 5. Partial Venezuelan Internet providers' similarity test results

Internet provider	18:00–20:00	20:00–22:00	22:00–24:00
AS52320	1.00	0.45	1.00
AS27807	1.00	0.79	0.99
AS7908	1.00	0.87	1.00
AS8048	1.00	0.88	1.00
AS27893	1.00	0.92	1.00
AS27891	1.00	0.92	1.00
AS17287	1.00	0.95	1.00

Table 6. Statistics of partial Venezuelan Internet providers

Internet provider	18:00–20:00	20:00–22:00	22:00–24:00
AS52320	95	93	93
AS27807	7	0	0
AS7908	19	17	17
AS8048	23	22	23
AS27893	3	0	0
AS27891	1	0	0
AS17287	1	0	0

Table 5 shows the network similarity statistics of the seven Internet providers with the greatest changes (lowest similarity) in Venezuela from 18:00 to 24:00 on March 7, 2019. Table 6 shows the edge numbers of the seven Internet providers mentioned above in time slice networks from 18 to 24 o'clock on March 7. According to the table, Networks relying on AS52320 are most severely affected. Venezuelan Internet providers' connectivity declined from 20:00 to 22:00, and there was still no improvement at 18:00 to 20:00.

6   Conclusion

In this paper, we propose a dynamic network representation learning method Egonet2Vec, then a dynamic network change detection method is carried out based on Egonet2Vec. Experiments on Enron email dataset and AS links datasets demonstrate the effectiveness of this method. One of our future works is to improve our method so that it can directly obtain the similarity of the time slice networks, in order to overcome the accuracy loss caused by taking the mean of the node similarity.

Acknowledgment. This work was supported by the National Key R&D Program of China (No. 2016YFB0801303, 2016QY01W0105), the National Natural Science Foundation of China (No.61309007, U1636219, 61602508, 61772549, U1736214, 61572052) and Plan for Scientific Innovation Talent of Henan Province (No. 2018JR0018).

References

1. Berlingerio, M., Koutra, D., Eliassirad, T., et al.: NetSimile: a scalable approach to size-independent network similarity. Comput. Sci. **12**(1), 28:21–28:28 (2012)
2. Miz, V., Ricaud, B., Benzi, K., et al.: Anomaly detection in the dynamics of web and social networks (2019)
3. Yu, W., Cheng, W., Aggarwal, C.C., et al.: Netwalk: a flexible deep embedding approach for anomaly detection in dynamic networks. In: Proceedings of the 24th ACM SIGKDD International Conference on Knowledge Discovery and Data Mining, pp. 2672–2681. ACM (2018)
4. Sun, J., Faloutsos, C., Faloutsos, C., et al.: GraphScope: parameter-free mining of large time-evolving graphs. In: Proceedings of the 13th ACM SIGKDD International Conference on Knowledge Discovery and Data Mining, pp. 687–696. ACM (2007)
5. Mikolov, T., Sutskever, I., Kai, C., et al.: Distributed representations of words and phrases and their compositionality. In: Advances in Neural Information Processing Systems, vol. 26, pp. 3111–3119 (2013)
6. Le, Q., Mikolov, T.: Distributed representations of sentences and documents. In: Proceedings of the International Conference on Machine Learning, pp. 1188–1196 (2014)
7. Perozzi, B., Al-Rfou, R., Skiena, S.: DeepWalk: online learning of social representations. In: Proceedings of the ACM SIGKDD International Conference on Knowledge Discovery and Data Mining (2014)
8. Grover, A., Leskovec, J.: node2vec: scalable feature learning for networks. In: Proceedings of the ACM SIGKDD International Conference on Knowledge Discovery and Data Mining (2016)
9. Jian, T., Meng, Q., Wang, M., et al.: LINE: large-scale information network embedding (2015)
10. Narayanan, A., Chandramohan, M., Chen, L., et al.: subgraph2vec: learning distributed representations of rooted sub-graphs from large graphs. arXiv preprint arXiv:160608928 (2016)
11. Narayanan, A., Chandramohan, M., Venkatesan, R., et al.: graph2vec: learning distributed representations of graphs (2017)

12. Nguyen, D., Luo, W., Nguyen, T.D., et al.: Learning graph representation via frequent subgraphs. In: Proceedings of the Proceedings of the 2018 SIAM International Conference on Data Mining. SIAM, pp. 306–314 (2018)
13. Priebe, C.E., Conroy, J.M., Marchette, D.J., Park, Y.: Scan statistics on enron graphs. Comput. Math. Organ. Theory 11(3), 229–247 (2005)
14. Views R. University of Oregon route views project [EB/OL]. http://www.routerviews.org/
15. BGPMon [EB/OL]. https://www.bgpmon.net/internet-outage-in-lebanon-continues-for-days/
16. CNN[EB/OL]. https://edition.cnn.com/2019/03/08/americas/venezuela-blackout-power-intl/index.html
17. Yan, X., Han, J.: gSpan: graph-based substructure pattern mining. In: Proceedings of the IEEE International Conference on Data Mining, vol. 721 (2002)
18. Araujo, M., et al.: Com2: fast automatic discovery of temporal ('Comet') communities. In: Tseng, V.S., Ho, T.B., Zhou, Z.-H., Chen, A.L.P., Kao, H.-Y. (eds.) PAKDD 2014. LNCS (LNAI), vol. 8444, pp. 271–283. Springer, Cham (2014). https://doi.org/10.1007/978-3-319-06605-9_23
19. Peel, L., Clauset, A.: Detecting change points in the large-scale structure of evolving networks. CoRR, abs/1403.0989 (2014)
20. Mongiovi, M., Bogdanov, P., Ranca, R., Singh, A.K., Papalexakis, E.E., Faloutsos, C.: NetSpot: spotting significant anomalous regions on dynamic networks. In: Proceedings of the 13th SIAM International Conference on Data Mining (SDM), Texas, Austin, TX (2013)

Robust RSS-Based Localization in Mixed LOS/NLOS Environments

Yinghao Sun, Gang Wang$^{(\boxtimes)}$, and Youming Li

Faculty of Electrical Engineering and Computer Science, Ningbo University,
Ningbo 315211, China
sunsunyinghao@163.com, {wanggang,liyouming}@nbu.edu.cn

Abstract. In this paper, we propose a robust received signal strength (RSS) based localization method in mixed line-of-sight/non-line-of-sight (LOS/NLOS) environments, where additional path losses caused by NLOS signal propagations are included. Considering that the additional path losses vary in a dramatic range, we express the additional path losses as the sum of a balancing parameter and some error terms. By doing so, we formulate a robust weighted least squares (RWLS) problem with the source location and the balancing parameter as unknown variables, which is, simultaneously, robust to the error terms. By employing the S-Lemma, the RWLS problem is transformed into a non-convex optimization problem, which is then approximately solved by applying the semidefinite relaxation (SDR) technique. The proposed method releases the requirement of knowing specific information about the additional path losses in the previous study. Simulation results show that the proposed method works well in both dense and sparse NLOS environments.

Keywords: Source localization · Received signal strength (RSS) ·
Line-of-sight/non-line-of-sight (LOS/NLOS) · Robust weighted least
squares (RWLS) · Semidefinite relaxation (SDR)

1 Introduction

In recent years, the development of wireless sensor network (WSN) is rapid because of its wide applications. One of the important functions of the WSN is to provide location estimate for some objects. However, the WSN is typically composed of cheap and small sensor nodes with limited communication range and computational ability, which limits its application in localization using time of arrival (TOA) [1] or time difference of arrival (TDOA) [2]. As such, received signal strength (RSS) is probably the most proper venue for source localization because of its low complexity and low cost [3,4]. In this paper, we address the RSS based source localization problem.

This work was supported in part by the National Natural Science Foundation of China under Grant 61571249, Zhejiang Provincial Natural Science Foundation under Grant LY18F010011, and the K. C. Wong Magna Fund in Ningbo University.

© ICST Institute for Computer Sciences, Social Informatics and Telecommunications Engineering 2020
Published by Springer Nature Switzerland AG 2020. All Rights Reserved
H. Gao et al. (Eds.): ChinaCom 2019, LNICST 312, pp. 659–668, 2020.
https://doi.org/10.1007/978-3-030-41114-5_49

In the previous study, the outdoor RSS measurement model is widely adopted in the RSS based source localization literature. The most common method to solve the problem is the maximum likelihood (ML) estimator formulated based on the outdoor measurement model. Unfortunately, the ML problem is nonlinear and non-convex, implying that the traditional iterative algorithm may fail to converge to the global optimum without good initial estimates [5]. Due to this, the linearization methods and convex relaxation methods have been proposed to solve the problem. The linearization methods usually have closed-form solutions, however, their performance may significantly degrade as the shadowing effect becomes severe [6,7]. The convex relaxation methods relax the ML or approximate problem into a convex semidefinite program (SDP). This kind of methods typically achieve better performance than the linearization methods, at the cost of higher complexity. Ouyang et al. [8] eliminated the logarithms firstly, and then relaxed the formulated problem based on MLE into an SDP. Wang et al. [9] proposed the least squares relative error (LSRE) method based on the least absolute relative error criterion, where the formulated problem was proven to be an approximation to the MLE. The formulated problem was also relaxed into an SDP. It was shown that this method performs better than several existing methods.

Traditionally, the model parameters, e.g., the transmit power and the path loss exponent (PLE), are estimated before performing localization, by a large amount of training data during the calibration phase. However, the calibration significantly increases the communication overhead and computational complexity. Instead of doing calibration, researchers proposed several methods which jointly estimate the model parameters and the source location. Wang et al. [10] formulated a non-convex weighted least squares (WLS) problem based on the unscented transformation (UT) to jointly estimate the source location and the transmit power. The method was extended to the case when the PLE is also unknown. Tomic et al. [11] proposed a three-step alternating estimation procedure to estimate the source location and the model parameters simultaneously, where the second-order cone relaxation was used to solve the non-convex problem.

In indoors and urban areas, the non-line-of-sight (NLOS) propagations may cause additional path losses. Hence, the outdoor RSS measurement model is not sufficient for modeling these environments. To cope with this, some additional path-loss terms are added to the original outdoor RSS measurement model [12,13]. The additional path losses can be computed by using some prior information. For example, in [12,13], the additional path losses are computed by assuming that the number of partitions and the attenuation of each partition in indoors are known. However, the prior information is generally difficult to obtain in practice. Even if this information can be obtained, it may not be accurate. To alleviate this problem, Tomic et al. [14,15] assumed that the additional path-loss terms were totally unknown. In [14], the path-loss terms were replaced by their mean, which was jointly estimated with the source location by formulating a generalized trust region sub-problem (GTRS). In [15], a worst-case robust method was proposed to mitigate the effect of the path-loss terms, where the path-loss terms were treated as nuisance parameters.

In a typical localization scenario, the additional path losses vary in a dramatic range. The additional path loss is very small if there is a line-of-sight (LOS) path between the sensor and the source, while it can be very large if there are many partitions/barriers in the path. In the worst-case robust method, e.g., [15], an accurate upper bound for the additional path losses is important. Obviously, the fixed upper bound does not fit all scenarios, which degrades the performance of the robust methods in the localization scenario with more line-of-sight (LOS) paths. To solve this problem, we propose to introduce a balancing parameter according to the additional path-loss terms, and express the additional path-loss terms as the sum of the balancing parameter and some other error terms. To alleviate the effect of the error terms, we formulate a worst-case robust weighted least squares (RWLS) problem with the balancing parameter and the source location as variables. The proposed RWLS problem is difficult minimax problem. To solve this problem, we need to eliminate the maximization part first. To do so, we employ the S-Lemma to eliminate the maximization part and then the semidefinite relaxation (SDR) technique to relax it into a tractable convex SDP.

Notations: Bold face lower case and bold face upper case letters are used to denote vectors and matrices, respectively. $A_{i,j}$ denotes the element at the ith row and jth column of matrix A and $A_{i:j,m:n}$ denotes the submatrix whose elements are the intersection of the ith to jth row and mth to nth column of matrix A.

2   System Model

Consider a k-dimensional ($k = 2$ or 3) WSN composed of N sensor nodes and one source node that needs to be located. The locations of the sensors and the source are denoted by $s_1, \ldots, s_N$, and x, respectively. Assume that the source emits signals to the sensors, which are able to compute the power from the received signals, i.e., the RSS. In outdoor environments, it is known that the RSS measurement at the ith sensor node can be denoted by:

$$P_i = P_0 - 10\gamma \log_{10} \frac{\|x - s_i\|}{d_0} + n_i, \ i = 1, \ldots, N, \tag{1}$$

where P_0 represents the received power at a reference distance d_0, γ the PLE, and n_i the shadowing effect modeled by a zero-mean Gaussian random variable with variance σ_i^2, i.e., $n_i \sim \mathcal{N}(0, \sigma_i^2)$.

However, the above model is not appropriate in indoors or urban areas due to the fruitful multipath fading and partitions/barriers, or, NLOS signal propagations, which cause additional path losses. To model the additional path loss, we add an additional term b_i into the above propagation model, yielding the following:

$$P_i = P_0 - b_i - 10\gamma \log_{10} \frac{\|x - s_i\|}{d_0} + n_i, \ i = 1, \ldots, N. \tag{2}$$

In the previous study [12,13], b_i is computed by assuming that the number of partitions and the attenuation of each partition are known. However, it is difficult to obtain this prior information in practice since a large amount of training data are required. Even if it can be obtained, it may not be accurate, yielding performance loss. Due to these, we treat b_i as a completely unknown variable and develop a robust localization method in this paper. The only assumption on b_i is that b_i is upper bounded by a known constant ρ_i, i.e., $0 \leq b_i \leq \rho_i$.

3   The RWLS Method

In this section, we detail the derivations of the proposed RWLS method. Without loss of generality, we consider the 2-D case in the following, i.e., $k = 2$. Extension to the 3-D case is straightforward.

According to the discussion in the Introduction, a balancing parameter $\bar{b}$ is introduced to the propagation model (2), giving:

$$P_i = P_0 - \hat{b}_i - \bar{b} - 10\gamma \log_{10} \|\boldsymbol{x} - \boldsymbol{s}_i\| + n_i, i = 1, \ldots, N \qquad (3)$$

where $\hat{b}_i = b_i - \bar{b}$ and $d_0 = 1$ without loss of generality.

In the following, we jointly estimate the source location $\boldsymbol{x}$ and the balancing parameter $\bar{b}$, and simultaneously, develop a robust method to eliminate the effect of the path-loss terms $\hat{b}_i$ ($i = 1, \ldots, N$). To this end, we first rewrite (3) into an equivalent form:

$$10^{\frac{P_0 - P_i}{10\gamma}} 10^{-\frac{\hat{b}_i}{10\gamma}} = 10^{\frac{\bar{b}}{10\gamma}} 10^{\log_{10} \|\boldsymbol{x} - \boldsymbol{s}_i\|} 10^{-\frac{n_i}{10\gamma}}, \ i = 1, \ldots, N. \qquad (4)$$

Applying the first-order Taylor-series expansion to the noise term on the right-hand side, we have

$$10^{\frac{P_0 - P_i}{10\gamma}} 10^{-\frac{\hat{b}_i}{10\gamma}} \approx 10^{\frac{\bar{b}}{10\gamma}} \|\boldsymbol{x} - \boldsymbol{s}_i\| (1 - \frac{\ln(10)}{10\gamma} n_i), \ i = 1, \ldots, N. \qquad (5)$$

Letting $d_i = 10^{\frac{P_0 - P_i}{10\gamma}}$, $\tilde{e}_i = 10^{-\frac{\hat{b}_i}{10\gamma}}$, and $\alpha = 10^{\frac{\bar{b}}{10\gamma}}$, we write (5) as a more concise form:

$$d_i \tilde{e}_i \approx \|\alpha \boldsymbol{x} - \alpha \boldsymbol{s}_i\| - \|\alpha \boldsymbol{x} - \alpha \boldsymbol{s}_i\| \frac{\ln(10)}{10\gamma} n_i,$$

$$= \|\boldsymbol{y} - \alpha \boldsymbol{s}_i\| - \|\boldsymbol{y} - \alpha \boldsymbol{s}_i\| \frac{\ln(10)}{10\gamma} n_i, \ i = 1, \ldots, N, \qquad (6)$$

where $\boldsymbol{y} = \alpha \boldsymbol{x}$.

According to (6), we can formulate the following worst-case RWLS problem:

$$\min_{\boldsymbol{g}, \boldsymbol{y}} \max_{\tilde{e} = [\tilde{e}_1, \ldots, \tilde{e}_N]^T} (A\tilde{e} - g)^T Q^{-1} (A\tilde{e} - g)$$

$$\text{s.t. } \boldsymbol{g} = [\|\boldsymbol{y} - \alpha \boldsymbol{s}_1\|, \ldots, \|\boldsymbol{y} - \alpha \boldsymbol{s}_N\|]^T, \qquad (7)$$

where $A = \text{diag}\{d_1, \ldots, d_N\}$, $\tilde{e} = [\tilde{e}_1, \ldots, \tilde{e}_N]^T$, and $Q = DRD^T$ with $D = \text{diag}\left\{\|y - \alpha s_1\|\frac{\ln 10}{10\gamma}, \ldots, \|y - \alpha s_N\|\frac{\ln 10}{10\gamma}\right\}$ and $R = \text{diag}\{\sigma_1^2, \ldots, \sigma_N^2\}$.

The weighting matrix Q^{-1} is unknown since it is related to the unknown variables y and α. Here, we replace the weighting matrix with an approximation denoted by $\hat{Q}^{-1}$, which is obtained by replacing $\|y - \alpha s_i\|$ with d_i for sufficiently small errors.

Problem (7) is a difficult non-convex minimax optimization problem. To solve this problem, we first eliminate the maximization part by employing the S-Lemma, and then use the SDR technique to relax it into a tractable convex SDP.

Assume that $\bar{b}$ is upper bounded by a given constant $\bar{\rho}$, i.e., $0 \leq \bar{b} \leq \bar{\rho}$, which implies that $-\bar{\rho} \leq \hat{b}_i \leq \rho_i - \bar{\rho}$. It follows from $\tilde{e}_i = 10^{-\frac{\hat{b}_i}{10\gamma}}$ that $10^{\frac{\bar{\rho}-\rho_i}{10\gamma}} \leq \tilde{e}_i \leq 10^{\frac{\bar{\rho}}{10\gamma}}$, from which we further obtain

$$\frac{10^{\frac{\bar{\rho}-\rho_i}{10\gamma}} - 10^{\frac{\bar{\rho}}{10\gamma}}}{2} \leq \tilde{e}_i - \frac{10^{\frac{\bar{\rho}-\rho_i}{10\gamma}} + 10^{\frac{\bar{\rho}}{10\gamma}}}{2} \leq \frac{10^{\frac{\bar{\rho}}{10\gamma}} - 10^{\frac{\bar{\rho}-\rho_i}{10\gamma}}}{2}. \quad (8)$$

By defining $\bar{v} = \frac{10^{\frac{\bar{\rho}}{10\gamma}}}{2}$ and $\hat{v}_i = \frac{10^{\frac{\bar{\rho}-\rho_i}{10\gamma}}}{2}$, (8) can be written into a more concise form:

$$|\tilde{e}_i - \bar{v} - \hat{v}_i| \leq \bar{v} - \hat{v}_i, \quad i = 1, \ldots, N. \quad (9)$$

Collecting $\hat{v}_i$ $(i = 1, \ldots, N)$ and $\bar{v} - \hat{v}_i$ $(i = 1, \ldots, N)$ into vectors $\hat{v} = [\hat{v}_1, \ldots, \hat{v}_N]^T$ and $\tilde{v} = [\bar{v} - \hat{v}_1, \ldots, \bar{v} - \hat{v}_N]^T$, respectively, we have

$$\|\tilde{e} - \bar{v}1_N - \hat{v}\|^2 \leq \|\tilde{v}\|^2, \quad (10)$$

where 1_N is an all-one column vector of length N.

Problem (7) can be equivalently written as the epigraph form:

$$\min_{g,y,\tau} \tau$$

$$\text{s.t.} \quad \max_{\tilde{e}} \{(A\tilde{e} - g)^T \hat{Q}^{-1}(A\tilde{e} - g)\} \leq \tau,$$

$$g = [\|y - \alpha s_1\|, \ldots, \|y - \alpha s_N\|]^T,$$

$$1 \leq \alpha \leq 10^{\frac{\bar{\rho}}{10\gamma}}, \quad (11)$$

where Q has been replaced by its approximation $\hat{Q}$.

By invoking (10), the first constraint in (11) implies that

$$\forall \tilde{e} \in \{\tilde{e} | \|\tilde{e} - \bar{v}1_N - \hat{v}\|^2 \leq \|\tilde{v}\|^2\} \Rightarrow (A\tilde{e} - g)^T \hat{Q}^{-1}(A\tilde{e} - g) \leq \tau, \quad (12)$$

i.e.,

$$\begin{bmatrix} \tilde{e} \\ 1 \end{bmatrix}^T \begin{bmatrix} I_N & -\bar{v}1_N - \hat{v} \\ (-\bar{v}1_N - \hat{v})^T & 4\bar{v}\sum_{i=1}^{N}\hat{v}_i \end{bmatrix} \begin{bmatrix} \tilde{e} \\ 1 \end{bmatrix} \leq 0 \Rightarrow$$

$$\begin{bmatrix} \tilde{e} \\ 1 \end{bmatrix}^T \begin{bmatrix} A^T\hat{Q}^{-1}A & -A^T\hat{Q}^{-1}g \\ -g^T\hat{Q}^{-1}A & g^T\hat{Q}^{-1}g - \tau \end{bmatrix} \begin{bmatrix} \tilde{e} \\ 1 \end{bmatrix} \leq 0. \quad (13)$$

According to the S-Lemma [16], there exists a $\lambda \geq 0$ such that

$$
\begin{bmatrix} A^T \hat{Q}^{-1} A & -A^T \hat{Q}^{-1} g \\ -g^T \hat{Q}^{-1} A & g^T \hat{Q}^{-1} g - \tau \end{bmatrix}
$$
$$
\preceq \lambda \begin{bmatrix} I_N & -\bar{v} 1_N - \hat{v} \\ (-\bar{v} 1_N - \hat{v})^T & 4\bar{v} \sum_{i=1}^N \hat{v}_i \end{bmatrix}. \tag{14}
$$

Thus, the RWLS problem (11) can be rewritten into

$$
\min_{y,g,\tau,\lambda} \quad \tau
$$
$$
\text{s.t.} \quad (14),\ \lambda \geq 0,
$$
$$
g = [\|y - \alpha s_1\|, \ldots, \|y - \alpha s_N\|]^T,
$$
$$
1 \leq \alpha \leq 10^{\frac{\bar{p}}{10\gamma}}, \tag{15}
$$

where the "max" part has been eliminated.

Problem (15) is still non-convex. We relax it as a tractable convex SDP in the following. By defining $G = gg^T$, $z = [y^T, \alpha]^T$, and $Z = zz^T$, problem (15) can be equivalently written as

$$
\min_{\substack{g,\tau,\lambda \\ Z,G}} \quad \tau
$$

$$
\text{s.t.} \quad \begin{bmatrix} A^T \hat{Q}^{-1} A & -A^T \hat{Q}^{-1} g \\ -g^T \hat{Q}^{-1} A & \text{tr}\{\hat{Q}^{-1} G\} - \tau \end{bmatrix}
$$
$$
\preceq \lambda \begin{bmatrix} I_N & -\bar{v} 1_N - \hat{v} \\ (-\bar{v} 1_N - \hat{v})^T & 4\bar{v} \sum_{i=1}^N \hat{v}_i \end{bmatrix}, \tag{16a}
$$
$$
\lambda \geq 0, \tag{16b}
$$
$$
G_{i,i} = \text{tr}\{Z_{1:2,1:2}\} - 2s_i^T Z_{1:2,3} + Z_{3,3}\|s_i\|^2,
$$
$$
i = 1, \ldots, N, \tag{16c}
$$
$$
1 \leq Z_{3,3} \leq 10^{\frac{\bar{p}}{5\gamma}}, \tag{16d}
$$
$$
Z \succeq 0, \tag{16e}
$$
$$
\text{rank}\{Z\} = 1, \tag{16f}
$$
$$
\begin{bmatrix} G & g \\ g^T & 1 \end{bmatrix} \succeq 0, \tag{16g}
$$
$$
\text{rank}\{G\} = 1, \tag{16h}
$$

where the following equivalences

$$
Z = zz^T \Leftrightarrow Z \succeq 0,\ \text{rank}\{Z\} = 1,
$$
$$
G = gg^T \Leftrightarrow \begin{bmatrix} G & g \\ g^T & 1 \end{bmatrix} \succeq 0,\ \text{rank}\{G\} = 1, \tag{17}
$$

have been used.

In (16), the only non-convex constraints are the rank-1 constraints. Dropping the rank-1 constraints, we can relax (16) as the following SDP

$$\min_{\substack{g,\tau,\lambda \\ Z,G}} \tau$$

$$\text{s.t.} \quad (16a), (16b), (16c),$$
$$(16d), (16e), (16g). \tag{18}$$

Solve the SDP problem (18) and denote the SDP solution of $\boldsymbol{Z}$ as $\boldsymbol{Z}^*$. The final estimate of the source location $\boldsymbol{x}^*$ can be extracted from $\boldsymbol{Z}^*$: $\boldsymbol{x}^* = \boldsymbol{Z}_{1:2,3}^*/Z_{3,3}^*$.

Finally, we give a hint for choosing the value of $\bar{\rho}$. Under dense NLOS conditions, a small $\bar{\rho}$ (and large $\rho_i - \bar{\rho}$) is required to make $\rho_i - \bar{\rho}$ be a proper upper bound for $\hat{b}_i$. On the other hand, $\bar{b}$ is small under sparse NLOS conditions, and hence, a small $\bar{\rho}$ is sufficient. Thus, we conjecture that a small $\bar{\rho}$ is proper for both dense and sparse conditions, which is consistent with the previous study in [17]. In the simulations, we set $\bar{\rho}$ as $\bar{\rho} = 0.4\frac{1}{N}\sum_{i=1}^{N}\rho_i$, i.e., a value smaller than half of the average value of ρ_i.

4   Simulation Results

In this section, simulations are conducted to show the performance of the proposed method (denoted by "RWLS"). For comparison, we also include the performance of the recently proposed GTRS method [15] and the LSRE method [9]. Note that LSRE is originally developed based on the outdoor RSS measurement model (1), where the additional attenuations b_i are not taken into account. The SDP (18) and that in [9] are solved using CVX [18], where the solver is SDPT3 [19] and the precision is "best".

We use eight sensor nodes ($N = 8$) to locate the unknown source. The sensors and the source are assumed to be randomly deployed in a square region with length 50 m. The root mean square error (RMSE), defined by RMSE $= \sqrt{\frac{1}{M}\sum_{i=1}^{M}\|\hat{\boldsymbol{x}}_i - \boldsymbol{x}_i\|^2}$, is used to evaluate the localization performance. Here, $\boldsymbol{x}_i$ and $\hat{\boldsymbol{x}}_i$ are the true source location and the source location estimate in the ith Monte Carlo (MC) run, respectively, and $M = 5000$ is the number of MC runs. The propagation model (2) is used to generate the RSS measurements, where $P_0 = 30\,\text{dBm}$, $d_0 = 1$, and $\gamma = 3$. For simplicity, we assume that $\sigma_i = \sigma$ for $i = 1,\ldots,N$. Without loss of generality, we further assume that $b_i = 0$ if there is an LOS path between the sensor and the source, and b_i follows the exponential distribution with fixed mean $\mu = 4$ otherwise. The upper bound of b_i, i.e., ρ_i, is set to $\mu\ln(10)$, i.e., $\rho_i = \mu\ln(10)$ for $i = 1,\ldots,N$, which implies that the probability of $0 \leq b_i \leq \rho_i$ is higher than 90%.

We first examine the scenario when the magnitude of the shadowing effect, i.e., the standard deviation (STD), varies. Assume that there are four randomly chosen NLOS paths (and also four LOS paths). Figure 1 shows the results. As expected, the performance of all the methods degrades as the STD increases.

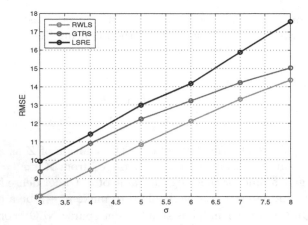

Fig. 1. RMSE versus the STD of the shadowing effect σ.

LSRE performs worst due to the fact that it does not deal with the additional attenuations from the NLOS propagations. Both GTRS and RWLS perform better since the effect of the additional attenuations is mitigated. The proposed RWLS method has the best performance by introducing an additional balancing parameter which improves the performance in mixed LOS/NLOS environments.

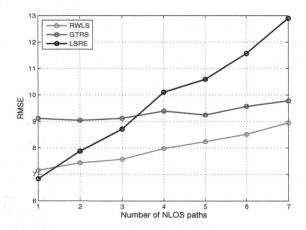

Fig. 2. RMSE versus the number of NLOS paths.

Next, we fix the STD of the shadowing effect $\sigma = 3$ and change the number of NLOS paths from 1 to 7. The results are shown in Fig. 2. Generally, LSRE performs well under very sparse NLOS conditions; however, its performance deteriorates dramatically as the number of NLOS paths grows. In comparison, the GTRS and RWLS methods perform stably regardless of whether the NLOS conditions are sparse or dense. RWLS still performs better than GTRS in this scenario, and performs only slightly worse as compared to LSRE in very sparse NLOS environments.

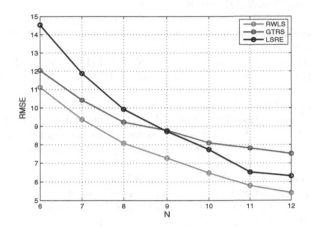

Fig. 3. RMSE versus the number of sensors.

Finally, we consider the scenario when the number of sensors varies, where $\sigma = 3$ and the number of NLOS paths is 4. Figure 3 shows the results. When the number of sensors is small, LSRE performs much worse than the other two methods. However, when the number of sensors is large enough, it performs better than GTRS. In comparison, the proposed RWLS method always performs best regardless of the number of sensors.

5   Conclusion

In this paper, a novel method has been proposed for RSS based source localization in indoors and urban areas, where some additional path losses are included. Under the condition of knowing the upper bounds on the additional path-loss terms, we have formulated an RWLS problem to mitigate the effect of the additional path-loss terms. Simulation results have confirmed the superior performance of the proposed method over the existing methods.

References

1. Cheung, K., So, H., Ma, W.-K., Chan, Y.T.: Least squares algorithms for time-of-arrival-based mobile location. IEEE Trans. Signal Process **52**(4), 1121–1130 (2004)
2. Yang, L., Ho, K.C.: An approximately efficient TDOA localization algorithm in closed-form for locating multiple disjoint sources with erroneous sensor positions. IEEE Trans. Signal Process **57**(12), 4598–4615 (2009)

3. Li, X.: RSS-based location estimation with unknown pathloss model. IEEE Trans. Wirel. Commun. **5**(12), 3626–3633 (2006)
4. Patwari, N., Ash, J.N., Kyperountas, S., Hero, A., Moses, R.L., Correal, N.S.: Locating the nodes: cooperative localization in wireless sensor networks. IEEE Signal Process. Mag. **22**(4), 54–69 (2005)
5. Vaghefi, R., Gholami, M., Buehrer, R., Strom, E.: Cooperative received signal strength-based sensor localization with unknown transmit powers. IEEE Trans. Signal Process. **61**(6), 1389–1403 (2013)
6. Chan, F.K.W., So, H.C., Zheng, J., Lui, K.W.K.: Best linear unbiased estimator approach for time-of-arrival based localization. IET Signal Process. **2**(2), 156–162 (2008)
7. So, H.C., Lin, L.: Linear least squares approach for accurate received signal strength based source localization. IEEE Signal Process. Lett. **59**(8), 4035–4040 (2011)
8. Ouyang, R., Wong, A.-S., Lea, C.-T.: Received signal strength based wireless localization via semidefinite programming: noncooperative and cooperative schemes. IEEE Trans. Veh. Technol. **59**(3), 1307–1318 (2010)
9. Wang, Z., Zhang, H., Lu, T., Gulliver, T.A.: Cooperative RSS-based localization in wireless sensor networks using relative error estimation and semidefinite programming. IEEE Trans. Veh. Technol. **68**(1), 483–497 (2019)
10. Wang, G., Chen, H., Li, Y., Jin, M.: On received-signal-strength based localization with unknown transmit power and path loss exponent. IEEE Wirel. Commun. Lett. **1**(5), 536–539 (2012)
11. Tomic, S., Beko, M., Dinis, R.: RSS-based localization in wireless sensor networks using convex relaxation: noncooperative and cooperative schemes. IEEE Trans. Veh. Technol. **64**(5), 2037–2050 (2015)
12. Wang, G., Yang, K.: A new approach to sensor node localization using RSS measurements in wireless sensor networks. IEEE Trans. Wirel. Commun. **10**(5), 1389–1395 (2011)
13. Oka, A., Lampe, L.: Distributed target tracking using signal strength measurements by a wireless sensor network. IEEE J. Sel. Areas Commun. **28**(7), 1006–1015 (2010)
14. Tomic, S., Beko, M., Tuba, M., Correia, V.M.F.: Target localization in NLOS environments using RSS and TOA measurements. IEEE Wirel. Commun. Lett. **7**(6), 1062–1065 (2018)
15. Tomic, S., Beko, M.: A robust NLOS bias mitigation technique for RSS-TOA-based target localization. IEEE Signal Process. Lett. **26**(1), 64–68 (2019)
16. Boyd, S., Vandenberghe, L.: Appendix. In: Convex Optimization, pp. 626–627. Cambridge University, Cambridge (2004)
17. Chen, H., Wang, G., Ansari, N.: Improved robust TOA-based localization via NLOS balancing parameter estimation. IEEE Trans. Veh. Technol. **68**(6), 6177–6181 (2019)
18. Grant, M., Boyd, S.: CVX: MATLAB software for disciplined convex programming, version 2.1, December 2018. http://cvxr.com/cvx
19. Toh, K.C., Todd, M.J., Tutuncu, R.H.: SDPT3: a matlab software package for semidefinite programming. Opt. Methods Softw. **11**(12), 545–581 (1999)

Primary Synchronization Signal Low Complexity Sliding Correlation Method

Huahua Wang[1], Dongfeng Chen[1(✉)], and Juan Li[2]

[1] School of Communication and Information Engineering, Chongqing University of Posts and Telecommunications, Chongqing 400065, China
chendongfengmr@foxmail.com
[2] School of Science College, Chongqing University of Posts and Telecommunications, Chongqing 400065, China

Abstract. With the development of technology, the mobile communication system has the characteristics of high rate and low delay. How to deal with the signal quickly and accurately has become a research hotspot. As the first step of the mobile communication system, the efficiency and performance of synchronization directly determine the follow-up signal Processing. In the mobile communication system, the terminal needs to synchronize the frequency and time of the received signal, that is, the synchronization signal is captured and processed. Frequency synchronization mainly carries on the digital down-conversion operation to the signal, the time synchronization is mainly through sliding the baseband signal with the locally generated synchronization sequence to determine the starting position of the synchronization signal, so as to achieve the time synchronization. Therefore, in this paper, taking LTE-A (Long Term Evolution Advanced) system as an example, a low-complexity sliding correlation method based on Fast Fourier Transform (FFT) is proposed in this paper, which can significantly reduce the computations in the synchronization process the complexity.

Keywords: LTE-A system · Primary synchronization signal · FFT · Sliding correlation

1 Introduction

LTE-A is an evolved version of LTE (Long Term Evolution). The system parameters of LTE-A are greatly improved compared with LTE, and can provide greater system capacity and lower system delay. With the improvement of LTE-A performance, it has become the new generation of mainstream mobile communication standard after 3G. After the user equipment UE (User Equipment) is powered on, a cell suitable for camping is selected to connect to the LTE-A network, and the base station eNodeB and the UE implement time-frequency synchronization, because the downlink transmission mode of the LTE-A system is OFDM, so this process is equivalent to the process of time-frequency synchronization of OFDM (Orthogonal Frequency Division Multiplexing) system [1–4].

© ICST Institute for Computer Sciences, Social Informatics and Telecommunications Engineering 2020
Published by Springer Nature Switzerland AG 2020. All Rights Reserved
H. Gao et al. (Eds.): ChinaCom 2019, LNICST 312, pp. 669–678, 2020.
https://doi.org/10.1007/978-3-030-41114-5_50

The primary synchronization signal PSS (Primary Synchronization Signal) implements this process in the LTE-A system. Since the primary synchronization signal is transmitted once every half frame (i.e., 5 ms), only the start position of the half frame in one radio frame can be determined, so the user terminal is not sure whether it is the first half frame or the second half frame [5]. Frame synchronization and cell ID group identification are implemented by a secondary synchronization signal SSS (Secondary Synchronization Signal). After the terminal synchronizes with the cell, the subsequent signal reception processing can be performed. The performance of the entire downlink depends on the synchronization performance. Therefore, as the first step of the cell search synchronization is crucial in the LTE-A system.

In this paper, based on FFT low complexity sliding correlation method, the synchronization signal is captured and processed, the algorithm complexity is reduced, the synchronization efficiency and performance have been improved, and the frequency and time of the received signal can be quickly synchronized.

2 Main Sync Signal

The primary synchronization signal of the LTE-A system uses a ZC (Zadoff-Chu) sequence [6] generation method with good autocorrelation in the frequency domain. This sequence is used to generate PSS [7] in the frequency domain. The three PSSs are distinguished by u, which is generated as follows:

$$d_u(n) = \begin{cases} e^{-j\frac{\pi un(n+1)}{63}} & n = 0, 1, \ldots, 30 \\ e^{-j\frac{\pi u(n+1)(n+2)}{63}} & n = 31, 32, \ldots, 61 \end{cases} \tag{1}$$

The sector number N(2) of the primary synchronization channel has an ID value of 0–2 corresponding to the ZC sequence root number $u \in \{25, 29, 34\}$ [8]. On the frequency, the main synchronization signal occupies a total of 72 subcarriers, the center of the bandwidth is used to allocate its frequency position, and the intermediate DC puncturing is used as the DC carrier. The guard interval occupies 5 resource elements on each side, and no signal is sent at this position. Reserved, its structure is shown in Fig. 1.

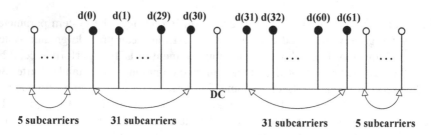

Fig. 1. Mapping of PSS sequence resources

3 Synchronization Algorithm

3.1 Traditional Synchronization Algorithm

The main synchronizing signal sequence has good cross-correlation characteristics, and the receiving sequence and the main synchronizing signal sequence time domain use sliding to complete symbol timing synchronization [9–11]. Three sets of different frequency domain PSS sequences are generated by the root sequence u ∈ {25, 29, 34}, and the relevant expressions are as follows:

$$r(n) = \sum_{m=0}^{N-1} x(n+m)y*(m) \tag{2}$$

In the expression (2), the received radio frame data is represented by x(n), M is a field length, the conjugate of y(n) is represented by y*(k), and the length of the local main synchronizing signal sequence is equal to N. The three sets of correlation results r(n) can be obtained by Eq. (2), and the value of the N(2) ID and the PSS position can be determined by the maximum value of the three sets of correlation results r(n). Because the x(n) sequence is relatively long and requires a large amount of storage space and running time to complete the time domain sliding correlation algorithm, the algorithm robustness [11–15] is lower.

3.2 Segmentation Correlation Synchronization Algorithm

The segment correlation synchronization is implemented by the local primary synchronization signal sequence y(n) and the received radio frame data x(n). The total number of segments is equal to D, and the segment-related synchronization expression is:

$$r(n) = \sum_{l=0}^{D-1} \sum_{m=0}^{N/D-1} x(n+m+Nd/D)y*(m+Nd/D) \tag{3}$$

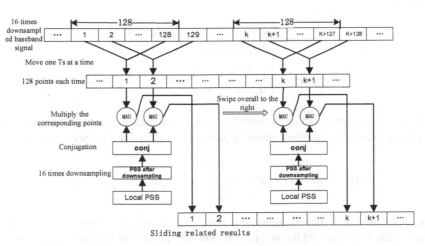

Fig. 2. Traditional sliding correlation method

The traditional sliding correlation method determines the N(2) ID and the position of the PSS by comparing the baseband signal with the local PSS and finding the maximum value of the sliding correlation result by comparison. The specific implementation scheme is shown in Fig. 2. Although the procedure is simple, the computational complexity and the number of correlations increase linearly, and the implementation complexity is still high.

3.3 Improved Low Complexity Sliding Correlation Method

In this paper, a low-complexity sliding correlation method based on fast Fourier transform is proposed. The linear correlation is replaced by the circular correlation theorem. The fast Fourier transform is segmented and transformed, and the fast linear correlation between long and short sequences is completed. The algorithm's anti-frequency offset performance improvement and time complexity are reduced. The method mainly includes six modules: data segmentation, adjacent data segment merging, FFT, corresponding point multiplication, accumulation, and IFFT. The time domain sliding correlation algorithm expression (2) of the main synchronization signal sequence is transformed:

$$r(n) = \sum_{m=0}^{N-1} x(m) y * (m - n) = x(n) y * (-n) \tag{4}$$

Expression (4) establishes the equivalent relationship between cross-correlation and linear convolution. Calculating the cross-correlation of two sequences is done by calculating the linear convolution method, so that $\tilde{y}(n)$ represents the inversion of $y*(n)$. The circular convolution theorem stipulates that linear convolution is equivalent to circular convolution after zero-complementing operations on $x(n)$ and $\tilde{y}(n)$. Replacing a linear correlation with a circular correlation is equivalent to using a fast Fourier transform method to find a linear correlation, where $L \geq M + N - 1$ and $L = 2\gamma$ (γ is a positive integer), make:

$$x(n) = \begin{cases} x(n), n = 0, 1, \ldots, M - 1 \\ 0, n = M, M + 1, \ldots, L - M \end{cases} \tag{5}$$

$$\tilde{y}(n) = \begin{cases} \tilde{y}(n), n = 0, 1, \ldots, N - 1 \\ 0, n = N, N + 1, \ldots, L - N \end{cases} \tag{6}$$

It can be seen from the circle correlation theorem that if $R(m) = X(m)\tilde{Y}(m)$, $x(n)$ and $\tilde{y}(n)$ are respectively represented by $X(m)$, $\tilde{y}(m)$ after fast Fourier transform:

$$r(n) = IDFT[R(m)] = \{\sum_{m=0}^{N-1} x(m)\tilde{y}[(m - n)]_N\} R_N(n) \tag{7}$$

It is known from the expression (7) that the cross-correlation operation of the sequence can be performed by the fast convolution method. $X(m)$ and $\tilde{y}(m)$ are obtained by zero-padding and FFT transformation of $x(n)$ and $\tilde{y}(n)$, and $R(m)$ is obtained by multiplying the frequency domain of X(m) and $\tilde{y}(m)$, R(m) After the IFFT transform, r(n) is the first $M + N - 1$ data.

Because the length M is long, the main synchronizing signal sequence needs to be complemented with zeros, so that long FFT transform is difficult and a large amount of computation is wasted. The above existing problem can be solved by the overlap addition method. First, x(n) is divided into multi-segment sequences of k length, and then the segmentation fast Fourier transform correlation calculation is performed, wherein the i-th segment of the x(n) sequence The sequence is represented by xi(n).

$$\begin{cases} x_i(n) = x(n), ik + 1 \leq n \leq (i+1)k \\ x(n) = \sum_{i=0}^{M/k-1} x_i(n) \end{cases} \tag{8}$$

After segmentation, the expression (2) is expressed as:

$$r(n) = \sum_{m=0}^{N-1} \left[\sum_{i=0}^{M/M_1-1} x_i(n+m) \right] y * (m)$$

$$= \sum_{i=0}^{M/M_1-1} \left[\sum_{m=0}^{N-1} x_i(n+m) y * (m) \right] = \sum_{i=0}^{M/M_1-1} r_i(n) \tag{9}$$

In the expression (9), the last output sequence r(n) is composed of the superposition of the $N - 1$ term after ri(n) and the $N - 1$ term of ri + 1(n).

In order to ensure the integrity of the main synchronization sequence at the time of segmentation, the expressions (7) and (9) can complete the fast correlation of the long and short sequences. Therefore, the superposition method and the fast convolution method can be used to quickly synchronize the frequency domain of the main synchronizing signal symbol.

3.4 Improved Algorithm Flow

The improved timing synchronization of the mobile communication system first segments the received sequence, and then performs adjacent splicing and merging of the adjacent data segments to perform FFT, and then segments, FFTs, and conjugates the local synchronization sequence again, and then receives the sequence. The frequency domain expression is multiplied by the corresponding point of the frequency expression of the local synchronization sequence, and finally the intermediate result is subjected to IFFT processing to obtain a sliding correlation result. Specific steps are as follows:

(1) The received signal is subjected to segmentation processing of length 1024, and the baseband signal is divided into data of a plurality of segments of 1024 lengths.
(2) The data in (1) is merged and merged adjacently, that is, the stitching of 1, 2, 2, 3, 3, 4, and so on.
(3) Perform a 2048-point FFT operation on each piece of data spliced in (2) to obtain a frequency domain expression after the baseband signal is segmented.

(4)   The local synchronization sequence is divided into two segments of data of length 1024, each segment of data is subjected to 2048-point FFT processing, and then the conjugate is obtained to obtain a segmentation frequency expression of the local synchronization sequence.

(5)   Multiplying the corresponding points of the results obtained by (3) and (4) to obtain the intermediate value of the correlation result.

(6)   When calculating the relevant intermediate values of the two or more stitching results, add the adjacent two related intermediate values, and then proceed to (7); otherwise, proceed to (3).

(7)   The addition result is 2048 points IFFT, and the first 1024 values are retained as relevant results. Repeat the above steps until the 153600 point (field) correlation values are calculated. The improved main synchronization algorithm flow is shown in Fig. 3.

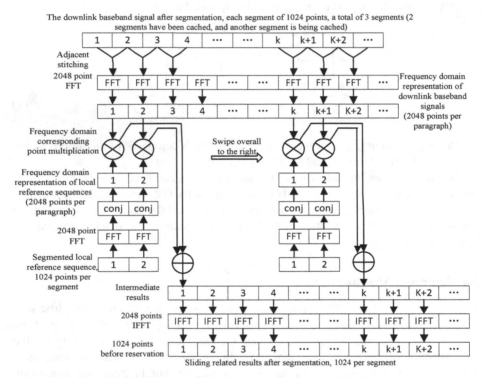

Fig. 3. Improved primary synchronization algorithm flow

4   Experimental Simulation and Analysis

4.1   Time Complexity Analysis

The computational complexity of this paper is mainly concentrated in the two processes of FFT and IFFT. The FFT calculation of N points consists of two parts: the number of complex additions is $N \log_2 N$, and the number of complex multiplications is $\frac{1}{2}N \log_2 N$. Therefore, it is derived that the computational complexity of the algorithm is $o(N \log_2 N)$. In this paper, the complexity of the algorithm is analyzed. The computational complexity is measured by the number of complex additions and complex multiplications required to find the position of the PSS in one field (153600 points).

Table 1. Half frame data complexity comparison.

Related programs	Complex multiplication	Complex addition
Traditional convolution algorithm	143718400	143718400
Traditional sliding correlation	7697408	14460928
Existing time domain correlation	5948544	13948544

It can be found from Table 1 that the computational complexity of the frequency domain correlation scheme designed in this paper is lower than that of the existing time domain correlation scheme, and there is no backtracking process in the implementation of the project, and the original signal is not stored, and the comparison decision process does not depend on the gate. Limit. The existing time-domain sliding related scheme can further reduce the computational complexity by setting the threshold value, but the signal fluctuation in the actual environment is large, and the threshold setting size will affect the correlation peak. In this paper, the effectiveness and correctness of the algorithm are verified by using simulation and measured data. The detailed simulation system environment configuration parameters are shown in Table 2.

Table 2. Simulation system environment.

System parameters	Parameter value
Channel bandwidth/MHz	20
Sampling frequency/MHz	30.72
FFT points	2048
CP type	Conventional CP
Channel model	AWGN channel

The improved algorithm divides the received sequence into segments and then merges them in the same way, which can reduce the duration and resource consumption in the implementation process. The performance is optimal when the segment length is 1024. Figure 4 shows the performance of the improved algorithm with SNR. The performance curve of the change, the segmentation process of the algorithm when the signal-to-noise ratio is low significantly reduces the time-consuming of the algorithm. It can be seen from the figure that the algorithm is significantly more time-consuming than the traditional algorithm.

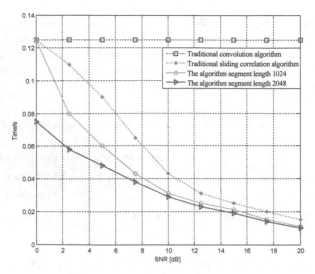

Fig. 4. Time performance comparison

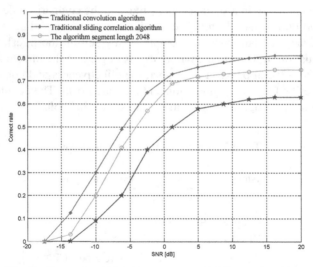

Fig. 5. Comparison of the correct rates of different algorithms

4.2 The Correctness of the Algorithm

Since the scheme designed in this paper does not depend on the threshold setting of the traditional scheme, the scheme has a higher correct signal to noise ratio than the traditional design scheme. It can be seen from Fig. 5 that the method is low in the letter. Better performance under noise ratio.

Figure 6 is a simulation result of correlation results of 4 frames of data length. In the environment where the frequency offset is 0, the signal-to-noise ratio is 0 dB and $u = 29$, the three sets of correlation results are obtained by the frequency domain fast synchronization algorithm. The symbol timing synchronization correlation results of $u \in \{25, 29, 34\}$ are t0, t2, and t3 in Fig. 5, respectively. It can be clearly observed that t0 and t2 do not show good correlation peaks, and the highest peak of related results does not exceed 4. The correlation result t1 has a distinct peak. In Fig. 5, the peak of t1 drops rapidly, and the correlation peak is close to 9, and the position of the peak is equivalent to the position of the main synchronization signal of the received data.

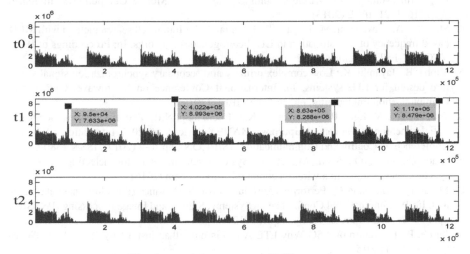

Fig. 6. Local three groups of PSS sequences

The value of the $N_{ID}^{(2)}$ ID and the position of the primary synchronization signal can be quickly and accurately located by the fast correlation method in the frequency domain, and the correctness of the synchronization algorithm is verified.

5 Conclusion

The acquisition and processing of synchronization signals is of utmost importance in LTE-A mobile communication systems, and it plays an important role in the reception and processing of subsequent signals. As the user activity range and the density of the LTE-A base station increase, the two processes of cell handover and cell reselection are performed more frequently. At present, there are some shortcomings in the synchronization algorithm. This paper presents a low-complexity sliding correlation method based on FFT for fast time-frequency synchronization, and the complexity is much lower than the traditional algorithm. This paper verifies the feasibility of the scheme by simulating the algorithm. The algorithm has the advantages of strong synchronization performance and low complexity. Since the cell search in the 5G system environment is also the synchronization process of the synchronization signal, the algorithm can meet the synchronization performance requirements of the future 5G system. The algorithm can be extended to apply. Cell search under 5G system has important reference application value for cell search in 5G environment.

References

1. Yang, X.M., Xiong, Y., Jia, G.Q.: Fast acquisition of primary synchronization signal in LTE systems. J. Appl. Sci. **30**, 14–18 (2012)
2. Berggren, F., Popović, B.M.: Primary synchronization signal for D2D communications in LTE-Advanced. IEEE Commun. Lett. **19**(7), 1241–1244 (2015)
3. Elsherif, A.R., Khairy, M.M.: Adaptive primary synchronization signal detection for 3GPP long term evolution. In: Wireless Communications and Mobile Computing Conference, pp. 1716–1721. IEEE (2013)
4. Shimura, A., Sawahashi, M., Nagata, S., Kishiyama, Y.: Initial cell search method with MLD based frequency offset estimation in LTE heterogeneous networks. In: Proceedings of IEEE VTC2017-Fall, September 2017
5. Shoba, B., Jayanthi, K.: Low complex primary and secondary synchronization signal structure design for LTE systems. In: International Conference on Microwave, Optical and Communication Engineering, pp. 467–470. IEEE (2016)
6. Timoshenko, A., Egor, B., Molenkamp, K., Molenkamp, N.B.: Zadoff-Chu sequence based initial synchronization for multipurpose MANET devices. In: 2017 International Siberian Conference on Control and Communications (SIBCON), pp. 1–4 (2017). ISSN 2380-6516
7. Xiao, C., Zhao, Q., Shen, M., et al.: Systems and methods for detecting a primary synchronization signal in a wireless communication system (2016)
8. Meidlinger, M., Wang, Q.: Performance evaluation of LTE advanced downlink channel estimators. In: 19th International Conference on Systems, Signals and Image Processing (IWSSIP), pp. 252–255. IEEE Press, Vienna, April 2012
9. Jarich, P.: The return of 4.5G-Why LTE-A Pro is more than just a silly name. FierceWirelessTech (11) (2015)
10. Ibrahim, B.: Design and implementation of synchroniation and cell search algorithms for LTE receiver. In: 32nd National Radio Science Conference. October University for Modern Sciences and Arts, Cairo (2015)
11. Shimura, A., Sawahashi, M., Nagata, S., Kishiyama, Y.: Effects of time and space diversity on physical cell ID detection for NB-IoT. In: Proceedings of the IEEE VTS APWCS 2017, August 2017
12. Sriharsha, M.: A complete cell search and synchronization in LTE. J. Wirel. Commun. Netw. **2017**(1), 101–106 (2017)
13. Shoba, B.: Low complex primary and secondary synchronization signal structure design for LTE systems. In: International Conference on Microwave. IIT, Varanasi (2015)
14. Lin, J.C., Sun, Y.T.: Initial synchronization exploiting inherent diversity for the LTE-A sector search process. IEEE Trans. Wireless Commun. **15**(2), 1114–1128 (2016)
15. Jeon, Y., Park, H., Choi, E.: Synchronization and cell search procedure in 3GPP 5G NR systems. In: 2019 21st International Conference on Advanced Communication Technology (ICACT), PyeongChang, Kwangwoon_Do, Korea (South), pp. 475–478 (2019)

Analysis of Frequency Offset Effect on PRACH in 5G NR Systems

Wenxi He$^{(\boxtimes)}$, Yifan Du, and Hang Long

Wireless Signal Processing and Network Lab, Key Laboratory of Universal Wireless Communication, Ministry of Education Beijing University of Posts and Telecommunications, Beijing, China
bupthewenxi@163.com

Abstract. Physical Random Access Channel (PRACH) in 5G new radio (NR) systems transmits random access preamble for the user equipment (UE) to access the network. In 5G NR systems, Zadoff-Chu (ZC) sequences are used as random access preamble sequences. Frequency offset severely affects the perfect autocorrelation properties of the preamble sequences, thereby affecting the preamble detection performance and timing accuracy. In this paper, frequency offset effect on PRACH preamble miss detection rate and timing error in 5G NR systems is analyzed. Firstly, the frequency offset effect on inter-carrier interference and the correlation of general sequences is derived. Then, based on the former derivation and characteristics of ZC sequences, the frequency offset effect on correlation of ZC sequences is derived. Moreover, PRACH preamble miss detection rate and timing error are analyzed. The analytical results show that for different random access UEs with different PRACH preamble numbers, the random access performances are differently affected by the same frequency offset. Besides, the higher miss detection rate, the smaller timing error. The simulation results show the rationality of the analysis.

Keywords: PRACH · Frequency offset · Correlation

1 Introduction

The random access procedure is of great importance for the user equipment (UE) to access the network and achieve timing synchronization with the gNodeB (gNB). As an initial step to connect to the network, one UE sends a preamble which carries access information (control and timing information) through Physical Random Access Channel (PRACH) [1], and the gNB needs to detect the preamble to identify the random access preamble number and obtain timing information to calculate timing advance (TA) value [2]. Then the UE can establish a connection with the network and achieve timing synchronization with the

Supported by China Unicom Network Technology Research Institute and project 61302088 which was supported by National Natural Science Foundation of China.

© ICST Institute for Computer Sciences, Social Informatics and Telecommunications Engineering 2020
Published by Springer Nature Switzerland AG 2020. All Rights Reserved
H. Gao et al. (Eds.): ChinaCom 2019, LNICST 312, pp. 679–692, 2020.
https://doi.org/10.1007/978-3-030-41114-5_51

base station [3]. The peak-to-average ratio (PAR) and peak position of correlation are usually used to detect PRACH preamble sequences and obtain timing information. Zadoff-Chu (ZC) sequences are used as random access preamble sequences in 5G new radio (NR) systems due to the good autocorrelation properties and periodic cross-correlation properties [4].

Frequency offset affects the orthogonality between subcarriers, thus affecting the accurate reception of preamble sequences and the correlation result at the receiver. Ultimately, frequency offset will affect the performance of preamble detection and timing accuracy. The high speed railway communication has been incorporated into 5G NR systems as a special scenario, so it is necessary to study frequency offset effect on PRACH and corresponding solutions in 5G NR Systems [5].

For solving the above problem, there are already some studies. Ref. [6] proposes a Peak Ratio based Estimation method to estimate the frequency offset between a mobile phone and the infrastructure based on PRACH preambles. This method use the ratio of the largest peak value over the second largest peak value to estimate frequency offset. However, this method does not take into account that frequency offset has different effect on detection performance of different preamble sequences. Ref. [7] introduces an analytical framework quantifying the ZC sequence's performance, and it demonstrates that the frequency offset immunity of a ZC sequence set can be controlled by shaping the spectrum of the ZC sequence set. But with the advancement of the 3GPP protocol, the type of restricted sets are determined to adapt to the high speed scenes, the above analytical framework is of little significance in 5G NR systems. So analysis of the frequency offset effect on the PRACH preamble sequences in 5G NR systems is needed.

In this paper, based on the analysis of the frequency offset effect on correlation of ZC sequences, the PRACH preamble detection performance and timing accuracy affected by the frequency offset are derived. Considering the average value of correlation does not change much when the signal and noise power are determined, the peak size is used to analyze the preamble detection performance in this paper. The analysis is performed in the frequency domain and based on the preamble transmit and receive processes in 5G NR systems. By analyzing the frequency offset effect on inter-carrier interference, general conclusion about frequency offset effect on the peak of correlation result is derived. Then, combining the characteristics of ZC sequences with the derived general conclusion, frequency offset effect on the PRACH is analyzed. The PRACH preamble detection Block Error Ratio (BLER) and Cumulative Distribution Function (CDF) of TA error are taken as two performance metrics. The analysis show that under the impact of frequency offset, the PRACH preamble detection performance and timing accuracy of different PRACH preamble sequences are different. The higher the PRACH preamble detection BLER, the lower TA error. Through simulation, the rationality of the whole analysis is verified.

The remainder of this paper is organized as follows. Section 2 mainly describes the system model, and Sect. 3 elaborates the analysis and inferences, including the frequency offset effect on subcarriers and the peak of correlation result. Section 4 deduces the specific effect of frequency offset on the PRACH. Section 5 shows the simulation results and proves the rationality of analysis. Finally Sect. 6 concludes this paper.

Notations: Sequences with uppercase letter Y denotes frequency-domain sequences, with lowercase letter x denotes time-domain sequences.

2   System Model

2.1   Preamble Transmitter

The general process of PRACH Preamble transmitter is shown in Fig. 1. Where $x(m)$ refers to the random-access preamble sequence, and its size is N_{seq}. $Y_1(n)$ refers to its frequency-domain representation and is calculated by DFT as

$$Y_1(n) = \sum_{m=0}^{N_{seq}-1} x(m)e^{-j\frac{2\pi mn}{N_{seq}}} \quad n = 0,1,\cdots,N_{seq}-1 \tag{1}$$

By mapping $Y_1(n)$ to the middle of N subcarriers, we can get a frequency-domain sequence $Y_2(n)$. $x_s(p)$ refers to the sending signal which is the time-domain representation of $Y_2(n)$, where the IFFT size is N.

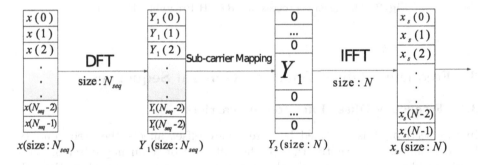

Fig. 1. The general process of PRACH Preamble transmitter.

2.2   Preamble Detector

At the receiver, the received time-domain preamble sequence $x_r(p)$ can be denoted as

$$x_r(p) = Hx_s(p)e^{j\frac{2\pi\Delta f}{f_s}p} + q(p) \quad p = 0,1,\cdots,N-1 \tag{2}$$

where H is the Line of Sight (LOS) channel gain, Δf refers to the Doppler shift, f_s is bandwidth of one subcarrier, and $q(p)$ refers to the noise [8]. The general process of PRACH Preamble detector is shown in Fig. 2. For the received sequence, after DFT and subcarrier de-mapping, we can get a frequency-domain sequence $Y_4(n)$. To facilitate calculation and analysis, we implement cross-correlation calculation between the received sequence and the root sequence in the frequency domain. In Fig. 2, $Y_{root}(n)$ refers to the frequency-domain representation of the root sequence $x_{root}(m)$, which is defined in 5G NR specifications. $Y_c(n)$ is calculated as

$$Y_c(n) = Y_4(n) \times Y_{root}(n)^* \tag{3}$$

$x_c(p)$ refers to the time-domain cross-correlation result between the received sequence and the root sequence, and its size is N. By detecting the peak size and peak position of the absolute value of $x_c(p)$, we can determine which UE send the preamble and obtain TA value.

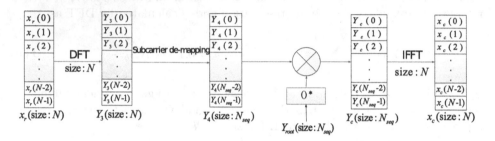

Fig. 2. The general process of PRACH Preamble detector.

3   Frequency Offset Effect on General Sequences

3.1   Frequency Offset Effect on Subcarriers

In this section, it is analyzed how frequency offset affects the orthogonality between subcarriers. Firstly, the specific influence of frequency offset on subcarriers will be analyzed by a simple frequency domain sequence, where the d-th entry is 1, and others are 0. Let

$$Y_2(z) = \begin{cases} 1 & z = d \\ 0 & \text{else} \end{cases} \quad z = 0, 1, \cdots, N-1 \tag{4}$$

According to Fig. 1, $x_s(p)$ can be obtained by IFFT as

$$x_s(p) = \frac{1}{N} e^{\frac{j2\pi dp}{N}} \tag{5}$$

Only consider frequency offset effect, set $H = 1$ and $q = 0$, according to (2), $x_r(p)$ is obtained as

$$x_r(p) = \frac{1}{N} e^{\frac{j2\pi(\Delta f + df_s)p}{Nf_s}} \tag{6}$$

After DFT, $Y_3(z)$ is obtained as

$$Y_3(z) = \frac{1}{N} \times \frac{\sin\left(\frac{\Delta f + df_s - zf_s}{f_s}\pi\right)}{\sin\left(\frac{\Delta f + df_s - zf_s}{Nf_s}\pi\right)} e^{j\left(\frac{\Delta f + df_s - zf_s}{f_s} - \frac{\Delta f + df_s - zf_s}{Nf_s}\right)\pi} \tag{7}$$

By comparing $Y_2(z)$ and $Y_3(z)$, it is known that only consider the impact of frequency offset, the received sequence $Y_3(z)$ can be expressed by $Y_2(z)$ as

$$Y_3(z) = \sum_{z_1=0}^{N-1} Y_2(z_1)K(z_1 - z) \tag{8}$$

where $K(z_1 - z)$ refers to the interference coefficient of inter-carrier interference and can be denoted as follows

$$K(l) = \begin{cases} \frac{1}{N}e^{j\theta_0} \left| \dfrac{\sin(\frac{\Delta f}{f_s}\pi)}{\sin(\frac{\Delta f + lf_s}{Nf_s}\pi)} \right| e^{j(\frac{-l}{N})\pi} & 0 \le l \le N-1 \\ \frac{1}{N}e^{j\theta_0} \left| \dfrac{\sin(\frac{\Delta f}{f_s}\pi)}{\sin(\frac{\Delta f + lf_s}{Nf_s}\pi)} \right| e^{j(\frac{-l}{N}+1)\pi} & -(N-1) \le l < 0 \end{cases} \tag{9}$$

$$\theta_0 = \frac{(N-1)\Delta f\pi}{Nf_s}$$

where θ_0 is the phase of $K(0)$, From (9), it is easier to get the following conclusions

- There is a sudden change of π between the phase of $K(-1)$ and θ_0.
- Regardless of the phase mutation, the phase difference between two adjacent items is $\frac{\pi}{N}$.
- The absolute value of $K(0)$ is the largest in $K(l)$, and the absolute value of $K(-1)$ is the second largest.
- The larger the absolute value of l, the smaller the absolute value of $K(l)$, so the farther a subcarrier is from the current subcarrier, the smaller the impact of the subcarrier on the current subcarrier.

Combine the above conclusions with (2), the received frequency-domain sequence after de-mapping affected by frequency offset can be denoted as

$$Y_4(n) = He^{j\theta_0}\left[\sum_{k=n}^{N_{seq}-1} Y_1(k)\,|K(k-n)|\, e^{j\frac{(n-k)\pi}{N}} - \sum_{k=0}^{n-1} Y_1(k)\,|K(k-n)|\, e^{j\frac{(n-k)\pi}{N}} \right]$$
$$+ Q(n) \tag{10}$$

According to (9) and (10), it is easier to get that the closer k is to n, the larger $|K(k-n)|$ is, and the closer $e^{j\frac{(n-k)\pi}{N}}$ is to 1. Considering that the size of IFFT N is often much larger than the size of preamble sequence N_{seq}, and

$|n - k|$ is smaller than N_{seq}. So the impact of $e^{j\frac{(n-k)\pi}{N}}$ can be ignored. Then $Y_4(n)$ can be simplified and approximated as

$$Y_4(n) \approx He^{j\theta_0}\left[|K(0)|Y_1(n) + \sum_{k=1}^{N_{seq}-1}|K(k)|Y_{1,k}(n) - \sum_{k=1-N_{seq}}^{-1}|K(k)|Y_{1,k}(n)\right]$$

$$+Q(n)$$

$$k = -(N_{seq} - 1), -(N_{seq} - 2), \cdots, -1, 1, 2, \cdots, N_{seq} - 2, N_{seq} - 1$$

$$(11)$$

where $Y_{1,k}(n)$ is the k-th entry interference and can be denoted by $Y_1(n)$ as

$$Y_{1,k}(n) = \left\{\begin{matrix} Y_1(n+k) & \max(0,\text{-}k) \le n \le \min(N_{seq} - 1, N_{seq} - 1 - k) \\ 0 & \text{else} \end{matrix}\right\} \quad (12)$$

So the received frequency-domain sequence affected by frequency offset is simply denoted by the sending sequence.

3.2   Frequency Offset Effect on Correlation

In the previous section, we analysis the frequency offset effect on subcarriers, and derive expression of the received frequency-domain sequence $Y_4(n)$ affected by frequency offset. In this section, it is theoretically analyzed how the peak of correlation result can be affected by the frequency offset. According to (3) and (11), $Y_c(n)$ is obtained as

$$Y_c(n) \approx He^{j\theta_0}\left[|K(0)|Y_1(n) + \sum_{k=1}^{N_{seq}-1}|K(k)|Y_{1,k}(n) - \sum_{k=1-N_{seq}}^{-1}|K(k)|Y_{1,k}(n)\right]$$

$$\times Y_{root}(n)^* + Q(n)Y_{root}(n)^*$$

$$(13)$$

where $e^{j\theta_0}$ has no effect on the absolute value of the cross-correlation result, and can be ignored. To compare the cross-correlation with or without affected by the frequency offset, set

$$Y_{c,pre}(n) = HY_1(n)Y_{root}(n)^*$$

$$Y_{c,interf}(n) = \sum_{k=1}^{N_{seq}-1}Y_{c,interf,k}(n) - \sum_{k=1-N_{seq}}^{-1}Y_{c,interf,k}(n) \quad (14)$$

$$Y_{c,interf,k}(n) = H|K(k)|Y_{1,k}(n)Y_{root}(n)^*$$

Then $Y_c(n)$ and $x_c(p)$ affected by the frequency offset can be denoted as

$$Y_c(n) = |K(0)|Y_{c,pre}(n) + Y_{c,interf}(n) + Q(n)Y_{root}(n)^*$$

$$x_c(p) = |K(0)|x_{c,pre}(p) + x_{c,interf}(p) + q_{cor}(p)$$

$$(15)$$

where $x_{c,pre}(p)$, $x_{c,interf}(p)$, $q_{cor}(p)$ are the time-domain representation of $Y_{c,pre}(n)$, $Y_{c,interf}(n)$, $Q(n)Y_{root}(n)^*$, respectively. Set the time-domain representation of $Y_{c,interf,k}(n)$ is $x_{c,interf,k}(p)$. Then it is clearly that $x_{c,pre}(p)$

is the time-domain cross-correlation without affected by the frequency offset, $x_{c,interf}(p)$ is the interference caused by the frequency offset and the k-th entry of it is $x_{c,interf,k}(p)$. Set m, m_{pre}, $m_{interf,k}$ are entries with the largest absolute value in $x_c(p)$, $x_{c,pre}(p)$, $x_{c,interf,k}(p)$, respectively. And the phases of $x_{c,pre}(m_{pre})$, $x_{c,interf,k}(m_{interf,k})$ are θ_{pre}, $\theta_{interf,k}$. So the peak position offset caused by the frequency offset can be denoted as the absolute value of m $-m_{pre}$.

If $m_{pre} \neq m_{interf,k}$, as shown in Fig. 3(a), the k-th entry interference will cause a large change in the peak size and peak position of the cross-correlation result. When $k < 0$, the closer $\theta_{interf,k}$ is to $\theta_{pre} + \pi$, the larger the peak size is, and the larger the peak position changes, the closer $\theta_{interf,k}$ is to θ_{pre}, the smaller the peak size is, and the smaller the peak position changes. When $k > 0$, changes are reversed.

If $m_{pre} = m_{interf,k}$, as shown in Fig. 3(b), frequency offset may cause a larger change in the peak size than $m_{pre} \neq m_{interf,k}$, but it can't change the peak position of the cross-correlation result. When $k < 0$, the closer $\theta_{interf,k}$ is to $\theta_{pre} + \pi$, the larger the peak size is, the closer $\theta_{interf,k}$ is to θ_{pre}, the smaller the peak size is. When $k > 0$, changes are reversed.

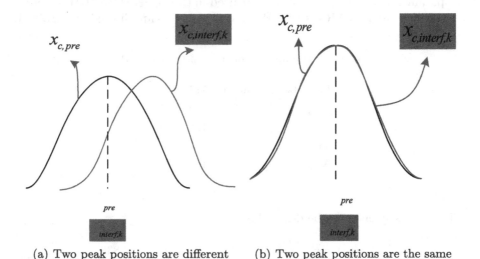

(a) Two peak positions are different   (b) Two peak positions are the same

Fig. 3. Peak position relationship between $x_{c,interf,k}(p)$ and $x_{c,pre}(p)$

According to the above analysis, it is known that for a sequence, if $m_{pre} \neq m_{interf,k}$, the peak of correlation will be greatly affected by frequency offset, and the larger the peak size is, the larger the peak position changes. If $m_{pre} = m_{interf,k}$, it can effectively avoid frequency offset effect on the peak position of correlation.

4   Frequency Offset Effect on the Correlation of ZC Sequences

In this section, the specific effect of frequency offset on the correlation of ZC sequences is analyzed based on the derivation of Sect. 3, and the PRACH preamble detection performance and TA accuracy are roughly predicted. According to the related specifications in 5G NR systems, the 64 preambles used in each time-frequency PRACH occasion can be determined by the root sequence number u and cyclic shift value C_v [1]. Since frequency offset usually is less than half subcarrier spacing, set the type of restricted sets is unrestricted in this paper. Then the 64 PRACH preambles can be obtained as

$$
\begin{aligned}
x^v(m) &= x_{root}[(m + C_v) \bmod N_{seq}] \\
x_{root}(m) &= e^{-j\frac{\pi u m(m+1)}{N_{seq}}} \\
C_v &= vN_{CS} \qquad v = 0,1,\cdots,63
\end{aligned}
\tag{16}
$$

where N_{CS} refers to the length of cycle shift and is determined by the higher-layer parameter [1]. The preamble format used in this paper is PRACH preamble format 0 defined in 5G NR systems. Related parameters are shown in the Table 1.

Table 1. Preamble parameters of the PRACH.

Preamble parameters	Values
N_{seq}	839
f_s	1.25 KHz
u	1
N_{CS}	13

The root sequence can be denoted as

$$
\begin{aligned}
x_{root}(m) &= e^{-j\frac{m(m+1)}{839}\pi} & m &= 0,1,\cdots,838 \\
Y_{root}(n) &= e^{j\left[1.750298+\frac{n(n+1)}{839}\right]\pi} & n &= 0,1,\cdots,838
\end{aligned}
\tag{17}
$$

And the preamble sequences can be denoted as

$$
\begin{aligned}
x^v(m) &= e^{-j\left[\frac{13v(13v+1)}{839}+\frac{26vm+m(m+1)}{839}\right]\pi} \\
Y_1^v(n) &= e^{j\left[1.750298+\frac{26vn+n(n+1)}{839}\right]\pi}
\end{aligned}
\tag{18}
$$

According to (14), $Y_{c,pre}^v(n)$ can be calculated as

$$
Y_{c,pre}^v(n) = He^{j\frac{26vn}{839}\pi}
\tag{19}
$$

After IFFT, $x_{c,pre}^v(p)$ is calculated as

$$x_{c,pre}^v(p) = \frac{H}{N} \frac{\sin\left[\left(13v + \frac{839p}{N}\right)\pi\right]}{\sin\left[\left(\frac{13v}{839} + \frac{p}{N}\right)\pi\right]} e^{j\left(\frac{13v}{839} + \frac{p}{N}\right)838\pi} \qquad p = 0, 1, \cdots, N-1 \quad (20)$$

where the entry with the largest absolute value $x_{c,pre}^v(m_{pre}^v)$ satisfies

$$\left[\left[\frac{13v}{839} + \frac{m_{pre}^v}{N}\right]\right] = 1$$

$$m_{pre}^v = N - \left[\left[\frac{13v}{839}N\right]\right] \qquad (21)$$

$$\left|x_{c,pre}^v(m_{pre}^v)\right| = \frac{H}{N} \left|\frac{\sin\left[\left(13v + \frac{839m_{pre}^v}{N}\right)\pi\right]}{\sin\left[\left(\frac{13v}{839} + \frac{m_{pre}^v}{N}\right)\pi\right]}\right|$$

where $[[\,]]$ denotes the round operator. Considering the interference caused by frequency offset, $Y_{c,interf,k}^v(n)$ is obtained as

$$Y_{c,interf,k}^v(n) = \begin{cases} H\,|K(k)|\,e^{j\left(\frac{26vn}{839} + \frac{26vk+2nk+k^2+k}{839}\right)\pi} & \begin{array}{l}\max(0, -k) \leq n \leq \\ \min(838, 838-k)\end{array} \\ 0 & \text{else} \end{cases} \qquad (22)$$

Then the k-th interference $x_{c,interf,k}^v(p)$ can be denoted as

$$x_{c,interf,k}^v(p) = \frac{H}{N}\,|K(k)|\,\frac{\sin\left[\left(\frac{13v+k}{839} + \frac{p}{N}\right)(839-|k|)\pi\right]}{\sin\left[\left(\frac{13v+k}{839} + \frac{p}{N}\right)\pi\right]} \qquad (23)$$
$$\times\,e^{j\left[\frac{(13v+k)(838-k)+26vk+k^2+k}{839} + \frac{p(838-k)}{N}\right]\pi}$$

where the entry with the largest absolute value $x_{c,interf,k}^v(m_{interf,k}^v)$ satisfies

$$\left[\left[\frac{13v+k}{839} + \frac{m_{interf,k}^v}{N}\right]\right] = 1$$

$$m_{interf,k}^v = N - \left[\left[\frac{13v}{839}N\right]\right] - \left[\left[\frac{k}{839}N\right]\right] \qquad (24)$$

So $m_{interf,k}^v$ has an offset of $\left[\left[\frac{Nk}{839}\right]\right]$ with respect to m_{pre}^v. According to (23), the bigger k is, the bigger the offset is, and the smaller $|K(k)|$ is. So it is reasonable to consider only two interferences ($x_{c,interf,1}^v$ and $x_{c,interf,-1}^v$) when analyzing frequency offset effect on the peak of ZC sequences correlation, then the final cross-correlation affected by frequency offset can be simplified as

$$x_c^v(p) \approx |K(0)|x_{c,pre}^v(p) + x_{c,interf,1}^v(p) + x_{c,interf,-1}^v(p) + q_{cor}(p) \qquad (25)$$

where the peak of final cross-correlation affected by frequency offset is related to the random access preamble number. According to the above calculations and general conclusion in Sect. 3, frequency offset has an impact on both the peak position and peak size of ZC sequences correlation results. Besides, the PRACH preamble miss detection rate and timing error of UEs with different random access preamble numbers are differently affected by the same frequency offset. The better the detection performance, the lower the TA accuracy.

5   Simulation Results and Analysis

In this section, simulations are performed to verify the rationality of the above analysis about frequency offset effect on the PRACH, including the PRACH preamble sequence detection performance and TA error. Simulation parameters are shown in the Table 2.

Table 2. Simulation parameters of the PRACH.

Simulation parameters	Values
The PRACH preamble format	Format 0
Antenna configuration	1Tx*2Rx
Carrier frequency	4 GHz
Bandwidth	40 MHz
Frequency offset	500 Hz
Channel model	AWGN
Sampling interval (dt)	0.0163 µs

In this part, the PRACH preamble detection BLER and CDF of TA error are taken as two performance metrics. The detection threshold is set according to the request that the false alarm probability shall be less than or equal to 0.001 [9], and the preamble detection BLER is counted by comparing the PAR of correlation with the detection threshold. TA error is denoted by the absolute value of m $-m_{pre}$. The peak size and peak position of the correlation result at the receiving end between the derived result in this paper and the simulation result are compared. Besides, the relationship between detection BLER and TA error is analyzed. Simulations are shown below. Where simulation represents the simulation result calculated by MATLAB according to Fig. 2, derivation denotes the derived result in this paper.

Firstly, peak sizes corresponding to different random access preamble numbers are shown as Fig. 4(a). As can be seen from Fig. 4(a), peak sizes of the simulation results and the derived results show the same trend with the change of v, and they are almost the same in a large range of v from 5 to 60. Besides, peak sizes of different preamble numbers are differently affected by the same frequency offset, which proves the rationality of the above calculations and analysis. Then, the preamble detection BLER is presented in Fig. 4(b), when $v = 0$,

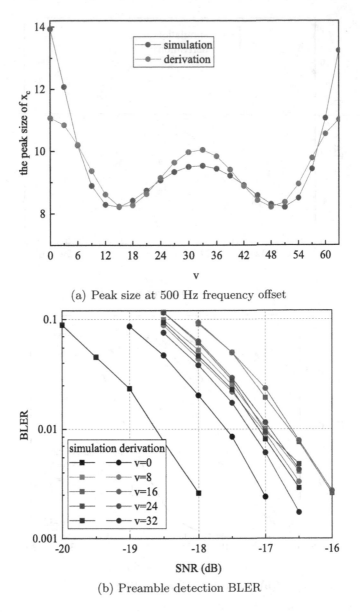

(a) Peak size at 500 Hz frequency offset

(b) Preamble detection BLER

Fig. 4. PRACH preamble detection performance

there is a significant difference in the detection BLER between the simulation results and the derived results. When v takes other values, there is basically no difference, which is consistent with the feature of peak size in Fig. 4(a).

Fig. 5(a) shows the TA error affected by 500 Hz frequency offset without considering the noise. It shows that the derived results are very close to the

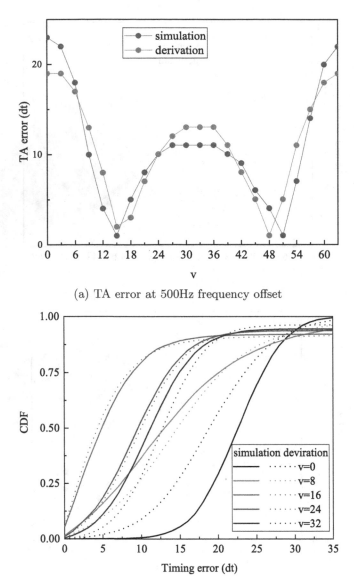

(a) TA error at 500Hz frequency offset

(b) TA error CDF at 18 dB SNR

Fig. 5. TA error

simulation results, and TA errors of different preambles are differently affected by the same frequency offset. Then, the TA error CDF at 18 dB SNR is presented in Fig. 5(b), which shows that the derived result is very close to the simulation results in most cases. Comparing Figs. 4(b) and 5(b), it can be found that under the frequency offset effect, for different preamble sequences, the lower the detection BLER, the larger the TA error, which proves the correctness of analysis in Sects. 3 and 4.

6   Conclusion

In this paper, the impact of frequency offset on PRACH in 5G NR systems is analyzed. Considering that preamble detection BLER and TA error are closely related to the peak of correlation result, this paper aims to analyze frequency offset effect on the peak of PRACH preamble correlation. Through derivation and calculation, the following analytical results are obtained. Inter-carrier interference coefficients of multiple interference entries caused by the frequency offset have almost the same phase. Correlation results of different sequences are differently affected by frequency offset, if frequency offset affects the peak position of correlation, the larger the peak size is, the larger the peak position changes. The preamble detection BLER and TA error of UEs with different random access preamble numbers are differently affected by the same frequency offset, the lower the detection BLER, the higher TA error. The simulation results show the rationality of analysis in this paper. The analytical method used in this paper plays a certain role in analyzing frequency offset effect on correlation. Moreover, the analytical results about the frequency offset effect on PRACH are helpful for studying how to effectively resist frequency offset. But there is room for improvement.

References

1. 3GPP TS 38.211, 3rd Generation Partnership Project, Technical Specification Group Radio Access Network, NR, Physical channels and modulation, Release 15 (2019)
2. 3GPP TS 38.213, 3rd Generation Partnership Project, Technical Specification Group Radio Access Network, NR, Physical layer procedures for control, Release 15 (2019)
3. Thota, J., Aijaz, A.: On performance evaluation of random access enhancements for 5G URLLC. In: IEEE Wireless Communications and Networking Conference (WCNC), Marrakech, Morocco, pp. 1–7 (2019)
4. Tao, J., Yang, L.: Improved Zadoff-Chu sequence detection in the presence of unknown multipath and carrier frequency offset. IEEE Commun. Lett. **22**(5), 922–925 (2018)
5. Tang, Q., Long, H., Yang, H., Li, Y.: An enhanced LMMSE channel estimation under high speed railway scenarios. In: 2017 IEEE International Conference on Communications Workshops, Paris, France, pp. 999–1004 (2017)
6. Cao, A., Xiao, P., Tafazolli, R.: Frequency offset estimation based on PRACH preambles in LTE. In: 2014 11th International Symposium on Wireless Communications Systems, Barcelona, Spain, pp. 22–26 (2014)
7. Hua, M., Wang, M., Yang, W., You, X., Shu, F., Wang, J., et al.: Analysis of the frequency offset effect on random access signals. IEEE Trans. Commun. **61**(11), 4728–4740 (2013)

8. Zhang, Y., Zhang, Z., Hu, X.: An improved preamble detection method for LTE-A PRACH based on Doppler frequency offset correction. In: Liu, X., Cheng, D., Jinfeng, L. (eds.) ChinaCom 2018. LNICST, vol. 262, pp. 573–582. Springer, Cham (2019). https://doi.org/10.1007/978-3-030-06161-6_56
9. 3GPP TS 38.104, 3rd Generation Partnership Project, Technical Specification Group Radio Access Network, NR, Base Station radio transmission and reception, Release 15 (2019)

Energy-Efficient Mode Selection for D2D Communication in SWIPT Systems

Jingjing Cui[1] and Jun Huang[2(✉)]

[1] School of Communication and Information Engineering,
Chongqing University of Posts and Telecommunications, Chongqing 400065, China
1596233657@qq.com
[2] Chongqing University of Posts and Telecommunications, Chongqing 400065, China
huangj@ieee.org

Abstract. To realized an energy-efficient mode selection, we apply simultaneous wireless information and power transfer (SWIPT) to D2D communications, so that D2D and cellular users can obtain energy from receiving information, and reduce the battery energy consumption in the communication process. We leverage the theory of stochastic geometry to analyze the ergodic energy harvesting (EEH) of D2D and cellular links in reuse, dedicated, and cellular communication modes. Based on the data transmission process, we obtain the expressions of the ergodic capacity (EC) of D2D and cellular users in three D2D communication modes with power splitting (PS) architectures of SWIPT, and based on this, we derive the system energy efficiency (EE). Finally, theoretical research is demonstrated through the simulation experiments. The mode selection mechanism is performed according to the energy-efficiency. The simulations show that the system EE is improved, especially for D2D communications in reuse mode by our proposed mode selection mechanism.

Keywords: Mode selection · Power splitting · EEH

1 Introduction

It is well-known that device-to-device (D2D) communications allow data to be transferred directly from one device to another without going through the base station. While the paradigm of D2D communications has many notable advantages such as improved spectral efficiency, enhanced system capacity, and accoladed performance [1,2], it, however, also faces some challenges. One of major challenges is the limited battery power in devices. Besides the regular routine battery replacement and/or battery recharge, on-site energy harvesting [3] is emerging as an additional effective method for resolving this energy shortage issue.

Mode selection [4] is one of the most direct and effective ways to address the energy and interference issues in D2D communication. The choice of D2D

H. Gao et al. (Eds.): ChinaCom 2019, LNICST 312, pp. 693–706, 2020.
https://doi.org/10.1007/978-3-030-41114-5_52

mode is related to the system spectrum utilization and the interference between D2D users and cellular users. D2D communications can work in: reuse mode, dedicated mode, and cellular mode. Reuse mode means that D2D users reuse uplink spectrum resources of the cellular link to communication, and this may cause interference between D2D users and cellular users, and among D2D users themselves as well. Dedicated mode refers to the case that the base station allocates the proprietary bandwidth to the D2D users, at this time, there is no interference between D2D users and cellular users. Cellular mode means that D2D users send and receive data through the base station, D2D users work in the same way as cellular users, and there is no interference. As such, the amount of interference experienced by D2D and cellular users in one mode will be different from that in another mode, which leads to different system capacities in these three modes. Therefore, the system energy consumption can be expected to be reduced by appropriately selecting a D2D communication mode.

Energy efficiency (EE) [5,6] is an important performance indicator for wireless networks. The EE of a system is essentially determined by the amount of energy consumed at the base station and at individual users in the system, both of which are aimed to be reduced. SWIPT [7] provides energy for communication devices while interacting with information between devices. In this paper, the power splitting method is used to use part of the power received by the receiver (sum of received power and interference power) for information decoding, and another part to charge the rechargeable battery, in order to reduce the energy consumption of the device during transmission, achieving the goal of improving EE and extending deceive standby time.

Currently, there is a large amount of studies dedicated to the SWIPT in wireless networks. Mohjazi [8] et al. evaluated the system throughputs for the time switching (TS) and power splitting (PS) mechanisms when the SIR is relatively low, according to outage probability and harvested energy, and by the differential modulation mechanism. Also, in [9], Mohjazi study the performance of the SWIPT relay network with non-coherent modulation and found that there is a unique PS ratio value that minimizes the systems outage probability, while this is not the case for the TS protocol. At lower SNR value, the performance of the TS protocol is superior to the PS protocol while ensuring maximum system throughput. In [10], when using the TS protocol and Non-Orthogonal Multiple Access (NOMA) technique, the outage probability expressions of all users are derived, and the system performance is evaluated by analyzing the system throughput. However, Maleki [11] et al. used amplify-and-forward EH relaying and hybrid EH protocol to obtain the systems outage probability and throughput, and computed the optimal values for TS and PS ratios that maximizes the system throughput.

When applying SWIPT to D2D communication, mode selection problem is manifested in the modeling of the channel fading for D2D users and cellular users, and more accurate mathematical calculations. In [12,13], the channel fading is always assumed to be Rayleigh no matter what communication mode the D2D and cellular users are in, however, this is not the case in practice because the distance between a D2D pair is of Los when the communication mode is in reuse mode or dedicated mode, therefore we assume that the channel fading for D2D users is Rician. Besides, the system throughput and EE computations may be inaccurate if the users distance to the base station is assumed to be a constant or the Shannon formula is directly used, as in [14]. To accurately simulate the randomness of the users, this paper uses stochastic geometry to model the users locations in a two-dimensional space, based on the distance to the energy harvesting and energy efficiency of the link for accurate calculation.

Although extensive studies have focused on interference management and EE, most studies have been largely conducted without considering SWIPT. Unlike the prior works, this paper proposes a mode selection mechanism based on PS using stochastic geometry, game theory, and SWIPT. It differs from existing studies in the following aspects: (1) Regarding the process of energy harvesting, both the PS architectures of SWIPT are considered and the corresponding closed-form formulas of the harvested energy for D2D and cellular users are derived by leveraging the theory of stochastic geometry. (2) In this paper, the channel fading of D2D links follows either Rician distribution or Rayleigh distribution, depending on whether or not the distance associated with the D2D pair is of line-of-sight (Los).

The rest of this paper is organized as follows. In Sect. 2, we introduce the system model. In Sect. 3, we analyze the EEH of all three modes under PS. In Sect. 4, we analyze the ergodic capacity of the link in the data transmission phase and propose the EE-based model selection strategy. Section 5 gives the simulation results to demonstrate the proposed model selection strategy. Section 6 concludes the paper.

2   System Model

We consider the scenario of multiple small cells. The sets of D2D users $\mathbf{D}$, cellular users $\mathbf{C}$, and BSs $\mathbf{B}$ are of independent and identically distributed PPP with densities λ_D, λ_C and λ_B, respectively. For any cellular user CUE and any D2D pair DTU-DRU, if the distance from CUE to the nearest BS is D_C, and the distance from DTU to DRU is D_D, then by the spatial probability of Poisson Point processes, the probability density functions of the cellular user and the D2D user are given as

$$f_{D_C}(D_C) = 2\pi\lambda_B D_C \exp(-\pi\lambda_B D_C{}^2) \tag{1}$$

and

$$f_{D_D}(D_D) = 2\pi\lambda_D D_D \exp(-\pi\lambda_D D_D{}^2) \tag{2}$$

respectively.

Since any CUE chooses to connect to its nearest BSs, there is a relative discrepancy in terms of distance from a CUE to its serving BS for all CUEs, thence all CUEs in each cell are separated into N tier. As illustrated in Fig. 1, the transmit power of CUEs in the i-th tier is $P_{C_i}(i = 1, 2, ..., N)$, with $P_{C_1} \neq$

$P_{C_2} \neq ... \neq P_{C_N}$. For the D2D link, in the case of reuse mode or dedicated mode, the difference between the distance of each D2D pair could be negligible, thus the transmit power for all DTUs is set to an average value P_D; In the cellular mode, DUEs, like CUEs, rely on BS to transmit data, so all DUEs will be stratified as well, and the transmit power of DTUs in the i-th tier is $P_{D_i}(i = 1, 2, ..., N)$. When BS becomes the transmitter as a data forwarding point in the small network, no matter which layer the receiver is on, the transmit power amplitude of BS varies slightly, so the base station transmits power is set to an average value P_B.

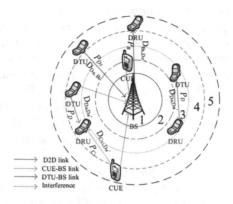

Fig. 1. Stratification model

In reuse mode, the uplink resources of CUEs are reused by DUEs, any DRU will experience both intra-cell and inter-cell interference caused by other DUEs or CUEs who are using the same spectrum used by this DRU; any CUE in one cell will experience both intra-cell and inter-cell interference caused by DUEs who are reusing the spectrum assigned to that CUE, and inter-cell interference caused by CUEs in other cells who are using the same spectrum. In dedicated and cellular modes, DUEs is interference-free to CUEs. In reuse and dedicated modes, due to the short and Los communication distance between D2D pairs, thence we assume that the D2D links follow the Rician fading. In cellular mode, DUEs, like CUEs, rely on BS to transmit data, so D2D links follow the Rayleigh fading with an exponential distribution of mean 1. In all three modes, since the distance of the transmission link from any CUE to its BS is of non-line-of-sight (NLos), thus cellular links follow the Rayleigh fading. Simultaneously, the distances of the interference links from any DTU to a non-pairing DRU, from any CUE to a DRU, and from any BS (BS does not serve the DRU in cellular mode) to a DRU are all of NLos, thus the interference links follow the Rayleigh fading. All signal largescale fading on any links can be modeled as $D^{-\alpha}$ and α is the path loss exponent for all links.

In this paper, we use PS in mode selection to extend device standby time and will analyze the two phases of energy harvesting and data transmission. In the energy harvesting phase, the receiver is subject to different interference, and the receiver acquires different energy in different modes of D2D communication. In the data transmission phase, we stipulate that the total spectrum resource in each cell is B Hz which will be split into various sub-spectrums for use by multiple CUEs. In reuse mode, D2D pairs will reuse all uplink spectrum resources of cellular users; in dedicated mode, a certain amount of bandwidth will be reserved for DUEs only, and the rest will be used by CUEs; in cellular mode, DUEs, just like CUEs, transmit all data through the BS, the cellular user can use the bandwidth B_1, and the remaining bandwidth $B_2(B_1 + B_2 = B)$ will be evenly distributed to the D2D uplink and downlink.

3   Energy Harvesting

In the energy harvesting phase, this paper does not consider the distinction between useful signals and interference and charges all of its absorption. We assume that the energy harvested by the cellular user is EEH_C, and the energy harvested by the D2D user is EEH_D. The signal received at the receiver is split into two signal streams for energy harvesting and information decoding. Let $\kappa \in [0,1]$ be the ratio of received power used for energy harvesting, then the energy harvested by D2D users and cellular users in all three modes is as follows.

3.1   D2D User Energy Harvesting

In reuse mode, there is co-channel interference between the cellular user and D2D user; in dedicated mode, there is no co-channel interference between cellular user and D2D user. Therefore, the total power of the signal that the receiver can receive will vary due to the size of the interference in reuse or dedicated mode of D2D communications. Also, D2D users need to forward data through the base station in cellular mode. Thus, the base station serves as the transmitter, and D2D serves as the receiver when the D2D user acquires energy.

EEH_D **in Reuse Mode:** In reuse mode, a D2D link $l_{D_a,D_{a'}}$ reuses the uplink spectrum resources of the cellular link, and the signal power received by the receiver is $S_D = P_D D_{D_a,D_{a'}}^{-\alpha} g_{D_a,D_{a'}}$, where P_D is the transmit power of D2D user, $D_{D_a,D_{a'}}$ is the distance between D2D pairs, $g_{D_a,D_{a'}}$ is the Rician power fading from the transmitter to the receiver. Interference power is $I = I_{C,D_{a'}} + I_{D-a,D_{a'}}$, $I_{C,D_{a'}} = \sum_{C_{i,j} \in C} \sum_{i=1}^{N} P_{C_i} D_{C_{i,j},D_{a'}}^{-\alpha} h_{C_{i,j},D_{a'}}$, $I_{D-a,D_{a'}} = \sum_{D_{a''} \in D_{-a}} P_D D_{D_{a''},D_{a'}}^{-\alpha} h_{D_{a''},D_{a'}}$, where P_{C_i} is the transmit power of cellular user, $D_{C_{i,j},D_{a'}}$ is the distance between DRU and cellular user, $h_{C_{i,j},D_{a'}}$ and $h_{D_{a''},D_{a'}}$ are respectively channel gain of the D2D link $l_{D_a,D_{a'}}$ with both $h_{C_{i,j},D_{a'}} \sim \exp(1)$ and $h_{D_{a''},D_{a'}} \sim \exp(1)$.

Theorem 1. *When D2D communications reuse the uplink resources of cellular users, the EEH of the D2D link is given by*

$$EEH_{D_a, D_{a'}} = \kappa\eta \left\{ P_D \left[d^{-\alpha}(-e^{-\pi\lambda_D d^2} + 1) + (\pi\lambda_D)^{\alpha/2}\Gamma\left(\frac{-\alpha+2}{2}, \pi\lambda_D d^2\right)\right] \right.$$
$$\left. \cdot(1+K) + \sum_{i=1}^{N} P_{C_i}\pi\lambda_C d^{-\alpha+2}\frac{\alpha}{\alpha-2} + P_D\pi\lambda_D d^{-\alpha+2}\frac{\alpha}{\alpha-2}\right\}.$$

(3)

where η is energy conversion efficiency.

Proof. $E\left(S_D + I\right) = P_D E\left(D_{D_{a,a'}}^{-\alpha}, g_{D_{a,a'}}\right) + E\left(I_{C,D_{a'}}\right) + E\left(I_{D_{-a}, D_{a'}}\right)$, where
$E\left(D_{D_{a,a'}}^{-\alpha}, g_{D_{a,a'}}\right) = E\left(D_{D_{a,a'}}^{-\alpha}\right) \cdot E\left(g_{D_{a,a'}}\right)$. We have

$$E\left(D_{D_{a,a'}}^{-\alpha}\right) = \int_0^\infty D_{D_{a,a'}}^{-\alpha} \cdot 2\pi\lambda_D D_{D_{a,a'}} \exp(-\pi\lambda_D D_{D_{a,a'}}^2) dD_{D_{a,a'}}$$

$$\overset{(a)}{=} \int_0^d d^{-\alpha} \cdot 2\pi\lambda_D D_{D_{a,a'}} \exp(-\pi\lambda_D D_{D_{a,a'}}^2) dD_{D_{a,a'}} + \int_d^\infty D_{D_{a,a'}}^{-\alpha} 2\pi\lambda_D$$

$$\cdot D_{D_{a,a'}} \exp(-\pi\lambda_D D_{D_{a,a'}}^2) dD_{D_{a,a'}}$$

$$= d^{-\alpha}\left(-e^{-\pi\lambda_D d^2} + 1\right) + (\pi\lambda_D)^{\alpha/2}\Gamma\left(\frac{-\alpha+2}{2}, \pi\lambda_D d^2\right).$$

Where step (a) is supported by the fact that when the integral range of $D_{D_{a,a'}}$ is $(0, \infty)$, $E\left(D_{D_{a,a'}}\right)$ will tend to infinity. To ensure the finiteness of the received power [15], we assume that the path loss is $d^{-\alpha}$ when $D_{D_{a,a'}} < d$ and $D_{D_{a,a'}}^{-\alpha}$ when $D_{D_{a,a'}} > d$.

$$E\left(g_{D_{a,a'}}\right) = \int_0^\infty g_{D_{a,a'}} \cdot \exp\left(-K - g_{D_{a,a'}}\right) \sum_{k=0}^\infty \frac{\left(K g_{D_{a,a'}}\right)^k}{(k!)^2} dg_{D_{a,a'}}$$

$$= \sum_{k=0}^\infty \exp\left(-K\right) \frac{K^k}{(k!)^2} \cdot \int_0^\infty g_{D_{a,a'}}^{k+1} \exp\left(-g_{D_{a,a'}}\right) dg_{D_{a,a'}}$$

$$= \sum_{k=0}^\infty \exp\left(-K\right) \frac{K^k}{(k!)^2} \cdot (k+1)!$$

$$= 1 + K,$$

$$E\left(I_{\mathbf{C},D_{a'}}\right) = E\left(\sum_{C_{i,j}\in\mathbf{C}}\sum_{i=1}^{N} P_{C_i}D_{C_{i,j},D_{a'}}^{-\alpha}h_{C_{i,j},D_{a'}}\right)$$

$$= \sum_{i=1}^{N} P_{C_i}E\left(\sum_{\substack{C_{i,j}\in\mathbf{C}\\ D_{C_{i,j},D_{a'}}>d}} D_{C_{i,j},D_{a'}}^{-\alpha} + \sum_{\substack{C_{i,j}\in\mathbf{C}\\ D_{C_{i,j},D_{a'}}<d}} D_{C_{i,j},D_{a'}}^{-\alpha}\right)$$

$$= \sum_{i=1}^{N} P_{C_i}\cdot\pi\lambda_C d^{-\alpha+2}\frac{\alpha}{\alpha-2}.$$

In a similar fashion, we can get

$$E\left(I_{\mathbf{D}_{-a},D_{a'}}\right) = P_D\pi\lambda_D d^{-\alpha+2}\frac{\alpha}{\alpha-2}.$$

EEH_D in Dedicated Mode: The difference in dedicated mode and reuse mode is that there is no co-channel interference between cellular user and D2D user in dedicated mode. Thus, the D2D user energy harvesting expression in dedicated mode can be given from the energy harvesting expression in reuse mode of D2D communications.

Theorem 2. *In dedicated mode, the EEH of the D2D link is given by*

$$EEH_{D_a,D_{a'}} = \kappa\eta\left\{P_D\left[d^{-\alpha}(-e^{-\pi\lambda_D d^2}+1)+(\pi\lambda_D)^{\alpha/2}\Gamma\left(\frac{-\alpha+2}{2},\pi\lambda_D d^2\right)\right]\right.$$
$$\left.\cdot(1+K)+P_D\pi\lambda_D d^{-\alpha+2}\frac{\alpha}{\alpha-2}\right\}.$$

$$(4)$$

Proof. Similar to that of Theorem 1.

EEH_D in Cellular Mode: In cellular mode, the communication process of the D2D user is divided into the uplink of DTU to BS and the downlink of BS to DRU. In the uplink, the base station serves as the receiver, just forward the data, so there is no energy harvesting, and in the downlink, DRU can perform data decoding and energy harvesting. In the cellular mode, the signal power received by a D2D downlink $l_{B_k,D_{a'}}$ receiver is $S_D = P_{B_k}D_{B_k,D_{a'}}^{-\alpha}h_{B_k,D_{a'}}$, interference power is $I = I_{\mathbf{B}_{-k},D_{a'}}$, $I_{\mathbf{B}_{-k},D_{a'}} = \sum_{B_{k'}\in B_{-k}} P_{B_{k'}}D_{B_{k'},D_{a'}}^{-\alpha}h_{B_{k'},D_{a'}}$, where $\mathbf{B}_{-k} = \mathbf{B}\setminus\{B_k\}$, P_{B_k} denotes the transmit power of B_k (B_k is the nearest base station to $D_{a'}$), $D_{B_k,D_{a'}}$ is the distance between B_k and $D_{a'}$, $h_{B_k,D_{a'}}$ is channel gain of the D2D link $l_{B_k,D_{a'}}$ with $h_{B_k,D_{a'}} \sim \exp(1)$, $P_{B_{k'}}$ denotes the transmit power of $B_{k'}$, $D_{B_{k'},D_{a'}}$ is the distance between $B_{k'}$ and $D_{a'}$.

Theorem 3. *In cellular mode, the EEH of the D2D downlink is given by*

$$EEH_{B_k,D_{a'}} = \kappa\eta\left\{P_{B_k}\left[d^{-\alpha}(1-e^{-\pi\lambda_B d^2}) + (\pi\lambda_B)^{\alpha/2}\Gamma\left(\tfrac{-\alpha+2}{2},\pi\lambda_B d^2\right)\right] + 2\pi\right.$$
$$\cdot\lambda_B P_{B_{k'}}\left[d^{-\alpha+2}(\tfrac{1}{2}+\tfrac{1}{\alpha-2})(1-e^{-\pi\lambda_B d^2}) + \tfrac{d^{-\alpha}}{2\pi\lambda_B}\left[(\pi\lambda_B d^2+1)e^{-\pi\lambda_B d^2}-1\right]\right.$$
$$\left.\left. + \tfrac{(\pi\lambda_B)^{\frac{\alpha}{2}-1}}{\alpha-2}\Gamma\left(\tfrac{-\alpha+4}{2},\pi\lambda_B d^2\right)\right]\right\}.$$

$$(5)$$

Proof.

$$E\left(I_{\mathbf{B}_{-k},D_{a'}}\right) = E_{\mathbf{B},h}\left(\sum_{B_{k'}\in\mathbf{B}_{-k}}P_{B_{k'}}D_{B_{k'},D_{a'}}^{-\alpha}h_{B_{k'},D_{a'}}\right)$$

$$\overset{(a)}{=} 2\pi\lambda_B P_{B_{k'}}\int_0^\infty\left\{\int_{D_D}^\infty\left[\max(D_{B_{k'},D_{a'}},d)\right]^{-\alpha}D_{B_{k'},D_{a'}}dD_{B_{k'},D_{a'}}\right\}$$

$$\cdot 2\pi\lambda_B D_D\exp(-\pi\lambda_B D_D^2)dD_D$$

$$= 2\pi\lambda_B\cdot P_{B_{k'}}\left[d^{-\alpha+2}\left(\frac{1}{2}+\frac{1}{\alpha-2}\right)\left(1-e^{-\pi\lambda_B d^2}\right) + \frac{d^{-\alpha}}{2\pi\lambda_B}\right.$$

$$\left.\cdot\left[(\pi\lambda_B d^2+1)e^{-\pi\lambda_B d^2}-1\right] + \frac{(\pi\lambda_B)^{\frac{\alpha}{2}-1}}{\alpha-2}\Gamma\left(\frac{-\alpha+4}{2},\pi\lambda_B d^2\right)\right].$$

For step (a), since the D2D user is connected to the nearest base station, the distance between the interfering base station and the D2D user is necessarily greater than the communication distance D_D of $l_{B_k,D_{a'}}$, so the integration range of the interference link distance is $(D_D,+\infty)$.

3.2 Cellular User Energy Harvesting

In the energy harvesting phase, when the cellular user obtains energy for charging, the base station acts as the transmitter, and the cellular user acts as the receiver to implement the charging process, which occurs on the cellular downlink. However, the D2D link reuses the spectrum resources of the cellular uplink in reuse mode. Therefore, regardless of the mode communication used by D2D, the energy available to the cellular user is unchanged, and the cellular user has the same energy as the D2D user in cellular mode.

Theorem 4. *The EEH of the cellular downlink is given by*

$$EEH_{B_k,C_i} = \kappa\eta\left\{P_{B_k}\left[d^{-\alpha}(1-e^{-\pi\lambda_B d^2}) + (\pi\lambda_B)^{\alpha/2}\Gamma\left(\tfrac{-\alpha+2}{2},\pi\lambda_B d^2\right)\right] + 2\pi\right.$$
$$\cdot\lambda_B P_{B_{k'}}\left[d^{-\alpha+2}(\tfrac{1}{2}+\tfrac{1}{\alpha-2})(1-e^{-\pi\lambda_B d^2}) + \tfrac{d^{-\alpha}}{2\pi\lambda_B}\left((\pi\lambda_B d^2+1)e^{-\pi\lambda_B d^2}-1\right)\right.$$
$$\left.\left. + \tfrac{(\pi\lambda_B)^{\frac{\alpha}{2}-1}}{\alpha-2}\Gamma\left(\tfrac{-\alpha+4}{2},\pi\lambda_B d^2\right)\right]\right\}.$$

$$(6)$$

Proof. Similar to that of Theorem 3.

4   Data Transmission

4.1   Ergodic Capacity

Combined with the system ergodic capacity part of the literature [16], the system ergodic capacity under SWIPT is analyzed. In the information transmission phase, the ratio of the power received by the receiver to the information decoding is $(1 - \kappa)$, so the capacity of each state of the D2D link and the cellular link in three modes is

EC in Reuse Mode: In reuse mode, when the D2D user uses the spectrum as B, the EC of D2D link is

$$
EC_{D_a,D_{a'}} = (1 - \kappa)B \left(\sum_{n=1}^{\infty} \sum_{m=0}^{n-1} \sum_{b=1}^{n-m} (-1)^{n-m} J(m,n) \beta_b^{n-m} \frac{\pi \lambda_D \alpha}{2} I_b \right.
$$
$$
\left. + \sum_{n=0}^{\infty} J(n,n) \frac{\alpha \pi \lambda_D}{2} I_0 \right), \tag{7}
$$

where
$$
I_b = \int_0^{\infty} \frac{t^{b + \frac{\alpha}{2} - 1} dt}{(\pi \lambda_D + t)^{b+1} \left(A^{\frac{\alpha}{2}} + t^{\frac{\alpha}{2}} \right)}, b = 0,1,2\ldots, \beta_b^{n-m} = \sum_{i=1}^{b} (-1)^i \binom{b}{i} \left(\frac{2i}{\alpha} \right)_{n-m},
$$
$$
C(\alpha) = \frac{2\pi/\alpha}{\sin(2\pi/\alpha)}, \mathcal{J}(m,n) = \frac{\frac{K^n m!}{e^K} \binom{n}{m}}{(n!)^2}, A = \pi C(\alpha) \left(\sum_{i=1}^{N} \left(\frac{P_{C_i}}{P_D} \right)^{2/\alpha} \lambda_C + \lambda_D \right).
$$

In reuse mode, when the cellular user uses the spectrum as B, the EC of cellular link is

$$
EC_{C_i,B_k} = \int_0^{\infty} \frac{(1 - \kappa)Bdt}{\frac{\lambda_C}{\lambda_B} \rho(e^t - 1, \alpha) + C(\alpha) \frac{\lambda_D}{\lambda_B} \left(\frac{P_D}{P_{C_\gamma}} (e^t - 1) \right)^{\frac{2}{\alpha}} + 1}, \tag{8}
$$

where $\rho(e^t - 1, \alpha) = \sum_{i=1}^{N} \int_{\left(\frac{P_{C_\gamma}}{(e^t-1)P_{C_i}} \right)^{2/\alpha}}^{\infty} \frac{1}{1+u^{\alpha/2}} \cdot \left(\frac{(e^t-1)P_{C_i}}{P_{C_\gamma}} \right)^{2/\alpha} du.$

EC in Dedicated Mode: In dedicated mode, when the D2D user uses the spectrum as B_1, the EC of D2D link is

$$
EC_{D_a,D_{a'}} = (1 - \kappa)B_1 \left(\sum_{n=1}^{\infty} \sum_{m=0}^{n-1} \sum_{b=1}^{n-m} (-1)^{n-m} J(m,n) \beta_b^{n-m} \frac{\pi \lambda_D \alpha}{2} I_b \right.
$$
$$
\left. + \sum_{n=0}^{\infty} J(n,n) \frac{\alpha \pi \lambda_D}{2} I_0 \right), \tag{9}
$$

where $A = \pi C(\alpha) \lambda_D$.

In dedicated mode, when the cellular user uses the spectrum as B_2, the EC of cellular link is

$$ EC_{C_i,B_k} = \int_0^\infty \frac{(1-\kappa)B_2 dt}{\frac{\lambda_C}{\lambda_B}\rho(e^t - 1, \alpha) + 1}. \tag{10} $$

EC in Cellular Mode: In cellular mode, when the D2D user uses the spectrum as B_1, the EC of D2D link is

$$ EC_{D_a,D_{a'}} = \frac{(1-\kappa)B_1}{2} \int_0^\infty SP_{D_a,D_{a'}}(e^t - 1)\, dt, \tag{11} $$

where $SP_{D_a,D_{a'}}$ is the success probability [16] of the D2D link $l_{D_a,D_{a'}}$.

In cellular mode, when the cellular user uses the spectrum as B_2, the EC of cellular link is

$$ EC_{C_i,B_k} = \int_0^\infty \frac{(1-\kappa)B_2 dt}{1 + \frac{\lambda_C}{\lambda_B}\rho(e^t - 1, \alpha)}. \tag{12} $$

4.2 Energy Efficiency

According to the energy harvesting of D2D user and cellular user in three modes, combined with the EC of D2D and cellular link in the data transmission part, the system energy efficiency in three modes using SWIPT can be obtained.

Theorem 5. *In reuse and dedicated modes, when cellular users are stratified into N tiers, the transmitting power of CUE at i tier is P_{C_i}, and the transmitting power of all DUEs is P_D, the system energy efficiency would be*

$$ \Delta_{EE} = \frac{\lambda_C \sum\limits_{i=1}^N EC_{C_i} + \lambda_D EC_D}{\lambda_C(\sum\limits_{i=1}^N P_{C_i} + P_{cir} - EH_C) + \lambda_D(P_D + P_{cir} - EH_D)}, \tag{13} $$

where P_{cir} denotes the average user device circuit power loss.

Theorem 6. *In cellular mode, the system energy efficiency would be*

$$ \Delta_{EE} = \frac{\lambda_C \sum\limits_{i=1}^N EC_{C_i} + \lambda_D \sum\limits_{i=1}^N EC_{D_i}}{\lambda_C(\sum\limits_{i=1}^N P_{C_i} + P_{cir} - EH_C) + \lambda_D(\sum\limits_{i=1}^N P_{D_i} + P_{cir} + P_{cir\_B} - EH_D)}, \tag{14} $$

where P_{cir-B} denotes the average BS circuit power loss.

5   Simulation Results

In this section, we conduct extensive simulations for the EEH and EE of D2D
users and cellular users investigated in the previous sections. The simulation
parameters are shown in Table 1.

Table 1. Parameters settings

Parameter	Value
Transmit power of BSs (P_B)	49 dBm
Transmit power of cellular users on tier 1 (P_{C_1})	27 dBm
Transmit power of cellular users on tier 2 (P_{C_2})	30 dBm
Transmit power of cellular users on tier 3 (P_{C_3})	33 dBm
Transmit power of D2D users on tier 1 in the cellular mode (P_{D_1})	20 dBm
Transmit power of D2D users on tier 2 in the cellular mode (P_{D_2})	24 dBm
Transmit power of D2D users on tier 3 in the cellular mode (P_{D_3})	28 dBm
Density of BSs λ_B (m^{-2})	$7 \cdot 10^{-6}$
Density of cellular users λ_C (m^{-2})	$4 \cdot 10^{-5}$
Density of D2D users λ_D (m^{-2})	$1 \cdot 10^{-4}$

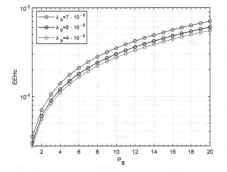

Fig. 2. Cellular users' energy harvesting   **Fig. 3.** D2D users' energy harvesting

As illustrated in Fig. 2, with PS, the energy harvested by the cellular user
in the energy harvesting phase increases as the base station transmit power P_B
and base station density λ_B. This is because when the transmission power P_B
increases, the power of the receiver receiving the useful signal increases, and
the co-channel interference signal increases. However, the receiver does not need
to distinguish between the useful signal and the interference when acquiring the
energy, and directly acquires all of them, so the harvested energy is consequently
increased; when λ_B increases, the co-channel interference will be significantly
enhanced, and the harvested energy will increase. Thus the cellular users energy
harvesting shows an increasing trend.

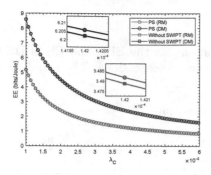 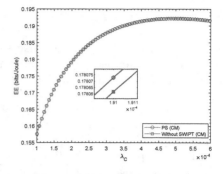

Fig. 4. λ_C vs EE in reuse and dedicated modes

Fig. 5. λ_C vs EE in cellular mode

Figure 3 shows the EEH of D2D users with PS in three different modes. With PS, the amount of energy harvested by a D2D user receiver in three different modes have the following rank: cellular mode > reuse mode > dedicated mode. In cellular mode, DRU obtains energy from the base station, so EEH has nothing to do with both P_D and λ_D, and BS transmit power is much greater than that of D2D transmitters, so that DRU receives more energy; in reuse and dedicated modes, the co-channel interference received by DRU in dedicated mode is less than that in reuse mode. Simultaneously, when λ_D increases, the energy harvesting by DRU will increase accordingly.

Figures 4 and 5 depict the correlation between λ_C and system energy efficiency with PS and without SWIPT under the three different communication modes. In reuse and dedicated modes, the system energy efficiency decreases with the increase of cellular user density, and the system EE in reuse mode is less than that in dedicated mode; in cellular mode, the system EE will reach its maximum value when λ_C is minimal. This can be attributed to the fact that a smaller number of cellular users leads to sufficient spectrum resources and low energy consumption of devices which leads to a larger EC and then EE, but an increased λ_C will lead to insufficient spectrum resources and increasing devices energy consumption which result in a decreased EE. Finally, note that these two figures show that the system EE can be improved with SWIPT, especially for D2D communications in reuse mode.

Figure 6 indicates that EE will increase as λ_D increases in reuse and dedicated modes; and in cellular mode, the increase of λ_D results in a decrease in EE. This can be interpreted as the result of the following fact. In reuse and dedicated modes, EC would increase when the number of available spectrum increases, and subsequently, EE will increase as well. In cellular mode, the base station is used as a relay in the D2D communications, and the energy consumed by the base station in the process of forwarding data is much larger than that of the user, and the EC of the D2D link is small compared to the cellular link, resulting in the entire system link EC is low.

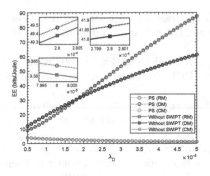

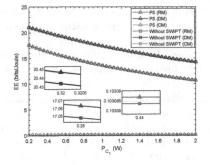

Fig. 6. λ_D vs EE   **Fig. 7.** PC_1 vs EE

Figure 7 demonstrate the EE of the system concerning the transmit power of cellular users with PS. In reuse and dedicated modes, the co-channel interference will increase as the value of PC_1 increases, leading to a decrease in EC and subsequently a decrease in EE as well. In cellular mode, the system EE increases over small values of PC_1 and decreases over the rest of PC_1. This owes to the fact that the transmit power of the cellular user is higher than the transmit power of the D2D user, and when the value of PC_1 is small, the interference caused between cellular users can be ignored. However, if PC_1 exceeds the threshold and continues to increase, it will affect EC due to excessive co-channel interference.

6   Conclusion

In this paper, we have investigated the mode selection for D2D communications from the perspective of energy saving. By utilizing the power splitting under SWIPT, the energy acquired by the cellular link and the D2D link can be used for communication, and energy can be effectively utilized while reducing energy consumption and extending the lifetime of the device. Then, according to DUEs and CTUs energy harvesting formulas in three modes, combined with the data transmission part, the expression of the system energy efficiency is obtained. Finally, our simulations demonstrate the impacting factors on the mode selection mechanism. In particular, ergodic energy harvesting of D2D and cellular links in-creases gradually as user transmit power increases in all three modes, and after using SWIPT, the system EE is improved, and the improvement is most obvious in reuse mode.

References

1. Huang, J., Huang, S., Xing, C., Qian, Y.: Game-theoretic power control mechanisms for device-to-device communications underlaying cellular system. IEEE Trans. Veh. Technol. **67**(6), 4890–4900 (2018)
2. Xu, Y., Wang, S.: Mode selection for energy efficient content delivery in cellular networks. IEEE Commun. Lett. **20**(4), 728–731 (2016)

3. Huang, J., Zhou, Y., Ning, Z., Gharavi, H.: Wireless power transfer and energy harvesting: current status and future prospects. IEEE Wirel. Commun. **26**(4), 163–169 (2019)
4. Kim, J., Kim, S., Bang, J., Hong, D.: Adaptive mode selection in D2D communications considering the bursty traffic model. IEEE Commun. Lett. **20**(4), 712–715 (2016)
5. Della Penda, D., Fu, L., Johansson, M.: Mode selection for energy efficient D2D communications in dynamic TDD systems. In: 2015 IEEE International Conference on Communications (ICC), pp. 5404–5409, June 2015
6. Huang, J., Huang, C., Xing, C., Chang, Z., Zhao, Y., Zhao, Q.: An energy-efficient communication scheme for collaborative mobile clouds in content sharing: design and optimization. IEEE Trans. Industr. Inf. **15**(10), 5700–5707 (2019)
7. Perera, T.D.P., Jayakody, D.N.K., Sharma, S.K., Chatzinotas, S., Li, J.: Simultaneous wireless information and power transfer (SWIPT): recent advances and future challenges. IEEE Commun. Surv. Tutorials **20**(1), 264–302 (2018)
8. Mohjazi, L., Muhaidat, S., Dianati, M., Al-Qutayri, M.: Outage probability and throughput of SWIPT relay networks with differential modulation. In: 2017 IEEE 86th Vehicular Technology Conference (VTC-Fall), pp. 1–6, September 2017
9. Mohjazi, L., Muhaidat, S., Dianati, M., Al-Qutayri, M.: Performance analysis of SWIPT relay networks with noncoherent modulation. IEEE Trans. Green Commun. Netw. **2**(4), 1072–1086 (2018)
10. Zaidi, S.K., Hasan, S.F., Gui, X.: Time switching based relaying for coordinated transmission using NOMA. In: 2018 Eleventh International Conference on Mobile Computing and Ubiquitous Network (ICMU), pp. 1–5, October 2018
11. Maleki, M., Hoseini, A.M.D., Masjedi, M.: Performance analysis of SWIPT relay systems over Nakagami-m fading channels with non-linear energy harvester and hybrid protocol. In: Iranian Conference on Electrical Engineering (ICEE), pp. 610–615, May 2018
12. Jia, X., Zhang, C., Kim, I.: Optimizing wireless powered two-way communication system with EH relays and Non-EH relays. IEEE Trans. Veh. Technol. **67**(11), 11248–11252 (2018)
13. Zaidi, S.K., Hasan, S.F., Gui, X.: Evaluating the ergodic rate in SWIPT-aided hybrid NOMA. IEEE Commun. Lett. **22**(9), 1870–1873 (2018)
14. Zhao, X., Xiao, J., Li, Q., Zhang, Q., Qin, J.: Joint optimization of an-aided transmission and power splitting for MISO secure communications with SWIPT. IEEE Commun. Lett. **19**(11), 1969–1972 (2015)
15. Huang, K., Lau, V.K.N.: Enabling wireless power transfer in cellular networks: architecture, modeling and deployment. IEEE Trans. Wirel. Commun. **13**(2), 902–912 (2014)
16. Huang, J., Zou, J., Xing, C.: Energy-efficient mode selection for D2D communications in cellular networks. IEEE Trans. Cogn. Commun. Netw. **4**(4), 869–882 (2018)

Research on OTFS Performance
Based on Joint-Sparse Fast Time-Varying
Channel Estimation

Wenjing Gao[1,2(✉)], Shanshan Li[1], Lei Zhao[1], Wenbin Guo[1,2], and Tao Peng[1]

[1] Wireless Signal Processing and Network Laboratory,
Beijing University of Posts and Telecommunications, Beijing 100876, China
{gaowenjing,lishanshan,leizhao,gwb,pengtao}@bupt.edu.cn
[2] Science and Technology on Information Transmission and Dissemination
in Communication Networks Laboratory, Beijing, China

Abstract. Contraposing the problem of high pilot overhead and poor estimation performance for OFDM system in fast time-varying channels, a novel channel estimation method based on joint-sparse basis expansion model is proposed. In order to resist the inter-carrier interference (ICI) of OFDM system over fast time-varying channel, we introduce the OTFS (Orthogonal Time Frequency Space) technique and propose an implementation scheme of OTFS system based on time-frequency domain channel estimation. Simulation results demonstrate that the proposed OTFS system has higher reliability and better adaptablity than the OFDM system in high dynamic scenarios.

Keywords: Time-varying channel estimation · OTFS · Joint-sparse basis expansion model · Compressed sensing

1 Introduction

Nowadays, the communication requirements in high mobility scenarios such as high-speed railway system have received increasing attention. In these scenarios, the channel parameters are no longer constant during each symbol period and this type of channel is called a fast time-varying channel. The amount of parameters to be estimated in each symbol over the fast-changing channel is much larger than the observable number. The Linear Time Varying (LTV) model [1,2] and Basis Expansion Model (BEM) [3] are two important models to effectively reduce the number of parameters. LTV models the channel taps of adjacent OFDM symbols as a piecewise linear time-varying relationship, it has a good approximation performance when the normalized Doppler shift is no more than 0.2. In BEM, channel taps are represented as a linear superposition of several two-dimensional basis functions and it has been widely studied [4–6] because it can better describe the nonlinear variation of channels. In addition, the fast time-varying channel exhibits sparsity in delay-Doppler domain. It has become a hot research topic to reduce pilot overhead by utilizing the channel sparsity [7,8].

© ICST Institute for Computer Sciences, Social Informatics and Telecommunications Engineering 2020
Published by Springer Nature Switzerland AG 2020. All Rights Reserved
H. Gao et al. (Eds.): ChinaCom 2019, LNICST 312, pp. 707–719, 2020.
https://doi.org/10.1007/978-3-030-41114-5_53

The OFDM system in fast time-varying channels suffers ICI due to its frequency offset sensitivity, which seriously affects the reliability of multi-carrier systems. Although some scholars have studied ICI cancellation or suppression methods [9, 10], they are of high complexity and cannot adapt to higher dynamic communication scenarios for instance that the future high-speed trains need to support a speed of 500 km/h. In order to solve the above problem, R. Hadani first proposed a new modulation method named Orthogonal Time Frequency Space (OTFS) [11, 12] to meet the requirements of high spectral efficiency in high Doppler scenarios while supporting the application of large-scale antennas. This modulation focuses on making the data itself subject to interference as small as possible rather than the subsequent interference elimination. It is worth considering whether to use the OFDM or the OTFS in the future mobile communication standards.

For the estimation problem of fast time-varying channels, a joint-sparse basis expansion model and a corresponding channel estimation method are proposed. This method converts the estimation of channel impulse response into an estimation of basis coefficients meanwhile considers the sparsity and joint sparsity of the coefficients. In order to improve the anti-interference ability of the system in fast time-varying channels, we propose an implementation of OTFS system based on time-frequency domain channel estimation. The simulation results manifest that the BER performance of the OTFS system using the proposed channel estimation method is significantly better than that of the OFDM system. The OTFS system can achieve high spectral efficiency and high reliability simultaneously and it has better adaptability over high dynamic channels.

The structure of this paper is organized as follows: In Sect. 2, the OFDM system model based on BEM model is derived. In Sect. 3, the proposed channel estimation method based on the joint-sparse BEM model is introduced in detail. In Sect. 4, the basic principles of the OTFS are described and an implementation scheme of the OTFS system is given. Simulation results are provided to compare the performance of OTFS and OFDM systems over fast time-varying channels in Sect. 5. The conclusion is presented in Sect. 6.

2 System Model

In this section, we will derive an OFDM system model over fast time-varying channel under the basis expansion model.

2.1 OFDM System-Basis Expansion Model with Pilots

In the case of fast time-varying channel, the ICI is unavoidable and the channel impulse response changes within each OFDM symbol period, which brings great difficulty to channel estimation. This paper introduces the basis expansion model to reduce the amount of estimation. Let the discrete form of the l-th channel tap at the n-th moment be $h(n, l)$, where $n = 0 \ldots N - 1, l = 0 \ldots L - 1$, under the basis expansion model, the l-th channel tap $\mathbf{h}_l$ can be written as:

$$\mathbf{h}_l = (\mathbf{b}_0, ..., \mathbf{b}_{Q-1}) \begin{bmatrix} g(0,l) \\ \vdots \\ g(Q-1,l) \end{bmatrix} + \xi_l = \mathbf{B}\mathbf{g}_l + \xi_l \tag{1}$$

where $\mathbf{h}_l \in \mathbb{C}^{N \times 1}$, $\mathbf{b}_q = [b(0,q), ..., b(N-1,q)]^T \in \mathbb{C}^{N \times 1}$ is the basis expansion vector, $\mathbf{B} = (\mathbf{b}_0, ..., \mathbf{b}_{Q-1}) \in \mathbb{C}^{N \times Q}$ is the basis function matrix, $\mathbf{g}_l = [g(0,l), ..., g(Q-1,l)]^T \in \mathbb{C}^{Q \times 1}$ is the BEM coefficient vector of the l-th channel tap, and $\xi_l \in \mathbb{C}^{N \times 1}$ is the model error vector. The model order Q satisfies $2f_{nds} + 1 \leqslant Q \ll N$, where f_{nds} is the normalized Doppler shift.

In the time-frequency domain, the transmission equation of OFDM system is:

$$\mathbf{Y} = \mathbf{F}\mathbf{H}_T\mathbf{F}^H\mathbf{X} + \mathbf{W} = \mathbf{H}_F\mathbf{X} + \mathbf{W} \tag{2}$$

where $\mathbf{X} \in \mathbb{C}^{N \times 1}$ and $\mathbf{Y} \in \mathbb{C}^{N \times 1}$ represent transmitted signal and received signal in the frequency domain, respectively, $\mathbf{H}_T \in \mathbb{C}^{N \times N}$ is the channel matrix in time domain, namely $[\mathbf{H}_T]_{i,j} = h(i, \mathrm{mod}(i-j, N))$, $\mathbf{F} \in \mathbb{C}^{N \times N}$ is the normalized Fourier transform matrix of N points, $\mathbf{H}_F \in \mathbb{C}^{N \times N}$ is called the channel matrix in frequency domain, and $\mathbf{W} \in \mathbb{C}^{N \times 1}$ is the frequency domain noise vector.

Combining (1) and (2), the received signal $\mathbf{Y}$ can be written as:

$$\begin{aligned} \mathbf{Y} &= \sum_{q=0}^{Q-1} \mathbf{F}diag(\mathbf{b}_q)\mathbf{F}^H diag(\mathbf{F}_L\mathbf{g}_q)\mathbf{F}\mathbf{F}^H\mathbf{X} + \mathbf{W} \\ &= \sum_{q=0}^{Q-1} \underbrace{\mathbf{F}diag(\mathbf{b}_q)\mathbf{F}^H}_{\mathbf{A}_q} diag(\mathbf{F}_L\mathbf{g}_q)\mathbf{X} + \mathbf{W} \end{aligned} \tag{3}$$

where $\mathbf{F}_L \in \mathbb{C}^{N \times L}$ represents the submatrix consisting of the first L columns of the Fourier transform matrix, and $\mathbf{W} \in \mathbb{C}^{N \times 1}$ represents the noise term including the model error. Using the commutative law $diag(\mathbf{F}_L\mathbf{g}_q)\mathbf{X} = diag(\mathbf{X})\mathbf{F}_L\mathbf{g}_q$, the above equation can be rewritten as:

$$\begin{aligned} \mathbf{Y} &= \sum_{q=0}^{Q-1} \mathbf{A}_q diag(\mathbf{X})\mathbf{F}_L\mathbf{g}_q + \mathbf{W} \\ &= [\mathbf{A}_0, ..., \mathbf{A}_{Q-1}] \{\mathbf{I}_Q \otimes [diag(\mathbf{X})\mathbf{F}_L]\} \mathbf{g} + \mathbf{W} \end{aligned} \tag{4}$$

where $\mathbf{I}_Q$ represents an identity matrix of size Q, $\otimes$ denotes the Kronecker product, and $\mathbf{g} = [\mathbf{g}_0, ..., \mathbf{g}_{Q-1}]^T \in \mathbb{C}^{LQ \times 1}$ is the complete form of the BEM coefficient vector.

Let the number of pilots be P, then the received signal at the pilot position $\mathbf{Y}_P \in \mathbb{C}^{P \times 1}$ can be represented as:

$$\begin{aligned} \mathbf{Y}_P &= [\mathbf{A}_{0,P}, ..., \mathbf{A}_{Q-1,P}] \{\mathbf{I}_Q \otimes [diag(\mathbf{X}_P)\mathbf{F}_P]\} \mathbf{g} \\ &\quad + [\mathbf{A}_{0,D}, ..., \mathbf{A}_{Q-1,D}] \{\mathbf{I}_Q \otimes [diag(\mathbf{X}_D)\mathbf{F}_D]\} \mathbf{g} + \mathbf{W}_P \end{aligned} \tag{5}$$

where $\mathbf{A}_{q,P} \in \mathbb{C}^{P \times P}$ denotes a submatrix of $\mathbf{A}_q$ formed by selecting P rows and P columns from where the pilots are located, $\mathbf{A}_{q,D} \in \mathbb{C}^{P \times (N-P)}$ represents the submatrix of $\mathbf{A}_q$ formed by selecting P rows where the pilots are located and $(N-P)$ columns where the data are located, $\mathbf{F}_P \in \mathbb{C}^{P \times L}$ and $\mathbf{F}_D \in \mathbb{C}^{(N-P) \times L}$ represent the submatrices of the Fourier transform submatrix $\mathbf{F}_L$ composed of selecting P rows where the pilot takes and $(N-P)$ rows where the data takes, respectively. The second term in the equation is the interference term which includes the system ICI. The interference term, model error and noise are synthesized into $\tilde{\mathbf{W}}_P$, then the BEM coefficient estimation equation of the j-th symbol in the OFDM system is:

$$\mathbf{Y}_P^j = \underbrace{\left[\mathbf{A}_{0,P}^j, ..., \mathbf{A}_{Q-1,P}^j \right] \left\{ \mathbf{I}_Q \otimes \left[diag(\mathbf{X}_P^j)\mathbf{F}_P^j \right] \right\}}_{\Phi_P} \mathbf{g}^j$$
$$+ \tilde{\mathbf{W}}_P^j = \Phi_P^j \mathbf{g}^j + \tilde{\mathbf{W}}_P^j \tag{6}$$

It can be seen that the basis expansion model reduces the estimated parameters of fast-changing channel from NL to QL and $Q << N$, hence the complexity of channel estimation can be effectively reduced.

3   Proposed Channel Estimation

In this section, the proposed joint-sparse basis expansion model is introduced first and then a channel estimation method based on the joint-sparse BEM is presented.

3.1   Joint-Sparse Basis Expansion Model

When the fast time-varying channel is fitted by basis expansion model, the sparsity of basis coefficient also characterizes the sparsity of the channel in the delay-Doppler domain [13]. Let Γ denotes a set containing all non-zero path positions of the channel, then

$$\mathbf{h}_l = [h(0,l), ..., h(N-1,l)]^T = \mathbf{0}^T, \ l \notin \Gamma \tag{7}$$

According to (1), when the model error is ignored, the BEM coefficient vector of the lth channel tap can be expressed as:

$$\mathbf{g}_l = (g[0,l], ..., g[Q-1,l])^T = \mathbf{B}^\dagger \mathbf{h}_l \tag{8}$$

where $\mathbf{B}^\dagger$ is the pseudo-inverse of the basis function matrix.

Combining (7) and (8) we can know that the basis coefficient satisfies the following characteristics: $g[0,l] = \cdots = g[Q-1,l] = 0$, $l \notin \Gamma$, that is, the basis coefficient vector $\mathbf{g} = [\mathbf{g}_0, ..., \mathbf{g}_{Q-1}]^T \in \mathbb{C}^{LQ \times 1}$ is a sparse vector and its sparsity is KQ at most, the specific sparsity S is related to the system Doppler frequency.

Although the channel amplitude changes within each OFDM symbol, the multipath structure of time-varying channel exhibits strong correlation between consecutive symbols [14]. In this paper, we assume that the multi-path delay structure of channel remains unchanged for consecutive J OFDM symbols, thus the corresponding J basis coefficient vectors exhibit joint sparsity. Based on this, a joint-sparse basis expansion model is established, let $\theta_g = [\theta_0, ..., \theta_l, ..., \theta_{QL-1}]^T \in \mathbb{C}^{LQ \times 1}$ denote a joint-sparse support set, then the joint-sparse basis expansion model is expressed as:

$$\mathbf{g}^j = \text{diag}(\theta_g)\mathbf{s}_g^j, j = 1, ..., J \tag{9}$$

The superscript j represents the serial number of the OFDM symbol, and $\mathbf{s}_g^j \in \mathbb{C}^{LQ \times 1}$ represents the amplitude of the basis coefficient corresponding to the j-th symbol. According to the joint-sparse basis expansion model, the joint multi-symbol channel estimation model of OFDM system for fast time-varying scenario can be derived as:

$$\begin{cases} \mathbf{Y}_P^1 = \mathbf{\Phi}_P^1 \mathbf{g}^1 + \tilde{\mathbf{W}}_P^1 \\ \mathbf{Y}_P^2 = \mathbf{\Phi}_P^2 \mathbf{g}^2 + \tilde{\mathbf{W}}_P^2 \\ \vdots \\ \mathbf{Y}_P^J = \mathbf{\Phi}_P^J \mathbf{g}^J + \tilde{\mathbf{W}}_P^J \end{cases} \tag{10}$$

The joint channel estimation model described above converts the estimation of the channel impulse response that changes within each symbol into an estimation of the invariant basis coefficient within each symbol, it reduces the amount of estimation and meanwhile fully considers to the sparsity of basis coefficients and the joint-sparse property between successive symbols, thus it can be used to guide channel estimation for low pilot overhead over fast-varying channels.

3.2 The Proposed Channel Estimation Scheme

The joint channel estimation problem shown in (10) is equivalent to solving the following optimization formula:

$$\hat{\mathbf{g}}^j = \arg \min \|\mathbf{g}^j\|_0 \text{ s.t. } \sum_{j=1}^{J} \left\|\mathbf{Y}_P^j - \mathbf{\Phi}^j \mathbf{g}^j\right\|_2^2 \leqslant \varepsilon \tag{11}$$

In this paper, the SOMP algorithm [15] of distributed compressed sensing is used to solve the channel BEM coefficients of J OFDM symbols. Furtherly according to (1), the estimated value of the corresponding channel impulse response is obtained by applying the following equation:

$$\hat{\mathbf{h}}^j = (\mathbf{B} \otimes \mathbf{I}_L)\hat{\mathbf{g}}^j \tag{12}$$

where $\hat{\mathbf{h}}^j = [\hat{h}(0,0), ..., \hat{h}(0, L-1), ..., \hat{h}(N-1,0), ..., \hat{h}(N-1, L-1)]^T \in \mathbb{C}^{NL \times 1}, j = 1, ..., J.$

We adopt the linear time varying model's derivative smoothing method–piecewise linear smoothing [16] to perform the subsequent processing of the initial channel estimation values obtained by the SOMP algorithm. The core idea of piecewise linear smoothing is using the correlation of channel amplitudes between successive symbols to reduce the model error further. In practical applications, the piecewise linear smoothing method adopts the sliding window in Fig. 2.

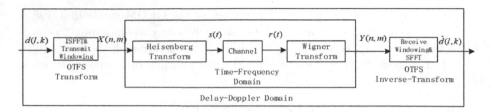

Fig. 1. OTFS system block diagram [17]

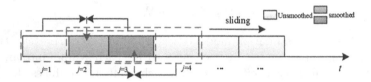

Fig. 2. Sliding window method of piecewise linear smoothing

4   Time-Frequency Domain Channel Estimation Based OTFS Scheme

In this section, we first introduce specific analysis of OTFS modulation and demodulation and then an implementation scheme of OTFS system based on time-frequency domain channel estimation is proposed.

4.1   OTFS Mod/demod Block Diagram

The block diagram of the OTFS system is shown in Fig. 1.

OTFS Modulation. The OTFS transform can be expressed as:

$$X[n, m] = w_{tx}[n, m] \cdot \text{ISFFT}(d[l, k])   \tag{13}$$

where $d[l, k]$ is the data symbol in delay-doppler domain, $X[n, m]$ is the symbol in time-frequency domain and $w_{tx}[n, m]$ is the transmitting window function.

Then $X[n, m]$ are mapped to a time domain waveform $s(t)$ by a time-frequency modulator which superposing the delay-and-modulate operation on the pulse waveform $g_{tx}(t)$, namely

$$s(t) = \sum_{n=-N/2}^{N/2} \sum_{m=0}^{M-1} X[n, m] g_{tx}(t - m\Delta t) e^{j2\pi n \Delta f(t - m\Delta t)} \tag{14}$$

The operation in (14) is called the Heisenberg transform of $X[n, m]$. Then the time domain waveform is transmitted through the wireless channel $h(\tau, \upsilon)$ and the received signal $r(t)$ is obtained as:

$$r(t) = \iint h(\tau, \upsilon) s(t - \tau) e^{j2\pi \upsilon(t - \tau)} d\upsilon d\tau \tag{15}$$

OTFS Demodulation. The OTFS demodulation includes two links of Wigner transform and OTFS inverse transform, wherein the Wigner transform is an inverse operation of Heisenberg transform and the OTFS inverse transform specifically includes windowing and SFFT transform.

Firstly, the time domain signal $r(t)$ is transformed back to the time-frequency domain via Wigner transform given by

$$Y[n, m] = A_{g_{rx}, r}(\tau, \upsilon)|_{\tau=mT, \upsilon=n\Delta f} \tag{16}$$

where $A_{g_{rx}, r}(\tau, \upsilon)$ is the cross ambiguity function given by

$$A_{g_{rx}, r}(\tau, \upsilon) \triangleq \int g_{rx}^*(t - \tau) r(t) e^{-j2\pi \upsilon(t - \tau)} dt \tag{17}$$

The above equation is sampled to obtain the discrete received signal $Y[n, m]$ of the matched filter output and its windowed by the receiving window function $w_{rx}[n, m]$ to obtain $Y_w[n, m]$:

$$Y_w[n, m] = w_{rx}[n, m] Y[n, m] \tag{18}$$

Then the $Y_w[n, m]$ are converted to symbols in the delay-Doppler domain via SFFT:

$$\hat{d}[l, k] = \mathrm{SFFT}(Y_w[n, m]) \tag{19}$$

The relation of input and output in OTFS modulation can be derived as:

$$\hat{d}[l, k] = \frac{1}{NM} \sum_{n=0}^{N-1} \sum_{m=0}^{M-1} d[l, k] h_w\left(\frac{k - m}{MT}, \frac{l - n}{N\Delta f}\right) \tag{20}$$

where

$$h_w\left(\frac{k - m}{MT}, \frac{l - n}{N\Delta f}\right) = h_w(\upsilon', \tau')|_{\upsilon'=\frac{k-m}{MT}, \tau'=\frac{l-n}{N\Delta f}} \tag{21}$$

and where $h_w(v', \tau')$ is the circular convolution of the channel response $\mathrm{h}(\tau, v)$ and the windowing function $w(v, \tau)$, given by

$$h_w(v', \tau') = \iint h(\tau, v)w(v' - v, \tau' - \tau)e^{-j2\pi v\tau}d\tau dv \tag{22}$$

where

$$w(v, \tau) = \mathrm{SFFT}(w_{tx}[n, m] \cdot w_{rx}[n, m]) \tag{23}$$

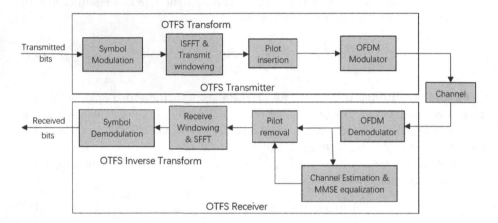

Fig. 3. Block diagram of OTFS system based on time-frequency domain channel estimation

4.2   Time-Frequency Domain Channel Estimation Based on OTFS Scheme

As shown in Fig. 3, an implementation scheme of OTFS system based on time-frequency domain channel estimation is presented which can take into account both the high spectral efficiency and reliability under the premise of compatible OFDM system.

If the number of system subcarriers is N and the number of multicarrier symbols is M, then the time-frequency domain and the corresponding delay-Doppler domain have a lattice size of $M \times N$. The transmitter obtains the constellation symbols by encoding and symbol modulation of the binary bits and maps them to the delay-Doppler domain to obtain the transmission sequence $d[l, k]l = 0 \ldots N - 1, k = 0 \ldots M - 1$, after which the OTFS transform completes the conversion from the delay-Doppler domain to the time-frequency domain. For the sake of simplicity, we adopt a rectangular window which can simplify the OTFS transform into an ISFFT transform:

$$\begin{aligned} X[n, m] &= \mathrm{ISFFT}(d[l, k]) \\ &= \frac{1}{\sqrt{MN}} \sum_{l=0}^{N-1} \sum_{k=0}^{M-1} d[l, k]e^{-j2\pi\left(\frac{nl}{N} - \frac{mk}{M}\right)} \end{aligned} \tag{24}$$

where m and n represent the time domain and frequency domain, respectively, $m = 0 \ldots M - 1, n = 0 \ldots N - 1$.

In this paper, the receiver adopts the proposed channel estimation method and the MMSE channel equalization as shown below:

$$\hat{X}[n,m] = \frac{Y[n,m]\hat{H}[n,m]^*}{\left|\hat{H}[n,m]\right|^2 + \sigma^2} \tag{25}$$

where $Y[n,m]$ and $H[n,m]$ represent the received signal and channel parameters in the time-frequency domain, respectively, and the noise power is σ^2. Then $\hat{X}[n,m]$ is converted to the delay-Doppler domain by SFFT and the estimated value of the transmitted constellation symbol is obtained, finally the binary information bits are restored by operations such as demodulation and decoding.

5   Simulation Results and Discussion

This section studies the performance of both OFDM and OTFS systems. Firstly, the BER performance of OFDM system under different channel estimation methods is simulated. Then, the BER performance of OTFS and OFDM system is compared using the proposed channel estimation method. The OFDM system compares four methods of compressed sensing channel estimation, all of which use random pilots and the pilots between the symbols in the joint multi-symbol estimation method are identical to each other. The algorithms for comparison are as follows: (1) OMP [18]: obtaining the BEM coefficients symbol by symbol according to (6); (2) OMP smooth: performing piecewise linear smoothing on the preliminary estimation of the channel obtained by (1); (3) SOMP: obtaining the BEM coefficients of $J = 5$ symbols jointly according to (10); (4) SOMP Smooth: performing the piecewise linear smoothing process on the initial value obtained in (3).

Table 1. Simulation parameters

Parameter	Value
Number of subcarrier	$N = 256$
Number of multi-carrier symbol	$M = 15$
CP length	$N_{CP} = 64$
Channel tap number	4
Channel length	$L = 64$
Modulation mode	QPSK
Subcarrier spacing	15 KHz
Carrier frequency	4 Ghz
Channel knowledge	unknown

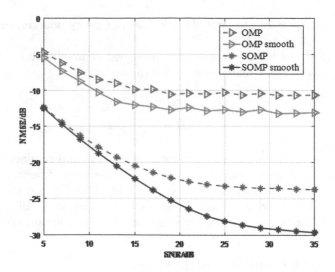

Fig. 4. OFDM NMSE performance of various channel estimation methods with $f_{nds} = 0.05$, 202.5 Kmph

We first generate channel based on the Jake's model. To describe the time variation of the channel, the definition of normalized Doppler shift (NDS) is given: $f_{nds} = f_d/\Delta f$, where f_d and Δf is the Doppler frequency and the system subcarrier spacing, respectively. The simulation adopts the DPS-BEM model with a model order of $Q = 3$, and other system parameters are shown in Table 1.

Figure 4 shows the normalized mean square error(NMSE) performance of OFDM system adopting different channel estimation methods when the f_{nds} is 0.05 (the corresponding maximum UE speed is 202.5 Kmph). It can be seen that the performance result is SOMP smooth>SOMP>OMP smooth>OMP. The performance of OMP algorithm is the worst and an error platform appears when SNR is above 10 dB. This is because OMP algorithm merely utilizes the sparsity of BEM coefficients without considering the correlation between consecutive symbols. After using the smoothing treatment, OMP gets a very limited performance boost. Our proposed channel estimation method gets the best performance because it makes full use of the sparsity of channel as well as reduces the model error by the smoothing treatment. Next, the BER performance of OTFS and OFDM will be simulated.

We simulate the BER performance of OFDM and OTFS using the proposed channel estimation method and MMSE channel equalization. The BER performance for both uncoded and (2,1,7) convolutional code are compared. Figure 5 shows the BER performance of OFDM and OTFS system using the SOMP smooth channel estimation method with a f_{nds} of 0.05. It can be seen that in the case of both coded and uncoded, the performance of OFDM is slightly better than that of OTFS in the relatively low SNR regime, while as SNR increases the advantages of OTFS becomes more prominent and the system performance

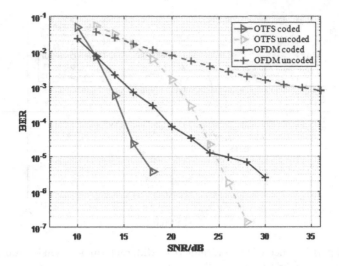

Fig. 5. BER performance of two systems with the proposed channel estimation method ($f_{nds} = 0.05$, 202.5 Kmph)

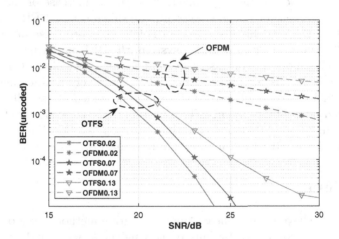

Fig. 6. BER performance of two systems over different time-varying channels (uncoded)

is far superior to OFDM, which indicates that OTFS can effectively resist system ICI. After adopting the proposed channel estimation method, it can obtain significantly superior BER performance and higher system reliability.

Figures 6 and 7 compare the BER performance of the OFDM system and the OTFS system with different normalized Doppler shifts (0.02, 0.07, 0.13) (the corresponding UE speed are 81 Kmph, 283.7 Kmph and 526.5 Kmph) in the case of uncoded and coded, respectively. For OFDM system, it can be seen that

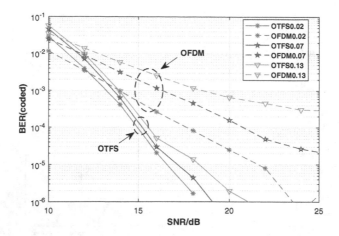

Fig. 7. BER performance of two systems over different time-varying channels (convolutional code with coding rate of 1/2)

the BER performance degrades significantly with the increase of channel time-variability. In the case of uncoded system, the difference of BER performance under the three Doppler shifts is about 4 dB (the signal-to-noise ratio when the BER is 1e-3). And in the case of coded system, the BER performance under the three f_{nds} differs more. In contrast, the BER performance of the OTFS system under the three f_{nds} is relatively stable. There is merely a difference of a few tenths of a dB in the case of coded OTFS system, which further illustrates the reliability and adaptability of the OTFS system over time-varying channels. In general, the simulation results indicate that our proposed OTFS implementation scheme outperforms OFDM in high dynamic scenarios.

6   Conclusion

In this paper, we have studied the channel estimation method based on the joint-sparse basis expansion model by fully exploiting the sparsity and correlation of fast time-varying channels. Based on the proposed fast time-varying channel estimation method, we study the performance of OTFS system and OFDM system. The simulation results illustrate that with the same multi-carrier parameters, the BER performance of OTFS system using the proposed channel estimation method is significantly superior than that of the OFDM system, which indicates that the OTFS system has higher reliability and better adaptability over high dynamic channel.

Acknowledgment. This work was partially supported by National Natural Science Foundation of China (NSFC 61271181, 61571054) and the Science and Technology on Information Transmission and Dissemination in Communication Networks Laboratory Foundation

References

1. Mostofi, Y., Cox, D.C.: ICI mitigation for pilot-aided OFDM mobile systems. IEEE Trans. Wirel. Commun. 4(2), 764–774 (2005)
2. Hlawatsch, F., Matz, G.: Wireless Communications Over Rapidly Time-Varying Channels (2001)
3. Rabbi, M.F., Hou, S.W., Ko, C.C.: High mobility orthogonal frequency division multiple access channel estimation using basis expansion model. IET Commun. 4(3), 353 (2010)
4. Deng, L., Chen, Z., Zhao, Y.: Basis expansion model for channel estimation in LTE-R communication system. Digit. Commun. Netw. 2(2), 92–96 (2016)
5. Wang, X., Wang, G., Fan, R., et al.: Channel estimation with expectation maximization and historical information based basis expansion model for wireless communication systems on high speed railways. IEEE Access 6, 72–80 (2018)
6. Wang, X., Wang, J., et al.: Doubly selective underwater acoustic channel estimation with basis expansion model. In: 2017 IEEE International Conference on Communications, pp. 1–6 (2017)
7. Ma, X., Yang, F., Liu, S., et al.: Sparse channel estimation for MIMO-OFDM systems in high-mobility situations. IEEE Trans. Veh. Technol. 67, 6113–6124 (2018)
8. Liu, T., Zheng, K., Wang, P.: Compressive sensing based channel estimation for scattered pilot OFDM Systems over doubly-selective Rician channel. In: 2016 25th Wireless and Optical Communication Conference (WOCC) (2018)
9. Le, T.B., Makula, P., Bui, T.T., et al.: Group successive ICI cancellation for MIMO-OFDM systems in underwater acoustic channels. In: International Conference on Mechatronics-Mechatronika. IEEE (2017)
10. Park, K., Kim, H., Lee, A., et al.: Iterative frequency-domain inter-carrier interference cancellation for coded spectrally efficient frequency division multiplexing. Electron. Lett. 53(19), 1333–1335 (2017)
11. Hadani, R., Rakib, S., Molisch, A.F., et al.: Orthogonal Time Frequency Space (OTFS) modulation for millimeter-wave communications systems. In: 2017 IEEE MTT-S International Microwave Symposium (IMS), pp. 681–683 (2017)
12. Hadani, R., Monk, A.: OTFS: a new generation of modulation addressing the challenges of 5G (2018)
13. Vahidi, V., Saberinia, E.: Channel estimation for wideband doubly selective UAS channels. In: International Conference on Unmanned Aircraft Systems. IEEE (2017)
14. Hu, D., Wang, X., He, L.: A new sparse channel estimation and tracking method for time-varying OFDM systems. IEEE Trans. Veh. Technol. 62(9), 4648–4653 (2013)
15. Tropp, J.A., Gilbert, A.C., Strauss, M.J.: Simultaneous sparse approximation via greedy pursuit. In: IEEE International Conference on Acoustics. IEEE (2005)
16. Qin, Q., Gui, L., Gong, B., et al.: Structured distributed compressive channel estimation over doubly selective channels. IEEE Trans. Broadcast. 62, 521–531 (2016)
17. Murali, K.R., Chockalingam, A.: On OTFS modulation for high-doppler fading channels. In: 2018 Information Theory and Applications Workshop (ITA), pp. 1–10 (2018)
18. Joel, A., Anna, C., et al.: Signal recovery from random measurements via orthogonal matching pursuit. IEEE Trans. Inf. Theory 53(12), 4655–4666 (2007)

Load Balancing Mechanism Based on Sparse Matrix Prediction in C-RAN Networks

Yang Liu[✉], Zhanjun Liu, Ling Kuang, and Xinrui Tan

School of Communication and Information Engineering,
Chongqing University of Posts and Telecommunications, Chongqing, China
liuzj@cqupt.edu.cn

Abstract. In order to solve the problem that the existing algorithms in large-scale networks have high complexity in adjusting power iteratively, a load balancing mechanism based on sparse matrix prediction is proposed to achieve load balancing in C-RAN architecture. In order to minimize the correlation degree of load transfer and the balance of load transfer, the optimal sparse matrix block is obtained combined with Ncut cutting algorithm to realize dimension reduction and zero removal of the load transfer matrix. After the block, the load transfer matrix of each block is recalculated, and the load transfer matrix is used to predict the load. Finally, combined with the predicted load, the power adjustment step size is determined, and the pilot signal power of each block is adjusted in parallel to achieve load balancing. The simulation results show that the load balancing mechanism can reduce the complexity of load balancing.

Keywords: Sparse matrix · Matrix block · Load balancing

1 Introduction

The scale of the mobile network based on C-RAN architecture tends to expand and complexity [1]. Followed by, the network load balancing technology faces new challenges. The existing load balancing algorithms based on iterative adjustment of transmission power achieves the maximum throughput but the complexity is very high [2]. As a essential method of reducing the complexity, sparse matrix technology is an important research direction of wireless network technology in the future and has a wide range of applications. The similarity matrix describing image pixels in image segmentation algorithm is a large-scale sparse matrix. The dimension of sparse Matrix can be reduced by establishing the corresponding

This work is supported by the National Natural Science Foundation of China (NSFC) (61801064), Chongqing Education Commission Project KJQN (201801908), and PHD Initialted Fund Project (A1029-17).

© ICST Institute for Computer Sciences, Social Informatics and Telecommunications Engineering 2020
Published by Springer Nature Switzerland AG 2020. All Rights Reserved
H. Gao et al. (Eds.): ChinaCom 2019, LNICST 312, pp. 720–728, 2020.
https://doi.org/10.1007/978-3-030-41114-5_54

relationship between large-scale sparse matrix and undirected graph and combined with the Normalized cutting Criterion (Ncut) in Graph Theory [3]. The sparse matrix is used in the spectral clustering image segmentation algorithm. The similarity matrix created is sparse and the theoretical analysis and the image segmentation experiment results show that the algorithm can effectively reduce the computational complexity of the spectral clustering, and improve the accuracy and the robustness of the segmentation [4]. With the increasing scale of the network, not all the nodes in the network are related. Although the order of the matrix describing the relationship between the network nodes is very high, the matrix has sparse characteristics. Therefore, the sparse matrix can be used to solve the problem of the high complexity of the network [5]. In order to predict the future load better, the commonly used time series models are the autoregression prediction model (AR), neural network prediction model, Markov prediction model and so on [6]. Load balancing can be realized by adjusting the power of the pilot signal. However, the power adjustment of the pilot signal directly relate to the performance of the system. To find the best adjustment power, absorbing game theory is used to establish the market buying and selling model in economics. To the same end, reinforcement learning is applied to the load balancing of the ad hoc network to determine the optimal transmission power by iterating. Moreover, markov decision can be utilized to adjust power [7–9]. C-RAN, as an access network of cloud processing model, contains a large number of RRU due to its distributed wireless network architecture [10]. However, it is not able to adapt to the development trend of a mobile communication network in the future because its high complexity of load balancing technology. In order to solve the problem of the high complexity of the above load balancing algorithm, a load balancing mechanism based on sparse matrix prediction is proposed inspired of load transfer matrix obtained in reference [11]. In this mechanism, the predicted load is obtained by the load transfer matrix predicted by sparse matrix, and then the power adjustment step size is determined. The pilot signal power of each block is adjusted in parallel to realize the load balance of the block cell. The simulation results show that the proposed load balancing mechanism can reduce the complexity of load balancing.

The paper is organized as follows. The system model of this paper is introduced in Sect. 2, including mathematical formulas and theoretical analysis. Load balancing optimization model based on sparse matrix prediction is specialized in Sect. 3. The new algorithm and the mechanism of innovation are proposed in Sect. 4. The performance of the proposed mechanism and comparisons with the existing algorithms is analyzed in Sect. 5. Finally, this paper is conclued in Sect. 6.

2 System Model

Consider a multi-cell multiuser system, which has a base station and serves a single antenna user. According to reference [12], a load of each base station over time is represented as a first-order markov prediction model:

$$L(n+1) = R(n) * L(n) \tag{1}$$

Where $L(n) = [l_1(n), l_2(n), \cdots, l_M(n)]^T$ represents the load condition of each base station at n time, and $R(n)$ represents the load state transition matrix of the network at n time, as follows:

$$R(n) = \begin{bmatrix} r_{11}(n) & r_{21}(n) & \dots & r_{M1}(n) \\ r_{12}(n) & r_{22}(n) & \dots & r_{M2}(n) \\ \dots & \dots & \dots & \dots \\ r_{1M}(n) & r_{2M}(n) & \dots & r_{MM}(n) \end{bmatrix} \tag{2}$$

Where $r_{ij}(n)$ represents the load transfer rate of the base station i at n time to the base station j at $n + 1$ time. The $M + 1$ network states are obtained by formula (1) to obtain $R(n)$. The load state of the next network is predicted by the load transfer matrix, and the load transfer matrix $R(n)$ is obtained by formula (3).

$$[L(n), L(n-1), \cdots, L(n-M+1)] = R(n) * [L(n-1), L(n-2), \cdots, L(n-M)] \tag{3}$$

The load transfer matrix $R(n)$ in large-scale C-RAN networks is a matrix with large sparsity. The division of zero and dimension reduction of $R(n)$ needs to be divided into blocks. Reasonable segmentation enhances the load transfer relationship within the block and weakens the load transfer relationship between blocks.

3   Load Balancing Optimization Model Based on Sparse Matrix Prediction

The above block problem can be transformed into the optimal segmentation problem of the undirected graph in graph theory. In order to find the most reasonable sparse matrix block, the following optimization model is established. The optimization goal is to minimize the load transfer correlation degree and load transfer balance. Therefore, the optimization model is established by means of joint optimization. The load transfer correlation degree is defined as the coupling degree of load transfer between blocks of an undirected graph, and the load transfer balance degree is defined as the mean square error of each block load after block segmentation of undirected graph.

Assume the base station set is $B = U_{m=1}^K * B_m, B_m \cap B_k = \Phi, \forall m \neq k(k = 1, 2, \cdots, K)$. K is divided into blocks, and the number of cells per block is represented by $N_k(k = 1, 2, \cdots, K)$. By using the parameters α and β, the load transfer correlation degree and load transfer balance degree are optimized jointly. And assume $V_j \in B_k$ if j cell is assigned to k block, then $x_{kj} = 1$, otherwise takes $x_{kj} = 0$. In order to meet reality, the number of cells in the block are not too small, so $N_k(k = 1, 2, \cdots, K) \geq 3$ and $K \geq 2$, The optimization model is established as follows:

$$G(x, \alpha, \beta) = \min[\alpha \cdot \sum_{k=1}^{K} \sqrt{(B_k - \bar{B})/K} + \beta \cdot \sum_{k=1}^{K} \frac{cut(B_k, B - B_k)}{vol(B_k)}]$$

$$\bar{B} = (\sum_{k=1}^{K} B_k)/K(K \geq 2)$$

$$B_k = \sum_{j=1}^{M} l_j \cdot x_{kj}(1 \leq k \leq K)$$

$$cut(B_m, B_k) = \sum_{i \in B_m, j \in B_k} r'_{ij}$$

$$vol(B_k) = \sum_{i \in B_k, j \in B} r'_{ij}$$

s.t.

$$\sum_{j=1}^{M} x_{kj} \geq 3$$

$$\sum_{k=1}^{K} x_{kj} = 1$$

$$x_{kj} = 0 \cup x_{kj} = 1$$

$$\alpha + \beta = 1(\alpha \geq 0, \beta \geq 0) \tag{4}$$

Where r'_{ij} represents the load transfer from the i cell to the j cell, corresponding elements in $R' = D - W$. W is $< R + R^T >$, R is the load transfer matrix and $< X >$ represents the zero-setting transformation of the main diagonal elements of the X matrix. $D = diag(d_1, d_2, \cdots, d_M)$ and $d_i = \sum_j w_{ij}$ represents the extent to which point i is associated with other nodes. w_{ij} is the element in an adjacent matrix W. $cut(B_m, B_K)$ represents the weighted sum of the associated edges of the subgraph B_m and the subgraph B_K, and $vol(B_K)$ represents the sum of the weights of the B_k edges of the subgraph. N_k is the total number of cells in the block k, K is the number of blocks, l_i is the load before cell i prediction, and r_{ij} is the element in the load transfer matrix after dimension reduction. B_k is the predicted load of the k block, and $\bar{B}$ is the average load of all blocks. M is the total number of system cells, l'_j is the load value of the predicted cell j.

4 Load Balancing Mechanism Based on Sparse Matrix Prediction

4.1 Solution Algorithm

The above optimization problem is a 0–1 integer programming problem. Using exhaustive method to obtain the optimal matrix block is with high complexity, so load balancing algorithm based on sparsity (SLBA) is designed combining with Ncut cutting algorithm to obtain the best matrix block. SLBA is as follow:

Algorithm 1. Load Balancing Algorithm Based on Sparsity (SLBA)

1: **Initialization:**input load transfer matrix R^{M*M}, and initial block number $k = 2$
2: **Output:**The block with the least load balance$\sigma = min(\sigma_2, \sigma_3, \cdots, \sigma_{[M/3]})$
3: Calculate adjacency matrix W and degree matrix D with $R + R^T$.
4: Eigenvalue decomposition of $D^{\frac{1}{2}}WD^{\frac{-1}{2}}$ and find out the eigenvector of the corresponding eigenvalue.
5: The feature vector $v_1, v_2, \cdots, v_k$ of the k maximum characteristic values are selected to form V^{M*k} by column
   repeat.
6: Cluster $y_i(i = 1, 2, \cdots, M)$ by k-means algorithm where y_i is the row vector of V^{M*k} to obtain the partition of graphs $C_1, C_2, \cdots, C_k$.
7: Calculate the load transfer matrix for each block $R_1, R_2, \cdots, R_k$ according to block case.
8: According to the load transfer matrix of each block, the load of the cell in the block is predicted and calculate load transfer balance σ_k by $\sigma = \Sigma_{k=1}^{K}\sqrt{(B_k - \bar{B})^2/K}$.
9: $k = k + 1$, then go to step 4, and calculate the load transfer balance under this block.
   until $k > [\frac{M}{3}]$.
10: Select the first block with the lowest load balance $\sigma = min(\sigma_2, \sigma_3, \cdots, \sigma_{[}M/3])$.

4.2   Load Balancing Mechanism

According to the proposed algorithm (SLBA), the above optimization problems are solved. Then the solution with the least load transfer balance is found in the finite feasible solution. Finally, the solution with the lowest load transfer balance and the least load transfer correlation degree is selected as the optimal solution. After the optimal cell block is obtained, the load balancing of each block is carried out to realize the load balancing of the whole network.

5   Simulation and Result Analysis

The simulation scene is mainly aimed at the isomorphism network under C-RAN architecture, and the occupation rate of PRB in the cell is taken as the load measurement index, and the initial network users are randomly uniform in each cell. In order to simulate the real load imbalance scene, Three cells are selected as hot spots. The speed of users is 5 km/h, 30 km/h and 60 km/h, respectively, which represents the speed of walking, bicycle and car. The algorithm, the load balancing mechanism of the iterative method and the mechanism which can't adopt load balancing compared and analyzed. Detailed configuration of system simulation parameters is shown in Table 1.

According to the parameters in the above table and the corresponding scenes, the proposed algorithm is simulated and compared with the existing algorithms in terms of system capacity, Jain's fairness index, PRB occupation ratio and so on.

Table 1. System simulation parameter configuration.

Parameter name	Parameter values
Number of base stations	19
Base station coverage radius (m)	500
Base station transmission power (w)	40
System bandwidth (MHZ)	10
Load balancing cycle (ms)	200
Background noise power (dBm)	-104
Service rate (kbit/s)	512
Overload threshold	0.9
Motor pattern (km/h)	speed [5,30,60] direction (0, 360)
Road loss model (dB)	$L = 128.1 + 37.6 * lg(d(km))$

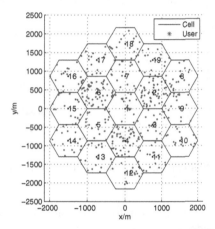

Fig. 1. Topology diagram of the base station and initial user distribution

Figure 1 is a scenario diagram for establishing a load balancing mechanism. It can be seen that the user density of each cell is different, so a reasonable load balancing mechanism is necessary to maximize throughput.

Figures 2 and 3 show the Jain fairness index and the relationship between system capacity and the total number of users, respectively. It can be seen from the diagram that the system capacity and fairness index of this mechanism are improved compared with the load balancing mechanism, and the system capacity and fairness index of this mechanism are slightly lower than those of the iterative load balancing mechanism. The capacity of the system is reduced by about $0.02\% - 0.1\%$, and the maximum reduction of fairness index is about 1.6%. This is because the load balancing mechanism is based on the established load forecasting, and there are always a small number of errors in the load forecasting. On the other hand, the sparse matrix block algorithm of the load

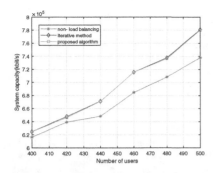

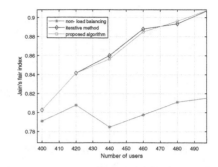

Fig. 2. System capacity and number of users

Fig. 3. Jain fairness index and number of users

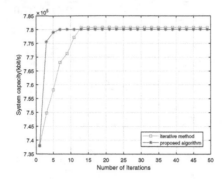

Fig. 4. System capacity and number of iteractions

balancing mechanism is the smallest load transfer correlation degree. But the load transfer between blocks still exists.

Figure 4 is a diagram of the system capacity varying with the number of iterations. It can be seen from the diagram that with the increase of the number of iterations, the load balancing mechanism of the iterative method and the proposed load balancing mechanism converge to the desired system capacity. However, the convergence speed of this load balancing mechanism is faster than that of iterative load balancing mechanism, which is because the load balancing mechanism is based on sparse matrix block. The number of cells in the block is smaller than the total number of cells in the network.

Figure 5 is a schematic diagram of PRB occupation ratio under different algorithms in each cell, and a straight line with a longitudinal coordinate of 0.9 represents the overload threshold. In this scenario, the total number of network users is 500. It can be seen from the diagram that compared with the unload balancing mechanism, the iterative method and the network of this algorithm do not exceed the overload threshold, and the proportion of PRB occupied by the iterative method is basically similar to that of the proposed algorithm.

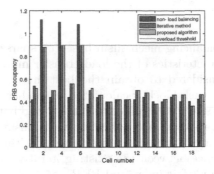

Fig. 5. Schematic diagram of PRB occupation ratio under different algorithms in each cell

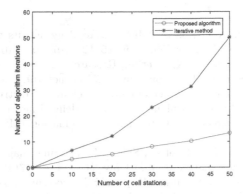

Fig. 6. Number of iterations and cell base stations

Figure 6 is the relationship between the number of iterations and the number of cell base stations. It can be seen that with the increase of the number of cell base stations, the number of iterations to achieve load balancing by the proposed algorithm (SLBA) is less than that by the iterative method. Moreover with the increase of the cell size, the number of iterations under the proposed algorithm increases more slowly, that is to say, the complexity of the proposed algorithm is lower.

From the above load balancing mechanism, it can be seen that if the load transfer matrix is not preprocessed, the complexity of the power adjustment algorithm is $O(M * N)$ directly by iteration, where M represents the total number of cells and N represents the number of iterations. If the sparseness of the load transfer matrix is used to block it, then load balancing is carried out in parallel. The complexity of the algorithm is $O(m * N)$, in which $m = max(N_1, N_2, \cdots, N_K)$ represents the number of cells of the largest block after block, and N represents the number of iterations of the algorithm. Obviously, m is smaller than M, especially in the case of large scale and a large number of blocks.

6   Conclusion

In this paper, a load balancing mechanism based on sparse matrix block is proposed. The sparse characteristics of the load transfer matrix and the Ncut cutting algorithm are considered to obtain the best matrix block, and then the load transfer matrix of each block is calculated to predict the load. Finally, the power adjustment step size is determined to achieve load balance. The simulation results show that the proposed load balancing mechanism can reduce the complexity of the load balance of the existing iterative algorithm under the condition that there is no difference between the existing iterative algorithm in ensuring the system capacity, jain's fair index and PRB.

References

1. Chai, T.S.: Brief introduction of C-RAN technology and its application scenario in mobile network. Chin. New Commun. **19**(12), 107–107 (2017)
2. Hao, Y.W., Wang, J.N., Li, X.X., et al.: Research on storage load balancing algorithm based on distributed environment. Inf. Technol. **09**, 55–58 (2016)
3. Cimorelli, F., Priscoli, F.D., Pietrabissa, A., et al.: A distributed load balancing algorithm for the control plane in software defined networking. In: 2016 24th Mediterranean Conference on Control and Automation (MED), pp. 1033–1040. Athens (2016)
4. Liu, Z.M., Li, Z.M., Li, B.H., et al.: Spectral clustering image segmentation algorithm based on sparse matrix. J. Jilin Univ. (Eng. Ed.) **47**(4), 1308–1313 (2017)
5. Zhang, Y., Roughan, M., Willinger, W., et al.: Spatio-temporal compressive sensing and internet traffic matrices. In: ACM SIGCOMM Conference on Data Communication, pp. 267–267. Barcelona (2009)
6. Ding, G., et al.: Spectrum inference in cognitive radio networks: algorithms and applications. IEEE Commun. Surv. Tutor. **20**(1), 150–182 (2018)
7. Liu, H.R.: Coverage control algorithm for wireless sensor networks based on non-cooperative game. J. Commun. **40**(1), 71–78 (2019)
8. Li, Y., Chen, Z.H., et al.: Research on LTE load balancing algorithm based on game. Telev. Technol. **37**(19), 141–144 (2013)
9. Zhang, X., Nakhai, M.R., Ariffin, W.N.S.F.W.: Adaptive energy storage management in green wireless networks. IEEE Signal Process. Lett. **24**(7), 1044–1048 (2017)
10. Duan, T.T., Zhang, M., Wang, Z.L., Song, C.: Inter-BBU control mechanism for load balancing in C-RAN-based BBU pool. In: 2016 2nd IEEE International Conference on Computer and Communications (ICCC), pp. 2960–2964. Chengdu (2016)
11. Kuan, L., Liu, Z.J., Tan, X., et al.: Prediction matrix algorithm based on sparsity in C-RAN networks. Telecommun. Technol. **59**(3), 255–259 (2019)
12. Ma, Q.C., Liu, Z.J., Peng, X., et al.: Brief introduction of C-RAN technology and its application scenario in mobile network. Multidimensional Markovian model of traffic forecast of wireless network in architecture of C-RAN. Video Eng. **39**(3), 148–152 (2015)

A Signaling Analysis Algorithm in 5G Terminal Simulator

Yu Duan[1]($\boxtimes$), Wanwan Wang[2], and Zhizhong Zhang[1]

[1] School of Communication and Information Engineering, Chongqing University of Posts and Telecommunications, Chongqing 400065, China
s170102001@stu.cqupt.edu.cn
[2] School of Data Science,
Chongqing Vocational College of Transportation, Chongqing 402247, China

Abstract. Focused on the issue that the low efficiency for 5G network signaling analysis and processing, a hash topology under a new architecture based on the traditional LTE-A signaling monitoring and analysis system was proposed, its main subsystems and specific functional modules were introduced in detail, provided support for 5G terminal emulator signaling analysis. Firstly, the Key of the signaling message was sorted according to the value by using a large top heap; Secondly, the Key was mapped to a hash table, and the position of the Key value in the linked list was determined according to the probability, and the probability was obtained. The larger Key value was placed in the hash table with less conflicts. Finally, the hash table record was accessed, and the same signaling process information of the same user was associated and synthesized. The experimental results show that the improved algorithm under the proposed new architecture reduces the time spent on signaling analysis by 55.66% compared with the traditional algorithm, so it is suitable for practical engineering applications.

Keywords: 5G network · Terminal simulator · Signaling analysis · Hash conflict · Heap sort

1 Introduction

With the rapid development of mobile communication networks, the global 5G enters the critical period of commercial deployment. On June 6, 2019, China's Ministry of Industry and Information Technology officially issued 5G commercial licenses to China Telecom, China Mobile, China Unicom and China Radio and Television, and accelerated the deployment of 5G trial commercials, which means that the era of 5G is coming.

According to the "5G Vision and Demand White Paper" released by the IMT-2020 (5G) Promotion Group in May 2014, the theoretical transmission speed of 5G networks can reach 10 Gb per second, which will be hundreds of times higher than 4G network transmission speed [1]. The existing Long Term Evolution-Advanced (LTE-A) air interface monitoring analyzer is difficult to handle such massive mobile data, and it is difficult to adapt to the 5G network structure [2], there is an urgent need for a more

© ICST Institute for Computer Sciences, Social Informatics and Telecommunications Engineering 2020
Published by Springer Nature Switzerland AG 2020. All Rights Reserved
H. Gao et al. (Eds.): ChinaCom 2019, LNICST 312, pp. 729–740, 2020.
https://doi.org/10.1007/978-3-030-41114-5_55

high-performance test [3]. The United States and the European Union are actively developing analog terminals for 5G testing [4]. Anritsu Corporation of Japan and South Korea Samsung Corporation development 5G terminal analog devices that support 5G NR full protocol stack connectivity testing. At present, most of the communication instrumentation produced in China is still a low-to-medium product [5]. Therefore, the development of new 5G terminal analog instruments with independent intellectual property rights can enhance the research and development capabilities of domestic high-end communication equipment, and promote the rapid development of China's 5G industry chain.

In the 5G terminal simulator, the signaling analysis technology is the core technology of the analog terminal signaling analysis system. Through the analysis of the signaling process, the specific location of the problem is obtained, and the data characteristics are used to solve the problem in the communication. In recent years, more and more researchers research for it. In [6, 7], a Multi-Protocol Correlation Analysis (MPCA) system based on the Uu interface of the LTE-Advanced network is proposed. The user data signaling process is associated with the user service data flow, and the same is not considered. The user's same signaling process is associated with the message; in [8, 9], it is proposed that the composite service call/transaction detail record (XDR) is multi-protocol association after the decoding synthesis process, but it is only applicable to the traditional Analysis of the LTE-A air interface monitor.

Therefore, this paper will combine the traditional LTE-A air interface monitor analysis signaling analysis technology in the process of 5G terminal simulator signaling analysis, and an improved signaling analysis algorithm based on the combination of chain address method and hash top stack processing hash to deal with hash conflicts is proposed and the new signaling analysis system architecture based on the algorithm is designed. The research focuses on decoding synthesis and multi-protocol association in the signaling analysis process to achieve accurate signaling monitoring in the signaling analysis system.

2   The Overall Structure of the System

The traditional LTE-A network is a centralized UMTS evolved umts terrestrial radio access (E-UTRAN) flattened and evolved packet core (EPC) centralized network. Point-to-point (P2P) communication [10]. The user equipment (UE) carries more control functions. The control plane equipment has a single function and the function modules are tightly coupled. This will result in low network-side data collection efficiency during signaling monitoring and analysis, and XDR cannot be decoded and synthesized. Efficient storage.

Combined with the signaling analysis technology in the LTE-A air interface monitoring analyzer, the 5G network is introduced based on the service-based architecture (SBA), and next generation core (NGC) is separated by the control plane and the transfer plane. The user plane is simplified to achieve efficient forwarding. The new radio (NR) is separated by a centralized unit/distribution unit (CU/DU) to achieve centralized coordination and control of radio resources, and the network function to close and couple. According to the requirements of 3GPP and related industry test specifications, the signaling analysis system in the 5G terminal simulator is divided into three subsystems:

L1L2 subsystem, L3 decoding synthesis subsystem, and reverse inspection subsystem. Figure 1 is a signaling analysis system framework in a 5G terminal emulator.

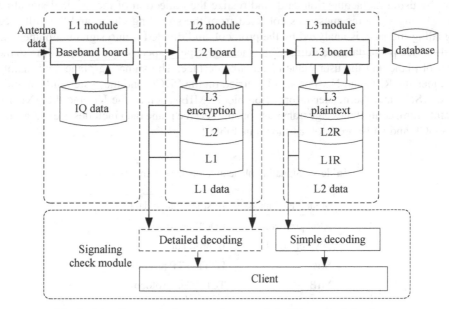

Fig. 1. Signaling analysis system framework in 5G terminal simulator.

The function of the L1L2 subsystem is mainly to complete the data acquisition and decoding, decryption and reorganization, and the L3 decoding and synthesis subsystem function is to complete the signaling plane and business plane decoding and synthesize the table, and the reverse check subsystem function is to complete the acquisition of the current page from the client. Message decoding result.

3 System Module Design

The 5G terminal simulator signaling analysis system draws on the design concept of micro service style (MSS) in the field of internet technology (IT), and introduces "service call" in signaling communication. According to the modular design idea, The network function is defined as a plurality of service modules that can be relatively independent and can be flexibly invoked. The signaling analysis mainly involves the baseband board collecting real-time data from the antenna and transmitting the L1 data to the layer two board; the layer two board stores the L1 data, and after completing the analysis of the MAC protocol, the RLC protocol, and the PDCP protocol, the output L2 is output. The data is transferred to the third board; the layer three board stores the L2 data to complete the protocol parsing; the decoding result is multi-protocol association, and the XDR is synthesized and stored in the database. The signaling analysis system can be divided into four modules: signaling acquisition module, decoding synthesis module, multi-protocol association module and synthetic output table and data back-checking module.

3.1 Signaling Acquisition Module

The function of the module is mainly to obtain the signaling data of the wireless port user by using the acquisition card, and realize the collection of the original signaling data. Using signaling messages collected from the signaling chain, and the collected signaling message is analyzed by the protocol, and divided it into signaling plane data and service plane data according to the message type, respectively corresponding to the control plane and the user plane of the air interface. The signaling plane data mainly includes the RRC and NAS protocols carried on the PDCP, and the system information block (SIB) and the master information block (MIB) such as the UE and the gNB for maintaining control message transmission. the service plane data includes user data such as PDCP and its IP protocol, as shown in Table 1.

Table 1. Signaling plane and business plane data.

Signaling plane data	Business plane data
RRC protocol	PDCP protocol
NAS protocol	IP protocol
SIB	HTTP, FTP protocol
MIB	TCP, UDP protocol

3.2 Decoding Synthesis Module

The signaling collection module obtains the L2 data from the Layer two board, and identifies the data as the signaling plane and the service plane according to the message type, respectively corresponding to the control plane and the user plane of the air interface, and respectively sent to the signaling plane lock-free queue and the tail of the service-side lock-free queue, the corresponding decoding synthesis module acquires data from the head of the queue and performs decoding synthesis. According to different types of protocols, different decoders are called, and the corresponding decoding function is called for decoding.

The decoding of the signaling plane mainly includes decoding of the NAS and RRC protocols, using the abstract syntax notation one (ASN.1) standard definition format, storing the protocol in a specific format in the description text, and then using the corresponding compiler to generate C++ code from the file and loop it to the top level data. The business plane decoding is mainly the decoding of user data including protocols such as IP, TCP, HTTP, UDP, DNS, and FTP. The specific decoding process is shown in Fig. 2(a). Protocol synthesis is to obtain information about each layer protocol according to the protocol type, according to different synthetic information to obtain user and signaling information, and combine them to form a complete signaling process.

The synthesis module needs to be initialized to obtain decoded data, and the decoded result is L3 data, which includes a field corresponding to the message of the MsgId and the CDR ID, traffic statistics information of the protocol, and storage protocol stack data. In addition, The respective protocol synthesizer needs to be defined for each layer of protocol. The key information of the message is used to search for a corresponding signaling flow message in the hash table and determine whether it exists. Update statistics if they exist, and create new XDR if they do not exist. At the same time, the timeout check is performed. If there is no time out, add that value of the corresponding key. When the end message is received, the synthetic table module is called to send the synthesized XDR and the statistics table to the multi-protocol association module for association. The specific synthesis process is shown in Fig. 2(b).

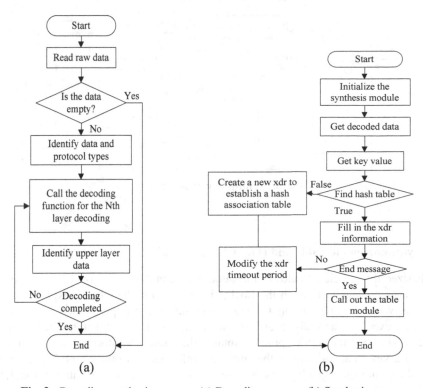

Fig. 2. Decoding synthesis process. (a) Decoding process. (b) Synthesis process

3.3 Multi-protocol Association Module

Multi-protocol association refers to the automatic association of network user information for real-time association backfilling. The complete signaling process is then synthesized by querying the temporary key correlation information Key value, and then synthesizing the complete signaling flow by means of the real Key value obtained by the detection system, and filled into XDR [4].

The system uses cell radio network temporary identifier (C-RNTI) as a user identifier, and combines messages associated with the same signaling process of the same user to form a complete signaling process. Synthesize the protocol transaction detail record according to the protocol type, and extract the protocol type, associated primary key and value, UE identification (userID), international mobile subscriber identification number (IMSIN), user IP address (UserIP), start time (Runtime), end time (Endtime) and other information used for correlation analysis. Finally, the signaling plane and the business plane data of the same user are matched and associated, and the multi-protocol association label is added to further synthesize the integrated XDR. The multi-protocol association process is shown in Fig. 3.

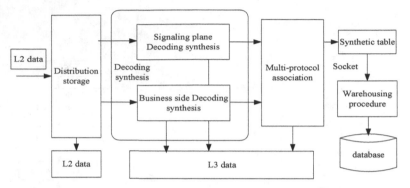

Fig. 3. Multi-protocol association.

3.4 Synthesizing the Table and Data Check Module

Synthesized the associated fields of the same user, and the synthesized XDR is sent to the storeroom program through the Socket interface, and the table is exported to the database. When the client wants to view the result, it first requests message statistics from the server, and the statistics are returned to the client. The client initiates a request to the service, and the service process obtains the summary information by searching for the L2 key data, and returns the summary information to the client. The user can check the composite signaling process after the multi-protocol association through the signaling reverse check.

4   Algorithm Design

4.1   Hash Signaling Analysis Algorithm

In the traditional hash signaling analysis algorithm (HSAA), the synthesis of the signaling and the multi-protocol association map the Key value of the signaling into the hash table [11]. Hash table is widely used because of its fast query speed in data query and convenient insertion and deletion operations [12]. When the signaling process information is associated with the XDR, the source IP, the source port number, the destination IP address, and the destination port number are selected as the Key value to construct a hash function, and the hash algorithm is used to search for the corresponding letter in the hash table by using the Key value of the signaling message. Let the process complete the relevant signaling process association [13].

In the form of hash index, the index value adopts a specific Key value, and different signaling processes have corresponding Key values. In the integrated signaling XDR synthesis process, the user's Key value may correspond to different Value [14]. At this time, the Key value with the same hash address will cause a conflict [15]. Its hash address is $p = H(Key)$, When a conflict occurs, it is the address that generated the conflict $H(Key)$ Find an address sequence:

$$H_0, H_1, H_2, \ldots, H_s (1 \le s \le m - 1) \tag{1}$$

Among:

$$H_0 = H(Key) \tag{2}$$

The general form of hash function is:

$$H_i = (H(Key) + di) \% m \ (i = 1, 2, \ldots s) \tag{3}$$

Where $H(Key)$ is a hash function, m is a table length and d_i is an incremental sequence.

The HSAA algorithm generally uses the open address method when dealing with hash collisions, but the open address method is prone to data accumulation problems. When the node size is large, it wastes a lot of space, consumes a large memory, and is not suitable for large-scale data storage, There may be multiple conflicts when inserting, and when the deleted element is one of multiple conflicting elements, the subsequent elements need to be processed, which is more complicated to implement.

In the HSAA algorithm, the value of the Key value of the signaling key message is sorted according to the direct insertion method, but the direct insertion method has more comparison times, greater time complexity, and lower efficiency.

4.2 Build a Hash Top Heap

In the signaling synthesis process, the HSAA algorithm is inefficient in dealing with hash collisions. in the improved signaling analysis algorithm, the hash table conflict is handled by the chain address method. Find the value in the hash table according to the hash Key value, and obtain the conflicting hash table entry pointing to the address of the linked list, and put all the Key values with the same hash address in the same synonym list, and store the head pointer of each linked list with an array. In the signaling analysis, a hash value key sequence of $\{K1, K2, K3, \ldots, Kn\}$ is assumed to be m, and a hash table that the chain address method handles conflicts is shown in Fig. 4.

In the process of signaling analysis to establish a hash table, based on the hash table address method, the Key value of the signaling message is sorted. This paper proposes a improved signaling analysis algorithm (ISAA). The same user signaling message has the Key value of the same Value, and the key top sorting method is used to sort the key words according to the probability of occurrence of Value, and the position in the linked

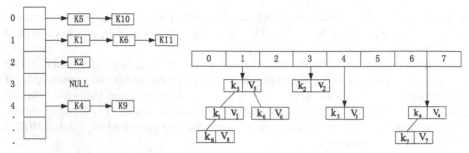

Fig. 4. Hash table when chain address method handles conflicts.

Fig. 5. Signaling message Key value hash big top heap.

list when the conflict is processed is determined according to the probability size, and increasing the look up efficiency in a hash-address conflict.

In the signaling analysis, assuming that the signaling message key sequence $\{(k_1, v_1), (k_2, v_2), (k_3, v_3), (k_4, v_4), (k_5, v_5), (k_6, v_6), (k_7, v_7), (k_8, v_8)\}$, the signaling message Key value hashes the top stack as shown in Fig. 5.

4.3 Analysis of Algorithms

In the signaling process synthesis of the signaling analysis, Judgment the corresponding signaling process message in the hash table is used to create the XDR by searching the key information of the message. The main operation is to compare the Key value of the key query. The average number of comparisons when the Key value is found successfully in the process is called Average Search Length (ASL). For the lookup table of n elements, the average search length is defined as:

$$ASL = \sum_{i=1}^{n} P_i C_i \tag{4}$$

Among them, P_i is the probability of the i-th data element in the lookup table, and C_i is the number of times that the i-th data element has been compared when it is found.

In the signaling message synthesis, based on the Value probability of finding the Key value of the signaling message, the Key value is mapped to a location in the hash table to access the record. the HSAA algorithm uses the direct insertion method to process hash collisions. The key message Key value is compared more frequently, and the time complexity is $O(n^2)$. The ISAA algorithm uses large top heap sorting when dealing with hash collisions. The number of comparisons in the search process is greatly reduced. In the worst case, the time complexity is $O(nlogn)$. Therefore, the search time is significantly reduced, and in the ISAA algorithm, the chain address method is used when processing hash collisions, the nodes in the linked list are dynamically applied, the processing conflict is simple, and there is no accumulation, and the average search length is short. It is more space-saving than the open address method, and it is convenient to insert a node in the head of the linked list and to delete a node, and only need to adjust the pointer without adjusting other conflicting elements. Therefore, for the ISAA algorithm, the larger the amount of data, the less time consuming, which improves the efficiency and accuracy of data processing, and also improves the reuse of dynamic memory resources.

5   Test Results and Analysis

5.1   Test Results

Test environment: Windows 10 operating system, the processor is Inter(R) Core(TM) i5-4460 CPU @ 3.20 GHz, and the platform with 8.00 GB of memory is installed. This paper uses the Visual Studio 2017 compile running environment, the test program is written in C++. In the test process, based on the TS38.331 protocol in 5G, a dynamic identifier C-RNTI allocated by the base station to the UE in the signaling message is used as the key message Key value. Since the value range of C-RNTI is 003D to FFF3, the analog data source is randomly generated within its range, and 5000 test cases are obtained by assignment. Through improving the ISAA algorithm, for example, looking up the corresponding value of the key information of the signaling flow message in the hash table, and judges its existence. the statistical information is updated, and the same signaling process information of the same user is associated and synthesized. As shown in Fig. 6, During the test, the diagnostic tools of the Visual Studio 2017 compiler can be used to view the memory resources and time spent by the algorithm program in real time.

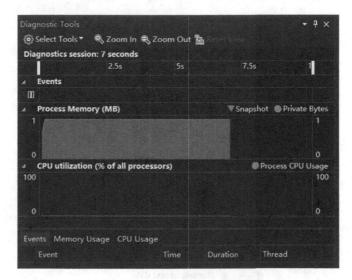

Fig. 6. Test process diagnosis.

5.2   Performance Analysis

By testing the above test cases, 5000 test cases were successfully tested. This paper compares the ISAA algorithm test results with the HSSA algorithm. As shown in Fig. 7, compared with HSSA, the improved ISAA by using the chain address method to handle hash collisions have no memory accumulation, realizing the dynamic reuse of memory resources, and save more memory resources.

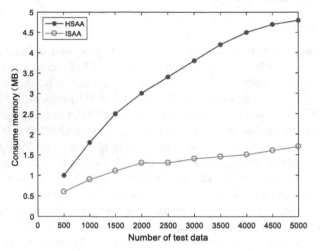

Fig. 7. Comparison of test signaling analysis consumes memory.

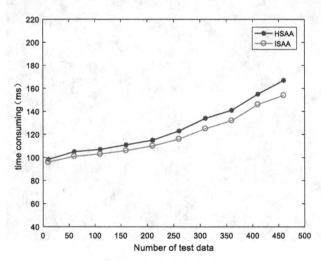

Fig. 8. Comparison of test signaling analysis consumes time of 500 data.

In the test process, as shown in Fig. 8, in the case of 50 to 500 test data, when the test data is 500, the traditional algorithm takes 167.4 ms, the improved algorithm takes 154.9 ms, and the time is reduced by 7.78%. Traditional algorithm and improvement the algorithm takes a small amount of time.

In the test results, as shown in Fig. 9, when the test data is 500, 2500, and 5000, the HSSA takes 167.4 ms, 393.1 ms, and 751.2 ms. ISAA takes 154.9 ms, 251.8 ms, and 333.5 ms, and reduced time by 55.66%. Compared to HSSA, the time required for the improved ISAA algorithm under the new architecture is significantly reduced.

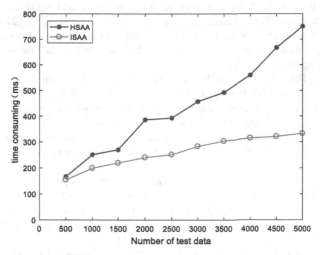

Fig. 9. Comparison of test signaling analysis consumes time of 5000 data.

The analysis rate of the signaling data of the HSSA algorithm is low, and when the amount of data is gradually increased, the analysis rate of the signaling data is slightly decreased; The signaling data analysis rate of the improved ISAA algorithm gradually increases with the amount of data, and can maintain a gradually increasing signaling analysis rate. This shows that the improved algorithm is very effective in signaling analysis.

6   Conclusion

Focused on the signaling analysis system in 5G terminal simulator, this paper designs a new signaling analysis system architecture. Compared with the traditional flat LTE-A network, it introduces the 5G network service system structure, According to the idea of modularization, the realization of centralized collaboration and control of wireless resources System, and network functions are tightly coupled moreover, in the signaling analysis process, when synthesizing XDR for signaling association, the user dynamic identification C-RNTI is selected as the Key value of the signaling message to construct a hash function, and advantages of combining the chain address method and the hash top heap sorting. An improved signaling analysis algorithm is proposed. The test results show that compared with the traditional signaling analysis system, the improved algorithm under the new architecture consumes significantly less time and memory, and the more the amount of data, the more obvious the effect. It shows that the system is effective and feasible, and it is of great significance for the optimization and testing of the 5G network to be commercialized.

References

1. IMT-2020 (5G) Program. White paper on 5G concept [S.l.:s.n.] (2015)
2. Hucheng, W., Hui, X., Zhimi, C.: Current research and development trend of 5G network technologies. Telecommun. Sci. **9**, 149–155 (2015)
3. Droste, H., Rost, P., Doll, M.: An adaptive 5G multiservice and multitenant radio access network architecture. Trans. Emerg. Telecommun. Technol. **27**(9), 1262–1270 (2016)
4. Padilla, P., Hirokawac, J., Foged, L.J., et al.: Future 5G millimeter-wave systems and terminals: propagation channel, communication techniques, devices, and measurements. IEEE Commun. Mag. **56**(7), 12–13 (2018)
5. Liu, T., Li, J., Feng, S., et al.: On the incentive mechanisms for commercial edge caching in 5G wireless networks. IEEE Wirel. Commun. **25**(3), 72–78 (2018)
6. Fan, Z.: The key technologies research of the signaling monitoring system correlation and correlation and refill. Telecommun. Netw. Technol. **10**, 56–59 (2011)
7. Wang, F., Jiao, M., Jia, Y.: Research and implementation of traffic monitoring technology on S1 interface in LTE network. J. Chongqing Univ. Posts Telecommun. Nat. Sci. **26**(3), 292–297 (2014)
8. Li, L., Zhang, Z., Xi, B.: Research and implementation of multi-protocol association scheme on Uu interface in LTE-Advanced network. Telecommun. Sci. **32**(6), 167–176 (2016)
9. Peng, L., Longhan, C., Zhizhong, Z.: Research and implementation of user behavior analysis system on Uu interface in LTE-Advanced network. Video Eng. **11**, 135–140 (2017)
10. Luo, F.L.: 5G new radio: standard and technology. ZTE Commun. **15**(s1) (2017)
11. Zhang, Z., Liu, Y.J.: Effective solution to hash collision. J. Comput. Appl. **30**(11), 2965–2966 (2010)
12. Collom, G., Redman, C., Robey, R.W.: Fast mesh to mesh remaps using hash algorithms. SIAM J. Sci. Comput. **40**(4), 450–476 (2018)
13. Fangfang, Z., Xungen, L.: Improved searching method of hash table. J. Hangzhou Dianzi Univ. (Nat. Sci. Ed.) **5**, 46–49 (2013)
14. Chevalier, Y., Kourjieh, M.: A symbolic intruder model for hash-collision attacks. In: Okada, M., Satoh, I. (eds.) ASIAN 2006. LNCS, vol. 4435, pp. 13–27. Springer, Heidelberg (2007). https://doi.org/10.1007/978-3-540-77505-8_2
15. Ndoundam, R., Karnel, J.: Collision-resistant hash function based on composition of functions. Comput. Sci. **14**, 167–183 (2011)

Design and Implementation of Assembler for High Performance Digital Signal Processor (DSP)

Peng Ding[1], Haoqi Ren[1], Zhifeng Zhang[1], Jun Wu[1(✉)], Fusheng Zhu[2], and Wenru Zhang[2]

[1] Tongji University, No.4800 Caoan Road, Jiading District, Shanghai, People's Republic of China
657799191@qq.com, {renhaoqi,zhangzf,wujun}@tongji.edu.cn
[2] GuangDong Communications & Networks Institute, Guangzhou, Guangdong Province, China
{zhufusheng,zhangwenru}@gdcni.cn

Abstract. With the rapid development of the fifth-generation mobile communication technology (5G), existing digital signal processors (DSP) on the market cannot efficiently provide the performance required by some applications. In this situation, we design a new DSP with faster speed, lower latency and higher performance. In this article, based on the new DSP which can adapt to the new technology of 5G, we designed an assembler called Swift Assembler (SA). Different from the traditional assembler, SA is based on the Gnu Architecture Description Language, (GADL). We perform semantic analysis on GADL description files and then with the help of flex, bison and Binutils, the assembler is compiled and generated. With the support of GADL, SA has a clearer architecture and better scalability. At the same time, it covered the underlying implementation. Benefit from this, programmers can modify its source code with no need to understand the underlying implementation process. In this way, the design of interdependent hardware and software can be more easily.

Keywords: 5G · DSP · GADL · SA

1 Introduction

Recently, the fifth-generation communication technology (5G) [1] has become a hot topic. With the continuous advancement of communication technology worldwide, 5G has developed rapidly and matured. Theoretically, 5G can provide a peak data rate of 20 Gbps with ultra-low latency of 1 ms. In smart grid, monitoring system, asset tracking, connected cars and more, it has a great application value. In the next few years, the market of wireless communication belongs to 5G. However, the existing data signal processor (DSP) cannot efficiently provide the qualified speed, latency and overall performance required by the upgrading of 5G in the application of LTE-Advanced Pro and Gigabit wireless networks. Because of this, there is an urgent need for a new DSP that can meet the

© ICST Institute for Computer Sciences, Social Informatics and Telecommunications Engineering 2020
Published by Springer Nature Switzerland AG 2020. All Rights Reserved
H. Gao et al. (Eds.): ChinaCom 2019, LNICST 312, pp. 741–751, 2020.
https://doi.org/10.1007/978-3-030-41114-5_56

requirements of ultra-high frequency and ultra-low power consumption, providing large-scale computing power, and supporting high-precession algorithms. We have done much work on the new DSP. In our design, the new DSP has a flexible architecture and a variety of optional features. Also, it implements new instructions for baseband processing, ultra-low transmission delay of the core and accelerator, and flexible customer provisioning and scaling to meet the needs of large-scale user management and multi-RAT (wireless access technology). At the same time with the research of hardware, our work on software have also made great progress. We have finished the work of toolchain based on the new DSP. In this article, the design of assembler will be introduced in detail.

The traditional assembler implementation usually builds a mapping of assembly code to machine code with the help of high-level programming languages. And someone may prefer to use existing assembly tools such as GNU Binutils to reduce the work of programming [2]. But int this way, it usually involves the underlying implementation in the design of the assembler. This will bring great difficulties to the use and modification of other programmers.

In our design of assembler, we used Gnu Architecture Description Language, (GADL) [3, 4] to help us complete the mapping of the assembly code to the machine code. In this way, we build a clear architecture of assembler, reduce the code we need to finish and make the whole project easy to read and modify for other programmers. We ported the Binutils toolset to help us to read in the assembly files and complete some relocation work. But for others, they don't need to understand how we do this work. They can use it and modify it for their own requirement through the upper layer codes.

2 Description of the New DSP

This new DSP is aimed to achieve high performance and low power consumption and its main application field is wireless communication. In addition to the most advantages of traditional DSP, it also has autonomously controllable high-performance instruction set architecture (ISA), dedicated acceleration instructions and high-performance DSP core microarchitecture for independent intellectual property rights and more.

This DSP support high parallelism single instruction multiple data (SIMD), providing a 640-bit SIMD unit that can perform vector operations of 16-channel-40-bit, 32-channel-20-bit and 64-channel-10-bit. At the same time, it can emit 8 instructions simultaneously in VLIW. To achieve this, we use a 10-stage pipeline as shown in Fig. 1.

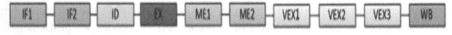

Fig. 1. A 10-stage pipeline

In the structure, the DSP includes a DSP core, a direct memory access (DMA) module, on-chip memory (I-MEM, D-MEM) and a debug module as the Fig. 2 shows.

The DSP core uses the LOAD/STORE instruction to directly access the data in the on-chip memory or to transfer data to and from external device and memories via the bus. And the on-chip memory transfers data through the DMA channel. The debug module provides an interface to the external debugger.

3   Description of GADL

Swift Assembler (SA) is an assembler based on the GADL. GADL is a highly scalable architecture description language presented by one of our members in our team. It's usually applied to the design of toolchain. The structure of GADL is described in Fig. 3.

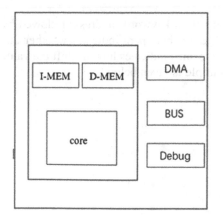

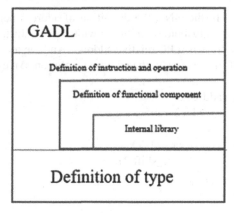

Fig. 2. A simplified structure of DSP   **Fig. 3.** Structure of GADL

Similar to lisp [5], the syntax of GADL uses a prefix expression. For example, the Backus-Naur Form (BNF) of the definition of an integer in the grammar is as follows.

- INT:: == '(' 'int_type' LIST ')'
- LIST:: = [LIST] DEC
- DEC:: == '(' NAME WIDTH FLAG ')'
- WIDTH:: = '(' 'width' NUMBER ')'
- FLAG:: == '(' 'flag' <signed | unsigned> ')'

An integer description begins with the keyword "int_type" followed by several definition lists (DEC). Each of the integer types begin with the type name followed by two attribute definitions: data width and data type (signed and unsigned). An example to help understanding is given below.

- (int_type
-    (bf5
-       (width 5)
-       (flag signed)
-    )
-)

In the example, we define a signed integer "bf5" and its width is 5-bits. Similarly, we can define address type with GADL as follows.

- ADDRESS:: == '(' 'address' LIST ')'
- LIST:: == [LIST] DEF
- DEF:: == '(' NAME WIDTH PCREL SHIFT ')'
- WIDTH:: == '(' 'width' NUMBER ')'
- PCRA:: == '(' 'pcra' < 'TURE' | 'FALSE'> ')'
- SHIFT:: == '(' < 'right_shift' | 'left_shift'> NUMBER ')'

In the BNF, the definition of address begins with keyword 'address' followed by three attribute definitions: width, pcra, shift. The attribute pcra indicates whether this address is a PC relative address. And the attribute shift indicates how to shift the value of the address in the address resolution. An example is given below.

- (address
-    (addr21rel
-       (width 21)
-       (pcra TURE)
-       (right_shift 2)
-    )
-)

With the help of these meaningful definitions, we can describe the instruction set completely. Based on the instruction set described, the design of the assembler is easily.

4 The Design of Assembler

The design of assembler usually contains two aspects. One is to transfer the instructions to the machine codes and the other is to identify assembly files. In the other word, just like compiler, the design of assembler can be divided into lexical analysis and semantic analysis [6, 7].

To implement the translation from instructions to machine codes, the most designs of traditional assemblers are to use lots of code to describe the mapping of instructions to machine codes [8]. In this way, the amount of code for the entire project is huge. And when we modified the ISA, it means we need to modified all the code we have finished before. To solve these problems, in our design of Swift Assembler, we use GADL to describe our ISA to separate the flow of mapping from the code. The design flow is as Fig. 4.

4.1 The Description of ISA with GADL

In the design, the description of ISA contains the instruction description, type description, register description and many other descriptions.

Before all the descriptions defined, we firstly defined enumeration description to contains all the keyword which may be used in the next work.

- (enum
-    (GR_E

- 'GR0' 'GR1' … 'GR31'
-)
- (VR_E
- ('VR0' 32) 'VR1' … 'VR15'
-)
- (BFEXT_E
- 'bfext' 'bfextu'
-)
- (…)
-)

After completing the enumeration type definition, we can go on our definitions of other descriptions.

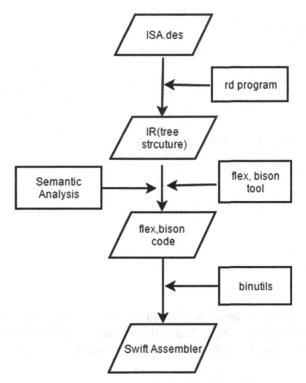

Fig. 4. The design flow of Swift Assembler

As mentioned above, the new DSP issues 8 instruction in parallel. So, we can define our instruction set with GADL like this.

- (instruction
- (top instrs
- (instrs

-         (= i slots_8)
-     )
-   )
- (code i)
- (binary i)
- (vliw 1 0)
-)

In the description above, 'code' indicates the assembly parameter and the 'binary' is the machine code of the assembly parameter. The first number in the 'vliw' column is a flag to indicate whether VLIW mode is supported. And the second means whether this instruction is the last in the VLIW package. And then we can continue to define 'slots_8' as follows.

- (slots_8
-     (= i slots0 empty)
-     (= j slots1 empty)
-     (...)
-     (= y slots7 empty)
-     (pack i j ... y)
-)
- (slot0
-     (= i NOP RET RTT JC JNC ...)
-     (code i)
-     (binary '000' i)
-)
- (...)
- (slot7
-     (...)
-     (code i)
-     (binary '111' i)
-)

As described above, we define 8 slots and specify the instruction that each slot can hold based on the hardware design. And next, we defined the assembly format for each instruction. To understand it easily, an example is provided.

- (BFEXT
-     (= i BFEXT_E)
-     (= rd GR_E)
-     (= rs GR_E)
-     (= bf0 imm5)
-     (= bf1 bf5)
-     (code i ' ' rd ' ' rs ' ' bf0 ' ' bf1)
-     (binary '110' '0' rd '0' rs bf0 bf1 '0' i '01')
-)

In this rule, we defined an assembly code "bfext rd rs bf0 bf1". This instruction is to achieve bit extraction. Similar to the examples given above, we can give many other definitions. All of them together describe the ISA with GADL.

4.2 The Semantic Analysis of GADL

Since GADL is a prefix expression, it is easy to create a LL1 read program rd. With the help of rd, we can convert from the text description to a tree structure.

- Class node {
-    int type;
-    Vector<node *> nodelist;
-    String str;
- }

When the value in the node is a string type with quotes or a variable, the parameter nodelist is invalid. Besides, when the value in the node is a vector, the parameter str is invalid. Then we need to perform semantic analysis on the resulting tree structure. The most important step in the semantic analysis process is the rule expansion.

The rules of GADL is similar to the rules of nML [9, 10], and we also provide sub-rules to avoid rewriting the same rules. So, in the rule expansion, we need to fill each sub-rule into the parent rule that reference it. In this process, we firstly build a hash table (VarTable) to save reserved word. The key of each item in the table is a string, and the value is its corresponding attribute which is saved by UnfoldedList. This UnfoldedList is the rule we may need to expand. Figure 5 shows the rule expansion

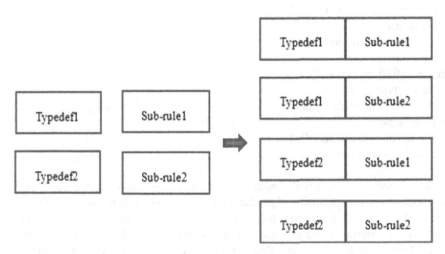

Fig. 5. Rule expansion

Since a rule may be expanded to contain a set of rules, we need to save it with a vector. Each rule is described by 7 sets of data, which are the expanded assembly description(code), binary(binary), variable(varName), the offset of the variable in the assembly description(offsetInBinary), the width of the variable after expansion(varLen), the declared name of enumerated type(enumName) and the information of relocation(relocInfo). The structure is as follows.

- class UnfoldedList {
-    vector <unfolded>lst;
- }
- class Unfolded {
-    string rulename;
-    vector<string>code;
-    vector<string>binary;
-    vector<string>offsetIncode;
-    vector<string>offsetInbinary;
-    vector<string>varName;
-    vector<string>varLen;
-    string enumName;
-    vector<int>relocInfo;
- }

The pseudo code of the rule expansion is given below.

- Unfold(nodePtr)
- nodename = node->str
- if nodeName in VarTable
- do return VarTable[nodename]
- switch type of (nodePtr)
- case instruction
- ret = unfoldinstr(nodePtr)
- case enum
- ret = unfoldenum(nodePtr)
- case int_type
- ret = unfoldint_type(nodePtr)
- case address
- ret = unfoldaddress(nodePtr)
- VarTable[nodeName] = ret

The pseudo code above will continue to call the relevant instruction expansion algorithm, enumerate the expansion algorithm and other algorithms to complete the development of the GADL description language. Of course, we also need to do some work required by the hardware. For example, in our design of the new DSP, the VLIW supports 8 slots. Apart from the VLIW end flag, we only have two bits to correspond to 8 slots. To solve this problem, in the rule expansion we need to declare that both slot0 and slot1 correspond to '00'. Similarly, slot2 and slot3 correspond to '01' and so on. Because the instructions are in order, we can tell which slot of the two adjacent slots the instruction belongs to by the order.

4.3 Porting of the Underlying Toolset of Binutils

In this step, we deeply analyzed the workflow of the mips assembler and referred to the implementation code of mips assembler code. By using Flex [11] and Bison [12] tools, the code needed is generated easily. All the descriptions completed with GADL above are transferred to the flex and bison code. Also, the BFD library code of Binutils according to the address type used by the instruction set is generated at the same time. The example is as follows.

GADL:

- enum(
- J_E(
- 'jmp' 'jc' 'jnc' 'call'
-)
-)

Flex:

- "jmp" return TOK_62
- "jc" return TOK_63
- "jnc" return TOK_64
- "call" return TOK_65

Bison:

- J_E: TOK_62 {$$=(char*) "00"
- TOK_63 {$$=(char*) "01"
- TOK_64 {$$=(char*) "10"
- TOK_65 {$$=(char*) "11"

At last, the flex and bison code is transferred to the cpp file which can be identified by the Binutils tool set. With the help of the Binutils tool set, the Swift Assembler is compiled and generated.

5 Results and Verification

In the current design, there are 186 basic assembly instructions for the new DSP. In addition, the processor supports 1 to 8 variable-length VLIW instructions. The description file of instruction set has 860 lines. All remaining files are less than 6000 lines containing much code generated by the flex and bison tools. Compared with other assemblers, the work on programming is easily.

To verify the correctness of the Swift Assembler, assembly code containing all instructions is tested and passed. The machine codes generated run normally on the new DSP. Figure 6 shows the working process of SA.

```
!nop|nop||||||!
00000000  000000a0
!addi GR2 GR2 0xfc84|||||||!
20a42098
!|addic GR5 GR6 0xfc84||||||!
  24a451b8
!|||||||store8 GR7 GR8 0xd5!
            a01a72ec
```

Fig. 6. Assembly process of SA

6 Conclusion and Future Work

This article presents the design and implementation of Swift Assembler of a new DSP with high performance. By using the GADL to describe the ISA of the new DSP, we present the semantic analysis of GADL and introduce the tools of flex, bison and Binutils. At last, we illustrate the actual working process of SA. Compared with traditional assemblers, SA has less coding and more flexible architecture. This bring great convenience to other colleagues in our team.

In the future, we will continue to optimize the design of assembler. And based on the GADL, we will go on our research for disassembler, simulator and debugger.

Acknowledgment. The authors thank the editors and the anonymous reviewers for their invaluable comments to help to improve the quality of this paper. This work was supported in part by the National Natural Science Foundation of China under Grant Nos. 61831018, 61571329 and 61631017, and Guangdong Province Key Research and Development Program Major Science and Technology Projects under Grant 2018B010115002.

References

1. Ji, X., Huang, K., Jin, L., Tang, H., Liu, C., et al.: Overview of 5G security technology. Sci. China (Inf. Sci.) **61**(08), 107–131 (2018)
2. GNU Binary Utilities. http://www.sourceware.org/binutils/
3. Clements, P.C.: A survey of architecture description languages. In: Proceedings of the Software Specification and Design. IEEE Computer Society, April 1996. https://doi.org/10.1109/iwssd.1996.501143
4. Shen, J.: A research on processor architecture description languages and implementation of tool-chain generation (unpublished)
5. McCarthy, J.: Recursive functions of symbolic expressions and their computation by machine. Technical report, Massachusetts Institute of Technology, Cambridge, MA, USA
6. Lin, T.J., Chen, S.K., Kuo, Y.T., et al.: Design and implementation of a high-performance and complexity-effective VLIW DSP for multimedia applications. J. Sig. Process. Syst. **51**(3), 209–223 (2008)
7. Hu, Y., Chen, S.: Preprocessing scheme of intelligent assembly for a high performance VLIW DSP. In: Second International Conference on Cloud & Green Computing (2013)

8. Hadjiyiannis, G., Hanono, S., Decadas, S.: ISDL: an instruction set description set processors for retargetability. In: Proceedings of the 34th Annual Design Automation Conference, pp. 299–302. ACM (1997)
9. Freericks, M.: The nML machine description formalism
10. Fau, A., Van Praet, J., Freericks, M.: Description instruction set processors using nML. In: Proceedings of the European Design and Test Conference, ED&TC 1995, pp. 503–507. IEEE (1995)
11. The Fast Lexical Analyzer. http://flex.sourceforge.net/
12. GNU Bison. http://www.gnu.org/software/bison/

Author Index

Printed in the United States
By Bookmasters